# A History of Russia

# A History of Russia

EIGHTH EDITION

Nicholas V. Riasanovsky
*University of California, Berkeley*

Mark D. Steinberg
*University of Illinois, Urbana-Champaign*

New York     Oxford
OXFORD UNIVERSITY PRESS
2011

Oxford University Press

Oxford   New York
Auckland   Bangkok   Buenos Aires   Cape Town   Chennai
Dar es Salaam   Delhi   Hong Kong   Istanbul   Karachi   Kolkata
Kuala Lumpur   Madrid   Melbourne   Mexico City   Mumbai
Nairobi   São Paulo   Shanghai   Taipei   Tokyo   Toronto

Published by Oxford University Press, Inc.
198 Madison Avenue, New York, New York, 10016

ISBN: 978-0-19-534197-3

Printing number: 9 8 7 6 5 4 3 2

Printed in the United States of America
on acid-free paper

To Our Students

# About the Authors

**Nicholas V. Riasanovsky** is Sidney Hellman Ehrman Professor Emeritus of European History at the University of California, Berkeley. One of the foremost Russian historians, Riasanovsky was elected to the American Academy of Arts and Sciences in 1987. He is the author of several books, including *The Image of Peter the Great in Russian History and Thought* (OUP, 1985) and *The Emergence of Romanticism* (OUP, 1992).

**Mark D. Steinberg** is Professor of History at the University of Illinois at Urbana-Champaign and editor of *Slavic Review*. Specializing in the cultural, intellectual, and social history of Russia in the late nineteenth and early twentieth centuries, his books include *Voices of Revolution, 1917* (2001) and *Proletarian Imagination: Self, Modernity, and the Sacred in Russia, 1910–1925* (2002).

# Contents

# Maps

# Illustrations

# New to the Eighth Edition

Improved balance between political/economic history and cultural/social history
- Updated for recent events, with extensive coverage of the Putin/Medvedev administrations
- More coverage of women
- More coverage of everyday life throughout
- Greatly expanded coverage of the 20th century and the first decade of the 21st century
- Completely re-designed maps and new full-color reference maps on the inside front and back covers

# Preface to the Eighth Edition

The eighth edition of *A History of Russia* has been substantially revised. The seventh edition, the first with Mark Steinberg's participation, saw considerable change in certain areas: we took account of new research and interpretations, especially for 1855 to the present; we greatly expanded coverage of the postcommunist years; and we chose many new images. In updating and revising this eighth addition, we have extensively revised the discussion of the long history before 1855 and have made additional revisions to the late imperial, Soviet and post-Soviet eras. Our goal has been to reflect new research and new questions and interpretations, as both Russian historiography and approaches to history generally have remained very lively. Yet the basic approach of *A History of Russia* has remained the same: careful attention to documentable facts, recognition of conflicting and changing interpretations, every attempt to ensure balance and fairness, and an inclusive and complex view of history that attends not only to the actions of rulers but also to political ideologies, economics, social relations, intellectual history, culture, and the arts. If anything, this diversity of actors and experiences has continued to grow with each successive edition, especially to include more attention to diverse social groups, women, dissenters, non-Russians, and the regions.

We want to express deep gratitude to colleagues at many colleges and universities who have commented on various parts of the book: Brian Boeck, DePaul University; Timothy Pursell, University of Alaska Fairbanks; Karl D. Qualls, Dickinson College; Gilbert C. Rappaport, University of Texas at Austin; Jennifer Spock, University of Eastern Kentucky; Glennys J. Young, University of Washington. Mark Steinberg wants especially to thank participants in the Russian Study Circle (the Kruzhok) at the University of Illinois and the historians who met at a workshop under the auspices of the Lazarski School in Warsaw, Poland. We are grateful to Brian Wheel, Danniel Schoonebeek, Charles Cavaliere, Julio Espin, Lauren Aylward, Michelle Kornegay and their colleagues at Oxford University Press and to Arlene Riasanovsky and Jane Hedges. Like its predecessors, the eighth edition of A History of Russia is dedicated to our students, who are always in mind as we write.

Nicholas V. Riasanovsky
*Berkeley, California*

Mark D. Steinberg
*Urbana, Illinois*

# A History of Russia

*Part I*

# INTRODUCTION

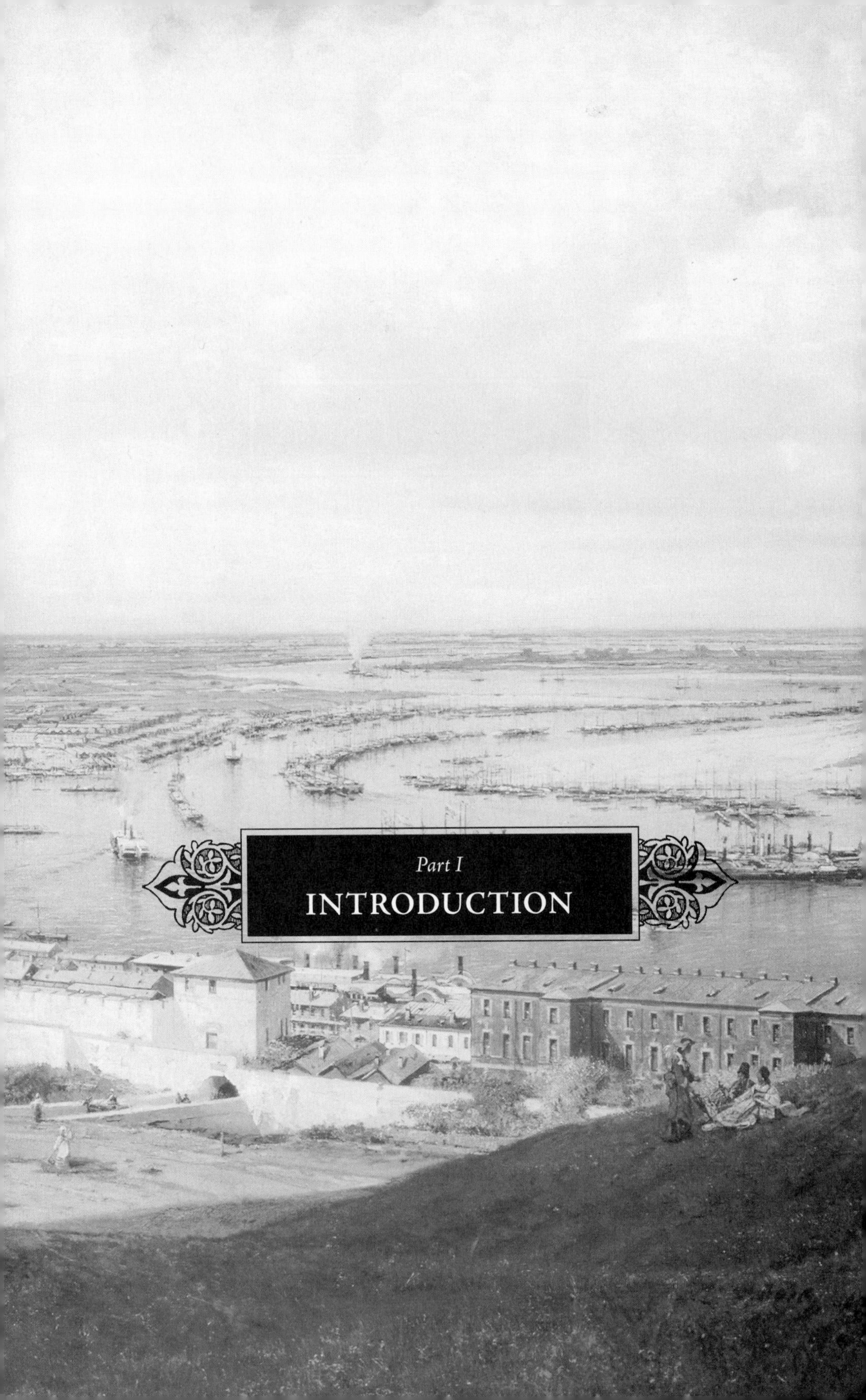

# Chapter I

# The Geographical Environment

Russia! what a marvelous phenomenon on the world scene! Russia—a distance of ten thousand versts* in length on a straight line from the virtually central European river, across all of Asia and the Eastern Ocean, down to the remote American lands! A distance of five thousand versts in width from Persia, one of the southern Asiatic states, to the end of the inhabited world—to the North Pole. What state can equal it? Its half? How many states can match its twentieth, its fiftieth part?...Russia—a state which contains all types of soil, from the warmest to the coldest, from the burning environs of Erivan to icy Lapland; which abounds in all the products required for the needs, comforts, and pleasures of life, in accordance with its present state of development—a whole world, self-sufficient, independent, absolute.

MIKHAIL POGODIN

Loe thus I make an ende: none other news to thee
But that the country is too cold, the people beastly bee
AMBASSADOR GEORGE TURBEVILLE REPORTING<br>TO ELIZABETH I OF ENGLAND

These poor villages,
This barren nature—
Native land of enduring patience,
The land of the Russian people!
FEDOR TIUTCHEV

Broad and spacious is my homeland,
Rich in rivers, fields, and woods,
I know no other land like this,
Where a man can breathe so free.
*SONG OF THE MOTHERLAND*, 1936

---

*A *versta* is not quite two-thirds of a mile, or a little over a kilometer.

Human societies, historians and geographers have long argued, cannot be understood apart from the natural environments in which they develop. Climate, soil, water, flora, fauna, mineral resources, and physical landscapes present human communities with limitations and opportunities. In turn, human history has often been a story of efforts to use, master, and even change environments. This dialogue—for neither is nature all-determining nor are humans able to completely free themselves from, much less conquer, nature— has been especially profound in Russian history, for it has occurred in a vast, difficult, and changing environment. At its imperial peak—as the Russian Empire and then the Union of Soviet Socialist Republics—Russia represented a land mass of over 8.5 million square miles, an area larger than the entire North American continent. To quote the leading Russian encyclopedia: "The Russian Empire, stretching in the main latitudinally, occupies all of eastern Europe and northern Asia, and its surface constitutes 0.42 of the area of these two continents. The Russian Empire occupies 1/22 part of the entire globe and approximately 1/6 part of its total land surface." Even after the loss of about a quarter of its territory when the Soviet Union broke up in 1991, the Russian Federation remains the largest country in the world geographically. This enormous territory is marked by a mixture of great homogeneity and rich variety, both of which helped shape Russia's history.

This enormous territory exhibits considerable homogeneity. Indeed, homogeneity helps to explain its size. The great bulk of Russia is an immense plain—at one time the bottom of a huge sea—extending from central and even western Europe deep into Siberia. Although numerous hills and chains of hills are scattered on its surface, they are not high enough or sufficiently concentrated to interfere appreciably with the flow of the mighty plain, the largest on the entire globe. The Ural Mountains themselves, ancient and weather-beaten, constitute no effective barrier between Europe and Asia, which they separate; besides, a broad gap of steppe land remains between the southern tips of the Ural chain and the Caspian and Aral seas. Only in vast northeastern Siberia, beyond the Enisei River, does the elevation rise considerably and hills predominate. But this area, while of a remarkable potential, has so far remained at best on the periphery of Russian history. Impressive mountain ranges are restricted to Russian borders or, at the most, borderlands. They include the Carpathians to the southwest, the high and picturesque Caucasian chain in the south between the Black Sea and the Caspian, and the mighty Pamir, Tien Shan, and Altai ranges farther east along the southern border.

Rivers have played a large role in Russian history—giving names to places and peoples, connecting distant places, and providing resources. Above all, Russia's broad and slow-moving rivers were the land's first important routes, carrying both goods and settlers. Most of these rivers carry their waters along a north-south axis and empty either into the Baltic and the Arctic Ocean or into the Black and the Caspian seas. In European Russia, such rivers as the Northern Dvina and the Pechora flow northward, while others, notably the Dniester, the Bug, and the larger Dnieper, Don, and Volga proceed south. The Dnieper and the Don empty into the Black Sea, the Volga into the Caspian. Siberian rivers, the huge Ob and Enisei, as well as the rapid Lena, the Indigirka, and the Kolyma, drain into the Arctic Ocean. The exception is the Amur, which flows eastward, serves during much of its course as the boundary between Russia and China, and empties into the Strait of Tartary. South of Siberia in Central Asia both the Amu Daria and the Syr Daria flow northwestward to the Aral Sea, although the former at one time used to reach the Caspian.

But while Russia abounds in rivers and lakes, it is essentially a landlocked country. By far its longest coastline opens on the icy Arctic Ocean. The neighboring seas include the Baltic and the Black, both of which must pass through narrow straits, away from Russian borders, to connect with broader expanses of water, and the Caspian and the Aral, which are totally isolated. Major Russian lakes include Ladoga and Onega in the European part of the country, and the huge and extremely deep Lake Baikal in Siberia. The Russian eastern coastline too is subject to cold and inclement weather, except for the southern section adjacent to the Chinese border.

Latitude and a landlocked condition largely determine Russian climate, which can be best described as severely continental. Northern and even central Russia are on the latitude of Alaska, while the position of southern Russia corresponds more to the position of Canada in the western hemisphere than to that of the United States. The Gulf Stream, which does so much to make the climate of western and northern Europe milder, barely reaches one segment of the northern coastline of Russia. In the absence of interfering mountain ranges, icy winds from the Arctic Ocean sweep across European Russia to the Black Sea. Siberian weather, except in the extreme southeastern corner, is more brutal still. Thus in northern European Russia the soil stays frozen eight months out of twelve. Even Ukraine is covered by snow three months every year, while the rivers freeze all the way to the Black Sea. Siberia in general and northeastern Siberia in particular belong among the coldest areas in the world. The temperature at Verkhoiansk has been registered at as low as –90°F. Still, in keeping with the continental nature of the climate, when summer finally comes—and it often comes rather suddenly—temperatures soar. Heat waves are common in European Russia and in much of Siberia, not to mention the deserts of Central Asia, which spew sand many miles to the west.

The long-term effects of climate, along with other environmental conditions (such as hydrology and erosion), created a variety of ecosystems across the Eurasian plain. As generations of migrants, settlers, and peasants learned firsthand, and as Russian scientists codified in nineteenth-century studies, Russia was divided into several natural "zones" extending east-west across the country, though there were overlapping transitional areas. Historically, the early history of Slavic and Scandinavian settlement was focused on the mixed forest zone that extends from the Baltic and western frontier toward the Ural Mountains; this region would remain, in terms of population, the heartland of Russia. In the medieval period, Russian peasants would begin to move north into the coniferous taiga, a harsh land that stretches from southern Scandinavia to the Pacific Ocean. Together, these two huge forested belts accounted for over half of the territory of the Russian Empire and the Soviet

Union. Still further north lies the tundra, a brutal land of swamps, moss, peat, and shrubs, reaching from the Kola Peninsula to the far northeastern edge of the Eurasian continent, and covering almost 15 percent of Russian territory. Few Russian settlers ventured there before the end of the seventeenth century. To the south is the steppe, or prairie, occupying southern European Russia and extending into Asia to the Altai Mountains. Russian colonization of the steppe was delayed by nomadic groups, many of which had come from farther east but would become extensive in the imperial period. Finally, the southernmost zone, that of semi-desert and desert, extends from the Caspian Sea through Central Asia. It occupies somewhat less than one-fifth of the total area of the former Soviet land mass.

These diverse patterns of climate and vegetation provided people with a variety of resources for subsistence and development, though relatively little first-rate agricultural land. Only an estimated one million square miles out of an area more than eight times that size are truly rewarding to the tiller of the soil. Much of the country suffers from short growing seasons, too little or too much precipitation, morainic deposits, and shallow and sandy topsoils. Even the best land in Ukraine and Russia, the excellent black soil of the southern steppe, offers agricultural conditions comparable to those on the great plains of Canada rather than those in warmer Iowa or Illinois. Russia, on the other hand, is fabulously rich in forests, more so than any other country in the world—rich not only in wood but also in game, berries, edible plants, and fish. And it possesses a great wealth and variety of natural resources, ranging from platinum to oil and from coal to gold. On the whole, however, these resources remained unused and even unexplored for a very long time. Adding to the everyday challenges faced by the working population, this was a land plagued by cold, flooding, famine, and fire. Still, even early settlers began to transform these environments: clearing forests for settlement and agriculture, burning steppe grasses, hunting and overhunting game, and damming rivers. With industrialization came even more radical efforts to bend nature to human needs and desires—not always successfully and not always with positive consequences.

Ever since Herodotus historians have been fascinated by the role of geographic factors in human history. Indeed the father of history referred to the broad sweep of the southern Russian steppe and to the adaptation of the steppe inhabitants, the Scythians, to their natural environment in his explanation of why the mighty Persians could not overcome them. Modern historians of Russia, including such leading Russian scholars as Vasilii Kliuchevsky and especially his teacher Sergei Soloviev, as well as such prominent Western writers as Robert Kerner and B. H. Sumner, have persistently emphasized the significance of geography for Russian history. More recently, the rise of environmental history and, in Russia, the influence of intellectuals like the geographer and historian Lev Gumilev, have revived attention to the influence of geographical environment on society and culture. Even if we reject environmental and geographic determinism (implicit in much older work) and refuse to speculate on such nebulous and precarious topics as the Russian national character and its dependence on the environment, some fundamental points have to be made.

For instance, it appears certain that the growth of the Russian state was affected by the geography of the area: a vast plain with very few natural obstacles to expansion. This setting notably made it easier for the Moscow state to spread across eastern Europe. Beyond the Urals, the Russians advanced all the way to the Pacific, and even to Alaska and California, a progression paralleled only by the great American movement west. As the boundaries of the Russian Empire ultimately emerged, they consisted of oceans to the north and east and, in large part, of seas, high mountains, and deserts to the south; only in the west, where the Russians merged with streams of other peoples, did the border seem unrelated to geography. The extremely severe climate contributed to the weakness of the tribes scattered in northern European Russia and of the various inhabitants of Siberia, leading to their utter inability to stem the Russian advance. Whereas the Russians could easily expand, they were well protected from outside attack. Russian distances brought defeat to many, although not all, invaders, from the days of the Persians and the Scythians to those of Napoleon and Hitler.

Occupied territory had to be governed. The problem of administering an enormous area, of holding the parts together, of coordinating local activities and efforts remained a staggering task for those in power, whether Ivan the Terrible, Nicholas I, or Stalin. And the variety of peoples on the great plain was bound to make such issues as centralization and federation all the more acute. Conquest and colonization of this vast land required the backing of state power, not only to overcome the sheer "friction of space," as geographers call it, but also to integrate diverse peoples into a common empire. One can appreciate, if not accept, the opinion of those thinkers, prominent in the Enlightenment and present in other periods, who related the system of government of a country directly to its size and declared despotism to be the natural form of rule in Russia.

The magnificent network of Russian rivers and lakes also left its mark on Russian history. It is sufficient to mention the significance of the Dnieper for Kievan Rus, or of the Volga and its tributaries for the Moscow state. The landlocked position of the country and the search for an access to the waterways of the world made the Russians repeatedly concerned with the Baltic, the Black Sea, and the Straits. Climate and vegetation basically affected the distribution of people in Russia and also their occupations. The poor quality of much agricultural land has led to endemic suffering among Russian peasants and has taxed the ingenuity of tsarist, Soviet, and post-Soviet ministers alike. Russian natural resources, since they began to be developed on a large scale, have added immeasurably to Soviet strength. Both the wealth of Russia and the geographic and climatic obstacles to a utilization of this wealth have remained a challenge even to the present.

The location of Russia on its two continents has had a profound impact on Russian history. The southern Russian steppe in particular served for centuries as the highway for Asiatic nomads to burst into Europe. Mongol devastation was for the Russians only the most notable incident in a long series, and it was followed by over 200 years of Mongol rule. In effect, the steppe frontier, open for centuries, contributed hugely to the militarization of Russian society, a trend reinforced by the generally unprotected and fluid nature of the western border of the country. But proximity to Asian lands led also to some less war-like contacts; furthermore, it enabled Russia later in turn to expand grandly in Asia without the need first to rule the high seas. The Eurasian school of historians, represented in the English language especially by George Vernadsky, tried to interpret the entire development of Russia in terms of its unique position in the Old World, as have neo-Eurasianists today.

Russian location in Europe may well be regarded as even more important than its connections with Asia. Linked to the West by language, religion, and basic culture, the Russians nevertheless suffered the usual fate of border peoples: invasion from the outside, relative isolation, and relative backwardness. Russia's location on the periphery of Europe, especially at a time when European power grew to dominate the globe, provided a challenge and a model, shaping Russia's emergence as both a nation and an empire. Hence, at least in part, the efforts to catch up, whether by means of Peter the Great's reforms or the Five-Year Plans or Yeltsin's "shock therapy." Hence also, among other things, the interminable debate concerning the nature and the significance of the relationship between Russia and the West.

As the preceding examples, which by no means exhaust the subject, indicate, geography does affect history. The influence of certain geographic factors tends to be especially persistent. Thus, while our modern scientific civilization does much to mitigate the impact of climate, a fact brilliantly illustrated in the development of such a northern country as Finland, so far we have not changed mountains into plains or created new seas, though some Soviet writers dreamed of just that. Still, it is best to conclude with a reservation: geography may set the stage for history; human beings make history.

# Chapter 2

# Russia before the Russians

We have only to study more closely than has been done the antiquities of South Russia during the period of migrations, i.e., from the fourth to the eighth century, to become aware of the uninterrupted evolution of Iranian culture in South Russia through these centuries....The Slavonic state of Kiev presents the same features...because the same cultural tradition—I mean the Graeco-Iranian—was the only tradition which was known to South Russia for centuries and which no German or Mongolian invaders were able to destroy.

MIKHAIL ROSTOVTZEFF

Yes, we are Scythians. Yes, we are Asiatics.
With slanting and greedy eyes.

ALEXANDER BLOK

Continuity is the very stuff of history. Although every historical event is unique, and every sequence of events, therefore, presents diversity, flux, and change, it is the connection of a given present with its past that makes the present meaningful and enables us to have history. The specifics of how we construct continuities, however, are arguments and are often controversial. The very title of this book, though seemingly straightforward, is an argument, for it groups many particular peoples, cultures, and histories under the heading "Russia"—including peoples speaking different languages and calling themselves by different names, some of whom would later, inspired by a consciousness of difference, win independence as nation-states and insist that their history is not Russian history. In contemporary Ukrainian and Polish historiography, for example, the tendency is to speak of the inhabitants of the Kievan Rus as Rus'ians or Ruthenians rather than as Russians. Other historians, too, warn that the term "Russia," read back historically into early times and extended geographically as far as the growing empire would reach, potentially obscures diversity and even legitimizes imperial domination. It is

## *Early Migrations*

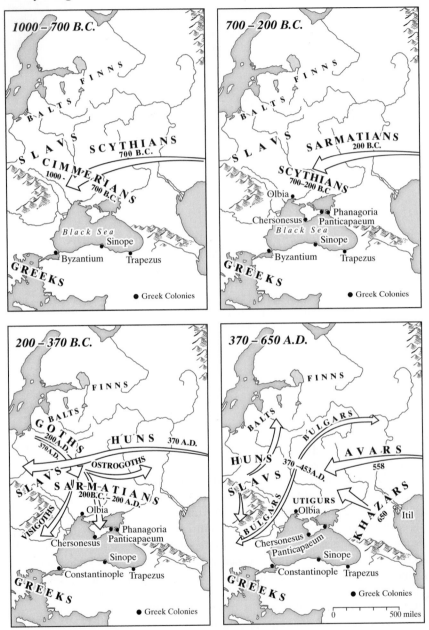

of considerable importance, as this chapter will show, that what came to be known as Russia emerged in a complex and shifting multiethnic space and would develop into a multiethnic empire. The history of Russia this book documents, therefore, cannot be the history of a simple "nation-state," though the role of Russians and ideas of Russian nationality would become powerful within it. But it is the job of the historian to seek both continuity and complexity. As such, this book, following long tradition, uses "Russia" very broadly in order to explore the continuities that comprise Russia's history. But we also insist on its persistent complexity and multiethnic diversity.

## Non-Slavic Peoples and Cultures

A number of ancient cultures developed in the huge territory that was to be enclosed within the boundaries of the USSR. Those that flourished in Transcaucasia and in Central Asia, however, exercised merely a peripheral influence on Russian history, the areas themselves becoming parts of the Russian state only in the nineteenth century and separating again in the late twentieth. As an introduction to Russian history proper, we must turn to the northern shore of the Black Sea and to the steppe beyond. These wide expanses remained for centuries on the border of the ancient world of Greece, Rome, and Byzantium. In fact, through the Greek colonies that began to appear in southern Russia from the seventh century before Christ and through commercial and cultural contacts in general, the peoples of the southern Russian steppe participated in classical civilization. Herodotus himself, who lived in the fifth century B.C., spent some time in the Greek colony of Olbia at the mouth of the Bug River and left us a valuable description of the steppe area and its population: Herodotus' account and other scattered and scarce contemporary evidence have been greatly augmented by excavations pursued first in tsarist Russia and subsequently, on an increased scale, in the Soviet Union. At present we know, at least in broad outline, the historical development of southern Russia before the establishment of the Kievan state. And we have come to appreciate the importance of this background for Russian history.

Archaeologists have documented hunter-gatherer communities on the Russian plain already in the upper Paleolithic Age (between 35,000 and 10,000 years ago), finding evidence of tools, weapons, mammoth-bone dwellings, jewelry, and art (possibly sacred). The Neolithic Age, beginning around 4,000 years before the Christian era, was a period of rich cultural development, especially in the valleys of the Dnieper, Bug, and Dniester rivers in the south. Its remnants testify to the fact that agriculture was then already entrenched in that area, and also to a struggle between the sedentary tillers of the soil and the invading nomads, a recurrent motif in southern Russian, and later Russian, history. This neolithic people also used domestic animals, engaged in weaving, and had a developed religion. The "pottery of spirals and meander" links it not only to the southern part of Central Europe, but also and especially, as Rostovtzeff insisted, to Asia Minor, although a precise connection is difficult to establish. At about the same time a culture utilizing metal developed in the Kuban valley north of the Caucasian range, contemporaneously with similar cultures in Egypt and Mesopotamia. Its artifacts of copper, gold, and silver, found in numerous burial mounds, testify to the skill and taste of its artisans. While the bronze age in southern Russia is relatively little known and poorly represented, that of iron coincided with, and apparently resulted from, new waves of invasion and the establishment of the first historic peoples in the southern Russian steppe.

The Cimmerians, about whom our information is very meager, are usually considered to be the earliest such people, again in large part thanks to Herodotus. They belonged to the Thracian subdivision of the Indo-European language family and ruled southern Russia from roughly 1000 B.C. to 700 B.C. At one time their dominion extended deep into the Caucasus. Recent historians have generally assumed that the Cimmerians represented the upper crust in southern Russia, while the bulk of the population consisted of indigenous elements who continued the steady development of culture on the northern shore of the Black Sea. The ruling group was to change several times during the subsequent centuries without destroying this fundamental cultural continuity.

The Scythians followed the Cimmerians, defeating them and destroying their state. The new invaders, who came from Central Asia, spoke an Iranian tongue and belonged thus to the Indo-European language family, although they apparently also included Mongol elements. They ruled southern Russia from the seventh to the end of the third century B.C. The Scythian sway extended, according to a contemporary, Herodotus, from the Danube to the Don and from the northern shore of the Black Sea inland for a distance traveled in the course of a twenty-day journey. At its greatest extent, the Scythian state stretched south of the Danube on its western flank and across the Caucasus and into Asia Minor on its eastern.

The Scythians were typical nomads: they lived in tentlike carriages dragged by oxen and counted their riches by the number of horses, which also served them as food. In war they formed excellent light cavalry, utilizing the saddle and fighting with bows and arrows and short swords. Their military tactics based on mobility and evasion proved so successful that even their great Iranian rivals, the mighty Persians, could not defeat them in their home territory. The Scythians established a strong military state in southern Russia and for over three centuries gave a considerable degree of stability to that area. Indigenous culture continued to develop, enriched by new contacts and opportunities. In particular, in spite of the nomadic and pastoral nature of the Scythians themselves, agriculture went on flourishing in the steppe north of the Black Sea. Herodotus who, in accordance with the general practice, referred to the entire population of the area as Scythian, distinguished, among other groups, not only "the royal Scythians," but also "the Scythian ploughmen."

The Scythians were finally defeated and replaced in southern Russia by the Sarmatians, another wave of Iranian-speaking nomads from Central Asia. The Sarmatian social organization and culture were akin to the Scythian, although some striking differences have been noted. Thus, while both peoples fought typically as cavalry, the Sarmatians used stirrups and armor, lances, and long swords in contrast to the light equipment of the Scythians. What is more important is that they apparently had little difficulty in adapting themselves to their new position as rulers of southern Russia and in fitting into the economy and the culture of the area. The famous Greek geographer Strabo, writing, in the first century A.D., mentions this continuity and in particular observes that the great east-west trade route through the southern Russian steppe remained open under the Sarmatians. The Sarmatians were divided into several tribes of which the Alans, it would seem, led in numbers and power. The Ossetians of today, a people living in the central Caucasus, are direct descendants of the Alans. The Sarmatian rule in southern Russia lasted from the end of the third century B.C. to the beginning of the third century A.D.

It was during the Scytho-Sarmatian period that the Graeco-Iranian culture developed on the northern shore of the Black Sea and in the Russian steppe. The Iranian element was represented in the first place by the Scythians and the Sarmatians themselves. They established large and lasting military states which provided the basic pattern of political organization for the area. They brought with them their languages, their customs, their religion emphasizing war, an original style in decorative art known as the Scythian animal style, and generally vigorous and varied art and craftsmanship, especially in metalwork. The enormously rich Greek civilization came to the area primarily through Greek colonies. These colonies began as fishing enterprises and grew into major commercial centers and flourishing communities. They included the already mentioned Olbia, founded as early as the middle of the seventh century B.C., Chersonesus in the Crimea near present-day Sevastopol, Tanais at the mouth of the Don, and Panticapaeum and Phanagoria on either side of the Strait of Kerch, which links the Sea of Azov to the Black Sea and separates the Crimea and the Caucasus. The Greeks engaged in varied trade, but especially significant was their importation of southern Russian grain into the Hellenic world. The settlements near the Strait of Kerch, enjoying a

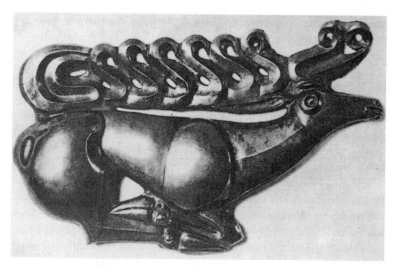

Scythian gold reindeer, sixth century B.C. Animal imagery was very strong in Scythian art and likely in their religion. (*Hermitage Museum*)

particularly favorable position for trade and defense, formed the nucleus of
the Bosporan kingdom which was to have a long and dramatic history. That
kingdom as well as other Greek centers in southern Russia fell in the first
century before Christ under the sway of Mithridates the Great of Pontus and,
after his ultimate defeat by the Romans, of Rome. Even after a retrenchment of
the Roman Empire and its eventual collapse, some former Greek colonies on
the northern shore of the Black Sea, such as Chersonesus, had another revival
as outposts of the Byzantine Empire.

Thus for many centuries the Iranians and the Greeks lived and worked
side by side. It has been noted that the Scythians and the Sarmatians made
no sustained effort to destroy Greek colonies in southern Russia, choosing
instead to maintain vigorous trade relations and other contacts with them.
Intermarriage, Hellenization of Iranians, and Iranization of Greeks proceeded
apace. The resulting cultural and at times political synthesis was such that
the two elements became inextricably intertwined. As Rostovtzeff explains
in regard to the Bosporan kingdom, a prize example of this symbiosis: "It is
a matter of great interest to trace the development of the new community. A
loosely knit confederation of cities and tribes in its beginning, it became gradually a political body of dual nature. The ruler of this body was for the Greeks
an elected magistrate, for the natives a king ruling by divine right." Today one
can readily appreciate some of the sweep and the glory of the ancient Graeco-
Iranian culture in southern Russia after visiting the appropriate rooms of the
Hermitage or of the historical museum in Moscow.

The Sarmatian rule in the steppe north of the Black Sea was shattered
by the Goths. These Germanic invaders came from the north, originally
from the Baltic area, reaching out in a southeasterly direction. In southern
Russia they split into the Visigoths and the Ostrogoths, and the latter eventually established under Hermanric a great state stretching from the Black Sea
to the Baltic. But the Gothic period in Russia, dated usually from A.D. 200 to
A.D. 370, ended abruptly with the appearance of new intruders from Asia, the
Huns. Furthermore, while the Goths proved themselves to be fine soldiers and
sailors, their general cultural level lagged considerably behind the culture of
southern Russia, to which they had little to contribute.

The Huns, who descended upon the Goths around A.D. 370, came in a mass
migration by the classic steppe road from Central Asia to southern Russia. A
remarkably mixed group when they appeared in European history, the Huns
were, on best evidence, a Turkic-speaking people supported by large Mongol
and Ugrian contingents. Later, as they swept into central and even western
Europe, they also brought with them different Germanic and Iranian elements
which they had overwhelmed and picked up on the way. Although one of the
most primitive peoples to come to southern Russia, the Huns had sufficient
drive and military prowess to conquer that area and, indeed, to play a key role
in the so-called period of great migrations in Europe. Even after their defeat in
the battle of Châlons, deep in France, in 451, they invaded Italy and, according
to tradition, spared Rome only because of the influence of Pope Leo I on their
leader, Attila. But with the sudden death of Attila in 453 the poorly organized

Hunnic state crumbled. Its successors included the large horde of the Bulgars and the smaller ones of the Utigurs and the Kutrigurs.

The next human wave to break into southern Russia consisted again of an Asian, Mongol- and Turkic-speaking, and relatively primitive people, the Avars. Their invasion is dated A.D. 558, and their state lasted for about a century in Russia and for over two and a half centuries altogether, at the end of which time it dissolved rapidly and virtually without trace, a common fate of fluid, politically rudimentary, and culturally weak nomadic empires. At the height of their power, the Avars ruled the entire area from eastern Russia to the Danubian plain, where they had their capital and where they remained after they had lost control in Russia. Avar armies threatened Byzantium, and they also waged major, although unsuccessful, wars against Charlemagne and his empire.

In the seventh century A.D. a new force emerged in southern Russia, to be more exact, on the lower Volga, in the northern Caucasus, and the southeastern Russian steppe in general: the Khazar state. The impact of the Khazars split the Bulgars sharply in two: one group definitely settled in the Balkans to dissolve in the Slavic mass and give its name to present-day Bulgaria; the other retreated to the northeast, eventually establishing a state at the confluence of the Volga and the Kama, with the town of Great Bulgar as its capital. The Utigurs and the Kutrigurs retrenched to the lands along the Sea of Azov and the mouth of the Don.

Although the Khazars were still another Turkic-speaking people from Asia, their historical role proved to be quite different from that of the Huns or of the Avars. To begin with, they fought bitter wars against the Arabs and served as a bulwark against the spread of Islam into Europe. When their own state assumed form in southeastern European Russia, it became notable for its commerce, its international connections, and the tolerance and enlightenment of its laws. Although a semi-nomadic people themselves, the Khazars promoted the building of towns, such as their capital of Itil—not far from the mouth of the Volga— Samandar, Sarkil, and certain others. The location at the crossroads of two continents proved to be of fundamental importance for the Khazar economy. In the words of a historian of the Khazars, Douglas Dunlop: "The prosperity of Khazaria evidently depended less on the resources of the country than on its favorable position across important trade-routes." The Khazar revenue, consequently, came especially from commercial imposts as well as from the tribute which increased as the Khazar rule expanded westward on the Russian plain. Pagans, Muslims, Christians, and Jews mingled in Khazaria, where all enjoyed considerable freedom and autonomy to live under their own laws. In the eighth and ninth centuries the Khazars themselves embraced Judaism, or at least their ruler, who bore the title of khagan, and the upper class did, thus adding another exceptional chapter to their unusual history. The Khazars have also been cited as one of the first peoples to institute a permanent paid armed force. The development of Khazaria, with its close links to the Arabic and Byzantine worlds, as well as to some other civilizations, its far-flung trade connections, and its general cosmopolitanism, well represents one line of political, economic, and cultural evolution on the great Russian plain at the time of the emergence of the Kievan state. It may be added that, while the Khazars were outstanding in commercial development, varied commercial intercourse on a large scale also grew farther north, in the country of the Volga Bulgars.

## The East Slavs

Cultures on the northern shore of the Black Sea and in the southern steppe, from the neolithic period to the time of the Khazars, form an essential part of the background of Kievan Rus. Yet it is true too that the people of the Kievan state who came to be known as the Rus or Russians were not Scythians, Greeks, or Khazars, much as they might have been influenced in one way or another by these and other predecessors and neighbors; they were overwhelmingly East Slavs. Therefore, East Slavs also demand our attention. The term itself is linguistic, as our better classifications of ancient peoples usually are. It refers to a group speaking the eastern variety of Slavic. With time, three distinct East Slavic languages developed: Great Russian, often called simply Russian; Ukrainian; and White Russian or Belorussian. Other branches of the Slavic languages are the West Slavic, including Polish and Czech, and the South Slavic, represented, for instance, by Bulgarian, Croatian, and Serbian. The Slavic languages, in turn, form a subdivision of the Indo-European language family that includes most of the tongues spoken today in Europe and some used in Asia.

Languages are organically and intrinsically related within the same subfamily and also within the same family. By contrast, no fundamental connection, as distinct from chance borrowing, has been firmly established between languages in different families, for example, the Indo-European and the Ural-Altaic. To explain the relatedness of the languages within a family and the much closer relationship in the languages of the same subfamily, scholars have postulated an original language and homeland for each family—such as for all Indo-European peoples whence they spread across Europe and parts of Asia—and later languages and homelands for different linguistic subfamilies before further separation and differentiation. Within the framework of this theory, the Slavs have usually been assigned a common homeland in the general area of the valley of the Vistula and the northern slopes of the Carpathians. Their split has been dated, by Alexei Shakhmatov and others, in the sixth century A.D., and the settlement by the East Slavs of the great plain of European Russia in the seventh, the eighth, and the ninth. It should be emphasized that in relying on original languages and their homelands one is dealing with languages, not races. The categories listed here are all linguistic, not racial, and do not necessarily correspond to any physical traits. Besides, intermarriage, conquest, imitation, as well as some other factors, have repeatedly changed the number and composition of those speaking a given language.

Recent scholarship has subjected the theory of original languages and homelands to a searching criticism. At present few specialists speak with any confidence about the historical homeland of the Indo-Europeans, and some reject it even as a theoretical concept. More important for students of Russian history, the Slavic homeland has also been thoroughly questioned. The revaluation has been largely instigated by discoveries of the presence of the Slavs at a much earlier time and over a much larger area in Russia than had been traditionally supposed. To meet new evidence, some scholars have redefined the original Slavic homeland to include parts of Russia. Others have postulated an earlier dispersal of the Slavs, some suggesting that it proceeded in several waves to explain both their ancient presence on the Russian plain and their later migration thither. Still others have given up the Slavic homeland altogether. While recent work concerning Slavic prehistory has produced many new facts, it has lacked a convincing general theory to replace that which has been found wanting.

The first extant written references to the Slavs belong to the classical writers early in our era, including Pliny the Elder and Tacitus. Important later accounts include those of the sixth century produced by the Byzantine historian Procopius and the Gothic Jordanes. The terms most frequently used to designate the Slavs were "Venedi" and "Antes," with the latter coming to mean the East Slavs—although "Antes" has also been given other interpretations, such as pre-Slavic Iranian inhabitants of southern Russia or Goths. Soviet archaeologists insist that Slavic settlements in parts of Russia, notably in the Don area, date at least from the middle of the first millennium B.C. It is now assumed by some historians that the Slavs composed a significant part, perhaps the bulk, of the population of southern and central Russia from the time of the Scythians. For instance, they may be hidden under various designations used by Herodotus, such as "Scythian ploughmen." It is known that the East Slavs fought against the Goths, were swept westward with the Huns, and were conquered by the Avars; certain East Slavic tribes were paying tribute to the Khazars at the dawn of Kievan history. At that time, according to our main written source, the Kievan *Primary Chronicle* of the early twelfth century, the East Slavs were divided into twelve tribes located on the broad expanses of the Russian plain, from the Black Sea, the Danube, and the Carpathian Mountains, across Ukraine, and beyond, northward to the Novgorod territory and eastward toward the Volga. Their neighbors included, in addition to some of the peoples already mentioned, Finnic elements scattered throughout northern and eastern Russia and Lithuanian tribes to the west.

By the ninth century A.D. East Slavic economy, society, and culture had already experienced a considerable development. Agriculture was well and widely established among the East Slavs. Other important occupations included fishing, hunting, apiculture, cattle raising, weaving, and pottery making, as well as other arts and crafts, such as carpentry. The East Slavs had known the use of iron for centuries. They had also been engaging in varied and far-flung commerce. They possessed a remarkable number of towns, some of which, such as Novgorod, Smolensk, and Kiev, a town belonging to the tribe of the Poliane, were to have long and important histories. Very little is known about the political organization of the East Slavs apart from a few scattered references to the rulers of the Antes and of some of the component tribes.

# CHAPTER 3

# The Origins of the Kievan State

They accordingly went overseas to the Varangian Russes.

*THE PRIMARY CHRONICLE*

The origins of the first state in Russian history, that of Kievan Rus, are exceedingly complex and controversial. Much of this early history exists in the foggy boundary zone between myth, legend, and verifiable fact. Central to this difficulty are our sources. Although archaeological evidence and a combination of textual sources—Latin, Byzantine, Islamic, and Slavic—have helped, we still depend a great deal on the *Tale of the Years of Time* (*Povest' vremennykh let*, also translated as *The Tale of Bygone Years*), more commonly known as the *Primary Chronicle*. Compiled by Kievan monks at the turn of the eleventh and twelfth centuries, this source is rich and colorful in narrative detail but, like the various texts it drew upon, is not restrained by modern notions of historical evidence. Even the dates of events, even their chronological order, are not all certain. More to the point, it was written from a distinct point of view and with distinct purposes, including, a close reading of the text would suggest, establishing a certain dynastic and territorial legitimacy for the ruling dynasty, creating a type of national history, and laying out ideal models for politics, society, and religion. Yet modern students of the subject, although they can by no means produce all the answers, should at least be able to avoid the cruder mistakes and oversimplifications of the past.

The first comprehensive, scholarly effort to explain the appearance of the Kievan state was made in the eighteenth century in terms of the so-called Norman theory. As formulated by Gottlieb Bayer, August Ludwig von Schlözer, and others, this view stressed the role of the Vikings from Scandinavia—that is, Norsemen, or, to follow the established usage in Russian historiography, Normans—in giving Russia government, cohesion, and, in large part, even culture. The Norman period of Russian history was thus postulated as the foundation for its subsequent evolution. In the course of over 200 years the Norman theory has been developed, modified, and changed by many prominent scholars. Other specialists, however, opposed it virtually from the very beginning, offering instead a dazzling variety of possibilities. More recently Soviet historians turned violently against it, and it remained largely out of bounds for Soviet scholarship until 1985 and *glasnost*.

In estimating the value of the Norman theory it is important to appreciate its drastic limitations in the field of culture. The original assertion of the Norman influence on Russia was made before the early history of southern Russia, outlined in the preceding chapter, had been discovered. With our present knowledge of that history there is no need to bring in the Norsemen to account for Kievan society and culture. What is more, Scandinavia itself, located in the far north, lay at that time much farther from cultural centers and crosscurrents than did the valley of the Dnieper. Not surprisingly, once the Kievan state emerged, its culture developed more richly and rapidly than that of its northern neighbor; whether we consider written literature and written law or coin stamping, we have to register their appearance in Kievan Rus a considerable time before their arrival in Scandinavia.

Detailed investigations of Scandinavian elements in Russian culture serve to emphasize their relative insignificance. Norman words in the Russian language, formerly supposed to be numerous, number actually only six or seven. Old Russian terms pertaining to navigation were often Greek, those dealing with trade, Asian or native Slavic, but not Scandinavian. Written literature in Kiev preceded written literature in Scandinavia, and it experienced clear Byzantine and Bulgarian rather than Nordic influences; under these circumstances, persistent efforts to link it to the Scandinavian epic fail to carry conviction. Claims of Norman contributions to Russian law have suffered a fiasco: while at one time scholars believed in the Scandinavian foundation of Russian jurisprudence, it has in fact proved impossible to trace elements of Kievan law back to Norman prototypes. Similarly, there is no sound evidence for Norman influence on Kievan paganism: Perun, the god of thunder and the chief deity of the East Slavic pantheon, far from being a copy of Thor, was described as the supreme divinity of the Antes by Procopius in the sixth century; a linguistic analysis of the names of East Slavic gods reveals a variety of cultural connections, but none of them with Scandinavia. Other assertions of Norman cultural influences, for instance, on the organization of the Kievan court or on Russian dress, tend to be vague and inconclusive, especially when compared to the massive impact of Byzantium and the tangible effects of some eastern cultures on Russia.

But, while the importance of Scandinavian culture for Russian culture no longer represents a major historical issue, the role of the Normans in the establishment of the Kievan state itself is on stronger ground, though remaining controversial. The question of the origin of the Kievan state is very closely connected with a group, tribe, or people known as the Rus, and it is also from the Rus that we derive the later name of the Russians. Almost everything connected with the Rus has become a subject of major controversy in Russian historiography. Under the year A.D. 862 the *Primary Chronicle* tells briefly about the arrival of the Rus following an invitation from the quarreling Slavic tribes of the Sloveni and the Krivichi and some Finnish tribes:

> They accordingly went overseas to the Varangian Russes: these particular Varangians were known as Russes, just as some are called Swedes, and others Normans, Angles, and Goths, for they were thus named. The Chuds, the Slavs and the Krivichians then said to the people of Rus, "Our whole land is great and rich, but there is no order in it. Come to rule and reign over us!" They thus selected three brothers, with their kinsfolk, who took with them all the Russes and migrated. The oldest, Rurik, located himself in Novgorod; the second, Sineus, in Byeloozero; and the third, Truvor, in Izborsk. On account of these Varangians, the district of Novgorod became known as the land of the Rus. The present inhabitants of Novgorod are descended from the Varangian race, but aforetime they were Slavs.*

The proponents of the Norman theory accepted the *Chronicle* verbatim, with the understanding that the Rus were a Scandinavian tribe or group, and proceeded to identify the *Rus-Ros-Rhos* of other sources with the Scandinavians. However, before long grave complications arose. A group called Rus could not be found in Scandinavia itself and were utterly unknown in the West. Although the *Chronicle* referred to Novgorod, *Rus* became identified with the Kievan state, and the very name came to designate the southern Russian state as distinct from the north, Novgorod included. Still more important was the discovery that the Rus had been known to some Byzantine and Asian writers before A.D. 862 and was evidently located in southern Russia. Finally, the *Primary Chronicle* itself came to be suspected and underwent a searching criticism.

As one of their first tasks, the supporters of the Norman view set out to find the Scandinavian origin of the name Rus. Their search, from the time of Schlözer to the present, has had mixed success at best. A number of derivations had to be abandoned. The deduction of *Rus* from the Finnish word for the Swedes, *Ruotsi,* developed by Vilhelm Thomsen and upheld by Adolph Stender-Petersen and others, seems linguistically acceptable, but it has been criticized as extremely complicated and unlikely on historical grounds.

One strong piece of evidence for Scandinavian influence, recent historians such as Jonathan Shepard have argued, is the *Bertinian Annals.* Written at the time, this text records under the year A.D. 839 the arrival from Byzantium at the court of Emperor Louis the Pious in Ingelheim of ambassadors calling themselves "Rhos" and identifying their king with the title of khagan. Suspicious that they were spies, Louis determined that they were actually "Swedes." Some historians have agreed, noting that although the odd usage of the title "khagan" might suggest Khazar rather than Norman influence, other evidence suggests that Scandinavian rulers might have adopted the title (along with other Khazar political practices) to bolster their power as they moved south

---

*We are using the standard English translation of the *Primary Chronicle* by Professor S. Cross (*The Russian Primary Chronicle, Laurentian Text.* Cambridge, Mass, 1930), although we are not entirely satisfied with it either in general or in this particular instance.

in search of silver and other sources of wealth and power. The early date has led some scholars to advance the hypothetical arrival of the Scandinavian Rus into Russia from A.D. 862 to "approximately A.D. 840." A slight change in the original chronology also enabled these specialists to regard as Scandinavian the Rus who staged an attack on Constantinople in A.D. 860 and who were described on that occasion by Patriarch Photius.

In the tenth century Bishop Liutprand of Cremona referred to the *Rusios* in his description of the neighbors of the Byzantine Empire. A controversy still continues as to whether Liutprand described his *Rusios* as Normans or merely as a northern people. Also in the tenth century the Byzantine emperor and scholar Constantine Porphyrogenitus gave the names of seven Dnieper rapids "in Slavic" and "in Russian." The "Russian" names, or at least most of them, can best be explained from Scandinavian languages. This evidence of "the language of the Rus" is rather baffling: there is no other mention of any Scandinavian tongue of the Rus; on the contrary, the *Chronicle* itself states that the Slavic and the Russian languages are one. The supporters of the Norman theory were quick to point to the Scandinavian names of the first Russian princes and of many of their followers listed in the treaties between Kievan Rus and Byzantium. Their opponents challenged their derivation of some of the names and stressed the fact that the treaties were written in Greek and in Slavic and that the Rus swore by Slavic gods.

Certain Arabic authors also mention and sometimes discuss and describe the Rus, but their statements have also been variously interpreted by different scholars. In general the Rus of the Arabic writers are a numerous people rather than a Viking detachment, "a tribe of the Slavs" according to Ibn-Khurdadhbih. The Rus had many towns, and its ruler bore the title of khagan. True, the Rus are often contrasted with the Slavs. The contrast, however, may refer simply to the difference between the Kievan Slavs and other Slavs to the north. Some of the customs of the Rus, described in Arabic sources, seem to be definitely Slavic rather than Norman: such are the posthumous marriage of bachelors and the suicide of wives following the death of their husbands. The Rus known to the Arabs lived most probably somewhere in southern Russia. Although Arabic writers refer primarily to the ninth century, the widespread and well-established relations of the Rus with the East at that time suggest an acquaintance of long standing.

Other evidence, it has been argued, also points to an early existence of the Rus in southern Russia. To mention only some of the disputed issues, the Rus, reportedly, attacked Surozh in the Crimea early in the ninth century and Amastris on the southern shore of the Black Sea between A.D. 820 and 842. Vernadsky derives the name of *Rus* from the Alanic tribe of the Roxolans. Other scholars have turned to topographic terms, ranging from the ancient word for Volga, *Rha,* to Slavic names for different rivers. An ingenious compromise hypothesis postulates both a Scandinavian and a southern derivation of *Rus-Ros* and the merger of the two.

The *Primary Chronicle,* a central source for the Norman theory, has been thoroughly analyzed and criticized by Shakhmatov and other specialists.

This criticism threw new light on the obvious inadequacies of its narrative and revealed further failings in it. The suspiciously peaceful establishment of Riurik and his brothers in northern Russia was related to similar Anglo-Saxon and other stories, in particular to a passage in Widukind's *Res gestae saxonicae*, to indicate, in the opinion of some scholars, the mythical character of the entire "invitation of the Varangians." Oleg's capture of Kiev in the name of Riurik's son Igor in A.D. 882, the starting point of Kievan history according to the *Chronicle*, also raised many issues. In particular it was noted that, due to considerations of age, Igor could hardly have been Riurik's son, and that no Kievan sources anterior to the *Primary Chronicle*, that is, until the early twelfth century, knew of Riurik, tracing instead the ancestry of Kievan princes only to Igor. Moreover, as we have noted, the *Chronicle* as a whole is no longer regarded as a naïve factual narrative. On the other hand, the proponents of the Norman theory argue plausibly that the *Chronicle* remains our best source concerning the origin of the Russian state, and that its story, although incorrect in many details, does on the whole faithfully reflect real events.

To sum up, the Norman theory can no longer be held in anything like its original scope. Most significantly, there is no reason to assert a fundamental Scandinavian influence on Kievan culture. But the supporters of the theory stand on a much firmer ground when they rely on archaeological, philological, and other evidence to substantiate the presence of the Normans in Russia in the ninth century, in pursuit of wealth and power. Shepard, for example, has concluded, based on both textual and archaeological evidence, that "what is certain is that by c. 838 some sort of political structure had been formed among the Rus," whom he calls "silver-seekers from the north," with a ruler based most likely in a fortified trading center near the mouth of Lake Ilmen. Only later in the century would the seat of this growing state shift to the Dnieper town of Kiev. The names of the first princes and of many of their followers in the treaties with Byzantium, along with material cultural evidence from archaeological sites, convince the majority of scholars today that the first Russian dynasty and their immediate retinue was Scandinavian. Another important variant, by the historian Omeljan Pritsak, rejects both the Normanist and Anti-Normanist positions as too simple and favors an interpretation of the "origins of Rus" as a "multiethnic and multilingual" social and economic entity involving Baltic, Mediterranean, eastern European, and other influences. Yet, even if we accept this view, it remains dangerous to interpret the role of the Vikings on the Russian plain by analogy with their much better known activities in Normandy or in Sicily. Historians can go beyond their evidence only at their own peril.

In any case, it is clear that structures of political authority (a "state") began to emerge in Russia in the ninth century, whether through internal evolution, outside intervention, or some combination of the two. Toward the end of that century, probably because of the lure of trade with Byzantium, the political and military locus of the Rus shifted toward the middle Dnieper, at which point we can begin to speak of the beginnings of a Kievan state and society.

# CHAPTER 4

# Kievan Rus: A Political Outline

In that city, in the city of Kiev....

THE FIRST LINE OF AN EPIC POEM

Kievan political history can be divided into three periods, though the boundaries are not precise. The first starts with Oleg's semi-legendary occupation of the city on the Dnieper in 882 and continues until 972 or 980. During that initial century of Kievan history, Kievan princes brought the different East Slavic tribes under their sway, successfully exploiting the position of Kiev on the famous road "from the Varangians to the Greeks"—that is, the very important trading route from the Scandinavian, Baltic, and Russian north of Europe to Constantinople—as well as connections with the inhabitants of both the forest and the steppe, and building up their domain into a major European state with wide regional ambitions. The second period, roughly 980 to 1054, was dominated by the reigns of two remarkable princes, St. Vladimir and Iaroslav the Wise. This was the period of Kiev's greatest development, prosperity, stability, and success. The third and last period of Kievan history was a history of decline and fall, though the precise dates are debated. Some scholars argue that the decline began with the passing of Iaroslav the Wise in 1054. Others date the "Golden Age" of Kievan Rus as extending through the reign of Vladimir Monomakh (1113–1125). There is even less consensus about the precise point at which foreign invasions, civil wars, and the general diminution in the significance of the city of Kiev brought this era to a close. One date, though, is particularly compelling: the year 1240, when Kiev, already a shadow of its former self in importance, was thoroughly destroyed by the Mongols, who established their dominion over conquered Russia. One more scholarly debate to mention: what we should call the Kievan state. Most scholars now prefer the archaic term "Rus" to the more modern "Russia," not only because Rus was the historical term, but also because it is a matter of intense dispute whether the Kievan state represents the early history of a *continuous* history of "Russia" or one of many separate histories of Slavic peoples in the region that would later be subsumed by an expanding Muscovite state. The use of the term "Rus" is also favored for emphasizing continuity with the history that preceded the establishment of a capital in Kiev.

## The Rise of the Kievan State

The city of Kiev was an East Slavic settlement probably ruled by the Khazars in the ninth century. According to the *Primary Chronicle,* a Varangian named Oleg occupied Kiev in 882, establishing it as the new capital, thus enabling closer connections with the important Byzantine markets. Since Oleg was not in the princely succession, he reigned in the name of Riurik's infant son Igor, who would take the throne after Oleg's death in 913. We can identify Oleg and Igor as historical figures, as opposed to largely legendary rulers like Riurik, but not unambiguously. As we noted in the previous chapter, many details are uncertain—including names, dates, and alleged relationships (in particular, historians strongly doubt that Igor had even been born in 882). What we do know is that Oleg was a key ruler in the early development and expansion of the Russian state. Assisted by his retainers, the *druzhina,* Oleg spread his rule from the territory of the Poliane to the areas of several neighboring East Slavic tribes. Some record of a subsequent bitter opposition of the Drevliane to this expansion has come down to our time; certain other tribes, it would seem, submitted with less struggle. Tribute became the main mark and form of their allegiance to Kiev. Still other tribes might have acted simply as associates of Oleg and his successor Igor in their various enterprises, without recognizing the supreme authority of Kiev. Toward the end of his life Oleg had gathered a sufficient force to undertake in 907 a successful campaign against Byzantium. Russian chronicles exaggerate Oleg's success and tell, among other things, the story of how he nailed his shield to the gates of Constantinople. Byzantine sources are strangely silent on the subject of Oleg's campaign. Yet some Russian victories seem probable, for in 911 Oleg obtained from Byzantium an extremely advantageous trade treaty.

Oleg's successor, Prince Igor, ruled Kievan Rus from 913 until his death in 945. Our knowledge of him comes from Greek and Latin, in addition to Russian, sources, and he stands out, by contrast with the semi-legendary Oleg, as a fully historical person. Igor had to fight the Drevliane as well as to maintain and spread Kievan authority in other East Slavic lands. That authority remained rather precarious, so that each new prince was forced to repeat in large part the work of his predecessor. In 941 Igor engaged in a major campaign against Constantinople and devastated its suburbs, but his fleet suffered defeat by the Byzantine navy which used the celebrated "Greek fire."* The war was finally terminated by the treaty of 944, the provisions of which

---

*The Greek fire was an incendiary compound projected through copper pipes by Byzantine sailors to set on fire the ships of their opponents. Its exact composition remains unknown.

were rather less favorable to the Rus than those of the preceding agreement of 911. In 943 the Rus campaigned successfully in the distant transcaspian provinces of Persia. Igor was killed by the Drevliane in 945 while collecting tribute in their land.

Oleg's and Igor's treaties with Byzantium deserve special attention. Their carefully worded and remarkably detailed provisions dealt with the sojourn of the Rus in Constantinople, Russian trade with its inhabitants, and the relations between the two states in general. What is clear is that connections with Byzantium were highly valued, especially as a source of trade—war was meant to protect and enhance these connections, not to alienate the Greeks. The allure of the "Byzantine connection," as historians have called it, likely motivated the Rus leaders to move their center to Kiev and would shape much subsequent foreign policy.

At the same time, inhabitants of the steppe continued to threaten the young Kievan state. The Khazar kingdom remained strong and the Kievan rulers were moving in on their domains—which meant threatening sources of tribute—leading to repeated armed conflicts. While Khazaria was a stabilized competitive force, Kiev was also threatened by various semi-nomadic tribes that pressed westward.

At the dawn of Kievan history, the Magyars, a nomadic horde speaking a Finno-Ugrian language and associated for a long time with the Khazar state, moved from the southern Russian steppe to enter, at the end of the ninth century, the Pannonian plain and lay the foundations for Hungary. But they were replaced and indeed in part pushed out of southern Russia by the next wave from the east, the ferocious and increasingly powerful Turkic Pechenegs or Patzinaks—in the mid-tenth century, Constantine Porphyrogenitus described "Patzinakia" as a vast realm "divided into eight provinces with the same number of great princes"—who began to carry out constant assaults on the Kievan state in the second half of the tenth century, after the decline of the Khazars.

Igor's sudden death at the hands of the Drevliane left his widow Olga in charge of the Kievan state, for their son Sviatoslav was still a boy. Olga rose to the occasion, ruling the land from 945 to about 962, becoming the first important female figure in Russian history. The *Primary Chronicle* focuses on Olga's devious and brutal revenge against the Drevliane; her persistent efforts to strengthen Kievan authority and collect tribute among other East Slavic tribes (again with much deviousness and brutality); her conversion to Christianity, possibly in 954 or 955; and her journey to Constantinople, possibly in 957, where she was received with great ceremony by the emperor Constantine Porphyrogenitus, who left us an account of her visit. Her visit helped strengthen political and commercial relations between Rus and Byzantium. Olga was also baptized there, although her personal conversion did not mean a conversion of her people, nor indeed of her son Sviatoslav—still, for her contribution in bringing Christianity to Russia she was later made a saint of the Orthodox church, "equal to the apostles."

The ten years of Sviatoslav's rule of Kievan Rus, 962 to 972, have been trenchantly called "the great adventure." If successful, the adventure might have given Russian history a new center on the Danube—we might then be writing a history of a quite different Danubian Rus with many consequences for the further course of Russian history. Even with their ultimate failure, Sviatoslav's daring campaigns and designs left their imprint all the way from Constantinople to the Volga and the Caspian Sea. Sviatoslav stands out in history as a classic warrior-prince, simple, severe, indefatigable, brave, sharing with his men uncounted hardships as well as continuous battles. He has been likened to the cossack hetmans and to the Viking captains as well as to leaders in other military traditions, and the cossack, if not the Viking, comparison has a point: Sviatoslav's appearance, dress, and manner of life all remind us of the steppe. In the words of the *Primary Chronicle*: "Upon his expeditions he carried with him neither wagons nor kettles, and boiled no meat, but cut off small strips of horseflesh, game, or beef, and ate it after roasting it on the coals. Nor did he have a tent, but he spread out a piece of saddle cloth under him, and set his saddle under his head."

In 964 Sviatoslav started out on a great eastern campaign, subjugating various Slavic, Finnic, and Turkic tribes; sacking the capital of the Volga Bulgars; and attacking the Khazar state. Sviatoslav's war against the powerful Khazars had a sweeping scope and impressive results: the Russians smashed the Khazar army; captured and sacked the Khazar capital, Itil; and took many key fortresses. Although the Khazar state lasted for another half century, it never recovered from these staggering blows. Sviatoslav returned to Kiev in 967. His remarkable eastern campaign completed the unification of the East Slavs around Kiev, attaching various groups to the southeast and bringing the entire flow of the Volga, and thus the great Volga–Caspian Sea trade route, under Kievan control. Yet the magnificent victory over the Khazars had its downside; it weakened decisively their effectiveness as a buffer against other eastern peoples, in particular the Pechenegs.

Sviatoslav's ambitions were also directed westward. In 968, the Byzantine emperor Nicephorus Phocas invited Sviatoslav to raid Bulgaria, offering payment in gold. Sviatoslav accepted and led a large army into the Balkans to attack the Bulgarian state in the Danubian valley. Once more the Russians achieved notable military successes, capturing the capital and taking prisoner their ruler Boris, although they had to interrupt the campaign to defeat the Pechenegs, who in 969, in the absence of Sviatoslav and his troops, had besieged Kiev. Sviatoslav, who thus came to control the territory from the Volga to the Danubian plain, began to imagine a vast Russian commonwealth—he assigned his sons to various cities—with its ruling center on the Danube. Russians were impressed by the fertility of the region but also by its strategic economic location. According to the *Chronicle,* Sviatoslav declared: "I do not care to remain in Kiev, but should prefer to live in Pereiaslavets on the Danube, since that is the center of my realm, where all riches are concentrated: gold, silks, wine, and various fruits from Greece, silver and horses from Hungary and Bohemia, and from Russia furs, wax, honey, and slaves." One can only speculate on the possible implications of such a change of capital for Russian history.

But the Byzantine state, still strong and ruled by the famous military leader Emperor John Tzimisces, thought the Russians were overstepping their bounds and threatening Byzantine control of the region. As Sviatoslav would not leave the Balkans, a bitter and fiercely fought war ensued in the spring of 971. By mid-summer, Sviatoslav was finally reduced to making peace with Byzantium on condition of abandoning the Balkans, as well as the Crimea, and promising not to challenge the Byzantine Empire in the future. On the other hand, Russia retained its right to continue to trade in Constantinople. On his way home, with a small retinue, Sviatoslav was intercepted and killed by the Pechenegs. Tradition has it that the Pecheneg khan had a gold-clad drinking cup made out of Sviatoslav's skull. The great adventure had come to its end. Sviatoslav's Balkan wars attract attention not only because of the issues involved but also because of the size of the contending armies and because of their place in military history; Byzantine sources indicate that Sviatoslav fought at the head of 60,000 troops, of whom 22,000 remained when peace was concluded.

After the death of his mother Olga in 969, Sviatoslav, constantly away with the army, entrusted the administration of the Kiev area to his eldest son Iaropolk, dispatched the second son Oleg to govern the territory of the Drevliane, and sent the third, the young Vladimir, with an older relative to manage Novgorod. A civil war among the brothers followed Sviatoslav's death. At first Iaropolk had the upper hand, Oleg perishing in the struggle and Vladimir escaping abroad. But in two years Vladimir returned and with foreign mercenaries and local support defeated and killed Iaropolk. About 980 he became the ruler of the entire Kievan realm.

*Vladimir, Sviatoslav's son.*

## Kiev at the Zenith

Vladimir, who reigned until 1015, continued on the path set by his predecessors but with some very important advances. First, he continued the political and military policies of establishing order and fealty to the Kievan state among the East Slavs, which had been badly shaken during the years of civil war, and expanding and defending Russian territory. He recovered Galician towns from Poland and, farther to the north, subdued the warlike Baltic tribe of the Iatviags, extending his domain in that area to the Baltic Sea. Vladimir also made a major and generally successful effort to contain the Pechenegs. He built fortresses and towns, brought settlers into the frontier districts, and managed to push the steppe border to two days, rather than a single day, of travel time from Kiev. Second, he established a more stable dynastic principle for ruling Kievan Rus, which would last for the next half a millennium. The Riurikid family (those who could claim descent from the legendary Riurik's recognized descendents) managed to establish itself as the only source of politically legitimate rule in Russia. Finally, and most famously, Vladimir's adoption of Christianity not only for himself but also the Rus state and society, had long lasting effects. As a prominent historian of Kievan Rus, Janet Martin, has recently summarized Vladimir's impact, his "policies thus laid

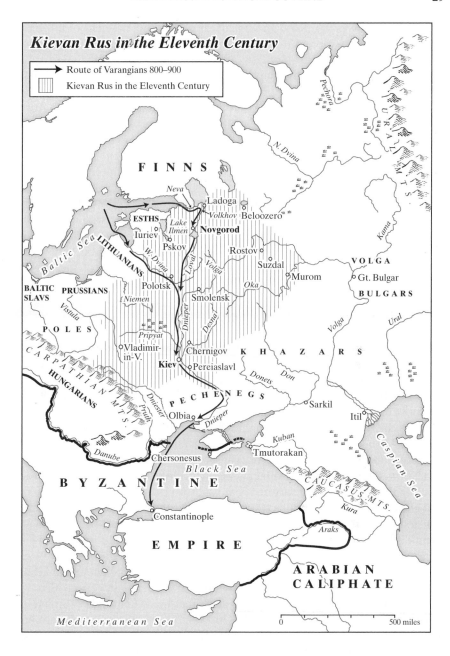

**Kievan Rus in the Eleventh Century**

→ Route of Varangians 800–900

▥ Kievan Rus in the Eleventh Century

the foundation for the transformation of his domain from a conglomeration of tribes, each of which separately paid tribute to him, into an integrated realm bound by a common religion and cultural ties as well as the political structure provided by a shared dynasty."

Vladimir's adoption of Christianity, historians conclude, was a political act, designed to integrate diverse peoples into a single society and to help legitimize his own reign and that of his dynasty with the help of a religion that emphasized one preeminent God to whom a prince might be compared and a church that allied itself with secular political authority. Christianization also facilitated further strengthening of the bonds with Byzantium. However, the significance of this choice long outlasted the specific political and cultural circumstances that led to the step. Interest in Christianity was not unprecedented among the Russians. In fact, there may even have been a Rus diocese of the Byzantine Church as early as 867, although not all scholars agree on this inference from a particular tantalizing passage in an early document Whether or not an early Christian Rus existed on the shores of the Sea of Azov, Kiev itself certainly experienced Christian influences before the time of Vladimir. A Christian church existed in Kiev in the reign of Igor, and we know that Olga, Vladimir's grandmother, became a Christian; Vladimir's brother Iaropolk has also been described as favorably inclined to Christianity. But it should be emphasized that Olga's conversion did not affect the pagan faith of her subjects and, furthermore, that, in the first part of the reign of Vladimir, Kievan Rus experienced a strong pagan revival. Vladimir's turnabout and the resulting "baptism of Russia" were accompanied by an intricate series of developments that has been given different explications and interpretations by scholars: Vladimir's military aid to Emperor Vasilii II of Byzantium, the siege and capture by the Rus of the Byzantine outpost of Chersonesus in the Crimea, and Vladimir's marriage to Anne, Vasilii II's sister. Whatever the exact import and motivation of these and certain other events, the Kievan Rus formally accepted Christianity from Constantinople in or around 988 and probably in or near Kiev, although some historians prefer Chersonesus.

The conversion of Kievan Rus to Christianity fits into a broad historical pattern. At about the same time similar conversions from paganism were taking place among some of the Baltic Slavs, and in Poland, Hungary, Denmark, and Norway. Christendom in effect was spreading rapidly across all of Europe. Nevertheless, it can well be argued that Vladimir's decision represented a real and extremely important choice. The legendary account of how the Russians selected their religion, spurning Islam because it prohibited alcohol—for "drink is the joy of the Russian"—and Judaism because it expressed the beliefs of a defeated people without a state, and opting for Byzantine liturgy and faith, contains a larger meaning: Rus did lie at cultural crossroads, and it had contacts not only with Byzantium and other Christian neighbors but also with the Muslim state of the Volga Bulgars and other more distant Muslims to the southeast as well as with the Jewish Khazars. But it was also consistent with a strong tendency, which we have already often seen, of Rus leaders looking more toward the west than the east. Thus, Vladimir and his associates chose to become the Eastern flank of Christendom rather than an extension into Europe of non-Christian civilizations. In doing so, they opened wide the gates for the highly developed Byzantine culture to enter their land. Kievan literature, art, law, manners, and customs experienced a fundamental impact of Byzantium. The most obvious result of the conversion was the appearance in Kievan Rus of the Christian Church itself, a new and extremely important institution which was to play a role similar to that of the Church in other parts of medieval Europe. But Christianity, as already indicated, remained by no means confined to the Church, permeating instead Kievan society and culture, a subject to which we shall return in later chapters. In politics too it gave the Kievan prince and state a stronger ideological basis, urging the unity of the country and at the same time emphasizing its links with Byzantium and with the Christian world as a whole. Francis Dvornik, Dimitri Obolensky, John Meyendorff, and many other scholars have given us a rich picture of the Byzantine heritage and of the Russian borrowing from it.

It must be kept in mind that Christianity came to Russia from Byzantium, not from Rome. Although at the time this distinction did not have its later significance and although the break between the Eastern and the Western Churches occurred only in 1054, the Russian allegiance to Byzantium determined or helped to determine much of the subsequent history of the country. It meant that Russia remained outside the Roman Catholic Church, and this in turn not only deprived Russia of what that Church itself had to offer, but also contributed in a major way to the relative isolation of Russia from the rest of Europe and its Latin civilization. It helped notably to inspire Russian suspicions of the West and the tragic enmity between the Russians and the Poles. On the other side, one can well argue that Vladimir's turn to Constantinople represented the richest and the most rewarding spiritual, cultural, and political choice that he could make at the time. Even the absence of Latinism and the emphasis on local languages had its advantages: it brought religion, in the form of a readily understandable Slavic rite, close to the people and gave a powerful impetus to the development of a national culture. In addition to being remembered as a mighty and successful ruler, Vladimir was canonized by the Church as the baptizer of the Russians, "equal to the apostles."

The violence that erupted between Vladimir's sons at the time of his death in 1015 revealed key weaknesses in the dynastic order Vladimir had established. While legitimacy was vested in the Riurikid family as a whole, its distribution among individuals and its structures of hierarchy and succession were not fixed. This system was made all the more unstable by the regional power of the princes. Vladimir had given each of his sons a regional base to ensure family control over tribute gathering. But this local source of strength and support combined with individual ambition within an ambiguous system of succession to undermine the ideal of orderly dynasticism. Initially, the eldest son, Sviatopolk, triumphed over several rivals and profited from strong Polish aid, only to be finally defeated in 1019 by another son, Iaroslav, who resumed the conflict from his base in Novgorod. Sviatopolk's traditional appelation in Russian history can be roughly translated as "the Damned," and his listed crimes—true or false, for Iaroslav was the ultimate victor—include the assassination of three of his brothers, Sviatoslav, Boris, and Gleb. The latter two became saints of the Orthodox Church.

The reign of Prince Iaroslav (1019–1054), known as Iaroslav the Wise, has been generally acclaimed as the high point of Kievan development and success, an age of stable political authority, a unified society, military security, economic prosperity, and the flowering of a new Russian Christian culture. In politics, at least, matters were more complex. Iaroslav had to contend with violent challenges to his authority by his brother Mstislav, with whom he was forced to divide the realm by an agreement of 1026. Only after the death of Mstislav in 1036 did Iaroslav become the ruler of the entire Kievan state. Indeed, it was really only when just one of Vladimir's sons remained alive and at liberty, namely Iaroslav, that we can speak of rulership as unified, secure, and stable. Besides fighting for his throne, Iaroslav had to suppress a whole series of local rebellions, ranging from a militant pagan revival in the Suzdal area to the uprisings of various Finnish and Lithuanian tribes. Success in establishing domestic order was matched by successful foreign wars, including an effort in 1031 to recover from Poland the southwestern section which that country had obtained in return for supporting Sviatopolk. By contrast, the campaign against Byzantium some twelve years later was unsuccessful and proved to be the last in the long sequence of Russian military undertakings against Constantinople. But especial significance attaches to Iaroslav's struggle with the attacking Pechenegs in 1037: the decisive Russian victory broke the might of the invaders and led to a quarter-century of relative peace on the steppe frontier, until the arrival from the east of new enemies, the Polovtsy.

At the time of Iaroslav the prestige of the Kievan state stood at its zenith; the state itself stretched from the Baltic to the Black Sea and from the mouth of the Oka River to the Carpathian Mountains, and the Kievan ruling family enjoyed close connections with many other reigning houses of Europe. Himself the husband of a Swedish princess, Iaroslav obtained the hands of three European princesses for three of his sons and married his three daughters to the kings of France, Hungary, and Norway; one of his sisters became the wife of the Polish king, another the wife of a Byzantine prince. Iaroslav offered asylum to exiled rulers and princes, such as the princes who fled from England and Hungary and St. Olaf, the king of Norway, with his son, and his cousin Harold Hardrada. It should be added that while the links with the rest of Europe were particularly numerous in the reign of Iaroslav, they were in general a rather common occurrence in Kievan Rus. Vernadsky has calculated, for instance, that six Kievan matrimonial alliances were established with Hungary, five with Bohemia, some fifteen with Poland, and at least eleven with Germany, or, to be more precise on the last point, at least six Russian princes had German wives, while "two German marquises, one count, one landgrave, and one emperor had Russian wives."

Iaroslav's great fame, however, rests more on his actions at home than on his activities in foreign relations. His name stands connected with an impressive religious revival and with Kievan law, education, architecture, and art. Iaroslav is credited with a major role in the dissemination and consolidation of Christianity in Russia. Rus was a province of the patriarchate of Constantinople—although there are some uncertainties and debates about the relations between the Russian Church and Byzantium in this period. The Church in Kiev was headed by a metropolitan, appointed or approved, as a rule, by Byzantium, and local districts were headed by bishops. As monasteries and churches were established, the numbers of monks and parish priests grew. The spread of bishoprics, monasteries, and local churches into the regions can be seen as a measure of the increasing success of Christianization among the population but also the reach of Kiev's political power, for the state and the Church spread together. Iaroslav's contributions were considerable. Notably, he had appointed the first native of Russia to serve as metropolitan, the able and educated Hilarion (c. 1051–1054). Most visibly, he supported the building of churches and monasteries on a large scale. From the moment of his sole rule, Iaroslav was determined to transform Kiev, especially through church construction, into a symbol of power and glory unrivaled in the Russian lands.

Iaroslav the Wise has the reputation also of a lawgiver, for he has generally been considered responsible for the first Russian legal code, *The Russian Justice* (*Russkaia Pravda*), an invaluable source for our knowledge of Kievan society and life. And he played a significant role in Kievan culture by such measures as his patronage of artists and architects and the establishment of a large school and a library in Kiev.

## The Decline and Fall of the Kievan State

Before his death Iaroslav assigned separate princedoms to his sons: Iziaslav, the eldest, received the Kiev and Novgorod areas; Sviatoslav, the second, the area centered on Chernigov; Vsevolod, the third, Pereiaslavl; Viacheslav, the fourth, Smolensk; and Igor, the fifth, Vladimir-in-Volynia—always with their surrounding territories. The princes, apparently, were expected to cooperate and to hold Kievan Rus together. Moreover, it would seem that when a vacancy occurred, they were to move up step by step, with the position in Kiev the summit. Some such moves did in fact take place, but the system—if indeed it can be called a system—quickly bogged down: Iaroslav's arrangement, based quite possibly on old clan concepts and relations still present in the ruling family, worked to break the natural link between a prince and his state, and it excluded sons from succession in favor of their uncles, their late father's brothers. Besides, with a constant increase in the number of princes, precise calculations of appropriate appointments became extremely difficult. At their meeting in Liubech in 1097 the princes agreed that the practice of succession from father to son should prevail. Yet the principle of rotation from brother to brother remained linked for a long time to the most important seat of all, that of the Grand Prince in Kiev.

The reigns of Iziaslav, Sviatoslav, and Vsevolod, the last of whom died in 1093, as well as that of Iziaslav's son Sviatopolk, who succeeded Vsevolod and ruled until his death in 1113, present a frightening record of virtually constant civil wars that failed to resolve with any degree of permanence the problem of political power in Kievan Rus. At the same time the Kievan state had to face a new major enemy, the Polovtsy, or the Cumans as they are known to Western authors. This latest wave of Turkic invaders from Asia had defeated the Pechenegs, pushing them toward the Danube, and had occupied the southeastern steppe. They attacked Kievan territory for the first time in 1061, and after that initial assault became a persistent threat to the security and even existence of Kievan Rus and a constant drain on its resources.

Although hard beset, the Kievan state had one more revival, under an outstanding ruler, Vladimir Monomakh. A son of Grand Prince Vsevolod, Vladimir Monomakh became prominent in the political life of the country long before he formally assumed the highest authority: he acted with and for his father in many matters and he took the lead at princely conferences, such as those of 1097 and 1100 to settle internecine disputes or that of 1103 to concert action in defense of the steppe border. Also, he played a major role in the actual fighting against the Polovtsy, obtaining perhaps his greatest victory over them, in 1111 at Salnitsa, before his elevation to the Kievan seat. As Grand Prince, that is, from 1113 until his death in 1125, Vladimir Monomakh fought virtually all the time. He waged war in Livonia, Finland, the land of the Volga Bulgars, and the Danubian area, repulsing the Poles and the Hungarians among others; but above all he campaigned against the Polovtsy. His remarkable *Testament* speaks of a grand total of eighty-three major campaigns and also of the killing of 200 Polovetsian princes; according to tradition, Polovetsian mothers used to scare their children with his name. Vladimir Monomakh distinguished himself as an effective and indefatigable organizer and administrator; a builder, for instance, possibly, of the town of Vladimir in the northeast on the river Kliazma, which was to become in two generations the seat of the grand prince; and also as a writer of note. Of special interest is his social legislation intended to help the poor, in particular the debtors.

Vladimir Monomakh was succeeded by his able and energetic son Mstislav (ruled 1125–32) and after him by another son, Iaropolk, who reigned until his death in 1139. But before long the Kievan seat became again the object of bitter contention and civil war that often followed the classic Kievan pattern of a struggle between uncles and nephews. In 1169 one of the contenders, Prince Andrew, or Andrei, Bogoliubskii of the northeastern principalities of Rostov and Suzdal, not only stormed and sacked Kiev but, after his victory in the civil war, transferred the capital to his favorite city of Vladimir. Andrew Bogoliubskii's action both represented the personal preference of the new grand prince and reflected a striking decline in importance of the city on the Dnieper. Kiev was sacked again in 1203. Finally, it suffered virtually complete destruction in 1240, at the hands of the Mongols.

## The Fall of Kiev: The Reasons

The decline and collapse of Kievan Rus have been interpreted in a number of different ways and ascribed to a number of factors. Indeed, many historians would question as overly simple phrases like "decline and fall," pointing instead to the century after the death of Vladimir Monomakh as a time of the rise and flourishing of local principalities, notably Volyn-Galicia to the west of

Kiev, and, to the northeast, Smolensk, Riazan, Vladimir-Suzdal, and Novgorod. While there was certainly rivalry and conflict as the rulers of these principalities sought to expand their territory and gain succession to the throne in Kiev, these regions were developing their own local interests and strengths. Many of these regions established independent relations with neighboring states and peoples, built commercial ties with neighbors and even more distant countries, and enjoyed a richly developing cultural life. One way to describe this, a view well developed by Soviet historians, emphasizes the loose nature of the Kievan state and its evolution in the direction of further decentralization and feudalism. In this interpretation, the Kievan state, very far from resembling its modern counterparts, represented in a sense a federation or association of a number of areas which could be effectively held together only for limited periods of time and by exceptionally able rulers. Huge distances and poor communications made the issue of centralization especially acute. Moreover, it is argued that Russia, as well as Europe in general, evolved toward natural economy, particularism, and feudalism. Therefore, the relatively slender unifying bonds dissolved, and Russia emerged as an aggregate of ten or twelve separate areas. We shall return to this view when we discuss the question of feudalism in Russia, and on other occasions. A related interpretation describes two opposing political trends existing simultaneously: on the one hand, the rise of powerful principalities and, on the other, the persistence of a sturdy dynastic structure in which Kiev remained the center of the realm—hence the fierce competition for its throne. In this light, it is worth keeping in mind the British historian Simon Franklin's argument that the very image of a Kievan "golden age" of political stability and unity was partly the invention of chroniclers who sought to idealize the accomplishments of their own prince, especially Iaroslav the Wise, or to highlight a Russia that was lost as the political order fragmented.

Soviet historians, as well as some other specialists, also pointed to social conflicts as a factor in the decline of Kiev. They refer in particular to the gradual enserfment of the peasants by the landlords and to the worsening position of the urban poor, as indicated by events at the time of Vladimir Monomakh. Slavery, which Kievan Rus inherited from earlier societies, has also been cited as an element of weakness.

Another essentially economic explanation of the fall of Kievan Rus stresses trade, or rather the destruction of trade. In its crude form it argues that the Kievan state arose on the great commercial route "from the Varangians to the Greeks," lived by it, and perished when it was cut. In a more limited and generally accepted version, the worsening of the Kievan position in international trade has been presented as one major factor in the decline of Kiev. The city on the Dnieper suffered from the change in trade routes which began in the eleventh century and resulted, largely through the activities of Italian merchants in the Mediterranean, in the establishment of closer connections between western and central Europe on the one hand and Byzantium and Asia Minor on the other, and a bypassing of Kiev. It was adversely affected by the Crusades, and in particular by the sacking of Constantinople by the

Crusaders in 1204, as well as by the decline of the Caliphate of Bagdad. The fact that certain Russian towns and areas, such as Smolensk and especially Novgorod, profited by the rearrangement of the commercial map of Europe and the rise of Italian and German cities only tended to make Kievan control over them less secure. Finally, Kiev experienced tremendous difficulty, and ultimately failed, in protecting from the steppe peoples the commercial line across the southern steppe to the Black Sea.

In addition to the economic and social analyses, one can turn to the political. A number of historians have placed much stress on the failure of the Kievan system of government which they consider a major, possibly decisive, cause of the collapse of Kievan Rus, rather than merely a reflection of more fundamental economic and social difficulties. There is a consensus that the Kievan princely political system did not function well, but no agreement as to the exact nature of that system. Of the two main interpretations, one considers it simply to be confusion worse confounded and a rule of force without broad agreement on principle, while the other gives full credence and weight to the practice of joint clan rule and of brother-to-brother rotation with such further provisions as the equation of the claims of the elder son of a prince to those of his father's third brother, his third uncle. In any case, the system did collapse in constant disputes and endemic internal strife. Mikhail Pogodin calculated that, of the 170 years following the death of Iaroslav the Wise witnessed civil war. Kievan princes have also been blamed for various faults and deficiencies and in particular for being too militant and adventurous and often lacking the more solid attributes of rulers. On this point it would seem, however, that their qualities in general were well suited to the age.

Towns added further complications to princely rule and princely relations. Towns in Kievan Rus had existed before princely authority appeared, and they represented, so to speak, a more fundamental level of political organization. As princely disputes increased and princely power declined, the towns proceeded to play an increasingly significant role in Kievan politics, especially in determining what prince would rule in a given town and area. The later evolution of Novgorod represents an extreme case of this Kievan political tendency.

At least one other factor must be mentioned: foreign pressure. While it can well be argued that Kievan economics, social relations, and politics all led to the collapse of the state, the fall of Kiev can also—perhaps paradoxically—be explained primarily in terms of outside aggression. For Kiev had to fight countless exhausting wars on many fronts, but above all in the southeast against the inhabitants of the steppe. The Pechenegs replaced the Khazars, and the Polovtsy the Pechenegs, but the fighting continued. After the Polovtsy and the Kievans virtually knocked each other out, the Mongols came to give the *coup de grâce.* In contrast to the wars of medieval Europe, these wars were waged on a mass scale with tremendous effort and destruction. It might be added that during the centuries of Kievan history the steppe had crept up on the forest, and deforestation has been cited as one development weakening the military defenses of Kiev. There exists an epic Russian tale about the destruction of the Russian land. It tells of the *bogatyri*, the mighty warriors of Kievan Rus, meeting the invaders head on. The bogatyri fought very hard; indeed they split their foes in two with the blows of their swords. But then each half would become whole, and the enemies kept pressing in ever-increasing numbers until they finally overwhelmed the Russians.

CHAPTER 5

# Kievan Rus: Economy, Society, Institutions

...merry-go-round, moving harmoniously and melodiously, full of joy.... This spirit permeates, this form marks everything that comes from Russia; such is our song itself, such is its tune, such is the organization of our Land.

KONSTANTIN AKSAKOV

The decisive factor in the process of feudalization proved to be the emergence of private ownership in land and the expropriation of the small farmer, who was turned into a feudal "tenant" of privately owned land, and his exploitation by economic or extra-economic compulsion.

PETR LIASHCHENKO

The traditional view of Kievan economy stresses the role of trade. Its classic document is an account of the activities of the Rus composed by the tenth-century Byzantine emperor and scholar Constantine Porphyrogenitus. Every November, writes Constantine Porphyrogenitus, the Kievan princes and their retainers went on a tour of the territories of different tributary Slavic tribes and lived on the fat of those lands during the winter. In April, after the ice on the Dnieper had broken, they returned, with the tribute, down the river to Kiev. In the meantime, Slavs, subject to the Rus, would fell trees, build boats, and in the spring, when rivers became navigable, take them to Kiev and sell them to the prince and his retinue. Having outfitted and loaded the boats, the Rus next moved down the Dnieper to Vitichev where they waited for more boats carrying goods from Novgorod, Smolensk, Liubech, Chernigov, and Vyshgorod to join them. Finally, the entire expedition proceeded down the Dnieper toward the Black Sea and Constantinople.

Kliuchevsky and other historians have expounded how this brief Byzantine narrative summarizes some of the most essential characteristics of Kievan Rus, and even, so to speak, its life cycle. The main concern of the prince and his retainers was to gather tribute from subject territories, either, as was just described, by visiting the different parts of the realm during the winter—a process called *poliudie* in Russian—or by having the tribute brought to them—*povoz*. The tribute in kind, which the prince obtained in his capacity as ruler and which consisted in particular of such items as furs, wax, and honey, formed the foundation of the commercial undertakings of the Rus. Slaves constituted another major commodity: the continuous expansion of the Kievan state connected with repeated wars enabled the prince constantly to acquire human chattel for foreign markets. The Kievan ruler thus acted as a merchant-prince on a grand scale. His retainers, the druzhina, emulated him as best they could: they helped him gather tribute in winter, and received their share of it, which they took for sale abroad with the great summer expedition of the Rus. Many other merchants from different parts of Kievan Rus with their merchandise joined the princely train to secure protection on the way and support for their interests at the end of the journey. The gathering of tribute, the construction of boats and their sale each spring near Kiev, the organization of the commercial convoy, and finally the expedition itself linked the entire population of the Dnieper basin, and even of Kievan Rus in the large, and constituted the indispensable economic foundation of the Kievan state. With regularity, coins from Byzantium or Bagdad found their way to the banks of the Oka or the Volkhov rivers.

Constantine Porphyrogenitus' account, it is further argued, explains also the foreign policy of the Rus which followed logically from their economic interests. The rulers in Kiev strove to gain foreign markets and to protect the lifelines of trade leading to those markets. The Kievan state depended above all on the great north-south commercial route "from the Varangians to the Greeks" which formed its main economic and political axis, and it perished with the blocking of this route. The famous Russian campaigns against Constantinople, in 860, under Oleg in 907, under Igor in 941 and 944, under Sviatoslav in 970, and in the reign of Iaroslav the Wise in 1043, demonstrate in an especially striking manner this synthesis between trade and foreign policy. Typically, wars began over such incidents as attacks on Russian merchants in Constantinople and ended with trade pacts. All the Russo-Byzantine treaties which have come down to us exhibit a commercial character. Furthermore, their provisions dealing with trade are both extremely detailed and juridically highly developed, constituting in fact an engaging chapter in the history of international relations and international law. Russian commercial interests, it may well be noted, obtained various advantages from these agreements; and they were considered in Constantinople not as private enterprise but as trade missions of the allied Kievan court.

Full evidence for a history of Kievan commerce goes, of course, far beyond the significant story of Russo-Byzantine relations. Its main points include trade routes and activities in southern Russia prior to the formation of the Kievan state, a subject expertly treated by Rostovtzeff and some other specialists. Attention must also be drawn to the widespread commercial enterprises of the East Slavs themselves long before the time of Oleg, as well as to the fact that at the dawn of Kievan history they already possessed many towns. Pavel Saveliev, for instance, estimates that the trade of the East Slavs with Asian peoples, which extended to the borders of China, dates at least from the seventh century A.D. Some Russian weights and measures were borrowed from the east, notably from Mesopotamia, while others came originally from Rome. Similarly, to the west at an early date the East Slavs established trade relations with their closer neighbors and also with some more remote European countries, like Scandinavia. With the flowering of the Kievan state, Russian trade continued to grow, and on an impressive scale. Its complexity and high degree of development find strong reflection, for example, in the eleventh-century legal code, *The Russian Justice*.

Whereas the traditional estimate of Kievan economy stresses commerce, more recent interpretations emphasize agriculture. Soviet historians, in particular, carefully delineated the early origin of agriculture in Russia and its great complexity and extent prior to as well as after the establishment of the Kievan state. In point of time, as mentioned earlier, agriculture in southern Russia goes back to the Scythian ploughmen and even to a neolithic civilization of the fourth millennium before Christ. The past of the East Slavs also testifies to their ancient and fundamental link with agriculture. For example, linguistic data indicate that from deep antiquity they were acquainted with various kinds of grains, vegetables, and agricultural tools and implements. Their pagan religion contained the cults of mother earth and the sun, and their different beliefs and rites connected with the agricultural cycle survived in certain aspects of the worship of the Virgin and of Saints Elijah, George, and Nicholas, among others. The East Slavic calendar had its months named after the tasks which an agricultural society living in a forest found it necessary to perform: the month when trees are cut down, the month when they dry, the month when burned trees turn to ashes, and so on. Archaeological finds similarly demonstrate the great antiquity and pervasiveness of agriculture among the East Slavs; in particular they include metallic agricultural implements and an enormous amount of various grains, often preserved in separate buildings.

Written sources offer further support of the case. "Products of the earth" were mentioned as early as the sixth century in a reference to the Antes. Slavic flax was reported on Central Asian markets in the ninth century, where it came to be known as "Russian silk." Kievan writings illustrate the central position of agriculture in Kievan life. Bread emerges as the principal food of people, oats of horses. Bread and water represent the basic ration, much bread is associated with abundance, while a drought means a calamity. It should be noted that the Kievan Rus knew the difference between winter grain and spring grain. The *Russian Justice*, for all its concern with trade, also laid extremely heavy penalties for moving field boundaries. Tribute and taxes too, while sometimes paid in furs, were more generally connected to the "plough" as the basic unit, which probably referred to a certain amount of cultivated land.

Boris Grekov and other Soviet historians argued further that this fundamental role of agriculture in Kievan economy determined the social character of the prince and his druzhina and indeed the class structure of Kievan society. They emphasized the connections of the prince and his retainers with the land, as shown in references to elaborate princely households, the spread of princely and druzhina estates throughout Kievan territory, and nicknames associated with the land. They considered that Kievan Rus was developing into a fully feudal society, in the definition of which they stressed the prevalence of manorial economy.

It can readily be seen that the evidence supporting the significance of trade in Kievan Rus and the evidence urging the importance of agriculture supplement, rather than cancel, each other. But the interrelationship of the two does present certain difficulties. One view holds that the bulk of the population supported itself by agriculture, whereas the prince and the upper class were mainly interested in trade. Other specialists stress the evolution in time, suggesting that, while Constantine Porphyrogenitus' account may be a valid guide for the middle of the tenth century, subsequent Kievan development tipped the scales increasingly in favor of agriculture. Indeed, it is mainly in the eleventh and twelfth centuries that we see princes, boyars, and members of their retinues claiming ownership of rural estates—though some scholars date the development of private ownership of land to earlier times.

Kievan exports, as has already been mentioned in the case of Byzantium, consisted primarily of raw materials, in particular furs, wax, and honey, and also, during the earlier part of Kievan history, of slaves. Other items for sale included flax, hemp, tow, burlap, hops, sheepskin, and hides. In return the Kievan Rus purchased such luxury goods as wines, silk fabrics, and objects of art from Byzantium, and spices, precious stones, and various fine fabrics from Asia. Byzantium also supplied naval stores, while Damask blades and superior horses came from the east. From the west the Kievan Rus imported certain manufactured goods, for instance textiles and glassware, as well as some metals and other items, such as Hungarian horses.

Russian merchants went abroad in many directions and foreign traders came in large numbers to Russia, where they established themselves, sometimes as separate communities, in Kiev, Novgorod, Smolensk, Suzdal, and other centers. The newcomers included Germans, Greeks, Armenians, Jews, Volga Bulgars, merchants from the Caucasus, and representatives of still other nationalities. Russian traders themselves were often organized in associations similar to Western guilds, not to mention less formal groupings. Financial transactions and commercial activity in general enjoyed a high level of development.

Internal trade, although less spectacular than foreign commerce, likewise dated from time immemorial and satisfied important needs. Kiev, Novgorod, and other leading towns served as its main centers, but it also spread widely throughout the land. Some of this domestic trade stemmed from the division of the country into the steppe and the forest, the grain-producing south and the grain-consuming north—a fact of profound significance throughout Russian history—and the resulting prerequisites for exchange.

Commerce led to a wide circulation of money. Originally furs were used as currency in the north and cattle in the south. But, beginning with the reign of St. Vladimir, Kievan minting began with, in particular, silver bars and coins. Foreign money too accumulated in considerable quantities in Kievan Rus.

Agriculture developed both in the steppe and in the forest. In the steppe it acquired an extensive, rather than intensive, character, the peasant cultivating new, good, and easily available land as his old field became less productive. In the forest a more complex process evolved. The trees had to be cut down—a process called *podseka*—and the ground prepared for sowing. Moreover, when the soil became exhausted, a new field could be obtained only after further hard work. Therefore, the *perelog* practice emerged: the cultivator utilized one part of his land and left the other fallow, alternating the two after a number of years. Eventually a regular two-field system grew out of the perelog, with the land divided into annually rotated halves. Toward the end of the Kievan period the three-field system appeared, marking a further important improvement in agriculture and a major increase in the intensity of cultivation: the holding came to be divided into three parts, one of which was sown under a spring grain crop, harvested in the autumn, another under a so-called winter grain crop, sown in the autumn and harvested in the summer; while the third was left fallow; the three parts were rotated in sequence each year. Agricultural implements improved with time; the East Slavs used a wooden plough as early as the eighth and even the seventh century A.D. Wheat formed the bulk of the produce in the south; rye, also barley and oats, in the north. With the evolution of the Kievan state, princes, boyars, and monasteries developed large-scale agriculture.

## Kievan Society

The bulk of the population, the so-called *smerdy*, were agricultural and rural. The majority of Kievan peasants seem to have been free at the dawn of Kievan history, and the free peasantry remained an important element throughout the evolution of the Kievan state. Free peasants lived in small communities, usually organized into territorial or clannic communes (*vervy* or *miry*). While not under the direct control of a prince or boyar, free peasants paid taxes or tribute. Various forms of bondage existed and increased over time. *Zakupy* were half-free peasants who had fallen into forced labor for a set period when they could not pay back a landlord's loan. At the bottom of the social pyramid were slaves—a condition that could be entered into by agreeing to work in a wealthy household, by selling oneself into slavery (often to pay a debt), by marrying a slave, and by birth.

As we have noted, Kievan society was also known for the great number and significance of towns and urban classes. Tikhomirov counted 89 towns in the eleventh century, 224 by the end of the twelfth, and nearly 300 at the time of the Mongol invasion—and he recognized that this was likely an underestimation. Many of these cities were impressively large. Scholars have estimated Kiev's population by the end of the twelfth century as between 40,000 and

Building Kiev. From a thirteenth-century illustrated manuscript. Note the indication of classes who command and classes who labor. *(University of Illinois Library)*

50,000 inhabitants, making the Rus capital comparable to Paris and London in that period. Novgorod may have had as many as 30,000 residents by the late twelfth century. At the top of urban society—and controlling Russian politics—stood the prince and the ever-increasing princely family with its numerous branches, followed by the prince's military retainers, the *druzhina*. The latter, divided according to their importance and function into the senior and the junior druzhina, together with the local aristocracy formed the upper class of the country, known in the *Russian Justice* and other documents of the time as the *muzhi*. With the evolution of the Kievan state, the prince's retainers, comprised of various ethnic groups, and the local Slavic nobility fused into a single group, which was to play an important role in Russian history under the name of the *boyars*.

The majority of the urban population, however, were *liudi* (Russian for "people"), mainly merchants, artisans, and laborers, and also differentiated into upper and lower strata. Because of the proliferation of towns and the urban economy in Kievan Rus, this middle class had considerable relative weight, more than its counterparts in other European countries at the time or in Russia in later periods. A special group consisted of people connected with the Church, both the clergy who married and had families and unmarried monks and nuns, together with others serving the huge ecclesiastical establishment in many different capacities. In addition to performing the fundamental religious functions, the Church operated hospitals and hostels, dispensed charity, and engaged in education, to mention only some of its activities. Finally, as part of the vitality of Kievan life, both urban and rural, were various groups living on the margins of established categories: criminals, minstrels (*skomorokhi*), freed slaves, freebooters, and others.

A measure of social status in Kievan society were the penalties for murder and injury in the *Russkaia Pravda*, translatable as both "Russian Justice" and "Russian Law," the Kievan compendium of East Slavic customary law and princely innovation. Many "injuries" involved physical insults to the dignity and honor of elites, such as cutting a man's beard or a slave striking a free man—as in other medieval societies honor was highly valued. All free men and women were protected to some degree, though the code clearly marked the higher value placed on men and elites. This is especially evident in monetary compensation that had to be paid to the kin of a murdered man (what in medieval England was called wergeld or bloodwite): 80 grivna for killing a member of the prince's druzhina, 40 grivna for a wealthy landowner or merchant, 5 grivna for a lower-class freeman. Free women in Kievan Rus had more rights than in many Western lands: they could own property and avenge insult (including rape), and their kin could claim a bloodwite—though fines for insult, injury, and death were only half that paid for men of their class.

## Kievan Institutions

The chief Kievan political institutions were the office of prince, the *duma* or council of the boyars, and the *veche* or town assembly, which have been linked, respectively, to the autocratic or monarchic, aristocratic, and democratic aspects of the Kievan state. While princes in Kievan Rus proliferated, the one in Kiev retained a special position. From the twelfth century he carried the title of the great, or grand, prince. Princely tasks included military leadership, the rendering of justice, and administration. In war the prince could rely first of all on his own druzhina, and after that on the regiments of important towns, and even, in case of need, on a mass levy. Kievan military history, as has already been mentioned, proved to be unusually rich, and the organization and experience of Kievan armies left a legacy for later ages.

In both justice and administration the prince occupied the key position. Yet he had to work with elected as well as his own appointed officials and in general coordinate his efforts with the local elements. To repeat a point made earlier, princely government came relatively late and had to be superimposed on rather well-developed local institutions, notably so in towns. The *Russian Justice* illustrates this complex relationship. In part the law, introduced by Iaroslav the Wise and developed through several versions until its most stable form in the thirteenth century, codified existing customary practices, but it also changed as society developed and as the power of the princes grew. A sign of the state's growing power to manage society can be seen in the changing responses to murder in the code: the earliest versions of the law endorsed the custom of violent revenge, while later editions, seeking to minimize societal violence and disorder, replaced this with fines. As we have partly seen, the law indicates a relatively high development of Kievan society, especially in the fields of trade and finance. It has also attracted attention for the remarkable mildness of its punishments, including a reliance on fines in preference to the death penalty. Canon law came with Christianity from Byzantium. Especially as the number of dioceses increased during the eleventh and twelfth centuries, Church courts had increasingly effective jurisdiction over sexual behavior, marriage, and family matters as well as particular matters involving religion and the Church—including the continual struggle against pagan priests, sorcerers, and folk healers.

The boyar duma developed, it would seem, from consultations and the joint work of the prince and his immediate retinue, the senior druzhina. It expanded with the evolution of Kievan Rus, reflecting the rise of the boyar class and also such developments as the conversion of Russia to Christianity, for the higher clergy found a place in the duma. While it would be quite incorrect to consider the boyar duma as analogous to a parliament—although it might be compared to its immediate predecessor, the *curia regis*—or even to claim for it a definite legal limitation of princely power, it remained an extremely important institution in its customary capacity as the constant adviser and collaborator of the prince. We know of a few occasions when the senior druzhina refused to follow the prince because he had failed to consult it.

Finally, the democratic element in the Kievan state found a certain expression in the veche or town meeting similar to the assemblies of freemen in the "barbarian" kingdoms of the West. All heads of households could participate in these gatherings, held usually in the market place and called to decide such basic issues as war and peace, emergency legislation, and conflicts with the prince or between princes. The frequently unruly veche practice of decision by unanimity can be described as an application of direct democracy, ignoring such principles as representation and majority rule. The veche derived from prehistoric times and thus preceded princely authority with which it never became fully coordinated. In the Kievan period, the veche in Kiev itself played an especially significant role, but there were other vecha in action all over Russia. In fact, the most far-reaching development of this institution was to occur a little later in Novgorod.

# CHAPTER 6

# Kievan Rus: Religion and Culture

Old customs and beliefs have left but the slightest trace in the documents of the earlier period, and no systematic attempt to record the national epic was made until the middle of the nineteenth century. Moreover, it is generally admitted that the survival of folklore has suffered important modifications in the course of time. Under these conditions any attempt to present a comprehensive survey of Russian cultural developments previous to the seventeenth century meets with insurmountable obstacles and is necessarily incomplete and one-sided. The sources have preserved merely the Christian literature, while the bulk of the national epic has been irretrievably lost....The early literary efforts of native origin were hardly more than slavish imitations of the Byzantine patterns.

MICHAEL FLORINSKY

Yet, Kievan Russia, like the golden days of childhood, was never dimmed in the memory of the Russian nation. In the pure fountain of her literary works anyone who wills can quench his religious thirst; in her venerable authors he can find his guide through the complexities of the modern world. Kievan Christianity has the same value for the Russian religious mind as Pushkin for the artistic sense: that of a standard, a golden measure, a royal way.

GEORGE FEDOTOV

It would be difficult to underestimate the importance of religion in Russian life, even before the momentous conversion to Christianity starting in the late tenth century. The pre-Christian East Slavic culture that Christians would call "pagan" was a deeply spiritual and mystical culture, and its influence would not entirely vanish with the rise of Christianity. A richly varied set of beliefs and practices, combining various Indo-European influences, included a cult of the dead (especially of ancestors), a view of the natural world as filled with gods and spirits, and a fluid sense of the boundaries between humans, animals, and nature. Early folklore often compared men to animals or plants, treated nature as a human-like force, and held particular reverence for "moist mother earth." Although East Slavic paganism lacked elaborate organization or institutional development, there is evidence of open air religious sites— especially marked by statues of gods atop hills (according to the *Chronicle* it was precisely these that Prince Vladimir demolished, having the statues of gods dragged to the river and beaten), where worship may have been led by priests. And we know of a large pantheon of deities, many with parallels in other Indo-European cultures, including some with similar names, such as Svarog, a god of the heavens, fire, and light; Dazhbog, a sun god; and Perun, a god of thunder and lightning. Unlike Greek or Roman paganism, however, gods were less powerful and influential than mysterious forces closer to home: the natural world and the living and the dead.

The question of the persistence of paganism after Christianization has long been a source of controversy. Some historians, notably Church historians, have declared that the new religion for centuries retained only a superficial hold on the masses, which remained stubbornly heathen in their true convictions and daily practices, incorporating many of their old superstitions into Christianity. Some scholars speak of *dvoeverie*, meaning a double faith, a term used originally by such religious leaders of the time as St. Theodosius to designate this troublesome phenomenon. Modern historians have tended to speak of syncretism rather than view Christianity as merely a superficial veneer over an essential paganism.

Kievan Christianity presents its own problems to the historian. Rich in content and relatively well known, it revealed the tremendous impact of its Byzantine origin and model as well as changes made to fit Russian circumstances. The resulting product has been both unduly praised as an organically Russian and generally superior type of Christianity and excessively blamed for its superficiality and derivative nature. In drawing a balance it should be made clear that in certain important respects Kievan Christianity could not even copy that of Byzantium, let alone surpass it. Thus theology and philosophy found little ground on which to grow in Kievan Rus and produced no major fruits. In fact, Kievan religious writings in general closely followed their Byzantine originals and made a minimal independent contribution to the Christian heritage. Mysticism too remained alien to Kievan soil. Yet in another sense Kievan Christianity did grow and develop on its own. It represented, after all, the religion of an entire, newly baptized people with its special attitudes, demands, and ethical and esthetic traditions. This Russification, so to speak, of Byzantine Christianity became gradually apparent in the emergence of Kievan saints, in the creative growth of church architecture and art, in the daily life of the Kievan Orthodox Church, and in its total influence on Russian society and culture.

Kievan saints, who, it might be added, were sometimes canonized with considerable delay and over pronounced opposition from Byzantium, which was apparently unwilling to accord too much luster to the young Russian Church, included, of course, Vladimir the baptizer of Russia, Olga the first Christian ruler of Kiev, and certain princes and religious leaders. Of these

princes, Boris and Gleb deserve special notice as reflecting both Kievan politics and in a sense—in their lives and canonization—Kievan mentality. As
mentioned before, the brothers, sons of St. Vladimir and his Bulgarian wife,
were murdered, allegedly, by their half-brother Sviatopolk, in the fratricidal
struggles preceding Iaroslav the Wise's accession to power. They were elevated to sainthood as innocent victims of civil war, but also, at least in the case
of Boris, because they preferred death to active participation in the deplorable conflict. St. Anthony, who lived approximately from 982 to 1073, and St.
Theodosius, who died in 1074, stand out among the canonized churchmen.
Both were monks and both are associated with the establishment of monasticism in Russia and with the creation and organization of the Monastery of
the Caves near Kiev. Yet they possessed unlike personalities, represented dis-
similar religious types, and left different impacts on Russian Christianity.
Anthony, who took his monastic vows on Mount Athos, and whose very name
recalled that of the founder of all monasticism, St. Anthony the Great, followed the classic path of asceticism and struggle for the salvation of one's soul.
His disciple, Theodosius, while extremely ascetic in his own life, made his
major contribution in developing the monastic community and in stressing
the social ideal of service to the needy, be they princes who required advice or
the hungry poor. The advice, if need be, could become an admonition or even
a denunciation. A number of St. Theodosius' writings on different subjects
have been preserved. Following the lead and the organizational pattern of the
Monastery of the Caves near Kiev, monasteries spread throughout the land,
although in Kievan Rus, in contrast to later periods of Russian history, they
clustered in and near towns.

At the end of the Kievan period the Russian Church, headed by the metropolitan in Kiev, encompassed sixteen dioceses, a doubling from St. Vladimir's
original eight. Two of them had the status of archbishoprics. The Russian
metropolitan and Church remained under the jurisdiction of the patriarch
of Constantinople. In the days of Kiev only two metropolitans are known
to have been Russians, Hilarion in the eleventh century and Clement in the
twelfth; especially at first, many bishops also came from Byzantium. The link
with Byzantium contributed to the strength and independence of the Russian
Church in its relations with the state. But in general the period witnessed a
remarkable cooperation, rather than conflict, between Church and state.

As already mentioned, the Church in Kievan Rus obtained vast holdings
of land and pre-empted such fields as charity, healing the sick, and sheltering
travelers, in addition to its specifically religious functions. Canon law extended
not only to those connected with the ecclesiastical establishment but, especially on issues of morality and proper religious observance, to the people at
large. The Church also occupied a central position, as we shall see, in Kievan
education, literature, and the arts. The overall impact of religion on Kievan
society and life is much more difficult to determine. Kievan Christianity has
been described, often in glowing terms, as peculiarly associated with a certain joyousness and affirmation of man and his works; as possessing a powerful cosmic sense and emphasizing the transfiguration of the entire universe,

perhaps under the influence of the closeness to nature of the pagan East Slavs; or as expressing in particular the kenotic element in Christianity, that is, the belief in the humble Christ and His sacrifice, in contrast to the Byzantine stress on God the Father, the ruler of heaven and earth. Whatever the validity of these and other similar evaluations of Kievan Christianity—and they seem to contain some truth in spite of the complexity of the issues involved and the limited and at times biased nature of our sources—Christian principles did affect life in Kievan Rus. Their influence can be richly illustrated from Kievan literature and especially its ethical norms, such as the striking concept of the good prince which emerges from Vladimir Monomakh's *Testament*, the constant emphasis on alms-giving in the writings of the period, and the sweeping endorsement of Christian standards of behavior.

## Language and Literature

The language of the Russians too was affected by their conversion to Christianity. The emergence among the Russians of a written language, using the Cyrillic alphabet, has been associated with the baptism of the country, the writing itself having been originally devised by St. Cyril and St. Methodius, the apostles to the Slavs, in the second half of the ninth century for the benefit of the Moravians. More precisely, the dominant view today is that St. Cyril invented the older Glagolithic alphabet and that the Cyrillic was a somewhat later development carried out by one of his disciples, probably in Bulgaria. While there exists some evidence, notably in the early treaties with Byzantium and in the fact that these treaties were translated into Slavic, that the Russians had been acquainted with writing before 988, the conversion firmly and permanently established the written language in Russia. To repeat, the liturgy itself, as well as the lesser services of the Church and its other activities, were conducted in Church Slavonic, readily understandable to the people, not in Greek, nor in Latin as in the West. A written literature based on the religious observances grew quickly and before long embraced other fields as well.

Kievan literature reached from oral creations to written works by particular authors or (mainly religious) communities, and from secular to sacred texts, though the boundaries could blur. Although it is likely that the great bulk of Kievan folklore has been lost, enough remains to demonstrate its richness and variety. This folklore was often very ancient but continued to develop in order to incorporate new Kievan experiences. Ritual songs to accompany agricultural work, festivals and holidays (both pagan and Christian), and especially life-cycle events such as marriage, childbirth, and death were very common and reveal much about everyday practices and attitudes. Wedding songs, for example, describe various conditions of becoming a bride: by consent, by purchase, by kidnapping. Kievan folklore also included folktales, sayings, proverbs, and riddles of different kinds.

Special interest attaches to the epic poems, the famous *byliny*. They represent one of the several great epic cycles of Western literature, comparable in many ways to the Homeric epic of the Greeks, or to the Serbian epic. The byliny narrate the activities of the bogatyri, the mighty warriors of ancient Russia, who can be divided into two categories: a few senior bogatyri and the more numerous junior ones. Members of the first group, concerning whom little information remains, belong to hoary antiquity, overlap with or even become part of mythology, and seem often to be associated with forces or phenomena of nature. The junior Kievan bogatyri, about whom we possess some 400 epic songs, reflect Kievan history much better, although their deeds too usually belong to the realm of the fantastic and the miraculous. Typically, they form the entourage of St. Vladimir, at whose court many byliny begin and end. They are always ready, and powerfully able, to defend the prince and the Russian land. But they are also not afraid to speak frankly to him and even abuse him for wrongdoing. They also tend to be less disciplined soldiers than rugged individualists. Above all, they fight the enemies of Rus. The Jewish Khazars may appear in the person of the legendary Zhidovin, the Jew, who is viewed with contempt; or Tugor Khan of the Polovtsy may become the dragon Tugarin. The junior bogatyri express the peculiarly Kievan mixture of a certain kind of knighthood, Christianity, and the unremitting struggle against the steppe peoples.

Ilia of Murom, Dobrynia Nikitych, and Alesha Popovich stand out as the favorite heroes of the epic. Ilia of Murom, the mightiest of them and in many respects the most interesting, is depicted as an invalid peasant who started on his great career of defending Kievan Rus against its enemies only at the age of thirty-three after a miraculous cure: his tremendous military exploits do not deprive him of a high moral sense and indeed combine with an unwillingness to fight, except as a last resort. If Ilia of Murom represents the rural masses of Kiev, Dobrynia Nikitych belongs clearly to the upper stratum: his bearing and manners strike a different note than those of the peasant warrior, and in fact he, more than other bogatyri, has links to an actual historical figure, an uncle and associate of St. Vladimir. Alesha Popovich, as the patronymic indicates, comes from the clerical class; his characteristics include bragging, greediness, and a certain shrewdness that often enables him to defeat his opponents by means other than valor. In addition to the great Kievan cycle, we know of some Novgorod byliny that will be mentioned later in a discussion of that city-state and a few stray epic poems not fitting into any cycle, as well as the artistically much less valuable historical songs of the Moscow period.

Kievan written literature, as already noted, developed in close association with the conversion to Christianity. It contained Church service books, collections of Old Testament narratives, canonical and apocryphal, known as *Palaea* after the Greek word for Old Testament, sermons and other didactic works, hymns, and lives of saints. Among the more prominent pieces one might mention the hymns composed by St. Cyril of Turov; a collection of the lives of the saints of the Monastery of the Caves near Kiev, the so-called *Paterikon*; and the writings of Hilarion, a metropolitan in the reign of Iaroslav the Wise and a leading Kievan intellectual, who has been described by Fedotov as "the best theologian and preacher of all ancient Russia, the Muscovite period included."

Hilarion's best-known work, a sermon *On Law and Grace*, begins with a skillful comparison of the law of Moses and the grace of Christ, the Old and the New Testaments, and proceeds to a rhetorical account of the baptism of Russia and a paean of praise to St. Vladimir, the baptizer. It has often been cited as a fine expression of the joyously affirmative spirit of Kievan Christianity.

The chronicles of the period deserve special notice. As we have noted, the chronicles were frequently written by monks and reflected a distinct point of view: the legitimacy and virtue of the Kievan rulers as well as ideals about proper Christian rule. At the same time, the chronicles belong more with the historical than the religious literature—though they are a model of history writing that both records the basic facts about the past and frames the narrative in arguments about good and evil and how people *should* behave. The very important *Primary Chronicle*, to which we have often referred and which formed the basis of most later chronicles, strongly influenced how Russia's early history would be viewed. Praised by specialists for its richness of detail and realism, it also established legends and interpretations. In narrating the famous story of the calling of the Varangians, for example, the chronicle explains that before the Varangians brought "order" the natives "lived in a bestial fashion." Likewise, the *Primary Chronicle* idealizes Kievan princes for military prowess, learning, piety, and devotion to the greatness and honor of Russia and blames them for their "sins," especially the "shamefulness" of fighting one another rather than the country's enemies.

Perhaps the most remarkable and revealing work of secular literature was the *Lay of the Host of Igor* (*Slovo o polku Igoreve*, often more simply translated as the *Tale of Igor's Campaign*), a brilliant poetic account of the unsuccessful Russian campaign against the Polovtsy in 1185. Although a number of scholars over the years have argued that it was a modern forgery, most specialists continue to regard it as a genuine, if in certain respects unique, expression of Kievan culture and of a rich secular poetic language. It would influence many later texts. The narrative shifts from the battlefront to Kiev, where Grand Prince Sviatoslav learns of the disaster, and to Putivl, where Igor's wife Iaroslavna speaks her celebrated lament for her lost husband. The story concludes with Igor's escape from his captors and the joy of his return to Russia. Its unknown author eulogizes warriors and appeals for unity among the princes in the face of constant threats from the east—indeed, scholars have described a type of nationalism in the *Lay's* devotion to "the Rus land" and its struggle against enemies. The *Lay* is written in magnificent language which reproduces in haunting sounds the clang of battle or the rustle of the steppe; and it also deserves praise for its impressive imagery, its lyricism, the striking treatment of nature—in a sense animate and close to man—and the vividness, power, and passion with which it tells its tale.

## Architecture and Other Arts

If Kievan literature divides naturally into the oral or popular and the written, Kievan architecture can be classified on a somewhat parallel basis as wooden

Head of St. Peter of Alexandria, from the fresco in the Church of the Savior on the Nereditsa, Novgorod, 1197. *(Sovfoto)*

or stone. Wooden architecture, like folk poetry, stems from the prehistoric past of the East Slavs. Stone architecture and written literature were both associated with the conversion to Christianity, and both experienced a fundamental Byzantine influence. Yet they should by no means be dismissed for this reason as merely derivative, for, already in the days of Kiev, they had developed creatively in their new environment and produced valuable results. Borrowing and adapting, to be sure, form the very core of cultural history.

Because wood is highly combustible, no wooden structures survive from the Kievan period, but some two dozen of the stone churches of that age have come down to our times. Typically they follow their Byzantine models in their basic form, that of a cross composed of squares or rectangles, and in many other characteristics. But from the beginning they also incorporate such Russian attributes as the preference for several and even many cupolas and, especially in the north, thick walls, small windows, and steep roofs to withstand the inclement weather. The architects of the great churches of the Kievan age came from Byzantium and from other areas of Byzantine or partly Byzantine culture, such as the Slavic lands in the Balkans and certain sections of the Caucasus, but they also included native Russians.

Cathedral of St. Dmitrii, 1194–97, in Vladimir. Architecturally, the cathedral repeats the features of the Church of the Intercession on the Nerl but is more richly decorated. The interior contains carved stone reliefs of saints, birds, lions, panthers, and plants. *(Mrs. Henry Shapiro)*

The Cathedral of St. Sophia in Kiev, built in 1037 and the years following, has generally been considered the most splendid surviving monument of Kievan architecture. Modeled after a church in Constantinople and erected by Greek architects, it follows the form of a cross made of squares, with five apses on the eastern or sanctuary side, five naves, and thirteen cupolas. The sumptuous interior of the cathedral contains columns of porphyry, marble, and alabaster, as well as mosaics, frescoes, and other decoration. In Novgorod another majestic and luxurious Cathedral of St. Sophia—a favorite Byzantine dedication of churches to Christ as Wisdom—built by Greeks around 1052, became the center of the life of that city and territory. But still more outstanding from the artistic point of view, according to Igor Grabar, was the St. George Cathedral of the St. George Monastery near Novgorod. Erected by a Russian master, Peter, in 1119–30, this building with its three apses, three cupolas, and unornamented walls of white stone produces an unforgettable impression of grace, majesty, and simplicity.

The architecture of the Kievan period achieved especially striking results in the twelfth and the first half of the thirteenth century in the eastern part of the country, the Vladimir-Suzdal area, which became at that time also the political center of Russia. The churches of that region illustrate well the blending of the native tradition with the Romanesque style of the West together with certain Caucasian and, of course, Byzantine influences. The best remaining examples include the two cathedrals in Vladimir, that of the Assumption of Our Lady, which later became the prototype for the cathedral by the same name in the Moscow Kremlin, and that of St. Dmitrii; the Cathedral of St. George in Iuriev Polskii, with its marked native characteristics; and the church of the Intercession of Our Lady on the Nerl River, near Vladimir, which has often been cited as the highest achievement of ancient Russian architecture. Built in 1166–71 and representing a rectangle with three apses and a single cupola, it has attracted unstinting praise for harmony of design and grace of form and decoration.

Other forms of art also flourished in Kievan Rus, especially in connection with the churches. Mosaics and frescoes richly adorned St. Sophia in Kiev and other cathedrals and churches in the land. Icon-painting too came to Russia with Christianity from Byzantium. Although the Byzantine tradition dominated all these branches of art, and although many masters practicing in Russia came from Byzantium or the Balkans, a Russian school began gradually to emerge. It was to have a great future, especially in icon-painting, in which St. Alipii of the Monastery of the Caves and other Kievan pioneers started what has often been considered the most remarkable artistic development in Russian history. Fine Kievan work in illumination and miniatures in general, as well as in different decorative arts, has also come down to our time. By contrast, because of the negative attitude of the Eastern Church, sculpture proper was banned from the churches, the Russians and other Orthodox peoples being limited to miniature and relief sculpture. Reliefs, however, did develop, reaching the high point in the Cathedral of St. Dmitrii in Vladimir, which has more than a thousand relief pieces, and in the cathedral in Iuriev

Polskii. Popular entertainment, combining music and elementary theater, was provided by traveling performers, the *skomorokhi*, whom the Church tried continuously to suppress as immoral and as remnants of paganism.

## Education. Concluding Remarks

The scope and level of education in Kievan Rus remain controversial subjects, beclouded by unmeasured praise and excessive blame. On the positive side, it seems obvious that the Kievan culture outlined here could not have developed without an educated layer of society. Moreover, as Kliuchevsky, Dmitrii Chizhevsky, and others have emphasized, Kievan sources, such as the *Primary Chronicle* and Vladimir Monomakh's *Testament*, express a very high regard for learning. As to specific information, we have scattered reports of schools in Kiev and other towns, of monasteries fostering learning and the arts, and of princes who knew foreign languages, collected books, patronized scholars, and generally supported education and culture. Beyond that, discoveries centering on Novgorod indicate a considerable spread of literacy among artisans and other broad layers of townspeople, and even to some extent among the peasants in the countryside. Still it would appear that the bulk of the Kievan population, in particular the rural masses, remained illiterate.

Even a brief account of Kievan culture indicates the variety of foreign influences that it experienced and their importance for its evolution. First and foremost stands Byzantium, but it should not obscure other significant contributions. The complexity of the Kievan cultural heritage would become even more apparent had we space to discuss, for example, the links between the Kievan and the Iranian epic, the musical scales of the East Slavs and of certain Turkic tribes, or the development of ornamentation in Kiev with its Scythian, Byzantine, and Islamic motifs. In general, these influences stimulated, rather than stifled, native growth—or even made it possible. Kievan Rus had the good fortune of being situated on the crossroads, not the periphery, of culture.

Perhaps too much emphasis has been placed on the destruction of Kievan civilization and the loss of its unique qualities. True, Kievan Rus, like other societies, went down never to reappear. But it left a rich legacy of social and political institutions, of religion, language, and culture that we shall meet again and again as we study the history of Russia.

Part III

# APPANAGE RUSSIA

# Chapter 7

# Appanage Russia: Introduction

> The grass bends in sorrow, and the tree is bowed down to earth by woe. For already, brethren, a cheerless season has set in: already our strength has been swallowed up by the wilderness.... Victory of the princes over the infidels is gone, for now brother said to brother: "This is mine, and that is mine also," and the princes began to say of little things, "Lo! this is a great matter," and to forge discord against themselves. And on all sides the infidels were victoriously invading the Russian land.
>
> "THE LAY OF THE HOST OF IGOR"
> (S. CROSS'S TRANSLATION)

In studying the complex transitional age known as the appanage period, we must return to the question of continuities and the controversies that always accompany this topic. It has long been the argument of Russian historians, and of this book, that the institutions and the culture of Kievan Rus created bonds of unity that prevented this age of division and defeat, in particular during the dark first hundred years following the Mongol conquest, from becoming a historical rupture and end. These bonds include a common religion, language, literature, and art—though with numerous regional and local modifications—along with a rich heritage in the economy, society, and politics. The metropolitan in Kiev headed the Church of the entire realm, and the grand prince, also in Kiev, occupied the seat of the temporal power of the state. Both offices outlived by centuries the society that had created them and both remained of major significance in Russian history, in spite of a shift in their locale and competition for preference among different branches of the huge princely clan. No less important, the concept of one common "Russian land," so dear to Kievan writers and preachers, persisted and grew. Indeed, it has been argued, the Kievan legacy ensured a type of national survival of the Russians and made possible their future historical role. Admittedly, the powerful Moscow state that would emerge on the eastern European plain looked, and often was, strikingly different from its Kievan predecessor. Yet, for most

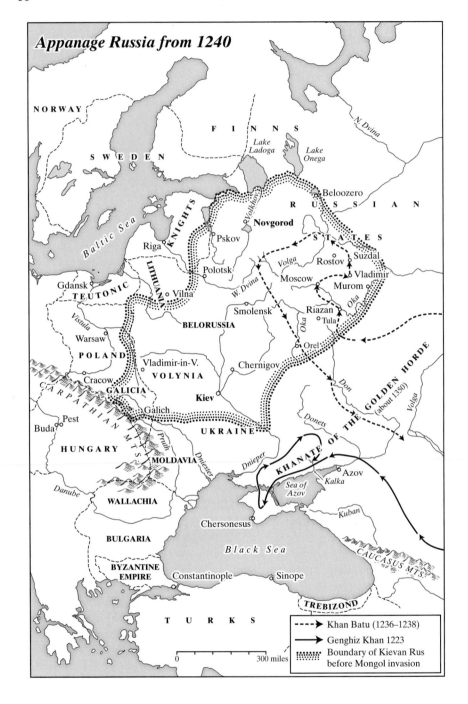

**Appanage Russia from 1240**

NORWAY

SWEDEN

FINNS

Lake Ladoga

Lake Onega

N. Dvina

RUSSIAN

Beloozero

KNIGHTS

Riga

Pskov

Novgorod

Volkhov

STATES

Polotsk

LITHUANIA

Vilna

W. Dvina

Volga

Rostov

Suzdal

Moscow

Vladimir

Murom

TEUTONIC

Gdansk

Vistula

Smolensk

Riazan

Oka

Tula

Oka

Warsaw

BELORUSSIA

POLAND

Vladimir-in-V.

VOLYNIA

Chernigov

Orel

Don

KHANATE OF THE GOLDEN HORDE
(about 1350)

Volga

Cracow

GALICIA

Galich

Kiev

Donets

CARPATHIAN MTS.

UKRAINE

Buda

Pest

HUNGARY

Prut

MOLDAVIA

Dnieper

KHANATE OF

Azov

Kalka

Danube

WALLACHIA

Dniester

Sea of Azov

Kuban

BULGARIA

Chersonesus

Black Sea

CAUCASUS MTS.

BYZANTINE EMPIRE

Constantinople

Sinope

TREBIZOND

TURKS

- - -▶ Khan Batu (1236–1238)
——▶ Genghiz Khan 1223
∙∙∙∙∙∙ Boundary of Kievan Rus
before Mongol invasion

0                300 miles

historians in any case, Muscovite Russia remains linked to Kievan Rus in many essential, as well as less essential, ways. And it affirmed and treasured at least a part of its Kievan inheritance. Critics, it bears noting, have seen a certain nationalist mythologizing in this narrative. Ukrainians, for example, see a different continuity: between Kievan Rus and their own emerging nation. And many historians today see the appanage era not only, or even mainly, as one of crisis and survival, but also one of transforming changes and of competition between alternative paths forward, each with their own inheritances in the Kievan past, out of which Moscow would prove dominant, crushing the others. A related perspective on the always thorny problem of historical periodization has been a growing tendency among historians to speak of the Kievan and appanage periods as "medieval Russia" and the establishment of the centralized Muscovite state as marking the beginning of the "early modern" period, thus deemphasizing the uniqueness of Russian developments in favor of comparability with broader European trends.

The twin terrors of Kievan Rus, internal division and invasion from abroad, prevailed in the age which followed the collapse of the Kievan state. The new period has been named after the *udel*, or appanage, the separate holding of an individual prince. And indeed appanages proliferated at that time. Typically, in his will a ruler would divide his principality among his sons, thus creating with a single act several new political entities. Subdivision followed upon subdivision, destroying the tenuous political unity of the land. As legal historians have emphasized, private law came to the fore at the expense of public law. The political life of the period corresponded to—some would say was determined by—the economic, which was dominated by agriculture and local consumption. Much Kievan trade, and in general a part of the variety and richness of the economy of Kievan Rus, disappeared.

The parceling of Russia in the appanage period combined with population shifts; a political, social, and economic regrouping; and even the emergence of new peoples. These processes began long before the final fall of Kiev, on the whole developing gradually. But their total impact on Russian history may well be considered revolutionary. As the struggle against the inhabitants of the steppe became more exhausting and as the fortunes of Kiev declined, migrants moved from the south to the southwest, the west, the north, and especially the northeast. The final terrible Mongol devastation of Kiev itself and southern Russia only helped to emphasize this development. The areas which gained in relative importance included Galicia and Volynia in the southwest, the Smolensk and Polotsk territories in the west, Novgorod with its huge holdings in the north, as well as the principalities of the northeast, notably Rostov, Suzdal, Vladimir, and eventually Moscow. Population movements led to a colonization of vast lands in the north and northeast of European Russia, although there too the continuity with the Kievan period persisted, for the new expansion radiated from such old Kievan centers as Novgorod, Rostov, and Suzdal.

Of special significance was the linguistic and ethnic differentiation of the Kievan Rus into three peoples: the Great Russians, usually referred to simply as Russian; the Ukrainians; and the Belorussians (or Belarusians) or White Russians. While certain differences among these groups go far back, the ultimate split was in part caused by the collapse of the Kievan state and the subsequent history of its population, in particular by the fact that southwestern and western Russia, where the Ukrainian and the Belorussian nationalities grew, experienced Lithuanian and Polish rule and influences, whereas virtually the entire territory of the Great Russians remained out of their reach.

Appanage Russia was characterized not only by internal division and differentiation but also by external weakness and, indeed, conquest. The Mongol domination over the Russians lasted from 1240 to 1380 or even 1480 depending on whether we include the period of a more or less nominal Mongol rule. But divided Russia became subject to aggression from numerous other quarters as well. As already mentioned, the western and southwestern parts of the country fell to the Lithuanians—whose state as we shall see represented in a sense a successor state to that of Kiev—and eventually fell to the Poles. Novgorod to the north had to fight constant wars against the German Knights, the Swedes, and the Norwegians, in addition to the Lithuanians. With the collapse of the Kievan state and the Mongol conquest, Russia lost its important international position, even though a few principalities, such as Novgorod, acted vigorously on the diplomatic stage. In general, in contrast to the earlier history of the country, a relative isolation from the rest of Europe became characteristic of appanage Russia, cut off from many former outside contacts and immersed in local problems and feuds. Isolation, together with political, social, and economic parochialism, led to stagnation and even regression, which can be seen in the political thought, the law, and most, although not all, fields of culture of the period. The exceptions, however, are also significant, including the development of alternative political models in Novgorod and other locations and a vital if conflicted resurgence in religious thought and art.

The equilibrium of appanage Russia proved to be unstable. The Russian economy would not permanently remain at the dead level of local agriculture. Politically, the weak appanage principalities constituted easy prey for the outside aggressor or even for the more able and ambitious in their own midst. Thus Lithuania and Poland obtained the western part of the country. In the rest, several states contended for leadership until the final victory of Moscow over its rivals. The successful Muscovite "gathering of Russia" marked the end of the appanage period and the dawn of a new age. Together with political unification came economic revival and steady, if slow, cultural progress, the entire development reversing the basic trends of the preceding centuries. The terminal date of the appanage period has been variously set at the accession to the Muscovite throne of Ivan III in 1462, or Vasilii III in 1505, or Ivan IV, the Terrible, in 1533. We shall adopt the last date.

# CHAPTER 8

# The Mongols and Russia

The churches of God they devastated, and in the holy altars they shed much blood. And no one in the town remained alive: all died equally and drank the single cup of death. There was no one here to moan, or cry—neither father and mother over children, nor children over father and mother; neither brother over brother, nor relatives over relatives—but all lay together dead. And all this occurred to us for our sins.

"THE TALE OF THE RAVAGE OF RIAZAN BY BATU"

And how could the Mongol influence on Russian life be considerable, when the Mongols lived far off, did not mix with the Russians, and came to Russia only to gather tribute or as an army, brought in for the most part by Russian princes for the princes' own purposes?...Therefore we can proceed to consider the internal life of Russian society in the thirteenth century without paying attention to the fact of the Mongol yoke....

SERGEI PLATONOV

A convenient method of gauging the extent of Mongol influence on Russia is to compare the Russian state and society of the pre-Mongol period with those of the post-Mongol era, and in particular to contrast the spirit and institutions of Muscovite Russia with those of Russia of the Kievan age....The picture changed completely after the Mongol period.

GEORGE VERNADSKY

The Mongols—or Tatars as they are called in Russian sources*—came upon the Russians like a bolt from the blue. They appeared suddenly in 1223 in

---

*"Tatars" referred originally to a Mongol tribe. But, with the expansion of the Mongol state, the Tatars of the Russian sources were mostly Turkic, rather than Mongol, linguistically and ethnically. We are using "Mongol" throughout in preference to "Tatar."

southeastern Russia and smashed the Russians and the Polovtsy in a battle near the river Kalka, only to vanish into the steppe. But they returned to conquer Russia, in 1237–40, and impose their long rule over it.

Unknown to the Russians, Mongolian-speaking tribes had lived for centuries in the general area of present-day Mongolia and in the adjoining parts of Manchuria and Siberia. The Chinese, who watched their northern neighbors closely, left us informative accounts of the Mongols. To quote one Chinese author:

...they are preoccupied exclusively with their flocks, they roam and they possess neither towns, nor walls, neither writing, nor books; they conclude all agreements orally. From childhood they practice riding and shooting arrows...and thus they acquire courage necessary for pillage and war. As long as they hope for success, they move back and forth; when there is no hope, a timely flight is not considered reprehensible. Religious rites and legal institutions they know not....They all feed on the meat of the animals which they kill...and they dress in their hides and furs. The strongest among them grab the fattest pieces; the old men, on the other hand, eat and drink what is left. They respect only the bravest; old age and feebleness are held in contempt.

While excellent fighters and warlike, the Mongols generally directed their efforts to fratricidal strife among the many tribes, their rivalries skillfully fanned by the Chinese. Only an extraordinary leader managed to unite the Mongols and suddenly transform them into a power of world significance. Temuchin, born probably in 1155 or 1162 and a son of a tribal chief, finally in 1206 after many years of desperate struggle became the head of all the Mongols with the title of Jenghiz Khan. One of the decisively important figures in history, Jenghiz Khan remains something of an enigma. It has been suggested that he was inspired by an urge to avenge the treasonable poisoning of his father and the subsequent humiliation of his family. With time, Jenghiz Khan apparently came to believe in his sweeping divine mission to re-establish justice on earth, and as in the case of some other great leaders, he seems to have had an unshakable conviction in the righteousness of his cause. The new Mongol ruler joined to this determination and sense of mission a remarkable intelligence and outstanding military, diplomatic, and administrative ability.

After uniting the Mongols, Jenghiz Khan subdued other neighboring tribes, and then in 1211 invaded the independent Chin Empire in northern China, piercing the Great Wall. What followed has been described as the conquest, in five years, of 100 million people by 100,000 soldiers. The western campaigns of Jenghiz Khan and his generals proved to be still more notable. In spite of bitter resistance, the Mongols smashed the Muslim states of Central Asia and reached the Caucasus. It was through Caucasian passes that they staged a raid into southern Russia to defeat the Russians and the Polovtsy on the river Kalka in 1223. Jenghiz Khan died in 1227. Before his death he had made provisions for succession, dividing the empire among four sons, although its substantial unity was to be preserved by the leadership of one of them with the title of "great khan," a position which fell to the third son, Ugedey. Jenghiz Khan's successors continued his sweeping conquests and spread Mongol rule to Turkestan, Armenia, Georgia, and other parts of the Caucasus, the state of the Volga Bulgars, Russia, Persia, Mesopotamia, Syria, Korea, and all of China. At the time of Kublai Khan, the founder of the Yuan dynasty in China who ruled as Great Khan from 1259 to 1294, Mongol dominion stretched from Poland and the Balkans to the Pacific and from the Arctic Ocean to Turkey, the Persian Gulf, and the southern borders of China. Moreover, the Mongols had penetrated deep into central Europe, defeating the Poles, the Germans, and the Hungarians in the process.

The remarkable success of Mongol armies can no longer be ascribed, as in the past, to overwhelming numbers. It stemmed rather from the effective strategy of the Mongols, their excellence as highly mobile cavalry, their endurance, and their disciplined and coordinated manner of fighting assisted by an organization which in certain ways resembled a modern general staff. These assets acquired particular importance because the military forces of the invaded countries, especially in Europe, were frequently cumbersome, undisciplined and uncoordinated. Espionage, terrorism, and superior siege equipment, borrowed from China and other lands, have also been cited as factors contributing to the amazing spread of Mongol rule. The Mongols held occupied territories with the aid of such devices as newly built roads, a courier system, and a crude census for purposes of taxation.

Batu, a grandson of Jenghiz Khan and a nephew of Ugedey, who succeeded his father Juchi to the greater part of Juchi's empire, directed the Mongol invasion of Europe. He had some 150,000 or 200,000 troops at his disposal and the veteran Subudey to serve as his chief general. The Mongols crossed the Urals in 1236 to attack first the Volga Bulgars. After that, in 1237, they struck at the Russian eastern principality of Riazan, coming unexpectedly from the north. In the Mongol strategy, the conquest of Russia served to secure their flank for a further major invasion of Europe. The Russian princes proved to be disunited and totally unprepared. Characteristically, many of them stayed to protect their own appanages rather than come to the aid of invaded principalities or make any joint effort. Following the defeat of a Russian army, the town of Riazan was besieged and captured after five days of bitter fighting and its entire population massacred. Next, in the winter of 1237/38, the Mongols attacked the Suzdal territory with its capital of Vladimir, the seat of the grand prince. The sequence of desperate fighting and massacre recurred on a larger scale and at many towns, the grand prince himself and his army perishing in the decisive battle near the river Sit. Thus, in a matter of several months, the Mongols succeeded in conquering the strongest section of the country. Furthermore, they attained their objectives by means of a winter campaign, the Mongol cavalry moving with great speed on frozen rivers—the only successful winter invasion of Russia in history. But a spring thaw that made the terrain virtually impassable forced the Mongols to abandon their advance on Novgorod and retreat to the southern steppe. They spent the next year and a half in preparation for a great campaign as well as in devastating and conquering some additional Russian territories, notably that of Chernigov.

The Mongol assault of 1240, continued in 1241 and the first part of 1242, aimed at more than Russia. In fact, it had been preceded by an order to the king of Hungary to submit to Mongol rule. The Mongols began by invading the Kievan area proper. Overcoming the stubborn defenders, they took Kiev by storm, exterminated the population, and leveled the city. The same fate befell other towns of the area, whose inhabitants either died or became slaves. After Kiev, the Mongols swept through the southwestern principalities of Galicia and Volynia, laying everything waste. Poland and Hungary came next. One Mongol army defeated the Poles and the Germans, the most important battle taking place at Liegnitz in Silesia in 1241, while another army smashed the Hungarians. Undeterred by the Carpathian Mountains, the Mongols occupied the Hungarian plain; their advance guard reached the Adriatic. Whereas campaigning in central Europe presented certain problems to the Mongols, particularly the need to reduce fortresses, many historians believe that only the death of Great Khan Ugedey saved a number of European countries. Concerned with internal Mongol politics, his nephew Batu decided to retrench; and in the spring of 1242 he withdrew his armies to the southern steppe, subjugating Bulgaria, Moldavia, and Wallachia on the way back. Although the Mongols thus retreated to the east, all of Russia, including the northwestern part that escaped direct conquest, remained under their sway.

Once this astonishing military campaign was concluded, the Mongol elite resumed, at least for part of each year, their nomadic and pastoral life. But rule of these vast lands also led to the establishment of new Mongol cities and the rebuilding of some Russian towns as administrative and commercial centers. Batu established his headquarters in the lower Volga area in what became the town of Old Sarai and the capital of the domain known as the Golden Horde. The Golden Horde constituted first a part of the Mongol Empire and later, as the central ties weakened, an independent state. A department in Old Sarai, headed by a *daruga*, handled Russian affairs. Cities like Old Sarai became cosmopolitan centers with growing numbers of officials, merchants, and craftsmen, as well as increasingly sedentary Mongol rulers. Along with the collection of tribute and taxes, local and international commerce became a key activity of the cities of the Golden Horde. By the reign of Khan Uzbeg (1313–41), the Golden Horde reached its zenith as a wealthy and powerful administrative and commercial state. Uzbeg also initiated the conversion of his people to Islam, which brought increasing ties to the larger Muslim world. Mongol dominion over Russia meant that the Russian rulers recognized the Mongol overlordship, that the Mongols, initially the great khan in Mongolia and subsequently the potentate of the Golden Horde, invested the Russian grand prince with his office, and that to be so invested the Russian prince had to journey to the Mongol headquarters and pay humble obeisance to his suzerain. Further, it meant that the Mongols collected tribute from the Russians, at first by means of their own agents and afterwards through the intermediacy of Russian princes. Also, the Russians occasionally had to send military detachments for the Mongol army. We know of several such levies and of Russians serving in the Mongol forces as far away from their homeland as China.

In general, although the Mongols interfered little in Russian life, they maintained an effective control over Russia for almost a century and a half, from 1240 to 1380. In 1380 the prince of Moscow Dmitrii succeeded in defeating the Mongols in a major battle on the field of Kulikovo. Although the Mongols managed to stage a comeback, their invincibility had been destroyed and their rule greatly weakened. Still, another century passed before the "Mongol yoke" was finally overthrown. Only in 1480 Ivan III of Moscow renounced his, and Russian, allegiance to the khan, and the Mongols failed to challenge his action seriously. Later yet, Russia expanded to absorb the successor states to the Golden Horde: the khanate of Kazan in 1552, of Astrakhan in 1556, and, at long last, that of Crimea in 1783.

## The Role of the Mongols in Russian History

The relationship between the Mongols and Russia, and the impact of Mongol rule on Russian history, has long been a topic of intense scholarly controversy. As the historian Donald Ostrowski commented in a recent review of the historiography, "on every major point, and most of the minor ones, there is ardent and passionate disagreement." Scholars argue about the reasons for Mongol success, the extent of the destruction, the nature of the Mongols and their rule, and especially the extent to which Mongols influenced Russian politics, society, and culture. The earliest interpretations, mainly in the Russian chronicles, emphasized the terrible devastation wrought by pagan savages on the Rus land and people as God's punishment "for our sins." The conversion of the Mongols to Islam intensified the narrative of alien rule, especially in Church sources. By the sixteenth century, this interpretation became fixed in the common notion of a "Mongol (or Tatar) yoke," a view increasingly secularized into an argument, most fully developed in late nineteenth-century Russian historiography, that Mongol rule had no influence on Russian life other than a "yoke" that would eventually be thrown off (see, for example, Sergei Soloviev and Vasilii Kliuchevsky) or that the impact of Mongol rule was only negative and destructive (see, for example, Sergei Platonov).

A thorough reconsideration of the problem of the Mongols and Russia occurred in the twentieth century among Russian émigré intellectuals. A new, so-called Eurasian, school proclaimed Russia's fundamental affiliation with parts of Asia, thus bringing the Mongol period of Russian history to the center of interest. The Eurasian school interpreted the Mongol impact largely in positive and creative terms, though the most influential version of this was George Vernadsky's more ambiguous account. While Vemadsky saw many positive influences that would leave their mark on the later Muscovite state—notably structures of administration, military organization and weaponry, and the system of taxation and fiscal administration—he also emphasized negative influences, including the destruction of the market for crafts, the favoring of large-scale manorial estates, the smashing of cities and urban democratic institutions, and the weakening of a potential aristocratic counterweight to a centralized state. Other historians, especially non-Russians, went further in exploring the negative affects of Mongol rule to argue that the despotism of the Russian autocracy was a direct result of Mongol rule: both due to the unity and force needed to overcome it, but also as a direct echo of brutal and authoritarian Mongol politics. More recent work, rooted in archive research, has tended to focus on the evidence, especially linguistic and institutional, of particular forms of influence and has tried to eschew a language of judgment about deep "positive" or "negative" effects and a language, which many consider nationalist and mythologizing, of "conquest" and "liberation."

One thing is quite clear: the Mongol invasion brought massive physical devastation. Although scholars debate the extent of the destruction and find that some regions and towns suffered more than others, there is no doubt that cities in the direct path of the invading Mongols were burnt and leveled, the population of these towns massacred to the point of extermination, and villages and fields ravaged. The papal legate to the Mongols and famous traveler, Friar (later Archbishop) John (or Joannes) of Plano Carpini, who crossed southern Russia in 1245–46 on his way to Mongolia, wrote as follows concerning the Mongol invasion of Russia:

> ...they went against Russia and enacted a great massacre in the Russian land, they destroyed towns and fortresses and killed people, they besieged Kiev which had been the capital of Russia, and after a long siege they took it and killed the inhabitants of the city; for this reason, when we passed through that land, we found lying in the field countless heads and bones of dead people; for this city had been extremely large and very populous, whereas now it has been reduced to nothing: barely two hundred houses stand there, and those people are held in the harshest slavery.

These and other similar contemporary accounts seem to give a convincing picture of the devastation of the Mongol invasion even if we allow for possible exaggeration.

In addition to the long-lasting effects of devastation and massacre, Mongol rule had other negative consequences. The Mongol occupation of the southern Russian steppe deprived the Russians for centuries of much of the best land and contributed to the shift of population, economic activity, and political power to the northeast. It also did much to cut Russia off from Byzantium and in part from the West, and to accentuate the relative isolation of the country typical of the time. It has been suggested that, but for the Mongols, Russia might well have participated in such epochal European developments as the Renaissance and the Reformation. The financial exactions of the Mongols laid a heavy burden on the Russians precisely when their impoverished and dislocated economy was least prepared to bear it. Rebellions against the Mongol taxes led to new repressions and penalties. The entire period, and especially the decades immediately following the Mongol invasion, acquired the character of a grim struggle for survival, with the advanced and elaborate Kievan style of life and ethical and cultural standards in rapid decline. We learn of new cruel punishments established by law, of illiterate princes, of an inability to erect the dome of a stone cathedral, and of other clear signs of cultural regression. Indeed, certain historians have estimated that the Mongol invasion and domination of Russia retarded the development of the country by some 150 or 200 years.

Constructive, positive contributions of the Mongols to Russian history were often of a quite specific and limited nature. Historians, especially on the evidence of various words of Mongol origin that entered Russian, have described a variety of institutional influences that persisted into the Muscovite era and beyond: military weaponry, strategy, and formations (especially the cavalry); structures of administration, taxation, and law; a system of postal stations; and various commercial and financial practices. More substantively, Charles Halperin and other recent historians have argued, Mongol interest in international commerce may have helped restore at least this part of the Russian economy.

But even many of these restricted Mongol influences have to be qualified. The financial measures of the Mongols together with the census and the Mongol roads added something to the process of centralization in Russia. Yet these taxes had as their aim an exaction of the greatest possible tribute and as such proved to be neither beneficial to the people nor lasting. The invaders replaced the old "smoke" and "plough" taxes with the cruder and simpler head tax, which did not at all take into account one's ability to pay. This innovation disappeared when Russian princes, as intermediaries, took over from the Mongol tax collectors. Thinking simply in terms of pecuniary profit, the Mongols often acted with little wisdom: they sold the position of grand prince to the highest bidder and in the end failed to check in time the rise of Moscow. Rampant corruption further vitiated the financial policy of the Mongols. As to military matters, where the invaders did excel, the fact remains that Russian armies and tactics of the appanage period, based on foot soldiers, evolved directly from those of Kiev, not from the Mongol cavalry. That cavalry, however, was to influence later Muscovite gentry horse formations. Similarly, the Mongols deserve only limited credit for bringing to Russia the postal service or the practice of keeping women in seclusion in a separate part of the house. A real postal system came to Russia as late as the seventeenth century, and from the West; the Mongols merely resorted to the Kievan practice of obligating the local population to supply horses, carriages, boats, and other aids to communication for the use of officials, although they did implement this practice widely and bequeath several words in the field of transportation to the Russians. The seclusion of women was practiced only in the upper class in Russia; it probably reflected the general insecurity of the time to which the Mongols contributed their part rather than the simple borrowing of a custom from the Mongols. The Mongols themselves, it might be added, acquired this practice late in their history when they adopted the Muslim faith and some customs of conquered peoples.

Turning to the key question of political, social, and cultural influences, many historians have also questioned how determining or essential these were. Historians in the past, and some still today, often blamed the Mongols for the Muscovite autocracy, which would long endure and define Russian politics: directly, by facilitating the primacy over their rivals of the Moscow princes, who allied with the Horde, and by contributing to Moscow key institutions of rule, and indirectly, by stimulating the formation of a powerful and disciplined force that could defeat the Mongols. However, even Halperin acknowledges that the Mongols only "facilitated" the rise of Moscow, which drew mainly on its "internal strength" and was shaped mainly by "internal processes of Russian history." Influence and borrowing, in this interpretation, is viewed as quite different than causation—agency is shifted much more to the Russian side. Likewise, the argument that the Mongols brought absolutism to Russia by undermining the "democratic" urban veche and the power of the boyar aristocracy has been criticized as not grounded in the evidence: the Mongols saw neither as a threat and generally ignored both. Similarly, the argument that the Muscovites learned cruelty, deceit, and oppression from the Mongols has been seen to be both unfair to the Mongols themselves and an overly rosy view of Kievan behavior. Even the argument that autocracy arose from the need to create a force strong enough to overthrow the Mongols has been criticized as reading post-Mongol developments, more the result of the internal history of Muscovy, backward into the Mongol period. As Halperin put this, "absolutism in Russia arose from domestic considerations and drew its theory and symbolic manifestations from Byzantium rather than Sarai." Moscow certainly made use of Mongol institutions; but, again, borrowing is not the same as causation.

Society and culture were even less influenced by the Mongols, who generally kept apart from the Russians, limiting their interest in their unwilling subjects to a few items, notably the exaction of tribute. Religion posed a formidable barrier between the two peoples, both at first when the Mongols were still pagan and later when the Golden Horde became Muslim. The Mongols, to repeat a point, were perfectly willing to leave the Russians to their own ways; indeed, they patronized the Orthodox Church. Mongol and Russian societies also bore little resemblance to each other. The Mongols remained nomads in the clan stage of development. Their institutions and laws were unsuitable for a much more complex agricultural society. A comparison of Mongol law, the code of Jenghiz Khan, to the Pskov *Sudebnik*, an example of Russian law of the appanage age, makes the difference abundantly clear. Even the increasing harshness of Russian criminal law of the period should probably be attributed to the conditions of the time rather than to borrowing from the Mongols.

The Eurasian argument also tends to misrepresent the nature of the Mongol states. Far from having been particularly well organized, efficient or lasting, they turned out to be relatively unstable and short-lived. Thus, in 1260 Kublai Khan built Peking and in 1280 he completed the conquest of southern China, but in 1368 the Mongol dynasty was driven out of China; the Mongol dynasty in Persia lasted only from 1256 to 1344; and the Mongol Central Asiatic state with its capital in Bukhara existed from 1242 until its destruction by Tamerlane in 1370. In the Russian case the dates are rather similar, but the Mongols never established their own dynasty in the country, acting instead merely as overlords of the Russian princes. While the Mongol states lasted, they continued on the whole to be rent by dissensions and wars and to suffer from arbitrariness, corruption, and misrule in general. Not only did the Mongols fail to contribute a superior statecraft, but they had to borrow virtually everything from alphabets to advisers from the conquered peoples to enable their states to exist. As one of these advisers remarked, an empire could be won on horseback, but not ruled from the saddle. True, cruelty, lawlessness, and at times anarchy in that period also characterized the life of many peoples other than the Mongols, the Russians included. But at least most of these peoples managed eventually to surmount their difficulties and organize effective and lasting states. Not so the Mongols, who, after their sudden and stunning performance on the world scene, receded to the steppe, clan life, and the internecine warfare of Mongolia.

When the Muscovite state emerged, its leaders looked to Byzantium for their high model and to Kievan Rus for their historical and still meaningful heritage. Historians too, whether they studied the growth of serfdom, the rise of the gentry, or the nature of princely power in Muscovite Russia, established significant connections with the Russian past and Russian conditions, not with Mongolia. Even for purposes of analogy, European countries stood much closer to Russia than did the Mongol states. In fact, from the Atlantic to the Urals absolute monarchies were in the process of replacing feudal division. Therefore, Vernadsky's affirming the importance of the Mongol impact by contrasting Muscovite with Kievan Rus appears to miss the point. There existed many other reasons for changes in Russia; and, needless to say, other countries changed during those centuries without contact with the Mongols.

# CHAPTER 9

# Lord Novgorod the Great

The Italian municipalities had, in earlier days, given signal proof of that force which transforms the city into the state.

JACOB BURCKHARDT

The men of Novgorod showed *Knyaz*\* Vsevolod the road. "We do not want thee, go whither thou wilt." He went to his father, into Russia.

"THE CHRONICLE OF NOVGOROD"
(R. MICHELL'S AND N. FORBES'S TRANSLATION)

Whereas Peter the Great cut a window through to Europe, in medieval Novgorod the door was already wide open.

BORIS KISELEV

Novgorod or, to use its formal name, Lord Novgorod the Great stands out as one of the most impressive and important states of appanage Russia and, many historians have argued, as an important political alternative to the centralized autocracy that would come with the growth and domination of the Muscovite state. Indeed, the memory of a relatively free, democratic, and cosmopolitan Novgorod would come to represent, for the Russian political opposition of the nineteenth century and after, a symbol of Russia's suppressed democratic heritage. No less, Novgorod's role in defending Russian lands from invasion by Western powers became part of its semi-mythic status in Russian history. When Kievan might and authority declined and economic and political weight shifted, Novgorod rose as the capital of northern Russia as well as the greatest trading center and, indeed, the leading city of the entire country. Located in a lake area, in the northwestern corner of European Russia, it came to rule enormous lands, stretching east to the Urals and north to the coast line. Yet, for the historian, the unusual political system of the principality of Novgorod and its general style of life and culture possess even greater interest than its size, wealth, and power.

---

\**Knyaz* means "prince".

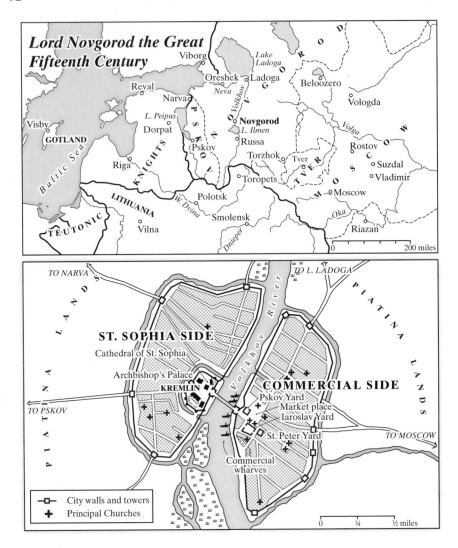

*Lord Novgorod the Great Fifteenth Century*

## The Historical Evolution of Novgorod

The vast Russian northwest was inhabited mainly by Finno-Ugric tribes until Slavic tribes moved into the region in the fifth and sixth centuries. Recent archaeological work finds evidence of numerous towns in the Novgorod region by the eighth century, possibly built cooperatively by both Slavs and Finno-Ugric peoples. In the ninth century, according to the chronicles, possibly due to conflicts between these tribes, the Scandinavian Prince Riurik was invited to rule. His men built up the town of Gorodishche, located three kilometers from Novgorod, which remained the residence of the Novgorod princes from the ninth to the fifteenth centuries. Novgorod itself began to develop in the early tenth century as a commercial center but also the residence of the landowning elites. Whether the story of Riurik's invitation is true—excavations at Gorodishche indicate that the coming of Scandinavian princes and the settlement of Gorodishche in the ninth century can be confirmed—the legend that the Novogorodians "invited" their prince remained part of the political culture of Novgorod, justifying continued insistence that the prince served at their pleasure.

During the hegemony of Kiev, Novgorod retained a position of high importance. It had not been destroyed by the Mongols and it was at the crossroads of the main eastern European trade routes—located on the Volkhov River, which flowed from the nearby Lake Ilmen to Lake Ladoga—Novgorod was both the northern base of the celebrated north-south route "from the Varangians to the Greeks" and was linked to the main east-west trade routes by means of the Volga River. Naturally, the ruling princes desired control of this important region. The city seems to have remained outside the regular Kievan princely system of succession from brother to brother. Instead, it was often ruled by sons of the grand princes of Kiev who, not infrequently, themselves later ascended the Kievan throne. St. Vladimir, Iaroslav the Wise, and Vladimir Monomakh's son Mstislav all were at some time princes of Novgorod. Iaroslav the Wise in particular came to be closely linked to Novgorod where he ruled for a number of years before his accession to the Kievan throne; even the *Russian Justice* has been considered by many scholars as belonging to the Novgorodian period of his activities. And Novgorod repeatedly offered valuable support to the larger ambitions and claims of its princes, for example, to the same Iaroslav the Wise in his bitter struggle with Sviatopolk for the Kievan seat.

The evolution of authority and power within Novgorod proved to be even more significant than the interventions of the Novgorodians on behalf of their favorite princes. While we know of a few earlier instances when Novgorod refused to accept the prince allotted to the city—in one case advising that the appointee should come only if he had two heads—it is with the famous expulsion of a ruler in 1136 that the Novgorodians embarked upon their peculiar political course. After that date the prince of Novgorod became in essence a hired official of the city with strictly circumscribed authority and prerogatives. His position resembled that of the *podestà* in Italian city-states, and it made some historians refer to Novgorod as a "commercial republic." In 1156 Novgorod obtained virtual independence in religious administration too by seizing the right to elect its own archbishop. To be exact, under the new system the Novgorodian veche selected three candidates for the position of archbishop; next, one of the three was chosen by lot to fill the high office; and, finally, he was elevated to his new ecclesiastical rank by the head of the Russian Church, the metropolitan. The emergence of Novgorod as an independent principality formed a part of the general process of collapse of the Kievan state accompanied by the appearance of competing regional entities which were frequently mutually hostile.

Novgorod's defense of Russian lands from foreign invasions, stemming from its location in the northwestern corner of Russia, might well have had a greater historical significance than its wars against other Russian principalities.

The most celebrated chapter of this defense is linked to the name of Prince Alexander, known as Alexander Nevskii, that is, of the Neva, for his victory over the Swedes on the banks of that river. Alexander became the prince of Novgorod and later the grand prince of Russia at a particularly difficult time in the history of his country. Born in 1219 and dying in 1263, Alexander had to face the Mongol invasion and the imposition of Mongol rule on Russia, and he was also forced to deal with major assaults on Russia from Europe. These assaults came from the Swedes and the Teutonic Knights, while neighboring Finnish and especially strong Lithuanian tribes applied additional pressure. The German attack was the most ominous: it represented a continuation and extension of the long-term German drive eastward which had already resulted in the Germanization or extermination of many Baltic Slavic and western Lithuanian tribes and which had spread to the Estonian, Latvian, and Lithuanian neighbors of Russia. The conversion of all these peoples to Roman Catholicism, as well as their subjugation and Germanization, constituted the aims of the Teutonic Knights who had begun as a crusading order in the Holy Land and later transferred their activities to the Baltic area.

In the year in which Kiev fell to the Mongols, 1240, Alexander seized the initiative and led the Novgorodians to a victory over the advancing Swedes on the banks of the Neva River. In the meantime the Teutonic Knights had begun their systematic attack on northwestern Russian lands in 1239, and they succeeded in 1241 in capturing Pskov. Having defeated the Swedes, Alexander Nevskii turned against the new invaders. In short order he managed to drive them back and free Pskov. What is more, he carried warfare into enemy territory. The crucial battle took place on April 5, 1242, on the ice of Lake Chud, or Peipus, in Estonia. It became known in Russian historical tradition as "the massacre on the ice" and has been celebrated in song and story—most famously in Prokofiev's music and Eisenstein's brilliant film *Alexander Nevskii*. The massed force of mailclad and heavily armed German knights and their Finnish allies struck like an enormous battering ram at the Russian lines; the lines sagged but held long enough for Alexander Nevskii to make an enveloping movement with a part of his troops and assail an enemy flank; a complete rout of the Teutonic Knights followed, the spring ice breaking under them to aid in their destruction.

Alexander Nevskii's victories were important, but they represented only a single sequence in the continuous struggle of Novgorod against its western and northwestern foes. Two Soviet specialists calculated that between 1142 and 1446 Novgorod fought the Swedes twenty-six times, the German knights eleven times, the Lithuanians fourteen times, and the Norwegians five times. The German knights then included the Livonian and the Teutonic orders, which merged in 1237.

Relations with the Mongols took a different turn. Although the Mongol invasion failed to reach Novgorod, the principality together with other Russian lands submitted to the khan. In fact, the great warrior Alexander Nevskii himself instituted this policy of cooperation with the Mongols, becoming a favorite of the khan and thus the grand prince of Russia from 1252 until his death in 1263. Alexander Nevskii acted as he did because of a simple and sound reason: he considered resistance to the Mongols hopeless. And it was especially because of his humble submission to the khan and his consequent ability to preserve the principality of Novgorod as well as some other Russian lands from ruin that the Orthodox Church canonized Alexander Nevskii in the sixteenth century.

Throughout the appanage period Novgorod remained one of the most important Russian principalities. It played a significant role in the rivalry between Moscow and Tver as well as in the struggle between Moscow and Lithuania. As Moscow "gathered" the Russian lands, declaring Novgorod an inseparable part of the Moscow grand prince's "patrimony," the position of Novgorod became increasingly difficult. Novgorodians began to call their city Great (Velikii) Novgorod as a defiant counterweight to the title of the Grand (also Velikii in Russian) Prince. By the 1470s, the conflict with Moscow approached its denouement. Ivan III of Moscow justified his anti-Novgorod policy by claiming that the Novgorod leadership planned to shift their alliance to the Grand Duchy of Lithuania and to renounce Orthodoxy. Indeed, in order to resist Moscow's pressures, many Novgorodian boyars sought such an alliance, though the draft agreement ensured religious independence and the protection of Orthodoxy. In 1471, Ivan III defeated the Novgorodian army and the city surrendered to him; the initiators of the alliance with Lithuania were executed. But the troubles, often violent, continued. According to a later Muscovite account (the *Nikonian Chronicle*), Novgorodians at veche assemblies "spoke senseless and depraved things," such as "we do not want to be called his patrimony. We are free people of Great Novgorod." But Moscow was not to be stopped, and complete subjugation came after a new assault in 1477–78. Muscovites severely suppressed all opposition, exiling many people, and incorporated the city organically into the Moscow state.

## Novgorod: Institutions and Way of Life

Novgorod was an impressive city. Its population at the time of its independence numbered more than 30,000. As already noted, this was a major commercial center connected to both north-south and east-west trade. Indeed, scholars have argued that Novgorod played a major role in revitalizing the entire Russian economy in the fourteenth century, especially through the import of European silver in return for products of agriculture, hunting, and fishing. One lasting effect of this important trade was the introduction in the late thirteenth century of a new monetary unit, the ruble, made of silver. Like other medieval towns, Novgorod suffered from crowding because everyone wanted to dwell within the walls. The rich families and their servants lived in large houses built in solid blocks and the poorer inhabitants used whatever area they could obtain. The Volkhov divided the city into two halves: the commercial side, where the main market was located, and that of St. Sophia. On the St. Sophia side stood, of course, the cathedral itself as well as the ancient kremlin, or citadel, of the city. The Novgorodians enjoyed the advantages of fire protection, streets ingeniously paved with wood, and a wooden water pipe system, the principles of which they had learned from Byzantium.

Local initiative, organization, and autonomy constituted the distinguishing traits of Novgorod. Several block houses in the city composed a street which already had the status of a self-governing unit with its own elected elder. Several streets formed a *sotnia*, that is, a hundred. Hundreds in their turn combined into quarters, or *kontsy*, which totaled five. Each *konets* enjoyed far-reaching autonomy: not only did it govern itself through its own veche and officials, but it also possessed separately a part of the *piatina* lands, a large area outside the city limits and subject to Novgorod. The piatina holdings of a particular konets usually radiated from its city boundary. It should be added that distant Novgorodian territories did not belong to the piatina lands and were managed by the city as a whole. Also, because of the autonomy of the kontsy, formal Novgorodian documents had to be confirmed at times with as many as eight seals: one for each of the five kontsy and three for central authorities.

Was Novgorod a democratic "republic," as some scholars have argued, or an oligarchy dominated by boyars, wealthy merchants, and other elites? Or did its politics evolve from rough mass democracy to oligarchy? Certainly, although the ruling prince formally commanded the army and played a central role in justice and administration, Novgorodians, especially after the 1136 uprising, restricted even these rights and imposed a growing set of severe and minute restrictions on the prince's power and activities. We have the precise terms of a number of such contracts between princes and the city, the earliest concluded with Alexander Nevskii's brother Iaroslav in 1265. As in most of these contracts, the prince promised to follow ancient Novgorodian custom in his government, to appoint only Novgorodians as administrators of the city's lands, not to dismiss officials without court action, and not to hold court without the *posadnik*, an elected official, or his delegate to represent the city. He had to establish his headquarters outside the city limits; he and his druzhina could not own land in Novgorod or trade with the Germans; his remuneration as well as his rights to hunt and to fish were all regulated in great detail. Thus, although in the course of time the grand prince of Moscow or at least a member of the Muscovite ruling family came to hold the office of prince in Novgorod, his power there remained quite limited.

The posadnik and the *tysiatskii*, elected by the veche, shared executive duties with the prince and, if need be, especially the posadnik protected the interests of the city from the prince. The posadnik served as the prince's main associate and assistant, who took charge of the administration and the army in the prince's absence. The tysiatskii, or chiliarch, had apparently at least two important functions: he commanded the town regiment or thousand—hence probably his name—and he settled commercial disputes. He has sometimes been regarded as a representative of the common people of Novgorod. The archbishop of Novgorod must also be mentioned, In addition to performing the highest ecclesiastical functions in the principality, he continuously played a leading role in political affairs, presiding over the Council of Notables, advising secular authorities, reconciling antagonistic factions, and sometimes heading Novgorodian embassies abroad.

As can be seen, the power of the Novgorodian veche, or town council, was considerable. It invited and dismissed the prince, elected the posadnik and the tysiatskii, and determined the selection of the archbishop by electing three candidates for that position. It decided the issues of war and peace, mobilized the army, proclaimed laws, raised taxes, and acted in general as the supreme authority in Novgorod. A permanent chancellery was attached to it. The veche could be called together by the prince, an official, the people, or even a single person, through ringing the veche bell. Thus the removal of the bell by the Muscovites in 1478 symbolized the end of the independence of Novgorod and of its peculiar constitution.

This power of the veche has led many scholars—and nostalgic anti-absolutist Russians throughout the centuries following—to describe Novgorod as a democratic republic, a view that sees the veche, made up of all the free people in the city, deciding key questions collectively. By contrast, the historian V. L. Ianin, perhaps the leading specialist today on the history of the region, calls Novgorod a "boyar republic," emphasizing elite domination of the veche and of town officials. Indeed, research indicates that voting members of the veche were most likely limited to boyars and other owners of large urban homesteads. But even Ianin acknowledges that the entire urban public had access to the veche assembly—which gathered in the open air near the Cathedral of St. Nicholas—and could influence (or feel that they influenced) discussions and decisions with loud cries of approval or dissent. Complicating the story still further, the veche frequently bogged down in violent factional quarrels promoted by its practices of direct democracy and unanimity of decision. The Novgorodians won respect as independent and self-reliant people who managed their own affairs. Yet the archbishop made many solemn appearances at the veche in a desperate effort to restore some semblance of order; and a legend grew up that the statue of the pagan god Perun, dumped into the river when the Novgorodians became Christian, reappeared briefly to leave a stick with which the townspeople have belabored one another ever since. The increasing challenges to their independence from Moscow and the growing wealth of boyars and other elites, along with this endemic disorder, may explain why, as will be seen, Novgorodian politics moved in an increasingly oligarchical direction.

The Council of Notables also rose into prominence in Novgorodian politics, both because the veche could not conduct day-to-day business efficiently and, still more fundamentally, as a reflection of the actual distribution of wealth and power in the principality. Presided over by the archbishop, it included a considerable number of influential boyars, notably present and past holders of the offices of posadnik and tysiatskii, as well as heads of the kontsy and of the hundreds. The Council elaborated the legislative measures discussed or enacted by the veche and could often control the course of Novgorodian politics. It effectively represented the wealthy, so to speak aristocratic, element in the principality.

The judicial system of Novgorod deserves special mention. It exhibited a remarkable degree of elaboration, organization, and complexity, as well as high juridical and humanitarian standards. The prince, the posadnik, the tysi-atskii, and the archbishop, all had their particular courts. A system of jury-men, *dokladchiki*, functioned in the high court presided over by the posadnik; the jurymen, ten in number, consisted of one boyar and one commoner from each of the five kontsy. Novgorodian jurisprudence also resorted frequently to mediation: the contending persons were asked to nominate two mediators, and only when the four failed to reach an agreement did court action follow. Judicial combat, after a solemn kissing of the cross, was used to reach the right decision in certain dubious cases. There seem to have been instances of such combat even between women. Novgorodian punishments remained characteristically mild. Although the death penalty was not unknown, they consisted especially of fines and, on particularly grave occasions, of banish-ment with the loss of property and possessions which could be pillaged at will by the populace. In contrast to the general practices of the time, torture occupied little, if any, place in the Novgorodian judicial process. Much evi-dence reflects the high regard for human life characteristic of Novgorod; the *Novgorodian Chronicle* at times refers to a great slaughter when it speaks of the killing of several persons.

Novgorod stood out as a great trading state. It exploited the enormous wealth of northern Russian forests, principally in furs, but also in wax and honey, for export to foreign markets, and it served, as already mentioned, as an intermediary point on extensive trade routes going in several directions. Manufactured goods, certain metals, and other items, such as herring, wine, and beer, were typical imports. Novgorod traded on a large scale with the island of Gotland and with the ports of the Baltic coast line, but its merchan-dise also reached England, Flanders, and other distant lands. Many mer-chants, especially from Gotland and Germany, came to Novgorod, where they enjoyed autonomy and a privileged position. Yet, the Novgorodians them-selves engaged for a long time in active trade—a point which some scholars failed to appreciate. They went to foreign lands and, on the basis of reciprocal treaties, established Novgorodian commercial communities abroad, as attested by the two Russian churches on the island of Gotland and other evidence. It was in the second half of the thirteenth century, with the beginnings of the Hanseatic commercial league of northern European cities and the growth of its special commercial ships vastly superior to the rather simple boats of the Novgorodians, that Novgorod gradually shifted to a strictly passive role in trade.

While merchants, especially prosperous merchants engaged in foreign trade, constituted a very important element in Novgorod, Soviet research emphasized the significance of landed wealth, together with the close links between the two upper-class groups. In any case, social differentiation in Novgorod increased with time, leading to political antagonisms, reminiscent again of Italian cities and their conflicts between the rich and the poor, the *populo grosso* and the *populo minuto*. Especially as the power of Moscow grew in the fourteenth and fifteenth centuries and threatened Novgorod's independence, the boyars consolidated their power, with a few powerful families controlling all high offices. Boyar consolidation of power was also a response to growing popular discontent, including an anti-boyar uprising in 1418. These social tensions were echoed in chronicle entries from the mid-fifteenth century that speak of "unjust boyars." Most important, these attitudes would have fateful consequences for boyar ability to win popular support in their efforts to resist Moscow.

At the time when social tensions inside Novgorod increased, the city also found it more difficult to hold its sprawling lands together. The huge Novgorodian territories fell roughly into two groups: the piatina area and the more distant semi-colonial possessions in the sparsely populated far north and east. In line with Novgorodian political practice, piatina towns, with their surrounding countryside, received some self-government, although their posadniki and tysiatskie were appointed from Novgorod rather than elected. Gradually decentralization increased, with Viatka, in fact, becoming independent in the late twelfth century and Pskov in the middle of the fourteenth. In addition, as has been noted, Novgorod had to struggle continuously for the security and allegiance of many of its territories against the princes of the northeast, who came to be ably represented by the powerful and successful Muscovite rulers.

Moscow finally destroyed Novgorod. The veche was banned, the election of the posadnik was abolished, and the veche bell was carted off to Moscow. The outcome of their conflict had been in a sense predetermined by the fact that Novgorod, in spite of its swollen size, had remained essentially a city-state. Devoted to its highly specific and particularistic interests, it flourished in the appanage period when it stood out because of its wealth and its strength and when it could utilize the rivalries of its neighbors. Furthermore, by controlling its prince it had escaped subdivision into new appanages. But it proved unable to compete with Moscow in uniting the Russian lands. Social conflict also contributed to this end. When Novgorod fell into the hands of the Moscow prince in 1478, it seems that the boyars found no defenders among the common people, who evidently preferred Ivan III to their own oligarchic government.

Novgorodian culture too developed in an impressive manner. The city had the good fortune to escape Mongol devastation. In contrast to other appanage principalities, it contained sufficient wealth to continue Kievan cultural traditions on a grand scale. And it benefited from its rich contacts with the West. While Russian culture in the appanage period will be discussed in a later chapter, it is appropriate to note here that Novgorod became famous for its church architecture and its icon-painting, as well as for its vigorous and varied literature.

Especially significant is evidence of widespread literacy in Novgorod and the surrounding region. It was long assumed that the population, even its elites, were illiterate. This presumption was radically revised, at least for Novgorod, by the discovery by Soviet archaeologists of hundreds of documents written on birch-bark. Continued archaeological work has now uncovered more than a thousand texts, dating from the eleventh to the fifteenth centuries, and many more certainly remain buried. The overwhelming majority come from Novgorod. Usually succinct businesslike messages, these documents reveal literacy extending from boyars to artisans to servants and including women. Since they were evidently rare in other towns, their preponderance here suggests that the peculiar political and social order in Novgorod also required a high cultural level. Novgorodian literature embraced the writings of such archbishops of the city as Moses and Basil; travelogues, in particular accounts of visits to the Holy Land; and extremely useful chronicles, together with an oral tradition that included a special cycle of byliny. The illuminated so-called *Ostromirovo Gospel* of 1056–57, of Novgorodian provenance, had long been considered the oldest surviving Russian, that is, Church Slavonic, manuscript, but in the year 2000 it lost its precedence to three wax tablets containing Psalms 67, 75, and 76, dating apparently from the first quarter of the eleventh century and found, again, in Novgorod. Indeed, as is frequently the case, the culture of Novgorod survived the political downfall of the city to exercise a considerable influence on Moscow and on Russia in general.

Specialists have cited certain characteristics of Novgorodian culture as reflecting the peculiar nature and history of that city-state. The *Chronicle of Novgorod* and other Novgorodian writings express a strong and constant attachment to the city, its streets, buildings, and affairs. Moreover, the whole general tone of Novgorodian literature has been described as strikingly realistic, pragmatic, and businesslike, even when dealing with religious issues. For example, Archbishop Basil adduced the following arguments, among others, to prove that paradise was located on earth rather than in heaven or in imagination: four terrestrial rivers flow from paradise, one of which, the Nile, Basil described with some relish; St. Macarius lived near paradise; St. Efrosimius even visited paradise and brought back to his abbot three apples, while St Agapius took some bread there; two Novgorodian boats once reached the paradise mountain as they sailed in a distant sea. Together with realism and practicality went energy and bustle, manifested, for example, in constant building—about 100 stone churches were erected in the city in the last two centuries of its independence. Visitors described the Novgorodians as an extremely vigorous and active people, whose women were equal to men and prominent in the affairs of the city.

The heroes of Novgorodian literature also reflect the life of the city. The main protagonists of the Novgorodian cycle of byliny included the extraordinary businessman and traveler, merchant Sadko, and the irrepressible and irresponsible young giant Vasilii Buslaev, whose bloody forays against his neighbors could be checked only by his mother. Buslaev's death illustrates well his behavior: given the choice by a skull to jump in one direction and live or to jump in another and perish, he naturally chose the second and cracked his head. Buslaev has been cited as a genuine representative of the free adventurers of Novgorod, who did so much to spread the sway of their city over enormous lands populated both by Russians and by Finnic-speaking and other tribes.

The history of Novgorod, remarkable in itself, attracts further attention as one variant in the evolution of the lands of Kievan Rus after the decline of Kiev. While it is usual to emphasize the peculiar qualities of Novgorod, it is important to realize also that these qualities stemmed directly from the Kievan—and to some extent pre-Kievan—period and represented, sometimes in an accentuated manner, certain salient Kievan characteristics. The urban life and culture of Novgorod, the important position of its middle class, its commerce, and its close contacts with the outside world all link Novgorod to the mainstream of Kievan history. The veche too, of course, had had a signifi-cant role in Kievan life and politics. In emphasizing further its authority and functions, the Novgorodians developed one element of the political synthesis of Kievan Rus: the democratic, at the expense of two others, the autocratic and the aristocratic, which, as we shall see, found a more fertile soil in other parts of the country.

## Pskov

The democratic political evolution characteristic of Novgorod also occurred in a few other places, especially in another northwestern Russian town, Pskov. Long subject to Novgorod, this extreme Russian outpost became in 1348 a small independent principality with a territory of some 250 by 75 miles. Pskov had a prince whose powers were even more restricted than those of the prince of Novgorod and a veche which in some ways exceeded that of the larger town in importance. Notably, the Pskovian veche, in addition to its other functions, acted as a court for serious crimes. The town had two elected posadniki as well as the elders of the kontsy, but no tysiatskii; and it was subdivided, much like Novgorod, into streets and kontsy. A council of elders also operated in Pskov.

Being much smaller than Novgorod, Pskov experienced less social differ-entiation and social tension. It has been generally described as more compact, democratic, and peaceful in its inner life than its "big brother." On the other hand, this "little brother"—a title given to Pskov by Novgorod at one point—participated fully in the high development of urban life and culture typical of Novgorod. In fact, Pskovian architects obtained wide renown, while the legal code issued by the Pskovian veche, the celebrated *Sudebnik* of 1397, with supplements until about 1467—mentioned earlier in contrasting the Russians and the Mongols—represents a most impressive compendium of highly devel-oped Russian medieval law.

Pskov's relations with Moscow differed from those of Novgorod. Never a rival of the Muscovite state, Pskov, on the contrary, constantly needed its help against attacks from the west, though Pskov was also actively connected to the west through trade, including association with the Hanseatic League. Thus, Pskov fell naturally under the influence of Moscow. Yet when the Muscovite state fully incorporated Pskov around 1511, the town, after suffering deportations, lost its special institutions, all of its independence, and, in the face of Muscovite taxes and regulations, its commercial and middle-class way of life.

In spite of brilliance and many successes, the historical development of Novgorod and Pskov proved to be, in the long run, abortive.

CHAPTER 10

# The Southwest and the Northeast

> At the end of the twelfth century the Russian land has no effective
> political unity; on the contrary, it possesses several important cen-
> ters, the evolutions of which, up to a certain point, follow different
> directions and assume diverse appearances.
>
> VENEDIKT MIAKOTIN

While the history of Novgorod represented one important variation on the
Kievan theme, two others were provided by the evolutions of the southwestern and the northeastern Russian lands. As in the case of Novgorod, these
areas formed parts of Kievan Rus and participated fully in its life and culture.
In fact, the southwest played an especially important role in maintaining close
links between the Russians of the Kievan period and the inhabitants of eastern and central Europe; whereas the northeast gradually replaced Kiev itself
as the political and economic center of the Russian state and also made major
contributions to culture, for instance, through its brilliant school of architecture which we discussed earlier. With the collapse of the Kievan state and the
breakdown of unity, the two areas went their separate ways. Like the development of Novgorod, their independent evolutions stressed certain elements in
the Kievan heritage and minimized others to produce strikingly different, yet
intrinsically related, societies.

## The Southwest

The territory directly west and southwest of the Kiev area was divided into
Volynia and Galicia. The larger land, Volynia, sweeps in a broad belt, west
of Kiev, from the foothills of the Carpathian Mountains into Belorussia. The
smaller, Galicia, which is located along the northern slopes of the Carpathians,
irrigated by such rivers as the Prut and the Dniester, and bordered by Hungary
and Poland, represented the furthest southwestern extension of the Kievan
state. During the Kievan period the southwest attracted attention by its international trade; its cities, such as Vladimir-in-Volynia and Galich, as well as

83

Volynia – Galicia c. 1250

many others, and in general by its active participation in the life and culture of the times. Vladimir-in-Volinia, it may be remembered, ranked high as a princely seat, while the entire area was considered among the more desirable sections of the state. The culture of Volynia and Galicia formed an integral part of Kievan culture, but it experienced particularly strong foreign, especially Western, influences. Indeed, some historians question whether this region, though once part of Kievan Rus, should be called "Russian" at all—a question shaped by distinctive local characteristics; by arguments, already noted, about the ambiguity of the term "Russia" when writing about the medieval era; by the strength of Western influences; and by the region's eventual division and incorporation into Poland and Hungary, and, later, modern Ukraine.

As Kiev declined, the southwest and several other areas rose in importance. In the second half of the twelfth century Galicia had one of its ablest and most famous rulers, prince Iaroslav Osmomysl, whose obscure appellation has been taken by some scholars to mean "of eight minds" and to denote his wisdom, and whose power was treated with great respect in the *Lay of the Host of Igor*. After Iaroslav Osmomysl's death in 1187, Andrew, king of Hungary, made an abortive effort to reign in the principality, which was followed by the rule of Iaroslav's son Vladimir who died in 1197. After Vladimir, Galicia obtained a strong and celebrated prince, Roman of Volynia, who united the two southwestern lands and also extended his sway to Kiev itself. Roman campaigned successfully against the Hungarians, the Poles, the Lithuanians, and the Polovtsy. Byzantium sought his alliance, while Pope Innocent III offered him a royal crown, which Roman declined. The chronicle of Galicia and Volynia, a work of high literary merit noted for its vivid language, pictured Roman as follows: "he threw himself against the pagans like a lion, he raged like a lynx, he brought destruction like a crocodile, and he swept over their land like an eagle, brave he was like an aurochs." Roman died in a Polish ambush in 1205, leaving behind two small sons, the elder, Daniel, aged four.

After Roman's death, Galicia experienced extremely troubled times marked by a rapid succession of rulers, by civil wars, and by Hungarian and Polish intervention. In contrast, Volynia had a more fortunate history, and from 1221 to 1264 it was ruled by Roman's able son Daniel. Following his complete victory in Volynia, which required a number of years, Daniel turned to Galicia and, by about 1238, brought it under his own and his brother's jurisdiction. Daniel also achieved fame as a creator of cities, such as Lviv (Lvov), which to an extent replaced Kiev as an emporium of east-west trade, a patron of learning and the arts, and in general as a builder and organizer of the Russian southwest. His rule witnessed, in a sense, the culmination of the *rapprochement* between Russia and the West. In 1253 Daniel accepted a king's crown from the pope—the only such instance in Russian history—while his son Roman married into the Austrian reigning house. Daniel's work, however, received a shattering blow from the Mongol invasion. The Mongols laid waste Galicia and Volynia, and the Russians of the southwest, together with their compatriots elsewhere, had to submit to the overlordship of the khan.

Following the death of Daniel in 1264 and of his worthy son and successor Leo in 1301, who had had more trouble with the Mongols, Volynia and Galicia began to decline. Their decline lasted for almost a century and was interrupted by several rallies, but they were finally absorbed by neighboring states. Volynia gradually became part of the Lithuanian state, which will be discussed in a later chapter. Galicia experienced intermittently Polish and Hungarian rule until the final Polish success in 1387. Galicia's political allegiance to Poland contributed greatly to a spread of Catholicism and Polish culture and social influences in the southwestern Russian principality, at least among its upper classes.

The internal development of Volynia and Galicia reflected the exceptional growth and power of the boyars. Ancient and well-established on fertile soil and in prosperous towns, the landed proprietors of the southwest often arrogated to themselves the right to invite and depose princes, and they played the leading role in countless political struggles and intrigues. In a most extraordinary development, one of the boyars, a certain Vladislav, even occupied briefly the princely seat of Galicia in 1210, the only occasion in ancient Russia when a princely seat was held by anyone other than a member of a princely family. Mikhail Vladimirsky-Budanov and other specialists have noted such remarkable activities of Galician boyars as their direct administration of parts of the principality, in disregard of the prince, and their withdrawal *in corpore* from the princedom in 1226 in their dispute with Prince Mstislav. By contrast with the authority of the boyars, princely authority in Galicia and Volynia represented a later, more superficial, and highly circumscribed phenomenon. Only exceptionally strong rulers, such as Iaroslav Osmomysl, could control the boyars. The veche in Galicia and Volynia, while it did play a role in politics and at least occasionally supported the prince against the boyars, could not consistently curb their power. It should be noted that the rise of the boyars in southwest Russia resembled in many respects the development of the landlord class in adjacent Poland and Hungary.

## The Northeast

The northeast, like the southwest, formed an integral part of the Kievan state. Its leading towns, Rostov and Suzdal and some others, belonged with the oldest in Russia. Its princes, deriving from Vladimir Monomakh, participated effectively in twelfth-century Kievan politics. In fact, as we have seen, when Kiev and the Kievan area declined, the political center of the state shifted to the northeast, to the so-called princedom of Vladimir-Suzdal which covered large territories in the central and eastern parts of European Russia. It was a ruler of this principality, Andrei Bogoliubskii, who sacked Kiev in 1169 and, having won the office of the grand prince, transferred its seat to his favorite town of Vladimir in the northeast. His father, the first independent prince of Suzdal and a son of Vladimir Monomakh, the celebrated Iurii Dolgorukii, that is, George of the Long Arm, had already won the grand princedom, but had kept it in Kiev; with Andrei, it shifted definitively to the northeast. Although Andrei Bogoliubskii fell victim to a conspiracy in 1174, his achievements of building up his principality and of emphasizing the authority of the princes of Suzdal in their own territory and in Russia, remained. His work was resumed in 1176 by Andrei's brother Vsevolod, known as Vsevolod III, because he was the third Russian grand prince with that name, or Vsevolod of the Large Nest because of his big family. Vsevolod ruled until his death in 1212 and continued to build towns, fortresses, and churches, to suppress opposition, and to administer the land effectively. At the same time, as grand prince, he made his authority felt all over Russia.

It will be remembered that the Mongol invasion dealt a staggering blow to the Russian northeast. The grand prince at the time, Iurii, a son of Vsevolod III, fell in battle, the Russian armies were smashed, and virtually the entire land was laid waste. Yet, after the Golden Horde established its rule in Russia, the northeastern principalities had some advantages. In contrast to the steppe of the south, they remained outside the zone directly occupied by the Mongols and on the whole could slowly rebuild and develop. A certain distance from the invaders, it might be added, gave them an advantage not only over the old Kievan south, but also over the southeastern principality of Riazan, which evolved along lines parallel to the evolution of the northeast, but experienced greater Mongol pressure. Moreover, the seat of the grand prince stayed in the northeast with the descendants of Vladimir Monomakh. To be more exact, after the death

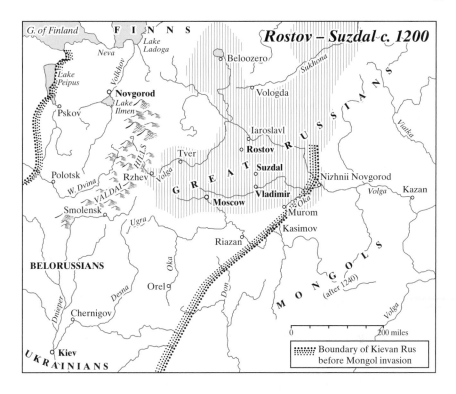

in 1263 of Alexander Nevskii, who, as mentioned earlier, had managed to stabilize relations with the Mongols, the office of the grand prince went successively to his brothers Iaroslav of Tver and Vasilii of Kostroma and to his sons Dmitrii and Andrei. Following the death of Andrei in 1304, Mikhail of Tver, Iaroslav's son and Alexander Nevskii's nephew, ruled as grand prince until he was killed by the Mongols at the court of the Golden Horde in 1319. Mikhail was succeeded by his rival, a grandson of Alexander Nevskii, Iurii, or George, who became the first prince of Moscow to assume the office of grand prince.

But, while the position of the grand prince, with its location in the northeast and the complicated Kievan practice of princely succession, continued as a symbol of Russian unity, in other respects division prevailed. Appanages multiplied as princes divided their holdings among their sons. On the death of Vsevolod III, the Vladimir-Suzdal princedom had already split into five principalities which proceeded to divide further. Ultimately some princes inherited tiny territories, while still others could not be provided for and had to find service with more fortunate members of the family. In the continuous shifting of political boundaries, four leading principalities emerged in the northeast in the first half of the fourteenth century: the princedoms of Vladimir, Rostov, Tver, and Moscow. A proliferation of appanages, characteristic of the northeast, occurred also in the western lands and in the southeastern principality of Riazan, in fact, everywhere in Russia, except in Novgorod which knew how to control its princes.

Whereas the evolution of Novgorod emphasized the role of the veche, and the evolution of Galicia and Volynia that of the boyars, the prince prevailed in the northeast. Although, as already mentioned, Rostov, Suzdal, and some other towns and areas of the northeast formed integral and important parts of Kievan Rus, they generally lay, in contrast to the southwest, in a wilderness of forests with no definite boundaries and hence with great possibilities of expansion to the north and the east. That expansion took place in the late Kievan and especially the appanage periods. This celebrated "colonization" of new lands was considered by S. Soloviev, Kliuchevsky, and some other specialists to have been decisive for subsequent Russian history. The princes played a major role in the expansion by providing economic support, protection, and social organization for the colonists. In the new pioneer society there existed little in the nature of vested interests or established institutions to challenge princely authority. It may be noted that Andrei Bogoliubskii had already transferred his capital from ancient Suzdal to the new town of Vladimir and that his chief political opponents were the boyars from the older sections of his realm. The Mongol invasion and other wars and disasters of the time also contributed to the growth of princely authority, for they shattered the established economic and social order and left it to the prince to rebuild and reorganize devastated territory. The increasing particularism and dependence on local economy, together with the proliferation of appanages, meant that the prince often acted simply as the proprietor of his principality, entering into every detail of its life and worrying little about the distinction between public and private law. With the passage of years, the role of the prince in the northeast came to bear little resemblance to that of the princes in Novgorod or in Galicia.

Kliuchevsky and other Russian historians seem to overstate the case when they select the evolution of the northeast as the only authentic Russian development and true continuation of Kievan history. It would seem better to consider Novgorod, the southwest, and the northeast, all as fully Kievan and as accentuating in their later independent growth certain aspects of the mixed and complicated Kievan society and system: the democratic veche, the aristocratic boyar rule, or the autocratic prince; the city or the countryside; trade or agriculture; contacts with the West or proximity to Asia. Nor should other Russian areas—not included in our brief discussion—such as those of Smolensk, Chernigov, or Riazan, be denied their full share of Kievan inheritance. But we should not minimize the significance of the northeast in Russian history. It was there, together with the Novgorodian north and other adjacent lands, that developed what would come to be defined as the Russian ethnic type, as distinct from Ukrainians and Belarusians (groups once distinguished as Great Russians, Little Russians, and White Russians). The conditions of its emergence, all characteristic of the northeast, included the breakdown of Kievan unity and the existence of a more primitive style of life in a forest wilderness inhabited also by Finnic-speaking tribes. And, of course, it was a northeastern principality, Moscow, that rose to "gather the Russian lands" and initiate a new epoch in Russian history.

# CHAPTER II

# The Rise of Moscow

...we can imagine the attitude towards the princedom of Moscow and its prince which developed amidst the northern Russian population.... 1) The senior Grand Prince of Moscow came to be regarded as a model ruler-manager, the establisher of peace in the land and of civil order, and the princedom of Moscow as the starting point of a new system of social relations, the first fruit of which was precisely the establishment of a greater degree of internal peace and external security. 2) The senior Grand Prince of Moscow came to be regarded as the leader of the Rus people in its struggle against foreign enemies, and Moscow as the instrument of the first popular successes over infidel Lithuania and the heathen "devourers of raw flesh," the Mongols. 3) Finally, in the Moscow prince northern Russia became accustomed to see the eldest son of the Russian church, the closest friend and collaborator of the chief Russian hierarch; and it came to consider Moscow as a city on which rests a special blessing of the greatest saint of the Russian land, and to which are linked the religious-moral interests of the entire Orthodox Russian people. Such significance was achieved, by the middle of the fifteenth century, by the appanage princeling from the banks of the Moscow River, who, a century and a half earlier, had acted as a minor plunderer, lying around a corner in ambush for his neighbors.

VASILII KLIUCHEVSKY

The unification of Great Russia took place through a destruction of all local, independent political forces, in favor of the single authority of the Grand Prince. But these forces, doomed by historical circumstances, were the bearers of "antiquity and tradition," of the customary-legal foundations of Great Russian life. Their fall weakened its firm traditions. To create a new system of life on the ruins of the old became a task of the authority of the Grand Prince which sought not only unity, but also complete freedom in ordering the forces and the resources of the land. The single rule of Moscow led to Muscovite autocracy.

ALEXANDER PRESNIAKOV

As the preceding quotation from the great nineteenth-century Russian historian Kliuchevsky suggests, during the century following the Mongol subjugation of Russia, the descendents of a minor princeling, based in what was still a modest rustic town in the fourteenth century, transformed the course of Russian history. In the fourteenth and fifteenth centuries, Moscow became the center of a mighty and expanding dynastic state, fortified by great wealth and extensive lands defined as the ruler's "patrimony," by centralized political power, by military victories over competitors and the Mongol Horde, and by an ideology grounded in both secular and religious notions of inheritance and destiny. Indeed, the traditional description of this process as a "gathering of the Russian lands" (*sobiranie russkikh zemel'*), with implications of necessity and national destiny, has long influenced much of the historiography of this process.

The name Moscow first appears in a chronicle under the year 1147, when Iurii Dolgorukii, a prince of Suzdal mentioned in the preceding chapter, sent an invitation to his ally Prince Sviatoslav of the eastern Ukrainian principality of Novgorod-Seversk: "Come to me, brother, to Moscow." And in Moscow, Iurii feasted Sviatoslav. Under the year 1156, the chronicler notes that Grand Prince Iurii Dolgorukii "laid the foundations of the town of Moscow," meaning—as on other such occasions—that he built the city wall. Moscow as a town is mentioned next under 1177 when Gleb, Prince of Riazan, "came upon Moscow and burned the entire town and the villages." It would seem, then, that Moscow originated as a princely village or settlement prior to 1147, and that about the middle of the twelfth century it became a walled center, that is, a town. Moscow was located in Suzdal territory, close to the borders of the principalities of Novgorod-Seversk and Riazan. In the fourteenth century, it possessed a modest wooden fortress (kremlin) flanked by a commercial and artisan settlement and farms.

## The Rise of Moscow to the Reign of Ivan III

We know little of the early Muscovite princes, who changed frequently and apparently considered their small and insignificant appanage merely as a stepping stone to a better position, although one might mention at least one Vladimir who was one of the younger sons of Vsevolod III and probably the first prince of Moscow in the early thirteenth century, and another Vladimir who perished when Moscow was destroyed by the Mongols in 1237. It was with Daniel (Daniil), the youngest son of Alexander Nevskii, who became the ruler of Moscow in the second half of the thirteenth century that Moscow acquired a separate family of princes who stayed in their appanage and devoted themselves to its development (hence historians write of the Daniilovichi, the descendents of Daniel). Daniel concentrated his efforts both on building up his small principality and on extending it along the flow of the Moscow River, of which he controlled originally only the middle course. Daniel succeeded in seizing the mouth of the river and its lower course from one of the Riazan princes; he also had the good fortune of inheriting an appanage from a childless ruler.

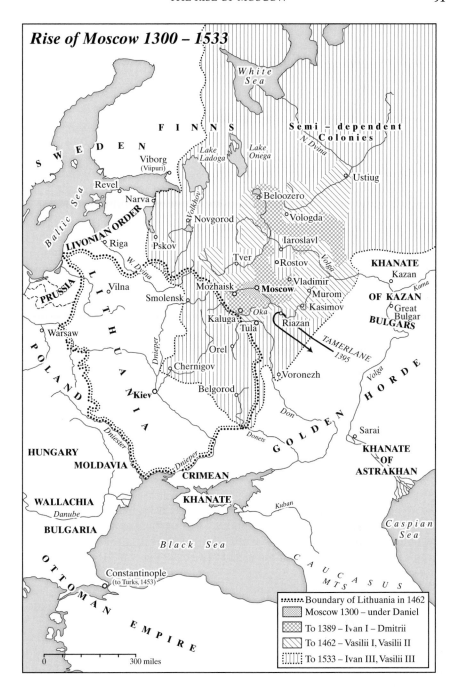

*Rise of Moscow 1300 – 1533*

**Legend:**

- ┅┅┅ Boundary of Lithuania in 1462
- ▨ Moscow 1300 – under Daniel
- ▦ To 1389 – Ivan I – Dmitrii
- ◫ To 1462 – Vasilii I, Vasilii II
- ▥ To 1533 – Ivan III, Vasilii III

Daniel's son Iurii, or George, who succeeded him in 1303, attacked another neighbor, the prince of Mozhaisk, and by annexing his territory finally established Muscovite control over the entire flow of the Moscow River. After that he turned to a much more ambitious undertaking: a struggle with Grand

Prince Michael of Tver for leadership in Russia. The rivalry between Moscow and Tver was to continue for almost two centuries, determined in large part which principality would unite the Russian lands, and also added much drama and violence to the appanage period. In 1317 or 1318 Iurii married a sister of the khan of the Golden Horde, the bride having become Orthodox, and received from the khan the appointment as grand prince. During the resulting campaign against Tver, the Muscovite army suffered a crushing defeat, and, although Iurii escaped, his wife fell prisoner. When she died in captivity, Iurii accused Michael of poisoning her. The Tver prince had to appear at the court of the Golden Horde, where he was judged, condemned, and executed. In consequence, Iurii was reaffirmed in 1319 as grand prince. Yet by 1322 the khan had made Michael's eldest son, Dmitrii, grand prince. Iurii accepted this decision, but apparently continued his intrigues, traveling in 1324 to the Golden Horde. There, in 1325, he was met and dispatched on the spot by Dmitrii, who was in turn killed by the Mongols. Dmitrii's younger brother, Alexander of Tver, became grand prince. However, he too soon ran into trouble with the Mongols. In 1327 a punitive Mongol expedition, aided by Muscovite troops, devastated Tver, although Alexander escaped to Pskov and eventually to Lithuania. In 1337 Alexander was allowed to return as prince of Tver, but in 1338 he was ordered to appear at the court of the Golden Horde and was there executed.

Following the devastation of Tver and Alexander's flight, Iurii's younger brother Ivan Kalita, prince of Moscow, obtained the position of grand prince, which he held from 1328, or according to another opinion from 1332, until his death in 1341. Ivan Kalita means "John the Moneybag," and Ivan I remains the prototype of provident Moscow princes with their financial and administrative talents. Always careful to cultivate the Golden Horde, he not only retained the office of grand prince, but also received the commission of gathering tribute for the khan from other Russian princes. He used his increasing revenue to purchase more land: both entire appanages from bankrupt rulers and separate villages. The princedom of Vladimir, which he held as grand prince, he simply added to his own principality, keeping the capital in Moscow. He ransomed Russian prisoners from the Mongols to settle them on Muscovite lands. All in all, Ivan Kalita managed to increase the territory of his princedom severalfold.

It was also in Ivan Kalita's reign that Moscow became the religious capital of Russia. After the collapse of Kiev, and in line with the general breakup of unity in the land, no ecclesiastical center immediately emerged to replace Kiev, "the cradle of Christianity in Russia." In 1326 the head of the Russian Church, Metropolitan Peter, died while staying in Moscow. He came to be worshipped as a saint and canonized, his shrine bringing a measure of sanctity to Moscow. Moreover, in 1328 Ivan Kalita persuaded Peter's successor, Theognost, to settle in Moscow. From that time on, the metropolitans "of Kiev and all Russia"—a title which they retained until the mid-fifteenth century—added immeasurably to the importance and prestige of the upstart principality and its rulers. Indeed, the presence of the metropolitan not only made Moscow the spiritual

center of Russia, but, as we shall see, it also proved time and again to be helpful to the princedom in diverse material matters.

Following the passing of Ivan Kalita in 1341, his son Simeon, surnamed
the Proud, was confirmed as grand prince by the khan of the Golden Horde.
Simeon's appellation, his references to himself as prince "of all Russia," and
his entire bearing indicated the new significance of Moscow. In addition to
emphasizing his authority over other Russian rulers, Simeon the Proud continued his predecessor's work of enlarging the Muscovite domain proper. He
died in 1353 at the age of thirty-six, apparently of the plague which had been
devastating most of Europe. In his testament Simeon the Proud urged his
heirs to obey a remarkable Russian cleric, Alexis, who was to become one of
the most celebrated Muscovite metropolitans.

Alexis, in fact, proceeded to play a leading role in the affairs of the
Muscovite state both during the reign of Simeon the Proud's weak brother
and successor, Ivan the Meek, which lasted from 1353 to 1359, and during the
minority of Ivan's son Grand Prince Dmitrii. Besides overseeing the management of affairs in Moscow and treating with other Russian princes, the metropolitan traveled repeatedly to the Golden Horde to deal with the Mongols.
Alexis's wise leadership of Church and state contributed to his enshrinement
as one of the leading figures in the Muscovite pantheon of saints. During Ivan
II's reign, beginning with 1357, civil strife erupted in the Golden Horde: no
fewer than twenty rulers were to change in bloody struggle in the next twenty
years. Yet, if Mongol power declined, that of Lithuania, led by Olgerd, grew;
and the Moscow princes had to turn increasing attention to the defense of
their western frontier.

Ivan the Meek's death resulted in a contest for the office of grand prince,
with Prince Dmitrii of Suzdal and Ivan's nine-year-old son Dmitrii as the
protagonists. In a sense, the new crisis represented a revival of old Kievan
political strife between "uncles" and "nephews": Dmitrii of Suzdal, who, as
well as Dmitrii of Moscow, was descended directly from Vsevolod III, was a
generation older than the Muscovite prince and claimed seniority over him.
Rapidly changing Mongol authorities endorsed both candidates. The rally of
the people of Moscow behind their boy-ruler and the principle of direct succession from father to son carried the day: Dmitrii of Suzdal abandoned his
headquarters in Vladimir without a fight, and Ivan the Meek's son became
firmly established as the Russian grand prince. The Kievan system of succession failed to find sufficient support in the northeast.

Grand Prince Dmitrii, known as Dmitrii Donskoi, that is, of the Don, after
his celebrated victory over the Mongols near that river, reigned in Moscow
for three decades until his death in 1389. The early part of his reign, with
Metropolitan Alexis playing a major role in the government, saw a continuing growth of Muscovite territory, while in Moscow itself in 1367 stone walls
replaced wooden walls in the Kremlin. It also witnessed a bitter struggle
against Tver supported by Lithuania. Indeed Prince Michael of Tver obtained
from the Golden Horde the title of grand prince and, together with the
Lithuanians, tried to destroy his Muscovite rival. Twice, in 1368 and 1372,

Olgerd of Lithuania reached Moscow and devastated its environs, although he could not capture the fortified town itself. Dmitrii managed to blunt the Lithuanian offensive and make peace with Lithuania, after which he defeated Tver and made Michael recognize him as grand prince. Muscovite troops also scored victories over Riazan and over the Volga Bulgars, who paid tribute to the Golden Horde.

But Dmitrii's fame rests on his victorious war with the Golden Horde itself. As Moscow grew and as civil strife swept through the Golden Horde, the Mongol hegemony in Russia experienced its first serious challenge since the time of the invasion. We have seen that Dmitrii had successfully defied the Mongol decision to make Michael of Tver grand prince and had defeated the Volga Bulgars, whose principality was a vassal state of the Golden Horde. A series of incidents and clashes involving the Russians and the Mongols culminated, in 1378, in Dmitrii's victory over a Mongol army on the banks of the Vozha River. Clearly the Mongols had either to reassert their mastery over Moscow or give up their dominion in Russia. A period of relative stability in the Golden Horde enabled the Mongol military leader and strong man, Mamai, to mount a major effort against Dmitrii.

The Mongols made an alliance with Lithuania, and Mamai set out with his troops to meet in the upper Don area with forces of Grand Prince Jagiello of Lithuania for a joint invasion of Muscovite lands. Dmitrii, however, decided to seize the initiative and crossed the Don, seeking to engage the Mongols before the Lithuanians arrived. Medieval sources—old chronicles and the epic poem *Zadonshchina*—dramatically magnify the size of the opposing forces. It was said that the Russians brought at least 150,000 men against at least 300,000 Mongol warriors. Modern historians believe the numbers were closer to 20,000–50,000 troops under Dmitrii and 90,000 under Mamai. The decisive battle, known as the battle of Kulikovo field, was fought on the eighth of September 1380 where the Nepriadva River flows into the Don, on a hilly terrain intersected by streams which the Russians selected to limit the effectiveness of the Mongol cavalry. The terrain was such that the Mongols could not simply envelop Russian positions, but had to break through them. Fighting of desperate ferocity—Dmitrii himself, according to one source, was knocked unconscious in combat and found after the battle in a pile of dead bodies— ended in a complete rout of Mamai's army when the last Russian reserve came out of ambush in a forest upon the exhausted and unsuspecting Mongols. Jagiello, whose Lithuanian forces failed to reach Kulikovo by some two days, chose not to fight Dmitrii alone and turned back. The great victory of the Russians laid to rest the belief in Mongol invincibility. What is more, the new victor of the Don rose suddenly as the champion of all the Russians against the hated Mongol oppressors. While certain important Russian rulers failed to support Dmitrii, and those of Riazan even negotiated with the Mongols, some twenty princes rallied against the common enemy in an undertaking blessed by the Church and bearing some marks of a crusade. The logic of events pointed beyond the developments of 1380 to a new role in Russian history for both the principality and prince of Moscow.

Nevertheless, the years following the great victory at Kulikovo saw a reversal of its results. In fact, only two years later, in 1382, the Mongols came back, led this time by the able Khan Tokhtamysh. While the surprised Dmitrii was in the north gathering an army, they besieged Moscow and, after assaults failed, managed to enter the city by a ruse: Tokhtamysh swore that he had decided to stop the fighting and that he and his small party wanted to be allowed within the walls merely to satisfy their curiosity; once inside, the Mongols charged their hosts and, by seizing a gate, obtained reinforcements and hence control of Moscow, which they sacked and burned. Although Tokhtamysh retreated, with an enormous booty, rather than face Dmitrii's army, the capital and many of the lands of the principality were desolated and its resources virtually exhausted. Dmitrii, therefore, had to accept the over-lordship of the Mongol khan, who in return confirmed him as the Russian grand prince. Still, after Kulikovo, the Mongol grip on Russia lacked its former firmness. Dmitrii Donskoi spent the last years of his reign in strengthening his authority among Russian princes, especially those of Tver and Riazan, and in assisting the rebuilding and economic recovery of his lands.

When Dmitrii Donskoi died in 1389 at the age of thirty-nine, his son Vasilii became grand prince without challenge either in Russia or in the Golden Horde. Vasilii I's long reign, from 1389 until his death in 1425, deserves attention for a number of reasons. The cautious and intelligent ruler continued very successfully the traditional policy of the Muscovite princes of enlarging their own principality and of making its welfare their first concern. Thus, Vasilii I acquired several new appanages as well as a number of individual towns with their surrounding areas. Also he waged a continuous struggle against Lithuania for western Russian lands. Although the warlike Grand Prince Vitovt of Lithuania scored some victories over his Russian son-in-law, Vasilii's persistent efforts led to a military and political deadlock in much of the contested area. It might be noted that, after the conclusion of a treaty with Lithuania in 1408, a number of appanage princes in the western borderlands switched their allegiance from Lithuania to Moscow.

Relations with the East presented as many problems as relations with the West. In 1395 Moscow barely escaped invasion by the army of one of the greatest conquerors of history, Tamerlane (Timur), who had spread his rule through the Middle East and the Caucasus and in 1391 had smashed Tokhtamysh. Tamerlane's forces actually devastated Riazan and advanced upon Moscow, only to turn back to the steppe before reaching the Oka River. Around 1400 Muscovite troops laid waste the land of the Volga Bulgars, capturing their capital Great Bulgar and other towns. In 1408 the Golden Horde, pretending to be staging a campaign against Lithuania, suddenly mounted a major assault on Moscow to punish Vasilii I for not paying tribute and for generally disobeying and disregarding his overlord. The Mongols devastated the principality, although they could not capture the city of Moscow itself. In the later part of his reign, Vasilii I, preoccupied by his struggle with Lithuania and Tver, maintained good relations with the khan and sent him "gifts."

The death of Vasilii I in 1425 led to the only war of succession in the history of the principality of Moscow. The protagonists in the protracted struggle were Vasilii I's son Vasilii II, who succeeded his father at the age of ten, and Vasilii II's uncle Prince Iurii, who died in 1434 but whose cause was taken over by his sons, Vasilii the Squint-eyed and Dmitrii Shemiaka. Prince Iurii claimed seniority over his nephew, and he represented, in some sense, a feudal reaction against the growing power of the grand princes of Moscow and their centralizing activities. By 1448, after several reversals of fortune and much bloodshed and cruelty—which included the blinding of both Vasilii the Squint-eyed and of Vasilii II himself, henceforth known as Vasilii the Blind—the Muscovite prince had prevailed. Dmitrii Shemiaka's final rebellion was suppressed in 1450. Indeed, having obtained sufficient support from the boyars and the people of Moscow, Vasilii II managed, although at a very heavy cost, not only to defeat his rivals but also to expand his principality at the expense of Vasilii the Squint-eyed and Dmitrii Shemiaka and also of some other appanage princes.

Relations with the Mongols continued to be turbulent as the Golden Horde began to break up and Moscow asserted its independence. In 1445 Vasilii II was badly wounded and captured in a battle with dissident Mongol leaders, although he soon regained his freedom for a large ransom. The year 1452 marked a new development: a Mongol prince of the ruling family accepted Russian suzerainty when the princedom of Kasimov was established. Vasilii II had taken into his service Mongol nobles with their followers fleeing from the Golden Horde, and he rewarded one of them, Kasim, a descendant of Jenghiz Khan, with the principality for his important assistance in the struggle against Dmitrii Shemiaka. The creation of this Mongol princedom subject to the grand prince of Moscow was only one indication of the decline of Mongol power. Still more significant was the division of the vast lands held directly by the Golden Horde, with the Crimean khanate separating itself in 1430, that of Kazan in 1436, and that of Astrakhan in 1466 during the reign of Vasilii II's successor, Ivan III. In 1475 the Crimean state recognized Ottoman suzerainty, with Turkish troops occupying several key positions on the northern shore of the Black Sea. Of course, the khans of the Golden Horde tried to stem the tide and, among other things, to bring their Russian vassal back to obedience. Khan Ahmad directed three campaigns against Moscow, in 1451, 1455, and 1461, but failed to obtain decisive results. For practical purposes, Moscow can be considered as independent of the Mongols after 1452 at least, although the formal and final abrogation of the yoke came only in 1480. In fact, Vernadsky regards the establishment of the principality of Kasimov as a decisive turning point in the relations between the forest and the steppe and thus in what is, to him, the basic rhythm of Russian history.

Vasilii II's long reign from 1425 to 1462 also witnessed important events in Europe which were to influence Russian history profoundly, although they did not carry an immediate political impact like that implicit in the breakup of the Golden Horde. At the Council of Florence in 1439, with Byzantium struggling against the Turks for its existence and hoping to obtain help from the West, the Greek clergy signed an abortive agreement with Rome, recognizing papal supremacy. The Russian metropolitan, Isidore, a Greek, participated in the Council of Florence and, upon his return to Moscow, proclaimed its results during a solemn service and read a prayer for the pope. After the service he was arrested on orders of the grand prince and imprisoned in a monastery, from which he escaped before long to the West. A council of Russian bishops in 1443 condemned the Church union, deposed Isidore, and elected Archbishop Jonas metropolitan. The administrative dependence of the Russian Church on the Byzantine came to an end. Furthermore, many Russians remained suspicious of the Greeks even after they repudiated the very short-lived Union of Florence. Then in 1453 Constantinople fell to the Turks, who proceeded to acquire complete control of the Balkan peninsula and of what used to be the Byzantine Empire. As we know, it was with Byzantium and the Balkan Slavs that ancient Russia had its most important religious and cultural ties, in the appanage period as well as in the days of Kiev. The success of the Turks contributed greatly to a weakening of these ties and, therefore, to a more complete isolation of Russia. As we shall see, it also strengthened Muscovite xenophobia and self-importance and various teachings based on these attitudes. It should be noted that this boost to Muscovite parochialism occurred at the very time when the northeastern Russian princedom was being transformed into a major state that was bound to play an important role in international relations and was in need of Western knowledge.

## The Reigns of Ivan III and Vasilii III

The long reign of Ivan III, which extended from 1462 to 1505, has generally been considered, together with the following reign of Vasilii III, as the termination of the appanage period and the beginning of a new age in Russian history, that of Muscovite Russia. These two reigns provide a fitting climax to the story of the rise of Moscow. Ivan III's predecessors had already increased the territory of their principality from less than 600 square miles at the time of Ivan Kalita to 15,000 toward the end of Vasilii II's reign. But it remained for Ivan III to absorb such old rivals as Novgorod and Tver and to establish virtually a single rule in what used to be appanage Russia. Also, it was Ivan III who, at the conclusion to the developments described earlier in this chapter, successfully asserted full Russian independence from the Mongols. And it was in his reign that the position and authority of the grand prince of Moscow, continuing their long-term rise, acquired attributes of majesty and formality unknown in the appanage period. Ivan III, also called Ivan the Great, suited his important role well: while sources differ concerning certain traits of his character, the general impression remains of a mighty figure combining the practical abilities of an appanage prince with unusual statesmanship and vision. Although only twenty-two years old at the time of Vasilii II's death, the new grand prince was fully prepared to succeed him, having already acted for several years as his blind father's chief assistant and even co-ruler.

Under Ivan III "the gathering of Russia" proceeded apace. The following catalogue of events might give some indication of the nature and diversity of

the process. In 1463—or about a decade later according to Lev Cherepnin—
Ivan III purchased the patrimony of the appanage princes of Iaroslavl, and
in 1474 the remaining half of the town of Rostov. In 1472 he inherited an
appanage, the town of Dmitrov, from his childless brother Iurii; and in the
same year he conquered the distant northeastern land of Perm, inhabited
by a Finnic-speaking people and formerly under the vague suzerainty of
Novgorod. In 1481 the Muscovite grand prince obtained another appanage
after the death of another brother, Andrew the Little. In 1485 he forced
Prince Michael of Vereia to bequeath to him Michael's principality, bypassing Michael's son, who had chosen to serve Lithuania. In 1489 he annexed
Viatka, a northern veche-ruled state founded by emigrants from Novgorod.
And in 1493 Ivan III seized the town of Uglich from his brother, Andrew
the Big, and imprisoned Andrew for failing to carry out his instructions to
march with an army to the Oka River, against the Mongols. Around 1500 the
Muscovite grand prince inherited, from Prince Ivan of Riazan, half of his
principality and was appointed warden of the other half bequeathed to Ivan
of Riazan's young son.

Ivan III's most famous acquisitions, however, were Novgorod and Tver.
Novgorod, which we discussed in an earlier chapter, collapsed because of
both the Muscovite preponderance of strength and its own internal weaknesses. After the treaty of 1456 imposed by Vasilii II on Novgorod, the boyar
party in the city—led by the Boretsky family which included Martha the
celebrated widow of a posadnik—turned to Lithuania as its last hope. The
common people of Novgorod, on the other hand, apparently had little liking either for Lithuania or for their own boyars. In the crucial campaign of
1471 Novgorodian troops made a poor showing, the archbishop's regiment
refusing outright to fight against the grand prince of Moscow. After winning the decisive battle fought on the banks of the Shelon River, Ivan III had
the Novgorodians at his mercy. They had to promise allegiance to the grand
prince and his son, pay a large indemnity, and cede to Moscow some of their
lands. The new arrangement, which meant a thorough defeat and humiliation of Novgorod but left its system and position essentially intact, could not
be expected to last. And indeed the authorities of Novgorod soon refused
to recognize Ivan III as their sovereign and tried again to obtain help from
Lithuania. In 1478 the angry grand prince undertook his second campaign
against Novgorod; because Lithuanian help failed to materialize (because the
Lithuanian ruler was shifting his geopolitical interests away from the Russian
north) and the Novgorodians split among themselves, the city finally surrendered without a battle to the besieging Muscovite army. This time Ivan
III executed some of his opponents as traitors, exiled others, and transferred
a considerable number of Novgorodian boyar families to other parts of the
country, seizing their lands. He declared, as quoted in a chronicle: "The veche
bell in my patrimony, in Novgorod, shall not be, a posadnik there shall not be,
and I will rule the entire state." In effect the entire Novgorodian system was
abolished. Further large-scale deportations took place in 1489, and Novgorod
became an integral part of the Muscovite state.

Tver's turn came next; this principality offered even less resistance than Novgorod. Another Tver prince named Michael also tried to obtain Lithuanian help against the expanding might of Moscow, signing an agreement in 1483 with Casimir IV of Lithuania and Poland. But when Ivan III marched on Tver, Michael repudiated the agreement and declared himself an obedient "younger brother" of the Muscovite ruler. Yet in 1485 he tried to resume relations with Lithuania; his messages to Casimir IV were intercepted and his plans discovered by Moscow. Thereupon, Ivan III promptly besieged Tver. Michael's support among his own followers collapsed, and he escaped to Lithuania, while the town surrendered without battle to the Muscovite army. When Michael died in Lithuania he left no heir, and in this manner ended the greatest rival family to the princes of Moscow. In contrast to Novgorod, the incorporation of Tver, which was a northeastern principality, presented no special problems to Muscovite authorities. The sum of Ivan III's acquisitions, large and small, meant that very few Russian appanages remained to be gathered, and as a rule even these few, such as Pskov or the last half of Riazan, survived because of their cooperation with the grand princes of Moscow.

Ivan III's ambitions were not limited to the remaining Russian appanages. The grand prince of Moscow considered himself the rightful heir to all the former Kievan lands, which in his opinion constituted his lawful patrimony. Ivan III made his view of the matter quite clear in foreign relations, and at home he similarly emphasized his position as the sole ruler of the whole country. In 1493 he assumed the title of Sovereign—*gosudar* in Russian—of All Russia. Ivan III's claim to the entire inheritance of the Kievan state represented above all else a challenge to Lithuania, which, following the collapse of Kiev, had extended its dominion over vast western and southwestern Russian territories. The Princedom of Lithuania, called by some the Lithuanian-Russian Princedom, which we shall discuss in a later chapter, arose in large part as a successor to Kiev: on the outcome of the struggle between Moscow on one side and Lithuania and Poland on the other depended the final settlement of the Kievan estate.

After Ivan III acquired Novgorod and Tver, a number of appanage princes in the Upper Oka area, a border region between Lithuania and Moscow, switched their allegiance from their Lithuanian overlord to him. Lithuania failed to reverse their decision by force and accepted the change in an agreement in 1494. But new defections of princes to Moscow, this time farther south, led to war again in 1500. The Russians won the crucial battle on the banks of the Vedrosha River, capturing the Lithuanian commander, artillery, and supplies. By the peace treaty of 1503, the Lithuanians recognized as belonging to the grand prince of Moscow those territories that his armies had occupied. Ivan III thus obtained parts of the Smolensk and the Polotsk areas and much of Chernigov-Seversk, a huge land in southern and central European Russia based on the old principality of Chernigov. Another peace treaty in 1503 ended the war which Moscow had effectively waged to defend the principality of Pskov against the Livonian Order. All in all, Ivan III's successes in other Russian states and in foreign wars enormously increased his domain.

The grand prince's growing power and prestige led him logically to a final break with the Mongols. This definitive lifting of the Mongol yoke, however, represented something of an anticlimax compared to the catastrophe of the Mongol invasion or the epic battle of Kulikovo. Ivan III became grand prince without being confirmed by the khan and, following the practice of his father Vasilii II, he limited his allegiance to the Golden Horde to the sending of "presents" instead of the regular tribute, finally discontinuing even those. Mongol punitive expeditions in 1465 and 1472 were checked in the border areas of the Muscovite state. Finally in 1480, after Ivan III publicly renounced any allegiance to the Golden Horde, Khan Ahmad decided on an all-out effort against the disobedient Russians. He made an alliance with Casimir IV of Lithuania and Poland and invaded Muscovite territory. Ivan III, in turn, obtained the support of Mengli-Geray, the Crimean khan, and disposed his forces so as to block the Mongol advance and above all to guard river crossings. The main Mongol and Muscovite armies reached the opposite banks of the Ugra River and remained there facing each other. The Mongols had failed to cross the river before the Muscovites arrived, and they did not receive the expected Lithuanian and Polish help because these countries had to concentrate on beating back the Crimean Tatars who had made a large raid into Lithuania. Strangely enough, when the river froze, making it possible for the cavalry of the Golden Horde to advance, and the Russians began to retreat, the Mongols suddenly broke camp and rushed back into the steppe. Apparently they were frightened by an attack on their home base of Sarai that was staged by a Russian and Tatar detachment. In any case, Khan Ahmad's effort to restore his authority in Russia collapsed. Shortly after, he was killed during strife in the Golden Horde, and around 1500 the Horde itself fell under the blows of the Crimean Tatars.

Another important event in Ivan III's reign was his marriage in 1472 to a Byzantine princess, Sophia, or Zoe, Paleologue. The marital alliance between the grand prince of Moscow and a niece of the last Byzantine emperor, Constantine XI, who had perished on the walls of Constantinople in the final Turkish assault, was sponsored by the Vatican in the hope of bringing Russia under the sway of the pope and of establishing a broad front against the Turks. These expectations failed utterly, yet for other reasons the marriage represented a notable occurrence. Specifically, it fitted well into the general trend of elevating the position of the Muscovite ruler. Ivan III added the Byzantine two-headed eagle to his own family's St. George, and he developed a complicated court ceremonial on the Byzantine model. He also proceeded to use the high titles of *tsar* and *autocrat* and to institute the ceremony of coronation as a solemn church rite. While *autocrat* as used in Moscow originally referred to the complete independence of the Muscovite sovereign from any overlord, and thus to the termination of the Mongol yoke, the word itself—although translated into the Russian as *samoderzhets*—and the attendant concept of power and majesty were Greek, just as *tsar* stemmed from the Roman, and hence Byzantine, *caesar*. Ivan III also engaged in an impressive building program in Moscow, inviting craftsmen from many countries to serve him. In 1497 he

Seal of Ivan III. The Moscow princes portrayed themselves as inheritors of the sacred mantle of the Byzantine throne. As a sign, Ivan combined the family crest, St. George killing the dragon, with the Byzantine double-headed eagle. (*Armory of the Kremlin, Moscow*)

promulgated for his entire land a code of law which counted the *Russian Justice* and the Pskov *Sudebnik* among its main sources. Apparently, the Muscovite ruler took the attitude of a distant superior toward his collaborators, especially after his Byzantine marriage. Or, at least, so the boyars complained for years to come.

Although Ivan III asserted his importance and role as the successor to the Kievan princes, he refused to be drawn into broader schemes or sacrifice any of his independence. Thus he declined papal suggestions of a union with Rome and of a possible re-establishment, in the person of the Muscovite ruler, of a Christian emperor in Constantinople. And when the Holy Roman Emperor offered him a kingly crown, he answered as follows: "We pray God that He let us and our children always remain, as we are now, the lords of our land; as to being appointed, just as we had never desired it, so we do not desire it now." Ivan III has been called the first national Russian sovereign.

Ivan III was succeeded by his son Vasilii III, who ruled from 1505 to 1533. The new reign in many ways continued and completed the old. Vasilii III annexed virtually all remaining appanages, such as Pskov, obtained in 1511, and the remaining part of Riazan, which joined the Muscovite state in 1517, as well as the principalities of Starodub, Chernigov-Seversk, and the upper Oka area. The Muscovite ruler fought Lithuania, staging three campaigns aimed at Smolensk before that town was finally captured in 1514; the treaty of 1522 confirmed Russian gains. Continuing Ivan III's policy, he exercised pressure on the khanate of Kazan, advancing the Russian borders in that direction and supporting a pro-Russian party which acted as one of the two main contending political factions in the turbulent life of the city and the state. Profiting from the new standing of Muscovite Russia, Vasilii III had diplomatic relations with the Holy Roman Empire—the ambassador of which, Sigismund von Herberstein, left an important account of Russia, *Rerum moscovitarum commentarii*—with the papacy, with the celebrated Turkish sultan Suleiman I, the Magnificent, and even with the founder of the great Mogul Empire in India, Babar. Ironically, in the case of this last potentate, of whom next to nothing was known in Moscow, the Russians behaved with extreme caution not to pay excessive honors to his empire and thus to demean the prestige of their ruler. Invitations to foreigners to enter Russian service continued. It was in the reigns of Ivan III and Vasilii III that a whole foreign settlement, the so-called German suburb, appeared in Moscow.

In home affairs too Vasilii III continued the work of his father. He sternly ruled the boyars and members of former appanage princely families who had become simply servitors of Moscow. In contrast to the practice of centuries, but in line with Ivan III's policy, the abandonment of Muscovite service in favor of some other power—which in effect came to mean Lithuania—was judged as treason. At the same time the obligations imposed by Moscow increased. These and other issues connected with the transition from appanages to centralized rule were to become tragically prominent in the following reign.

## Explanations and Interpretations

As we have noted, contemporaries had every reason to be surprised (and written sources suggest they were) at the spectacular rise of Moscow and its transformation of the political landscape. Moscow, after all, began with very little and for a long time could not be compared to such flourishing principalities as Novgorod or Galicia. Even in its own area, the northeast, it started as a junior not only to old centers like Rostov and Suzdal but also to Vladimir, and it defeated Tver in a long struggle which it appeared several times to have lost. In explaining the rise of Moscow, historians have emphasized several factors, many of which have already become apparent in our brief narrative.

One of the earliest and most basic explanations is geographical, an argument already developed by S. Soloviev. Moscow's geographic advantage included location at the crossing of three roads, the most important of which being the route from Kiev and the entire declining south to the growing northeast, which brought both settlers and trade. Even more important at that time, Moscow was also at the crossroads of water communications that spanned and united European Russia. Moscow had the rare fortune of being located near the headwaters of four major rivers: the Oka, the Volga, the Don, and the Dnieper. This offered marvelous opportunities for expansion across the flowing plain, especially as there were no mountains or other natural obstacles to hem in the young principality.

In another sense too Moscow benefited from a central position. It stood in the midst of lands inhabited by the Russian, and especially the Great Russian, people, which, so this traditional argument runs, provided a proper setting for natural growth in all directions. In fact, some specialists have tried to estimate precisely how close to the geographic center of the Russian people Moscow was situated, noting also such circumstances as its proximity to the line dividing the two main dialects of the Great Russian language. Central location within Russia, to make an additional point, cushioned Moscow from outside invaders. Thus, for example, it was Novgorod, not Moscow, that continuously had to meet enemies from the northwest, while in the southeast Riazan absorbed the first blows, a most helpful situation in the case of Tamerlane's invasion and on some other occasions. All in all, the considerable significance of the location of Moscow for the expansion of the Muscovite state cannot be denied, although this geographic factor certainly is not the only one and indeed has generally been assigned less relative weight by recent scholars.

The economic argument is linked in part to the geographic. The Moscow River served as an important trade artery, and as the Muscovite principality expanded along its waterways it profited by and in turn helped to promote increasing economic intercourse. Soviet historians in particular treated the expansion of Moscow largely in terms of the growth of a common market. Another economic approach emphasizes the success of the Muscovite princes in developing agriculture in their domains and supporting colonization. These princes, it is asserted, clearly outdistanced their rivals in obtaining peasants to settle on their lands, their energetic activities ranging from various inducements to free farmers to the purchase of prisoners from the Mongols. As a further advantage, they managed to maintain in their realm a relative peace and security highly beneficial to economic life.

The political argument focuses partly on the condition and policies of the Mongol horde and the clever policies of the Moscow princes in dealing with the khans. Good timing, however, was as important as good policy. From the fourteenth century on, the Mongol Empire was slowly fracturing and weakening, though it experienced periods of revival. Devastations by the Black Plague, a fraying commercial network due to problems in the Balkans and China, and violent conflicts for power within the horde created opportunities for Russian princes. The Moscow princes played this well. While the Mongols retained their strength, the princes of Moscow demonstrated complete obedience to the khans, and indeed eagerly cooperated with them. In this manner they became established as grand princes after helping the Mongols to devastate the more impatient and heroic Tver and some other Russian lands to their own advantage. In addition, they collected tribute for the Mongols, thus acquiring some financial and, indirectly, judicial authority over other Russian princes. Indeed, the khans handed over to the Muscovite princes entire appanages that were unable to pay their tribute. Symbolically, even at the end of the fourteenth century, coins were still being struck in Moscow that testified to this inter-dependent relationship: for example, a coin produced under Dmitrii Donskoi after 1382 featured on one side the words, "Grand Prince Dmitrii Ivanovich," and on the other side, "Sultan Tokhtamysh: Long may he live." As the horde fractured and Moscow strengthened, the relationship changed. To be sure, new Muscovite princes continued to present themselves to the khan to receive a patent for the throne, until Vasilii II named his son heir without asking for the khan's approval. But, as we have seen, many of the the rituals and tangible manifestations of homage and fealty were increasingly being ignored. When Ivan III finally renounced allegiance to the horde, he completed this gradual but transformative process, which the Mongols no longer had the strength to stop or undo.

As this suggests, a major factor in the success of Moscow were its ruling princes. Moscow has generally been considered fortunate in its princes, and in a number of ways. Sheer luck constituted a part of the picture. For sev-eral generations the princes of Moscow, like the Capetian kings who united France, had the advantage of continuous male succession without interruption or conflict. In particular, for a long time the sons of the princes of Moscow were lucky not to have uncles competing for the Muscovite seat. When the classic struggle between "the uncles" and "the nephews" finally erupted in the reign of Vasilii II, direct succession from father to son possessed sufficient standing and support in the principality of Moscow to overcome the chal-lenge. The princedom has also been considered fortunate because its early rulers, descending from the youngest son of Alexander Nevskii and thus rep-resenting a junior princely branch, found it expedient to devote themselves to their small appanage instead of neglecting it for more ambitious undertakings elsewhere.

It is generally believed that the policies of the Muscovite princes made a major and massive contribution to the rise of Moscow. From Ivan Kalita to Ivan III and Vasilii III these rulers stood out as "the gatherers of the Russian land," as skillful landlords, managers, and businessmen, as well as war-riors and diplomats. They all acted effectively even though, for a long time, on a petty scale. Kliuchevsky distinguishes five main Muscovite methods of obtaining territory: purchase, armed seizure, diplomatic seizure with the aid of the Golden Horde, service agreements with appanage princes, and the settlement by Muscovite population of the lands beyond the Volga. The rela-tive prosperity, good government, peace, and order prevalent in the Muscovite principality attracted increasingly not only peasants but also, a fact of great importance, boyars, as well as members of other classes, to the growing grand princedom.

Politically the development of the Muscovite state followed the pattern mentioned earlier in our general discussion of the northeast: in a relatively primitive society and a generally fluid and shifting situation, the prince became increasingly important as organizer and owner as well as ruler—with little distinction among his various capacities—while other elements of the Kievan political system declined and even atrophied. We know, for instance, that Vasilii Veliaminov, the last Muscovite tysiatskii, died in 1374 and that thenceforth that office was abolished. On the other hand, scholars have recently argued, Muscovite authoritarianism, at least before Ivan the Terrible, required cooperative relations with two major sources of domestic power: the boyars and the Church. While Ivan III and Vasilii III completed the process of incorporating rival princes into their own aristocracy and army—first making them into "service princes," as some historians have called them, and then merging them into the boyars—this expanded boyar estate was treated carefully. In order to ensure boyar loyalty, the early Moscow princes consulted with them about matters of state and ensured their considerable local wealth and power as landed magnates.

Good relations with the Church were also essential. One can argue that the Church, in fact, led the way in unifying Russia. While the various princes, in the wake of the Mongol invasion, concerned themselves with their own appanages or with developing and expanding in the northeast, the hierarchs of the Church strove to unite the entire ecclesiastical realm of Orthodox Rus, including Lithuania and the Kievan southwest. By the time of Metropolitan Cyprian (d. 1406), the Church could again justifiably speak of a single metropolitanate of "Kiev and all Rus." Ecclesiastical unity pointed logically toward the idea of political unity. In the early fourteenth century, the seat of the metropolitan moved to Moscow, making this city a religious capital long before it could claim any effective political domination over most of the country. If the metropolitan was seen as heir of the Church of Kievan Rus, should not the Moscow prince be seen as inheriting the mantle of his Kievan ancestors? Not least, the prince could represent himself, and be so blessed by the Church, as protector of the entire Orthodox community. Moscow was also the city of St. Alexis and especially St. Sergius, whose monastery, the Holy Trinity-St. Sergius Monastery north of Moscow, was a fountainhead of a broad monastic movement and quickly became a most important religious center, rivaled in all Russian history only by the Monastery of the Caves near Kiev. Church leaders appear to have supported Moscow's efforts to unite the Russian lands politically—although there is controversy among historians about this. The greatest service of the religious leadership to this cause consisted probably in their frequent intervention in princely quarrels and struggles, through advice, admonition, and occasionally even excommunication; this intervention was usually in favor of Moscow.

The construction of new myths and symbols of political legitimacy was also a crucial aspect of Moscow's success. It is important to remember that the Moscow princes' claim of all Russian rule violated the traditional rules of succession of the Kievan era—which required brothers to inherit the throne of grand prince before sons. Thus, according to dynastic traditions, the Daniilovichi were illegitimate rulers. They used the backing of the khan to help them overcome this obstacle, but this was a weak and fading source of legitimacy. Hence, it is not surprising that Vasilii II, Ivan III, and their successors sought every form of legitimacy they could find. As Richard Wortman has argued, until the nineteenth century Russian sources of political sacrality were mainly borrowed, quite explicitly, from recognized foreign civilizations, especially ancient Rome, Byzantium, and universal Christianity. As we have seen, the Moscow princes vigorously and creatively emphasized their ties to Byzantium, indeed their inheritance of its sacred mantle after Constantinople fell to the Turks in 1453. Ivan III's marriage to Sophia Paleologue, his creation of a new state seal combining the Byzantine double-headed eagle with the Muscovite crest of St. George killing the dragon, and his adoption of the titles tsar and autocrat were all part of this process. It was also during the reigns of Ivan III and Vasilii III that additional myths of descent were developed and propagated, including that Christianity was brought to Russia by St. Andrew the Apostle, that Muscovite princes could trace their ancestry back to the Roman emperors, and that the regalia worn by the ruler had been given to the Rus princes by the Byzantine emperor. The doctrine of Moscow as the Third Rome, to be discussed later, served similar purposes. More tangibly, Ivan III hired Italian architects to rebuild the Moscow Kremlin as a sign of Moscow's new preeminence, both as a symbol and as a means to impress Russians and foreigners alike.

Judgments of the nature and import of the rise of Moscow are even more controversial than descriptions and explanations of that process. Most pre-revolutionary Russian historians praised it as a great and necessary achievement of the princes of Moscow and of the Russian people, who had to unite to survive outside aggression and to play their part in history. Soviet historians came to share the same view, and this argument has been enshrined in the official post-Soviet history curriculum and in statements about the national past by Russian leaders. On the other hand, this interpretation—a "nationalist myth" in the eyes of critics—has often been questioned, including by prerevolutionary Russian historians like Alexander Presniakov, by many contemporary Western scholars today, and, understandably, by Polish, Lithuanian, and Ukrainian historians. These writers have emphasized in particular that the vaunted "gathering of Russia" consisted, above all, in a skillful aggression by the Muscovite princes against both Russians, such as the inhabitants of Novgorod and Pskov, and eventually various non-Russian nationalities, which deprived them of their liberties, subjugating everyone to Muscovite despotism. As is frequently the case in major historical controversies, both schools are substantially correct, stressing as they do different aspects of the same complicated phenomenon. Without necessarily taking sides on this or other related issues, we shall appreciate a little better the complexity and the problems of the period after devoting some attention to the economic, social, and cultural life of appanage Russia.

# CHAPTER 12

# Appanage Russia: Economy, Society, Institutions

Thus our medieval boyardom in its fundamental characteristics of territorial rule; the dependence of the peasants, with the right of departure; manorial jurisdiction, limited by communal administration; and economic organization, characterized by the insignificance of the lord's own economy: in all these characteristics our boyardom represents an institution of the same nature with the feudal seigniory, just as our medieval rural commune represents, as has been demonstrated above, an institution of the same essence with the commune of the German Mark.

NIKOLAI PAVLOV-SILVANSKY

...the "service people" was the name of the class of population obligated to provide service (court, military, civil) and making use, in return, on the basis of a conditional right, of private landholdings. The basis for a separate existence of this class is provided not by its rights, but by its obligations to the state. These obligations are varied, and the members of this class have no corporate unity.

MIKHAIL VLADIMIRSKY-BUDANOV

Whereas the controversy continues concerning the relative weight of commerce and agriculture in Kievan Rus, scholars agree that tilling the soil represented the main occupation of the appanage period. Rye, wheat, barley, millet, oats, and a few other crops continued to be the staples of Russian agriculture. The centuries from the fall of Kiev to the unification of the country under Moscow saw a prevalence of local, agrarian economy, an economic parochialism corresponding to political division. Furthermore, with the decline of the south and the Mongol invasion, the Russians lost much of their best land and had to establish or develop agriculture in forested areas and under severe climatic conditions. Mongol exactions further strained the meager Russian economy. In Matvei Liubavsky's words: "A huge parasite attached itself to the popular organism of northeastern Russia; the parasite sucked the juices of the organism, chronically drained its life forces, and from time to time produced great perturbations in it." In addition to the impact of Mongol conquest and exactions, the bubonic plague (or Black Death) reached northeast Russia in the mid-fourteenth century and would recurrently appear over the next hundred years; some scholars estimate a loss to the plague of as much as 25 percent of the population.

Notwithstanding the terrible effects of conquest and plague, the northeast, to which many fled, experienced a slow economic recovery, with trade as a driving force. The Mongol invasion produced new mobility in the population, with some towns, such as Moscow and Tver, benefitting from the arrival of migrants. By the fourteenth century, we see a new growth in such towns of artisanal manufacturing, including carpentry, tanning, weaving, and metalwork—mainly to provide local needs—and a growth in urban construction, notably churches and fortifications. Luxury and artistic crafts sharply declined, largely because of the poverty characteristic of the age, but they survived in some places, principally in Novgorod; with the rise of Moscow, the new capital gradually became their center.

Commerce was the main reason for economic recovery. Even apart from lands such as Galicia, not to mention the city and principality of Novgorod, where trade retained great importance, in the northeast too we see signs of new development by the fourteenth century. The Mongol Empire established a commercial network that extended from China to the Mediterranean, and Russian princes and cities were drawn into this trade. Further, the Mongols, in the interests of enhancing their own wealth, scholars argue, encouraged Russian trade with the Baltic states, along the ancient Volga trade artery, along the Don River, and with Genoese and Venetian colonies that appeared by the Black Sea. Russians continued to export such items as furs and wax and to import a wide variety of products, including textiles, wines, silverware, gold objects, and other luxuries. By the late fifteenth century, Moscow became the dominant power controlling and benefiting from this growing merchant trade network. Still, we should not forget that the vast majority of the population tilled the soil and that even most magnates earned their wealth from control of agricultural land and people. Commercial interests and the middle class in general had remarkably little weight in the history of the rising Muscovite state.

## The Question of Russian Feudalism

The question of the social structure of appanage Russia is closely tied to the issue of feudalism in Russian history. Although most recent histories of this era no longer show much interest in this concept for interpreting appanage society, it still deserves consideration as a means of viewing Russia in a comparative European frame. Until the early twentieth century, specialists treated the absence of feudalism in Russia as a key sign of a social development significantly different from that of other European countries. Then Nikolai Pavlov-Silvansky offered a brilliant and detailed defense of the idea that Russia too had experienced a feudal stage. Pavlov-Silvansky's thesis became an object of heated controversy in the years preceding the First World War. After the Revolution, Soviet historians proceeded to define "feudal" in extremely broad terms and to apply this concept to the development of Russia all the way from the days of Kiev to the second half of the nineteenth century. Outside the Soviet Union, a number of scholars, while disagreeing with Pavlov-Silvansky on important points, nevertheless accepted at least a few feudal characteristics as applicable to medieval Russia.

Pavlov-Silvansky argued that three traits defined feudalism and that all three were present in appanage Russia: division of the country into independent and semi-independent landholdings, the seigniories; inclusion of these landholdings into a single system by means of a hierarchy of vassal relationships; and the conditional quality of the possession of a fief. Russia was indeed divided into numerous independent principalities and privileged boyar holdings, that is, seigniories. As in western Europe, the vassal hierarchy was linked to the land: the *votchina*, which was an inherited estate, corresponded to the seigniory; the *pomestie*, which was an estate granted on condition of service, to the benefice. Pavlov-Silvansky, it should be noted, believed that the pomestiia, characteristic of the Muscovite period of Russian history, already represented a significant category of landholding in the appanage age. The barons, counts, dukes, and kings of the West found their counterparts in the boyars, service princes, appanage princes, and grand princes of medieval Russia. Boyar service, especially military service, based on free contract, provided the foundation for the hierarchy of vassal relationships. Special ceremonies, comparable to those in the West, marked the assumption and the termination of this service. Appanage Russia knew such institutions as feudal patronage, commendation—personal or with the land—and the granting of immunity to the landlords, that is, of the right to govern, judge, and tax their peasants without interference from higher authority. Vassals of vassals appeared, so that one can also speak of sub-infeudation in Russia.

Pavlov-Silvansky's opponents, however, presented strong arguments on their side. They stressed the fact that throughout the appanage period Russian landlords acquired their estates through inheritance, not as compensation for service, thus retaining the right to serve whom they pleased. The estate of an appanage landlord usually remained under the jurisdiction of the ruler in whose territory it was located, no matter whom the landlord served. Furthermore, numerous institutions and even entire aspects of Western feudalism either never developed at all in Russia, or, at best, failed to grow there beyond a rudimentary stage. Such was the case, for example, with the extremely complicated Western hierarchies of vassals, with feudal military service, or with the entire phenomenon of chivalry. Even the position of the peasants and their relationship with the landlords differed markedly in the East and in the West, for serfdom became firmly established in Russia only after the appanage period.

In sum, it would seem that a precise definition of feudalism, with proper attention to its legal characteristics, would not be applicable to Russian society. Yet, on the other hand, many developments in Russia, whether we think of the division of power and authority in the appanage period, the economy of large landed estates, or even the later pomestie system of state service, bear important resemblances to the feudal West. As already indicated, Russian social forms often appear to be rudimentary, or at least simpler and cruder, versions of Western models. Therefore, a number of scholars speak of the social organization of medieval Russia as incipient or undeveloped feudalism. That feudalism proved to be particularly weak when faced with the rising power of the grand princes and, especially, of the autocratic tsars.

Today, scholars who emphasize the comparability of pre-Muscovite Russia to many aspects in the history of western Europe—and not only similarities but also influential interactions across the continent—are more likely to use the term "medieval" than "feudal" and often extend this back into the Kievan era as well. This more open term, with its sense of betweenness and transition, sees many commonalities without forcing Russia into the straightjacket of having to be identical to European societies in social and political form, without ignoring continual change across Europe east and west, and without losing sight of the variety of medieval societies. Indeed, scholars of western European history, with the exception of traditional Marxists, tend now to avoid the term "feudalism" precisely because its rigid definition masks important differences and processes of change within western Europe itself. Still, questions of periodization and definition remain very important. Thus, among historians of early Russia, the question of when Russia ceased to be medieval and became "early modern" has become a more preoccupying question than whether it was or was not "feudal."

## Appanage Society and Institutions

The social structure of appanage Russia represented a continuation and a further evolution of the society of the Kievan period, with no sharp break between the two. The princes occupied the highest rung on the social ladder. The already huge Kievan princely family proliferated and differentiated further during the centuries that followed the collapse of a unitary state. The appanage period naturally proved to be the heyday of princes and princelings, ranging from grand princes to rulers of tiny principalities and even to princes who had nothing to rule and were forced to find service with their relatives. It might be added that in addition to the grand princes "of Moscow and all Russia," grand princes emerged in several other regional centers, notably Tver and Riazan, where the lesser members of a particular branch of the princely family paid a certain homage to their more powerful elder. The expansion of Moscow ended this anarchy of princes, and with it the appanage period.

Next came the boyars, followed by the less aristocratic "free servants" of a prince who performed a similar function. The boyars and the free servants made contracts with their prince, and they were at liberty to leave him and seek another master. The boyars had their own retinues, sometimes quite numerous. For instance, in 1332 a boyar with a following of 1,700 persons entered the service of the grand prince of Moscow, while shortly after his arrival another boyar with a retinue of 1,300 left it. As already emphasized, members of the upper classes of appanage Russia were landlords. They acted as virtual rulers of their large estates, levying taxes and administering justice, although it is worth noting that, as Moscow rose, the immunities they received to govern their lands no longer extended to jurisdiction in cases of major crimes.

With the rise of the Moscow state came an important change in the pattern of land ownership. Through most of the appanage period, apart from court and Church lands, the dominant form of land tenure was the hereditary form known as votchina, private lands that could be bought, sold, or inherited. Under Ivan III and after, conditional pomestie landholding became increasingly common—including when the Moscow grand prince seized votchiny and either changed their tenure or replaced the owner with one with conditional tenure. Pomestiia were given at the complete discretion of the prince in return for military service. As long as a pomestie owner remained in the prince's service or could ensure that a brother or son could provide service after his death, pomestiia remained in a family. But unlike a votchina, a pomestie could not be sold or mortgaged to raise money. The key purpose of the pomestie system was for Ivan III and his successors to provide a livelihood for their military servitors and to ensure their loyalty.

Traders, artisans, and the middle class as a whole experienced a decline during the appanage period. Except in Novgorod and a few other centers, members of that layer of society were relatively few in number and politically ineffective.

Peasants constituted the bulk of the population. It is generally believed that their position worsened during the centuries following the collapse of the Kievan state. Political division, invasions, and general insecurity increased the peasant's dependence on the landlord and consequently his bondage, thus accelerating a trend that had already become pronounced in the days of Kiev. As a larger and larger percentage of the peasants ceased to be free farmers and found themselves on the estates of magnates or monasteries, traditional freedoms were reduced. They owed various forms of service, mainly of two types: the as yet relatively little developed *barshchina,* or corvée, that is, work for the landlord, and *obrok,* or quitrent, that is, payment to the landlord in kind or in money. Evidence that peasants valued their traditional freedoms, and that these were under assault, can be seen in acrimonious court cases against landlords. Most important, though, were efforts to restrict peasant movement. Peasants had traditionally moved to new lands as old ones grew less productive. In the fifteenth century, in order to ensure a reliable supply of labor for landlords, various state regulations began to limit this practice. Most significantly, the 1497 law code (*Sudebnik*) stipulated that a peasant could leave his master only during a two-week period once a year, around St. George's day in the late autumn, after the harvest, provided his accounts had been settled. In the sixteenth and seventeenth centuries, restrictions on movement would

expand, tying peasants to privately held land as serfs. It should be noted, however, that many peasants, especially in the north, had no private landlords, a
fortunate situation for them, even though they bore increasingly heavy obligations to the state.

The slaves, *kholopy,* of the Kievan period continued to play a significant
role in the Russian economy, performing all kinds of tasks in the manorial
households and estates. In fact, a small upper group of kholopy occupied
important positions as managers and administrators on the estates. Indeed
Mikhail Diakonov suggested that in the Muscovite principality, as in France,
court functionaries and their counterparts in most noble households were
originally slaves, who were later replaced by the most prominent among the
free servitors.

In the period which followed the fall of Kiev, the Church in Russia maintained and developed its strong and privileged position. In a time of division it profited from the best and the most widespread organization in the
country, and it enjoyed the benevolence of the khans and the protection of
Russian, especially Muscovite, princes. Ecclesiastical lands received exemptions from taxation and sweeping immunities; also, as in the West—although
this is a controversial point—they probably proved to be more attractive to
the peasants than other estates because of their relative peace, good management, and stability. The Church, or rather individual monasteries and monks,
often led the Russian penetration into the northeastern wilderness. Disciples
of St. Sergius alone founded more than thirty monasteries on or beyond the
frontier of settlement. But the greatest addition to ecclesiastical possessions
came from continuous donations, in particular the bequeathing of estates or
parts of estates in return for prayers for one's soul, a practice similar to the
granting of land in free alms to the Catholic Church in the feudal West. It has
been estimated that at the end of the appanage period the Church in Russia
owned over 25 percent of all cultivated land in the country. As we shall see,
these enormous ecclesiastical, particularly monastic, holdings created major
problems both for the religious conscience and for the state.

The unification of Russia under Moscow meant a victory for a northeastern political system characterized by the dominant position of the prince,
indeed of a system in which Russia was treated as the grand prince's personal
"patrimony." On the other hand, many recent scholars have argued, princely
authority, even in Moscow, was not as absolute as the grand princes might
have wished and as they often tried to demonstrate. Princes, of course, played
a major social role throughout the appanage period. They acted as managers and even proprietors of their principalities, as illustrated in the celebrated
princely wills and testaments that deal indiscriminately with villages and
winter coats. Indeed, princely activities became more and more petty; public rights and interests became almost indistinguishable from private. With
the rise of Moscow to national dominance, the role of the princes was subordinated to the power and interests of the "tsar" and "autocrat" of "Moscow
and all Russia." Yet, for all their exalted majesty, the Moscow tsars retained
much from their northeastern princeling ancestry, combining in a formidable

manner sweeping authority with petty despotism and public goals with proprietary instincts. Their power proved all the more dangerous because it faced few effective counterweights. After the absorption of Novgorod, Pskov, and Viatka, the veche disappeared from Russian politics. Competing princes were reduced to serving boyars. And the so-called boyar duma, as will be seen in later chapters, ultimately supported rather than circumscribed the authority of the ruler.

One should not exaggerate autocratic power, however, especially in these early years. Many historians now caution that beneath the surface of growing autocracy—what Nancy Shields Kollmann provocatively called the "facade of autocracy," which she applied even to later Muscovite history—was the persistence of a ruling class of grand princes and high boyars who ruled by consultation and consensus-building. Treaties, trade agreements, military actions, and law codes had to be witnessed by the leading boyars and agreed to by these assembled magnates. Thus, according to this influential but still controversial argument, formulaic statements in legal decisions under Ivan III and Vasilii III, such as "the Grand Prince decreed with the boyars..." or (as in the opening words of the 1497 law code) "The Grand Prince of all Rus, Ivan Vasilievich, with his sons and boyars, compiled a code of law..." should be viewed not as mere formality, but as reflecting a complex structure of negotiated power relations.

CHAPTER 13

# Appanage Russia: Religion and Culture

The Mongol yoke, which dealt a heavy blow to the manufactures of the Russian people in general, could not but be reflected, in a most grievous manner, in the artistic production and technique closely related to manufacturing.... The second half of the thirteenth and the entire fourteenth century were an epoch "of oppression of the life of the people, of despair among the leaders, of an impoverishment of the land, of a decline of trades and crafts, of a disappearance of many technical skills."

DMITRII BAGALEI

If we consider nothing but its literature, the period that extends from the Tatar invasion to the unification of Russia by Ivan III of Moscow may be called a Dark Age. Its literature is either a more or less impoverished reminiscence of Kievan traditions or an unoriginal imitation of South Slavonic models. But here more than ever it is necessary to bear in mind that literature does not give the true measure of Old Russian culture. The fourteenth and fifteenth centuries, the Dark Age of literature, were at the same time the Golden Age of Russian religious painting.

D. S. MIRSKY

The Russian icon was the most significant artistic phenomenon of ancient Russia, the fundamental and preponderant means, and at the same time a gift, of its religious life. In its historical origin and formation the icon was an expression of the highest artistic tradition, while in its development it represented a remarkable phenomenon of artistic craftsmanship.

NIKODIM KONDAKOV

Although it is clear that the religion and culture of appanage Russia, like its economy and society, developed directly out of the Kievan period, historians have viewed its condition and direction quite differently, as the epigraphs for this chapter suggest. More precisely, historians have documented contradictory trends. Certainly, the hard centuries that followed the collapse of a unitary state witnessed a certain retardation, and even regression, in many fields of culture. Impoverishment and relative isolation had an especially adverse effect on education in general and on such costly and difficult pursuits as large-scale building in stone and certain luxury arts and crafts. Indeed, many crafts and skills seem to have been completely lost. Literature too seemed to have lost much of its former artistry and *élan*. As the noted Russian historian Dmitrii Likhachev observed, "the writing of chronicles became paler, laconic, and lacking the broad Russia-wide horizon" of eleventh- and twelfth-century chronicles. Yet this decline in many areas of activity coincided with probably the highest achievements of Russian creative genius in a few fields, including wooden architecture and, especially, icon painting. Indeed, some writers have described such great vitality in religious life, especially in the fourteenth and fifteenth centuries, as to speak of a "Russian spiritual renaissance" expressed in religious art, the flowering of monasticism, and intense concern (and conflict) with questions of faith and morals.

Religion in appanage Russia reflected, in its turn, the strong and weak points, the achievements and failings of the period, as it continued to occupy a central position in the life and culture of the people. In an age of division, the unity and organization of the Church stood out in striking manner. In the early fifteenth century the Orthodox Church in Russia had, in addition to the metropolitan in Moscow, fifteen bishops, of whom three, those of Novgorod, Rostov, and Suzdal, had the title of archbishop. In 1448, after suspicions of the Greek clergy had been aroused in Russia by the Council of Florence, Jonas became metropolitan without the confirmation of the patriarch of Constantinople, thus breaking the old Russian allegiance to the Byzantine See and inaugurating the autocephalous, in effect independent, period in the history of the Russian Church. Administrative unity within the Russian Church, however, finally proved impossible to preserve. The growing division of the land and the people between Moscow and Lithuania resulted in the establishment, in Kiev, of a separate Orthodox metropolitanate for the Lithuanian state, the final break with Moscow coming in 1458.

As we know, the Church, with its enormous holdings and its privileged position, played a major role in the economic and political life of appanage Russia, influencing almost every important development of the period, from the rise of Moscow to the colonization of the northeastern wilderness. But the exact impact of the Church in its own religious and spiritual sphere remains difficult to determine. It has been frequently, and on the whole convincingly, argued that the ritualistic and aesthetic sides of Christianity prevailed in medieval Russia, finding their fullest expression in the liturgy and other Church services, some of which became extremely long and elaborate. Fasting, celebrating religious holidays, and generally observing the Church calendar provided further occasions for the ritualism of the Russian people, while icon painting and church architecture served as additional paths in their search for beauty. Still, the ethical and social import of Russian Christianity should not be underestimated in this period any more than during the hegemony of Kiev. Many specialists credit the teaching of the Church with the frequent manumission of slaves by individual masters, realized often by means of a provision in last wills and testaments. And, in a general sense, Christian standards of behavior remained at least the ideal of the Russian people.

Saints continued to reflect the problems and aspirations of the Russians. Figures of the appanage period who became canonized ranged from princes, such as Alexander Nevskii, and ecclesiastical statesmen exemplified by Metropolitan Alexis, to obscure hermits. But the strongest impression on the Russian religious consciousness was made by St. Sergius of Radonezh. St. Sergius, who died in 1392 at the age of about seventy-eight, began as a monk in a forest wilderness and ended as the recognized spiritual leader of Russia. His blessing apparently added strength to Grand Prince Dmitrii and the Russian army for the daring enterprise of Kulikovo, and his word could on occasion stop princely quarrels. Although he refused to be metropolitan, he became in effect the moral head of the Russian Church. As already mentioned, the monastery that St. Sergius founded north of Moscow and that came to be known as the Holy Trinity-St. Sergius Monastery became one of the greatest religious and cultural centers of the country and the fountainhead of a powerful monastic movement. For centuries after the death of St. Sergius tens and hundreds of thousands of pilgrims continued to come annually from all over Russia to his burial place in one of the churches in the monastery. They still come. As in the case of many other saints, the chief explanation of the influence of St. Sergius lies in his ability to give a certain reality to the concepts of humility, kindness, brotherhood, and love which remain both beliefs and hopes of the Christians. It might be added that St. Sergius tried constantly to help all who needed his help and that he stressed work and learning as well as religious contemplation and observance.

The disciples of St. Sergius, as already mentioned, spread the Christian religion to vast areas in northern Russia, founding scores of monasteries. St. Stephen of Perm, the most distinguished of the friends of St. Sergius, brought Christianity to the Finnic-speaking tribes of the Zyriane: he learned their tongue and created a written language for them, utilizing their decorative designs as a basis for letters. Thus, following the Orthodox tradition, the Zyriane could worship God in their native language.

Intellectual life in medieval Russia, as in medieval Europe as a whole, centered on matters of religion, although their concerns often encompassed many other areas of human activity. Thus, the appanage era was marked by a religious ferment around a series of dissenting trends—heresies, from the perspective of the established Church—that concerned key questions of theology and faith but also of everyday life and social morality. While, in the main, Russia stayed outside the rationalist and reforming currents that developed in Western Christendom, it did not remain totally unaffected by them. Significantly, Russian religious movements stressing rationalism and radical reform emerged in western parts of the country and especially in Novgorod. As early as 1311 a Church council condemned the heresy of a certain Novgorodian priest who denounced monasticism. In the second half of the fourteenth century, in Novgorod, the teaching of the so-called *strigolniki* acquired prominence. These radical sectarians, quite similar to the evangelical Christians in the West, denied the authority of the Church and its hierarchy, as well as all sacraments except baptism, and wanted to return to the time of the apostles; an extreme faction within the movement even renounced Christ and sought to limit religious observances to prayer to God the Father. It might be noted that the protest began apparently over the issue of fees for the sacraments, and that the dissidents came rapidly to adhere to increasingly radical views. All persuasion failed, but violent repression by the population and authorities in Novgorod and Pskov, together with disagreements among the strigolniki, led to the disappearance of the sect in the early fifteenth century.

Later in the century, however, new heretics appeared, known as the Judaizers. Their radical religious movement has been linked to the arrival in Novgorod in 1470 of a Jew Zechariah, or Skharia, and to the spread of his doctrines. The Judaizers in effect accepted the Old Testament, but rejected the New, considering Christ a prophet rather than the Messiah. Consequently they also denounced the Church. Through the transfer of two Novgorodian priests to Moscow, the movement obtained a foothold in the court circles of the capital. Joseph of Volok, an abbot of Volokolamsk, led the ecclesiastical attack on the heretics. They were condemned by the Church council of 1504, and Ivan III, finally ceding to the wishes of the dominant Church party, cruelly suppressed the Judaizers, having their leaders burned at the stake.

Controversies within the Russian Orthodox Church at the time had an even greater historical significance than did challenges to the Church from the outside. The most important and celebrated dispute of the age pitted the "possessors" against the "non-possessors," with Joseph of Volok again occupying a central position as the outstanding leader of the first-named faction. Joseph of Volok and the possessors believed in a close union of an autocratic ruler and a rich and powerful Church. The prince, or tsar, was the natural protector of the Church with all its lands and privileges. In return, he deserved complete ecclesiastical support, his authority extending not only to all secular matters but also to Church administration. The possessors emphasized, too, a formal and ritualistic approach to religion, the sanctity of Church services, rituals, practices, and teachings, and a violent and complete suppression of all dissent.

The non-possessors, who because of their origin in the monasteries of the northeast, have sometimes been called the "elders from beyond the Volga," had as their chief spokesman Nil Sorskii—or Nilus of Sora—a man of striking spiritual qualities. The non-possessors, as their name indicates, objected to ecclesiastical wealth and in particular to monastic landholding. They insisted that the monks should in fact carry out their vows, that they must be poor, must work for their living, and must remain truly "dead to the world." The Church and the state should be independent of each other; most especially, the state, which belonged to a lower order of reality, had no right to interfere in religious matters. The non-possessors stressed contemplation and the inner spiritual light, together with a striving for moral perfection, as against ecclesi-astical formalism and ritualism. Furthermore, by contrast with the possessors, they differentiated in the teaching of the Church among Holy Writ, tradition, and human custom, considering only Holy Writ—that is, God's command-ments—as completely binding. The rest could be criticized and changed. But even those who challenged the foundations of the Church were to be met with persuasion, never with force.

The Church council of 1503 decided in favor of the possessors. Joseph of Volok and his associates cited Byzantine examples in support of their position and also argued, in practical terms, the necessity for the Church to have a large and rich establishment in order to perform its different functions, including the exercise of charity on a large scale. Their views, especially on relations of Church and state, suited on the whole the rising absolutism of Moscow, although it seems plausible that Ivan III sympathized with the non-possessors in the hope of acquiring monastic lands. After Joseph of Volok died in 1515, subsequently to be proclaimed a saint, other high clerics continued his work, notably Daniel, who became metropolitan in 1521. At the councils of 1524 and 1531, and even as late as 1554–55, some of Nil Sorskii's chief followers were declared to be heretics. Nil Sorskii himself, however, was canonized.

In explaining the controversy between the possessors and the non-possessors, many scholars, including Soviet historians as a group, have emphasized that the possessors championed the rise of the authority of the Muscovite rulers and the interests of those elements in Russian society which favored this rise. The non-possessors, on the other hand, with their high social connections, reflected the aristocratic opposition to centralization. In a differ-ent context, that of the history of the Orthodox Church, the non-possessors may be considered to have derived from the mystical and contemplative tradi-tion of Eastern monasticism, especially as practiced on Mount Athos. However, in a still broader sense, the possessors and the non-possessors expressed two recurrent attitudes that devoted Christians have taken toward things of this world, burdened as they have been by an incompatibility between the tem-poral and the eternal standards and goals of behavior. The non-possessors, thus, resemble the Franciscans in the West as well as other religious groups that have tried hard to be in, and yet not of, this world. And even after all the sixteenth-century councils they remained an important part of the Russian Church as an attitude and a point of view. Indeed, this medieval religious and moral debate about the proper balance between living in the social world and seeking to better it through moral action and charity or following a path (though also to heal and save the world) of withdrawal, self-denial, contempla-tion, and prayer would reappear often in times of dynamism and uncertainty in Russian history, notably at the beginning of the twentieth century and after the collapse of communism.

The seemingly secular intellectual problem of political authority, the question of the position and power of the ruler, also often acquired a religious coloring. This became especially important as Moscow rose to "gather Russia" and as its princes turned into autocratic tsars. As already mentioned, a number of legends and doctrines were developed to justify and buttress the growing power and realm of the Moscow princes. Especially important were markers of succession from both Byzantium and ancient Rome and of Moscow's role as a legitimate new center of universal Christendom. For example, one tale about the princes of Vladimir, which originated, apparently, in the first quarter of the sixteenth century, related how Vladimir Monomakh of Kiev, the celebrated ancestor of the Muscovite princes, received from his maternal grandfather, the Byzantine emperor Constantine Monomakh, certain regalia of his high office, including a famous crown that came to be known as the "cap [*shapka*] of Monomakh" (most likely, in fact, a work of thirteenth-century Tatar craftsmanship). Still more grandly, the princes of Moscow came to be connected to the Roman emperors. According to the new genealogy, Augustus, a sovereign of Rome and the world, in his old age divided his possessions among his relatives, placing his brother Prus as ruler on the banks of the Vistula. Riurik was a fourteenth-generation descendant of this Prus, St. Vladimir a fourth-generation descendant of Riurik, and Vladimir Monomakh a fourth-generation descendant of St. Vladimir. Concurrently with this revision of the genealogy of the princes of Moscow, Christianity in Russia was antedated and St. Andrew, the apostle, was proclaimed its true originator.

But the most interesting doctrine—and one that has received divergent interpretations from scholars—was that of Moscow as the Third Rome. Its originator, an abbot from Pskov named Philotheus or Filofei, wrote a letter to Vasilii III in 1510 which described three Romes: the Church of Old Rome, which fell because of a heresy; the Church of Constantinople brought down by the infidels; and finally the Church in Vasilii III's own tsardom which, like the sun, was to illumine the entire world—in Philotheus's words, "all the Christian realms have come to an end and have been reduced to the single realm of our Sovereign.... For two Romes have fallen, the Third stands, and there shall be no fourth." Some scholars have stressed the secular political implications of this notion of Moscow's universal role, including connecting it to the growth of Russian authoritarianism and imperialism. It is, therefore, necessary to emphasize that Philotheus thought, in the first place, of Churches, not states, and that he was concerned with the preservation of the true faith, not political expansion. Also, Philotheus, like many churchmen of his age, included a warning to ambitious secular rulers. As he wrote in a letter to Ivan III, "if thou rulest thine empire rightly, thou wilt be the son of light and a citizen of the heavenly Jerusalem.... [T]ake care and take heed." In any case, the Muscovite rulers in their foreign policy never endorsed the view of Moscow as the Third Rome, remaining, as already mentioned, quite uninterested in the possibility of a Byzantine inheritance, while at the same time determined to recover the inheritance of the princes of Kiev.

## Literature and the Arts

The literature of the appanage period has generally been rated rather low. This judgment applies with full force only to the extant written works, although the oral, folkloristic tradition too, while it continued to be rich and varied, failed to produce tales equal in artistry to the Kievan byliny. As a qualification it might be added that, in the opinion of certain scholars, surviving material is insufficient to enable us to form a definitive view of the scope and quality of appanage literature.

The Mongol conquest of Russia gave rise to a number of factual narratives as well as semi-legendary and legendary stories. These dwelt on the bitter fighting, the horror, and the devastation of the invasion and interpreted the events as divine punishment for the Russians' sins. The best artistic accounts of the catastrophe can be read in the series dealing with the Mongol ravage of Riazan and in the *Lay of the Destruction of the Russian Land*, written early in the appanage period about the middle of the thirteenth century, of which only the beginning has survived. The victory of Kulikovo in turn found reflection in literature. Thus the *Story of the Massacre of Mamai*, written with considerable artistry some twenty years after the event, tells about the departure of Prince Dmitrii from Moscow, the grief of his wife, the visit of the prince to the blessed Sergius of Radonezh, the eve of the battle, and the battle itself. Another well-known account of Kulikovo, the *Zadonshchina* composed at the end of the fifteenth century, is a weak imitation, both in its poetic devices and in its ideological advocacy of the necessary unification of Russia against its enemies, of the *Lay of the Host of Igor*. The expansion of Moscow, as seen from the other side, inspired the *Tale about the Capture of Pskov*, written by a sorrowing patriot of that city. Chronicles in Novgorod and elsewhere continued to give detailed and consecutive information about developments in their localities.

Accounts of the outside world can be found in the sizeable travel literature of the period. Foremost in this category stands Afanasii Nikitin's celebrated *Wanderings beyond the Three Seas*, a narrative of this Tver merchant's journey to Persia, Turkey, and India from 1466 to 1472. Particular value attaches to the excellent description of India, which Nikitin saw some twenty-five years before Vasco da Gama. Other interesting records of travel during the period include those of a Novgorodian named Stephen to the Holy Land in 1350, of Metropolitan Pimen to Constantinople in 1389, and of a monk Zosima to Constantinople, Mount Athos, and Jerusalem in 1420 and also two accounts of journeys to the Council of Florence.

Church literature, including sermons, continued to be produced on what must have been a considerable scale. Hagiography deserves special notice. Lives of saints composed in the thirteenth and fourteenth centuries, for example, of Abraham of Smolensk, Alexander Nevskii, Michael of Chernigov, and Metropolitan Peter, are characterized by simplicity and biographical detail. Unfortunately for the historian, a new style, artificial, pompous, and opposed to realistic description, came to the fore with the fifteenth century. This style came from the southern Slavs and was introduced by such writers as Cyprian in his life of St. Peter the Metropolitan, and Epiphanius the Wise, who dealt with St. Sergius of Randonezh and St. Stephen of Perm. The southern Slavs, it should be added, exercised a strong influence on appanage literature and thought, as for example in the formulation of the doctrine of Moscow as the Third Rome.

In contrast to literature, architecture has frequently been considered one of the glories of the appanage period in spite of the fact that the age witnessed relatively little building in stone. Russian wooden architecture, to say the least, represents a remarkable achievement. Although it dates, without doubt, from the Kievan and the pre-Kievan eras, no buildings survive from those early times. It is only with the appanage and the Muscovite periods that we can trace the consecutive development of this architecture and study its monuments.

A *klet* or *srub*, a rectangular structure of stacked beams, each some twenty or twenty-five feet long, constituted the basis of ancient Russian wooden architecture. The walls were usually eight or nine feet high. A steep, two-slope roof offered protection and prevented an accumulation of snow, while moss and later hemp helped to plug cracks and holes. At first the floors were earthen, later wooden floors were constructed. A klet represented the living quarters of a family. Another, usually smaller, klet housed livestock and supplies. Generally the two were linked by a third small structure, a passageway, which also contained the door to the outside. A peasant household thus consisted of three separate, although connected, units. As the owner became more prosperous, or as his sons started families of their own, additional kleti were built and linked to the old ones, the ensemble growing, somewhat haphazardly, as a conglomeration of distinct, yet joined, structures.

After the Russians accepted Christianity, they adapted their wooden architecture to the Byzantine canons of church building. The three required parts of a church were erected as follows: the sanctuary, always on the eastern side, consisted of a small klet; the main section of the church, where the congregation stood, was built as a large double klet, one on top of the other; finally, another small klet on the western side constituted the *pritvor*, or separate entrance hall, where originally catechumens waited for the moment to enter the church proper. The high two-slope roof of the large klet was crowned with a small cupola topped by a cross. Churches of this simple ancient type can be seen on old icons, and a few of them in northern Russia—built, however, in the seventeenth century—have come down to our times.

Various developments in church architecture followed. In particular, the roofs of the churches became steeper and steeper, until many of them resembled wedges. In contrast to the Byzantine tradition of building churches with one or five cupolas, the Russians, whether they worked in stone or in wood, early demonstrated a liking for more cupolas. It might be noted that St. Sophia in Kiev had thirteen cupolas, and another Kievan church, that of the Tithe, had twenty-five. Numerous wooden churches also possessed many cupolas, including a remarkable one with seventeen and another with twenty-one.

The Russians not only translated Byzantine stone church architecture into another medium, wood, but they also developed it further in a creative and varied manner. Especially original and striking were the so-called tent, or pyramidal, churches, of which some from the late sixteenth and the seventeenth centuries have escaped destruction. In the tent churches the main part of the church was a high octagon—although occasionally it had six or twelve sides—which provided the foundation for a very high pyramidal, sometimes conical, roof, capped by a small cupola and a cross. The elevation of these roofs ranged from 125 to well over 200 feet. The roofs of the altar and the pritvor were, by contrast, usually low. To quote Grabar, a distinguished historian of Russian architecture and art, concerning tent churches:

> Marvelously strict, almost severe, in their majestic simplicity are these giants, grown into the earth, as if one with it....The idea of the eternity and immensity of the church of Christ is expressed here with unbelievable power and utmost simplicity. The simplicity of outline has attained in them the highest artistic beauty, and every line speaks for itself, because it is not forced, not contrived, but absolutely necessary and logically inevitable.

Weidle wrote of undeveloped Gothic in Russia, an approach not unrelated to the general concept of undeveloped Russian feudalism.

By contrast, architecture in stone, as already indicated, experienced a decline in the appanage period, although stone churches continued to be built in Novgorod and in lesser numbers in some other centers. To illustrate regression, historians have often cited the inability of Russian architects in the 1470s to erect a new Cathedral of the Assumption, the patron church of Moscow, using the Cathedral of the Assumption in Vladimir as their model. Yet this incident also marked the turning point, for Ivan III invited foreign specialists to Moscow and initiated stone building on a large scale. The most important result of the revival of stone architecture was the construction of the heart of the Kremlin in Moscow, a fitting symbol of the new authority, power, and wealth of the Muscovite rulers.

Beginning in 1474, Ivan III sent a special agent to Venice and repeatedly invited Italian architects and other masters to come to work for him in Moscow. The volunteers included a famous architect, mathematician, and engineer, Aristotle Fieravanti, together with such prominent builders as Marco Ruffo, Pietro Solario, and Alevisio. Fieravanti, who lived in Russia from 1475 to 1479, erected the Cathedral of the Assumption in the Kremlin on the Vladimir model, but with some differences. In 1490 architects from Pskov constructed in the same courtyard the Cathedral of the Annunciation, a square building with four inside pillars, three altar apses, five cupolas, and interesting decorations. It reflected the dominant influence of Vladimir architecture, but also borrowed elements from the tradition of Novgorod and Pskov and from wooden architecture. Next, still working on the Kremlin courtyard, Ivan III ordered the construction of a new Cathedral of the Archangel in place of the old one, just as he had done earlier with the Cathedral of the Assumption. Alevisio accomplished this task between 1505 and 1509, following the plan of the Cathedral of the Assumption, but adding such distinct traits as Italian decoration of the facade. The three cathedrals of the Annunciation, the Assumption, and the Archangel Michael became, so to speak, the sacred heart of the Kremlin and served, among other functions, respectively, as the place for the weddings, the coronations, and the burials of the rulers of Russia.

Stone palaces also began to appear. As with the cathedrals, probably the greatest interest attaches to the palace in the Kremlin in Moscow. It was

Cathedral of the Assumption, Moscow Kremlin, 1475–79. Designed by Aristotle Fieravanti on the model of the twelfth-century Cathedral of the Assumption in Vladimir, which was seen as the classic statement of "Russian" style.   (*Mark Steinberg*)

constructed by Ruffo, Solario, Alevisio, and other Italian architects, but following the canons of Russian wooden architecture: the palace was a conglomerate of separate parts, not a single building. Indeed stone structures often replaced the earlier wooden ones piecemeal. Italian architects also rebuilt walls and erected towers in the Kremlin, while Alevisio surrounded it with a moat by joining the waters of the rivers Moscow and Neglinnaia.

More than architecture, icon painting has frequently been considered the medieval Russian art par excellence, the greatest and most authentic expression of the spirituality and the creative genius of the Russians of the appanage period. As we have seen, icon painting came to Russia with Christianity from Byzantium. However, apparently quite early the Russians proceeded to modify their Byzantine heritage and to develop the rudiments of an original style. In the centuries which followed the collapse of the Kievan state several magnificent Russian schools of icon painting came into their own. To understand their role in the life and culture of the Russians, one should appreciate the importance of icons to a believer who finds in them a direct link with the other world and, in effect, a materialization of that other world. If, on the one hand, icons might suggest superstition and even idolatry, they represent, on the other, one of the most radical and powerful attempts to grapple with such fundamental Christian doctrines as the incarnation and the transfiguration of the universe. And, in the appanage period, pictorial representation provided otherwise unobtainable information and education for the illiterate masses.

The first original Russian school of icon painting appeared in Suzdal at the end of the thirteenth century, flourished in the fourteenth, and merged early in the fifteenth with the Muscovite school. Like the architecture of Suzdal, the icons are characterized by elegance, grace, and fine taste and can also be distinguished, according to Grabar, by "a general tone, which is always cool, silvery, in contrast to Novgorodian painting which inevitably tends towards the warm, the yellowish, the golden." The famous icon of Saints Boris and Gleb and that of Archangel Michael on a silver background provide excellent examples of the icon painting of Suzdal.

"The warm, the yellowish, the golden" Novgorodian school deserves further notice because of its monumentality and generally bright colors. The icons are often in the grand style, large in size, massive in composition, and full of figures and action. "The Praying Novgorodians" and "The Miracle of Our Lady," also known as "The Battle between the Men of Suzdal and the Novgorodians," illustrate the previously mentioned points. The Novgorodian school reached its highest development around the middle of the fifteenth century, and its influence continued after the fall of the city.

In the second half of the fourteenth century a distinct school formed in and around Moscow. Soon it came to be led by the most celebrated icon painter of all times, Andrei Rublev, who lived approximately from 1370 to 1430. The few extant works known to be Rublev's, especially his masterpiece, a representation of the so-called Old Testament Holy Trinity, demonstrate exquisite drawing, composition, rhythm, harmony, and lyricism. Pavel Muratov, stressing the influence of St. Sergius on the artist, describes Rublev's chef d'oeuvre as follows:

> This masterpiece is imbued with a suave and mystical spirituality. The composition is simple and harmonious; following its own rhythm, free from any emphasis or heaviness, it obeys a movement clearly discernible and yet hardly noticeable. The impression of harmony, peace, light and integrity which this icon produces, is a revelation of the spirit of St. Sergius.

Other scholars have emphasized the "humanistic" side of Rublev's work, suggesting comparisons to European Renaissance artists such as Giotto and

The Holy Trinity by Andrei Rublev, early fifteenth century. Scholars have noted the unusually gentle portrayal of Father, Son, and Holy Spirit (based on the Old Testament story of three angels who visited Abraham and Sarah), its emphasis on God as contemplative, peaceful, and loving.   (*Tretiakov Gallery, Sovfoto*)

Fra Angelico, and even Raphael. This interpretation emphasizes the beauty, gentleness, harmony, and human intimacy in Rublev's images of Christ and other sacred figures.

Dionysus, who was active in the first decade of the sixteenth century, stood out as the greatest continuer of the traditions of Rublev and the Muscovite school. Contemporaries mentioned his name immediately after Rublev's, and his few remaining creations support this high esteem. The icons of Dionysus are distinguished by a marvelous grace, especially in the delineation of figures, and by a certain perfection and polish. For subjects he often chose the Virgin Mary, the protectress of the city of Moscow, and the Holy Family. It should be noted that the works of Rublev and Dionysus set the high standard of icon paintings, not only in Russia, but also generally in the Orthodox East.

On the other hand, it has been argued, these were high points more than turning points in Russian art, for these achievements were too little built upon by later Russian painters.

In addition to the icons, some very valuable frescoes have come down to us from the appanage period. Located in old churches, they include works possibly of Rublev and certainly of Dionysus and his followers. The art of the miniature also continued to develop, achieving a high degree of excellence in the fifteenth century. The so-called Khitrovo Gospels of the beginning of the fifteenth century and some other manuscripts contained excellent illustrations and illumination. By contrast with all these forms of painting, sculpture was stifled because the Orthodox Church continued its ban on statuary, although, contrary to a popular misconception, even large-scale sculpture was not unknown in ancient Russia. Miniature sculpture, which was permitted, developed in a remarkable manner. Cutting figures one inch and less in height, Russian artists managed to represent saints, scenes from the Gospels, and even trees, hills, and buildings as background. The most famous practitioner of this difficult art was the monk Ambrosius, whose work is linked to the Holy Trinity-St. Sergius Monastery. In spite of general poverty, certain artistic crafts, especially embroidery, also developed brilliantly in the appanage period.

We should not neglect the vitality of popular culture. To be sure, we know relatively little about popular songs, stories, and games, for much of this culture was oral and ephemeral and thus few sources were left to us. One outstanding exception are the *skomorokhi*, or minstrels. Persisting since Kievan times, these secular entertainers joined the migration of people to the northeast. Illustrations in manuscripts in the fourteenth and fifteenth centuries show musicians, dancers, actors, jugglers, and animal trainers performing in flamboyant costumes. The unstable conditions of the appanage era evidently suited them. It appears that these traveling performers found greater tolerance in the appanage northeast than they had in Kievan Rus or would later find in Muscovite Russia, where the power of the state was strong enough to ban them in 1648. Still, the Church continued to fight against the skomorokhi, condemning their public performances as sinful acts linked to paganism, witchcraft, and Satanism. As such, skomorokhi often found it safer to remain on the road moving from town to town and village to village.

## Education

In the appanage period, education was in eclipse. As already indicated, the Mongol devastation and the relative isolation and poverty characteristic of the age led to a diminution in culture and learning. The decline of Russian towns played an especially significant role in this process, because Kievan culture had been essentially urban. Studying documents of the appanage period, we find mention of illiterate princes, and we note repeated complaints on the part of the higher clergy of the ignorance of priests. The masses of people, of course, received no education at all, although an important qualification of that statement might be in order on the basis of the already mentioned Novgorodian birchbark documents. Yet some learning and skills did remain to support the cultural development outlined in this chapter. They were preserved and promoted largely by the monasteries—as happened earlier and under comparable conditions in the West—not only by the great Holy Trinity-St. Sergius Monastery north of Moscow, but also by such distant ones as that of St. Cyril on the White Lake or the Solovetskii on the White Sea. The first century after the Mongol invasion seems to have been the nadir. With the rise of Moscow, education and learning in Russia likewise began a painful ascent.

# CHAPTER 14

# The Lithuanian-Russian State

And one more trait distinguishing the grand princedom of Lithuania from its origin revealed itself. This state from the very beginning was not simply Lithuanian, but Lithuanian-Russian.

MATVEI LIUBAVSKY

Lithuania's expansion, almost unique in its rapid success, thus proved beyond the real forces of the Lithuanians alone and of a dynasty which in spite of the unusual qualities of many of its members was too divided by the petty rivalries of its various branches to guarantee a joint action under one chief....A union of Poland with Lithuania and her Ruthenian lands, added to those already connected with Poland, could indeed create a new great power, comprising a large and crucial section of East Central Europe and strong enough to check both German and Muscovite advance. The amazing success of a plan which would seem almost fantastic was a turning point in the history not only of that region but also of Europe.

OSCAR HALECKI

The ideological center of the new commonwealth of Poland and Lithuania was to be found in the political model that was taking shape within the Polish Kingdom, especially involving growing privileges and political rights for the nobility. These privileges and rights, or, in stronger terms, freedoms, constituted the foundation of ideological union, binding the new territories to the Polish center without war. The guarantee that this expansion and the resultant union would be successful was found not mainly in the authority and charisma of the ruler, or in the administrative and military apparatus, but in the creation of a relatively broad and united elite, which was capable of further growth by admitting representatives of new countries and ethnic groups. In this political model, the source of "charisma" was those very rights and privileges that would allow a gradual evolution from subjects to citizens.

ANDRZEJ NOWAK

Whereas by the reign of Vasilii III the Muscovite rulers had managed to bring a large part of the former territory of the Kievan state under their authority, another large part of the Kievan inheritance remained in the possession of the grand princes of Lithuania. In effect, the history of the western Russian lands was linked for centuries to the social systems and fortunes of Lithuania and Poland. Some historians have even argued that the growing power of Lithuania, especially after its increasing association with Poland and the adoption of Polish political models, represented an alternative for Russia—its partisans say a more democratic and Western alternative—to the model represented by autocratic Moscow. These differences and rivalry would play an important role in Russian history.

## The Evolution of the Lithuanian State

The Lithuanians, whose language belongs to the Baltic subfamily of the Indo-European family, appeared late on the historical scene, although for a very long time they had inhabited the forests of the Baltic region. Situated between Catholic Poland, the Teutonic Knights, Orthodox Russia, and the Mongols, the pagan Lithuanians deftly preserved their independence, established a growing state of their own, and dramatically expanded to the east and south. It was apparently the pressure of the Teutonic Knights—the same who attacked Novgorod—that finally forced a number of Lithuanian tribes into a semblance of unity under the leadership of Mindovg, or Mindaugas, whose rule is dated approximately 1240–63. Mindovg accepted Christianity and received a crown from Pope Innocent IV only to sever his Western connections and return to paganism. A period of internal strife and rapidly changing rulers followed his assassination. However, toward the end of the thirteenth century Viten, or Vytenis, managed to unite the Lithuanians again. He ruled as grand prince (or grand duke) from 1295 to 1316, acted energetically at home and in foreign relations, and perished fighting the Teutonic Knights.

Viten's brother Gedymin (Gediminas), who reigned from 1316 to 1341, has been called the true founder of the Lithuanian state. He completed the unification of the Lithuanian tribes and strove hard to organize his possessions into a viable political unit. What is more, he extended his dominion to the southeast. Some Kievan territories, notably in the Polotsk area, had already become parts of the Lithuanian principality under Mindovg; with Gedymin, that principality began a massive expansion into Russia. Vilna—Vilnius in Lithuanian—became the capital of the growing state.

Gedymin's famous son Olgerd, or Algirdas, who died in 1377, carried the work of his father much further. Assisted by his valiant brother Keistut, or Kestutis, who undertook the heavy task of blocking the formidable Teutonic Order in the west, Olgerd expanded eastward with a stunning rapidity. The lands that he brought under his authority included, among others, those of Volynia, Kiev, and Chernigov, and a large part of Smolensk. In the process, he defeated the Polish effort to win Volynia and fought successfully against the Mongols. Lithuanian sway spread from the Baltic to the Black Sea. Indeed,

Olgerd wanted to rule all of Russia. Three times he campaigned against the Muscovite state, and twice he besieged Moscow itself, although he failed to capture it or to force the issue otherwise.

The sweeping Lithuanian expansion into Russia has more explanations than one. Obviously, internal division and foreign invasions had made the Russian power of resistance extremely low. But it should also be noted that the attacks of the Lithuanians could not be compared in destruction and brutality to the invasions of the Mongols or the Teutonic Knights, and that their domination, in a sense, did not represent foreign rule for the Russians. Indeed, many historians speak, on good evidence, of a Lithuanian-Russian state. Population statistics help to illustrate the situation: it has been estimated that, after the expansion of the Lithuanian state virtually to the Black Sea, two-thirds or even three-fourths and more of its people were Russians, if we group together the still little distinguished Great Russians, Little Russians (later known as Ukrainians), and White Russians (later Belorussians or Belarusians). Also, very little social displacement took place: the towns retained their Russian character; the Russian boyars and the Orthodox Church kept their high positions and extensive privileges; Russian princes continued to rule in different appanages next to Lithuanian princes, all subject to the Lithuanian grand prince; and intermarriage between the two aristocracies was quite common. It is especially interesting that the Lithuanian rulers, though pagan, sought ecclesiastical endorsement of their role as rulers of Orthodox people by seeking and winning from the patriarch in Constantinople a new metropolitanate for Lithuania, Kiev, and the western Orthodox lands, though the Russian grand princes fought vigorously against this. In addition, the Lithuanian rulers found much of value in the more developed culture of Kievan Rus. The Lithuanian army, administration, legal system, and finance were organized on the Russian pattern, and Russian became the official language of the new state. As Platonov insisted in the case of Grand Prince Olgerd of Lithuania: "In relation to different nationalities, it can be said that Olgerd's entire sympathy and attention concentrated on the Russian nationality. By his opinions, habits, and family connections, Olgerd belonged to the Russian nationality and served as its representative in Lithuania." Not surprisingly, then, the Lithuanian state could well be considered another variation on the Kievan theme and an heir to Kiev, rather than a foreign body imposed upon Russia. And this made its rivalry with Moscow, the other successful heir, all the more fundamental and significant.

Soon after Olgerd's death a new major factor complicated this situation: an alliance between Lithuania and Poland. These two expanding states had been rivals over control of both territory and commercial markets and routes in the region. In 1386, following the dynastic agreement of Krewo of 1385, Olgerd's son and successor Jagiello, or Jogaila—who reigned from 1377 to 1434—married Queen Jadwiga of Poland. Because the Polish Piast ruling family had no male members left, Jagiello became the legitimate sovereign of both states, with the Polish name of Wladyslaw II. The states remained distinct, and the union personal. In fact, in 1392 Jagiello had to recognize his cousin, Keistut's son Vitovt, or Vytautas, as a separate, although vassal, grand prince of Lithuania, an arrangement extended in 1413 to subsequent rulers of the two states. Yet both positions came to be occupied by the same man again when, in 1447, Casimir IV ascended the Polish throne without relinquishing his position as grand prince of Lithuania. Whether with the same or different rulers, Poland exercised a major and increasing influence on Lithuania after 1385.

The late fourteenth and early fifteenth century was a remarkable period in the history of the Lithuanian state. Within the decade from 1387 to 1396, Moldavia, Wallachia, and Bessarabia accepted Lithuanian suzerainty. Vitovt's rule, which lasted from 1392 to 1430, witnessed the greatest extension of the Lithuanian domain, with still more alluring possibilities in sight, as Lithuania continued to challenge Moscow for supremacy on the great Russian plain. Relations with Moscow were not entirely hostile, though. Vasilii I married Vitovt's daughter and generally recognized and cooperated with expanding Lithuanian rule in the region—with the important exception of the struggles over Novgorod and Pskov. By the end of Vitovt's rule, Lithuania directly controlled much of the original Rus lands and was continuing to move eastward, as evident in treaties with Tver and Riazan pledging service to Lithuania and the Lithuanians' growing influence in Novgorod. In addition, in 1410 Vitovt personally led his army in the crucial battle of Tannenberg, or Grünwald, where the joint forces of Poland and Lithuania crushed the Teutonic Knights, thus finally eliminating this deadly threat to both Slav and Lithuanian. The Lithuanian prince's great defeat came in 1399, when his major campaign against the Mongols met disaster at their hands. Some historians believe that had Vitovt won rather than lost on the banks of the Vorskla, he could then have asserted his will successfully against both Moscow and Poland and given a different direction to eastern European history.

Jagiello's marriage, in the last analysis, proved more important for Lithuania than Vitovt's wars or the Lithuanian-Muscovite marriage alliance (Vasilii II was Vitovt's grandson, it will be recalled). It marked the beginning of a Polonization of the country. Significantly, in order to marry Jadwiga, Jagiello forsook Orthodoxy for Roman Catholicism. Moreover, he had his pagan Lithuanians converted to Catholicism. The clergy, naturally, came to Lithuania from Poland, and the Church became a great stronghold of Polish influence. It has been noted, for instance, that three of the first four bishops of Vilnius were definitely Poles, and that the Poles constituted the majority in the Vilnius chapter even at the end of the fifteenth century. Education followed religion: the first schools were either cathedral or monastic schools, and their teachers were mainly members of the clergy. To obtain higher education, unavailable at home, the Lithuanians went to the great Polish university at Cracow, which provided the much-needed training for the Lithuanian elite. Russian historians, who stress the cultural impact of the Russians on the Lithuanians and see Polonization as forcibly imposed, often fail to appreciate the powerful attraction of Polish culture of the late Middle Ages and the Renaissance. Naturally the Lithuanians were dazzled by what Poland had to offer. Naturally too, Polish specialists, ranging from architects and artists to diplomats, appeared in Lithuania. Even Polish colonists came. But, to return to the Church, its influence extended, of course, beyond religion proper, education, and culture, to society, economics, and politics. Church estates grew, and they remained exempt from general taxation. The bishops sat in the council of the grand prince, while many clerics, highly esteemed for their education, engaged in the conduct of state business.

Polonization was the most extensive at the court and among the upper classes. Poland, with its sweeping privileges and freedom for the gentry, proved to be extremely attractive to Lithuanian landlords. Indeed, many western Russian landlords as well were Polonized, to complicate further the involved ethnic and cultural pattern of the area and contribute another element for future conflicts. Polish language and Polish customs and attitudes, stressing the independence and honor of the gentry, came gradually to dominate Lithuanian life. For example, in 1413 forty-seven Polish noble families established special relations with the same number of Lithuanian aristocratic families, each Polish family offering its coat of arms to its Lithuanian counterpart. It should also be emphasized that between 1386, that is, the marriage of Jagiello and Jadwiga and the beginning of a close relationship between Lithuania and Poland, and 1569, the year of the Union of Lublin, the Lithuanian upper classes underwent a considerable change: in general their evolution favored the development of a numerous gentry, similar to the Polish *szlachta,* while the relative importance of the great landed magnates declined.

## The Union of Lublin: The Polish-Lithuanian Commonwealth

As Lithuania grew closer to Poland, historians have argued, it ultimately ceased to be a successor state to Kievan Rus. The Union of Lublin of 1569 formally cemented this relationship in a confederation of two states. While this may be seen as a logical culmination of the historical evolution of the Lithuanian principality and the appeal of Polish culture, wealth, and politics, it did not occur without resistance from Lithuanian magnates (including Slavs who became part of the Lithuanian elite) who feared losing power and status; petty gentry, by contrast, expected to benefit. Only when Sigismund II Augustus, the King of Poland and Grand Duke of Lithuania, proceeded to detach a large section of Russian territories from Lithuania and incorporate them into Poland, did the Lithuanian magnates accept his proposals for unification.

The Union of Lublin created a new and unusual state. Formally known as the Kingdom of Poland and Grand Duchy of Lithuania, it was more commonly known as the Polish-Lithuanian Commonwealth (Rzeczpospolita in Polish), though foreigners often referred to it simply as Poland, especially as time passed. The alliance lasted, in various forms, until the partitions of Poland in the eighteenth century. Historians have much debated the nature of political and social relations in this new multiethnic, two-state confederation, which was a crucial event in the histories of several peoples. Admirers of the Commonwealth (and there have been many, and not only Polish nationalist historians), emphasize the unique rights and liberties of the combined class of Polish and Lithuanian noblemen, which mainly involved extending the "golden liberties" belonging to the Polish szlachta to nobles in the Lithuanian lands. The political order of the Commonwealth was built on a strong aristocracy with many rights and privileges and a weak king. The parliament or diet, known as the Sejm, was the main institution enacting noble rule. Through the Sejm, the Polish-Lithuanian szlachta elected the king (though from the ruling dynasty) and could oppose any royal decree. In fact, any single member of the Sejm could exercise veto power (the famous *liberum veto),* which protected the rights of minorities but also created a certain chaos in governance. Scholars often describe Poland-Lithuania as a noble "republic."

Critics have underscored the elements of national inequality in the alliance of Poland and Lithuania, even before 1569. Notwithstanding the formal equality between Lithuania and Poland and the grant of vast autonomy to the Lithuanians, the new arrangement can still be seen as fundamentally a Polish victory. The Kingdom of Poland kept the Russian lands that it had just annexed from Lithuania, which constituted the entire southern section of the principality and over a third of its total territory, including some of the richest areas. Kievans were especially resentful of the loss of self-governance they had long enjoyed until Polish centralization of authority (begun already before 1569). Because each county sent two representatives of the nobility to the Sejm and because there were many more counties in Poland than in Lithuania, the Poles outnumbered the Lithuanians in the Sejm by a ratio of three to one (though various rules, including the *liberum veto,* tried to mitigate this imbalance). Perhaps still more important, Polish culture (including Roman Catholicism) was a dominant and spreading force, though formally there was a policy of tolerance for the multiple religions of the Commonwealth. In a word, notwithstanding the many protections and rights granted Lithuanians, Poland was naturally the senior partner in the new commonwealth. Some historians have suggested that Poland had become a type of empire. Russian, Ukrainian, and Belarusian historians have paid particular attention to the fate of the non-Polish Slavic populations in this new state. Poland's annexation of Kiev, Volynia, and other southern areas of the Lithuanian principality meant that the Orthodox Slavic population found themselves with less autonomy and under the rule and influence of a largely Polish and Catholic authority. Not least, despite the many privileges that the Polish system gave the nobility, the vast majority of the population lacked any such rights. Peasants, as always, faced little but oppression.

## The Lithuanian State and Russian History

From the standpoint of Russian history, the Lithuanian, or Lithuanian-Russian, princedom presents particular interest as the great, unsuccessful rival of Moscow for the unification of the country. A major line of argument, developed by Liubavsky and others, attributes the victory of Moscow and the failure of Vilna to the differences in the evolution and structure of central authority in the two states. In a word, princely absolutism in Moscow trumped decentralized power and weak central authority in Lithuania. Though critics have characterized this argument as merely a justification of authoritarianism, and many might find the Lithuanian model more politically attractive than autocracy, it cannot be so easily dismissed. Limited by the interests of powerful boyars and largely self-governing towns, the grand princes of Lithuania turned into elected, constitutional monarchs who granted ever-increasing rights and privileges to their subjects: first they came to depend on the sanction of their aristocratic council; after the statutes of 1529 and 1566 they also needed the approval of the entire gentry gathered in a diet. Thus, as the Muscovite autocracy reached unprecedented heights in the reign of Ivan the Terrible, the authority of the Lithuanian grand princes sank to a new low. Whereas the Muscovite rulers strove, successfully on the whole, to build up a great central administration and to control the life of the country, those of Lithunia increasingly relied on, or resigned themselves to, the administration of local officials and the landlord class in general. In the showdown, for better or worse, the Muscovite system proved to be the stronger.

Important causes, of course, lay behind the contrasting evolutions of the two states. To refer to our earlier analysis, the princedom of Moscow arose in a relatively primitive and pioneer northeast, where rulers managed to acquire a dominant position in a fluid and expanding society. The Lithuanian principality, on the other hand, as it emerged from the Baltic forests, came to include primarily old and well-established Kievan lands. It encompassed much of the Russian southwest, and its economic, social, and political development reflected the southwestern pattern, which we discussed in a preceding chapter and which was characterized by the great power of the boyars as against the prince. Detailed studies indicate that in the princedom of Lithuania the same noble families frequently occupied the same land in the seventeenth as in the sixteenth or fifteenth centuries, that at times they were extremely rich, even granting loans to the state, and that the votchina landholding remained dominant, while the pomestie system played a secondary role. The rulers found this entrenched landed aristocracy, as well as, to a lesser degree, the old and prosperous towns, too much to contend with and had to accept restrictions on princely power. The Lithuanian connection with Poland contributed to the same end. Poland served as a model of an elective monarchy with sweeping privileges for the gentry; in fact, it presented an entire gentry culture and way of life. While the social and political structure of Lithuania evolved out of its own past, Polish influences supported the rise of the gentry, supplying it with theoretical justifications and legal sanctions. Ethnic and religious diversity in Lithuania also had a large influence. Muscovy was still a relatively homogeneous nation in the sixteenth century: the vast majority of its inhabitants were Orthodox Great Russians, and non-Russians and non-Orthodox still represented only small and peripheral groups. By contrast, expanded Lithuania was a multiethnic and multiconfessional polity that included Orthodox, Catholics, pagans, Jews, and Muslims speaking a great variety of languages. This, too, encouraged the formation of a federal rather than a unitary state. In the end, as already indicated, it became a junior partner to Poland rather than a serious contender for the Kievan succession.

No less important for historians of Russia, though even more controversial, is the effect of the history of the Lithuanian principality on the linguistic and ethnic division of East Slavs into Great Russians, Ukrainians, and Belorussians (now Belarusians). Scholars (and not only nationalists) still debate the relationships between old Ruthenian, the ancestor of modern Belarusian and Ukrainian, and the Russian then spoken in the northeast. All were likely descended from the old East Slavic of Kievan Rus (though some argue for even older distinctions), raising the question of when these dialects or languages became distinct. Scholars generally agree that the separation was fully visible in the fourteenth century, even if the roots of differentiation extended further back. Certainly, many influences altered these tongues, not least the fragmentation of the appanage era and the deepening divide between Lithuanian and Polish controlled lands and Muscovite Russia. As such, the Great Russians came to be associated with the Muscovite realm, the Ukrainians and the Belorussians with Lithuania and Poland. One can speculate that events would have taken a different shape had Russians preserved their political unity in the Kievan state or had Lithuania-Russia become the new center rather than Moscow. Political separation tended also to promote cultural differences, although all started with the same Kievan heritage. Strong Latin European influence by way of Poland in the areas now known as Ukraine and Belarus would prove crucial in helping to nurture a distinct identity there. The Russian Orthodox Church too, as we.know, finally split administratively, with a separate metropolitan established in Kiev to head the Orthodox in the Lithuanian state. The division of the Russians into the Great Russians, the Ukrainians, and the Belorussians, reinforced by centuries of separation, became a major factor in subsequent Russian history.

Part IV

# MUSCOVITE RUSSIA

# CHAPTER 15

# The Reigns of Ivan the Terrible, 1533–84, and of Theodore, 1584–98

There is nothing more unjust than to deny that there was a principle at stake in Ivan's struggle with the boyars or to see in this struggle only political stagnation. Whether Ivan IV was himself the initiator or not—most probably he was not—yet this "oprichnina" was an attempt, a hundred and fifty years before Peter's time, to found a personal autocracy like the Petrine monarchy.... Just as the "reforms" had been the work of a coalition of the bourgeoisie and the boyars, the coup of 1564 was carried out by a coalition of the townsmen and the petty vassals.

MIKHAIL POKROVSKY

The new system which he [Ivan the Terrible] set up was madness, but the madness of a genius.

BERNARD PARES

Ivan's life and reign should convince us that Muscovite politics was as autocratic as its ritual and ideology declared it to be....[However,] Muscovite politics was more complex than simple autocracy. Admittedly, no social force but the sovereign dynasty possessed a legitimate claim to power....But Muscovy, unlike Europe, did not define political relations as corporate privileges and legal rights. Rather it relied on personal loyalties to structure politics, and maintained a complex political reality behind a facade of political simplicity. The complexity of Muscovite politics lies therein: boyar factions shared with the grand prince decision-making and leadership, but all participants in political life cultivated a facade of autocracy in ritual and in ideology.

NANCY SHIELDS KOLLMANN

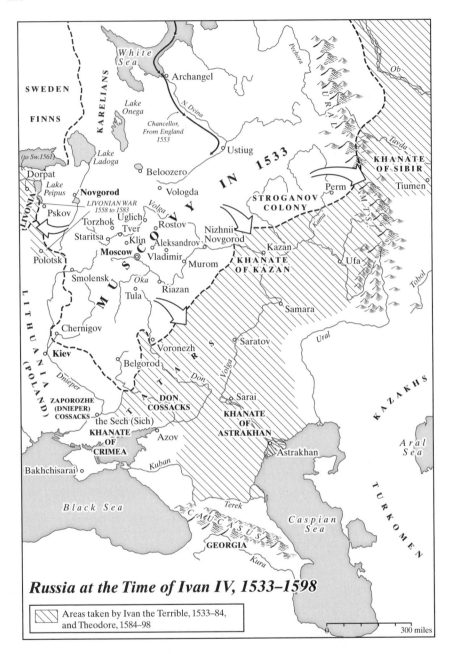

**Russia at the Time of Ivan IV, 1533–1598**

⫽⫽⫽ Areas taken by Ivan the Terrible, 1533–84, and Theodore, 1584–98

0                                                    300 miles

With the reign of Ivan IV, the Terrible, Muscovite absolutism came fully into its own. Ivan IV was the first Muscovite ruler to be crowned tsar, to have this action approved by the Eastern patriarchs, and to use the title regularly and officially both in governing his land and in conducting foreign relations. In calling himself also "autocrat" he emphasized his complete power at home as well as the fact that he was a sovereign, not a dependent, monarch. Nevertheless, it was Ivan the Terrible's actions, rather than his titles or ideas, that offered a stunning demonstration of the new arbitrary might of the Muscovite, and now Russian, ruler. Indeed, Ivan the Terrible remains the classic Russian tyrant in spite of such successors as Peter the Great, Paul I, and Nicholas I.

This image of Ivan the tyrant has been accompanied, however, by a great deal of debate among historians, as our epigraphs begin to suggest. Was there a "rational" first part of the reign defined by the pursuit of "reform" followed by a deranged second part defined by "terror," or was terror a continuation of reform by more radical means? Can we compare Ivan IV's reign to that of other early modern state-builders and define his actions as a characteristically modern effort, if at times excessive, to overcome "feudal fragmentation" (a term favored especially by Soviet historians), integrate diverse territories into a single state, and advance the centralization and systematization of government? Did the influence of boyar clans and customs remain strong, or did Ivan finally rid the state, as he seemed to want, of boyar influence? And what do we know, especially given limited and biased contemporary sources, of Ivan's personality, psychology, and thinking, even of many of his actions? In a word, was he essentially pathological or rational? It should be noted that Ivan's later honorific title, "the Terrible," is more ambiguous in Russian than English: the Russian term "groznyi" denoted a complex and largely positive mixture of severity and awesome might, especially in battle, where a groznyi ruler strikes fear in the hearts of Russia's enemies.

## Ivan the Terrible's Childhood and the First Part of His Rule

Ivan IV was only three years old in 1533 when his father, Vasilii III, died, leaving the government of Russia to his wife—Ivan's mother Helen, of the Glinsky family—and the boyar duma. The new regent acted in a haughty and arbitrary manner, disregarding the boyars and relying first on her uncle, the experienced Prince Mikhail Glinsky, and after his death on her lover, the youthful Prince Telepnev-Obolensky. In 1538 she died suddenly, possibly of poison. Boyar rule—if this phrase can be used to characterize the strife and misrule which ensued—followed her demise. To quote one brief summary of the developments:

> The regency was disputed between two princely houses, the Shuiskys and the Belskys. Thrice the power changed hands and twice the Metropolitans themselves were forcibly changed during the struggle, one of them, Joseph, being done to death. The Shuiskys prevailed, and three successive members of this family held power in turn. Their use of it was entirely selfish, dictated not even by class interests but simply by those of family and favour.

Imprisonments, exiles, executions, and murders proliferated.

All evidence indicates that Ivan IV was a sensitive, intelligent, and precocious boy. He learned to read early and read everything that he could find, especially Muscovite Church literature. He became of necessity painfully aware of the struggle and intrigues around him and also of the ambivalence of his own position. The same boyars who formally paid obeisance to him as autocrat and treated him with utmost respect on ceremonial occasions, neglected, insulted, and injured him in private life. In fact, they deprived him at will of his favorite servants and companions and ran the palace, as well as Russia, as they pleased. Bitterness and cruelty, expressed, for instance, in his torture of animals, became fundamental traits of the young ruler's character.

At the age of thirteen Ivan IV suddenly turned on Andrei Shuisky, who was arrested and dispatched by the tsar's servants. The autocrat entered into his inheritance. The year 1547 is commonly considered the introduction to Ivan IV's effective reign. In that year, at the age of sixteen, he decided to be crowned, not as grand prince, but as tsar. While earlier rulers had occasionally used the term "tsar," Ivan's coronation with this title was groundbreaking, as was the entire ceremony itself and the special mass that followed. Ivan (or, more likely, the metropolitan Macarius) understood what historians today often highlight: the importance of ritual and myth in politics. The elaborate and awe-inspiring coronation ceremony was adapted from the Byzantine ritual, serving both to endow the tsar with sacred authority and to indicate his legitimate descent from the sacred rulers in Byzantium. On the other hand, Ivan was not anointed at the coronation, as the Byzantine emperors were, and the metropolitan advised Ivan that his great power was not unlimited: to enter heaven he needed to be a moral and Christian ruler, protecting faith and Church and listening to wise advisors.

In the same year Ivan IV married Anastasia of the popular Romanov boyar family: again, he acted with great seriousness and deliberation in selecting Anastasia from a special list of eligible young Russian ladies after he had considered and dismissed the alternative of a foreign marital alliance, though the choice of a Romanov fit well with a tradition of "marriage politics" that was solicitous of powerful boyar clans. The marriage turned out to be a very happy one. Still in the same year, a great fire, followed by a riot, swept Moscow. As the city burned, and even the belfry of Ivan the Great in the Kremlin collapsed, crazed mobs killed an uncle of the tsar and imperiled the tsar's own life before being dispersed. The tsar himself experienced one of the psychological crises which were periodically to mark his explosive reign. He apparently believed the disaster to be a punishment for his sins: he repented publicly in Red Square and promised to rule in the interests of the people.

What followed has traditionally been described as the first, the good, half of Ivan IV's rule. The young tsar, beneficially influenced by his kind and attractive wife, worked with a small group of able and enlightened advisers, the Chosen Council, which included Metropolitan Macarius, a priest named Sylvester, and a court official of relatively low origin, Alexei Adashev. In 1549 he called together the first full *zemskii sobor*, an institution similar to a gathering of the representatives of estates in other European countries, which will be discussed in a later chapter. While our knowledge of the assembly of 1549 remains fragmentary, it seems that Ivan IV solicited and received its approval for his projected reforms, notably for a new code of law and for changes in local government, and that he also used that occasion to hear complaints and learn the opinions of his subjects concerning various matters. The general purpose of his many reforms, as will be seen, was not to overturn traditional political relationships but to systematize and regularize them.

In 1551 a great Church council, known as the Council of a Hundred Chapters. (Stoglav), took place. Its decrees did much to regulate the position of the Church in relation to the state and society as well as to regulate ecclesiastical affairs proper. Significantly, the Church lost the right to acquire more land without the tsar's explicit permission, a regulation which could not, however, be effectively put into practice. In general, Metropolitan Macarius and his associates accomplished a great deal in tightening and perfecting the organization of the Church in the sprawling, but now firmly united, Russian state. One interesting aspect of this process was their incorporation of different regional Russian saints—with a number of new canonizations in 1547 and 1549—into a single Church calendar.

Ivan also presented to the Church council his new legal code, the *Sudebnik* of 1550, and the local government reform, and received its approval. The new law code signified the regime's determination to establish more effective rule by systematizing administrative and legal practices. However, this was a reform that mainly brought order to existing norms rather than rejecting them. Notably, Article 98 restated the traditional rule that the monarch must consult with his boyars when considering new laws. The institution of a novel scheme of local government deserves special attention as one of the more daring attempts in Russian history to resolve this perennially difficult problem. The new system aimed at the elimination of corruption and oppression on the part of centrally appointed officials by means of popular participation in local affairs. Various localities had already received permission to elect their own judicial authorities to deal, drastically if need be, with crime. Now, in areas whose population guaranteed a certain amount of dues to the treasury, other locally elected officials replaced the centrally appointed governors. And even where the governors remained, the people could elect assessors to check closely on their activities and, indeed, impeach them when necessary. But we shall return to the Muscovite system of government in a later chapter.

In 1556 Ivan IV established general regulations for military service of the gentry. While this service had existed for a long time, it remained without comprehensive organization or standardization until the new rules set a definite relationship between the size of the estate and the number of warriors and horses the landlord had to produce on demand. It should be noted that by the middle of the sixteenth century the distinction between the hereditary votchina and the pomestie, granted for service, had largely disappeared: in particular, it had become impossible to remain a landlord, hereditary or otherwise, without owing service to the tsar. In 1550 and thereabout Ivan the Terrible and his advisors also engaged in an army reform, which included new emphasis on artillery and engineering as well as development of the southern defense line. Moreover, the first permanent, regular regiments, known because of their chief weapon as the *streltsy* or musketeers, were added to the Russian army.

The military improvements came none too soon, for in the 1550s the Muscovite state was already engaging in a series of wars. Most important, a new phase appeared in the struggle against the peoples of the steppe. After Ivan IV became tsar, just as in the time of his predecessors, Russia remained subject to constant large-scale raids by a number of Tatar armies, particularly from the khanates of Kazan, Astrakhan, and the Crimea. These repeated invasions in search of booty and slaves cost the Muscovite state dearly, because of the havoc and devastation which they wrought and the immense burden of guarding the huge southeastern frontier. Certain developments in the early years of Ivan the Terrible's reign indicated that the Tatars were increasing their strength and improving their coordination. In 1551, however, the Russians began an offensive against the nearest Tatar enemy, the khanate of Kazan, conquering some of its vassal tribes and building the fortress of Sviiazhsk near Kazan itself. But as soon as the great campaign against Kazan opened in 1552, the Crimean Tatars, assisted by some Turkish janissaries and artillery, invaded the Muscovite territory, aiming for Moscow itself. Only after they had been checked and had withdrawn to the southern steppe could the Russians resume their advance on Kazan. The tsar's troops surrounded the city by land and water, and after a siege of six weeks stormed it successfully, using powder to blow up some of the fortifications. The Russian heroes of the bitter fighting included commanders Prince Mikhail Vorotynsky and Prince Andrei Kurbsky, who led the first detachment to break into the city. It took another five years to establish Russian rule over the entire territory of the khanate of Kazan.

Following the conquest of Kazan on the middle Volga, the Russians turned their attention to the mouth of the river, to Astrakhan. They seized it first in 1554 and installed their candidate there as khan. After this vassal khan established contacts with the Crimea, the Russians seized Astrakhan once more in 1556, at which time the khanate was annexed to the Muscovite state. Thus of the three chief Tatar enemies of Russia, only the Crimean state remained, with its Ottoman suzerain looming behind it. Crimean forces invaded the tsar's domain in 1554, 1557, and 1558, but were beaten back each time. On the last occasion the Russians counter-attacked deep into the southern steppe, penetrating the Crimean peninsula itself.

Another major war was waged at the opposite end of the Russian state, in the northwest, against the Livonian Order. It started in 1558 over the issue of Russian access and expansion to the Baltic beyond the small hold on the coastline at the mouth of the Neva. The first phase of this war, to 1563, brought striking successes to the Muscovite armies. In 1558 alone they captured some twenty Livonian strongholds, including the greatest of them, the town of Dorpat, originally built by Iaroslav the Wise and named Iuriev. In 1561 the Livonian Order was disbanded, its territories were secularized, and its last master, Gotthard Kettler, became the hereditary Duke of Courland and a vassal of the Polish king. Yet the resulting Polish-Lithuanian offensive failed, and the Russian forces seized Polotsk from Lithuania in 1563.

Ivan IV and his assistants had many interests in the outside world other than war. As early as 1547 the Muscovite government sent an agent, the Saxon

Ivan IV in a psychological portrait by Victor Vasnetsov, 1897.    *(Sovfoto)*

Slitte, to western Europe to invite specialists to serve the tsar. Eventually over 120 doctors, teachers, artists, and different technicians and craftsmen from Germany accepted the Russian invitation. But when they reached Lübeck, authorities of the Hanseatic League and of the Livonian Order refused to let them through, with the result that only a few of their number ultimately came to Russia on their own. In 1553 an English captain, Richard Chancellor, in search of a new route to the East through the Arctic Ocean, reached the Russian White Sea shore near the mouth of the Northern Dvina. He went on to visit Moscow and establish direct relations between England and Russia. The agreement of 1555 gave the English great commercial advantages in the Muscovite state, for they were to pay no dues and could maintain a separate organization under the jurisdiction of their own chief factor. Arkhangelsk—Archangel in English—on the Northern Dvina became their port of entry. Ivan IV valued his English connection highly. Characteristically, the first Russian mission to England returned with some specialists in medicine and mining. As a result of Ivan's reforms, wars, and diplomatic initiatives, historians have argued, Russia was becoming a modern state, an empire, and a world power.

## The Second Part of Ivan the Terrible's Rule

This history became much more complicated and troubled, though, as Ivan the Terrible launched an increasingly fierce struggle against the boyars. He broke with the Chosen Council and turned violently against many of his advisers and their associates, and then, as his suspicion and reach expanded, against the boyars as a whole. Indeed, it can be argued, the second part of Ivan's reign reflected a radical effort to overcome the conservative tradition of Russian politics grounded in family relations, consensus among the ruling elite, and established custom. Ivan was fighting, in this view, for a personal and absolute rule that, notwithstanding its roots in previous reigns, was a departure from the past in both political theory and governmental practice. Whether he was fully successful is another matter. What is certain is that his efforts proved, at least in the short term, devastating to political life, society, and the economy.

In a sense, a conflict between the tsar and the boyars followed logically from preceding history. As Muscovite absolutism rose to its heights with Ivan the Terrible, the boyar class, constantly growing with the expansion of Moscow, represented one of the few possible checks on the sovereign's power. Furthermore, the boyars remained partly linked to the old appanage order, which the Muscovite rulers had striven hard and successfully to destroy. The size and composition of the Muscovite boyardom reflected the rapid growth of the state. While in the first half of the fifteenth century some 40 boyar families served the Muscovite ruler, in the first half of the sixteenth the number of the families had increased to over 200. The Muscovite boyars included descendants of former Russian or Lithuanian grand princes, descendants of former appanage princes, members of old Muscovite boyar families, and, finally, members of boyar families from other parts of Russia who had transferred their service to Moscow. The first two groups, the so-called service princes, possessed the greatest influence and prestige and also the strongest links with the past: they remained at least to some extent rulers in their own localities even after they became servitors in Moscow. The power of the Muscovite boyars, however, should not be overestimated. They showed little initiative and lacked solidarity and organization. In fact, they constantly engaged in petty squabbles and intrigues against one another, a deplorable situation well illustrated during the early years of Ivan the Terrible's reign. The Muscovite system of appointments, the notorious *mestnichestvo*, based on a hierarchical ranking of boyar families, as well as of the individual members within a given family, added to the boyar disunity, while also severely constraining the ruler's freedom to appoint state officials and military commanders.

Alongside the interpretation of Ivan's brutal turn against his advisers and the boyars as part of his continuing, if frustrated, effort to build a centralized state free of the anachronistic influences of family and custom, is a more personal and psychological interpretation, though still connected to problems of political rule. Indeed, the most common interpretation of Ivan's changed attitudes focuses on personal events in Ivan's life that may have profoundly disturbed him. In 1553 the tsar fell gravely ill and believed himself to be on his deathbed. He asked the boyars to swear allegiance to his infant son Dmitrii, but met opposition even from some of his closest associates, such as Sylvester, not to mention a considerable number of boyars: they apparently resented the merely boyar, not princely, family of Ivan the Terrible's wife, were afraid of more misfortunes for the Muscovite state during another reign of a minor, and favored Ivan the Terrible's cousin, Prince Vladimir of Staritsa, as tsar. Although the oath to Dmitrii was finally sworn, Ivan the Terrible never forgot this troubling experience. Shortly afterwards some boyars were caught planning to escape to Lithuania. New tensions resulted from the Livonian War. In fact it led to the break between the tsar and his advisers, Sylvester and Adashev, who disapproved of the proposed offensive in the Baltic area, preferring an assault against the Crimean Tatars.

In 1560 Ivan the Terrible's young and beloved wife Anastasia died suddenly. Convinced that Sylvester and Adashev had participated in a plot to poison her, the tsar had them condemned in extraordinary judicial proceedings, in the course of which they were not allowed to appear to state their case. The priest was apparently exiled to a distant monastery; the layman thrown into jail where he died. Before long Ivan the Terrible's wrath descended upon everyone connected with the Chosen Council. Adashev's and Sylvester's relatives, associates, and friends perished without trial. Two princes lost their lives merely because they expressed disapproval of the tsar's behavior. At this turn of events, a number of boyars fled to Lithuania. The escapees included a famous commander and associate of the tsar, Prince Andrei Kurbsky, who spent the rest of his life organizing forces and coalitions against his former sovereign. Kurbsky is best known, however, for the remarkable letters which he exchanged with Ivan the Terrible in 1564–79 and which will demand our attention when we deal with the political thought of Muscovite Russia.

In late 1564 Ivan IV suddenly abandoned Moscow for the small town of Aleksandrov some sixty miles away. A month later two letters, addressed to the metropolitan, arrived from the tsar. In them Ivan IV expressed his desire to retire from the throne and denounced the boyars and the clergy. Yet, in the letter to be read to the masses, he emphasized that he had no complaints against the common people. In confusion and consternation, the boyars and the people of Moscow begged the tsar to return and rule over them. Ivan the Terrible did return in February 1565, after his two conditions had been accepted: the creation of a special institution and subdivision in the Muscovite state, known as the *oprichnina*—from the word *oprich*, that is, *apart, beside*—to be managed entirely at the tsar's own discretion; and an endorsement of the tsar's right to punish evil-doers and traitors as he saw fit, executing them when necessary and confiscating their possessions. After the tsar returned to Moscow, it became apparent to those who knew him that he had experienced another shattering psychological crisis, for his eyes were dim and his hair and beard almost gone.

The oprichnina acquired more than one meaning. It came to stand for a separate jurisdiction within Russia which consisted originally of some twenty towns with their countryside, several special sections scattered throughout the state, and a part of Moscow where Ivan the Terrible built a new palace. Eventually it extended to well over a third of the Muscovite realm. The tsar set up a separate state administration for the oprichnina, paralleling the one in existence which was retained for the rest of the country, now known as the *zemshchina*. Much later there was even established a new and nominal ruler, a baptized Tatar prince Simeon, to whom Ivan the Terrible pretended to render homage. Our knowledge of the structure and functioning of the oprichnina administration remains fairly limited. Platonov suggested that after the reform of 1564 the state had actually one set of institutions, but two sets of officials. In any case, new men under the direct control of Ivan the Terrible ran the oprichnina, whereas the zemshchina stayed within the purview of the boyar duma and old officialdom. In fact, many landlords in the territory of the oprichnina were transferred elsewhere, while their lands were granted to the new servitors of the tsar. The term *oprichnina* also came to designate especially this new corps of servants to Ivan the Terrible—called *oprichniki*— who are described sometimes today as gendarmes or political police. The oprichniki numbered at first 1,000 and later as many as 6,000. Their purpose was to destroy those whom the tsar considered to be his enemies. According to various accounts, they dressed in black and rode black horses, to which they affixed the head of a dog and a brush—symbols of biting the tsar's enemies and sweeping them away.

A reign of terror followed. Boyars and other people linked to Prince Kurbsky, who had escaped to Lithuania, fell first. The tsar's cousin, Prince Vladimir of Staritsa, perished in his turn, together with his relatives, friends, and associates. The circle of suspects and victims kept widening: not only more and more boyars, but also their families, relatives, friends, and even servants and peasants were swept away in the purge. The estates of the victims and the villages of their peasants were confiscated by the state, and often plundered or simply burned. Ivan the Terrible brooked no contradiction. Metropolitan Philip, who dared remonstrate with the tsar, was thrown into jail and killed there by the oprichniki. Entire towns, such as Torzhok, Klin, and, especially, in 1570, Novgorod, suffered utter devastation and ruin. It looked as if a civil war were raging in the Muscovite state, but a peculiar civil war, for the attackers met no resistance. It might be added that the wave of extermination engulfed some of the leading oprichniki themselves. In 1572 Ivan the Terrible declared the oprichnina abolished, although division of the state into two parts lasted at least until 1575.

Following the death of his first wife, Ivan the Terrible appeared to have lost his emotional balance. His six subsequent wives never exercised the same beneficial influence on him as had Anastasia. The tsar was increasingly given to feelings of persecution and outbreaks of wild rage. He saw traitors everywhere. After the oprichnina began its work, Ivan the Terrible's life became part of a nightmare which he had brought into being. With Maliuta Skuratov and other oprichniki the sovereign personally participated in the investigations and the horrific tortures and executions, which, if contemporary observers can be believed, included dismemberings, crucifixions, skinning victims, and worse. Some contemporary accounts of the events defy imagination. In 1581, in a fit of violence, Ivan the Terrible struck his son and heir Ivan with a pointed staff and mortally wounded him. It has been said that from that time on he knew no peace at all. Adding to the strangeness of Ivan's personal behavior and outlook, he combined brutality with religiosity: he prayed constantly, read holy books and promoted new saints, and would seek repentance, asking that the names of all those killed be collected (officially 4,095) so that he could personally ask for prayers for their souls. This paradoxical mix of cruelty and piety was echoed in the images of Ivan the Terrible in folklore. Elaborating on the notion of Ivan as a "groznyi tsar"—in the sense of *groza* (the noun form of the adjective groznyi) as a mixture of severity, fearsomeness, and awe-inspiring power—popular songs and stories portray a ruler who could be wrathful, despotic, cruel, unjust, and terrifying, but also merciful, forgiving, generous, just, and respectful of subordinates and comrades, even when they cross him with good advice. The tsar died in March 1584. A Soviet autopsy of his body indicated poisoning, though most historians today doubt these findings.

While the oprichnina was raging inside Russia, enemies pressed from the outside. Although the Crimean Tatars failed to take Astrakhan in 1569, in 1571 Khan Davlet-Geray led them to Moscow itself. Unable to seize the Kremlin, they burned much of the city. They withdrew from the Muscovite state only after laying waste a large area and capturing an enormous booty and 100,000 prisoners. Famine and plague added to the horror of the Tatar devastation. The following year, however, a new invasion by the Crimean Tatars met disaster at the hands of a Russian army.

The Muscovite unpreparedness for the Crimean Tatars resulted largely from the increasing demands of the Livonian War (1558–83). The war was started by Ivan the Terrible with the aim, according to the traditional interpretation, of expanding Russia to the Baltic sea in order to develop overseas trade, though recent scholars have argued that his purpose was limited to gaining tribute to replenish the treasury. After a series of victories in the late 1550s, the situation changed dramatically in the early 1560s after Poland-Lithuania, Sweden, and Denmark partitioned Livonia among themselves and joined to stop Russian efforts in this region. After the death of Sigismund II in 1572, Poland had experienced several turbulent years: two elections to the Polish throne involved many interests and intrigues, with the Habsburgs making a determined bid to secure the crown, and Ivan the Terrible himself promoted as a candidate by another party; also, the successful competitor, Henry of Valois, elected king in 1573, left the country the following year to succeed his deceased brother on the French throne. The situation changed after the election in 1575 of the Hungarian Prince of Transylvania, Stephen Báthory,

as King of Poland. The new ruler brought stability and enhanced his reputation as an excellent general. In 1578 the Poles started an offensive in southern
Livonia. The following year they captured Polotsk and Velikie Luki, although,
in exceptionally bitter combat, they failed to take Pskov. On their side, in 1578,
the Swedes smashed a Russian army at Wenden. By the treaties of 1582 with
Poland and 1583 with Sweden, Russia had to renounce all it had gained during the first part of the war and even cede several additional towns to Sweden.
Thus, after some twenty-five years of fighting, Ivan the Terrible's move to the
Baltic failed dismally. The Muscovite state lay prostrate from the internal ravages of the oprichnina and continuous foreign war.

In concluding the story of Ivan the Terrible, we must consider his major
contribution to the transformation of Russia into a multiethnic empire—
indeed, a Russian Orthodox state whose subjects included non-Slavic, non-
Christian indigenous peoples—a move pregnant with consequences for
the rest of Russia's history. The first key step was Moscow's conquest of the
Tatar khanates of Kazan and Astrakhan, which also gave Russia control of
the important Volga region. The next stage, especially after movement west
was hampered, was eastward expansion into Siberia. This was not entirely
a new direction of interest for Russia. Even prior to the Mongol invasion the
Novgorodians had penetrated beyond the Urals. The Russians used northern
routes to enter Siberia by both land and sea and, by the middle of the sixteenth century, had already reached the mouth of the Enisei. The initiative for
greater penetration and conquest of Siberia, however, came not from the state
but from the Stroganov family. In the sixteenth century, with support from
the Muscovite state, the Stroganovs developed large-scale industries, including the extracting of salt and the procurement of fish and furs, in northeastern European Russia, especially in the Ustiug area. After the conquest of
Kazan, the Stroganovs obtained from the government large holdings in the
wild upper Kama region, where they maintained garrisons and imported
colonists. Their quest for furs led them increasingly to look to the forests
across the Ural Mountains, in other words, to Siberia. The indigenous peoples
of the region, mostly shamanist tribes, resisted these incursions, encouraged
by their nominal suzerain, the so-called khan of Sibir, or Siberia. In 1582 the
Stroganovs sent an expedition against the Siberian khanate. It consisted of
perhaps 1,650 cossacks and other volunteers, led by a cossack commander,
Ermak. Greatly outnumbered, but making good use of their better organization, firearms, and daring, the Russians defeated the natives in repeated
engagements and seized the headquarters of the Siberian Khan Kuchum.
Ivan the Terrible appreciated the importance of this unexpected conquest,
accepted the new territories into his realm, and sent reinforcements. Although
Ermak perished in the struggle in 1584 before help arrived and although the
conquest of the Siberian khanate had to be repeated, the Stroganov expedition marked in effect the beginning of the establishment of Russian control in
western Siberia. Tiumen, a fortified town, was built there in 1586, and another
fortified town, Tobolsk, was built in 1587 and subsequently became an important administrative center.

## Explanations and Interpretations

As we noted at the outset, the eventful and tragic reign of Ivan the Terrible has received different interpretations and evaluations. In general, the judgments of historians have fallen into two categories. The most traditional view emphasizes the tsar's pathological character, indeed madness, focusing on the division of the reign into a first, good, half, when the tsar listened to his advisers, and a second, bad, half, when he became an insane, bloodthirsty tyrant. This view derives from the accounts of Andrei Kurbsky and some other contemporaries. Karamzin adopted this view in his extremely influential history of the Russian state, and it was accepted by many later scholars. Many scholars today, while often acknowledging Ivan's increasingly "disordered personality" and much that was irrational, tyrannical, and cruel in his rule, focus on explaining his actions, even his brutality, in the context of fundamental Muscovite needs and problems, and thus in terms of a larger purpose. But debate does not end here. Even non-pathological arguments emphasize different purposes and logics.

Disagreement about the first part of Ivan's reign mainly concerns how to interpret the efforts at standardization and centralization. Some see evidence of political "modernization" in the development, for example, of a larger and more efficient central administration, a more coherent set of legal rules and procedures, a stronger army, a loyal middle service class, and a functioning and loyal local administration. But other scholars have argued that these were efforts mainly at political "mobilization," not modernization. This was not a freer society, nor one developing a Western-style independent civic sphere, but a society better harnessed to the state's needs.

Turning to the second part of Ivan's reign, the oprichnina evokes particularly heated historiographical debate. Various rational purposes have been identified: freeing the state from the power of boyar special interests; responding to real threats to the independent power of the monarchy, especially from old princely clans; bypassing the rigid mestnichestvo system so that the tsar could bring to the fore servicemen from among the gentry; and, generally, creating a new class of servitors who depended entirely on the monarch for their lands and therefore would be absolutely loyal. Even the bitterness and cruelty of the struggle have been seen as stemming less from the tsar's character than from the difficulty of the task and the extent of noble resistance. It can be argued, in this regard, that the tsar began with relatively mild measures and turned to severe punishments only after boyar opposition continued. Thus, it would seem, Ivan the Terrible's reign can be seen as parallel to those of Louis XI in France or Henry VIII in England, who similarly suppressed their aristocracies. Critics, however, note that there were no *real* domestic threats to the monarchy and that the boyars and even the old princely clans were already largely under control, and the evidence is that their position would only continue to decline. In other words, Ivan was attacking political "problems" that his predecessors had already solved by less dramatic means.

On the other hand, as Nancy Shields Kollmann has influentially argued, when Ivan came to the throne as a minor, he discovered real boyar power at the Moscow court. This was not, she argues, the stereotypical view of boyar power—the one seen in many textbooks and, most famously, in Sergei Eisenstein's two-part film in the 1940s—as a venal, obstructionist, and disorderly force against which Ivan was determined to act, heroically at first and more insanely as his frustrations grew or his mind become disordered. Not surprisingly, this model of heroic struggle by the monarch against selfish boyars was also the official view that appeared in Muscovite chronicles and histories. Rather, Kollmann argues, following early Muscovite tradition, "boyars had a dynamic and legitimate role in politics." They advised the sovereign and provided military and administrative leadership. This was not an ideal and harmonious system—though this is how its boyar defenders portrayed it. It was marked by interest groups, rival factions, disagreements over policy, and much balancing of power. For this system to work, it required two things: a complex structure of hierarchies that were respected by all parties (hence, mestnichestvo) and a charismatic dynastic ruler who could resolve differences and ensure functional harmony. As such, the many symbols and rituals of autocracy were signs of the unity of the kingdom and set a limit on conflict among the boyars. This was a messy political system with lots of jockeying for influence and a ruler who was required both to present a public face of absolute rule and to constantly persuade, cajole, and maneuver. Many historians would argue that it was not dysfunctional. But it may have seemed that way to Ivan and to gentry and servitors not in the boyar elite. The oprichnina, in this case, can be seen as an effort to break out of this restrictive system. When considering Ivan's experience as a child monarch faced by powerful and quarrelling boyars, the historian Robert Crummey has suggested that "the contrast between ritual omnipotence and actual powerlessness must have been jarring indeed!" This clash between real Muscovite politics and the idea of autocratic power might be extended to the whole of Ivan's experience until he launched the oprichnina.

Yet, after all the able and valuable explanations of Ivan the Terrible's actions in the context of Russian history and comparative politics, grave doubts remain. If we accept the argument that there was no real threat to his power and that boyar influence was not really dysfunctional, then the best remaining explanation is that these threats and deficiencies seemed real to Ivan. This, in turn, leads us to either what might be called the ideological and semiotic explanation or to the psychological. The first argues that Ivan believed so fully in the myth of the tsar's absolute power—embodied in so many rituals and symbols—that he wished to make it real. The second, and still widespread, argument focuses on Ivan's inner demons. Even Soviet scholars, who did the most to interpret Ivan the Terrible in terms of a purposeful, modern state overcoming resistant remnants of feudal fragmentation, recognized Ivan's pathological suspiciousness and cruelty. Few historians doubt that Ivan's childhood experiences had a troubling influence on him. But all this takes us onto the hazardous terrain of historical psychoanalysis, before which the historian is wise to stop. Still, few would disagree that Ivan IV was a disturbed and erratic figure. People of such character have brought about many private tragedies. Ivan the Terrible, however, was not just a private person but the ruler of a huge state, with very few institutionalized limitations on his power to act.

## The Reign of Theodore

The reign of Ivan IV's eldest surviving son Theodore, or Fedor, 1584–98, gave Russia a measure of peace. Physically weak and extremely limited in intelligence and ability, but well meaning as well as very religious, the new tsar relied entirely on his advisers. Fortunately, these advisers, especially Boris Godunov, performed their task fairly well.

An important and extraordinary event of the reign consisted in the establishment of a patriarchate in Russia in 1589. Largely as a result of Boris Godunov's skillful diplomacy, the Russians managed to obtain the consent of the patriarch of Constantinople, Jeremiah, to elevating the head of the Russian Church to the rank of patriarch, the highest in the Orthodox world. Later all Eastern patriarchs agreed to this step, although with some reluctance. Boris Godunov's friend, Metropolitan Job, became the first Muscovite patriarch. The new importance of the Russian Church led to an upgrading and enlargement of its hierarchy through the appointment of a number of new metropolitans, archbishops, and bishops. This strengthening of the organization of the Church proved to be significant in the Time of Troubles.

Foreign relations in the course of the reign included Theodore's unsuccessful candidacy to the Polish throne, following Stephen Báthory's death in 1586, and a successful war against Sweden, which ended in 1595 with the return to the Muscovite state of the towns and territory near the Gulf of Finland which had been ceded by the treaty of 1583. The pre-Livonian War frontier was thus re-established. In 1586 an Orthodox Georgian kingdom in Transcaucasia, beset by Muslims, begged to be accepted as a vassal of the Russian tsar. While Georgia lay too far away for more than a nominal, transitory connection to be established in the sixteenth century, the request pointed to one direction of later Russian expansion.

Theodore's reign also witnessed, in 1591, the death of Prince Dmitrii of Uglich in a setting which made it one of the most famous detective stories of Russian history. Nine-and-a-half-year-old Dmitrii, the tsar's brother and the only other remaining male member of the ruling family, died, his throat slit, in the courtyard of his residence in Uglich. The populace rioted, accused the child's guardians of murder and killed them. An official investigating commission, headed by Prince Vasilii Shuisky, declared that Dmitrii had been playing with a knife and had injured himself fatally while in an epileptic fit. Many contemporaries and later historians concluded that Dmitrii had been murdered on orders of Boris Godunov who had determined to become tsar himself. Platonov, however, argued persuasively against this view: as a son of Ivan the Terrible's seventh wife—while canonically only three were allowed— Dmitrii's rights to the throne were highly dubious; the tsar, still in his thirties, could well have a son or sons of his own; Boris Godunov would have staged the murder much more skillfully, without immediate leads to his agents and associates. Later Verndansky established that no first-hand evidence of an assassination exists at all, although accusations of murder arose immediately following Prince Dmitrii's apparently accidental death. But, whereas scholars may well remain satisfied with Platonov's and Verndansky's explanation, the general public will, no doubt, prefer the older version, enshrined in Pushkin's play and Musorgsky's opera, *Boris Godunov.*

Even if Boris Godunov did not murder Dmitrii, he made every other effort to secure power. Coming from a Mongol gentry family which had been converted to Orthodoxy and Russified, himself virtually illiterate, Boris Godunov showed uncanny intelligence and abilities in palace intrigue, diplomacy, and statecraft. He capitalized also on his proximity to Tsar Theodore, who was married to Boris's sister, Irina. In the course of several years Boris Godunov managed to defeat his rivals at court and become the effective ruler of Russia in about 1588. In addition to power and enormous private wealth, Boris Godunov obtained exceptional outward signs of his high position: a most impressive and ever-growing official title; the formal right to conduct foreign relations on behalf of the Muscovite state; and a separate court, imitating that of the tsar, where foreign ambassadors had to present themselves after they had paid their respects to Theodore. When the tsar died in 1598, without an heir, Boris Godunov stood ready and waiting to ascend the throne. His reign, however, was to be not so much a successful consummation of his ambition as a prelude to the Time of Troubles.

# CHAPTER 16

# The Time of Troubles, 1598–1613

O God, save thy people, and bless thine heritage..., preserve this city and this holy Temple, and every city and land from pestilence, famine, earthquake, flood, fire, the sword, the invasion of enemies, and from civil war....

AN ORTHODOX PRAYER

The Time of Troubles—*Smutnoe Vremia*, in Russian—refers to a particularly turbulent, confusing, and painful segment of Russian history at the beginning of the seventeenth century, or, roughly, from Boris Godunov's accession to the Muscovite throne in 1598 to the election of Michael as tsar and the establishment of the Romanov dynasty in Russia in 1613. Following the greatest student of the Time of Troubles, Platonov, we may subdivide those years into three consecutive segments on the basis of the paramount issues at stake: the dynastic, the social, and the national. This classification immediately suggests the complexity of the subject. Likewise, since Platonov, who wrote at the very end of the nineteenth century, scholars have debated how best to define the events of this troubled era: in particular, whether it was mainly a social and class conflict (a "peasant war" in the classic Marxist definition) or a "civil war," a view that emphasizes vertical over horizontal divisions. These two models also downplay the importance of foreign intervention—a key feature in both prerevolutionary Russian and Stalin-era Soviet historiography—and see the conflict as rooted chiefly in internal problems.

The dynastic aspect stemmed from the fact that with the passing of Tsar Theodore the Muscovite ruling family died out. For the first time in Muscovite history there remained no natural successor to the throne. The problem of succession was exacerbated because there existed no law of succession in the Muscovite state, because a number of claimants appeared, because Russians looked in different directions for a new ruler, and because, apparently, they placed a very high premium on some link with the extinct dynasty, which opened the way to fantastic intrigues and impersonations.

While the dynastic issue emerged through the accidental absence of an heir, the national issue resulted largely from the centuries-old Russian struggle in the west and in the north. Poland, and to a lesser extent Sweden, felt compelled to take advantage of the sudden Russian weakness. The complex involvement of Poland, especially, reflected some of the key problems and possibilities in the history of eastern Europe.

But it is the social element that demands our main attention. For it was the social disorganization, strife, and virtual collapse that made the dynastic issue so critical and opened the Muscovite state to foreign intrigues and invasions. The Time of Troubles can be understood only as the end product of the rise of the Muscovite state with its attendant dislocations and tensions. It has often been said that Russian history, by comparison with the histories of western European countries, has represented a cruder or simpler process, in particular that Russian social structure has exhibited a certain lack of complexity and differentiation. While this approach must be treated circumspectly, it must not be dismissed. We noted earlier that it might be appropriate to describe appanage Russia in terms of an incipient or undeveloped feudalism. The rise of Moscow meant a further drastic simplification of Russian social relations.

To expand and to defend its growing territory, the Muscovite state relied on service people, that is, on men who fought its battles and also performed the administrative and other work for the government. The service people— eventually known as the service gentry, or simply gentry—were supported by their estates. In this manner, the pomestie, an estate granted for service, became basic to the Muscovite social order. After the acquisition of Novgorod, in its continuing search for land suitable for pomestiia, the Muscovite government confiscated most of the holdings of the Novgorodian boyars and even half of those of the Novgorodian Church. Hereditary landlords too, it will be remembered, found themselves obligated to serve the state. The rapid Muscovite expansion and the continuous wars on all frontiers, except the north and northeast, taxed the resources of the government and the people to the breaking point. Muscovite authorities made frantic efforts to obtain more service gentry. "Needing men fit for military service, in addition to the old class of its servitors, free and bonded, nobles and commoners, the government selects the necessary men and establishes on pomestiia people from everywhere, from all the layers of Muscovite society in which there existed elements answering the military requirements." Thus, for example, small landholders in the areas of Novgorod and Pskov and an ever-increasing number of Mongols, some of whom had not even been converted to Christianity, became members of the Muscovite service gentry.

When Moscow succeeded in the "gathering of Russia" and the appanages disappeared, the princes and boyars failed to make a strong stand against Muscovite centralization and absolutism. Many of them, indeed, were slaughtered, without offering resistance, by Ivan the Terrible. But the relatively easy victory of the Muscovite despots over the old upper classes left problems in its wake. Notably, it has been argued that the Muscovite government displaced the appanage ruling elements all too rapidly, more rapidly than it could provide effective substitutes. The resulting weakening of the political and social framework contributed its share to the Time of Troubles. And so did the boyar reaction following the decline in the tsar's authority after Boris Godunov's death.

As the Muscovite state expanded, centralizing and standardizing administration and institutions and subjugating the interests of other classes to those of the service gentry, towns also suffered. They became administrative and military centers at the expense of local self-government, commercial elements, and the middle class as a whole. This transformation occurred most strikingly in Novgorod and Pskov, but similar changes affected many other towns as well.

Most important, however, was a deterioration in the position of the peasants, who constituted the great bulk of the people. They, of course, provided the labor force on the estates of the service gentry, and, therefore, were affected immediately and directly by the rise of that class. Specifically, the growth of the service gentry meant that more and more state lands and peasants fell into gentry hands through the pomestie system. Gentry landlords, themselves straining to perform burdensome state obligations, squeezed what they could from the peasants. Furthermore, the ravages of the oprichnina brought outright disaster to the already overtaxed peasant economy of much of central Russia. Famine, which appeared in the second half of Ivan the Terrible's reign, was to return in the frightful years of 1601–3.

Many peasants tried to escape. The Russian conquest of the khanates of Kazan and Astrakhan opened up fertile lands to the southeast, and at first the government encouraged migration to consolidate the Russian hold on the area. But this policy could not be reconciled with the interests of the service gentry, whose peasants had to be prevented from fleeing if their masters were to retain the ability to serve the state. Therefore, in the last quarter of the sixteenth century, Muscovite authorities made an especially determined effort to secure and guarantee the labor force of the gentry. Legal migration ceased. The state also tried to curb Church landholding, and especially to prevent the transfer of any gentry land to the Church. Furthermore, serfdom as such finally became fully established in Russia. While the long-term process of the growth of serfdom will be discussed later, it should be mentioned here that the government's dedication to the interests of the service gentry at least contributed to it.

Hard-pressed economically and increasingly deprived of their rights, the peasants continued to flee to the borderlands in spite of all prohibitions. The shattering impact of the oprichnina provided another stimulus for the growth of that restless, dislocated, and dissatisfied lower-class element which played such a significant role during the Time of Troubles. Moreover, some fugitive peasants became cossacks. The cossacks, first mentioned in the chronicles in 1444, represented free or virtually free societies of warlike adventurers that began to emerge along distant borders and in areas of overlapping jurisdictions and uncertain control. Combining military organization and skill, the spirit of adventure, and a hatred of the Muscovite political and social system, and linked socially to the broad masses, the cossacks were to act as another major and explosive element in the Time of Troubles.

Dissatisfied elements in the Russian state included also a number of conquered peoples and tribes, especially in the Volga basin. The gentry itself, while a privileged class, had many complaints against the exacting government. Finally, it should be emphasized that conditions and problems varied in the different parts of the huge Muscovite state, and that the Time of Troubles included local as much as national developments. The Russian north, for example, had no problem of defense and very few gentry or serfs. Since a brief general account can pay only the scantest attention to these local variations, the interested student must be referred to more specialized literature, beginning with the writings of Platonov.

## The Dynastic Phase of the Time of Troubles: Boris Godunov and the First False Dmitrii

With the passing of Theodore, the Muscovite dynasty died out and a new tsar had to be found. While it is generally believed that Boris Godunov remained in control of the situation, he formally ascended the throne only after being elected by a specially convened zemskii sobor and implored by the patriarch, the clergy, and the people to accept the crown. He proved to be, or rather continued to be, an intelligent and able ruler. Interested in learning from the West, Boris Godunov even thought of establishing a university in Moscow, but abandoned this idea because of the opposition of the clergy. He did, however, send eighteen young men to study abroad. In foreign policy, Boris Godunov maintained peaceful relations with other countries and promoted trade, concluding commercial treaties with England and with the Hansa.

But, in spite of these efforts, Boris Godunov's brief reign, 1598–1605, witnessed tragic events. In 1601 drought and famine brought disaster to the people. The crops failed again in 1602 and also, to a considerable extent, in 1603. Famine reached catastrophic proportions; epidemics followed. Although the government tried to feed the population of Moscow free of charge, direct supplies to other towns, and find employment for the destitute, its measures availed little against the calamity. It has been estimated that more than 100,000 people perished in the capital alone. Starving people devoured grass, bark, cadavers of animals and, on occasion, even other human beings. Large bands of desperate men that roamed and looted the countryside and sometimes gave battle to regular troops appeared and became a characteristic phenomenon of the Time of Troubles.

At this point rumors to the effect that Boris Godunov was a criminal and a usurper and that Russia was being punished for his sins began to spread. It was alleged that he had plotted to assassinate Prince Dmitrii; it was alleged further that in reality another boy had been murdered, that the prince had escaped and would return to claim his rightful inheritance. The claimant soon appeared in

*The Time of Troubles 1598 – 1613*

person. Most historians believe that False Dmitrii was in fact a certain Grigorii Otrepiev, a young man of service class origin, who had become a monk and then left his monastery. Very possibly he believed himself to be the true Prince Dmitrii. Apparently he lived in Moscow in 1601 and early 1602, but escaped to the cossacks when authorities became interested in his assertions and decided to arrest him. Next he appeared in Lithuania, where he reiterated his claim to

be Ivan the Terrible's son Prince Dmitrii. The Polish government gave him no
official recognition. Though False Dmitrii met with the king in Cracow and
promised to convert the Russians to Roman Catholicism, the Sejm refused to
support a military adventure in support of False Dmitrii. But he did win the
support of the Jesuits for his commitment to spreading Catholicism and certain Lithuanian and Polish aristocrats. These bonds were strengthened by his
betrothal to Marina Mniszech, the daughter of a powerful Polish aristocrat, and
possibly his own adoption of Catholicism. By contrast, the role of the Muscovite
boyars in the rise of False Dmitrii remains less clear. Yet, in spite of the pau-
city and frequent absence of evidence, many scholars have become convinced
that important boyar circles secretly supported False Dmitrii in order to destroy
Boris Godunov. Indeed, the entire False Dmitrii episode has been described as a
boyar stratagem. Boris Godunov, on his part, in an effort to defend his position,
turned violently against the boyars around the throne, instituting in 1601 a veritable purge of them. In October 1604, False Dmitrii invaded Russia at the head of
some 1,500 cossacks, Polish soldiers of fortune, and other adventurers.

Most surprisingly, the foolhardy enterprise succeeded. False Dmitrii's
manifestoes proclaiming him to be the true tsar had their effect, in spite of Boris

"False Dmitrii." Note the use of Latin and his presentation in Polish dress.
(*Tsartvuiushchii dom Romanovykh*)

Godunov's attempts to confirm that Prince Dmitrii was dead and to brand the pretender as an impostor and a criminal by such means as his excommunication from the Church and the testimony of Grigorii Otrepiev's uncle. Much of southern Russia, including such large centers as Chernigov, welcomed False Dmitrii; in a number of places authorities and population wavered in their stand, but failed to offer firm resistance. Dissatisfaction and unrest within the Muscovite state proved to be more valuable to the pretender's cause than Polish and Lithuanian aid. False Dmitrii's motley forces suffered repeated defeats, but regrouped and reappeared. Still, False Dmitrii probably owed his victory to a stroke of luck: in April 1605, when the military odds against the pretender appeared overwhelming, Boris Godunov suddenly died. Shortly after his death his commander, Fedor Basmanov, went over to False Dmitrii's side, Boris Godunov's wife and his young son and successor Theodore were deposed and murdered in Moscow, and on June 20, 1605, False Dmitrii entered the capital in triumph.

The people rejoiced at what they believed to be the miraculous return of the true tsar to ascend his ancestral throne. On the eve of the riots that overthrew the Godunovs, Vasilii Shuisky himself had already publicly reversed his testimony and claimed that in Uglich Prince Dmitrii had escaped the assassins, who killed another boy instead. In July 1605, Prince Dmitrii's mother, who had become a nun under the name of Martha, was brought to identify her alleged long-lost child: in the course of a tender meeting she proclaimed him her own. Followers of False Dmitrii, such as Fedor Basmanov, succeeded the supporters of Godunov around the throne. A Greek cleric, Ignatius, who had been among the first to side with the pretender, replaced Boris Godunov's friend Job as patriarch. The new tsar returned from disgrace, prison, or exile the boyars who had suffered during the last years of his predecessor's reign. Those regaining favor included Philaret, formerly Fedor Romanov, the abbot of a northern monastery whom Boris Godunov had forced to take holy orders and exiled. Philaret became the metropolitan in Rostov.

False Dmitrii has been described as an unprepossessing figure with no waistline, arms of unequal length, red hair that habitually stood up, a large wart on his face, a big ugly nose, and an expression both unsympathetic and melancholy. Assessments of his achievements as tsar have been hampered by the lack of sources (much was burned after his overthrow). Some scholars have seen him as a modernizer who ran afoul of conservative boyars. Others have described him as relying closely on the boyars and even as beginning to establish a model of gentry influence according to the Polish model. Likewise, there is little evidence for claims that his social policies favored peasants. His main concern, it seems, was to protect the interests of his most loyal noble servitors, not to improve the conditions of their bondsmen. He refused to be anyone's puppet, and in particular failed to honor his promises concerning the introduction of Catholicism into Russia. Instead of acting on these promises, he propounded the grandiose project of driving the Turks out of Europe.

Their new ruler's manners upset the Muscovites. False Dmitrii repeatedly failed to observe the established traditions and etiquette. He would not attend church services, and did not take a nap in the afternoon, but instead wandered on his own in the city, dressed as a Pole. The tsar's Polish entourage proved still more disturbing: these Poles, loud and prominent, generally despised the Russians, who in turn suspected and hated them as enemies and heretics. But the main argument against False Dmitrii, in the opinion of Platonov and many other specialists, rested simply in the fact that he had already served his purpose. The boyars had utilized him successfully against the Godunovs and now made arrangements to dispose of him in his turn.

It would seem that almost immediately after False Dmitrii's victory Vasilii Shuisky and his brothers began to spread rumors to the effect that the new tsar was, after all, an impostor. Caught and condemned to death, they were instead exiled and, after several months, entirely pardoned by the clement tsar—a sure sign in the opinion of some specialists that False Dmitrii believed himself to be the true heir to the throne. The next important event of the reign, the tsar's marriage to Marina Mniszech, increased tensions. The wedding was celebrated in Moscow on May 8, 1606. Marina, however, remained a Catholic, and she brought with her another large group of Poles. Arguments and clashes between the Poles and the Russians increased.

Having prepared the ground, Prince Vasilii Shuisky, Prince Vasilii Golitsyn, and other boyars on the night of May 26 led into Moscow a very large military detachment stationed nearby. Their coup began under the slogan of saving the tsar from the Poles, but as it progressed the tsar himself was denounced as an impostor. The defenders of the palace were overwhelmed. False Dmitrii tried to escape, but was handed over to the rebels and death by a guard of the streltsy, apparently after they had been persuaded by the mother of Prince Dmitrii of Uglich, the nun Martha, that their tsar was an impostor. Fedor Basmanov and 2,000–3,000 other Russians and Poles perished. The Patriarch Ignatius was deposed.

Both the Godunovs and their rival had thus disappeared from the scene. Prince Vasilii Shuisky became the next tsar with no greater sanction than the wishes of his party and the endorsing shouts of a Muscovite crowd. The new ruler made certain revealing promises: he would not execute anyone without the decision of the boyar duma; innocent members of a family would not suffer because of a guilty relative; denunciations would not be given credence without a careful investigation; and false informers would be punished. Although historians who see in Vasilii Shuisky's declaration an effective limitation of autocracy seem to overstate the case, the tsar's assurances did reflect his ties to the boyars as well as the efforts of the latter to obtain minimal guarantees against the kind of persecution practiced by such rulers as Ivan the Terrible and Boris Godunov. Moreover, it appears that the boyars acquired a certain freedom under the new monarch and often behaved willfully and disobediently in their relations with him.

The government tried its best to assure the people that False Dmitrii had been an impostor who had won the throne by magic and had forced the nun Martha and others to recognize him as the authentic prince. The body of False Dmitrii was exposed in Red Square and then burned. Legend has it that the ashes were fired from a cannon in the direction of Poland. In addition to this, and to Vasilii Shuisky's and Martha's denunciations of False Dmitrii, another novel attempt at persuasion was made: in June 1606 Prince Dmitrii of Uglich was canonized and his remains were brought to Moscow.

## The Social Phase: The Bolotnikov Revolt and the Second False Dmitrii

With the deposition and murder of False Dmitrii, state authority in the land was further weakened, whereas the forces of discontent and rebellion grew in size and strength. Indeed, the Russians had seen four tsars—Boris and Theodore Godunov, False Dmitrii, and Vasilii Shuisky—within thirteen and a half months, and the once firm government control and leadership had collapsed in intrigue, civil war, murder, and general weakness. Then too, whatever advantages the changes brought to the boyars, the masses had gained nothing, and their dissatisfaction grew. In effect, Vasilii Shuisky's unfortunate reign, 1606–10, had no popular sanction and very little popular support, representing as it did merely the victory of a boyar clique.

Opposition to the government and outright rebellion took many forms. An enemy of Vasilii Shuisky, Prince Grigorii Shakhovskoy, and others roused southern Russian cities against the tsar. Disorder swept towns on the Volga, and in Astrakhan in the far southeast the governor, Prince Ivan Khvorostinin, turned against Vasilii Shuisky. Similarly in other places local authorities refused to obey the new ruler. Rumors persisted that False Dmitrii had escaped death, and people rallied to his mere name. Serfs and slaves started numerous and often large uprisings against their landlords and the state. On occasion they joined with indigenous peoples, such as the Finnic-speaking Mordva, who on their part also sought to overturn the oppressive political and social system of Muscovite Russia.

The rebellion in the south, led by Shakhovskoy and by Bolotnikov, presented the gravest threat to the government and in fact to the entire established order. Ivan Bolotnikov was a remarkable person who was thrown into prominence by the social turmoil of the Time of Troubles: he claimed to be a former military slave and cossack and a former captive of Tatars and Turks, from whom he escaped and returned to Russia by way of Poland. He told Shakhovskoy that in Poland he had met Tsar Dmitrii, who had survived Vasilii Shuisky's attempt to kill him and who had appointed Bolotnikov commander of his army, a claim that Shakhovskoy accepted. Beyond fighting in the name of the rightful tsar, the rebel armies rallied the lower classes in a war against authority and property. Some sources—largely based on the testimony of pro-Shuisky forces, so this is uncertain—identify manifestoes calling on the poor to fight for their own interests, to rise up and kill their masters, for which they would be rewarded with their lands, wives, and high offices. In October 1606, the southern armies came to the gates of Moscow, where, however, they were checked by government forces commanded by the tsar's brilliant young nephew, Prince Mikhail Skopin-Shuisky. Perhaps inevitably, the rebels split.

The gentry armies of Riazan, led by the Liapunov brothers, and those of Tula, led by Filip Pashkov, broke with the social rebel Bolotnikov and even in large part went over to Vasilii Shuisky's side. The tsar also received other reinforcements. In 1607 a huge government army surrounded the rebels in Tula and, after a bitter four-month siege and a partial flooding of the town, forced them to surrender. Shakhovskoy was exiled to the north; Bolotnikov was also exiled and, shortly afterwards, blinded and drowned.

The rebels were also undermined by their inability to produce Tsar Dmitrii in person. Briefly, however, they did acquire a different pretender, False Peter, who claimed to be Tsar Theodore's son, born allegedly in 1592, although this son never existed. False Peter was hanged after the capture of Tula. As order collapsed and disorganization spread, more and more pretenders appeared. The cossacks in particular produced them in large numbers and with different names, claiming in that strange manner, it would seem, a certain legal sanction for their bands and movements. But it was another False Dmitrii, the second, who became a national figure. Although he emerged in August 1607, shortly before the fall of Tula and thus too late to join Shakhovskoy and Bolotnikov, he soon became a center of attraction in his own right.

The new False Dmitrii, who claimed to be Prince Dmitrii of Uglich and also the Tsar Dmitrii who defeated the Godunovs and was deposed by a conspiracy of the boyars, resembled neither. In contrast to the first pretender, he certainly realized that he was an impostor, and his lieutenants also had no illusions on that score. Nothing is known for certain about the second False Dmitrii's identity and background. The earliest mention in the sources locates him in a Lithuanian border town, in jail. Yet, in spite of these unpromising beginnings, the new pretender quickly gathered many supporters. After the defeat of Shakhovskoy and Bolotnikov he became the focal point for forces of social discontent and unrest. He attracted a very large following of cossacks, soldiers of fortune, and adventurers, especially from Poland and Lithuania, including several famous Polish commanders. Marina Mniszech recognized him as her husband and later bore him a son; the nun Martha declared him her child.

Vasilii Shuisky made the grave mistake of underestimating his new enemy and of not acting with vigor in time. In the spring of 1608 the second False Dmitrii defeated a government army under the command of one of the tsar's brothers, Prince Dmitrii Shuisky, and approached Moscow. He established his headquarters in a nearby large village called Tushino—hence his historical appellation, "The Felon of Tushino." Prince Mikhail Skopin-Shuisky again prevented the capture of the capital, but he could not defeat or dislodge the pretender. A peculiar situation arose: in Tushino the second False Dmitrii organized his own court, a boyar duma, and an administration, parallel to those in Moscow; he collected taxes, granted lands, titles, and other rewards, judged, and punished. Southern Russia and a number of cities in the north recognized his authority. Moscow and Tushino, so close to each other, maintained a constant clandestine intercourse. Many Russians switched sides; some families served both rulers at the same time. The second False Dmitrii suffered a setback, however, when his forces tried to capture the well-fortified Holy Trinity-St. Sergius Monastery, one of the gateways to northern Russia. A garrison of 1,500 men, reinforced later by another 900, withstood for sixteen months the siege of a force numbering, according to traditional accounts, up to 30,000 troops. Also, the Felon of Tushino's rule in those northern Russian cities which had recognized his authority proved to be ephemeral once they had a taste of his agents and measures.

In his desperate plight, Vasilii Shuisky finally, in February 1609, made an agreement with Sweden, obtaining the aid of a detachment of Swedish troops 6,000 strong, commanded by Jakob De la Gardie, in return for abandoning all claims to Livonia, ceding a border district, and promising eternal alliance against Poland. Throughout the rest of the year and early in 1610, Prince Mikhail Skopin-Shuisky, assisted by the Swedes, cleared northern Russia of the Felon of Tushino's troops and bands, lifted the siege of the Holy Trinity-St. Sergius Monastery, and finally relieved Moscow of its rival Tushino neighbor. The pretender and a part of his following fled to Kaluga. After his departure, and before the entire camp disbanded, the Russian gentry in Tushino asked King Sigismund III of Poland to let his son Wladyslaw, a youth of about fifteen, become the Russian tsar on certain conditions.

Sigismund III granted the request and signed an agreement in February 1610 with Russian emissaries from Tushino, who by that time had ceased to represent any organized body in Russia. The Polish king had become deeply involved in Russian affairs in the autumn of 1609, when he declared war on the Muscovite state on the ground of its anti-Polish alliance with Sweden. His advance into Russia, however, had been checked by a heroic defense of Smolensk. It would seem that from the beginning of his intervention Sigismund III intended to play for high stakes and obtain the most from the disintegration of Russia: his main goal was to become himself ruler of Russia as well as Poland. The invitation to Wladyslaw, however, gave him an added opportunity to participate in Muscovite affairs.

In March 1610 the successful and popular Prince Mikhail Skopin-Shuisky triumphantly entered Moscow at the head of his army. But his triumph did not last long. In early May he died suddenly, although he was only about twenty-four years old. Rumor had it that he had been poisoned by Dmitrii Shuisky's wife, who wanted to assure the throne to her husband after the death of childless Tsar Vasilii. New disasters soon followed. The Polish commander, Stanislaw Zolkiewski, defeated Dmitrii Shuisky when the latter tried to relieve Smolensk, and marched on Moscow. In the area occupied by Polish troops, the population swore allegiance to Wladyslaw. At this turn of events, the Felon of Tushino too advanced again on Moscow, establishing himself once more near the capital. In July 1610 Vasilii Shuisky finally lost his throne: he was deposed by an assembly of Muscovite clergy, boyars, gentry, and common people, and forced to become a monk. The boyar duma in the persons of seven boyars, with Prince Fedor Mstislavsky as the senior member, took over the government, or what there was left of it. The interregnum was to last from 1610 to 1613.

## The National Phase

The national phase of the Time of Troubles began as opposition grew within Russian society against Polish, and soon Swedish, involvement in these political and social struggles, especially Polish occupation of Moscow. The great rally of the Russian people, as it has long been described in traditional Russian accounts of how the Time of Troubles was overcome, found inspiration in an essentially national and religious determination to save the country from foreign and heretical rulers. This increasing prominence of the national and religious struggle also explains the important role of the Church during the last years of the Time of Troubles. Yet, needless to say, dynastic and social issues retained their significance during those years. In fact any neat classification of the elements which, together, produced the fantastically complicated Time of Troubles is of necessity arbitrary and artificial.

The condition of the country prevented the calling of a zemskii sobor. Yet some decision had to be taken, and urgently. At the gathering of Muscovite boyars, clergy, and ranking service gentry opinions differed. Those proposed for the throne included Prince Vasilii Golitsyn, and a boy, Michael Romanov, Metropolitan Philaret's son; however, the candidacy of the Polish prince Wladyslaw, which found backing especially among the boyars, prevailed. Probably Wladyslaw profited from a general lack of enthusiasm for another boyar tsar. But, more importantly, he was one of the only two strong and active candidates in the field, the other being the Felon of Tushino who had much support among the lower classes and probably in Moscow itself. In late August 1610, the Muscovites reached an agreement with the Polish commander Zolkiewski concerning the invitation to Wladyslaw to rule Russia; Russian conditions, which stressed that Wladyslaw was to become Orthodox, resembled in most respects those offered to the Polish prince earlier by the Tushino group, although they acquired a boyar, rather than gentry, coloring. Ten days later Moscow swore allegiance to Wladyslaw. An impressive embassy headed by Prince Vasilii Golitsyn, Metropolitan Philaret, and other dignitaries departed for Sigismund III's headquarters near Smolensk to confirm the new arrangement with the Polish king. The Felon of Tushino fled again to Kaluga, while Zolkiewski's troops entered Moscow.

At this point, when the Muscovite state appeared finally to be settling its affairs and obtaining a firm government, another reversal occurred: unexpectedly Sigismund III rejected the Russian offer. He objected especially to the conversion of Wladyslaw to Orthodoxy and to the lifting of the siege of Smolensk. But—beyond these and other specified issues—his real intention was to become the Russian ruler himself and without conditions. No agreement could be reached. Finally, contrary to international usage, Sigismund III arrested the Russian representatives, except those few who endorsed his claims, and sent them to Poland where they were to remain for nine years. Then he proceeded openly to develop his campaign to win the Russian throne by arms, diplomacy, and propaganda.

The autumn of 1610 saw the Muscovite state in utterly desperate straits. The Poles were again enemies of the Russians, and they held Moscow as well as a large area in the western part of the country. The Swedes had declared war on the Russians after Moscow had sworn allegiance to Wladyslaw. They advanced in the north, threatened Novgorod, and before long claimed the Muscovite throne for their own candidate, Prince Philip. With the collapse of Wladyslaw's candidacy, the Felon of Tushino again increased his following, much of eastern Russia turning to him for leadership. Innumerable bands of lawless men were roaming and devastating the land. Yet—as if to illustrate the Russian proverb "there is no evil, but that it brings some good"—at least the issues gradually became clearer. Sigismund III's rejection of the arrangement to put Wladyslaw on the Russian throne eliminated one major alternative for the Russians. More important still, Swedish and especially Polish aggression led to a national rally. Moreover, the cause of Russian unity received an unexpected and mighty boost in December 1610 when the Felon of Tushino was killed by one of his men in a settlement of personal accounts.

In the absence of a tsar and because of the impotence of the boyar duma and other branches of government in Polish-occupied Moscow, the Church headed the rally. Patriarch Hermogen in Moscow declared the Russians released from allegiance to Wladyslaw; and through trusted emissaries he sent manifestoes to other towns, urging them to organize an army and liberate the capital. The patriarch's appeals had a strongly religious as well as national character, for the Poles were Catholic, and Hermogen feared especially the extension of the Uniate jurisdiction to Muscovite territories—a subject to be examined later when we discuss Ukraine. Other clerics and laymen joined the patriarch in trying to arouse the people. The first response came from Riazan, where Procopius Liapunov formed an army of gentry, peasants, certain remnants of Skopin-Shuisky's troops and other elements. As Liapunov's army marched on Moscow in early 1611, it was joined by other forces, including even former troops of the Felon of Tushino who came from Kaluga, notably a mixed group commanded by Prince Dmitrii Trubetskoy, and the cossacks led by Ivan Zarutsky. It should be noted that this so-called first national army, headed by Procopius Liapunov, Trubetskoy, and Zarutsky, acted also as the government of the Muscovite state. In particular, it contained a council of representatives who concerned themselves with state legislation and policy as well as with the more immediate demands of the campaign.

The Poles, who had but a small garrison in Moscow, retreated under pressure, burned most of the city, and entrenched themselves principally in the Kremlin. The large Russian army appeared to be in control of the situation. But once more social antagonisms asserted themselves. The cossacks, furious because certain legislative measures in the interest of the gentry were passed, especially on the subject of land, fugitive serfs, and cossack brigandage, and also possibly believing a false document manufactured by the Poles, killed Procopius Liapunov in July 1611. Deprived of its leader and unwilling to cooperate with the cossacks, the gentry army disbanded. The men of Trubetskoy and Zarutsky, on the other hand, stayed around Moscow to continue the siege and seized the government machinery of the defunct first national army. In June 1611 the main Polish army finally captured Smolensk, the population of the town having been reduced, according to traditional accounts, from 80,000 to 8,000 in the course of the siege. In July the Swedes took Novgorod by a stratagem. And in Pskov, a new pretender appeared, sometimes called the third False Dmitrii. In Kaluga Marina Mniszech and her son by the Felon of Tushino, known as the Little Felon, constituted another center of attraction for dissatisfied elements.

Yet the Russians did not collapse under all these blows. They profited from a certain lack of energy and initiative on the part of their enemies: instead of advancing with a large army, Sigismund III sent merely a cavalry detachment to the relief of the Poles in Moscow, and that detachment was blocked by the cossacks; the Swedes, after the capture of Novgorod, appeared to rest on their laurels. Still, the magnitude of the Russian recovery should not be underestimated. Stimulated again by the appeals of Patriarch Hermogen, of Abbot Dionysus of the Holy Trinity-St. Sergius Monastery, and of others, the new liberation movement began in the town of Nizhnii Novgorod, on the Volga. It found a remarkable leader in Kuzma Minin, a local butcher and elected representative of the townspeople. He took charge of raising the needed resources for a new national army. The people of Nizhnii Novgorod donated a third of their possessions to the cause and, together with other northeastern towns, soon organized a large army. Command was entrusted to a veteran warrior, Prince Dmitrii Pozharsky, who was convalescing near Nizhnii Novgorod from wounds received as a general in Liapunov's army. The entire movement marked a religious, as well as a national, revival, accompanied by fasting and prayer. The second national army, just like its predecessor, acted as the government of the Muscovite state as well as its military force. It too apparently contained an assembly of representatives from different localities, something in the nature of a traveling zemskii sobor.

In early September 1612, the second national army reached Moscow and besieged the Poles. The cossacks blockading the city remained neutral; eventually one part of them joined Minin and Pozharsky, while another, with Zarutsky, went to the borderlands to continue their rebellion. In early November the Russians stormed Moscow and, after bitter fighting, captured Polish positions in the heart of the city, in particular in the Kremlin. Moscow was free at last of the enemy. All Polish efforts, finally led by Sigismund III himself, to come to the aid of the Polish garrison in Moscow failed.

The first aim of the victors was to elect a tsar and thus establish a firm, legitimate government in Russia and end the Time of Troubles. The specially called zemskii sobor which met for that purpose in the beginning of 1613 consisted of 500 to perhaps 700 members, although only 277 signatures have come down to us on the final document. It included the clergy, the boyars, the gentry, the townspeople, and even some representatives of peasants, almost certainly of the state peasants of northern Russia rather than of serfs. Twelve of the signatures belonged to peasants. While we have no records of the assembly and very little information about its deliberations, we know that the number

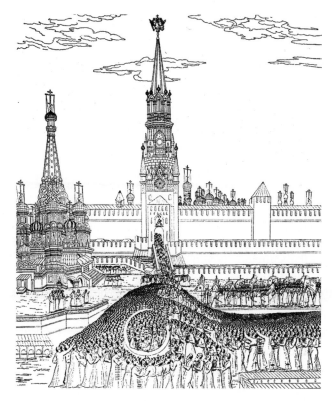

Zemskii sobor elects Michael Ramanov. According to the original caption, "on Red Square after the zemskii sobor, the Muscovite people (narod) are asked who they want for ruler." *(Tsarstvuiushchii dom Romanovykh)*

of possible candidates for tsar was first reduced by the decision to exclude foreigners. From a half dozen or more Russians mentioned, the assembly selected Michael Romanov to be tsar, and the Romanov family ruled Russia for over 300 years, from 1613 to 1917.

Historians have adduced a number of reasons for this choice. Through Ivan the Terrible's marriage to Anastasia Romanova, Michael Romanov was related to the old dynasty. The family enjoyed popularity with the masses. In particular, the people remembered Anastasia, Ivan the Terrible's good first wife, and her brother, Nikita Romanov, who dared defend some of the victims of the violent tsar. Metropolitan Philaret, Nikita's son and Michael's father, who was a prisoner of the Poles at the time of the zemskii sobor, added to the advantageous position of the family. In particular, Paul Miliukov and others have stressed that he stood closer to the Tushino camp and had much better relations with the cossacks than other boyars. Michael's youth too counted in his favor: only sixteen years old, he had not been compromised by serving the Poles or the pretenders, and he generally remained free of the extremely complicated and painful entanglements of the Time of Troubles. Michael

Romanov also gained stature as Patriarch Hermogen's choice, although the patriarch himself did not live to see the election, having perished as a prisoner of the Poles shortly before the liberation of Moscow.

Thus, in February 1613, the zemskii sobor decided in favor of Michael Romanov. Next, special emissaries were dispatched to different parts of the Muscovite state to sound local opinion. When they reported the people's strong endorsement of the decision, Michael Romanov was elected to rule Russia as tsar, and the title was to pass on to his future descendants. It took additional time to persuade his mother and him to accept the offer. Finally, Michael Romanov was crowned tsar on July 21, 1613. In Platonov's words: "According to the general notion, God himself had selected the sovereign, and the entire Russian land exulted and rejoiced." As this suggests, we should pay close attention to how this political outcome was justified. The "election" of a tsar by representatives of the whole nation was certainly not endorsed as a political principle, nor was rule justified by ideas about the will of the nation and thus popular sources of sovereignty. The "election" was a result of divine intervention, it was suggested. Moreover, it was emphasized at the coronation and after that Michael Romanov was a legitimate heir to the throne, a descendent of Riurik and St. Vladimir.

## The Nature and Results of the Time of Troubles

As this suggests, in spite of everything that happened between 1598 and 1613, autocracy as a principle and as a political order survived essentially unimpaired. If anything, at the end of it all, autocracy may have appeared more than ever the only legitimate form of government and the only certain guarantee of peace and security. State centralization was certainly strengthened in the wake of these years of political and social disorganization. The local self-government that had developed in Ivan the Terrible's reign did not outlast the Time of Troubles. The Church, too, gained authority and prestige as the great champion of the interests of the country and the people and the most effective organization in the land that had survived the collapse of the secular order. As for popular opposition, it can be seen that these movements were still attached to notions of a better tsar not a different form of rule altogether. At the same time, the brutal violence and looting committed by followers of the various pretenders likely discredited, at least for a time, the idea of a new popular movement led by a new alternative tsar.

Most historians share this general emphasis on the persistence and strengthening of autocracy but emphasize different elements of continuity and change. Scholars are not in accord, for example, about which social groups most benefitted. According to Platonov and many other historians, the big losers were the boyars and the common people, while the main winners were the autocratic state and the middle service nobility. The boyars attained their greatest power in the reign of Vasilii Shuisky and the period immediately following his deposition. Their desires found expression in the remarkably mild "conditions" associated with the accession of Vasilii Shuisky, that is in his promise not to purge the boyars arbitrarily, and in the Muscovite invitation to Wladyslaw, which changed the earlier Tushino stipulations to exclude promotion according to merit and the right to study abroad and insisted that foreigners must not be brought in over the heads of the Muscovite princely and boyar families. But boyar influence failed to last and the state returned with its former authority, while the boyars, many of their families further decimated during the Time of Troubles, became unequivocally servants of the tsar. Recent scholarship, though, has questioned this interpretation and argued that the old princely-boyar aristocracy persisted in maintaining high influence in the state, notwithstanding the formal "facade of autocracy."

No one doubts, though, that the common people lost. The serfs, slaves, fugitives, vagabonds, and the uprooted, together with the cossacks, fought for Bolotnikov, for the various pretenders, and also in countless lesser armies and bands. Although they left little written material behind them, their basic demand seems clear enough: a destruction of the oppressive Muscovite social and economic order, though not, it would seem, the political one: they focused their dreams on the coming of a benevolent but still all-powerful tsar. Yet the old social order survived and strengthened. The decades that followed the Time of Troubles saw a final and complete establishment of serfdom in Russia and in general a further subjugation of the toiling majority to the interests of the gentry.

The middle service gentry, along with the richest merchants, were perhaps the biggest social beneficiaries, though this was less a change than a continuation of social-political relationships already in place in the sixteenth century. We have some sense of further changes this class may have desired from documents such as the invitation to ascend the Muscovite throne sent to Wladyslaw by the service gentry in Tushino. The conditions of the offer included full protection of the Orthodox Church in Russia and freedom of religion, for Wladyslaw was a Catholic; rule with the help of the boyar duma and the zemskii sobor; no punishment without trial in court; the preservation and extension of the rights of the clergy, the service gentry, and to a degree the merchants; the rewarding of servitors according to merit; the right to study abroad; and at the same time a prohibition against serfs leaving their masters and a guarantee that slaves would not be freed. This attempt by the Tushino gentry to establish a government failed. Still, it has been argued, the gentry succeeded in defending its interests during the Time of Troubles and in preserving and in part re-establishing a political and social order in which it already occupied the central position.

Perhaps, therefore, the most important consequence of the Time of Troubles, as we have already noted, was the state's heightened authority and legitimacy. The historian S. Soloviev, for example, argued that this era helped bring about the victory in Russia, at long last, of the concept of state over that of family and clan. No less important, though much more complex in its long-term potential, the Time of Troubles nurtured a newer sense of national identity—at least in how these events would be remembered, mythologized, and utilized in the coming years. The Slavophiles—whom we shall consider when we discuss

Russian thought in the nineteenth century—were probably the most enthusiastic about the positive effect of the Time of Troubles in revealing the greatness of the Russian people, who survived the hardest trials and tribulations, overcame all enemies, saved their faith and country, and re-established the monarchy. Many historians, including Platonov, would similarly point to the important growth of national sentiment in the fight against foreign intervention, aristocratic reaction, and popular anarchy. For Platonov, this had the beneficial effect of nurturing a new recognition of public, as against private, rights and duties by sovereign and subject alike. Not every historian has been so sanguine, of course. Many liberal writers have viewed the survival of autocratic power, and its reinforcement by modern ideas of state and nation, as making alternative political paths less likely and contributing to the social and political subordination of the majority of Russian subjects, and of non-Russians, as the empire expanded. From a related perspective, the Russian historian Kliuchevsky emphasized the long-term significance of the social upheavals of the Time of Troubles, though not in the same positive way as Soviet historians would later do. Kliuchevsky noted the abandonment of the tradition of patient suffering by the common people, and the legacy of devastation and discord that pointed to the great popular rebellions of later years. The peculiar role and importance of the pretenders, he added, demonstrated the Russians' political immaturity.

# CHAPTER 17

# The Reigns of Michael, 1613–45, Alexis, 1645–76, and Theodore, 1676–82

The seventeenth century cannot be separated either from the preceding or the succeeding epoch. It is the continuation and the result of the past just as it is the preparation for the future. It is essentially an age of transition, which lays the groundwork, and rapidly, for the reforms of Peter.

PAUL MILIUKOV

In Nikolai Kostomarov's words, "Few examples can be found in history when a new sovereign ascended the throne in conditions so extremely sad as those in which Mikhail Fedorovich, a minor, was elected." And indeed Michael Romanov assumed power over a devastated country with the capital itself, as well as a number of other towns, burned down. The treasury was empty, and financial collapse of the state appeared complete. In Astrakhan, Zarutsky, who had Marina Mniszech and the Little Felon in his camp, rallied the cossacks and other malcontents, continuing the story of pretenders and social rebellion so characteristic of the Time of Troubles. Many roaming bands, some of them several thousand strong, continued looting the land. Moreover, Muscovy remained at war with Poland and Sweden, which had seized respectively Smolensk and Novgorod as well as other Russian territory and promoted their own candidates to the Muscovite throne, Prince Wladyslaw and Prince Philip.

Under the circumstances, the sixteen-year-old tsar asked the zemskii sobor not to disband, but to stay in Moscow and help him rule. The zemskii sobor, while its personnel changed several times, in fact participated in the government of Russia throughout the first decade of the new reign. Platonov and others have pointed to the naturalness of this alliance of the "stable" classes of the Muscovite society with the monarchy which they had established. Michael also worked very closely with the boyar duma. Some historians even believe that at his accession he had given the duma certain promises limiting autocracy—an interesting supposition that has not been corroborated by the evidence. The tsar's advisers, few of whom showed ability, at first included especially members of the Saltykov family, relatives on his mother's side. In 1619, however, Michael's father, Metropolitan Philaret, returned from imprisonment in Poland, was made patriarch, and became the most important man in the state. In addition to his ecclesiastical dignities, Philaret received the title of Great Sovereign, with the result that the country had two great sovereigns and documents were issued in the names of both. But Philaret's real power lay in his ability and experience and especially in his forceful character that enabled him to dominate his rather weak son. Philaret died in 1633, almost eighty years old.

In 1613 and the years following, the most pressing problems were those of internal disorder, foreign invasion, and financial collapse. Within some three years the government had dealt effectively with the disorder, in spite of new rebellions. Authorities made certain concessions to the cossacks and amnestied all bandits, provided they would enroll in the army to fight the Swedes. Then they proceeded to destroy the remaining opponents, group by group. One of Michael's first tasks was to send troops to defeat his most dangerous opponents, the cossack leader Zarutsky, Marina Mniszech, and her three-year-old son by the first False Dmitrii, the Little Felon, who has been described as "an involuntary pretender by birth." In 1614, government troops seized Astrakhan, whose citizens had already rebelled against Zarutsky's brutal rule, and soon captured the three. Zarutsky was impaled, the Little Felon hanged, and Mniszech soon died in prison.

Everything considered, Tsar Michael's government could also claim success in checking foreign aggression and stabilizing international relations, although at a price. Sweden, with its new king Gustavus II, or Gustavus Adolphus, occupied elsewhere in Europe, concluded peace in Stolbovo in 1617. According to the agreement, the Swedes returned Novgorod and adjacent areas of northern Russia, but kept the strip of territory on the Gulf of Finland, thus pushing the Russians farther from the sea. In addition, Sweden received 20,000 rubles. The Poles had greater ambitions; however, an understanding was attained after Wladyslaw's campaign of 1617–18 reached but failed to capture Moscow. By the truce of Deulino of 1618, which was to last for fourteen years, Poland kept Smolensk and certain other gains in western Russia. It was by the terms of this agreement that Russian prisoners, including Philaret, were allowed to return home. At the termination of the treaty in 1632, hostilities were resumed. But in 1634 peace was made: Poland again kept its gains in western Russia and, besides, received 20,000 rubles, while Wladyslaw finally withdrew his claims to the Muscovite throne.

During Michael's reign important events also occurred south of the Muscovite borders. In 1637 Don cossacks, on their own, seized the distant Turkish fortress of Azov by the sea of the same name. In 1641 a huge Turkish army and navy returned, but in the course of an epic siege of four months could not dislodge the intruders. Having beaten back the Turks, the cossacks offered Azov to Tsar Michael. Acceptance meant war with Turkey. At the especially convened zemskii sobor of 1642 the delegates of the service class opted for war, but those of the merchants and the townspeople argued that financial stringency precluded large-scale military action. The tsar endorsed the latter opinion, and the cossacks had to abandon Azov. In the Azov area, as in the area of the Gulf of Finland, the next Russian effort was to be led by Peter the Great.

Financial stability proved to be more difficult to attain than security at home or peace abroad. Miliukov and others have pointed out that the catastrophic financial situation of the Muscovite state resulted from its

Tsar Alexis wearing the royal regalia, symbolizing some of the sources of legitimation favored by the Russian throne: the barmy (shoulder coverings) equivalent to the shoulder pieces of the Byzantine emperor, the "Life-Giving Cross" believed to contain a piece of wood from the cross of the crucifixion; the Crown of Monomakh, supposedly given by the Byzantine emperor to an earlier Moscow ruler; the orb and scepter, traceable to both Rome and Byzantium; and the double-headed eagle.   (*Tsarstvuiushchii dom Romanovykh*)

overextension, from the fact that its needs and requirements tended to exceed the economic capacity of the people. The Time of Troubles caused a further depletion and disorganization. In a desperate effort to obtain money, Tsar Michael's government tried a variety of measures: collection of arrears, new taxes, and loans, including successive loans of 3,000, 16,000, and 40,000 rubles from the Stroganovs. In 1614 an extraordinary levy of "the fifth money" in towns, and of corresponding sums in the countryside, was enacted. While specialists dispute whether this impost represented one-fifth of one's possessions or one-fifth of one's income, its Draconian nature is obvious. On two later occasions the government made a similar collection of "the tenth money." On the whole, enough funds were obtained for the state to carry on its activities; but at the end of Michael's reign, as in the beginning, the financial situation remained desperate. Finances were to plague the tsar's successors with further crises.

## The Reigns of Alexis and Theodore

Michael died in 1645 at the age of forty-eight, and his only son Alexis or Aleksei, a youth of sixteen, succeeded him as tsar. Known as *Tishaishii*, the Quietest One, in spite of his outbursts of anger and general impulsiveness, Alexis left a favorable impression with many contemporaries, as well as with subsequent historians. In his brilliant reconstruction of the tsar's character Kliuchevsky called Alexis "the kindest man, a glorious Russian soul" and presented him both as the epitome of Muscovite culture and as one of the pioneers of the new Russian interest in the West. Even if we allow for a certain exaggeration and stylization in Kliuchevsky's celebrated analysis, there remains the image of an attractive person, remarkably sensitive and considerate in his relations with other people, an absolute ruler who was not at all a despot. Alexis had been brought up in the Muscovite religious tradition, and he continued to be a dedicated and well-informed churchgoer and to observe fasts and rituals throughout his life. At the same time he developed an interest in the West and Western culture, including architecture and also the theatre, which was an innovation for Russia. The tsar liked to write and left behind him many fascinating letters.

Alexis's long reign, 1645–76, was by no means quiet. Old crises and problems persisted and some new ones appeared. Not least, he was faced with major popular uprisings, including in Moscow itself. Making matters worse, the tsar was a weak ruler and much depended, especially in the earlier years of rule, on relatives and other advisers, who often failed him. The boyar Boris Morozov, Alexis's Western-oriented tutor who married a sister of Alexis's wife, and Prince Ilya Miloslavsky, Alexis's father-in-law, became especially prominent after the accession of the new sovereign. Morozov acted with intelligence and ability, but his efforts to replenish the treasury by such means as an increase in the salt tax and the sale of the hitherto forbidden tobacco, to which the Church objected, antagonized much of the urban population. Also, some of his protégés and appointees robbed the people. Narrow selfishness, greed, and corruption characterized the behavior of Miloslavsky and his clique.

In May and June 1648 the exasperated inhabitants of Moscow staged a large rebellion. Begun by artisans and tradesmen, they were soon joined by soldiers (*streltsy*) and some gentry. Townsmen presented the young Tsar Alexis with a petition protesting the poor administration of the city and especially the high tax burden. Contrary to paternalistic tradition, Alexis refused to accept the petition of the people and instead ordered arrests. Soon, large crowds were in the streets attacking homes and property of the ruling elite. A number of officials were brutally lynched by the crowd or executed—notably, the head of the chancellery that managed the city, though both Morozov and Miloslavsky survived. Fires, of disputed origin, burned down large sections of Moscow. Often inspired by news of the Moscow rebellion, uprisings swept through many other towns. In 1650, new rebellions against rich merchants and city officials arose in Novgorod and Pskov, suppressed by troops sent from the capital.

Discontent and rebellion continued, however, especially in response to the government's continuing efforts to raise money, needed particularly to fund new wars. Not only were taxes raised but the government attempted to increase its currency by debasing silver coinage with copper. This reform proved no more successful than similar efforts in other countries; it led to counterfeiting and inflation. It also inspired the huge "copper coin riot" of 1662. But the greatest rebellion of the reign, headed by Stepan, or Stenka, Razin, and long remembered and romanticized in Russian folklore, occurred in 1670–71. Razin, a chieftain (ataman) of a community of Don cossacks, first attracted attention as a daring freebooter who raided Persia and other lands along the Caspian Sea and along the lower Volga. Among the cossacks of the Don River region discontent with Moscow had been growing, partly due to strong government pressure to return runaway serfs who fled to cossack lands and material sanctions for failing to do this. In the spring of 1670, Razin led his cossacks up the Volga with the declared aim of eradicating the "boyar-traitors" in Moscow. His movement attracted many followers with a rather vague but incendiary ideology that pointed forward to later cossack and peasant rebellions more than backward to the Time of Troubles: the goal was, in the name of the "good tsar," to expel from power the "wicked" men among the rich and powerful (not as a "class" but as individuals according to their presumed actions) who interfered with, indeed were "traitors" to, the sovereign's purposes and oppressed the common people, and thus to give the common folk "freedom." As one English traveler described Razin's claims, "he promised Liberty and redemption from the Yoke of the Boyars or Nobles, which he said were the oppressors of the Country." All accounts agree on the ferocious brutality of the insurgents—though no less brutal than the government's suppression of this and other rebellions—who would literally tear their enemies apart and defile their corpses. Along with widespread burning and looting, these violent acts have been seen as symbolic gestures, typical of many popular revolutions, to cleanse society of privilege and oppression and to redistribute both wealth and symbolic power. This cossack rebellion attracted a large and diverse following: not only more cossacks but also garrison soldiers, and townspeople (who often welcomed the rebels), including some women, peasants, and non-Russian and non-Christian people living in the Volga region, especially Chuvash, Mordva, Mari, and Tatars. In different ways, it has been argued, all these rebels shared resentment against the growing Muscovite state and the traditional freedoms that the state was eroding. At its greatest extent, the rebel army may have reached 20,000 people. The rebels seized Volga towns from Astrakhan to the outskirts of Simbirsk, where regular Muscovite troops, which included several regiments trained in the Western manner, finally stopped this motley force. Razin and some of his followers escaped to the Don, but in 1671 he was seized by loyal cossack authorities and sent to Moscow, where he was tortured and then executed by quartering in Red Square. Several months later Astrakhan, the last center of the rebellion, surrendered.

In addition to suppressing uprisings, the government took steps to improve administration and justice in order to assuage popular discontent. Of major importance was the introduction of a new legal code, the *Ulozhenie* of 1649. Approved in principle by the especially convened zemskii sobor of 1648 and produced by a commission elected by the sobor, the new code provided the first systematization of Muscovite laws since 1550. It marked a great improvement over its predecessors, though it also finally made serfdom complete, and was not to be superseded until 1835.

The extension of Muscovite jurisdiction to Ukraine in 1654 represented an event of still greater and more lasting significance. As we remember, that land after 1569 found itself under Polish, rather than Lithuanian, control. Association with Poland meant increasing pressure of the Polish social order—based on the exclusive privileges of the gentry and servitude of the masses—as well as pressure of Catholicism on the Orthodox Ukrainian people. The religious issue became more intense after 1596. That year marked the Union of Brest and the establishment of the so-called Uniate Church, that is, a Church linked to Rome but retaining the Eastern ritual, the Slavonic language in its services, and its other practices and customs—though in common use at the time, the term "Uniate" is seen as derogatory by many today, who prefer terms such as Eastern Catholics, Byzantine Rite Catholics, or Greek Catholics. Athough the Orthodox community split violently on the subject of union, each side anathemizing the other, the Polish government chose to proceed as if the union had been entirely successful and the Uniate Church had replaced the Orthodox in the eastern part of the realm. Yet, in fact, although most Orthodox bishops in the Polish state favored the union, the majority of the Orthodox people did not. Two churches, therefore, competed in Ukraine: the Uniate, promoted by the government but often lacking other support, and the Orthodox, opposed and sometimes persecuted by authorities but supported by the majority. Lay Orthodox brotherhoods and a small, diminishing, but influential group of Orthodox landed magnates helped the Church of the people.

The cossacks also entered the fray. Around the middle of the sixteenth century the Dnieper cossacks, the most celebrated of all cossack "hosts," had established their headquarters, the *Sech*—*Sich* in Ukrainian—on an island in the Dnieper beyond the cataracts. They proceeded to stage unbelievably daring raids in all directions, but especially against the Crimean Tatars and Turkey—as described in detail by Mykhailo. Hrushevsky and other Ukrainian historians. The cossacks developed a distinctive society, both military and democratic, for their offices were elective and a general gathering of all cossacks made the most important decisions. The Polish government faced difficulties in trying to control the cossacks. Stephen Báthory and his successors allowed them very considerable autonomy, but also established a definite organization for the "host" and introduced the category of registered, that is, officially recognized, cossacks to whom both autonomy and the new organization applied. All other cossacks were to be treated simply as peasants. The Polish policy had some success in that it helped to develop economic and social ties between the cossack upper stratum and the Polish gentry. Yet the same well-established cossacks retained ethnic and, especially, religious links with the Ukrainian people and generally supported the Ukrainians against Polish rule. There was much ambivalence, however, especially among commanders. The hetmans and registered cossacks, who after the expansion in 1625 numbered 6,000 men, obtained certain advantages from their association with Poland and found themselves often with divided loyalties. However, the unrecognized cossacks, who were several times more numerous, as well as the peasants, viewed Polish rule as bringing only serfdom and Catholicism.

From 1624 to 1638 a series of cossack and peasant rebellions swept Ukraine. Only with great exertion and after several defeats did the Polish army and government at last prevail. The ruthless Polish pacification managed to force obedience for no longer than a decade. In 1648 the Ukrainians rose again under an able leader Bogdan, or Bohdan, Khmelnitsky in what has been called the Ukrainian War of Liberation. After some brilliant successes, achieved with the aid of the Crimean Tatars, and two abortive agreements with Poland, the Ukrainians turned again to Moscow. Earlier, in 1625, 1649, and 1651, the Muscovite government had failed to respond to the Ukrainian request, which, if acceded to, would have meant war against Poland. However, the zemskii sobor of 1653 urged Tsar Alexis to take under his sovereign authority Hetman Bogdan Khmelnitsky and his entire army "with their towns and lands." Specialists suggest that Moscow's willingness finally to support Khmelnitsky in war against Poland-Lithuania may have been due to Poland's relative weakness militarily after losses to the cossacks and especially the desire to regain Russian lands that had been lost to Lithuania, which, because of the war, were now relatively undefended.

In Pereiaslavl (or Pereiaslav) in January 1654, an important but controversial treaty was signed that brought the Ukrainian cossack host and its lands into a union with Moscow. The agreement was signed by a representative *rada*, or council, headed by Khmelnitsky, and representatives of the Moscow tsar. No final text has survived and scholars continued to debate, sometimes vociferously, what was actually agreed to and the underlying intentions and assumptions on each side. We know that Khmelnitsky had considered and even negotiated other options, including joining the Polish-Lithuanian

Commonwealth or becoming a protectorate of the Ottoman Empire. The most promising option seemed to be loyalty to the Moscow tsar. In return for this union, many historians argue, the cossacks retained considerable autonomy and rights—more than could have been won from Poland or Turkey. The historian Serhii Plokhy has described this as the "confirmation of the corporate privileges of Cossackdom and international recognition of cossack statehood." Other historians have insisted that the new arrangement represented unconditional acceptance of the authority of Moscow. Certainly, this seems to be how Moscow understood the deal: complete Cossack "submission and loyalty," in the words of the oath Alexis had insisted on for new hetmans. In subsequent decades and centuries, Ukrainians acquired good reasons to complain of the Russian government, which eventually abrogated entirely the considerable autonomy granted to Ukrainians after they had sworn allegiance to the Muscovite tsar, and which imposed, or helped to impose, upon them many heavy burdens and restrictions, including serfdom and measures meant to arrest the development of Ukrainian literary language and culture. At the same time, Ukrainians would play a very important part in Muscovite government and culture, not least because of greater closeness to the West. In particular, many Ukrainians distinguished themselves as leading supporters of Westernizing reforms in Russia.

In response to the new cossack-Muscovite alliance, Poland-Lithuania declared war on Russia. The brutal Thirteen-Years War, which included intervention by Sweden at one point, ended in 1667 with the Treaty of Andrusova. A very important effect of this war, as reflected in the treaty, was a further expansion of the Moscow state. The Dnieper became the new boundary between Poland-Lithuania and Muscovy, with Ukraine on the left bank being ceded to Moscow and right-bank Ukraine remaining under Poland. Kiev, on the right bank, was an exception, for it was to be left for two years under Muscovite rule. Actually Kiev stayed under Moscow beyond the assigned term, as did Smolensk, granted to the tsar for thirteen and a half years; and the treaty of 1686 confirmed the permanent Russian possession of the cities. The Muscovite state also fought an inconclusive war against Sweden that ended in 1661 and managed to defend its new possessions in Ukraine in a long struggle with Turkey that lasted until 1681. In Ukrainian history the period following the Union of Pereiaslavl, Bogdan Khmelnitsky's death in 1657, and the Treaty of Andrusovo is vividly described as "the Ruin," and its complexities rival those of the Russian Time of Troubles. Divided both physically and in orientation and allegiance, the Ukrainians followed a number of competing leaders who usually, in one way or another, played off Poland against Moscow; Hetman Petr Doroshenko even paid allegiance to Turkey. Constant and frequent fratricidal warfare decimated the people and exhausted the land. Yet the Muscovite hold on left-bank Ukraine remained, and the arrangement of 1654 acquired increasing importance with the passage of time.

Significant events in the second half of Alexis's reign include the ecclesiastical reform undertaken by Patriarch Nikon and the resulting major split in the Russian Orthodox Church. Nikon himself certainly deserves notice. Of peasant origin, intelligent, and possessing an extremely strong and domineering character, he attracted the favorable attention of the tsar, distinguished himself as metropolitan in Novgorod, and, in 1652, became patriarch. The strong-willed cleric proceeded to exercise a powerful personal influence on the younger and softer monarch. Alexis even gave Nikon the title of Great Sovereign, thus repeating the quite exceptional honor bestowed upon Patriarch Philaret by his son, Tsar Michael. The new patriarch, expressing a viewpoint common in the Catholic West, but not in the Orthodox world, claimed that the church was superior to the state and endeavored to assert his authority over the sovereign's. Charged with papism, he answered characteristically: "And why not respect the pope for that which is good." Nikon pushed his power and position too far. In 1658 Alexis quarreled with his exacting colleague and mentor. Finally, the Church council of 1666–67, in which Eastern patriarchs participated, deposed and defrocked Nikon. The former Great Sovereign ended his days in exile in a distant monastery.

The measures of Patriarch Nikon that had the most lasting importance concerned a reform of Church books and practices that resulted in a permanent cleavage among Russian believers. While this entire subject, the fascinating issue of the Old Belief, will be considered when we discuss religion in Muscovite Russia, it might be mentioned here that the same ecclesiastical council of 1666–67 that condemned Nikon entirely upheld his reform. The last decade of Tsar Alexis's reign passed in religious strife and persecution.

Alexis's successor Theodore, his son by his first wife, became tsar at the age of fourteen and died when he was twenty. He was a sickly and undistinguished person, whose education, it is interesting to note, included not only Russian and Church Slavonic, but also Latin and Polish taught by a learned theologian and writer, Simeon of Polotsk. Theodore's brief reign, 1676–82, has been noted for the abolition of mestnichestvo. It was in 1682 that this extremely cumbersome system of service appointments at last disappeared, making it easier later for Peter the Great to reform and govern the state. The mestnichestvo records were burned.

# CHAPTER 18

# Muscovite Russia: Economy, Society, Institutions

After he inherits the throne, the Tsar, or Grand Prince, alone rules the whole country; all his subjects, the noblemen and the princes as well as the common people, townsmen, and peasants, are his serfs and slaves, whom he treats as the master of the house does his servants.... If one keeps in mind the basic distinction between a legitimate and a tyrannical order, that the first subserves the welfare of the subjects and the second the personal wants of the sovereign, then the Russian government must be considered closely related to tyranny.

ADAM OLEARIUS, 1647

The key to Muscovy's achievement, and the secret of the success of the Muscovite princes (or of those who chose to rule in their name), was in the development of a stable political system in which these princes became the focal point—and the hostages—(herein the true secret) of an oligarchy of boyar clans. For it was these clans, closely organized extended families of tradition-bound cavalrymen, that provided the crucial nucleus of the military forces of the Muscovite princes, it was these clans that effected, and benefited from, the mobilization of the available resources of the Russian village, and it was these clans, or rather certain superclans, that controlled, and were the principle players in, the game of politics at the Muscovite court.

EDWARD KEENAN

In the interstices of the autocratic state, society developed many spheres of autonomy, and people conducted their lives in ways quite unconnected with the controlling agenda of the tsarist regime.

VALERIE KIVELSON

For the vast majority of Muscovite Russians, agriculture stood at the center of their economic lives. Rye, wheat, oats, barley, and millet constituted the basic crops. Farming technology remained as it had been for centuries. Implements included wooden or iron ploughs, harrows, scythes, and sickles. Oxen and horses provided draft power and manure served as fertilizer. Cattle-raising, vegetable-gardening, and, particularly in the west, the growing of more specialized crops such as flax and hemp, as well as hunting, fishing, and apiculture, constituted some other important peasant occupations. But these years also witnessed a major change in agricultural life: as the Muscovite state expanded and peasants were prevented from moving, the old system of slash-and-burn agriculture, which depended on the availability of free lands, gave way to a stationary three-field system. This was accompanied by the rise of strip farming, whereby villages divided fields into long narrow strips and distributed these among families in order to spread the risks and coordinate land with available labor. In most of the country, yields remained low, due to both primitive implements and poor soil and weather conditions. This was all made much worse by a terrible economic crisis in the second half of the sixteenth century, brought on by the effects of the oprichnina, deadly epidemics, civil war, and growing gentry exploitation of peasants. Many peasants fled to the borderlands, making labor shortages and thus exploitation even worse.

The sixteenth-century economic depression also affected trade, crafts, manufacturing, and urban life generally. After the Time of Troubles, however, we see impressive new growth, largely stimulated by the demands of the expanding Moscow state, though all accounts agree that the Russian economy remained far less developed than in Western Europe at that time. Russia continued to sell raw materials to other countries, and its foreign trade received a boost from the newly established relations with the English and the Dutch. The Russians, however, lacked a merchant marine, and their role in the exchange remained passive. Domestic trade increased, especially after the Time of Troubles, and profited from a rather enlightened new commercial code promulgated in 1667. The mining of metal and manufacturing had to provide, first of all, for the needs of the army and the treasury. Industrial enterprises belonged either to the state or to private owners; among the latter were the Stroganov family which engaged in various undertakings, especially in extracting salt, and the Morozovs, so prominent in Alexis's reign, who developed a huge business in potash. Foreign entrepreneurs and specialists played a leading role in the growth of Muscovite mining and manufacturing, and we shall return to them when we discuss Western influences on Muscovy. As a result of intensified and more varied economic activity, regional differentiation increased. For example, metalwork developed in the Urals, the town of Tula, and Moscow, while the salt enterprises centered principally in the northeast.

## Serfdom. Muscovite Society

Serfdom was the foundation of the Muscovite economic and social system. Serf labor supported the gentry and thus the entire structure of the state. As we have seen, peasant bondage had a long history, reaching back to the days of Kiev. It seems that earlier peasant dependence, including slavery, was primarily the result of contracts: in return for a loan of money, grain, or agricultural tools, the peasant would promise to pay dues, the quitrent or *obrok,* to the landlord and perform work, the corvée or *barshchina,* for him. Although made for a period ranging from one to ten years, the agreements tended to continue, for the peasant could rarely pay off his obligations. Indeed his annual contributions to the landlord's economy often constituted merely interest on the loan. In turn, the need to ensure a reliable source of agricultural labor, especially the gentry service class, led to demands for limitations on peasant mobility. Gradually it became possible for the peasant to leave his master only once a year, around St. George's day in late autumn, provided, of course, his debts had been paid.

While these development preceded the rise of the Moscow state, enserfment remained incomplete until the seventeenth century. The growth of pomestie agriculture meant that bondage spread rapidly as lands with peasants were granted by the tsar to his gentry servitors. The government continued to promote the interests of the gentry, in particular by its efforts to limit or eliminate peasant transfer and to stop peasant flights. While no law directly establishing serfdom was ever issued, certain legislative acts contributed to that end. In particular the government proclaimed forbidden years, that is, years when the peasants could not move—or, more realistically, be moved by those who paid their obligations—even around St. George's day. We know, for example, of such legislation in regard to many categories of peasants in 1601 and 1602. Also, in response to repeated petitions from the gentry, the government proceeded to lengthen the period of time after which a fugitive serf could no longer be returned to his master: from five years at the end of the sixteenth century to an indefinite term, as we find it in the *Ulozhenie* of 1649. Further, in 1607 and other years, the state legislated penalties for harboring fugitive serfs; while the first census, taken from 1550 to 1580, as well as later ones, also helped the growth of serfdom by providing a record of peasant residence and by listing children of serfs in the same category as their parents.

With the *Ulozhenie* of 1649, the defining essence of serfdom was now enshrined in law and could be effectively enforced: a peasant could not move without the lord's permission. The new code eliminated any statute of limitations for fugitives and imposed heavy penalties for harboring runaways. The government also established special teams to search the countryside for fugitives. Although a few highly special exceptions remained, the *Ulozhenie* in essence assumed the caste principle "once a serf always a serf" and gave full satisfaction to the gentry. Vladimirsky-Budanov and others have argued convincingly that after 1649 the government continued to consider the serfs its responsible subjects rather than merely gentry property; nevertheless, in fact their position in relation to their masters deteriorated rapidly. Their obligations undefined, the serfs were at the mercy of the landlords, who came to exercise increasing judicial and police authority on their estates. By the end of the century, the buying, selling, and willing of serfs had developed; that is, they were treated virtually as slaves. It is worth noting that serfdom in Russia appeared simultaneously with a centralized monarchy not with any kind of feudalism. It resulted from two major factors: the old and growing economic dependence of the peasant on the landlord, and the activity of the Muscovite government in support of the gentry.

Richard Hellie estimated that as much as 85 percent of the population of Muscovy in the seventeenth century were serfs—including smaller numbers of state peasants and monastery peasants, who owed service to the state or the Church rather than to private landlords and were likely to be treated less harshly. Perhaps 10 percent of the population were slaves, who continued to play a significant role in large households and on large estates. More people joined this category during the disturbances and disasters of the late sixteenth and early seventeenth centuries by selling themselves into slavery. With the growth and final triumph of serfdom, the distinction between slaves and serfs became less and less pronounced. State peasants constituted the bulk of the population in the north and the northeast.

Towns played a key role in control and development of the lands of the expanding Russian state. The main classes of townspeople were merchants, subdivided into several hierarchical groups, and artisans. The 1649 *Ulozhenie* regulated urban life in the interests of order and especially taxation; indeed, the government levied the greater part of its taxes in the towns. In response to petitions from urban communities, who were responsible for a collective tax payment, the law abolished tax-exempt ("white") suburbs, which were mainly controlled by the Church or wealthy merchants, merging all urban groups into the "black" town of taxpayers. The government also granted a monopoly on urban trade and manufacturing to the tax-paying community (though the state retained a monopoly on foreign trade and on certain products sold at home, such as wine and tobacco, as well as holding the greatest single interest in the fur trade). Along with these benefits, the *Ulozhenie* also effectively enserfed townsmen: they were forbidden from leaving the tax-paying community without the town's permission, and the statute of limitations for recovering runaway townsmen was abolished. Merchants and artisans, like peasants, had become a closed and hereditary caste, with sons following the occupation of their fathers, and an immobile one.

Landlords can be considered the upper class of Muscovite Russia. They ranged from extremely rich and influential boyars to penniless servitors of the tsar who frequently could not meet their service obligations. Yet, as already indicated, with the growth of the pomestie system and the uniform extension and standardization of state service, differences diminished in importance and the landlords gradually coalesced into a fairly homogeneous class of service gentry.

The history of mestnichestvo, or precedence, illustrates well the adaptation of ancient Russian princely and boyar families to Muscovite state service and their complex relation to the ruler and the state. Mestnichestvo was a system of state and military appointments, dating from a genealogical registration of all boyar families in the Muscovite service in 1475, in which a person's position had to correspond to the standing of his family and to his own place in the family; nobody who ranked lower on the mestnichestvo scale could be appointed above him. Matters of family standing and honor, based on histories of service, were far more important than experience or ability. The boyars valued their own and their families' "honor" and "just position" extremely highly. Some boyars even dramatically determined to eat sitting on the floor rather than at a position at the table they considered below their rank.

Until recently, most historians were uniformly negative about mestnichestvo, and thus viewed its abolition in 1682 as a logical move by an absolutist state that required greater simplicity and uniformity in state service and the possibility of rewarding merit. These historians tended to describe precedence quarrels as undermining the modernizing authority of the state and also preventing the aristocracy from uniting as a proper social estate. More recent research by historians such as Crummey and Kollmann, often developing arguments of early twentieth-century scholars like A. Presniakov and S. Veselovskii, has emphasized the positive functionality of mestnichestvo as ensuring elite loyalty and thus political cohesion and stability through an orderly system of hierarchical appointments. Also, research suggests, the state may have had more flexibility in appointments than critics of the system have suggested. The government proclaimed certain military campaigns exempt from precedence rules and the tsar made various appointments outside the mestnichestvo system (naming positions as *bez mest,* or "without place"). Still, it can be argued, these measures did not alter the fundamental rigidity of a system that made it extremely difficult for a man of talent who did not belong to a leading aristocratic family to receive an important position in the state or the military. Thus, this conservative arrangement can be seen as producing stability but not progress. Debates over the reasons mestnichestvo was abolished reflect similar points of view. The traditional explanation is that it was discarded in favor of a more rational system based on principles of uniformity, efficiency, and merit, which better served the interests of both the state and the lesser gentry. Others argue that the system simply grew ineffective as more and more ranks and campaigns were declared to be "without place," as the dying out of clans made precedence calculations increasingly difficult and as large numbers of new men flooded into state and military service and thus into mestnichestvo. In any case, it has been argued, the elite were finding new ways to protect their privilege, status, and honor.

As can be seen, our generalizations about social groups have mainly been about men. We know relatively little about women in peasant, artisanal, or merchant families in the sixteenth and seventeen centuries. Religious teachings and popular culture, as in other medieval societies in the West, taught that women were a dangerous temptation, impure, and morally weak, and thus must be subordinated to men, but also that women played an essential role in social life as mothers. Contemporary prescriptive texts suggest women's highly constrained domestic role—the ideal of women as "meek, silent, and obedient," in the words of the early seventeenth-century hagiographic biography of the holy woman Iuliana Osorina. But the actual everyday lives of women are largely invisible to us. More evident, indeed famously so, because it so fascinated visiting foreigners, is the seclusion of elite women. Elite women in Muscovy were required to live in separate quarters from men and were excluded from public life. Marriage was mainly a way of building family alliances, especially when these could lead to greater political power for a man and his clan. Some scholars have argued that this gave women a certain hidden power in linking key families, conveying information, and smoothing conflicts between intermarried clans. Seclusion, in this view, gave elite women a type of status and power. It was also the case that women in Russia could own their own property, which was rare in Europe.

## Muscovite Political Culture and Institutions

The traditional view of Muscovite politics, which is still strong, is that the Russian state had become effectively autocratic, absolutist, and patrimonial (the idea that the whole of state and society is the private property of the ruler), even a type of "oriental despotism." In other words, in the often repeated formula spoken by Russians when addressing the tsar, this was a system in which all Muscovites, even the highest, were the tsar's "slaves" (*kholopy*). Today, many specialists on Muscovy are likely to look behind what they view as the formal and ritualized face of absolutism, where they see a complex but stable "game of power politics" involving political maneuvering by powerful boyar clans, an inner circle of families with hereditary rights to be present at court, a process of collective consultation between the tsar and clan elites, and local autonomy outside the court. From this perspective, the kowtowing of the tsar's "slaves" should be interpreted not literally but as a ritualized assertion of "rights" of membership and participation in this polity, a way of making real claims on the government while symbolically respecting the tsar's elevated status.

Autocratic ideology itself can be seen as allowing different interpretations of the power of the tsar. On the one hand, as we have seen, rituals, symbols, and public rhetoric powerfully emphasized the ruler's absolute and sacred power. On the other hand, these same rituals and symbols reminded everyone that the tsar was required to be a truly Christian ruler, governing in consultation with his best men, and always acting for the good of his people. In other words, the tsar's legitimacy was grounded in both divine selection and religious and moral obligation. The complexity of the tsar's formally autocratic power can also be seen in one of the most important court rituals in the seventeenth century. On Palm Sunday, the tsar, on foot, led an ass bearing the patriarch, symbolically reenacting Christ's arrival in Jerusalem. One interpretation is that this symbolized the tsar's subservience before Christ and the Church and the subordination of the secular to religious government. On the other hand—or, perhaps, at the same time—we can see, as Michael Flier has argued, the tsar's ritual act as revealing not subservience but his absolute and sacred authority in the earthly political realm. In other words, his humility was a pious deed *(podvig)* that demonstrated his sacred status and thus elevated his authority.

The complexity of Muscovite politics—and the need to examine both the official appearance of things and actual practice—can be seen when we turn to the main institutions of government. While the Muscovite tsars could truthfully claim to be absolute rulers of perhaps ten to fifteen million subjects, they did not exercise their high authority alone: the boyar duma, or council, persisted as their constant companion, and a new important state institution appeared, the zemskii sobor, or assembly of the land. Though the terms themselves are probably of eighteenth- or nineteenth-century coinage, and the institutions have been much romanticized, it is clear that the boyar duma and the zemskii sobor existed and deserve our attention, both as part of the complex structure of Muscovite "autocracy" and for their suggestive resemblances to Western institutions.

The boyar duma of the Muscovite tsars represented, of course, a continuation of the boyar duma of the Muscovite grand princes. However, in the conditions of a new age, it gradually underwent certain changes. Thus although it still included the great boyars, an increasing portion of the membership were less aristocratic people brought in by the tsar, a bureaucratic element so to speak. The duma membership grew, to cite Diakonov's figures, from 30 under Boris Godunov to 59 under Alexis and 167 under Theodore. Large size interfered with work in spite of the creation of various special committees. The boyar duma met very frequently, usually daily, and could be considered as continually in session. It dealt with virtually every kind of state business. Kliuchevsky and others have demonstrated convincingly that the boyar duma was essentially an advisory body and that it did not limit autocracy. But, on the other hand, the ever-present boyar duma formed in effect an integral part of the supreme authority of the land rather than merely a government department or agency. The celebrated Muscovite formula for state decisions, "the sovereign directed and the boyars assented," reminds one strongly of the English legal phrase "King in Council," while the boyar duma itself bears resemblance to royal councils in different European monarchies. The boyar duma assumed the directing authority in the absence of the tsar from Moscow or in case of an interregnum, such as that which followed the deposition of Vasilii Shuisky.

The nature of the zemskie sobory and their relationship to the Muscovite autocracy present even more complicated problems than does the boyar duma. Again, one should bear in mind that Muscovite political practice showed little evidence of the clear disjunctions of modern political theory and that it was based on custom, not written constitutions. The zemskie sobory, as we had occasion to see earlier, were essentially sporadic gatherings convened by the tsar when he wanted to discuss and decide a particularly important issue "with all the land." They had much in common with certain Western institutions and especially with the so-called Estates General. In fact, their chief characteristic, in the opinion of most scholars, consisted precisely in their inclusion of at least three estates: the clergy, the boyars, and the gentry servitors of the tsar. These were usually supplemented by the townspeople and, on at least one occasion, in 1613, by the peasants. The representation was by estates. Sometimes, as in the West, the estates would first meet separately, for instance, in the boyar duma or a Church council, and afterwards present their opinion to the entire zemskii sobor.

The assembly of 1471, called by Ivan III before his campaign against Novgorod, has usually been listed as a "forerunner" of the zemskie sobory. The first full-fledged zemskie sobory occurred in the reign of Ivan the Terrible, in 1549, 1566, 1575, and possibly 1580, and dealt with such important matters as the tsar's program of reforms and the Livonian War. Immediately after Ivan the Terrible's death, in 1584, another zemskii sobor confirmed his son Theodore as tsar, a step possibly suggested by the fact that Ivan the Terrible had left no testament and no formal law of succession existed in Muscovite Russia. In 1598 a zemskii sobor offered the throne to Boris Godunov. The celebrated zemskii sobor of 1613, which we discussed earlier, elected Michael Romanov and his successors to rule Russia. As we know, at the time of Tsar Michael, the zemskie sobory reached the peak of their activity: they met almost continually during the first decade of the reign; later, in 1632–34, 1636–37, and 1642, they convened to tackle the issue of special taxes to continue war against Poland and the problem of the Crimea, Azov, and relations with Turkey. In 1645 a zemskii sobor confirmed Alexis's accession to the throne, while during his reign one zemskii sobor dealt with the *Ulozhenie* of 1649, another in 1650 with the disturbances in Pskov, and still another in 1651–53 with the Ukrainian problem. Many historians add to the list of zemskie sobory the gathering or gatherings of 1681–82 connected with the abolition of the mestnichestvo and the accession of a new ruler. Unknown zemskie sobory may yet be uncovered. But, in any case, the zemskie sobory belonged dearly to Muscovite Russia, and the period of their activity corresponded roughly to its chronological boundaries. They found no place in Peter the Great's reformed empire.

The key controversial issue in the literature on the zemskie sobory has been the scope of their authority and their exact position in the Muscovite order of things. Kliuchevsky and some other leading specialists have shown that the zemskie sobory aided and supported the policies of the tsars but did not limit their power. The question of restricting the sovereign's authority never arose at their gatherings. Moreover, at least in the sixteenth century, the members were appointed by the government rather than elected. Although in the Time of Troubles, with the collapse of the central government and an interregnum, the elective principle appeared and a zemskii sobor emerged as the highest authority in the country, it proved only too eager to hand over full power to a new tsar. In the seventeenth as in the sixteenth century, membership in a zemskii sobor continued to represent obligation and service to the sovereign, rather than rights or privileges against the crown. At most the participants could state their grievances and petition for redress; the monarch retained full power of decision and action.

A different view of the situation was emphasized by Mikhail Tikhomirov and other Soviet historians, as well as by certain Western scholars such as

J. L. H. Keep. They point out that the zemskie sobory, after all, dealt with most important matters, and often dealt with them decisively: the succession to the throne, war and peace, major financial measures. It should also be noted that during a large part of Michael's reign no subsidy was levied or benevolence extorted without the consent of zemskie sobory; thus they had a hand on the purse strings, if they did not actually control state finances. Many edicts carried the characteristic sentence: "By the desire of the sovereign and all the land." Again, such epoch-making decisions as the extension of the tsar's jurisdiction to Ukraine depended on the opinion of a zemskii sobor. Besides, particularly in the seventeenth century, with the elective principle persisting after the Time of Troubles and asserting itself in the composition of several of the zemskie sobory, these assemblies acted by no means simply as rubber stamps for the tsars. For example, it has been argued that the *Ulozhenie* of 1649 represented the decision and initiative of a zemskii sobor that it forced on the government. In fact, the argument proceeds, the tsars and their advisers in the second half of the seventeenth century began to convene the zemskie sobory less and less frequently precisely because of their possible threat to the position of the monarch. The assertion of tsarist absolutism in Russia against the zemskie sobory corresponded to parallel developments in a number of other European countries, such as France, where the Estates General did not meet between 1614 and 1789, and England, where the seventeenth century witnessed a great struggle between the Stuarts and Parliament. But, whether the story of the zemskie sobory resembles its Western counterparts closely or only faintly—critics remind us that unlike European bodies the role of the zemskii sobor was not defined by law or even custom—we know that its continued development was arrested. By the eighteenth century, the state saw no need to convene any such representative of "the land," even for consultation.

The expansion of the Muscovite state brought with it centralization and standardization. Law was at the center of the seventeenth-century drive for centralized regulation of society and the mobilization of resources, though the state's ambition often exceeded its real capacity. Many areas and groups remained outside the tsar's laws: for example, lords had nearly absolute power over serfs (indeed, the law endorsed this), the Church was exempt from most rules, and as the empire expanded, many local particularities were allowed to persist. Still, the uncounted legal peculiarities and local practices of the appanage era largely disappeared and central control increased as a result of the law codes (*sudebniki*) of 1497 and 1550 and later redactions and especially the very important codification of 1649, the *Ulozhenie*. This massive work, with 965 articles, was declared to be the law of "all the people of the Muscovite state, from the highest to lowest rank." It was also the first law code to be issued in print and widely disseminated. And this was not the end of new legislation: by one account, more than 1,500 decrees were issued in the second half of the century. The goal of law was to regulate society. As we have seen, peasants and townsmen lost any remaining rights to move, and people were bound to a limited number of social ranks. Social hierarchy was fixed in law—thus, punishments for insulting a person's honor varied by the victim's social status.

Punishments for crimes became harsher, unorthodox religious practices such as witchcraft or sorcery were vigorously suppressed, and attacks even on the symbols of the tsar's authority were prosecuted as crimes.

As the reach and interests of the state expanded, so did the bureaucracy. The central administration developed through rather haphazard growth of different departments and bureaus. By the seventeenth century these agencies, which came to be known as chancelleries or *prikazy*—singular *prikaz*—already numbered about fifty and they continued to proliferate, as did the numbers of officials working in them, many of whom were quite literate and skilled. The authority of a prikaz extended over certain types of affairs, such as foreign policy in the case of the ambassadorial prikaz; certain categories of people, such as the slaves and the streltsy; or a certain area, such as Siberia and the former khanates of Kazan and Astrakhan. Overlapping and confusion increased with time, although some scholars see in the unwieldly Muscovite arrangement the wise intention to maintain mutual supervision and checks.

Local government constituted one of the weakest parts of the Muscovite political system. The problem, of course, became enormous as the state grew to gigantic size. As a ruler of Moscow acquired new territories, he sent his representatives, the *namestniki* and *volosteli,* to administer them. The appointments, known as *kormleniia,* that is, feedings, were considered personal awards as well as public acts. The officials exercised virtually full powers and at the same time enriched themselves at the expense of the people. Although both custom and law regulated "feeding" relationships, setting limits on the amount of cash, goods, and services the population had to provide for its administrators, this "political economy of corruption," as it has been called (and direct bribes were also a feature), persisted, not least because local communities often viewed "feedings" as a useful way to draw administrators into a system of mutual obligation.

As we have seen, however, local administration developed strongly in the sixteenth century. In addition to the locally elected judicial and police officials—the so-called *gubnye* officials—who were already functioning to combat crime, the enactments of that year provided for local *zemskii* institutions concerned with finance, administration, and justice. Where the population guaranteed a certain amount of dues to the treasury, locally elected town administrators—*gorodovye prikazchiki*—replaced centrally appointed officials; and even where the latter remained, the population could elect assessors to check closely on their activities and, indeed, impeach them when necessary. Unfortunately, although historians have shown the considerable development and broad competence of the institutions of local self-government in sixteenth-century Muscovy, these institutions did not last. After the Time of Troubles self-government was replaced by a centralized system of appointed governors, the *voevody,* who were all servitors of high Moscow rank with extensive military and civil powers. At the same time, the *voevoda* administration became an increasingly modern bureaucracy, following codified law and practicing regular accounting and reporting procedures. Also, research on the provincial gentry has shown a growing sense of local allegiance and community; but this in no way challenged central state authority, as it mainly involved gentry promoting their local material interests. The demise of self-government in the localities, a weakness that would plague later reforming rulers, reminds us of the continued centralization of the Moscow state and of the weak development of social independence, initiative, and education in old Russia.

## The Emergence of Empire

The expansion of the Muscovite state in the seventeenth century brought under the tsar's scepter lands and peoples to the west, north, south, and east of the old Muscovite principality. While many historians have long argued that the expansion in the west, notably the agreement of 1652 that brought most of Ukraine under Russian rule, was a reunification with ancient Russian lands, most agree that expansion to the east and southeast had a "colonial" quality. The advance into the southern steppe continued after the conquest of the khanates of Kazan and Astrakhan. It has been estimated that between 1610 and 1640 alone the Russian military line and colonists moved 300 miles farther into the steppe, under conditions of continuous struggle with the Crimean Tatars and other nomads. But the most spectacular expansion occurred in the direction of the less settled east, where, in the course of the same three decades, the Russians advanced 3,000 miles from the Ob River to the Pacific, exploring and conquering the expanse of Siberia, though actual settlement developed more slowly. Russians met relatively little resistance because there were no strong political communities and local elites could easily be co-opted. Yet just as Russian expansion was limited in the west and north by the strong and ambitious states of Sweden and Poland-Lithuania and in the south by the Persian and Ottoman empires, the Chinese stood against Russian expansion outside of northern Asia. As Russian colonists reached the borders of imperial China in the Amur region, the Chinese sent troops who forced the Russians to dismantle forts and step back from this frontier.

Furs presented the main attraction in Siberia, where sable, ermine, beaver, and other valuable fur-bearing animals abounded. Furs constituted an extremely important item in Muscovite finance and foreign trade. As Russian rule spread among the thinly scattered natives in Siberia, they were required to pay the *iasak*, a tax in furs, to their new sovereign. Also the central authorities expended great effort to limit the private acquisition of furs by the administrators in Siberia. In general, the annexation of Siberia, which has been compared to the European exploration of Africa and the American advance westward, was a highly profitable undertaking for the Muscovite state. Siberia also acquired importance as a land to which one might escape. With very few gentry and endless spaces for the fugitive, Siberia escaped serfdom, and the state's reach was always modest. As Siberian society developed, profiting from an assimilation of natives—intermarriage was common—as well as from migration from European Russia, it came to represent a freer and more democratic social system than the one across the Urals and to exhibit certain qualities of

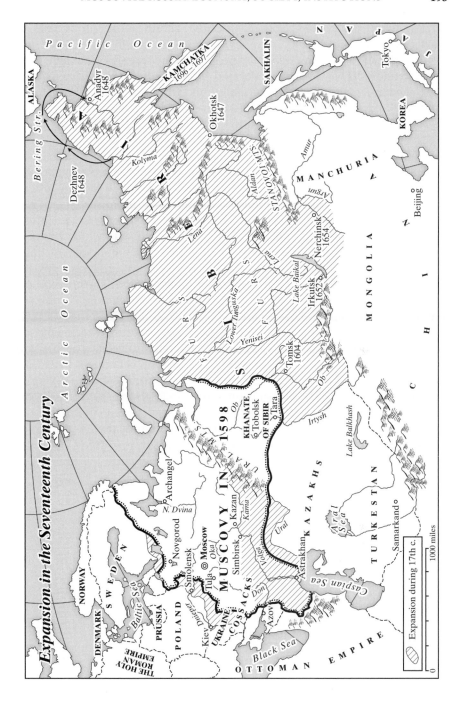

Expansion in the Seventeenth Century

sturdiness and independence often associated with the American frontier. In this light, Siberia acquired a certain mythic status in Russian culture.

The question of how Russia ruled its many non-Russian and non-Orthodox subjects has been much debated, though only recently have scholars researched this history closely, especially concerning the south and east. It is important to distinguish the more aggressive imperial policies of later centuries, however, from seventeenth-century practices, the difference likely being due to both limited capacity and a different approach to ruling non-Russians. The policy of the Muscovite state in Siberia, along with that of the Church, was oriented toward a mixture of toleration of local difference, co-optation of local elites, and gradual integration. In the early stages of conquest, Moscow placed great weight on winning over indigenous elites with promises of rewards, payments, and protection of their traditional power and privileges. Natives were not forcibly baptized, though if they became Orthodox, which was welcomed, they were treated as Russians—a condition that, among other things, excused them from paying the iasak and thus might have given the government second thoughts about the desirability of conversion. The government also tried to determine local needs and problems, to develop the local economy, and to extend paternalistic care to both natives and Russian settlers, as Lantzeff and others have described. But Moscow was very far away, whereas the local situation encouraged extreme exploitation and cruelty on the part of officials and other Russians. In general, as Russian settlement increased, indirect rule through local elites gave way to direct administrative authority from Moscow. Still, most new lands remained undergoverned, with Moscow preferring incentives and other noncoercive policies to the sort of interference and control that would come with the modernization of the empire in the eighteenth century.

# CHAPTER 19

# Muscovite Russia:
# Religion and Culture

The Emperor was seated upon an Imperiall Throne, with Pillars of silver and gold, which stood 3 or 4 stepps high, an Imperiall Crowne upon his Head, his Scepter in his right hand and his Globe in his left. And so he sate without any motion that I could perceave, till such time as I had repeated all the King my Masters titles and his owne, and given him greeting in his Majesties name.... As I was to goe out of the roome, I observed betwixt 20ty and 30ty great Princes and Councellors of State, sitting upon the left hand of the Emperor, who were all in long Roabes of Cloth of gold, imbrodered with Pearles and Precious Stones, and high Capps either of Sables or Black Foxe about three quarters of a yard high upon their heads. To them, at my going out of the Doore, I bowed myself and they all rose up and putt of their Capps unto me.

SIMON DIGBY TO SIR JOHN COKE

O you Teachers of Christendom! Rome fell away long ago and lies prostrate, and the Poles fell in the like ruin with her, being to the end the enemies of the Christian. And among you orthodoxy is of mongrel breed; and no wonder—if by the violence of the Turkish Mahound you have become impotent, and henceforth it is you who should come to us to learn. By the gift of God among us there is autocracy; till the time of Nikon, the apostate, in our Russia under our pious princes and tsars the orthodox faith was pure and undefiled, and in the Church was no sedition.

AVVAKUM (J. HARRISON'S AND H. MIRRLEES'S TRANSLATION)

Muscovy appeared strange to foreigners. Visitors from the West, such as Guy de Miege, secretary to the embassy sent to Alexis by Charles II of England, as well as many others, described it as something of a magic world: weird, sumptuous, colorful, unlike anything they had ever seen, and utterly barbarian.

Foreign emissaries noticed the rich costumes, especially the furs, the striking grey beards, the elaborate court ceremonial, the lavish banquets and the tremendous drinking. Of more importance were the fundamental characteristics of Muscovy that the visitors quickly discovered: the enormous power and authority of the tsar and the extreme centralization which required that even insignificant matters be referred for decision to high officials.

The view of Muscovy as a strange world apart contains some truth. Muscovite Russia existed in relative isolation by contrast, for example, with Kievan Rus. Moreover, it developed a distinctive culture based on religion and ritualism and assumed a tone of self-righteousness and suspicion toward any outside influence. But the case should not be overstated. In reality the main elements of Muscovite culture—religion, language, law, and others—served as links to the outside world. In terms of time, too, Muscovy represented, not simply a self-contained culture, but a transitional culture, where tradition vied with innovation and native culture interacted with foreign influences. And, after all, it was the Muscovites themselves, led by Peter the Great, who transformed their country and culture—the fairy land and at times the nightmare of Western travelers—into one of the great states of modern Europe.

## Religion and Church. The Schism

Religion pervaded every aspect of life in Muscovite Russia. Religious belief, identity, and ritual played a powerful role in the growth and consolidation of the state, in arguments about Russia's relation to the larger world, in art and literature, and in everyday social life. Religion contributed both to a narrow-minded, self-satisfied pride and the recognition of the need for reform. As already mentioned, the expansion and strengthening of the Muscovite state found a parallel in the evolution of the Church in Muscovy. The Church councils of 1547, 1549, 1551, and 1554 strove to improve ecclesiastical organization and practices and eliminate various abuses. In 1547 twenty-two Russians were canonized, and in 1549 seventeen more. The resulting consolidated national pantheon of saints represented a religious counterpart to the political unification. The Hundred-Chapter (Stoglav) council of 1551 dealt, as its name indicates, with many matters in the life of the Church. The council of 1554 condemned certain Russian heretics and heresies which had roots either in Protestantism or in the teachings of the non-possessors. None of them, it might be noted, gained popular support.

The rising stature of the Russian Church at a time when many other Orthodox Churches, including the patriarchate of Constantinople itself, fell under the sway of the Muslim Turks increased Muscovite confidence and pride. References to the holy Russian land, to Holy Russia, date from the second half of the sixteenth century. In 1589, as we know, Muscovy obtained its own patriarch, as a result of considerable political pressure on Constantinople. As we have also seen, some later incumbents of this position would play major historical roles, as Hermogen, for example, did during the Time of Troubles and Philaret did during the reign of his son, Michael. The seventeenth-century

Church did much to enhance its power and cultural influence. Officially, state and Church were united in a "symphony" of authority, though these years saw a good deal of maneuvering over whether the tsar or the patriarch was more important; thus, Philaret adopted the title Great Sovereign (Velikii Gosudar), previously used only by tsars. The Church also fought to limit the competition of Catholicism and Protestantism in the Russian lands, a growing threat as Muscovy expanded westward and as foreign specialists came to Russia in increasing numbers. The Church began printing religious books to help spread and standardize faith and ritual and endeavored to gain better control of far-flung monasteries and parish priests, not to mention the often less than knowledgeable laity, who continued to mix Christian and traditional folk beliefs and practices. It should be added that the Church, especially the monasteries, enjoyed enormous wealth in land and other possessions in spite of the repeated efforts of the government to curb its holdings and particularly to prevent its encroachments on the gentry.

The great split or schism in the seventeenth century—*raskol* in Russian—revealed serious weaknesses in the apparently mighty and monolithic Muscovite Church. A growing awareness among the Church leadership of the need for reform in Russian religious life was the key historical context for the schism. Church leaders, sometimes in response to petitions from parish clergy, noticed many deviations from the purity of the faith: a tendency in many churches to shorten services (which had, indeed, become very long, especially as Orthodox stand during the service) by chanting several parts of the liturgy simultaneously; continued lay celebrations of pre-Christian festivals; the persistent popularity of "pagan" folk minstrels (*skomorokhi*); immorality in everyday life, including among the clergy; and various inaccuracies and deviations from the Greek originals that had crept into Russian texts and practices. Little was done, however, before the reign of Alexis, who was an active supporter of reform. These were years of religious and moral revival in the Russian Orthodox Church, which sought to improve the celebration of the liturgy and to bring a higher moral and spiritual tone to parish life. Some historians have compared this to contemporary reform movements in the Protestant West and especially to the Catholic Reformation. Key figures were a group of clergymen known in history as the Zealots of Piety. These included the tsar's confessor, Stefan Vonifatiev; the celebrated archpriest Avvakum, or Habakkuk; and many other influential clergy. They advocated better preaching, proper celebration of the liturgy, and bringing the moral teachings of Christ into everyday life. Tsar Alexis made many of these policies into law, including banning skomorokhi and requiring the full-length service. Reform often led to opposition, sometimes violent, among laity and local priests. Avvakum recalls in his autobiography being beaten up and chased more than once from provincial towns by large mobs of "priests, peasants, and goodwives" who were enraged by his moralizing accusations against them.

The movement for reform turned a fateful corner after Nikon, who had been close to the Zealots of Piety, was named patriarch in 1652. A strong-willed administrator, a confidant of the tsar, and an ally of the reformers,

Nikon became controversial both for his insistence that the Church was superior to the state in promoting Russia's spiritual well-being (Nikon also called himself "Great Sovereign") and for his high-handed promotion of reform in the Church. He continued efforts to promote greater piety and purity in religious life, such as prohibiting vodka on holy days. Problems arose, however, over his efforts to bring Orthodox worship into conformity with the rest of Eastern Orthodoxy. In 1653 and 1654, after extensive consultation with Greek specialists and old texts, Nikon ordered new, corrected editions of liturgical service books (*sluzhebniki*) and other texts and ordered quite drastic corrections in ritual and liturgy: replacing the Russian two-fingered sign of the cross (only the index and middle fingers) with the Greek three-fingered sign (with the thumb held against extended index and middle fingers), changing the spelling of Jesus from Isys to Iisus, requiring a Greek tripling rather than the Russian doubling of the "Hallelujah" after certain prayers, changing the number of deep bows and the direction of certain processions, revising a few words in the Nicene Creed, altering the cross on the communion wafer, and other changes of this sort. For a religion in which ritual and tradition were so central, these were not trivial changes.

Indeed, with these reforms, and their backing by state power, the schism began in earnest. Many of the reformers turned against Nikon, complaining of his arrogance and intransigence in forcing these reforms and of his abandonment of Russian traditions. In return, with his usual aggressive manner, Nikon excommunicated, imprisoned, and exiled these former allies. Harsher punishments awaited those who continued to resist. To defeat the opposition, the patriarch sought the highest possible authority in support of his reforms: Russian Church councils approved his changes, as did a council convened by the patriarch of Constantinople. In 1658, however, Nikon broke with the tsar. In turn, Alexis grew impatient with the patriarch's imperious manner and growing influence and wealth. Part of the conflict certainly centered on Nikon's continued insistence on the Church's superiority to the secular state—comparing the Church to the sun and secular government to the moon, for example, would not have endeared him to the autocrat. Important Church councils in 1666 and 1667, which included representatives of other eastern churches, resolved the question of both the reforms and Nikon's place: Nikon was deposed and the supremacy of the state over the Church was reiterated, but the reforms were completely endorsed. Dissenters were ordered to submit or be in defiance of both Church and state.

Although no dogmatic or doctrinal differences were involved, priests and laymen in considerable numbers refused to obey. The Old Believers or Old Ritualists—*starovery* or *staroobriadtsy*—rejected the changes and hence rejected the established Church. For them, rituals were themselves a manifestation of the divine and could not be changed, even in the name of greater uniformity with the rest of the Orthodox community. Georg Michels and other scholars have argued that the schism resulted from not merely the reforms but a larger crisis involving "deep alienation between ordinary Russians and their church." Persecutions of Old Believers were vigorous and brutal.

Patriarch Nikon. Here portrayed instructing the clergy. A painting from 1665. (*Ukrainskaia portretnaia zhivopis' XVII–XVIII vv.*)

Avvakum himself—whose stunning autobiography represents the greatest document of Old Belief and one of the great documents of human faith—perished at the stake in 1682. The Solovetskii Monastery in the far north had to be captured by a siege that lasted from 1668 to 1676. Apocalyptic views, which had been growing throughout Russian society in these years, became especially strong among the early Old Believers, who saw in the Church reform the end of the world and in Nikon the Antichrist. When government forces attacked Old Believer monasteries and villages, dissenters sometimes committed suicide by fire rather than submit. It has been estimated that between 1672 and 1691 over 20,000 of them burned themselves alive in thirty-seven known communal conflagrations.

Yet the Old Belief survived. Reorganized in the eighteenth century by a number of able leaders, especially by the Denisov brothers, Andrei and Semen, it claimed the allegiance of millions of Russians up to the Revolution

of 1917 and after. It exists today. With no canonical foundation and no independent theology to speak of, the Old Belief divided again and again, but it
never disappeared. The main cleavage came to be between the *popovtsy* and
the *bespopovtsy*, those who had priests and those who had none. Old Believers
soon found themselves without priests and thus without the liturgy, and without most of the sacraments: bishops were required for elevation to the priesthood, and no bishops joined the Old Belief. Some dissenters, the popovtsy,
bent all their efforts to obtain priests by every possible means, for instance, by
enticing them away from the established Church. The priestless, on the other
hand, accepted the logic of their situation and organized their religious life
along different lines. It is from the priestless Old Believers that many Russian
sects derive. But all this takes us well beyond the Muscovite period of Russian
history.

The raskol constituted the only major schism in the history of the
Orthodox Church in Russia. In an important sense it was the opposite of
the Reformation: in the West, Christians turned against their ecclesiastical authorities because they wanted changes; in Russia, believers revolted
because they refused to accept even minor modifications of the traditional
religious usage. Many scholars have tried to explain the raskol. Thus Afanasii
Shchapov and numerous others have stressed the social composition of the
Old Believers and the social and economic reasons for their rebellion. The
dissenters were originally and continued to be mostly well-established peasants and traders. Their action could, therefore, be interpreted as a protest
against gentry domination and the entire oppressive Muscovite system.
More immediately, they reacted against the increased ecclesiastical centralization under Nikon which led to the appointment of priests—formerly they
had been elected in northern parishes—and to the loss of parish autonomy
and democracy. In addition to being democrats—so certain historians have
claimed—the Old Believers expressed the entrepreneurial and business acumen of the Russian people. Over a period of time they made a remarkable
record for themselves in commerce. Some parallels have even been drawn
with the Calvinists in the West. As to the other side, the drive for reform has
been ascribed, in addition to the obvious reason, to the influence of the more
learned Ukrainian clergy, and to the desire of the Muscovite Church and
state to adapt their practices to include the Ukrainians and Belorussians. It
has been argued that Alexis gave Ukrainian, Belorussian, and Greek scholars important roles as intellectual leaders of the Church as part of a bid for
Russian leadership of the whole of ecumenical Orthodoxy and perhaps,
according to S. Zenkovsky, in preparation for a possible expansion to the
Balkans and Constantinople.

Even more rewarding as an explanation of the raskol has been the emphasis on the fundamental formalism, ritualism, and traditionalism of Muscovite
culture. Form and tradition in religion were part of its power and legitimacy
and could not be compromised. Religious ceremony and ritual served as a
great unifying bond for believers, a connection to the past, and a part of the
foundation of daily life. This and the related belief in the superiority of the

Muscovite Church and its practices go far to explain the rebellion. The reformers exhibited a similar formalism. In spite of the advice of such high authorities as the patriarch of Constantinople, Nikon and his followers refused to allow any local practice or insignificant variation to remain, thus on their part, too, confusing the letter with the spirit. The raskol can thus be considered a tribute to the hold that Muscovite culture had on the people. Others have seen it as marking the dead end of that culture.

Miliukov and others have argued that, because of the split, the Russian Church lost its most devoted and active members and, in effect, its vitality: those who had the courage of their convictions joined the Old Belief; the cowardly and the listless remained in the establishment. Even if we allow for the exaggeration implicit in this view and note further that many of the most ignorant and fanatical must also have joined the dissenters, the loss remains great. It certainly made it easier for Peter the Great to treat the Church in a high-handed manner.

## Muscovite Thought and Literature

In addition to the issue of the true faith, the issue of the proper form of government preoccupied certain Muscovite minds. This discussion of the nature and the new role of autocracy continued the intellectual trend clearly observable in the reigns of Ivan III and Vasilii III. Such publicists as Ivan Peresvetov, who wrote in the middle of the sixteenth century, upheld the new power and authority of the tsar, while the events of the Time of Troubles provided variations on this theme of proper government. Panegyrics often likened the ruler to Christ: humble, pious, and chaste but also endowed with sacred power. The most famous debate on politics took place between Ivan the Terrible and Prince Andrei Kurbsky in two letters from the tsar and five from the fugitive nobleman, written between 1564 and 1579—though Edward Keenan famously argued that the exchange was fabricated in the early seventeenth century. With great vigor, Ivan the Terrible defended his actions on the basis of the sacredness and necessity of autocracy: his power came from "the will of God and the blessing of our ancestors," from his duty to defend the true Church against its enemies, and from the proven historical necessity of a strong ruler who could control the selfish andSS quarrelsome boyars. He declared that, even if he were a tyrant, Kurbsky's only alternative, as a Christian and a faithful subject, remained patient suffering. The prince, on his part, bitterly attacked Ivan for his "leprous conscience," "sophistic" arguments, and sinful pride. Yet his views, too, represented a system of political belief: they harkened back to an earlier order of things, when no great gulf separated the ruler from his chief lieutenants, and when an aristocrat enjoyed more freedom and more respect than Ivan IV wanted to allow.

In foreign relations, as in domestic matters, Ivan the Terrible and other tsars reiterated the glory of autocracy and demanded full respect for it. They considered the Polish kings degraded because the latter had been put on their throne by others, and thus could not be regarded as hereditary or rooted rulers. They asked why Swedish monarchs treated their advisers as companions. Or, to quote the frequently mentioned bitter letter of Ivan the Terrible to Elizabeth of England, written in 1570: "We had thought that you were sovereign in your state and ruled yourself, and that you saw to your sovereign honor and to the interests of the country. But it turns out that in your land people rule besides you, and not only people, but trading peasants."

Literary life in Muscovy was rather meager compared with the riches of the contemporary West or even compared to Muscovite architecture and other arts, though comparison with the West should not be the only way of interpreting Russian culture. Certainly, by the measure of "book culture," Muscovy was far behind the West. Printing arrived in Russia only in the 1560s, more than a century after Gutenberg, and produced far fewer volumes and far fewer secular works. But the lack of printed books is not the only measure of culture or even cultural change. Old forms were often finding new life and accommodating new content. The most widespread literature continued traditional popular forms: lives of saints, miracle tales, heroic byliny, and folk songs and stories commemorating historical events, including contemporary ones such as the capture of Kazan, the conquest of Siberia, or Stenka Razin's rebellion. Pilgrims and beggars composed religious poems at venerated shrines, and the skomorokhi continued entertaining people, in spite of all prohibitions. Recent historians of popular Christianity have described a complex mixture of Christian teachings with folklore and magic, producing a vision of the world filled with otherworldly spirits of all sorts, both good and evil, and a rich body of ideas and practices about how to cope with trouble in this world, including prayers, magic incantations and charms, and miracle-working icons. This vital popular culture, it should be noted, was not limited to the village or the poor.

The *Domostroi*, or "house manager," constituted one of the most noteworthy works of Muscovite Russia. Attributed to Sylvester and dating in its original version from about 1556, it intends in sixty-three didactic chapters to instruct the head of a Muscovite family and its other members how properly to run their households and lead their lives. The *Domostroi* teachings reflect the ritualism, piety, severity, and patriarchal nature of Muscovite society. Possibly the most often cited directive reads:

> Punish your son in his youth, and he will give you a quiet old age, and restfulness to your soul. Weaken not beating the boy, for he will not die from your striking him with the rod, but will be in better health: for while you strike his body, you save his soul from death. If you love your son, punish him frequently, that you may rejoice later.

If the *Domostroi* is considered by some to be a kind of Muscovite *summa*, other events in literature, especially in the seventeenth century, pointed in new directions. Of particular note were innovations in literary language, such as the development of a "chancellery language," based on the Muscovite spoken idiom, in which official documents were written, and also the gradual penetration of popular language into literature in place of the bookish Slavonic-Russian. Avvakum's autobiography of the early 1670s, a milestone in Russian literature, was written in an earthy spoken idiom. Religious writings flourished in the seventeenth century. They included hagiography and, in particular, menologia, that is, calendars with the lives of saints arranged under the dates of their respective feasts, the most important of which was compiled by Metropolitan Macarius. They also included theological and polemical works, sermons, and other items. After Ukraine joined Muscovy, the more learned and less isolated Ukrainian clerics began to play a leading role in a Russian literary revival.

Gradually the lay literature of the West spread to Russia. Indeed, scholars have seen the emergence, in the sixteenth and seventeenth centuries, of a literary culture for the elite linked to European trends. Coming through Poland, Ukraine, the Balkans, and sometimes more directly, the stories assumed a romantic, didactic, or satirical character and were usually full of adventure, which, as a rule, the religious writings of ancient Russia lacked. Often, through the vehicle of such recurrent themes as the tales of the seven wise men or of Tristan and Isolde, the stories acquainted Muscovites with the world of knighthood, courtly love, and other concepts and practices unknown in the realm of the tsars. Soon, Russian tales following Western models made their appearance: for instance, stories about Savva Grudtsyn, who sold his soul to the devil, and about the rogue Frol Skobeev. Many of these tales enjoyed great popularity.

Syllabic versification also came from the West, from the Latin and Polish languages, largely through the efforts of Simeon of Polotsk, who died in 1680. It remained the dominant form in Russian poetry until the middle of the eighteenth century. After some productions of plays arranged by private individuals, Tsar Alexis established a court theater in 1672 under the direction of a German pastor, Johann Gregory. Before long, a few Russian plays enriched the repertoire, which was devoted primarily to biblical subjects.

Not only forms were changing. Literary historians have described significant, even radical, cultural changes in late sixteenth-century and especially seventeenth-century Russian literature, especially concerning the individual and the inward self. Dmitrii Likhachev made a strong case for the "discovery of the value of the human personality" and the rise of "individualism" in Russian literature and art. Relatively secular tales, such as stories about Grudtsyn and Skobeev, and religious "Lives," such as the biography of Iuliana Osorina and the autobiography of Avvakum, reveal a new more realistic concern with everyday experience, individual morality, human emotions, and personal suffering. Victor Zhivov, who has also described a new consciousness of self seventeenth-century Russian literature—new attention to moral integrity, the suffering individual, and personal courage—has added that for understanding early Russian literature and culture it would be misleading to treat the secular and the religious as separate, for both were always present and interconnected.

## The Arts

Architecture in both wood and stone flourished in the sixteenth and seventeenth centuries, largely continuing and elaborating older styles. The boyars'
wooden houses and the rulers' wooden mansions—the so-called *khoromy*—
evolved into remarkable conglomerations of independent units that compensated for their lack of symmetry with an abundant variety of parts.
Outstanding examples of this type of building included the khoromy of the
Stroganovs in Solvychegodsk and Tsar Alexis's huge summer palace in the village of Kolomenskoe near Moscow. Furthermore, it was especially during the
Muscovite age that the principles of Russian wooden architecture found rich

St. Basil's Cathedral, Moscow. Commissioned by Ivan the Terrible to commemorate the victory over the Mongols at Kazan in 1552, the cathedral was named the
Cathedral of the Intercession of the Virgin. A small chapel was later built as the
burial site of the revered "holy fool" St. Basil. This has become the popular name for
the entire cathedral.   (Olearius, *Voyages*, 1662)

expression in stone, notably in churches. The church of St. Basil the Blessed at one end of Red Square, outside the Kremlin wall, provides the most striking illustration of this wooden type of construction in stone. Built in 1555–60 by two architects from Pskov, Barma and Posnik, it has never ceased to dazzle visitors and to excite the imagination. This church, known originally as the Cathedral of the Intercession of the Virgin, consists in fact of nine separate churches on a common foundation. All nine have the form of tall octagons—a narrower octagon on top of a broader one in each case—and the central church, around which the other eight are situated, is covered by a tent roof. Striking and different cupolas further emphasize the variety and independence of the parts of the church. Bright colors and abundant decorations contribute their share to the powerful, if somewhat idiosyncratic, impression.

In the second half of the seventeenth century the baroque style reached Muscovy through Ukraine and quickly gained popularity, developing into the so-called Muscovite, or Naryshkin, baroque—the last name referring to the boyar family that sponsored it. Developing the popular ornamental trend in a new direction, Moscow baroque replaced the asymmetrical mixtures in older buildings with complex symmetries and replaced "Russian" ornamentation with columns, pediments, volutes, gables, and other classical forms. The church built in 1693 in the village of Fili, now part of Moscow, provides an interesting example of Russian baroque.

The great Russian tradition of icon painting continued during the sixteenth and seventeenth centuries but then was effectively terminated. Two prominent new schools emerged: the Stroganov school and the school of the tsar's icon-painters. The first, supported by the great merchant family of the northeast, was active from 1580 to 1630, approximately. Its characteristics included bright backgrounds, rich colors, elaborate and minute design, and a penchant for decorative elements and gold, for instance gold contours. In fact, the Stroganov icons tended to become miniatures, "lovely and highly precious objects, if no longer great works of art" in the words of one critic. Procopius Chirin, who later joined the tsar's icon-painters and even became Tsar Michael's favorite artist, was an outstanding member of the Stroganov group.

The tsar's icon-painters dominated the scene in the second half of the seventeenth century. They found patronage in the so-called *Oruzheinaia Palata* or Armory, headed by an able and enlightened boyar, Bogdan Khitrovo. The Oruzheinaia Palata began early in the sixteenth century as an arsenal, but, to quote Arthur Voyce: "It became successively a technical, scientific, pedagogical, and art institute, and contained shops and studios of icon and portrait painting, gold and silversmith work, keeping at the same time its original purpose—the manufacture of arms." The tsar's icon-painters developed a monumental style and reflected the influence of the West with its knowledge of perspective and anatomy. Simon Ushakov, who lived from 1626 to 1686, approximately, was the school's celebrated master. He pioneered the use of new techniques and images in icon painting, including chiaroscuro shading on faces and realistic depiction of contemporary buildings and people. At the same time, his work remained imbued with Orthodox religiosity. However, the school of the tsar's icon-painters marked the end of a long road. Ushakov and his companions have been praised for their ability to combine Byzantine and Western elements, but before long the West swept over the East. Icon painting would, of course, persist, but it ceased to be a creative and leading art.

New forms of painting would take its place. In the seventeenth century already we see the rise of secular painting. Ushakov himself organized a workshop for nonreligious painting at the Armory; this work ranged from maps to furniture decoration. A very important, if still rare, development was the appearance of portrait painting toward the end of the seventeenth century. Although stylistically imitative of Polish styles—indeed, Polish and Ukrainian artists play a large role—these portraits of rulers and especially boyars, some of them shaven and wearing Polish styles, have been interpreted as a sign not only of the Westernization of Russian art but also of the growing cultural and social regard for the individual.

Other arts also flourished in Muscovy, especially fresco painting and book illumination, along with artistic crafts such as religious wood-block prints (*lubki*), carving in wood (notably of church iconostases), ceramics, enamel, precious metal work, and jewelry. Here too, we see increasing evidence of Western influences.

## Literacy and Education

The extent of literacy in pre-Petrine Russia remains controversial, not least because we lack good sources to measure it. Foreign observers at the time and many critical Russian elites described well-nigh total illiteracy and ignorance, and many historians have agreed. By contrast, historians like the late-nineteenth-century specialist Alexei Sobolevsky found widespread ability to read and write: 75 percent literacy among landlords, 50 percent among townsmen, and 15 percent among peasants. There is good reason to be skeptical of both extremes. In this case, as in so many others, one has to strive for a balanced judgment. Certainly, Muscovy lacked any formal system of primary schooling. But literacy was acquired from small schools in churches or monasteries or from relatives and tutors, including foreign ones, especially among the elite. Archival research has found a considerable growth in the production of primers and abecedaria in the late seventeenth century, though the numbers printed would have only served a small minority of people. On the basis of such evidence, Gary Marker has concluded that literacy was growing but that "reading was the privilege of the few and writing the domain of a tiny minority." Studies of the swelling bureaucracy in the seventeenth century have concluded that most chancellery employees could read and write well enough to do their jobs. Certainly, the Muscovite culture that we have discussed in this chapter could not have existed without some enlightenment.

Especially significant was the appearance in the seventeenth century of some advanced schools, especially after the acquisition of Ukraine by

Muscovy. In Kiev in Ukraine, which was more open to the West, and where Orthodoxy had to defend itself against Catholicism, Metropolitan Peter Mogila, or Mohila, founded an Academy modeled on Jesuit colleges in 1631. In Moscow in 1648–49, a boyar Fedor Rtishchev built a monastery and invited some thirty Kievan monks to teach Slavonic, Latin, Greek, rhetoric, philosophy, and other disciplines. In 1666 Simeon of Polotsk established a school where he taught Latin and the humanities. After his death the school was reestablished by his student, Sylvester Medvedev. In 1683 a school that offered Greek was opened in conjunction with a printing office and eventually contained up to 230 students. Later in the 1680s the Medvedev and the printing press schools combined to form the Slavonic-Greek-Latin Academy, headed by learned Greek monks, the Lichud brothers, Ioannicius and Sofronius. As planned, the Academy was to protect the faith and to control knowledge as well as disseminate it. While Kiev and Moscow clearly stood out as centers of Russian enlightenment, some relatively advanced teaching also went on in such places as the Holy Trinity-St. Sergius Monastery and the cities of Novgorod and Kharkov.

The Muscovite school curriculum closely resembled that of medieval Europe at corresponding levels. In particular, it included almost no study of science and technology. Of the humanities, history fared best. In the sixteenth and, especially, the seventeenth centuries Russian textbooks in such fields as arithmetic, history, and grammar, dictionaries, and even elementary encyclopedias made their appearance, and toward the end of the period Sylvester Medvedev compiled the first Russian bibliography.

## Western Influences. The Beginnings of Self-Criticism

Even if we make full allowance for Muscovite enlightenment, the fact remains that in a great many ways Muscovy lagged behind the West. Russia experienced no Renaissance and no Reformation, and it took no part in the maritime discoveries and the scientific and technological advances of the early modern period. Deficiencies became most apparent in war and in such practical matters as medicine and mining. They extended, however, into virtually every field. It should be noted that the Muscovite government showed a continuous and increasing interest in the West and in the many things that it had to offer. Muscovite society too, in spite of all the parochialism and prejudice, began gradually to learn from "the heretics."

Diplomacy constituted one obvious contact between the Muscovite state and other European countries. Although we traced the highlights of Russian foreign relations in preceding chapters, we should note here that these relations repeatedly included distant lands, such as England and Holland, as well as neighbors like Poland and Sweden, and that they dealt with many matters. For instance, an English merchant, Sir John Merrick, helped to negotiate the Treaty of Stolbovo between Sweden and Russia. Or, less happily, after the execution of Charles I, Tsar Alexis restricted English traders to Archangel, and he helped the king's son, later Charles II, with money and grain.

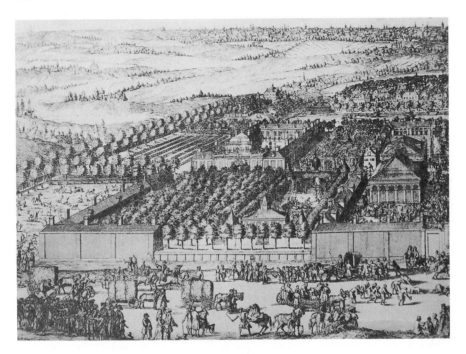

The foreign settlement (Nemetskaia sloboda) in Moscow during the reign of Alexis. As a special quarter in the city, it was a sign of both increased Western influence in Moscow and efforts to contain it.    (Alekseeva, *Graviura petrovskogo vremeni*)

Many foreigners came to Muscovy and stayed. The number continued to increase after the first large influx in the reign of Ivan III. At the end of the sixteenth century foreigners in Muscovite service could be counted in hundreds, and even thousands if we include Poles, Lithuanians, and Ukrainians, while the foreign section of the tsar's army consisted of 2,500 men. The Time of Troubles reduced these numbers, but with the reign of Michael the influx of foreigners resumed. In 1652 Tsar Alexis assigned them a northeastern suburb of Moscow, the so-called *Nemetskaia Sloboda*, or German Suburb. Incidentally, the Russian word for *German, nemets*, derived from the Russian for *dumb, nemoi*, came to mean all Europeans except Slavs and Latins. A visitor in the 1670s estimated that about 18,000 foreigners lived in Muscovy, mostly in the capital, but also in Archangel and other commercial centers, and in mining areas.

The importance of the foreign community, in particular for the economic development of the country, far exceeded its numbers. In addition to handling Russia's foreign trade, the newcomers began to establish a variety of manufactures and industries. Sir John Merrick, already mentioned as a diplomat, concentrated on producing hemp and fiber. Andrew Vinius, a Dutchman, organized the industrial processing of iron ore and built the first modern ironworks in Muscovy. A Swede established a glass factory near Moscow. Others manufactured such items as gunpowder and paper. Second-generation foreigners often proved particularly adept at advancing both the economy of

Russia and their own fortunes. Foreigners also acted as military experts, physicians, and other specialists.

Russian elites were slowly and hesitatingly turning to Western ways. Thoroughly Westernized men such as Prince Vasilii Golitsyn, even at the end of the seventeenth century, remained rare. But signs of change were widespread, even within the bounds of what remained a deeply religious society. As we have seen, Russians were reading and even writing secular stories, constructing baroque buildings, and painting portraits. Some began to eat salad and asparagus, to snuff and smoke tobacco in spite of all the prohibitions, and to cultivate roses. Western clothing gained in popularity; some audacious men also trimmed their hair and beards. In 1664 the postal service appeared, based on a Western model. And in the reign of Tsar Theodore a proposal was advanced to deal with the poor "according to the new European manner."

The stage was set for Peter the Great. In conclusion, however, it might be added that the reformer's wholesale condemnation of the existing order, although highly unusual, also had certain precedents in the Muscovite past. Not to mention the religious jeremiads, the secular writers often complained that there was no justice in the land even when praising the Muscovite form of government, as in the case of Peresvetov. More radical critics included Prince Ivan Khvorostinin (who died in 1625 and has been described as the first Russian free-thinker), Juraj Križanić, and Grigorii Kotoshikhin. Križanić, a Croatian and a Catholic priest, spent eighteen years in the realm of the tsars, from 1659 to 1677, and wrote there some nine books on religious, philosophical, linguistic, and political subjects. He combined an extremely high regard for Russia as the natural leader and savior of Slavdom with a sweeping condemnation of its glaring defects and, above all, its abysmal ignorance. Križanić's writings were apparently known to the Russian ruling circles. Kotoshikhin, an official in the foreign office, escaped to Sweden in 1664 after some personal trouble. There—before being executed in 1667 for the murder of his landlord—he wrote a sweeping denunciation of his native land. Kotoshikhin emphasized Muscovite pride, deceit, and, again, the isolation and ignorance of the people. As it turned out, the system that he condemned did not long outlast him, and its transformation came from forces born within this Muscovite life and culture.

# CHAPTER 20

# The Reign of Peter the Great, 1682–1725

Our people are like children, who, out of ignorance, will never get down to learning their alphabet unless the master forces them to do so.

PETER THE GREAT

Entire Russia is your statue, reshaped by your expert skill.

FEOFAN PROKOPOVICH

If we consider the matter thoroughly, then, in justice, we must be called not *Russians,* but *Petrovians.*...Russia should be called *Petrovia,* and we *Petrovians.*...

COUNT EGOR KANKRIN

We became citizens of the world but ceased in certain respects to be citizens of Russia. The fault is Peter's.

NIKOLAI KARAMZIN

Peter I replaced the antiquated landlord rule of Russia with a European chancellery regime; everything that could be copied from Swedish and German legal codes...was transported. But the unwritten part, which restrained authority morally, the instinctive recognition of the rights of the individual, the rights of thought, of truth, could not come over and did not come over....The state was growing, improving, but the individual was not gaining.

ALEXANDER HERZEN

Peter the Great's reign began a new epoch in Russian history, known variously as the Imperial Age because of the new designation of ruler and land, the St. Petersburg Era because of the new capital, or the All-Russian Period because the state came to include more and more peoples other than the Great

Russians, that is, the old Muscovites. This was an age of radical change that has been interpreted in dramatically different ways: as an era of rationality and enlightenment and of unprecedented economic, social, and cultural progress; as an era of harsh absolutist rule, perhaps for the sake of modernization, or perhaps only for the sake of power itself; as an era of expansionist wars that made Russia a great power but also deepened the subjugation of non-Russians. Peter has been seen as both a great Russian hero and as betraying and defiling Russian traditions. Likewise, many have argued that Peter broke decisively with the backward Muscovite past, while many others have argued that he built on Muscovite achievements and often used old methods in the service of new goals. What no one doubts is Peter the Great's enormous impact. As a mark of his personal role in establishing this modern era, the entire epoch of Russian history that began with his rule and ended abruptly in 1917 has often been called by historians simply Petrine Russia and the age preceding it "Pre-Petrine."

## The Beginnings: Russian History from 1682 to 1694

Although the chronological boundaries of Imperial Russia are much clearer than those of earlier epochs, the precise beginning of Peter the Great's reign itself can be variously dated. The reformer, who died on February 8, 1725, attained supreme power in stages, and with reversals of fortune: in 1682 as a boy of ten he was proclaimed at first tsar and later that same year co-tsar with his elder but unwell half-brother Ivan; in 1689 he, or rather his family and party, regained effective control of the government; in 1694 Peter's mother died and he started to rule in fact as well as in name; finally in 1696 Ivan died, leaving Peter the only and absolute sovereign of Muscovy. Before turning to the celebrated history of the reformer and his activities, we must consider these years when Peter's authority remained at best nominal.

Tsar Alexis had been married twice, to Maria Miloslavskaia from 1648 to 1669, and to Natalia Naryshkina from 1671 until his death in 1676. He had thirteen children by his first wife, but of the sons only two, Theodore and Ivan, both of them sickly, survived their father. Peter, strong and healthy, was born on June 9, 1672, about a year after the tsar's second marriage. Theodore, as we know, succeeded Alexis and died without an heir in 1682. In the absence of a law of succession, the two boyar families, the Miloslavskys and Naryshkins, competed for the throne. The Naryshkins gained an early victory: supported by the patriarch, a majority in the boyar duma, and a gathering of the gentry, Peter was proclaimed tsar in April 1682. Because of his youth, his mother became regent, while her relatives and friends secured leading positions in the state. However, as early as May, the Miloslavsky party, led by Alexis's able and strong-willed daughter Sophia, Peter's half-sister, inspired a rebellion of the regiments of the streltsy, or musketeers, concentrated in Moscow. Leading members of the Naryshkin clique were murdered—Peter witnessed some of these murders—and the Miloslavskys seized power. At the request of the streltsy, the boyar duma declared Ivan senior tsar, allowed Peter to be junior

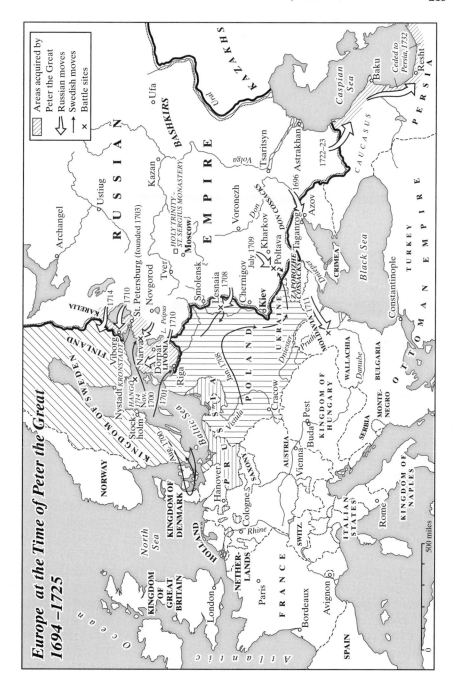

Europe at the Time of Peter the Great 1694–1725

Areas acquired by Peter the Great
Russian moves
Swedish moves
× Battle sites
Ceded to Persia, 1732

KAZAKHS

Baku

Caspian Sea

PERSIA

Resht

1722–23

CAUCASUS

Ufa

BASHKIRS

Ural

Astrakhan

Tsaritsyn

1696

Kazan

Volga

EMPIRE

Ustiug

Archangel

RUSSIA

Voronezh

Don

Azov

Taganrog

Kharkov

ZAPOROZHE COSSACKS

DON COSSACKS

CRIMEA

Black Sea

TURKEY

OTTOMAN EMPIRE

Constantinople

HOLY TRINITY–ST. SERGIUS MONASTERY

Moscow

St. Petersburg (founded 1703)

Novgorod

Tver

Smolensk

Chernigov

Poltava
July 1709 ×

Kiev

Lesnaia
× 1708

KARELIA

FINLAND

1714
1710

Viborg

KRONSTADT

St. Petersburg

Stockholm

KINGDOM OF SWEDEN

Nystadt

HANGO
Nov. 1714 ×

Narva ×

Dorpat

LIVONIA

L. Peipus

1710

1701

1700

Riga

Baltic Sea

UKRAINE

POLAND

PRUSSIA

Dnieper

Dniester

Prut

MOLDAVIA
1711
×

Jan. 1708

Vistula

Cracow

WALLACHIA

Danube

BULGARIA

SERBIA

MONTE-NEGRO

KINGDOM OF HUNGARY

Buda
Pest

AUSTRIA

Vienna

Hanover

SAXONY

Cologne

Rhine

SWITZ.

ITALIAN STATES

Rome

KINGDOM OF NAPLES

NORWAY

KINGDOM OF DENMARK

North Sea

KINGDOM OF GREAT BRITAIN

London

NETHER-LANDS

HOLLAND

FRANCE

Paris

Bordeaux

Avignon

SPAIN

Atlantic Ocean

500 miles
0

The symbolic portrayal of Peter the Great as a warrior in Western armor began already in the 1690s. The use of the Latin title "imperator" appeared in portraits before he officially adopted it in 1721.   (*Sovfoto*)

tsar, and, a little later, made Sophia regent. It might be added that the streltsy, strongly influenced by the Old Belief, proceeded to put more pressure on the government and cause further trouble, but in vain: the new regent managed to punish the leaders and control the regiments.

From 1682 to 1689 Sophia and her associates governed Muscovy, with Ivan V incapable of ruling and Peter I, together, with the entire Naryshkin party, kept away from state affairs. Russia's first female ruler, Sophia helped extend Russia's relations with Europe and was increasingly receptive to new ideas and influences from abroad. Prince Vasilii Golitsyn, her foreign minister and possibly her lover, played a particularly important role. An enlightened and humane person who spoke several foreign languages and arranged his own home and life in the Western manner, Golitsyn cherished vast projects of improvement and reform including the abolition of serfdom and education on a large scale. He did liberalize the Muscovite penal code, even if he failed to implement his more ambitious schemes. Golitsyn's greatest success came in 1686 when Russia and Poland signed a treaty of "eternal peace" that confirmed the Russian gains of the preceding decades, including the acquisition of Kiev. Yet the same treaty set the stage for the war against the Crimean Tatars, who were backed by Turkey. This war, led by Golitsyn, proved disastrous to Muscovite arms and contributed to Sophia's downfall.

As Peter grew older, his position as a tsar without authority became increasingly invidious. Sophia, on her part, realized the insecurity of her office and desired to become ruler in her own right. In 1689 Fedor Shaklovity, appointed by Sophia to command the streltsy, apparently tried to incite his troops to stage another coup, put Sophia on the throne, and destroy her opponents. Although the streltsy failed to act, a denouement resulted. Frightened by the report of a plot, Peter escaped in the dead of night from the village of Preobrazhenskoe, near Moscow, where he had been living, to the Holy Trinity-St. Sergius Monastery. In the critical days that followed, the patriarch, many boyars and gentry, the military units trained in the Western manner and commanded by General Patrick Gordon, and even several regiments of the streltsy, rallied behind Peter. Many others wavered, but did not back Sophia. In the end the sister capitulated to the brother without a fight and was sent to live in a convent. Shaklovity and two of his aides were executed; several other officers and boyars, including Vasilii Golitsyn, suffered exile. Thus, in August 1689, Peter won acknowledgment as the effective ruler of Russia, although Ivan retained his position as co-tsar. Still, at seventeen, Peter showed no desire to take personal charge of affairs. Instead the government fell into the hands of his mother Natalia and her associates, notably her brother, the boyar Lev Naryshkin, Patriarch Joachim, and, after his death in 1690, Patriarch Hadrian. What followed has been described as a traditionalist reaction against the Westernizing direction of Sophia's reign. The restoration of traditional religious norms was encouraged. Foreigners seeking to come to Russia were interrogated, and those already there were viewed with suspicion. It was even forbidden to train troops in the Western manner. Thus, the years 1689–94 witnessed the last flowering of Muscovite religiosity, ritualism, parochialism, and suspicion of everything foreign. But in 1694 Natalia died, and Peter I finally assumed the direction of the state at the age of twenty-two.

## Peter the Great: His Character, Childhood, and Youth

The impression that Peter I commonly made on his contemporaries was one of enormous strength and energy. Almost seven feet tall and powerfully built, the tsar possessed astonishing physical strength and vigor. This restless energy was a personality trait emblematic of his whole reign. Like no Russian ruler before him, Peter was positive and active, and this translated into politics: he believed that government had a positive and active role to play in a nation's life. Willful and determined, he recovered quickly from even the worst defeats. Related was his personal love of physical work: he was constantly making things with his hands, including model boats, furniture, crockery. He even fancied himself a good dentist and pulled the teeth of his own courtiers. He was personally involved in every aspect of statecraft and war.

He studied the professions of soldier and sailor from the bottom up, serving first in the ranks and learning the use of each weapon before promoting himself to his first post as an officer. The monarch attained the rank of full general after the victory of Poltava and of full admiral after the successful conclusion of the Great Northern War. Characteristically, he wanted to be everywhere and see everything for himself, traveling indefatigably around his vast state as no Muscovite monarch had ever done. In a still more unprecedented manner he went twice to the West to learn, in 1697–98 and in 1717. Peter I's mind can best be described as active and practical, able quickly to grasp problems and devise solutions. He turned to the West for skills and techniques, not theories. Or rather, he viewed Western civilization as a useable culture of rationality and technology, not refinement or liberal values.

At the same time, and not entirely unrelated to his imposing political persona, Peter could be violent, crude, and cruel. He personally beat nobles, friends, and other members of his court with his own cudgel when he felt this was needed. Of more political significance, he did not shy away from the bloody suppression of dissent. In external relations, as will be seen, he styled himself a royal warrior. On a personal level, he reveled in public horseplay and could drink prodigiously when in company, demanding that others keep up. Perhaps the most notorious expression of this excess was his "All-Mad, All-Jesting, All-Drunken Assembly." Together with his closest advisors, Peter performed elaborate mock rituals of state and Church, sometimes lasting for days. Interpretations of the Assembly have often viewed it as a way to ridicule tradition in preparation for overcoming it. In practical political terms, it can also be seen as a way of promoting camaraderie and bonding among Peter's associates, as a way, through humor and liquor, of uniting the men who would be leading Peter's efforts to transform Russia. It also reflected Peter's characteristic excess.

That said, Peter the Great must not be confused with Ivan the Terrible, whom he, incidentally, admired. The reformer never lost himself in the paranoid world of megalomania and delusions of persecution, and he even refused to identify himself with the state. To mention one significant detail, when reforming the army, Peter I crossed out "the interests of His Tsarist Majesty" as the object of military devotion and substituted "the interests of the state." He consistently made every effort to serve his country, to bring to it change and enlightenment. As the sovereign wrote in the last month of his life, in connection with dispatching Vitus Bering's first expedition: "Having ensured the security of the state against the enemy, it is requisite to endeavor to win glory for it by means of the arts and sciences." Or, to support Peter the Great's emphasis on education with another quotation—and one especially appropriate in a textbook—"For learning is good and fundamental, and as it were the root, the seed, and first principle of all that is good and useful in church and state."

Peter received no systematic education, barely being taught to read and write. Instead, from a very early age he began to pick things up on his own and pursue a variety of interests. He devoted himself in particular to war games with a mixed assortment of playmates. These games, surprisingly enough, developed over a period of years into a serious military undertaking and resulted in the formation of the first two regiments of the guards, the *Preobrazhenskii*—for Peter lived in the village of Preobrazhenskoe—and the *Semenovskii*, named after a nearby village. Similarly, the young tsar showed an early interest in the navy. At first he built small vessels, but as early as 1694 he established a dockyard in Archangel and constructed a large ship there all by himself. For information and instruction Peter went to the foreign quarter in Moscow. There he learned from a variety of specialists what he wanted to know most about military and naval matters, geometry and the erection of fortifications. There too, in a busy, informal, and unrestrained atmosphere, the tsar apparently felt much more at ease than in the conservative, tradition-bound palace environment, which he never accepted as his own. The smoking, drinking, love-making, rough good humor, and conglomeration of tongues, first discovered in the foreign quarter in Moscow, became an enduring part of Peter the Great's life. The determined attempt of Peter's mother to make him mend his ways by marrying him to Eudoxia Lopukhina in 1689 failed completely to accomplish the desired purpose.

## Peter's Assistants

After Peter took over the conduct of state affairs and began to reform Muscovy, he found few collaborators. His own family, the court circles, and the boyar duma overwhelmingly opposed change. Because he discovered little support at the top of the state structure, and also because he never attached much importance to origin or rank, the sovereign proceeded to obtain assistants wherever possible. Before long an extremely mixed but on the whole able group emerged. To quote Kliuchevsky's colorful summary:

> Peter gathered the necessary men everywhere, without worrying about rank and origin, and they came to him from different directions and all possible conditions: one arrived as a cabin-boy on a Portuguese ship, as was the case of the chief of police of the new capital, de Vière; another had shepherded swine in Lithuania, as it was rumored about the first Procurator-General of the Senate, Iaguzhinsky; a third had worked as a clerk in a small store, as in the instance of Vice-Chancellor Shafirov; a fourth had been a Russian house serf, as in the case of the Vice-Governor of Archangel, the inventor of stamped paper, Kurbatov; a fifth, i.e., Ostermann, was a son of a Westphalian pastor. And all these men, together with Prince Menshikov, who, the story went, had once sold pies in the streets of Moscow, met in Peter's society with the remnants of the Russian boyar nobility.

Among foreigners, the tsar had the valuable aid of some of his old friends, such as Patrick Gordon and the Swiss, Francis Lefort, who played a prominent role until his early death in 1699. Later such able newcomers from Germany as the diplomat, Andrew Ostermann, and the military expert, Burkhard Münnich, joined the sovereign's entourage. Some of his numerous foreign assistants, for example, the Scot James Bruce who helped with the artillery, mining, the navy and other matters, had been born in Russia and belonged to the second generation of foreign settlers in Muscovy.

Russian assistants to Peter ranged over the entire social gamut. Alexander Menshikov, Pavel Iaguzhinsky, Petr Shafirov, and Alexei Kurbatov, among others, came from the lower classes. A large group belonged to the service gentry, of whom only two examples are the chief admiral of the reign, Fedor Apraksin, and Chancellor Gavril Golovkin. Even old aristocratic families contributed a number of important figures, such as Field Marshal Count Boris Sheremetev and Senator Prince Iakov Dolgoruky. The Church too, although generally opposed to reform, supplied some able clerics who furthered the work of Peter the Great. The place of honor among them belongs to Archbishop Theophanes, or Feofan, Prokopovich, who, like many other promoters of change in Russia, came from Ukraine. Of all the "fledglings of Peter's nest"—to use Pushkin's expression—Menshikov acquired the greatest prominence and power. This son of a corporal or groom came closest to being the sovereign's alter ego and participating in the entire range of his activity. Beginning as the boy tsar's orderly in the Preobrazhenskii regiment, Menshikov rose to be Generalissimo, Prince in Russia, and Prince of the Holy Roman Empire, to mention only his most outstanding titles. Vain and thoroughly corrupt, as well as able and energetic, he constituted a permanent target for investigations and court proceedings and repeatedly suffered summary punishment from Peter the Great's cudgel, but somehow managed to maintain his position. At the same time, Paul Bushkovitch has argued, Peter may have never entirely freed himself from the traditional elite. He benefitted from the contributions of both old and new men and was limited, like his predecessors, by the need to maintain a balance in court politics.

## War, the Grand Embassy to Europe, Rebellion

War against Turkey was Peter I's first major action after he took the government of Russia into his own hands in 1694, following the death of his mother. In fighting Turkey, the protector of the Crimean Tatars and the power controlling the Black Sea and its southern Russian shore, the new monarch followed in the steps of his predecessors. However, before long it became apparent that he managed his affairs differently. The war began in 1695, and the first Russian campaign against Azov failed: supplied by sea, the fortress remained impregnable to the Muscovite army. Then, in one winter, the tsar built a fleet in Voronezh on the Don River. He worked indefatigably himself, as well as ordering and urging others, and utilized to the best advantage the knowledge of all available foreign specialists along with his own previously acquired knowledge. By displaying his tremendous energy everywhere, Peter the Great brought thirty sea-going vessels and about a thousand transport barges to Azov in May 1696. This time besieged by sea as well as by land, the Turks surrendered Azov in July.

With a view toward a further struggle against Turkey and a continuing augmentation and modernization of the Russian armed forces, the tsar next sent fifty young men to study, above all shipbuilding and navigation, in Holland, Italy, and England. Peter dispatched groups of Russians to study abroad several more times in his reign. After the students returned, the sovereign often examined them personally. In addition to experts, the tsar needed allies to prosecute war against Turkey. The desire to form a mighty coalition against the Ottoman Empire, and an intense interest in the West, prompted Peter to organize a large embassy to visit a number of European countries and—a most unusual act for a Muscovite ruler—to travel with the embassy.

Headed by Lefort, the party of about 250 men set out in March 1697. The sovereign journeyed incognito under the name of Peter Mikhailov. His identity, however, remained no secret to the rulers and officials of the countries he visited or to the crowds which frequently gathered around him. The tsar engaged in a number of important talks on diplomatic and other state matters. But, above all, he tried to learn as much as possible from the West. He seemed most concerned with navigation, but he also tried to absorb other technical skills and crafts, together with the ways and manners and, in fact, the entire life of Europe as he saw it. As the so-called Grand Embassy progressed across the continent and as Peter Mikhailov also took trips of his own, most notably to the British Isles, he obtained some first-hand knowledge of the Baltic provinces of Sweden, Prussia, and certain other German states, and of Holland, England, and the Habsburg Empire. From Vienna the tsar intended to go to Italy, but instead he rushed back to Moscow at news of a rebellion of the streltsy. Altogether Peter the Great spent eighteen months abroad in 1697–98. At that time over 750 foreigners, especially Dutchmen, were recruited to serve in Russia. Again in 1702 and at other times, the tsar invited Europeans of every nationality to come to his realm, promising to subsidize passage, provide advantageous employment, and assure religious tolerance and separate law courts.

The streltsy had already caused trouble for Peter and suffered punishment on the eve of the tsar's journey to the West—in fact delaying the journey. Although the new conspiracy that was aimed at deposing Peter and putting Sophia in power had been effectively dealt with before the sovereign's return, the tsar acted with exceptional violence and severity. After investigation and torture more than a thousand streltsy were executed, and their mangled bodies were exposed to the public as a salutary lesson. Sophia was forced to become a nun, and the same fate befell Peter's wife, Eudoxia, who had sympathized with the rebels.

If the gruesome death of the streltsy symbolized the destruction of the old order, many signs indicated the coming of the new. After he returned from the West, the tsar began to demand that beards be cut and foreign dress be worn by courtiers, officials, and the military. (In 1705 this became law for all "men of rank," including merchants and artisans. Those who refused to cut their beards could pay a tax; even peasants visiting the city had to pay a small fee to keep their beards. With the beginning of the new century, the sovereign changed the Russian calendar: henceforth years were to be counted from the birth of Christ, not the creation of the world, and they were to commence on the first of January, not the first of September.

More important, Peter the Great rapidly proceeded to reorganize his army according to the Western pattern.

## The Great Northern War

The Grand Embassy failed to further Peter the Great's designs against Turkey. But, although European powers proved unresponsive to the proposal of a major war with the Ottomans, other political opportunities emerged. Before long Peter joined the military alliance against Sweden organized by Augustus II, ruler of Saxony and Poland. The interests of the allies, Denmark, Russia, and Poland-Saxony, clashed with those of Sweden, which after its extremely successful participation in the Thirty Years' War had acquired a dominant position on the Baltic and in the Baltic area. The time to strike appeared ripe, for Charles XII, a mere youth of fifteen, had ascended the Swedish throne in 1697. While Peter I concentrated on concluding the long-drawn-out peace negotiations with Turkey, Augustus II declared war on Sweden in January 1700, and several months later Denmark followed his example. On July 14 the Russo-Turkish treaty was finally signed in Constantinople: the Russians obtained Azov and Taganrog as well as the right to maintain a resident minister in Turkey. On August 19, ten days after Peter the Great learned of the conclusion of the treaty with the Porte and the day after he officially announced it, he declared war on Sweden. Thus Russia entered what came to be known as the Great Northern War.

Immediately the Russians found themselves in a much more difficult situation than they had expected. With utmost daring Charles XII crossed the straits and carried the fight to the heart of Denmark, quickly forcing the Danes to surrender. Having disposed of Denmark, the Swedish king promptly attacked the new enemy. Transporting his troops across the Baltic to Livonia, on November 30, 1700, he suddenly assaulted the main Russian army that was besieging the fortress of Narva. In spite of the very heavy numerical odds against them the Swedes routed the Russian forces, killing or capturing some 10,000 troops and forcing the remaining 30,000 to abandon their artillery and retreat in haste. In the words of one historian summarizing the Russian performance at Narva: "The old-fashioned cavalry and irregulars took to flight without fighting. The new infantry levies proved 'nothing more than undisciplined militia,' the foreign officers incompetent and unreliable. Only the two guards and one other foot regiment showed up well."

It was believed by some at the time and has been argued by others since that after Narva Charles XII should have concentrated on knocking Russia out of the war and that by acting in a prompt and determined manner he could have accomplished this purpose. Instead, the Swedish king for years underestimated and neglected his Muscovite opponent. After lifting the Saxon siege of Riga in the summer of 1701, he transferred the main hostilities to Poland, considering Augustus II his most dangerous enemy. Again Swedish arms achieved notable successes, but for about six years they could not force a decision. In the meantime, Peter made utmost use of the respite he received. Acting with his characteristic energy, the tsar had a new army and artillery ready within a year after the debacle of Narva. Conscription, administration, finance, and everything else had to be strained to the limit and adapted to the demands of war, but the sovereign did not swerve from his set purpose. The melting of church bells to make cannons has remained an abiding symbol of that enormous war effort.

Peter I used his reconstructed military forces in two ways: he sent help to Augustus II, and he began a systematic advance in Livonia and Estonia, which Charles XII had left with little protection. Already in 1701 and 1702 Sheremetev at the head of a large army devastated these provinces, twice defeating weak Swedish forces, and the Russians began to establish themselves firmly on the Gulf of Finland. The year 1703 marked the founding of St. Petersburg near the mouth of the Neva, initially as a fortified outpost for fighting the Swedes and soon as the new capital of the Russian empire; it was named in honor of Peter's patron saint but also to signal Peter's love of all things Dutch—the original spelling of the name was Sankt Pieter Burkh, gradually modernized into Sankt Peterburg. The following year Peter the Great built the island fortress of Kronstadt to protect his future capital, while the Russian troops captured the ancient city of Dorpat, or Iuriev, in Estonia and the stronghold of Narva itself. The tsar rapidly constructed a navy on the Baltic, his southern fleet being useless in the northern war, and the new ships participated effectively in amphibious and naval operations.

But time finally ran out for Augustus II. Brought to bay in his own Saxony, he had to sign the Treaty of Altranstädt with Charles XII in late September, 1706: by its terms Augustus II abdicated the Polish crown in favor of pro-Swedish Stanislaw Leszczynski and, of course, withdrew from the war. Peter the Great was thus left alone to face one of the most feared armies and one of the most successful generals of Europe. The Swedish king began his decisive campaign against Russia in January 1708, crossing the Vistula with a force of almost 50,000 men and advancing in the direction of Moscow.

Peter I's position was further endangered by the need to suppress rebellions provoked both by the exactions of the Russian government and by opposition to the tsar's reforms. In the summer of 1705 a monk and one of the streltsy started a successful uprising in Astrakhan aimed against the upper classes and the foreign influence. It was even rumored in Astrakhan that all Russian girls would be forced to wed Germans, a threat which led to the hasty conclusion of many marriages. The town was recaptured by Sheremetev only in March 1706, after bitter fighting. In 1707 Konrad Bulavin, a leader of the Don cossacks, led a major rebellion in the Don area. Provoked by the government's determination to hunt down fugitives and also influenced by the Old Belief, Bulavin's movement followed the pattern of the great social uprisings of the past. At its height, the rebellion spread over a large area of southern Russia, including dozens of towns, and the rebel army numbered perhaps as many as 100,000 men. As usual in such uprisings, however, this huge force lacked organization and discipline. Government troops managed to defeat the rebels decisively a year or so before the war with Sweden reached its climax in the summer of 1709. Still another rebellion, that of the Turkic Bashkirs who opposed the Russian disruption of their way of life as well as the heavy exactions of the state, erupted in the middle Volga area in 1705 and was not finally put down until 1711.

Some historians believe that Charles XII would have won the war had he pressed his offensive in 1708 against Moscow. Instead he swerved south and entered Ukraine. The Swedish king wanted to rest and strengthen his army in a rich land untouched by the fighting before resuming the offensive, and he counted heavily on Hetman Ivan Mazepa, who had secretly turned against Russia. His calculations failed: Mazepa could bring only some 2,000 cossacks to the Swedish side—with a few thousand more joining later—while a general lack of sympathy for the Swedes together with Menshikov's energetic and rapid countermeasures assured the loyalty of Ukraine to Peter the Great. Also, Charles XII's move south made it easier for a Russian force led by the tsar to intercept and smash Swedish reinforcements of 15,000 men and a huge supply train at Lesnaia. Largely isolated from the people, far from home bases, short of supplies, and unable to advance their cause militarily or diplomatically, the Swedish army spent a dismal, cold winter in 1708–9 in Ukraine. Yet Charles XII would not retreat. The hour of decision struck in the middle of the following summer when the main Russian army finally came to the rescue of the small fortress of Poltava besieged by the Swedes, and the enemies met in the open field.

The Swedish army was destroyed on July 8, 1709, in the battle of Poltava. The Swedes, numbering only 22,000 to 28,000 as against over 40,000 Russians, and vastly inferior in artillery, put up a tremendous fight before their lines broke. Most of them, including the generals, eventually surrendered either on the field or several days later near the Dnieper, which they could not cross. Charles XII and Mazepa did escape to Turkish territory. Whereas in retrospect the outcome of Poltava occasions no surprise, it bears remembering that a few years earlier the Swedes had won at Narva against much greater odds and that Charles XII had acquired a reputation as an invincible commander. But, in contrast to the debacle at Narva, Russian generalship, discipline, fighting spirit, and efficiency had dramatically improved. Peter the Great, who had himself led his men in the thick of battle, appreciated to the full the importance of the outcome. And indeed he had excellent reasons to celebrate the victory and to thank his captive Swedish "teachers" for their most useful "lessons."

Yet not long after Poltava the fortunes of Peter I and his state reached perhaps their lowest point. Instigated by France, as well as by Charles XII, Turkey, which had so far abstained from participation in the hostilities, declared war on Russia in 1710. Peter acted rashly, underestimating the enemy and relying heavily on the problematical support of the vassal Ottoman principalities of Moldavia and Wallachia and of Christian subjects of the sultan elsewhere, notably in Serbia and Montenegro. In July 1711, the tsar found himself at the head of an inadequate army in need of ammunition and supplies and surrounded by vastly superior Turkish forces near the Pruth River. Argument persists to this day as to why the Turks did not make more of their overwhelming advantage. Suggested answers have ranged from the weariness and losses of the Turkish troops to skillful Russian diplomacy and even bribery. In any case Peter the Great signed a peace treaty, according to which he abandoned his southern fleet, returned Azov and other gains of 1700 to the Turks, promised not to intervene in Poland, and guaranteed to Charles XII safe passage to Sweden. But, at the price of renouncing acquisitions to the south, he was enabled to extricate himself from a catastrophic situation and retain a dominant hand in the Great Northern War.

That war, decided in effect in 1709, dragged on for many more years. After Poltava, the tsar transferred his main effort to the Baltic, seizing Viborg—or Vlipuri—Riga, and Reval in 1710. The debacle of Charles XII in Ukraine led to a revival of the coalition against him. Saxony, Poland, Denmark, Prussia, and Hanover joined Russia against Sweden. In new circumstances, Peter the Great developed his military operations along two chief lines: Russian troops helped the allies in their campaigns on the southern shore of the Baltic, while other forces continued the advance in the eastern Baltic area. Thus in 1713–14 the tsar occupied most of Finland. The new Russian navy became ever more active, scoring a victory under Peter's direct command over the Swedish fleet off Hangö in 1714.

The sudden rise of Russia came as something of a shock to other European countries, straining relations, for example, between Great Britain and Russia. It also led to considerable fear and worried speculations about the intentions and future steps of the northern giant; this was reflected later in such forgeries as the purported testament of Peter the Great which expressed his, and Russia's, aim to conquer the world. In 1717 the tsar traveled to Paris, and, although he failed to obtain any diplomatic results beyond the French promise not to help Sweden, once more he saw and learned much. In December 1718, Charles XII was killed in a minor military engagement Norway. His sister Ulrika Eleonora and later her husband Frederick I succeeded to the Swedish throne. Unable to reverse the course of the war and, indeed, increasingly threatened, for Peter the Great proceeded to send expeditions into Sweden proper in 1719–21, the Swedes finally admitted defeat and made peace.

On August 30, 1721, Sweden concluded the Treaty of Nystadt with Russia. Russia acquired Livonia, Estonia, Ingermanland, part of Karelia, and certain islands, although it returned the bulk of Finland and paid 2 million rix-dollars. In effect it obtained the so-called Baltic provinces which were to become, after the Treaty of Versailles, the independent states of Estonia and Latvia and also obtained southeastern Finnish borderlands located strategically next to St. Petersburg and the Gulf of Finland. The capture and retention of the fortress of Viborg in particular gave Russia virtual control of the Gulf.

In modern European history the Great Northern War was one of the important wars and Poltava one of the decisive battles. The Russian victory over Sweden and the resulting Treaty of Nystadt meant that Russia became firmly established on the Baltic, acquiring its essential "window into Europe," and that in fact it replaced Sweden as the dominant power in the north of the continent. Historians have argued that these victories marked the true founding of Russia as an empire. Moreover, Russia not only humiliated Sweden but also won a preponderant position vis-à-vis its ancient rival Poland, became directly involved in German affairs—a relationship that included marital alliances arranged by the tsar for his and his half-brother Ivan V's daughters—and generally stepped forth as a major European power. The two other wars of Peter's reign, the Azov Campaigns against Turkey and the Persian Campaign, though both were less successful, shared with the Great Northern War a common goal: a desire for commercial and naval ports. Russia's interest in Central Asia, though mainly nonmilitary, reflected interest in expanding relations and trade with India and China.

Celebrations of these victories symbolically elevated Russia and the ruler to new heights. In words and imagery, as Richard Wortman has shown, Peter was compared to classical and biblical heroes and gods, including Mars, Hercules, Samson, and David. The Senate prevailed upon Peter I to accept the titles "Great," "Father of the Fatherland," and "Emperor," especially in the older sense of *imperator* as a great military leader. The imagery of glory and power was not only secular, however. At the Poltava celebration, Peter was honored with a chant normally reserved for the patriarch performing the role of Christ in the Palm Sunday ritual, "Blessed is He who cometh in the name of the Lord, Hosanna in the highest, the Lord God appear before us." Archbishop Prokopovich expressed certainty that the battle of Poltava, which took place on the feast day of St. Samson, occurred "not, I imagine, without the watchfulness of God."

## The Reforming of Russia: Introductory Remarks

In regard to internal affairs during the reign of Peter the Great, we find that scholars have taken two extreme and opposite approaches. On the one hand, the tsar's reforming of Russia has been presented as a series, or rather a jumble, of disconnected ad hoc measures necessitated by the exigencies of the moment, especially by the pressure of the Great Northern War. Contrariwise, the same activity has been depicted as the execution of a comprehensive, radically new, and well-integrated program. In a number of ways, the first view seems closer to the facts. As Kliuchevsky pointed out, only a single year in Peter the Great's whole reign, 1724, passed entirely without war, while no more than another thirteen peaceful months could be added for the entire period. Connected to the enormous strain of war was the inadequacy of the Muscovite financial system, which was overburdened and in a state of virtual collapse even before Peter the Great made vastly increased demands upon it. The problem for the state became simply to survive, and survival exacted a heavy price. Under Peter the Great the population of Russia might have declined. Miliukov and other scholars have shown how military considerations repeatedly led to financial measures, and in turn to edicts aiming to stimulate Russian commerce and industry, to changes in the administrative system without whose

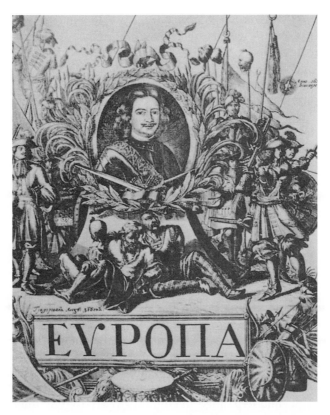

An image of Peter I from a map of Europe, portraying his triumphs over rebellious streltsy and over enemy Turks and Tatars. *(Alekseeva, Graviura Petrovskogo vremeni)*

improvement these and other edicts proved ineffective, to attempts to foster education in whose absence a modern administration could not function, and on and on. It has further been argued, on the whole convincingly, that in any case Peter the Great was not a theoretician or planner, but an intensely energetic and practical man of affairs.

Yet a balanced judgment has to allow something to the opposite point of view as well. Although Peter the Great was preoccupied during most of his reign with the Great Northern War and although he had to sacrifice much else to its successful prosecution, his reforming of Russia was by no means limited to hectic measures to bolster the war effort. In fact, he wanted to Westernize and modernize all of the Russian government, society, life, and culture. Even if his efforts fell far short of this stupendous goal and left huge gaps, the basic pattern is clear. Countries of the West served as models in the work of the emperor and his associates, though they chose among a rich variety of European states and societies and tried to adapt Western institutions to Russian needs and possibilities. Although the reformer was no theoretician, he had the makings of a visionary. With characteristic boldness and optimism he saw ahead the image of a modern, powerful, prosperous, and educated country. Clearly, then, both the needs of the moment and longer range aims must be considered in evaluating the reforms. Also, as time passed, Peter became more interested in general issues and larger patterns.

There is much we can argue about in interpreting Peter the Great's vision, however. What was the relationship of reforms to the Russian past? What changes occurred as Western forms evolved in Russian conditions? What did progress and civilization actually mean to Peter and his allies: was it mainly rationalization and technical progress or a deeper vision of a more enlightened and cultured society in which human lives were improved? Did the means used in this "revolution from above," as many historians have called it, affect the ends? How enduring were the reforms? And at what human cost were change and progress made? What is not debated is that Peter the Great transformed Russia.

## The Army and the Navy

Military reforms stemmed most directly from the war. In that field Peter the Great's measures must be regarded as radical, successful, and lasting, as well as imitative of the West; and he has rightly been considered the founder of the modern Russian army. The emperor's predecessors had large armies, but these were poorly organized, technically deficient, and generally of low quality. They assembled for campaigns and disbanded when the campaign ended. Only gradually did "regular" regiments, with Western officers and technicians, begin to appear. Even the streltsy, or musketeers, founded by Ivan the Terrible and expanded to contain twenty-two regiments of about a thousand men each, represented a doubtful asset. Stationed mainly in Moscow, they engaged in various trades and crafts and constituted at best a semi-professional force. Moreover, as mentioned earlier, the streltsy became a factor in Muscovite politics, staged uprisings, and were severely punished and then disbanded by Peter the Great. The reformer instituted general conscription and reorganized and modernized the army. The gentry, of course, had been subject to personal military service ever since the formation of the Muscovite state. Under Peter the Great this obligation came to be much more effectively and, above all, continuously enforced. Except for the unfit and those given civil assignments, the members of the gentry were to remain with their regiments for life. Other classes, with the exception of the clergy and members of the merchant guilds, who were needed elsewhere, fell under the draft. Large numbers were conscripted, especially in the early years of the Great Northern War. In 1715 the Senate established the norm of one draftee from every seventy-five serf households. Probably the same norm operated in the case of the state peasants, while additional recruits were obtained from the townspeople. All were to be separated from their families and occupations and to serve for life, a term which was reduced to twenty-five years only in the last decade of the eighteenth century.

Having obtained a large body of men, Peter I went on to transform them into a modern army. He personally introduced a new and up-to-date military manual, became proficient with every weapon, and learned to command units the smallest to the largest. He insisted that each draftee, aristocrat and serf alike, similarly work his way from the bottom up, advancing exactly as fast and as far as his merit would warrant. Important changes in the military establishment included the creation of the elite regiments of the guards, and of numerous other regular regiments, the adoption of the flintlock and the bayonet, and an enormous improvement in artillery. By the time of Poltava, Russia was producing most of its own flintlocks. The Russian army was the first to use the bayonet in attack—a weapon originally designed for defense against the charging enemy. As to artillery, Peter the Great developed both the heavy siege artillery, which proved very effective in 1704 in the Russian capture of Narva, and, by about 1707, light artillery, which participated in battles alongside the infantry and the cavalry. The contrast between the bearded, xenophobic, and archaically trained streltsy who rebelled in 1698 and the clean-shaven, modern trained, and Western clad guards, often commanded by foreigners, symbolized how much had changed. So did, of course, the victory over Sweden.

The guards were more than the elite of Peter's army; they had, so to speak, grown up with the emperor, and contained many of his most devoted and enthusiastic supporters. Especially in the second half of his reign, Peter the Great frequently used officers and noncommissioned officers of the guards for special assignments, bypassing the usual administrative channels. Often endowed with summary powers, which might include the right to bring a transgressing governor or other high official back in chains, they were sent to speed up the collection of taxes or the gathering of recruits, to improve the functioning of the judiciary or to investigate alleged administrative corruption and abuses. Operating outside the regular bureaucratic structure, these emissaries could be considered as extensions of the ruler's own person. Later emperors, such as Alexander I and Nicholas I, continued Peter the Great's novel practice on a large scale, relying on special, and usually military, agents to obtain immediate results in various matters and in general to supervise the workings of the government apparatus.

To an even greater extent than the army, the modern Russian navy was the creation of Peter the Great. One can fairly say it was one of his passions. He began from scratch—with one vessel of an obsolete type, to be exact—and left to his successor 48 major warships and 787 minor and auxiliary craft, serviced by 28,000 men. He also bequeathed to those who followed him the first Russian shipbuilding industry and, of course, the Baltic ports and coastline. Moreover, the navy, built on the British model, had already won high regard by defeating the Swedish fleet. The British considered the Russian vessels comparable to the best British ships in the same class, and the British government became so worried by the sudden rise of the Russian navy that in 1719 it recalled its men from the Russian service.

## Administrative Reforms: Central Government, Local Government, the Church

Although mainly occupied with military matters, Peter reformed the central and local government in Russia as well as Church administration and finance, and he also effected important changes in Russian society, economy, and culture. Peter I ascended the throne as Muscovite tsar and autocrat and he proved to be one of the most powerful and impressive absolute rulers of his age, or any age. Yet comparisons with Ivan the Terrible or other Muscovite predecessors can be misleading. Peter the Great believed in enlightened despotism as preached and to an extent practiced in Europe during the so-called Age of Reason. He borrowed his definition of autocracy and of the relationship between the ruler and his subjects from Sweden, not from the Muscovite tradition. In contrast to Ivan the Terrible, Peter the Great had the highest regard for law, and he considered himself the first servant of the state. Yet, again in accord with his general outlook, he had no use for the boyar duma, or the zemskii sobor, and treated the Church in a much more high-handed manner than his predecessors had. Thus the reformer largely escaped the vague, but nevertheless real, traditional hindrances to absolute power in Muscovy. In their place, he built a completely new structure of governing institutions.

In 1711, before leaving on his campaign against Turkey, Peter the Great published two orders which created the Governing Senate. The Senate was founded as the highest state institution to supervise all judicial, financial, and administrative affairs. Originally established only for the time of the monarch's absence, it became a permanent body after his return. The number of senators was first set at nine and in 1712 increased to ten. A special high official, the Ober-Procurator, served as the link between the sovereign and the Senate and acted, in the emperor's own words, as "the sovereign's eye." Without his signature no Senate decision could go into effect; any disagreements between the Ober-Procurator and the Senate were to be settled by the monarch. Certain other officials and a chancellery were also attached to the Senate. While it underwent many subsequent changes, the Senate became one of the most important institutions of imperial Russia, especially in administration and law.

In 1717 and the years immediately following, Peter the Great established *collegia*, or colleges, in place of the old, numerous, overlapping, and unwieldy prikazy. The new agencies, comparable to the later ministries, were originally nine in number: the colleges of foreign affairs, war, navy, state expenses, state income, justice, financial inspection and control, commerce, and manufacturing. Later three colleges were added to deal with mining, estates, and town organization. Each college consisted of a president, a vice-president, four councilors, four assessors, a procurator, a secretary, and a chancellery. At first a qualified foreigner was included in every college, but as a rule not as president. At that time collegiate administration had found considerable favor and application in Europe. Peter the Great was especially influenced by the example of Sweden and also, possibly, by Leibniz's advice. It was argued that government by boards assured a greater variety and interplay of opinion, since decisions depended on the majority vote, not on the will of an individual, and that it contributed to a strictly legal and proper handling of state affairs. More bluntly, the emperor remarked that he did not have enough trustworthy assistants to put in full charge of the different branches of the executive and had, therefore, to rely on groups of men, who would keep check on one another. The colleges lasted for almost a century before they were replaced by ministries in the reign of Alexander I.

Local government also underwent reform. In 1699 towns were reorganized to facilitate taxation and obtain more revenue for the state. This system, run for the government by merchants, took little into account except finance and stemmed from Muscovite practices rather than Western influences. In 1720–21, on the other hand, Peter the Great introduced a thorough municipal reform along advanced European lines. Based on the elective principle and intended to stimulate the initiative and activity of the townspeople, the ambitious scheme failed to be translated into practice because of local inertia and interests.

Provincial reform provided probably the outstanding example of a major reforming effort of Peter's come to naught. Again, changes began in a somewhat haphazard manner, largely under the pressure of war and a desperate search for money. After the reform of 1708 the country was divided into huge *gubernii*, or governments, eight, ten, and finally eleven in number. But with the legislation of 1719 a fully developed and extremely far-reaching scheme appeared. Fifty provinces, each headed by a *voevoda*, became the main administrative units. They were subdivided into *uezdy* administered by commissars. The commissars, as well as a council of from two to four members attached to the voevoda, were to be elected by the local gentry from their midst. All officials received salaries and the old Muscovite practice of *kormleniia*—"feedings"— went out of existence. Peter the Great went beyond his Swedish model in charging provincial bodies with responsibility for local health, education, and economic development. And it deserves special notice that the reform of 1719 introduced into Russia a separation of administrative and judicial power. But all this proved to be premature and unrealistic. Local initiative could not be aroused, nor suitable officials found. The separation of administration and justice disappeared by about 1727, while some other ambitious aspects of the reform never came into more than paper existence.

The reign witnessed a strengthening of government control in certain borderlands. After the suppression of Bulavin's great revolt, the emperor tightened his grip on the Don area, and that territory came to be more closely linked to the rest of Russia. The cossacks, however, did retain a distinct administration, military organization, and way of life until the very end of the Russian Empire and even into the Soviet period. Similarly, Mazepa's defection to Charles XII led to a tightening of Russian control of Ukraine. Among other policies we see an early example of what would later be called imperial Russification: an order in 1714 emphasized the desirability of mixing the Ukrainians and the Russians and of bringing Russian officials into Ukraine, buttressing its argument with references to successful English policies vis-à-vis Scotland, Wales, and Ireland.

Peter's Church reforms essentially made the Church into a branch of government, run along similar lines. When the conservative patriarch Hadrian died in 1700, the tsar kept his seat vacant, and the Church was administered for over two decades by a mere *locum tenens*, the very able moderate supporter of reform Metropolitan Stephen Iavorsky. Finally in 1721, the so-called Spiritual Reglament, apparently written mainly by Archbishop Theophanes Prokopovich, established a new organization of the Church. The Holy Synod, consisting of ten, later twelve, clerics, replaced the patriarch. A lay official, the Ober-Procurator of the Holy Synod, was appointed to see that that body carried on its work in a perfectly legal and correct manner. Although the new arrangement fell under the conciliar principle widespread in the Orthodox Church and although it received approval from the Eastern patriarchs, the reform belonged—as much as did Peter the Great's other reforms—to Western, not Muscovite or Byzantine, tradition. In particular, it tried to reproduce the relationship between Church and state in the Lutheran countries of northern Europe. Although it did not make Russia Byzantine as some writers assert, nor even caesaropapist—for the emperor did not acquire any authority in questions of faith—it did enable the government to exercise effective control over Church organization, possessions, and policies. If Muscovy had two supreme leaders, the tsar and the patriarch, only the tsar remained in the St. Petersburg era. The Holy Synod and the domination of the Church by the government lasted until 1917.

Other policies toward the Church and religion reflected Peter's general outlook. He expected the Church to serve the public good and the interests of the state and empire as a whole. He tried to strengthen and broaden Church schools and charged the Church with organizing welfare institutions such as almshouses. While he sought to improve the lot of the impoverished secular clergy, he considered monks to be shirkers and wastrels and undertook steps to limit ecclesiastical possessions and control ecclesiastical wealth, though he stopped short of secularizing Church lands. The government also ordered priests to report any talk of sedition heard during confession. As one might expect, the reformer exhibited more tolerance toward those of other denominations than had his Muscovite predecessors, on the whole preferring Protestants to Catholics. In 1721 the Holy Synod permitted intermarriage between the Orthodox and Western Christians. The emperor apparently felt no religious animosity toward the Old Believers and favored tolerance toward them. They, however, proved to be bitter opponents of his program of reform. Therefore, the relaxation in the treatment of the Old Believers early in the reign gave way to new restrictions and penalties, such as special taxation.

An evaluation of the total impact of Peter the Great's administrative reforms presents certain difficulties. These reforms copied and adapted Western models, trying to import into Russia the best institutions and practices to be found anywhere in Europe. Efforts to delimit clearly the authority of every agency, to separate powers and functions, to standardize procedure, and to spell out each detail could well be considered revolutionary from the old Muscovite point of view. On the surface at least the new system seemed to bear a greater resemblance to Sweden or the German states than to the realm of the good Tsar Alexis. The very names of the new institutions and the offices and technical terms associated with them testified to a flood of Western influences and a break with the Muscovite past. Yet reality differed significantly from this appearance. Even where reforms survived—and sometimes, as in the case of the local government, they did not—the change turned out to be not nearly as profound as the emperor had intended. Statutes, prescriptions, and precise rules looked good on paper; in actuality in the main cities and especially in the enormous expanses of provincial Russia, everything depended as of old on the initiative, ability, and behavior of officials. The kormleniia could be abolished, but not the all-pervasive bribery and corruption. Personal and largely arbitrary rule remained, in sum, the foundation of Russian administration. Of course, the reforms themselves, being so closely associated with Peter's own vision and drive to transform Russia, perpetuated the Russian tradition of personal rule. Also, the reformer's frantic efforts to craft a new system—a process too complicated and involved to discuss fully here—produced an order that was new but lacked integration, coordination, and cohesion. In fact a few scholars, such as Platonov, have argued that the administrative order established by Peter the Great proved to be more disjointed and disorganized than that of Muscovite Russia.

## Financial and Social Measures

The difficulty of transforming Russian reality into something new and Western becomes even more evident when we consider Peter the Great's social legislation and his overall influence on Russian society. Before turning to this topic, however, we must mention briefly the emperor's financial policies, for they played an important and continuous part in his plans and actions.

Peter the Great found himself constantly in dire need of money, and at times the need was utterly desperate. The only recourse was to squeeze still more out of the Russian masses, who were already overburdened and strained almost to the breaking point. According to one calculation, the revenue the government managed to exact in 1702 was twice, and in 1724 five and a half times, the revenue obtained in 1680. In the process it taxed almost everything, including beehives, mills, fisheries, beards, and bathhouses; and it also extended the state monopoly to new items. For example, stamped paper, necessary for legal transactions, became an additional source of revenue for the state, and so did oak coffins. In fact, finding or concocting new ways to augment government funds developed into a peculiar kind of occupation in the course of the reign. Another and perhaps more significant change was in the main form of direct taxation; in 1718 Peter the Great introduced the head, or poll, tax in place of the household tax and the tax on cultivated land.

One purpose of the head tax was to catch shirkers who combined households or failed to till their land. It was levied on the entire lower class of the population and it represented a heavy assessment—considerably heavier than the taxes that it replaced—and it had to be paid in cash. From 1718 to 1722 a census, a so-called revision, of the population subject to the head tax took place. Initially the census included only serfs and slaves who tilled the soil on private estates. Then came orders to add household slaves and all dependent people not on the land, and finally even vagrants. Each person registered during the census had to pay the same set head tax. On estates, landlords were held responsible for the prompt flow of money to the treasury. Scholars have stressed that the head tax finally erased all differences between serfs and slaves, merging all peasants into one bonded mass. Of course, we have already seen that the arbitrary power of the landlord and the weakness of the peasant made Russian serfdom differ little from slavery. After the revision the serfs were allowed to leave the estate only with their master's written permission, a measure which marked the beginning of a passport system. The head tax, it might be added, proved to be one of the emperor's lasting innovations.

On the whole Peter the Great had to accept and did accept Russian society as it was, with serfdom and the economic and social dominance of the gentry. The emperor, however, made a tremendous effort to bend that society to serve his purposes: the successful prosecution of war, Westernization, and reform. Above all, the government needed money and men. The head tax presents an excellent example of an important social measure passed for financial reasons. But whereas the head tax affected the lower classes, other social groups also found themselves subject to the insatiable demands of the emperor and his growing state. For example, the merchants, the few professional people, and other middle-class elements, who were all exempt from the head tax, had to work harder than ever before to discharge their obligations to the state in the economic domain and other fields of activity.

In so many areas, as we can see, the emperor insisted on service. This especially applied to the gentry. As we know, state service constituted an ancient obligation of that class. But, as we have already seen with the army, under Peter the Great it became a more regular and continuous as well as much heavier obligation. Every member of the gentry was required to serve from about the age of sixteen to the end of his days, and the sovereign himself often gave an examination to boys as young as fourteen or even ten and assigned them to schools and careers. After an inspection, held usually in Moscow, the gentry youths were divided roughly two-thirds to one-third between the military and the civilian branches of service. Peter the Great insisted that in the civilian offices as in the regiments or aboard ships all novices must start at the bottom and advance only according to their merit. The Table of Ranks, promulgated in 1722, is the most vivid and famous expression of these principles of orderly and universal service. The Table listed in hierarchical order a ladder of fourteen ranks through which servitors could climb in parallel columns of service: army, navy, civil service, and the court. The impressive names of the ranks were generally borrowed or adapted from foreign ranks. The Table managed to both reward merit and continue to recognize nobles as leaders of society. Individuals who advanced beyond a certain level were granted personal nobility. Those who reached a still higher level—rank eight for civil service and rank twelve in the military—were given hereditary nobility, which could be passed on to their descendents. Peter also began to grant titles of nobility, including "prince," for extraordinary achievements, and later emperors continued this practice. The Table of Ranks served as the foundation of the imperial Russian bureaucracy and lasted, with modifications, until 1917.

Peter the Great's handling of the gentry represented something of a tour de force, and it proved successful to the extent that the emperor did obtain a great deal of service from that class. But the reformer's successors could not maintain his drastic policies. In fact, we shall see how in the course of the eighteenth century the gentry gradually escaped from its service obligations. At the same time entry into that class became more difficult, so that Peter the Great's effort to open the road to all talents was somewhat diminished. It might be added that some of the emperor's social legislation failed virtually from the start. Thus, for example, in 1714, in opposition to the established Russian practice of dividing land among sons, the reformer issued a law of inheritance according to which the entire estate had to go to one son only—by choice, and to the elder son if no choice had been made—the others thus being forced to exist, as in the case of the British nobility, solely by service. But this law turned out to be extremely difficult to enforce even during Peter the Great's reign, and it was repealed as early as 1731.

## The Development of the National Economy

The emperor, characteristically, thought first of war and its immediate demands in his determination to develop the Russian economy. But, in addition, from about 1710 he strove to develop industries not related to military needs, to increase Russian exports, and in general to endow the country with a more varied and active economy. Peter the Great made every effort to stimulate private enterprise, but he also acted on a large scale directly through the state. Ideologically the emperor adhered to mercantilism, popular in Europe at the time, with its emphasis on the role of the government, a favorable balance of trade, and the protection of home industries as reflected in the Russian tariff of 1724. One account gives the figure of 200 manufacturing establishments founded in Peter the Great's reign—86 by the state and 114 by private individuals and companies—to add to the 21 in existence in Russia by 1695; another account mentions 250 such establishments in operation at the time of the emperor's death. The greatest development occurred in metallurgy, mining, and textiles. In effect, the emperor created the Russian textile industry, while he developed mining and metallurgy impressively from very modest beginnings, establishing them, notably, in the Urals. He promoted many other industries as well, including the production of china and glass.

To facilitate trade Peter the Great built canals and began the construction of a merchant marine. For instance, a canal was built between 1703 and 1709 to connect the Neva with the Volga. Indeed, the Volga-Don canal itself, finally completed by the Soviet government after the Second World War, had been one of the reformer's projects. In the course of Peter the Great's reign Russian foreign trade increased fourfold, although it continued to be handled in the main by foreign rather than Russian merchants. To be sure, this rapid development exacted a heavy social price, especially in the burdened and bonded lives of the lower classes. And some of his projects failed. But on the whole, Peter the Great exercised a major and creative influence on the development of the Russian economy, a foundation that would be built upon by later generations. There was no turning back.

## Education and Culture

There could be no turning back in culture either. In a sense Peter the Great's educational and cultural reforms proved to be the most lasting of all, for they pushed Russia firmly and irrevocably in the direction of the West. While these measures will be discussed in more detail in the chapter dealing with Russian culture in the eighteenth century, it should be pointed out here that they fitted well into the general pattern of the emperor's activity. Utilitarian in his approach, the sovereign stressed the necessity of at least a minimum education for service; and he also encouraged schools that would produce specialists, such as the School of Mathematics and Navigation established in 1701. His broader plans included compulsory education for the gentry—which could not be translated into practice at the time—and the creation of the Academy of Sciences to develop, guide, and crown learning in Russia. This academy did come into existence a few months after the reformer's death. Throughout his life Peter the Great showed a burning interest in science and technology as well as some interest in other areas of knowledge.

In bringing the civilization of the West to his native land, the emperor tried to introduce Western dress, manners, and usages, often by fiat and against strong opposition. The shaving of beards is a celebrated and abiding symbol of the reign. While the government demanded it "for the glory and comeliness of the state and the military profession"—to quote from Sumner's excellent little book on Peter the Great—the traditionalists objected on the ground that shaving impaired the image of God in men and made the Russians look like such objectionable beings as Lutherans, Poles, Kalmyks, Tatars, cats, dogs, and monkeys. Similarly it was argued that the already-mentioned calendar reform stole time from God and that the new simplified civil script should not be allowed to replace Church Slavonic. The *assemblées* or society parties that women attended also aroused a storm. These elegant gatherings of women and men in Western dress demonstratively ended the Muscovite tradition of secluding women of the elite, thus suggesting a radical new view of the place of women in the public sphere, even if at this stage their inclusion was still largely ornamental. Yet by the end of Peter's reign members of the civil service, army, and navy, of the upper classes, and to some extent even of the middle classes, particularly in the two leading cities, were shaven and wore foreign dress. Other Western innovations also generally succeeded in winning more adherents with time. Critics have long argued that Peter the Great split Russian society in two between a

Westernized elite and a traditional majority. Of course, even if he had wanted to (we do not really know), the cultural transformation of the majority would have been unrealistic. Changing the elite was difficult enough. It was left to his successors to try to bridge this growing gap, if they tried at all.

## The Problem of Succession

The conflict between old Muscovy and new imperial Russia was played out in the sovereign's own family. Both Peter the Great's mother and Eudoxia, the wife chosen for him by his mother, whom Peter forced to become a nun in 1698, belonged to the unreformed. In 1690 Eudoxia gave Peter a son, Alexis. The boy lived with his mother until her seclusion and later with aunts, in the old Muscovite palace. The emperor had little time for his son and never established a rapport with him. Instead Alexis became the hope of the opponents of the new order and their rallying point. In 1711 Peter the Great married Alexis to a German princess. In 1712 the emperor himself married for the second time, taking as his wife an illiterate Livonian peasant woman named Martha, who took the name Catherine when converting to Orthodoxy. Peter had found Catherine in his friend Menshikov's household, where she had been living with Menshikov happily for a few years and bore him children. She proved to be a good companion to the emperor. She evidently shared his tastes for alcohol and parties. Understanding and energetic, she also accompanied him on military campaigns. After the marriage, Peter declared Catherine to be his legal spouse and "sovereign tsaritsa."

In 1715, Alexis's wife died after giving birth to a son, Peter. At about this time, Peter the Great warned Alexis that he would rather appoint a "worthy stranger" to succeed him than an unworthy legal heir and demanded that Alexis either endorse his reforms or renounce his rights to the throne. With characteristically passive resistance, Alexis agreed to give up his rights. Soon after that, in 1716, when Peter the Great, then in Denmark, called for his son, Alexis used the opportunity to escape to Austria and ask the protection of Emperor Charles VI, who had married a sister of Alexis's late wife. Reports suggested that a conspiracy was hatched there to depose and assassinate Peter the Great. Lured back to Moscow in 1718 with a pardon, on the condition that he renounce his rights to the throne and name those who urged him to escape, Alexis was brought before an investigatory commission, which brought to light a great deal of opposition to and hatred of the new order. As a result, the pardon was withdrawn and a trial set. Over a hundred high dignitaries of the state acted as the special court that condemned Alexis to death for treason and attempted regicide. But before the execution could be carried out Alexis expired in the fortress of Peter and Paul in the summer of 1718, probably from shock and also torture used during the questioning. Nine of his associates were executed, nine sentenced to hard labor, while many others received milder punishments.

Catherine bore Peter ten children, but only two girls survived beyond early childhood. Possible heirs, therefore, included the emperor's grandson

Peter, the emperor's daughters and those of his half-brother Tsar Ivan V, and the emperor's wife Catherine. In 1722 Peter the Great passed a law of succession which disregarded the principle of hereditary seniority and proclaimed instead that the sovereign could appoint his successor. Once more position was to be determined by merit and will! But the emperor never used his new law. His powerful organism worn out by disease, strain, and an irregular life, he died on February 8, 1725, without designating a successor to his gloriously victorious, multinational, modernizing, shaken, and exhausted empire.

## Evaluations of Peter the Great

In his own time and at the time of his death, Peter the Great was compared to Jupiter, Mars, Neptune, and Hercules and to David, Moses, and Samson. Like them, he was said to have brought Russia victory over its enemies and the rule of law and reason. But he also had enemies, as we have seen, who hated what he had done to Russia. Rumors spread and legends grew that the reformer was not a son of Tsar Alexis, but a foreigner who had substituted himself for the true tsar during the latter's journey abroad, that he was an imposter, a usurper, indeed the Antichrist. Peter himself contributed to the polarization of opinion. He too saw things in black and white, hating old Muscovy and believing himself to be the creator of a new Russia. And we must not neglect the dark sides of his rule. In the name of civilization he was intolerant of his critics and did not hesitate to use compulsion and violence to achieve his ends. These too were hallmarks of his reign.

Through most of the eighteenth and nineteenth centuries, Peter was similarly either revered as a bold champion of light against darkness, as an enlightened ruler who had replaced savagery with civilization, or as a crude tyrant who undermined and perverted Russia's distinct national spirit and imported the alien spirit of Western rationalism. It took a sensitive poet like Alexander Pushkin to draw a balance, emphasizing the necessity and the greatness of Peter's reforms, while at the same time lamenting their human cost.

In many ways, St. Petersburg was a fitting symbol of these contradictions. It was an act of as much symbolic as practical significance that Peter was determined to convert borderland marshes, won in war, into a brilliant Western imperial capital. To do so, he brought to St. Petersburg thousands of serfs, convicts, and war prisoners to drain the marshes, drive oak piles into the ground, and construct a great city. The terribly high death toll from overwork and illness, probably greater than the losses at Poltava, became a lasting part of the legend of the city: in the words of the historian and poet Nikolai Karamzin, writing in 1811, "Petersburg was founded upon tears and corpses." In Russian cultural history, Petersburg became the embodiment of contradiction: a place of modern progress and modern suffering, of civilization and its discontents, of authoritarian power and personal freedom, of elegant architecture and decrepit slums, of bright open spaces and fog and dirt.

Historians have often echoed these old debates about Peter the Great, though documentary research and more modern notions of the historian's craft have allowed for more balanced and complex interpretations. Without minimizing the reformer's accomplishments, Russian historians of the late nineteenth century like Sergei Soloviev and Vasily Kliuchevsky already did much to demythologize Peter, though both admired Peter's achievements and understood the necessity of modernization. Later historians would continue the effort to historicize Peter's rule. Thus, since Soloviev, scholars have deemphasized Peter's originality, recognizing the many close connections between Peter the Great and the Muscovite past. In foreign policy and social policy, for example, relatively little changed. And, of course, the central issue, the process of Westernization, had begun long before the reformer and had gathered momentum rapidly in the seventeenth century. Historians have also recognized the often chaotic, piecemeal, and ineffective side of Peter's reforming drive, as well as the brutality, violence, and suffering brought by change, however necessary change might have been. The most recent scholarship has tended to deepen complexity and move further away from the long tradition of either adulating or vilifying Peter. Studies have shown, for example, the emperor's use of religion to legitimize his rule, the complex meanings of court ritual and ceremony, and his dependence on networks of both established and new elites.

Quite possibly Russia was destined to be Westernized, but Peter the Great cannot be denied the role of the chief executor of this fate. Or, as one modern scholar has written, Peter the Great marked Russia's transition from an unconscious to a conscious following of its historical path. At the very least the emperor's reign brought a tremendous speeding up of the process of Westernization and put this path in the hands of state policy and control, where formerly individual choice and chance had prevailed. However, since Peter the Great was practical, and a utilitarian, it may be better to conclude this discussion with a more mundane assessment of Peter's impact, rather than with a discussion of historical destiny. Mikhail Pogodin, a nineteenth-century conservative historian and journalist, wrote:

> Yes, Peter the Great did much for Russia. One looks and one does not believe it, one keeps adding and one cannot reach the sum. We cannot open our eyes, cannot make a move, cannot turn in any direction without encountering him everywhere, at home, in the streets, in church, in school, in court, in the regiment, at a promenade—it is always he, always he, every day, every minute, at every step!

> We wake up. What day is it today? January 1, 1841—Peter the Great ordered us to count years from the birth of Christ; Peter the Great ordered us to count the months from January.

> It is time to dress—our clothing is made according to the fashion established by Peter the First, our uniform according to his model. The cloth is woven in a factory which he created; the wool is shorn from the sheep which he started to raise.

> A book strikes our eyes—Peter the Great introduced this script and himself cut out the letters. You begin to read it—this language became a written language, a literary language, at the time of Peter the First, superseding the earlier church language.

> Newspapers are brought in—Peter the Great introduced them.

You must buy different things—they all, from the silk neckerchief to the sole of your shoe, will remind you of Peter the Great; some were ordered by him, others were brought into use or improved by him, carried on his ships, into his harbors, on his canals, on his roads.

At dinner, all the courses, from salted herring, through potatoes which he ordered grown, to wine made from grapes which he began to cultivate, will speak to you of Peter the Great.

After dinner you drive out for a visit—this is an *assemblée* of Peter the Great. You meet the ladies there—they were admitted into masculine company by order of Peter the Great.

Let us go to the university—the first secular school was founded by Peter the Great.

You receive a rank—according to Peter the Great's Table of Ranks.

The rank gives me gentry status—Peter the Great so arranged it.

I must file a complaint—Peter the Great prescribed its form. It will be received—in front of Peter the Great's mirror of justice. It will be acted upon—on the basis of the General Reglament.

You decide to travel abroad—following the example of Peter the Great; you will be received well—Peter the Great placed Russia among the European states and began to instill respect for her; and so on, and so on, and so on.

# CHAPTER 21

# Russian History from Peter the Great to Catherine the Great: The Reigns of Catherine I, 1725–27, Peter II, 1727–30, Anne, 1730–40, Ivan VI, 1740–41, Elizabeth, 1741–62, and Peter III, 1762

She came, the God-chosen autocrat, who has adorned the All-Russian throne with Her kindness and Her beauty. And all wish, with one voice and one heart, with the grace and blessing of God, that She rule Her fatherland for innumerable years in endless joy and eternal prosperity.

ARCHBISHOP AMBROSII OF NOVGOROD, ORATION ON
EMPRESS ELIZABETH'S VISIT TO MOSCOW, 1742

The period between the death of Peter the Great and the accession of Catherine the Great, 1725 to 1762, has been considered by some historians as an era of shallowness, confusion, and decay, whereas others attribute to it much of Russia's spiritual growth and political advancement. The truth seems to lie on both sides. Rapid and violent changes, as under Peter, were discontinued, but slowly the process of Westernization went on, gaining in depth and leading to a better proportion between the ambitions and the actual potentialities of the country.

WALTER KIRCHNER

Russian history from the death of Peter the Great to the accession of Catherine the Great has been undeservedly neglected. Moreover, the treatments available turn out not infrequently to be superficial in nature and derisive in tone. Sandwiched between two celebrated reigns, this period—"when lovers ruled Russia," to quote one writer—offers little to impress, dazzle, or inspire. Rather it appears to be taken up with a continuous struggle of unfit candidates for the crown, with the constant rise and fall of their equally deplorable favorites, with court intrigues of every sort, with Biron's police terror, Elizabeth's absorption in French fashions, and Peter III's imbecility. In the course of thirty-seven years Russia had, sardonic commentators remark, six autocrats: three women, a boy of twelve, an infant, and a mental weakling.

And yet, Westernization continued to spread into broader areas of Russian life. Foreign relations brought Russia into an ever-closer relationship with other European powers. And the gentry were able to increase their advantages and free themselves from the mandate of state service. Some recent historians have argued that the role of women as rulers in the eighteenth century—after Peter the Great's death in 1725, women ruled for all but seven of the remaining years of the century—brought a new spirit to Russian political life marked by at least the expectation that power should be "gracious" and "loving" and bring "happiness" to the country. Of course, the reason women sat on the Russian throne reflected other conditions as well, including Peter the Great's notion that a monarch should be able to choose a successor based on merit and reason; the power and influence of court nobles and aristocratic guards' regiments, who likely thought that women would be more pliable; and, not least, a shortage of adult, able, and healthy male successors.

## Catherine I. Peter II

When the first emperor died without naming his successor several candidates for the throne emerged. The dominant two were Peter, Alexis's son and Peter the Great's grandson, and Catherine, Peter the Great's second wife. The deceased sovereign's daughters, Anne and Elizabeth, and his nieces, daughters of his half-brother Tsar Ivan V, Catherine and Anne, appeared as more remote possibilities at the time, although before very long two of them were to rule Russia, while descendants of the other two also occupied the throne. Peter was the only direct male heir and thus the logical successor to his grandfather. He had the support of the old nobility, including several of their number prominent in the first emperor's reign. Catherine, who had been crowned empress in a special ceremony in 1724—in the opinion of some, a clear indication of Peter the Great's intentions with regard to succession—possessed the backing of "the new men," such as Iaguzhinsky and especially Menshikov, who had risen with the reforms and dreaded everything connected with Peter's son Alexis and old Muscovy. The Preobrazhenskii and Semenovskii guard regiments decided the issue by demonstrating in favor of the empress. Opposition to her collapsed, and the dignitaries of the state proclaimed Catherine the sovereign of Russia, "according to the desire of Peter the Great." The guards, as we shall see, were subsequently to play a decisive role in determining who ruled Russia on more than one occasion.

Catherine's reign, during which Menshikov played the leading role in the government, lasted only two years and three months. The empress's most important act was probably the creation, in February 1726, of the Supreme Privy, or Secret, Council to deal with "matters of exceptional significance." The six members of the council, Menshikov and five others, became in effect constant advisers and in a sense associates of the monarch, a departure from Peter the Great's administrative organization and practice. Catherine I died in 1727, having appointed young Peter to succeed her and nominated as regent the Supreme Privy Council, to which Anne and Elizabeth, her daughters and the new ruler's aunts, were added.

Peter II, not yet twelve when he became emperor, fell into the hands of Menshikov, who even transferred the monarch from the palace to his residence and betrothed him to his daughter. But Peter II did not like Menshikov; he placed his confidence in young Prince Ivan Dolgoruky. The Dolgoruky family used this opportunity to have Menshikov arrested. The once all-powerful favorite and the closest assistant of Peter the Great died some two years later in exile in northern Siberia, and the Dolgorukys replaced him at the court and in the government. Two members of that family sat in the Supreme Privy Council, and late in 1729 the engagement of Peter II to a princess Dolgorukaia was officially announced. But again the picture changed suddenly and drastically. Early in 1730, before the marriage could take place and when Peter II was not quite fifteen years old, he died of smallpox.

## Anne. Ivan VI

The young emperor had designated no successor. Moreover, with his death the male line of the Romanovs came to an end. In the disturbed and complicated deliberations which ensued, the advice of Prince Dmitrii Golitsyn to offer the throne to Anne, daughter of Ivan V and childless widow of the Duke of Courland, prevailed in the Supreme Privy Council and with other state dignitaries. Anne appeared to be weak and innocuous, and thus likely to leave power in the hands of the aristocratic clique. Moreover, the Supreme Privy Council, acting on its own, invited Anne to reign only under certain rigid and highly restrictive conditions. The would-be empress had to promise not to marry and not to appoint a successor. The Supreme Privy Council was to retain a membership of eight and to control state affairs: the new sovereign could not without its approval declare war or make peace, levy taxes or commit state funds, grant or confiscate estates, or appoint anyone to a rank higher than that of colonel. The guards as well as all other armed forces were to be under the jurisdiction of the Supreme Privy Council, not of the empress. These drastic conditions, which had no precedent in Russian history, stood poles apart from Peter the Great's view of the position and function of the monarch and his translation of this view into practice. But Anne, who had very little to lose, accepted the limitations, thus establishing constitutional rule in Russia.

Russian constitutionalism, however, proved to be extremely short-lived. Because the Supreme Privy Council had acted in its narrow and exclusive interest, tension ran high among the gentry. Some critics spoke and wrote of extending political advantages to the entire gentry, while others simply denounced the proceedings. Anne used a demonstration by the guards and other members of the gentry, shortly after her arrival, to tear up the conditions she had accepted, asserting that she had thought them to represent the desires of her subjects, whereas they turned out to be the stratagem of a selfish cabal. And she abolished the Supreme Privy Council. Autocracy came back into its own.

Empress Anne's ten-year reign left a bitter memory. Traditionally, it has been presented as a period of cruel and stupid rule by individual Germans and even "the German party" in Russia. And while this interpretation should not be overdone—for, after all, the 1730s, in foreign policy, in social legislation, and in other major respects constituted an integral part of the Russian evolution in the eighteenth century rather than anything specifically German—it remains true that Anne brought with her from Courland a band of favorites, and that in general she patronized Germans as well as other foreigners and distrusted the Russian high nobility, whose influence she did all she could to restrict. Anne was disinclined to take an active role in government and so relied on a close circle of officials and advisors.

Certain departments, such as the foreign office with Ostermann at the head and the army with Münnich, profited from able German leadership of the Petrine vintage; but many new favorites had no qualifications for their positions, acted simply in their personal interest, and buttressed their remarkable ignorance of Russia with their disdain for everything Russian. Ernst-Johann Biron, the empress's lover from Courland, acquired the highest honors and emoluments and became the most hated figure and symbol of the reign. *Bironovshchina*—that is, Bironism—refers especially to the police persecution and political terror during the reign, which led to the execution of several thousand people and to the exile of some 20,000 or 30,000 to Siberia. Although many of the victims were Old Believers and even common criminals rather than political opponents, and although the cruelty of Biron and his associates perhaps should not be considered exceptional for the age, the persecutions excited the popular imagination and made the reign compare unfavorably, for example, with the rule of Elizabeth that was to follow it. It might be added that after the abolition of the Supreme Privy Council Anne did not restore the Senate to its former importance as the superior governing institution but proceeded to rely on a cabinet of two or three members to take charge of state affairs.

Anne died in the autumn of 1740. Shortly before her death she had nominated a two-month-old infant, Ivan, to be her successor on the throne. Ivan was a great-grandson of Ivan V and a grandson of Anne's elder sister, Catherine, who in 1716 had married the Duke of Mecklenburg, Charles Leopold. A daughter from this marriage, Anna Leopoldovna, became the wife of Duke Anthony Ulric of Brunswick-Bevern-Lüneburg. The new emperor was the child of Anna Leopoldovna and Anthony Ulric. But, although both of his parents resided at the Russian court, Empress Anne appointed Biron as regent. The arrangement failed to last. First, within a month Biron was overthrown by Münnich and Anna Leopoldovna became regent. Then, in another year, late in 1741, Ivan VI, Anna Leopoldovna, and the entire "German party" were tumbled from authority and power. This last coup was executed by the guards led by Peter the Great's daughter Elizabeth, who then ascended the throne as Empress Elizabeth of Russia.

## Elizabeth. Peter III

Just as Anne and her reign have been excessively blamed in Russian historiography, Elizabeth has received more than her fair share of praise, though this has echoed in part the adulation she received in her own day. Beautiful, young, and charming, the new monarch symbolized to many contemporaries and later commentators the end of the brutal and scandalous "foreign" domination associated with Biron and even, to an extent, a return to the glorious days of Peter the Great, an association that the empress herself stressed as much as she could. Elizabeth seemed to promise respect for Russians and the Russian elite and a new gentleness in Russian politics. In a way, perhaps, she was too charming: unlike her energetic and forceful father, Empress Elizabeth, though by no means stupid, was notoriously indolent, undisciplined, and pleasure-loving.

Elizabeth, or at least her administration, did much to continue Peter the Great's legacy. The Senate was restored to its former authority and her reign saw further rationalization of government institutions. Her government sought to stimulate the economy by abolishing most domestic custom barriers and encouraging private entrepreneurship. She supported artistic and cultural development, including the establishment of the University of Moscow. And, in foreign policy, her armies demonstrated Russia's status as a European great power by helping to defeat Prussia as part of the Seven Years' War and even briefly occupying Berlin. In social life, the abolition of capital punishment was a striking development in light of the practices of Anne's government but also much Russian tradition, though it pales beside the enormous, persistent, and, in fact, growing evil of serfdom.

The rise in public political discourse of imagery of the ruler as a kind and loving monarch (for all the adulation of Peter the Great, no one in his time would have called him kind) who brings joy and happiness to the nation was indeed something new and significant, though more a sign of changing political ideology than changing political practice. In part, this new standard grew out of comparison with the Bironovshchina that Elizabeth's coup ended. But it was also an echo of evolving European notions of enlightened authority. Elizabeth was continually praised, not only as a "native" empress who had overthrown the Germans, but as a ruler who would replace all the "oppressions and insults" of the old with a new "age of gold." As the historians Stephen Baehr and Richard Wortman have shown, a new "iconography of happiness" became widespread in political rituals, texts, and sermons. Elizabeth was continually portrayed as bringing happiness and pleasure to her subjects, who were said to love her for her commitment to this national good.

Elizabeth. Portraits invariably emphasized Elizabeth's femininity and gentleness, a
key part of her public image.   *(Tsarstvuiushchii dom Romanovykh)*

This cult of pleasure and love was echoed, in a quite different but not irrel-
evant way, in Elizabeth's private life. Without a husband, she went through a
succession of lovers, all very visible and public. Indeed, this was treated as a
matter of right and of the value she placed on pleasure. Generally, Elizabeth
relied extensively on favorites and their relatives in her administration, as
Empress Anne had, though Elizabeth's group proved on the whole more competent and attractive than the one sponsored by Empress Anne.

Alexei Razumovsky, who may have been morganatically married to
Elizabeth, was closest to the monarch. He was a simple cossack who had
tended the village flock in his native Ukraine. Because of his magnificent
voice, the future favorite was brought to the court as a singer. Elizabeth
fell in love with him, and her attachment lasted until her death. Yet, while
Razumovsky became a very close associate, he showed little interest in state

affairs, preferring the acquiring of titles and decorations to the daily work of government. By contrast, the Shuvalovs, the brothers Petr and Alexander and their cousin Ivan, were energetic and influential.

Ivan Shuvalov, the empress's favorite, left behind him an almost unique reputation for integrity and kindness, for refusing honors and rewards, and for selfless service in several capacities, especially in promoting enlightenment in Russia. The University of Moscow, which he founded, remains his lasting monument. Petr Shuvalov was made Count by the empress—a title Ivan Shuvalov refused—and used his strong position at the court to have a hand in every kind of state business, in particular in financial and economic matters and in the military establishment. Able, but shamelessly corrupt and cynical, Petr Shuvalov contributed much to the ruinous financial policy of the reign and has been credited with saying that debased coinage would be less of a load to carry and that the tax on vodka suited a time of distress because people would then want to get drunk.

Elizabeth's own extravagant love of beauty contributed to the state's financial crisis. She commissioned the building of the extremely expensive Winter Palace, and the acquisition of, reportedly, 15, 000 dresses added greatly to the financial crisis. A French milliner finally refused further credit to the Russian empress! Of much more importance is the fact that the financial chaos, together with the fundamental and overwhelming burden of serfdom, led to the flight and uprisings of peasants that became characteristic of the age.

The German orientation that had been overthrown by Elizabeth—her circle, by the way, was more attracted to French culture and to France—came back with a vengeance, if only briefly, when Peter III ascended the throne. When Elizabeth died in late 1761 or early 1762—depending on whether we use the Russian or European calendars—Peter, Duke of Holstein-Gottorp, who had been nominated by the empress as her successor as early as 1742, became Emperor Peter III. The new ruler was a son of Elizabeth's older sister, Anne—therefore a grandson of Peter the Great—and of Charles Frederick, Duke of Holstein-Gottorp. Having lost his mother in infancy and his father when a boy, Peter was brought up first with the view of succeeding to the Swedish throne, for his father was a son of Charles XII's sister. After Elizabeth's decision, he was educated to succeed to the throne of the Romanovs. Although he lived in Russia from the age of fourteen, Peter III never adjusted to his new country. Extremely limited mentally, as well as crude and violent in his behavior, he continued to fear and despise Russia and the Russians while he held up Prussia, and in particular Frederick II, as his ideal. His reign of several months, best remembered in the long run for the law abolishing the compulsory state service of the gentry, impressed many of his contemporaries as a violent attack on everything Russian and a deliberate sacrifice of Russian interests to those of Prussia. While not given to political persecution and in fact willing to sign a law abolishing the security police, the new emperor threatened to disband the guards, and even demanded that icons be withdrawn from churches and that Russian priests dress like Lutheran pastors, both of which orders the Holy Synod did not dare execute. In foreign policy Peter III's admiration for

Peter III. Even official portraits seem to hint at Peter's notorious arrogance and boorishness.   (Brikner, *Illustrirovannaia istoriia Ekateriny vtoroi*)

Frederick the Great led to the withdrawal of Russia from the Seven Years' War, an act that probably saved Prussia from a crushing defeat and deprived Russia of great potential gains. Indeed, the Russian emperor refused to accept even what Frederick the Great was willing to give him for withdrawing and proceeded to make an alliance with the Prussian king.

While Peter III rapidly made enemies, his wife Catherine, who had married him in 1745 and who was originally a princess of the small German principality of Anhalt-Zerbst, behaved with far greater intelligence and understanding. Isolated and threatened by her boorish husband, who had a series of love affairs and wanted to marry one of his favorites, she adapted herself to her difficult environment, learned much about the government and the country, and found supporters. In mid-summer 1762 Catherine profited from the general dissatisfaction with Peter III to lead the guards in another palace revolution. The emperor was easily deposed and shortly after killed, very possibly by one of the leaders of the insurrection, Alexei Orlov, in a drunken argument. Catherine became empress, bypassing her son Paul, born in 1754 during her marriage with Peter III, who was proclaimed merely heir to the throne. Although the coup of 1762 appeared to be simply another in a protracted sequence of overturns characteristic of Russian history in the eighteenth century, and although Catherine's chances of securing her power seemed, if anything, less promising than those of a number of her immediate predecessors, in fact her initial success marked the beginning of a long and celebrated reign.

## The Gains of the Gentry and the Growth of Serfdom

While rulers changed rapidly and favorites constantly rose and fell in Russia between 1725 and 1762, basic social processes went on. Most important was the growth of the power and standing of the gentry together with its complementary process, a further deterioration in the position of the serfs. As we know, Peter the Great's insistence that only one son inherit his father's estate could hardly be enforced even in the reformer's reign and was formally repealed in 1731. Empress Anne began giving away state lands to her gentry supporters on a large scale, the peasants on the lands becoming serfs, and Elizabeth enthusiastically continued the practice. These grants were no longer connected to service obligations.

In 1731 Empress Anne opened a cadet school for the gentry in St. Petersburg. Graduates of this school could become officers without serving in the lower ranks, a privilege directly opposed to Peter the Great's intentions and practice. As the century progressed the gentry came to rely increasingly on such cadet schools for both education and advancement in service. Also to their advantage was the Gentry Bank established by Empress Elizabeth in St. Petersburg, with a branch in Moscow, to supply the landlords with credit at a moderate rate of interest. The gentry became increasingly class-conscious and exclusive. An order of 1746 forbade all but the gentry to acquire "men and peasants with and without land." In 1758 the members of other classes who owned serfs were required to sell them. A Senate decision of 1756 affirmed that only those who proved their gentry origin could be entered into gentry registers, while decisions in the years 1758–60 in effect eliminated the opportunity to obtain hereditary gentry status through state service, thus destroying another one of Peter the Great's characteristic arrangements. At the same time "personal," or nonhereditary, members of the class came to be rigidly restricted in their gentry rights.

The most significant evolution took place in regard to the service obligations of the gentry to the state. In 1736 this service, hitherto termless, was limited to twenty-five years––the gentry themselves had asked for twenty years––with a further provision exempting one son from service so he could manage the estates. Immediately following the publication of the law and in subsequent decades, many members of the gentry left service to return to their landholdings. Moreover, some landlords managed to be entered in regimental service early in their lives. Finally, on February 18, 1762, in the reign of Peter III, compulsory gentry service was abolished. Henceforth members of the gentry could serve the state, or not serve it, at will, and they could even serve foreign governments abroad instead, if they so desired. The edict also impressed upon the gentry the importance of education and proper care of their estates, in other words, to be of use even when not serving the government directly.

The law of 1762 has attracted much attention from historians. To many older scholars, exemplified by Kliuchevsky, it undermined the basic structure of Russian society, in which everyone served: the serfs served the landlords, the landlords served the state. In equity the repeal of compulsory gentry service should have been followed promptly by the emancipation of the serfs. Yet—again to cite Kliuchevsky—although the abolition of serfdom did take place on the following day, the nineteenth of February, that day came ninety-nine years later. The serfs themselves, it would seem, shared the feeling that an injustice had been committed, for the demand for freedom of the peasants, to follow the freedom of the gentry, became a recurrent motif of their uprisings. By contrast, some specialists have emphasized the positive results of the law of 1762: it represented the acquisition of an essential independence from the state by at least one class of Russian society, and thus the first crucial step taken by Russia on the road to liberalism; besides, it contributed to the growth of a rich gentry culture and, beyond that, to the emergence of the intelligentsia.

As the gentry rose, the serfs sank to a greater depth of misery. In the reign of Peter II they were already prohibited from volunteering for military service and thus escaping their condition. By a series of laws under Empress Anne peasants were forbidden to buy real estate or mills, establish factories, or become parties to government leases and contracts. Later, in the time of Elizabeth, serfs were ordered to obtain their master's permission before assuming financial obligations. Especially following the law of 1731, landlords acquired increasing financial control over their serfs, for whose taxes they were held responsible. After 1736 serfs had to receive the permission of their masters before they could leave for temporary employment elsewhere. Landlords obtained further the right to transfer serfs from one estate to another and, by one of Elizabeth's laws, even to exile delinquent serfs to Siberia and to fetch them back, while the government included these exiles in the number of recruits required from a given estate. The criminal code of 1754 listed serfs only under the heading of property of the gentry. Russian serfdom, although never quite the same as slavery and in the Russian case not concerned with race or ethnicity, came to approximate it closely.

## The Foreign Policy of Russia from Peter to Catherine

Russian foreign policy from Peter the Great to Catherine the Great followed certain clearly established lines. The first emperor, as we know, brought Russia forcefully into the community of European nations as a major power that was concerned with the affairs of the continent at large, not, as formerly, merely with the activities of its neighbors, such as Turkey, Poland, and Sweden. From the time of Peter the Great, permanent—rather than only occasional—representatives were exchanged between Russia and other leading European states.

As Michael Karpovich, to mention one historian, has pointed out, Russian foreign policy from 1726 to 1762, and immediately before and after, approached what has been called the checkerboard system: Russia was to a considerable degree an enemy of its neighbors and a friend of its neighbors' neighbors, with other relations affected by this basic pattern. France, for example, consistently remained an antagonist of Russia, because in its struggle for the mastery of the continent it relied on Turkey, Poland, and Sweden to envelop and weaken its arch-enemy, the Habsburgs. Russia, of course, had repeatedly fought against the three eastern European allies of France.

Austria, ruled by the Habsburgs, stood out, by contrast, as the most reliable Russian ally. The two states shared hostility toward France, and, more importantly for Russia, also toward Turkey and Sweden, which, beginning with its major intervention in the Thirty Years' War, acted repeatedly in Germany against the interests of the Habsburgs. In Poland also both Russia and Austria found themselves opposed to the French party. The first alliance between these two eastern European monarchies was signed in 1726, and it remained, with certain exceptions, a cornerstone of Russian foreign policy until the Crimean War in the mid-nineteenth century. In Poland, Russia and Austria also sought to displace French influence. As the Polish-Lithuanian Commonwealth deteriorated, Russia steadily increased its influence there. Indeed, some historians have described the power of Russia in Poland by the middle of the eighteenth century as equivalent to that of a protectorate.

Prussia, the other leading German power, represented a threat to Russia rather than a potential ally. Prussia's rise to great power rank under Frederick the Great after 1740, together with Russia's rise under Peter the Great, which had just preceded it, upset the political equilibrium in Europe. Count Alexei Bestuzhev-Riumin was one of the first continental statesmen to point to the Prussian menace. He worried especially about the Russian position on the Baltic, called Frederick the Great "the sudden prince," and spoke in a typically eighteenth-century doctrinaire manner of Russia's "natural friends," Austria and Great Britain, and its "natural enemies," France and Prussia. The hostile Russian attitude toward Prussia lasted, with some interruptions, until the time of Catherine the Great and the partitions of Poland, which satisfied both monarchies and brought them together.

In the period under consideration, Great Britain could well be called a "natural friend" of Russia. After the scare occasioned by the achievements of Peter the Great and his navy, no serious conflicts arose between the two until the last part of the century. On the contrary, Great Britain valued Russia both as a counterweight to France and as a trading partner from which it obtained raw materials, including naval stores, in exchange for manufactured goods.

Thus it is no surprise that Russia concluded its first modern commercial treaty with Great Britain.

In line with its interests and alliances, Russia participated in five wars between 1725 and 1762. In 1733–35 Russia and Austria fought against France in the War of the Polish Succession, which resulted in the defeat of the French candidate Stanislaw Leszczynski and the coronation of Augustus II's son as Augustus III of Poland. In 1736–39 Russia, again allied to Austria, waged a war against Turkey who was supported by France. Münnich and other Russian commanders scored remarkable victories over the Ottoman forces. However, because of Austrian defeats and French mediation, Russia, after losing approximately 100,000 men, gained very little according to the provisions of the Treaty of Belgrade: a section of the steppe between the Donets and the Bug, and the right to retain Azov, captured during the war, on condition of razing its fortifications and promising not to build a fleet on the Black Sea. In 1741–43, Russia, supported by Austria, fought Sweden, who was supported by France. Sweden started the war to seek revenge, but was defeated, and by the Treaty of Åbo ceded some additional Finnish territory to Russia.

In its new role as a great power Russia also became involved in wars fought away from its borders over issues not immediately related to Russian interests. The most important was Russian intervention in the Seven Years' War, 1756–63, fought again largely over Silesia. At one point, in 1760, Russian troops even briefly held Berlin. Moreover, Russia and its allies managed to drive Prussia to the brink of collapse. Only the death of Empress Elizabeth early in 1762, and the accession to the throne of Peter III, who admired Frederick the Great, saved the Prussian king. Russia withdrew without any compensation from the war and made an alliance with Prussia, which in turn was discontinued when Catherine the Great replaced Peter III.

Although Russian foreign policy between 1725 and 1762 has been severely criticized for its cost in men and money, its meddling in European affairs that had no immediate bearing on Russia, and its alleged sacrifice of national interests to those either of Austria or of the "German party" at home, these criticisms on the whole are not convincing. In its new role Russia could hardly disengage itself from major European affairs and conflicts. In general Russian diplomats successfully pursued the interests of their country, and the wars themselves brought notable gains, for example, the strengthening of the Russian position in Poland and the defeat of the Swedish challenge, even though Peter III did write off in a fantastic manner the opportunities produced by the Seven Years' War. Catherine the Great would continue the basic policies of her predecessors. Militarily the Russians acquitted themselves well. The Russian army, reorganized, improved, and tempered in the wars, scored its first major victories against Turkey in 1736–39, and played its first major part in the heart of Europe in the course of the Seven Years' War. Such famous commanders as [Petr] Rumiantsev and Alexander Suvorov began their careers in this interim period between two celebrated reigns.

# CHAPTER 22

# The Reigns of Catherine the Great, 1762–96, and Paul, 1796–1801

Russia is a European State...The Sovereign is absolute, for no authority but the power centered in his single person can act with the vigor proportionate to the extent of such a vast dominion...All other forms of government whatsoever would not only have been prejudicial to Russia, but would have proved its entire ruin...What is the true goal of monarchy? Not to deprive people of their natural liberty but to correct their actions in order to attain the supreme good. Therefore the form of government that best attains this goal, and at the same time sets fewer limits than others on natural liberty, is the one coinciding best with the views and purposes of rational creatures...God preserve that after this legislation, no nation will be more just and consequently flourish more...such that the people of Russia, as human beings, will be rendered the most happy of any nation on earth.

CATHERINE THE GREAT, FROM HER *INSTRUCTION (NAKAZ)*

Catherine the Great was thirty-three years old when she ascended the Russian throne. She had acquired considerable education and experience. Born a princess in the small German principality of Anhalt-Zerbst, the future empress of Russia grew up in modest but cultured surroundings. The court in Anhalt-Zerbst, like many other European courts in the eighteenth century, was strongly influenced by French culture, and Catherine started reading French books in childhood. In 1744, at the age of fifteen, she came to Russia to marry Peter of Holstein-Gottorp and prepare herself to be the wife of a Russian sovereign.

The years from 1744 to 1762 were hard on Catherine. Peter proved to be a miserable husband, while the German princess's position at the imperial court could be fairly described as isolated and even precarious. To add to Catherine's difficulties, her mother was discovered to be Frederick the Great's

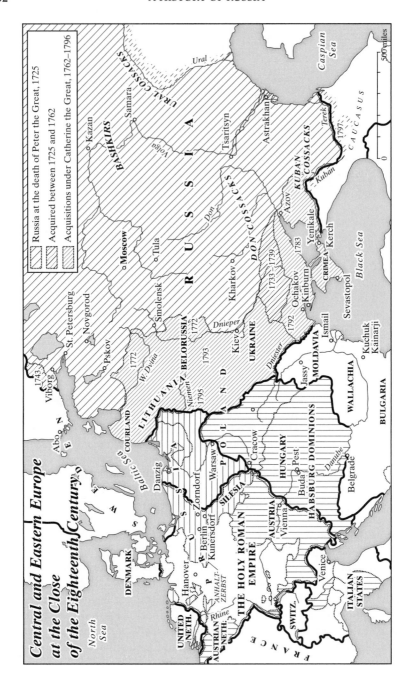

*Central and Eastern Europe at the Close of the Eighteenth Century*

agent and had to leave Russia. Yet the future empress accomplished much more than merely surviving at court. In addition to becoming Orthodox in order to marry Peter, she proceeded to learn Russian language and literature well and to obtain some knowledge of her new country. Simultaneously she turned to the writings of the *philosophes*, Voltaire, Montesquieu, and others, for which she had been prepared by her earlier grounding in French literature. As we shall see, Catherine the Great's interest in the Enlightenment was to constitute an important aspect of her reign. The young princess adapted herself skillfully to the new environment, made friends, and won a measure of affection and popularity in court circles. While simulating innocence and submissiveness, she participated in political intrigues and plots, carefully covering up her tracks, however, until she led the successful coup in mid-summer 1762, which brought deposition and death to her husband and made her Empress Catherine II.

Catherine the Great's personality and character impressed many of her contemporaries as well as later commentators. The empress possessed high intelligence, a natural ability to administer and govern, a remarkable practical sense, energy to spare, and an iron will. Along with her determination went courage and optimism: Catherine believed that she could prevail over all obstacles, and more often than not events proved her right. Self-control, skill in discussion and propaganda, and a clever handling of men and circumstances to serve her ends were additional assets of that unusual monarch. The empress herself asserted that it was ambition that sustained her. The historian can agree, provided that ambition is understood not merely as a desire to snatch the crown, or attain glory by success in war, or gain the admiration of the *philosophes*, but as a constant, urgent drive to excel in everything and bring everything under one's control. For the first time since Peter the Great, Russia acquired a sovereign who worked day and night, paying personal attention to all kinds of matters, great and small.

Yet, together with her formidable virtues, Catherine the Great had certain weaknesses. Indeed the two were intrinsically linked. Determination easily became ruthlessness, ambition fed vanity just as vanity fed ambition, skill in propaganda would not stop short of asserting lies. Foreign observers often noted her insatiable desire to impress others, both with her physical presence and her intellect. Many believed she always played a part. Ultimately, it has been argued, she was a supreme egoist, with few beliefs or standards of value outside her own overpowering wishes. Her relationship to the Enlightenment may be the most controversial subject in the historiography of her reign: though Catherine often declared adherence to the principles of the Age of Reason, many historians have argued that it is difficult to be certain exactly what the empress actually believed, or whether she believed anything. Even Catherine II's admirers sometimes noticed that she lacked something, call it charity, mercy, or human sympathy. Typical of the time, contemporaries sometimes viewed her traits in terms of assumptions about gender: she combined manly strength and obstinacy with feminine vanity and love of flattery.

Catherine II leading the troops, on June 29, 1762, against her husband
Peter III. Catherine is dressed in male military attire (here as a colonel in the
Preobrazhensky guard), with saber unsheathed, riding her beloved stallion Brilliant
(although the gender of the horse has been obscured in this etching of a famous
painting).   (Brikner, *Illiustrirovannaia istoriia Ekateriny vtoroi*)

Incidentally, some thought that she looked her best in masculine attire, which
she occasionally chose to wear.

She was also said to have a feminine "propensity to voluptuousness,"
in the words of the British ambassador. Catherine the Great's notorious love
affairs have certainly become one of the lasting memories of her rule in popular imagination. This too, it would seem, reflected her driven, passionate,
and vain personality. It has been suggested that her first lover was forced on
Catherine, so that she would have a son and Russia an heir, and that Paul
resulted from that liaison rather than from the marriage to Peter. In any case,
Catherine soon took matters into her own hands. The empress allegedly had
twenty-one known lovers, the last after she had turned sixty. The favorites

included Grigorii Orlov, an officer of the guards who proved instrumental in elevating Catherine the Great to the throne and whose brother may have killed Peter III; Stanislaw Poniatowski, a Polish nobleman whom the empress made King of Poland; and, most important, Grigorii Potemkin. Potemkin came to occupy a unique position both in the Russian government, to the extent that he can be considered the foremost statesman of the reign, and in the empress's private life. Some specialists believe he married her; he certainly continued to be influential after the rise of other favorites.

## The First Years of the Reign. The Legislative Commission

Catherine II had to behave carefully during her first years on the throne. Brought to power by a palace revolution and without a legal title to the crown, the empress had the enthusiastic support of guardsmen such as the Orlov brothers, but otherwise little backing. Elder statesmen looked at her with some suspicion. There persisted the possibility that another turn of fortune would make her son Paul sovereign and demote Catherine to the position of regent or even eliminate her altogether. In addition, she was threatened by some early crises in her reign: a failed attempt in 1764 to liberate Ivan VI from his confinement in the Schlüsselburg fortress, which ended in Ivan's guards murdering him and the later execution of the conspirator, and a rebellion by some Church leaders in 1763–64 when Catherine secularized Church lands. But Catherine II gradually consolidated her position. She distributed honors and rewards on a large scale, in particular state lands with peasants, who thus became serfs. She traveled widely all over Russia, reviving Peter the Great's practice, both to learn more about the country and to win popularity. She selected her advisers carefully and well. Time itself worked for the empress: with the passage of years memories of the coup of 1762 faded, and the very fact that Catherine II continued to occupy the throne gave the reign a certain legitimacy.

In late 1766 Catherine felt ready to introduce into Russia important changes based on the precepts of the Enlightenment, and for that purpose she called the Legislative Commission. The aim of the Commission was to codify laws, a task last accomplished in 1649, before the Westernization of the country. Moreover, Catherine the Great believed that the work of the Commission would go a long way toward rationalizing and modernizing Russian law and life. In preparation for the Commission, Catherine drafted a remarkable document to guide the discussions of the delegates, her lengthy *Instruction*, or *Nakaz*, in which she laid out her vision of how Russia should be governed and how society should be organized. The text, composed by Catherine personally over a period of eighteen months, drew heavily on her favorite reading, especially Montesquieu's *Spirit of the Laws* (1748), which the empress referred to as her prayer book and used for general political principles, and Cesare Beccaria's *On Crimes and Punishments* (1763), which inspired Catherine's thinking about the possibility of a less brutal way to treat criminals. It should be noted that Catherine adapted these works to how she understood Russian conditions. Thus, critics have argued, she abandoned much that was essential in Montesquieu, such as the division of powers, which in Catherine's version was reduced to an administrative arrangement meant to improve the functioning of autocracy. Certainly she had no intention of ending autocracy in Russia. She strongly believed that autocracy was the only feasible form of government for holding together and ensuring the progress of an enormous country like Russia, though central power must be grounded in fundamental laws and the advancement of the "supreme good" if it were not to become tyranny. Of course, this view of government was shared by many Enlightenment thinkers. Likewise, she hesitated to recommend ending serfdom, though she claimed to find it morally offensive. In fact, she had written strong words on the matter for an early draft, but was advised to remove these. The final version of the *Instruction* merely contains a pious wish that masters would not abuse their serfs. As to the influence of Beccaria, Catherine the Great explicitly rejected his ideas of government based on social contract but found very useful his criticisms of arbitrariness and cruelty in penal law. Thus, the *Instruction* denounced capital punishment as well as torture and argued for crime prevention. On the whole, the *Instruction* is a strikingly liberal document, so much so that it was banned in France.

The Legislative Commission, which opened deliberations in the summer of 1767, consisted of 564 deputies, 28 appointed and 536 elected. The appointees represented the state institutions, such as the Senate. The elected deputies comprised delegates from different segments of the population of the empire: 161 from the landed gentry, 208 from the townspeople, 79 from the state peasants, and 88 from the cossacks and national minorities. Yet this numerous gathering—an "all-Russian ethnographic exhibition," to quote Kliuchevsky—excluded large bodies of the Russian people; the serfs, obviously, but also, in line with the secular tendency of the Enlightenment, the clerical class, although the Holy Synod was represented by a single appointed deputy. Delegates received written instructions or mandates from their electorates, including the state peasants, who, together with the cossacks and national minorities, supplied over a thousand such sets of instructions. Taken together, the instructions of 1767 offer the historian insight into the Russian society of the second half of the eighteenth century comparable to that obtainable for France in the famous *cahiers* of 1789. Alexander Kizevetter and other scholars have emphasized the following well-nigh universal characteristics of the instructions: a practical character; a definite acceptance of the existing regime; a desire for decentralization; complaints of unbearable financial demands and, in particular, requests to lower the taxes; and a wish to delineate clearly the rights and the obligations of all classes of society.

The Legislative Commission met for a year and a half, holding 203 sessions; in addition, special committees were set up to prepare the ground for dealing with particular issues. But all this effort came to naught. The commission proved unwieldy, not enough preliminary work had been done, often there seemed to be little connection between the French philosophy of the empress's *Instruction* and Russian reality. Most important, however, the members of the commission split along class lines. For example, gentry delegates argued with merchant representatives over serf ownership and rights to engage in trade and industry. More ominously, gentry deputies clashed with those of the peasant class on the crucial issue of serfdom. No doubt Catherine the Great quickly realized the potential danger of such confrontations. The outbreak of war against Turkey in 1768 provided a good occasion for disbanding the Legislative Commission. Some committees continued to meet for several more years until the Pugachev rebellion, but again without producing any practical results. Still, the abortive convocation of the commission served some purpose: it gave Catherine the Great considerable information about the country and influenced both the general course of her subsequent policy and certain particular reforms.

## Pugachev's Rebellion

Social antagonisms that simmered in the Legislative Commission exploded in the Pugachev rebellion. Emelian Pugachev was a Don cossack, though alienated from the cossack establishment because of their growing acceptance of Moscow's authority. A veteran of several wars, he was then a deserter. In November 1772, he arrived among Ural cossacks and peasants claiming to be tsar Peter III come to deliver them from oppression; many peasants believed Peter had been murdered because he intended to free the serfs. The revolt quickly spread up and down the Ural (then Yaik) River and westward to the Volga basin. At its height the rebellion encompassed a huge territory in eastern European Russia, including such important cities as Kazan. By January 1774, his forces were said by observers to have numbered around 30,000 followers.

The uprising was built upon social discontents that were widespread in imperial Russia. What began as a cossack movement quickly attracted serfs, state peasants, serfs "ascribed" to mines and factories, poorer town dwellers, Old Believers, and non-Russians, including Bashkirs, Tatars, Kalmyks, and others. All these groups felt, in one way or another, that they had lost traditional freedoms. The violent ferocity of the rebellion suggests the intensity of discontent. Looting, pillaging, beatings, and murders of the rich were common when towns were attacked. Assaults on rural estates resulted in the death of a great many landlords.

In speeches and proclamations, "Peter III" promised his followers the end of serfdom (more precisely, that all peasants would work on lands owned by the tsar rather than for private landlords), free use of all the land without payment, exemption from taxes and military recruitment, and, when addressing Old Believers, the return of the old religious traditions ("the old cross and prayers, heads and beards, liberty and freedom"). Religious language pervaded the proclamations, sometimes portraying Pugachev as a savior who had come, in Christ's name, "to free Russia from the yoke of servile labor." Above all, proclamations promised retribution against oppressors, complete freedom, and happiness: "With the extermination of these enemies . . . everyone will be able to enjoy a quiet and peaceful life, which will continue evermore."

The weak military presence in these regions, partly due to a war with Turkey, allowed the movement to grow unopposed. Once well-trained army troops arrived, the rebel army was soon defeated. In late 1774, following the defeat of his troops and his escape back to the Ural area, Pugachev's own men handed him over to government forces. Chained and brought in a cage to Moscow, he was tried and executed in the manner reserved for such social rebels: decapitated and quartered, his head was stuck on a pike and the parts of his body were displayed around the old capital as a warning. A government commission was convened to look into the causes of the rebellion. When Catherine II read Pugachev's proclamations, she dismissed these as promising "castles in the air." As a rationalist, she could not see the power such dreams of revenge, deliverance, and perfect freedom can have to mobilize people. The rebellion was also an influential political shock. While the sharp division of Catherine's reign into early liberal years and a later period of conservatism and reaction appears none too convincing, the revolt, combined with the experience of the Legislative Commission, may have helped disillusion Catherine, revealing the chasm between French philosophy and Russian reality. And although she had never intended to act against the interests of the

The rebel and pretender Pugachev, shown after his capture. (Brikner/*Illiustrirovannaia istoriia Ekateriny vtoroi*)

landed nobility, the rebellion helped cement the alliance between crown and gentry, to make it more explicit and even militant. Yet Catherine the Great was too intelligent to become simply a reactionary. She intended instead to combine oppression and coercion with a measure of reform and a great deal of propaganda.

## Reforms. The Gentry and the Serfs

The new system of local government introduced by Catherine the Great in 1775 was closely related to the frightening collapse of local authority during the Pugachev rebellion, although it was also an attempt to fix the perennial problem that the localities were poorly and inadequately governed. Scholars debate whether the purpose of these reforms was to create a more rational, efficient, and effective structure of local administration—which was certainly needed—or to promote a radically different model of local political life based on principles of participation and autonomy. Both aspects can be seen in the Statute on Provincial Administration of 1775, which distributed administrative powers and functions more clearly but also decentralized control and mandated local gentry participation. Both aspects can also be seen in Catherine's statements about the need for both "orderly" administration and active involvement by her subjects.

The scope of these reforms was great. She reorganized the administrative geography of the country, establishing fifty *gubernii*—"governments" or "provinces"—each subdivided into some ten *uezdy*, or districts. Every province contained between 300,000 and 400,000 inhabitants and every district between 20,000 and 30,000; historical and regional considerations were completely disregarded in the drawing of these "orderly" boundaries. Each province was to be run by an appointed governor and a network of institutions and officials, divided, in principle, by executive, legislative, and judicial functions. Most important, Catherine expected active participation by the local gentry, who were urged to display initiative and energy. To facilitate this gentry involvement, she established noble assemblies and authorized the gentry to elect a marshal of the nobility in each district and, on the recommendation of the governor, a district judge and "land captain." In the towns, the reform similarly stipulated elected mayors and town officials. Catherine also reorganized the provincial court system, explicitly on a class basis, with different courts and procedures for different estates. And she expanded the range of local responsibility. Provincial administrations were told to organize new Bureaus of Public Welfare to establish schools, hospitals, almshouses, madhouses, and other institutions for the poor.

The process of recognizing the corporate identity of the nobility and strengthening the status and role of landlords in Russian life reached its full development in the Charter to the Nobility of 1785. According to the Charter, the "service, fidelity, and zeal" that had defined the history of the Russian nobility as a service class had been transformed "into dignity," into hereditary honor, though it was still expected that nobles would serve the country even if not enrolled in state service. The rights and privileges of this estate reached a highwater mark. The incorporated gentry of a province, through the new Assemblies of the Nobility, could petition the monarch directly "regarding its corporate needs and interests," a right denied the rest of the population. The Charter confirmed earlier privileges and added new ones. Members of the gentry remained free from obligations of personal service and taxation, and they became exempt from corporal punishment. They could lose their gentry standing, estates, or life only by court decision. The property rights of the landlords reached a new high; members of the gentry were recognized as full owners of their estates, without any restriction on the sale or exploitation of land, forests, or mineral resources; in case of forfeiture for crime, an estate remained within the family.

As earlier, a rise in the position of the gentry meant an extension and strengthening of serfdom, a development that characterized Catherine the Great's entire reign. Serfdom spread to new areas, and in particular to Ukraine. Although Catherine's government in essence confirmed an already existing system in Ukraine, it does bear the responsibility for helping to legalize serfdom in Ukraine and for, so to speak, standardizing that evil throughout the empire. A series of laws, fiscal in nature, issued in 1763–83, forbade Ukrainian peasants to leave an estate without the landlord's permission and in general directed them "to remain in their place and calling." Catherine the Great personally extended serfdom on a large scale by her frequent and huge grants of state lands and peasants to her favorites, beginning with the leaders of the coup of 1762. The total number of peasants who thus became serfs has been variously estimated, but it was on the order of several hundred thousand working males—the usual way of counting peasants in imperial Russia—and well over a million persons. The census of 1794–96 indicated this growth of serfdom, with the serfs constituting 53.1 percent of all peasants and 49 percent of the entire population of the country. As to the power of the masters over their serfs, little could be added, but the government nevertheless tried its best: it became easier for the landlords to sentence their peasants to hard labor in Siberia, and they were empowered to fetch the peasants back at will, the serfs were forbidden, under a threat of harsh punishment, to petition the empress or the government for redress against the landlords. Catherine the Great also instituted firmer control over the cossacks, abolishing the famed Sech on the Dnieper in 1775 and limiting the autonomy of the Don and the Ural "hosts."

Other government measures relating to land and people included a huge survey of boundaries and titles—an important step in legalizing and confirming landholdings—the above-mentioned final secularization of vast Church estates with some 2 million peasants who became subject to the so-called College of Economy, and a program of colonization. Colonists were sought abroad, often on very generous conditions and at great cost, to populate territories newly won from Turkey and other areas, because serfdom and government regulations drastically restricted the mobility of the Russian people. Elizabeth had already established Serbian communities in Russia. Catherine the Great sponsored many more colonies of foreigners, especially of Germans along the Volga and in southern Russia.

Catherine II's efforts to promote the economy, education, and culture in Russia will be discussed in more detail in later chapters. But the extent of her activity needs to be recognized here. In economic life the empress turned in certain respects from rigid mercantilism to the newly popular ideas of free enterprise and trade and tried to stimulate economic activity with loans and incentives to noble farmers and business owners. In cultural life, she saw it as her mission to civilize Russia; she wished to make, in her words, "better people." She promoted free public primary and secondary schools and authorized private publishing and printing for the first time in Russian history. With the same missionary zeal she founded hospitals, led in the struggle against infectious diseases, and decreed that Russia begin to produce its own medicines and surgical instruments. She also pioneered, if modestly, in social welfare, introducing some measures to help the underprivileged, for example, widows and orphans.

## Foreign Affairs: Introductory Remarks

Catherine the Great also sought success and glory, for herself and her country, in expanding the empire and advancing Russia's place as a great power in the system of European states. Assisted by such statesmen as Nikita Panin and Potemkin and such generals as Rumiantsev and Suvorov, the empress scored triumph after triumph on the international stage, resulting in a major extension of the boundaries of the empire, the addition of millions of subjects, and Russia's rise to a new importance and eminence in Europe. However, Catherine the Great's foreign policy was by no means a novel departure. New ideas did appear: for example, Panin's early doctrine of a northern accord or alliance of all leading northern European states to counterbalance Austria, France, and Spain; and Potemkin's celebrated "Greek project," which we shall discuss in its proper place. But, in fact, these ideas proved ephemeral, and Russia continued on her old course. As Russian historians like to put it, Peter the Great had solved one of the three fundamental problems of Russian foreign relations: the Swedish. Catherine the Great settled the other two: the Turkish and the Polish.

Important events in Russia's foreign policy under Catherine clustered in two segments of time. The years 1768–74 witnessed the First Turkish War, together with the first partition of Poland in 1772. Between 1787 and 1795 Russia participated in the Second Turkish War, 1787–92, an inconclusive war with Sweden after they attacked Russia in 1788, and the second and third partitions of Poland, 1793 and 1795. One other development of note was Catherine's success, during Britain's war with its rebellious American colonies, in promoting the doctrine of free commerce at sea for noncombatants, which led to the formation of the League of Armed Neutrality in 1780. The French Revolution of 1789 created additional worries. At first, Catherine tried to minimize the significance of the events in France and to dissociate them from her beloved Enlightenment. But as the Revolution became more radical, the empress reacted with bitterness and hostility. At home she turned against critical intellectuals and indeed against much of the cultural climate she herself had striven so hard to create. After the execution of Louis XVI in 1793, she broke off relations with France entirely and was considering a military coalition against France. But the French Revolution and other distractions for the West may also have helped Catherine: Great Britain was immersed in a conflict with its North American colonies during the latter part of the First Turkish War, while during the second crucial sequence of years all powers had to shift their attention to revolutionary France.

## Russia and Turkey

In their struggle against Turkey, the Russians aimed to reach the Black Sea and thus attain what could be considered their natural southern boundary as well as recover fertile lands that had been part of the Kievan state but were lost to invaders from the east. The Crimean Tatars, successors to the Golden Horde in that area, had recognized the suzerainty of the Sultan of Turkey. In pushing south, Catherine the Great followed the time-honored example of Muscovite tsars and such imperial predecessors as Peter the Great and Anne. The First Turkish War, 1768–74, was fought both on land and, more unusual for Russia, on sea. A Russian army commanded by Rumiantsev advanced into Bessarabia and the Balkans, scoring impressive victories over large Turkish forces and appealing to the Christians to rise against their masters; another Russian army invaded and eventually captured the Crimea. A Russian fleet under Alexei Orlov sailed from the Baltic to Turkish waters and sank the Ottoman navy in the Bay of Chesme on July 6, 1770; however, it did not dare to try to force the Straits. In spite of the fact that the Russian drive into the Balkans had bogged down, Turkey was ready in the summer of 1774 to make peace.

By the Treaty of Kuchuk Kainarji, a humiliating blow to the once-powerful Ottomans, Russia gained access to the Black Sea and other strategic points, including the Crimean ports of Yenikale and Kerch, the fortress at Kinburn, and part of the Black Sea coast, reaching almost to the foot of the Caucasian range and including Azov. The Crimean Tatars were proclaimed independent, although they recognized the sultan as caliph, that is, the religious leader of Islam. Russia obtained the right of free commercial navigation in Turkish waters, including permission to send merchantmen through the Straits. Moldavia and Wallachia were returned to Turkey, but they were to be leniently ruled, and Russia reserved the prerogative to intervene on their behalf. Also, Russia acquired the right to build an Orthodox church in Constantinople, while the Turks promised to protect Christian churches and to accept Russian representations on behalf of the new church to be built in the capital. The provisions of the treaty relating to Christians and Christian worship became the basis of many subsequent Russian claims in regard to Turkey.

Although the First Turkish War in Catherine the Great's reign marked Russia's first decisive defeat of Turkey and although the Treaty of Kuchuk Kainarji reflected the Russian victory, Russian aims had received only partial satisfaction. Some of the northern littoral of the Black Sea remained Turkish, while the Crimea became independent. From the Ottoman point of view, the war was a disaster that could only be remedied by exaction of revenge and by restoration of Turkey's former position by force of arms. The unstable political situation in the Crimea added to the tension. In 1783 Russia moved to annex the Crimea, causing many Crimean Tatars to flee to the sultan's domain. By 1785 Russia had built a sizable fleet in the Black Sea, with its main base in Sevastopol.

Potemkin worked intensively to develop the newly annexed Crimea: to colonize it with settlers, develop the economy, build towns, and establish a navy for the Black Sea. In 1787, Catherine toured the region by boat, accompanied by French, English, and Austrian ambassadors. Potemkin did all he could to impress the visitors: decorating villages along the way and ensuring stops at the most picturesque villages, where happy singing peasants were presented. Gossip at court exaggerated the stage managing, suggesting that villages along the shore were only painted facades and the singing peasants were moved as the visitors moved. These stories are the source for the famous expression "Potemkin villages." But as historians have shown, without ignoring Potemkin's showmanship, the progress in developing this southern region of the empire was very real.

At that time Potemkin and Catherine the Great nursed very far-reaching aims that came to be known as "the Greek project." Roughly speaking, the project involved conquering the Ottomans, or at least their European possessions, and establishing—re-establishing the sponsors of the project insisted—a great Christian empire centered at Constantinople. Catherine the Great had her second grandson named Constantine, entrusted him to a Greek nurse, and ordered medals struck with a reproduction of St. Sophia! Austria finally agreed to allow the project after receiving assurance that the new empire would be entirely separate from Russia and after an offer of compensations in the Balkans and other advantages. Yet, like many other overly ambitious schemes, the Greek project proved to be ephemeral. Neither it nor its chief promoter Potemkin survived the Second Turkish War.

Turkey declared war on Russia in 1787 after the Russians rejected an ultimatum demanding that they evacuate the Crimea and the northern Black Sea littoral. The Porte enjoyed the sympathy of several major European powers, especially Great Britain, which almost entered the war in 1791, and before long Sweden gave active support by attacking Russia. Catherine the Great had Austria as her military ally. The Second Turkish War, 1787–92, was confined to land action. Russian troops led by Suvorov scored a series of victories over Turkish forces, notably in 1790 when Suvorov stormed and won the supposedly impregnable fortress of Ismail. Incidentally, it was Mikhail Kutuzov, the hero of 1812, who first broke into Ismail. At the end of the war, Suvorov was marching on Constantinople. By the Treaty of Jassy, signed on January 9, 1792, Russia gained the fortress of Ochakov and the Black Sea shore up to the Dniester River, while Turkey recognized Russian annexation of the Crimea. Russia had reached what appeared to be its natural boundaries in the south; the Turkish problem could be considered essentially solved.

## The Partitioning of Poland

The partitioning of Poland, an important European state, represented a greater tour de force of imperial expansion than the capture of a huge segment of a largely uninhabited steppe from the Ottomans. But, whereas the settlement with Turkey proved definitive and, as many scholars have insisted, logical and natural, the same could not be asserted by any stretch of the imagination in the case of Poland. Indeed, the partitioning of that country left Russia and Europe with a constant source of pain and conflict.

Weakness and disorder in the political system in Poland—properly speaking, in the Polish-Lithuanian Commonwealth—from about the middle of the seventeenth century was a factor leading to this catastrophe. As we have seen, Poland-Lithuania was dominated by a very strong aristocracy, expressing its authority through the Sejm (parliament or diet), and a weak, elected king. To be sure, like monarchs elsewhere, rulers tried to expand their power, but unsuccessfully. For its part, the Sejm, composed of instructed delegates from provincial parliaments, resembled in its procedure a diplomatic congress more than a national legislature. The right of any member of parliament to veto any law and even dissolve the Sejm—the famous, or notorious, *liberum veto*—and growing corruption and foreign interference (including by an increasingly influential Russia) created frequent political chaos. The main traditional recourse to the Sejm being dissolved was to proclaim a confederation, a gathering of the adherents of a given position. A confederation could not be obstructed by a *liberum veto*, and it might try to impose its views by force. This political system has been described as "anarchy tempered by civil war." Partisans have admired the democratic qualities of this system; or, at least, they admire its role in preventing absolutism, for the vast majority of the population was not enfranchised. Most historians, however, have noted that given the growing political stability and centralization of neighboring states, this was a fatal path.

Of course, Poland did not partition itself: it was dismembered by three powerful and greedy neighbors. This deserves emphasis, for Poland might have survived its problems absent outside interference. Polish society, in the eighteenth century, experienced an intellectual and cultural revival that began to spread to politics. Given time, Poland might well have successfully reformed its political system to create more order and effectiveness. But its neighbors were determined that Poland would not have the time. Indeed, historians have argued, they encouraged Poland's internal problems in order to take advantage of them. The last king of Poland—and Catherine the Great's former lover—Stanislaw Poniatowski, who reigned from 1764 to 1795, tried to introduce certain reforms but failed to obtain firm support from Russia and Prussia, which had agreed in 1764 to cooperate in influencing Polish affairs. In 1766–68, the allies reopened the issue of tolerance for

## Poland 1662–67 and Partitions of Poland

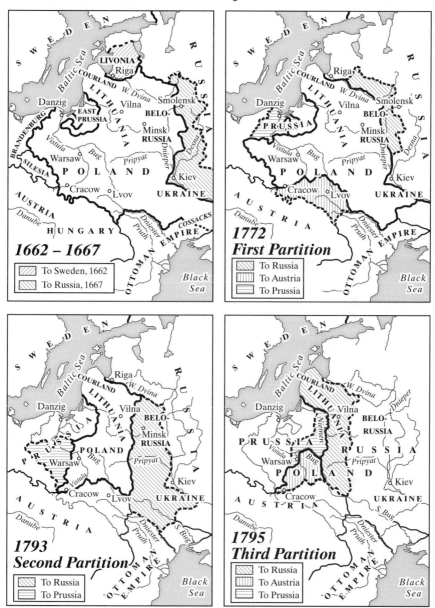

the Orthodox and the Protestant minorities and forced the Polish government to grant them equal rights with Catholics. Critics argue that this was a deliberate effort to weaken Polish unity rather than a defense of religious tolerance as a principle. In any case, the concession led to violent protests against the reform, Poniatowski, and Russian interference in Poland. This, in turn, led to the formation of the Bar Confederation and civil war, with France lending some support to the Confederation and Turkey using the pretext of defending "Polish liberties" to declare war on Russia. Eventually Russian troops subdued the Confederates, and the first partition of Poland came in 1772.

Great power politics played a large role in this unusual attempt to solve the Polish problem. Russia's success in the Turkish War alarmed Austria. Frederick the Great of Prussia proposed the partition of a part of Poland as a way to satisfy Catherine the Great's expansionist ambitions and at the same time to provide compensation for Austria—which in effect had taken the initiative in 1769 by seizing and "re-incorporating" certain Polish border areas—as well as to obtain for Prussia certain long-coveted Polish lands that separated Prussian dominions. By the first partition of Poland, Russia obtained Belorussian and Latvian Lithuania to the Dvina and the Dnieper rivers with some 1.3 million inhabitants; Austria received the region they called Galicia, with a total population of 2.65 millon, including Lwow (Lvov in Russian, Lviv in Ukrainian), or Lemberg as it would be renamed, but not Cracow; Prussia took the so-called Royal, or Polish, Prussia, except Gdansk (Danzig) and Torun (Thorn). Although the Prussian acquisition was smallest in size and population, it represented the most valuable gain of the three from the political, military, and economic points of view. In all, Poland lost about one-third of its territory and more than a third of its population.

This disaster spurred the Poles to enact long-needed reforms, though these would be halted by neighbors who worried about a revitalized Commonwealth. Changes were begun in 1773 and culminated in the work of the celebrated Four Years' Sejm of 1788–92 and in the constitution of May 3, 1791. The monarchy was to become hereditary, and the king to have effective executive power; legislative authority was to be vested in a two-chamber Sejm with the lower chamber in a dominant position; the Sejm was to include representatives of the middle classes; the dysfunctional *liberum veto* was abolished in favor of majority rule; and a cabinet of ministers, organized along modern lines, was created and made responsible to the Sejm. The Polish reform party profited from the benevolent attitude of Prussia, which apparently hoped to obtain further concessions from a new Poland. Formally, Russia and Austria also accepted the constitution. But all of this tolerance was tactical and temporary. In May 1792, Russia instigated the organization of the Confederation of Targowica in defense of the old order and sent armies into Poland in support of this Confederation. At this point, the Prussians reversed themselves and joined the invaders. The second partition of Poland followed in January 1793. This time Russia took more of Lithuania and most of western Ukraine, with a total of 3 million inhabitants, and Prussia seized Danzig, Thorn, and Great Poland, with a combined population of 1 million; Austria did not participate. In addition, Russia obtained the right to move its troops into what remained of Poland and control its foreign policy.

The Poles responded in March 1794 with a great national uprising led by Tadeusz, or Thaddeus, Kosciuszko. In spite of their courage, their fight was hopeless. The Poles were crushed by the Russians, commanded by Suvorov, and the Prussians. Austria rejoined her allies to participate in the third partition of Poland in October 1795. By its provisions, Russia acquired the remainder of Lithuania and Ukraine, with more than 1 million inhabitants, as well as the Duchy of Courland; Prussia took Mazovia, including Warsaw, with 1 million people; Austria appropriated the rest of Little Poland, with Cracow, and another 1.5 million inhabitants. Poland ceased to exist as an independent state.

The partitioning of Poland brought tragedy to the Poles. Its impact on the successful aggressors is more difficult to assess. On the one hand, Prussia, Russia, and Austria scored a remarkable, indeed virtually unprecedented, diplomatic and military coup. They dismembered and totally destroyed a large European state, eliminating an old enemy, rival, and source of conflicts, while at the same time adding greatly to their own lands, resources, and populations. Eastern Europe fell under their complete control, with France deprived of her old ally. Significantly, for a long time after the division of Poland, the three east European monarchies cooperated closely on the international scene—partners in crime, if you will.

On the other hand, the partitions left a legacy of trouble with lasting consequences. In particular, we might date the beginning of the "national problem" in the Russian Empire from the partitions. Most Russian scholars like to emphasize that, in the three partitions of Poland, Russia took only old Russian lands, once part of the Kievan state, populated principally by Orthodox Ukrainians and Belorussians, whereas the two German powers grabbed ethnically and historically Polish territory. This view, while factually correct, neglects a great deal. First, the brutal Russian policy toward Poland had to allow for the interests of other aggressors and indeed led to further repartitioning, with Warsaw and the very heart of Poland attached to Russia in 1815. Second, while the peasantry in the annexed lands of Poland-Lithuania were indeed mainly Lithuanians, Belorussians, and Ukrainians, the nobility was generally Polish by language and culture. In any case, Catherine the Great showed she was not mainly concerned about the faith or the ethnic origins of her new subjects. Thus, after suppressing the Bar Confederation, Russian troops also suppressed a desperate uprising of Ukrainian peasants against their Polish and Polonized landlords. In fact, some Ukrainian historians have argued that oppression by Polish landlords only increased under Russian occupation, as the strong Russian government maintained law and order more successfully than had the weak Polish authorities.

In other words, the partitions, for all their benefits to Russia, also brought to the growing empire several potential sources of national conflict and anti-Russian nationalism. For the short term, the most worrisome for the Russian state were Catholic Poles and Jews. Most Poles, of course, refused to accept the dismemberment of their nation and foreign rule. Polish elites already had a high level of national consciousness, such as would arise only later among other peoples in the Russian Empire, and they had strong connections with the West. In some respects, then, the "Polish problem" was made worse by partition. The dismemberment of Poland also brought into the empire an even larger group of religious "aliens," long viewed with hostility and carefully kept out of Russia: Jews. Indeed, the Russian Empire now absorbed a great part of one of the largest and oldest Jewish communities in Europe.

## Evaluations of Catherine the Great

Catherine the Great, in her own time and in the writing of history, has received a great deal of both praise and criticism. Her admirers focus mainly on her achievements in advancing Russia's Westernization and international position. Her detractors dwell on her failures to achieve many of her stated goals and especially on the continued growth of serfdom. Critics have been repelled by the contrast between her professedly enlightened views and the ease and thoroughness of her accommodation to this great social evil. More generally, historians debate how real and deep were her commitments to the principles of the Enlightenment. Was this merely vanity—a desire to impress foreigners, her elites, and her own self-regard—or sincere conviction? Or, in accord with the traditional argument, did a naive, youthful commitment to Enlightenment ideas of freedom and equal rights, nurtured by knowledge of the French philosophers but ignorance of Russia, deteriorate under the pressures of hostile nobles, peasant rebellion, and then the frightening example of revolution in France?

These arguments are too simple. A more balanced assessment—though much research still needs to be done on the actual working and effects of her policies before a final judgment is possible—avoids these easy dichotomies. Isabel de Madariaga has argued that what defined, and limited, Catherine's vision of politics was "her sensitivity to the possible." As such, it can be argued, Catherine believed in her reforms but also recognized harsh realities. She believed, as she wrote in her *Instruction*, that human beings are "rational creatures" with natural dignity and liberty but also that they need to be educated. She believed in the necessity of an active society, even local initiative, but also in a strong and active state regulating action in pursuit of "the supreme good." In a word, as de Madariaga and other recent historians have argued, she was not a liberal or a democrat but neither was she an enlightened despot, much less a hypocritical one. Her ideal, drawn from both the French Enlightenment and German cameralism and from her own observations and instincts, was a regulated and orderly polity in which everyone performed their functions well and in the interests of the common good.

There were many inadequacies, inconsistencies, and brutalities in her long reign. And Catherine's extreme self-confidence did not always guide her well. But most historians would agree that her achievements were considerable. She continued many trends begun before her: advancing Russia as a great power, expanding the empire, modernizing administration, and fostering learning and the arts. As such, her reign was a culmination. But she also steered the ship in a new direction. By encouraging greater social initiative and local engagement (some scholars have even seen here the idea of a modern civil society), by making the idea of national discussion and debate conceivable, by promoting new concepts of legality and justice, she fostered, carefully and even hesitatingly, the promise of a new relationship between rulers and ruled. As such, she set the stage for the nineteenth century.

## The Reign of Paul

When Emperor Paul ascended the throne in 1796, he made undoing his mother's work a salient feature of his brief reign, which ended in his death in 1801 in a palace coup. During her reign Catherine had kept Paul away from power. He, in turn, came to hate his mother, her favorites, her advisers, and everything she stood for. Symbolically, Paul had his murdered father, Peter III, dug up from his modest resting place and reburied with pomp. He also freed from prison and exile those punished by his mother, including liberal and radical intellectuals and leaders of the Polish rebellion such as Kosciuszko, though he would replace them in time with his own perceived enemies. In ideology and policy, he was suspicious of all independent social activity, especially by the nobles. He revoked the Charter to the Nobility and the Charter to the Towns and promoted a military model for both state and society. He also banned French fashions, foreign books, and foreign travel. Paul's politics was also shaped by his personality and character. Historians have variously described Paul as "capricious," "neurotic," "manic," even a "crowned psychopath." Highly suspicious, irritable, and given to frequent outbreaks of rage, the emperor promoted and demoted his assistants with dazzling rapidity and often for no apparent reason. Above all, he loved all things military. He spent huge amounts of time on the parade ground. He personally changed the drill and redesigned the uniforms of the Russian army; imperial military reviews inspired terror in the participants. Most important, the emperor insisted on his autocratic power and majesty even in small things like dancing at a palace festival and saluting. As Paul reportedly informed the French ambassador, the only important person in Russia was the one speaking to the emperor, and only while he was so speaking. With the same concept of the majesty of the Russian monarchy in mind, and also reacting, no doubt, to his own long and painful wait for the crown, Paul changed the law of succession to the Russian throne at the time of his coronation in 1797: primogeniture in the male line replaced Peter the Great's provision of free selection by the reigning monarch. Russia finally acquired a strictly legal and stable system of succession to the throne, but also one that explicitly excluded women.

The emperor's views and attitudes found reflection in his treatment of the crucial problem of serfdom and the gentry. On the one hand Paul continued Catherine the Great's support and promotion of serfdom by spreading it to extreme southern Russia, so-called New Russia, in 1797, and by distributing state lands and peasants to his favorites at an even faster rate than had his mother. Also, he harshly suppressed all peasant disturbances and tolerated no disobedience or protest on the part of the lower classes. Yet, as Paul did not share his mother's confidence in and liking for the gentry, he tried for the first time to regulate and limit the obligations of the serfs to their masters by proclaiming in 1797 that they should work three days a week for their landlords and three days for themselves, with Sunday sanctified as a day of rest. Although Paul's new law was not, and possibly could not be, enforced, it did represent a turning point in the attitude of the Russian government toward serfdom. From that time on, limitation and, eventually, abolition of serfdom became real issues of state policy. The emperor gave further expression to his displeasure with the gentry through such measures as the restoration of corporal punishment for members of that class as well as for the townspeople, and through increased reliance on the bureaucracy in preference to the gentry in local self-government and in general administration.

It was in the field of foreign policy and especially of war that Paul's reign left its most lasting memory. Just before her death, Catherine the Great had come close to joining an anti-French coalition. Paul began with a declaration of the Russian desire for peace, but before long he too, provoked by French victories and certain mistakes of tact on the part of France, turned to the enemies of the revolutionary government. Russia entered the war against France as a member of the so-called Second Coalition, organized in large measure by Paul and composed of Russia, Great Britain, Austria, Naples, Portugal, and Turkey. In the campaigns that followed, a Russian fleet under the command of Fedor Ushakov sailed through the Straits, seized the Ionian Islands from the French, and established there a Russian-controlled republic under the protectorate of Turkey. Russian influence extended even further west in the Mediterranean, for Paul had accepted his election as the grand master of the Knights of Malta and thus ruler of that strategic island.

The main theater of operations, however, remained on land. Russian troops joined allied armies in the Low Countries and in Switzerland, but their most effective intervention took place in northern Italy. There a force of 18,000 Russians and 44,000 Austrians led by Suvorov drove out the French in the course of five months in 1798–99. Suvorov wanted to invade France. Instead, because of defeats on other fronts and the change of plans in the allied high command, he had to retreat in 1799–1800 to southern Germany through the Swiss Alps held by a French force. His successful management of the retreat has been considered one of the great feats of military history. On the whole, Suvorov, who died very shortly after the Swiss campaign at the age of seventy, is regarded as the ablest military commander Russia ever produced. The qualities of this eccentric and unpredictable general included heavy reliance on speed and thrust and remarkable psychological rapport with his soldiers.

Disgusted with Austria and also with Great Britain, which failed to support Russian troops adequately in the Netherlands, Paul abandoned the coalition. In fact, in 1800 he switched sides and joined France, considering the rise of Napoleon to be a guarantee of stability and the end of the revolution. The new alignment pitted Russia against Great Britain. Having lost Malta to the British, Paul, in a fantastic move, sent the Don cossacks to invade distant India over unmapped territory. The emperor's death interfered at this point, and Alexander I promptly recalled the cossacks.

Paul was killed in a palace revolution in March 1801. His rudeness, violent temperament, and unpredictable behavior helped the conspiracy to grow even among the emperor's most trusted associates and indeed within his family. His preference for the troops trained at his own estate of Gatchina antagonized, and seemed to threaten, the guards. The emperor's turning against Great Britain produced new enemies. Count Petr Pahlen, the military governor of St. Petersburg, took an active part in the plot, and Grand Duke Alexander, Paul's son and heir, apparently assented to it. It remains uncertain whether murder was part of the original plans of the conspirators—Alexander, it seems, had not expected it—or whether it occurred by accident.

# CHAPTER 23

# The Economic and Social Development of Russia in the Eighteenth Century

Serfdom in its fullness lasted longer in Russia than in Western countries because its economic disadvantages did not earlier outweigh its advantages; because the increase of population did not cause sufficiently acute land shortage among the peasantry until the first half of the nineteenth century; because the middle classes were weak in comparison with the serf-owners; because humanitarian and other ideas of the value of the individual spirit were little developed; because the reaction against the ideas of the French Revolution strengthened the *vis inertiae* inherent in any long-established institution; lastly, because serfdom was not merely the economic basis of the serf-owners but also a main basis of the Russian state in its immense task of somehow governing so many raw millions.

B. H. SUMNER

It is significant that none of the contemporary western European authors who have written on Russian economics in the late eighteenth century and the early nineteenth speaks of Russia as an economically backward country. In fact, during some part of the eighteenth century, Russian industry, at least in some branches, was ahead not only of all the other Continental countries but of England as well.

MICHAEL KARPOVICH

The notion of Russian "backwardness" has long been a seductive metaphor for telling the history of Russia, not least in discussing the economy. But economic historians have emphasized the extent to which the eighteenth century—notwithstanding the persistent weight of harsh climate and poor soil in suppressing productivity—was a time of radical transformations, dramatically rising prices for grain, robust development of trade and markets, a growing money economy, and even an increasingly vital peasant economy. The reforms of Peter the Great and Catherine the Great played no small part in facilitating this development. On the other hand, as will be seen, this progress was often contradictory. While agriculture thrived and landlords made greater and greater profits, serfdom became stronger than ever, the tax burden on the poor grew, and towns and urban manufacture languished.

One important sign of Russian development were changes in the population curve, which, it might be added, paralleled the curves in other European countries: whereas the population of Russia apparently remained largely stationary for a century and longer prior to the time of Peter the Great, and whereas it might have decreased during the reformer's hard reign, it rose rapidly from then on. Within the Russian boundaries of 1725 there lived some 13 million people in that year, 19 million in 1762, and 29 million in 1796. Counting approximately 7 million new subjects acquired as a result of expanding the empire's boundaries, Russia had by the end of the eighteenth century over 36 million inhabitants.

In addition to the immediate increase in population, the expansion of the Russian Empire in the eighteenth century produced a number of other results important for the economic life of the country. Peter the Great's victory in the Great Northern War gave his state access to the Baltic; and citizens of such ports as Riga, who were more proficient in navigation and commerce than the Russians, were then brought into the empire. "A window into Europe" referred as much to economic affairs as to culture or politics. Catherine the Great's huge gains from the partitions of Poland also brought Russia closer to other European countries and included towns and areas with a relatively more developed economy. Both the German landlords of the Baltic region and the Polish or Polonized gentry of what came to be known as the western provinces were in certain respects more advanced than their Russian counterparts. The acquisitions to the south proved similarly significant. Catherine the Great's success in the two Turkish wars opened vast fertile lands of southern Russia—a further extension of what had been obtained in the preceding decades and centuries—for colonization and development and established the empire firmly on the Black Sea. Although serfdom restricted mobility, population in the south grew rapidly by means of voluntary migration and the transfer of serfs and state peasants.

## Agriculture and Other Occupations

Differentiation accompanied expansion. The fertile, mostly "black-earth," agricultural areas of the south became more and more distinct from the more barren regions of the center and north. The system of barshchina, that is, of work for one's master, prevailed in the south, that of obrok, or payments to the landlord in kind or money, in the north. On the rich black earth of the south the serfs tilled their masters' fields as well as their own plots, and they also performed other tasks for the master such as cutting firewood or mowing hay.

In addition to the increase in grain and other agricultural products, cattle-raising developed on a large scale. The landlords generally sold the products of their economy on the domestic market, but toward the end of the century export increased.

In the provinces of the center and north, where the earth was not so fertile, the obrok, or quitrent, practice grew. There only modest harvests of rye and other grains suitable to the rigorous climate could be obtained from the soil, so that the peasant population had to find different means to support itself and to discharge its obligations to the landlord and the state. Special crafts developed in various localities. In some places peasants produced iron implements, such as locks, knives, and forks; in others they made wooden utensils, spoons, cups, plates, toys, and the like, or leather goods. Where no such subsidiary local occupations emerged, many peasants left their homes periodically, especially for the winter, to find work elsewhere. Often groups of peasants sought employment together in associations known as *arteli*—singular *artel*—and became carpenters, house-painters, or construction workers. Others earned money in industrial production, transportation, or petty trade. These varied earnings, together with their meager agriculture, made it possible for a large number of peasants to pay their quitrent to the landlord, meet their obligations, and support themselves and their families—although at a very low standard of living. It has been estimated that about one-quarter of the peasant population of the less fertile provinces left their villages for winter employment elsewhere.

The great extent and the continuing expansion of agriculture in Russia did not mean that it was modern in technique or very productive. Russian agriculture remained rather primitive, and, because of the backward technique of cultivation, even excellent land gave relatively low yields. Serfdom contributed heavily to the inefficient use of labor and to rural overpopulation. In agriculture Westernization came very slowly indeed. By the end of the century, in spite of the efforts of the Free Economic Society established in 1765 and a few other groups as well as certain individuals, no substantial modernization had occurred. As Soviet historians repeatedly emphasized, serfdom with its abundant unskilled labor still could effectively satisfy the needs of the rather sluggish and parochial Russian rural economy in the eighteenth century.

## Industry and Labor Force

In a sense, the Russians during that period made greater advances in industry. The number of factories grew from 200 or 250 at the time of Peter the Great's death to 1,200 by the end of the century, to cite one opinion, or possibly even over 3,000, if the smallest manufacturing establishments are included. The total number of workers rose to a considerable figure variously estimated between 100,000 and 225,000. Many factories employed hundreds of hands, with the highest known number in the neighborhood of 3,500. The vitally important mining and metal industries developed so spectacularly as to give Russia a leading position in Europe in this type of production. The Ural area produced at that time some 90 percent of Russian copper and some 65 percent of pig iron. Lesser centers of metal industry existed in Olonets, near the Finnish border, and in Tula, south of Moscow. The textile industry flourished in and around Moscow and in some neighboring provinces and, to a lesser extent, in the St. Petersburg area. A number of other industries also developed in eighteenth-century Russia.

However, in the context of Russian society, the acquisition of a suitable labor force often created special problems; Russian manufacturing establishments reflected and in turn affected the social structure of the empire. Thus, in addition to owning and operating some factories outright, the state established in areas of scarce labor supply numerous "possessional factories," which were operated by merchants and to which state peasants were attached as "possessional workers." They were, in fact, industrial serfs, but they belonged to a factory, not to an individual. These possessional factories acquired special prominence in heavy industry. Some landlords, in their turn, set up manorial factories, especially for light industry, where they utilized the bonded labor of their serfs. Nevertheless, free labor also played an increasingly important role in the industrial development of Russia in the eighteenth century. Even when it represented, as it often did, the labor of someone else's serfs out to earn their quitrent, it led to new, more "capitalistic," relationships in the factories. For instance, in the middle of the century merchants owned some 70 percent of textile factories in Russia as well as virtually the entire industry of the Moscow and St. Petersburg regions.

In addition to government managers, merchants, and gentry entrepreneurs, businessmen of a different background, including peasants and even serfs, made their appearance. In a number of instances, peasant crafts were gradually industrialized and some former serfs became factory owners, as, for example, in the case of the textile industry in and around Ivanovo-Voznesensk in central European Russia. The state engaged directly in industrial development but also encouraged private enterprise. This encouragement was plainly evident in such measures as the abolition of various restrictions on entering business—notably making it possible for the gentry to take part in every phase of economic life—and the protective tariffs of 1782 and 1793.

## Trade

Trade also grew in eighteenth-century Russia. Domestic commerce was stimulated by the repeal of internal tariffs that culminated in Empress Elizabeth's legislation in 1753, by the building of new canals following the example of Peter the Great, by territorial acquisitions, and especially by the quickened tempo and increasing diversity of economic life. In particular, the fertile south sent its cultural surplus to the center and the north in exchange for products of industries and crafts, while the countryside as a whole supplied the cities and towns with grain and other foods and raw materials. Moscow was the most important center of internal commerce as well as the main distribution and transit point for foreign trade. Other important domestic markets included

St. Petersburg, Riga, Archangel, towns in the heart of the grain-producing area such as Penza, Tambov, and Kaluga, and Volga ports like Iaroslavl, Nizhnii Novgorod, Kazan, and Saratov. In distant Siberia, Tobolsk, Tomsk, and Irkutsk developed as significant commercial as well as administrative centers. Many large fairs and uncounted small ones assisted the trade cycle. The best known among them included the celebrated fair next to the Monastery of St. Macarius on the Volga in the province of Nizhnii Novgorod, the fair near the southern steppe town of Kursk, and the Irbit fair in the Ural area.

Foreign trade developed rapidly, especially in the second half of the century. The annual ruble value of both exports and imports more than tripled in the course of Catherine the Great's reign, an impressive achievement even after we make a certain discount for inflation. After the Russian victory in the Great Northern War, the Baltic ports such as St. Petersburg, Riga, and Libau "Liepaja" became the main avenue of trade with Russia, and they maintained this dominant position into the nineteenth century. Russia exported to other European countries timber, hemp, flax, tallow, and some other raw materials, together with iron products and certain textiles, notably canvas for sails. Also, the century saw the beginning of the grain trade that was later to acquire great prominence. This trade became possible on a large scale after Catherine the Great's acquisition of southern Russia and the development of Russian agriculture there as well as the construction of the Black Sea ports, notably Odessa, which was won from the Turks in 1792 and transformed into a port in 1794. Russian imports consisted of wine, fruits, coffee, sugar, and fine cloth, as well as manufactured goods. Throughout the eighteenth century exports greatly exceeded imports in value. Great Britain remained the best Russian customer, accounting for something like half of Russia's total European trade. The Russians continued to be passive in their commercial relations with the West: foreign businessmen who came to St. Petersburg and other centers in the empire handled the transactions and carried Russian products away in foreign ships, especially British and Dutch. Russia also engaged in commerce with Central Asia, the Middle East, and even India and China, channeling goods through the St. Macarius Fair, Moscow, Astrakhan, and certain other locations. A considerable colony of merchants from India lived in Astrakhan in the eighteenth century.

## Imperial Society

Eighteenth-century Russia was overwhelmingly rural. In 1724, 97 percent of its population lived in the countryside and 3 percent in towns; by 1796 the figures had shifted slightly to 95.9 percent as against 4.1 percent. The great bulk of the people were, of course, peasants. They fell into two categories, roughly equal in size, serfs and state peasants. Toward the end of the century the serfs constituted 53.1 percent of the total peasant population. As outlined in earlier chapters, the position of the serfs deteriorated from the reign of Peter the Great to those of Paul and Alexander I and reached its nadir around 1800. In addition to a growing tax burden—the head tax as well as taxes on products bought and sold—peasants faced increasing economic exploitation, made worse by the virtual complete dependence of serfs on the will of their masters, without even the right to petition for redress. It has been estimated that the obrok increased two and a half times in money value between 1760 and 1800, while the barshchina grew from three to four and in some cases even five or more days a week. It was this striking expansion of the barshchina that Emperor Paul tried to stem with his ineffectual law of 1797. Perhaps the most unfortunate were the numerous household serfs who had no land to till, but acted instead as domestic servants or in some other capacity within the manorial household. This segment of the population expanded as landlords acquired new tastes and developed a more elaborate style of life. Indeed, some household serfs became painters, poets, or musicians, and a few even received education abroad. But, as can be readily imagined, it was especially the household serfs who were kept under the constant and complete control of their masters, and their condition could barely be distinguished from slavery. State peasants fared better than serfs, although their obligations, too, increased in the course of the century. At best, they maintained a reasonable degree of autonomy and prosperity. At worst, as exemplified by possessional workers, their lot could not be envied even by the serfs.

As we have seen, peasants were not entirely silent about their misery. Even apart from major rebellions such as those associated with Bulavin in Peter the Great's reign and with Pugachev under Catherine the Great, peasants, like bondsmen everywhere, expressed their discontent in everyday ways, such as slow and sloppy work during barshchina or petty theft from estate fields. Many fled to the frontiers, where government was weak. When particularly riled, often by some new demand on their labor, peasants occasionally gathered together locally to petition their landlord, or even the tsar, though this was forbidden by law.

By contrast, the eighteenth century, especially the second half during the reign of Catherine the Great, has been considered the golden age of Russian gentry. Constituting a little over 1 percent of the population, this class certainly dominated the life of the country and enjoyed growing wealth in this favorable economy. Their style of life became increasingly elaborate and costly, requiring servants, elegant furniture, imported books and art, costly balls, the finest education for their children, and travel abroad. While many noblemen, with the lessening and finally abolition of their service obligations, focused on enjoying this life, many landlords took a greater interest in their estates, and some of them also pursued other lines of economic activity, such as manufacturing. The State Lending Bank, established by Catherine the Great in 1786, had as its main task the support of gentry landholding. The nobility can also be credited with facilitating Russian Westernization and developing modern Russian culture. And, of course, the gentry continued to surround the throne, to supply officers for the army, and to fill administrative posts.

While the gentry prospered, the position of the clergy and their dependents declined. This sizable group of Russians, about 1 percent of the total—it should be remembered that Orthodox priests marry and raise families—suffered

from the anti-ecclesiastical spirit of the age and especially from the secularization of Church lands in 1764. Never rich, Russian priests became poorer and
more insecure financially after 1764. They had to depend almost entirely on
fees and donations from their usually impoverished parishioners, often producing resentment. The style of life of priests and their families, especially in
the countryside, frequently differed little from that of peasants, often inspiring contempt. In addition, as Gregory Freeze has shown, the eighteenth century saw the disintegration of the parish community. Where the boundaries of
religious and secular activities had once overlapped, the local church forming
a unifying center, these were now split apart, leaving the church as only a
religious institution.

The bulk of the town inhabitants were divided into three legal categories:
merchants, artisans, and workers. These classes were growing: for instance,
peasants who established themselves as manufacturers or otherwise successfully entered business became merchants. Nevertheless, none of these classes
was numerous or prominent in eighteenth-century Russia. As usual, it was
the government that tried to stimulate initiative, public spirit, and a degree
of participation in local affairs among the townsmen by such means as the
creation of guilds and the charter of 1785 granting urban self-government. As
usual, too, these efforts failed.

Women, outside the charmed circle of privilege enjoyed by the Westernized
and often educated wives of the elite (not to mention the empresses), tended to
share in the experience and burdens of their menfolk, with the added burden of
domestic responsibilities and patriarchical family hierarchies. Women labored
in the fields, worked as servants, occasionally engaged in commerce, ran their
households, cared for children, and worried about having enough food and
paying increasing taxes. Echoing Muscovite concerns, the government made
a special effort to control women's sexuality, confining "debauched" women
in special institutions and sometimes punishing them. On the other hand,
Catherine the Great hoped to spread elementary education to girls.

The dramatic increase in the number of non-Russians and non-Orthodox
living under the rule of the Russian crown was one of the defining social
changes in the eighteenth century. Whatever the reasons for the expansion of
empire—historians have spoken of an "urge to the sea," of natural boundaries
not yet reached, of unstable borderlands, of Messianic ambition, of international competition—the effect was the forced entry into Russian life of people
representing many different ethnicities and religions. As the German-Russian
economist Heinrich Storch observed in 1797, "the inhabitants of the Russian
empire comprise at least eighty distinct nations.... To see such an extraordinary number of peoples and ethnic groups united in a single body of a state
is a most rare occurrence, a second example of which we would look for in
vain in the history of the world." While some groups had little in the way of
autonomous organization, other groups, such as Polish nobles, Cossack leaders, Baltic Germans, Jews, and Muslims, had already developed institutions
and a strong sense of separate identity. As we have seen, some ethnic groups,

especially in the south and east, fought against the encroachments of Russian power.

Policies toward different groups varied widely, usually depending on how much the state valued their potential service to crown and country, though this was also influenced by existing prejudices. In general, the tendency was to incorporate and assimilate elites and disregard local peculiarities. Following Muscovite tradition, and also influenced by study of the Ottoman experience, the imperial government in the eighteenth century generally tolerated local differences in language, religion, and communal organization. Tolerance did not include, however, Uniate Ukrainians and Belorussians, for they were viewed as heretics from the true faith; and, as a rule, Jews and Muslims were viewed with suspicion. Catherine the Great also made some effort to absorb new subjects into the Russian social hierarchy and to replace local communal institutions with a uniform system of local administration. Still, compared to the age of nationalism in the nineteenth century, Russian policy toward non-Russian ethnic and religious groups, as historians such as Andreas Kappeler have shown, remained remarkably pragmatic, flexible, and tolerant. There were many reasons for this, including the rationalist philosophy of viewing people according to their utility, the great distances of the empire and the weakness of local government, and native resistance to interference in their traditional ways. But we cannot neglect the fact that Russian ethnicity and Orthodox religion were not yet treated by the state as the unifying and stabilizing foundation of Russian politics and society. Such nationalism, on both sides of the relationship, would come later. As such, Kappeler has argued, Russia was still, at the start of the nineteenth century, a "pre-modern" empire. Yet the potential for conflict and protest was there, making the multiethnicity of the empire a destabilizing reality that would be of growing concern to the imperial state.

Clearly, we can never ignore the state in discussing Russia's economy and society. The state's ambitions in the eighteenth century required squeezing people and resources. Although a poor, underdeveloped, and illiterate country, Russia had a large and glorious army, a complex bureaucracy, and one of the most splendid courts in Europe. With the coming of Westernization, the tragic, and as it turned out fatal, gulf between the small enlightened and privileged segment at the top and the vast majority living near to the bottom became wider than ever. We shall consider this again when we deal with Russian culture in the eighteenth century and, indeed, throughout our discussion of imperial Russian history.

CHAPTER 24

# Russian Culture in the Eighteenth Century

...A mixture of tongues,
The language of France with that of Nizhnii Novgorod.
ALEXANDER GRIBOEDOV

On the one hand, the eighteenth century marked a decisive break with the Muscovite past. Peter the Great's violent activity was perhaps most revolutionary in the domain of culture. All of a sudden, skipping entire epochs of scholasticism, Renaissance, and Reformation, Russia moved from a parochial, ecclesiastical, quasi-medieval civilization to the Age of Reason. On the other hand, Russian culture of the eighteenth century also differed significantly from the culture of the following periods. From the beginning of Peter the Great's reforms to the death of Catherine the Great, the Russians applied themselves to the huge and fundamental task of learning from the West. The eighteenth century in Russia then was an age of apprenticeship and imitation par excellence. It has been said that Peter the Great, during the first decades of the century, borrowed Western technology; that Empress Elizabeth, in the middle of the period, shifted the main interest to Western fashions and manners; and that Catherine the Great, in the course of the last third of the century, brought Western ideas into Russia. Although much too simple, this scheme has some truth. It gives an indication of the stages in the Russian absorption of Western culture, and it suggests that by 1800 the process had spread to everything from artillery to philosophy.

## The Russian Enlightenment

The culture of the Enlightenment, which Russia borrowed, had a number of salient characteristics. It represented notably the triumph of secularism and thus stood in sharp contrast to the Church-centered civilization of Muscovy. To be sure, Orthodoxy remained in imperial Russia and even continued, in a

"Allegory of Mathematics," 1703. In Peter's time, visual allegories, often appearing in books, were common expressions of ideas. This image suggests the high value placed on scientific and technical knowledge. The name of God, in Hebrew, hovers above this temple to mathematics, with its feminine personification holding the key to many sciences, ranging from astronomy to fortifications. (Alekseeva, *Graviura Petrovskogo vremeni*)

sense, to be linked to the state and occupy a high position. But instead of being central to Russian life and culture, it became, at least as far as the government and the educated public were concerned, a separate and rather neglected compartment. Moreover, within this compartment, to follow George Florovsky and other specialists, one could detect little originality or growth. The secular philosophy that dominated the stage in eighteenth-century Europe emphasized reason, education, and the ability of enlightened men to advance the interests of society. The last point applied especially to rulers, who had the greatest means at their disposal to direct the life of a country. These views fitted imperial Russia remarkably well.

In addition to the all-pervasive government sponsorship, Enlightenment came to Russia through the educated gentry. After the pioneer years of Peter the Great, with his motley group of foreign and Russian assistants, the gentry, as we know, increasingly asserted itself to control most phases of the development of the country. Despite some striking individual exceptions, modern Russian culture emerged as gentry culture and maintained that character well into the nineteenth century. It became the civilization of an educated, aristocratic elite, with its salons and its knowledge of French, a civilization that showed more preoccupation with an elegant literary style and proper manners than with philosophy or politics. Nonetheless, this culture constituted the first phase of modern Russian intellectual and cultural history and the foundation for its subsequent development.

## Education

The glitter of the age of Catherine the Great was still far away when Peter the Great began his work of educating the Russians. Of necessity, his efforts were aimed in many directions and dealt with a variety of fundamental matters. As early as 1700 he arranged for publication of Russian books by a Dutch press; several years later the publishing was transferred to Russia. Six hundred different books published in the reign of the reformer have come down to our time. In 1702 the first Russian newspaper, *Vedomosti* or *News*, began to be published, the monarch himself editing its first issue. Next Peter the Great took part in reforming the alphabet to produce what came to be known as the civil Russian alphabet. Composed of Slavonic, Greek, and Latin letters, the new alphabet represented a considerable simplification of the old Slavonic. The old alphabet was allowed for Church books, but, following a decree in early 1710, all other works had to use the new system. Also, Peter the Great introduced Arabic numerals to replace the cumbersome Slavonic ones.

Peter the Great sent, altogether, hundreds of young Russians to study abroad, and he opened schools of new types in Russia. For example, as early as 1701 he established in Moscow a School of Mathematical and Navigational Sciences. Essentially a secondary school, that institution stressed the teaching of arithmetic, geometry, trigonometry, astronomy, and geography. The number of its students reached 500 by 1715, and two elementary schools were founded to prepare Russian boys to enter it. In 1715 a Naval Academy for 300 pupils opened in St. Petersburg. Moscow, in turn, received an artillery and an engineering academy of the same general pattern. Some other special schools, such as the so-called "admiralty" and "mathematical" ones, also appeared in the course of the reign. In 1716, in an attempt to develop a broader educational system, the government opened twelve elementary "cypher" schools in provincial towns. By 1723 their number had increased to forty-two. In 1706 a medical school with a student body of 50 began instruction in Moscow; in 1709 another medical school, this time with 30 students, started functioning in St. Petersburg. Peter I also organized small classes to study such special subjects as Chinese and Japanese and the languages of some non-Russian peoples within the empire. In addition to establishing state schools, the reformer tried to improve and modernize those of the Church. Finally, education in Russia began to expand by means of private schools. , which began to appear in the course of his reign.

Peter the Great's measures to promote enlightenment in Russia also included the founding of a museum of natural science and a large general library in St. Petersburg. Both were opened free to the public. But the reformer's most ambitious cultural undertaking was the creation of the Imperial Academy of Sciences. Although the Academy only came into being some months after Peter the Great's death, it represented the realization of a major project of the reformer's last years. The Academy had three departments, the mathematical, physical, and historical, as well as a section for the arts. The academicians gave instruction, and a high school was attached to the Academy to prepare students for this advanced education. Although the Academy operated at first on a small scale and consisted of only seventeen specialists, all of them foreigners, it became before long, as intended, the main directing center of science and scholarship in the Russian Empire. It has been noted repeatedly, sometimes with an unbecoming derision, that Russia obtained an Academy of Sciences before it acquired elementary schools—a significant comment on the nature of Peter the Great's reforms and the role of the state in eighteenth-century Russian culture.

After the death of Peter the Great, there followed a certain decline in education in Russia. Once the government relaxed its pressure, state schools tended to empty and educational schemes to collapse. Church schools, which were much less dependent on the reformer, survived better. They were to produce many trained Russians, some of whom became prominent in a variety of activities in the eighteenth and subsequent centuries. On the whole, however, Church schools served Church needs, that is, the training of the clergy, and stood apart from the main course of education in Russia. With the rise of the gentry in the eighteenth century, exclusive gentry schools whose graduates were given certain privileges became increasingly important. Peter the Great's artillery and engineering academies were restricted to members of that class, while new kadet schools were opened under Empress Anne and her successors to prepare sons of the nobility to assume the duties of army officers, in contrast to the first emperor's insistence on rising through the ranks. Home education, often by foreign tutors, also developed among the gentry. Increasing attention was given to good manners and the social etiquette that the Russians began to learn from the West at the time of Peter the Great's reforms: the first emperor had a manual on social etiquette, *A Mirror for Youth,* translated from the German as early as 1717. In the education of the gentry much time and effort were devoted to such subjects as proper bearing in society, fencing, and dancing, as well as to French and sometimes to other foreign languages. As noted in the scheme mentioned earlier, Western manners and fashions came to occupy much of the attention of educated Russians.

While Russian schools showed relatively little vitality or development between the reigns of Peter I and Catherine II, the government did take at least one decisive step forward: in Moscow in 1755 the first Russian university came into existence. Promoted by Ivan Shuvalov and Mikhail Lomonosov, this first Russian institution of higher learning was to be, all in all, the most important one in the history of the country, as well as a model for other universities. Responsible directly to the Senate and endowed with considerable administrative autonomy, the university possessed three schools: law, medicine, and philosophy. The school of philosophy included both the humanities and sciences, much as reflected in the range of the present-day degree of Doctor of Philosophy. The University of Moscow started with ten professors and some assistants to the professors; of the ten, two were Russians, a mathematician and a rhetorician. In a decade the number of professors about doubled, with Russians constituting approximately half of the total. Originally instruction took place in Latin; but in 1767 Russian began to be used in the university. In 1756 the university started to publish a newspaper, the *Moskovskie Vedomosti* or *Moscow News*. Higher education in Russia, both at the Academy and in the University of Moscow, had a slow and hard beginning, with few qualified students and in general little interest or support. Indeed at one time professors attended one another's lectures! Still, in this field, as in so many others, the eighteenth century bequeathed to its successor the indispensable foundations for further development.

Catherine the Great's reign, or roughly the last third of the century, witnessed a remarkable growth and intensification of Russian cultural life. For instance, we know of 600 different books published in Russia in the reign of Peter the Great, of 2,000 produced between 1725 and 1775, and of 7,500 that came out in the period from 1775 to 1800. Catherine the Great's edict of 1783, licensing private publishing houses, contributed to the trend. The rise of the periodical press proved even more striking. Although here too the origins went back to Peter the Great, there was little development until the accession of Catherine II. It was the empress's personal interest in the propagation of her views, together with the interests and needs of the growing layer of educated Russians, that led to the sudden first flowering of Russian journalism. By 1770 some eight periodicals entered the field to comment on the Russian and European scene, criticize the foibles of Russian society, and engage in lively debate with one another, a debate in which Catherine the Great herself took an active part. Societies for the development and promotion of different kinds of knowledge, such as the well-known Free Economic Society, multiplied in Catherine II's reign.

In the sphere of education we can see clearly both Catherine's sweeping ambition to transform society and a shift in emphasis from Peter the Great's primarily technical and professional orientation to a broadly liberal and humanist approach. Catherine shared the Enlightenment view that human beings, hence society, could be improved through education. Her main collaborator, who shared her philosophical interests, was Ivan Betskoy. Their optimistic goal was nothing less than to "bestow new existence" and form "a new kind of person." This meant developing individuals both intellectually and morally, giving them knowledge and skills but also fostering a sense of civic responsibility and a love of virtue. Following Rousseau, they believed this required isolating students from their corrupting environments. Hence, Catherine and Betskoy relied on select boarding schools, including the new Smolny school for noble girls, the first and the most famous state school for girls in the history of the Russian Empire.

Catherine and her collaborators could see the weakness and limitations in these efforts. Boarding schools for the elite, after all, reached very few people.

Yet their ambitions were greater: they wanted to extend enlightenment deeply into society, even to nurture an educated "third estate." Also, even for the select few, the walls of boarding schools evidently could not keep out the cultural environment; students often failed to become paragons of virtue and enlightenment. Therefore, other approaches, broader in scope but more limited in purpose, had to be tried. The empress became especially interested in the system of popular education instituted in the Austrian Empire in 1774 and explained to her by Emperor Joseph II himself. In 1782, following the Austrian monarch's advice, she invited the Serbian educator Theodore Iankovich de Mirievo from Austria and formed a Commission for the Establishment of Popular Schools. The Commission approved Iankovich de Mirievo's plan of a network of schools on three levels and of the programs for the schools. The Serbian educator then concentrated on translating and adapting Austrian textbooks for Russian schools and also on supervising the training of Russian teachers. A teachers' college was founded in St. Petersburg in 1783. Its first hundred students came from Church schools and were graduated in 1786. In that year a special teachers' seminary began instruction. It was to produce 425 teachers in the course of its fifteen years of existence. Relying on its new teachers, the government opened twenty-six more advanced popular schools in the autumn of 1786 and fourteen more in 1788, all of them in provincial centers. It also proceeded to put popular elementary schools into operation in district towns: 169 such schools, with a total of 11,000 pupils, began to function in 1787; at the end of the century the numbers rose to 315 schools and 20,000 students.

Everything considered, Catherine the Great deserves substantial credit in the field of education. Her valuable measures ranged from pioneering in providing education for girls to the institution of the first significant teacher training program in Russia and the spreading of schools to many provincial and district towns. Of course, the government's limited efforts did not represent all of Russian education. Church schools continued, and education of the gentry advanced in the last third of the eighteenth century. When not attending exclusive military schools of one kind or another, sons of the nobility received instruction at home by private teachers, augmented, with increasing frequency, by travel abroad. The French Revolution, while it led to the exclusion of France from Russian itineraries, brought a large number of French émigrés to serve as tutors in Russia.

The long-term effects of educating and Westernizing the elite were considerable. First, the growing number of young educated Russians were a class of people imbued with advanced notions about society and the person, often burning to apply their ideas to Russia's realities. We will see the consequences of this, neither intended nor desired by the state, in the early nineteenth century, especially. Second, it has been argued, education and cultural reform were producing the first signs of a "public sphere" in Russia—that important social space between the state and private life, where individuals can come together to discuss matters of general concern. By the late eighteenth century, this argument maintains, we see precisely this, though never entirely free of government involvement, in places like the university, the academies, and the Masonic lodges; around the new independent press; and in salons held in the homes of the rich.

The history of education also reminds us of the glaring division of Russian society. The eighteenth-century cultural revolution left the majority of the population largely untouched. If the dominant cultural trend among the elite was increasing secularization, the culture of the peasantry was thoroughly imbued with the religious, the spiritual, and the mystical—and with tradition. But we should not exaggerate this. Although the evidence is scattered, important signs of connection and change can be seen. Scholars have traditionally viewed the peasantry as a world apart. Educated Russians in the late eighteenth century shared this view and began to collect folklore as evidence of a timeless culture. But the research of historians like Marina Gromyko has shown that peasants were not entirely isolated. Folklore, for example, included stories about contemporary wars—peasants were the soldiers, after all—and other events. Rumors about the monarchy that circulated orally among peasants reveal both their awareness of the larger world and the power of the ideal of a just monarch who would bring freedom to the people, for this was often their subject. Even printing had an impact. Cheap, often garishly colored *lubki*, or popular prints, circulated in both cities and villages, often illustrating folkloric themes, exotic events, or bawdy situations; these might be sold alongside printed religious images and texts, which were also popular.

## Language

The adaptation of the Russian language to new needs in the eighteenth century constituted a major problem for Russian education, literature, and culture in general. It will be remembered that on the eve of Peter the Great's reforms Russian linguistic usage was in a state of transition as everyday Russian began to assert itself in literature at the expense of the archaic, bookish, Slavonicized forms. This basic process continued in the eighteenth century, but it was complicated further by a mass intrusion of foreign words and expressions that came with Westernization and had to be dealt with somehow. The language used by Peter the Great and his associates was in a chaotic state, and at one time apparently the first emperor wanted to solve the problem by having educated Russians adopt Dutch as their tongue!

In the course of the century the basic linguistic issues were resolved, and modern literary Russian emerged. The battle of styles, although not entirely over by 1800, resulted in a definitive victory for the contemporary Russian over the Slavonicized, for the fluent over the formal, for the practical and the natural over the stilted and the artificial. Nikolai Karamzin, who wrote in the last decades of the eighteenth and the first of the nineteenth century, contributed heavily to the final decision by effectively using the new style in his own highly popular works. As to foreign words and expressions, they were either rejected or gradually absorbed into the Russian language, leading to a great increase in its vocabulary. The Russian language of 1800 could handle many series of terms and concepts unheard of in Muscovy. That the Russian linguistic evolution of the eighteenth century was remarkably successful can best be seen from the fact that the golden age of Russian literature, still the standard of linguistic and literary excellence in modern Russian, followed shortly after. Indeed Pushkin was born in the last year of the eighteenth century.

The linguistic evolution was linked to a conscious preoccupation with language, to the first Russian grammars, dictionaries, and philological and literary treatises. These efforts, which were an aspect of Westernization, contributed to the establishment of modern Russian literary culture. Mikhail Lomonosov deserves special praise for the first effective Russian grammar, published in 1755, which proved highly influential. A rich dictionary composed by some fifty authors including almost every writer of note appeared in six volumes in 1789–94. Theoretical discussion and experimentation by Vasilii–Trediakovsky, Lomonosov, and others led to the creation of the now established system of modern Russian versification.

## Literature

Modern Russian literature must be dated from Peter the Great's reforms. While, to be sure, the Russian literary tradition goes back to the Kievan age in the *Lay of the Host of Igor* and other works, and even to the prehistoric past in popular song and tale, the reign of the first emperor marked a sharp division. Once Russia turned to the West, it joined the intellectual and literary world of Europe, which had little in common with that of Muscovy. In fact, it became the pressing task of educated eighteenth-century Russians to introduce and develop in their homeland such major forms of Western literary expression as poetry, drama, and the novel. Naturally, the emergence of an original and highly creative Russian literature took time, and the slowness of this development was emphasized by the linguistic evolution. The century had to be primarily imitative and in a sense experimental, with only the last decades considerably richer in creative talent. Nevertheless, the pioneer work of eighteenth-century writers made an important contribution to the establishment and development of modern Russian literature.

Antioch Kantemir, 1709–44, a Moldavian prince educated in Russia and employed in Russian diplomatic service, has been called "the originator of modern Russian *belles lettres*." Kantemir produced original works as well as translations, poetry and prose, satires, songs, lyrical pieces, fables, and essays. Mikhail Lomonosov, 1711–65, had a greater poetic talent than Kantemir. In literature he is remembered especially for his odes, some of which are still considered classics of their kind, in particular when they touch upon the vastness and glory of the universe. Alexander Sumarokov, 1718–77, a prolific and influential writer, has been honored as the father of Russian drama. In addition to writing tragedies and comedies as well as satires and poetry and publishing a periodical, Sumarokov was the first director of a permanent Russian theater. Sumarokov wrote his plays in the pseudo-classical manner characteristic of the age, and he often treated historical subjects.

The reign of Catherine the Great witnessed not only a remarkable increase in the quantity of Russian literature, but also considerable improvement in its quality. Two writers of the period, not to mention Nikolai Karamzin, who belongs to the nineteenth century as well as to the eighteenth, won permanent reputations in Russian letters. The two were Gavriil Derzhavin and Denis Fonvizin. Derzhavin, 1743–1816, can in fairness be called Catherine the Great's official bard: he constantly eulogized the vain empress and such prominent Russians of her reign as Potemkin and Suvorov. Like most court poets, he wrote too much; yet at his best Derzhavin produced superb poetry, both in his resounding odes, exemplified by the celebrated "God," and in some less-known lyrical pieces. The poet belonged to the courtly world that inspired him and even served as minister of justice in the government of Alexander I.

Fonvizin, 1745–92, has received wide acclaim as the first major Russian dramatist, a writer of comedies to be more exact. Fonvizin's lasting fame rests principally on a single work, the comedy whose title has been translated as *The Minor,* or *The Adolescent*—in Russian *Nedorosl.* Pseudo-classical in form and containing a number of artificial characters and contrived situations, the play, nevertheless, achieves a great richness and realism in its depiction of the manners of provincial Russian gentry. The hero of the comedy, the lazy and unresponsive son who, despite his reluctance, in the changing conditions of Russian life has to submit to an elementary education, and his doting, domineering, and obscurantist mother are apparently destined for immortality. In addition to *The Minor,* Fonvizin translated, adapted, or wrote other plays, including the able comedy *The Brigadier,* in which he ridiculed the excessive admiration of France in Russia; he also produced a series of satirical articles and a noteworthy sequence of critical letters dealing with his impressions of foreign countries.

While classicism, or neo-classicism, represented the dominant trend in the European literature of the eighteenth century, other currents also came to the fore toward the end of that period. Again, the Russians eagerly translated, adapted, and assimilated Western originals. Nikolai Karamzin, 1766–1826, can be called the founder of sentimentalism in Russian literature. His sensitive and lacrimose *Letters of a Russian Traveler* and his sensational story *Poor Liza,* both of which appeared at the beginning of the last decade of the century, marked the triumph of the new sensibility in Russia. Karamzin, it might be added, succeeded also as a publisher, and generally helped to raise the stature of the professional writer in Russian life. One important new trend, as shown by Hans Rogger's study of "national consciousness" in eighteenth-century Russia, was a new interest in folklore, a concern with the history of the country, and an emphasis on things Russian as opposed to Western.

## Social Criticism

The history of ideas cannot be separated from literary history, least of all in the Russian setting. Social criticism constituted the dominant content of both in eighteenth-century Russia. This didactic tendency, highly characteristic of the Age of Reason, found special application in Russia, where so much had to be learned so fast. Kantemir, "the originator of modern Russian literature," wrote satires by preference, while his translations included Montesquieu's *Persian Letters*. Satire remained a favorite genre among Russian writers of the eighteenth century, ranging from the brilliant comedies of Fonvizin to the pedestrian efforts of Catherine the Great and numerous other aspiring authors. The same satire, the same social criticism inspired journalism; in fact, no clear line divided the two fields. Russian writers and publicists inveighed against the backwardness, boorishness, and corruption of their countrymen, and they neglected no opportunity to turn them toward civilization and light. At the same time they noticed that on occasion "the ungainly beasts" began to admire the West, in particular France, too much and to despise their own country, and that in turn was satirized and denounced throughout the century.

The spirit of criticism developed especially in the reign of Catherine the Great and was aided by the sponsorship and example of the empress herself. Indeed, she gave, so to speak, official endorsement to the far-reaching critiques and views of the *philosophes*. The Free Economic Society even awarded its first prize to a work advocating the abolition of serfdom. A certain kind of Russian Voltairianism emerged, combining admiration for the sage of Ferney with a skeptical attitude toward many aspects of Russian life. Although some historians dismiss this Voltairianism as a superficial fashion, it no doubt served for some Russians as a school of criticism.

Freemasonry became another school of criticism and thought for the Russians, and a more complicated one, for it combined disparate doctrines and trends. It came to Russia, of course, again from the West, from Great Britain, Germany, Sweden, and France. Although the first fraternal lodges appeared at the time of Empress Elizabeth, the movement became prominent only in the reign of Catherine the Great. At that time it consisted of about 100 lodges located in St. Petersburg, Moscow, and some provincial towns and of approximately 2,500 members, almost entirely from the gentry. In addition to the contribution made by Freemasonry to the life of polite society, which constituted probably its principal attraction to most members, specialists distinguish two main trends within that movement in eighteenth-century Russia, growing out of the double obligation all Freemasons were expected to assume. The first was personal and often mystical: spiritual contemplation and self-perfection, the effort to know God and to realize in one's own personal life the principle that all human beings are created in the divine image. The second was a duty to one's fellow human beings: to help others realize their God-given dignity, not through humiliating charity but by uplifting people through education, including through the printed word. Many of these more socially oriented Freemasons were centered around the University of Moscow. They engaged in education and publishing, establishing a private school and the first large-scale program of publication in Russia outside of the government. They contributed heavily to the periodical literature and its social criticism. Catherine

Nicholas Novikov. An etching based on the famous painting of 1797 by Levitsky, who also painted Catherine the Great. Note the hand extended and mouth slightly parted as if in reasoned argument.   (Brikner/*Illiustrirovannaia istoriia Ekateriny vtoroi*)

the Great expressed contempt for the mysticism of the Freemasons, but, until the 1790s, she encouraged their social activism.

Nikholai Novikov, 1744–1818, was a leader in this effort. Sometimes compared to a contemporary American Freemason, Benjamin Franklin, Novikov established a private printing and publishing firm, edited and contributed essays to many journals, promoted the Russian book trade, and established the first series of children's books in Russia. His early writings, which Catherine the Great admired, were mainly gentle, humorous satires—especially against landlords who felt vain pride in their noble rank but contributed little to the common good and were cruel to their peasants. His later writings were weighty and biting essays on moral and ethical problems. He chastised "weakness, imperfection, and vice" in Russian life and appealed to society to recognize that man is not a "a rotten and putrid vessel of original sin" (in the language of the traditional Church) but the majesty of God's creation; hence all men are naturally equal in dignity and rights.

Of the many things to be criticized in Russia, serfdom loomed largest. Yet that institution was both so well accepted and so fundamental to Russian life that few in the eighteenth century dared challenge it. Numerous writers criticized certain individual excesses of serfdom, such as the cruelty of one master or the wastefulness of another, but they did not assail the system itself. Novikov and a very few others went further: their image of serf relations could not be ascribed to individual aberrations, and it cried for reform.

Still, it remained to Alexander Radishchev to make the condemnation of serfdom total and unmistakably clear. It was Radishchev's attack on serfdom that broke through the veneer of cultural progressivism and well-being typical of the reign of Catherine the Great and served as the occasion for a sharp break between the government and critical intellectuals.

Radishchev, 1749–1802, was educated at the University of Leipzig as well as in Russia and acquired a wide knowledge of eighteenth-century thought. In particular, he experienced the impact of Rousseau, Mably, and the entire egalitarian, and generally more radical, tendency of the later Enlightenment. A member of the gentry, an official, and a writer of some distinction, Radishchev left his mark on Russian history with the publication in 1790 of his stunning *Journey from Petersburg to Moscow*. Following the first section called "the departure," twenty-odd chapters of that work, named after wayside stations, depicted specific and varied horrors of serfdom. The panorama included such scenes as serfs working on a Sunday, because they could till their own land only on that day, the rest of the week being devoted to the barshchina; the sale at an auction of members of a single family to different buyers; and the forced arrangement of marriages by an overly zealous master. Moreover, Radishchev combined his explicit denunciation of serfdom with a comprehensive philosophical, social, political, and economic outlook, reflected in the *Journey* and in other writings. He assailed Russian despotism and administrative corruption and suggested instead a republic with full liberties for the individual. And he actually drew up a plan for serf emancipation and an accompanying land settlement.

Radishchev's philippic resulted in his being sentenced to death, changed fortunately to ten-year imprisonment in Siberia. Frightened by the French Revolution, Catherine the Great finally turned against the ideas of the Enlightenment, which she had done so much to promote. Novikov and his fellow Masons in Moscow also suffered—in 1792, she had Novikov arrested as a "subversive" and sentenced without trial to fifteen years' imprisonment in the Schlisselberg fortress near St. Petersburg—and their educational and publishing work came to an abrupt end. Edicts against travel and other contacts with the revolutionary West multiplied, reaching absurd proportions in Paul's reign. But the import of the issue proved even more profound than a reaction to the French Revolution. Until 1790 the state led Russia on the path of enlightenment. From that year on, it began to apply the brakes. Radishchev's *Journey* meant the appearance of a radical intellectual protest in Russia, a foretaste of the radical intelligentsia.

## Science and Scholarship

While secular philosophy, literary debates, and social criticism stood in the center of the Enlightenment, other aspects of culture also developed at that time. Following the West as usual, Russia proceeded to assimilate modern science, scholarship, and the arts. Science took root slowly in Russia, and for a number of decades the Russians had relatively little in this field, except a number of scholars invited from abroad, some of them of great merit. But—to underline the danger of generalizations and schemes—the one great Russian scientist of the eighteenth century appeared quite early on the scene; moreover, his achievements were rarely if ever to be matched in the entire annals of science in Russia. This extraordinary man was Mikhail Lomonosov, born in a peasant family in the extreme northern province of Archangel and educated both in Russia and for five years in Germany, most of that time at Marburg University. Lomonosov, 1711–65, who has already been mentioned as a pioneer grammarian, an important literary scholar, and a gifted poet, was also a chemist, a physicist, an astronomer, a meteorologist, a geologist, a mineralogist, a metallurgist, a specialist in navigation, a geographer, an economist, and a historian, as well as a master of various crafts and a tireless inventor. Pushkin was to refer to him, appropriately, as the first Russian university. In considering the work of Lomonosov, we should remember that he lived before the time of extreme scientific specialization, when a single mind still could master many disciplines, and indeed advance them. Lomonosov represented, in other words, the Russian counterpart of the great encyclopedic scholars of the West.

Lomonosov probably did his best work in chemistry, physics, and the border area between these two sciences. In fact, he developed and in 1751 taught the first course of physical chemistry in the world, and in 1752 he published a textbook in that field. The Russian scientist's other most outstanding achievements included the discovery of the law of the preservation of matter and of energy long before Lavoisier, the discovery of atmosphere on Venus, brilliant studies in electricity, the theory of heat, and optics, and the establishment of the nature and composition of crystals, charcoal, and black earth. Lomonosov's scientific work unfortunately proved far ahead of his time, especially in Russia, where it found no followers and was fully rediscovered only by Vasilii Menshutkin and other twentieth-century scholars.

Although Lomonosov remained essentially an isolated individual, the eighteenth century was also noteworthy in Russian history for large-scale, organized scientific effort. That effort took the form of expeditions to discover, explore, or study distant areas of the empire and sometimes neighboring seas and territories. Geography, geology, mineralogy, botany, zoology, ethnography, and philology, as well as some other disciplines, all profited from these well-thought-out and at times extremely daring undertakings. Begun by Peter the Great, the expeditions led to important results even in the first half of the century. For example, Alaska was discovered in 1732. The so-called First Academic Expedition, which lasted from 1733 to 1742 and included 570 participants, successfully undertook the mammoth task of mapping and exploring the northern shore of Siberia. Numerous expeditions, often of great scholarly value, followed later in the century.

The Russians also applied themselves to what can be called the social sciences and the humanities. Mention has already been made of new Russian scholarship in connection with language and literature. Modern Russian study of economics dates from Peter the Great. Ivan Pososhkov, a wealthy peasant, an extraordinary critic and admirer of the first emperor, and the author of a remarkable treatise, *Books about Poverty and Wealth*, has often been cited as its originator. Pososhkov found his inspiration in Peter the Great's reforms and in the issues facing Russia, not in Western scholarship, of which he was ignorant. The study of history too developed quickly in Russia, with the Russians profiting throughout the century from the presence of foreign scholars, such as the outstanding German historian August-Ludwig von Schlözer. Eighteenth-century Russian historians included an important administrator and collaborator of Peter the Great, Vasilii Tatishchev; Prince Mikhail Shcherbatov, who argued the case for the rights of the gentry in Catherine the Great's Legislative Commission and produced a number of varied and interesting works; and Major-General Ivan Boltin. From the time of Tatishchev, Russian historians understandably tended to emphasize the role of the monarch and the state.

## The Arts. Concluding Remarks

Architecture flourished in eighteenth-century Russia because of the interest and liberality of Peter the Great and his successors. Catherine the Great proved a passionate builder, and the same was true of Paul, as well as of Alexander I and Nicholas I in the nineteenth century. St. Petersburg, which rose from the swamps to become one of the truly beautiful and impressive cities of the world, remains the best monument of this imperial devotion to architecture. Baroque at the beginning of the century and the neo-classical style toward the

The Winter Palace in St. Petersburg. Commissioned by Elizabeth, although only completed after her death, and designed by Rastrelli, the palace was a residence of the Russian emperors and empresses until the 1917 revolution. It was then opened to the public as part of the Hermitage museum, originally established by Catherine the Great as a wing of the palace. (*Sovfoto*)

end of the century dominated European and Russian architecture. The builders in the empire of the Romanovs included a number of gifted foreigners,
notably Count Bartolomeo Rastrelli, who came as a boy from Italy to Russia,
when his sculptor father was invited by Peter the Great, and who designed the
Winter Palace and the Smolny Institute in St. Petersburg and the great palace
in Tsarskoe Selo, together with many other buildings. Some excellent Russian
architects, such as Vasilii Bazhenov and Matvei Kazakov, emerged in the second half of the century.

Other arts also grew and developed. In the 1750s the art section of the
Academy of Sciences became an independent Academy of Arts. In the field of
painting, portrait painting fared best, as exemplified by the work of Dmitrii
Levitsky, 1735–1822—a Ukrainian whose father was a priest and religious
artist. Fedot Shubin, 1740–1805, like Lomonosov a peasant from the extreme
north, was the first important Russian sculptor. Having received his initial
training in his family of bone carvers, he went on to obtain the best artistic
education available in St. Petersburg, Italy, and France and to win high recognition abroad as well as at home. Shubin's sculptures are characterized by
expressiveness and realism.

The eighteenth century also witnessed the appearance in Russia of modern music, notably the opera, as well as ballet and the theater. All of these
arts came from the West. But, as in so much, imitation and apprenticeship
developed into mastery and, with time, originality. As to theater, while Peter
the Great invited German actors and later sovereigns sponsored French and
Italian troupes, a native Russian theater became established only in the 1750s.
Its creator was a merchant's son, Fedor Volkov, who organized a successful
theater in Iaroslavl on the Volga and was then requested to do the same in
the capital. By the end of the century Russia possessed several public theaters, a theatrical school, and a periodical, *The Russian Theater,* which began
to appear in 1786. Furthermore, theater had won popularity among the great
landlords, who maintained some fifteen private theaters in Moscow alone.
Recent scholars have argued not only that theater played a key part in the
civilizing mission of the Russian Enlightenment but also that the new private
world of theater audiences was one of the key new sites of nongovernmental
civic activity and sociability in Russia, potentially so important for the development of a civil society.

Russian culture of 1800 bore little resemblance to that of 1700. There were,
of course, continuities, not least the continuing influence of religious belief.
The cultural world of the common people had changed little, a bourgeoisie
was still missing, and the few dissenting voices could be easily silenced.
But much had changed. Above all, the educated upper class had become
Westernized. As Karamzin would later argue, influenced by early nineteenth-
century notions of national identity and genius, "we became citizens of the
world but ceased in certain respects to be citizens of Russia." Like Karamzin,
many Russians worried about this wholesale borrowing from the West. A
large number of writers, especially Soviet historians, minimized the role of
the West, insisting that anything alien to the national spirit was discarded and

emphasizing native Russian achievements and originality. Wounded national pride, although common, is an unfortunate and usually unjustified sentiment. To be sure, in contrast to Russia's famous contributions to world culture in the nineteenth century, no eighteenth-century writers or artists are much known outside Russia, and not primarily because of unfair neglect. Russian culture was indeed still too imitative. This was not so exceptional, though: of European countries, only England and France can claim a full continuity of intellectual, literary, and cultural development, and even they, of course, experienced any number of foreign influences. More to the point, Russians borrowed from the West, but they also assimilated, adapted, and developed Western culture. The sources of a heritage should be important to the historian, but how it was used may well be considered still more significant. We have seen something of that use in this chapter and shall see much more of it in our subsequent discussions of Russian culture.

# CHAPTER 25

# The Reign of Alexander I, 1801–25

You shine like a divine angel
With goodness ancl beauty,
And your first words promise
Catherine's golden age,
Days of happiness, joy, glory,
When wise legislation
Preserved our domestic tranquility
And abroad Russia was glorified.

NIKOLAI KARAMZIN

TO ALEXANDER I, 1801

We must show them that we are not bears.

ALEXANDER I, 1815

If, during the two centuries which divide the Russia of Peter the Great from the Bolshevik revolution, there was any period in which the spell of the authoritarian past might have been overcome, the forms of the state liberalized in a constitution, and the course of Russian development merged with the historic currents of the west, it is the earlier part of the reign of Alexander I. Or so, for a moment, one is tempted to think.

RICHARD CHARQUES

The accession of twenty-three-year-old Alexander I to the throne, following the overthrow and assassination of his father, was met with jubilation and high hopes. His youth, enlightened education, and first statements as ruler seemed to justify these expectations. Some later historians, as the epigraph by the British historian Charques suggests, have viewed Alexander's reign as holding the potential to finally push Russia off the path of authoritarianism; conservative contemporaries, in fact, feared that this was precisely Alexander's intention. But most often historians have approached Alexander I as mystifyingly contradictory: "the enigmatic tsar," a "sphinx," and a "crowned Hamlet." Contemporary accounts also differed dramatically. He was hailed as a liberal by many writers, Thomas Jefferson among them, and denounced as a reactionary by numerous others, including Lord Byron. He was glorified as a pacifist, as the originator of the Holy Alliance, and in general as a man who did his utmost to

Alexander I. This contemporary painting captures both sides of Alexander I's image: his devotion to Russia's political and military might and his gentleness and good intentions, which led to him being offered the title "blessed" and being called, at the time of his death, "our angel." (*Tsarstvuiushchii dom Romanovyh*)

establish peace and a Christian brotherhood on earth. Yet this "angel"—an epithet frequently applied to Alexander I—was also a drill sergeant and a parade ground enthusiast. Some accounts see continual vacillation; others a shift from liberalism to reaction between the beginning and end of his reign.

A common explanation for the contradictory image of the emperor is psychological: his unstable, uncertain, and contradictory personality. Though psychology is a hazardous terrain for the historian, it can be observed that Alexander may have belonged with those exceedingly sensitive, charming, and restless individuals whose lives display a constant irritation, search, and disappointment. They lack balance, consistency, and firmness of purpose. They are essentially contradictory. Alexander I's inability to come to terms with himself and to pursue a steady course, it has been argued, explains his actions better than do allegations of cynicism or Machiavellianism. As is characteristic of the type, personal problems grew with the passage of time: the emperor became more and more irritable, tired, and suspicious of people; more dissatisfied with life; more frantically in search of transcendent answers.

A related explanation focuses on his upbringing. There was, to begin with, Alexander's difficult childhood and boyhood, in particular his ambiguous relations with his father, Paul, and his grandmother, Catherine the Great, who hated each other. Alexander spent more time with Catherine than with his parents, and he learned early the arts of flattery, dissimulation, and hypocrisy, or at least so his boyhood letters indicate. The empress took a great liking to Alexander from the very beginning and apparently wanted to make him her successor, bypassing Paul. Quite possibly only the suddenness of her death upset this plan.

Education also influenced the future emperor's character, views, and activities. Catherine the Great took a personal interest in Alexander's upbringing, which was guided by the ideas of the Enlightenment. Catherine personally and repeatedly instructed him in the principles that should define an ideal monarch, including Stoic self-control to enable the higher voice of reason to be heard, compassion and accessibility, and commitment to the common good. These lessons were elaborated by the tutor Catherine chose for the grand duke, a Swiss *philosophe* and professed republican named Frédéric-César de La Harpe, who showed Alexander classical examples of the virtuous ruler, guided by reason, working for the good of his people, but also elaborated on the ideal of a "civil society" in which the natural equality of human beings is respected and citizens participate actively in civic life. La Harpe had Alexander read all of the great books of the Enlightenment, both classical and modern, along with histories of every European nation and of the new republic of the United States. Catherine also arranged for a religion tutor who advocated a personal and universalistic faith that focused on the contemplative search for God's truth and the belief that God's main desire was for the happiness of all humanity. The problem, historians have argued, is that La Harpe's teaching had little in common with Russian reality. Some scholars believe that the contrast between theory and practice characteristic of Alexander I's reign stems from this one-sided education.

The circumstances of Alexander I's accession to the throne have also been analyzed for their effect on the sovereign's character and rule. Alexander found himself in a precarious position during Paul's reign, especially because Paul thought of divorcing his wife and of disinheriting Alexander and his other sons by her. The young grand duke almost certainly knew of the conspiracy against his father, but the murder of Emperor Paul was apparently a surprise and a shock. Certain critics attribute Alexander I's strong feeling of guilt and his later mysticism and lack of balance to the tragedy of his accession.

Finally, the contradictoriness of Alexander's reign can also be explained in terms of history and political culture. We have already often seen the tension between the ideal of a tsar as loving, benevolent, and devoted to the good of Russia and the ideal of the tsar as awesome (*groznyi*) and almighty in his power. In theory, there is no contradiction: absolute power is essential to unite the country and advance the common good. It requires strong central power to ensure, in Karamzin's words at the time of Alexander's accession, "happiness, joy, and glory." In practice, as we have often seen and will see again, these principles can be at odds.

The autocrat died in 1825, only forty-eight years old. However, as if to continue the mystery of Alexander I, some specialists insist that he did not die, but escaped from the throne to live in Siberia as a saintly hermit Theodore, or Fedor, Kuzmich. Based on such circumstantial evidence as the emperor's constant longing to shed the burdens of his office, and a court physician's refusal to sign the death warrant, this supposition needs further proof, although it cannot be entirely dismissed. Suicide might offer another explanation for a certain strangeness and confusion associated with the sovereign's death.

## Liberalism and Reform

Alexander I himself, on coming the throne, gave good cause for the hope among educated Russians that he would rule in the spirit of the Enlightenment. His manifesto on the occasion of his coronation proclaimed his self-ideal as a caring and virtuous ruler: "how sincerely we wish the happiness of our people, how pleasant it is for us to attest before the true sons of the fatherland to our love for the fatherland and attention to its good." The new emperor's first acts also encouraged liberal hopes. An amnesty restored to their former positions up to 12,000 men dismissed by Paul; the obnoxious restrictions on travel abroad and on the entry into Russia of foreigners as well as of foreign books and periodicals were abrogated; the censorship was relaxed, and private publishing houses were again allowed to open; torture in investigation was abolished; and the charters granted by Catherine the Great to the gentry and to towns regained their full force. But, of course, these welcome measures marked at best only the beginning of a liberal program. The key issues to be faced included serfdom and autocracy, together with the general backwardness of the country and the inadequacy and corruption of its administrative apparatus. One of the striking things about Alexander's reign is how much talk of reform there was but how little was actually accomplished. Unlike his predecessors, Alexander

*Лицевая сторона.*

*Оборотная сторона.*

Coronation Medal of Alexander I. The reverse side reads "Happiness to Each and Everyone." On the crowned column is the word "Law."  (*Tsarstvuiushchii dom Romanovykh*)

was willing to consider limiting autocracy and abolishing serfdom. But he was unwilling, or unable, to effect any substantial change.

It is generally said that there were two "liberal" periods in the reign of Alexander I, from 1801 to 1805 and from 1807 to 1812, each, incidentally, followed by war with France. The first period of reform, following immediately upon Alexander I's acquisition of the crown, was the most far-ranging in purpose and the most hopeful. The new emperor decided to transform Russia with the help of four young, cultivated, intelligent, and liberal friends, the so-called Unofficial Committee. The members of the committee, Nikolai Novosiltsev, Count Pavel Stroganov, Count Viktor Kochubey, and a Polish patriot Prince Adam Czartoryski, reflected the enlightened opinion of the period, ranging from Anglophilism to Jacobin connections. While they could not be classified as radicals, the four did represent a new departure after Paul's administration. The emperor spoke of them jokingly as his "Committee of Public Safety," a reference to the French Revolution that would have made his predecessors shudder. He met with the committee informally and frequently, often daily over coffee.

Our information about the work of the Unofficial Committee—which includes Stroganov's notes on the meetings—suggests that at first Alexander I intended to abolish autocracy and serfdom. However, the dangers and difficulties associated with these issues, as well as the unpreparedness for reform of the administration and the mass of people, quickly became apparent. Serfdom represented, so to speak, the greatest single interest in the empire, and its repeal was bound to affect the entire Russian society, in particular the extremely important gentry class. As to autocracy, the emperor himself, although at one time he had spoken of a republic, hesitated in practice to accept any diminution of his authority. Characteristically, he became disillusioned and impatient with the proceedings and called the Unofficial Committee together less and less frequently. The war of 1805 marked the conclusion of its activities. Russia, thus, went unregenerated and unreformed. Even more limited projects such as the proclamation of a Russian charter of rights failed to be translated into practice.

In fact, recent scholars have argued, Alexander I may never have seriously contemplated abolishing autocracy. Yes, he spoke often of a "constitution," but the question is how he understood this. As Marc Raeff and other historians have argued, Alexander I, and at least most of his advisors, probably did not mean limiting the power of the executive through a democratic balance of power. Rather, as elsewhere in Europe at the time, he thought of a constitution as primarily bringing an orderly system of administration and law, free of arbitrariness and willful caprice, enhanced perhaps by representation from various social estates. In a word, the ideal was a *Rechtsstaat,* a state based on "law," which meant a strong central government based on rationalized written procedures and clear and rational division of functions. In other words, like Peter the Great and Catherine the Great, Alexander believed in the necessity of a strong and rational central state that could guarantee order and happiness and be a dynamic force for change. In this view, his jealous protection of his prerogatives as an autocrat can be seen as neither hypocrisy nor vacillation but as the reflection of a certain philosophy of politics.

Although no great reforms ever materialized from all these discussions, the first years of Alexander's reign witnessed the enactment of some important specific measures. For example, the Senate was restored, or perhaps promoted, to a very high position in the state: it was to be the supreme judicial and administrative institution in the empire, and its decrees were to carry the authority of those of the sovereign, who alone could stop their execution. Peter the Great's colleges, which had a checkered and generally unhappy history in the eighteenth century, were gradually replaced in 1802 and subsequent years by ministries, with a single minister in charge of each. At first there were eight: the ministries of war, navy, foreign affairs, justice, interior, finance, commerce, and education. Later the ministry of commerce was abolished, and the ministry of police appeared. The reasoning, as expressed in an 1810 decree defining the responsibilities of the ministries, was characteristically rationalistic: "to introduce a more equal division of state affairs and more uniformity in their execution, and to simplify and make easier their functioning in order that the limits of authority and responsibility may be precisely defined."

The government also undertook some limited social legislation. In 1801 the right to own estates was extended from the gentry to other free Russians. In 1803 the so-called "law concerning the free agriculturists" went into effect. It provided for voluntary emancipation of the serfs by their masters, assuring that the emancipated serfs would be given land and establishing regulations and courts to secure the observance of all provisions. The newly emancipated serfs were to receive in many respects the status of state peasants, but, by contrast with the latter, they were to enjoy stronger property rights and exemption from certain obligations. Few landlords, however, proved eager to free their peasants. To be more exact, under the provisions of the law concerning the free agriculturists from the time of its enactment until its suspension more than half a century later on the eve of "the great reforms," 384 masters emancipated 115,734 working male serfs together with their families.

Russian backwardness and ignorance became strikingly apparent to the monarch and his Unofficial Committee as they examined the condition of the country. Education, therefore, received a high priority in the official plans and activities of the first years of the reign. Fortunately too this effort did not present quite the dangers and obstacles that were associated with the issues of serfdom and autocracy. Spending large sums of money on education for the first time in Russian history, Alexander I founded several universities to add to the University of Moscow, forty-two secondary schools, and considerable numbers of other schools. Education in Russia during the first half of the nineteenth century will be discussed in a later chapter, but it should be noted here that Alexander I's establishment of institutions of learning and his entire school policy were distinctly liberal for his time. Indeed, they have been called the best fruits of the monarch's usually hesitant and brittle liberalism.

The second period of reform in Alexander I's reign, 1807–12, corresponded to the French alliance and was dominated by the emperor's most remarkable assistant, Mikhail Speransky. Speransky, who lived from 1772 to 1839, was fully a self-made man. In contrast to the members of the Unofficial Committee as well as to most other associates of the sovereign, he came not from the aristocracy but from poor village clergy. It was Speransky's intelligence, ability to work, and outstanding administrative capacity that made him for a time Alexander I's prime minister in fact, if not in name, for no such formal office then existed. As most specialists on Speransky believe, that unusual statesman sought to establish in Russia a strong monarchy firmly based on law and legal procedure, and thus free from arbitrariness, corruption, and confusion. In other words, Speransky found his inspiration in the vision of a *Rechtsstaat*, not in advanced liberal or radical schemes. Still, Marc Raeff, the best author on the subject, goes too far when he denies that the Russian statesman was at all liberal. In Russian conditions Speransky's views were certainly liberal, as his contemporaries fully realized. Furthermore, they could have been developed more liberally, if the opportunities had presented themselves.

In 1809, at the emperor's request, Speransky submitted to him a thorough proposal for a constitution. In his customary methodical manner, the statesman divided the population into three categories: the gentry; people of "the middle condition," that is, merchants, artisans, and peasants or other small proprietors who owned property of a certain value; and, finally, working people, including serfs, servants, and apprentices. The plan also postulated three kinds of rights: general civil rights; special civil rights, such as exemption from service; and political rights, which depended on a property qualification. The members of the gentry were to enjoy all the rights. Those belonging to the middle group received general civil rights and political rights when they could meet the property requirement. The working people too obtained general civil rights, but they clearly did not own enough to participate in politics. Russia was to be reorganized on four administrative levels: the *volost*—a small unit sometimes translated as "canton" or "township"—the district, the province, and the country at large. At each level there were to be the following institutions: legislative assemblies—or *dumy*—culminating in the state duma for all of Russia; a system of courts, with the Senate at the apex; and administrative boards, leading eventually to the ministries and the central executive power. The state duma, the most intriguing part of Speransky's system, showed the statesman's caution, for in addition to the property restriction imposed on its electorate, it depended on a sequence of indirect elections. The assemblies of the volosti elected the district assemblymen, who elected the provincial assemblymen, who elected the members of the state duma, or national assembly. Also the activities of the state duma were apparently to be rather narrowly restricted. But, on the other hand, the state duma did provide for popular participation in the legislative process. That, together with Speransky's insistence on the division of functions, strict legality, and certain other provisions such as the popular election of judges, if successfully applied, would have in time transformed Russia. Indeed, it has been observed that Speransky's fourfold proposal of local self-government and a national legislative assembly represented a farsighted outline of the Russian future. That future, however, took extremely long to materialize, offering—in the opinion of many specialists—a classic example of too little and too late. Thus Russia received district and provincial self-government by the so-called zemstvo reform of 1864; a national legislature, the Duma, in 1905–6; and volost self-government in 1917.

In 1809 and the years following, Alexander I failed to implement Speransky's proposal. The statesman's fall from power in 1812 resulted from the opposition of officialdom and the gentry evoked by his measures and projects in administration and finance, from the emperor's fears, suspicions, and vacillations, and also from the break with Napoleon, Speransky having been branded a Francophile. Although Speransky was later to return to public office and accomplish further useful and important work, he never again had the opportunity to suggest fundamental reform on the scale of his plan of 1809. The second liberal period of Alexander I's reign, then, like the first, produced no basic changes in Russia.

Yet, again like the first, the second liberal period led to some significant legislation of a more limited nature. In 1810, on the advice of Speransky—actually this was the only part of the statesman's plan that the monarch translated into practice—Alexander I created the Council of State modeled after Napoleon's *Conseil d'Etat*, with Speransky attached to it as the Secretary of State. This body of experts appointed by the sovereign to help him with the legislative work in no way limited the principle of autocracy; moreover, the Council tended to be extremely conservative. Still, it clearly reflected the emphasis on legality, competence, and correct procedure so dear to Speransky. And, as has been noted for the subsequent history of the Russian Empire, whereas "all the principal reforms were passed by regular procedure through the Council of State, nearly all the most harmful and most mischievous acts of succeeding governments were, where possible, withdrawn from its competence and passed only as executive regulations which were nominally temporary." Speransky also reorganized the ministries and added two special agencies to the executive, one for the supervision of government finance, the other for the development of transport. A system of annual budgets was instituted, and other financial measures were proposed and in part adopted. Perhaps still more importantly, Speransky did yeoman's service in strengthening Russian bureaucracy by introducing something in the nature of a civil service examination and trying in other ways to emphasize merit and efficient organization.

Speransky's constitutional reform project represented the most outstanding but not the only such plan to come out of government circles in the reign of Alexander I. One other should be noted here, that of Novosiltsev. Novosiltsev's *Constitutional Charter of the Russian Empire* emphasized very heavily the position and authority of the sovereign and bore strong resemblance to Speransky's scheme in its stress on legality and rights and its narrowly based and weak legislative assembly. Novosiltsev differed, however, from Speransky's rigorous centralism in allowing something to the federal principle: he wanted the Russian Empire, including Finland and Russian Poland, to be divided into twelve large groups of provinces which were to enjoy a certain autonomy. The date of Novosiltsev's project deserves attention: its second and definitive version was presented to Alexander I in 1820, late in his reign. Furthermore, the monarch not only graciously accepted the plan, but—it has been argued—proceeded to implement it in small part. Namely, by combining several provinces, he created as a model one of the twelve units proposed by Novosiltsev. Only after Alexander I's death in 1825 was Novosiltsev's scheme completely abandoned, and the old system of administration re-established in the experimental provinces. The story of Novosiltsev's *Charter*, together with certain other developments, introduces qualifications into the usual sharp division of Alexander I's reign into the liberal first half and the reactionary second half and suggests that a constitution remained a possible alternative for Russia as long as "the enigmatic tsar" presided over its destinies.

## Foreign Policy, Wars, and the Expansion of Empire, 1801–12

One explanation for the failure of reform is Alexander I's preoccupation with diplomacy and war, especially the difficult, even cataclysmic, wars against Napoleon. Alexander's reign began with declarations of peaceful intentions and a certain isolationism. Around 1805, however, influenced by Czartoryski (to whom Alexander confessed some regret over the partition of Poland and hope it could be reversed), an isolationist policy, based on the assumption that Russia's interests were best served by protecting the existing balance of powers, gave way to an activist policy, based on the assumption that Russia's strategic advantages gave it the responsibility to lead the continent to true peace, which was threatened by French expansionism.

After succeeding Paul, who had both fought France and later joined it against Great Britain, the new emperor proclaimed a policy of neutrality. Yet Russia could not long stay out of the conflicts raging in Europe. Not surprisingly, Alexander I joined the opponents of France. Economic ties with Great Britain, and traditional Russian friendship with Austria and Great Britain, together with the equally traditional hostility to France, contributed to the decision. Furthermore, Alexander I came early to consider Napoleon as a menace to Europe, all the more so because the Russian sovereign had his own vision of a new European order. An outline of the subsequent Holy Alliance and concert of Europe, without the religious coloration, can be found in the instructions issued in 1804 to the Russian envoy in Great Britain.

The War of the Third Coalition broke out in 1805 when Austria, Russia, and Sweden joined Great Britain against France and its ally, Spain. The combined Austrian and Russian armies suffered a crushing defeat at the hands of Napoleon on December 2, 1805, at Austerlitz. Although Austria was knocked out of the war, the Russians continued to fight and in 1806 even obtained a new ally, Prussia. But the French armies, in a nineteenth-century version of the *Blitzkrieg*, promptly destroyed the Prussian forces in the battles of Jena and Auerstädt, and, although they could not destroy the Russians, finally succeeded in inflicting a major defeat on them at Friedland. The treaties of Tilsit between France and Russia and France and Prussia followed early in July 1807. The Franco-Prussian settlement reduced Prussia to a second-rate power, saved from complete destruction by the insistence of the Russian sovereign. The agreement between France and Russia was a different matter, for, although Alexander I had to accept Napoleon's redrawing of the map of Europe and even had to support him, notably against Great Britain, Russia emerged as the hegemon of much of eastern Europe and the only major power on the continent other than France.

It was the temporary settlement with France that allowed the Russians to fight several other opponents and expand the boundaries of the empire in the first half of Alexander's reign. In 1801 the eastern part of Georgia, an ancient Orthodox country in Transcaucasia, joined Russia, and Russian sway was extended to western Georgia in 1803–10. Hard-pressed by their powerful Muslim neighbors, the Persians and the Turks, the Georgians had repeatedly asked and occasionally received Russian aid. Especially as Iran and the Ottoman Empire weakened, Russian expansion represented the logical culmination of a process. To be sure, Georgian disillusionment with Russian rule would later develop; but the official Russian view at the time that this was a voluntary entry into the empire is consistent with the facts. This also marked the first step in the extension of Russian imperial authority across the great Caucasian mountain range. In response, Britain and France began to view Russia as a colonial rival.

As expected, the annexation of Georgia by Russia led to a Russo-Persian war, fought from 1804 to 1813. The Russians proved victorious, and by the Treaty of Gulistan Persia had to recognize Russian rule in Georgia and cede to its northern neighbor the areas of Daghestan and Shemakha in the Caucasus. The annexation of Georgia also served as one of the causes of a Russo-Turkish war that lasted from 1806 to 1812. Again, Russian troops, this time led by Kutuzov, scored a number of successes. The Treaty of Bucharest, hastily concluded by Kutuzov on the eve of Napoleon's invasion of Russia, added Bessarabia and a strip on the eastern coast of the Black Sea to the empire of the Romanovs, and also granted Russia extensive rights in the Danubian principalities of Moldavia and Wallachia. Finally, in 1808–9 Alexander I fought and defeated Sweden, with the result that the Peace of Frederikshamn gave Finland to Russia. Finland became an autonomous grand duchy with the Russian emperor as its grand duke.

The first half of Alexander's reign also witnessed a continuation of Russian expansion in North America, which had started in Alaska in the late eighteenth century. New forts were built not only in Alaska but also in northern California, where Fort Ross was erected in 1812.

## 1812

The days of the Russian alliance with Napoleon were numbered. The agreement that the two emperors reached in Tilsit in 1807, and which was renewed at their meeting in Erfurt in 1808, failed in the long run to satisfy either side. The Russians, who were forced to accept it because of their military defeat, resented Napoleon's domination of the continent, his disregard of Russian interests, and, in particular, the obligation to participate in the so-called continental blockade. That blockade, meant to eliminate all commerce between Great Britain and other European countries and to strangle the British economy, actually helped Russian manufactures, especially in the textile industry, by excluding British competition. But it did hurt Russian exporters and thus the powerful landlord class. Russian military reverses at the hands of the French cried for revenge, especially because they came after a century of almost uninterrupted Russian victories. Also, Napoleon, who had emerged from the fearful French Revolution, who had upset the legitimate order in

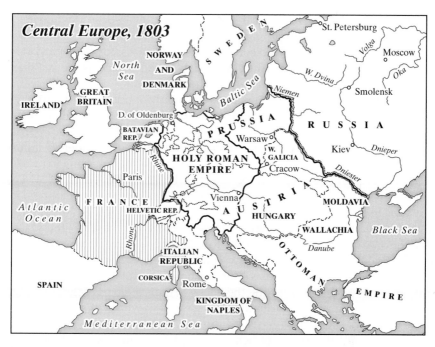

Central Europe, 1803

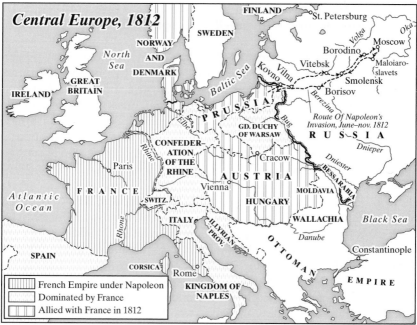

Central Europe, 1812

French Empire under Napoleon
Dominated by France
Allied with France in 1812

Europe on an unprecedented scale, and who had even been denounced as Antichrist in some Russian propaganda to the masses, appeared to be a peculiar and undesirable ally. Napoleon and his lieutenants, for their part, came to regard Russia as an utterly unreliable partner and indeed as the last major obstacle to their complete domination of the continent.

Tensions and crises multiplied, involving a mix of traditional competition between state powers and newer elements of imperial and colonial rivalry. The French protested the Russian perfunctory, and in fact feigned, participation in Napoleon's war against Austria in 1809, and Alexander I's failure, from 1810 on, to observe the continental blockade. The Russians expressed bitterness over the development of an active French policy in the Near East and over Napoleon's efforts to curb rather than support the Russian position and aims in the Balkans and the Near East: the French opposed Russian control of the Danubian principalities, objected to Russian bases in the eastern Mediterranean, and would not let the Russians have a free hand in regard to Constantinople and the Straits. Napoleon's political rearrangement of central and eastern Europe also provoked Russian hostility. Notably his deposing the Duke of Oldenburg and annexing the duchy to France, a part of the rearrangement in Germany, offended the Russian sovereign, who was a close relative of the duke. Still more ominously for Russia, in 1809 after the French victory over Austria and the Treaty of Schönbrunn, West Galicia was added to the Duchy of Warsaw, a state created by Napoleon from Prussian Poland. This change appeared to threaten in turn Russia's hold on the vast lands that it had acquired in the partitions of Poland.

In June 1812, having made the necessary diplomatic and military preparations, Napoleon invaded Russia. France had obtained the support of a number of European states, allies, satellites, including Austria and Prussia: the twelve invading tongues in the popular Russian tradition. Russia had just succeeded in making peace with Turkey, and it had acquired active allies in Sweden and Great Britain. Scholars continue to debate the exact size of the opposing armies, but none doubt the overwhelming size of the French invasion force. Napoleon crossed the Nieman River into Russia with from 450,000 to 600,000 troops to face perhaps 200,000 Russian soldiers and cossacks, an army that grew with reinforcements to no more than 400,000 troops. The Russian force was divided into two separate armies, one commanded by Prince Michael Barclay de Tolly and the other by Prince Peter Bagration. In addition to its tremendous numbers, Napoleon's army had the reputation of invincibility and what was considered to be an incomparably able leadership. Yet all the advantages were not on one side. Napoleon's *Grande Armée* contained a surprisingly small proportion of veterans. Also, Frenchmen constituted less than half of it, while of the allied troops only the Poles, who fought for a great independent Poland, acquitted themselves with distinction. With the return of the Russian forces from the Turkish front, the arrival of other Russian reinforcements, and the extension of French lines of communication which had to be protected, the French advantage of greater numbers was much reduced. Moreover, on the whole the country rallied solidly behind Alexander I, and the Russian soldiers fought with remarkable tenacity. Indeed, Napoleon's expectations that their early defeats would force the Russians to sue for peace proved groundless. An early and exceptionally cold winter contributed its share to the Russian cause. But, above all, problems of logistics involved in the French campaign turned out to be much more difficult to resolve than Napoleon and his assistants had foreseen.

Napoleon advanced into the heart of Russia along the Vilna-Vitebsk-Smolensk line, just as Charles XII had done a century earlier. The Russians could not stop the invaders and lost several engagements to them, including the bloody battle of Smolensk. However, Russian troops inflicted considerable losses on the enemy, and near Smolensk the two separate Russian armies managed to effect a junction and thus present a united front to the invaders. Under the pressure of public opinion incensed by the continuous French advance, Alexander I put Prince Mikhail Kutuzov in supreme command of the Russian forces. A disciple of Suvorov and a veteran of many campaigns, the sixty-seven-year-old Kutuzov did agree in fact with Barclay de Tolly's policy of retreat. Still, he felt it incumbent upon him and his army to fight before surrendering Moscow, and so gave Napoleon a major battle on the seventh of September near the village of Borodino, seventy-five miles from the great Russian city. The battle of Borodino had few equals in history for the severity of the fighting. Although it lasted but a single day, the extent of the bloodshed was staggering. The number of dead and wounded in the Russian army (and many would later die of their wounds) likely numbered around 40,000 men out of about 100,000 who went into battle. French casualties were approximately 28,000 out of 120,000 combatants. The casualties included scores of generals and thousands of officers, with Prince Bagration and other prominent commanders among the dead or fatally wounded. By nightfall the Russians in the center and on the left flank had been forced to retreat slightly, while they held fast on the right. Kutuzov, however, decided to disengage and to withdraw southeast of Moscow. On the fourteenth of September Napoleon entered the Kremlin.

His expectations of final victory and peace were cruelly deceived. In a rare demonstration of tenacity, Alexander I refused even to consider peace as long as a single French soldier remained on Russian soil. Far from providing sumptuous accommodations for the French emperor and his army, Moscow, still constructed largely of wood, burned down during the first days of the French occupation. It is possible that Count Fedor Rostopchin, the Russian governor and military commander of the city, deliberately started the conflagration—as most French and some Russian specialists assert—but this remains a disputed issue. Unable to obtain peace from Alexander and largely isolated in the Russian wasteland, Napoleon had to retreat before the onset of winter. The return march of the *Grande Armée,* which started on October 19, gradually became a rout. To begin with, the action of the Russian army at Maloiaroslavets prevented the French from taking a new road through fertile areas untouched by war and forced them to leave the way they had come. As Napoleon's soldiers marched slowly westward, winter descended upon them and they were constantly pressed by the pursuing Russian forces—although Kutuzov chose to avoid a major engagement—and harassed by cossacks and other irregulars, including peasant guerrillas. The French and their allies perished in droves, and their discipline began to break down. Late in November, as the remnants of the *Grande Armée* crossed the Berezina River, they were lucky to escape capture through the mistake of a Russian commander. Out of the total force of perhaps, from 30,000 to 50,000 men finally struggled out of Russia.

The catastrophic French defeat can be ascribed to a number of factors: the fighting spirit of the Russian army, Kutuzov's wise decisions, Napoleon's crucial mistakes, Alexander's determination to continue the war, the winter, and others. But the breakdown of the transportation and supply of the *Grand Armée* should rank high among the reasons for its collapse. More of Napoleon's soldiers, died from hunger and epidemics than from cold, for the supply services, handicapped by enormous distances, insecure lines of communication, and bad planning, failed on the whole to sustain the military effort. It should be mentioned that, contrary to legend, historians have established that the Russian high command had no "Scythian policy" of retreat with the intention of enticing Napoleon's army deep into a devastated country. The French advance resulted rather from Russian inability to stop the invader and from Napoleon's obsession with seizing Moscow. In many respects, the war of 1812 deserves its reputation in Russian history as a popular, patriotic war. Except for certain small court circles, no defeatism appeared in the midst of the Russian government, educated public, or people. Moreover, the Russian peasants not only fought heroically in the ranks of the regular army but also banded into guerrilla detachments to attack the enemy on their own, an activity unparalleled at the time except in Spain. Indeed, not included in the numbers of causalities previously mentioned were large numbers of civilians, both partisans and ordinary villagers along the path of war.

## Russian Foreign Policy, 1812–25

Alexander I carried the war beyond the boundaries of Russia. Prussia and, several months later, Austria switched sides to join Russia, Sweden, and Great Britain. The combined forces of Austria, Prussia, and Russia finally scored a decisive victory over Napoleon in the tremendous Battle of Leipzig, known as the "Battle of the Nations," fought from October 16-19, 1813. Late that year they began to cross the Rhine and invade France. After more desperate fighting and in spite of another display of the French emperor's military genius, the allies entered Paris triumphantly on March 31, 1814. Alexander I referred to that day as the happiest of his life. Napoleon had to abdicate unconditionally and retire to the island of Elba. He returned on March 1, 1815, rapidly won back the French throne, and threatened the allies until his final defeat at Waterloo on June 18.

The French emperor's abortive comeback thus failed to undo the new settlement for Europe drawn by the victors at the Congress of Vienna. The

Congress, which lasted from September 1814, until the Act was signed on June 9, 1815, constituted one of the most impressive and important diplomatic gatherings in history. Alexander I himself represented Russia and played a leading role at the Congress together with Metternich of Austria, Castlereagh of Great Britain, Hardenberg of Prussia, and, eventually, Talleyrand of France. The great powers, assembled in Vienna, redrew the political map of Europe and resolved certain conflicts over colonial territories in Africa and Asia, all with the goal of promoting greater stability as well as protecting and advancing their gains. Russia's geopolitical ambitions were focused especially on Poland, one of the most contentious issues at the conference. Alexander I wanted to establish a large kingdom of Poland in personal union with Russia, that is, with himself as king. His reasons likely included not only further geopolitical expansion but also a way of undoing the unjust partition of Poland and creating a testing ground for liberal reform. As compensation he offered to support the Prussian claim to all of Saxony. The Prussians agreed, but Great Britain and Austria strongly opposed the plan. Talleyrand used this opportunity to bring France back into the diplomatic picture, on the side of Great Britain and Austria. The conflict almost provoked a war. Alexander was forced to compromise—which angered many Russians who expected "gratitude" for "liberating Europe from Napoleon." He obtained his Kingdom of Poland, but reduced in size, while Prussia acquired about three-fifths of Saxony. More precisely, the Kingdom of Poland contained most of the former Grand Duchy of Warsaw, with Warsaw itself as its capital, but Prussia regained northwestern Poland, and Austria retained most of its earlier share of the country; Cracow became a free city-state under the joint protection of Russia, Austria, and Prussia. New Poland received a liberal constitution from Alexander I. He thus combined the offices of autocratic Russian emperor, constitutional Finnish grand duke, and constitutional Polish king. It might be added that he also favored constitutionalism in France, where the Bourbons returned to the throne as constitutional, not absolute, monarchs.

Alexander I's elated, mystical, and even messianic mood at the time of the Congress of Vienna—a complex sentiment that the Russian sovereign apparently shared in some measure with many other Europeans in the months and years following the shattering fall of Napoleon, expressed itself best in a remarkable and peculiar document known as the Holy Alliance. Signed on September 26, 1815, by Russia, Austria, and Prussia, and subsequently by the great majority of European powers, the alliance simply appealed to Christian rulers to live as brothers and preserve peace in Europe. While the Holy Alliance had deep roots in at least two major Western traditions, Christianity and international law, it had singularly little relevance to the international problems of the moment and provided no machinery for the application or enforcement of Christian brotherhood. Indeed, Castlereagh could well describe it as a piece of sublime mysticism and nonsense, while the pope remarked drily that from time immemorial the papacy had been in possession of Christian truth and needed no new interpretation of it.

But, if the Holy Alliance had no practical consequences, the Quadruple Alliance, and the later Quintuple Alliance with which it came to be confused, did. The Quadruple Alliance represented a continuation of the wartime association of the allies and dated from November 20, 1815. At that time Great Britain, Austria, Russia, and Prussia agreed to maintain the settlement with France and in particular to prevent the return of Napoleon or his dynasty to the French throne. The alliance was to last for twenty years. Moreover, its sixth article provided for periodic consultations among the signatory powers and resulted in the "government by conference," also known as the Congress System or Confederation of Europe. Conferences took place at Aix-la-Chapelle in 1818, Troppau and Laibach in 1820–21, and Verona in 1822. At Aix-la-Chapelle, with the payment of the indemnity and the withdrawal of allied occupation troops, France shed its status as a defeated nation and joined the other four great European powers in the Quintuple Alliance.

After an impressive start, the Congress System failed to work. A fundamental split developed between Great Britain, which, as the British state paper of May 5, 1820, made plain, opposed intervention in the internal affairs of sovereign states, and Austria, Prussia, and Russia, who, as the Protocol of Troppau spelled out, were determined to suppress revolution, no matter where it raised its head. Also, Britain increasingly viewed Russia as a menacing rival to its interests in Europe and in overseas colonies, and the British public viewed the repressive tendencies of the Russian autocracy with distaste. France occupied something of an intermediate position, although it did invade Spain to crush the liberal regime there. Metternich tended to dominate the joint policies of the eastern European monarchies, especially in the crucial years of 1820–22 when Alexander I, frightened by a mutiny in the elite Semenovskii guard regiment and other events, followed the Austrian chancellor in his eagerness to combat revolution everywhere. Thus, when the Orthodox Greeks rose against their Ottoman rulers in 1821, Metternich convinced Alexander that preserving monarchical legitimacy, even of a despised Muslim ruler, overrode the rights of national minorities, even Christian ones. The conservative European powers succeeded in defeating a series of liberal revolutions on the continent of Europe, though these victories proved to be short-lived, as the subsequent history of Europe in the nineteenth century was to demonstrate.

The Congress System has been roundly condemned by many historians as a tool of reaction, both noxious and essentially ineffective in maintaining order and stability in Europe. Yet at least one positive aspect of that unusual political phenomenon and of Alexander I's role in it deserves notice. The architects of the Congress System may have created, at its best, more than a mere diplomatic alliance of the great powers. A British historian writing about the Congress of Aix-la-Chapelle called it "a European representative body" and even "a sort of European Supreme Court, which heard appeals and received petitions of all kinds from sovereigns and their subjects alike." This European harmony did not last, of course, and "the Confederation of Europe" seems too grand a designation for the alliance following the Congress of Vienna.

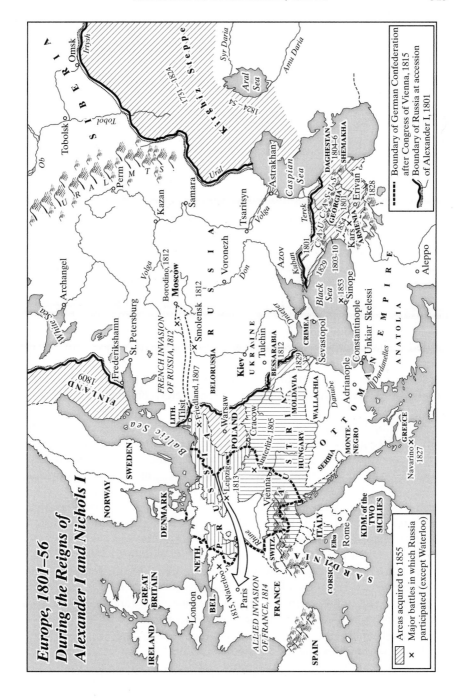

*Europe, 1801–56
During the Reigns of
Alexander I and Nichols I*

Boundary of German Confederation
after Congress of Vienna, 1815

Boundary of Russia at accession
of Alexander I, 1801

Areas acquired to 1855

× Major battles in which Russia
participated (except Waterloo)

Yet, it can be argued, the Congress System can be seen as an early, in a sense prophetic, predecessor to the still evolving European Union of our time. And it was Alexander I who, more than any other European leader, emphasized the broad construction of the Quadruple and the Quintuple alliances and tried to develop cooperation and unity in Europe. He even proposed forming a permanent international army to guarantee the European settlement and offered Russian troops for that purpose, but the suggestion was speedily rejected by Castlereagh and Metternich. He also proposed, again unsuccessfully, disarmament.

## The Second Half of Alexander's Reign

While "the emperor of Europe" attended international meetings and occupied himself with the affairs of foreign countries, events in Russia took a turn for the worse. The second half of Alexander's reign, that is, the period after 1812, saw virtually no progressive legislation and few plans in that direction; Novosiltsev's constitutional project formed a notable exception. In Poland the constitutional regime, impressive on paper, did not function well, largely because Alexander I proved to be a poor constitutional monarch because he quickly became irritated by criticism or opposition and repeatedly disregarded the law. Serfs were emancipated in the Baltic provinces, but, because they were freed without land, the change turned out to be a doubtful blessing for them. Serfdom remained undiminished and unchallenged in Russia proper, although apparently to the last the sovereign considered emancipating the serfs.

While Speransky was Alexander I's outstanding assistant in the first half of the reign, General Alexei Arakcheev came to occupy that position in the second half—and the difference between the two men tells us much about the course of Russian history in the first quarter of the nineteenth century. Arakcheev, once a faithful servant of Emperor Paul and a distinguished specialist in artillery and military matters in general, was brutal, rude, and a martinet of the worst sort. He became Alexander's minister of war and eventually prime minister, without the title, reporting to the sovereign on almost everything of importance in the internal affairs of Russia and entrusted with every kind of responsibility. Yet the rather common image of the evil genius Arakcheev imposing his will on the emperor badly distorts the relationship. In fact, it was precisely the general's unquestioning and prompt execution of Alexander's orders that made him indispensable to the monarch.

In the years following the Napoleonic wars, Alexander became increasingly attached to the ideal of discipline and order, often linked to his growing regard for his own sacred authority and mission. Military parades and architecture exemplified principles of orderliness and cleanliness, demonstrating, in Richard Wortman's words, "the emperor's invincible power over refractory reality." Arakcheev well suited these inclinations. A perfect—and perfectly flawed—expression of this cult of orderliness were the so-called military settlements, or military colonies, that are often the main thing remembered about Arakcheev. The project, however, was evidently Alexander's idea, though it was executed by Arakcheev. The plan was largely inspired by the precision and order on Arakcheev's own estate, which Alexander had visited in 1810. Arakcheev combined on his lands intense supervision of serfs and draconian punishments—it was said that among other regulations, every married woman was commanded to bear a child every year—with a certain vision of rural well-being: he replaced village huts with barracks arrayed in symmetrical order. Alexander admired "the symmetry and elegance" and "cleanliness" of it all. Applied to the military, the idea was to combine military service with farming, both to reduce the cost of the army and to enable soldiers to lead a normal family life, for this was also a humanitarian endeavor. The reform began in 1810, was interrupted by war, and attained its greatest impetus and scope between 1816 and 1821, with at least one-third, possibly as much as a half, of the peacetime Russian army established in military settlements, where soldiers lived in orderly barracks arranged in squares with a watchtower at the center. Everything was said to be in "good order." Scholars have described the settlements as an experimental "utopia" of ordered, rationalized, and supervised men and space. Troubles and uprisings in the settlements, however, checked their growth. After the rebellion of 1831, Nicholas I turned definitely against the reform, but the last settlements were abolished only much later. Alexander I's and Arakcheev's scheme failed principally because of the extreme regimentation and minute despotism that it entailed, which became unbearable. Richard Pipes has argued further that Russian soldiers proved particularly poor material for this venture in state direction and paternalism, resenting even useful sanitary regulations.

In the final years of Alexander's reign, there are signs that he was losing confidence in this faith in rational order as the best path to happiness. He began to voice doubts that mortals could actually end the sufferings and evils of the world. He became more and more pious and mystical and came to see religious faith rather than secular change as the best means of ensuring the people's happiness—hence his support for the Russian Bible Society's massive campaign to distribute bibles and for education officials who tried to purge higher education of the pernicious influences of the Age of Reason. He began to show less interest in government. He even lost his old charm and became testy and peremptory. Partly to escape the capital city but also to show the people his care for their needs, Alexander spent much time in his final years traveling around Russia. He was warmly received and praised as a tender and loving tsar, a humble man willing to walk among his people. But the backwardness and suffering he saw on his travels only seem to have reinforced his anxieties and doubts. A key moment was the gigantic flood in St. Petersburg in 1824, which wreaked terrible destruction and death. In its wake, Alexander toured the city and viewed the carnage. It is said that at one point he got out of his carriage, stood, and wept. Pushkin was soon to make this flood culturally famous as a symbol of the hubris of the imperial state's rationalist project to control nature and impose order on the world. We do not know if this is how Alexander understood the disaster. Reportedly, though, when someone suggested that the flood was God's punishment for the sins and failings of the people, he replied, "No, for mine." The discrepancy between myth and reality had reached a crossroads.

## The Decembrist Movement and Rebellion

Disappointment with the course of Alexander I's reign played an important role in the emergence of the first Russian revolutionary group, which came to be known after its unsuccessful uprising in December 1825 as the Decembrists. Most of the Decembrists were army officers, often from aristocratic families and elite regiments, who had received a good education, learned French and sometimes other foreign languages, and obtained a first-hand knowledge of the West during and immediately after the campaigns against Napoleon.

Initially, these young men sympathized with Alexander I's enlightened purposes, but they grew disenchanted, first with the lack of positive results and then with the growing conservatism. The Decembrists were essentially liberals in the tradition of the Enlightenment and the French Revolution; they wanted to establish constitutionalism and basic freedoms in Russia and to abolish serfdom. They produced a variety of statements and programs, indicating the range of liberal opinion among educated Russians in the early nineteenth century. The most moderate, reflected in the "constitution" drafted by Nikita Muraviev, envisioned a Russia ruled by a hereditary monarch who shared power with an elected legislature. The most radical document, Colonel Pavel Pestel's *Russian Justice* (*Russkaia pravda*), favored a Jacobin-style dictatorship for the first ten years after the revolution and then a strongly centralized republic. As can be seen, all agreed on the necessity of a strong state to ensure progress. At the very minimum, it was the responsibility of this revolutionary state to defend the rights of individuals, abolish serfdom (the ultimate violation of the natural freedom and dignity of the individual), advance education and social welfare, and ensure basic civil rights, especially freedom of speech, press, religion, and assembly. While the Decembrists included some of the most gifted and prominent Russian youth and enjoyed the sympathy of many educated Russians, including such literary luminaries as Pushkin and Griboedov, they had little social backing for their rebellion. Russian liberalism was still far from the broad social movements seen in England or France. The feebleness and backwardness of the Russian middle class was one of many key differences.

The first societies formed by the future Decembrists, such as the Union of Salvation, founded in St. Petersburg in 1816, and the Union of Welfare that replaced it the following year, still wished to cooperate with Alexander I and were concerned with the development of philanthropy, education, and the civic spirit in Russia rather than with military rebellion. But as reaction grew and hopes for a liberal transformation from above faded, some of these idealistic young men begin to think seriously of revolution. The movement acquired two centers, St. Petersburg in the north, where the Union of Salvation had become in 1821 the more political and conspiratorial Northern Society, and the radical Southern Society, led by Pestel, located in Tulchin, the headquarters of the Second Army, in western Ukraine. Organizationally, the Southern Society was especially effective and increasingly large. It soon incorporated the Society of the United Slavs—a less aristocratic alliance of lower-ranking army officers who shared the general aims of the Decembrists with the additional goal of a democratic federation of all Slavic peoples—and established contacts with a Polish revolutionary group. When the hour of rebellion suddenly arrived, however, the Southern Society, handicapped by Pestel's arrest, proved to be little better prepared than the Northern.

A dynastic crisis created the opportunity to act. When Alexander I died unexpectedly in December 1825, it was not entirely clear who should ascend to the throne. Since the late emperor had no sons or grandsons, according to Paul's law of succession, the next in line was Alexander's eldest brother Constantine. However, he had renounced his rights to the throne five years earlier when he married a Polish aristocrat who was not of royal blood. A manifesto by Alexander recognized this in 1822 and named Nicholas, the third brother, heir to the throne. But the manifesto had remained unpublished, and only a few people had received exact information about it. The problem was not simply uncertainty, of course. In much of educated society, Nicholas was viewed as a reactionary, whereas Constantine was thought to have more liberal views. In any case, the capital and the army swore allegiance to the new emperor Constantine I, Constantine reaffirmed his position renouncing that claim, Nicholas published Alexander's 1822 manifesto, and then guard's regiments in St. Petersburg were told to swear allegiance to the new ruler for a second time, this time to Nicholas I.

At this moment, the Northern Society of the Decembrists staged its rebellion. Realizing that they had a unique chance to act, the conspiring officers used their influence with the soldiers to start a mutiny in several units by entreating them to defend Constantine's rightful interests against his usurping brother. Altogether about 3,000 misled rebels came in military formation to Senate Square in the heart of the capital. Although the government was caught unprepared, the mutineers were soon faced by troops several times their number and strength. The two forces stood opposite each other for several hours. The Decembrists failed to act because of their general confusion and lack of leadership; the new emperor hesitated to start his reign with a massacre of his subjects, hoping that they could be talked into submission. But, as verbal inducements failed and dusk began to gather on the afternoon of that northern winter day, artillery was brought into action. Several canister shots dispersed the rebels, killing sixty or seventy of them. Large-scale arrests followed. In the south, too, an uprising was easily suppressed. Eventually five Decembrist leaders, including Pestel and the firebrand of the Northern Society, the poet

Kondratti Ryleev, were executed, while almost 300 other participants suffered exile to Siberia and other punishments. Here began the reign of Nicholas I, who would become famous for tightening authoritarian power. So, too, might we date the beginnings of Russia's revolutionary movement with the rise and fall of the Decembrist rebellion.

# CHAPTER 26

# The Reign of Nicholas I, 1825–55

Here [in the army] there is order, there is a strict unconditional legality, no impertinent claims to know all the answers, no contradiction, all things flow logically one from the other; no one commands before he has himself learned to obey; no one steps in front of anyone else without lawful reason; everything is subordinated to one definite goal, everything has its purpose. That is why I feel so well among these people, and why I shall always hold in honor the calling of a soldier. I consider the entire human life to be merely service, because everybody serves.

NICHOLAS I

The most consistent of autocrats.
THEODORE SCHIEMANN

As man and ruler Nicholas I had little in common with his brother Alexander I. By contrast with his predecessor's psychological paradoxes, ambivalence, and vacillation, the new sovereign displayed determination, singleness of purpose, and an iron will. He also possessed ah overwhelming sense of duty and a great capacity for work. In character, and even in his striking and powerful appearance, Nicholas I seemed to be the perfect absolute monarch. Appropriately, he was always a soldier at heart, finding pleasure and strength amidst the disciplined order of the army. He was devoted to military drills, the parade ground, and uniforms down to the last button—in fact, as emperor he ordered alterations of the uniforms, even changing the number of buttons. In the same spirit, the autocrat insisted on arranging and ordering minutely and precisely everything around him. Indeed, for Nicholas, the parade ground was a model for society and politics. Engineering, especially the construction of defenses, was Nicholas's other enduring passion. Even as a child "whenever he built a summer house, for his purse or his governess, out of chairs, earth, or toys, he never forgot to fortify it with guns—for protection." Later, specializing in fortresses, he became head of the army corps of engineers and thus the chief military engineer of his country; still later, as emperor, he staked all on making the entire land an impregnable fortress.

Complicating this personality, Nicholas was also a religious, moral, and domestic man—or, at least, he cultivated this public image alongside his public persona as fierce autocrat. His religion, however, was not like that of his brother Alexander and other educated Russians of the time: not a restless searching for truth but simple and unquestioning faith, "in the manner of a peasant," as Nicholas himself put it. His moral sense was also mainly a commitment to values like discipline, order, and loyalty. Finally, perhaps surprisingly, he saw himself and was portrayed publicly as a family man: images of the tsar and his family were widely distributed for the first time in Russia.

Nicholas I. Shown here in the uniform of the Polish army, Nicholas I was often admired for his physical beauty and majesty. The American diplomat Andrew White described him as "colossal in stature; with a face such as one finds on a Greek coin, but overcast with a shadow of Muscovite melancholy." (*Tsarstvuiushchii dom Romanovykh*)

And he constructed for himself a cozy and idyllic domesticity at his family retreat, the "Cottage" at Peterhof.

In a country and at a time when powerful men were of more consequence than laws and institutions, these questions of the tsar's personality and taste were of more than trivial significance. Moreover, his character fit very well with his ideology of power and rule. Born in 1796, the new ruler was brought up, not in the atmosphere of the late Enlightenment like his older brother, but in that of wars against Napoleon and of growing conservatism. His was also an age of nationalism, and Nicholas was increasingly inclined to view his great personal power as rooted in Russian traditions of patriarchal authoritarianism rather than in Western notions of enlightened despotism. The best expression of this ideology was the doctrine later called "Official Nationality." Formally proclaimed in 1833 by Count Sergei Uvarov, the tsar's minister of education, Official Nationality contained three principles: Orthodoxy, autocracy, and nationality. The order was significant and unvarying, even when different terms were used, such as "faith, tsar, and fatherland." This basic set of principles, with variations, would long remain influential in Russian politics, including today.

These were not three separate ideas, Uvarov said; they formed a "unified spirit." Orthodoxy (*Pravoslavie*) highlighted both the role of the official Church and the ultimate source of ethics and ideals. In many ways, this was a repudiation of the Age of Reason, a rejection of the prime place given to human reason and human capacities. In its place rose an insistence on "the mystery and unfathomableness" of life and thus the vanity of reason. As a political principle, this meant rejecting human efforts to perfect society but also sanctifying existing authority as coming from God. As it was said, each "must serve God in his own place." The principle of autocracy (*samoderzhavie*) as sacred authority follows from this. In addition, assuming that human beings were inherently weak and sinful—"a despicable and ungrateful tribe" in the words of a leading publicist of the day, Nikolai Grech—the strong hand of government was needed to keep order. Advocates of Official Nationality also viewed the history of Russia as reinforcing this lesson. At the same time, and also following tradition, they considered the autocracy the best means of ensuring Russia's progress and happiness. As such, autocracy was said to be not despotism but a paternal power united in love with the people. Thus, again and again, the Russian polity was described as a "family" in which the tsar was the stern but benevolent father and the people were obedient and loving children, though often in need of discipline and help.

Finally, but not least, nationality (*narodnost*) referred to the special nature of the Russian people. In part this was simply the reverse side of autocracy: a view of Russians as uniquely loving and obedient subjects but also in need of a strong hand. This was certainly Nicholas I's view. After the Decembrist rebellion, for example, he insisted that "this design did not correspond to the character...or ways of the Russian people.... Love for the monarch and devotion to the Throne are based on natural traits of the people." Likewise, during a military uprising in 1831, he insisted that ordinary soldiers were not against him: "Observe, that, except for Orlov and Chernyshev [high officials], I was alone among them; and all lay flat, their faces to the ground! That's the Russian people for you!" As can be seen, this ideal of nationality had its roots both in Russian traditions and in European thought of the day, especially the Romantic nationalist idea that each nation has its own unique genius, its distinctive history, institutions, language, temperament, and virtues. Russia's genius, it was felt, was the unique bond of love and devotion between the people and the tsar.

## Nicholas's "System"

The Decembrist rebellion at the beginning of Nicholas I's reign only hardened the new emperor's basic views as well as his determination to fight revolution to the end. No doubt it also contributed to the emperor's mistrust of the gentry, and indeed of independence and initiative on the part of any of his subjects. Characteristically, Nicholas I showed minute personal interest in the arrest, investigation, trial, and punishment of the Decembrists, and this preoccupation with the dangers of subversion remained with him throughout his reign. The new regime became preeminently one of militarism and bureaucracy. The emperor surrounded himself with military men to the extent that in the later part of his reign there were almost no civilians among his immediate assistants. Also, he relied heavily on special emissaries, most of them generals of his suite, who were sent all over Russia on particular assignments, to execute immediately the will of the sovereign. Operating outside the regular administrative system, they represented an extension, so to speak, of the monarch's own person. In fact, the entire machinery of government came to be permeated by the military spirit of direct orders, absolute obedience, and precision, at least as far as official reports and appearances were concerned. Corruption and confusion, however, lay immediately behind this façade of discipline and smooth functioning.

In his conduct of state affairs Nicholas I often bypassed regular channels, and he generally resented formal deliberation, consultation, or other procedural delay. The importance of the Committee of Ministers, the State Council, and the Senate decreased in the course of his reign. Instead of making full use of them, the emperor depended more and more on special bureaucratic devices meant to carry out his intentions promptly while remaining under his immediate and complete control. As one favorite method, Nicholas I made extensive use of ad hoc committees standing outside the usual state machinery. The committees were usually composed of a handful of the emperor's most trusted assistants, and, because these were very few in number, the same men in different combinations formed these committees throughout Nicholas's reign. As a rule, the committees carried on their work in secret, adding further complication and confusion to the already cumbersome administration of the empire.

The work of most of these committees was painstaking, but the results were generally negligible, including the committee with the broadest mandate, headed by Count Kochubey and meeting from December 1826 until 1832, which was asked to reconsider virtually all major aspects of government and social organization in Russia and to propose improvements. Indeed, the laborious futility of this first ad hoc committee became the characteristic pattern of most of the subsequent committees during the reign of Nicholas I, in spite of the fact that the emperor himself often took an active part in their proceedings. The failure of one committee to perform its task merely led to the formation of another. For example, some nine committees tried to deal with the issue of serfdom.

As an effective means to exercise personal authority outside the regular structures of bureaucracy and law, His Majesty's Own Chancery was much more useful than the special committees. Organized originally as a bureau to deal with matters that demanded the sovereign's personal participation and to supervise the execution of the emperor's orders, the Chancery grew rapidly in the reign of Nicholas I. As early as 1826, two new departments were added to it: the Second Department was concerned with the codification of law, and the Third with the administration of the newly created corps of gendarmes. In 1828 the Fourth Department was created for the purpose of managing the charitable and educational institutions under the jurisdiction of the Empress Dowager Mary. Eight years later the Fifth Department was created and charged with reforming the condition of the state peasants; after two years of activity it was replaced by the new Ministry of State Domains. Finally, in 1843, the Sixth Department of His Majesty's Own Chancery came into being, a temporary agency assigned the task of drawing up an administrative plan for Transcaucasia. The departments of the Chancery served Nicholas I as a major means of conducting a personal policy that bypassed the regular state channels.

The Third Department of His Majesty's Own Chancery, the political police—which for many Russians came to symbolize the reign of Nicholas I—acted as the autocrat's main weapon against subversion and revolution and as his principal agency for controlling the behavior of his subjects and for distributing punishments and rewards among them. Its assigned fields of activity ranged from "all orders and all reports in every case belonging to the higher police" to "reports about all occurrences without exception"! The new guardians of the state, dressed in sky-blue uniforms, were incessantly active:

> In their effort to embrace the entire life of the people, they intervened actually in every matter in which it was possible to intervene. Family life, commercial transactions, personal quarrels, projects of inventions, escapes of novices from monasteries—everything interested the secret police. At the same time the Third Department received a tremendous number of petitions, complaints, denunciations, and each one resulted in an investigation, each one became a separate case.

The Third Department also prepared detailed, interesting, and remarkably candid reports of all sorts for the emperor, supervised literature—an activity ranging from minute control over Pushkin to ordering various "inspired" articles in defense of Russia and the existing system—and fought every trace of revolutionary infection. The two successive heads of the Third Department, Count Alexander Benckendorff and Prince Alexsi Orlov, probably spent more time with Nicholas I than any of his other assistants; they accompanied him, for instance, on his repeated trips of inspection throughout Russia. Yet most of the feverish activity of the gendarmes seemed to be to no purpose. Endless investigations of subversion, stimulated by the monarch's own suspiciousness, revealed very little. Even the most important radical group uncovered during the reign, the Petrashevtsy, fell victim not to the gendarmerie but to its great rival, the ordinary police, which continued to be part of the Ministry of the Interior.

The desire to control in detail the lives and thoughts of the people and above all to prevent subversion, which constituted the main aims of the Third Department, also guided the policies of the Ministry of Education—which we shall discuss in a later chapter—specifically in censorship; and, indeed, in a sense they guided the policies of Nicholas's entire regime. As in the building of fortresses, the emphasis was defensive: to hold fast against the enemy and to prevent his penetration. The sovereign himself worked indefatigably at shoring up the defenses. He paid the most painstaking attention to the huge and difficult business of government, did his own inspecting of the country, rushed to meet all kinds of emergencies, from cholera epidemics and riots to rebellion in military settlements, and bestowed special care on the army. Beyond that, the emperor wanted to embody the ideal of the tsar as father to his people, physically present everywhere so that the people could be reassured and inspired. Illustrative of the changed political style and mood at the top is the contrast between Alexander I's uncertain and tragic reaction to the St. Petersburg flood of 1824 and Nicholas I's boldness during the cholera epidemic in Moscow in 1830, where he confidently appeared on the scene to take charge of the countermeasures—Count Benckendorff wrote, presumably without irony, that "it seemed to all that the disease itself would capitulate to his omnipotence."

## The Issue of Reform

However, as already indicated, all the efforts of the emperor and his government bore little fruit, and the limitations of Nicholas's approach to reform revealed themselves with special clarity in the crucial issue of serfdom. Nicholas I personally disapproved of that institution: in the army and in the country at large he saw only too well the misery it produced, and he remained constantly apprehensive of the danger of insurrection; also, the autocrat had no sympathy for aristocratic privilege when it clashed with the interests of the state. Yet, as he explained the matter in 1842 in the State Council: "There is no doubt that serfdom, as it exists at present in our land, is an evil, palpable and obvious to all. But to touch it now would be a still more disastrous evil.... The Pugachev rebellion proved how far popular rage can go." In fact throughout his reign the emperor feared, at the same time, two different revolutions. There was the danger that the gentry might bid to obtain a constitution if the government decided to deprive the landlords of their serfs. On the other hand, an elemental, popular uprising might also be unleashed by such a major shock to the established order as the coveted emancipation.

In the end, although the government was almost constantly concerned with serfdom, it achieved very little. New laws either left the change in the serfs' status to the discretion of their landlords, thus merely continuing Alexander's well-meaning but ineffectual efforts, or they prohibited only certain extreme abuses connected with serfdom such as selling members of a single family to different buyers. Even the minor concessions granted to the peasants were sometimes nullified. Following the European revolutions of 1848, the meager and hesitant government solicitude for the serfs came to an end. Only the bonded peasants of western Russian provinces obtained substantial advantages in the reign of Nicholas I. As we shall see, they received this preferential treatment because the government wanted to use them in its struggle against the Polish influence that was prevalent among the landlords of that area.

Determined to preserve autocracy, afraid to abolish serfdom, and suspicious of all independent initiative and popular participation, the emperor and his government could not introduce in their country the much-needed fundamental reforms. In practice, as well as in theory, they looked backward. Important developments did nevertheless take place in certain areas where change would not threaten the fundamental political, social, and economic structure of the Russian Empire. Especially significant proved to be the codification of law and the far-reaching reform in the condition of the state peasants. The new code, produced in the late 1820s and the early 1830s by the immense labor of Speransky and his associates, marked, despite defects, a tremendous achievement and a milestone in Russian jurisprudence. In January 1835 it replaced the ancient *Ulozhenie* of Tsar Alexis, dating from 1649, and it was destined to last until 1917.

The reorganization of the state peasants followed several years later after Count Pavel Kiselev became head of the new Ministry of State Domains in 1837. Kiselev's reform, which included the shift of taxation from persons to land, additional allotments for poor peasants, some peasant self-government, and the development of financial assistance, schools, and medical care in the villages, received almost universal praise from prerevolutionary historians. The leading Soviet specialist on the subject, Druzhinin, however, claimed, on the basis of impressive evidence, that the positive aspects of Kiselev's reform had a narrow scope and application, while fundamentally it placed an extremely heavy burden on the state peasants, made all the more difficult to bear by the exactions and malpractices of local administration.

## The Last Years

But even limited reforms became impossible after 1848. Frightened by European revolutions, Nicholas I became completely reactionary. Russians were forbidden to travel abroad, an order that hit teachers and students especially hard. The number of students without government scholarships was limited to 300 per university, except for the school of medicine. Uvarov had to resign as minister of education in favor of an entirely reactionary and subservient functionary, who on one occasion told an assistant of his: "You should know that I have neither a mind nor a will of my own—I am merely a blind tool of the emperor's will." New restrictions further curtailed university autonomy and academic freedom. Constitutional law and philosophy were eliminated from the curricula; logic and psychology were retained, but were to be taught by professors of theology. In fact, in the opinion of some historians, the universities themselves came close to being eliminated and only the timely intervention of certain high officials prevented this disaster. Censorship reached ridiculous proportions, with new agencies appearing, including "a censorship over the censors." The censors, to cite only a few instances of their activities, deleted "forces of nature" from a textbook in physics, probed the hidden meaning of an ellipsis in an arithmetic book, changed "were killed" to "perished" in an account of Roman emperors, demanded that the author of a fortune-telling book explain why in his opinion stars influence the fate of men, and worried about the possible concealment of secret codes in musical notations. Literature and thought were virtually stifled. Even Mikhail Pogodin, a right-wing professor of history and a leading exponent of the doctrine of Official Nationality, was impelled in the very last years of the reign to accuse the government of imposing upon Russia "the quiet of a graveyard, rotting and stinking, both physically and morally." It was in this atmosphere of suffocation that Russia experienced its shattering defeat in the Crimean War.

## Foreign Policy and Empire

If the Crimean debacle represented, as many scholars insist, the logical termination of Nicholas I's foreign policy and reign, it was a case of historical logic unique for the occasion and difficult to follow. For, to begin with, the Russian emperor intended least of all to fight other European powers. Indeed, a dedicated supporter of autocracy at home, he became a dauntless champion of legitimism abroad. Nicholas I was determined to maintain and defend the existing order in Europe, just as he considered it his sacred duty to preserve the archaic system in his own country. He saw the two closely related as the whole and its part, and he thought both to be threatened by the same enemy: the many-headed hydra of revolution, which had suffered a major blow with the final defeat of Napoleon but refused to die. Indeed it rose again and again, in 1830, in 1848, and on other occasions, attempting to reverse and undo the settlement of 1815. True to his principles, the resolute tsar set out to engage the enemy. In the course of the struggle, this "policeman of Russia" assumed added responsibilities as the "gendarme of Europe." The emperor's assistants in the field of foreign policy, led by Count Karl Nesselrode, who served as foreign minister throughout the reign, on the whole shared the views of their monarch and bent to his will.

Shortly after Nicholas I's accession to the throne, Russia fought a war against Persia that lasted from June 1826 to February 1828. The hostilities, which represented another round in the struggle for Georgia, resulted in the defeat of Persia. While the Treaty of Turkmanchai gave Russia part of Armenia with the city of Yerevan, exclusive rights to have a navy on the Caspian Sea, commercial concessions, and a large indemnity, Nicholas I characteristically refused to press his victory. In particular, he would not support a native movement to overthrow the shah and destroy his rule.

A few weeks after making peace with Persia, Russia declared war on Turkey. This conflict marked the culmination of an international crisis that had begun with the rebellion of the Greeks against their Turkish masters in 1821, the so-called Greek War of Independence. The Russian government vacillated in its attitude toward the Greek revolution for, on one hand, the Russians sympathized with the Orthodox Greeks and were traditionally hostile to the Turks, while, on the other hand, Russia was committed to the support of the status quo in Europe. Moreover, the Greek crisis had unusually complicated diplomatic ramifications and possibilities. Other European powers also found it difficult to maintain a consistent policy toward the struggle of the Greeks against the Turks. Acting more firmly than his brother, Nicholas I tried, first with Great Britain and France, and then on his own, to restrain Turkey and settle the Balkan conflict. On October 20, 1827, in the battle of Navarino, the joint British, French, and Russian squadrons destroyed the Egyptian fleet that had been summoned to help its Turkish overlord. But it was not until April 1828 that the Russo-Turkish hostilities officially began. Although the Porte proved to be more difficult to defeat than the Russian emperor had expected, the second major campaign of the war brought decisive, if costly, victory to the Russian army and forced the Ottoman state to agree to the Treaty of Adrianople in 1829.

That settlement gave Russia the mouth of the Danube as well as considerable territory in the Caucasus; promised autonomous existence, under a Russian protectorate, to the Danubian principalities of Moldavia and Wallachia; imposed a heavy indemnity on Turkey; guaranteed the passage of Russian merchant ships through the Straits; and, incidentally, assured the success of the Greek revolution, which the tsar continued to detest. But in spite of these and other Russian gains embodied in the treaty, it has often and justly been considered an example of moderation in international affairs. The Russian emperor did not try to destroy his former opponent, regarding Turkey as an important and desirable element in the European balance of power. In fact, the decision to preserve the Ottoman state represented the considered judgment of a special committee appointed by Nicholas I in 1829 to deal with the numerous problems raised by the defeat of Turkey and the changing situation in the Balkans. And the committee's report to the effect that "the advantages offered by the preservation of the Ottoman Empire in Europe exceed the inconveniences which it presents," received the Russian sovereign's full endorsement.

The revolution in Paris in July 1830 came as a great shock to the tsar, and its impact was heightened by the Belgian uprising in September and by unrest in Italy and Germany. Rebellion against the system created by the Congress of Vienna was clearly underway and spreading. Nicholas I was determine to crush it. He sent a special emissary to Berlin to coordinate action with Prussia and tried to assemble an army in Poland to march west. When the regime of Louis-Philippe was promptly accepted by other European governments, the Russian emperor still withheld official recognition for four months and then treated the new French ruler in a grudging and discourteous manner. The revolution of the Belgians against the Dutch similarly provoked the anger of the Russian autocrat who regarded it as another assault on the sacred principle of legitimacy and, in addition, as a clear violation of the territorial provisions of the Treaty of Vienna. Once again failing to obtain diplomatic support from other powers, Nicholas I had to subscribe to the international settlement of the issue, which favored the rebels, although he delayed the ratification of the Treaty of London for several months and did not establish regular diplomatic relations with the new state until 1852. It should be added that the early plans for a Russian military intervention in western Europe might well have been realized, except for the Polish revolution, which broke out late in November 1830 and which took the Russian government approximately a year to suppress.

Resentment of Russian rule in Poland continually grew after the partitions. The settlement of 1815 had created a Kingdom of Poland (also known as Congress Poland) ruled by the Russian emperor. Many Poles resented what they saw as a "fourth partition" rather than the reestablishment of their historic state. This was a constitutional monarchy, however, with its own legislature, army, currency, school system, and administration. And all official business was conducted in Polish. These rights and autonomy were sometimes violated by Alexander I and especially by his brother Grand Duke Constantine, who ruled Poland on behalf of the emperor. But Nicholas I's intense anti-constitutionalism seemed a greater threat, though the new emperor took no steps to abrogate the constitution. When revolutions broke out in Europe, rumors that the tsar was planning to use his Polish army to suppress these uprisings likely precipitated the Polish revolt, which began among the officer corps in Warsaw in November 1830. Quickly, perhaps due to Nicholas I's rejection of any compromise, the movement magnified into a national uprising for Polish independence and freedom. Russia soon lost control of both the government and the army in Poland and had to reconquer Poland in a full-fledged war. Russian troops, led by General Ivan Paskevich, vastly outnumbered Polish forces, though it took many months for Paskevich's forces to eradicate patriotic detachments and bands in the dense Polish forests. But there were also failings on the Polish side. Some Polish historians have argued that there was a real chance for success. But the leadership was far from well organized or even sufficiently determined. Most important, like the Decembrist uprising in St. Petersburg, the Polish revolt remained an upper-class affair without support from Polish peasants, much less Ukrainian and Belorussian peasants.

The result was another tragedy for Poland. The Polish constitution of 1815 was replaced by the Organic Statute of 1832 that made Poland "an indivisible part" of the Russian Empire. The Statute itself, with its promises of civil liberties, separate systems of law and local government, and widespread use of the Polish language, remained in abeyance while Poland was administered in a brutal and authoritarian manner by its conqueror, the new Prince of Warsaw and Nicholas's viceroy, Marshal Paskevich, The monarch himself carefully directed and supervised his work. The estates of the insurgents were confiscated; Polish institutions of higher learning were closed; the lands of the Catholic Church were secularized and the clergy given fixed salaries. At the same time, Poland was forced more and more into the Russian mold in legal, administrative, educational, and economic matters. The Russian language reigned in the secondary schools as well as in the administration, while a stringent censorship banned the works of most of the leading Polish authors as subversive. In turn, rebellion and its suppression stimulated a more radical Polish nationalism, including a mass emigration of educated Poles who would establish an important émigré community in the West, largely committed to independence for Poland.

A Russification more thorough than in Poland developed in the western and southwestern provinces, with their Belorussian and Ukrainian peasant population and Polonized landlord class. Even prior to the insurrection of 1830–31 the government of Nicholas I had moved toward bringing that territory into closer association with Russia proper, a process connected with the emperor's general penchant for centralization and standardization. After the revolution was suppressed, assimilation proceeded swiftly under the direction of a special committee. Rebels from Lithuanian, Belorussian, and Ukrainian provinces were denied the amnesty offered to those from Poland. It was in this territory that the Orthodox Church scored its greatest gain when, in 1839, the Uniates severed their connection with Rome and came into its fold. In 1840 the Lithuanian Statute was repealed in favor of Russian law. Because the landlords represented the Polish element, Nicholas I and his assistants changed the usual policy to legislate against their interests. They went so far as to introduce in some provinces "inventories" that defined and regularized the obligations of the serfs to their masters, and in 1851 to establish compulsory state service for the gentry of the western region. Thousands of poor or destitute families of the petty gentry were reclassified as peasants or townspeople, some of them being transferred to the Caucasus.

As ideas of national identity, influenced by German Romanticism, grew in the western borderlands of the Russian Empire during the 1830s and 1840s, Nicholas I was determined that these not be allowed to challenge Russian national unity and rule. This can be seen especially in Ukraine, where the imperial government crushed the secret Brotherhood of Cyril and Methodius—described as the first attempt by Ukrainian intellectuals to move from cultural to political activism—and harshly punished its members, especially the great Ukrainian Romantic poet Taras Shevchenko.

Relative stabilization in Europe was followed by new troubles in the Near East and more Russian intervention. In 1832, Mohammed Ali of Egypt, having failed to win Syria as a reward for supporting the Ottoman sultan, his nominal suzerain, in the Greek war, sent an army that conquered Syria and invaded

Anatolia, smashing Turkish forces. No European capital answered the sultan's desperate appeals for help with the exception of St. Petersburg. Nicholas I's eagerness to aid the Porte in its hour of need found ample justification in the political advantages that Russia could derive from this important intervention. But such action also corresponded perfectly to the legitimist convictions of the Russian autocrat, who regarded Mohammed Ali as yet another major rebel. On February 20, 1833, a Russian naval squadron arrived at Constantinople and, several weeks later, some 10,000 Russian troops landed on the Asian side of the Bosporus—the only appearance of Russian armed forces at the Straits in history. Extremely worried by this unexpected development, the great powers acted in concert to bring Turkey and Egypt together, arranging the Convention of Kutahia between the two combatants and inducing the sultan to agree to its provisions. The Russians withdrew immediately after Orlov had signed a pact with Turkey, the Treaty of Unkiar Skelessi, on July 8, 1833. That agreement, concluded for eight years, contained broad provisions for mutual consultation and aid in case of attack by any third party; a secret article at the same time exempted Turkey from helping Russia in exchange for keeping the Dardanelles closed to all foreign warships. Although, contrary to wide-spread supposition at the time and since, the Treaty of Unkiar Skelessi did not provide for the passage of Russian men-of-war through the Straits—a point established by Philip Mosely—it did represent a signal victory for Russia: the empire of the tsars became the special ally and, to a degree, protector of its ancient, decaying enemy, thereby acquiring important means to interfere in its affairs and influence its future.

The events of 1830–31 in Europe, and to a lesser extent recurrent conflicts in the Near East, impressed on Nicholas I the necessity for close cooperation and joint action of the conservative powers. Austria and in a certain measure Prussia felt the same need, with the result that the three eastern European monarchies drew together by the end of 1833. Agreements were concluded at meetings at Münchengrätz and Berlin. Russia came to a thorough understand-ing with the Habsburg Empire, especially regarding their common struggle against nationalism and their desire to maintain Turkish rule in the Near East. Similarly, the Russian agreement with Prussia stressed joint policies in relation to partitioned Poland. More far-reaching in its provisions and its implications was the Convention of Berlin signed by all three powers on October 15, 1833, which "recognize[d] that eaeh independent Sovereign has the right to call to his aid, in case of internal troubles as well as in case of an external threat to his country, every other independent Sovereign" and stipulated that if "any power" tried with the force of arms to prevent Austria, Prussia, or Russia from offering "material help" to one another, "these three Courts" would consider such hostile action "as directed against each one of them." The agreements of 1833 were thus meant to protect, not only the immediate interests of the signatory powers, but also the entire conservative order in Europe. Nicholas I in particular proved eager to police the continent. After the 1846 uprising in Cracow, it was the Russian emperor who insisted to the somewhat slow and reluctant Austrian government that this remnant of free Poland must become a part of the Habsburg state, as had been previously arranged among the eastern European monarchies.

The revolution of February 1848 in France opened a new chapter in the struggle between the old order and the rising forces of modern liberalism, nationalism, and socialism in nineteenth-century Europe, including the political consequences of rapid economic, social, and intellectual changes in Europe. While the famous story or Nicholas I telling his guests at a ball to saddle their horses because a republic had just been proclaimed in France is not exact, the Russian autocrat did react immediately and violently to the news from Paris. Although delighted by the fall of Louis-Philippe, whom he hated as a usurper and traitor to legitimism, the tsar could not tolerate a revolution, so he broke diplomatic relations with France and assembled 300,000–400,000 troops in western Russia in preparation for a march to the Rhine. But rebellion spread faster than the Russian sovereign's countermeasures: in less than a month popular rebellions broke out in Prussia, Austria, and other German states, and the entire established order on the continent rapidly began to crumble into dust.

In the trying months that followed, Nicholas I rose to his full stature as the defender of legitimism in Europe. The remarkable ultimate failures of the initially successful revolutions of 1848 and 1849 can best be explained in terms of the specific political, social, and economic conditions of the different countries involved. Still, the Russian monarch certainly did what he could to tip the balance in favor of reaction. On March 14, he issued a thunderous manifesto against revolution, described as threatening "to overthrow legal authority and all social institutions," appealing to "every Russian to respond joyfully to the call of their Sovereign," and to "our ancient cry, 'for faith, Tsar, and fatherland,'" to end this threat. He tried to use every resource at his disposal to oppose the numerous uprisings that had gripped the continent. For example, the Russian government supplied Austria with a loan of 6 million rubles and pointed out to Great Britain that, if an outside power were to support an Italian state against the Habsburgs, Russia would join Austria as a full-fledged combatant. The first Russian military intervention to suppress revolution occurred in July 1848 in the Danubian principalities of Moldavia and Wallachia, where Russia acted for itself and for Turkey to defeat the Romanian national movement. The most important action took place in the summer of 1849, when Nicholas I heeded the Austrian appeal, on the basis of the agreements of 1833, to help combat the revolt in Hungary, assigning Paskevich and almost 200,000 troops for the campaign. The successful Russian intervention in Hungary—which earned the undying hatred of the Hungarians—was directed in part against the Polish danger, as Polish revolutionaries were fighting on the Hungarian side. But its chief rationale lay in the Russian autocrat's determination to preserve the existing order in Europe, for the Austrian Empire was one of the main supports of that order.

The impressive and in certain ways dominant position that Russia gained with the collapse of the revolutions of 1848–49 on the continent failed to last. In fact, the international standing of the "gendarme of Europe" and the country he ruled was much stronger in appearance than in reality: liberalism and nationalism although defeated, were by no means dead, and they carried European public opinion from Poland and Hungary to France and England; even the countries usually friendly to the tsar complained of his interference with their interests, as in the case of Prussia, or at least resented his overbearing solicitude, as was true of Austria. On the other hand, Nicholas I himself—in the opinion of some specialists—reacted to his success by becoming more blunt, uncompromising, doctrinaire, and domineering than ever before. The stage was set for a debacle.

## The Crimean War

When the debacle did come, however, the accompanying circumstances proved to be exceedingly complex, and they were related especially to issues in the Near East. There the resumption of hostilities between Turkey and Egypt in 1839–40 undid the Treaty of Unkiar Skelessi. European powers acted together to impose a settlement upon the combatants, under terms of the Treaty of London of July 15, 1840, and they also signed the Straits Convention of July 13, 1841. The Convention, in which Great Britain, Austria, Prussia, Russia, and France participated, reaffirmed the closure of the Bosporus and the Dardanelles to all foreign warships in time of peace, substituting an international guarantee of the five signatories for the separate treaty between Russia and Turkey. Nicholas I proved willing to cooperate with the other states, and, in the same spirit, made a particular effort during the years following to come to a thorough understanding with Great Britain. In the summer of 1844 he personally traveled to England and discussed the Near Eastern situation and prospects with Lord Aberdeen, the foreign secretary. The results of these conversations were summarized in an official Russian memorandum, prepared by Nesselrode, which the British government accepted as accurate. According to its provisions, Russia and Great Britain were to maintain the Turkish state as long as possible, and, in case of its impending dissolution, the two parties were to come in advance to an understanding concerning the repartitioning of the territories involved and other problems.

Although the crucial Russo-British relations in the decades preceding the Crimean War have been variously explicated and assessed by different scholars, several elements in the situation stand out clearly. Nicholas I's apparently successful agreement with Great Britain had an illusory and indeed a dangerous character. The two main points of the understanding—the preservation and the partitioning of Turkey—were, in a sense, contradictory, and the entire agreement was, therefore, especially dependent on identical, or at least very similar, interpretation by both partners of developments in the Near East, a degree of harmony never to be achieved. Moreover, the form of the agreement also contributed to a certain ambivalence and difference of opinion: while Nicholas I and his associates considered it to be a firm arrangement of fundamental importance, the British apparently thought of it more as a secret exchange of opinions not binding on the subsequent premiers and foreign ministers of Her Majesty's government. Also, we should not underestimate the influence of public Russophobia in England, often shared by high officials, which grew especially as Russia's influence in Turkey grew.

Russia's seeming invincibility after 1848 blinded Nicholas to growing distrust and hostility to Russia in Europe, even among allies. And the complex and unfortunate entanglement with Great Britain encouraged Nicholas I's mistaken belief that his Near Eastern policy had strong backing in Europe. None of this made war inevitable, though. The precipitating event was a dispute in the Holy Land between Catholics and Orthodox in regard to certain rights connected with some of the most sacred shrines of Christendom. Countering Napoleon III's championing of the Catholic cause, Nicholas I acted in his usual direct and forceful manner by sending Prince Alexander Menshikov, in February 1853, with an ultimatum to the Turks: the Holy Land controversy was to be settled in favor of the Orthodox, and the Porte was to recognize explicitly the rights of the vast Orthodox population of its empire. When Turkey accepted the first series of demands, but would not endorse Russian interference on behalf of the Orthodox subjects of the Porte, considering it to be an infringement of Turkish sovereignty, Menshikov terminated the discussion and left Constantinople. Russian occupation of the Danubian principalities as "material guarantees" added fuel to the fire. There is little doubt that Nicholas I's rash actions precipitated war, although it is probable that he wanted to avoid a conflict. After the first phases of the controversy described earlier, the Russian government acted in a conciliatory manner, accepting the so-called Vienna Note as a compromise settlement, evacuating the principalities, and repeatedly seeking peace even after the outbreak of hostilities. The war guilt at this later stage should be divided principally among Turkey, France, Great Britain, and even Austria, who pressed increasingly exacting demands on Russia. In any case, after fighting between Russia and Turkey started in October 1853, and the Russians destroyed a Turkish fleet and transports off Sinope on November 30, Great Britain and France joined the Porte in March 1854, and Sardinia intervened the next year. Austria stopped just short of hostilities against Russia, exercising strong diplomatic pressure on the side of the allies. Nicholas I found his country fighting alone against a European coalition.

The Russian emperor's Near Eastern policy, which culminated in the Crimean War, has received various interpretations. Many historians have emphasized Russian aggressiveness toward Turkey, explaining it by the economic requirements of Russia, such as the need to protect grain trade through the Black Sea or to obtain markets in the Near East, by the strategic imperative to control the Straits, or simply by a grand design of political expansion more or less in the footsteps of Catherine the Great. Yet, as we had occasion to observe, the tsar's attitude toward the Ottomans long retained the earmarks of his basic belief in legitimism. Even his ultimate decision to partition the Turkish Empire can be construed as a result of the conviction that the Porte could not survive in the modern world, and that therefore the leading European states had to arrange for a proper redistribution of possessions and power in the

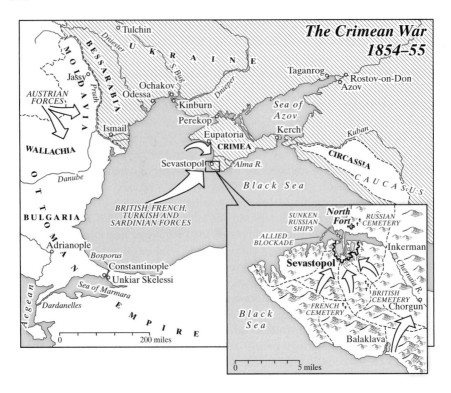

Balkans and the Near East in order to avoid anarchy, revolution, and war. In other words, Nicholas's approach to Great Britain can be considered sincere, and the ensuing misunderstanding thus all the more tragic. One other factor must also be weighed in an appreciation of Nicholas I's Near Eastern policy, however: Orthodoxy. Obviously, the Crimean War was provoked partially by religious conflicts. And the tsar himself retained throughout his reign a certain ambivalence toward the sultan. He repeatedly granted the legitimacy of the sultan's rule in the Ottoman Empire, but remained, nevertheless, uneasy about the sprawling Muslim state with numerous Orthodox subjects. Once the conflict began, Nicholas I readily proclaimed himself the champion of the Cross against the infidels.

Although the Crimean War involved several major states, its front was narrowly restricted. After Austrian troops occupied Moldavia and Wallachia separating the Russians from the Turks in the Balkans, the combatants possessed only one common border, the Russo-Turkish frontier in the Caucasus, and that distant area with its extremely difficult terrain was unsuited for major operations. The allies controlled the sea and staged a number of naval demonstrations and minor attacks on the Russian coasts from the Black, the Baltic, and the White seas to the Bering Sea. Then, in search of a decisive front, they landed in the Crimea in September 1854. The war became centered on the allied effort to capture the Crimean naval base of Sevastopol. Except for the

Crimea, the fighting went on only in the Caucasus, where the Russians proved rather successful and even seized the important Turkish fortress of Kars. Sevastopol held out for eleven and a half months against the repeated bombardments and assaults of French, British, Turkish, and Sardinian forces with their superior weapons. While the Russian supply service broke down and the high command showed little initiative, the soldiers and the sailors of the Black Sea fleet led by such dedicated officers as the admirals Pavel Nakhimov and Vladimir Kornilov—both, incidentally, killed in combat—fought desperately for their city. Colonel Count Eduard Totleben, the chief Russian military engineer at Sevastopol, proved to be a great improviser of defenses, who did more than any other man to delay the allied advance. The hell and the heroism of the Crimean War were best related by Lev Tolstoy, himself an artillery officer in the besieged city, in his *Sevastopol Tales*. It might be added that this conflict, which many scholars consider the unnecessary result of misunderstandings, was the more tragic since typhus and other epidemics caused even more deaths than did the actual fighting.

The Russian forces finally abandoned Sevastopol on September 11, 1855, sinking their remaining ships—others had been sunk earlier to block the harbor—and blowing up fortifications. Nicholas I had died in March, and both his successor, Alexander II, and the allies, effectively supported by Austrian diplomacy, were ready early in 1856 to make peace. An impressive international congress met in Paris for a month, from late February until late March. Its work resulted in the Treaty of Paris, signed on March 30. By the provisions of the Treaty, Russia ceded to Turkey the mouth of the Danube and a part of Bessarabia and accepted the neutralization of the Black Sea—that is, agreed not to maintain a navy or coastal fortifications there. Further, Russia gave up its claims to a protectorate over the Orthodox in the Ottoman Empire. The Danubian principalities, the basis for the future state of Romania, were placed under the joint guarantee of the signatory powers, and an international commission was established to assure safe navigation of the Danube. The Treaty of Paris marked a striking decline of the Russian position in southeastern Europe and the Near East, and indeed in the world at large.

Nicholas I died on February 18, 1855, evidently after a brief but severe illness, watching his beloved military colossus fail against the modern armies of the West. As the military historian William Fuller has written, echoing a near consensus among historians, "the Crimean War exploded one of the principle justifications for autocracy—its ability to beget military power and security." One version of the death of Nicholas I, though likely only a legend, is that the shocked and disillusioned emperor poisoned himself.

## Concluding Remarks

Historians agree that Nicholas I and his firm beliefs strongly influenced Russian history, but he did not give it new direction. On the contrary, he clung with a desperate determination to the old system and the old ways. The creator of the doctrine of Official Nationality, Count Uvarov, once remarked that he would die with a sense of duty fulfilled if he could succeed in "pushing Russia back some fifty years from what is being prepared for her by the theories." In a sense, Nicholas I and his associates accomplished just that: they froze Russia as best they could for thirty—although not fifty—years, while the rest of Europe was changing. The catastrophe of the Crimean War underlined the pressing need for fundamental reforms in Russia as well as the fact that the hour was late. Alexander II's "great reforms" reflected a new recognition of necessary change. But these reforms also reflected changes within Russia's economy, society, and culture, to which we now turn. Indeed, in those fields, by contrast with Nicholas's politics, movement prevailed over stagnation.

# CHAPTER 27

# The Economic and Social Development of Russia in the First Half of the Nineteenth Century

Only in the nineteenth century did the money economy begin to evolve into its second stage of development, when a majority of the people becomes engulfed in the trade cycle, works for the market, and to satisfy its own needs buys products of someone else's labor, also brought to the market as merchandise.

NIKOLAI ROZHKOV

For many foreign observers at the time and most early historians, Russian economic and social life in the first half of the nineteenth century is defined by overwhelming backwardness, stagnation, and oppression. This view was challenged by later historians, especially Soviet specialists and Russian émigré scholars, who stressed Russian achievements during those difficult decades: not only the brilliance of Russian literature and culture during that period but also the penetration of capitalism into the country, certain technological improvements, the development of railroads and the cotton industry, expanding trade, and the growing middle class. Indeed, the old structure of society was breaking down, advancing social groups that poorly fit into the established structure of traditional social groups, namely nobles, clergy, merchants, townspeople, and peasants.

And yet, we cannot ignore the fact that the Russian economy and society failed to keep pace with other European countries. The forces of capitalism that were affecting Russia were revolutionizing Great Britain, Belgium, and France. Serfdom and state control of society undoubtedly held back Russia's economic development. Russian industry was less important in the total European and

world picture in 1860 than in 1800, and it had to be protected by high tariffs. Although the Russian urban classes rose rapidly, they remained small
and weak compared to the bourgeoisie in much of western Europe. Whereas
the country obtained some steamships and railroads, its transportation system failed to serve adequately either the peacetime needs or the needs of the
Crimean War. Russian weapons and military equipment proved inferior to
those of their European opponents; the Black Sea fleet, composed of wooden
sailing vessels, could not compete with the steam-propelled warships of the
allies. In the nineteenth century, Russia could afford such relative backwardness even less than at the time of Peter the Great. To be sure, as postcolonial
historians today argue, Europe should not be the only measure of modernity.
But for countries like Russia in the nineteenth century, the European model
and standard could be ignored only at its peril.

## Agriculture, Landowners, and Peasants

The second half of the eighteenth century marked the zenith of manorial economy and serf agriculture in Russia, but the first decades of the nineteenth witnessed significant changes in the economic picture. Russian estates sent more
and more produce to the market, at home and even abroad, as southern Russia
began to export grain via the Black Sea. New opportunities for marketing,
together with a continuing growth of population, led to a strong and steady
rise in land prices. Yet, most landlords, entirely unprepared for the task by
their education and outlook, failed to adjust effectively to competition and to
establish efficient production on their estates. In the first half of the nineteenth
century, the proportion of nongentry landownership grew, despite the fact that
only members of the gentry could own serfs. In addition, the indebtedness of
the gentry to the state increased rapidly, acquiring tremendous proportions by
the middle of the century. It has been estimated that on the eve of the emancipation of the serfs in 1861 the state held in mortgage two-thirds of all the
serfs. Small estates were especially hard hit. While substantial landlords on
the whole adjusted more or less effectively to the new conditions, their poorer
brethren, lacking capital or other sufficient assets, lost out in the competition.
The first half of the century thus saw a concentration of gentry landholding,
and a decline, often pauperization, of small gentry landowners. Indeed, the
increasing differentiation of the gentry, from successful landed magnates at
one extreme to numerous poor and even destitute gentry at the other, has been
seen as an unmistakable sign, not so long after the "golden age" of the late
eighteenth century, of looming decline among the nobility as a class.

Serfdom, of course, lay at the heart of prereform Russian agriculture.
Considerable evidence indicates that the landlords first responded to the
new market opportunities and the generally rising tempo of economic life by
trying to obtain a greater yield from their own fields. Barshchina, therefore,
increased in scope and became more demanding, a process culminating in
the 1840s. But more intensive exploitation of serf labor offered no solution to
the problem of achieving efficient, improved production. Not only were serfs

ignorant of modern techniques and resistant to change, but they had no incentive to work any harder on estate lands. Since very few landlords were interested in taking a direct role in agricultural management—using their greater education and resources to improve farming methods and equipment—the best option seemed to be to let peasants farm and market as they wished and demand higher payments. Hence, in the 1840s and especially in the 1850s obrok increased at the expense of barshchina. Peasants had to pay their masters perhaps ten times as much obrok in 1860 as in 1800. Serfs received additional land in return for obrok, but also, to make these escalating payments, more and more serfs earned additional income by working in factories, transportation, and other occupations, including as hired agricultural labor away from their home. Significantly, more and more free labor came to be hired in agriculture, especially in the Volga region and the Black Sea provinces.

There were signs of positive change in agriculture. Some estates became successful "capitalist" producers, making use of machinery, fertilizers, and more modern methods of farming. Overall, productivity increased somewhat as Russian agriculture became more intensive. Also, the produce gradually became more diversified. Old staple crops, notably rye and wheat, continued to be grown on a large scale. But certain new items rose to positions of some importance in the agriculture of the country, including potatoes and sugar beets, and, in the south, wine, the successful production of which required considerable knowledge and skill. The production of potatoes quintupled in the 1840s, the production of wine tripled between the early 1830s and 1850, and the spread of sugar beets in Russia can be gauged by the number of sugar beet factories: 7 in 1825, 57 in 1836, 206 in 1844, 380 in the early 1850s. The culture of silk and certain vegetable dyes developed in Transcaucasia, Fine wool began to be produced with the introduction into Russia of a new and superior breed of sheep in 1803. With government aid, the number of these sheep increased from 150,000 in 1812 to some 9 million in 1853.

As in the past, peasants found many ways of coping with the material hardships and uncertainties of their lives, from their deeply religious view of the world to minor and major acts of resistance, as we have seen. It is important to emphasize here—for it would be increasingly challenged by reformers—how much autonomy Russian peasants enjoyed. Although legally little distinguished from slaves, socially their lives were very different from the slaves in the southern United States in the early 1800s. Because Russian landlords, as Peter Kolchin has shown, preferred to manage their estates from afar, the major institution in peasant life was not the landlord and his agent—though these representatives made clear what landlords expected and freely used corporal punishment to ensure obedience—but the peasant commune or *obshchina* (also sometimes called the *mir*, which usually denoted the periodic communal assembly of heads of households). The commune was responsible for peasant relations with landlords and the state and with establishing rules for community welfare. Major decisions were made in communal assembly—usually of heads of households though sometimes involving the whole community, including women—while daily communal business was handled by chosen

officials. The commune collected taxes owed to the state and obrok owed to
landlords, maintained order in the village (punishing individuals who violated communal rules and norms), decided who should serve in the army, and,
most important, organized fieldwork (peasants did not work family homesteads but farmed strips scattered over estate and peasant lands) and periodically redistributed these strips to ensure that every family had an appropriate
amount of land, given the size of its family. While scholars argue over whom
the commune served—the authorities or the peasants themselves—it can be
seen that it had a double function: to serve the interest of the landlords and
state and to protect and promote the interests of peasants. As Steven Hoch has
shown, the commune did make the village a place of idyllic harmony: there
were richer and poorer peasants, though mainly due to family and individual
circumstances rather than any structure of peasant classes; male patriarchs
tended to dominate women and the young; and there were endemic problems
of resentment, anger, and petty crime.

## Industry and Labor

Industry, no less than agriculture, was affected by the growth of a market
economy. Russian manufacturing establishments, counting only those that
employed more than fifteen workers, increased in number from some 1,200
at the beginning of the century to 2,818 by 1860. The labor force expanded
even faster: from between 100,000 and 200,000 in 1800 to between 500,000 and
900,000 on the eve of the "great reforms".

The pervasiveness of contractually forced industrial labor in Russia
was in striking difference to industrial development in western Europe.
"Possessional" and "ascribed" workers—state peasants bound to a factory
and obliged to toil long hours in private or state enterprises—had flourished
since Peter the Great's time. Serf owners could also contract their serfs out to
non-noble manufacturers until this practice was banned in the early 1820s.
Beginning in the 1830s, however, the number of freely hired factory workers
was on the rise, especially in the rapidly growing cotton textile industry. The
output of this relatively new industry increased sixteen times over the course
of the half-century. A major stimulus was a decision by the British government in 1842 to end the ban on exporting cotton-spinning machinery. Russian
manufacture of industrial machinery was still little developed, so most industrial labor was still handwork, and often outwork. But now, at least in cotton
spinning (mechanization of weaving would come decades later) hand-labor
and outwork could be replaced by true factories: workers under a single roof
laboring with direct supervision on machines powered by steam.

On the whole, free labor gained steadily over bonded labor, and "capitalist" factories over both possessional and manorial ones. According to one
count, by 1825 "capitalist" factories constituted 54 percent of all industrial
establishments.

As mentioned, the use of machinery was fueled by a massive increase
in imported equipment. Thus, Russians imported machinery to the value of

42,500 silver rubles in 1825, 1.164 million silver rubles in 1845, and 3.103 million in 1860. Moreover, they began to build their own machines: the country possessed 19 machine-building factories with their annual output valued at 500,000 rubles in 1851, and 99 with an output worth 8 million rubles in 1860. Russian industry, however, remained largely restricted to the Urals, the Moscow area, the rapidly growing St. Petersburg-Baltic region, and several other already well-established centers. In particular, none had as yet arisen in the vast Russian south.

## Trade and Transportation

Trade also reflected the quickening tempo of economic life in Russia in the first half of the nineteenth century. Internal trade experienced marked growth. The differentiation of the country into the grain-producing south and the grain-consuming center and north became more pronounced, providing an ever stronger basis for fundamental, large-scale exchange. Thus the north and the center sent the products of their industries and crafts south in return for grain, meat, and butter. Certain areas developed their own specialties. For example, the northwestern region produced flax for virtually all of Russia. A district in the distant Archangel province raised a special breed of northern cows. Several Ukrainian provinces became famous for their horses, while the best sheep were bred in southern Russia, between the Volga and the Don. Even such items as woolen stockings became objects of regional specialization. A number of scholars have noted how, in the first half of the nineteenth century, purchased clothing began gradually to displace the homespun variety among the peasants.

Merchant capital grew and fairs expanded. The famous fair near the Monastery of St. Macarius in Nizhnii Novgorod province was transferred in 1817 to the town of Nizhnii Novgorod itself and there attained new heights. In 1825 goods worth 12.7 milllion rubles were sold at that fair; in 1852 the sum rose to 57.5 million. A number of other fairs also did a very impressive business.

Transportation also developed, if rather slowly. Rivers and lakes continued to play an extremely important role in trade and travel. A number of canals, especially those constructed between 1804 and 1810, added to the usefulness of the water network, by linking, for instance, the western Dvina to the Dnieper and St. Petersburg to the Volga, thus making it possible to send goods from the upper Volga to the Baltic Sea. The first steamship appeared in Russia in 1815, on the Neva. In 1820 regular steam navigation commenced on the Volga to be extended later to other important rivers and lakes. Following by several years the construction of a small private railroad to serve the needs of a factory, the first public Russian railroad, joining St. Petersburg and the suburban imperial residence of Tsarskoe Selo was opened to traffic in 1837. In 1851 the first major Russian railroad went into operation, linking St. Petersburg and Moscow on a remarkably straight line as desired by Nicholas I. The Russians even proceeded to establish a railroad industry and build their own locomotives and cars, a development in which Americans, including George Whistler, the father of the painter James McNeill Whistler, played a prominent part. But, considering the size of the country, the systems of transportation remained thoroughly inadequate. In particular, in 1850 Russia possessed only a little over 3,000 miles of first-class roads. The Russian army in the Crimea proved to be more isolated from its home bases than the allied forces, which were supplied by sea, from theirs.

Foreign trade—about which we have more precise data than we have concerning domestic commerce—grew swiftly in the first half of the nineteenth century. The annual value of Russian exports on the eve of the "great reforms" has been estimated at 230 million rubles, and of imports at 200 million, compared to only 75 and 52 million, respectively, at the beginning of the century. Russia continued to export raw materials, such as timber and timber products, hemp, flax, tallow, and increasing quantities of grain. The grain trade resulted from the development of agriculture, notably the raising of wheat, in southern Russia; from the organization of grain export, largely in Greek ships, via the Black Sea; and from the pressing demand for grain in industrializing western Europe. From bare beginnings at the turn of the century, the grain trade rose to 35 percent of the total value of Russian exports in 1855. It led to the rapid rise of such ports as Odessa and Taganrog and made the Black Sea rival the Baltic as an avenue for commerce with Russia. Russian manufactures, by contrast, found no demand in the West, but—a foretaste of the future—they attracted some customers in Turkey, Central Asia, Mongolia, and China. The Russian imports consisted of tropical produce, such as fruits and coffee, and factory goods, including machinery, as has already been noted.

## Social Diversification

The population continued to increase rapidly throughout this period, from 36 million people in 1796, to 45 million in 1815, to 67 million in 1851. At the same time, society became more diverse. While the serfs multiplied in the eighteenth century to constitute, according to Jerome Blum, 49 percent of the total population of Russia in 1796 and as much as 58 percent in 1811, by 1858 they composed only 44.5 percent of the total. Crushing conditions of existence were certainly a factor—though recent historians have questioned older arguments about the extent of peasant impoverishment. No less important was the growth of other groups in society. The urban population, in particular, grew both in absolute numbers and as a proportion of the total population between 1800 and the "great reforms." Townspeople constituted about 4.1 percent of the inhabitants of the empire at the turn of the century and 7.8 percent in 1851.

Of particular importance was the growth of people "in between" the traditional social groups, often designated, by a state determined to define and contain everyone, as *raznochintsy*, literally, people of various ranks or origins. These included civil servants beneath the lowest rank in the Table of Ranks and the children born to servitors who had not gained hereditary nobility, nonnoble students in gymnasia and universities, non-noble scholars and artists, sons of priests who did not follow their father's profession, entrepreneurs of various sorts not registered as merchants, soldiers' wives and sons (freed from the normal strictures of serfdom), and others. As Elise Wirtschafter has argued, "try as it might to contain society's development within hereditary social categories, the imperial government's need to mobilize human and material resources also created legal opportunities for the crossing of social boundaries." In addition to the government's need for educated and trained servicemen, this growing middle class was built by the energy, talent, and initiative of many commoners who advanced themselves through education and effort.

As a result of continued imperial expansion, the Russian population continued to become more diverse in ethnicity, language, and religion. The conquest of Transcaucasia, which began with the annexation of Georgia in 1801 and soon extended to Armenia and Azerbaijan, brought one of the most ethnically and religiously diverse places on earth into the Russian Empire. A sign of growing official awareness of what would later be called the national problem was the new designation, starting with Nicholas I's reign, of the non-Christian peoples of Siberia as *inorodtsy*, or "aliens," a term that would continually expand in its application. Other signs of concern included government efforts to weaken Jewish communal institutions and the beginning of Russification in the western borderlands, especially in Poland after the insurrection. In turn, Russian rule faced growing resistance by some of its subject peoples, in Poland most spectacularly, but also by other groups, ranging from independent national cultural development among educated Ukrainians to a guerilla war against Russian rule by mountain peoples of the Caucasus.

In different ways, these patterns of differentiation and difference—rural economic pressures, the rise of new industries and free labor (and restrictions on this development), growing possibilities for geographic and social mobility, and troubled ethnic diversity—all point toward trends that would increasingly define Russian society in the nineteenth century and beyond.

# CHAPTER 28

# Russian Culture in the First Half of the Nineteenth Century

Pushkin. This name, this sound, fills our days. There are the gloomy names of emperors, military commanders, inventors of weapons of murder, torturers, and martyrs. And beside them, one bright name: Pushkin.

ALEXANDER BLOK

We do not belong to any of the great families of the human race. We are neither of the West nor of the East, and we have the traditions of neither. We stand, as it were, outside of time.... We move so oddly in time that, as we advance, the immediate past is irretrievably lost to us. That is but a natural consequence of a culture that is wholly imported and imitative.... We have not added a single idea to the sum total of human ideas. We have not contributed to the progress of the human spirit. And what we have borrowed of this progress we have distorted.

PETR CHAADAEV, 1829

Fresh forces are seething and struggling for expression, but weighted down by onerous oppression and, finding no outlet, these forces merely induce dejection, weariness, and apathy. Literature alone, despite the Tatar censorship, still lives and moves forward. That is why we hold the title of writer in such esteem.... With us the title of poet and writer has long since eclipsed the tinsel of epaulettes and gaudy uniforms.

VISSARION BELINSKY, 1847

The Russian people, having renounced the political realm and given unlimited political powers to the government, reserved for themselves *life*—their moral and communal freedom, the high purpose of which is to achieve a Christian society.

KONSTANTIN AKSAKOV, 1855

The early nineteenth century has been called the beginning of Russia's literary "golden age." No less, philosophical, social, and political thought grew and developed in spite of autocracy and strict censorship. Architecture, painting, music, and theater also thrived. And science and scholarship made important advances. The eighteenth century had mainly been a period of learning from the West. This continued and intensified in the early nineteenth century. But simple borrowing also gave way to creative adaptation and originality. Perhaps the most remarkable and original cultural development in the early nineteenth century was the rise of an "intelligentsia." This term—though coined only later in the 1860s—denoted not simply educated people or even people devoted to a life of ideas but educated and intellectually engaged individuals who, in the name of absolute principles, which tended to derive from contemporary European thought but were shaped by the Russian experience, stood against what they saw as a repressive and restrictive political and social order.

This culture was still mainly gentry culture. Its spirit and tone have been preserved in such brilliant works of memory and literature as Tolstoy's *War and Peace*, Turgenev's *A Gentry Nest*, Sergei Aksakov's family chronicle, and Alexander Herzen's brilliant memoir. This culture grew in a rich and rarified world—one supported by the labor of serfs. The educated gentry enjoyed a cosmopolitan upbringing at home, with emphasis on French, and to a lesser extent German, language and literature, aided by a small army of foreign and Russian tutors. Their estates often contained valuable libraries. They followed developments in the West and frequently traveled abroad. The sons of the gentry often attended select military schools before entering the army as officers, where again the French language and proper social manners were emphasized. More and more of them attended universities, both at home and in western Europe. Gentry women too, though unable to attend university, often received extensive cosmopolitan educations, spoke foreign languages, and played music.

## Education

University education, as well as secondary education in state schools, became more readily available after Alexander I's reforms. With the creation of the Ministry of Education in 1802, the empire was divided into six educational regions, each headed by a curator. The plan called for a university in every region, a secondary school in every provincial center, and an improved primary school in every district. By the end of the reign the projected expansion had been largely completed: Russia then possessed 6 universities, 48 secondary state schools, and 337 improved primary state schools. Alexander I founded universities in Kazan, Kharkov, and St. Petersburg—the latter first being established as a pedagogical institute—transformed the "main school," or academy, in Vilna into a university, and revived the German university in Dorpat, which with the University of Moscow made a total of six. In addition, a university existed in the Grand Duchy of Finland: originally in Åbo—called Turku in Finnish—and from 1827 in Helsingfors, or Helsinki. Following a traditional European pattern, Russian universities enjoyed a broad measure of autonomy. While university enrollments usually numbered a few hundred or less each, and the total of secondary school students rose only to about 5,500 by 1825, these figures represented undeniable progress for Russia. Moreover, private initiative emerged to supplement the government efforts. It played an important part in the creation of the University of Kharkov, and it established two private institutions of higher education that were eventually to become the Demidov Law School in Iaroslavl and the Historico-Philological Institute of Prince Bezborodko in Nezhin. Finally, it may be noted that the celebrated Imperial Lyceum in Tsarskoe Selo, which Pushkin attended, was also founded during the reign of Alexander I.

During the last years of Alexander's rule, education officials undertook a series of obscurantist purges of several universities. Most extreme were Mikhail Magnitsky's effort to turn the University of Kazan into a kind of monastic barracks: he purged the faculty and the library, flooded the university with Bibles, and instituted severe discipline among the students, demanding mutual spying and compulsory attendance at religious services. These extreme policies ended with Magnitsky's fall from grace. But this did not rescue education from this threat. Nicholas I's influence on education was ultimately much more damaging. During the thirty years of Official Nationality, with Uvarov himself serving as minister of education from 1833 to 1849, the government tried to centralize and standardize education; to limit the individual's schooling according to his social background, so that each person would remain in his assigned place in life; to foster the official ideology exclusively; and, above all, to eliminate every trace or possibility of intellectual opposition or subversion. The emperor's view of the universities may be suggested by a story that on passing by Moscow University in his carriage, he said to a companion, "There is a wolf's den."

Nicholas I and his associates did everything in their power to introduce absolute order and regularity into the educational system of Russia. The state even extended its minute control to private schools and indeed to education in the home. By a series of laws and rules issued in 1833–35, private institutions, which were not to increase in number in the future except where public schooling was not available, received regulations and instructions from central authorities, while inspectors were appointed to assure their compliance. "They had to submit to the law of unity which formed the foundation of the reign." Home education came under state influence through rigid government control of teachers: Russian private tutors began to be considered state employees, subject to appropriate examinations and enjoying the same pensions and awards as other comparable officials; at the same time the government strictly prohibited the hiring of foreign instructors who did not possess the requisite certificates testifying to academic competence and exemplary "moral" character. Nicholas I himself led the way in supervising and inspecting schools in Russia, and the emperor's assistants followed his example.

The restrictive policies of the Ministry of Education resulted logically from its social views and aims. In order to assure that each class of Russians obtained only "that part which it needs from the general treasury of enlightenment," the government resorted to increased tuition rates and to such requirements as special certificates of leave that pupils belonging to the lower layers of society had to obtain from their village or town before they could attend secondary school. Members of the upper class, by contrast, received inducements to continue their education, many boarding schools for the gentry being created for that purpose. Ideally, in the government's scheme of things—and reality failed to live up to the ideal—children of peasants and of lower classes in general were to attend only parish schools or other schools of similar educational level, students of middle-class origin were to study in the district schools, while secondary schools and universities catered primarily, although not exclusively, to the gentry. Special efforts were made throughout the reign to restrict the education of the serfs to elementary and "useful" subjects. Schools for girls, which were under the patronage of the empress dowager and the jurisdiction of the Fourth Department of His Majesty's Own Chancery, served the same aims as those for boys.

The inculcation of the true doctrine, that of Official Nationality, and a relentless struggle against all pernicious ideas constituted, as we know, essential activities of the Ministry of Education. Only officially approved views received endorsement, and they had to be accepted without question rather than discussed. Teachers and students, lectures and books were generally suspect and required a watchful eye. In 1834 full-time inspectors were introduced into universities to keep vigil over the behavior of students outside the classroom. Education and knowledge, in the estimate of the emperor and his associates, could easily become subversion! As already mentioned, with the revolutionary year of 1848 unrelieved repression set in.

Still, the government of Nicholas I made some significant contributions to the development of education in Russia. Thus, it should be noted that the Ministry of Education spent large sums to provide new buildings, laboratories, and libraries, and other aids to scholarship such as the excellent Pulkovo observatory; that teachers' salaries were substantially increased—extraordinarily increased in the case of professors, according to the University Statute of 1835; that, in general, the government of Nicholas I showed a commendable interest in the physical plant necessary for education and in the material well-being of those engaged in instruction. Nor was quality neglected. Uvarov in particular did much to raise educational and scholarly standards in Russia in the sixteen years during which he headed the ministry. Especially important proved to be the establishment of many new chairs, the corresponding opening up of numerous new fields of learning in the universities of the empire, and the practice of sending promising young Russian scholars abroad for extended training. The Russian educational system, with all its fundamental flaws, came to emphasize academic thoroughness and high standards. Indeed, the government utilized the standards to make education more exclusive at all levels of schooling. Following the Polish rebellion, the Polish University of Vilna was closed; in 1833 a Russian university was opened in Kiev instead. The government of Nicholas I created no other new universities, but it did establish a number of technical and "practical" institutions of higher learning, such as a technological institute, a school of jurisprudence, and a school of architecture, as well as schools of arts and crafts, agriculture, and veterinary medicine.

## Science and Scholarship

With the expansion of higher education, science and scholarship grew in Russia. Mathematics led the way. Nikolai Lobachevsky, who lived from 1793 to 1856 and taught at the University of Kazan, was the greatest Russian mathematician of that, or indeed any, period. The "Copernicus of geometry" left his mark in the history of thought by formulating a non-Euclidian geometry, within which the Euclidian scheme represented but a single instance. While Lobachevsky's revolutionary views received scant recognition from his contemporaries either in Russia or in other countries—although, to be exact, he was not quite alone, for a few Western scholars were approaching similar conclusions at about the same time—they nevertheless represented a major breakthrough in the direction of the modern development of mathematics and the physical sciences. Several other gifted Russian mathematicians of the first half of the nineteenth century also contributed to the growth of their subject.

Astronomy too fared exceptionally well in Russia in the first half of the nineteenth century. In 1839 the celebrated Pulkovo observatory was constructed near St. Petersburg. Directed by one of the leading astronomers of the age, who was formerly professor at the University of Dorpat, Frederick Georg Wilhelm von Struve, and possessing the largest telescope in the world at that time and in general the most up-to-date equipment, Pulkovo quickly became not only a great center of astronomy in Russia but also a valuable training ground for astronomers from other European countries and the United States. Struve investigated over 3,000 double stars, developed methods to calculate the weight of stars and to apply statistics to a study of them, and dealt with such problems as the distribution of stars, the shape of our galaxy, and the absorption of light in interstellar space. Struve's associates and students—in fact, several other members of the Struve family—further expanded the study of astronomy in Russia.

Other natural sciences also developed in these decades, including physics (Vasilii Petrov being a particularly noteworthy experimental physicist), chemistry (notably, the influential organic chemist Nikolai Zinin), and biology (such as the great Baltic German embryologist Karl Ernst von Baer). As in the eighteenth century, and in other imperial powers, the natural sciences were enriched by expeditions and discoveries. Russians continued to explore Siberia and the northern seas but also organized expeditions to circumnavigate the globe. Russian explorers were the first Europeans to encounter numerous islands in the Pacifc Ocean, though the Russian government did not choose to claim them. And, from 1819 to 1821, Faddei Bellingshausen led an expedition to the south polar region, where he was one of the first Europeans to see the continent of Antarctica.

The humanities and the social sciences evolved similarly. Again, Russia's imperial and global interests had a strong affect. Russia's location in both Europe and Asia encouraged the development of "Oriental studies." An Asian Museum was established in St. Petersburg in 1818, and similar institutes were established at many universities. Contributions in this field ranged from early ethnographic descriptions of Central Asian peoples to Father Iakinf Bichurin's extensive research on China. In this age of nationalism, it was natural that history writing should have developed strongly and gained a new public.

Nikolai Karamzin, who must be mentioned more than once in connection with the evolution of the Russian language and literature, also became the first widely popular historian. His richly documented twelve-volume *History of the Russian State*, which began to appear in 1816 but was left unfinished in the account of the Time of Troubles when the author died in 1826, won the enthusiastic acclaim of the educated public, who enjoyed Karamzin's extremely readable reconstruction of the colorful Russian past. But Karamzin's purposes were not mainly to entertain—he had an important political and national argument to make: that autocracy and a strong state made Russia great and must remain inviolable. In 1811 Karamzin had expressed similar views succinctly in his secret *Memoir on Ancient and Modern Russia* given to Alexander I to counteract Speransky's reformist influence. In Russian universities new chairs were founded in history. Mikhail Pogodin, a proponent of Official Nationality, became in 1835 the first professor of Russian history proper at the University of Moscow.

## Language and Literature

The Russian language evolved further, and so did linguistic and literary studies. If the writings of Karamzin marked the victory of the new style over the old, those of Pushkin already represented the apogee of modern Russian language and literature and became their classic model. The simplicity, precision, grace, and flow of Pushkin's language testify to the enormous development of the Russian literary language since the time of Peter the Great. Such opponents of this process as the reactionary Admiral Alexander Shishkov, who served from 1824 to 1828 as minister of education, fought a losing battle. While writers developed the Russian language, scholars studied it. The first decades of the nineteenth century witnessed the work of the remarkable philologist Alexander Vostokov and the early studies of several other outstanding linguistic scholars. Literary criticism rose to a new prominence. The critics ranged from conservative university professors, typified by Stepan Shevyrev of the University of Moscow, who adhered to the doctrine of Official Nationality, to the radical firebrand Vissarion Belinsky. Indeed, we shall see that with Belinsky literary criticism in Russia acquired sweeping social, political, and generally ideological significance.

Literature constituted the glory of Russian culture in the first half of the nineteenth century. Karamzin's sentimentalism, mentioned in an earlier chapter, which was popular at the end of the eighteenth and in the first years of the nineteenth century, gradually lost its appeal. New literary trends included what prerevolutionary and Soviet scholars described as Romanticism and realism, though the definitions and usefulness of these categories are debated. Romanticism attracted a number of gifted poets and writers and also contributed to the artistic growth of such luminaries as Pushkin, Lermontov, and Gogol. Vasilii Zhukovsky deserves particular mention. Zhukovsky, who lived from 1783 to 1852, reflected in his poetry certain widespread Romantic moods and traits: sensitivity and concern with subjective feelings, an interest in and idealization of the past, and a penchant for the mysterious, ghostly, and strange. On the whole the poet represented the humane, elegiac, and contemplative, rather than the "demonic" and active, aspects of Romanticism.

Nineteenth-century and Soviet critics insisted on the greater value of Russian "realism." In their view, with realism Russian literature finally achieved true independence and originality and established a firm foundation for lasting greatness. A difficult concept to use, the term realism has been applied to a variety of literary developments in Russia in the first half of the nineteenth century. Paradoxically, Ivan Krylov, the writer of fables, has been described as an exemplary realist. Krylov, who lived from 1768 to 1844, but began to write fables only in his late thirties after concentrating unsuccessfully on comedy, tragedy, and satire, achieved something like perfection in his new genre, rivaling such world masters of the fable as Aesop and La Fontaine. Krylov's approximately 200 fables, which became best sellers as they appeared during the author's lifetime and have remained best sellers ever since, win the reader by the richness and raciness of their popular language, the vividness, precision, and impeccable wording of their succinct narrative, and their author's power of human observation and comment. While animals often act as protagonists, their foibles and predicaments serve as apt illustrations both of Krylov's Russia and of the human condition in general.

Alexander Griboedov, whose life began in 1795 and ended violently in 1829 when a Persian mob killed him in the Russian legation in Teheran, achieved immortality as a realist through one work only: the comedy *Gore ot uma*, translated into English as *Woe from Wit* or as *The Misfortune of Being Clever*. This masterpiece was finished in 1824, but, because of its strong criticism of Russian high society, was put on the stage only in 1831 and then with numerous cuts. *Gore ot uma* is neo-classical in form and contains very little action, but it overflows with wit. It consists almost entirely of sparkling, grotesque, or caustic statements and observations by its many characters, from a saucy maid to the embittered hero Chatsky—all set in the milieu of Muscovite high society. Its sparkle is such that Griboedov's play possesses an eternal freshness and effervescence, while many of its characters' observations—like many lines from Krylov's fables—have become part of the everyday Russian language. Nor, of course, does a "comic form exclude serious content. *Gore ot uma* has been praised as the outstanding critique of the leading circles of Russian society in the reign of Alexander I, as a perspicacious early treatment of the subject of the conflict of generations—a theme developed later by Turgenev and other Russian writers—and as providing in its main character, Chatsky, a prototype of the typical "superfluous" hero of Russian literature, at odds with his environment.

Like Griboedov, Alexander Pushkin, the greatest Russian writer of the age, was born near the end of the eighteenth century and became famous in the last years of Alexander I's reign. Again like Griboedov, Pushkin had but a short life to live before meeting violent death. He was born in 1799 and was killed in a duel in 1837. Between 1820, which marked the completion of his first major poem, the whimsical and gently ironic *Ruslan and Liudmila*, and his death, Pushkin established himself permanently as, everything considered, the greatest Russian poet and one of the greatest Russian prose writers, as a master of the lyric, the epic, and the dramatic forms, and even as a literary critic, publicist, and something of a historian and ethnographer. Pushkin's early works, such as *The Fountain of Bakhchisarai* and *The Prisoner of the Caucasus*, magnificent in form, reflected a certain interest in the unusual and the exotic that was characteristic of the colonial age. However, as early as *Eugene Onegin*, written in 1822–31, Pushkin turned to a penetrating and remarkably realistic treatment of Russian educated society and its problems. Onegin became one of the most effective and compelling figures in modern Russian literature, while both he and the heroine of the poem, Tatiana Larina, as well as their simple story, were to appear and reappear in different variations and guises in the works of Lermontov, Turgenev, Goncharov, and many other writers. While *Eugene Onegin* was written in most elegant verse, Pushkin also contributed greatly to the development of Russian prose, especially by such tales as the celebrated *A Captain's Daughter*. In his prose even more than in his poetry Pushkin has been considered a founder of realism in Russia. Pushkin's deeply sensitive and versatile genius ranged from unsurpassed personal lyrics to

Alexander Pushkin. *(New York Public Library)*

historical themes—for example, in the tragedy *Boris Godunov* and in the long poem, *Poltava*, glorifying his recurrent hero, Peter the Great—and from realistic evocations of the Russia of his day to marvelous fairy tales in verse. He was busily engaged in publishing a leading periodical, *The Contemporary*, and in historical studies when he was killed.

Pushkin's genius has often been described as "classical." Its outstanding characteristic consisted in an astounding sense of form, harmony, and measure, which resulted in perfect works of art. The writer's fundamental outlook reflected something of the same classical balance: it was humane, sane, and essentially affirmative and optimistic. Not that it excluded tragedy. A long poem, *The Bronze Horseman*, perhaps best expressed Pushkin's recognition of tragedy in the world. It depicted a disastrous conflict between an average little man, Eugene, and the bronze statue of the great founder of St. Petersburg, who built his new capital on virtually impassable terrain, where one of the recurrent floods killed Eugene's beloved: a conflict between an individual and the state, human desire and necessity, man and his fate. Yet—although a minority of specialists reject this reading of the poem—*The Bronze Horseman*, too, affirms Peter the Great's work, modern Russia, and life itself.

After his death, even more than during his short life, Pushkin achieved a unique status as Russia's "national poet," a phrase already used by Nikolai Gogol while Pushkin was alive: "Pushkin's name calls to mind the thought of a Russian national poet....Pushkin is a manifestation of the Russian spirit....In him, the Russian nature, the Russian soul, the Russian language, the Russian character are reflected." For Fedor Dostoevsky, in his speech at the unveiling of a monument to Pushkin in Moscow in 1880 (a speech met, according to Dostoevsky, with "wails of rapture"), Pushkin was most Russian precisely in being a "universal man," able to express the spirit of any nation. As such, his voice, like Russia itself, had a unique prophetic and salvational power "to reconcile European conflicts once and for all, to show the way out of European ennui in our universally human and unifying Russian soul." Such arguments would become a full-blown Pushkin myth, which developed very strongly in the late 1800s and in Stalin's Soviet Union. Pushkin himself, though, some scholars have demonstrated, was less certain about how well he fit into Russian life. His African origins and swarthy looks—his great-grandfather was Ibrahim Hannibal, who, according to family legend, was the son of an Abyssinian prince, given as a gift to Peter the Great by a Russian envoy who acquired him from the Turkish sultan—was one reason Pushkin sometimes felt himself to be an outsider. So was his discontent with Russian authoritarianism, which led him to openly sympathize with the Decembrists and earned him Nicholas I's undying suspicion. On the other hand, Pushkin was part of the very elite of privileged society in Russia, and, as his poems show, he clearly reveled in society life. But his works also reveal the darker sides of society life, especially for the sensitive individual. Poems like *The Bronze Horseman* show some understanding of the suffering of commoners as well. There is scattered evidence that Pushkin expressed a desire to emigrate to the West.

Mikhail Lermontov, though never celebrated in the way Pushkin was, should not be allowed to fall into Pushkin's shadow. Born in 1814 and killed in a duel in 1841, Lermontov began writing at a very early age and left behind him a literary legacy of considerable size and richness. Very different in temperament and outlook from Pushkin, Lermontov came closest to being the leading Romantic genius of Russian letters, the "Russian Byron." His life was a constant protest against his environment, a protest that found expression both in public gestures, such as his stunning poem condemning Russian high society for the death of Pushkin, and in private troubles, which resulted in his own death. Lermontov often chose fantastic, exotic, and highly subjective themes set in the grandeur of the Caucasus, where he spent some time in the army. Throughout most of his life he kept writing and rewriting a magnificent long poem called *A Demon*, in which he explores his own troubled self through the figure of a demon, who embodies the spirit of difference and alienation.

> I am he, whose gaze withers hope
> At the moment hope blossoms;
> I am he, whom no one loves,
> Accursed by every living soul.
> I am the scourge of my earthly slaves,
> I am tsar of knowledge and freedom,
> I am the enemy of the heavens and the evil of nature.

Yet to describe Lermontov as a Romantic poet does not do him full justice. Through his prose writings, particularly his short novel *A Hero of Our Times*, he became one of the founders of the Russian realistic novel, in subject matter as well as in form. Such a discerning critic as Dmitrii Mirsky considered Lermontov's superbly powerful, succinct, and transparent prose superior even to Pushkin's. Lermontov, no doubt, could have done much more had he not been shot dead at the age of twenty-six.

Nikolai Gogol's early venture into poetry proved an unmitigated disaster. But as a prose writer Gogol had few equals and no superiors. Gogol, who lived from 1809 to 1852, came from provincial Ukrainian gentry, and the characteristic society of his stories and plays stood several rungs lower on the social ladder than the world of Chatsky and Onegin. Gogol's first collection of tales, *Evenings on a Farm near Dikanka*, which came out in 1831 and received immediate acclaim, sparkled with a generally gay humor and the bright colors of Ukrainian folklore. The gaiety and the folklore, as well as a certain majestic tone and grand manner—much admired by some critics, but considered affected by others—were to appear in Gogol's later works, for example, the famous cossack prose epic, *Taras Bulba*, which dealt with the struggle of the Ukrainians against the Poles. However, gradually, the real Gogol emerged in literature: the Gogol of the commonplace and the mildly grotesque, which he somehow shaped into an overwhelming psychological world all his own; the Gogol who wrote in an involved, irregular and apparently clumsy style, which proved utterly irresistible. Occasionally, for instance in the stories *Notes of a*

*Madman* and *A Nose*, strange content paralleled these magical literary powers. More frequently, as in the celebrated play *The Inspector General* and in Gogol's masterpiece, the novel *Dead Souls*, the subject matter contained nothing out of the ordinary and the plot showed little development.

*Dead Souls*, published in 1842, demonstrates the scope and might of Gogol's genius and serves as the touchstone for different interpretations of Gogol. That simple story of a scoundrel, Chichikov, who proceeded to visit provincial landlords and buy up their dead serfs—serfs were called "souls" in Russia—to use them in business deals as if they were alive, has been hailed, and not at all unjustly, by critics from Belinsky to Soviet and post-Soviet scholars as a devastating, realistic, satirical picture of rural Russia under Nicholas I. But there seems to be much more to Gogol's novel. The landlords of different psychological types whom Chichikov meets, as well as Chichikov himself, appear to grow in vitality with the years, regardless of the passing of that society which they are supposed to mirror faithfully, for, indeed, they are "much more real than life." Russian formalist critics and such writers as Dmitrii Merezhkovsky and Vladimir Nabokov deserve credit for emphasizing these other "non-realistic" aspects and powers of Gogol. The great novelist himself, it might be added, probably did not know what he was doing. His withering satire, applauded by the opponents of the existing system in Russia, stemmed directly from his strange and troubled genius, not from any ideology of the Left. In fact, in the second volume of *Dead Souls* Gogol tried to reform his characters and save Russia. That project, of course, failed. Still trying to resurrect Russian society, Gogol published in 1847 his naïve and reactionary *Selected Passages from Correspondence with Friends*, which suggested, for example, that serfs should remain illiterate and shocked educated Russia. Gogol also attempted to find salvation for himself—and, by extension, for Russia—in religious experience, but to no avail. He died in 1852 after a shattering nervous breakdown when he burned much of the sequel to the first volume of *Dead Souls*.

Karamzin, Zhukovsky, Krylov, Griboedov, Pushkin, Lermontov, and Gogol were by no means the only Russian authors in the reigns of Alexander I and Nicholas I. Pushkin was the outstanding member of a brilliant generation of poets. And prose writers included, in addition to those already mentioned, the magnificent narrator of provincial gentry life, Sergei Aksakov, and other gifted authors. Moreover, prereform Russia saw the first publications of such giants of Russian and world literature as Turgenev, Dostoevsky, and Tolstoy. It was a golden age.

## Ideologies

Alexander Herzen described the first half of the nineteenth century as a remarkable age of outward political slavery and inward intellectual emancipation. Again, Russia profited from its association with the West and from the great development of cosmopolitan and secular education and culture in Russia over the previous century. Ideologically, Enlightenment liberalism and radicalism persisted into the early 1800s, notably among groups as different as Alexander I's Unofficial Committee and the Decembrists. But on the whole the intellectual orientation among educated Russians shifted toward German idealistic philosophy and Romanticism. The new intellectual *Zeitgeist* affirmed deep, comprehensive knowledge—often with mystical or religious elements—in opposition to mere rationalism, an organic view of the world as against a mechanistic view, and the historical approach to society in contrast to a utilitarian attitude with its vision limited to the present. It also emphasized such diverse doctrines as struggle and the essential separateness of the component parts of the universe in place of the Enlightenment ideals of harmony, unity, and cosmopolitanism. And it stressed the supreme value of art and culture. Questions of the meaning and mission of the individual, the nation, and the world—though certainly present among eighteenth-century thinkers such as Novikov and among the Decembrists—acquired great force in this era.

Romanticism and idealistic philosophy penetrated Russia in a variety of ways. For example, a number of professors, typified by Mikhail Pavlov, who taught physics, mineralogy, and agronomy at the University of Moscow, presented novel German ideas in their lectures in the first decades of the nineteenth century. Educated Russians continued to read voraciously and were strongly influenced by Schiller and other brilliant Western Romanticists. Of course, the subjects of the tsar were also Europeans and thus could not help but be part of European intellectual movements. While some Russians showed originality in developing different currents of Western thought, and while in general the Russian response to Romantic ideas can be considered creative rather than merely imitative, there is no convincing reason for dissociating Russian intellectual history of the first half of the nineteenth century from that of the rest of Europe, whether in the name of the alleged uniquely religious nature of the ideological development in Russia or in order to satisfy a Russian nationalism.

In particular, two German philosophers, Schelling first and then Hegel, exercised strong influence on the Russians. Schelling affected certain professors and a number of poets—the best Russian expression of some Schellingian views can be found in Fedor Tiutchev's unsurpassed poetry of nature—and also groups of intellectuals and even schools of thought, such as the Slavophile. It was largely an interest in Schelling that led to the establishment of the first philosophic "circle" and the first philosophic review in Russia. In 1823 several young men who had been discussing Schelling in a literary group formed a separate society with the study of German idealistic philosophy as its main object. The circle chose the name of "The Lovers of Wisdom" and came to contain a dozen members and associates, many of whom were to achieve prominence in Russian intellectual life. It published four issues of a journal, *Mnemosyne*. The leading Lovers of Wisdom included a gifted poet, Dmitrii Venevitinov, who died in 1827 at the age of twenty-two, and Prince Vladimir Odoevsky, 1803–69, who developed interesting views concerning the decline of the West and the great future of Russia to issue from the combination

and fruition of both the pre-Petrine and the Petrine heritages. The Lovers of
Wisdom reflected the Romantic temper of their generation in a certain kind of
poetic spiritualism that pervaded their entire outlook, in their worship of art,
in their pantheistic adoration of nature, and in their disregard for the "crude"
aspects of life, including politics. The group disbanded after the Decembrist
rebellion in order not to attract police attention.

A decade later, the question of the nature and destiny of Russia was powerfully and shockingly presented by Petr Chaadaev. In his *Philosophical Letter*,
written in French in 1829 and circulated by hand until its first publication in
the *Telescope* in 1836, Chaadaev argued, in effect, that Russia had no past, no
present, and no future. It had never really belonged to either the West or the
East, and it had contributed nothing to culture. In particular, Russia lacked
the dynamic social principle of Catholicism, which constituted the basis of
the entire Western civilization. Indeed, Russia remained "a gap in the intellectual order of things." Chaadaev, who was officially proclaimed deranged
by the incensed authorities after the publication of the letter, later modified
his thesis in his *Apology of a Madman*. Russia, he now argued did enter history
through the work of Peter the Great and could obtain a glorious future by
throwing all of its fresh strength into the construction of the common culture
of Christendom.

Spurred by Schelling, by an increasing Hegelian influence, and by German
Romantic thought in general, as well as by the new importance of Russia in
Europe ever since the cataclysm of 1812 and by the blossoming of Russian culture, several ideologies emerged to compete for the favor of the educated public. Conservative thought was strong and persistent. Karamzin's 1811 *Memoir
on Ancient and Modern Russia*, already mentioned, used an argumentative
survey of Russian history to show the dangers of social division (especially
the "many headed hydra of aristocracy") and the necessity of strong central
government, especially when tempered by virtue and moral purpose. To be
certain that Alexander I understood the message, he warned him that limiting autocracy was both dangerous and illegitimate: "You may do everything,
but you may not limit your authority by law!" Among ideological justifications of autocracy, the most influential was "Official Nationality," which we
discussed in the previous chapter. It found influential spokesmen among a
number of professors and writers, not to mention censors and other officials,
notably in education and in the Church. Its most nationalistic wing, typified
by Mikhail Pogodin, a professor of history at Moscow University, was influenced by German Romanticism. But Romanticism also strongly influenced
radical thought on the Left, especially the two most important independent,
as opposed to government-sponsored, schools of thought: the Slavophiles and
the Westernizers—*slavianofily* and *zapadniki* in Russian. It should be mentioned
that these terms were coined by each side as a slightly ironic and mocking
definition of the other, and thus are caricatures rather than accurate definitions of their main views.

The Slavophiles formulated a comprehensive and remarkable ideology
centered on their belief in the superior nature and supreme historical mission of

Orthodoxy and of Russia. The leading members of the group, all of them land-lords and gentlemen-scholars of broad culture and many intellectual interests, included Alexei Khomiakov, who applied himself to everything from theology and world history to medicine and technical inventions; Ivan Kireevsky, who has been called the philosopher of the movement; his brother Petr, who collected folk songs and left very little behind him in writing; Konstantin Aksakov, a specialist in Russian history and language; Konstantin's brother Ivan, later prominent as a publicist and a Pan-Slav; and Georgii Samarin, who was to have a significant part in the emancipation of the serfs and who wrote especially on certain religious and philosophical topics, on the problem of the borderlands of the empire, and on the issue of reform in Russia. This informal group, gathering in the salons and homes of Moscow, flourished in the 1840s and 1850s until the death of the Kireevsky brothers in 1856 and of Khomiakov and Konstantin Aksakov in 1860.

Slavophilism expressed a fundamental vision of integration, peace, and harmony among people. On the religious plane it produced Khomiakov's concept of *sobornost*, an association of believers joined in love, freedom, and truth, which Khomiakov considered the essence of Orthodoxy. Historically, so the Slavophiles asserted, a similar harmonious integration of individuals could be found in the social life of the Slavs, notably in the peasant commune—described as "a moral choir" by Konstantin Aksakov—and in such other ancient Russian institutions as the zemskii sobor. Again, the family represented the principle of integration in love, and the same spirit could pervade other associations of human beings. As against love, freedom, and cooperation stood the world of rationalism, necessity, and compulsion. It too existed on many planes, from the religious and metaphysical to that of everyday life. Thus it manifested itself in the Roman Catholic Church—which had chosen rationalism and authority in preference to love and harmony and had seceded from Orthodox Christendom—and, through the Catholic Church, in Protestantism and in the entire civilization of the West. Moreover, Peter the Great introduced the principles of rationalism, legalism, and compulsion into Russia, where they proceeded to destroy or stunt the harmonious native development and to seduce the educated public. The Russian future lay in a return to native principles, in overcoming the Western disease. After being cured, Russia would take its message of harmony and salvation to the discordant and dying West. It is important to realize that the all-embracing Slavophile dichotomy represented—as pointed out by Fedor Stepun and others—the basic Romantic contrast between the Romantic ideal and the Age of Reason. In particular, as well as in general, Slavophilism fits into the framework of European Romanticism, although the Slavophiles showed considerable originality in adapting Romantic doctrines to their own situation and needs and although they also experienced the influence of Orthodox religious thought and tradition.

Some scholars, such as Andrzej Walicki, have described the complex Slavophile ideology as a paradoxical "retrospective utopianism"—in other words, the Slavophiles imagined a future based on a past that was itself largely imagined. Certainly, in its application to the Russia of Nicholas I the

Slavophile teaching often produced paradoxical results, antagonized the government, and baffled Slavophile friends and foes alike. In a sense, the Slavophiles were religious anarchists, for they condemned all legalism and compulsion in the name of their religious ideal. Yet, given the sinful condition of man, they granted the necessity of government and even expressed a preference for autocracy: in addition to its historical roots in ancient Russia, autocracy possessed the virtue of placing the entire weight of authority and compulsion on a single individual, thus liberating society from that heavy burden; besides, the Slavophiles remained unalterably opposed to Western constitutional and other legalistic and formalistic devices. Yet this justification of autocracy remained historical and functional, therefore relative, never religious and absolute. Furthermore, the Slavophiles desired the emancipation of the serfs and other reforms, and, above all, insisted on the "freedom of the life of the spirit," that is, freedom of conscience, speech, and publication. As Konstantin Aksakov tried to explain to the government: "Man was created by God as an intelligent and a talking being." Also, Khomiakov and his friends opposed such aspects of the established order as the death penalty, government intrusion into private life, and bureaucracy in general. "Thus the first relationship of the government and the people is the relationship of mutual non-interference." No wonder Slavophile publications did not escape censorship and prohibition for long.

The Westernizers were much more diverse than the Slavophiles, and their views did not form a single, integrated whole. Even socially the Westernizers consisted of different elements, ranging from Mikhail Bakunin, who came from a gentry home like those of the Slavophiles, to Vissarion Belinsky, whose father was an impoverished doctor and grandfather a priest, and Vasilii Botkin, who belonged to a family of merchants. Yet certain generally held opinions and doctrines gave a measure of unity to the movement.

Like the Slavophiles, Westernizers built their arguments on a foundation of German idealistic philosophy. Indeed, it can be argued that they shared a common group culture as emerging intelligentsia: a culture defined by devotion to ideas and principles, concern with the good of others (the nation, the common people), opposition to a repressive and restrictive political and social order, and a belief that enlightened individuals must consecrate themselves to the higher cause. They also shared a certain Romantic mood: they were not to be jaded and aloof, like ordinary upper-class youths, but passionate, emotional, and enthusiastic, especially about ideas, but also about human relationships. Many were friends and met to discuss ideas, but they came to very different conclusions. Certainly, a key difference was how they viewed Russia and the West. While Khomiakov and his friends affirmed the superiority of true Russian principles over those of the West, the Westernizers argued that Russia could accomplish its mission only in the context of Western civilization. They viewed Russia's Westernization as positive, but criticized the established order for its failures to follow this path fully. However, the differences ran more deeply than views of Russia and the West—in fact, Westernizers could be quite critical of the West for failing to live up to its own high ideals. A deeper difference was how each group viewed the individual human person. The Slavophiles idealized a world in which people were all bonded together in a natural community (well expressed in the concept of *sobornost*). The Westernizers, as we shall see, idealized the individual and were concerned above all with the rights and dignity of the person. These groups also differed in their attitudes toward religion. Slavophiles anchored their entire ideology in an interpretation of Orthodoxy. Westernizers, though they believed in a universal moral code and even spoke of this as exemplified by Christ's teachings, attached little importance to religion as such. Even those who did not turn toward atheism viewed existing religion as an insult to reason. The most moderate Westernizers were essentially idealistic liberals, emphasizing gradualism and popular enlightenment. These moderates were typified by Nikolai Stankevich, who brought together a famous early Westernizer circle but died in 1840 at the age of twenty-seven before the movement really developed, and by Professor Timofei Granovsky, who lived from 1813 to 1855 and taught popular courses in European history at the University of Moscow. The radical Westernizers, however, largely through Hegelianism and Left Hegelianism, came to challenge religion, society, and the entire Russian and European system and to call for a revolution. Although few in number, their impact on history would be great. The major figures were Vissarion Belinsky, 1811–48, Alexander Herzen, 1812–70, and Mikhail Bakunin, 1814–76.

Belinsky became widely known and very influential as a literary critic. He had the good fortune to write at a remarkable time in Russian letters: he could comment on the writings of Pushkin, Lermontov, and Gogol and welcome the debuts of Dostoevsky, Turgenev, and Nekrasov. More important, his literary criticism was famous for its passion, invective, and eulogy; for his ability to see works of literature as expressions of their time; and for a view of literature that liberated it from mere aesthetics. For Belinsky, art should inspire and awaken people, regenerate and ennoble them. It should express "truth." As Nekrasov later put it, for Belinsky one did not have to be a poet, but one must be a citizen. Following Belinsky's insight and example, literature and literary criticism in Russia would indeed become the freest place in Russia for examining social and political conditions and imagining change. Although Belinsky, due to his social background, lacked the education enjoyed by noblemen like Herzen and Bakunin, he made up for this in intellectual commitment and fervor. This became the essence of his intellectual style: "For me, to think and feel, to understand and suffer, are one and the same thing." Above all, the notion of the human person—*lichnost* in Russian—was key to his thought. Convinced, as many were, that the individual person possessed natural dignity and rights, he built on this foundation a sweeping critique of existing society. He rejected an abstract approach to philosophy: "What is it to me that the Universal exists when the individual personality [*lichnost*] is suffering." He bitterly criticized autocracy and serfdom as "trampling upon everything that is even remotely human and noble." He condemned, on the same basis, poverty, prostitution, drunkenness, bureaucratic coldness, and cruelty toward the less powerful (including women). To be sure, Belinsky's views underwent a series of crises and changes. But, as Isaiah Berlin noted, "his consistency was moral, not intellectual."

Herzen's autobiography, *My Past and Thoughts*, is one of the most remarkable Russian texts written in the nineteenth century—a blend of memoir, literature, philosophy, and political criticism. He was an incisive writer and a complex thinker, sensitive to how intractable were the problems of human existence. Like Belinsky, he continually stressed the dignity and freedom of the individual and the oppression of the personality in Russia. As such, he hated despotism but he also feared the absolutism of the radical Left. And he was not blind to the inadequacies of Western life. He left Russia in 1847, eventually settling in London, where he was able to organize a major center of Russian dissident publishing and journalism. But he quickly grew disillusioned with Western bourgeois liberalism. He suggested that the dominant spirit in western Europe had become that of the "petite bourgeoisie," whose guiding principle was not the human person (*lichnost*) but property. He became attracted to the ideas of socialism. Like the Slavophiles, he began to see the Russian peasant commune as a possible source for a new social order. But his socialism was always tempered by his commitment to individual freedom and a good deal of skepticism about any simple solutions.

Bakunin has been described as a "founder of nihilism and apostle of anarchy"—Herzen said he was born not under a star but under a comet—but he began peacefully enough as an enthusiast of German thought, especially Hegel's. Several years earlier than Herzen, Bakunin too left Russia. Before long he turned to Left Hegelianism and moved beyond it to anarchism and a sweeping condemnation of state, society, economy, and culture in Russia and in the world. Bakunin emphasized destruction, proclaiming in a signal early article that the passion for destruction was itself a creative passion. While Herzen bitterly witnessed the defeat of the revolution of 1848 in Paris, Bakunin attended the Pan-Slav Congress in Prague and participated in the revolution in Saxony. After the Austrian government handed him over to the Russian authorities, he was to spend over a decade in fortresses and in Siberian exile.

Many small radical groups emerged in these years, inspired by a variety of ideologies. Most famous perhaps, not least because of the traumatic experience of the young Dostoevsky while associated with this circle, were the Petrashevtsy. This informal group of two score or more men, who from late 1845 until their arrest in the spring of 1849 gathered on Fridays at the home of Mikhail Butashevich-Petrashevsky in St. Petersburg, espoused especially the teaching of the French Utopian socialist Charles Fourier. Fourier preached the peaceful transformation of society into small, well-integrated, and self-supporting communes, which would also provide for the release and harmony of human passions. Many Petrashevtsy, however, added to Fourierism political protest, demand for reform, and general opposition to the Russia of Nicholas I. The government took such a serious view of the situation that it condemned twenty-one men to death, although it changed their sentence at the place of execution in favor of less drastic punishments.

As a member of the Petrashevtsy, Dostoevsky faced imminent execution and later went to Siberia. The Petrashevtsy, it should be noted, generally came from lower social strata than did the Lovers of Wisdom, the Slavophiles, and the Westernizers and included mostly minor officials, junior officers, and students.

We can see that as educated Russians grew more critical of the established order and more committed to radical change, the abstractions of German idealism and even the vague spirit of revolt born of Romanticism disintegrated. The talk became more critical of current realities, and some turned to action, ranging from Herzen's publication of free and defiant words at his press in London to Bakunin's armed defiance of the establishment on Europe's revolutionary barricades. Also, as the movement grew, its social reach expanded beyond the nobility. What began in the 1830s and 1840s as fervent intellectual struggle and searching among small circles of mainly privileged young men became in historiography the "birth of the intelligentsia." As this often-heard phrase suggests, this was the beginning of a process that would have a profound impact on the rest of Russian history. In some accounts, this was the beginning of the "Russian revolution."

## The Arts

Architecture flourished in the early nineteenth century, much of it still sponsored by the government. Neo-classical and Empire style, often skillfully adapted to native traditions, reached its height in Russia during the time of Alexander I. It strongly affected the appearance of St. Petersburg, Moscow, and other towns, as well as countless manor houses all over the empire. Leading architects included Andreian Zakharov, who created the remarkable Admiralty building in St. Petersburg; Andrei Voronikhin, of serf origin, who constructed the Kazan Cathedral in the capital and a number of imperial palaces; and Carlo Rossi (he came to Russia from Italy as a child), who designed many important squares and buildings in the capital, including the Alexandrinsky theater and square. Under Nicholas I, neo-classicism gave way to an eclectic mixture of styles. August de Montferrand's St. Isaac's Cathedral is a major example; it has been described by specialists as both grand and majestic and fundamentally tasteless and inelegant.

Russian music, largely owing to the brilliance of Mikhail Glinka, 1804–57, finally achieved originality and stature. Historians have long viewed Glinka as the "father of Russian national music," especially with his extensive use of folkloric melodies and motifs and his interests in Russian history and myth as narrative sources. His patriotic opera about the Time of Troubles, *Ivan Susanin (A Life for the Tsar)*, which premiered in 1836, has been described as a perfect reflection of Uvarov's ideas of Official Nationality; Nicholas I certainly lavished praise on it. Music-historical critics of this view, however, agree that Glinka was patriotic but argued that he composed fully in a European tradition, using folk-songs not to create a new national music but simply to denote when folk characters were present.

Among other arts, painting, largely guided by the Academy of Arts, evolved gradually from neo-classicism toward Romanticism, a transition exemplified by Karl Briullov's vast apocalyptic canvas *The Last Day of Pompeii*. Theater flourished as well, due to the new availability of Russian plays, which included such masterpieces as *Woe from Wit* and *The Inspector General*, and the emergence of some excellent actors. Landlords continued to establish private theaters on their estates, with serfs as actors. More important, public theaters arose in many towns. Ball was particularly favored by the state and the elite. And as the skillfullness of dancers grew the training of French and Italian masters, a new sense of ballet as a Russian art began to emerge.

Chaadaev's claim that Russia was a blank in the cultural order of things and had contributed nothing to "the progress of the human spirit," already extreme when these words appeared in print in 1836, would have found even less justification in 1855 or 1860. And yet, as Chaadaev had tried to express with his outburst of frustration and pain over the conditions of Russian life, and as the Slavophiles, Belinsky, Herzen, Bakunin, and other critically minded Russians would continue to insist, not all was well in the land of the tsars: an enormous gulf separated educated society from the people, and even many of the fortunate few at the top of the social pyramid felt suffocated and ashamed by serfdom and autocracy.

# CHAPTER 29

# The Reign of Alexander II, 1855–81

The same enthusiasm was in the streets. Crowds of peasants and educated men stood in front of the palace, shouting hurrahs, and the Tsar could not appear without being followed by demonstrative crowds running after his carriage....I was in Nikolskoe in August, 1861, and again in the summer of 1862, and I was struck with the quiet, intelligent way in which the peasants had accepted the new conditions. They knew perfectly well how difficult it would be to pay the redemption tax for the land, which was in reality an indemnity to the nobles in lieu of the obligations of serfdom. But they so much valued the abolition of their personal enslavement that they accepted the ruinous charges—not without murmuring, but as a hard necessity—the moment that personal freedom was obtained....When I saw our Nikolskoe peasants, fifteen months after the liberation, I could not but admire them. Their inborn good nature and softness remained with them, but all traces of servility had disappeared. They talked to their masters as equals talk to equals, as if they never had stood in different relations.

PETR KROPOTKIN

Alexander II succeeded his father, Nicholas I, on the Russian throne at the age of thirty-seven. He had received a rather good education as well as considerable practical training in the affairs of state. Alexander's teachers included the famous poet Zhukovsky, who has often been credited with developing humane sentiments in his pupil. To be sure, Grand Duke Alexander remained an obedient son of his strong-willed father and showed no liberal inclinations prior to becoming emperor. Indeed he retained an essentially conservative mentality and attitude throughout his life. Nor can Alexander II be considered a strong or a talented man. Yet, forced by the logic of the situation, the new monarch decided to undertake, and actually carried through, fundamental

Alexander II. *(Tsarstvuiushchii dom Romanovykh)*

reforms unparalleled in scope in Russian history since Peter the Great. These reforms, although extremely important, failed to cure all the ills of Russia and in fact led to new problems and perturbations, which resulted, among other things, in the assassination of the "Tsar-Liberator."

## The Emancipation of the Serfs

The last words of Alexander II's manifesto announcing the end of the Crimean War promised reform, and this produced a strong impression on the public. The new emperor's first measures, enacted even before the termination of hostilities, included the repeal of some of the Draconian restrictions of Nicholas I's final years, such as those on travel abroad and on the number of students attending universities. All this represented a promising prologue; the key issue, as it was for Alexander I, the last ruler who wanted to transform Russia, remained serfdom. However, much had changed in regard to serfdom during the intervening fifty or fifty-five years. Human bondage, as indicated in an earlier chapter, satisfied less and less effectively the economic needs of the Russian Empire. With the growth of a money economy and competition for markets, the deficiencies of low-grade serf labor became ever more obvious. Many landlords, especially those with small holdings, could barely feed their serfs; and the gentry accumulated an enormous debt. As we know, free labor, whether really free or merely the contractual labor of someone else's serfs, became more common throughout the Russian economy during the first half of the nineteenth century. Interpretations of the Russian economic crisis in mid-nineteenth century range from Ivan Kovalchenko's emphatic restatement, with the use of quantitative methods, of the thesis of the extreme and unbearable exploitation of the serfs to Pavel Ryndziunsky's stress on the general loosening of the social fabric. Economic liberals at the time, and generations of historians since, have agreed that serfdom was becoming increasingly anachronistic. But this was likely not the main reason for reform. First, some scholars have recently questioned the evidence behind arguments about the economic failure of serfdom or the decline in peasant living standards. In any case, perception and opinion are usually more determining than facts alone. Whatever the economic facts, it is clear that the majority of government officials and most of the landowning nobility did not share the view that serfdom must be abolished for economic reasons. So we must consider other reasons.

The fear of peasant rebellion has often been identified as a key reason the state finally acted to end serfdom. Oppressed and exasperated beyond endurance, the serfs kept rising against their masters. While no nineteenth-century peasant insurrection could rival the Pugachev rebellion, the uprisings became more frequent and on the whole more serious. Vasilii Semevsky, using official records, had counted 550 peasant uprisings in the nineteenth century prior to the emancipation. A Soviet historian, Inna Ignatovich, raised the number to 1,467 and gave the following breakdown: 281 peasant rebellions, that is, 19 percent of the total, in the period from 1801 to 1825; 712 rebellions, 49 percent, from 1826 to 1854; and 474 uprisings, or 32 percent, in the six years and two months of Alexander II's reign before the abolition of serfdom. Ignatovich emphasized that the uprisings also increased in length, in bitterness, in the human and material losses involved, and in the military effort necessary to restore order. Semen Okun and other Soviet scholars further expanded Ignatovich's list of uprisings. Soviet scholarship claimed that peasant rebellions played the decisive role in the emancipation of the serfs, and that on the eve of the "great reforms" Russia experienced in effect a revolutionary situation. Although exaggerated, this view cannot be entirely dismissed. Interestingly, it was the Third Department, the gendarmerie, that had stressed the danger of serfdom during the reign of Nicholas I. Besides rising in rebellion, serfs ran away from their masters, sometimes by the hundreds and even by the thousands. On occasion large military detachments had to be sent to intercept them. Mass flights of peasants, for example, would follow rumors that freedom could be obtained somewhere in the Caucasus, while crowds of serfs tried to join the army during the Crimean War, because they mistakenly believed that they could thereby gain their liberty.

A growing sentiment for emancipation, based on moral grounds, also contributed to the abolition of serfdom. The Decembrists, the Slavophiles, the Westernizers, the Petrashevtsy, some supporters of Official Nationality, together with other thinking Russians, all wanted the abolition of serfdom. As education developed in Russia, and especially as Russian literature came into its own, humane feelings and attitudes became more widespread. Such leading writers as Pushkin and particularly Turgenev, who in 1852 published in book form his magnificent collection of stories, *Sportsman's Sketches*, where serfs were depicted as full-blown, and indeed unforgettable, human beings, no doubt exercised an influence. In fact, on the eve of the abolition of serfdom in Russia—in contrast to the situation with slavery in the American South—virtually no one defended that institution; the arguments of its proponents were usually limited to pointing out the dangers implicit in such a radical change as emancipation.

Finally, the Crimean War provided additional evidence of the deficiencies and dangers of serfdom that found reflection both in the poor physical condition and listlessness of the recruits and in the general economic and technological backwardness of the country. Besides, as Alfred Rieber emphasized, Russia had essentially to rely on a standing army without a reserve, because the government was afraid to allow soldiers to return to villages.

At the time of the coronation, about a year after his assumption of power, Alexander II, addressing the gentry of Moscow, made the celebrated statement that it would be better to begin to abolish serfdom from above than to wait until it would begin to abolish itself from below, and asked the gentry to consider the matter. Although the government experienced great difficulty in eliciting any initiative from the landlords on the subject of emancipation, it finally managed to seize upon an offer by the gentry of the three Lithuanian provinces to discuss emancipation without land. The ensuing imperial rescript made it clear that emancipation was indeed official policy and, furthermore, that emancipation would have to be with land.

A remarkable aspect of the coming of emancipation was the publicity and public discussion that surrounded this process. The government announced its plans and invited discussion and suggestions—a process of openness and publicity known as *glasnost*. Noble assemblies were asked to discuss how the reform should be implemented, and they sometimes opened their sessions to non-nobles. Restrictions on discussing the abolition of serfdom in the press were lifted. At the same time, Alexander asked the police to submit weekly reports on the public's attitude and mood, and warnings and even arrests could result when overly critical opinion was voiced. Some historians have argued that the government, at least its more liberal members, deliberately wished to "awaken public opinion," since nurturing a modern civil society was the deeper goal of the "great reforms." Others have insisted that the government really had no choice—the public was already aroused and had to be recognized. In any case, a wave of expectation and enthusiasm swept the country after the publication of the rescript. Even Herzen exclaimed to Alexander II: "Thou hast conquered, O Galilean!"

Eventually, in 1858, gentry committees were established in all provinces to consider emancipation, while a bureaucratic Main Committee of nine members was set up in St. Petersburg. Except for a few diehards, the landlords assumed a realistic position and accepted the abolition of serfdom once the government had made its will clear, but they wanted the reform to be carried out as advantageously for themselves as possible. The gentry of southern and south-central Russia, with its valuable, fertile soil, wanted to retain as much land as possible and preferred land to a monetary recompense; the gentry of northern and north-central Russia, by contrast, considered serf labor and the resulting obrok as their main asset and, therefore, while relatively willing to part with much of their land, insisted on a high monetary payment in return for the loss of serf labor. Gentry committees also differed on such important issues as the desirable legal position of the liberated serfs and the administration to be provided for them.

The opinions of provincial committees went to the Editing Commission— actually two commissions that sat together and formed a single body— created at the beginning of 1859 and composed of public figures interested in the peasant question, such as the Slavophiles Georgii Samarin and Prince Vladimir Cherkassky, as well as of high officials. After twenty months of work the Editing Commission submitted its plan of reform to the Main Committee, whence it went eventually to the State Council. After its quick consideration by the State Council, Alexander II signed the emancipation manifesto on March 3, 1861—February 19 on the Russian calendar. Public announcement followed twelve days later.

Throughout its protracted and cumbersome formulation and passage the emancipation reform faced the hostility of conservatives in government and society. That a far-reaching law was finally enacted can be largely credited to the determined efforts of so-called "enlightened bureaucrats" and "liberals," including officials such as Nikolai Miliutin, the immediate assistant to the minister of the interior and the leading figure in the Editing Commission, and participants from the public like Samarin. Two members of the imperial family, the tsar's brother Grand Duke Constantine and the tsar's aunt Grand Duchess Helen, belonged to the "liberals." More important, Alexander II himself, repeatedly sided with them, while his will became law for such devoted bureaucrats as Iakov Rostovtsev—a key figure in the emancipation—who cannot be easily classified as either "conservative" or "liberal." The emperor in effect forced the speedy passage of the measure through an antagonistic State Council, which managed to add only one noxious provision to the law, that permitting a "pauper's allotment," which will be mentioned later. Whereas the conservatives defended the interests and rights of the gentry, the "liberals" were motivated by their belief that the interests of the state demanded a thoroughgoing reform and by their views of what would constitute a just settlement.

The law of the nineteenth of February abolished serfdom. Thenceforth human bondage was to disappear from Russian life. It should be noted, however, that, even if we exclude from consideration certain temporary provisions that prolonged various serf obligations for different periods of time, the reform failed to give the peasants a status equal to that of other social classes: they had to pay a head tax, were tied to their communes, and were judged on the basis of customary law. In addition to landowners' serfs, the new freedom was extended to peasants on the lands of the imperial family and to the huge and complex category of state peasants.

Together with their liberty, serfs who had been engaged in farming received land: household serfs did not. While the detailed provisions of the land settlement were extremely complicated and different from area to area, the peasants were to obtain roughly half the land, that part which they had been tilling for themselves, the other half staying with the landlords. They had to repay the landlords for the land they acquired and, because few serfs could pay anything, the government compensated the gentry owners by means of treasury bonds. Former serfs in turn were to reimburse the state through redemption payments spread over a period of forty-nine years. As an alternative, serfs could take one-quarter of their normal parcel of land, the so-called "pauper's allotment," and pay nothing. Except in Ukraine and a few other areas, land was given, not to individual peasants, but to a peasant commune.

The emancipation of the serfs can be called a great reform, although an American historian probably exaggerated when he proclaimed it to be the greatest legislative act in history. It directly affected the status of some 52 million peasants, over 20 million of them serfs of private land owners. That should be compared, for example, with the almost simultaneous liberation of 4 million black slaves in the United States, obtained as a result of a huge Civil War, not by means of a peaceful legal process. The moral value of the emancipation was no doubt tremendous, if incalculable. The specific provisions of the new settlement have also been defended and even praised, especially on the basis of the understanding that the arrangement had to be a compromise, not a confiscation of everything the gentry owned. Thus, the emancipation of serfs in Russia has been favorably compared to the largely landless emancipation in Prussia at the beginning of the nineteenth century, and the land allotments of Russian peasants, to allotments in several other countries.

And yet the emancipation reform also deserves thorough criticism. The land allotted to the former serfs turned out to be insufficient. While in theory they were to retain the acreage that they had been tilling for themselves prior to 1861, in fact they received 18 percent less land. Moreover, in the fertile southern provinces their loss exceeded the national average, amounting in some cases to 40 percent or more of the total. Also, in the course of the partitioning, former serfs often failed to obtain forested areas or access to a river, with the result that they had to assume additional obligations toward their onetime landlords to satisfy their needs. Liashchenko summarized the settlement as follows: "The owners, numbering 30,000 noblemen, retained ownership over some 95 million dessyatins of the better land immediately after the Reform, compared with 116 million dessyatins of suitable land left to the 20 million 'emancipated' peasants." Other scholars have stressed the overpopulation and underemployment among former serfs, who, at least after a period of transition, were no longer obliged to work for the landlord and at the same time had less land to cultivate for themselves. State peasants, although by no means prosperous, received, on the whole, better terms than did the serfs of private owners.

The financial arrangement proved unrealistic and impossible to execute. Although liberated serfs kept meeting as best they could the heavy redemption payments, which were not related to their current income, the arrears kept mounting. By the time the redemption payments were finally abolished in 1905, former serfs paid, counting the interest, 1.5 billion rubles for the land initially valued at less than a billion. It should be noted that while officially the serfs were to redeem only the land, not their persons, actually the payments included a concealed recompense for the loss of serf labor. Thus, more had to be paid for the first unit of land, the first desiatina, than for the following units. As a whole the landlords of southern Russia received 340 million rubles for land valued at 280 million; those of northern Russia, where obrok prevailed, 340 million rubles for land worth 180 million rubles. The suspect Polish and Polonized landlords of the western provinces constituted an exception, for they were given slightly less money than the just price of their land.

The transfer of land in most areas to peasant communes rather than to individual peasants has been judged another major error, although this is an extremely complex issue. Arguments in favor of the commune ranged from the Slavophile admiration of the moral aspects of that institution to the desire on the part of the government to have taxes and recruits guaranteed by means of communal responsibility and to the assertion that newly liberated peasants would not be able to maintain themselves but could find protection in the commune. While some of these and other similar claims had a certain validity—indeed, as a practical matter the government could hardly have been expected to break up the commune at the same time the serfs were being freed and peasants themselves were deeply attached to the commune as both a practical necessity for survival and a moral value in defining proper social relationships in the village—the economic disadvantages of the commune may have outweighed its advantages. Of most importance was the fact that the commune sustained a subsistence ethos (whereby community survival stands above all other values), which perpetuated low productivity, resistance to innovation, and overpopulation in the countryside precisely when Russian agriculture drastically needed improvement and modernization.

The emancipation reform disappointed Russian radicals, who considered it inadequate. More important, it disappointed peasants who evidently believed that they had a right to all the land they worked without payment. A rash of agrarian disturbances followed the abolition of serfdom, and the misery, despair, and anger in the countryside remained a powerful threat to imperial Russia until the very end of imperial rule.

## Other "Great Reforms"

The emancipation of the serfs made other fundamental changes much more feasible. Alexander II and his assistants turned next to the reform of local government, to the establishment of the so-called zemstvo system. For centuries local government had remained a particularly weak aspect of Russian administration and life. The arrangement that the "Tsar-Liberator" inherited dated from Catherine the Great's legislation and combined bureaucratic management with some participation by the local gentry; the considerable manorial jurisdiction of the landlords on their estates formed another prominent characteristic of the prereform countryside. The new law, enacted in January 1864, represented a strong modernization and democratization of local government, as well as a far-reaching effort on the part of the state to meet the many pressing needs of rural Russia and to do this largely by stimulating local initiative and activity. Institutions of self-government, zemstvo assemblies and boards, were created at both the district and provincial levels—the word zemstvo itself connotes land, country, or people, as distinct from the central government. The electorate of the district zemstvo assemblies consisted of three categories: the towns, the peasant communes, and all individual landowners, including those not from the gentry. Representation was proportional to landownership, with some allowance for the possession of real estate in towns. The elections were indirect. Members of district assemblies, in turn, elected from their own midst, regardless of class, delegates to their provincial assembly. Whereas the district and provincial zemstvo assemblies, in which the "zemstvo" authority resided, met only once a year to deal with such items as the annual budget and basic policies, they elected zemstvo boards to serve continuously as the executive agencies of the system and to employ professional staffs. A variety of local needs fell under the purview of zemstvo institutions: education, medicine, veterinary service, insurance, roads, the establishment of food reserves for emergency, and many others.

The zemstvo system has legitimately been criticized on a number of counts. For example, for a long time it encompassed only the strictly Russian areas of the empire, some thirty-four provinces, not the borderlands. Also, it possessed a limited, many would say insufficient, right to tax. In broader terms, it represented merely a junior partner to the central government, which retained police and much administrative control in the countryside; a governor could in various ways interfere with the work of a zemstvo, but not vice versa. The smallest zemstvo unit, the district, proved too large for effective and prompt response to many popular needs, and the desirability of further zemstvo subdivision soon became apparent. The democracy of the system too had its obvious limitations: because they owned much land, members of the gentry were very heavily represented in the district assemblies, and even more so in the provincial assemblies and the zemstvo boards, where education, leisure, and means to cover the expenses incurred favored gentry delegates. Thus, according to one count, the gentry generally held 42 percent of the district assembly seats, 74 percent of the seats in the provincial assemblies, and 62 percent of the positions on the zemstvo boards. Yet, even such a system constituted a great step toward democracy for autocratic and bureaucratic Russia. It might be added that the zemstvo institutions functioned effectively also in those areas, such as large parts of the Russian north, where there were no landlords and where peasants managed the entire system of local self-government.

Yet, in spite of its deficiencies, the zemstvo system accomplished much for rural Russia from its establishment in 1864 until its demise in 1917. Especially valuable were its contributions to public education and health. In effect, Russia obtained a kind of socialized medicine through the zemstvo long before other countries, with medical and surgical treatment available free of charge. As George Fischer and other scholars have indicated, the zemstvo system also served, contrary to the intentions of the government, as a school for radicalism and especially liberalism which found little opportunity for expression on the national, as distinct from local, scene until the events of 1905 and 1906.

In 1870 a municipal reform reorganized town government and applied to towns many of the principles and practices of the zemstvo administration. The new town government, which was "to take care of and administer urban economy and welfare," consisted of a town council and a town administrative board elected by the town council. The town council was elected by all property owners or taxpayers; but the election was according to a three-class system, which gave the small group on top that paid a third of the total taxes a third of the total number of delegates, the middle taxpayers another third, and the mass at the bottom that accounted for the last third of taxes the remaining third of delegates.

At the end of 1864, the year that saw the beginning of the zemstvo administration, another major change was enacted into law: the reform of the legal system. The Russian judiciary needed reform probably even more than the local government did. Archaic, bureaucratic, cumbersome, corrupt, based on the class system rather than on the principle of. equality before the law, and relying entirely on a written and secret procedure, the old system was thoroughly hated by informed and thinking Russians. Radicals attached special importance to a reform of the judiciary. A conservative, the Slavophile Ivan Aksakov, reminisced: "The old court! At the mere recollection of it one's hair stands on end and one's flesh begins to creep!"

The most significant single aspect of the reform was the separation of the courts from the administration. Instead of constituting merely a part of the bureaucracy, the judiciary became an independent branch of government. Judges were not to be dismissed or transferred, except by court action. Judicial procedure acquired a largely public and oral character instead of the former bureaucratic secrecy. The contending parties were to present their cases in court and have adequate legal support. In fact, the reform virtually created the class of lawyers in Russia, who began rapidly to acquire great public prominence. Two legal procedures, the general and the abbreviated one, replaced the chaos of twenty-one alternate ways to conduct a case. Trial by jury was introduced for serious criminal offenses, while justices of the peace were established to deal with minor civil and criminal cases. The courts were organized into a single unified system with the Senate at the apex. All Russians were to be equal before the law and receive the same treatment. Exceptions to the general system were the military and ecclesiastical courts, together with special courts for peasants who lived for the most part by customary law.

The reform of the judiciary, which was largely the work of the Minister of Justice Dmitrii Zamiatnin, his extremely important assistant Sergei Zarudny, and several other enlightened officials, proved to be the most successful of the "great reforms." Almost overnight it transformed the Russian judiciary from one of the worst to one of the best in the civilized world. Later the government tried on occasion to influence judges for political reasons; and, what is more important, in its struggle against radicalism and revolution it began to withdraw whole categories of legal cases from the normal procedure of 1864 and to subject them to various forms of the courts-martial. But, while the reform of the judiciary could be restricted in application, it could not be undone by the imperial government; and, as far as the reform extended, modern justice replaced arbitrariness and confusion. Russian legal reform followed Western, especially French, models, but, as Samuel Kucherov and others have demonstrated, these models were skillfully adapted to Russian needs. It might be added that the courts, as well as the zemstvo institutions, acquired political significance, for they served as centers of public interest and enjoyed a somewhat greater freedom of expression than was generally allowed in Russia.

A reorganization of the military service in 1874 and certain changes within the army have usually been grouped as the last "great reform." Inspired by military needs and technically complex, the reform nevertheless exercised an important general impact on Russian society and contributed to the modernization and democratization of the country. It was executed by Minister of War Dmitrii Miliutin, Nikolai Miliutin's brother, who wanted to profit by the example of the victorious Prussian army. He introduced a variety of significant innovations, of which the most important was the change in military service. The obligation to serve was extended from the lower classes alone to all Russians, while at the same time the length of active service was drastically reduced—from twenty-five years in the beginning of Alexander II's reign to six after the reform of 1874—and a military reserve was organized. Recruits were to be called up by lot; different exemptions were provided for hardship cases; and, in addition, terms of enlistment were shortened for those with education, a not unwarranted provision in Russian conditions. Miliutin also reformed military law and legal procedure, abolished corporal punishment in the army, strove to improve the professional quality of the officer corps and to make it somewhat more democratic, established specialized military schools, and, a particularly important point, introduced elementary education for all draftees. Measures similar to Miliutin's were carried out in the navy by Grand Duke Constantine.

Other reforms under Alexander II included such financial innovations as Valerii Tatarinov's establishment of a single state treasury, publication of the annual budget, and the creation in 1866 of the State Bank to centralize credit and finance, as well as generally liberalizing steps with regard to education and censorship.

The "great reforms" went a long way toward transforming Russia. Vastly important in themselves, the government's reforms also stimulated continued and sometimes dramatic changes in the economy and in social relations, to be discussed in a later chapter. The development of capitalism, the decline of the gentry, the rise of a middle class (especially educated professionals), new mobility for the peasantry, the growth of a working class, and the development of a public sphere—all were affected by the reforms. Indeed, Russia began to take long strides on the road to becoming a modern society. To be sure, Alexander II's Russia remained an autocracy. Indeed, it was autocracy that forced through many of these changes. But change was also making this authoritarian political order increasingly anachronistic and, in the eyes of many Russians, a brake on continued progress.

## The Difficult Sixties

Although the government could not restore the old social and legal order, it could stop advancing on the new road and try to restrict and limit the effectiveness of the changes. And in fact it attempted to do so in the second half of Alexander II's reign, under Alexander III, and under Nicholas II until the Revolution of 1905. While the need for reforms had been apparent, the rationale of reaction proved less obvious and more complicated. For one thing, the reforms, as we know, had their determined opponents in official circles and among the Russian gentry, who did their best to reverse state policy. Special circumstances played their part, such as peasant uprisings, student disturbances, the unexplained fires of 1862, the Polish rebellion of 1863, and Dmitrii Karakozov's attempt to assassinate the emperor in 1866. More important was the fact that the government failed to resolve the fundamental dilemma of change: where to stop. The "great reforms," together with the general development of Russia and the intellectual climate of the time, led to pressure for further reform. Possibly the granting of a constitutional monarchy and certain other concessions would have satisfied most of the demand and provided stability for the empire. But neither Alexander II nor certainly his successors were willing to go that far. Instead they turned against the proponents of more change and fought to preserve the established order. The "great reforms" had come only after the Crimean War had demonstrated the total bankruptcy of the old system, and they owed little to any far-reaching liberalism or vision on the part of Alexander II and his immediate associates. The sequel showed how difficult it was for the imperial government to learn new ways.

After the political stillness and immobility of Nicholas I's reign, and stimulated by the "great reforms," the early 1860s in Russia were loud and active. Peasant riots occurred with great frequency and on a large scale. In 1861 and 1862 disturbances, provoked largely by the clumsy and authoritarian policies of the new minister of education, Count Admiral Evfimii Putiatin, swept Russian universities. In 1862 the provincial assembly of the Tver gentry, led by Alexei Unkovsky, renounced its gentry privileges and demanded the convocation of a constituent assembly representing the entire people to establish a new order in Russia. And in the same year of 1862 a series of mysterious fires broke out in St. Petersburg and in a number of towns along the Volga. Also, in 1861 and 1862 leaflets urging revolution began to appear in different Russian cities. In 1863 Poland erupted in rebellion.

The challenge of anti-imperial nationalism to Russian policies, and the limits of government reformism when it came to the national question, was again highlighted by the problem of Poland. In Poland too, Alexander II was viewed with hope as a reformer, though his famous remark on a visit there in 1856 suggested his hesitations: "Pas de rêveries, messieurs" ("No daydreams, gentlemen"), he warned the Poles. Still, his early policies, which partly restored Polish autonomy, pointed to the possibility of greater change. As Norman Davies summarized the situation, Alexander II "gave an inch and his Polish subjects immediately thought of taking a mile." Hoping to contain the situation, the emperor put Marquis Alexander Wielopolski in charge of the Polish administration. His rule combined cultural autonomy for Poland with social reforms and repression of dissent, a mixture of reform and repression that would also often be seen in Russia. But this satisfied neither the moderate nationalist "Whites" nor the socially radical "Reds." When, following a series of disorders, the imperial government took steps to draft into the army thousands of young Polish men, mostly students (seen as a source of trouble), rebellion erupted. In contrast to the situation in 1831, the Poles possessed no regular army and had to fight for the most part as guerrilla bands. Yet the insurrection grew quickly, spread to Lithuanian and Belorussian lands, and lasted from January 1863 until it was finally suppressed in May 1864. Great Britain, France, and Austria tried to aid the Polish cause with diplomatic interventions but were rebuffed by Russia.

As a result of the rebellion, Poland lost the limited autonomy it had recently regained. The terms of the emancipation of the serfs and the accompanying land settlement in Poland functioned at least in part to undermine the rebellious gentry: peasants received more and landlords less than elsewhere in the empire. In general, the government increased centralization, police control, and Russification, with the Russian language made compulsory in Polish schools. A still more intense Russification developed in the western borderlands of Russia, where every effort was made to eradicate the Polish influence. A 10 percent assessment was imposed there on Polish estates, the use of the Polish language was forbidden, and the property of the Catholic Church was confiscated. In 1875 the Uniates in Poland proper were forcibly reconverted to Orthodoxy.

In interpreting the "great reforms" and Alexander II's rule as a whole, scholars have remarked on the vacillations and inconsistencies. One argument, which we have seen before in the histories of other Russian rulers, focuses on change over time: he began in a liberal mood and turned increasingly conservative. One turning point were the troubles of the early 1860s, though we can also see movement in the opposite direction. For example, while the authorities penalized disaffected Russian students and punished severely those connected with the revolutionary agitation, a considerably more liberal official,

Alexander Golovnin, replaced Admiral Putiatin in 1862 as minister of education, and a new and much freer University Statute became law in 1863. A more decisive turning point, in the opinion of many historians, came in 1866, after an attempt by an emotionally unbalanced student, Dmitrii Karakozov, to assassinate the emperor. In that year the reactionary Count Dmitrii Tolstoy took charge as minister of education, and the government proceeded gradually to revamp schooling in Russia, intending that stricter controls and heavy emphasis on the classical languages would discipline students and keep their attention away from the issues of the day. Over a period of years reaction also expressed itself in the curbing of the press, in restrictions on the collection of taxes by the zemstvo and on the uses to which these taxes could be put, in the exemption of political and press cases from regular judicial procedure, in continuing Russification, in administrative pressure on magistrates, and the like. On the other hand, despite the reactionary nature of the period, the municipal reform took place in 1870 and the army reform as late as 1874.

Another argument focuses less on change over time than on deeper sources of inconsistency. One approach focuses on Alexander II personally: his lack of strong convictions, either reformist or reactionary. Thus, he often chose as his ministers and advisors men whose views were completely opposed to one another. A less personalized argument sees contradiction in the nature of "great reforms" themselves, a certain structural ambivalence, as it were. When we look at what reformers—the tsar and his ministers—were saying about reform, not to mention what they were doing, we see a certain dualism. On the one hand, their goal was to modernize Russian society and politics in the interests of national strength: to ensure that government was based on regular procedures and the rule of law and especially to free people from restrictions so that they might become active citizens helping to advance the country's interests. On the other hand, their goals contained the characteristically ambivalent political logic of the modernizing state: to preserve the creative power (autocracy in the Russian case) that brought about these changes and to protect the social structures needed to prevent change turning into disorder and revolution. In other words, we see the already familiar Russian tradition of reform: an effort to balance progress and power, change and order, stability and modernity.

## New Radicalism and the Revolutionary Movement

Russian history came increasingly to be dominated by a struggle between the government Right and the radical and revolutionary Left, with the moderates and the liberals in the middle powerless to influence the fundamental course of events. The Polish rebellion, which was hailed on the Left, stimulated conservative Russian nationalism and helped push conservatives closer to the government—though the partnership between the Right and the government would never be fully amicable or trusting. In 1863, the onetime liberal Westernizer, the journalist Mikhail Katkov, came out emphatically in support of the government and Russian national interests. Katkov's stand proved very popular during the Polish war. In a sense Katkov and his fellow patriots who enthusiastically defended the Russian state acted much like the liberals in Prussia and Germany when they swung to the support of Bismarck. Yet, in the long run, it proved more characteristic of the situation in Russia that, although leftist revolutionaries remained a small minority, they attracted the sympathy of broad layers of the educated public.

While the intellectual history of Russia in the second half of the nineteenth century will be summarized in a later chapter, some aspects of Russian radicalism of the 1860s and 1870s must be mentioned here. Following Turgenev, it has become customary to speak of the generation of the 1860s as "sons" and "nihilists" and to contrast these "sons" with the "fathers" of the 1840s. A powerful contrast does emerge. The transformation in Russia formed part of a broader change in Europe that has been described as a transition from Romanticism to realism. In Russian conditions the shift acquired an exaggerated and violent character.

Whereas the "fathers" grew up on German idealistic philosophy and Romanticism in general, with its emphasis on the metaphysical, religious, aesthetic, and historical approaches to reality, the "sons," led by such young radicals as Nikolai Chernyshevsky, Nikolai Dobroliubov, and Dmitrii Pisarev, hoisted the banner of utilitarianism, positivism, materialism, and especially "realism." "Nihilism"—and also in large part "realism," particularly "critical realism"—meant above all else a fundamental rebellion against accepted values and standards: against abstract thought and family control, against lyric poetry and school discipline, against religion and rhetoric. The earnest young men and women of the 1860s wanted to cut through every polite veneer, to get rid of all conventional sham, to get to the bottom of things. What they usually considered real and worthwhile included the natural and physical sciences—for that was the age when science came to be greatly admired in the Western world—simple and sincere human relations, and a society based on knowledge and reason rather than ignorance, prejudice, exploitation, and oppression. The casting down of idols—and there surely were many idols in mid-nineteenth-century Russia, as elsewhere—emancipation, and freedom constituted the moral strength of nihilism.

It has been noted that the rebels of the 1860s, while they stood poles apart from the Slavophiles and other idealists of the 1830s and 1840s, could be considered disciples of Herzen, Bakunin, and to some extent Belinsky, in their later, radical, phases. True in the very important field of doctrine, this observation disregards the difference in tone and manner: as Samarin said of Herzen, even the most radical Westernizers always retained "a handful of earth from the other shore," the shore of German idealism and Romanticism, the shore of their youth; the new critics came out of a simpler and cruder mold. Socially too the radicals of the 1860s differed from the "fathers," reflecting the progressive democratization of the educated public in Russia. Many of them belonged to a group known in Russian as *raznochintsy*, that is, people of mixed background below the gentry, such as sons of priests who did not follow the calling of their fathers, offspring of petty officials, or individuals from the masses who made their way up through education and effort. The participation of women in this movement was another very important social change. The effects of continuing education for women, combined with the iconoclastic rejection among educated youth in the 1860s and 1870s of traditional norms of gender, sex, and family, brought many women into the arena of radical thought and revolutionary politics. The word and concept "intelligentsia," which came to be associated with a critical approach to the world and a protest against the existing Russian order, acquired currency during that portentous period.

The Russian revolutionary movement can be traced to the revolutionary propaganda and circles of the 1860s. It first became prominent, however, in the 1870s. By that time the essentially individualistic and anarchic creed of nihilism, with its stress on total personal emancipation, became combined with and in part replaced by a new faith, populism—*narodnichestvo*—which gave the "critical realists" their political, social, and economic program. While populism also has a broad meaning that could include as adherents Dostoevsky, Tolstoy, certain ideologists of the Right, and other diverse Russian figures, in the narrow sense it came to be associated with the teachings of such intellectuals as Herzen, Bakunin, Chernyshevsky, Petr Lavrov, and Nikolai Mikhailovsky—who will be discussed in a later chapter—and the main trend of the Russian radical and revolutionary movement in the last third of the nineteenth century. If nihilists gloried in their emancipation, independence, and superiority to the rotten world around them, populists felt compelled to turn to the masses, which in Russia meant the peasants. They wanted to repay their debt for acquiring education—which had brought the precious emancipation itself—at the expense of the sweat and even the blood of the *muzhik*, the peasant, and to lead the people to a better future. The intellectuals, it must be added, desired to learn as well as to teach. In particular, following Herzen and Bakunin, they believed in the unique worth and potential of the peasant commune, which could serve as an effective foundation for the just social order of the future. In one way or another most populists hoped to find in the people that moral purity and probity—truth, if you will—which their own environment had denied them. Whether their search stemmed from reason and critical "realism," irrational and utopian dreams, or a deep moral and emotional desire for a more just and happy world is a question of perspective and argument.

The climax came in 1873, 1874, and the years immediately following. When in 1873 the imperial government ordered Russian students to abandon their studies in Switzerland—where Russians, especially women, could often pursue higher education more easily than in their fatherland—and return home, a considerable number of them, together with numerous other young men and women who had stayed in Russia, decided to "go to the people." And they went to the villages, some 2,500 of them, to become rural teachers, scribes, doctors, veterinarians, nurses, or storekeepers. Some meant simply to help the people as best they could. Others nurtured vast radical and revolutionary plans. In particular, the followers of Bakunin put their faith in a spontaneous, elemental, colossal revolution of the people that they had merely to help start, while the disciples of Lavrov believed in the necessity of gradualism, more exactly, in the need for education and propaganda among the masses before they could overturn the old order and establish the new.

The populist crusade failed. The peasants did not respond. The only uprising that the populists produced resulted from an impressive but forged manifesto in which the tsar ordered his loyal peasants to attack his enemies, the landlords. Indeed the muzhiks on occasion handed over the strange new-comers from the cities to the police. The police, in turn, were frantically active, arresting all the crusaders they could find. Mass trials of the 193 and of the 50 in 1877 marked the sad conclusion of the "going to the people" stage of populism.

Yet, one more possibility for struggle remained: the one advocated by another populist theoretician, Petr Tkachev, and by an amoral and dedicated revolutionist, Sergei Nechaev, and given the name "Jacobin" in memory of the Jacobins who seized power to transform France during the great French Revolution. If the peasants would not act, the revolutionaries should them-selves fight the government, and their successes would also show the masses that the government was vulnerable and serve as an inspiration in deeds where words had not worked. Several years of revolutionary conspiracy, ter-rorism, and assassination ensued. The first instances of violence occurred more or less spontaneously, sometimes as countermeasures against brutal police officials. Thus, early in 1878 Vera Zasulich shot and wounded the mil-itary governor of St. Petersburg, General Fedor Trepov, who had ordered a political prisoner to be flogged (he had earlier distinguished himself in help-ing to suppress both Polish uprisings). A jury refused to convict her, though she never denied shooting Trepov—on the contrary, her defense was that her act was morally justified in order, as she later wrote, "to prove that no one who abused a human being that way could be sure of getting away with it." In the wake of this humiliation for the government, political cases were withdrawn from regular judicial procedure. But before long an organization emerged that consciously put terrorism at the center of its activity. The conspiratorial revo-lutionary society "Land and Freedom," founded in 1876, split in 1879 into two groups: the "Black Partition," or "Total Land Repartition," which emphasized gradualism and propaganda, and the "People's Will," which mounted an all-out terroristic offensive against the government. Members of the "People's Will" believed that, because of the highly centralized nature of the Russian state, a few assassinations could do tremendous damage to the regime, as well as to inspire the population: this was "propaganda of the deed." They selected the emperor, Alexander II, as their chief target and condemned him to death. What followed has been described as an "emperor hunt" and in certain ways it defies imagination. The Executive Committee of the "People's Will" included only about thirty men and women, led by such persons as Andrei Zheliabov, who came from the serfs, and Sofia Perovskaia, who came from Russia's high-est administrative class, but it fought the Russian Empire. Although the police made every effort to destroy the revolutionaries and although many terrorists perished, the "People's Will" made one attempt after another to assassinate the emperor. Time and again Alexander II escaped through sheer luck. Many people were killed when the very dining room of his palace was blown up, while at one time the emperor's security officials refused to let him leave his suburban residence, except by water!

After the explosion in the Winter Palace and after being faced by strikes, student disturbances, and a remarkable lack of sympathy on the part of the educated public, as well as by the dauntless terrorism of the "People's Will," the emperor finally decided on a more moderate policy that could lead to a *rapprochement* with the public. He appointed General Count Mikhail Loris-Melikov first as head of a special administrative commission and several months later as minister of the interior. Loris-Melikov was to suppress terrorism, but also to propose reforms. Several moderate or liberal ministers replaced a number of reactionaries. Loris-Melikov's plan called for the participation of representatives of the public, both elected and appointed, in considering administrative and financial reforms—not unlike the pattern followed in the abolition of serfdom. On March 13, 1881, Alexander II indicated his willingness to consider Loris-Melikov's proposal. That same day he was finally killed by the remaining members of the "People's Will."

## Foreign Policy

The foreign policy of Alexander II's reign, while perhaps not quite as dramatic as its internal history, also deserves careful attention. It began with the termination of the Crimean War and the Treaty of Paris, possibly the nadir of the Russian position in Europe in the nineteenth century, and it did much to restore Russian prestige. Notably, the Russians fought a successful war against Turkey and largely redrew the map of the Balkans. Also, in the course of the reign, the empire of the Romanovs made a sweeping expansion in the Caucasus, Central Asia, and the Far East. But not everything went well. Russia experienced important diplomatic setbacks as well as victories. Moreover, the changing pattern of power relations in Europe—fundamentally affected by the unification of Germany, which the tsarist government helped more than hindered—was in many ways less favorable to the state of the Romanovs in 1881 than it had been fifty years earlier.

The Crimean War meant the collapse of the world of Nicholas I, the world of legitimism with himself as its leader. Specifically, it left the Russian government and public bitterly disappointed with Austria, which, in spite of the crucial Russian help in 1849, did everything to aid Russia's enemies short of actually fighting. As Tiutchev insisted, no "Austrian Judas" could be allowed to pay last respects to Nicholas I on behalf of the Habsburgs! When the new minister of foreign affairs, Prince Alexander Gorchakov, surveyed the situation, he turned to France as a possible ally, and Napoleon III indicated reciprocal interest. Yet at that time—in contrast to what happened thirty years later—the Franco-Russian *rapprochement* foundered on the Polish rebellion of 1863. As already mentioned, both the French ruler and his people sympathized with the Poles, and, as in the case of Great Britain and Austria, France intervened diplomatically on behalf of the Poles, arguing that from the time of the Congress of Vienna and the creation of the Kingdom of Poland the fate of that country was of international concern and not simply an internal Russian affair. The imperial government could reject the argument of these powers and rebuff their intervention only because of the strong support that it obtained from the Russian public and also from Prussia. Bismarck, who realized the danger of Polish nationalism for Prussia and wanted to secure the goodwill of the tsar, sent Count Constantin von Alvensleben to promise the Russians cooperation against the Polish rebels and to sign a convention to that effect. Bismarck's astute handling of the Russians contributed, no doubt, to the rather benevolent attitude on the part of the tsarist government toward the unification of Germany under Prussia, which involved the defeat of Austria in 1866 and of France in 1870. In retrospect, the fact that Russia did nothing to prevent the emergence of Germany as the new continental giant has been called the worst mistake that tsarist diplomacy ever made. To qualify that charge, it should at least be noted that Russian statesmen were not the only ones in that crucial decade totally to misjudge the situation and prospects in Europe. Also, Russia did obtain some compensation through the abrogation of the Black Sea provisions of the Treaty of Paris: at a time when European attention centered on the Franco-Prussian war, Gorchakov, with Bismarck's backing, repudiated the vexatious obligation not to have a warfleet or coastal fortifications on the Black Sea that Russia had assumed under the Treaty. The British protested and an international conference was held in London in March 1871, but the Russian action was allowed to stand, although the principle of general consent of the signatories as against unilateral action was reaffirmed.

When in the 1870s the tsarist government looked again for allies, it once more found Prussia, or rather Germany, and Austria, which had become Austria-Hungary. For a century the Hohenzollerns had remained, on the whole, the best friends of the Romanovs; as to the Habsburgs, the Russian rancor against them, generated by their behavior at the time of the Crimean War, had somewhat subsided in the wake of Austrian defeats and other misfortunes. The new alliance, the so-called Three Emperors' League, was formed in 1872 and 1873. Russia's part in it involved a military convention with Germany, according to which each party was to assist with 200,000 troops if its partner were attacked by a European power, and a somewhat looser agreement with Austria-Hungary. The League could be said to represent a restoration of the old association of conservative eastern European monarchies determined to preserve the established order. But, in contrast to earlier decades when Alexander I and Nicholas I led the conservative coalition, the direction of the new alliance belonged to Bismarck. In fact, the Russian government was grateful to be admitted as a partner. Moreover, Russian and German interests did not correspond in some important matters. The lack of harmony became obvious in 1875 when Russia and Great Britain exercised strong pressure on Germany to assure that it would not try a preventive war against France.

The Three Emperors' League finally collapsed over the issue of Turkey and the Balkans, which in the 1870s led to a series of international crises and

**The Balkans, 1877–78**

0     300 miles

········· Boundary of Ottoman Empire, 1877
〜 Proposed boundary of Bulgaria by Treaty of San Stefano, 1878
— Boundaries after Treaty of Berlin, 1878

to war between Russia and the Ottoman Empire. Beginning with the insurrection against Turkish rule in Herzegovina and Bosnia in July 1875, rebellion swept the Balkans. The year 1876 witnessed a brutal Turkish suppression of a Bulgarian uprising, as well as fighting and massacres in other parts of the peninsula, and the declaration of war on the Porte by Serbia and Montenegro. The Russian public reacted strongly to these developments. Pan-Slavism— hitherto no more than a vague sentiment, except for certain small circles of intellectuals—for the first time became an active force. Pan-Slav committees sent up to 5,000 volunteers, ranging from prominent members of society to simple peasants and including about 800 former Russian army officers, to fight in the Serbian army, which had been entrusted to another Russian volunteer, General Mikhail Cherniaev. But the Turks defeated the Serbs; hence the last hope of Balkan nationalities in their uneven contest with the Ottomans rested on Russian intervention. The imperial government considered intervention carefully and without enthusiasm. The international situation, with Great Britain and Austria-Hungary hostile to Russia, argued against war; and so did the internal conditions, for reforms were in the process of enactment, notably in the military and financial domains, and there was populist unrest. Besides, Gorchakov and other responsible tsarist officials did not believe at all in Pan-Slavism, the exception being the Russian ambassador to Constantinople, Count Nikolai Ignatiev. However, as the Balkan struggle continued, as international diplomacy failed to bring peace, and as Russia became gradually more deeply involved in the conflict, the tsarist government, having come to an understanding with Austria-Hungary, declared war on Turkey on April 24, 1877.

The difficult, bitter, and costly war resulted in a decisive Russian victory. The tsarist troops were approaching Constantinople when the fighting ceased. The Treaty of San Stefano, signed in March 1878, reflected the thorough Ottoman defeat: Russia obtained important border areas in the Caucasus and southern Bessarabia; for the latter, Romania, which had fought jointly with Russia at Plevna and elsewhere, was to be compensated with Dobrudja; Serbia and Montenegro gained territory and were to be recognized, along with Romania, as fully independent, while Bosnia and Herzegovina were to receive some autonomy and reform; moreover, the treaty created a large autonomous Bulgaria reaching to the Aegean Sea, which was to be occupied for two years by Russian troops; Turkey was to pay a huge indemnity.

But the forces of international diplomacy turned Russia's victory into a new humiliation. Austria-Hungary and Great Britain forced Russia to reconsider the settlement. Austria-Hungary was particularly incensed by the creation of a large Slavic state in the Balkans, Bulgaria, which Russia had specifically promised not to do. The reconsideration took the form of the Congress of Berlin, which met for a month in the summer of 1878 and redrew the map of the Balkans. While, according to the arrangements made in Berlin, Serbia, Montenegro, and Romania retained their independence and Russia held on to southern Bessarabia and most of her Caucasian gains, such as Batum, Kars, and Ardakhan, other provisions of the Treaty of San Stefano were changed beyond recognition. Serbia and Montenegro lost some of their acquisitions. More important, the large Bulgaria created at San Stefano underwent division into three parts: Bulgaria proper, north of the Balkan Mountains, which was to be autonomous; Eastern Rumelia, south of the mountains, which was to receive a special organization under Turkish rule; and Macedonia, granted merely certain reforms. Also, Austria-Hungary acquired the right to occupy, although not to annex, Bosnia, Herzegovina, and the Sanjak of Novi Bazar, while Great Britain took Cyprus. The diplomatic defeat of Russia reflected in the Berlin decisions made Russian public opinion react bitterly against Great Britain, Austria-Hungary, and, less justifiably, Bismarck, the "honest broker" of the Congress.

## Expansion in Asia

Whereas Russian dealings with European powers in the reign of Alexander II brought mixed results, the empire of the tsars continued to expand in Asia, turning the already multinational Russian Empire into a truly colonial power. Indeed, many scholars assert the existence of a positive correlation between

Russian isolation or rebuffs in the west and the eastward advance. In turn, Russia's colonial expansion made England and other colonial powers increasingly nervous. Be this as it may, there can be no doubt that the third quarter of the nineteenth century witnessed enormous Russian gains in Asia, notably in the Caucasus, in Central Asia, and in the Far East. Also, in 1867, the tsarist government withdrew from the Western hemisphere by selling Alaska to the United States for $7.2 million.

As mentioned earlier, Georgian recognition of Russian rule and successful wars against Persia and Turkey in the first decades of the nineteenth century had brought Transcaucasia and thus all of the Caucasus under the sway of the tsars. But imperial authority remained nominal or nonexistent as far as numerous mountain tribes were concerned. The determination to subdue the mountaineers produced a series of wars against Circassians, Abkhazians, Osetians, Chechens, and others, beginning in the 1810s. The mountaineers, mostly Muslims, responded to attempts at Russian domination by uniting in a prolonged jihad, or holy war, in defense of their freedom and faith. The complete "pacification" of the Caucasus, therefore, took decades, and military service in that majestic land seemed for a time almost tantamount to a death warrant. Beginning in 1857, however, Russian troops commanded by Prince Alexander Bariatinsky, using a new and superior rifle against the nearly exhausted mountaineers, staged another, this time decisive, offensive. In 1859 Bariatinsky captured the legendary Shamil, who for twenty-five years had been the military, spiritual, and political leader of Caucasian resistance to Russia. That event has usually been considered as the end of the fighting in the Caucasus, although more time had to pass before order could be fully established there. A large number of Muslim mountaineers chose to migrate to Turkey.

The conquest of Central Asia began in earnest only during the reign of Alexander II, with a series of daring military expeditions in the period from 1865 to 1876. Thus in the course of a decade the Russians conquered the khanates of Kokand, Bokhara, and Khiva, and finally, in 1881, also annexed the Transcaspian region. Russian expansion into Central Asia bears a certain resemblance both to colonial wars elsewhere and to the American westward movement. Central Asia was attractive for commercial reasons, as a source of raw materials, notably cotton, and as a market for Russian manufactured goods. Also, expansion had a security logic: to stabilize the frontier and to defend Russian settlements in the borderlands from predatory neighbors. Ideologically as well, these years saw the development of thinking that much resembled Western imperialism, especially the view that Russia, as a civilized nation, had the duty to control backward peoples and bring them order. While natives of Central Asia were viewed as alien and inferior "others"—literally, *inorodtsy*—the establishment of Russian rule usually interfered little with the native economy, society, law, religion, or customs. Russia's imperial approach in Central Asia, as in the Caucasus, was still focused on control more than on assimilation.

The Russian Far Eastern boundary remained unchanged from the Treaty of Nerchinsk in 1689 until Alexander II's reign, though the Russian population in Siberia had increased considerably. In 1847 the energetic and ambitious Count Nikolai Muraviev—known later as Muraviev-Amursky, that is, of the Amur—became governor-general of Eastern Siberia. He promoted Russian advance in the Amur area and took advantage of the desperate plight of China, at war with Great Britain and France and torn by a rebellion, to obtain two extremely advantageous treaties from the Chinese Empire: in 1858, by the Treaty of Aigun, China ceded to Russia the left bank of the Amur River, and in 1860, by the Treaty of Peking, the Ussuri region. The Pacific coast of the Russian Empire began gradually to be settled by Russian soldiers and colonists.

Russia's renewed expansion into the Far East, as into the Caucasus and Central Asia, was inspired by economic and security interests but also by an imperial self-image as a modern empire, comparable to other colonial empires, particularly Britain. Writers spoke of Russia's "civilizing mission" in Asia and of the prestige that this gave to the civilizers. As Dostoevsky wrote in 1881, "In Europe we were hangers-on and slaves, while in Asia we are masters. In Europe we were Tatars, while in Asia we are Europeans." One of the most important new cities on the Pacific coast was Vladivostok, or "the rule of the east," established in 1860. Its name signaled the commanding achievement of an empire that had now reached the very eastern edge of the Asian continent. And this would not be its last move in Asia.

CHAPTER 30

# The Reign of Alexander III, 1881–94, and the First Part of the Reign of Nicholas II, 1894–1905

The natural conclusion is that Russians live in a period which Shakespeare defined by saying, "The time is out of joint."

MAKSIM KOVALEVSKY

Politically, the reign of Alexander III and the reign of Nicholas II until the Revolution of 1905 formed a period of deepening crisis and intensifying efforts to preserve the traditions of autocratic monarchical power. At the same time, this increasingly conservative monarchy recognized the need to modernize the economy and did all it could to stimulate industrial development. In fact, the 1880s and 1890s were a period in Russian history defined by both rapid change in the economic and social spheres and strong reaction in the political arena. One view of the 1905 revolution is that this was the moment when this impossible contradiction finally broke down. At the very end of his reign, as we saw, Alexander II considered further reform as a possible path away from crisis. In the wake of his assassination and continuing social and political turmoil, Alexander III and Nicholas II rejected the path of political reform. Convinced of the sacredness and necessity of unlimited personal power remaining in the hands of the tsar, they not only rejected further reform but also did their best to limit the effectiveness of many changes that had already taken place. Thus they instituted what have come to be known in Russian historiography as "counterreforms." The official estimate of Russian conditions and needs became increasingly unreal. The government relied staunchly on the gentry, although that class was in decline. It held high the banner of "Orthodoxy-autocracy-nationality," in spite of the fact that Orthodoxy could hardly cement together peoples of many faiths in a multinational empire or unite even the many formally Orthodox Russians for whom religion was no longer central to their lives and identities or had become a more personal and variable form of sacred belief and value; that autocracy was bound to be even more of an anachronism and obstacle to progress in the twentieth than in the nineteenth century; and that a nationalism still grounded in a paternalistic ideal of the mystical bond of love and devotion between tsar and people little satisfied the political and social desires of ordinary Russians and, to the extent that it had come to include Russification, could only split a multinational state. Whereas the last two Romanovs to rule Russia agreed on principles and policies, they differed in character. Alexander III was a strong man, Nicholas II a weak one; under Nicholas confusion and indecision complicated further the government's fundamentally harmful efforts.

Alexander III, born 1845, was full of strength and vigor when he ascended the Russian throne after the assassination of his father. The new ruler was determined to suppress revolution and to maintain autocracy, a point that he made clear in a manifesto of May 11, 1881, which led to the resignation of Loris-Melikov, Dmitrii Miliutin, Grand Duke Constantine, and the minister of finance, Alexander Abaza. Yet it took a number of months and further changes at the top before the orientation represented by Loris-Melikov was entirely abandoned and the government embarked on a course away from all reform. The promoters of reaction included Konstantin Pobedonostsev, formerly a noted jurist at the University of Moscow, who had served as tutor to Alexander and had become in 1880 the Ober-Procurator of the Holy Synod; Dmitrii Tolstoy, who returned to the government in 1882 to head the Ministry of the Interior; and Ivan Delianov, who took charge of the Ministry of Education in the same year. Pobedonostsev, the chief theoretician as well as the leading practitioner of reaction in Russia in the last decades of the nineteenth century, characteristically emphasized the weakness and viciousness of man and the fallibility and dangers of human reason, hated the industrial revolution and the growth of cities, and even wanted "to keep people from inventing things." The state, he believed, had as its high purpose the maintenance of law, order, stability, and unity among men. In Russia that aim could be accomplished only by means of autocracy and the Orthodox Church.

"Temporary Regulations" to protect state security and public order, issued late in the summer of 1881, gave officials in designated areas broad authority in dealing with the press and with people who could threaten public order. Summary search, arrest, imprisonment, exile, and trial by courts-martial became common occurrences. The "Temporary Regulations" were aimed primarily at the "People's Will," which lasted long enough to offer the new ruler peace on conditions of political amnesty and the convocation of a constituent assembly! Although the "People's Will" had been largely destroyed even before the assassination of the emperor and although most of its remaining members soon fell into the hands of the police, the "Temporary Regulations" were not rescinded, but instead applied, as their vague wording permitted, to virtually anyone whom officials suspected or simply disliked. For many years after the demise of the "People's Will," terrorism died down in Russia, although occasional individual outbreaks occurred. Yet the "Temporary Regulations," introduced originally for three years, were renewed. Indeed, the tsarist government relied on them during the rest of its existence, with the result that Russians lived under something like a partial state of martial law.

Alexander III's government also enacted "counterreforms" meant to curb the sweeping changes introduced by Alexander II and to buttress the centralized, bureaucratic, and class nature of the Russian system. New press regulations made the existence of radical journals impossible and the life of a mildly liberal press precarious. The University Statute of 1884, which replaced the more liberal statute of 1863, virtually abolished university autonomy and also emphasized that students were to be considered "individual visitors," who had no right to form organizations or to claim corporate representation. In fact most policies of the Ministry of Education—which will be summarized in a later chapter—whether they concerned the emphasis on classical languages

Alexander III in 1889. Known for the strength of his conservative convictions, as well as his physical strength, Alexander III was described as a "mountain of stone." He was the first Russian ruler since Peter the Great to grow a beard. *(Treasures of Russia Exhibition)*

in secondary schools, the drastic curtailment of higher education for women, or the expansion of the role of the Church in elementary teaching, consciously promoted the radically conservative aims of the regime.

The tsar and his associates used every opportunity to help the gentry and to stress their leading position in Russia, as, for example, by the creation in 1885 of the State Gentry Land Bank. At the same time they imposed further restrictions on the peasants, whom they considered essentially wards of the state rather than mature citizens. The policies of bureaucratic control of the peasants and of emphasizing the role of the gentry in the countryside found expression in the most outstanding "counterreform" of the reign, the establishment in 1889 of the office of *zemskii nachalnik*, zemstvo chief, or land captain. That official—who had nothing to do with the zemstvo self-government—was appointed and dismissed by the minister of the interior following the recommendation of the governor of the land captain's province. His assigned task consisted in exercising direct bureaucratic supervision over the peasants and, in effect, in managing them. Thus the land captain confirmed elected peasant officials as well as decisions of peasant meetings, and he could prevent the officials from exercising their office, or even fine, arrest, or imprison them, although the fines imposed by the land captain could not exceed several rubles and the prison sentences, several days. Moreover, land captains received vast judicial powers, thus, contrary to the legislation of 1864, again combining administration and justice. In fact, these appointed officials replaced for the peasants, that is, for the vast majority of the people, elected and independent justices of peace. The law of 1889 stipulated that land captains had to be appointed from members of the local gentry who met a certain property qualification. Each district received several land captains; each land captain administered several volosti, that is, townships or cantons. Russia obtained in this manner a new administrative network, one of land captaincies.

The following year, 1890, the government made certain significant changes in the zemstvo system. The previous classification of landholders, that of 1864, had been based on a form of property that did not distinguish members of the gentry from other Russians who happened to hold land in individual ownership. In 1890 the members of the gentry became a distinct group—and their representation was markedly increased. Peasants, on the other hand, could thenceforth elect only candidates for zemstvo seats; the governor making appointments to district zemstvo assemblies from these candidates, as recommended by land captains. In addition, the minister of the interior received the right to confirm chairmen of zemstvo boards in their office, while members of the boards and zemstvo employees were to be confirmed by their respective governors. In 1892 the town government underwent a similar "counterreform," which, among other provisions, sharply raised the property requirement for the right to vote. After its enactment, the electorate in St. Petersburg decreased from 21,000 to 8,000, and that in Moscow from 20,000 to 7,000.

The reign of Alexander III also witnessed increased pressure on non-Orthodox denominations and a growth of the policy of Russification. Even Roman Catholics and Lutherans, who formed majorities in certain western areas of the empire and had unimpeachable international connections and recognition, had to face discrimination: for instance, children of mixed marriages with the Orthodox automatically became Orthodox, and all but the dominant Church were forbidden to engage in proselytizing. Old Believers and Russian sectarians suffered greater hardships. The government also began to oppose non-Christian faiths such as Islam and Buddhism, which had devoted adherents among the many peoples of the empire.

Russification went hand in hand with militant Orthodoxy, although the two were by no means identical, for peoples who were not Great Russians such as the Ukrainians and the Georgians belonged to the Orthodox Church. Although Russification was practiced earlier against the Poles, especially in the western provinces following the rebellions of 1831 and 1863 and to a somewhat lesser extent in Poland proper, and was also apparent in the attempts to suppress the budding Ukrainian nationalism, it became a general policy of the Russian government only late in the nineteenth century. It represented in part a reaction against the growing national sentiments of different peoples of the empire with their implicit threats to the unity of the state and in part a response to the rising nationalism among Russians themselves. Alexander III has often been considered the first nationalist on the Russian throne, though the Official Nationality of Nicholas I was also a type of Russian nationalism. Certainly, during Alexander III's reign, measures of Russification began to be extended not only to the rebellious Poles, but, for example, to the Georgians and Armenians in Transcaucasia and even gradually to the loyal Finns.

Jews, who were very numerous in western Russia as a result of the invitation policy of late medieval Polish kings, were bound to suffer in the new atmosphere of aggressive Orthodoxy and Russification. And indeed old limitations came to be applied to them with a new force, while new legislation was enacted to establish additional curbs on them and their activities. Thus, in contrast to the former lax enforcement of rules, Jews came to be rigorously restricted to residence in the "Pale of Jewish Settlement," that is, the area in western Russia where they had been living for a long time, with the added proviso that even within the Pale they could reside only in towns and smaller settlements inhabited by merchants and craftsmen, but not in the countryside. Educated or otherwise prominent Jews could usually surmount these restrictions, but the great bulk of the poor Jewish population was tied to its location. In 1887 the government established quotas for Jewish students in institutions of higher learning: 10 percent of the total enrollment within the Pale of Jewish Settlement, 5 percent in other provinces, and 3 percent in Moscow and St. Petersburg. In 1881, pogroms—the sad word entered the English language from the Russian—that is, violent popular outbreaks against the Jews, occurred in southwestern Russian towns and settlements, destroying Jewish property and sometimes taking Jewish lives. They were to recur sporadically until the end of imperial Russia. Local authorities often did little to prevent pogroms and on occasion, it is rather clear, even encouraged them. As Pobedonostsev allegedly remarked, the Jewish problem in Russia was to be solved by the conversion to Orthodoxy of one-third of the Russian Jews, the emigration of one-third, and the death of the remaining third. It should be added that the Russian government defined Jews according to their religion; Jews who converted to Christianity escaped the disabilities imposed on the others, though prejudice against them often persisted.

Alexander III was not entirely opposed to all change and reform. Like all modern Russian rulers, he recognized the need for progress, if only to maintain and develop the strength of the nation and the state. What was new was the belief that economic and social change could be separated from political change. Progressive economic measures were largely the work of a series of ministers responsible for finance and the economy. We will look more closely at economic and social history in a later chapter. But it should be noted that Nikolai Bunge, who headed the Ministry of Finance from 1881 to 1887, hoping to stimulate economic development and lessen the burdens and dangers of poverty, established a Peasant Land Bank, abolished the head tax, introduced the inheritance tax, and also began labor legislation in Russia. His pioneering factory laws included the limitation of the working day to eight hours for children between twelve and fifteen, the prohibition of night work for children and for women in the textile industry, and regulations aimed at assuring the workers proper and regular pay from their employers, without excessive fines or other illegitimate deductions. Factory inspectors were established to supervise the carrying out of the new legislation. It is significant that Bunge had to leave the Ministry of Finance because of the strong opposition to his measures and accusations of socialism. His successors, Ivan Vyshnegradsky, 1887–92, and Sergei Witte, 1892–1903, would become even more celebrated for their efforts to stimulate industrial growth and modernization, including a massive program of state railroad building and the promotion of heavy industry through high tariffs, state contracts and subsidies, and other means.

## Nicholas II

Nicholas II, Alexander III's eldest son, who was born in 1868, became the autocratic ruler of Russia after his father's death in 1894. The last tsar possessed personal qualities that many have admired, such as modesty, self-discipline, faith, patriotism, a deep sense of duty, and devotion to his family. But these virtues mattered little in a situation that demanded strength, adaptability, and vision. It may well be argued that another Peter the Great could have saved the Romanovs and imperial Russia. There can be no doubt that Nicholas II did not. In fact, he proved unable to remove his traditionalist political blinders even when circumstances forced him into entirely new situations with great potentialities, and at the same time unable to manage even reaction effectively. Everything about Nicholas II's upbringing, experience, intellect, and personality led him to believe deeply in a polity based on the most traditional notions of power (often deriving from a nostalgic image of pre-Petrine Russia). Nicholas believed explicitly that the unrestricted personal power of the tsar was the only assurance of Russia's might, stability, and even progress as a nation. This was, however, a moral power. This was autocracy linked with Orthodoxy and nationality. The ruler, Nicholas believed, was blessed and guided by God. Typically, he loved the traditional saying, "the heart of the tsar is in the hand of God." And the Russian ruler enjoyed, he believed, a special bond of almost mystical love of the people. Even when forced, reluctantly, to respond to massive public unrest in 1905 by agreeing to demands for a national representative assembly, he continued to cast his vision of even a reformed political order in traditionalist terms: "Let there be established as in olden time, the union between Tsar and all Rus, the communion between Me and the people of the land, which lies at the foundation of an order that corresponds to unique Russian principles." At the same time, Nicholas loved orderliness and discipline. His model and inspiration was the military, whose rituals he always loved. At the same time, complicating these convictions,

Nicholas II in seventeenth-century dress for a masked ball at the Winter Palace in 1903. Nicholas admired what he viewed as a more national and healthy spirit in Russia before Peter the Great. *(New York Public Library)*

he revealed what many saw as signs of deeper uncertainty and even weakness. The emperor struck many observers as peculiarly automatic in his attitudes and actions, without the power of spontaneous decision. Various, often unworthy, ministers made crucial decisions that the sovereign failed to understand fully or to evaluate. Later in the reign the empress, Alexandra, a German-born convert to Orthodoxy whose devotion to old Russian traditions, moral conservatism, mysticism, and contempt for the reformist ideas of intellectuals were perhaps even more stubborn than Nicholas's, became the tsar's closest confident and advisor. Perhaps the most notorious sign of Nicholas's poor judgment, and Alexandra's baneful influence, was that such an incredible person as Rasputin could rise to the position of greatest influence in the state. On top of all this, Nicholas was notably fatalistic. He was often quoted as saying, "God knows what is good for us, we must bow down our heads and repeat the sacred words 'Thy will be done.'" It has been argued that Nicholas may have been a good man, even a saintly one (indeed, he was canonized in 2000 by the Orthodox Church in Russia), but that he was a miserable ruler lost in the moment of crisis. At a time when so much was changing in Russia and the world and so many Russians were convinced that the time had come for new political relationships based on limited central government, civil rights, democratic participation, and the rule of law, it appears that the autocracy was retreating into a stubborn, even blind, faith in Russia's ancient political traditions: the ideal of absolute personal rule by a divinely anointed and inspired monarch bound to his people through mystical love rather than modern democratic institutions. Lev Trotsky and other determinists have insisted that the archaic, rotten Russian system could not logically produce a leader much different from that ineffective relic of the past. Or, as an old saying has it, the gods blind those whom they want to destroy.

## Reaction under Nicholas II

In the face of expectations that he would relax the restrictive policies of his father and possibly embark on needed reforms, Nicholas II hastened to make clear to society where he stood politically. Addressing a gathering of representatives of the gentry, zemstvos, and cities in January 1895, he bluntly declared (in words widely reported in the press), "It is known to Me that voices have been heard of late, in some zemstvo assemblies, by persons carried away by senseless dreams of participation of representatives of the zemstvos in the affairs of internal administration. Let all know that, in devoting all my strength to the people's well-being, I will preserve the principles of autocracy as firmly and unswervingly as did my late unforgettable father." Policy followed accordingly. Himself a former pupil of Pobedonostsev, Nicholas relied on the Ober-Procurator of the Holy Synod and on other reactionaries such as his ministers of interior Dmitrii Sipiagin and Viacheslav Plehve. The government continued to apply and extend the "Temporary Regulations," to supervise the press with utmost severity, and as best it could to control and often restrict education. The zemstvo and municipal governments experienced further curtailments of their jurisdictions. For example, in 1900 the limits of zemstvo taxation were strictly fixed and the stockpiling of food for emergency was taken away from zemstvo jurisdiction and transferred to that of the bureaucracy. Moreover, the authorities often refused to confirm elections of zemstvo board members or appointments of zemstvo employees, trying to assure that only people of unimpeachable loyalty to the regime would hold public positions of any kind.

Official Russian nationalism, closely linked to these conservative political values, meant both constant talk about the "loving communion" of the tsar and his true Russian people and restrictions and persecution for those defined as outside the national fold. These policies were not without some ambiguity. The state sometimes celebrated, as in the ceremonies marking Nicholas's accession, the variety of the empire's subjects (though emphasizing Russian leadership), tolerated local customs and native languages, and even encouraged a circumscribed role in administration or education for non-Russians themselves, though all in the pursuit of the integration of diverse peoples into a common imperial polity. But intolerance for difference was also quite evident and brutal. Religious persecution grew. Russian sectarians suffered the most, in particular those groups that refused to recognize the state and perform such state obligations as military service. Many of them were exiled from central European Russia to the Caucasus and other distant areas. It was as a result of the policies of the Russian government that the Dukhobory and certain other sects—helped, incidentally, by Lev Tolstoy—began to emigrate in large numbers to Canada and the United States. The state also confiscated the estates and charity funds of the Armenian Church and harassed other denominations in numerous ways. The position of the Jews too underwent further deterioration. Additional restrictions on them included a prohibition from acquiring real estate anywhere in the empire except in the cities and settlements of the Jewish Pale, while new pogroms erupted in southwest Russia, including the horrible one in Kishinev in 1903.

But the case of Finland represented in many respects the most telling instance of the folly of Russification. As an autonomous grand duchy from the time it was won from Sweden in 1809, Finland received more rights from the Russian emperor, who became the Grand Duke of Finland, than it had had under Swedish rule, and remained a perfectly loyal, as well as a relatively prosperous and happy, part of the state until the very end of the nineteenth century and the introduction of a policy of Russification. Finnish soldiers helped suppress the Poles, and in general the Finns participated actively and fruitfully in almost every aspect of the life of the empire. Yet the new nationalism demanded that they too be Russified. While some preliminary measures in that direction had been enacted as early as in the reign of Alexander III, real Russification began with the appointment of General Nikolai Bobrikov as governor-general of Finland and of Plehve as state secretary for Finnish affairs in 1898. Russian authorities argued that Finland could remain different from Russia only as far as local matters were concerned, while it had to accept the general system in what pertained to the entire state. With that end in view, a manifesto concerning laws common to Finland and Russia and a new statute dealing with the military service of the Finns were published in 1899. Almost overnight Finland became bitterly hostile to Russia, and a strong though passive resistance developed: new laws were ignored, draftees failed to show up, and so on. In 1901 freedom of meetings was abrogated in Finland. In 1902 Governor-General Bobrikov received the right to dismiss Finnish officials and judges and to replace them with Russians. In 1903 he was vested with extraordinary powers to protect state security and public order, which represented a definitive extension of the "Temporary Regulations" of 1881 to Finland. In 1904 Bobrikov was assassinated. The following year the opposition in Finland became part of the revolution that spread throughout the empire.

## Witte and the Ministry of Finance

However, under Nicholas II, as in the reign of Alexander III, the Ministry of Finance was the location of a very different orientation toward change, which affected many aspects of the Russian economy and life. The minister, Sergei Witte, was an economic planner and manager of the type exceedingly rare in the high officialdom of imperial Russia. Witte devoted his remarkable energy and ability especially to the stabilization of finance, the promotion of heavy industry, and the building of railroads. In 1897, after accumulating a sufficient gold reserve, he established a gold standard in Russia, a measure that did much to add stability and prestige to Russian economic development, and in particular to attract foreign capital. Witte encouraged heavy industry by virtually every means at his command, including government orders, liberal credits, unceasing efforts to obtain investments from abroad, tariff regulations, and improved transportation. As to railroads, the minister, who had risen to prominence as a railroad official, always retained a great interest in them and saw the potential contribution of railroads to stimulating the economy, unifying the empire, and even advancing foreign policy. The Russian railroad network doubled in mileage between 1895 and 1905, and the additions included the enormous Trans-Siberian line, built between 1891 and 1903—except for a section around Lake Baikal completed later.

## Russian Foreign Policy after the Congress of Berlin

Russian foreign policy had been undergoing important changes in the decades that followed the Congress of Berlin. The most significant developments were the final rupture with Austria-Hungary and Germany and the alliance with France. Although the Three Emperors' League had foundered in the Balkan crisis, a new Alliance of the Three Emperors was concluded in June 1881 for three years and renewed in 1884 for another three years. Its most essential provision declared that if one of the contracting powers—Germany, Austria-Hungary, or Russia—engaged in war with a fourth power, except Turkey, the other two were to maintain friendly neutrality. But, because of their conflicting interests in the Balkans, it proved impossible for Russia and Austria-Hungary to stay in the same alliance. The next major crisis occurred over Bulgaria where—as

Charles Jelavich and other specialists have demonstrated—Russia destroyed a great amount of popularity and goodwill by an overbearing and stupid policy. The Russian quarrel with the Bulgarian ruler, Alexander of Battenberg, and the Russian refusal to sanction the unification of Bulgaria and Eastern Rumelia in 1885 failed to stop the unification but resulted in the abdication of Alexander of Battenberg and the election by the Bulgarian Assembly of the pro-Austrian Ferdinand of Saxe-Coburg to the Bulgarian throne. Bulgaria abandoned the Russian sphere of influence and entered the Austrian, leaving the empire of the tsars virtually without Balkan allies. At the same time tension in relations between Russia and Austria-Hungary increased almost to the breaking point. However, Germany, by contrast with Austria-Hungary and despite the fact that in 1879 it had become a close partner of the Habsburg state, tried at first to retain the Russian connection. Thus when the Alliance of the Three Emperors expired in 1887, Germany and Russia concluded in secret the so-called Reinsurance Treaty, Bismarck's "wire to St. Petersburg" and a veritable *tour de force* of diplomacy: each party was to remain neutral in case the other fought a war, with the exception of an aggressive war of Germany against France or of Russia against Austria-Hungary—the exception making it barely possible for Germany to square the Reinsurance Treaty with its obligations to Austria-Hungary. Nevertheless, following Bismarck's forced resignation in 1890, Germany discontinued the Reinsurance Treaty and thus severed its connection with Russia.

The Russian rupture with the Germanic powers and the general isolation of Russia appeared all the more ominous because of Anglo-Russian tension over the expansion of the Russian Empire in Central Asia, which, the British felt, threatened India. That tension attained its high point in 1885 when the Russians, having reached as far south as the vague Afghan border, clashed with the soldiers of the amir. Although an Anglo-Russian war was avoided and the boundary settled by compromise, Great Britain and Russia remained hostile to each other well past the turn of the century as they competed for influence and control in vast lands south of Russia, especially in Iran.

Political realities pointed to a Franco-Russian alliance—Bismarck's nightmare and the reason behind the Reinsurance Treaty—for France was as isolated as Russia and more threatened. Alexander III, his cautious foreign minister Nikolai Giers, and other tsarist high officials reached that conclusion reluctantly, because they had no liking for the Third Republic and no confidence in it, and because the traditional German orientation in Russian foreign policy died hard. Yet France remained the only possible partner, and it had much to offer. In particular, Paris alone provided a great market for Russian state loans—the Berlin financial market, it might be added, was closed to Russia in 1887—and thus the main source of foreign financial support much needed by the imperial government. In fact, Frenchmen proved remarkably eager to subscribe to these loans as well as to invest directly in the Russian economy. Economics thus joined politics, although it would be fair to say that politics led the way. The alliance was consolidated in several stages, beginning with the diplomatic understanding of 1891 and ending with the military convention of

Nicholas II blessing troops leaving for the front in the Russo-Japanese War, 1905.
Nicholas often spoke of the Russian common people's traditional love and devotion
for their tsar and described moments like these as deeply moving.   (*Terra Publishers*)

December 1893–January 1894. Boris Nolde, William Langer, and other scholars
have indicated how through the drawn-out negotiations the French pressed
for an ever firmer and more binding agreement, gradually forcing the hand
of the hesitant Russians. In its final form the alliance provided that if France
were attacked by Germany, or by Italy supported by Germany, Russia would
employ all available forces against Germany; and if Russia were attacked
by Germany, or by Austria-Hungary supported by Germany, France would
employ all available forces against Germany. Additional articles dealt with
mobilization, the number of troops to be contributed, and other specific military plans. The Franco-Russian agreement was to remain in force for the dura-
tion of the Triple Alliance of Germany, Austria-Hungary, and Italy.

Nicholas II approved Alexander III's foreign policy on the whole and
wanted to continue it. However, as we shall see, the new emperor proved to
be less steady and more erratic than his father in international relations as
in domestic affairs. Also, while Alexander III relied on the careful and experienced Giers throughout his rule, Nicholas II had several foreign ministers
whose differences and personal preferences affected imperial diplomacy.
In addition, the reign of the last tsar witnessed more than its share of court
cliques and cabals, which on occasion exercised a strong and at the same time
irresponsible influence on the conduct of Russian foreign policy.

Nicholas II appeared prominently on the international scene in 1899, when
he called together the first Hague Peace Conference attended by representatives

of twenty-six states. Although instigated by Russian financial stringency and in particular by the difficulty of keeping up with Austrian armaments, this initiative was in accord with the emperor's generally peaceful views. While the Conference failed to agree on disarmament or compulsory arbitration of disputes, it did pass certain "laws of war"—later often disregarded in practice, as in the case of the temporary injunction against the use of "projectiles thrown from balloons"—and set up a permanent court of arbitration, the International Court of Justice at the Hague. More important, it became the first of a long series of international conferences on disarmament and peace. The Second Hague Peace Conference, in 1907, was also attended by Russian representatives, but again it could not reach agreement on the major issues under discussion.

## The Russo-Japanese War

Nicholas II's own policy, however, did not always contribute to peace. Aggressiveness and adventurous involvement characterized Russian behavior in the Far East around the turn of the century, which culminated in the Russo-Japanese War of 1904–5. The construction of the Trans-Siberian railroad between 1891 and 1903, entirely justified in terms of the needs of Siberia, served also to link Russia to Manchuria, China, Korea, and even, indirectly, to Japan. Japan had just gone through a remarkable modernization and in 1894–95 it fought and defeated China, obtaining by the Treaty of Shimonoseki the Chinese territories of Formosa, the Pescadores Islands, and the Liaotung Peninsula, together with other gains, including the recognition of full independence for Korea. Before Japan could profit from the Liaotung Peninsula, Russia, France, and Germany forced her to give it up. Next Russia concluded a secret agreement with China, whereby in return for guaranteeing Chinese territory against outside aggression, it obtained the right to construct a railroad through Manchuria to the coast. Although the new railroad, the East China Railway, belonged nominally to a private company with a large Chinese participation, it marked in effect the establishment of a Russian sphere of influence in northern Manchuria, an influence centered in Harbin and extending along railroad tracks and properties guarded by a special Russian railroad guard.

While Russia had legitimate commercial and other interests in Asia—for one thing, selling the products of its factories in the East when they could not compete in the West—and while up to that point Russian imperialism in the Far East had limited itself to peaceful conquest, the situation became increasingly tense. Moreover, Russia responded to new opportunities more and more aggressively. Thus, when the murder of two German missionaries in November 1897 led to the German acquisition of Kiao-chow through a ninety-nine-year lease, Nicholas II demanded and obtained a twenty-five-year lease of the southern part of the Liaotung Peninsula with Port Arthur—in spite of Witte's opposition to that move and in flagrant disregard of the Russian treaty with China. Witte in turn proceeded to make the most of the situation

*Russo-Japanese War 1904–5*

and rapidly develop Russian interests in southern Manchuria. Following the
so-called Boxer rebellion of the exasperated Chinese against foreigners in
1900–1901, which Russian forces helped to suppress, tsarist troops remained
in Manchuria on the pretext that local conditions represented a threat to the
railroad. In addition, a group of adventurers with strong connections at the
Russian court began to promote a scheme of timber concessions on the Yalu
River meant to serve as a vehicle for Russian penetration into Korea. Witte,
who objected energetically to the dangerous new scheme, had to leave the
Ministry of Finance; the Foreign Office failed to restrain or control Russian
policy in the Far East; and Nicholas II himself sided cheerfully with the adventurers, apparently because he believed in a Russian national mission in Asia
and, in common with almost everyone else, grossly underestimated Japan.

Japan proved to be the more skillful aggressor, notwithstanding the
contempt often expressed in the boulevard press for the Japanese as "yel-
low monkeys." Offering partition, which would give the Russians northern

Manchuria and the Japanese southern Manchuria and Korea, the Japanese gauged the futility of negotiating, chose their time well, and on February 8, 1904, attacked successfully the unsuspecting Russian fleet in the outer harbor of Port Arthur—thus accomplishing the original Pearl Harbor. What followed turned out to be a humiliating war for the Russians. The Russian colossus suffered defeat after defeat. This outcome, so surprising at the time, resulted from ample causes: Japan was ready, well-organized, and in effect more modern than Russia, while Russia was unprepared, disorganized, troubled at home, and handicapped by a lack of popular support and even by some defeatism; Japan enjoyed an alliance with Great Britain and the favor of world public opinion, Russia found itself diplomatically isolated; Japan used short lines of communication, Russian forces had to rely on the enormously long single-track Trans-Siberian railroad, with the section around Lake Baikal still unfinished. The Japanese destroyed the Russian navy in the Far East, besieged and eventually captured Port Arthur, and gradually, in spite of bitter engagements near Mukden and elsewhere, pushed the main Russian army north in Manchuria. Finally, on May 27–29, 1905, in the battle of Tsushima Strait, they annihilated Admiral Zinovii Rozhdestvensky's antique fleet which had been sent to the Far East all the way from the Baltic.

An armistice followed soon after Tsushima. The Russians had suffered numerous defeats, and the government had to cope with revolutionary unrest at home. The Japanese had exhausted their finances and, despite their victories, could not destroy the main Russian army or force a conclusion. In response to a secret Japanese request, President Theodore Roosevelt arranged a peace conference at Portsmouth, New Hampshire, in August 1905. The provisions of the Treaty of Portsmouth reflected the skillful diplomacy of Witte, who headed the Russian delegation, and represented, everything considered, a rather satisfactory settlement for Russia: Russia acknowledged a paramount Japanese interest in Korea and ceded to Japan its lease of the Liaotung Peninsula, the southern part of the railroad up to Changchun, and the southern half of the island of Sakhalin; both countries agreed to restore Manchuria to China; in spite of strong Japanese insistence, there was no indemnity.

The Russian government ended the war against Japan none too soon, for, as fighting ceased, the country was already in the grip of what came to be known as the Revolution of 1905.

CHAPTER 31

# The Last Part of the Reign of Nicholas II: The Revolution of 1905 and the Constitutional Period, 1905–17

Russia at the dawn of the twentieth century knew no more magic word than "revolution." The idea of revolution was viewed with fear and hatred by the propertied classes of the population, and was loved and revered by all who dreamed of liberty. To the Russians who longed for a new life, there was enchantment in the very sound of the word. Even as they conceived it, even as they pronounced the sacred words, "Long Live the Revolution," Russians felt obscurely that they were already halfway to liberation.

ISAAC STEINBERG

The main weakness of the Russian monarchy of the imperial period consisted not at all in representing the interests of a *"minority,"* restricted in this or that manner, but in the fact that it represented *no one* whatsoever.*

GEORGE FLOROVSKY

The critical years from the turn of the century to the eve of the First World War were a time of uncertainty and crisis for Russia's old political, social, and cultural order, but also a time of possibility, imagination, and daring. In many respects, the Revolution of 1905 was a turning point. The social transformation of Russia—especially the rise of an urban working class and the proliferation of professionals and businessmen—together with the continued growth of

---

*Italics in the original

**400**

political opposition made revolution in 1905 possible. We will examine social and ideological developments more closely in the following chapters. But it is essential here to make particular note of three developments: the rise of liberalism, the development of Marxism, and growing labor unrest. Of course, behind dissatisfied bourgeois, critical intellectuals, and angry workers spread the human ocean of impoverished and dissatisfied peasants—an ocean that had risen in uncounted storms through centuries of Russian history.

The opposition began to organize in these years, though much of this was necessarily outside of and against the law. The terrible famine of 1891–92 marked the end of a certain lull in Russia and the resumption of social and political activity with emphatic criticism of the regime. For the first time, liberals were in the vanguard. Liberalism in Russia grew especially among middle-class professionals, whose growth reflected social change but also the "great reforms": the judicial reform of 1864 had virtually created a class of lawyers, and the introduction of the zemstvo system provided numerous openings for doctors, veterinarians, teachers, statisticians, and many other specialists, the "third element" of the zemstva (the other two elements were the elected representatives of local gentry and peasants and the appointed representatives of the central state). Liberalism found particularly propitious circumstances for development among the professionals, though also among some gentry landlords and educated urban elites. On the eve of 1905, though their social base remained small, liberals could boast of many prominent names in their ranks. Organizationally, they established a Union of Liberation in 1903, with its organ, *Liberation*, published abroad by the noted economist Petr Struve. In 1905 they organized the Constitutional Democratic Party—or "Kadet," a word based on the two initial letters in the Russian name—led by the historian Pavel Miliukov.

Liberals were a diverse group ideologically, ranging from constitutional monarchists to republicans, from moderate reformists to radical democrats. But they shared a common set of goals for transforming Russia: the rule of law, basic civil rights, an elected parliament, local self-government, and social reforms to ensure social stability and justice, including the extension of public education, moderate land reform, and protective labor legislation. Socialists shared the liberals' democratic goals and even the philosophical logic underpinning liberal democracy: that political and social change ought to promote the freedom and dignity of the individual by removing social, cultural, and political constraints. But socialists approached this ideal with the radical insistence that only the root and branch transformation of all social and political relationships could set Russia on the path to true emancipation. Various underground socialist organizations emerged in the early years of the century. Populist socialists were organized after 1901 around the Socialist Revolutionary Party. Ideologically, they viewed the whole laboring common people (the *narod*) as their constituency and socialism as a future society embodying the ethical values of community and liberty. Marxists, or Social Democrats, were increasingly numerous and influential starting in the 1880s and were often closely associated with the labor movement. Georgii Plekhanov had organized the first major Marxist group among émigrés in 1883, the Emancipation of Labor group. The first significant Marxist group in Russia was formed in 1895 in St. Petersburg, the Union of Struggle for the Emancipation of the Working Class, led by young intellectuals including Vladimir Ulianov, known by his party pseudonym Lenin, and Yulii Tsederbaum, who called himself Martov. Most of its members were soon arrested. The founding congress of the Russian Social Democratic Workers' Party took place in Minsk in 1898. Arrests also followed swiftly, though in 1903 the party was reestablished at a congress in Brussels and London. The party also split at that meeting, however, mainly over organizational questions, into the Bolsheviks, led by Lenin, who wanted a disciplined organization of professional revolutionaries, and the Mensheviks, led by Martov, who favored a more open association. In time, the ramifications of that initial difference acquired great importance.

As the twentieth century opened, Russia was in turmoil. Workers' demonstrations and strikes spread throughout the country. Student protests and disturbances became more frequent, constituting an almost continuous series from 1898 on. Sporadic peasant disturbances kept the tension high in rural areas and offered increased opportunities to the Socialist Revolutionaries, just as the growth of the labor movement encouraged the Social Democrats. In 1902, 1903, and early 1904, committees dealing with the national economy, conferences of teachers and doctors, and other public bodies all demanded reforms. Moreover, the Socialist Revolutionaries resumed the terrorist tactics of their predecessors such as the "People's Will." Their "Battle Organization" assassinated a number of important officials, including the two especially reactionary ministers of the interior, Sipiagin in 1902 and Plehve in 1904, and early in 1905 Grand Duke Sergei, commanding officer of the Moscow military region and Nicholas II's second cousin and brother-in-law. The war against Japan and resulting defeats added fuel to the fire. The government was not entirely unresponsive. Plehve was replaced as minister of the interior by Prince Dmitrii Sviatopolk-Mirsky, who spoke openly as few tsarist officials had before of finding ways for the voice of "society" to be heard, initiating what many expectantly called a political "spring" in relations between state and society. But this only further stimulated civic demands for reform. In November and December 1904, liberals staged a "banquet campaign," inspired by the French example of 1847–48, featuring fervent speeches and resolutions calling for democratizing political change. In November, a zemstvo congress, meeting in St. Petersburg, demanded a representative assembly and civil liberties. The same demands were made with increasing frequency by numerous other public bodies. In particular, professional organizations, such as unions of doctors and teachers, and other associations spread rapidly throughout Russia and made their voices heard.

## The Revolution of 1905

The revolution was ignited by a shocking act of repressive government violence. On January 22, 1905 (January 9 on the Russian calendar), the police of the capital fired on a huge demonstration of workers marching toward the Winter Palace with a petition for the tsar, killing, according to the official estimate, 130 persons and wounding several hundred. "Bloody Sunday," as it came to be known in Russian history, set in motion an unprecedented political and social upheaval throughout the empire. The march had been led by Father Georgii Gapon, a charismatic priest who had organized workers throughout the city into an "Assembly of Russian Factory Workers." Ironically, Gapon's union had begun in 1904 as part of a police effort to lure workers away from socialists and nurture their loyalty to autocracy through inexpensive tea-rooms, edifying lectures, and concern for their everyday material needs. What resulted was an organization whose meetings were marked by a mixture of social criticism, moral fervor, and sacred purpose, and which began to act with increasing vigor to help and defend workers. Ironically too, the workers were converging on the Winter Palace—ignorant of the fact that Nicholas II was not there—with icons and the tsar's portraits, as faithful subjects, nay, children, of their sovereign, begging him for redress and help. The massacre led to a great outburst of indignation in the country and gave another boost to the revolutionary movement. In particular, as many authorities assert, it meant a decisive break between the tsar and those numerous workers who had until that "Bloody Sunday" remained loyal to him.

Under ever-increasing pressure, Nicholas II declared early in March his intention to convoke a "consultative" assembly; in further efforts toward

Social Democrats demonstrate in 1905. Banners read "Proletarians of All Countries, Unite!," "Russian Social-Democratic Workers' Party," "We Demand a Constituent Assembly," and "Down with Autocracy." (*Russian State Archive of Film and Photographic Documents*)

pacification, he proclaimed religious tolerance and repealed some legislation against ethnic minorities; nevertheless, the revolutionary tide kept rising. The revolution had many faces: workers' and students' strikes, demonstrations stretching through city streets, vandalism and other periodic violence, naval mutinies (most famously the rebellion on the battleship *Potemkin* on the Black Sea), peasant unrest in many provinces, and nationalist movements in the imperial borderlands. On August 19 an imperial manifesto created an elective Duma with consultative powers, but that too failed to satisfy the educated public or the masses. The revolutionary movement culminated in a mammoth general strike which lasted from the twentieth to the thirtieth of October and has been described as the greatest, most thoroughly carried out, and most successful strike in history. Russians seemed to act with a single will, as they made perfectly plain their unshakable determination to end autocracy. To bolster their demands, society had become more organized than ever before. In May, fourteen professional unions united to form a huge Union of Unions led by the liberal Kadets. Industrial workers established, without seeking official approval, trade unions, in which socialist workers and intellectuals often played leading roles. During strikes, factory-based and industry-wide strike committees proliferated, and business owners also began to organize. In addition, many organizations began to publish their own newspapers. During the October general strike, and in order to direct it, workers and socialists in St. Petersburg organized a *soviet*, or council—a harbinger of the then unknown future. Paralyzed in their essential activities and forced at last to recognize the immensity of the opposition, Nicholas II and his government finally capitulated. On October 30, the emperor, as advised by Witte, issued the October Manifesto. That brief document guaranteed civil liberties to the Russians, announced a Duma with the true legislative function of passing or rejecting all proposed laws, and promised a further expansion of the new order in Russia. In short, the October Manifesto made the empire of the Romanovs a constitutional monarchy.

It also split the opposition. Liberals were divided over whether these reforms were sufficient. The left-liberal Kadets considered the government's concessions positive but inadequate. A new party, the Union of 17 October, or Octobrists, felt that enough had been granted and feared that demands for further change would reignite popular violence and challenge the whole social order. Even more consequential was the split between almost all liberals and the popular movement. Socialists continued to encourage this mass movement and viewed the reforms as simply creating better opportunities to fight for a true democratic transformation of Russian politics and society. Thus divided, the opposition lost a great deal of its former power. In the middle of December the government arrested the members of the St. Petersburg Soviet. The Soviet's appeal for revolution found effective response only in Moscow where workers and some other radicals fought bitterly against the police and the soldiers, including a guards' regiment, from December 22 until January 1, 1906.

The year 1905 thus ended in Russia in bloody fighting. In the course of the winter, punitive expeditions and summary courts-martial restored order

NICHOLAS II: 1905–17 405

in many troubled areas. The extreme Right joined the army and the police; Rightist active squads, known as the "Black Hundreds," beat and even killed Jews, liberals, and other intellectuals. Proto-fascist in nature, this newly awakened Right thrived on ethnic and religious hatreds and appealed especially to wealthy peasants and to members of the lower middle class in towns.

## The Fundamental Laws

On May 6, 1906, virtually on the eve of the meeting of the First Duma, the government promulgated the Fundamental Laws. These laws provided the framework of the new Russian political system; the October Manifesto had merely indicated some of its guiding lines. According to the Fundamental Laws, the emperor retained huge powers. He continued in complete control of the executive, the armed forces, foreign policy—specifically making war and peace—succession to the throne, the imperial court, imperial domains, and so forth. He maintained unchanged his unique dominating position in relation to the Russian Church. And he even retained the title of autocrat. He was to call together the annual sessions of the Duma and to disband the Duma, in which case, however, he had to indicate the time of the election and of the meeting of the new Duma. He had veto power over legislation. Moreover, in case of emergency when the Duma was not in session, he could issue *ukazes* with the authority of laws, although they had to be submitted for approval to the next session of the Duma no later than two months after its opening.

The Duma, to be sure, received important legislative and budgetary rights and functions by the Fundamental Laws, but these rights were greatly circumscribed. Notably, almost 40 percent of the state budget, encompassing such items as the army, the navy, the imperial court, and state loans, stayed outside the purview of the Duma, while the remainder, if not passed by the Duma, was re-enacted in the amounts of the preceding year. Ministers and the entire executive branch remained responsible only to the emperor, although the Laws did contain complicated provisions for interpellation, that is, questioning of ministers by the Duma. Furthermore, the State Council, which had functioned since its creation by Alexander I as an advisory body of dignitaries, became rather unexpectedly the upper legislative chamber, equal in rights and prerogatives to the Duma and meant obviously as a conservative counterweight to it. "No more than half" of the membership of the upper house was to be appointed by the emperor—appointed not even for life but by means of annual lists—and the other half elected by the following groups: 56 with very high property standing by the provincial zemstva, 18 by the gentry, 12 by commerce and industry, 6 by the clergy, 6 by the Academy of Sciences and the universities, and 2 by the Finnish Diet. Legislation also extended the October Manifesto's promises of reform into social policy. Unions and even strikes were legalized—it was at this point that employers began to organize—though police retained extensive authority to monitor union activities and to close unions for engaging in illegal political activities. Greater press freedom was guaranteed, but in practice the press was carefully monitored and subject to punitive fines and even closure for overstepping the bounds of tolerated free speech.

Personally, Nicholas II increasingly regretted the power he ceded in 1905–6, and he would do what he could in the coming years to undo the concessions he had made under duress. Nicholas's letters and conversations in the months and years following 1905 make it clear that he had taken Witte's advice to issue the October Manifesto out of desperation, but that he had not and never would compromise his fundamental political values. He refused to accept as a principle, as distinct from an expedient for the sake of stability, limitations on the tsar's personal authority—hence his insistence that his title as autocrat be preserved and that so much power remain in his hands. But this had perilous consequences. It has been argued that Nicholas II, along with prominent conservative figures who supported and advised him, ultimately became a source of instability in the emerging political order of late Imperial Russia. While ministers like Witte and Stolypin and the legislators of the Duma worked to construct a stable polity around the ideal of a modernized autocracy ruling, however firmly, according to law and over a society of citizens, Nicholas II was at the forefront of those embracing a political vision that insisted on situating legitimate state power in the person of the emperor. As Wortman has argued, "rather than accommodating the monarchy to the demands for a civic nation," Nicholas II clung tenaciously to a tradition, established most strongly with Nicholas I, that "redefined the concept of nation to make it a mythical attribute of the monarch." The tsar's insistent attachment to this increasingly archaic political vision, it has been argued, could only have harmful consequences for Russia.

## The First Two Dumas

Whereas the Fundamental Laws introduced numerous restrictions on the position and powers of the Duma, the electoral law emphasized its representative character. The electoral system, despite its complexities and limitations, such as the grouping of the electorate on a social basis, indirect elections, especially in the case of the peasants, and a gross underrepresentation of urban inhabitants, allowed almost all Russian men to participate in the elections to the Duma, thus transforming overnight the empire of the tsars from a country with no popular representation to one which practiced virtually universal manhood suffrage. The relatively democratic nature of the electoral law resulted partly from Witte's decision in December 1905, at the time when the law received its final formulation, to make concessions to the popular mood. More significantly, it reflected the common assumption in government circles that the peasants, the simple Russian people, would vote for their tsar and for the Right. After a free election, the First Duma convened on May 10, 1906.

Contrary to its sanguine expectations, the government had suffered a decisive electoral defeat. According to Walsh, the 497 members of the First Duma could be classified as follows: 45 deputies belonged to parties of the Right; 32 belonged to various national and religious groups, for example, the

Poles and the Muslims; 184 were Kadets; 124 were representatives of different groups of the Left; and 112 had no party affiliation. The Kadets with 38 percent of the deputies thus emerged as the strongest political party in the Duma, and they had the added advantage of an able and articulate leadership well-versed in parliamentary procedure. Those to the Left of the Kadets, on the other hand, lacked unity and organization and wanted mainly to fight against the regime, purely and simply. The cause of the Left in the First Duma had been injured by the fact that both the Socialist Revolutionaries and the Social Democrats had largely boycotted the election to the Duma. The deputies with no political affiliation were mostly peasants who refused to align themselves permanently with any of the political groupings, but belonged in a general sense to the opposition. The government received support only from the relatively few members of the unregenerate Right and also from the more moderate Octobrists.

Not surprisingly, the government and the Duma could not work together. The emperor and his ministers clearly intended the Duma to occupy a position subordinate to their own, and they further infuriated many deputies by openly favoring the extreme Right. The Duma, in its turn, also proved quite intractable. The Left wanted merely to oppose and obstruct. The Kadets, while much more moderate and constructive, seem to have overplayed their hand: they demanded a constituent assembly, they considered the First Duma to be, in a sense, the Estates-General of 1789, and they objected to the Fundamental Laws, thus in effect telling the government to abdicate. Similarly, while they insisted on a political amnesty, they refused to proclaim their opposition to terrorism, lest their associates to the Left be offended. But the most serious clash came over the issue of land: the Duma wanted to distribute to the peasants the state, imperial family, and Church lands, as well as the estates of landlords in excess of a certain maximum, compensating the landlords; the government proclaimed alienation of private land inadmissible, even with compensation. The imperial regime continued to the last to stand on the side of the landlords. After seventy-three days and forty essentially fruitless sessions, Nicholas II dissolved the First Duma.

The dissolution had a strange sequel. Some 200 Duma deputies, over half of them Kadets, met in the Finnish town of Viborg and signed a manifesto that denounced the government and called for passive resistance by the people. It urged them not to pay taxes or answer the draft call until the convocation of a new Duma. Although the Viborg Manifesto cited as its justification certain irregularities in the dissolution of the First Duma, in itself it constituted a rash and unconstitutional step. And it turned out to be a blunder as well, for the country failed to respond. The Viborg participants were sentenced to three months in jail. More important, they lost the right to stand for election to the Second Duma which was thus deprived of much of its potential leadership.

In contrast to the first election, the government exerted all possible pressure to obtain favorable results in the election to the Second Duma, and it was assisted by the fact that much of Russia remained in a state of emergency. But the results again disappointed the emperor and his associates. Although—as one authoritative calculation has it—the Duma opposition, including mainly the Kadets and the Left, might have declined from 69 to 68 percent of the total number of deputies, it also became more extreme. In fact, a polarization of political opinion, with both wings gaining at the expense of the center, constituted the most striking aspect of the election. More specifically, the Kadet representation declined from 184 to 99 deputies, while the Social Democrats and the Socialist Revolutionaries, who this time participated fully in the election, gained respectively 64 and 20 seats. The entire Left membership in the Duma rose from 124 to 216 deputies. Significantly, the number of unaffiliated deputies declined by about 50 percent in the Second Duma.

The Second Duma met on March 5, 1907, and lasted for a little more than three months. It also found itself promptly at an impasse with the government. Moreover, its special opponent, the prime minister, was no longer the nonentity Ivan Goremykin—who had replaced the first constitutional prime minister, Witte, early in 1906—but the able and determined Petr Stolypin. Before it could consider Stolypin's important land reform, he had the Second Duma dissolved on June 16, using as a pretext its failure to comply immediately with his request to lift the immunity of fifty-five, and particularly of sixteen, Social Democratic deputies whom he wanted to arrest for treason.

## The Change in the Electoral Law and the Last Two Dumas

On the same day, June 16, 1907, Nicholas II and his minister arbitrarily and unconstitutionally changed the electoral law. The tsar mentioned as justification his historic power, his right to abrogate what he had granted, and his intention to answer for the destinies of the Russian state only before the altar of God who had given him his authority! The electoral change was, of course, meant to create a Duma that would cooperate with the government. The peasant representation was cut by more than half and that of the workers was also drastically cut, whereas the gentry gained representation quite out of proportion to its number. Also, Poland, the Caucasus, and some other border areas lost many deputies; and the representation of Central Asia was entirely eliminated on the ground of backwardness. At the same time the election procedure became more indirect and more involved, following in part the Prussian model. In addition, the minister of the interior received the right to manipulate electoral districts. It has been calculated that the electoral change of June 1907 produced the following results: the vote of a landlord counted roughly as much as the votes of 4 members of the upper bourgeoisie, or of 65 average middle-class people, or of 260 peasants, or of 540 workers. To put it differently, 200,000 members of the landed gentry were assured of 50 percent of the seats in the Duma.

The electoral change finally provided the government with a cooperative Duma. And indeed, by contrast with the first two Dumas, which lasted but a few months each, the Third Duma served its full legal term of five years, from 1907 to 1912, while the Fourth also continued for five years, from 1912 until the revolution of February 1917, which struck just before the Fourth Duma was to end. In the Third Duma the government had the support of some 310 out of the total of 442 deputies: about 160 representatives of the Right and about 150 Octobrists. The opposition, reduced to 120 seats, encompassed 54 Kadets, smaller numbers of other moderates, and only 33 deputies of the former Left. The Socialist Revolutionaries, it might be noted, boycotted the Third and Fourth Dumas. To indicate another aspect of the change, it has been calculated that whereas non-Great Russians had composed almost half of the membership of the First Duma, in the Third there were 377 Great Russians and 36 representatives of all the other nationalities of the empire.

In the election of 1912 the government made a determined effort to obtain a Right majority that would eliminate its dependence on the Octobrist vote, but it could not quite accomplish its purpose. The Fourth Duma contained approximately 185 representatives of the Right, 98 Octobrists, and 150 deputies to the left of the Octobrists. Because of their crucial central position, the Octobrists continued to play a major role in the Duma, although their number had been drastically diminished. For the rest, the gain of the Right found a certain counterbalance in the gain of the Left.

The Octobrists, who had replaced the Kadets after the electoral change of June 1907 as the most prominent party in the Duma, represented both the less conservative country gentry and business circles. While their Left wing touched the Kadets, Right Octobrists stood close to the old-fashioned Right. The party enjoyed the advantages of skillful leadership, in particular the leadership of Alexander Guchkov, and operated well in a parliament. The Octobrist deputies, it might be noted, were the wealthiest group in the last two Dumas. The Kadets, who became the loudest voice of the Duma opposition, were, above all, the party of professional people, although their influence extended to large layers of the middle class, especially perhaps of the upper middle class, as well as to some landlords and other groups. The Right, which consisted of more than one party, defended to the limit the interests of the landlords, although it also made demagogic efforts to obtain broader support and paraded some priests and peasants in the Dumas. Bitter dissatisfaction, widespread among the Russian masses, found a modicum of expression in the Duma Left.

## Stolypin's Policy

With the Duma under control, the government could develop its own legislative program. The architect of the program, Stolypin, has been described as the last truly effective and important minister of imperial Russia. Indeed, Abraham Asher has argued that Stolypin's "drive and persistence" and "commanding presence" were decisive in shaping the government's policies in the years 1906–11. Stolypin's aim consisted of "pacification" and reform. "Pacification" meant an all-out struggle against the revolutionaries, for, although the mass opposition movements characteristic of 1905 no longer threatened the regime, terrorism continued on a large scale. Practiced especially by the Battle Organization of the Socialist Revolutionaries and by the

Prime Minister Petr Stolypin. Contemporaries and historians have viewed Stolypin variously as the Russian leader doing the most to avert revolution through reform in the years after 1905 and as undermining progress by weakening the Duma and brutally repressing dissent. *(Central State Archive of Film, Photographic, and Sound Documents of St. Petersburg)*

Socialist Revolutionaries-Maximalists who had split from the main party, terrorism caused some 1,400 deaths in 1906 and as many as 3,000 in 1907. The victims included police officers and agents, various officials, high and low, and numerous innocent bystanders. In August 1906, for example, the Maximalists blew up Stolypin's suburban residence, killing 32 persons and wounding many others, including the prime minister's son and daughter, but not the prime minister himself.

Stolypin acted with directness and severity. By the end of 1906, 82 areas in the Russian Empire had been placed under different categories of special regulations; also, the publication of 206 newspapers had been stopped, and over 200 editors had been brought to court. Moreover, Stolypin introduced summary courts-martial, consisting of officers without juridical training, which tried those accused of terrorism and rebellion. The trials and the execution of sentences were carried out within a matter of some two days or even a few hours. Although the special courts-martial lasted only several months—because Stolypin never submitted the law creating them to the Duma and it expired two months after the Second Duma had met—they led to the execution of well over a thousand persons. "Stolypin's necktie"—the noose—became proverbial in Russia. The policy of "pacification" succeeded on the whole. The Maximalists and many other terrorists were killed or executed, while numerous revolutionaries escaped abroad. A relative quiet settled upon the country.

It should be added that Stolypin continued to sponsor police infiltration of the revolutionary movement and an extremely complex system of agents and informers. Such police practices led, among other things, to the emergence of remarkable double agents, the most notorious of whom, the unbelievable Evno Azeff, successfully combined the roles of the chief informer on the Socialist Revolutionaries and of leader of their Battle Organization. In the latter capacity he arranged the assassination of Plehve and other daring acts of terrorism.

Stolypin intended his "pacification" to constitute a prelude to important changes, especially to a fundamental agrarian reform. That reform, introduced by an imperial legislative order in the autumn of 1906, approved by the Third Duma in the summer of 1910, and developed by further legislative enactments in 1911, aimed at a break-up of the peasant commune and the establishment of a class of strong, independent, individual farmers—Stolypin's so-called wager on the strong and the sober. The emergence of a large group of prosperous and satisfied peasants would, presumably, transform the Russian countryside from a morass of misery and a hotbed of unrest into a conservative bulwark of the regime.

The new legislation divided all peasant communes into two groups: those that did not and those that did engage in land redistribution. In the first type all peasants simply received their landholdings in personal ownership. In the communes with periodic redistribution every householder could at any time request that the land to which he was entitled by redistribution be granted to him in personal ownership. He could also press the commune to give him the land not in scattered strips, but in a single location; the commune had in effect to comply with this request if separation occurred at the time of a general communal redistribution of land, and it had to meet the request "in so far as possible" at other times. Similarly, the commune had to divide its land into consolidated individual plots if requested to do so by not less than one-fifth of the total number of householders. Moreover, separated peasants invariably retained rights to common lands, meadows, forests, and the like. Indeed a partitioning even of pastures and grazing lands was permitted in 1911. Finally, the commune could be entirely abolished: by a majority vote in the case of non-repartitional communes, and by a two-thirds vote in the case of those that engaged in a redistribution of land. It is significant that the reform made the household elder the sole owner of the land of the household, replacing the former joint family ownership which remained only in the case of households containing members other than the elder's lineal descendants.

Stolypin's reform made peasants more equal legally to other classes and gave them greater potential freedom of mobility. The government also undertook other reforms, often in cooperation with the Dumas, including measures to develop popular education; in fact, a law of 1908 foresaw schooling for all Russian children by 1922. The government also broadened labor legislation, worked to strengthen the army and national defense, and engaged in a variety of other useful activities.

However, all this fell short of fundamental reform. Only Stolypin's controversial agrarian legislation attempted a sweeping change in the condition of the Russian people, and even that legislation had perhaps too narrow a scope, for Stolypin was determined not to confiscate any gentry land, even with recompense. Moreover, progressive measures remained intertwined with reaction. Thus constitutional Russia witnessed a terrorism of the Right—for example the assassinations in 1906 and 1907 of two Kadet deputies to the First Duma—as well as a terrorism of the Left, and the terrorism of the Right usually went unpunished. Stolypin, himself from the western borderlands, acted as a nationalist and a Russificator, for one thing reviving the ill-fated policy of trying to Russify Finland. Besides, the government lacked stability. The prime minister, who was after all something of a constitutionalist, antagonized much of the Right in addition to the Left. He managed to have one important piece of legislation enacted only by having the emperor prorogue the legislature for three days and suspend two leading members of the State Council; his highhanded tactics made the Octobrist leader Guchkov resign as chairman of the Third Duma. On September 14, 1911, Stolypin was fatally shot by a police agent associated with a revolutionary group. Stolypin's successor, Count Vladimir Kokovtsov, possessed intelligence and ability, but not his predecessor's determination or influence within the government. After a little more than two years he was replaced by the weak and increasingly senile Goremykin, who thus became prime minister for the second time. Goremykin assumed the leadership of the government in early 1914; in a matter of a few months he and Russia had to face the devastating reality of the First World War.

## Empire and Nation

The difficult question of Russian nationhood in an imperial context was a source of continuing official concern and policy. As we know, Russia was not an ethnic nation but an empire that included large numbers of other ethnicities, some of whom claimed independent national histories and others who were discovering and inventing themselves as nations. Non-Russian "minorities," based on native language, were already a slight majority in the empire at the time of the 1897 census: excluding Finland, which was not included in this census, only 44.9 percent of the population of the empire spoke Russian as their native language—of course, contemporaries viewed the Belorussian and Ukrainian languages as subcategories of Russian, so their inclusion restored a "Russian" majority. Many ethnic and religious minorities were active in urban centers, especially in business and the professions.

Scholars have debated whether or not it is useful to interpret empire in Russia with terms like imperialism, colonialism, orientialism, frontier, and borderlands—which suggest useful comparisons to Western histories and practices. At the level of state policy, certainly, it would be misleading to apply any single model: the treatment of Jews, Catholic Poles, Orthodox Ukrainians, Muslim Tatars, and "pagan" Evenks, for example, was not uniform. Also, local policies, shaped by imperial administrators and educators who often better understood local needs and possibilities, could differ from the policy directives coming from St. Petersburg. And individuals were treated differently depending on their professions and their degree of assimilation. In the words of one recent historian, the state's policy toward the empire's peoples was "enormously ambiguous, variable, uncertain, and contested."

On the one hand, the government of Nicholas II, like that of his father, promoted a renewed Russian nationalism that often had dire consequences for those defined as outside the national fold. Official images of the tsar's communion with his "people" pointedly excluded non-Russian nationalities. This exclusion grew especially strong after the disturbances of 1905, which Nicholas II blamed explicitly on non-Russians, especially Jews and Poles. Nicholas II also continued his father's policies of Russification among the non-Russian nationalities: insisting on Russian as the language of education and administration, promoting the settlement of ethnic Russians in the borderlands, supporting active Orthodox missionary work throughout the empire, tightening quotas on Jews and some other groups in higher education, tolerating anti-Jewish violence (some argue that the state instigated pogroms), reducing the representation of non-Russian national parties in the Duma, and suppressing radical nationalist parties and demonstrations.

But the government's approach to empire and nation was not a simple matter of Russian nationalist revivalism and the repression of the "other." The state also followed a policy, especially after 1905, of relative religious tolerance and greater possibilities for native leaders to play active roles in civic life. The effort to assimilate various ethnic groups into a common imperial polity could sometimes mean in practice respect for local customs and education in native languages. Imperial diversity was sometimes visibly celebrated in rituals such as when the tsar or imperial dignitaries visited the borderlands. But celebration of the empire's many peoples was often entwined with the ideology of national hierarchy and mission: the idea of Russia as a "civilized" nation bringing "order" and "culture" to "backward" peoples. Overall, the Russian imperial vision in these years was one of integration and uniformity. This was sometimes practiced in generous and inclusive ways. Most often, especially in the final years of the empire, the model was a polity that accepted difference only when it reinforced traditional authorities and imperial unity.

## Russian Foreign Policy, 1905–14

Like the other powers, Russia stumbled into the First World War. The tsarist government contributed its share to international alignments, tensions, and crises, and in the fateful summer of 1914 it decided to support Serbia and thus resort to arms. Yet its part of the infamous "war guilt" should not be exaggerated or singled out. Russian ambitions and eagerness for war were no greater than those of other countries, while Russian preparedness for an armed conflict proved to be less. The empire of the tsars took no part in the race for colonies overseas that constituted an important aspect of the background of the First World War. Russian interests and schemes in the Balkans and the Near East were paralleled by those of Austria-Hungary and eventually also to some extent by those of Germany. Even the early Russian mobilization found its counterpart in the Austrian. Finally, it has been argued, with the possible exception of Austria-Hungary, no one desired war in the summer of 1914; and Austria merely thought of a quick destruction of Serbia, not of a continental conflagration. Once war began, however, various aggressive desires, including Russian ones, were quickly brought into play. Along with rivalry and ambition, war broke out largely because Europe at the time lacked an effective system to resolve interstate conflicts. Also, no one foresaw how devastating and politically catastrophic a new continental war would be.

The years that followed the Russo-Japanese War witnessed an alienation or Russia from Germany, a virtual breakdown of Russo-Austrian relations, and at the same time a further *rapprochement* between Russia and France as well as the establishment of an Anglo-Russian Entente. The agreement with Great Britain, signed on August 31, 1907, was a landmark in Russian foreign policy, for it transformed a relationship of traditional and often bitter hostility into one of cordiality. That result was achieved through compromise in those areas where the interests of the two countries clashed: in Persia, Russia was assigned a large sphere of influence in the northern part of the country, and Great Britain a smaller one in the southeastern section, while the central area was declared neutral; Russia agreed to consider Afghanistan outside its sphere of influence and to deal with the Afghan ruler only through Great Britain, Great Britain in turn promising not to change the status of that country or interfere in its domestic affairs; both states recognized the suzerainty of China over Tibet. Because Great Britain and France had reached an agreement in 1904, the new accord marked the emergence of the Triple Entente of France, Russia, and Great Britain, poised against the Triple Alliance of Germany, Austria-Hungary, and Italy. It should be added that the alignment with France and Great Britain gained in popularity in Russia in the years preceding the First World War. It attracted the support of liberals, of many radicals, of business circles closely linked to French and British capital, and also of numerous conservatives who veered toward Pan-Slavism or suffered from tariff wars with Germany and objected to tariff arrangements with that country as detrimental to Russian agriculture.

Alexander Izvolsky, the Russian minister of foreign affairs from 1906 to 1910, also developed an active policy in the Balkans and the Near East. In fact he, his successor Sergei Sazonov, who headed the ministry from 1910 to 1916, and their various subordinates have been described as a new generation of Russian diplomats eager to advance Russian interests against Turkey and Austria-Hungary after a quarter-century of quiescence. To be sure, as early as 1896 the Russian ambassador in Constantinople, Alexander Nelidov, had proposed to his government that Russia seize the Straits, but that proposal was never implemented. Izvolsky devised a different scheme. In September 1908, in Buchlau, Moravia, he came to an agreement with the Austrian foreign minister, Count Alois von Aehrenthal: Russia would accept the Austrian annexation of Bosnia and Herzegovina, which Austria had been administering according to a decision of the Congress of Berlin; Austria-Hungary in turn would not object to the opening of the Straits to Russian warships. Austria-Hungary proceeded to annex Bosnia and Herzegovina before Russia could prepare diplomatically the desired reconsideration of the status of the Straits—a betrayal of the mutual understanding, according to Izvolsky, but not according to Aehrenthal. Betrayed or not, Russia was left holding the bag, because other powers, especially Great Britain, proved unwilling to see Russian warships in the Straits. The tsarist government experienced further humiliation when it hesitated to endorse the Austrian coup but was finally forced to do so after receiving a near-ultimatum from Germany.

The years following witnessed repeated tensions, crises, and conflicts in the Balkans and the Near East. Like Austria-Hungary and Russia, Germany also pursued a forward policy in that area. Two important Balkan wars were fought in 1912 and 1913. First Bulgaria, Serbia, Greece, and Montenegro combined to defeat Turkey and expand at Turkish expense. Next, the victors quarreled and the Bulgarians suffered a defeat by the Serbians, the Greeks, and the Montenegrins, as well as by the Romanians and by the Turks, who resumed hostilities to regain some of their losses. The Balkan wars left a legacy of tensions behind them, in particular making Bulgaria a dissatisfied and revisionist state and further exacerbating the relations between Austria-Hungary and Serbia.

When the heir to the Habsburg throne, Archduke Francis Ferdinand, was assassinated by Serbian patriots on June 28, 1914, and Austria delivered a crushing ultimatum to Serbia, the Russian government decided to support Serbia—the alternative was another, and this time complete, defeat in the Balkans. With the alliances operating almost automatically, Germany backed Austria-Hungary, while France stood by Russia. Austria-Hungary declared war on Serbia on July 28, Germany on Russia on August 1 and on France on August 3. The German attack on Belgium brought Great Britain to the side of France and Russia on August 4. Europe entered the First World War.

## Russia in the First World War

Wars have always been moments of truth in Russian history, revealing the country's strengths and weaknesses and thereby shaping politics. The Great

War, as it was then called in English, was no ordinary war. It was a protracted modern military conflict requiring unprecedented mobilization of society and economy as well as of military machinery and manpower. Russia had never been through such a trial. Initially, however, the outbreak of war in August 1914 quieted political and social protest, focusing hostilities against an external enemy. But this patriotic unity did not last long. Hostility toward the German Kaiser and the desire to defend their land and their lives did not necessarily translate into enthusiasm for the tsar or the government. For some, the war fed suspicions that the rich and powerful were pursuing their own interests, not those of the poor. As one peasant-soldier described attitudes among many soldiers already in 1914: "the war will do nothing for us and the Germans will give us a beating." By contrast, Russia's generals spoke with pride about the brave and righteous enthusiasm of the nation's fighting men and of their own good spirits.

Before very long, many Russians began to speak of the war as a catastrophe. Casualty rates were the most vivid sign of the disaster. By the end of 1914, only five months into the war, nearly 400,000 Russian men had lost their lives and nearly a million were injured. Far sooner than expected, scarcely trained recruits had to be called to active duty, a process repeated throughout the war as staggering losses continued to mount. The huge losses on the battlefields were not limited to men. The army quickly ran short of rifles and ammunition, and even uniforms and food. By mid-1915, as many as 25 percent of Russian soldiers were being sent to the front without arms, with instructions to pick up what they could from the dead. With good reason, soldiers began to complain that they were treated not as human beings or even as valuable soldiers but as raw material to be squandered by the rich and powerful. By the spring of 1915, the army was in steady retreat. It was not always orderly. Desertion, chaotic flight, and plunder were not uncommon.

By 1916, however, the situation improved. Russian troops ceased retreating and there were some modest successes in offensives staged that year, though at great loss of life. Also, the problem of shortages was largely solved by a major effort to increase domestic production. And yet, by the end of 1916, morale among soldiers was even worse than during the great retreat of 1915. The fortunes of war may have improved, but the fact of the war, still draining away the strength of the country and the lives of so many families and individuals, remained an oppressive fact. The crisis in morale, as Allan Wildman, a leading historian of the Russian army in war and revolution, argued, "was rooted fundamentally in the feeling of utter despair that the slaughter would ever end and that anything resembling victory could be achieved."

The war was devastating not only to the army. By the end of 1915, there were many signs that the economy was breaking down under the heightened strain of wartime demand. The main problems were food shortages and rising prices. Many conditions combined to produce these problems: labor shortages at the largest estates caused by the draft, falling supplies and rising prices for basic consumer goods, the preferences of smallholding peasants to produce for their own needs rather than for the market, and the government printing huge amounts of new money to pay for military production. Although the causes were complex, the effects were simple and clear, especially for the urban lower and middle classes. Inflation rapidly forced down real incomes, and shortages made it difficult to buy even what one could afford. Shortages were a problem especially in the capital—patriotically renamed Petrograd— where distance from supplies and poor transportation networks made matters particularly bad. Shops closed early or entirely for lack of bread, sugar, meat, and other provisions. And lines grew for what remained. It became increasingly difficult both to find and afford food. Not surprising strikes increased steadily from the middle of 1915. And so did crime. But mostly people suffered and endured: scouring the city for food (working-class women in Petrograd reportedly spent about forty hours a week in food lines), begging, turning to prostitution or crime, tearing down wooden fences to keep stoves heated for warmth, grumbling about the rich, and wondering when and how this would all end. With good reason, government officials responsible for public order worried about how long people's patience would last. A report in October 1916 by the Petrograd branch of the security police, the Okhrana, warned bluntly of "the possibility in the near future of riots by the lower classes of the empire enraged by the burdens of daily existence."

While the Russian command made its share of military mistakes, the political mistakes of the Russian government proved to be both greater and more damaging. Nicholas II and his ministers failed to utilize the national rally that followed the outbreak of the war. In fact, they continued to rely on exclusively bureaucratic means to mobilize the resources of the nation, and they proceeded to oppress ethnic and religious minorities in the areas temporarily won from Austria as well as in home provinces. Russian defeats, the collapse of Russian supply, and the utter incompetence of the war minister, General Vladimir Sukhomlinov, as well as of some other high officials, did lead, to be sure, to certain adjustments. The Duma was finally called together in August 1915 for a short session, Sukhomlinov and three of his colleagues had to resign, and the government began to utilize the efforts of society to support the army. These efforts, it should be added, which were led by public figures and industrialists such as Guchkov, had developed on a large scale, ranging from work in the Red Cross to widespread measures to increase production of military materiel. The Zemstvo Union and the Union of Towns, which joined forces under the chairmanship of Prince Georgii Lvov, and the War Industry Committee, led by Guchkov, became especially prominent.

But the *rapprochement* between the government and the educated public turned out to be slight and fleeting. Nicholas II would not cooperate with the newly created, moderate Progressive Bloc led by Miliukov, which included the entire membership of the Duma, except the extreme Right and the extreme Left, and which won majority support even in the State Council. Instead he came to rely increasingly on his wife Empress Alexandra and on her extraordinary advisor, the peasant holy man Grigorii Rasputin, whose exalted

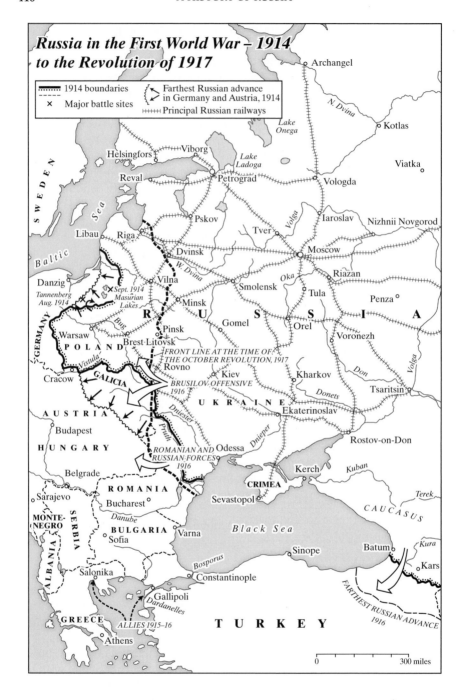

Russia in the First World War – 1914 to the Revolution of 1917

Grigorii Rasputin. A contemporary caricature, titled "The Russian Ruling House," portraying Rasputin as the puppeteer controlling Nicholas and Alexandra. Many such images were in circulation, often in the form of postcards—including some suggesting an immoral intimate relationship between Rasputin and Alexandra. (Fülöp-Miller, *Rasputin*)

position resulted from the empress's belief that he could protect their son from hemophilia and that he had been sent by God to guide her, her husband, and Russia. Making matters worse, Nicholas II, confident of God's guidance and the inspiring effect his presence would have among officers and troops, left for the front to take personal command of the armed forces. As a result, it seemed to many Russians that the levers of government had fallen into the hands of the "German" empress and the "dissolute" Rasputin. The following description by a historian echoes the view of many contemporaries: "a narrow-minded, reactionary, hysterical woman and an ignorant, weird peasant...had the destinies of an empire in their hands." Ministers changed rapidly in what was described as "ministerial leapfrog," and each was more under Rasputin's power than his predecessor. In general, the abysmal quality of these high-level appointments—rumors were widespread that Interior Minister Alexander Protopopov was demented from advanced syphilis—made the political unaccountability of the ministers all the more grating. In December 1916, Rasputin was assassinated. The long and gruesome murder was engineered by a leader of the extreme Right, a member of the imperial family, and an aristocrat related to the imperial family by marriage. Their goal was to save the dynasty and Russia. As the year 1917 began, there were discussions of a palace coup to restore sanity and leadership to the imperial government. But a popular revolution came first.

# CHAPTER 32

# The Economic and Social Development of Russia from the "Great Reforms" until the Revolutions of 1917

Life is movement....Telegraph wires encircle the world, causing every heart to beat with common human interest. Only local circumstances vary.

THE NEWSPAPER COLUMNIST "SKITALETS" (THE
WANDERER) IN *GAZETA-KOPEIKA*, JULY 1911

Our reality is dismal. The year's results are nil. And hope has flown away from us. What, for example, might we recall about the year that has just passed into eternity? We met the new year with noisy wishes of "new happiness," but when the year ended there was little to show for it. What did it bring us? What remained? Nothing. Nothing besides bitterness and disillusionment. Not only no "new happiness" but no happiness at all.

"SKITALETS" IN *GAZETA-KOPEIKA*, JANUARY 1913

Every social class felt the impact of the "great reforms" and of their aftermath. The gentry, to be sure, remained the dominant social group in the country. In fact, as already indicated, both Alexander III and Nicholas II made every effort to strengthen the gentry and to support its interests. Court circles consisted mainly of great landlords. The bureaucracy that ran the empire was closely linked on its upper levels to the landlord class. The ministers, senators, members of the State Council, and other high officials in the capital and the governors, vice-governors, and heads of various departments in the provinces belonged predominantly to the gentry. With the establishment in 1889 of land captains to be appointed from the local gentry, Russia obtained a new network of gentry officials who effectively controlled the peasants. A year later the zemstvo "counterreform" greatly strengthened the role of the gentry in local self-government and emphasized the class principle within that government. In the army most high positions were held by members of the landlord class, while virtually the entire officer corps of the navy belonged to the gentry. The government supported gentry agriculture by such measures as the establishment in 1885 of the State Gentry Land Bank, which provided funds for the landlords on highly favorable terms.

Nevertheless, the gentry class declined after the "great reforms." Members of the gentry owned 73.1 million *desiatin** of land according to the census of 1877, 65.3 million according to the census of 1887, 53.2 in 1905 according to a statistical compilation of that year, and only 43.2 million desiatin in 1911 according to Nikolai Oganovsky's calculations. At the same time, to quote Geroid Robinson: "The average size of their holdings also diminished, from 538.2 *desiatinas* in 1887 to 488 in 1905; and their total possession of work horses from 546,000 in 1888–1891, to 499,000 in 1904–6—that is, by 8.5 percent." Although the emancipation settlement was on the whole generous to the gentry, it should be kept in mind that a very large part of the wealth of that class had been mortgaged to the state before 1861 and that, therefore, much of the compensation that the landlords received as part of the reform went to pay debts, rather little remaining for development and modernization of the gentry economy. Moreover, most landlords failed to make effective use of their resources and opportunities. Deprived of serf labor and forced to adjust to more intense competition and other harsh realities of the changing world, members of the gentry had little in their education, outlook, or character to make them successful capitalist farmers. A considerable number of landlords, in fact, preferred to live in Paris or Nice, spending whatever they had, rather than face the new conditions in Russia. Others remained on their estates and waged a struggle for survival, but, as statistics indicate, frequently without success. Uncounted "cherry orchards" left gentry possession. The important fact, much emphasized by Soviet scholars, that a small segment of the gentry did succeed in making the adjustment and proceeded to accumulate great wealth in a few hands does not fundamentally change the picture of the decline of a dominant class.

## The Industrialization of Russia

If the "great reforms" helped push the gentry down a steep incline, they also led to the rise of a Russian middle class, and in particular of industrialists, businessmen, and technicians—both results, to be sure, were not at all intentional. It is difficult to conceive of a modern industrial state based on serfdom, although, of course, the elimination of serfdom constituted only one prerequisite for the development of capitalism in Russia. Even after the emancipation

---

*A *desiatina* equals 2.7 acres.

Count Sergei Witte in St. Petersburg in 1905.   *(Terra Publishers)*

the overwhelmingly peasant nature of the country convinced many observers that the empire of the tsars could not adopt the Western capitalist model as its own. The populists argued that the Russian peasant was self-sufficient, producing his own food and clothing, and that he, in his egalitarian peasant commune, did not need capitalism and would not respond to it. Perhaps more to the point, the peasant was miserably poor and thus could not provide a sufficient internal market for Russian industry. Also the imperial government, especially the powerful Ministry of the Interior, preoccupied with the maintenance of autocracy and the support of the gentry, for a long time in effect turned its back on industrialization.

Nevertheless, Russian industry continued to grow, and in the 1890s it shot up at an amazing rate, estimated by Alexander Gerschenkron at 8 percent a year on the average. Russian industrialists could finally rely on a better system of transportation, with the railroad network increasing in length by some 40 percent between 1881 and 1894 and doubling again between 1895 and 1905. In addition to Russian financial resources, foreign capital began to participate on a large scale in the industrial development of the country: foreign investment in Russian industry has been estimated at 100 million rubles in 1880, 200 million in 1890, and over 900 million in 1900. Most important, the Ministry of Finance under Witte, in addition to building railroads and trying to attract capital from abroad, did everything possible to develop heavy industry in Russia. To subsidize that industry Witte increased Russian exports, drastically curtailed imports, balanced the budget, introduced the gold standard, and used heavy indirect taxation on items of everyday consumption to squeeze the necessary funds out of the peasants. Thus, in Russian conditions, the state played the leading role in bringing large-scale capitalist enterprise into existence.

Toward the end of the century Russia possessed eight basic industrial regions, to follow the classification adopted by Liashchenko. The Moscow industrial region, comprising six provinces, contained textile industries of every sort, as well as metal processing and chemical plants. The St. Petersburg region specialized in metal processing, machine building, and textile industries. The Polish region had textile, coal, iron, metal processing, and chemical industries. The recently developed south Russian Ukrainian region supplied coal, iron ore, and basic chemical products. The Ural area continued to produce iron, nonferrous metals, and minerals. The Baku sector in Transcaucasia contributed oil. The southwestern region specialized in beet sugar. Finally, the Transcaucasian manganese-coal region supplied substantial amounts of its two products.

The new Russian industry displayed certain striking characteristics. Because Russia industrialized late and rapidly, the Russians borrowed advanced Western technology wholesale, with the result that Russian factories were often more modern than their Western counterparts. Yet this progress in certain segments of the economy went together with appalling backwardness in others. Indeed, the industrial process frequently juxtaposed complicated machinery and primitive manual work performed by a cheap, if unskilled, labor force. For technological reasons, but also because of government policy, Russia acquired huge plants and large-scale industries almost overnight. Before long the capitalists began to organize: a metallurgical syndicate was formed in 1902, a coal syndicate in 1904, and several others in later years. Russian entrepreneurs and employers, it might be added, came from different classes—from gentry to former serfs—with a considerable admixture of foreigners. Their leaders included a number of old merchant and industrialist families who were Old Believers, such as the celebrated Morozovs. As to markets, since the poor Russian people could absorb only a part of the products of Russian factories, the industrialists relied on huge government orders and also began to sell more abroad. In particular, because Russian manufactures were generally unable to compete successfully in the West, export began on a large scale to the adjacent Middle Eastern and Asian countries of Turkey, Persia, Afghanistan, Mongolia, and China. Again Witte and the government helped all they could by such means as the establishment of the Russo-Persian Bank and the Russo-Chinese Bank, and the building of the East China Railway, not to mention the Trans-Siberian. As already indicated, Russian economic activity in the Far East was part of the background of the Russo-Japanese War.

The great Russian industrial upsurge of the 1890s ended with the depression of 1900, produced by a number of causes, but perhaps especially by the "increasing weakness of the base," the exhaustion of the Russian peasantry. The depression lasted several years and became combined with political unrest and finally with the Revolution of 1905. Still, once order had been restored and the Russians returned to work, industrialization resumed its course. In fact, the last period of the economic development of imperial Russia, from the calling of the First Duma to the outbreak of the First World War, witnessed rapid industrialization, although it was not as rapid as in the 1890s, with an annual industrial growth rate of perhaps 6 percent compared to the 8 percent of the earlier period. The output of basic industries again soared, with the exception of the oil industry. Thus, counting in millions of *pudy** and using 1909 and 1913 as the years to be compared, the Russian production of pig iron rose from 175 to 283, of iron and steel from 163 to 246, of copper from 1.3 to 2.0, and of coal from 1,591 to 2,214.

The new industrial advance followed in many ways the pattern of the previous advance, for instance, in the emphases on heavy industry and on large plants. Yet it exhibited some significant new traits as well. With the departure of Witte, the government stopped forcing the pace of industrialization, decreased the direct support of capitalists, and relaxed somewhat the financial pressure on the lower classes. Russian industry managed to make the necessary adjustments, for it was already better able to stand on its own feet. Also, industry often had the help of banks, which began to assume a guiding role in the economic development of the country. But, financial capital aside, Russian industrialists themselves were gradually gaining strength and independence. Also, it can well be argued that during the years immediately preceding the First World War Russian industry was becoming more diversified, acquiring a larger home market, and spreading its benefits more effectively to workers and consumers.

To be sure, the medal had its reverse side. In spite of increasing production in the twentieth century, imperial Russia was falling further behind the leading states of the West—or so it is claimed by many analysts. Just as the Russian government relied on foreign loans, Russian industry remained heavily dependent on foreign capital, which rose to almost two and a quarter billion rubles in 1916/17 and formed approximately one-third of the total industrial investment. The French, for example, owned nearly two-thirds of the Russian pig iron and one-half of the Russian coal industries, while the Germans invested

---

*A *pud* equals 36 pounds.

heavily in the chemical and electrical engineering industries, and the British in oil. On the basis of investment statistics some analysts have even spoken of Russia's "semi-colonial" status. More ominously, Russian industry rose on top of a bitter and miserable proletariat and a desperately poor peasant mass.

## The Peasant Question

The vast majority of Russians were peasants: at 85 percent of the total population, according to a statistical report of 1913, Russia had the highest proportion of rural dwellers in Europe at that time. Although peasant emancipation was the greatest of the "great reforms," the condition of the freed peasants remained one of the gravest problems in Russia. As mentioned, the emancipation provisions proved to be insufficient to develop a healthy peasant economy. Peasants themselves, scholars have argued, felt not only the impossibility of their new situation but also its injustice. The widespread belief among peasants that the land ought to belong to those who work it made any settlement that left in place large private land owners using hired labor likely disappointing. But it especially grated that the emancipation did not even give to peasants all of the land that they had formerly been farming for themselves.

A great deal of everyday peasant life changed little after the abolition of serfdom in 1861. Work, community, family, and religion remained the hallmarks of everyday life in the village. Subsistence family farming and handicraft manufacture were still central to daily experience, little changed by technological innovation. Village life was largely controlled by the commune (*obshchina* or *mir*), acting most often through its assembly of male heads of household. The family remained the foundational unit of everyday peasant social and economic life. Within the family, the male head of household exercised enormous power: controlling, sometimes brutally, the behavior of family members; representing the family at assemblies of the village commune; and holding village administrative, police, and judicial posts. In this patriarchal world, women were relegated to domestic and some farming work and to ceremonial life. Religious life, in which women had the largest role to play, was an Orthodoxy (though Old Belief was strong in many areas of the country and sectarianism common) that, as of old, complexly blended folk, magical, and Church traditions.

Evidence of profound change in the experiences and expectations of peasants in these years was no less significant. Most frightening to elites, some peasants were becoming engaged politically. In the midst of the national upheavals of 1905–7, when the possibilities for change seemed high, peasants voiced their discontent and desires openly in petitions to the government and through new political organizations such as the All-Russian Peasant Union. Even larger numbers took direct action, seizing land, taking and redistributing grain, pillaging landlords' property, and burning manor houses. More subtle but no less important changes in peasant society and culture were also occurring. With enormous consequence, peasants were becoming less and less a "world apart." Partly, this resulted from the policies of the government,

A staged photograph taken around 1900 by British photographer Netta Peacock of a meeting of the peasant commune (the mir), comprising heads of households. The mir has been interpreted variously as an instrument of the state for taxing and controlling peasants, a means of collective survival, an expression of peasant notions of moral order and justice, a form of primitive socialism on which basis a socialist society could be created in Russia, a backward hindrance to modern rural economic development, and a means for male patriarchs to exercise domination in the village. (*Victoria and Albert Museum*)

which began, after the turn of the century, to remove some of the disabilities that marked peasants as a distinct and legally inferior social estate: collective responsibility for tax payment was ended in 1903, corporal punishment was abolished in 1904, and Stolypin's reforms began to free peasants from the rule of the commune. In addition, various outsiders to the village—educated reformers, teachers, clergy, and others—were an increasing presence, organizing cooperatives, mutual assistance organizations, lectures and readings, theaters, and temperance societies. The expansion of schooling and literacy, to be discussed in the next chapter, and the huge rise in newspapers and literature directed at common people, which even the illiterate could hear read and discussed in village taverns and tearooms, exposed peasants in unprecedented ways to knowledge of the larger world. Perhaps most important, Russia's continuing economic development made it possible for many peasants to leave the village for industrial and urban work. This experience affected the lives of millions of peasants—not only the migrants themselves but also their kin and fellow villagers when these individuals returned to the countryside after seasonal or temporary industrial or commercial work, on holidays, or after becoming sick or aged. In quite tangible ways, peasant everyday life was changing. Many peasants, especially younger men and women who had been to the city, demonstrated new social values (for example, in personal and sexual relations), began wearing urban-style clothing, and purchased, or at least desired, commodities such as clocks, urban furniture, stylish boots and hats, porcelain dishes, and cosmetics. Raised expectations and stimulated desire, of course, could also bring greater frustration. What was said of peasant women who had worked in the city can be said of many individual peasants in these years whose lives were no longer confined by tradition: they were "distinguished by livelier speech, greater independence, and a more obstinate character." These changes brought pleasure and stimulated expectations and desires but could also bring frustration and danger, especially given peasant economic realities.

As we have seen before, the commune stood at the center of the peasant economy as well as peasant society. After emancipation, the communes were given control of peasant lands and were made responsible for taxes and recruits and were in general intended to serve as bulwarks of order and organized life in the countryside. As a result, the commune became more important than ever in the lives of peasants. Acting through the periodic assembly of male heads of household, the commune made the major decisions about land use—what work should be done in each field, when it should be done, and by which methods—and periodically, according to tradition, redistributed the holdings, which were divided into scattered strips among peasant families on the basis of a calculus of hands to work and mouths to feed. The commune also carried out a wide range of administrative functions to sustain the village community. In addition to collecting taxes and designating military recruits, the commune controlled who had permission to work away from the village, investigated and punished petty crimes, maintained roads and bridges, kept up the local church or chapel, and cared for needy members of the community, especially widows and orphans without kin and the aged. No doubt they helped many peasants keep their bearings in post-reform Russia, and they usually provided at least minimal security for their members.

The economic price of communal authority in agriculture may have been high, however. In the view of most contemporaries (and most historians, though debate continues), the commune tended to keep productivity low—and hence peasant need for more land high—by perpetuating backward, indeed archaic, agricultural production. To be sure, some circumstances were beyond the peasants' control, such as shortages in draft animals and fertilizer, the continued use of less efficient equipment such as wooden plows, and the lack of investment capital. But, it has been argued, low productivity was also the "fault" of communal agriculture. Since the land a peasant family worked might eventually belong to some other family through redistribution, individuals had little incentive to improve their soil through modern techniques such as fertilization, deep plowing, or crop diversification. The division of land into small strips in each field, in order to allow each household to receive land of every quality, resulted in much unused land between strips, led to inefficient use of time, and compelled conformity with the practices of one's neighbors. More generally, the heads of household who dominated the commune tended to see custom, not innovative scientific advice, as the best guide. At the same time communes greatly hampered peasant mobility and promoted ever-increasing overpopulation in the countryside. Members of a commune frequently found it difficult to obtain permission to leave, because their departure would force the commune to perform its set obligations to the state with fewer men. Also, where communes periodically redivided the land among the households, the head of the household could prevent the departure of one of its members on the ground that that would result in a smaller allotment of land to the household at the next reapportionment.

Population in Russia grew rapidly after the emancipation: from over 73 million in 1861 to over 125 million according to the census of 1897 and almost 170 million in 1917. Land prices more than doubled between 1860 and 1905, and almost doubled again between 1905 and 1917. In spite of the fact that peasants purchased much of the land sold over a period of time by the gentry, individual peasant allotments kept shrinking. Russian economic historians have calculated that 28 percent of the peasant population of the country could not support itself from its land allotments immediately after the emancipation, and that by 1900 that figure had risen to 52 percent. That the allotments still compared reasonably well with the allotments of peasants in other countries proved to be cold comfort, for with the backward conditions of agriculture in Russia they plainly did not suffice. The average peasant ownership of horses also declined sharply, with approximately one-third of peasant households owning no horses by 1901. The peasants, of course, tried a variety of ways to alleviate their desperate plight, from periodic employment in the cities to migration, but with limited success at best. They worked as hard as they could, exhausting themselves and the land, and competing for every bit of it. In this marginal economy droughts became disasters, and the famine of 1891 was a shattering catastrophe. But even without outright famine peasants died rapidly. At the beginning of the twentieth century, the annual death rate for European Russia, with the countryside leading the cities, stood at 31.2 per 1,000, compared to 19.6 in France and 16 in England. Naturally, conditions differed in the enormous Russian Empire, with Siberian peasants, for example, reasonably prosperous. On the other hand, perhaps the worst situation prevailed in the thickly populated provinces of central European Russia—caused by the so-called "pauperization of the center." How the peasants themselves felt about their lot became abundantly clear in the agrarian disturbances culminating in the massive upheavals of 1905–7.

To appreciate the burden that the Russian peasant had to carry, we should take further note of the fiscal pressures on peasants. Thus, an official inquiry indicated that after the emancipation the peasants paid annually to the state in taxes, counting redemption payments, ten times as much per desiatina of land as did members of the gentry. And even after the head tax was abolished in

1886 and the redemption payments were finally canceled in 1905, the impoverished masses continued to support the state by means of indirect taxes.
These taxes, perennially the main source of imperial revenue, were levied on
domestic and imported items of everyday consumption such as vodka, sugar,
tea, tobacco, cotton, and iron. The tax on alcohol, which Witte made a state
monopoly in 1894, proved especially lucrative. While relentless financial pressure forced the peasants to sell all they could, the government, particularly
Witte, promoted the export of foodstuffs, notably grain, to obtain a favorable
balance of trade and finance Russia's industrialization. Foodstuffs constituted
almost two-thirds in value of all Russian exports in the first years of the twentieth century compared to some two-fifths at the time of the emancipation.

However, the last years of imperial Russia, the period from the Revolution
of 1905 to the outbreak of the First World War, brought some hope and
improvement—many authorities claim much hope and great improvement—
into the lives of the Russian peasants, that is, the bulk of the Russian people.
The upswing resulted from a number of factors. As already indicated, the
industrialization of Russia no longer demanded or obtained the extreme sacrifices characteristic of the 1890s, and the new Russian industry had more to offer
to the consumer. The national income in fifty provinces of European Russia
rose, according to Sergei Prokopovich's calculation, from 6,579.6 million rubles
in 1900 to 11,805.5 million in 1913. In 1913 the per capita income for the whole
Russian Empire amounted to 102.2 rubles, a considerable increase even if highly
inadequate compared to the figures of 292 rubles for Germany, 355 for France,
463 for England, or 695 for the United States. Luckily, the years preceding the
First World War witnessed a series of bountiful harvests. Russian peasants
profited, in addition, from a remarkable growth of the cooperative movement,
and from government sponsorship of migration to new lands. Cooperatives
multiplied from some 2,000 in 1901 and 4,500 in 1905 to 33,000 at the outbreak
of the First World War, when their membership extended to 12 million people.
Credit and consumers' cooperatives led the way, although some producers'
cooperatives, such as Siberian creamery cooperatives, also proved highly successful. As to migration, the government finally began to support it after the
Revolution of 1905 by providing the necessary guiding agencies and also by
small subsidies to the migrants, suspension of certain taxes for them, and the
like. In 1907 over half a million people moved to new lands and in 1908 the
annual number of migrants rose to about three-quarters of a million. After
that, however, it declined to the immediate pre-war average of about 300,000
a year. Land under cultivation increased from 88.3 million desiatin in 1901–5
to 97.6 million in 1911–13. Also as mentioned earlier, the Peasant Land Bank
became much more active, helping peasants to purchase over 4.3 million desiatin of land in the decade from 1906 to 1915, compared to 0.96 million in the preceding ten years. State and imperial family lands amounting to about a million
and a quarter desiatin were offered for sale to the peasants.

Stolypin's land reform could well be considered the most important factor in the changing rural situation, because it tried to transform the Russian
countryside. Stolypin's legislation of 1906, 1910, and 1911—outlined in the

preceding chapter—aimed at breaking up the peasant commune and at creating a strong class of peasant proprietors. These peasant proprietors were to have their land in consolidated lots, not in strips. In a relatively brief span of years, the reform had considerable impact, though historians still debate how deep the changes went and what the precise effects of the changes were. Most agree that by January 1, 1916, only 24 percent of formerly communal households completed their legal withdrawal from the commune, thus transforming their lands into personal ownership. But many scholars emphasize greater spread and potentiality of the reform. Although only 470,000 households in non-repartitional communes had time to receive legal confirmation of their new independent status, the law of 1910 made in effect all householders in such communes individual proprietors. Two million would thus be a more realistic figure than 470,000. If we make this adjustment and if we add to the newly established independent households the 3 million or more hereditary tenure households in areas where communal ownership had never developed, we obtain for European Russia at the beginning of 1916 over 7 million individual proprietary households out of the total of 13 or 14 million. In other words, peasant households operating within the framework of the peasant commune had declined to somewhat less than half of all peasant households in Russia. Consolidation of strips, a crucial aspect of the reform, proceeded much more slowly than separation from the commune, but it too made some progress. One important set of figures indicates that of the almost 2.5 million households that had left communes somewhat more than half had been provided with consolidated farms by 1916.

Still, these impressive statistics do not necessarily indicate the ultimate wisdom and success of Stolypin's reform. True, Stolypin has received much praise from many specialists, including post-Soviet Russian historians and such American scholars as Donald Treadgold, who believe that the determined prime minister was in fact saving the empire and that, given time, his agrarian reform would have achieved its major objective of transforming and stabilizing the countryside. But critics have also been numerous and by no means limited to populists or other defenders of the commune as such. They have pointed, for example, to the limited scope of Stolypin's reform, which represented, in a sense, one more effort to save gentry land by making the peasants redivide what they already possessed, and to the element of compulsion in the carrying out of the reform. They argued that the reform had largely spent itself without curing the basic ills of rural Russia. Moreover, it added new problems to the old ones, in particular by helping to stratify the peasant mass and by creating hostility between the stronger and richer peasants whom the government helped to withdraw from the commune on advantageous terms and their poorer and more egalitarian brethren left behind.

## The Working Class

The most visible sign of Russia's industrialization and urban development since the middle of the nineteenth century was the large numbers of industrial workers, most of them recently uprooted from the countryside and left to fend for themselves in the harsh world of the city. Russian industrial workers numbered over 2 million in 1900 and perhaps 3 million out of a population of about 170 million in 1914. Not impressive in quantity in proportion to total population, the proletariat was more densely massed in Russia than in other countries. Because of the heavy concentration of Russian industry, over half the industrial enterprises in Russia employed more than 500 workers each, with many employing more than 1,000 each. The workers thus formed large and closely knit groups in industrial centers, which included St. Petersburg and Moscow.

Working conditions were eased in the late 1800s by labor legislation. Minister of Finance Bunge tried to eliminate or curb certain glaring abuses of the factory system and established factory inspectors to supervise the carrying out of new laws. More legislation followed later, with a law in 1897 applicable to industrial establishments employing more than 20 workers that limited day work of adults to eleven and a half hours and night work to ten hours. The ten-hour day was also to prevail on Saturdays and on the eve of major holidays, while no work was allowed on Sundays or the holidays in question. Adolescents and children were to work no more than ten and nine hours a day respectively. A pioneer labor insurance law, holding the employers responsible for accidents in connection with factory work, came out in 1903, but an improved and effective labor insurance act, covering both accidents and illness, appeared only in 1912. Unions were finally allowed in 1906, and even then exclusively on the local, not the national, level.

However, in spite of labor legislation, and also in spite of the fact that wages probably increased in the years preceding the First World War, Russian workers remained in general in miserable condition. Workers endured overcrowded housing with often deplorable sanitary conditions, an exhausting workday (ten hours a day, six days a week, even after the reforms of the late nineteenth century), widespread disease (notably tuberculosis) and high rates of premature mortality (made worse by pervasive alcoholism), constant risk of injury from poor safety conditions, harsh workplace discipline, and inadequate wages. The positive benefits of urban industrial life also affected the lives of urban workers, though these could be just as dangerous to the social and political status quo. Acquiring new skills and learning to cope with city life often gave workers a new sense of self-respect and confidence, which in turn tended to raise desires and expectations. The expanding array of consumer goods could provide new pleasures and hope, but with very limited incomes workers were just as likely to feel envy and anger. Also, urban workers were more likely than peasants to be or to become literate, exposing them to a range of new experiences and ideas. Indeed, the very act of reading and becoming "cultured" encouraged many commoners to feel a sense of self-esteem that made the ordinary deprivations, hardships, and humiliations of lower-class life more difficult to endure.

Not surprisingly, workers began to organize to better their lot. Indeed, they exercised at times sufficient pressure to further labor legislation, notably

Alexei Medvedev, a compositor, around 1903. A worker in a Moscow printing house, Medvedev was one of the organizers of a printers' strike in 1903 and of an illegal trade union, one of the first in Russia. Dressing in "bourgeois" fashion was a common gesture among "conscious" workers, meant to signal respectability and a recognition of their own human dignity, the violation of which was a central theme in workers' protests. (*Moskovskie pechatniki v 1905 godu*)

in the case of the law of 1897, and they were not deterred by the fact that unions remained illegal until after the Revolution of 1905 and were still hampered and suspected by the government thereafter. The first significant strikes occurred in St. Petersburg in 1878 and 1879 and at a Morozov textile factory near Moscow in 1885. The short-lived but important Northern Workers' Union, led by a worker and populist, Stepan Khalturin, helped to organize the early labor movement in the capital. Major strikes took place in the 1890s, not only in St. Petersburg, but also in Riga, in industrial areas of Russian Poland, and in new plants in the Ukraine. In addition, railwaymen struck in several places. The strike movement again gathered momentum in the first years of the twentieth century, culminating, as we know, in the Revolution of 1905. Strikes broke out in almost every industry and every part of the country. Trade unions and soviets proliferated. The government legalized strikes in December 1905 and unions in March 1906, clearly hoping that legalizing strikes and unions and allowing workers to vote for representatives to the new State Duma would lead the labor movement onto a more peaceful path. Initially, this appeared to be precisely what happened. Thousands of workers joined the legal unions and concentrated on attaining better economic conditions. For their leaders, workers tended to choose activists from the more moderate wing of Social Democrats, the Mensheviks, who emphasized, at least for the short term, legal struggle for realizable and mainly liberal-democratic gains. This moderation of the labor movement did not continue, however. The fault was partly the government's. Although trade unions were authorized by law, they remained under very close surveillance and control by the police, who regularly closed meetings, arrested leaders, and shut down union papers. Meanwhile, employers formed their own strong organizations and endeavored, often with success, to take back economic gains workers had made in 1905. When the strike movement revived in 1910–14, workers' frustrations were sharply visible, not only in the stubborn persistence of strikers and the revival of political demands, but also in the growing popularity of the more radical Bolsheviks. Many unions elected Bolshevik majorities to their governing boards. And in the fall of 1912, Bolsheviks won a majority of workers' votes to the Duma in almost all industrial electoral districts. Strikes became especially frequent after the massacre of workers in the Lena gold fields in April 1912, when police fired into a crowd of protesting workers killing and wounding more than a hundred of them. In 1912, 725,000 workers went out on strike, 887,000 in 1913, and more than 1.25 million from January to July 1914. In July 1914, only days before the outbreak of war, a large and sometimes violent strike broke out in St. Petersburg, echoing a strike in the Baku oil fields.

Workers' strike demands often combined the economic with the political, but they also very often included what historians have called moral demands for decent treatment that respected workers' "dignity." At the same time, labor protest could contain a great deal of bitter resentment and anger, even violence. Of course, evidence of labor protest is not the whole story of working-class mentalities. Many activists among workers, and many "conscious" workers themselves, regularly complained that, most of the time, the average working-class man lived a debased life marked by drunkenness, passivity before fate, and crass tastes in boulevard fiction, the music hall, and (by the eve of the war) low-brow popular cinema. Working-class women, in turn, were viewed as victims—of men's lies about wages spent on drink or of men's fists—and as lost in even deeper "backwardness" than most male workers. Some historians have argued that such mentalities, tastes, and behaviors were a type of defiance against elite moral norms, even a form of protest against class domination. But labor activists at the time, both intellectuals and workers themselves, constantly worried that such "rebellion" did not point to any solution other than escape.

## Civil Society

One of the most consequential developments in Russian life after the Great Reforms, recent scholarship has emphasized, was the expansion of the public sphere in the late 1800s and early 1900s. The growth of a civic space in which organized associations mediate between the individual and the state, citizens communicate with one another on matters of general interest, and public opinion takes shape dramatically altered the social terrain in Russia, with enormous implications for politics. A major site for the development of civil society were voluntary associations, which proliferated in the late 1800s and after. These included learned societies, literacy and temperance societies, business and professional associations, philanthropic and service organizations, workers' mutual assistance funds, and varied cultural associations and circles. Already before the de facto press freedom of 1905 and the official freeing of the press from preliminary censorship in 1906, newspapers (including a mass circulation daily press), magazines, journals, and books had become pervasive and powerful media for disseminating and exchanging information and ideas. In addition, universities, public schools, law courts, organizations of local rural and urban self-government, and even the Church stood on the uncertain boundaries of being at once state and civil institutions, though offering an important space for individuals to be involved in the emerging public life. The Revolution of 1905, as we have seen, unleashed civic opinion and organization as never before. The increase of civil rights resulting from 1905 gave these further impetus, including enabling the formation of legal political parties and other new types of civic associations. While most of these organizations concerned themselves with everyday secular matters, religion also thrived in this expanding public sphere, though often running outside the official channels of the established Church. For example, a series of Religious-Philosophical Meetings in St. Petersburg, begun at the end of 1901, brought together prominent intellectuals and clergy to discuss the meaning of religion in public life. After 1905, religious associations such as the Spiritualist Society and the Russian Theosophical Society formed. We also see a revival of religious enthusiasm and organization among the urban middle and lower classes, including gatherings in taverns to talk about religion, the charismatic movement known as the "Brethren," Tolstoyans, and growing and increasingly visible congregations of religious dissenters, ranging from Baptists to well-established Russian groups like the Molokany ("milk drinkers") or Skoptsy ("castrates") to new sectarian groups.

These years also saw the rise of public movements to extend rights to disadvantaged groups. We have already described the rise of the labor movement. Also in these years arose organized efforts to promote women's rights and emancipation. During 1905, women were often heard at meetings appealing for respect as human beings and for equal rights as citizens. A series of

The *Passazh* on Nevsky prospect, St. Petersburg, 1901. Palaces of commerce, department stores were not only economically central to the rise of a consumer life in Russia but characteristically modern locations as sites for public display (of both products and people) and desire. (*Central State Archive of Film, Photographic, and Sound Documents of St. Petersburg*)

women's organizations and publications emerged to promote the cause, such as the All-Russian Union for Women's Equality, and feminist and women's groups joined together in a series of women's congresses (on women's rights, the struggle against prostitution, and women's education).

In the non-Russian areas of the empire, but also among ethnic and religious minorities living in the major Russian cities, these were years of widespread nationalist activism. Many groups—Poles, Ukrainians, Finns, Balts, Jews, Georgians, Armenians, Muslims, and others—defined themselves as "nations" (a modern concept gaining increasing resonance), and activists organized movements seeking cultural autonomy and perhaps an independent nation state. Changes in the lives and expectations of non-Russians, however, were not limited to the history of political and nationalist movements. For many non-Russian communities, these were also years of exploring new possibilities and new identities—likely more than we know, as historians are still only beginning to research this non-Russian side of Russian history. Among Jews, for example, we see the rise around the turn of the century and after of schools promoting Hebrew or Yiddish along with growing numbers of Russian-educated Jews, the emergence of a new Jewish literature and a Jewish periodical press, increasing secular studies in traditional Jewish schools, and organized political movements of both Jewish socialism, which sought a transformed Russian Empire, and Zionism, which sought salvation in a new land. We see similar movements of national revival and organization, especially after 1905, among Russia's Muslims—Tatars, Azeris, Central Asians, and others. Muslim organizations proliferated—including libraries, charities, credit unions, national congresses, and political unions and parties—expressing ideologies ranging from liberalism and socialism to Pan-Islamism and Pan-Turkism.

The daily newspaper, itself an institution at the center of Russia's increasingly vital civic life, reminded readers of how deeply contradictory this life was. On the one hand, newspapers reported the best of what modern life produced: scientific and technical knowledge, opportunities for upward mobility, increasing numbers of institutions of culture (museums, schools, libraries, exhibitions, theaters), and civic organizations of all sorts. Regular ads as well as daily reportage pointed to Russia's emerging consumer life, most evident in the rise of department stores, like Moscow's famous Muir and Merrilies, and glass-covered arcades like the St. Petersburg "Passage," which displayed goods designed not only to cater to material needs but to stimulate new notions of being visibly fashionable and respectable. The papers also kept readers informed about the many public entertainments available to those with at least some disposable income (though even workers saved for such pleasures), such as music halls, nightclubs, outdoor summer "pleasure gardens," and theaters at all price levels. At the same time, the press reminded readers of the dark sides of modern public life: the egoistic and predatory practices of some merchants and employers, frightening attacks on respectable citizens and civic order by irrational "hooligans," the pervasive dangers and depredations of con-artists, thieves, and burglars, sexual licentiousness and debauchery, murder and suicide, widespread public drunkenness, neglected and abandoned children (who often turned to street crime and vice), and the spread of diseases such as syphilis, tuberculosis, and cholera that were seen as nurtured by the very conditions of urban public life.

## Conclusion

Historians have long debated whether the Russian economy and society in the decades before the Great War were heading toward inevitable crisis and revolution or toward a viable civil society and a reformed political order. "Optimists," mainly earlier historians, emphasize the many signs of progress: economic modernization and development, social reforms, the rise of the middle class, and other changes. "Pessimists," who included most Soviet historians and a large proportion of historians today, conclude that despite great effort Russia was not solving its main problems. To be sure, regardless of whether conditions improved or declined in the years leading to the war, they remained desperately hard for the bulk of the population, aggravated by a limited and faltering parliamentary system, an increasingly conservative ruler, and persistent social disorder and conflict. At the same time, historians need not oversimplify for the sake of taking sides in a debate. We can also recognize a great deal of characteristically modern uncertainty and ambiguity in Russian society. This was a time, as many contemporaries said, of both progress and collapse, of both possibility and crisis. Of course, danger lay in this contradictoriness, too. It has been said that revolutions occur not when the people are utterly destitute, oppressed beyond all measure, and deprived of hope—crushing conditions are more likely to lead to blind and fruitless rebellions—but when there is growth, advancement, and high expectation, hampered, however, by an archaic and rigid established order.

# CHAPTER 33

# Russian Culture from the "Great Reforms" until the Revolutions of 1917

Tell everyone that the future will be radiant and beautiful. Love it, strive toward it, work for it, bring it nearer, transfer into the present as much as you can from it.

NIKOLAI CHERNYSHEVSKY, 1863

The physical, mental, and moral development of the individual, the incorporation of truth and justice in social relationships—this is the brief formula that encompasses, I believe, everything that can be regarded as progress.

PETR LAVROV, 1870

Art is not, as the metaphysicians say, the manifestation of some mysterious idea, of beauty, of God. . . . It is not the expression of emotions by external signs. It is not the production of pleasing objects. Above all, it is not pleasure. It is a necessity for life, for movement toward the well-being of individuals and humanity, for sociability among people, uniting them with one and the same feelings.

LEV TOLSTOY, 1897–98

Reaction is triumphant, executions have not ceased, but society is as silent as a tomb. . . . [In the past], a youth did not have to take the risk of defining the purpose of life for himself; he found it ready-made. . . . All the filth and disorder in personal and social life was blamed on the autocracy—the individual was absolved of responsibility. . . . Now we are entering a new era fraught with many difficulties. . . . Each will have to determine for themselves the meaning and direction of their lives. . . . The tyranny of civic activism over young people will be shattered for a long time, until such time as the human personality [*lichnost*], after plumbing its own depths, emerges with a new form of social idealism.

MIKHAIL GERSHENZON IN *VEKHI* (SIGNPOSTS), 1909

The decades that elapsed between the emancipation of the serfs and the revolutions of 1917 constituted an active, fruitful, and fascinating period in the history of Russian culture, but also a cultural time of troubles. Education continued to grow at all levels, in spite of obstacles and even governmental "counterreforms"; in the twentieth century the rate of growth increased sharply. Russian science and scholarship, already reasonably well established at the time of Nicholas I's death, developed further and blossomed out. In a word, Russia became a full-fledged contributor to and partner in the intellectual and academic efforts of the Western world. Russian literature continued its "golden age," although primarily in prose rather than in poetry and largely through the achievements of a handful of great writers, such as Turgenev, Tolstoy, and Dostoevsky. Later, when the giants died or, as in the case of Tolstoy, stopped writing fiction and the "golden age" came to its end, Chekhov, Gorky, and some other outstanding authors maintained the tradition of Russian prose. Moreover, the very end of the nineteenth century and the first part of the twentieth witnessed another literary and artistic revival, designated often as the "silver age." In literature that renaissance meant the appearance once again of superb poetry, the introduction of a wide variety of new trends, and the emergence of exceptionally high standards of culture and craftsmanship. The "silver age" also extended to the theater, music, ballet, painting, and sculpture, and in effect to every form of creative expression. In the history of ideas, as well as in literature and art, the period can be divided into two parts: from the 1860s to the end of the century and indeed to the revolutions of 1917, the creed of radicalism, utilitarianism, and materialism first proclaimed by left-wing Westernizers dominated student and other active intellectual circles, finding its best expression in nihilism, different forms of populism, and Marxism; yet with the turn of the century and the "silver age" in culture members of the intellectual elite began to return to idealistic metaphysics and religion. The First World War and later the revolutions struck when Russian intellectual and cultural life was exhibiting more vitality, diversity, and sophistication than ever before. At the same time, especially as the twentieth century began, literature, art, and even widely circulating newspapers and magazines dwelled on a deepening sense of cultural crisis. Numerous writers spoke of "these times," especially after 1905, as "times of trouble," marked by widespread feelings of uncertainty, groundlessness, and disenchantment. A review of Russian poetry on the eve of the war found little besides "pain, melancholy, and death." In the view of many, society and culture were physically and spiritually sick, perhaps dying.

## Education

The death of Nicholas I and the coming of the "great reforms" meant liberalization in education as in other fields. The university statute of 1863 reaffirmed the principle of university autonomy, while Nicholas I's special restrictions on universities were among the first regulations to disappear in the new reign. The zemstvo reform of 1864 opened vast opportunities to establish schools in the countryside. In towns or rural areas, the increasing thirst for knowledge on the part of the Russians augured well for education in a liberal age. However, as already mentioned, official liberalism did not last long, and reaction logically, if unfortunately, showed a particular concern for education. As a result, the growth of education in Russia, while it could not be stopped, found itself hampered and to an extent deformed by government action.

After Dmitrii Tolstoy replaced Alexander Golovnin in 1866 as minister of education, the ministry did its best to control education and to direct it into desirable channels. As in the days of Uvarov, high standards were used in universities and secondary schools to keep the number of students down, hindering especially the academic advancement of students of low social background. In secondary education, the emphasis fell on the so-called classical *gymnasia*, which became the only road to universities proper, as distinct from more specialized institutions of higher learning. These gymnasia concentrated on teaching the Latin and Greek languages, to the extent of some 40 percent of the total class time. Largely because of the rigorous demands, less than one-third of those who had entered the gymnasia were graduated. In addition to the natural obstacles that such a system presented to "socially undesirable" elements, ministers of education made direct appeals in their circulars to subordinates to keep "cook's sons" out of the gymnasia, as did one of Dmitrii Tolstoy's successors, Ivan Delianov, in 1887. In general, the government tried to divide education into airtight compartments that students as a rule could not cross. Under Alexander III and Pobedonostsev, Church schools received special attention. Following the statute of 1884 concerning Church-parish schools, an effort was made to entrust elementary education as much as possible to the Church, the number of Church-parish schools increasing from 4,500 in 1882 to 32,000 in 1894. While inferior in quality, these educational institutions were considered "safe." By contrast, advanced education for women, barely begun in Russia, came to be increasingly restricted. And in all schools and at all levels the Ministry of Education emphasized "conduct" and tried to maintain iron discipline.

Yet in spite of all the vicissitudes, education continued to grow in Russia as a result of sustained efforts by the state, the Church, and, especially, the zemstva. Compared to 1856, when official data list only about 8,000 primary schools in the Russian Empire enrolling 450,000 pupils (less than 1 percent of the population, although an estimated 9 percent was school-aged), forty years later in 1896 there were ten times this number of schools enrolling 3.8 million pupils (approximately one-third of all school-age children), and by 1911, 6.6 million children were in Russian schools, which meant nearly half of full enrollment, according to Ben Eklof's calculations. In addition to the exclusive classical gymnasia, *Realschule*, which taught modern languages and science in place of Greek and Latin, provided a secondary education that could lead to admission to technical institutions of higher learning. Other kinds of schools also developed. In addition to the activities of the ministries of education, war, navy, and of the Holy Synod, Witte promoted commercial schools under the jurisdiction of the Ministry of Finance, establishing some 150 of them between 1896 and 1902, and well over 200 altogether. In 1905 these schools were transferred to the Ministry of Trade and Industry. Moreover, after the Revolution of 1905 schools in Russia profited from a more liberal policy as well as from an increasing interest in education on the part of both the government and the public. As mentioned earlier, plans were drawn to institute schooling for all Russian children by 1922, or, according to a revised estimate following the outbreak of the First World War, by 1925. Educational prospects had never looked brighter in Russia than on the eve of the revolutions of 1917.

The problem, however, remained immense. On the eve of the 1917 revolutions, the majority of Russians remained illiterate. Yet, enormous progress had been made since the end of serfdom. According to data compiled by Adolf Rashin, literacy in Russia had increased from only about 6 percent in the 1860s to an estimated 28 percent by 1913. But such aggregate data obscure the significant unevenness of the social geography of literacy in Russia. As revealed by the invaluable 1897 census, literacy rates were higher than average among males, city dwellers (but also peasants living near large cities), workers, youth, and people living in the European parts of the empire. Thus, in place of a simple national aggregate of literacy, it is more telling, for example, that still only 17 percent of peasants in European Russia could read in 1897, while 54 percent of industrial and commercial workers could, or that fully 74 percent of male workers in St. Petersburg were literate in 1897. It is also important to underscore, as recent scholars have, that the impact of literacy on individuals was quite varied. Among the lower classes, for example, literacy could mean no more than a rough skill needed to function better at work or could be an important source of pride and self-esteem and of exposure to new ideas and possibilities.

At the other end of the educational ladder, universities increased in number, although slowly. The so-called Novorossiiskii University—referring to the name of the area, *Novorossiia*, or New Russia—was founded in Odessa in 1864, the University of Tomsk in Siberia in 1888, the University of Saratov in 1910, of Perm in 1915, and of Rostov-on-Don in 1917. That gave Russia a total of twelve universities, all of them belonging to the state. However, in 1917 the empire also possessed more than a hundred specialized institutions of higher learning: pedagogical, technological, agricultural, and other. Gradually it became possible for women to obtain higher education by attending special "courses" set up in university centers, such as the "Guerrier courses," named after a professor of history, Vladimir Guerrier, which began to function in 1872 in Moscow, and the "Bestuzhev courses," founded in 1878 in St. Petersburg and named after another historian, Konstantin Bestuzhev-Riumin. The total number of students in Russian institutions of higher learning in 1917 has been variously estimated between 100,000 and 180,000. It should be noted that while the university statute of 1884 proved more restrictive than that of 1863 and over a period of time led to the resignation of a number of noted professors, most of the restrictions disappeared in 1905. In general, and especially after 1905, the freedom and variety of intellectual life in imperial Russian universities invite comparison with Western universities.

## Science and Scholarship

The Academy of Sciences, the universities, and other institutions of higher learning developed, or rather continued to develop, science and scholarship in Russia. In fact, in the period from the emancipation of the serfs until the revolutions of 1917, Russians made significant contributions in almost every area of knowledge. In mathematics, while no one quite rivaled Lobachevsky, a considerable number of outstanding Russian mathematicians made their appearance, including Pafnutii Chebyshev in St. Petersburg and a remarkable woman, Sofia Kovalevskaia, who taught at the University of Stockholm. Chemistry in Russia achieved new heights in the works of many talented scholars, the most celebrated of them being the great Dmitrii Mendeleev, who lived from 1834 to 1907 and whose periodic table of elements, formulated in 1869, both organized the known elements into a system and made an accurate forecast of later discoveries. Leading Russian physicists included the specialist in magnetism and electricity, Alexander Stoletov, and the brilliant student of the properties of light, Petr Lebedev, as well as such notable pioneer inventors as Pavel Iablochkov, who worked before Edison in developing electric light, and Alexander Popov, who constructed the first radio receiver in 1895, shortly before Marconi. Russian inventors, like Russian scholars in general, frequently had little international influence and thus received less than their due recognition because of Russia's isolation, ignorance abroad of the Russian language, and the inability or failure in Russia to utilize these inventions.

Advances in the biological sciences rivaled those in the physical. Alexander Kovalevsky produced classic works in zoology and embryology, while his younger brother, Vladimir, the husband of the mathematician, made important contributions to paleontology—and, incidentally, was much appreciated by Darwin. The famous embryologist and bacteriologist Ilya Mechnikov, who did most of his work in the Pasteur Institute in Paris, concentrated on such problems as the function of the white corpuscles, immunity, and the process of aging. Medicine developed well in Russia during the last decades of the empire, both in terms of quality and, after the zemstvo reform, in terms of accessibility to the masses. Following the lead of an outstanding anatomist, surgeon, teacher, and public figure, Nikolai Pirogov, who died in 1881, and others, Russian doctors exhibited a remarkable civic spirit and devotion to their work and their patients.

Russian contributions to physiology were especially striking and important, and they overlapped into psychology. Ivan Sechenov, who taught in several universities for about half a century and died in 1905, did remarkable research on gases in the blood, nerve centers, and reflexes and on other related matters. Ivan Pavlov, who lived from 1849 to 1936 and whose epoch-making experiments began in the 1880s, established through his studies of dogs' reactions to food the existence and nature of conditioned reflexes, and, further developing his approach, contributed enormously to both theory and experimental work in physiology and to behavioral psychology.

The social sciences and the humanities also prospered. Russian scholars engaged fruitfully in everything from law to oriental studies and from economics to folklore. In particular, Russian historiography flourished in the last decades of the nineteenth and the first of the twentieth century. Building on the work of Sergei Soloviev and other pioneers, Vasilii Kliuchevsky, Sergei Platonov, Matvei Liubavsky, Pavel Miliukov, and their colleagues in effect established Russian history as a rich and many-sided field of learning. Other Russians made notable contributions to the histories of other countries and ages, as did the medievalist Pavel Vinogradov and the specialist in classical antiquity Mikhail Rostovtzeff. While Russian historiography profited greatly from the sociological emphasis characteristic of the second half of the nineteenth century, the "silver age" stimulated the history of art, which could claim in Russia such magnificent specialists as Nikodim Kondakov, Alexander Benois, and Igor Grabar, and it led to a revival of philosophy, aesthetics, and literary criticism.

## Literature

After the "great reforms" as before them, literature continued to be the chief glory of Russian culture, and it also became a major source of Russian influence on the West, and indeed on the world. The three outstanding figures, of course, were Ivan Turgenev, Fedor Dostoevsky, and Lev Tolstoy.

Ivan Turgenev lived from 1818 to 1883 and became famous around 1850 with the gradual appearance of his *Sportsman's Sketches*. He responded to the trends of the time and depicted with remarkable sensitivity the intellectual life of Russia, but he failed eventually to satisfy the Left. Six novels, the first of which appeared in 1855 and the last in 1877, described the evolution of Russian educated society and Russia itself as Turgenev, a gentleman of culture, had witnessed it. These novels are, in order of publication, *Rudin*, *A Gentry Nest*, *On the Eve*, the celebrated *Fathers and Sons*, *Smoke*, and *Virgin Soil*. Turgenev depicted Russia from the time of the iron regime of Nicholas I, through the "great reforms," to the return of reaction in the late 1860s and the 1870s. He concerned himself especially with the idealists of the 1840s and the later liberals, nihilists, and populists. Indeed, it was Turgenev's hero, Bazarov, who gave currency to the concept "nihilist" and to the term itself. Although he was a consistent Westernizer and liberal, who was appreciative of the efforts of young radicals to change Russia, Turgenev advocated gradualism, not revolution; in particular he recommended patient work to develop the Russian economy and education. And he refused to be one-sided or dogmatic. In fact, critics debate to this day whether Rudin and Bazarov are essentially sympathetic or unsympathetic characters. Besides, Turgenev's novels were by no means simply *romans à thèse*. The reader remembers not only the author's ideological protagonists, but also his remarkable, strong heroines, the background,

Fedor Dostoevsky. *(New York Public Library)*

the dialogue, and, perhaps above all, the consummate artistry. As a writer, Turgenev resembled closely his friend Flaubert. In addition to the famous sequence of novels, Turgenev wrote some plays and a considerable number of stories—he has been described as a better story writer than novelist.

Fedor Dostoevsky, who lived from 1821 to 1881, also became well known before the "great reforms." He was already the author of a novel, *Poor Folk,* which was acclaimed by Belinsky when it was published in 1845, and of other writings, when he became involved, as already mentioned, with the Petrashevtsy and was sentenced to death, the sentence being commuted to Siberian exile only at the place of execution. Next the writer spent four years at hard labor and two more as a soldier in Siberia before returning to European Russia in 1856, following a general amnesty proclaimed by the new emperor. Dostoevsky recorded his Siberian experience in a remarkable book, *Notes from the House of the Dead,* which came out in 1861. Upon his return to literary life, the one-time member of the Petrashevtsy became an aggressive and prolific right-wing journalist, contributing to a certain Slavophile revival, Pan-Slavism, and even outright chauvinism. His targets included the Jews, the Poles, the Germans, Catholicism, socialism, and the entire West. While Dostoevsky's journalism added to the sound and fury of the period, his immortal fame rests on his late novels, four of which belong among the greatest ever written. These were *Crime and Punishment, The Idiot, The Possessed,* and *The Brothers Karamazov,* published in 1866, 1868, 1870–72, and 1879–80, respectively. In fact, Dostoevsky seemed to go from strength to strength and was apparently at the height of his creative powers in working on a sequel to *The Brothers Karamazov* when he died.

Dostoevsky has often been represented as the most Russian of writers and evaluated in terms of Russian messiahship and the mysteries of the Russian soul—an approach to which he himself richly contributed. Yet, a closer study of the great novelist's so-called special Russian traits demonstrates that they are either of secondary importance at best or even entirely imaginary. To the contrary, Dostoevsky could be called the most international or, better, the most human of writers because of his enormous concern with and penetration into the nature of man. The strange Russian author was a master of depth psychology before depth psychology became known. Moreover, he viewed human nature in the dynamic terms of explosive conflict between freedom and necessity, urge and limitations, faith and despair, good and evil. Of Dostoevsky's several priceless gifts the greatest was to fuse into one his protagonists and the ideas—or rather states of man's soul and entire being—that they expressed, as no other writer has ever done. Therefore, where others are prolix, tedious, didactic, or confusing in mixing different levels of discourse, Dostoevsky is gripping, in places almost unbearably so. As another Russian author, Gleb Uspensky, reportedly once remarked, into a small hole in the wall, where the generality of human beings could put perhaps a pair of shoes, Dostoevsky could put the entire world. One of the greatest anti-rationalists of the second half of the nineteenth century, together with Nietzsche and Kirkegaard, Dostoevsky became with them an acknowledged prophet for the twentieth, inspiring existential philosophy, theological revivals, and scholarly attempts to understand the catastrophes of our time—as well as, of course, modern psychological fiction.

Lev Tolstoy is not only one of Russia's greatest fiction writers, but one of the most remarkable and influential men in modern Russian life. We have already heard the frequent Russian argument in the nineteenth century that writers should do more than entertain, that they must also speak the truth and take a stand as moral witnesses against evil in the world. Tolstoy combined both great literary talent and, especially in his later years, the stance of moral critic and prophet, for which he was both idolized and vilified in his own time.

Born in 1828 into an ancient and high noble family, Count Tolstoy enjoyed a youth filled with privilege, an excellent education (at home and at Kazan University), and typical aristocratic dissipation. After dropping out of university he spent the next few years drinking, dancing, and gambling his way around Moscow and St. Petersburg. In 1851, he decided to join his brother in the army and served as an officer in the Crimean War. While in the army, he began writing fiction. His first writings were well received and he decided to pursue this career. Here begins the second period of his life, that of the great novelist. His major works, known throughout the world, include his autobiographical trilogy of the 1850s, *Childhood, Boyhood, and Youth*; his great epic of individuals and families during the Napoleonic wars, *War and Peace*, published in 1869; and *Anna Karenina*, a tragic story about two marriages and the search for true love and happiness in an often corrupt and crushing society, published in 1876. The third period in Tolstoy's life began around 1878, when he experienced a religious crisis and "conversion" to a truer Christianity. He then devoted his life to propagating his new religious views and a social ethics

Lev Tolstoy.   (*New York Public Library*)

of simplicity and nonviolence. At the same time, he tried to exemplify these ideals in his own everyday life: he tried to live simply, in touch with nature and physical labor. During his final years, Tolstoy often thought of becoming a hermit or a pilgrim. With this aim in mind, in 1910, at the age of eighty-two, he fled his estate, his family, and the world. On the road, he fell ill and died at a modest train station.

These three periods of Tolstoy's long life were less separate than they appear at first glance. Even as a young man, he was obsessed with self-perfection, as can be seen in his self-castigating diaries filled with rules for himself. Later and more seriously, the search for self-understanding and moral perfection can be seen throughout his stories and novels. His autobiographical trilogy explores his favorite theme at that time: psychological self-analysis of his own developing consciousness. Self-examination and self-perfection can also be seen in the lives of characters—sometimes minor ones, to be sure—in his great novels. Also, long before his religious conversion, he began to seek solutions to the problems of "civilization." Already in the 1850s, inspired by the conviction that human beings were born innocent but were ruined by the institutions of civilization, and especially Western-style education, which separated children from natural moral and spiritual truths, Tolstoy organized educational reform efforts on his own estate. He also featured characters in his novels, such as Pierre Bezukhov in *War and Peace* and Konstantin Levin in *Anna Karenina,* who recognize their alienation from the natural truths that children and common people still understand.

These and other early ideas fed Tolstoy's new thinking about religion. His ideas, in fact, become so different, and so influential, that the Russian Orthodox Church excommunicated him in 1901. According to Tolstoy, official Christianity masked, crushed, and perverted the real meanings of life: the universal truths that all people knew by nature, and that Jesus Christ knew, but were hidden behind arcane rituals and absurd mystical beliefs. Tolstoy rejected the need for priests, sacraments, and liturgy, and most of the Church's theological dogma: all that is needed is an ethical commitment to reject evil; the only true sacrament is the everyday practice of moral good. As the dramatic conclusion of his life revealed, however, Tolstoy was never fully certain he had escaped the baneful effects of civilization and found truth. In retrospect, it is difficult to say whether Tolstoy was more influential as a novelist or as a teacher of nonviolence, an unmasker of modern civilization, and whether *Anna Karenina* or *A Confession*—an account of his spiritual crisis— had the greater impact. In late imperial Russia at least, Tolstoy's position as a major voice of moral criticism of the status quo, which the government dared not silence, appeared at times even more extraordinary and precious than his literary creations, though these were masterpieces of art and empathy.

The Russian novel, which in the second half of the nineteenth century won a worldwide reputation because of the writings of Turgenev, Dostoevsky, and Tolstoy, had other outstanding practitioners as well. Ivan Goncharov, who lived from 1812 to 1891, produced at least one great novel, *Oblomov*, published two years before the emancipation of the serfs and representing in a sense a farewell, spoken with mixed feelings, to the departing patriarchal Russia, and a welcome, again with mixed feelings, to the painfully evolving new order. Oblomov himself snored his way to fame as one of the most unforgettable as well as most "superfluous" heroes of Russian literature. Other noteworthy novelists of the period included Nikolai Leskov, who developed a highly individual language and style and wrote about the provincial clergy and similar topics associated with the Church and the people, and Gleb Uspensky, a populist and a pessimist, deeply concerned with peasant life as well as with the intelligentsia. An able satirist, Mikhail Saltykov, who wrote under the pseudonym of N. Shchedrin, fitted well into that critical and realistic age and acquired great popularity. A highly talented dramatist, Alexander Ostrovsky, wrote indefatigably from about 1850 until his death in 1886, creating much of the basic repertoire of the Russian theater and contributing especially to the depiction of merchants, minor officials, and the lower middle class in general.

Toward the end of the nineteenth century and in the early twentieth new writers came to the fore to continue the great tradition of Russian prose. Vladimir Korolenko, a populist and optimist, was the author of charming stories expressing his belief in people's fundamental goodness and in the ultimate victory of truth and justice, even in the face of harsh natural and social conditions. The restless Alexei Peshkov, better known as Maxim Gorky, wrote often of the lives and struggles of outcasts, tramps, and rebels and featured strong and restless plebeian heroes challenging both oppressive authorities

Anton Chekhov.    *(New York Public Library)*

and the slavish submissiveness of the masses. Anton Chekhov, who lived from 1860 until 1904, left a lasting imprint on Russian and world literature. A brilliant playwright, he had the good fortune to be writing just as the Moscow Art Theater was rising to its heights. He is even more important as one of the founders and a master craftsman of the modern short story, the literary genre that he usually chose to make his simple, gentle, restrained, and yet wonderfully effective comments on the world.

Poetry remained enormously popular among readers in the years between the "great reforms" and the turn of the century, though a relative lack of originality and innovation and a predominance of realism have led many critics to see these decades as an "unpoetic age." Two trends competed for attention in these years: "art for art's sake" and "civic poetry." Among those inclined toward the first, the best was Afanasii Fet, whose beautiful impressionistic verses, mostly about nature and love, reflected the view, much influenced by the pessimism of Schopenhauer, that reality is ugly and the role of art is to transcend and overcome this world through pure beauty. Utilitarian critics like Chernyshevsky heaped abuse and mockery on Fet, contributing to his silence as a writer during most of the 1860s and 1870s. Likewise, the great lyricist Fedor Tiutchev, perhaps the world's outstanding poet of late love and of nature in its Romantic, pantheistic, and chaotic aspects, died in 1873, an isolated figure. The dominant trend in these years was civic poetry. Realistic, even naturalistic, in portraying the world and optimistic about the possibilities of improving the human condition, the civic poets, encouraged by critics like Chernyshevsky, were determined to use literature to awaken consciences and change the world. With pathos, satire, or sarcasm, using echoes of rough folk speech or soaring moral passion, they described various abuses in Russian life, especially the sufferings of the common people. The leading civic poet was Nikolai Nekrasov, whose poetic voice could range from poignant realism to eloquent lyricism, often echoing Russian folk songs. His many influential poems were inspired both by the beauty of Russian nature and moral outrage at the poverty and suffering of ordinary Russians.

The "silver age" in Russian literature, which dawned toward the turn of the century, brought new vitality and creativity to Russian culture. Foreshadowed by certain literary critics and poets in the 1890s, the new period has often been dated from the appearance in 1898 of a seminal periodical, *The World of Art*, put out by Sergei Diaghilev and Alexander Benois. What followed was a cultural explosion. Almost overnight there sprung up in Russia a rich variety of literary and artistic creeds, circles, and movements. As Mirsky and other specialists have noted, these different and sometimes hostile groups had little in common, except their denial of "civic art" and their high standards of culture and craftsmanship. Form-conscious impressionism and symbolism pushed aside rationalism, positivism, and didactic realism. Aestheticism, mysticism, decadence, sensualism, idealism, and pessimism all intertwined in different combinations. Some critics have found in "silver age" writing a tendency toward pretentiousness, obscurity, or artificiality. But even when flawed, the works of the "silver age" indicated a new refinement, richness, and maturity in Russian culture.

In literature, the new trends resulted in a great revival of poetry and literary criticism, although some remarkable prose was also produced, for example, by Boris Bugaev, known as Andrei Bely. Among the poets, the symbolist Alexander Blok, who lived from 1880 to 1921 and wrote verses of stunning magic and melody to the mysterious Unknown Lady and on other topics, has been justly considered the greatest of the age and one of the greatest in all Russian literature. But Russia suddenly acquired many brilliant poets; other symbolists, for example, Innokentii Annensky, Bely, Valerii Briusov, and Konstantin Balmont; "acmeists," such as Nikolai Gumilev and Osip Mandelstam; futurists, such as Velemir Khlebnikov and Vladimir Mayakovsky; or peasant poets, such as Sergei Esenin. The poet and novelist Boris Pasternak, who died in 1960, and the poet Anna Akhmatova, who lived until 1966, also belong fully to the "silver age."

The "silver age" was a sign not only of Russia's cultural florescence but also, it has been argued, of a troubled cultural spirit of the age. Literary scholars have spoken of a characteristic *fin-de-siècle* sense of uncertainty and disintegration, of deep skepticism about all received truths and certainties, and a pessimistic foreboding (prescient, it turned out), though also hopeful anticipation, of an approaching "end." A major preoccupation was the self—self-discovery, self-development, self-fulfillment. Some writers, such as Gorky, presented the individual human self as a moral ideal upon which society should be constructed

Anna Akhmatova.  *(Zephyr Press, Brookline, MA)*

and focused their writings on the sufferings and assertions of their characters' inward and social beings. Other writers found meaning for the self, amidst the whirlwind of modern life, in aestheticist (some called it decadent) evocations of love, beauty, and sadness, as in the highly personal and beautifully crafted poetry of Akhmatova and other "acmeists." Still other writers and cultural critics, such as Andreev, Bely, Briusov, Hippius, Merezhkovsky, Rozanov, and Sologub, dwelled on the darker, egoistic, Dionysian side of the awakened modern self. Typically, these writers both admired and dreaded the creative powers of the all-too-human ego and id—the influences of Nietzsche and Freud were widely evident—and explored, in a complex psychological and philosophical frame, sensuality, lust, cruelty, depravity, madness, disease, death, and other drives, passions, and experiences.

The uncertainties and pessimism so characteristic of the silver age nurtured its characteristic aestheticism. Many artists, it was said, felt that the old world was dying, but they were determined at least that it be a beautiful death. By contrast, futurists took a stance of iconoclastic rebellion in the name of new and modern meanings. Writers like Khlebnikov and Mayakovsky loudly and visibly challenged the conventional values of what they called "philistine" culture; their most famous manifesto spoke of offering a "slap in the face to public taste." They appeared in public with absurd pictures painted on their faces, peculiarly invented clothing, seashell earrings, and radishes or spoons in their buttonholes. And their works deliberately echoed the noisy confusion and chaos of modern life. Truth and beauty, they insisted, lay not in the creative subjects or vocabularies of past work but in the new noise of factories and the marketplace and in the primitive and transcendent sounds of "transrational" words.

## The Arts

In art, as in literature, "realism" dominated the second half of the nineteenth century, only to be enriched and in large part replaced by the varied new currents of the "silver age." In painting the decisive turning to realism can even be precisely dated: in 1863 fourteen young painters, led by Ivan Kramskoy and constituting the entire graduating class of the Academy of Arts, refused to paint their examination assignment, "A Feast in Valhalla." Breaking with the stifling academic tradition, they insisted on painting realistic pictures. Several years later they organized popular circulating exhibitions of their works and came to be known as the "itinerants." With new painters joining the movement and its influence spreading, "critical realism" asserted itself in Russian art just as it had in Russian literary criticism and literature. In accord with the spirit of the age, the "itinerants" and their disciples believed that content was more important than form, that art had to serve the higher purpose of educating the masses and championing their interests, and they depicted such topics as the exploitation of the poor, the drunken clergy, and the brutal police. Vasilii Vereshchiagin, for example, observed wars at firsthand until he went down with the battleship *Petropavlovsk* when it was sunk by the Japanese. He painted numerous and often huge canvases on the glaring inhumanity of wars, characteristically dedicating his "Apotheosis of War," a pyramid of skulls, "to all great conquerors, present, past, and future." Realistic painting was not limited to blunt social commentary, however. Such talented artists as Kramskoy, Ilya Repin, Vasilii Surikov, Nikolai Ge, Vasilii Perov, Isaak Levitan, and Valentin Serov—largely unfamiliar in the West but deserving attention—produced many compelling portraits, landscapes, and historical paintings. These works are often introspective and psychological (this was the age of great interest in the self), lyrical and beautiful, and rich in light and texture. Of course, it can be argued that the sympathetic humanism in this work was also a type of social and even political commentary.

The development of music followed a somewhat different pattern. It, too, responded to the social concerns of the age, as seen, for example, in Modest Mussorgsky's emphasis on content, realism, and closeness to the masses and in the nationalism inspiring many composers. But music, by its very nature, also reached far beyond social and political argument. And the second half of the nineteenth century was a period of great musical talent and originality. The spread of musical education aided this process, with a conservatory established in St. Petersburg in 1862, headed by the noted composer and magnificent pianist Anton Rubinstein; another one in Moscow in 1866, headed by

Modest Mussorgsky.   *(Sovfoto)*

Anton Rubinstein's younger bromer, Nikolai; and still other musical schools in other cities in subsequent years. Moreover, quite a number of outstanding Russian composers came to the fore at that time. The most prominent of them included Petr Tchaikovsky and the celebrated "Mighty Bunch" or "Mighty Handful" (*Moguchaia kuchka*): Modest Mussorgsky, Nikolai Rimsky-Korsakov, Alexander Borodin, Caesar Cui, and Milii Balakirev. Importantly, this was an age when composers sought to discover and construct a truly Russian classical music, influenced by Western technique and form but also growing organically from Russia's native traditions, often including Russia's links to "the Orient." This musical nationalism was connected especially to the adaptation of folk songs, melodies, tales, and legends and to a romanticized vision of the Russian past. Some of the most brilliant musical work of that age occurred in opera, as in Mussorgsky's *Boris Godunov*, Borodin's *Prince Igor*, and Rimsky-Korsakov's *Sadko*—all works exploring national themes. Tchaikovsky stood out in many ways, not least for developing an elegiac, subjective, lyrical, and psychological approach all his own.

During the "silver age," we see the same remarkable vitality, experimentation, and searching for the new and the true in the visual and performing arts as in literature. In music, the work of composers like Sergei Rachmaninov, Alexander Scriabin, and Igor Stravinsky ranged from the lyrical and elegiac to the mystical, Dionysian, and even apocalyptic. Rachmaninov's work exudes

Petr Tchaikovsky. *(New York Public library)*

gentle and lyrical spirituality, aestheticism, melancholy, and fatalism. By contrast, Scriabin's music—influenced by an eclectic mixture of Chopin, Wagner, Nietzsche, symbolism, and religious mysticism—offers a mix of Dionysian emotions, mystical spirituality, and pure sound. One of the most remarkable artistic collaborations was Diaghilev's famous "Ballets Russes." Founded in St. Petersburg in 1909, the Ballets Russes brought together some of Russia's most innovative painters, dancers, choreographers, and composers. Diaghilev and his company soon relocated to France, where there was greater artistic freedom and a more sophisticated modern audience, but also where money could be made catering to audiences fascinated by the exoticness of Russian culture. Echoing other "decadent" trends in Russian and European culture, the Ballets Russes placed aestheticism (beauty for beauty's sake) and sensualism (ranging from love of the body to suggestions of sexuality) at the center, often with exotic "Oriental" overtones.

The most remarkable achievement in Russian visual arts was the innovative modernism of such artists as Marc Chagall, Vasilii Kandinsky, and Kazimir Malevich, still renowned throughout the world for their originality and influence. Various trends arose. Some artists took a revivalist turn, evoking a seemingly stable and authentic time of pure national identity before Russia's Westernization or crafted nostalgic recollections of the elegance of the eighteenth century. Many were attracted to the ideal of beauty for its own

Vaslav Nijinsky represented a new type of male ballet artist: central to the performance rather than simply assisting ballerinas, openly erotic, sexually ambiguous.   (*New York Public Library*)

sake and to efforts to create "pure painting" that embodied emotion above all. Others sought truth and beauty in other places. Futurist artists, like Mikhail Larionov, Natalia Goncharova, and Malevich, experimented with images of modern machines in motion, with primitivism in style and subject, with evocations of "Oriental" forms in Russian culture, and with an abstraction of dynamically interacting rays or geometric blocks of primal color.

Theater, like the ballet a combination of arts, also developed in the "silver age." In addition to the fine imperial theaters, private ones came into prominence. The Moscow Art Theater, directed by Konstantin Stanislavsky, achieved the greatest and most sustained fame and exercised the strongest influence on acting in Russia and abroad through his emphasis on psychological realism. But it is important to realize that it represented only one current in the theatrical life of a period remarkable for its variety, vitality, and experimentation.

Exhibition room of "suprematist" paintings by Kazimir Malevich at "0.10: The Last Futurist Painting Exhibition," held in Petrograd in 1915. While most reviewers voiced incomprehension and even scorn in viewing these experiments in abstraction as a new way of seeing, a sympathetic reviewer praised this exhibit as a stand against the "stupidity and vulgarity covering the world." Note the position of the "Black Square" in the traditional icon corner.  *(Mark Steinberg)*

Russian art as well as Russian literature in the "silver age" formed an inseparable part of the art and literature of the West, profiting hugely, for example, from literary trends in France or from German thought, and in turn contributing in quite original ways to virtually every form of literary and artistic argument and creative expression. In a sense, Russian culture was less directly imitative but also more "Western" than ever on the eve of 1917.

## Ideologies and Social Thought

As already mentioned, the radicals of the generation of the 1860s, Turgenev's "sons," found their spiritual home first in "nihilistic" ideologies, which rejected established political and social authorities in the name of an often vague program of radical change. As their spokesman, the gifted young literary critic Dmitrii Pisarev, 1840–68, said: "What can be broken, should be broken." The new radical spirit reflected both the general materialistic and realistic character of the age and special Russian conditions, such as a reaction to the stifling of intellectual life under Nicholas I, the autocratic and oppressive nature of the regime, the weak development of the middle class or other elements of moderation and compromise, and a gradual democratization of the educated public.

While nihilism emancipated the young Russian radicals from any allegiance to the established order, it was, to repeat a point, more individualistic than social in its spirit of total personal emancipation and lacked much of a positive program, though proclamations produced by radical student groups in the 1860s suggest a vague general commitment to "freedom" embodied in such principles as an end to monarchy, a decentralized society based on communes, cooperative ownership and work in the economy, women's equality, and the rights of nationalities to independence. A more elaborate social creed came with a vengeance in the form of *narodnichestvo*, or populism, which arose in the 1860s and 1870s to dominate much of Russian radicalism until the Soviet era. We have already seen its political impact in such events as the celebrated "going to the people" of 1874, the terrorism of the "Peoples' Will," and the activities of the Socialist Revolutionary party. Ideologically, populism was defined by devotion to the common people (improving their lives but also inspiring them to revolution), a rejection of capitalism, the belief that Russia had a special historical opportunity to avoid the evils of capitalism thanks to the strength of the peasant commune, and insistence that social revolution was even more essential than political change. Populism also openly reasserted moral argument. Not unlike the generation of Herzen and Belinsky, populists insisted on universal moral truths grounded in human nature, at the heart of which was the natural equality and dignity of all human beings and hence the right to a life of respect and opportunity for personal development. Bakunin's violent anarchism inspired many of the more impatient populists. Anarchism, it might be added, appealed to a variety of Russian intellectuals, including such outstanding figures as Tolstoy and Prince Petr Kropotkin, a noted geographer, geologist, and radical, who lived from 1842 to 1921 and devoted most of his life to spreading anarchism. Kropotkin's activities, including a fantastic escape from a prison-hospital, were described in his celebrated *Memoirs of a Revolutionist* written in English for *The Atlantic Monthly* in 1898–99.

Whereas Herzen and Bakunin were émigrés, populist leaders also arose in Russia after 1855. Nikolai Chernyshevsky, whose views and impact were not limited to populism, but who nevertheless exercised a major influence on Russian populists, deserves special attention. Born in 1828, Chernyshevsky actually enjoyed only a few years of public activity as journalist and writer, especially as editor of a leading periodical, *The Contemporary*, before his arrest in 1862. He returned from Siberian exile only in 1883 and died in 1889. It was probably Chernyshevsky more than anyone else who contributed to the spread of utilitarian, positivist, and in part materialist views in Russia. Drawing on Ludwig Feuerbach's materialism and Jeremy Bentham's utilitarianism, Chernyshevsky argued that individual needs and individual happiness must be the basis of all morality, and thus of society, but that this egoism must be tempered with the rational knowledge that true self-interest lay in seeing the greatest benefit among the largest number of people. From this he argued for the necessity of an economy and society based on equality and cooperation. A man of vast erudition, Chernyshevsky concerned himself with aesthetics—developing further Belinsky's ideas on the primacy of life over art—as much as with economics, and wrote on nineteenth-century French history, demonstrating the failure of liberalism, as well as on Russian problems. His extremely popular novel, *What Is to Be Done?*, dealt with the new generation of "critical realists," their ethics and their activities, and sketched both the revolutionary hero and forms of cooperative organization. As to the peasant commune, Chernyshevsky showed more reserve than certain of his contemporaries. Yet he generally believed that it could serve as a direct transition to socialism in Russia, provided socialist revolution first triumphed in Europe. For a time Chernyshevsky collaborated closely in spreading his ideas with an able radical literary critic, Nikolai Dobroliubov, who died in 1861 at the age of twenty-five.

Chernyshevsky's and Dobroliubov's work was continued, with certain differences, by Petr Lavrov and Nikolai Mikhailovsky. Lavrov, 1823–1900, another erudite adherent of positivism, utilitarianism, and populism, emphasized in his *Historical Letters* of 1870, which many young radicals claimed to have read with "hot tears of idealistic enthusiasm," and in other writings the crucial role of "critically thinking individuals" in the revolutionary struggle and the transformation of Russia. Philosophically, he voiced the need for an ethical system that could guide action and argued that the proper center of such a practical philosophy must be the principle of the human person: society must be judged by whether it enhanced or restricted the dignity and development of individuals. Mikhailovsky, a literary critic who lived from 1842 to 1904, employed the "subjective method" in social analysis to stress moral values rather than mere objective description and to champion the peasant commune, which provided for harmonious development of the individual, by contrast with the industrial order, which led to narrow specialization along certain lines and the atrophy of other aspects of personality. The populist defense of the peasant commune became more desperate with the passage of time, because Russia was in fact developing into a capitalist country and because an articulate Marxist school arose to point that out as proof that history was proceeding according to Marxist predictions. In the early twentieth century, the populist tradition was continued mainly by the Socialist Revolutionaries, led by Viktor Chernov. While they borrowed some ideas from the Marxists, they remained distinct in their insistence on popular unity and democracy (they rejected arguments that there was a class divide between workers and peasants that required the rural majority to be subordinate to the urban minority) and their tendency to view socialism as derived more from morality and ethics than from the rational logics of science and history.

Marxists proved to be strong competitors and opponents of populists. The actual development of Russia seemed to follow the Marxist rather than the populist blueprint. Beginning with the 1890s Marxism made important inroads among Russian intellectuals, gaining adherents both among scholars and in the radical and revolutionary movement. While Marxism will be discussed in a later chapter, it should be kept in mind that Marxism offered its followers an "objective knowledge" of history instead of a mere "subjective method" and a quasi-scientific certainty of victory in lieu of, or rather in addition to, moral earnestness and indignation. Still, Russian Marxists were divided over fundamental questions. The occasion for the split between Bolsheviks and Mensheviks, we have seen, was over how open or disciplined the revolutionary party should be. But there were deeper divisions. The leader of the Mensheviks, Iulii Martov, for example, was attracted to Marxism, not only by its "scientific" arguments about the natural progress of history toward socialism, but also by its compelling moral arguments about the justice of ending inequality and suffering. By contrast, the Bolshevik leader Lenin repeatedly voiced his contempt for the political moralizing so common to Russian socialism. Different sensibilities were reflected in different politics. Whereas Martov and the Mensheviks emphasized the value to workers' consciousness of the struggle itself, Lenin and the Bolsheviks emphasized the guidance and leadership workers needed—hence the difference in their visions of the party. And whereas Marxists like Martov viewed the socialist goal of democracy as an inherent value, Marxists like Lenin saw democracy as mainly a means to facilitate the struggle for socialism.

For liberals, by contrast, freedom and democracy were absolutes. Michael Karpovich, George Fischer, and other scholars have argued that Russian liberalism was by no means a negligible quantity, even though its main social bases in the professions and the zemstvo system remained small. It gained strength steadily and produced able ideologists and leaders such as Pavel Miliukov and Petr Struve. Although divided over strategy and tactics, liberals shared a common set of goals for transforming Russia into a strong and modern polity: the rule of law instead of the arbitrary will of the state; freedom of conscience, religion, speech, and assembly as "rights" for all citizens of the empire; a democratic parliament; strong local self-government; and social reforms to ensure social stability and justice. They also believed in the need for personal transformation: individuals should develop in themselves the virtues of initiative, self-reliance, self-improvement, discipline, and rationality. It should be noted that liberals viewed themselves as acting for the national good rather than the interests of any particular class. This was especially true of the Constitutional Democrats, who vehemently insisted that they were "above class" and even "above party." The good they sought to promote was, of course, the good of the individual—a liberal touchstone—but also the development of a national community founded on free association and patriotic solidarity. Some liberals felt themselves to be "above nation" also: alongside Struve's liberal nationalism, for example, stood Miliukov's arguments that human progress meant that modern national consciousness would give way to a critical social consciousness.

Not all thinking and outspoken Russians were liberals or socialists; and conservatism, even reaction, was not the property of the autocratic state. Conservatives tended toward Russian nationalism, belief in the need for an absolutist state, anti-individualism, and a philosophical skepticism about the possibility of human-made happiness on earth. Within the government,

the leading intellectual proponent of official conservatism was Konstantin
Pobedonostsev, whose anxieties about the direction of the modern world
and insistence on the saving power of Orthodoxy, autocracy, and nationality
we have encountered already. Outside of government, though able to influence both public opinion and state policy through his newspapers and journals, the leading conservative voice was Mikhail Katkov. A leader among
Russian nationalists and Pan-Slavists, Katkov was a vehement advocate of the
Russification of non-Russians but also of the necessary superiority of Russians
within the empire. Among the more extreme (and interesting) Russian conservatives was Nikolai Danilevsky, whose magnum opus, *Russia and Europe*
(1869), predicted that a unified Slavdom was destined by history to be the next
great and dominant civilization in the world. A related but different vision
of the Slavic mission and future belonged to Konstantin Leontiev. He viewed
Western liberalism, egalitarianism, and materialism as catastrophically harmful to humanity and saw Russia's salvation in its traditional "Byzantinism"—
Orthodoxy, autocracy, and a hierarchical society—and its union with countries
of the East.

The "woman question" was a social issue that engaged almost everyone,
from conservatives to socialists. The "emancipation of women" was a central
theme in the writings of Chernyshevsky and other radicals in the 1860s and
after, though the issue gained particular prominence and urgency during and
after the 1905 revolution. Liberal and socialist activists, both men and women,
regularly challenged the traditionally subordinate status and role of women in
Russian life and targeted the particular humiliations women endured: sexual
harassment, domestic violence, prostitution, lack of education, lack of training
for employment, lower wages, undeveloped social support for maternity and
child care, and the lack of legal protections or civil rights. Ideologically, the
women's movement was as divided as the larger political world. Many activists fought directly to overcome women's inferior status; others, especially
socialists, distanced themselves from such feminism, insisting that women
should focus on the "larger" cause, since women's position would change only
when all people were freed from the old order.

The "national question" also concerned everyone. We have seen that
official, conservative, and much liberal thought included arguments about
Russian identity and destiny. Art and music, too, were filled with Russian
national concerns. A large part of this question concerned the place of Russia
and Russians within their multinational and multiethnic empire. Mark Bassin
has described three main models for this relationship: Russia as a "European
empire" bringing civilization to non-Europeans; Russia as an "anti-European"
empire with its own native qualities and virtues, often linked to Asia; and,
though this conception emerged only in the late 1800s, Russia as a "national
empire" that should gradually assimilate non-Russians as imperial citizens
into a culture defined by Russian traditions.

The empire's non-Russian nationalities themselves explored the meanings of their own ethnic and national experiences. We have already noted the
rise of nationalist movements. Most were also concerned with the cultural

question of defining their ethnic and religious identities for modern times. Thus, for example, Jewish communities, often through new Yiddish-language magazines, argued intensely over questions such as religious faith versus secular knowledge, and cultural assimilation versus the cultivation of separateness (including through Zionism and emigration to America). We see similar debates among Muslims, notably in the movement for cultural reform. The Jadid (new-method) movement in Islamic education, studied by Adeeb Khalid and others, sought to create a new modern Muslim steeped both in a revitalized and "purified" Islam and in modern cosmopolitan knowledge. A major sign and catalyst of change was the growth of native-language publishing, including influential magazines like the satirical *Mulla Nasreddin* from Tiflis, which elaborated a new hybrid discourse that blended the worldview of Western modernity—thus, for example, satirizing Muslim "backwardness" and advocating women's rights—with Muslim identities and values.

One of the most significant shifts in Russian thought and culture, reaching from the heights of philosophy to popular culture, was the turn toward spirituality and religion. In Russian philosophy, the "silver age," in particular, marked a return to metaphysics, and often to religious belief itself. Among intellectuals, a most influential figure was Vladimir Soloviev, the son of the historian Sergei Soloviev. He lived from 1853 until 1900 and wrote on a variety of philosophical and theological subjects. A trenchant critic of the radical positivism of the age, as well as of chauvinism and reaction, Soloviev remained a rather isolated figure during his lifetime but came to exercise a profound influence on the intellectual elite of the "silver age." Another influential thinker who challenged the dominant rationalism and positivism of the late nineteenth century was the brilliant philosopher Lev Shestov. In his 1905 book, *Apotheosis of Groundlessness*, Shestov asserted the liberating possibilities of modern "disenchantment," "doubt," "indeterminacy," "lack of clarity," and "disorder." The most important intellectual act of turning away from the rationalist traditions of the Russian intelligentsia occurred in 1909, when a group of intellectuals, several of them former Marxists, published a sensation-creating volume of essays under the title *Vekhi* (Signposts or Landmarks). Their essays bluntly repudiated the materialism, atheism, and collectivism that had dominated the thought of the intelligentsia for generations as leading inevitably to failure and moral disaster, advocating instead a philosophy of individuality, spirituality, and morality.

Extending and broadening this turn away from narrow rationalism was a remarkable upheaval in spiritual searching and crisis, often called a "religious renaissance" by historians. In the years after 1900, and especially after the excitement and disappointment of 1905, many educated Russians returned to the Church to revitalize their faith. Many others were drawn to private prayer, mysticism, spiritualism, theosophy, and Eastern religions—a movement known as "God-Seeking." As we have seen, religious associations proliferated among both the educated and the urban poor. Urban movements such as the "Brethren," for example, attracted workers and others with their charismatic preaching, ideas of moral living (to realize the dignity befitting human beings as carriers of the flame of the Holy Spirit), and promises of salvation in this life. Among the peasantry, historians have discovered growing interest in spiritual-ethical literature, an upsurge in pilgrimage and devotions to miracle-working icons, and the proliferation of what the Orthodox establishment branded as "sectarianism." A few individual clergy sought to revitalize Orthodox faith, most famously the charismatic Father John (Ioann) of Kronstadt, who, until his death in 1908 (though his followers remained active long after), emphasized Christian living and sought to restore fervency and the presence of the miraculous in liturgical celebration. Many artists and writers as well were attracted to the spiritual and the sacred. Thus, many "silver age" poets sought in their writings to penetrate appearances to discover the spiritual essence of things and sometimes voiced apocalyptic visions of a transformed world. Visual artists were also drawn toward a spiritual understanding of the power and function of images, including explicitly religious ones but also abstract forms. Alexander Benois, the leader of the World of Art movement, observed in 1902 that in all the arts there was a widespread feeling that the reigning "materialism" of the age was too "astonishingly simple" to answer questions about life or to express ideals and feelings. Discontent with materialism and the allure of religious and mystical perceptions reached even the most unexpected places: around 1908–9, a group of Marxists, including the future Soviet Commissar of Enlightenment, Anatolii Lunacharsky, and the writer Maxim Gorky, elaborated a re-enchanted Marxism known as "God-Building." Feeling the cold rationalism, materialism, and determinism of traditional Marxism inadequate to inspire a revolutionary mass movement, they insisted on the need to appeal to the subconscious and the emotional, to recapture for the revolution, in Lunacharsky's words, the power of "myth," in order to create a new faith that placed humanity where God had been but retained a religious spirit of passion, moral certainty, and the promise of deliverance from evil and death.

Russian cultural life was not entirely filled with high-minded concerns about politics, society, philosophy, morality, and religion. Modern city life was filled with opportunities, especially for those with some disposable income, for what many intellectuals viewed as quite unenlightened public pleasure: music halls, nightclubs, *cafés chantants*, outdoor "pleasure gardens," cheap theaters, increasing numbers of cinemas, and popular public divertissements like car races or wrestling bouts. Popular reading tastes also seemed far from uplifting. Newspapers, it was said, "pandered to crude instincts" with stories of "scandal" and sensation—though for popular readers this was a fascinating window into the bustling modern world—while widely available popular fiction, it was feared, eroded traditional popular and national values and tastes in favor of preoccupations with adventure, individual daring, exotic locales, and material success. The enormously popular cinema contributed to this changing popular culture with its ethos of spectacle and sensation and its narratives of melodramatic conflict over values in a changing society, materialist consumption, and the often troubled pursuit of pleasure.

## Concluding Remarks

We can return, in thinking about cultural life, to the question of whether or not Russia was heading toward crisis and revolution. Cultural life, like social and political life, seemed to point in many directions. "Optimists" could highlight the richness of cultural and intellectual developments, the spread of democratic ideas, heightened respect for human dignity, and the religious and spiritual discovery of universal values and truths. Pessimists could emphasize artistic defiance of established norms, decadent artistic tastes and interests, widespread public depression and disillusionment, the rise of socialism and other radical ideologies, and intellectual and cultural fragmentation. Of course, the historian cannot neglect the deep chasm between the few and the many: the brilliant cultural achievements this chapter has described touched the majority of Russians very little if at all. But we must also recognize, again, the contradiction and uncertainty—Russia did indeed seem to be heading in multiple directions at once. We cannot really be sure of what might have happened in the absence of the devastating war that began in the summer of 1914. A working-class writer named Nikolai Liashko, looking back on the prerevolutionary years through the wake of the war, revolution, and civil war that followed, recognized the contradictions of those years: this was a time marked by "unexpected pains and joys," a time when "people sicken, go mad from exhaustion, but really live." The same would be said for the revolutionary epoch to which we now turn.

# CHAPTER 34

# The Revolutions of 1917

"Long live free Russia."
The joyous cry floods my soul.
"Long live our freedom,"
The red flag stills my heart.
A leaden weight has fallen,
The world dreams a shining dream ...
I'm young again, my body drunk,
My soul replete with feelings.
With feelings as vast and endless
As drops in the cup of the sea.

MIKHAIL SERAFIMOVICH, PRIVATE IN THE
CAVALRY RESERVE, MARCH 1917

The revolution has accomplished its business: right away it turned off the road the old regime was going down, that camp of stuffed, greasy, gluttonous living, but very soon after it returned to that same rut as before under the monarchist order, where the same animals cart the unbearable, tortuous weight, the same wolves govern us only in sheep's clothing and the same words are spoken and promises made about the good life.

A. KUCHLAVOK, SOLDIER, AUGUST 1917

As has been indicated in preceding chapters, the constitutional period of Russian imperial history has continued to evoke much controversy. Optimistic students of the development of Russia from the Revolution of 1905 to the First World War and the revolutions of 1917 have emphasized that Russia had finally left autocracy behind and was evolving toward liberalism and political freedom. The change in 1907 in the electoral law indicated that the Duma could no longer be abolished. Moreover, the reformed Russian legislature proceeded to play an important part in the affairs of the country and to gain ever-increasing prestige and acceptance at home, among both government officials and the people, as well as abroad. As an Englishman observed, "the atmosphere and instincts of parliamentary life" grew in the empire of the Romanovs. Besides, continue the optimists, Russian society at the time was much more progressive and democratic than the constitutional framework alone would indicate, and was becoming increasingly so every year. Modern education spread rapidly at different levels and was remarkably humanitarian and liberal—as were Russian teachers as a group—not at all likely to serve as a buttress for antiquated ideas or obsolete institutions. Russian universities enjoyed virtually full freedom and a rich creative life. Elsewhere, too, an energetic discussion went on. Even the periodical press, in spite of various restrictions, gave some representation to every point of view, including the Bolshevik. Government prohibitions and penalties could frequently be neutralized by such simple means as a change in the name of a publication or, if necessary, by sending the nominal editor to jail, while important political writers continued their work. To be sure, grave problems remained, in particular, economic backwardness and the poverty of the masses. But, through industrialization on the one hand and Stolypin's land reform on the other, they were on the way to being solved. Above all, Russia needed time and peace.

Pessimistic critics have drawn a different picture of the period. Many of them refuse even to call it "constitutional" because, both according to the Fundamental Laws and in fact, the executive branch of the government and the ministers in particular were not responsible to the Duma. Limited in power and limited in representativeness by a highly unequal electoral system (especially after the arbitrary electoral change of 1907), the Duma functioned, it is argued, less as an effective channel for the popular redress of grievances than as a constantly frustrating reminder of the autocracy's unwillingness to accept real political reform. Indeed, Nicholas II's hostility to the participation of organized society in Russia's political life seemed to be growing all the more intense in these final years. The power of nonentities, like Goremykin and Sukhomlinov, and the fantastic Rasputin himself, were logical end products of the bankruptcy of the regime. Meanwhile, society appeared to be heading toward crisis. Social discontent, the pessimists argue, was growing not lessening as the economy modernized. They point to ominous signs: the peasants' persistent desire to possess all they land they work as both the practical solution to their poverty and a necessary act of justice, continuing workers' protests against low wages and harsh working conditions and the frequency with which these demands were combined with demands for political change, growing popular support for radical socialists (especially among workers concentrated in St. Petersburg and Moscow), political terrorism both of the Left and the Right, and the widespread influence of the languages of class hostility and democratic freedoms. Assumedly positive developments like urbanization, the growing availability of consumer goods, and widening literacy seemed more likely to generate frustration with the status quo than to lessen social tensions. Even cultural life pointed toward crisis, as artists rejected all tradition as bankrupt and philistine or were drawn toward "decadent" fascination with sex, evil, demons, shadows, and a coming apocalypse. Russia was headed for catastrophe.

The optimists, thus, believe that imperial Russia was ruined by the First World War. The pessimists maintain that the war provided merely the last mighty push to bring the whole rotten structure tumbling down. Certainly it added an enormous burden to the load borne by the Russian people. Human losses were staggering. To cite Nikolai Golovin's figures, in the course of the war the Russian army mobilized 15.5 million men and suffered greater casualties than did the armed forces of any other country involved in the titanic struggle: 1.65 million killed, 3.85 million wounded, and 2.41 million taken prisoner. The destruction of property and other civilian losses and displacement escaped count. The Russian army tried to evacuate the population as it retreated, adding to the confusion and suffering. It became obvious during the frightful ordeal that the imperial government had again failed in its tasks, as in the Crimean War and the Russo-Japanese War, but on a much larger scale. In addition to the army, the urban population suffered as a result of this because it experienced serious difficulties obtaining food and fuel. Inflation ran rampant. Worst of all, the government refused to learn any lessons: instead of liberalizing state policies and relying more on the public, which was eager to help, Nicholas II held fast to his anachronistic political faith in unfettered autocracy. He dismissed appeals by organized civic organizations to be allowed a larger role in the mobilization effort and showed nothing but contempt for demands that he appoint a cabinet of ministers that would enjoy "the confidence of the public." And he ignored all warnings, including blunt reports in the first weeks of 1917, by police agents assigned to keep watch over public opinion, of "a wave of animosity against those in authority in wide circles of the population."

## The February Revolution and the Provisional Government

The imperial regime died with hardly a whimper. Popular revolution, which came suddenly, was totally unprepared. In the course of the momentous days of February 23 to 27 (March 8–12 on the Western calendar) riots and demonstrations in the capital—renamed "Petrograd" instead of the German-sounding "St. Petersburg" during the war—occasioned by a shortage of bread and coal assumed a more serious character. On February 23 (March 8), thousands of women textile workers walked out of their factories—partly in commemoration of International Women's Day but mainly to protest the severe shortages of bread. Already large numbers of men and women were on strike or idled by fuel shortages or lockouts. The numbers of strikers continued to grow, as did the size and vehemence of street demonstrations, at which banners and speeches voiced demands ranging from bread (the most common shout heard from the crowds) to an end to the war to the abolition of autocracy. On February 25 reserve battalions sent to suppress the crowds fraternized with them instead, and there were no other troops in the city. Resolute action, such as promptly bringing in loyal forces from elsewhere, might have saved the imperial government, at least temporarily. Instead, with Nicholas II away at the front, authority simply collapsed and many officials went into hiding.

Seemingly with one mind, the population of Petrograd turned to the Duma for leadership.

On February 26 members of the Duma sidestepped an imperial dissolution decree, and the next day they created a Provisional Government, composed of a score of prominent Duma leaders and public figures. Prince Georgii Lvov, formerly chairman of the Union of Zemstva and Towns, assumed the positions of chairman of the Council of Ministers, that is, prime minister, and of minister of the interior. His more important colleagues included the Kadet leader Miliukov as minister of foreign affairs—the Octobrist leader Guchkov as minister of war and of the navy, and Alexander Kerensky, the only socialist in the cabinet—associated with the Socialist Revolutionary party—as minister of justice. The new government closely reflected the composition and views of the Progressive Bloc in the Duma, with the Kadets obtaining the greatest single representation.

Nicholas II bowed to the inevitable and on March 2 adicated for himself and his only son, Alexis, in favor of his brother, Michael, who in turn abdicated the next day in favor of the decision of the constituent assembly, or in effect in favor of the Provisional Government pending that decision. Nicholas II, on his side, had appointed Lvov prime minister before renouncing the throne. Thus ended the rule of the Romanovs in Russia. The Provisional Government was quickly recognized, and hailed, by the United States and other Western democracies.

From the first, the Provisional Government faced a serious rival: the Petrograd Soviet of Workers' and Soldiers' Deputies, which claimed to represent the will of workers and soldiers and could, in fact, mobilize and control these groups during the early months of the revolution. The Soviet was modeled on the workers' councils of 1905. When workers began electing deputies during the February 1917 strikes, socialist activists, mostly Mensheviks and Socialist Revolutionaries (SRs), established a citywide council, calling for elections in all factories and in the garrisons. The first meeting of the Petrograd Soviet took place on the evening of February 27 in the Tauride Palace, the same building where the new government was taking shape. The leaders of the Soviet hesitated, though, to act beyond what they considered their legitimate authority: they believed that they represented particular classes of the population, not the whole nation. Dominated by moderate socialists until the fall of 1917, the Soviet had no desire to wrest power from the "bourgeoisie," for its leaders considered Russia too backward for socialism. Still, they acted boldly in the interests, as they saw them, of the popular masses. Notably, on March 1 the Soviet issued its famous Order No. 1, which amounted to a charter of soldiers' power and rights. Military units were to establish soldiers' committees of elected representatives from the lower ranks and send deputies to the Petrograd Soviet, which was to be the final authority controlling the actions of the military. Weapons, vehicles, and other materiel were to be taken from the control of officers and put under the authority of soldiers' committees. Symbolically, soldiers were no longer obliged to salute officers when not on duty (for soldiers were now free citizens in their civic life) nor, even when on

duty, to address them with honorific titles like "your Excellency," and officers were forbidden to be "rude" toward soldiers or to address them with the
familiar *ty*. Following the Petrograd lead, Soviets began to be formed all over
Russia. The first All-Russian Congress of Soviets, which met in the capital on
June 3, contained representatives from more than 350 local units. The delegates
included 285 Socialist Revolutionaries, 245 Mensheviks, and 105 Bolsheviks,
as well as some deputies from minor socialist parties. The Congress elected
an executive committee that became the supreme Soviet body. Soviets stood
much closer to restless workers, soldiers, and peasants than did Lvov and his
associates and thus enjoyed a large and immediate following.

The Provisional Government lasted approximately eight months: from
February 27 until October 25, 1917 (March 12 to November 7). This was almost
certainly the most liberal government in the world at that time. Committed
to ideals of democracy, freedom, and the unity of all classes and peoples, the
Provisional Government immediately launched a radical program of reform.
In a matter of weeks, they freed thousands of political prisoners and exiles;
proclaimed freedom of speech, press, assembly, and association and the right
to strike; abolished flogging, exile to Siberia, and the death penalty; removed
legal restrictions based on nationality or religion (and promised Poland independence); granted women the right to vote and run for office; began preparing for elections to a Constituent Assembly on the basis of universal, secret,
direct, and equal suffrage; and started work on land reform. Rhetorically,

The first "cabinet of ministers" of the Provisional Government. Prince Georgii Lvov
is first on the left Kerensky is third and Miliukov sixth from the left. By April 1917
crowds in the streets would be calling for the removal of these "bourgeois ministers" (excluding Kerensky). (*Russian State Archive of Film and Photographic Documents*)

the liberal leaders of the new government articulated a broad and embracive notion of the revolution that made the individual citizen the foundation of the new order. This was an ideal of citizenship that disregarded class interests or particularistic needs in favor of ideals of national unity and concord. And, consistent with their long years of struggle against autocracy, they deemphasized the state as the key force in transforming the country in favor of an active civil society.

Although the Provisional Government demonstrated what liberalism might have done for Russia, it failed to overcome the quite extraordinary difficulties that beset the country, and those who ruled it, in 1917. The new government continued the war in spite of the fact that support for the war continued to decline among the people and that the army became daily less able to fight on. While convinced that all available land should belong to the peasants, it made no definitive land settlement, leaving that to the constituent assembly and thus itself failing to satisfy the peasantry. It proved unable to check inflation, restore transportation, or increase industrial production. In fact, the Russian economy continued to disintegrate.

A large part of this failure stemmed from the limited authority and power of the new regime. It had little in the way of an effective administrative apparatus, the tsarist police in particular having largely gone into hiding. As already mentioned, it had at all times to contend with the Soviet. While the high command of the army supported the government, enlisted men remained an uncertain quantity; the Petrograd garrison itself was devoted to the Soviet. What is more, the Provisional Government had to promise the Soviet not to remove or disarm that garrison. Kerensky's derisive appellation, "persuader-in-chief," was in part a reflection of his unenviable position.

The government also made mistakes. It refused to recognize the catastrophic condition of the country and misjudged the mood of the people. Of course, many of the government's "mistakes" were understandable given their liberal political values. Thus, as mentioned, it continued the war, believing that the Russians, like the French at the time of the great French Revolution, would fight better than ever because they were finally free men. They also sincerely believed that abandoning the democratic allies France and Great Britain in their struggle against authoritarian Germany would have betrayed their political principles and Russia's best interests as a new democracy. In internal affairs, a moderate and liberal position, generally difficult to maintain in times of upheaval, proved quixotic in a country of desperately poor and largely illiterate peasants who wanted the gentry land above all else. The government's temporary, "provisional," nature constituted a special weakness. Its members were deeply conscious of the fact that they had acquired their high authority by chance and that the Duma itself had been elected by the extremely restricted suffrage of 1907. Believing deeply in the rule of law, they insisted that fundamental questions of Russia's future could only be settled by a fully democratic constituent assembly. Such basic decisions as those involved in the land settlement and in the future status of the national minorities had, therefore, to be left to that assembly. Yet, if a constituent assembly meant so much to the members of the Provisional Government, they made perhaps their worst mistake in not calling it together soon enough. While some of the best Russian jurists tried to draw a perfect electoral law, time slipped by. When a constituent assembly finally did meet, it was much too late, for the Bolsheviks had already come to power.

The Bolshevik victory in 1917 cannot be separated from the person and activity of Lenin. He returned to Russia thanks to the amnesty the new government granted to exiles, arriving at the Finland Station in Petrograd on April 3, 1917. The German government had let Lenin and his associates pass from Switzerland though Germany in a sealed train in hopes they would disorganize the Russian war effort; this journey would soon lead to rumors that Lenin was in the pay of the Germans. On the following day, Lenin issued an appeal that amazed even most Bolsheviks: the time had come to turn the bourgeois revolution into a socialist revolution. These "April Theses," as they would be titled a few days later when published in the party newspaper *Pravda*, were a dramatic call for revolution against the "bourgeois" Provisional Government, all political power to the Soviets, an immediate end to the war, nationalization of land and its distribution to the peasants, and industry under the control of workers' councils. Many of his comrades thought he had simply fallen out of touch with political realities, having been out of Russia so long. But Lenin found growing rank-and-file support in the party and soon won over most party leaders.

The crushing burden of the war and increasing economic dislocation made the position of the Provisional Government constantly more precarious. Also, enthusiasm for the new freedoms mixed with growing distrust of the new rulers, who were variously labeled the rich, the upper classes, and the bourgeoisie. The first open crisis occurred in late April 1917 in connection with the government's war policy. Pressured from the Petrograd Soviet to renounce annexationist war aims, the Provisional Government issued to Russian citizens a "Declaration on War Aims" that insisted on a purely defensive war. Further pressure forced the government to send a diplomatic note to the allies declaring the same. But when this note was made public, the effect was catastrophic. On April 20, the newspapers published the text of the note that Foreign Minister Miliukov had sent to the allies: it assured them that Russia would fight to victory and was fully ready to impose "guarantees and sanctions" after the war, which the public widely understood as implying, among other things, that Russia intended to continue to demand control of Constantinople and the Dardanelle straits, as had been agreed upon with the allies in 1915. This clearly contradicted the foreign policy the Petrograd Soviet had been demanding and even contradicted the government's own "Declaration on War Aims." It seemed to many that the Declaration was now shown to have been political deceit and hypocrisy. The next day, large crowds of protesters, including soldiers with arms, were in the streets of Petrograd and Moscow denouncing "Miliukov-Dardanelskii," the "capitalist ministers," and the "imperialist war." To calm the furor, Miliukov was forced to resign and the cabinet was reorganized to include five socialists rather than one, with

Kerensky taking the ministries of war and the navy. The government declared itself committed to a strictly defensive war and to a peace "without annexations and indemnities." Yet, to drive the enemy out, Kerensky and General Alexei Brusilov started a major offensive on the southwestern front late in June. Initially successful, it soon collapsed because of confusion and lack of discipline. Entire units simply refused to fight. The Germans and Austrians in turn broke through the Russian lines, and the Provisional Government had to face another disaster. The problem of national minorities became ever more pressing as ethnic and national movements mushroomed in the disorganized former empire of the Romanovs. The government continued its increasingly hazardous policy of postponing political decisions until the meeting of a constituent assembly. Nevertheless, four Kadet ministers resigned in July because they believed that too broad a recognition had been accorded to the Ukrainian movement. Serious tensions and crises in the cabinet were also demonstrated by the resignation of the minister of trade and industry, who opposed the efforts of the new Social Democratic minister of labor to have workers participate in the management of industry, and the clash between Lvov and Viktor Chernov, the Socialist Revolutionary leader who had become minister of agriculture, over the implementation of the land policy. The crucial land problem became more urgent as peasants began to appropriate the land of the gentry on their own, without waiting for the constituent assembly.

Growing popular frustration and discontent helped produce the next big crisis, the so-called "July Days," in which tens of thousands of armed soldiers, sailors, and workers took to the streets of the capital, starting on July 3. Nothing like this had been seen since the February revolution. But the differences from February were striking. These crowds in the streets lacked the embracive multiclass character of the February Days. And, by all accounts, the mood was much more grim and angry. By July 4, shootings were reported all over the city, and the numbers of injured and dead began to rise. Violence erupted whenever cossacks or other forces of authority were encountered. Even many socialists felt that the "excesses" of the crowd were the actions of a mob that had, as Maxim Gorky wrote at the time, "absolutely no idea of what they were doing." But documents from the time also show that people knew what they were against: the war, the new offensive, the bourgeoisie. And they knew what they were for: Soviet power. What was not clear was how to achieve this end, especially when the Soviet itself refused to be forced to take power. In one famous scene, when the Soviet leaders sent out Chernov to calm the crowd, an angry demonstrator shook his fist and shouted at Chernov, "Take power, you son of a bitch, when it is handed to you." The moderate leaders of the Soviet blamed the Bolsheviks for all this. The Bolsheviks themselves, though tempted and at first uncertain how to respond, also refused to lead this street movement to power. Historians still argue about whether the Bolsheviks organized these events and, if so, to what purpose. Certainly, the goal of overthrowing the Provisional Government was on the Bolshevik agenda. The question was when. It is reasonable to argue that, whatever role the Bolsheviks played in fomenting these demonstrations, a justifiable fear of failure stayed their hand. Without leadership from either the Soviets or the Bolsheviks the movement disintegrated. A heavy rainfall on the evening of July 4 finally drove the last of the crowds off the streets.

The government responded with repression against participating troops and organizations. The Bolsheviks were accused of treason—of having taken money and instructions from the German government—and hundreds of Bolshevik leaders were arrested. Lenin, and a few others, went into hiding or fled abroad. In addition, some civil liberties were restricted in the interests of greater social order. The death penalty was restored for military personnel at the front convicted by field courts of treason, desertion, flight from battle, refusal to fight, incitement to surrender, disobeying orders, and mutiny. Street processions in Petrograd were banned until further notice. On July 18, Kerensky appointed as the new commander in chief Lavr Kornilov, a tough-minded cossack general already greatly admired in conservative circles for his strong advocacy of military and civic discipline. In this new atmosphere, various right-wing and conservative groups became more active and bolder. A new coalition government was also formed, headed by Kerensky and comprised of ten socialists (SRs, Mensheviks, and Trudoviks) and seven liberals (mostly Kadets). It continued efforts to restore authority and order in the country, though many argued that the government should have pressed their victory and entirely eliminated the radical opposition.

The crisis continued to deepen. The government, hoping to unite the country around its authority and program, convened in Moscow a national "State Conference" in mid-August, to which every type of civic organization was invited to send representatives. The conference accomplished little but did reveal the deep social and political rifts in Russian life. Before the meeting, many groups on the Right were already calling for a "strong unified national government" that would "save Russia" through greater order and unity. Socialists, by contrast, were blaming Russia's sufferings on the greed of the bourgeoisie and warned of the threat of counterrevolution. These mutual suspicions and charges filled the conference hall.

The famous "Kornilov affair" grew directly out of the rising summer flood of talk about disorder, betrayal, and danger and about the need for discipline, unity, and strong authority. The affair itself alternated between the ominous and the absurd, forged as much by confusion and misunderstanding as by conspiracy. The consequences, however, were enormous. The new commander in chief, Kornilov, was inclined to share the view on the Right that Kerensky and the government had become a prisoner of the Soviet and the Left. In turn, Kornilov saw himself as the man who could rescue the government and Russia, a self-regard encouraged by the conservative press, right-wing leaders, and increasingly well-organized associations of military officers, businessmen, and landowners. Kornilov appears to have believed, not without reason, that Kerensky also wished to end the power of the Left and was prepared to support a temporary military dictatorship that could impose civil order and create strong government. However, there is also a good deal of evidence of mutual misunderstanding between the two men, or perhaps deliberate mutual deception—the historical record is full of contradictory claims. In any case, when Kornilov dispatched troops to the capital to "protect" the revolution, which seemed to have included dispersing the Soviet, Kerensky appealed to the people to "save the revolution" from Kornilov's conspiracy to take power. In the final days of August, the population of the capital mobilized for defense, while the advancing troops, faced with a railroad strike, encountering general opposition, and short of supplies, became demoralized and bogged down without reaching the destination; their commanding officer committed suicide. Only the Bolsheviks really gained from the episode. Their leaders were let out of jail, and their followers were armed to defend Petrograd. After the Kornilov threat collapsed, they retained the preponderance of military strength in the capital, winning ever more adherents among the increasingly radical masses.

The Provisional Government, on the other hand, came to be bitterly despised by the Right for having betrayed Kornilov—whether the charge was entirely justified is another matter—while many on the Left suspected it of having plotted with him. The cabinet experienced another crisis and was finally able to reconstitute itself—for the third and last time—with ten socialist and six nonsocialist ministers, Kerensky remaining at the head. It should be added that the Kornilov fiasco, followed by the arrest of Kornilov and several other generals, led to a further deterioration of military discipline, making the position of officers in many units untenable.

## Social Revolution

Research on the social history of the revolution has added much to our knowledge of the role workers, soldiers, and peasants played in the coming to power of the Bolsheviks and to our understanding of what these events meant to ordinary Russians. It seems likely that Lenin's arguments would have remained only a footnote to the history of 1917 had not so many people found Bolshevik promises so appealing and had not continuing social discontent and anger undermined Russia's fragile new order. Of course, the erosion of order was in large measure caused by continued economic collapse, especially the abysmal material conditions in the cities and at the front. It seemed to many lower-class Russians, deeply distrustful of existing political and social authorities, that the only solution to this crisis was greater power over their own everyday lives. Thus, factory workers demanded that their elected committees be allowed to supervise production, oversee supplies and fuel, monitor fines and other disciplinary measures, and supervise hiring and firing. As economic conditions worsened and distrust of employers grew, "workers' control" evolved from supervision to demands for complete managerial power by workers. Workers also took revenge on those who had claimed power over their lives in the past, whether simply by being insolent and insubordinate with foremen and employers or through more elaborate rituals in which supervisors or owners were carted out of factories in wheelbarrows. Soldiers and sailors similarly disregarded orders, mocked officers (even beat them), elected new ones (especially when old officers tried to resist the growing demands of soldiers' committees), or simply deserted in increasingly large numbers. Peasants, beginning in the spring, seized and divided up livestock and tools belonging to large landowners, cut wood in private forests, forced independent peasant farmers to return to the communal rules of the village, seized land from both the gentry and richer peasants without waiting for legal sanction, and tried to

Soldiers at a funeral on Mars Field in Petrograd for those who fell in the February Revolution. Banners read "Eternal and Glorious Memory to the Fallen Comrade Fighters for Freedom," "Long Live the Democratic Republic," and "In Organization Is Strength." Use of symbols such as the rising sun, broken chains, and female personifications of liberty was common.  (*Russian State Archive of Film and Photographic Documents*)

expel landlords from the countryside by attacking and burning their homes. On the streets of every major town, crowds of workers, soldiers, students, and other townspeople repeatedly took control of public squares, boulevards, and streets for meetings, funeral processions, and demonstrations. Alongside these acts of social defiance was a good deal of drunkenness, hooliganism, robbery, and criminal violence. By the fall of 1917, even many moderate socialists viewed these upheavals with horror as an upwelling of dark popular instincts and destructive class hatred, leading Russia toward a nightmarish abyss of violence and anarchy.

The motivations, goals, and moods of the aroused population were complex and contradictory. Judging by the torrent of words, spoken and written, that accompanied this social revolution, certain ideas seem to have been most pervasive. Freedom pervades the language of almost everyone in the months after the February Revolution, often cast in near religious terms as something "sacred," as enabling the "resurrection" of the Russian people. But freedom was understood variously: negatively as the end of a long history of subjugation, lack of rights, and repression; positively as one of the fundamental "rights of man"; and quite tangibly as a good that would bring such social benefits as food, land, free education, and an end to the war. Political power also preoccupied people. Side by side with talk of freedom, most Russians also seemed to believe in the need for strong and unified political authority to restore order to the country, especially to the economy. But this must be a political power that would serve the interests of the majority against the minority, of the poor against the rich. Such "democratic" authority, embodied for many in the idea of Soviet power, would, for example, establish a bread monopoly to prevent hunger, distribute land to the poor, introduce workers' control in industry, fix prices to control inflation, expropriate "super-profits," and even suppress opposition to such popular power. As can be seen, social class pervaded popular thinking. Most lower-class Russians distrusted the rich and powerful and tended to blame them for the failures of the revolution since February, even to brand them as "enemies of the people" and "traitors" to Russia and the revolution. Complicating all this, the language of popular revolution was also suffused with moral language and feeling. Talk of "good" and "evil" were common currency in 1917. And ethical notions of honor and dignity, and of the social rights these entailed, were pervasive. The revolution, it was said, was about ending "humiliation and insult" and creating a social and political order defined by the "respect" it gave to ordinary people. Whether this is what the Bolshevik revolution accomplished is another story.

## The Bolshevik Revolution

The Bolsheviks had good reason to believe that their moment on the historical stage had arrived. Bolsheviks were gaining in popularity and support. The patience of workers, soldiers, and peasants had run out, Lenin argued (in person, as he had returned in disguise to Petrograd from Finland in early October). They were ready to support an armed rising against the government.

And given the Bolshevik program—especially immediate peace and land to the peasants immediately—this would be a government "that nobody can overthrow." Against much doubt in his own party, it was decided at a meeting of the Bolshevik central committee on October 10, 1917, to organize the immediate armed overthrow of the government.

The rising popularity of the Bolsheviks, who benefited from the deepening political polarization in the country and from being the only major organized opposition party outside the government, is unquestionable. Evidence was already visible before the Kornilov affair, especially in Moscow and Petrograd: they made dramatic gains (and often won majorities) in elections to local factory committees and trade unions, in elections to district and city Soviets, in elections to the Moscow and Petrograd city councils, in growing readership for the Bolshevik press, and in growing party membership. After the Kornilov affair, which intensified fear of counterrevolution and frustration with the moderate socialists, Bolshevik influence grew even more rapidly. By September 25, the Bolsheviks had a majority in the Petrograd Soviet, allowing them to elect a Bolshevik majority to the presidium and to elect Lev Trotsky chairman. At roughly the same time, Bolsheviks won control of the Moscow Soviet. The weeks following brought more of the same, culminating in the opening in Petrograd of the Second Congress of Soviets of Workers' and Soldiers' Deputies on October 25, 1917. With approximately 300 out of 670 delegates, the Bolsheviks did not have a majority, but half of the 193 SRs were "Left SRs," who supported the Bolsheviks. An overwhelming majority of delegates agreed that the time had come to transfer "all power to the Soviets."

Lenin worried, however, and with good reason, that the congress might tie the Bolsheviks' hands by insisting on a Soviet government that included all the socialist parties. Lenin's plan was to present the Soviet Congress with an accomplished fact: the overthrow of the Provisional Government by Bolshevik forces, though in the name of the Soviets not the Bolshevik party, a tactical move on which Trotsky insisted. On October 25 (November 7)—a date that would be officially celebrated as the anniversary of the Revolution for more than seventy years—Bolshevik "Red Guards" seized control of major streets and bridges, government buildings, railway stations, post and telegraph offices, the telephone exchange, the electric power station, the state bank, and police stations. In the face of this insurrection, the ministers of the Provisional Government barricaded themselves inside the poorly defended Winter Palace (without Kerensky, however, who had fled, possibly in disguise, on the morning of the 25th). After the new Soviet leadership was installed, Menshevik and SR speakers took the podium to denounce the Bolshevik action as a "criminal political adventure" and to call for democratic unity. Trotsky famously mocked proposals for compromise as the pleas of "bankrupts" whose role had been played out and now belonged "on the trash heap of history." Most of these socialist opponents walked out of the congress in protest of Bolshevik actions, leaving Lenin's party with an even larger majority. In the predawn hours of October 26, with news that the palace had been stormed and the ministers were under arrest, the Soviet congress approved Lenin's declaration of the transfer of state authority into its own hands and all local power into the hands of local Soviets of workers', soldiers', and peasants' deputies. The Congress also declared its commitment to propose immediate peace to all nations, to safeguard the transfer of land into the control of peasants' committees, to establish workers' control in industry, and to ensure the convocation of the Constituent Assembly. Within days, Soviets of many other cities endorsed the revolution. Large numbers of Russians across the political spectrum expressed outrage at this violent seizure of power. And very many people voiced certainty that this undemocratic adventure would surely fail, and soon.

*Part VI*

**SOVIET RUSSIA**

# CHAPTER 35

# Soviet Russia: An Introduction

The philosophers have only *interpreted* the world in various ways;
the point however is to *change* it.[*]

KARL MARX

Class struggle, which for a historian schooled in Marx is always in
evidence, is a fight for the crude and material things without which
no refined and spiritual things could exist. But these latter things,
which are present in class struggle, are not present as a vision of
spoils that fall to the victor. They are alive in this struggle as confidence, courage, humor, cunning, and fortitude, and have effects that
reach far back into the past. They constantly call into question every
victory, past and present, of the rulers.

WALTER BENJAMIN

When Lenin and the Bolsheviks took power in 1917 they faced almost
incomprehensible obstacles: a catastrophic war, continuing economic disintegration, social support among only a minority of the population, a world of
states hostile to socialism, and the failure of revolutions to break out in other
countries. And very soon they faced civil war. The brutal struggle to survive
changed the party, its leaders, and their thinking about many things. And
the pressures never let up. The whole of Soviet history is a story of great difficulties, crises, and conflicts—some of them, to be sure, caused by their own
actions—though also of survival and accomplishment. This history of troubles and adaptations is the subject of the following chapters. But to say that
Soviet history was mainly a product of circumstances would miss a key quality that makes this history so remarkable and distinctive. Perhaps more than
any other modern state, the Communists (as they would begin to call themselves) were driven by an all-encompassing ideology, which they would call

---

[*]Italics in the original.

Marxism-Leninism or dialectical materialism. The ideology itself evolved and changed—and was misused, some would say "betrayed"—but it remained the lens through which every circumstance and decision had to be viewed.

Debates among Western historians about Soviet history—and these debates have, at times, been vociferous, especially during the Cold War—have partly concerned this question of the varying weight of circumstance and ideology in shaping the Soviet system. Other, partly related, questions have also been at stake. Early historians told a story almost entirely centered on the state and the party, and often mainly on the leaders of these institutions. These studies were often attached to the overarching interpretation of the Soviet Union as "totalitarian"—famously defined by Carl Friedrich and Zbigniew Brzezinski as a polity ruled by a pervasive ideology, a single and highly centralized party, a terroristic police, a monopoly on communications, state control of all weapons, and a centrally directed economy. Later work, aided by greater access to archival sources, shifted attention to institutions, economic relations, and, especially, social groups and their experiences. Attention also began to be paid to groups on the margins or otherwise ignored: provincials, women, non-Russians. This shift tended to displace the "totalitarian paradigm" with a picture of a complex, inconsistent, fractured, and conflict-ridden society. Still more recent work has examined the "cultural" history of Soviet society and politics—looking closely, for example, at rituals, myths, memory, subjectivity, and emotion—and has suggested that this can change our telling and understanding of history. The collapse of Communist rule in 1991, which brought greater opening of the archives, stimulated continued development in our knowledge and interpretations of Soviet history, including new appreciation for the ubiquitous and overwhelming power of ideology and the brutality of a dictatorial state, but also for the fantastic variety of social experience and behaviors and the persistence of change even in the most totalitarian times. Soviet history, like history as a discipline, remains a dynamic and still changing field of study.

## Ideological Roots: Marxism

As we enter this new historical terrain, we must first look backward, as Soviet Communists often did, at a key intellectual source of revolutionary vision: Marxism. Working for several decades, beginning in the 1840s, Karl Marx and Friedrich Engels constructed a huge and comprehensive, although not entirely consistent, system of philosophical, social, and political thought. The roots of Marxism include the eighteenth-century Enlightenment, classical economics, pre-Marxist socialism, and German idealistic philosophy—in other words, some of the main traditions of Western thought. As Bertrand Russell wrote, Marx was "the last of the great system-builders, the successor of Hegel, a believer, like him, in a rational formula summing up the evolution of mankind." Most important, this was to be a practical formula that could be used to change a world judged to be filled with inequality, injustice, and suffering. It was an optimistic theory that saw the dark sides of social life creating the conditions for their own overcoming.

The philosophical heart of the whole system, as it was understood and named by Soviet ideologists, was "dialectical materialism," for it brought together Hegel's dialectics and more recent "materialist" theories of existence. We can offer a summary, though this necessarily oversimplifies; also, this is a summary that echoes how these ideas were taught in the Soviet Union, for that is their relevance here. Materialism, in contrast to philosophical idealism, takes its stand on a "scientific" understanding of the world to assert that only matter exists and that consciousness derives from it. In Marxism, this developed into an emphasis on the primacy of economic relations in shaping human society, culture, and history. As Marx wrote in 1859, "The mode of production of the material means of existence conditions the whole process of social, political, and intellectual life. It is not the consciousness of men that determines their existence, but, on the contrary, it is their social existence that determines their consciousness." The dialectic adds change, conflict, and history to this theory, and especially, the centrality of class struggle. Dialectics reminds us that everything always changes, that everything exists in dynamic contradiction to other things, that gradual change will eventually result in a leap of qualitative change (revolutions), and that change is positive, such that the world progresses through contradiction and revolution. A common theoretical formulation involves the thesis, the antithesis, and the synthesis. A given condition, the thesis, produces opposition within itself, the antithesis, and the tension between the two is resolved by a leap to a new condition, the synthesis. The synthesis in turn becomes a thesis producing a new antithesis, and the dialectic continues.

In Marxism, the driving force in this movement is class struggle. "The material productive forces of a society," always developing, "come into contradiction with the existing productive relationships," and social strife ensues. Eventually revolution leads to a transformation of society, only to become itself the new established order producing a new antithesis. In this manner the bourgeoisie overthrew feudalism and the proletariat would overthrow capitalism. Each revolutionary class is nurtured by the very conditions of the system they are destined to destroy so that history can progress. As Marx wrote in *Capital*, his massive study of capitalism:

> Along with the constantly diminishing number of the magnates of capital, who usurp and monopolize all advantages of this process of transformation, grows the mass of misery, oppression, slavery, degradation, exploitation; but with this too grows the revolt of the working class, a class always increasing in numbers, and disciplined, united, organized by the very mechanism of the process of capitalist production itself....Centralization of the means of production and socialization of labor at last reach a point where they become incompatible with their capitalist husk. This husk is burst asunder. The knell of capitalist private property sounds. The expropriators are expropriated.

Significantly though, and, some would argue, illogically, the proletarian revolution marks the end of this historic process. In Marx's famous words, "the history of all *hitherto* existing society is the history of class struggles." The victory of the oppressed majority will end history as we have known it and allow humankind to pass, though not without the need to violently overcome resistance from the minority who benefits from the old order, into a new realm of freedom and equality, free of conflict. This is "communism."

## Leninism

Lenin did a great deal to adapt Marxism to conditions in the world that were quite different than those in Marx's time, including the power of imperialism and colonialism, which required adjusting theories of capitalism to an increasingly global economy, the surprising conservatism of the working class, and the need to apply Marxism to largely peasant countries like Russia. Among Lenin's arguments, those on the party, democracy, the revolution, and the dictatorship of the proletariat, together with those on the peasantry and on imperialism, deserve special attention. As already mentioned, it was a disagreement on the nature of the party that split the Russian Social Democrats into the Lenin-led Bolsheviks and the Mensheviks in 1903. The Mensheviks favored a party open to any who shared its Marxist goals. Lenin insisted on a tightly knit body of dedicated professional revolutionaries, with clear lines of command and a military discipline. Behind these different conceptions of the party lay deeper differences, which would have long-term effects on Soviet politics. One difference concerned the place of workers in the working-class movement. While Mensheviks tended to believe strongly in the consciousness-raising benefits of the experience of struggle itself, Lenin emphasized the need for guidance and leadership by more "conscious" activists. As he famously argued in *What Is to Be Done?* (1902), workers left to themselves would be unable to see beyond the economic struggle and understand that their interests lie in overthrowing the existing social system. A vanguard party was necessary to ensure that socialists did more than "gaze with awe upon the 'posterior' of the Russian proletariat."

More generally, Lenin differed from many other Russian Marxists in thinking about democracy. The Mensheviks, and even many Bolsheviks before 1917, were attracted to Marxism precisely for its democratic promise to give all people equal political representation and civil freedom, though they believed this political democracy would need to be supplemented by the democracy of social rights. Lenin, by contrast, was among those who insisted that democracy had no inherent value apart from its usefulness in promoting the cause of the socialist transformation of society. The Bolsheviks, he liked to say, make no "fetish" of democracy. With characteristic determination and believing in the imminent worldwide overthrow of the capitalist system, Lenin decided in 1917 that he and his party could then stage a successful revolution in Russia, although at first virtually no one, even among the Bolsheviks, agreed. After the Bolsheviks did seize power in the October Revolution, Lenin's Bolshevik party, renamed the Communist Party, drew on these ideas about the party and democracy to shape the new Soviet state.

Lenin's revolutionary optimism stemmed in part from his reconsideration of the role of the peasantry in bringing about the establishment of the

V. I. Lenin in 1917. *(Gosizdat)*

new order. Marx, Engels, and Marxists in general have neglected the peasants in their teachings and relegated them, as petty proprietors, to the bourgeois camp. Lenin, however, came to the conclusion that, if properly led by the proletariat and the party, poor peasants could be a revolutionary force: indeed later he proclaimed even the middle peasants to be of some value to the socialist state. The same *April Theses* that urged the transformation of the bourgeois revolution into a socialist one stated that poor peasants were to be part of the new revolutionary wave.

Lenin also expanded Marxism to view class struggle under capitalism in a global setting shaped by imperialism. In his book *Imperialism, the Highest Stage of Capitalism*, written in 1916 and published in the spring of 1917, Lenin concluded that in its ultimate form capitalism becomes imperialism, with monopolies and financial capital ruling the world. Cartels replace free competition, and export of capital becomes more important than export of goods.

An economic and political partitioning of the world follows in the form of a constant struggle for economic expansion, spheres of influence, and colonies. International alliances and counteralliances arise. The disparity between the development of the productive forces of the participants and their shares of the world is settled among capitalist states by wars. Thus, instead of the original Marxist vision of the victorious socialist revolution as the simple expropriation of a few supercapitalists, Lenin described the dying stage of capitalism as an age of gigantic conflicts. Still more important, this externalization, so to speak, of the capitalist crisis brought colonies and underdeveloped areas in general prominently into the picture. The capitalists were opposed not only by their own proletariats, but also by the colonial peoples whom they exploited, more or less regardless of the social order and the stage of development of those peoples. Therefore, the proletarians and the colonial peoples were natural allies. Lenin, it is worth noting, paid much more attention to Asia than did Western Marxists. Eventually, this would be elaborated into a theory that socialist revolutions were most likely to break out, as one had in Russia, at the "weakest links" in the chain of imperialism: countries, mainly on the peripheries, exploited by colonialism, where capitalism was most paradoxical and unstable.

Besides Marxism, it has been argued, Lenin also drew on Russian populist traditions. Born in 1870, Lenin grew up admiring Chernyshevsky; and his oldest brother, Alexander, was executed in 1887 for his part in a populist plot to assassinate Alexander III. Though Lenin would later violently condemn populist ideology, this should not obscure a certain indebtedness to it. Lenin objected to the populists' moralism—as a Marxist, he insisted in grounding revolutionary ideology in a scientific view of the world—and their utopian faith that capitalism could be avoided in Russia and socialism built on the foundation of peasant communes. But he shared with populists a belief in the creative and heroic power of individuals to change history. Chernyshevsky called them "new people." Lavrov called them "critically thinking individuals." Lenin called them "conscious" and "professional" revolutionaries. Also, partly inspired by the terrorism of the populist People's Will, Lenin and the Bolsheviks liked to portray themselves as tough-minded and "hard" and to romanticize revolutionary violence. Lenin, in particular, insisted the Bolsheviks were not afraid of using "plebian methods": fists, revolvers, and "the guillotine."

## The Allure of Truth and Justice

As an ideology, Marxism-Leninism was founded on the certainty that it is the only truth, for it is built upon scientific laws. Appropriately, the Bolshevik and later Communist Party's newspaper was known simply as *Pravda*—a term meaning "justice" and "law" but especially "truth." This was also, it has been argued, an intolerant and exclusionary ideology, inherently prone to violence. Communists were inspired by the conviction that the world evolved through struggle against enemies whose material interests placed them inevitably and permanently at odds with the interests of the proletariat and socialism. Very often, too, this required struggle against internal enemies who were believed to deviate from the truth.

At the same time, Marxism and Leninism, especially as it was used by people other than Marx and Lenin, contained quasi-religious qualities. Of course, the Soviet Communists hoped to eliminate religion from modern consciousness and frequently persecuted clergy and believers. Yet, as scholars have shown, the language of socialist revolution appealed to many ordinary Russians precisely because it resonated so strongly with religious notions of truth, righteousness, and salvation. And the party and government itself, especially in the early years, often framed the socialist dream in sacred and messianic terms. As a leading Russian historian of the 1917 revolution has written, "from the Revolution was often expected not only concrete social and political changes, but a Miracle—rapid and universal purification and 'resurrection.'" Berdiaev and other commentators have emphasized the extent to which Marxism, especially in Soviet hands, functioned in religious terms as the ultimate and total truth and the measure of good and evil, and offered a guarantee of salvation. Even in the original Marxism something less than pure scientific reason may have been involved in the prediction of the transcendence of history as class struggle—what Engels famously called "the ascent of man from the kingdom of necessity into the kingdom of freedom."

As this suggests, communism could easily be an attractive ideology, for both intellectual elites and ordinary working people. The spread of Marxism-Leninism and communist revolutions throughout the world in the twentieth century suggests how effectively this ideology served as a means to protest the inequalities and injustices of capitalism and colonialism. Perhaps its greatest strength lies in its explanation of human exploitation and misery and in its promise that the combined effort of people and history would inevitably end both. In the face of so many reasons in the twentieth century to despair of modem civilization, communism was brilliantly optimistic. It promised, in the often heard Soviet phrase, a "bright future," no matter how dark the present. Different scholars have variously emphasized the role of reason and emotion in this promise and appeal. Isaiah Berlin, for example, emphasized Marxism's largely rational force: its claim to comprehensiveness and to scientific authority, its appeal to a natural constituency (the poor and oppressed), and its reasoned optimism about the direction of history. Other scholars have emphasized more psychological and moral aspects: the condemnation of the capitalist system for denying affection and care to the individual and giving unfair advantage to some individuals over others, the ability to raise expectations and fire the imagination, the psychological benefits of association with the prestige of science, and a focus on future time, which helped isolate Marxism from the disappointments of the present. Of course, as time passed, many of Marxism's promises seemed disproved by the facts, especially the growing polarization of capitalist society into a handful of rich capitalists and a vast, impoverished majority. Thus, it has been argued, "Marxism possesses no invincible logic, and no scientific certainty; it does provide an elaborate intellectual rationalization and a splendid intellectual facade for those who subscribe to the teaching for nonintellectual reasons." Whatever the reasons, this optimistic, elaborate, totalizing, and malleable philosophy would make its weight felt in every aspect of Soviet life.

# CHAPTER 36

# War Communism, 1917–21, and the New Economic Policy, 1921–28

You will never be alive again,
Never rise from the snow:
Twenty-eight bayonet,
Five fire wounds.
A bitter new garment
I sewed for my friend.
It does love, does love blood—
The Russian earth.

ANNA AKHMATOVA

Yes, we are living through a storm of dark passions....All that is vile and despicable on earth has been and is being done by us, and all that is beautiful and intelligent, for which we are striving, lives within us....In these days of revolt, blood, and hostility, days that are terrifying for many people, one should not forget that, through great torments and unbearable trials, we are moving toward the rebirth of man....Yes, now, at this very moment when people, deafened by the preaching of equality and brotherhood, are robbing their neighbor in the streets, stripping him bare....in these days of monstrous contradiction a new Russia is being born.

MAXIM GORKY

Although the Bolsheviks seized power easily in Russia in November 1917, they managed to consolidate their new position only after several years of bitter struggle. In a desperate effort to survive, the Bolsheviks mobilized the population and resources in the area that they controlled and instituted a drastic regime that came to be known as "War Communism." Communist rule did survive, although at a tremendous price. To revive an utterly exhausted, devastated, and starving country, the so-called New Economic Policy replaced War Communism and lasted from 1921 to 1928, until the beginning of Stalin's

First Five-Year Plan. The period of the New Economic Policy has been rightly contrasted with that of War Communism as a time of relaxation and compromise. Yet, on the whole the Soviet government showed more continuity than change in its policies and pursued its set goals with intelligence and determination—as a brief treatment of the first decade of Communist rule should indicate.

## The New Government. Lenin

The Soviet government was organized two days after the October Revolution, on October 27, 1917, under the name of the Council of People's Commissars. Headed by Lenin as chairman, the Council contained such prominent members of the Bolshevik Party as Trotsky, who became commissar for foreign affairs; Alexei Rykov, who became commissar of the interior; and Iosif Dzhugashvili, better known as Stalin, who assumed charge of national minorities. Lenin thus led the government as well as the party and was recognized as by far the most important figure of the new regime in Russia.

Lenin was born in an intellectual family—his father was a school inspector—in 1870 in a town on the Volga named Simbirsk, later Ulianovsk. Vladimir Ulianov proved to be a brilliant student both in secondary school and at the University of Kazan, where he studied law. He early became a radical—the execution of his eldest brother in 1887 for participating in a plot to assassinate Alexander III has sometimes been considered a turning point for him—and then became a Marxist, suffering imprisonment in 1896 and Siberian exile for the three years following. He participated in the publication of a Social Democratic newspaper, *The Spark*, which was printed abroad beginning in 1900, and in other revolutionary activities, often under the pseudonym of *N. Lenin*. At first awed by the "father of Russian Marxism," Plekhanov, Lenin before long struck out on his own, leading the Bolshevik group in the Social Democratic Party split in 1903. We have already met Lenin as an important Marxist theoretician. But practice meant more than theory for the Bolshevik leader. Most of his writings in fact were polemical, brief, and to the point: they denounced opponents or deviationists in ideology and charted the right way for the faithful. As Lenin remarked when events in 1917 interrupted his work on a treatise, *The State and Revolution:* "It is more pleasant and more useful to live through the experience of a revolution than to write about it."

The October Revolution, masterminded by Lenin, gave him power that he continued to exercise in full until largely incapacitated by a stroke in May 1922. After that he still kept some control until his death on January 21, 1924. Moreover, in contrast to Stalin's later terror, Lenin's leadership of the party did not depend on the secret police, but rather on his own personality, ability, and achievement. Perhaps appropriately, whereas Stalin's cult experienced some remarkable reversals of fortune shortly after his demise, that of Lenin kept, if anything, gaining in popularity throughout the communist world until its collapse in the late 1980s.

ПРИЗРАК БРОДИТ ПО ЕВРОПЕ, ПРИЗРАК КОММУНИЗМА

"A Specter Is Haunting Europe—the Specter of Communism," 1920. Picturing Lenin in a characteristic pose, the phrase is a quotation from the *Communist Manifesto* of Marx and Engels. *(Victoria Bonnell)*

The communist myth of Lenin is not far removed from reality in many respects. For Lenin was a dedicated Bolshevik who lived and breathed revolution and communism. He combined high intelligence, an ability for acute theoretical thinking, and practical sense to become a great Marxist "realist." The amalgam proved ideal for communist purposes: Lenin never wavered in his Marxist faith; yet he knew how to adapt it, drastically if need be, to circumstances. Other outstanding qualities of the Bolshevik leader included exceptional will power, persistence, courage, and the ability to work extremely hard. Even Lenin's simple tastes and modest, almost ascetic, way of life were transposed easily and appropriately from the actual man to his mythical image. At the same time, devotion to an exclusive doctrine led to narrow vision. Ruthlessness followed from Lenin's conviction that he, and sometimes only he, knew the right answer.

At the same time, Lenin and the Bolsheviks came to power without a clear blueprint for ruling the country and building socialism or even a clear strategy for governing. On the one hand, Lenin spoke of the revolution creating a "commune state" by releasing the "energy, initiative and decisiveness" of the people, who could perform "miracles." In a speech in November 1917, for example, he called on "all working people" to "remember that you yourselves are now administering the state" and to "take matters into your own hands below, waiting for no one." At the same time, Lenin never tired of reminding people that "a revolution is the most authoritarian thing imaginable," and after October he spoke often, and quite explicitly, of the need for strict control, ruthless suppression, iron discipline, and even dictatorship. Some historians have argued that Lenin's talk about popular participation was a deceitful fig leaf covering his authoritarian and even tyrannical nature. Others have argued that this contradictory language reflected a contradictory political ideology, which, at least in these early years, combined sincere ideals about popular initiative and creativity with strong convictions about the importance of leadership, discipline, and central control. Whatever Lenin's actual views, much of the first decade of Soviet rule was a history of debates and conflicts over how to balance these two principles.

## The First Months

Relying on local Soviets, Bolshevik power spread quickly across the country in the weeks and months following the October Revolution. The first serious challenge to the Bolshevik government occurred in January 1918, when the Constituent Assembly finally met. It should be remembered that the Assembly had been awaited for months by almost all political groups in Russia as the truly legitimate and definitive authority in the country. Lenin himself had denounced the Provisional Government for failing to summon it promptly. With Bolshevik support, polling took place across the country in mid-November (though not in Poland or other regions under German occupation, and in some areas votes were incomplete or left uncounted). As the results slowly rolled in, it became increasingly clear that the Bolsheviks would not have a majority. On the one hand, the socialist idea was triumphant. Of more than 40 million votes cast, Social Revolutionaries (not including the scattered dissident Left SR lists) won 38 percent of the vote (Ukrainian SRs won another 8 percent), Bolsheviks 24 percent, Mensheviks 3 percent, and other socialist parties another 3 percent, giving socialists approximately three-quarters of the total vote. Nationalist parties (Muslim, Armenian, German, Jewish, and others, some of which had socialist orientations) won approximately 8 percent of the total. The liberal Kadets polled less than 5 percent. Other nonsocialists won only an additional 3 percent. Not only was this a victory for socialism, broadly understood, but Bolshevik success was impressive, especially in large cities (and not only among their base, the working class), the northern industrial regions, and the army. Still, the elections left the Bolsheviks a minority party, which meant that they could not justify their monopoly control of the government on electoral grounds. The Bolsheviks attempted to delay the opening of the Constituent Assembly, warned of danger to the revolution, arrested some liberals and conservatives, and argued that changed circumstances (such as the split in the SR party) had made the elections no longer a true reflection of reality. Still, the Bolsheviks decided to let the assembly open on the morning of January 5, 1918, and then to disperse it the next day with troops. Thousands demonstrated in support of the assembly, despite a ban on demonstrations. But these gatherings were easily dispersed with force and no major protests followed. The lack of response to the disbanding of the assembly resulted in part from the fact that it had no organized force behind it, and in part from the fact that on the very morrow of the revolution the Soviet government had declared its intention to make peace and also had in effect granted the peasants gentry land, thus taking steps to satisfy the two main demands of the people. The Bolsheviks also had the cooperation of the Left Socialist Revolutionaries who received three cabinet positions, including the ministry of agriculture.

But the making of peace proved both difficult and extremely costly, with the very existence of the Soviet state hanging in the balance. The Allies failed to respond to the Soviet bid for peace and in fact ignored the Soviet government, not expecting it to last. Discipline in the Russian army collapsed entirely, with soldiers sometimes massacring their officers. After the conclusion of an armistice with the Germans in December 1917, the front simply disbanded in chaos, most men trying to return home by whatever means they could find. The Germans proved willing to negotiate, but they offered Draconian conditions of peace. Trotsky, who as commissar for foreign affairs represented the Soviet government, felt compelled to turn them down, proclaiming a new policy: "no war, no peace!" The Germans then proceeded to advance, occupying more territory and seizing an enormous amount of military materiel. In Petrograd many Bolshevik leaders as well as the Left Socialist Revolutionaries agreed with Trotsky that German demands could not be accepted. Only Lenin's authority and determination swung the balance in favor of the humiliating peace. By sacrificing much else, Lenin in all probability saved Communist rule in Russia, for the young Soviet government was in no position whatsoever to fight Germany.

The Soviet-German Treaty of Brest-Litovsk was signed on March 3, 1918. To sum up its results in Vernadsky's words:

> The peace conditions were disastrous to Russia. The Ukraine, Poland, Finland, Lithuania, Estonia, and Latvia received their independence. Part of Transcaucasia was ceded to Turkey. Russia lost 26 percent of her total population; 27 percent of her arable land; 32 percent of her average crops; 26 percent of her railway system; 33 percent of her manufacturing industries; 73 percent of her iron industries; 75 percent of her coal fields. Besides that, Russia had to pay a large war indemnity.

Or to put it in different terms, Russia lost over 60 million people and over 5,000 factories, mills, distilleries, and refineries. Puppet states dependent on Germany were set up in the separated border areas. Only the ultimate German defeat in the First World War prevented the Brest-Litovsk settlement from being definitive, and in particular made it possible for the Soviet government to reclaim Ukraine.

Since Lenin's firm direction in disbanding the Constituent Assembly and capitulating to the Germans had enabled the Soviet government to survive, the Soviet leader and his associates proceeded rapidly to revamp and even transform Russia politically, socially, and economically, a process that had begun in the first days of Bolshevik power. Many of the earliest acts of the government, it has been argued, reflected a need to secure popular support but also a working out in practice of the emancipatory, even libertarian, side of Bolshevik ideology. Peasants were given complete local control over the use of the land through communes and local Soviets and workers' committees were given the power to supervise their own managers—though these developments were more the results of a social revolution the Bolsheviks could not control than of Bolshevik policy. The existing judicial system was abolished and replaced by elected revolutionary tribunals and people's courts. To democratize local government, Soviets were given extensive powers and workers and soldiers were recruited by the thousands as local officials. National minorities were told they had the right to complete self-determination, a policy decision that was also as much recognition of revolutionary realities as a matter of ideological principle. Many early policies were directed at undermining the position of those who formerly held power and status in Russia. Titles and ranks were abolished. As the state gradually assumed control over the scarce housing and other material aspects of life, those who belonged to the upper and middle classes often lost their property, suffered discrimination, and were considered by the new regime to be suspect by definition. Church property was confiscated and religious instruction in schools terminated. Even time changed. The Gregorian or Western calendar—New Style—was adopted on January 31, 1918. At the same time, much early Soviet policy expressed the Bolsheviks' centralizing and authoritarian approach to transforming Russia, even before the disbanding of the Constituent Assembly. In November 1917, the press was placed under state control and many "bourgeois" and even moderate socialist papers were closed down. To centralize control of the economy, banks and large factories were immediately nationalized, foreign trade was made a state monopoly, and, in December, a committee was formed to develop a national economic plan. Also in December 1917, the government established the Extraordinary Commission to Combat Counterrevolution, Sabotage, and Speculation, the dreaded "Cheka," headed by Felix Dzerzhinsky, which fought against both ordinary hooliganism and looting, which became common after October, and suspected anti-regime activities. From that time on, the political police became a fundamental reality of Soviet life. After the closing of the Constituent Assembly, the government ominously declared the liberal Constitutional Party to be a "party of enemies of the people" and treated even many Mensheviks and Socialist Revolutionaries—except for the Left Socialist Revolutionaries until their break with the Bolsheviks in March 1918—as dangerous opponents of the new order.

## War Communism and New Problems

By the summer of 1918, with armed opposition to Bolshevik rule already underway and the economy in shambles, a radical policy of mobilization that some called War Communism began to take shape. The nationalization of industry, which began shortly after the revolution, was extended by the law of June 28, 1918. To cite Carr's listing, the state appropriated "the mining, metallurgical, textile, electrical, timber, tobacco, resin, glass and pottery, leather and cement industries, all steam-driven mills, local utilities and private railways together with a few minor industries." Eventually private industry disappeared almost entirely. Compulsory labor was introduced. Private trade was gradually suppressed, to be replaced by rationing and by government distribution of food and other necessities of life. On February 19, 1918, the nationalization of land was proclaimed: all land became state property to be used only by those who would cultivate it themselves. The peasants, however, had little interest in supplying food to the government because, with state priorities and the breakdown of the economy, they could not receive much in return. Therefore, under the pressure of the Civil War and of the desperate need to obtain food for the Red Army and the urban population, the authorities finally decreed a food levy, in effect ordering the peasants to turn over their entire harvest, except for a minimal amount to be retained for their own sustenance and for sowing. As the peasants resisted, forcible requisitioning and repression became common.

The rigors of War Communism on the home front largely resulted from and paralleled the bitter struggle the Soviet regime was waging with its external enemies. Beginning in summer of 1918 the country entered a major, many-faceted, and cruel Civil War, when the so-called Whites—who had rallied initially to continue the war against the Germans—rose to challenge the Red control of Russia. In addition, as will be discussed later, numerous nationalities asserted their independence from Russian authority. Also, a number of foreign states intervened by sending armed forces into Russia and supporting local opposition movements and governments, as well as by blockading Soviet Russia from October 1919 to January 1920. It certainly appeared to the Bolsheviks that Soviet Russia was isolated in the world and faced serious enemies at home. This only stimulated greater Bolshevik determination and vigilance.

At the same time, paradoxically, War Communism was an era of unbridled utopianism, a time when radicals imagined it was possible to make a sudden leap to real "communism," the long dreamed of free society without classes. Here, again, we see the strange but persistent intertwining in Bolshevism of violent authoritarianism with efforts at radical emancipation. Thus, side by side with increasing dictatorship (including reducing the power of such popular and semi-autonomous institutions as Soviets, factory committees, and Red Guard units) and a "Red Terror" against all enemies (idealized as virtuous violence), the Civil War was a time of utopian experimentalism. We will describe this more in a later chapter, but it included, for example, efforts to liberate women from all restrictions, to create "new people," to introduce a classless and moneyless economy, to radically redesign every aspect of society and culture from education to law, and to invent new forms of art and music.

## The Civil War

The counterrevolutionary forces, often called vaguely and somewhat misleadingly the White movement, constituted the greatest menace to Soviet rule, because, in contrast to various border nationalities, which had aims limited to particular regions, and to the intervening Allied powers, which had no clear aims, the Whites meant to destroy the Reds. The counterrevolutionaries drew their strength from army officers and cossacks, from the "bourgeoisie," including a large number of secondary school students and other educated youth, and from political groups ranging from the far Right to the Socialist Revolutionaries. Such prominent former terrorists as Boris Savinkov fought against the Soviet government, while the crack units of the White Army included a few worker detachments. Most intellectuals joined or sympathized with the White camp.

After the Soviet government came to power, civil servants staged an unsuccessful strike against it. Following their break with the Bolsheviks in March 1918 over excessive authoritarianism and Bolshevik determination to promote class struggle in the villages, the Left Socialist Revolutionaries attempted an abortive uprising in Moscow in July. At about the same time and in part in response to the action of the Left SRs, counterrevolutionaries led by the local military commander seized Simbirsk, while Savinkov raised a rebellion in the center of European Russia, capturing and holding for two weeks the town of Iaroslavl on the Volga. These efforts collapsed, however, because of the insufficient strength of the counterrevolutionaries once the Soviet government could concentrate its forces against them. Indeed, it became increasingly clear that the Communist authorities, in particular the Cheka, had a firm grip on the central provinces and ruthlessly suppressed all opponents and suspected opponents. True to their tradition, the Socialist Revolutionaries tried terrorism, assassinating several prominent Bolsheviks, such as the head of the Petrograd Cheka, and seriously wounding Lenin himself in August 1918. Earlier, in July, a Left Socialist Revolutionary had killed the German ambassador, producing a diplomatic crisis. Yet even the terrorist campaign could not shake Soviet control in Moscow—which had again become the capital of the country in March 1918—Petrograd, or central European Russia. And it provoked frightful reprisals, a veritable reign of terror, during which huge numbers of "class enemies" and others suspected by the regime were killed.

The borderlands, on the other hand, offered numerous opportunities to the counterrevolutionaries. The Don, Kuban, and Terek areas in the south and southeast all gave rise to local anti-Bolshevik cossack governments. Moreover, the White Volunteer Army emerged in southern Russia, led first by Alekseev, next by Kornilov, and after Kornilov's death in combat by an equally prominent general, Anton Denikin. Other centers of opposition to the Communists sprang up in the east. In Samara, on the Volga, Chernov headed a government composed of members of the Constituent Assembly. Both the Ural and the Orenburg cossacks turned against Red Moscow. The All-Russian Directory of five members was established in Omsk, in western Siberia, in September 1918, as a result of a conference attended by anti-Bolshevik political parties and local governments of eastern Russia. Following a military coup the Directory was replaced by another anti-Red government, that of Admiral Alexander Kolchak.

**Revolution and Civil War in European Russia 1917–22**

Red Army moves, 1919–21
Deepest penetration of White Army forces, 1919–20
Allied intervention, 1918–20
Boundaries after 1922
1914 boundaries
Areas lost by Russia after World War I

A commander of the cossacks of Transbaikalia, Grigorii Semenov, ruled a part of eastern Siberia with the support of the Japanese. New governments also emerged in Vladivostok and elsewhere. Russian anti-Bolshevik forces in the east were augmented by some 40,000 members of the so-called Czech Legion composed largely of Czech prisoners of war who wanted to fight on the side of the Entente. These soldiers were being moved to Vladivostok via the Trans-Siberian Railroad when a series of incidents led to their break with Soviet authorities and their support of the White movement. In the north a prominent anti-Soviet center arose in Archangel, where a former populist, Nikolai Chaikovsky, set up a government supported by the intervening British and French. And in the west, where the non-Russian borderlands produced numerous nationalist movements in opposition to the Soviet government, General Nikolai Iudenich established a White base in Estonia to threaten Petrograd.

The Civil War, which broke out in the summer of 1918, first went favorably for the Whites. In late June and early July the troops of the Samara government captured Simbirsk, Kazan, and Ufa. Although the Red Army managed to eliminate that threat, it immediately had to face a greater menace: the forces of Kolchak, supported by the Czechs, and those of Denikin, aided by cossacks. Kolchak's units, advancing from Siberia, took Perm in the Urals and almost reached the Volga. At this time, on July 16, Nicholas II, the empress, their son and four daughters, along with a family doctor and three loyal servants, were killed—possibly in compliance with Lenin's secret order—by local Bolsheviks in Ekaterinburg, where they had been confined, when the Czechs and the Whites approached the town. Denikin's army, after some reversals of fortune, resumed the offensive, and its right wing threatened to link with Kolchak's army in the spring of 1919. While Kolchak's forced retreat eliminated this possibility, Denikin proceeded to occupy virtually all of Ukraine and to advance on Moscow. In the middle of October his troops took Orel and approached Tula, the last important center south of Moscow. At the same time Iudenich advanced from Estonia on Petrograd, seizing Gatchina, only thirty miles from that city, on October 16, and besieging Pulkovo on its outskirts. As a historian of these events has commented: "In the middle of October it appeared that Petrograd and Moscow might fall simultaneously to the Whites."

But the tide turned. Iudenich's offensive collapsed just short of the former capital. Although the Red Army had had to be created from scratch, it had constantly improved in organization, discipline, and leadership under Commissar of War Trotsky, and it managed finally to turn the tables on both Kolchak and Denikin. The admiral, who had assumed the title of "Supreme Ruler of Russia" and had received recognition from some other White leaders, suffered a crushing defeat in late 1919 and was executed by the Bolsheviks on February 7, 1920. The general was driven back to the area of the Sea of Azov and the Crimea by the end of March 1920. At that point a Soviet-Polish war gave respite to the southern White Army and even enabled Denikin's successor General Baron Petr Wrangel to recapture a large section of southern Russia. But with the end of the Polish war in the autumn, the Red Army concentrated again on the southern front. After more bitter fighting, Wrangel, his remaining army, and a considerable number of civilians, altogether about 100,000 people, were evacuated on Allied ships to Constantinople in mid-November. Other and weaker counterrevolutionary strongholds, such as that in Archangel, had already fallen. By the end of 1920 the White movement had been effectively defeated.

## Allied Intervention

The great Civil War in Russia was complicated by Allied intervention, by the war between the Soviet government and Poland, and by bids for national independence on the part of a number of peoples of the former empire of the Romanovs who were not Great Russians. The intervention began in 1918 and involved fourteen countries; the Japanese in particular sent a sizeable force into Russia—over 60,000 men. Great Britain dispatched altogether some 40,000 troops, France and Greece two divisions each, and the United States about 10,000 men, while Italy and other countries—except for the peculiar case of the Czechs—sent smaller, and often merely token, forces. The Allies originally wanted to prevent the Germans from seizing war matériel in such ports as Archangel and Murmansk, as well as to observe the situation, while the Japanese wanted to exploit the opportunities presented in the Far East by the collapse of Russian power. Japanese troops occupied the Russian part of the island of Sakhalin and much of Siberia east of Lake Baikal. Detachments of American, British, French, and Italian troops followed the Japanese into Siberia, while other Allied troops landed, as already mentioned, in northern European Russia, as well as in southern ports such as Odessa, occupied by the French, and Batum, occupied by the British. Allied forces assumed a hostile attitude toward the Soviet government, blockaded the Soviet coastline from October 1919 to January 1920, and often helped White movements by providing military supplies—such as some British tanks for Denikin's army—and by their very presence and protection. But they often avoided actual fighting. This fruitless intervention ended in 1920 with the departure of Allied troops, except that the Japanese stayed in the Maritime Provinces of the Russian Far East until 1922 and in the Russian part of Sakhalin until 1925.

## The War against Poland

The Soviet-Polish war, which lasted from February 1919 to March 1921, was shaped by desires and illusions on both sides. The political and military leader of Poland, Josef Pilsudski, started the war as part of his "promethean" plan to create a federation of independent states, allied with Poland, from the Baltic, through Belorussia, to Ukraine. Some historians argue that the goal was to protect Poland from Russia; others see this as an effort to reclaim historic lands and re-create something like the pre-partition Polish-Lithuanian Commonwealth. On the Soviet side, the war was viewed in the context of a desperate hope that sympathetic revolutions would erupt in the West, especially in Germany. By 1920, emboldened by Red Army victories over the Whites, the Communist leadership was feeling optimistic and Poland seemed to be the portal to the West. Thus, though the Polish war began as a defensive war to push back Polish advances to the east, it seemed a perfect opportunity to spread the revolution into Europe, first inspiring Polish workers to join the cause and then continuing on to Germany. The Red Army, led by Mikhail Tukhachevsky and others, managed to reach the outskirts of Warsaw in August and prepared to take the Polish capital. But the Poles, helped by

French credits and Allied supplies, defeated the onrushing Soviet army: the Battle of Warsaw became known in Poland as the "Miracle at the Vistula." Of course, the Soviet hope that Polish workers would rise in support proved illusory: they viewed the invaders as Russian imperialists, not revolutionary liberators. Russia sued for peace and complicated peace negotiations followed. Among the many controversies that still surround this war include mutual charges of atrocities, questions of responsibility for anti-Jewish pogroms, and the relationship of the new border achieved by the Treaty of Riga on March 18, 1921, to the Polish ethnic border: some emphasize Poland's gain of large non-Polish populations and others emphasize that many Poles were left on the Soviet side of the border. What is clear is that both Pilsudski's vision of a line of new states and Lenin's vision of spreading revolution were crushed.

## National Independence Movements

The political disintegration and radicalization of citizens during the First World War in the three great land-based empires of Europe—the Russian, Austro-Hungarian, and Ottoman empires—along with the promotion by the allies of the nation-state formation in this region encouraged nationalist movements to move from demands for autonomy to demands for independence. The history of these movements, and of changing Soviet policy toward the nationalities, has been the subject of a number of excellent studies in recent years: with the collapse of the Soviet Union into a number of new states, the origins of the Union of Soviet Socialist Republics (USSR) as a reconstructed "empire" has attracted considerable scholarly attention. This is a complex history: here we can only highlight key developments. Departure from the Russian Empire came quickly after the fall of the autocracy. In 1917, Finland, Latvia, Lithuania, and Belorussia declared their independence, followed in 1918 by Estonia, Ukraine, Poland, and the Transcaucasian Federation (to be dissolved into the separate states of Georgia, Armenia, and Azerbaijan). The fourth congress of Central Asian Muslims, held in December 1917, declared autonomy for Turkestan and various small republics emerged in Central Asia. Apart from Poland and Lithuania, these were independent states for the first time in their history. While the liberal Provisional Government had feared the break up of the empire would weaken the country, the Bolsheviks had insisted, while contending for power, on the principle that every nation has the "right to self-determination." Once in power, the new Soviet government said the same. The "Decree on Peace," for example, insisted that all nationalities who felt themselves to be oppressed should have the right to decide by democratic elections if they wished to establish independent nation-states. But the Bolshevik leaders also hoped to hold the lands of the empire together, theoretically in the spirit of proletarian solidarity. Thus, advocates of national independence were often condemned as bourgeois nationalists opposed to the interests of the people and socialism. Those peoples that were successful in asserting their independence, that is, the Finns, the Estonians, the Latvians, and the Lithuanians, as well as the Poles, did so in spite of the Soviet

БОРЬБА КРАСНОГО РЫЦАРЯ С ТЕМНОЙ СИЛОЮ.

"The Struggle of the Red Knight against the Dark Force," 1919. Civil War–era images and texts often cast the revolutionary struggle in terms of good and evil. "Dark forces" is also the term used in Russian to speak of devils and other evil spirits. (*Gosizdat*)

government and local Soviets. Often, nationalists had to suppress their own Communists, sometimes, as in the case of Finland, after a full-fledged civil war. In a number of areas, the Red Army and local Communists combined to prevent or destroy independence. In general, Communist nationalities policy, once in power, was far less tolerant of nationalism than suggested by the theory of "self-determination." Each particular history had its own distinctive complications.

In Ukraine, the local government, the Rada or central council, proclaimed an independent Ukrainian republic after the fall of the Provisional Government in Petrograd. Soviet authorities recognized the new republic, but in February 1918 the Red Army overthrew the Rada. Soviet rule, established in the spring of 1918, was in turn overthrown by the advancing German army.

The Germans at first accepted the Rada, but before long they replaced it with a right-wing government under Pavlo Skoropadsky. After the Germans left, the Directory of the Rada deposed Skoropadsky in December 1918, only to be driven out themselves in short order by Denikin's White forces. Following Denikin's withdrawal in the autumn of 1919, the Red Army restored Soviet authority in Ukraine. Next the Directory of the Rada made an agreement with the Poles, only to be left out at the peace treaty terminating the Soviet-Polish war, which simply divided Ukraine between Soviet Russia and Poland. Ukrainians supported different movements and fought in different armies as well as in radical peasant movements. Political divisions survived the collapse of the Ukrainian bid for independence and later divided Ukrainian émigrés. Yet it remains an open question to what extent the young Ukrainian nationalism, nurtured especially among Ukrainian intellectuals and professionals, had reached the peasant majority of the country, who were still primarily concerned about material questions of survival and land ownership.

Among the peoples living to the south and southeast of European Russia, many of whom had been joined to the Russian Empire as late as the nineteenth century, numerous independence movements arose and independent states were proclaimed. The new states included the Crimean Tatar republic: the Transcaucasian republics of Georgia, Armenia, and Azerbaijan; the Bashkir, Kirghiz, and Kokand republics; the emirates of Bokhara and Khiva; and others. Time and again local interests clashed and bitter local civil wars developed. In certain instances foreign powers, such as Turkey, Germany, and Great Britain, played important roles.

The traditional interpretation of Soviet nationality policy in these years emphasizes the use of military force to suppress independence efforts and support power by local Communists. This account is part of the story almost everywhere, though it is most accurate in Georgia, where a popular and effective Menshevik government was toppled by the Red Army in 1921. Elsewhere, this basic scenario was complicated by a variety of factors that undermined the strength of the nationalists. In many of these regions, ethnic Russians lived and worked there and opposed separation from Russia. Also, many non-Russians, especially peasants and workers, found Bolshevik promises of land reform and radical social change appealing, especially when combined with promises of respect for local national cultures. Finally, some non-Russians saw strategic advantages to be had in remaining within the empire. In Armenia, notably, the nationalist Dashnaks viewed Soviet rule as a hedge against invasion by Turkey—however, when Dashnak-led rebels overthrew the new Soviet government after a few months, the Red Army restored Soviet power.

On December 30, 1922, the USSR came into being as a federation of Russia, Ukraine, Belorussia, and Transcaucasia. Later in the 1920s, three Central Asian republics received "Union Republic" status. Compared to the empire of the Romanovs, the new Soviet Union had lost Finland, Estonia, Latvia, Lithuania, and the Polish territories, all of which had become independent, and had lost western Ukraine and western Belorussia to Poland, Bessarabia to Romania, and the Kars-Ardakhan area in Transcaucasia to Turkey. Also, as already mentioned, Japan evacuated all of the Siberian mainland of Russia only in 1922 and the Russian half of the island of Sakhalin in 1925. In spite of these reductions, the USSR emerged as a large and potentially powerful country.

Recent historians have sometimes spoken of a new "Soviet Empire." The Bolsheviks themselves, however, were concerned not to repeat the tsarist empire's colonial domination of the peripheries. They hoped that Soviet socialism would be a model for colonial peoples around the world. Thus, the question of how to rule immediately became a very important one. Iosif Stalin, the commissar responsible for nationalities policy, favored close unity with Russia and an active policy of socialist social and economic development. Lenin hesitated, fearing that this would alienate local nationalities. The legal form of the Soviet Union as, in theory, a federation of equals reflected this approach. Even more important was a reliance on local elites and efforts by the ruling state to nurture national and ethnic identity. This policy of *korenizatsiia*—a term highlighting the planting of local "roots" (*koren* means root) and loosely translatable as indigenization—included the promotion of natives in employment, education, and the Party (Terry Martin has suggested that this was a type of Soviet "affirmative action") and the encouragement of national languages and cultures. Some historians have argued that these actions were concessions resulting from Bolshevik weakness. Others have seen a more visionary policy of trying to move national identity from bourgeois nationalism to new Soviet forms.

## Reasons for the Red Victory

Few observers believed that the Bolsheviks would survive the ordeal of Civil War, national independence movements, war against Poland, and Allied intervention. Lenin himself, apparently, had serious doubts on that score, especially if international revolution did not bring support and aid to Soviet Russia. Indeed, in March 1918, Lenin told a Communist Party congress that "it is an absolute truth that without a German revolution we are doomed." But he also understood, and continually reminded his sometimes despairing comrades, that they had no choice but to fight for the survival of Soviet power. Victory in the Civil War, therefore, became a legendary Communist epic, as important as the revolution itself. Yet, a closer look allows us to explain the Bolshevik victory without recourse to Marxist theories of inevitability or the superhuman qualities of Red fighters. To begin with, Allied intervention—the emphatic Soviet view to the contrary notwithstanding—represented anything but a determined and coordinated effort to strangle the new Communist regime. Kennan, Ullman, and other scholars have shown how much misunderstanding and confusion went into the Allied policies toward Russia, which never amounted to more than a half-hearted support of White movements. Allied soldiers and sailors, it might be added, saw even less reason for intervening than did their commanders. The French navy mutinied in the Black Sea, while the efficiency of American units was impaired by unrest as well as by a fervent desire to return home. The Labor Party in Great Britain and various groups elsewhere exercised what pressure they could against intervention. Ill-conceived and poorly executed, the Allied intervention produced in the end little or no result. The Poles, by contrast, knew what they wanted and obtained it by means of a successful war. Their goals, however, did not include the destruction of the Soviet regime in Russian territory proper. National independence movements also had aims limited to their localities, and were, besides, usually quite weak. The Soviet government could, therefore, defeat many of them one by one and at the time of its own choosing, repudiating its earlier promises when convenient, as in the cases of Ukraine and the Transcaucasian republics.

The White movement did pose a deadly threat to the Reds. Ultimately there could be no compromise between the two sides. The White armies were many, contained an extremely high proportion of officers, and often fought bravely. The Reds, however, had advantages that in the end proved decisive. The Soviet government controlled the heart of Russia, including both Moscow and Petrograd, most of its population, much of its industry, and the great bulk of military supplies intended for the First World War. The White armies constantly found themselves outnumbered and, in spite of Allied help, more poorly equipped. Also, the Red Army enjoyed the inner lines of communication, while its opponents had to shift around on the periphery. Still more important, the Reds possessed a strict unity of command, whereas the Whites fought, in fact, separate and uncoordinated wars.

Ultimately, however, it was probably the political failure of the White movement that ensured Red victory. Politics divided the Whites no less than geography did. Anti-Bolshevism represented the only generally accepted tenet in this camp, which encompassed everyone from monarchists to Socialist Revolutionaries. But there were also policy choices that limited their bases of support. One of these was open hostility to the desires of non-Russian nationalities. Most White leaders believed strongly in "Russia one and indivisible"—a principle shared from the moderate liberal Left to the reactionary Right—and not only rejected separatism but also fought against it. Thus, for example, Denikin antagonized the Ukrainians by his measures to suppress the Ukrainian language and schools, and Iudenich weakened his base in Estonia because he would not promise the Estonians independence.

The Whites failed even more to win over the Russian population. White leaders were often quite clear that if restored to power, the radical land reform that peasants had enacted on their own by seizing estate lands, an outcome that the Bolsheviks wisely endorsed, would be reversed in the name of law and the principle of private property. Thus, whereas the upper and middle classes generally favored the Whites, and the vast majority of workers backed the Reds, the peasants, the great majority of the people, tended to support neither side enthusiastically but were likely to be more hostile to the Whites. There were plenty of reasons for peasants to view both sides with hostility. Both Red and White armies forced peasants into their armies, requisitioned grain and horses, and used terror against suspected opponents. But what mattered most to peasants was land, and the Whites were associated in their minds—not unjustly—with a return of the landlords and a restoration of the old order, a possibility that evoked hatred and fear in the Russian village. One sign of peasant hostility to both camps, however, was the "Green" movement during the Civil War. In many rural areas, Green armies violently attacked both armies and defended peasants against both the draft and forced requisitioning. A number of Green leaders were associated with the anarchists, who rejected any form of central state control over local lives; this was a view peasants naturally found congenial.

## The Crisis

At the end of the Civil War Soviet Russia was exhausted and ruined. The droughts of 1920 and 1921 and the frightful famine during that last year added the final, gruesome chapter to the disaster. In the years following the originally "bloodless" October Revolution, epidemics, starvation, fighting, executions, and the general breakdown of the economy and society had taken something like 20 million lives. Another 2 million had left Russia—with Wrangel, through the Far East, or in numerous other ways—rather than accept Communist rule, the émigrés including a high proportion of educated and skilled people. War Communism might have saved the Soviet government in the course of the Civil War, but it also helped greatly to wreck the national economy. With private industry and trade proscribed and the state unable to perform these functions on a sufficient scale, much of the Russian economy ground to a standstill. It has been estimated that the total output of mines and factories fell in 1921 to 20 percent of the pre–World War level, with many crucial items experiencing an even more drastic decline; for example, cotton fell to 5 percent, iron to 2 percent, of the prewar level. The peasants responded to requisitioning by refusing to till their land. By 1921 cultivated land had shrunk to some 62 percent of the prewar acreage, and the harvest yield was only about 37 percent of normal. The number of horses declined from 35 million in 1916 to 24 million in 1920, and cattle from 58 to 37 million during the same span of time. The exchange rate of an American dollar, which had been 2 rubles in 1914, rose to 1,200 rubles in 1920.

This unbearable material situation, combined with growing resentment at Communist authoritarianism and brutality, which had intensified in the course of the Civil War, sparked uprisings in the countryside and unrest and strikes in the factories. Already during the Civil War, peasants had occasionally attacked detachments of Communists and workers come to requisition grain. But once no longer faced with the threat of White victory, viewed as the return of the landlords, peasants turned against Bolshevik interference in their economic lives. Grain requisitioning teams were ambushed and other representatives of state authority in the countryside were attacked. In some regions, notably western Siberia, the middle Volga, Tambov province, and Ukraine, massive uprisings broke out starting in late 1920. The goals of these movements varied, and social rebellion often mixed with brigandage, but the basic message was clear: no more grain requisitioning, a restoration of free trade, and the guarantee of complete peasant control of the land they worked. Some peasants also demanded the reconvening of the Constituent Assembly. Although rural unrest was the greatest threat to Communist power, politically more unsettling was the unrest among urban workers that broke out in early 1921. Meetings, demonstrations, and even strikes made clear that discontent was widespread among what was left of the proletariat (the economic devastations of the Civil War era having reduced the number of industrial workers by half). Workers' complaints mainly concerned matters of simple physical survival: larger food rations, distribution of shoes and warm clothing, allowing workers to barter with peasants for food (peasants should be free to sell the produce of their own labor). But economic grievance brought to the surface political discontent. Workers often demanded also the restoration of civil rights, the end of coercive management practices in factories (strict one-man management had been introduced in 1918, effectively ending workers' control), and even the calling of a Constituent Assembly. Finally, in March 1921, the Kronstadt naval base, celebrated by the Communists as one of the sources of the October Revolution, rose in rebellion against Communist rule. It is worth noting that the sailors and other Kronstadt rebels demanded free Soviets, an end to one-party rule, freedom of speech and press, the summoning of a Constituent Assembly, and an end not only to forced grain requisitioning but also to all state control of the economy. "Down with the Commissarocracy" was an often heard slogan. Although Red Army units ruthlessly suppressed the uprising, the well-nigh general dissatisfaction with Bolshevik rule could not have been more forcefully expressed. Complicating this crisis still further, Communists who felt that the idealistic purposes of the Revolution were being lost sight of were increasingly outspoken in these months. This was not the first time dissident factions had arisen within the party. In 1918, "Left Communists" opposed the Brest-Litovsk treaty as a betrayal of world revolution and criticized Lenin's proposals to introduce strict labor discipline into industry to revive the economy. In 1919, a similarly short-lived "Military Opposition" opposed Trotsky's plans for a Red Army that would employ traditional discipline and make use of former tsarist officers. But once the Civil War had ended, criticism of party policy became more open and vehement. "Democratic Centralists" criticized growing centralization and bureaucratization and demanded freer discussion within the party and the election of local party officials. The "Workers' Opposition" opposed the imposition of traditional discipline in industry, the use of "bourgeois specialists" in management, and efforts in 1920 to subordinate completely the trade unions to the state.

Against this background of utter devastation and discontent, Lenin, who, besides, had finally to admit that a world revolution was not imminent, proceeded in the spring of 1921 to inaugurate his New Economic Policy (NEP) in place of War Communism. Once more Lenin proved to be the realist who had to overcome considerable doctrinaire opposition to have his views prevail in the party and, therefore, in the entire country.

## The New Economic Policy

The New Economic Policy was a compromise, a temporary retreat on the road to socialism, in order to give the country an opportunity to recover. It was, in Lenin's words, a "peasant Brest-Litovsk." The Communist Party, of course, retained full political control; the compromise and relaxation never extended to politics. Indeed, peasant rebellions and the Kronstadt uprising were violently crushed, protesting workers were met with lockouts and mass arrests, and critics within the party were forced into silence with a ban on factions in March 1921. Discipline, Lenin insisted, was essential when an army was retreating. And NEP was that necessary retreat. But this was not a complete retreat. The state kept its exclusive hold on the "commanding heights'" of the economy, that is, on finance, on large and medium industry, on modern transportation, on foreign trade, and on all wholesale commerce. Private enterprise, however, was allowed in small industry, which meant plants employing fewer than twenty workers each, and in retail trade. The government's change of policy toward the peasants was perhaps still more important. Instead of requisitioning their produce, as had been done during War Communism, it established a definite tax in kind, particularly in grain, replaced later by a money tax. The peasants could keep and sell on the free market what remained after the payment of the tax, and thus they were given an obvious incentive to produce more. Eventually the authorities even permitted a limited use of hired labor in agriculture and a restricted lease of land. The government also revamped and stabilized the financial system, introducing a new monetary unit, the *chervonets;* and it put into operation new legal codes to help stabilize a shattered society.

The New Economic Policy proved to be a great economic success. After the frightful starvation years of 1921 and 1922—years, incidentally, when many more Russians would have perished, but for the help received from the American Relief Administration headed by Herbert Hoover, from the Quakers, and from certain other groups—the Russian economy revived in a remarkable manner. In 1928 the amount of land under cultivation already slightly exceeded the pre–World War area. Industry on the whole also reached the prewar level. It should be added that during the NEP period, in contrast to the time of War Communism, the government demanded that state industries account for costs and pay for themselves. It was highly characteristic of NEP that 75 percent of retail trade fell into private hands. In general, the so-called Nepmen, the small businessmen allowed to operate by the new policy, increased in number in towns, while the *kulaki*—or kulaks, for the term has entered the English language—gained in the villages. *Kulak,* meaning "fist," came to designate a prosperous peasant, a man who held tightly to his own; the prerevolutionary term, used by Soviet sources, also has connotations of exploitation and greed.

These social results of the New Economic Policy naturally worried many Communists. The Eleventh Party Congress declared as early as 1922 that no further "retreat" could be tolerated. In 1924 and 1925 the government introduced certain measures to restrict the Nepmen, and in 1927 to limit the kulaks. At the same time, scholars have argued, many Bolsheviks, including Lenin himself, began to view NEP less as a temporary retreat and more as a unique path to socialism in a backward peasant country like Russia. Notions of a decades-long evolution to socialism, based on gradually raising the cultural and economic level of the population and teaching the benefits of socialist cooperation, began to compete with notions of returning to Civil War strategies of forcing the country into socialism. These debates came to be closely linked to personalities and to the struggle for power that gained momentum after Lenin's death in January 1924.

## The Struggle for Power after Lenin's Death

Two main points of view competed among Soviet Communists during the 1920s. The so-called Left position, best developed by Trotsky, emphasized the need to overcome rapidly Russian backwardness (both in the economy and in the cultural level of the population) through the active leadership of the party and state. These principles produced vigorous criticism of current party policies in both economics and inner-party administration. Rapid industrialization was urgent, the Left argued, if the socialist ideals of Soviet Russia were not to drown in the country's massive petit bourgeois peasant population. This required aggressive state economic planning and the accumulation of capital for investment by squeezing the peasants and the private sector through high taxes and high industrial prices, but also through wage controls and low investment in consumer goods. At the same time, the Communist "vanguard" leading this effort must be improved by fighting against "bureaucracy" in the party and the state. The Left condemned the widespread practice of appointing local party secretaries, accused the party of nurturing a political culture of "passive obedience" and "careerism," and called for greater freedom of debate and more mass participation in party affairs. Stalin came in for particular criticism, for, as general secretary of the party, he was in charge of appointments. Such prominent Communist leaders as Grigorii Zinoviev—born Radomyslsky—and Lev Kamenev—born Rosenfeld—essentially shared Trotsky's view.

Nikolai Bukharin was the chief opponent of the Left, representing the position of the party majority, including Stalin, until the late 1920s. Bukharin and the Right, as they would be called later when Stalin turned against them, agreed with the Left that Russia's backwardness was the most serious obstacle to building socialism in Russia. But they drew quite different conclusions from this. Bukharin mocked the Left for trying to create a "Genghis Khan plan" that would require such a massive apparatus and such use of coercion that economic growth would be impeded. He agreed that industrialization was essential but insisted that this must be based not on a production model that squeezed the private sector but on a consumption model that used the workings of the market. His objections to the plans of the Left were as much political as economic, however. One must teach the peasants to love socialism, not force them along a socialist path, which would only lead to alienation,

Nikolai Bukharin around 1917. Unlike many other Bolshevik leaders during the Civil War and after, Bukharin eschewed the style of wearing military dress. In Lenin's letter to the party congress in December 1922 ("Lenin's testament"), he called Bukharin "the favorite of the whole party."   *(Stephen Cohen)*

resentment, and possibly rebellion. In his words, the road to socialism must be "peaceful" and "bloodless," not marked by "the clanging of metal weapons." Stalin, it is clear, never felt entirely comfortable with such arguments, and neither did many of the more militant Communists. But only after defeating the Left did Stalin turn against the "Right Deviation," partly, it is argued, by co-opting the Left's economic program.

As has often been described and analyzed, the struggle for power that followed Lenin's death was decided by Stalin's superior control of the party membership. Acting behind the scenes, Stalin managed to build up a following strong enough to overcome Trotsky's magnificent rhetoric and great prestige, as well as Kamenev's party organization in Moscow and Zinoviev's in Petrograd—named Leningrad after Lenin's death. Stalin intrigued skillfully,

Lev Trotsky. In his 1922 "testament," Lenin called Trotsky "personally perhaps the most capable person" in the Central Committee of the party.  (*New York Public Library*)

first allying himself with Kamenev and Zinoviev against Trotsky, whom they envied and considered their rival for party leadership; then with the Right group against the Left; and eventually, when sufficiently strong, suppressing the Right as well. He kept accusing his opponents of factionalism, of disobeying the established party line and splitting the party. Final victory came at the Fifteenth All-Union Congress of the Communist Party, which on December 27, 1927, condemned all "deviation from the general party line" as interpreted by Stalin. The general secretary's rivals and opponents recanted or were exiled; in any case, they lost their former importance. Trotsky himself was expelled from the Soviet Union in January 1929 and was eventually murdered in exile in Mexico in 1940, almost certainly on Stalin's orders.

Still, although Stalin's rise to supreme authority can well be considered an impressive, if gruesome, study in power politics, its ideological aspect should not be forgotten. Stalin built a following by appealing not only to the careerist

Iosif Stalin. Lenin's view of Stalin in his 1922 letter was that he "has, becoming General Secretary, concentrated boundless power in his hands, and I am not certain he will always be capable of using that power with sufficient caution." (*Sovfoto*)

aspirations of many Communists but also to widespread desires for the Soviet Union to take a more idealistic and activist path. Two related characteristics of Stalin's political approach attracted allies and admirers. First, he simplified and even sacralized ideology for the masses of ordinary Communists. His popular 1924 book *Foundations of Leninism* reduced Communist ideology to its simplest terms, and after Lenin's death Stalin took the lead in treating Lenin's works as dogma and dissent as heresy. Second, Stalin consistently emphasized optimism, hope, and even faith. When Trotsky, for example, argued (as Lenin had) that, in the long term, the success of socialism in Russia would depend on revolutions bringing socialists to power in more advanced Western countries, Stalin mocked this theory of "permanent revolution" as a theory of "permanent hopelessness," which showed too little "faith" in the Russian proletariat. Offering an alternative theory of "socialism in one country," Stalin argued that Russia did not depend on others to achieve heroic goals. Indeed, he offered an appealingly voluntarist interpretation of Leninism as "neither knowing nor recognizing obstacles." Only Stalin offered a sweeping program and a majestic goal to be achieved by Soviet efforts alone. This heroic spirit would attract many to his side as he launched his economic and social "revolution from above." The same party congress that condemned all deviations from Stalin's line enthusiastically adopted measures that signified the end of the New Economic Policy and the beginning of the First Five-Year Plan.

CHAPTER 37

# The Stalin Era

It [the First Five-Year Plan] asked no less than a complete transformation from backward agricultural individualism to mechanized collectivism, from hothouse subsidized industry to self-sufficient industry on the greatest, most modern scale, from the mentality of feudalism, far behind the Western industrial age, to socialism still ahead of it.

WALTER DURANTY

Life has become better comrades, life has become more joyous, and when you are living joyously, work turns out well.

IOSIF STALIN, 1935

The trials brought to light the fact that the Trotsky-Bukharin fiends, in obedience to the wishes of their masters—the espionage services of the bourgeois states—had set out to destroy the Party and the Soviet state, to undermine the defensive power of the country, to assist foreign military intervention, to prepare the way for the defeat of the Red Army, to bring about the dismemberment of the USSR, to hand over the Soviet Maritime Region to the Japanese, Soviet Belorussia to the Poles, and Soviet Ukraine to the Germans, to destroy the gains of the workers and collective farmers, and to restore capitalist slavery in the USSR....These Whiteguard insects forgot that the real masters of the Soviet country were the Soviet people, and that the Rykovs, Bukharins, Zinovievs, and Kamenevs were only temporary employees of the state, which could at any moment sweep them out from its offices as so much useless trash. These contemptible lackeys of the fascists forgot that the Soviet people had only to move a finger, and not a trace of them would be left.

HISTORY OF THE ALL-UNION COMMUNIST PARTY (BOLSHEVIKS):
SHORT COURSE, 1938

"When a forest is cut down, splinters fly." Of course, it is unfortunate to be a splinter.

THE REMARK OF A SOVIET CITIZEN TO NICHOLAS<br>
RIASANOVSKY IN THE SUMMER OF 1958

Stalin's rule began with his sweeping victory at the Fifteenth Party Congress
in 1927 and lasted for a quarter of a century. The Stalin era—some even speak
of a Stalinist revolution—was a time of enormous change and suffering but
also great achievement. These years saw massive, forced industrialization,
which resulted in displacement, hardship, and economic growth. These years
experienced the sudden collectivization of all agriculture, resulting in famine,
death, and anger but also modernization. And, especially in the late 1930s, the
Stalin era was marked by a "great terror" in which "enemies" of all sorts were
purged and executed. As will be seen, historians have debated this period
intensely. Some historians have compared Stalin to Hitler in his dictatorial
control and brutality, while others have argued that Stalin could not and did
not rule through coercion and terror alone. Scholars continue to investigate
and debate how best to define this system, how to measure its effects, and
how to understand what it meant for the people who participated in and lived
through it.

## Stalin

Stalin began his life and career humbly enough. In fact, it has often been mentioned that he was one of the few Bolshevik leaders of more or less proletarian origin. Born a son of a shoemaker in 1879 in the little town of Gori
near the Georgian capital of Tiflis—or Tbilisi—Iosif Dzhugashvili attended a
Church school in Gori until 1894 and then went to the theological seminary
in Tiflis. In 1899, however, he was expelled from the seminary for reasons that
are not entirely clear. By that time, apparently, Stalin had become acquainted
with some radical writers and in particular with Marx and Lenin. He joined
the Social Democratic Party and when it split in 1903 sided firmly with the
Bolsheviks. Between 1902 and 1913 Dzhugashvili, or rather Stalin as he came
to be known, engaged in a variety of conspiratorial and revolutionary activities, suffering arrest and exile several times. He managed to escape repeatedly from exile, which has suggested police collusion to certain specialists.
Stalin's last exile, however, continued from 1913 until the February Revolution.
Apparently the Georgian Bolshevik first attracted Lenin's attention when he
organized a daring raid to seize funds for the party. Stalin's revolutionary
activity developed in such Transcaucasian centers as Tiflis, Batum, and Baku,
as well as in St. Petersburg. In contrast to many other Bolshevik leaders, Stalin
never lived abroad, leaving the Russian Empire only to attend a few meetings.
Because of Stalin's Bolshevik orthodoxy and Georgian origin, the party welcomed him as an expert on the problem of nationalities, a subject to which he
devoted some of his early writings.

One of the first prominent Bolsheviks to arrive in Petrograd, Stalin participated in the historic events of 1917, and after the October Revolution he became

the first commissar for national minorities. As a member of the Revolutionary Military Council of the Southern Front he played a role in the Civil War, for example, in the defense of Tsaritsyn against the Whites. Incidentally, Tsaritsyn was renamed Stalingrad in 1925 and Volgograd in 1961. It might be noted that in the course of executing his duties he quarreled repeatedly with Trotsky. But Stalin's real bid for power began in 1922 with his appointment as general secretary of the party, a position that gave him broad authority in matters of personnel. The long-time official Soviet view of Stalin as Lenin's anointed successor distorts reality, for, in fact, the ailing Bolshevik leader came to resent the general secretary's rigidity and rudeness and in his so-called testament warned the party leadership against Stalin. But Stalin's rivals failed to heed Lenin's late forebodings, and, before too long, Stalin's party machine rolled over all opponents. The complete personal dictatorship which began in 1928 was to last until the dictator's death in 1953.

Interpreting Stalin and Stalinism has for many years been the subject of sometimes fierce scholarly debate. In part, the heated arguments can be explained by the Cold War (and its lingering influence), which made the interpretation of Soviet history also a matter of ideology and even morality. But serious analytical questions have also been at the heart of the debate: What was the defining character of the Stalinist order, its model of rule? What kept Stalin in power all those years? One answer to this question—long the predominant one outside the Soviet Union and now in post-Soviet Russia—is to view Stalin's regime as "totalitarian." The focus here is on Stalin himself (though scholars have debated whether he was a rational actor or was inspired by unreasonable paranoia, obsession with his own heroic role in history, or even a pathological personality) and on a system of party-state rule in which indoctrination, repression, and terror held all of Soviet political, social, and cultural life in an iron grip and in which social groups and individuals were passive victims. Scholars like Merle Fainsod, Robert Conquest, Adam Ulam, and Robert Tucker have offered excellent, well-documented, and often nuanced examples of this approach. Starting in the 1970s, "revisionist" historians, notably Sheila Fitzpatrick, have questioned the one-sidedness of the totalitarian paradigm. Without denying the repressiveness and violence of the regime (though some have deemphasized its extent and centrality), these scholars have argued that the Stalinist system could not and did not rule only through coercion and terror. Reinvestigating the relationship between state and society—facilitated by growing opportunities for research in the Soviet Union—these scholars point to support within the population for many of Stalin's policies and argue that the party and state were often responsive to people's desires and values. The opening of the archives after the end of Communist rule has not resolved these debates, though some revisionists have been surprised at how extensive and often arbitrary the brutality was. But overall, the evidence highlights the contradictoriness of the Stalin era: belief in a presumably infallible ideology, a great deal of coercion, force, and terror (sometimes more brutal and systematic than we knew), subtle forms of cultural and psychological control, and support and enthusiasm for Stalin and the Soviet system.

## The First Five-Year Plan

The First Five-Year Plan and its successors hit the Soviet Union with tremendous impact. The USSR became a great industrial nation: from being the fifth country in production when the plans began, it was eventually second only to the United States. In agriculture individual peasant cultivation gave way to a new system of collective farming. Indeed 1928 and 1929 have been described as the true revolutionary years in Russia: it was then that the mode of life of the peasants, the bulk of the people, underwent a radical change, whereas until the First Five-Year Plan they continued to live much as they had for centuries. A vast social transformation accompanied the economic, while at the same time the entire Soviet system as we came to know it acquired its definitive form in the difficult decade of the 1930s.

A number of considerations explain the regime's decision to force rapid industrialization. Ideologically, Marxism did not provide a plan for the industrialization of a peasant country, for industrialization was assumed to be a precondition of socialist revolution, not the result of it. This precondition had to be produced after the fact, as it were. The "dictatorship of the proletariat" over a largely rural population needed to be corrected quickly if the revolution was not to drown in this alien class environment. Industry and workers needed to be created. Likewise, the collectivization of agriculture represented the very important step from an individual and, therefore, bourgeois system of ownership and production to a collective economy and, therefore, to socialism. As already mentioned, after the October Revolution the Soviet government proceeded to nationalize Russian industry. Lenin showed a special interest in electrification, popularizing the famous slogan: "Electrification plus Soviet power equals communism." In 1921 the State Planning Commission, known as *Gosplan,* was organized to draft an economic plan for the entire country. It studied resources and proposed production figures; eventually it drew up the five-year plans.

Why was the New Economic Policy, which Communists like Bukharin and some later historians have seen as a viable alternative to Stalinism, abandoned? First, NEP raised serious economic problems. While by 1928 Russian industry had regained its pre–World War level, a further rapid advance appeared quite uncertain. With the industrial plant restored and in operation—a relatively easy accomplishment—the Soviet Union needed investment in the producer goods industries and a new spurt in production. Yet the "socialist sector" of the economy lacked funds, while the "free sector," particularly the peasants, failed to rise to government expectations. The Soviet economy in the 1920s continued to be plagued by pricing problems, beginning with the disparity between the low agricultural prices and the high prices of manufactured consumers' goods, resulting in the unwillingness of peasants to supply grain and other products to the government and the cities—a situation well described as the "scissors crisis." Alexander Gerschenkron and other specialists have argued that the Bolsheviks had good reason to fear that a continuation of NEP would stabilize a peasant society at the point where it was interested in obtaining more consumer goods, but neither willing nor able to support large-scale industrialization. On top of these economic pressures for changing course, there were political pressures. Many rank-and-file Communists, young people, and workers were deeply hostile to the social results of NEP. The persistence of capitalism, the continuation of poverty, the visible social presence of petty capitalists in the city ("Nepmen") and rich peasants in the countryside ("kulaks"), and the unheroic gradualism offered by even those who defended NEP as a path to socialism frustrated and angered many. A character in Fedor Gladkov's 1925 novel *Cement* captured these sentiments by comparing the present society to the brutal but heroic Civil War: "I don't know where the nightmare is: in those years of blood, misery, and sacrifice or in this bacchanalia of rich shop windows and drunken cafes! What was the good of mountains of corpses?...So that scoundrels and vampires should again enjoy all the good things in life, and get fat by robbery?" Many were ready for this "retreat," as NEP was originally called, to end and longed for a new heroic march forward. Stalin's "revolution from above" seemed to provide just that. Stalin's Five-Year Plan also proved attractive because it promised that the Soviet Union could become a truly socialist country without waiting for world revolution. "Socialism in one country" gripped many imaginations and became the new Bolshevik battle cry.

Once the Plan went into operation, the economic factors involved in its execution acquired great significance, all the more so because the planners set sail in essentially uncharted waters and often could not foresee the results of their actions. In particular, according to Gerschenkron, Alexander Erlich, and certain other scholars, the fantastically rapid collectivization of agriculture came about as follows: while the Plan had called for a strictly limited collectivization, set at 14 percent, the unexpectedly strong resistance on the part of the peasants led to an all-out attack on individual farming; moreover, the government discovered that the collectives, which finally gave it control over the labor and produce of the peasants, enabled it to squeeze from them the necessary funds for industrial investment. It has been estimated that the Soviet state paid to the collectives for their grain only a distinctly minor part of the price of that grain charged the consumer; the remaining major part constituted in effect a tax. That tax, plus the turnover or sales tax that the Soviet state charged all consumers, together with the ability of the government to keep real wages down while productivity went up, produced the formula for financing the continuous industrialization of the Soviet Union.

In addition to ideology and economics, other factors entered into the execution of the five-year plans. Many scholars assign major importance to considerations of foreign policy and of internal security and control. Preparation for war, which affected all major aspects of the five-year plans, began in earnest after Hitler came to power in Germany in 1933, and while Japan was further developing its aggressive policies in the Far East. The stress on internal security and control in the five-year plans is more difficult to document. Yet it might well be argued that police considerations were consistently uppermost in the minds of Stalin and his associates. Collectivization, from that

"Full Speed Ahead with Shock Tempo: The Five-Year Plan in Four Years,"
1930. (*Lenizogiz*)

point of view, represented a tremendous extension of Communist control over
the population of the Soviet Union, and it was buttressed by such additional
measures—again combining economics and control—as the new crucial role
of the Machine Tractor Stations, the MTS, which will be mentioned later.

The First Five-Year Plan lasted from October 1, 1928, to December 31, 1932,
that is, four years and three months. The fact that Soviet authorities tried to
complete a five-year plan in four years is a significant comment on the enormous speed-up typical of the new socialist offensive. Very high targets were
set and then revised upward to fantastic levels. As one economic historian has
observed, "in the absence of divine intervention it is hard to imagine" how
these goals could have been achieved. The intent of these goals, it has therefore been suggested, was more to inspire by their daring than to offer rational
targets. The main goal of the Plan was to develop heavy industry, including machine-building, and that emphasis remained characteristic of Soviet

industrialization from that time on. According to Alexander Baykov's calculation, 86 percent of all industrial investment during the First Five-Year Plan went into heavy industry. Whole new branches of industry, such as the chemical, automobile, agricultural machinery, aviation, machine tool, and electrical, were created from slight beginnings or even from scratch. Over 1,500 new factories were built. Gigantic industrial complexes, exemplified by Magnitostroi in the Urals and Kuznetsstroi in western Siberia, began to take shape. Entire cities arose in the wilderness. Magnitogorsk, for instance, acquired in a few years a population of a quarter of a million.

The First Five-Year Plan was proclaimed a great success: officially it was fulfilled in industry to the extent of 93.7 percent in four years and three months. Furthermore, heavy industry, concerned with means of production, exceeded its quota, registering 103.4 percent, while the light or consumer goods industry produced 84.9 percent of its assigned total. Of course, Soviet production claims included great exaggerations, difficult to estimate because of the limited and often misleading nature of Soviet statistics for the period. To put it very conservatively and without percentages: "The fact remains beyond dispute that quantitatively, during the years covered by the F.Y.P., industrial production did increase and very substantially." Quality, however, was often sacrificed to quantity, and the production results achieved varied greatly from item to item, with remarkable overfulfillments of the plan in some cases and underfulfillments in others. Besides, the great industrial spurt was accompanied by shortages of consumer goods, rationing, and various other privations and hardships that extended to all of the people, who at the same time were forced to work harder than ever before. The whole country underwent a quasi-military mobilization reminiscent of War Communism. Indeed, the language of war was pervasive. Speeches and articles in the press described industry as a battlefield with "fronts," "campaigns," and "breakthroughs," workers were organized into "shock troops," and those who dissented or failed in their tasks were treated as if traitors in wartime. The economic utopianism of the First Five-Year Plan was also reflected in a popular military metaphor, which Stalin especially liked: "there are no fortresses Bolsheviks cannot storm."

The First Five-Year Plan was clearly about more than economics. The "Great Turn," as it was called, was a revolution that sought to transform all aspects of society. Public trials of "bourgeois experts," starting in 1928 with the trial of engineers in the Shakhty coal mines for sabotage and conspiring with imperialists, was the most visible incitement to renewed class struggle. Throughout society, Communists were encouraged to challenge the authority of established experts, especially if they were from "alien" class backgrounds. A storm of purges was unleashed against non-Communist and nonworker engineers, foremen, teachers, journalists, state officials, writers, and others. This "cultural revolution," as it was called, was initiated by the state and party, but it had its enthusiasts throughout Soviet society. Class hatred for "bourgeois" specialists was widespread among working-class Communists. And social purges, as well as special efforts to educate and promote proletarians, created enormous opportunities for upward mobility for workers and

Communists. This cultural revolution also brought to the fore radical ideas about transforming society. For example, educators envisioned a system of school communes in which labor and study would be combined. And city planners imagined cities of both hyper-modernity (electrical towns planned by "bio-geometrics") and closeness to nature (linear "green cities").

The greatest transformation probably occurred in the countryside. As already mentioned, the collectivization of agriculture, planned originally as a gradual advance, became a flood. Tens of thousands of trusted Communists and proletarians—the celebrated "25,000" in one instance, actually 27,000—were sent from towns into villages to organize kolkhozes and establish social-ism. Local authorities and party organizations, with the police and troops where necessary, forced peasants into collectives. "Kulaks" were officially to be "eliminated as a class" in this process, but most scholars now see collectiv-ization as a war against the entire peasantry as a traditional social group. In turn, peasants were generally united against the regime and engaged in mas-sive resistance, including direct violence against representatives of the state and the mass slaughter of their own cattle and horses rather than hand them over to the collective farm. Anyone who resisted collectivization was branded a kulak. Kulaks lost their property and were arrested, along with their fami-lies, and sent to labor camps in far-off Siberia or Central Asia. The victims of this anti-kulak campaign numbered in the millions. In 1932 a terrible fam-ine swept Ukraine, the North Caucasus, and parts of central Russia, caused by the disruptions of collectivization, excessive procurement quotas, and bad harvests. Some historians, especially Ukrainians, have seen in this famine a deliberate policy of genocide against the Ukrainian people. By the time the famine eased in late 1933, over 5 million people may have died of starvation.

Stalin himself applied the brakes to his own policy after the initial fifteen months. In his remarkable article, "Dizzy with Success," published in March 1930, he criticized the collectivizers for excessive enthusiasm and reempha-sized that collectives were to be formed on the voluntary principle, not by force. At the same time he announced certain concessions to collective farm-ers, in particular their right to retain a small private plot of land and a limited number of domestic animals and poultry. The new stress on the voluntary principle produced striking results: whereas 14 million peasant households had joined collective farms by March 1930, only 5 million remained in collec-tives in May. But before long their number began to increase again when the authorities resorted to less direct pressure, such as a temporary suspension of taxes and priority in obtaining scarce manufactured goods. By the end of the First Five-Year Plan more than 14 million peasant households had joined the kolkhoz system. According to one count, at that time 68 percent of all culti-vated land in the Soviet Union was under kolkhoz agriculture, and 10 percent under sovkhoz agriculture, while only 22 percent remained for independent farmers. The Plan could well be considered overfulfilled.

A sovkhoz is essentially an agricultural factory owned by the state, with peasants providing hired labor. Although sovkhozes, serving as experimen-tal stations, as enormous grain producers in newly developed regions, and in many other crucial assignments, were more important for the Soviet economy than their number would indicate, Communist authorities refrained from establishing them as the basic form of agricultural organization in the country. Instead they relied on the kolkhoz as the norm for the Soviet countryside. A kolkhoz—*kollektivnoe khoziaistvo,* collective economy or farm—was owned by all its members, although it had to deliver the assigned amount of produce to the state and was controlled by the state. Significantly, the produce of a collective farm was generally allocated as follows: first, the part required by the state, both as taxes and as specified deliveries at set prices; next, the seed for sowing and the part to serve as payment to the Machine Tractor Station that aided the kolkhoz; after that, members of the collective received their shares calculated on the basis of the "workdays"—a unit of labor to be distinguished from actual days—that they had put in for the kolkhoz; finally, the remainder went into the indivisible fund of the collective to be used for its social, cultural, and other needs. The members also cultivated their small private plots—and with remarkable intensity and success. The Machine Tractor Stations, finally abolished in 1958, provided indispensable mechanized aid to the collectives, notably at harvest time, helping to coordinate the work of different kolkhozes and acting as another control over them. While it might be noted that the Soviet government found it easier to introduce collective farms in those regions where communal agriculture prevailed than in areas of individual proprietors, such as Ukraine, the kolkhoz bore very little resemblance to the commune. Members of a commune possessed their land in common, but they farmed their assigned lots separately, undisturbed, and in their own traditional way. Organization and regimentation of labor became the very essence of the kolkhoz.

## The Second and Third Five-Year Plans

The Second Five-Year Plan, which lasted from 1933 through 1937, and the Third, which began in 1938 and was interrupted by the German invasion in June 1941, continued on the whole the aims and methods of the initial Plan. They stressed the development of heavy industry, completed the collectivization of agriculture, and did their best to mobilize the manpower and other resources of the country to attain the objectives. The Soviet people lived through eight and a half more years of quasi-wartime exertion. Yet these plans also differed in certain ways from the first and from each other. The Second Five-Year Plan, drawn on the basis of acquired knowledge more expertly than the first, tried to balance production to avoid extreme over- or underfulfillment. It emphasized "mastering the technique," including the making of especially complicated machine tools, precision instruments, and the like. Also, it allowed a little more for consumer goods than the first plan did. However, in the course of the Second Five-Year Plan, and especially during the third, military considerations became paramount. Military considerations linked to ideology had of course always been present in the planning of Soviet leaders. From the beginning of industrialization, Stalin and his associates had insisted that they had

"Long Live Our Happy Socialist Motherland. Long Live Our Beloved Great Stalin," 1935. Stalin and Voroshilov (commissar for defense) stand upon Lenin's Mausoleum on Red Square. The airplanes flying overhead bear the names of Lenin, Stalin, Gorky, Kalinin, Molotov, and other Soviet leaders. The planes in the distance spell out "Stalin." *(Victoria Bonnell)*

to build a powerful socialist state quickly, perhaps in a decade, or be crushed by capitalists. In the 1930s the threat became increasingly real and menacing. Soviet leaders did what they could to arm and equip Red forces, and they accelerated the development of industries inland, east of the Volga, away from the exposed frontiers.

Both the Second Five-Year Plan and the Third, as far as it went, were again proclaimed successes, and again the official claims, in spite of their exaggeration, had some sound basis in fact. Industry, especially heavy industry, continued to grow. On the basis of official—and doubtful—figures, the Soviet share in world production amounted to 13.7 percent in 1937, compared to 3.7 in 1929 and to 2.6 for the Russian Empire in 1913. In the generation of electrical power, for example, the Soviet Union advanced from the fifteenth place among the countries of the world to the third, and it was second only to the United States in machine building, tractors, trucks, and some other lines of production. Moreover, the Soviet Union made its amazing gains while the rest of the world experienced a terrible depression and mass unemployment.

In agriculture collectivization was virtually completed and, except for the wilderness, the Soviet countryside became a land of kolkhozes and sovkhozes. Slightly less than 250,000 kolkhozes replaced over 25 million individual farms. The famine and other horrors of the First Five-Year Plan did not recur. In fact, agricultural production increased somewhat, and food rationing was abolished in 1935. Still, the economic success of Soviet agricultural policy remained much more doubtful than the achievements of Soviet industrialization. Peasants regularly failed to meet their production quotas. They showed far greater devotion to their small private plots than to the vast kolkhoz possessions. In other ways, too, they remained particularly unresponsive to the wishes of Communist authorities. A full evaluation of Soviet social engineering should also take account of the costs.

## An Evaluation of the Plans

Any overall judgment of the first three five-year plans is of necessity a complicated and controversial matter. The plans did succeed—and succeed strikingly—in developing industry, particularly heavy industry, and in collectivizing agriculture. Skepticism as to the feasibility of the plans, extremely widespread outside the Soviet Union, turned to astonishment and sometimes admiration. To repeat, not only did production greatly increase, but entire new industries appeared, while huge virgin territories, including the distant and difficult far north, began to enter the economic life of the country. Red armed forces, by contrast with the tsarist army, obtained a highly developed industrial and armaments base, a fact that alone justifies the five-year plans, in the opinion of some critics. Moreover, the entire enormous undertaking was carried out almost wholly by internal manpower and financing, except for the very important contribution of several thousand Western specialists in all fields who were invited to help, and some short-term credit extended to the Soviet government by German and other suppliers during the first years of industrialization. Considered by many as Stalin's chimera, the five-year plans proved to be an effective way—if not necessarily the only or the best way—to industrialize a relatively backward country.

Yet the cost was tremendous. Soviet authorities could accomplish their aims only by imposing great hardships on the people and by mobilizing the country in a quasi-military manner for a supreme effort. Piece work became common and wage differentials grew by leaps and bounds. The new emphasis on "socialist competition" culminated in the Stakhanov movement. In 1935 Alexei Stakhanov, a coal miner in the Donets Basin, was reported to have over-fulfilled his daily quota by 1,400 percent in the course of a shift hewing coal. "Stakhanovite" results were soon achieved by other workers in numerous branches of industry. Rewarding the Stakhanovites, whose accomplishments stemmed in different degrees from improved technique, enormous exertion, and cooperation by their fellow workers, the government used their successes to raise general production norms over a period of time. Most workers must have resented this speed-up—some Stakhanovites were actually killed—but they could not reverse it. After the October Revolution, and especially in the 1930s labor unions, to which almost all workers belonged, served as agencies of the state, to promote its policies and rally the workers behind them, rather than as representatives of labor interests and point of view. Hardships of Soviet life included a desperate shortage of consumer goods, as well as totally inadequate housing combined with a rigid system of priorities. As a result the black market flourished, and indeed remained an essential part of the Soviet economic system. Criticisms of the first three five-year plans—in fact, of their successors as well—have also pointed to top-heavy bureaucracy and excessive red tape, to a relatively low productivity per worker and production per inhabitant, to the frequently poor quality of the items produced, and to numerous weaknesses, perhaps outright failure, in agriculture. It can legitimately be asked whether a different regime could have industrialized the country better and with less pain.

For extreme painfulness emerged as a fundamental aspect of the first three five-year plans. While all suffered to some extent, some groups of the population suffered beyond all measure. One such group, as already mentioned, was the kulaks and their families. Another, overlapping but by no means identical with the kulaks, was the inmates of the forced-labor camps. Having begun in the early 1930s the system encompassed millions of human beings on the eve of the Second World War, in spite of the extremely high mortality rate in the camps. Forced labor was used especially on huge construction projects, such as the Baltic–White Sea and other canals, and for hard work under primitive conditions in distant areas, as in the case of the lumber and gold industries. The political police—from 1922 to 1934 known as the GPU and the OGPU rather than the Cheka, after 1934 as the NKVD after the People's Commissariat of Internal Affairs, subsequently as MVD and MGB, and after 1954 as KGB—which guarded and administered forced labor, developed veritable concentration camp empires in the European Russian and Siberian far north, in the Far East, and in certain other areas of the Soviet Union.

## The Great Purge

The great purge of the 1930s helped to fill forced-labor camps and formed another major, although perhaps unnecessary, aspect of the five-year plans. It also marked Stalin's extermination of all opposition or suspected opposition and his assumption of complete dictatorial power. Although earlier some engineers and other specialists, including foreigners, had been accused of sabotaging or wrecking the industrialization of the country, the real purge began in December 1934 with the assassination of one of the party leaders who was boss in Leningrad, Sergei Kirov, and reached high intensity from 1936 to 1938.

A 1934 newspaper cartoon depicts an old peasant cart marked "deviationists" carrying Bukharin, Kamenev, and Zinoviev toward a massive tank identified as the Communist Party. *(Mark Steinberg)*

The purge eventually became enormous in scope; it was directed primarily against party members, not against the White Guards or other remnants of the old regime as repressive practices had been before.

The assassin of Kirov, proclaimed to be a member of the Left Opposition, was shot, together with about a hundred alleged accomplices. (Revelations at the Twenty-second Party Congress strengthened the suspicions of some specialists that Stalin himself was apparently responsible for Kirov's murder.) A party purge followed. While uncounted people disappeared, the three great public trials featured sixteen Bolshevik leaders, notably Zinoviev and Kamenev, in 1936, another seventeen in 1937, and twenty-one more, including Bukharin and Rykov, in 1938. The accused were charged variously with espionage, "wrecking," and terrorism on behalf of imperialists, fascists, and Trotsky, and specifically with plotting to murder Stalin, overthrow the Soviet state, restore capitalism, and dismember the USSR with the help of Germany and Japan. Invariably they confessed to the fantastic charges and in all but four cases received the death penalty. Observers and scholars have been trying since to find reasons for the staggering confessions in everything from torture to heroic loyalty to Soviet communism.

The purge spread and spread, affecting virtually all party organizations and government branches, the army, where Marshal Tukhachevsky and seven other top commanders perished at the same time, and almost every other prominent institution, including the political police itself. Everywhere, party members were expected to denounce enemies of the regime at their places of work. Soon, the movement to expose enemies reached well beyond the party. Swept up in the terror were large numbers of government officials, military officers, engineers, scientists, intellectuals, artists, and writers. Children were encouraged to denounce their parents for criticizing the regime. Entire groups were specially targeted, notably foreign communists (who had often fled to the Soviet Union from German and Italian fascism), non-Russian nationalities suspected of nationalism, and religious believers. Justified by an expectation of war, the NKVD launched special national operations among Germans, Poles, and other groups to root out alleged "diversionary and espionage groups." Before the purge had run its course, Nikolai Ezhov himself and many of his henchmen fell victim to it. Those caught up in the widening circle of accusations and denunciations would likely be expelled from the party, fired from work, imprisoned, perhaps tortured (starting in the middle of 1937), sent to a labor camp, or perhaps shot. The great purge reached its height when Ezhov— hence *Ezhovshchina*—directed the NKVD from late September 1936 until the end of July 1938.

The full scope of the "Great Terror" is difficult to measure, given the lack of reliable statistics, but we can have some idea of its dimensions. Almost the entire prerevolutionary Bolshevik leadership was exterminated between 1936 and 1938. Certainly, anyone who had ever participated in one of the many opposition groups within the party or had simply criticized Stalin perished. But even Stalin's own elite was decimated: 80 percent of the members of the Central Committee of 1934 were executed or driven to suicide. The rank and file of the party did only slightly better: of the 2.8 million party members in 1934, perhaps as many as a million were arrested. The total numbers who suffered, of course, are unknown, but most agree that at least 1.5 million people were arrested. Many were executed after a summary trial or sent to the growing network of NKVD prison camps known as the "Gulag," the acronym for the Main Directorate of Corrective Labor Camps. Scholarly estimates of the number who died during the terror are quite varied. A recent study by the Russian organization Memorial, using declassified archives, identifies 724,000 people sentenced to execution during the peak period between October 1936 and November 1938. Many scholars argue that many more were shot without record or died in the camps without formally being sentenced to death. Thus, for example, S. G. Wheatcroft and R. W. Davies, using demographic and NKVD data, concluded that repression deaths in 1937–38 were about

1–1.5 million, while Robert Conquest argued that the actual number killed was 2–3 million. Of course, the effects of the terror were felt not only by the immediate victim, but also by friends and especially by family members. And as Merle Fainsod argued, one should not underestimate the brutal shock of being accused falsely, as most were:

> Most of the prisoners were utterly bewildered by the fate which had befallen them. The vast resources of the NKVD were concentrated on one objective—to document the existence of a huge conspiracy to undermine Soviet power. The extraction of real confessions to imaginary crimes became a major industry. Under the zealous and ruthless ministrations of NKVD examiners, millions of innocents were transformed into traitors, terrorists, and enemies of the people.

Suggesting the arbitrariness of the purge, in many areas of the country and among many groups, arrests and executions were by quota. It was decided a priori that a certain percentage of the population were enemies of the people. Archive documents show that when Stalin received these quota lists, he sometimes raised the targets.

## Stalin's System

The great purge assured Stalin's dictatorial control of the party, the government, and the country. As frequently pointed out, the Old Bolsheviks, members of the party before 1917 and thus not creatures of the general secretary, suffered enormous losses. Except for a few lieutenants of Stalin, such as Viacheslav Molotov, born Skriabin, almost no leaders of any prominence were left. For example, with the exception of Stalin himself and of Trotsky, who was murdered in 1940, Lenin's entire Politburo had been wiped out. Absolute personal dictatorship set in. While the Politburo remained by far the most important body in the country, because its fourteen or so members and candidate members were the general secretary's immediate assistants, there is much evidence that they, too, implicitly obeyed their master. Other party organizations followed the instructions they received as best they could to the letter. Significantly, no party congress was called between 1939 and 1952. The so-called democratic centralism within the party, that is, the practice of discussing and debating issues from the bottom up, but, once the party line had been formed, executing orders as issued from the top down, became a dead letter: even within the Communist Party framework no free discussion could take place in the Soviet Union, and almost every personal opinion became dangerous.

Through the Communist Party apparatus and the several million party members, as well as through the political police, Stalin supervised the government machine and controlled the people of the country. The peculiar relationship between the party and the government in the Soviet Union, in which the party is the leading partner as well as a driving force in carrying out state policies, has been elucidated in many studies. Not in vain did Article 126 of the Soviet Constitution of 1936 declare:

> ...the most active and most politically conscious citizens in the ranks of the working class and other sections of the working people unite in the Communist Party

A 1934 poster depicting a happy peasant family. An award for excellent work hangs on the wall. On the bookshelf are works by Gorky, Lenin, and Stalin and on tractors, agricultural technology, and setting up rural reading rooms. Note the centrality in this poster of electric light and the phonograph. Stalin is quoted: "Any peasant, collective farmer, or individual farmer can now live like a human being, as long as he is willing to work honestly, not loaf, not wander about the country, and not loot the property of the collective farm." *(Victoria Bonnell)*

of the Soviet Union (Bolsheviks), which is the vanguard of the working people in their struggle to strengthen and develop the socialist system and is the leading core of all organizations of the working people, both public and state.

The party, as will be shown in a later chapter, in fact dominated the social and cultural, as well as the political and economic, life in the Soviet Union.

At the same time, recent scholars have argued, Stalin's system could not rely solely on iron-fisted control, repression, and fear. As we have seen, enthusiasm for socialist construction, class hostility to "bourgeois" specialists, and personal ambition to rise in the hierarchy at the expense of ideological or social aliens could win the regime allies and supporters. There were also concrete rewards. Especially after the end of the First Five-Year Plan, mobilization for its own sake gave way to a tendency to promise material benefits as well. Stakhanovite workers, for example, were shown being rewarded with new clothes, bicycles, phonographs, radios, china, linen, and pianos and portrayed spending their leisure time not only at party or production meetings but also at parties and dances. Indeed, happiness became a pervasive theme in public life. In 1936, Stalin introduced a new guiding slogan for the day: "Life has become better, life has become more joyous." Movies, popular entertainment, music, art, and literature all held out this promise of a happy life, however allusive it remained for so many and however contradicted by the brutalities of the age. Newspapers were filled not only with stories about enemies and purges but also with advertisements for attractive new hats and shoes and reports of dances and carnivals in the parks. This too was part of Stalin's system.

## The Constitution of 1936

The Stalinist Constitution of 1936, which replaced the constitution of 1924 and was officially hailed as marking a great advance in the development of the Union of Soviet Socialist Republics, retained in effect the "dictatorship of the proletariat," exercised by the Communist Party and its leadership, specifically Stalin. At the same time it was meant to reflect the new "socialist" stage achieved in the Soviet Union, based on collective ownership of the means of production and summarized in the formula: "From each according to his ability, to each according to his work." It gave the ballot to all Soviet citizens—for no "exploiters" remained in the country—and made elections equal, direct, and secret. In fact, it emphasized democracy and contained in Chapter X a long list of civil rights as well as obligations. Yet, as has often been demonstrated, the permissiveness of the new constitution never extended beyond the Communist framework. Thus Chapter I affirmed that the basic structure of Soviet society could not be challenged. The civil liberty articles began: "In conformity with the interests of the working people, and in order to strengthen the socialist system..."—and could be considered dependent on this condition. The Communist Party, specifically recognized by the Constitution, was the only political group allowed in the Soviet Union. Still more important, the niceties of the Constitution of 1936 mattered little in a country ruled by an absolute dictator, his party, and his police. Ironically, the height of the great purge followed the introduction of the Constitution.

The Union of Soviet Socialist Republics remained a federal state, its component units being increased to eleven: the Russian Soviet Federated Socialist Republic and ten Soviet Socialist Republics, namely, Ukraine, Belorussia or White Russia, Armenia, Georgia, and Azerbaijan in Transcaucasia and the Kazakh, Kirghiz, Tajik, Turkmen, and Uzbek republics in Central Asia. While the larger nationalities received their own union republics, smaller ones obtained, in descending order, autonomous republics, autonomous regions, and national areas. Altogether, fifty-one nationalities were granted some form of limited statehood. Yet, like much else in the constitution, this arrangement was largely a sham: while important in terms of cultural autonomy—a subject to be discussed in a later chapter—as well as in terms of administration, in fact it gave no political or economic independence to the local units at all. The Soviet Union was one of the most highly centralized states of modern times.

A bicameral Supreme Soviet replaced the congresses of Soviets as the highest legislative body of the land. One chamber, the Union Soviet, represented the entire Soviet people and was to be elected in the proportion of one deputy for every 300,000 inhabitants. The other, the Soviet of Nationalities, represented the component national groups and was to be elected as follows: twenty-five delegates from each union republic, eleven from each autonomous republic, five from each autonomous region, and one from each national area. The two chambers received equal rights and parallel functions, exercising some of them jointly and some separately. Elected for four years—although with the Second World War intervening the second Supreme Soviet was not elected until 1946—the Supreme Soviet met twice a year, usually for no more than a week at a time. In the interims between sessions a Presidium elected by the Soviet had full authority. Almost always, Supreme Soviets unanimously approved all actions taken by their Presidiums. In the words of one commentator: "The brevity of the sessions, already noted, the size of the body, and the complexity of its agendas are all revealing as to the actual power and place of the Supreme Soviet." Still more revealing was the acquiescence and obsequiousness of the Soviet legislature in its dealings with Soviet rulers.

In the Constitution of 1936 the executive authority continued to be vested in the Council of People's Commissars, which had to be confirmed by the Supreme Soviet. Commissariats were of three kinds: Union—that is, central—Republican, and a combination of the two. Their number exceeded the number of ministries or similar agencies in other countries because many branches of the Soviet economy came to be managed by separate commissariats. In general, heavy industry fell under central jurisdiction, while light industry was directed by Union-Republican commissariats.

The Soviet legal system, while extensive and complicated, served party and state needs both explicitly and implicitly and had only an extremely limited independent role in Soviet society. Besides, the political police generally operated outside even Soviet law. It might be added that the Soviet central government served as the model for the governments of the union republics, although the latter established single-chamber, rather than bicameral, legislatures by omitting a chamber of nationalities. Stalin's Soviet regime, which took its definitive shape in the 1930s, was to undergo before long the awesome test of the Second World War. In a sense it passed the test, although it can well be argued that the war raised more questions about the regime than it settled. But, before turning to the Second World War, it is necessary to summarize Soviet foreign policy from the time of Brest-Litovsk and Allied intervention to the summer of 1941.

CHAPTER 38

# Soviet Foreign Policy, 1921–41, and the Second World War, 1941–45

From Great Moscow to the farthest borderland,
From the southern mountains to the northern seas,
A person can feel he is the master
Of his own unbounded Motherland.

"HOW BROAD IS MY NATIVE LAND,"

A POPULAR SONG

The Russian by nature is gentle, passionate, easily pacified, ready to understand and forgive....Hatred was never one of the traits of the Russians. It did not drop from the skies. No, this hatred our people now evince has been born of suffering. At first many of us thought that this was a war like other wars, that pitted us against mere human beings dressed only in different uniforms....Now everybody in our country knows that this war does not in any way resemble the wars that went before it. For the first time our people have found pitted against them not human beings but vile, malicious monsters, savages, armed with everything that modern science can give....Now our hatred is ripe. It no longer goes to the head like young wine; it has become cold and deliberate. We have realized that the world is too small a place to hold both us and the fascists....The question at issue is plain and simple: our right to exist.

ILYA EHRENBURG, 1942

Our Government committed no few mistakes; at times our position was desperate, as in 1941–42, when our army was retreating, abandoning our native villages and towns in Ukraine, Belorussia, Moldavia, the Leningrad Region, the Baltic Region, and the Karelo-Finnish Republic, abandoning them because there was no other alternative. Another people might have said to the government: You have not come up to our expectations. Get out. We shall appoint another government, which will conclude peace with Germany and ensure tranquillity for us. But the Russian people did not do that, for they were confident that the policy their Government was pursuing was correct; and they made sacrifices in order to ensure the defeat of Germany. And this confidence which the Russian people displayed in the Soviet Government proved to be the decisive factor which ensured our historic victory over the enemy of mankind, over fascism.

I thank the Russian people for this confidence!

To the health of the Russian people!

STALIN

Soviet foreign policy could only partly be shaped by Marxist ideology. Marxism provided no explicit guidance for the foreign relations of a Communist state in a capitalist world, just as it did not indicate how Communists should rule and develop a rural society. That the Bolsheviks had to conduct international relations in a largely hostile world was one of several major paradoxes of their position. The hoped-for solution was international socialist revolution. Especially in the early years after 1917, Lenin and his associates regularly predicted that revolution in the West would destroy capitalism, and they regularly expressed the fear that without it Russian socialism was doomed. But when revolutions failed to arise in the West, Lenin insisted that, while these would certainly occur one day, one had in the meantime to adapt realistically to circumstances. Lenin's ideas about global imperialism helped explain both the failure of revolution in the West—colonial exploitation enabled the Western bourgeoisie to buy off their proletariats with material benefits—and focused attention on the potential for revolution in the colonialized East and South. But the main task was to preserve Soviet power.

The Bolshevik government inherited an international position and national interests that had little in common with their ideological desires and values. They did their best to break with tsarist Russia, repudiating treaties and debts and publishing secret diplomatic documents. But they could not entirely divest the country of its past and of national interest. In fact, as the Soviet regime developed and after Soviet Russia became the self-proclaimed center of international Communism, Soviet foreign policy evolved, in the opinion of many scholars, in the direction of traditionalism, nationalism, and imperial expansionism. It acquired, as it were, a pronounced "Russian" character. Likewise, it has been argued, as a multinational country ruled from Moscow, the Soviet Union was also a type of empire. But Soviet foreign policy can also be viewed in a different interpretive context: the USSR can be analyzed as a huge modern state with rational interests in the world, and thus its foreign policy can be understood as a product of such considerations of Realpolitik as security, rather than considerations of Marxist ideology or of national tradition.

## Soviet Foreign Policy in the Twenties

When Trotsky became commissar of war in 1918, his assistant, Georgii Chicherin, replaced him as commissar of foreign affairs. Chicherin was to occupy that position until 1930; because of Chicherin's ill health, however, his eventual successor, Maxim Litvinov, directed the commissariat from 1928. Chicherin was of gentry origin and for many years of Menshevik, rather than Bolshevik, affiliation. In fact, he never entered the narrow circle of Communist leaders. Nevertheless, because of his ability and special qualifications for the post—Chicherin had originally begun his career in the tsarist diplomatic service and was a fine linguist with an excellent knowledge of the international scene—he was entrusted for over a decade with the handling of Soviet foreign policy, although, to be sure, he worked under the close supervision of Lenin, Stalin, and the Politburo. As mentioned previously, positions of real power in the Soviet system have been at the top of the party hierarchy, not in any of the commissariats.

One of Chicherin's main tasks was to obtain recognition for the Soviet Union and to stabilize its position in the world. In spite of transitory successes in Hungary and Bavaria, Communist revolutions had failed outside Soviet borders. On the other hand, with the defeat of the White movement and the end of Allied intervention, the Bolshevik regime appeared to be firmly entrenched in Russia. "Coexistence" became a reality, and both sides sought a suitable modus vivendi. Yet the Soviet Union supported the Third or Communist International—called the Comintern—established in 1919 with Zinoviev as chairman, and it refused to pay tsarist debts or compensate foreigners for their confiscated property, demanding in its turn huge reparations for Allied intervention. In particular the Comintern, composed of Communist parties scattered throughout the world, who were bent on subversion and revolution and were clearly directed from the Soviet Union in Soviet interests, constituted a persistent obstacle to normal diplomatic relations. Most other states, on their side, looked at Soviet Russia with undisguised hostility and suspicion.

The Soviet Union gradually broke out of its isolation after the end of the Civil War and the start of the New Economic Policy. In March 1921, the USSR and Great Britain concluded an economic accord. In 1922, a Soviet delegation participated in an international economic conference, held in Genoa. Although the conference itself produced no important results, bogging down on the aforementioned issues of debts and reparations, among others, Soviet representatives used the occasion to reach an agreement with Germany. The Treaty of Rapallo of April 16, 1922, supplemented later by a commercial agreement, established economic cooperation between the Soviet Union and Germany and even led to some political and military ties. It lasted until after Hitler's advent to power. While the Treaty of Rapallo produced surprise and indignation in many quarters, its rationale was clear enough and, as in the case of most other Soviet agreements, it had nothing to do with the mutual sympathy or antipathy of the signatories: both Soviet Russia and Germany were outcasts in the post-Versailles world, and they joined hands naturally for mutual advantage.

Early in 1924 Great Britain formally recognized the Soviet Union; it was followed by France, Italy, Austria, Sweden, Norway, Denmark, Greece, Mexico, and China before the end of the year. In 1925 Japan established normal relations with the USSR, evacuating at last the Russian part of the island of Sakhalin, although retaining certain oil, coal, and timber concessions there. The recognition of Soviet Russia by many states simply marked their acceptance of the existence of the Bolshevik regime, accompanied sometimes by hopes of improving trade relations, rather than any real change in their attitude toward the USSR. Lloyd George's remark on trading even with cannibals has often been quoted. Moreover, other countries, including notably the United States and most Slavic states of eastern Europe, continued to ignore the Soviet Union and refuse it recognition. Still, all in all, Chicherin succeeded in bringing Soviet Russia into the diplomatic community of nations.

That the course of Soviet foreign policy could be tortuous and even paradoxical became clear in the case of China. There Stalin chose to support the Kuomintang, the nationalist movement of Sun Yat-sen and Sun's successor Chiang Kai-shek, sending hundreds of military specialists to help the Nationalists and directing the Chinese Communists to follow "united front" tactics. For a time Communist infiltration appeared successful, and Soviet position and prestige stood high in China. But in 1927 as soon as Chiang Kai-shek had assured himself of victory in the struggle for the control of the country, he turned against the Communists, massacring them in Shanghai and evicting Soviet advisers. When the Chinese Communists, on orders from Moscow, retaliated with a rebellion in Canton, they were bloodily crushed. Yet, although defeated in China, the Soviet Union managed to establish control over Outer Mongolia after several changes of fortune. Also, in the mid-1920s it concluded useful treaties of neutrality and friendship with Turkey, Persia, and Afghanistan. It should be added that the Bolshevik regime renounced the concessions and special rights obtained by the tsarist government in such Asian countries as China and Persia. But it held on to the Chinese Eastern Railway, weathering a conflict over it with the Chinese in 1929.

## Soviet Foreign Policy in the Thirties

Chicherin's efforts in the 1920s to obtain recognition for his country and to stabilize Soviet diplomatic relations developed into a more ambitious policy in the 1930s. Devised apparently by Stalin and the Politburo and executed by Maxim Litvinov, who served as commissar for foreign affairs from 1930 until 1939, the new approach aimed at closer alliances with status quo powers in an effort to check the mounting challenges to the postwar order and the growing threat of aggression. It culminated in the Soviet entrance into the League of Nations and Litvinov's emphasis on disarmament and collective security. To appreciate the shift in Soviet tactics, it should be realized that the Bolshevik leadership had for a long time been predicting a great confrontation between the socialist and capitalist worlds and regarded Great Britain and France as their main enemies and the League of Nations as the chief international agency of militant imperialism. Indeed, the Politburo placed its hopes, it would seem, in the expected quarrels among leading capitalist powers, and in particular in a war between Great Britain and the United States! Under the circumstances, the Japanese aggression that began on the Chinese mainland in 1931 and especially the rise of Hitler to power in Germany in January 1933, together with his subsequent policies, came as rude shocks. Anxieties about the threat posed by fascism increased during the 1930s and became a major theme in speeches by party leaders, in the press, and, as we have seen, in the purge trials. Thus, in 1934, Soviet diplomacy dramatically changed directions and pursued collective security, which focused on convincing England, France, and the United States to unite with the USSR to contain German expansion. Communist parties all over the world were ordered to support this new "line." Hence the celebrated "popular fronts" of the 1930s and the strange *rapprochement* between the USSR and Western democracies as well as a new cordiality between the USSR and Chiang Kai-shek. Based on dire expediency rather than on understanding or trust and vitiated by mistakes of judgment on all sides, including the preference of the Western powers for appeasement over containment, the *rapprochement* with the West collapsed in a catastrophic manner in 1938 and 1939 to set the stage for the Second World War.

As early as 1929 the Soviet Union used the occasion of the making of the Kellogg-Briand Pact outlawing war to formulate the Litvinov Protocol, applying the pact on a regional basis. Poland, Romania, Latvia, Estonia, Lithuania, Turkey, Persia, and the Free City of Danzig proved willing to sign the Protocol with the USSR. In 1932 the Soviet Union concluded treaties of nonaggression with Poland, Estonia, Latvia, and Finland, as well as with France. In 1933 the United States finally recognized the Soviet Union, obtaining from the Soviets the usual unreliable promise to desist from Communist propaganda in the United States. In the spring of 1934 the nonaggression pacts with Poland and the Baltic states were expanded into ten-year agreements. In the summer of that year the Soviet government signed treaties with Czechoslovakia and Romania—the establishment of diplomatic relations with the latter country marked the long delayed, temporary Soviet reconciliation to the loss of Bessarabia. And in the autumn of 1934 the USSR joined the League of Nations.

The following year witnessed the conclusion of the Soviet-French and the Soviet-Czech alliances. Both called for military aid in case of an unprovoked attack by a European state. The Soviet-Czech treaty, however, added the qualification that the USSR was obliged to help Czechoslovakia only if France, which had concluded a mutual aid treaty with the Czechs, would come to their assistance. France, it is worth noting, failed to respond to Soviet pressure for a precise military convention, while neither Poland nor Romania wanted to allow the passage of the Red Army to help the Czechs in case of need.

Also in 1935 the Third International, which had become somewhat less active as a revolutionary force in the course of the preceding years, at its Seventh Congress proclaimed the new policy of popular fronts: Communist parties, reversing themselves, were to cooperate in their respective countries with other political groups interested in checking fascist aggression, and they were to support rearmament. In its turn the Soviet government demanded in the League of Nations and elsewhere that severe sanctions be applied to aggressors and that forces of peace be urgently mobilized to stop them. Yet both the League and the great powers individually accomplished little or nothing. Italy completed its conquest of Ethiopia, while Japan developed its aggression on the Asian mainland. In the summer of 1936 a great civil war broke out in Spain, pitting Franco's fascist rebels and their allies against the democratic and left-wing republican government. Once more, the Soviet Union proved eager to stop fascism, while France and Great Britain hesitated, compromised, emphasized nonintervention, and let the Spanish republic go down. Whereas Italian divisions and German airmen and tankmen aided Franco, none but Soviet officers and technicians were sent to assist the Loyalists, while the international Communist movement mobilized its resources to obtain and ship volunteers who fought in the celebrated "international brigades." Soviet intervention in Spain has long been a controversial topic. Declassified archival documents have added fuel to these debates, as they reinforce arguments both that the Soviet effort to defeat Franco was sincere and determined and that the Soviet government acted cynically and duplicitously in pursuit of greater Soviet influence in Spain, indeed to "Sovietize" Spain, even when this meant attacking their Republican allies and international leftists who had joined the anti-fascist effort.

The position and prospects of the Soviet Union became graver and graver in the course of the 1930s. In November 1936, Germany and Japan concluded the so-called Anti-Comintern Pact aimed specifically against the USSR. Italy joined the Pact in 1937 and Spain in 1939. In the Far East in 1935 the Soviet Union sold its dominant interest in the Chinese Eastern Railway to the Japanese puppet state of Manchukuo, thus eliminating one major source of conflict. But relations between Japan and the USSR remained tense, as Japanese expansion and ambitions grew, while the Soviet leaders continued to send supplies to Chiang Kai-shek as well as to direct and support Communist movements in Asia. In fact, in 1938 and again in 1939 Japanese and Soviet troops fought actual battles on the Manchurian and Mongolian borders, the Red Army better than holding its own and hostilities being terminated as abruptly as they had begun. Hitler's Germany represented an even greater menace to the Soviet Union than Japan. The Führer preached the destruction of Communism and pointed to the lands in the east as the natural area of German expansion, its legitimate *Lebensraum.* Again, as in the cases of Japan and Italy, the Western powers failed to check the aggressor. Following the remilitarization of the Rhineland in 1936, Hitler annexed Austria to the Third Reich in March 1938, making a shambles of the Treaty of Versailles.

## Soviet Foreign Policy from September 1938 until June 1941

The climax of appeasement came in September 1938 at Munich. Great Britain and France capitulated to Hitler's demand for Germany's annexation of the Sudetenland, a largely ethnically German area of Czechoslovakia; Chamberlain and Daladier flew to Munich and sealed the arrangement with Hitler and Mussolini. The unpreparedness and unwillingness of the Western democracies to fight, rather than any collusion of the West with Hitler against the USSR, motivated the Munich surrender. Still, the extreme Soviet suspicion of the settlement can well be understood, especially since the Soviet government was not invited to participate in it. Although it had expressed its readiness to defend Czechoslovakia, the Soviet Union had been forced to remain a helpless bystander when France failed to come to the aid of the Czechs and Prague had to accept its betrayal by the great powers. Moreover, after Munich the Franco-Russian alliance appeared to mean very little, and the USSR found itself, in spite of all its efforts to promote collective security, in highly dangerous isolation.

His appetite whetted by appeasement. Hitler in the meantime developed further aggressive designs in eastern Europe. In March 1939 he disposed of what remained of Czechoslovakia, establishing the occupied German protectorate of Bohemia and Moravia and a puppet state in Slovakia. This step both destroyed the Munich arrangement and made plain Nazi determination to expand beyond ethnic German boundaries. Next Hitler turned to Poland, demanding the cession of Danzig to Germany and the right of extraterritorial German transit across the Polish "corridor" to East Prussia. The alternative was war.

Poland, however, did not stand alone against Germany in the summer of 1939. France and Great Britain finally saw the folly of appeasement after Germany had seized the remainder of Czechoslovakia. At the end of March they made clear their determination to fight if Poland were attacked. As war clouds gathered, the position of the Soviet Union became all the more significant. In May Molotov replaced Litvinov as commissar for foreign affairs, retaining at the same time his office of Chairman of the Council of People's Commissars, equivalent to prime minister, as well as his membership in the Politburo. Thus for the first time since Trotsky in 1918 a Communist leader of the first rank took charge of Soviet foreign policy. Moreover, in contrast to his predecessor Litvinov, Molotov had not been personally committed to collective security and, therefore, could more easily undertake a fresh start. In retrospect commentators have also noted that Molotov, again in contrast to Litvinov, was not Jewish. After an exchange of notes in the spring of 1939, Great Britain and France began in the summer to negotiate with the USSR concerning the formation of a joint front against aggression. But the Western powers failed to come to terms with the Soviet Union, or even to press the negotiations, sending a weak and low-ranking mission to Moscow. The Soviet government, for its part, remained extremely suspicious of the West, especially after the Munich settlement, and eagerly sought ways of diverting impending hostilities away from its borders. On August 23 the German-Soviet Non-Aggression Treaty (variously known as the Nazi-Soviet Pact, the Hitler-Stalin Pact, and the Molotov-Ribbentrop Pact) was signed in Moscow—secret talks had begun as early as May—an event that produced surprise and shock in the world. Fortified by the pact, Hitler attacked Poland on the first of September 1939. On the third, Great Britain and France declared war on Germany. The Second World War began.

The Bolsheviks and the Nazis hated each other and considered themselves irreconcilable enemies. That no illusions were involved in their agreement is indicated, among many other things, by the fact that Molotov, who signed the treaty for the Soviet Union and thus represented the "pro-German orientation," retained his position and Stalin's favor after Hitler attacked the USSR. Yet both parties to the pact expected to gain major advantages by means of it. Germany would be free to fight Western powers. The Soviet Union would escape war, at least for the time being. No less important, the pact enabled the Soviet Union to advance its perceived interests in eastern Europe. The agreement was accompanied by a secret protocol that divided Poland and the Baltic states into mutual "spheres of influence." Whether the aim was to create a "buffer zone" to protect the USSR in the case of a later German attack or to expand Soviet power into the region is still a subject of scholarly dispute. What is not in doubt is how quickly the Soviets took advantage of the opportunity.

The Red Army occupied eastern Poland, incorporating its Belorussian and Ukrainian areas into the corresponding Soviet republics. Next the Soviet government signed mutual assistance pacts with Estonia, Latvia, and Lithuania, obtaining a lease of Baltic bases. But in July 1940 these states were occupied by Soviet troops, and, following a vote of their beleaguered parliaments, they were incorporated into the USSR as union republics—a procedure that the Western democracies refused to recognize. Finland was more troublesome: the Finnish government turned down the Soviet demand that they move the Finnish boundary some twenty miles farther away from Leningrad, abandoning a Finnish defense line, in exchange for a strip of Karelia; a war between the two countries resulted and lasted from the end of November 1939 until mid-March 1940. In spite of the heroic Finnish defense and the surprising early reverses of the Red Army, the Soviet Union eventually imposed its will on Finland. Finally, in the summer of 1940 the USSR utilized its agreement with Germany to obtain from Romania, by means of an ultimatum, the disputed region of Bessarabia as well as northern Bukovina. The new Moldavian Soviet Socialist Republic was formed from the territory acquired from Romania. For "security" reasons, large numbers of native elites and intellectuals were systematically deported eastward from annexed regions. In April 1941 the Soviet Union signed a five-year nonaggression treaty with Japan, which had chosen to expand south rather than into Siberia.

But, although the Soviet government did not know it, time was running short for its efforts to strengthen its position on the European and Asian continents. Following his stunning victory in the west in the summer of 1940, Hitler decided to invade the Soviet Union. In December he issued precise instructions for an attack in May 1941. The defeat that Germany suffered in the autumn in the aerial Battle of Britain apparently only helped convince the Nazi dictator that he should strike his next major blow in the east. The schedule, however, could not quite be kept. A change of government in Yugoslavia made the Germans invade Yugoslavia as well as Greece, which had stopped an earlier Italian offensive. While brilliantly successful, the German campaign in the Balkans, together with a certain delay in supplying the German striking force with tanks and other vehicles, postponed by perhaps three weeks the invasion of Soviet Russia. The new date was June 22, and on that day German troops aided by Finnish, Romanian, and other units attacked the USSR along an enormous front from the Baltic to the Black Sea.

## The Soviet Union in the Second World War

The blow was indeed staggering. Hitler threw into the offensive some 175 divisions, including numerous armored formations. A huge and powerful air force closely supported the attack. Moreover, perhaps surprisingly, the German blow caught the Red Army off guard. Apparently, although Stalin and the Politburo were preparing for war, they had ignored Western warnings as well as their own intelligence and did not expect such an early, sudden, and powerful offensive. Stalin disappeared from public sight for more than a week—leading to rumors about nervous shock. Only on July 3 did he return, with a grim but confident radio address about the need to fight heroically against what he described as Germany's intent to make "slaves" of the Soviet peoples and destroy its "national culture." The Germans aimed at another Blitzkrieg, intending to defeat the Russians within two or three months or in any case before winter. Although it encountered some determined resistance, the German war machine rolled along the entire front, particularly in the north toward Leningrad, in the center toward Moscow, and in the south toward Kiev and Rostov-on-Don. Entire Soviet armies were smashed and taken prisoner at Bialystok, Minsk, and Kiev, which fell in September. The southern wing of the invasion swept across Ukraine. In the north, Finnish troops pushed to the Murmansk railroad, and German troops reached, but could not capture, Leningrad. The city underwent a two-and-a-half-year siege, virtually cut off from the rest of the country; its population was decreased by starvation, disease, and war from 4 to 2.5 million. Yet the city would not surrender, and it blocked further German advance north.

The central front proved decisive. There the Germans aimed their main blow directly at Moscow. But they were delayed in fierce fighting near Smolensk. The summer *Blitzkrieg* became a fall campaign. Hitler increased the number of his and his allies' divisions in Russia to 240 and pushed an all-out effort to capture the Soviet capital. In the middle of October German tanks broke through the Russian lines near Mozhaisk, some sixty miles from Moscow. Stalin and the government left the city for Kuibyshev, formerly Samara, on the Volga. Yet, instead of abandoning Moscow as in 1812, its defender, Marshal Georgii Zhukov, had his troops fall slowly back on the capital, reducing the German advance to a crawl. The Germans proceeded to encircle the city on three sides, and they came to within twenty miles of it, but no farther. Late in November the Red Army started a counteroffensive against the extremely extended German lines on the southern front, recapturing Rostovon-Don at the end of the month. In early December it struck on the central front, attacking both north and south of Moscow as well as in the Moscow area itself. The Germans suffered enormous losses and had to retreat. Winter came to

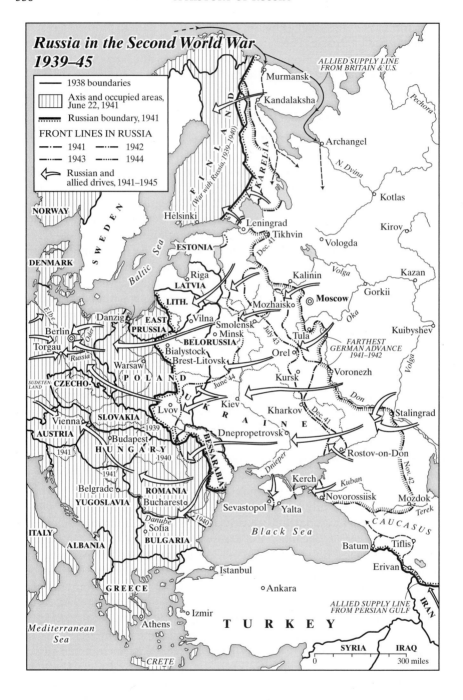

*Russia in the Second World War
1939–45*

1938 boundaries

Axis and occupied areas,
June 22, 1941

Russian boundary, 1941

FRONT LINES IN RUSSIA
---- 1941     ---- 1942
---- 1943     ---- 1944

Russian and
allied drives, 1941–1945

play havoc with unprepared German troops and to assist the Russians. On January 20 the Red Army recaptured Mozhaisk, thus eliminating any immediate threat to Moscow. But German troops had to retreat much farther west before they could stabilize the front. In fact, its lines overextended, its troops unequipped for cold weather and exhausted, the German army probably came near complete collapse in the winter of 1941/42. Some specialists believe that only Hitler's frantic determination to hold on prevented a catastrophic withdrawal. As it was, the German army gave up about 100,000 square miles of Soviet territory, but retained 500,000 when fighting finally quieted down.

In retrospect it seems clear that, in spite of its many victories, the great German campaign of 1941 in Russia failed. The Red Army remained very much in the field, and the Blitzkrieg turned into a long war on an enormous front. Quite possibly Hitler came close to crushing the Soviet Union in 1941, but he did not come close again. Taking into account Soviet resources and the determination to resist, the Nazis had to win quickly or not at all. German losses in their initial eastern campaign, large in quantity, were still more damaging in quality: the cream of German youth lined the approaches to Moscow.

Furthermore, although the Soviet Union bore the brunt of Nazi armed might from the summer of 1941 until the end of the Second World War in Europe, it certainly did not fight alone. Churchill welcomed Soviet Russia as an ally the day of the German attack—although shortly before he had been ready to wage war against the USSR in defense of Finland. Great Britain and the United States arranged to send sorely needed supplies to the Soviet Union; and after the Japanese strike at Pearl Harbor on December 7, 1941, the United States became a full-fledged combatant. In spite of German submarines and aircraft and the heavy losses they inflicted, British convoys began to reach Murmansk and Archangel in the autumn of 1941, while American aid through Persia started to arrive in large quantity in the spring of 1942. More important, the Axis powers had major enemies to fight in Africa, and eventually in southern and western Europe, as well as in the east.

The second great German offensive in Russia, unleashed in the summer of 1942, was an operation of vast scope and power, even though it was more limited in its sweep and resources than the original attack of 1941: in 1942 the Germans and their allies used about 100 divisions and perhaps a million men in an attack along the southern half of the front, from Voronezh to the Black Sea. Having occupied the Kerch area and captured Sevastopol after a month of bitter fighting, the Germans opened their main offensive early in July. They struck in two directions: east toward the Volga, and south toward the Caucasus. Blocked on the approaches to Voronezh, the German commander, Marshal Fedor von Bock, had his main army of over 300,000 men cross the Don farther south and drive to the Volga. At the end of August the Nazis and their allies reached Stalingrad.

That industrial city of half a million people, strung along the right bank of the Volga, had no fortifications or other defensive advantages. Yet General Vasilii Chuikov's 62nd Army, supported by artillery massed on the other bank, fought for every house and every foot of ground. Reduced to rubble, the city became only more impassable to the invaders in spite of all their weapons and aircraft. Both sides suffered great losses. Hitler, who had assumed personal command of the German army in December 1941 and possibly saved his troops from catastrophe in the winter of 1941/42, began to make disastrous strategic errors. He kept pounding at Stalingrad for fruitless weeks and even months and, disregarding professional opinion, would not let his troops retreat even when a Soviet counteroffensive began to envelop them. Eventually, at the end of January 1943, Marshal Friedrich Paulus and some 120,000 German and Romanian troops surrendered to the Red Army, their attempt to break through to the Volga thus ending in a complete fiasco. The German offensive southward had captured Rostov-on-Don once more and had swept across the northern Caucasus, the attackers seizing such important points as the port of Novorossiisk and the oil center of Mozdok. But again the extended German lines crumbled under Zhukov's counteroffensive in December. The invaders had to retreat fast into southern Ukraine and the Crimea and were fortunate to extricate themselves at all.

After some further retreats and counterattacks in the winter of 1942/43, the Germans tried one more major offensive in Russia the following summer. They struck early in July in the strategic watershed area of Kursk, Orel, and Voronezh with some forty divisions, half of them armored or motorized, totaling approximately half a million men. But after initial successes and a week or ten days of tremendous fighting of massed armor and artillery the German drive was spent, and the Red Army in its turn opened an offensive. Before very long the Red drive gathered enough momentum to hurl the invaders out of the Soviet Union and eventually to capture Budapest, Vienna, Prague, and Berlin, stopping only with the end of the war. The smashing Soviet victory was made possible by the fact that the German forces had exhausted themselves. Their quality began to decline probably about the end of 1941, while the increasing numbers of satellite troops pressed into service, notably Romanians, could not at all measure up to the German standard. Hitler continued to make mistakes. Time and again, as in the case of Stalingrad, he would not allow his troops to retreat until too late. The Red Army, on the other hand, in spite of its staggering losses, improved in quality and effectiveness. Its battle-tested commanders showed initiative and ability; its weapons and equipment rolled in plentiful supply both from Soviet factories, many of which had been transported eastward and reassembled there, and through Allied aid, while the German forces suffered from all kinds of shortages. As long as they fought on Soviet soil, the Germans had to contend with a large and daring partisan movement in their rear as well as with the Red Army. And they began to experience increasing pressure and defeat on other fronts, as well as from the air, where the Americans and the British mounted a staggering offensive against German cities and industries. The battle of Stalingrad coincided with Montgomery's victory over Rommel in Egypt and Allied landings in Morocco and Algeria. Allied troops invaded Sicily in the summer of 1943 and the Italian mainland that autumn. Finally, on June 6, 1944, the Americans, the British, and the Canadians landed in Normandy to establish the long awaited, promised, and delayed "second front." As the Russians began to invade the Third Reich from the east, the Allies were pushing into it from the west.

The Red Army recovered much of occupied Soviet territory in the autumn of 1943 and in the winter of 1943/44. On April 8, 1944, Marshal Ivan Konev crossed the Pruth into Romania. In the following months Soviet armies advanced rapidly in eastern and central Europe, while other armies continued to wipe out the remaining German pockets on Soviet soil. Romania and Bulgaria quickly changed sides and joined the anti-German coalition. The Red Army was joined by Tito partisans in Yugoslavia and in September 1944 entered Belgrade. After some bitter fighting, Red forces took Budapest in February 1945 and Vienna in mid-April. In the north, Finland had to accept an armistice in September 1944. The great offensive into Germany proper began in the autumn of 1944 when Red forces, after capturing Vilna, penetrated East Prussia. It gained momentum in January 1945 when large armies commanded by Konev in the south, Zhukov in the center, and Marshal Konstantin Rokossovsky in the north invaded Germany on a broad front. On April 25, 1945, advanced Russian units met American troops at Torgau, on the Elbe, near Leipzig. On May 2, Berlin fell to Zhukov's forces after heavy fighting. Hitler had already committed suicide. The Red Army entered Dresden on the eighth of May and Prague on the ninth. On that day, May 9, 1945, fighting ceased: the Third Reich had finally surrendered unconditionally to the Allies, first in Rheims on the seventh of May and then formally in Berlin on the eighth.

Urged by its allies and apparently itself eager to participate, the Soviet Union entered the war against Japan on August 8, 1945, three months after the German surrender. By that time Japan had already in fact been defeated by the United States and other powers. The American dropping of an atomic bomb on Hiroshima on the sixth of August and on Nagasaki on the ninth, which instantly killed tens of thousands of people, led the Japanese government to surrender, though scholars continue to debate whether the atomic bombings were necessary for this end. In spite of subsequent claims of Soviet historians and propagandists, the role of the USSR in the conflict in the Far East and the Pacific was, therefore, fleeting and secondary at best. Yet it enabled the Red forces to occupy Manchuria, the Japanese part of the island of Sakhalin, and the Kurile Islands and to capture many prisoners—all at the price of considerable casualties.

## Wartime Diplomacy

Diplomacy accompanied military operations. In the course of the war the Soviet Union established close contacts with its allies, in particular with Great Britain and the United States. It accepted the Atlantic Charter formulated by Roosevelt and Churchill in August 1941, which promised freedom, self-determination, and equality of economic opportunity to all countries, and it participated fully in the preparation and the eventual creation of the United Nations Organization. It concluded a twenty-year agreement with Great Britain "for the joint achievement both of victory and of a permanent peace settlement" in June 1942 and later made a treaty with France.

Of the various high-level conferences of the Allies during the war, the three meetings of the heads of state were the most important. They took place at Teheran in December 1943, at Yalta in the Crimea in February 1945, and at Potsdam near Berlin in July and August 1945. Stalin, who had assumed the position of prime minister and generalissimo, that is, chief military commander, while remaining the general secretary of the party, represented the Soviet Union on all three occasions. Roosevelt headed the American delegation at Teheran and Yalta, and Truman, after Roosevelt's death, at Potsdam. Churchill and later Attlee spoke for Great Britain. The heads of the three world powers devoted large parts of their conferences to a discussion of such major issues of the Second World War as the establishment of the "second front" and the eventual entry of the Soviet Union into the struggle against Japan. But, especially as victory came nearer, they also made important provisions for the time when peace would be achieved. These included among others: the division of Germany into zones of occupation, with Berlin receiving special status; the acceptance of the incorporation of the Königsberg district of East Prussia into the Soviet Union; the determination of the Polish eastern frontier, which was to follow roughly the Curzon Line (which had been proposed, but rejected, in 1920 by the British foreign secretary as a Polish-Soviet border that allegedly came closest to the ethnic line), Poland being granted an indefinite compensation in the west; the decision to promote the establishment of democratic governments based on free elections in all restored European countries; and provisions concerning the formation of the United Nations. Many eastern European historians argue that the Yalta conference deserves particular attention—and opprobrium—as the place where the Western powers implicitly agreed to give Stalin a free hand in the region, though this interpretation is much debated. At the very least, the Western powers misjudged Stalin's intentions. Roosevelt exuded optimism. Even Churchill, generally more skeptical than Roosevelt, famously commented after Yalta, "Poor Neville Chamberlain believed he could trust Hitler. He was wrong. But I don't think I'm wrong about Stalin." These conferences produced considerable, if largely deceptive, harmony.

Yet even during the war years important disagreements developed among the Allies. The Soviet Union was bitterly disappointed that the Western powers did not invade France in 1942 or in 1943. In spite of the importance of contacts with the West and the enormous aid received from Western countries, Soviet authorities continued to supervise closely all relations with the outside world and to restrict the movement and activities of foreigners in the Soviet Union. Perhaps more important, early difficulties and disagreements concerning the nature of postwar Europe became apparent. Poland served as a striking case in point. After Germany attacked the Soviet Union, Soviet authorities established relations with the Polish government in exile in London. But the cooperation between the two broke down before long. A Polish army formed in the Soviet Union was transferred to Iran and British auspices, while the Soviet leadership proceeded to rely on a smaller group of left-wing Poles who eventually organized the so-called Lublin government in liberated Poland. The Nazi-Soviet Pact and the course of the war exacerbated long-standing resentment in Poland over Russian behavior toward their country. Russian policies toward Poles reflected their own deep suspicions and anxieties. In historical memory, especially, two dark events of these years stand out. The first was the massacre of thousands of Polish officers in the Katyn Forest near Smolensk, which the German radio announced to the world in April 1943 after their own invading troops captured this area. This charge, which led to the break in relations between Moscow and the Polish government in London, was long denied by the Soviet government, though it has since been confirmed. Second, when the Red Army reached the Vistula in August 1944, it failed to cross the river to assist an uprising against the Germans in Warsaw, which was finally crushed in October. In this manner, the Soviets witnessed (intentionally, critics argue) the annihilation of the anti-German, but also the anti-Soviet, Polish underground. Some evidence supports the official explanation that Red troops could not advance because they had exhausted their supplies and needed to rest and regroup; but Soviet authorities would not even provide airstrips for Allied planes to help the Poles. Against this background, Yalta seemed like the final betrayal. The Allies agreed at Yalta to recognize the Lublin government expanded by several representatives of the London Poles. They also agreed that free elections would be held to establish a democratic government in Poland, though no mechanisms were established to ensure this. In essence, many historians argue, the Yalta agreement amounted to Western surrender to Soviet wishes.

## The Soviet Union in the Second World War: An Evaluation

The Soviet performance in the Second World War presents a fascinating picture of contrasts. Seldom did a country and a regime do both so poorly and so well in the same conflict. Far from purposely enticing the Germans into the interior of the country or executing successfully any other strategic plan, the Red Army suffered catastrophic defeat in the first months of the war. Indeed, the Russians were smashed as badly as the French had been a year earlier, except that they had more territory to retreat to and more men in reserve. Moreover, while the German army was at the time the best in the world, Soviet forces did not at all make the most of their admittedly difficult position. Some top Red commanders, such as the Civil War cavalry hero Marshal Semen Budenny, proved as incompetent as the worst tsarist generals. The fighting spirit of Soviet troops varied greatly: certain units fought heroically, while others hastened to surrender. The enormous number of prisoners taken by the Germans testified not only to their great military victory, but also in part to the Soviet unwillingness to fight. Even more significantly, the Soviet population often welcomed the Germans. This was strikingly true in the recently acquired Baltic countries and in large areas of Ukraine and Belorussia, but it also occurred in Great Russian regions near Smolensk and elsewhere. After a quarter of a century of Communist rule many inhabitants of the USSR greeted invaders, any invaders, as liberators. In addition to Red partisans there developed anti-Soviet guerrilla movements, which were at the same time anti-German. In Ukraine, nationalist bands continued resisting Red rule even long after the end of the Second World War. To the great surprise of the Western democracies, tens of thousands of Soviet citizens liberated by Allied armies in Europe did all they could not to return to their homeland.

But the Soviet regime survived. Indeed, in many respects the war strengthened Communist rule, especially by creating a sense of besieged national unity and providing the government with a source of legitimacy as defender of the homeland. In spite of its staggering losses, the Red Army did finally hold the Germans and then gradually push them back until their defeat became a rout. Red infantry, artillery, cavalry, and tanks all repeatedly distinguished themselves in the Second World War. Uncounted soldiers

"Avenge Us!" 1942.   (*Sovetskoe iskusstvo*)

acted with supreme heroism. The names of such commanders as Zhukov and Rokossovsky became synonymous with victory. In addition to the regular army, daring and determined partisans also fought the invader to the death. The government managed under most difficult conditions to organize the supply of the armed forces. It should be stressed that while Soviet military transportation depended heavily on vehicles from Lend-Lease, the Red Army was armed with Soviet weapons. The centralized structure of the Soviet economy enabled it quickly to mobilize resources and adapt production to war needs. The mass evacuation of factories and workers to the east—an impressive organizational feat—was essential in keeping Soviet war industries out of German hands. Although many people died of starvation in Leningrad and elsewhere, government control remained effective and morale did not break on the home front. Eventually the Soviet Union won, at an enormous cost, it is true, a total victory.

Much has been written to explain this victory. Certainly, improved military command and the mobilization of economic resources were critical. But the mobilization of human resources may be the more compelling explanation. The Nazis themselves contributed to this. It has been argued that to win the war the Nazis had merely to arm Soviet citizens and let them fight against their own government. Instead, the Nazis treated the Soviet population with contempt and brutality, as documented in Alexander Dallin's study and in other works. Instead of liberating peasants from collective farms, the Nazis used the kolkhozy as convenient structures for their own purposes. They deported as many as 3 million civilians—Russians, Belorussians, Poles, and especially Ukrainians—to forced labor camps in Germany. Millions of Jews, Roma (gypsies), and Communists were executed on the spot or sent to German death camps. Partisans were tortured and the population of whole villages were murdered if they were suspected of helping the partisans. War prisoners were starved, frozen to death, and experimented on. These policies were not merely a mistake: they reflected official Nazi thinking about Slavic peoples, whom they viewed, not as human beings to be liberated, but as *Untermenschen* (subhumans) to be exploited in the interests of a greater Germany. The leader of the SS, Heinrich Himmler, echoed this perspective in a speech in 1941: "Whether ten thousand Russian females fall from exhaustion while building an antitank ditch interests me only insofar as the antitank ditch gets finished for Germany's sake." And this was only the beginning. The stated Nazi war aim in the East was the colonization of eastern Europe and Russia, which foresaw not only complete economic and political subjugation in the interests of the German fatherland but also the extermination of millions of people, including the complete annihilation of "useless races" especially Jews and gypsies. Their purpose was certainly not to free Soviet subjects from tyranny much less encourage them to free themselves. As the historian Timothy Synder has written, "Auschwitz is only an introduction to the Holocaust, the Holocaust only a suggestion of Hitler's final aims." The bloody signs of these plans in Nazi behavior greatly contributed to the enthusiasm with which Russians fought during the war.

Ultimately, it can be argued, it was this popular determination to resist Nazi aggression and brutality that was the decisive element in Soviet victory. The government wisely associated itself with and encouraged this. Official propaganda during the war was filled with true tales of heroism, courage, and sacrifice. One can argue that, as the Nazi onslaught advanced, the Soviet Union became more united than ever before. What united Soviets behind the war efforts however, was not class struggle or world revolution but nation, home, and family. The Communist government consciously utilized the prestige of Russian military heroes of the past and the manifold attractions of nationalism. Wartime speeches, journalism, political posters, and literature all emphasized the inhuman brutalities of the enemy and the need to defend the nation (vaguely defined as both Soviet and Russian) and the lives of one's wife and children. The government also took practical measures to strengthen popular support of the war effort, such as making concessions to the practice of religion and giving collective farmers more freedom to market products grown on private plots. And there were implied promises of further changes in political and social relations. The government spoke of a new and better life that would follow the end of the war. In other words, the war helped the Soviet regime create a new patriotic political culture. The significance of this went beyond the war. This new solidarity born of suffering and struggle would help bolster the legitimacy and even popularity of the Soviet regime more than any other event in Soviet history. It is not surprising, therefore, that remembrance of the "Great Patriotic War" would remain a permanent part of Soviet culture and that it would become a key element in post-Soviet nostalgia. But mobilization of popular support to free the Soviet Union from the Nazi threat carried with it political risks. As we shall see, disappointment with expectations that the regime had changed during the war, and that people would be rewarded for their sacrifices, would feed new discontent.

# CHAPTER 39

# Stalin's Last Decade, 1945–53

Stalin! No name is nearer or dearer to millions of people—the builders of Communism.

Stalin! No name is more respected and esteemed by the laboring millions in the People's Democracies, liberated from fascist fetters by the valiant Soviet Army and now happily laying the foundations of Socialism.

Stalin! The eyes of all the common men and women the world over, of all those who cherish freedom and true democracy, of all those who hate war and dream of durable and lasting peace, are now turning to him with hope.

BORIS POLEVOI, 1950

We demand that our comrades, both as leaders in literary affairs and as writers, be guided by the vital force of the Soviet order—its politics. Only thus can our youth be reared, not in a devil-may-care attitude and a spirit of ideological indifference, but in a strong and vigorous revolutionary spirit

ANDREI ZHDANOV

The matches were ready to burn with shame for the factory that produced them, but they couldn't.

THE SATIRICAL MAGAZINE *KROKODIL*

The Second World War brought tremendous human losses and material destruction to the Soviet Union. In addition to the millions of soldiers who died, millions of civilians perished in the shifting battle zone and in German-occupied territory. Scholars continue to debate the numbers who perished due to the war. The most recent calculations, based on newly available archival material and demographic research, estimate approximately 25 million war dead, with more civilian than military deaths. Soviet citizens died, often under horrific conditions, as slave laborers in Germany, as prisoners of war, and in Nazi concentration camps. Partisan warfare led to horrible reprisals against the population. In contrast to the First World War, most atrocity stories of the Second World War were true. Because Hitler's war in the East was one of annexation and extermination—in large part the work of the notorious *Einsatzgruppen*—mass shootings and mass deportations to death camps were common. While the general Nazi goal of depopulating Ukraine and Russia encouraged murderous brutality, particular groups were targeted for complete annihilation, especially Jews, Roma (gypsies), and Communists. To the dead may be added perhaps another 20 million for the children that were not born in the decade of the 1940s. Complicating efforts to count the war dead, scholars have noted that conditions in Stalin's labor camps also contributed to higher than normal mortality rates, though it is also argued that most deaths in the Gulag were due to conditions created by the war. Of those alive at the start of the war, nearly one in five were dead at its end. Many of the survivors were physically crippled and emotionally scarred. All told, the war was a time of catastrophic human loss.

Material losses were similarly enormous. In addition to the destruction suffered in the fighting, huge areas of the country were devastated—frequently more than once—at the hands of the retreating Red Army or the withdrawing Germans. The Red Army followed the scorched-earth policy, trying to destroy all that could be of military value to the enemy. The Nazis, when they were forced to abandon Soviet territory, attempted to demolish everything, and often did so with remarkable thoroughness. For example, they both flooded and wrecked mines and developed special devices to blow up railroad tracks. Much of the Soviet Union became an utter wasteland. Scholars debate how to measure the devastation, but the general picture is clear. Thousands of towns and villages ceased to exist. Millions of buildings were destroyed, including tens of thousands of factories, schools, and libraries. The Soviet economy lost thousands of tractors and combine harvesters and millions of horses, cattle, hogs, sheep, and goats. It is likely that the economy lost about two-thirds of the reproducible wealth in occupied Soviet areas and one-quarter of the reproducible wealth of the Soviet Union as a whole.

The war affected Soviet Russia in other ways as well. It led to a strong upsurge of patriotism and nationalism, promoted by the Communist government itself which did all it could to mobilize the people for supreme effort and sacrifice. The army acquired new prominence and prestige, whereas from the time of the Civil War it had been kept in the background in the Soviet state. Religion, as already mentioned, profited from a more tolerant attitude on the part of the authorities. In addition, a striking religious revival developed in German-occupied territory. While the Soviet government maintained control over the people, in certain respects it somewhat relaxed its iron grip. Many Soviet citizens apparently felt freer than before the war. In particular, some kolkhozes simply collapsed, the peasants dividing the land and farming it in private. On the whole, because of lessened controls and a great demand for food, many peasants improved their position during the war years. In the German zone of occupation the people immediately disbanded the collectives.

The Nazis, however, later in part reintroduced them as useful devices to control peasants and obtain their produce. The war also led to closer and friendlier relations with Western allies and made widespread contacts between the Soviet and the non-Soviet world inevitable. Moreover, millions of Soviet citizens, prisoners of war, deportees, escapees, and victorious Red Army soldiers had their first look at life outside Soviet borders. Other millions, the inhabitants of the Baltic countries, eastern Poland, Bessarabia, and northern Bukovina, brought up under non-Communist systems and in different circumstances, were joined to the Soviet Union.

Another obvious result of the Second World War was the great rise in the Soviet Union's position and importance in the world. The USSR came to dominate eastern Europe, except for Greece, and much of central Europe. Barring the Allied expeditionary forces, it had no military rival on the entire continent. The international Communist movement, which had reached its nadir with the Soviet-German treaty and Hitler's victory in the west, was experiencing a veritable renaissance. After the German attack on the USSR, Communists had played major roles in numerous resistance movements, and they emerged as a great political force in many European countries, including such important Western states as France and Italy. With the total defeat and unconditional surrender of Germany and Japan, the earlier defeat of Italy, and the collapse of France, only exhausted Great Britain and the United States remained as major obstacles to Soviet ambitions in the world.

In a sense, Stalin and the Politburo had their postwar policy cut out for them. They had to rebuild the Soviet Union and to continue the industrial and general economic advance. They had to reimpose a full measure of socialism on the recalcitrant peasant and to supervise and control closely such non-Marxist sources of inspiration and belief as religion and nationalism. They had to combat the "contamination" that had come to their country from the non-Soviet world, and they had to make all their people, including the inhabitants of the newly acquired territories, into good Soviet citizens. They had to maintain complete control over the army. They had to exploit the new position of the USSR and the new, sweeping opportunities open to the Soviet Union and international communism in the postwar world. Those numerous observers who were surprised by the course of Soviet politics at home and abroad from 1945 until Stalin's death in the spring of 1953 for the most part either had failed to understand Stalin and the nature of the Soviet system or believed that they had undergone a fundamental change during the Second World War.

## Reconstruction and Economic Development

To repair war damage and resume the economic advance, Stalin and the Politburo resorted, characteristically, to a five-year plan, and indeed to a sequence of such plans. The Fourth Five-Year Plan, which lasted from 1946 to 1950 and was proclaimed overfulfilled in four years and three months, was cut out of the same cloth as its predecessors. It stressed heavy industry, which absorbed some 85 percent of the total investment, particularly emphasizing the production of coal, electrical power, iron, steel, timber, cement, agricultural machinery, and trucks. The demobilization of more than 10 million men provided the needed additional manpower, for the total number of workers and employees had declined from 31 million in 1940 to 19 million in 1943. The rebuilding of devastated towns and villages, which had begun as soon as the Germans had left, gathered momentum after the inauguration of the Plan. But the Fourth Five-Year Plan aimed at more than restoration: Russian industry, especially heavy industry, was supposed to achieve new heights of production, while labor productivity was to rise 36 percent, based on an increase in the amount of capital per worker of about 50 percent. As usual, every effort was made to force the Soviet people to work hard. A financial reform of December 1947 virtually wiped out wartime savings by requiring Soviet citizens to exchange the money they had for a new currency at the rate of ten to one. Piece work and bonuses received added emphasis. Official retail prices went up, although the concurrent abolition of rationing and of certain other forms of distribution alleviated somewhat the hardships of the consumer. Foreign economists noted a certain improvement in the urban standard of living as well as a redistribution of real income within the urban population, primarily against the poorer groups.

The Fourth Five-Year Plan obtained a great boost from reparations and other payments collected from defeated Germany and its allies. In 1947, for example, three-fourths of Soviet imports came from eastern Europe and the Soviet zone of Germany, that is, from the area dominated by Red military might. The total value of Soviet "political" imports, including reparations, especially favorable trade provisions, and other economic arrangements, as well as resources spent by different countries for the support of Red Army troops stationed in those countries, has been estimated at the extraordinary figure of over 20 billion dollars. Some reparations were made in the form of complete factories that were dismantled, transported to the Soviet Union, and reassembled there.

In the end the Plan could well be considered a success in industry, much like its predecessors, in spite of the frequently inferior quality of products and uneven results, which included underfulfillments of the plan, overproduction (materials that could not be used), and products that simply did not work but met the numerical targets. While industry was rebuilt and even expanded in Ukraine and other western areas, the Plan marked a further industrial shift east, which grew in relative economic importance compared to the prewar period. By mobilizing resources the Soviet Union managed to maintain during the Fourth and Fifth Five-Year Plans the very high annual industrial growth rate characteristic of the first three plans and estimated by Western economists at some 12 to 14 percent on average—a figure composed of much higher rates in the late 1940s and much lower in the early 1950s. The Fifth Five-Year Plan lasted from 1951 to 1955 and thus continued beyond Stalin's rule. Similar to all the others in nature and accomplishments, it apparently made great advances in such complex fields as aviation and armament industries and atomic energy. Its completed projects included the Volga-Don canal.

Agriculture, as usual, formed an essential aspect of the plans and, again as usual, proved particularly difficult to manage successfully. The war, to repeat, produced sweeping destruction, a further sharp decline in the already insufficient supply of domestic animals, and at the same time a breakdown of discipline in many kolkhozes, where members proceeded to divide the land and farm it individually or at least to expand their private plots at the expense of the collective. Discipline was soon restored. By September 1, 1947, about 14 million acres had been taken away from the private holdings of members of collectives as exceeding the permissible norm. Moreover, the Politburo and the government mounted a new offensive aimed at turning the peasants at long last into good socialists. This was to be done by greatly increasing the size of the collectives—thereby decreasing their number—and at the same time increasing the size of working units in a collective, in the interests of further mechanization and division of labor. Nikita Khrushchev, who emerged as one of the leaders in postwar Soviet agriculture, even spoke of grouping peasants in *agrogoroda*, veritable agricultural towns, which would do away once and for all with the diffusion of labor, the isolation, and the backwardness characteristic of the countryside. The agrogoroda proved unrealistic, or at least premature, but authorities did move to consolidate some 250,000 kolkhozes into fewer than 100,000 larger units. In spite of all these efforts—some hostile critics believe largely because of them—peasants failed to satisfy the demands of Soviet leaders, and insufficient agricultural production remained a major weakness of the Soviet economy, as Khrushchev in effect admitted after Stalin's death.

## Administration, Politics, and Control

As already mentioned, the Soviet Union acquired five new republics during the time of the Nazi-Soviet Pact. They were lost, together with other large territories, when Germany invaded the USSR and reacquired when the Red Army advanced west. The five Soviet Socialist Republics, the Estonian, Latvian, Lithuanian, Karelo-Finnish, and Moldavian, raised the total number of component units of the USSR to sixteen. In July 1956, however, the Karelo-Finnish SSR was downgraded to its prewar status of an autonomous republic within the RSFSR, reducing the number of union republics to fifteen. The Karelo-Finnish Republic, consisting both of some older Soviet lands and of territory acquired from Finland in 1940 and again in 1944, largely failed as an expression of Finnish culture and nationality; in particular, because the inhabitants had a choice of staying or moving to Finland, virtually no people remained in the area that the Soviet Union annexed from Finland. The downgrading, therefore, seemed logical, although it might have been connected with the desire to Russify that strategic area still more effectively. While the number of union republics increased as a result of the Second World War, the number of autonomous republics was reduced: five of the latter, the Volga-German Autonomous Republic and four in the Crimea, the northern Caucasus, and adjacent areas were disbanded for sympathizing with or assisting the Germans, their populations being transported to distant regions.

As this suggests, the pursuit of conformity and control amidst the great diversity of the Soviet Union—combined with long-standing prejudice and even paranoia about ethnic and national difference—led to especially brutal policies toward certain Soviet nationalities during the war and after. Already in the 1930s, "national operations" had persecuted Poles, Germans, Finns, Cossacks, and Koreans to root out alleged nationalism. During the war, many groups, accused of sympathy for or collaboration with the Nazis, faced sudden mass deportations to Siberia or Central Asia, carried out by the NKVD. This included ethnic Germans from the Volga region, Chechens and Ingush from the north Caucasus, Crimean Tatars, Kalmyks, Meskhetian Turks from Georgia, and others. Large numbers of people died on these forced journeys. Although these deported nations were usually allowed to return to their homelands after Stalin's death, the disruptions and resentments would linger for a very long time. The newly incorporated areas faced particular violence, since the goal was to rapidly assimilate them to the Soviet system. The occupation of these lands in 1940, and reoccupation as the Red Army advanced against the Nazis, was accompanied by deportations, arrests, and executions. Intellectuals, army officers, government officials, landowners, and clergy were especially targeted. In Stalin's last years, the Soviet labor camp empire bulged at the seams. At the same time, nationalities not judged as suspect were often courted during the war: national units were established, the unity of all the peoples of the USSR was emphasized, and national and native religions were allowed more freedom. On the other hand, both during the war and especially afterward, the leadership and contributions of the Russian people were insistently emphasized.

The political system changed little during these years. Union-wide elections were held in 1946 for the first time since 1937, and again in 1950. The new Supreme Soviets acted, of course, as no more than rubber stamps for Stalin and the government. Republican and other local elections also took place. The minimum age for office holders was raised from eighteen to twenty-three. In 1946 people's commissariats became ministries. More important, their number was reduced in the postwar years and they were more strongly centralized in Moscow. Shortly before his death, Stalin carried out a potentially important change in the top party administration: the Politburo as well as the Organizational Bureau were abolished and replaced by the Presidium, which was to consist of ten Politburo members, the eleventh being dropped, plus another fifteen high Soviet leaders. But Stalin died without calling together the Presidium. After his death its announced membership was reduced to ten, so that as an institution it differed from the Politburo only in name, and even the name was restored after Khrushchev's fall.

The postwar years also witnessed militant reaffirmation of Communist orthodoxy in ideology and culture. While more will be said about this subject in a later chapter, it might be noted here that scholarship, literature, and the arts all suffered from the imposition of a party straitjacket. Moreover, Andrei Zhdanov, a member of the Politburo and the party boss of Leningrad during the frightful siege, who led the campaign to restore orthodoxy, emerged as

Stalin's most prominent lieutenant from 1946 until Zhdanov's sudden death in August 1948. That death—engineered by Stalin in the opinion of some specialists—again left the problem of succession wide open. The aging dictator was surrounded during his last years by a few surviving old leaders, his long-time associates, such as Molotov, Marshal Klement Voroshilov, Lazar Kaganovich, and Anastas Mikoyan, as well as by some younger men who had become prominent after the great purge, notably Beria, Khrushchev, and Georgii Malenkov. Malenkov in particular appeared to gain consistently in importance and to loom as Stalin's most likely successor.

## Foreign Policy

Stalin's last decade saw extremely important developments in Soviet foreign policy. Crucial events of the postwar years included the expansion of Soviet power in eastern Europe, the breakdown of the wartime cooperation between the USSR and its Western allies, and the polarization of the world into the Communist and the anti-Communist blocs, headed by the Soviet Union and the United States, respectively. Scholars have much debated the origins of the "cold war." Many have placed the blame chiefly on the Soviet side. That the Soviet Union proved intractable in its dealings with the West, that it did what it could to expand its own bloc (including, as the West saw it, betraying the promise of freedom and democratic elections in eastern Europe), and that it received support from Communist movements all over the world followed logically from the nature and new opportunities of Soviet communism. Other scholars have pointed to a deep tradition of anticommunism in the West, especially in the United States, and to America's own ambitions for a dominant role in the postwar world. A related argument emphasizes Soviet anxieties about Western, especially American, intentions after the war, specifically fears that the capitalist West (naturally hostile to communism and emerging from the war with America's new atomic power in hand) would take advantage of the Soviet Union's economic debility in the wake of the war. Stalin understood that Russia was not yet ready to survive a major new attack against it. To protect Soviet power against the capitalist West, it is argued, the Soviet Union needed Communist allies on its western borders and to project an image of strength (which required not only showing what the Red Army could do in eastern Europe but also erecting barriers to keep information about real conditions in Russia as hidden as possible). The postwar break between Russia and the West can also be explained by short-term considerations. The Soviet leaders, too, had prepared little for the postwar period, and in their preparation they had concentrated on such objectives as rendering Germany permanently harmless. The sweeping Soviet expansion in eastern Europe occurred at least in part because of special circumstances: the rapid Western withdrawal of forces and demobilization, the fact that it became apparent that free elections in most eastern European countries would result in anti-Soviet governments, and the pressure of local Communists as well as, possibly, the urging of the more activist group within the Soviet leadership.

ПОД ВОДИТЕЛЬСТВОМ ВЕЛИКОГО СТАЛИНА—ВПЕРЕД К КОММУНИЗМУ!

"Under the Leadership of the Great Stalin—Forward to Communism," 1951. Stalin, the "father of the peoples," stands with representatives of varied Soviet nationalities and before a map showing plans for massive canals and hydroelectric projects. (*Victoria Bonnell*)

The Soviet Union and the Allies cooperated long enough to put into operation their arrangement for dividing and ruling Germany and to bring top Nazi leaders to trial before an international tribunal at Nuremberg in 1946. Also, in February 1947, the victorious powers signed peace treaties with Italy, Romania, Bulgaria, Hungary, and Finland. The Soviet Union confirmed its territorial gains from Romania and Finland, including a lease of the Finnish base of Porkkala, and obtained extensive reparations. Rounding out its acquisitions, the USSR obtained the so-called Carpatho-Ruthenian area from friendly Czechoslovakia in 1945. While most inhabitants of that region spoke Ukrainian, they had not been connected with any Russian state since the days of Kievan Rus.

But on the whole cooperation between the USSR and the Western powers broke down quickly and decisively. No agreement on the international control of atomic energy could be reached, the Soviet Union refusing to participate in the Atomic Energy Commission created by the United Nations in 1946. In the same year a grave crisis developed over the Soviet government's efforts to obtain significant concessions from Persia, or Iran, and its refusal to follow the example of Great Britain and the United States and withdraw its troops from that country after the end of the war. Although, as a result of Western pressure and the airing of the question in the United Nations, Soviet forces did finally leave Iran, the hostility between former allies became increasingly apparent.

The Communist seizure of power in eastern Europe contributed very heavily to the division of the world into two opposed blocs. While many details of the process varied from country to country, the end result in each case was the firm entrenchment of a Communist regime cooperating with and dominated by the Soviet Union. The same happened in eastern Germany. Only Greece and Finland managed to escape Communist rule. Liberated Greece fell into the British rather than the Soviet sphere, and its government, supported by Great Britain and the United States, managed to win a bitter civil war against the Communist-led Left. The fact that Finland survived as an independent nation remains puzzling. It could be that Moscow first overestimated the strength of Finnish Communists, who did play a prominent part in the government of the country immediately after the war, and then decided not to force the issue in a changing international situation after the Finnish Communists failed to seize power. In particular, the Soviet Union probably wanted to avoid driving Sweden into the camp of Soviet enemies. Similarly—at a greater distance from the USSR—the large and strong Communist and allied parties in France and Italy, very prominent in the first years following the war, were forced out of coalition governments and had to limit themselves to the role of an opposition bent largely on obstruction.

It has frequently been said that communism won in Europe only in countries occupied by the Red Army, and that point deserves to be kept in mind. Yet it does not tell the whole story. Whereas in Poland, for example, native Communists were extremely weak, in Yugoslavia and Albania they had led resistance movements against the Axis powers and had attained dominant positions by the end of the war (though strong indigenous Communist movements also made these countries, especially Yugoslavia, more difficult to control). Perhaps more important, the Soviet Union preferred to rely in all cases on local party members, while holding the Red Army in readiness as the ultimate argument. Usually, the "reactionary" elements, including monarchs where such were present and the upper classes in general as well as fascists, would be forced out of political life and a "united front" of "progressive" elements formed to govern the country. Next the Communists destroyed or at least weakened and neutralized their partners in the front to establish in effect, if not always in form, their single-party dictatorship even though the party might be known as the "workers'" or "socialist unity" party rather than simply "Communist." It is worth noting that the eastern European Communists had the most trouble with agrarian parties, just as the Bolsheviks had met their most dangerous rivals in the Socialist Revolutionaries. In Roman Catholic countries, such as Poland and Hungary, they also experienced strong and persistent opposition from the Church. The Communist seizure of power in Czechoslovakia proved particularly disturbing to the non-Communist world, because it occurred as late as 1948 and disposed of a regime headed by President Beneš which had enjoyed popular support and maintained friendly relations with the Soviet Union. The new Communist governments in eastern Europe proclaimed themselves to be "popular democracies." They followed the Soviet lead in introducing economic plans, industrializing, collectivizing agriculture—sometimes gradually, however—and establishing minute regulation over all phases of life, including culture. As in the USSR, the political police played a key role in social transformation and control. Local scholars in these countries have argued strongly that for most of Communist eastern Europe, with the notable exception of Poland, occupation by Moscow was harsher than occupation by Nazi Germany.

Winston Churchill, at the time out of office, was among the first Western statesmen to speak openly of the danger of Communist influence in eastern Europe. In a speech at Westminster College in Fulton, Missouri, in March 1946, he described an "iron curtain" separating the "Soviet sphere" from the rest of the continent. The foreign policies of the United States soon reflected this sense of global divide and a "cold war"—a term that began to be used in the United States around this time. When another year of negotiations with the USSR produced no results, President Truman appealed to Congress for funds to provide military and economic aid to Greece and Turkey, whose independence was threatened directly or indirectly by the Communist state; this policy came to be known as the Truman Doctrine. In June 1947 the Marshall Plan was introduced to help rebuild the economies of European countries devastated by war. Because the Soviet Union and its satellites would not participate, the plan became a powerful bond for the Western bloc. Next, in 1949, twelve Western countries, the United States, Great Britain, Canada, France, Belgium, the Netherlands, Luxembourg, Norway, Denmark, Iceland, Italy, and Portugal, signed the Atlantic Defense Pact of mutual aid against aggression. A permanent North Atlantic Treaty Organization (NATO) and armed force were subsequendy created, under General Eisenhower's command. Also in 1949, the U.S. Congress passed a broad Mutual Defense Assistance Program to aid American allies all over the world. With these agreements and with numerous bases girding the USSR, the United States and other countries organized to meet the perceived Soviet threat.

The Communist bloc also organized. In 1947 the Communist Information Bureau, known as Cominform, replaced the Communist International, which had been disbanded in 1943. Bringing together the Communist parties of the USSR, eastern Europe, France, and Italy, the Cominform aimed at better coordination of Communist efforts in Europe. Zhdanov, who represented the Soviet party, set the unmistakably militant tone of the organization. But Communist cooperation was dealt a major blow by the break between Yugoslavia and the USSR, backed by its satellites, in the summer of 1948. Tito chose to defy Stalin because he wanted to retain full effective control of his own country and resented the role assigned to Yugoslavia in the economic and other plans of the Soviet bloc. He succeeded in his bold undertaking because he had a strong organization and support at home in contrast to other eastern European Communist leaders, many of whom were simply Soviet puppets, and because the Soviet Union did not dare invade Yugoslavia, apparently from fear of the probable international complications. Tito's unprecedented defection created the new phenomenon of "national" communism, independent of the Soviet bloc. It led to major purges of potential heretics in other eastern

European Communist parties, which took the lives of some of the most important Communists of eastern Europe and resembled in many respects the great Soviet purge of the 1930s.

The Western world confronted the Soviet in many places and on many issues. Continuous confrontation in the United Nations resulted in little more than Soviet Russia's constant use of its veto power in the Security Council. Thus, of the eighty vetoes cast there in the decade from 1945 to 1955, seventy-seven belonged to the Soviet Union. The two sides also faced each other in Germany. Because of the new enmity of the wartime allies, the Allied Control Council in Germany failed to function almost from the beginning, and no agreement could be reached concerning the unification of Germany or the peace treaty with that country. Finally, the Federal Republic of Germany with its government in Bonn was established in the Western-occupied zones in May 1949, while the German Democratic Republic was created in the Soviet-held area in October of the same year. The first naturally sided with the West and eventually joined NATO. The second formed an integral part of the Soviet bloc. Cold war in Germany reached its height in the summer of 1948 when Soviet authorities stopped the overland supply of the American, British, and French sectors of Berlin. Since that city, located 110 miles within the Soviet zone, was under the jurisdiction of the four powers, three of them Western, it, or rather West Berlin, remained a highly provocative and disturbing "window of freedom" in rapidly Stalinized eastern Germany and eastern Europe. But Soviet hopes of forcing the Western powers to abandon their part of the city failed: a mammoth airlift was maintained for months by American and British planes to keep West Berlin supplied until the Soviet Union discontinued its blockade.

Postwar events in Asia were as important as the developments in Europe. Communists made bids to seize power in such different areas as Indonesia, Malaya, and Burma. They succeeded in China. The great Chinese civil war ended in 1949 with Chiang Kai-shek's evacuation to Formosa—or Taiwan—and the proclamation of the Communist Chinese People's Republic, with Mao Zedong at its head, on the mainland. Although the Soviet Union took no direct part in the Chinese war and at first apparently even tried to restrain Mao, it helped Chinese Communists with supplies and fully backed Mao's new regime. And indeed Communist victory in a country of great size inhabited by some half a billion people meant an enormous accretion of strength to the Soviet bloc, although it also created serious problems: China could not be expected to occupy the role of a satellite, such as Bulgaria or Czechoslovakia, and the Communist world acquired in effect a second center of leadership. By an agreement concluded in 1950, the USSR ceded to Communist China its railroad possessions in Manchuria, although briefly retaining a naval base at Port Arthur.

In Korea cold war turned to actual hostilities. There, as in Germany, no agreement could be reached by the victorious powers, and eventually two governments were formed, one in American-occupied southern Korea and the other in the Soviet north, the thirty-eighth parallel dividing the two. At the end of June 1950, North Korea attacked South Korea. In the ensuing years of fighting, which resulted in the two sides occupying approximately the same positions when the military action stopped as they had in the beginning, U.S. forces and some contingents from other countries came to the assistance of South Korea in execution of a mandate of the United Nations, whereas tens and even hundreds of thousands of Chinese "volunteers" intervened on the North Korean side. The Soviet army itself did not participate in the war, although the North Koreans and the Chinese used Soviet-made aircraft and weapons, and although Soviet advisers, as well as Soviet pilots and other technicians, were in North Korea. Although the front became stabilized in the summer of 1951, no armistice could be concluded until the summer of 1953, after Stalin's death.

## The End of Stalin

Stalin's final years were also marked by an intensified "cult of personality," as Khrushchev would brand it. Statues and pictures of the "great leader" proliferated, songs and poems were written in his honor, public ceremonies honored him, his every pronouncement was treated as sacred truth, and his eulogists vied with one another to find greater superlatives with which to describe this "greatest genius of humankind" who brought nothing but joy to every decent Soviet person and struck terror in the hearts of all the enemies of socialist happiness. At the same time, Stalin grew increasingly distrustful of all around him. Stalin's final months, especially, had a certain weird quality to them. It could be that the madness that kept peering through the method during his entire rule asserted itself with new vigor. With international tensions high, dark clouds gathered at home. In January 1953, nine doctors were accused of having assassinated a number of Soviet leaders, including Zhdanov, and of planning to murder others. Seven of the arrested doctors were Jewish, and anti-Semitism, visibly on the rise in the postwar years (including anti-Jewish purges in some institutions), especially after the establishment of the State of Israel in 1948, was clearly evident in reporting about the "doctor's plot." But Jews were only one of the targets. Beria's police were charged with insufficient vigilance. The press whipped up a campaign against traitors. Everything pointed to another great purge. Then on March 4 it was announced that Stalin had suffered a stroke on the first of the month, and on the morning of the sixth the news came that he had died the previous night. Some of the dictator's entourage especially close to him disappeared at the same time.

# CHAPTER 40

# The Soviet Union after Stalin, 1953–85

We must seriously consider and correctly analyze this question in order to preclude any possibility of repeating in any form whatsoever that which took place during the time of Stalin, who was completely intolerant of collectivity in leadership and in work and who deployed brutal force against not only everyone who contradicted him but against anyone who seemed to him, given his capricious and despotic character, to contradict his way of thinking....Comrades, we must decisively, once and for all, dethrone the cult of the personality....For this purpose, it is necessary: First, in a Bolshevik manner to condemn and eradicate the cult of the personality as alien to Marxism-Leninism and inconsistent with the principles of party leadership and the norms of party life....Second, systematically and consistently to continue the work done by the party's Central Committee in recent years to ensure strict compliance in all party organizations, from the bottom to the top, with Leninist principles of party leadership, which are characterized, above all, by the highest principle of collective leadership, by adherence to the norms of party life as fixed in the statutes of our party, and by expanding the practice of criticism and self-criticism. Third, to restore completely the Leninist principles of Soviet socialist democracy, expressed in the Constitution of the Soviet Union, and to fight against the willful arbitrariness of individuals who abuse their power.

NIKITA KHRUSHCHEV, SPEECH TO THE
TWENTIETH PARTY CONGRESS, 1956

With every year and with every month that passes, with every day one may say, the active peace-loving policy of the Soviet Union and other countries of socialism gives the peoples of the earth ever new convincing proof that the concepts of socialism and peace are indivisible....Our people are working under the banner of peace and are carrying on the struggle for peace in the cause of the

emancipation of labor. Under the red banner of peace and labor we
have scored outstanding successes that are admired by all honest
people of the world. Under this banner we shall score great new
victories....Permit me from the bottom of my heart to wish all citizens of our great country, all builders of communism, every Soviet
family, every Soviet person, the greatest success in their noble work
and the greatest happiness.

LEONID BREZHNEV, MAY DAY 1973

Stalin's stroke—if its official date is to be believed—was followed by three days
of silence from the Kremlin and, in all probability, by hard bargaining among
top Soviet leaders. When the dictator's demise was announced, the new leadership proclaimed itself ready to govern the country, emphasizing the solidarity of its members as well as its unity with the people. The shrill tone and the
constant repetition of both assertions must have covered many suspicions and
fears. Malenkov emerged clearly in the chief role, for he became presumably
both the senior party secretary, which had been Stalin's most important office,
and prime minister. Beria and Molotov stood next to Malenkov, forming a
triumvirate of successors to the dictator. The three, in that order, were the key
living figures during Stalin's burial in the Lenin Mausoleum in Red Square on
March 9, making appropriate speeches on the occasion.

## The Rise, Rule, and Fall of Nikita Khrushchev

As early as the middle of March, however, it was announced that Malenkov
had resigned as the party secretary, although he remained prime minister
and continued to be treated as the top personage in the Soviet Union. The new
Presidium of the party was reduced to ten members. Later it was announced
that Khrushchev had been promoted to the position of first party secretary,
the title used instead of that of general secretary associated with Stalin. In the
summer of 1953, Beria was arrested and then executed in secret, with a number of his followers, on charges of treason and conspiracy; or, as Khrushchev
related to some visitors, Beria was killed at the Presidium meeting at which
he had expected to assume full power. In any case, it would seem that in the
race to dispose of one another Beria had narrowly lost out. Beria's fall marked
a certain weakening in the power of the political police. In February 1955,
Malenkov resigned as prime minister, saying that he was guilty of mistakes
made in the management of Soviet agriculture and of having incorrectly
emphasized the production of consumer goods at the expense of heavy industry. Nikolai Bulganin, a prominent Communist leader who had been a member of the Politburo since 1948, replaced Malenkov as head of the government.
Bulganin and Khrushchev, the chief of the government and the chief of the
party, then occupied the center of the Soviet stage and also held the limelight
in international affairs, suggesting to some observers the existence of something resembling a diarchy in the USSR. Marshal Zhukov, a great hero of the
Second World War who had been reduced by Stalin to provincial commands
and had returned to prominence after Stalin's death, took over Bulganin's

Stalin's funeral. From right: Khrushchev, Beria, Chou En-Lai, Malenkov, Voroshilov, Kaganovich, Bulganin, Molotov.   *(Sovfoto)*

former office of minister of defense. Zhukov's rise marked the first appearance of an essentially military, rather than party, figure in high governing circles in Soviet Russia.

The struggle in the Kremlin continued. Probably its most astounding event—though its significance reached far beyond the struggle for power—was Khrushchev's speech to a closed session of the Twentieth Party Congress in February 1956, in which the new first secretary denounced his predecessor, Stalin, as a cruel, irrational, and bloodthirsty tyrant. Stalin was accused of creating a "personality cult" around himself, of ruling in arbitrary and tyrannical ways, of violating the principles of Marxism-Leninism, of violating the norms of collective leadership, of imagining enemies and then exterminating them, of killing many party activists and leaders, of decimating the army leadership, of failing to ensure Soviet preparedness for the war, and of unjustified mass deportations of nationality groups. At the same, these colossal crimes were viewed as a deviation from the essentially correct norms and policies of Marxism-Leninism and rectified by the collective leadership that replaced the despot. Khrushchev's explosive speech—though known as the "secret speech," it was either read or summarized to millions of party members and most of the text soon made its way into the Western press—remains difficult to explain: after all, these breathtaking revelations were certain to produce shock among Communists after years of endless adulation of Stalin and public lies and perhaps harm the Communist cause internationally. Besides, Khrushchev could not help but implicate himself and other leading Communists, at least indirectly, in Stalin's crimes and errors. One answer to the riddle of the speech lies in the exigencies of the struggle for power among Soviet leaders. Khrushchev's denunciation of Stalin struck at some "old Stalinists," his main competitors. No less important, Khrushchev and his allies may have been trying to save communism from Stalinism by blaming the worst aspects of the Soviet past on one individual rather than on the system itself, on the party as an institution, or on its guiding ideology. In practice, the revelations of Stalin's crimes, a process that would continue unevenly in the coming years, did undermine the faith of some people in the system that produced Stalin.

The conflict at the top reached its culmination in the spring and early summer of 1957, after the Hungarian rebellion of the preceding autumn and certain other events at home and abroad had raised grave questions concerning the orientation and activities of the new Soviet administration and indeed concerning the stability of the whole Soviet system. Defeated in the Presidium of the party, Khrushchev took his case to its entire Central Committee, successfully reversing the unfavorable decision and obtaining the ouster from the Presidium and other positions of power of the "anti-party group" of Malenkov, Molotov, Kaganovich, and Dmitrii Shepilov, a recent addition to the Soviet front ranks. While Khrushchev's enemies were dropped from the Presidium, its membership was increased to fifteen, giving the general secretary further opportunities to bring his supporters into that extremely important body. Finally in March 1958, Bulganin, who had been disloyal to Khrushchev the preceding year, resigned as head of the government. Khrushchev himself replaced Bulganin, thus combining the supreme effective authority of the party and of the state.

Khrushchev's biography and personality shaped his actions and policies. He was born in 1894 into a poor peasant family in a southern Russian village. His father became a migrant worker. Starting in 1908, Khrushchev lived in the Donbas (Donetsk Basin) region of Ukraine, where he became a skilled metalworker with ambitions to become an engineer. His education included no more than four years of primary school, though, after the revolution, he briefly attended a special school for workers and gained some additional technical training. During the revolution and Civil War, he became involved in Bolshevik politics and entered a career in the Soviet state and the Communist Party, first in Ukraine, then in Moscow, where he became the city's party boss, then back to Ukraine as party leader in 1938, and then again to Moscow in 1949 when Stalin recalled him to join the top leadership. Throughout the 1930s and 1940s, Khrushchev was a devoted Stalinist of a practical bent: he supervised construction of the Moscow metro, devoted much energy to developing Ukrainian industry and agriculture, and participated actively in the purges. He took great pride in helping to build socialism. But he also later admitted that his arms were "up to the elbows in blood." In this light, the "secret speech" can be seen as the act of a devoted Communist and pragmatist and as a type of repentance. Khrushchev was a complex figure: a devoted Stalinist who became a driven de-Stalinizer, a reformer and practical builder but also a figure of limited capacities and irrational methods. As William Taubman, who has written the best biography of Khrushchev, concluded, "despite his miraculous rise, his doubts about both his capacities and his sins remained, exacerbated by domestic and foreign-policy troubles that came crowding in on him, troubles to which he responded with increasingly desperate and reckless actions which, rather than consolidating and extending his achievement, ultimately ensured his defeat." On the other hand, we should remember that "the reforms of the Khrushchev period, awkward and erratic though they were, allowed a nascent civil society to take shape where Stalinism had created a desert."

Khrushchev's reforms involved significant initiatives in a number of areas, though many produced unexpected results or simply failed. His first priority was agriculture, where he tried to stimulate production through administrative reorganizations, by encouraging more active party involvement in production, and through various heroic "campaigns" such as the "virgin lands" campaign, the meat and milk campaign, and the corn campaign. He tried to encourage better industrial management and more production of consumer goods, again through administrative reorganizations and campaigns. A massive boom in housing construction was also initiated. These policies, as will be discussed later, resulted in an advancing economy and substantial improvements in people's everyday material lives. Perhaps the most consequential reform was de-Stalinization of culture. After the long winter of Stalinist cultural politics—the required adherence in all the arts to the strictures of Stalinist "socialist realism—a "thaw" began. Writers and artists, but also scholars and journalists, were able to speak more openly of the crimes of the past, to criticize inadequacies in Soviet life, and, especially, to pay more attention to the experiences and needs of the individual rather than only the collective, the party, and building socialism.

The remarkable Twenty-second Party Congress held in the second half of October 1961 gave ready approval to the new leader's twenty-year program of "building communism" and denounced his enemies at home and abroad. Another old leader, Voroshilov, was linked to the "anti-party group." In a much more unexpected development, however, Khrushchev and the Congress returned to the grizzly issue of Stalinism, detailing and documenting many of its atrocities. The removal of Stalin's body from the mausoleum in Red Square, the renaming of the cities named after Stalin, with Stalingrad becoming Volgograd, and the publicity given for the first time to certain aspects of the great purge must have had a powerful impact on many Soviet minds.

In retrospect, although Khrushchev seemed triumphant at the party congress in 1961, his fortunes were in decline. The year 1958 was probably his zenith. That year followed Khrushchev's decisive defeat of his competitors for power in the "anti-party group" and the sensational Soviet inauguration of the space age with the launching of the first Sputnik. There was a bounteous harvest and industrial production continued to grow at a strong rate. The ebullient Khrushchev could readily believe, and every indication is that he did believe, his own declarations that the USSR would very soon "catch up and overtake" the United States, that every citizen would at last enjoy the good life

Nikita Khrushchev.   (*Sovfoto*)

that socialism had always promised, and even that the Utopia of communism was only a couple of decades over the horizon.

But problems and disillusionments followed in rapid succession. Economic development went sour; Khrushchev's exhortations, and his economic, administrative, and party reorganizations, together with his hectic campaigns to remedy particular deficiencies—to be discussed later in this chapter—were increasingly ineffective in resolving the crisis. In his last years and months in office Khrushchev saw the rate of industrial growth decline sharply while he had to resort to an unprecedented purchase of Canadian wheat to forestall hunger at home. De-Stalinization or, more broadly, a certain "liberalization" of Soviet life seemed to produce as many problems as it resolved. It led in effect to soul-searching and instability rather than to any outburst of creative communist energy. The world situation—also to be discussed later—deteriorated even more sharply from the Soviet point of view. In 1960 the conflict with China, which dated back at least to Khrushchev's original de-Stalinization of 1956, burst into the open, and from about 1963 the break between the former allies seemed irreparable. In the relations with the West, Khrushchev's aggressive enthusiasm, spurred by the successes of Soviet space technology, received repeated checks in Germany and finally suffered a smashing defeat in October 1962 in the crucial confrontation with the United States over the Soviet missiles in Cuba. Khrushchev's survival of the catastrophe of his apparently largely personal foreign policy might be considered a sign of the continuing power of the single leader in the Soviet authoritarian system. But this system, too, was weakening. The party elite was deeply wary of allowing a new dictator. And the leader, in turn, no longer had at his command the mechanisms of power that Stalin had. Observers noted that although the Twenty-second Party Congress confirmed and extended Khrushchev's victory over the "anti-party group" these enemies of the leader were not even expelled from the party. It would seem that during this time Khrushchev made the mistake of acting in an increasingly autocratic and arbitrary manner even though his power was not nearly as great as Stalin's had been.

On October 15, 1964, it was announced in Moscow that Nikita Sergeevich Khrushchev had been "released" from both his party and his government positions, because of "advanced age and deterioration of his health."

## The Brezhnev Era

In many ways, Khrushchev's relatively brief reign was a culmination of a long history of revolutionary politics. Khrushchev oriented his government and the party toward "building communism" domestically and internationally and he pursued these goals through dramatic (and erratic) campaigns and reforms. His successors brought a very different spirit and purpose to rule: the guiding principle was stability not change, order not revolution. It is significant that the new collective leadership that came to power in 1964—with Leonid Brezhnev, chosen as party leader, quickly emerging as the dominant figure—was the first generation of rulers to come of age after 1917. They were children during the revolution; most received technical educations; all were promoted rapidly through the party and the state during the First Five-Year Plan; all benefitted from the Great Purge, which opened opportunities to enter the higher ranks. Overall, they were practical men concerned with stable power and effective policies of economic development. Political scientists studying the regime described the years that this steadily aging and increasingly conservative generation were in power as a time of "oligarchical petrification," but also, no less importantly, as a time of the "modernization" of government. Close studies of Soviet politics after Khrushchev paid less attention to the formal claims of ideology and more to how Soviet institutions actually worked. This led to interpretations such as Jerry Hough's notion of a "return to normalcy" involving rational administration, institutional pluralism, and political interest groups. What scholars did not see was true revolutionary purpose. Or at least, as Stephen Hanson has argued, there was a "routinization of Soviet revolutionary modernity."

The new leaders—especially Brezhnev as party head, Alexei Kosygin as prime minister, Mikhail Suslov as chief party ideologist, Nikolai Podgorny as chairman of the Supreme Soviet, and others—moved quickly to undo most of Khrushchev's reforms. His administrative reorganizations were canceled. The radical ideas of limiting terms in office and encouraging public criticism of bureaucracy were replaced by a conservative policy that ensured job stability for the bureaucracy. The ideal of rational and orderly government was expressed in denunciations of Khrushchev's "hare-brained schemes," "mad improvisations," "voluntarism," and "subjectivism." Economic experiments that had tried to spur local initiative were replaced by central control from Moscow (though plans to decentralize management of enterprises, to emphasize the production of consumer goods, and to rely more on consumer demand were considered in the early Brezhnev years). The Twenty-third Party Congress held in the spring of 1966, a giant affair with around 5,000 delegates, approved many of these measures. The Congress also agreed to allow the Presidium to again be called, as in the days of Stalin, the Politburo, and the first secretary of the party to again be called the general secretary. In the years that followed, Brezhnev and his associates also brought the cultural "thaw" to an end: the crimes of the past were to be ignored and critical writers were silenced. The power and role of the KGB grew rapidly, though mass terror, viewed as dangerous to the system, was not reinstated. Ideologically, rhetoric shifted from talking about the coming of "communism" to a focus on the achievements of the past that had created a society of "developed socialism" in the present. Of course, socialist rhetoric did not disappear, especially when criticizing Western capitalism and imperialism. But, Stephen Hanson has argued, "Brezhnevian stability," especially by the 1970s, "had degenerated into a 'neo-traditional' form of rule in which Marxism-Leninism became a set of quasi-religious rituals."

The later years of Brezhnev's rule were famously described by Mikhail Gorbachev as the "era of stagnation." One very visible aspect of this was the dramatic aging of the leadership: by the late 1970s, most of the Soviet Union's leaders, in virtually every institution, were men (rarely women) in their sixties and seventies. Many, like Brezhnev himself, were physically ailing. Similarly, the growth of the economy was slowing and society, as we shall see, was increasingly alienated from the government and the whole socialist project. Nonetheless, the Soviet leadership launched important initiatives in these years, including strengthening Soviet military might, economic policies emphasizing development in such crucial sectors as agriculture and energy, and an international policy of "détente," which sought to maintain the superpower status of the USSR with less political danger and economic cost.

At the heart of domestic politics during the Brezhnev years, and key to the regime's stability, it has been argued, was a generous policy of catering to the interests of elites combined with a growing welfare state for the population at large. In 1965, the Brezhnev leadership took as its motto the phrase "trust in cadres." In practice, this meant, for example, that greater job security than ever before was assured. Material interests were also taken into account. Institutional interests were respected by providing their departments with good budgets. Most important, personal interests and desires were catered to with extensive privileges in such areas as consumer goods, housing, medical

Soviet leaders at Kremlin Meeting of the Supreme Soviet Celebrating the Fiftieth Anniversary of the Bolshevik revolution, November 4, 1967. From left: Brezhnev, Kosygin, Podgorny, Suslov.    (*World Wide Photos*)

care, and travel abroad. The effect, scholars have argued, was to create a loyal managerial class, one of the keys to the stability of the system.

At the same time, the Soviet welfare state grew, partly as a means to ensure popular toleration of this increasingly hierarchical society. Individuals were offered opportunities for upward mobility—even the opportunity to join the privileged elite—through hard work and political loyalty. But efforts were also made to ensure broader benefits. Political scientists have spoken of an implicit "social contract" between the government and the population. Repression remained (for publicly criticizing policies, for spending unauthorized time with foreigners, for damaging or stealing socialist property, for illegal buying and selling) but it was not random or inexplicable. Most important, material promises were made and partly fulfilled: free medical care for all citizens (though quality was often low), the complete lack of unemployment, guaranteed pensions at retirement, more housing so that families could live in their own apartments, subsidized prices for essential food products, and a growing consumer economy. Indeed, living standards measurably rose, and some commentators began to write of a Soviet version of consumer attitudes and a consumer society. This is not to say that Soviet citizens did not notice or resent the growing privileges of the elite. Anecdotes, a widespread form of subtle everyday critique of the systems, often spoke of this inequality. In one, Brezhnev's uneducated mother, at the sight of her son's splendid collection of motor cars, voiced concern: "That is fine, my dear son, but what if the Bolsheviks return?" As the Soviet economic situation became more difficult in the late 1970s and early 1980s, this system of rewards and welfare became more difficult to sustain. Yet, the Brezhnev government attempted essentially palliatives rather than fundamental reform. As described by a Western specialist, the decision had been made "to settle for short-run solutions to long-term problems."

When Brezhnev died, finally, on November 10, 1982, at the age of seventy-five, he had outlived such near-peers as Kosygin, by about two years, and the chief party ideologist, Suslov, by less than a year; Podgorny had been ousted from the leadership in 1977; Brezhnev's long-time lieutenant, Andrei Kirilenko, slightly older than his patron, lost his Politburo position in 1982, whether for political or medical reasons. Yet the remaining leaders still belonged to the same well-established group and were of comparable age and, as far as one could tell, orientation. Nikolai Tikhonov, who replaced Kosygin as prime minister, was born, like Brezhnev, in 1906; Konstantin Chernenko, probably closest to Brezhnev at the time of the latter's death, was only five years younger; Dmitrii Ustinov, the man in charge of what may be described as the Soviet military-industrial complex, was born in 1908. That the general Secretaryship of the party went to Iurii Vladimirovich Andropov, sixty-eight, was not unexpected, although some observers were surprised by the rapidity and smoothness of the transition. Credited with uncommon intelligence and general ability, as well as a certain sophistication, Andropov became well-

Brezhnev on a skimobile, probably near his country house. Among the many material benefits of power he enjoyed, Brezhnev had a particular fondness for motor vehicles of all sorts. In particular, he had a large collection of luxury and imported cars. (*V. Musaelyan*)

known as the head of the KGB, the political police, for the fifteen years before he switched in May 1982 to work in the party secretariat. Andropov's earlier service included the position of ambassador to Hungary in 1954–57, when he became linked, apparently, both to the brutal suppression of the Hungarian revolt and to the institution of a liberal economic policy in Hungary in its wake. A sharp critic of the stagnation and corruption under Brezhnev, Andropov addressed himself immediately to purging the administrative apparatus and to strengthening labor discipline by such spectacular measures as police searches in public places for absentee workers. But his activity was cut short by kidney failure, and he died after only about a year and three months in office. Andropov was replaced by Chernenko, Brezhnev's intended heir and already a sick man, who lived for barely another year. Then, on March 11, 1985, Mikhail Sergeevich Gorbachev, Andropov's fifty-four-year-old protégé, was elected by the Politburo to the general secretaryship of the party.

## Economic Development and Stagnation

A significant change in Soviet economic life occurred in 1957, when Khrushchev, in a move aimed at a geographic dispersion, or deconcentration—although not organizational decentralization—of authority, transferred the direction of a good proportion of industry from the ministries in Moscow to regional Economic Councils. Reflecting the constant Soviet search for the most effective and efficient economic organization, this reform was nevertheless considered by many observers as primarily political in motivation: it removed from Moscow large economic managerial staffs which, it would seem, had supported Malenkov in the struggle for power within the Kremlin. Another aim might have been to give the local party bosses more authority in economic matters and thus to stimulate local initiative.

The Sixth Five-Year Plan, scheduled to run from 1956 to 1960, was cut short in 1958, replaced by a Seven-Year Plan to last from 1959 through 1965. The official explanation for the change stressed the discovery of vast new natural resources that altered Soviet economic prospects. The more likely reason was that the Sixth Five-Year Plan had fallen considerably behind its assigned norms of production and the Soviet leadership decided to try a fresh start. Western economists such as Robert Campbell and Naum Jasny judged the industrial goals of the Seven-Year Plan to be quite realistic. While concentrating as usual on heavy industry, with special attention paid to, for example, further electrification and development of the chemical industry, the plan called for a rate of industrial growth approximately 20 percent slower than that achieved during the Fifth Five-Year Plan. In this sense it was also less ambitious than the abortive Sixth Five-Year Plan. In results, the Soviet economy continued to gain in relative output on the American economy, helped by such developments as the recession in the United States and the Western world in general in the 1970s and 1980s.

Although concentrating on capital goods, the Seven-Year Plan allowed somewhat more for the everyday needs of the people than had generally been true of previous Soviet industrialization. Especially interesting was the ambitious housing and general building program of the plan, which aimed to increase total Soviet building investment by 83 percent. Even when executed not in its entirety and with buildings of inferior quality, this aspect of the Seven-Year Plan constituted a major contribution to the improvement of the Soviet standard of living. Superior quality and unflagging attention were devoted, by contrast, to such advanced technical fields as atomic energy, rockets, missiles, and space travel. From the launching of the first artificial satellite, Sputnik I, in October 1957, the USSR achieved a remarkable series of pioneering successes in rockets and space travel.

Important developments took place in Soviet agriculture during the Khrushchev years. Indeed, frantic efforts to raise agricultural production constituted, together with certain concessions to the consumer, the salient new features of Soviet economic policy. The magnitude of the Soviet farm problem can be seen from the fact that, by contrast with industrial achievements, the gross output of agriculture in 1952 was only some 6 percent above 1928. In 1954 Khrushchev set into full operation his sweeping "virgin lands" project: huge expanses of arid lands in Soviet Asia, eventually totaling some 70 million acres, were to be brought under cultivation. This undertaking, supported by great exertion as well as by a mighty propaganda effort, gave remarkably mixed results from year to year, depending in large part on weather conditions, but did not live up to expectations. The new first secretary also started a huge corn-planting program. He further decided to boost drastically the production of such foods as meat, milk, and butter. These items came to rival electric power and steel in Soviet propaganda and to serve as significant gauges in "surpassing America."

Yet the condition of Soviet agriculture remained bad. Official claims and promises, especially the latter, differed sharply from reality. Indeed, the mass planting of corn, often in unsuitable conditions, and even the huge gamble on the virgin lands, which were difficult to cultivate, might have been unwise. To increase production Soviet authorities resorted to the old method of further socialization. Between 1953 and 1957 the number of sovkhozes increased while the number of kolkhozes declined, reducing the kolkhoz share of land under cultivation from 84 to 72 percent. As late as September 1958, Khrushchev, other leaders, and the propaganda machine still spoke of the more truly socialist nature, as well as of the technical superiority, of the sovkhoz system of agriculture over that of the kolkhoz. Yet, apparently because of the strength of peasant resistance, especially of the passive kind, the first secretary stopped the attack on kolkhozes in early 1959 at the Twenty-first Party Congress.

The official policy toward the collective farms continued to be ambivalent. There is a consensus among experts that the income of the members of the kolkhozes, extremely low at the time of Stalin's death, increased markedly in subsequent years. The collectives themselves also gained in strength. In 1958, in an abrupt reversal of previous policy, the government enacted measures to disband the Machine Tractor Stations, enabling the kolkhozes to obtain in ownership all the agricultural equipment they needed. On the other hand, state and party pressure on the kolkhozes continued and in certain respects even gained momentum. The years witnessed a great stress on increasing the "indivisible fund" of a collective—that is, that part of its revenue which belongs to the entire kolkhoz and is not parceled out among individual members—and on using this fund for such "socially valuable" undertakings as building schools and roads in the locality. Also, Khrushchev and other leaders returned to the theme that the private plots of the members of a kolkhoz are meant merely to augment a family's food supply rather than to produce for the market and that they should become entirely unnecessary with further successes of socialist agriculture.

Moreover, the Seven-Year Plan goals of increasing agricultural production by 70 percent and raising labor productivity in the kolkhozes by 100 percent and in the sovkhozes by 60 to 65 percent proved impossible to attain. Perhaps they had been predicated on a further drastic socialization of Soviet agriculture, and in particular on the elimination or near elimination of the 20 million small private plots of the members of the collectives, which the leadership did not dare carry out.

In the opinion of Abram Bergson and other Western observers, the agricultural goals adopted by the Twenty-second Party Congress as part of the program of creating a "material basis" for communism by 1980 seemed fantastically optimistic and quite unreal—an estimate that did not apply to nearly the same extent to the industrial goals. Khrushchev's frantic efforts after the Congress to bolster farm production—this time demanding the abolition of the grass rotation system in favor of planting feed crops such as sugar beets, corn, peas, and beans—served to emphasize further the crisis in Soviet agriculture. It is also probably in connection with the economic, especially the agricultural, crisis that Khrushchev enacted, in 1962, his strangest reorganizational measure: the across-the-board division of the hitherto monolithic Communist Party into two party hierarchies, one to deal with industry and the other with agriculture.

As we have mentioned, Khrushchev enthusiastically promised that communism, which was to replace socialism as the culminating phase in the evolution of Soviet society, was within reach. The Twenty-second Party Congress, in October 1961, paid much attention to this issue, proclaiming that the preconditions for communism should be established in the USSR by 1980. Although the details of communist society were somewhat vague, in general terms it was to be an economy of abundance that would satisfy all the needs of the population. "Of course, when we speak of satisfying people's needs," Khrushchev added, "we have in mind not whims or claims to luxuries, but the healthy needs of a culturally developed person." Great equality was assumed. Not only would income differentials vanish and people live according to the classic communist ideal of "from each according to their abilities, to each according to their wants," but communism would finally eliminate the inequalities between town and country, industrial and agricultural work, mental and manual labor. Members of the new society would be "broad-profile workers" that is, persons trained in two or three related skills who would, in addition, engage without pay in one or more other socially useful occupations in their leisure hours. This was meant to approximate Karl Marx's famous description of "communist society" as one in which "nobody has one exclusive sphere of activity but each can become accomplished in any branch he wishes, society regulates the general production and thus makes it possible for me to do one thing today and another tomorrow, to hunt in the morning, fish in the afternoon, rear cattle in the evening, criticize after dinner, just as I have a mind, without ever becoming hunter, fisherman, herdsman or critic."

Collectivism was a defining ideal for everything. Even some of the abundant consumer goods would be available in the form of "appliance pools" of refrigerators, washing machines, or vacuum cleaners. Apparently, Khrushchev objected to the last to private automobile ownership and projected instead public car pools. On a still broader scale, life would become increasingly socialized. Free public health services and transportation would be followed, for example, by free public meals, which would virtually eliminate kitchen drudgery for women. The Academician Stanislav Strumilin and others constructed models of communal cities of the future, with parents allowed a daily visit to their children, who would live separately under the care of a professional staff. Indeed communism would seem to imply a great diminution in the role of the family, if not its abolition. By contrast, the role of the school would expand, and so would the roles of labor brigades, comrades' courts, and other public organizations.

Khrushchev's successors, we have mentioned, ended the discussion of the imminent building of communism and abandoned many of Khrushchev's "schemes." But they remained committed, if less and less effectively, to economic development. In the middle and late 1960s fundamental measures were enacted to bolster Soviet agriculture. Collective farmers finally received a guaranteed wage, which made their position comparable to that of the sovkhoz workers, whereas earlier they had the last claim in the distribution of gain, frequently rendering their very existence marginal. Also, pensions and social services were extended to the kolkhoz members. Over a period of years the state greatly increased the amount of resources devoted to agriculture so that investment in agriculture came to constitute over a third in the allocation of the total national investment. Another 4.5 percent of the national income was assigned to subsidize retail food prices, to keep these down despite heavy production costs. Still other large sums went into agricultural research. If one adds to these huge expenses some 5 billion dollars spent by the Soviet Union in 1975–76 alone to buy grain abroad, more money to buy meat and butter, as well as similar huge purchases later, one can get an idea of the enormous effort mounted by the Soviet leadership to develop the agricultural sector and to supply the Soviet public with increasing amounts of food at more or less stable prices but also the generally miserable condition of Soviet agriculture.

The new Five-Year Plan, 1966–70—eventually designated as the Eighth— presented by Kosygin to the Twenty-third Party Congress in the spring of 1966, reset a number of Khrushchev's economic goals from 1965 to 1970. The economy was to strive for a 49–52 percent increase in the output of heavy industry and a 43–46 percent increase in consumer goods, with the annual growth rate of 85 percent and 7.7 percent, respectively—a very high figure for consumer goods in relation to heavy industry, although in line with Khrushchev's thought on the matter on the eve of his fall. Subsequently the Soviet government signed contracts with Italian and French companies to help develop the automobile industry in the Soviet Union.

The Eighth, Ninth, and Tenth Five-Year Plans, covering the years from 1966 to 1980, testify to the slowdown of the Soviet economy, accentuated by disastrous crop failures in 1972 and especially 1975, which necessitated massive purchases of grain abroad. Western economists reported that the plans' targets were "generally—sometimes widely—missed, affected as the USSR has been by declining reserves of labor and other retardational forces," and successive plans tended to set lower targets, also often not reached. Almost every area fell far short of expectations: agriculture, consumer goods, civilian equipment, capital formation, and labor productivity. Only Soviet heavy industries and military production seemed to grow at high rates. Despite these problems, Alexander Dallin observed in 1977, "no liberalizing reforms seem to be in the offing; rather, there is strong emphasis on centralism in planning and management, with further mergers of enterprises into rather large units and computerization. Still, the industrial basis of Soviet power—including military might—will certainly continue to grow at a pace that would be creditable for any advanced industrial power."

Since the fall of Khrushchev and in general since the death of Stalin, the standard of living of the urban, and especially of the poverty-stricken rural, population apparently continued to improve. During the 1960s and 1970s, wages and salaries steadily increased (and there was little inflation), food supplies improved, the amount and variety of consumer goods grew, and new housing continued to be built. Additional needs could often be satisfied in the growing "second economy" (the "black market" or "unofficial economy"), where one could purchase foreign products, illegally (i.e., privately) manufactured goods, scarce Soviet goods purchased legally and then resold, goods obtained illegally (for example, by truck drivers or by store managers), and services. As the economy began to falter in the 1970s and early 1980s, however, these improvements slowed. At the same time, the Soviet Union was bearing very heavy military expenditures, exemplified by the deployment of antimissile ballistic systems and by the tremendous growth of the Soviet navy. Economic activities in the USSR spread out, and the economic map of the country underwent constant change. Illustrations of this change include the rise of Novosibirsk as a great scientific and technological center in Siberia, the Bratsk Dam, the Baikal-Amur mainline railway, the new problem of the industrial pollution of Lake Baikal, and the shift in the center of oil production since the Second World War from its long-time location in the Caucasus to new fields between the Volga and the Urals, and also to oil and natural gas fields beyond the Urals.

The new leadership also resorted to economic reform, described generally as an economic "liberalization" and associated with the name of a Kharkov economist, Evsei Liberman. Faced with an economic slowdown, characterized by a drop in the growth rate of the gross national product and by a marked decline in the return on investment and in the growth of productivity of labor as well as by a great loss accruing from an underutilization of capital and labor resources, the government decided to shift the emphasis and the incentives from the sheer volume of production, where they had been from the inauguration of the First Five-Year Plan, to sales and profits. Under the new system managerial bonuses were to depend, not on output as such, but on sales and profits, the latter factor finally giving serious recognition to the element of cost in Soviet production. In January 1966 forty-three enterprises from seventeen industries, with a total of 300,000 workers, were switched to the new system. Others followed in subsequent months and years. Some economic reform was realized in industry, transportation, and retail trade, and it spread to the sovkhozes and to the construction sector. Yet, ambivalent and probably insufficient to begin with, it was emasculated in the process of implementation, with the result that there proved to be very little difference between the new system and the old system. More prominent was the new emphasis on material incentives, on the provision of more and more differentiated rewards. However, although widely applied, these incentives did not lead to an important improvement in performance.

Indeed, the Tenth Five-Year Plan, 1976–80, and the Eleventh that succeeded it, although on the whole less ambitious than their predecessors, witnessed repeated inability of the Soviet economy to meet set goals, a decline in the increase of labor productivity, and other signs of stagnation. Some specialists considered 1979, the first of the unprecedented four successive years of bad grain harvests, a disastrous turning point. Then and in the years immediately following, seemingly everything, from transportation bottlenecks and difficulty in maintaining the supply of energy to ever-increasing alcoholism and inflation, combined to retard Soviet economic development and to emphasize the seriousness of Soviet economic problems. Other observers wrote more generally of the first successful period of the Brezhnev regime, when the growth of Soviet military and industrial might went hand in hand with a sharp rise in living standards, and of the last stagnant and disappointing years with their ubiquitous shortages of food and consumer goods.

An economic assessment of the development of the Soviet economy under Brezhnev's stewardship, from 1964 to 1982, written at the time of his death, described the following conditions, in comparison with the United States. On the one hand, there was

Steady growth of aggregate output over the eighteen-year period, averaging 3.8 percent per year, with industrial output growing at an average annual rate of 4.9 percent.

Steady increase in living standards of the Soviet population, with per capita consumption rising at an average annual rate of 2.7 percent.

Significant growth in Soviet military power in absolute terms as well as in relative terms vis- à-vis the United States.

Reduction of the gap in aggregate and per capita output (GNP) between the Soviet Union and the United States. Whereas in 1965 Soviet GNP was only about 46 percent that of the United States (38 percent on a per capita basis), by 1982 it was 55 percent (47 percent on a per capita basis).

Reduction of the gap in productivity between the Soviet Union and the United States. While in 1965 the productivity of an average Soviet worker was only 30 percent that in the United States, by 1982 it was 41 percent.

Increase in the output of major industrial commodities to the point where, at the beginning of the 1980s, the physical output of many key commodities in the Soviet Union equaled or exceeded that of the United States.

On the other hand, there also was

Steady deceleration in the growth of the Soviet economy. The average annual growth of GNP declined from the peak of 5.2 percent during 1966–70 to 3.7 percent during 1971–75, to 2.7 percent during 1976–80, and to an estimated 2.0 percent during 1981–82.

Steady deceleration in the growth of living standards, with the average annual growth of per capita consumption declining from a peak of 4.3 percent during 1966–70 to 2.6 percent during 1971–75, to 1.7 percent during 1976–80, and to an estimated 1.2 percent during 1981–82.

Failure to achieve satisfactory growth in Soviet agriculture. Over the eighteen-year period the average growth rate of GNP originating in agriculture amounted to only 1.7 percent.

Lack of growth of agricultural productivity both in absolute terms and in relative terms vis-à-vis the United States. While in 1965 the productivity of an average Soviet farm worker was only 14 percent that in the United States (in the Soviet Union one worker supplied six persons; in the United States one worker supplied forty-three persons), by 1981 it actually declined to a mere 12 percent (in the Soviet Union one worker supplied eight people; in the United States the corresponding figure was sixty-five).

Although a significant effect of *long-term* weather cycles on grain output in the Soviet Union cannot be ruled out, the most significant failure of the Brezhnev era appears to be grain harvests, which after 1972 repeatedly fell far short of expectations and needs.... The Brezhnev reign was characterized by the highest priority being given to the growth of investment and defense spending except during the period 1964–70. As a result, the per capita consumption of an average Soviet citizen today is still not much more than one-third that in the United States.

But while the facts and the statistics seemed reasonably reliable, explanations of them differed. Possibly the most important issue was to what extent Soviet economic difficulties were of a temporary and relatively remediable character and to what extent they were intrinsic to the system.

## "The Thaw"

Khrushchev's "secret speech" to the Twentieth Party Congress in 1956 was the most dramatic gesture in the process of de-Stalinization of Soviet life—though it was also, as noted, part of the struggle for power within the party leadership. One thing was clear to Stalin's successors: they could not rule as he had—if only because they lacked his charisma (and perhaps his ruthlessness) but also because the Soviet people were expecting so much more. For the system to survive, it needed to be more responsive to the needs and wishes of the population. This was especially evident, as we have seen, in economic policies, which paid much more attention than in the past to raising the material standard of living. The renunciation of terror was another essential step away from the past. Stalin's death and especially Beria's fall in the summer of 1953 resulted in a considerable diminution in the role and power of the political police. Immediate steps were taken to assure the population, and especially the party, that terror would no longer be part of the Soviet system of rule. The "doctors' plot" was declared to be a fabrication. New regulations and supervisory structures limited the autonomy of the political police. Immediate work began on a new legal code, promulgated in 1958, which offered citizens more legal protections. And of course, Khrushchev's 1956 speech openly castigated the state's security apparatus for mistakes and crimes, leading to the posthumous vindication ("rehabilitation" in the language of the time) of some of its most prominent victims. Living victims benefited as well. Thousands, perhaps millions, of political prisoners were released from the notorious Gulag of forced labor camps. Still, dissent was not tolerated. It seems that Soviet citizens gradually lost the immediate and all-pervasive dread of the political police that they had acquired under Stalin. But, although milder, the Soviet Union remained a police state.

As we shall see in a later chapter, Stalin's death was also followed by some relaxation of party control in the field of culture. Khrushchev's denunciation of the late dictator in itself suggested the need for a thorough reevaluation of a great many former assumptions and assertions. It also created much confusion. For a number of months in 1956 some Soviet writers exercised remarkable freedom in their approach to Soviet reality and their criticism of it. But, after the Polish crisis and the Hungarian uprising in the autumn of that year, restrictions reappeared. Khrushchev's successors assumed a much harder line against dissent, as illustrated by the arrest, trial, and sentencing of Andrei Siniavsky and Iulii Daniel in 1965–66 and numerous other instances of cultural suppression.

The amount of covert opposition and bitterness that this control and the Soviet system in general created can only be surmised. Yet it should be noted that uprisings against Communist regimes took place not only in East Germany, Poland, Czechoslovakia, and Hungary, but also in the USSR itself, mainly to protest food shortages, price increases, and other changes in living and working conditions, though protests also often revealed deep resentment of state officials and of the larger conditions of Soviet life. These included uprisings in the Vorkuta and Kengir forced-labor camps in 1953 and 1954; nationalist protests in Tbilisi, the capital of Georgia, in 1956; protests by Russian construction workers in Temirtau in Kazakhstan in 1959; and a workers' uprising in Novocherkassk in 1962. Sporadic riots, strikes, and student demonstrations also occurred in later years. The government invariably responded to these protests with severe repression.

The thawing of Soviet society and the emerging of opposition views gave rise to blossoming of a striking and varied *samizdat*, that is, self-published, illegally produced, reproduced, and distributed literature, and to the appearance of dissenting intellectuals and even groups of intellectuals on the fringes of official cultural life. Numerous dissident groups and trends emerged in these years: religious study-prayer groups (Orthodox, Protestant, Jewish, Buddhist, and others), nonconformist artists displaying their works in private apartments, dissident poets and songwriters, feminists, liberals, socialists, and anarchists. Harassed and suppressed in many ways, including on occasion incarceration in dreadful mental hospitals, the opposition nevertheless kept delivering its message, or rather messages, ranging from a kind of conservative nationalism and neo-Slavophilism to former hydrogen-bomb physicist, the late Andrei Sakharov's, progressive, generally Westernized, views and the late Andrei Amalrik's personal, catastrophic, almost Chaadaev-like vision, to the dissident Marxism of Roy Medvedev. And it produced the phenomenon of Alexander Solzhenitsyn. Whatever one thinks of that writer in terms of literary stature, ideological acumen, or scholarly precision, most of his works, especially the *Gulag* volumes, are likely to be linked as indissolubly to the way we remember the Russia of Stalin as Pushkin's *Eugene Onegin* and Turgenev's *Gentry Nest* have been linked to the Russia of the landed gentry. Isolated, weak, armed only with a belief in individual moral regeneration, the intellectual opposition remained a highly troublesome element in Soviet society but also a sign of the complexity of that society and of its own sources for change.

Jewish self-affirmation, protest, and massive migration to Israel (about 235,000 emigrants up to 1985, some 10 percent of the total Jewish population of the USSR, with many more applying)—together with the permitted emigration of some non-Jews—represented another development to disturb the post-Stalin Soviet scene, a development closely linked to the intellectual opposition, although also quite distinct. One suspects that the decision to let numerous dissatisfied Soviet citizens leave, while solving the immediate problem of dealing with those people as well as responding in a conciliatory way to world public opinion, potentially raised more questions for the Soviet system than it settled. Complete alienation from the established order among Soviet Jews cannot be explained by deep Jewish identity, widespread anti-Semitism, or Zionism: most Soviet Jews were quite assimilated and even relatively successful. Their alienation from Soviet society was little different from their non-Jewish fellow citizens. The main difference was their opportunity to leave. A Soviet joke heard in the early 1980s is suggestive: While swimming in the Black Sea Brezhnev begins to drown. A strong Soviet woman grabs him and brings him to shore. "You have saved my life, comrade. I am a powerful man. What wish can I grant you?" She answers: "Open the borders of the Soviet Union and let all the peace-loving progressive people of the world who love the USSR enter and all the anti-Soviet elements leave."

Brezhnev pauses and then laughs, "I understand you, dearest, you just want to be alone with me."

The post-Stalin relaxation of restrictions appeared especially striking in an area that spans domestic and foreign policies: foreign travel and international contacts in general. Modifying the former Draconian regulations, which had made a virtually impenetrable "iron curtain" between the Soviet people and the outside world, Soviet authorities began to welcome tourists, including Americans, and allow increasing numbers of their citizens to travel abroad. Always strong on organization, they proceeded to arrange numerous "cultural exchanges," ranging from advanced study in many fields of learning to motion pictures and books for children. Soviet scientists, scholars, athletes, dancers, and musicians, not to mention the astronauts, drew deserved attention in many countries of the world. At the same time Soviet citizens welcomed distinguished visitors from the West and vigorously applauded their performances. In 1976, following the Helsinki agreements of the preceding year, foreign travel and cultural exchange gained further strength, supplying the USSR with more international contacts than had been the case at any time since the discontinuation of NEP. Bit by bit, Soviet citizens were becoming better acquainted with the West and the world.

## Foreign Relations and the Cold War

Soviet foreign policy became much more nuanced and complex after Stalin's death. The simple view of the world as filled with enemies was replaced, in Ted Hopf's words, "by a continuum of difference" that recognized a wide range of different interests and positions among nations, but also by recognition that some difference was not harmful to the Soviet Union. This led to greater tolerance of divergence within the Communist bloc—though only to a point—and to the new dogma that the capitalist and socialist worlds could coexist and resolve their differences without war. In the nuclear age, of course, détente was a quite rational policy. At the same time, beside this greater flexibility and tolerance—reflecting also greater self-confidence and security—were important perspectives on foreign relations that reflected a persistent Stalinist approach, which would lead to new conflicts. The Soviet Union viewed itself, with good cause, as a "great power" with its own sphere of influence and interests. Indeed, the Soviet Union hoped to expand this sphere by fomenting socialist revolutions in other countries, which hopefully would bring them new allies. To be sure, as the evidence of relations with eastern Europe, China, and the revolutionary movements of the Third World show, but also Moscow's relations with the national republics of the USSR, these comrades were not equals: the Soviet Union must stand at the commanding apex of this international movement. Still, this domination was handled, most of the time, with far more subtlety and effectiveness than in the past.

Stalin's death and Malenkov's assumption of the leading role in the Soviet Union immediately marked some lessening of international tensions as well as some relaxation at home. The new prime minister asserted that all disputed questions in foreign relations could be settled peacefully, singling out the United States as a country with which an understanding could be reached. In the summer of 1953 an armistice was finally agreed upon in Korea. In the spring of 1954 an international conference ended the war in Indo-China by partitioning it between the Communist Vietminh in the north and the independent state of Vietnam in the south. Although the Soviet Union had not participated directly in the Indo-Chinese conflict, that local war had threatened to become a wider conflagration, and its termination enhanced the chances of world peace. In January 1954, the Council of Foreign Ministers of the four powers, inoperative for a long time, met in Berlin to discuss the German and Austrian treaties, but without result. The Soviet Union joined the United Nations Educational, Scientific, and Cultural Organization, or UNESCO, and the International Labor Organization, or ILO, that April. Malenkov spoke of a further improvement of international relations and of a summit meeting.

That a policy of even moderate relaxation had its dangers for the Soviet bloc became, however, quickly apparent. In early June 1953, demonstrations and strikes erupted in Czechoslovakia, assuming a dangerous form in Pilsen—or Plzeň—where rioters seized the city hall and demanded free elections. In the middle of the month East Berlin and other centers in East Germany rose in a rebellion spearheaded by workers who proclaimed a general strike. Soviet troops reestablished order after some bitter fighting. Beria's fall that summer might have been affected by these developments, for the police chief had stressed relaxation and legality since the death of Stalin. Malenkov's resignation from the premiership in February 1955 ended the role of that former favorite of Stalin on the world scene.

Bulganin, who replaced Malenkov as head of the government, became the most prominent Soviet figure in international affairs, although he usually traveled in the company of and acted jointly with the party chief, Khrushchev. Molotov, in the meantime, continued in charge of the foreign office. "B. and K." diplomacy, as it came to be known, included much showy journeying on goodwill missions in both Europe and Asia. The Soviet Union paid special court to India and other neutralist countries, which had formerly been condemned as lackeys of imperialism. At the same time the two Soviet leaders claimed to be ready to settle the points at issue with the United States and the West. And, indeed, in May 1955 the great powers managed to come to an agreement and conclude a peace treaty with Austria, which included the permanent neutralization of that state as well as certain Austrian payments and deliveries to the USSR in recompense for the Soviet return of German property in Austria to the Austrian government. The height of the détente was reached at the summit conference in Geneva in July 1955. While no concrete problems were solved at that meeting, the discussion took place in a remarkably cordial atmosphere, with both Bulganin and Eisenhower insisting that their countries would never engage in aggressive action. The following month Soviet authorities announced a reduction of their armed forces by 640,000 men. In September the USSR returned the Porkkala base to Finland and concluded a treaty of friendship with the Finns for twenty years. yet in the autumn of 1955, as soon as the ministers of foreign affairs tried to apply the attitude of accommodation and understanding expressed by their chiefs to the settlement of specific issues, a deadlock resulted, with Molotov not budging an inch from the previous Soviet positions and demands. The "spirit of Geneva" proved to be an enticing dream rather than a reality.

Since the *rapprochement* between the USSR and the West failed to last, the polarization of the world continued. Following the Communist victory in northern Indo-China, the Manila pact of September 1954 created the Southeast Asia Treaty Organization, or SEATO. Great Britain, France, Pakistan, and Thailand joined the four countries already allied, the United States, Australia, New Zealand, and the Philippines, to establish a new barrier to Communist expansion in Asia. In Europe, West Germany rose steadily in importance as an American ally and a member of the Western coalition. The Soviet Union in its turn concluded the so-called Warsaw Treaty with its satellites in May 1955 to unify the Communist military command in Europe.

The year 1956 was a remarkable one, especially in eastern Europe. The first sign of a new policy toward the rest of the socialist world came when Khrushchev, Bulganin, and a large delegation visited Belgrade to essentially admit Stalin's mistakes in his intolerance of Tito and the Yugoslav path. As long as Belgrade accepted its status as a younger brother to the Soviet Union— though this would become a source of tension—Moscow would tolerate their different approach to socialist construction. In April 1956, the Cominform was dissolved, and Molotov, who had opposed these softer policies, was replaced as foreign minister by Shepilov. Khrushchev's not-so-secret speech in February 1956, which was summarized or even read at meetings of Communists in eastern Europe, was a particular stimulus of trouble. Moscow's recognition of Stalin's errors and crimes seemed to authorize demands for systemic reform. Political explosions in Poland and Hungary reflected these rapidly changing conditions.

In Poland, in late June 1956, workers took to the streets in the city of Poznan. When Polish troops were sent against them, scores of people were killed. At the same time, Polish intellectuals were calling for a relaxation of controls. The Communist Party in Poland was itself divided, with many Communists favoring a distinctive Polish path to socialism. In October, Wladyslaw Gomulka, who had been imprisoned as a "reactionary," was reinstated as party secretary, and Khrushchev and other Soviet leaders flew to Warsaw to settle the crisis. In spite of extreme tension—Khrushchev called the Poles traitors and Gomulka blamed Khrushchev for his imprisonment—an understanding was reached: the USSR accepted Gomulka and a liberalization of the Communist system in Poland and agreed to withdraw Soviet military advisors from the country. The day after the Soviet leaders left, hundreds of thousands of people took to the streets in Warsaw in support of Gomulka.

Hungary went further. As Hopf observed, "Poland had just missed violating the boundaries of permissible difference; Hungary would not." Partly influenced by the events in Poland, a revolution broke out in late October 1956.

After the Twentieth Party Congress, Hungarian demonstrators demanded reform and the return to power of the reformist prime minister Imre Nagy, who had been forced out of the party and the government in 1955 by the Stalinist party leader, Matyas Rakosi. In July, Moscow sent Mikoyan, a supporter of Khrushchev's de-Stalinization, to Budapest to remove Rakosi. By October, inspired by the events in Poland, demonstrators in the streets, mostly students, were demanding the restoration of Nagy to power, the complete withdrawal of Soviet troops from the country, complete freedom of speech, and democratic elections. Nagy was restored, but the demonstrations continued and grew increasingly violent as students encountered security forces and the military. At the end of October, Nagy formed a coalition government that included non-Communists and began negotiations to withdraw Hungary from the Warsaw Pact. The Soviet leadership, memoirs and archival documents show, were frightened of the implications of showing "weakness" in the face of such disorder and disloyalty. This could spread through the whole region—indeed, there were signs it was already spreading—and give opportunity to the Western powers. Mikoyan reported from Budapest that the Hungarian army could not be relied upon to restore order. The Soviet leaders decided to send troops to crush the rebellion. On November 4, Soviet tanks and troops began their assault on Budapest, the center of the rebellion. Witnesses describe great brutality as soldiers attacked anyone on the streets and tanks fired at buildings. It is estimated that over 2,500 Hungarians and 722 Soviet troops were killed in the fighting. Nagy was arrested and would be executed in 1958. Although the Western powers were reluctant to intervene, the moral shock of the Hungarian intervention stimulated Western hostility toward the Soviet Union. It also led to a crisis among Western Communists: the revelations after 1953 along with the violent repression of the Communist reform movement in Hungary encouraged movements for change within many parties but also led large numbers of individual Communists to quit the movement altogether.

Khrushchev's behavior on the international scene showed a certain pattern. He remained essentially intransigent, pushing every advantage he had, be it troubles in newly independent states, such as the Congo, or Soviet achievements in armaments and space technology. Nevertheless, he talked incessantly in favor of coexistence and summit conferences to settle outstanding issues. Also, he paid friendly visits to many countries, including the United States in 1959. The summit conference in the summer of 1960 was never held, for two weeks before it was scheduled to begin Khrushchev announced that an American U-2 spy plane had been brought down deep in Soviet territory. But in 1961 Khrushchev met the new American president, John F. Kennedy, in Vienna. In the summer of 1962 both aspects of Soviet foreign policy stood in bold relief: fanned by the USSR, a new Berlin crisis continued to threaten world peace; yet, on the other hand, Khrushchev emphasized more than ever coexistence abroad and peaceful progress at home, having made that his signal theoretical contribution to the program that was enunciated at the Twenty-second Party Congress. To be sure, as officially defined in the Soviet Union, coexistence meant economic, political, and ideological competition with the capitalist world until the final fall of capitalism. But that fall, Soviet authorities came to assert, would occur without a world war.

In the autumn of that same year, however, Khrushchev overreached himself and brought the world to the brink of a thermonuclear war The confrontation between the United States and the USSR in October 1962 over the Soviet missiles in Cuba, which resulted in a stunning Soviet defeat, can be explained, at least in part, by the Soviet leader's enthusiasm and his conviction that the United States and capitalism in general were on the decline and would retreat when hard pressed. The outcome, no doubt, strengthened the argument for peaceful coexistence and emphasized caution and consultation in foreign policy, symbolized by the celebrated "hot line" between Washington and Moscow.

The Soviet Union proceeded to measure carefully its reactions and its involvement even in such complicated and entangling crises as the Israeli-Arab wars of 1967 and 1973 and the Vietnam War. In the latter conflict, the Soviet Union denounced "American imperialism" and provided extremely valuable matériel to North Vietnam, but it avoided escalation. Yet, following the complete victory of communism in Indo-China in 1975 and the shattering impact of the catastrophic American policy in Vietnam on the American public, the Soviet Union might have felt that it had a freer hand on the international stage, in Angola or elsewhere.

With the Soviet Union as well as the United States acquiring a second-strike capability, that is, the ability to retaliate and inflict "unacceptable damage" on the enemy after absorbing a nuclear blow, a true balance of terror settled on the world. Ever-improving technology made virtually all established strategic concepts obsolete. Numerous bases and indeed whole sections of the globe lost their importance in terms of the possible ultimate showdown between the two nuclear giants.

From the mid-1970s it was authoritatively estimated in the West that the USSR had caught up with the United States in overall nuclear military strength, and indeed had perhaps moved slightly ahead; on the other hand, evidence available since 1991 has led some specialists to conclude that these estimates were based on successful Soviet efforts to exaggerate the size and effectiveness of their forces. Yet the enormous economic burden, terror, and inconclusiveness of the arms race did not lead to a full negotiated settlement. Important results were achieved, to be sure. Following the earlier banning of nuclear tests in the atmosphere, the nuclear nonproliferation agreement was signed by the two superpowers and other states in early 1968. Other agreements were reached concerning outer space, where 1975 witnessed the celebrated joint effort of the Russians and the Americans. The crucial issue of military limitations itself was tackled in numerous negotiations, but these remained inconclusive. Moreover, as Edward Teller and other scientists have pointed out, the difficulty in the negotiations resided not only in the entire complex of aims, attitudes, and policies of the two superpowers, but also in the very nature of scientific and technological advance, which rapidly makes prearranged schemes of limitation obsolete.

The very closely related but even larger issue of détente between the Soviet Union and the United States also sailed to an uncertain future. Détente scored a resounding success at the Helsinki conference in the summer of 1975, where the United States and other Western countries accepted in effect the Communist redrawing of the map of central and eastern Europe following the Second World War in exchange for unsubstantiated promises of greater contacts between the two worlds and a greater degree of freedom in those contacts. But a comprehensive economic agreement between the USSR and the United States failed over the questions of the most favored nation clause, credits, and the American concern with the fate of Soviet Jews. Furthermore, before long détente was again swamped by new international developments, to be detailed later in this chapter.

Ironically, while Soviet-American relations improved and became more stable after the Cuban confrontation, and while the Soviet leaders found welcome in Gaullist France and other capitalist countries, their standing in the Communist world deteriorated. The conflict with China broke out into the open around 1960 and widened and deepened thereafter. After the abrupt withdrawal of Soviet personnel from China in August of that year and the discontinuance of assistance, relations between the two countries quickly became extremely antagonistic. To the sound of violent mutual denunciations the two states and parties competed with each other for the leadership of world communism, the Chinese usually championing their revolutionary position against Soviet "revisionism." Moreover, China became an atomic power and formulated large claims on Soviet Asian territory. Observers noted that international crises such as the war in Vietnam only intensified the hostility between the two great Communist states. Although China remained far behind the USSR in industrial and technological development and although it was fully preoccupied with a "cultural revolution," its aftermath, and other internal problems, it was still viewed as posing a major threat to the Soviet Union in the future, if not in the immediate present.

Problems in eastern Europe proved to be more pressing. The twelve years that followed the suppression of the Hungarian revolution witnessed Soviet attempts to adjust to changing times, to allow for a Communist pluralism with a considerable measure of institutional and eventually even ideological diversity. In Zbigniew Brzezinski's phrase, satellites were to become junior allies. Even Tito usually received a kind of fraternal recognition, and he spoke with authority. Yet tensions persisted and indeed increased, both between the different East European countries and the Soviet Union and within those countries as most of them proceeded with de-Stalinization, economic liberalization, and other important changes. The break with China led in 1961 to the unexpected departure of Albania into "the Chinese camp." Romania under its new leader, Nicolae Ceausescu, showed a remarkable, even stunning, independence from the Soviet Union, although it remained barely within the Communist bloc and continued a hard-line policy at home. Poland, belying the promise of 1956, had its progress toward freedom arrested, and concentrated its energy on trying to contain, by petty and persistent persecution, the

Catholic Church, liberal intellectuals and students, and other forces favoring change.

Then came the "Prague Spring" of 1968 and another armed intervention by Soviet troops into a "fraternal" socialist country. In the years before 1968, there was a growing desire among Czechoslovak intellectuals and reformist party members for more rapid de-Stalinization and reform. After a visit to Prague at the end of 1967, Brezhnev supported removing the unpopular party leader Antonin Novotny, who was replaced by a representative of the reformist wing of the party, Alexander Dubček. Dubček announced a dramatic program of change that included freedom of the press, reducing the power of the political police, greater market freedom in the economy, and, after a transition period, free elections. Immediately, relatively free discussion was allowed in the press. These reforms, confirmed and extended at a party congress, led to consternation in the governing circles of the Soviet Union, East Germany, Poland, and Bulgaria. The Soviet leaders tried to limit the reforms, and an unprecedented face-to-face discussion between the members of the Politburos of the Soviet Union and Czechoslovakia seemed to resolve the conflict. Then on August 20, Soviet troops, assisted by the troops of Warsaw Pact allies, invaded Czechoslovakia with half a million soldiers and occupied the country.

By now it was clear that the Soviet Union was determined to insist on the control of dissent, maintenance of a planned economy, and subordination to the Soviet Union. The Czech invasion was justified as an act of "socialist internationalism" necessary to prevent "capitalist restoration." In time, this implied policy become known as the "Brezhnev Doctrine": the socialist community led by the USSR has a duty and right to intervene where and when, as Brezhnev put it in a speech in Warsaw in November 1968, "internal and external forces that are hostile to socialism try to turn the development of some socialist country towards the restoration of a capitalist regime." The repercussions of the intervention lasted long after the summer of 1968 and not only in the emergence of the Brezhnev doctrine. Still more European socialists turned away from the Soviet Union after 1968 and the Western powers grew increasingly wary.

It may have been in Poland, though, that evidence of a crisis in the Communist world—including economic stagnation, social discontent, political alienation, and resentment of Soviet domination—pointed most strongly toward the eventual collapse of Soviet power in eastern Europe. In the late 1970s, after dissident intellectuals offered support to striking workers, a unique alliance of workers and intellectuals emerged that would become a major threat to Communist power in Poland and beyond. Indeed, it has been argued that this movement, out of which the "Solidarity" trade union would emerge, was the beginning of the end of Communist rule in eastern Europe. Already in the 1970s, a growing underground of labor and dissident organizations and publications began to develop. This movement was given a boost in 1978 when the Archbishop of Cracow, Karol

Wojtyla, was elected to the papal throne as Pope John Paul II. His visit to Poland a year later has been described by participants as a brief national festival of liberation. His public masses were attended by millions (and the government and police dared not interfere). He spoke openly of the need for human rights and national and religious freedom. His spiritual and moral stature as Pope and his support for change inspired many Poles. The movement continued to grow. The government hesitated to suppress the opposition, in part at least, because of Poland's heavy dependence on continuing Western loans, which were required to keep the troubled economy solvent.

In the wake of a massive and successful strike of workers at the Lenin Shipyard in Gdansk, supported by dissident intellectuals and other worker groups, a nationwide independent labor union calling itself "Solidarity" was established, led by the electrician and labor activist Lech Walesa. Very quickly, Solidarity took the form of a social movement seeking fundamental change. Its stated goals were not only economic improvements in the lives of workers but also "justice, democracy, truth, legality, human dignity, freedom of convictions, and the repair of the republic." In their view, economic protest was "social protest" and social protest was "moral protest." The government was effectively losing control of the situation—one sign of which were the thousands of opposition publications being printed without censorship. The Soviet leadership could not tolerate this threat. But rather than an invasion, a military coup was planned, for this time Moscow had reliable allies able to command a strong armed force. The coup took place, in close cooperation with the Soviet authorities, on December 13, 1981. Its leader, General Wojciech Jaruzelski, had been given increasing authority in the preceding months; at this point he was simultaneously minister of defense, prime minister, and first secretary of the party. He declared martial law, created a ruling Military Council of National Salvation, arrested Solidarity's leaders and supporters, and expanded censorship.

Active resistance against the overwhelming force of the regime was quite limited, and, from a military standpoint, the operation was carried out rather effectively. Nevertheless, the "success" of General Jaruzelski's junta was very dubious. Although thousands of Solidarity activists, including Walesa and other dissidents, were arrested and placed in internment camps, some leaders of the movement escaped arrest and an underground opposition began to form. Western economic sanctions and continuing passive resistance to the regime in the factories, offices, schools, and universities were making the task of running the country extremely difficult for the Jaruzelski regime. By the end of 1982, there appeared to be two clear choices before the military government of Poland: either to continue with the martial law administration, further alienating the population and risking a total economic collapse of the country, or to end martial law and attempt to open the few remaining channels of contact with the great majority of the Polish population in an effort to reduce tensions and improve the performance of the economy. The choice was not an easy one for the Polish Communist authorities—and their Soviet sponsors.

The Soviet invasion of Afghanistan in late December 1979 may have been the most damaging decision of the Brezhnev era, both for the Soviet Union's international reputation and for the Soviet system itself. The invasion was in support of a Communist government in Afghanistan that had overthrown a military dictator in 1978 and embarked on a series of social reforms, including collectivization of agriculture, unveiling and educating women, and attacking influential religious leaders. These radical measures stimulated an Islamic rebellion that threatened the Afghan government but also, when viewed alongside the 1979 revolution in Iran, raised the specter of Islamic uprisings in Central Asia and elsewhere in the Soviet Union. The Afghan government repeatedly asked for Soviet military support. By contrast, in much international opinion, the Afghan invasion was a sign of Soviet expansionism: it was the first direct Soviet use of military force outside "its own" eastern European empire since the Second World War, and it was interpreted as a first step in a bid for the oil of the Middle East and a general takeover of that region. In the wake of the invasion, the United States took a much harsher stance toward the Soviet Union and offered material support to the rebels. The invasion also damaged the USSR's reputation in the postcolonial world, where the image of the Soviet Union as a force for "national liberation" was being eclipsed by evidence of Soviet "imperialism." Perhaps even more important, the war was damaging domestically. The brutal ten-year war became a "bleeding wound," as Gorbachev would call it before ending the war in failure in 1989. Unable to defeat the mujahideen rebels, who enjoyed much popular support and operated on rugged lands they knew well, Soviet losses were enormous. About 14,000 soldiers died during the war and a great many more were wounded and disabled. The war was also psychologically devastating: many returning Afghan veterans suffered from mental illness and drug addiction.

As of 1985, tension between the Soviet Union and the United States, the East and the West, was not confined to the crucial problems of Afghanistan and Poland. Rather, the two sides opposed each other all over the world, from Central America to southern Africa, Lebanon, and Cambodia. To be sure, western European countries, in spite of strong United States objections and even sanctions against particular companies, continued to support the building of a natural-gas pipeline from western Siberia to western Europe. But they were also apparently prepared to proceed with the installation of United States middle-range missiles to counteract the already established Soviet ones, an installation most especially opposed for years by Brezhnev. The very important Soviet-American disarmament negotiations remained deadlocked. SALT II was not ratified by the United States Senate, and its future chances appeared slim, especially after the departure of Carter from the presidency. In fact, numerous critics accused the tougher anti-Soviet policies of the Reagan administration of largely precluding adjustment and agreement. Yet the administration itself and others claimed that it was precisely this firmer approach, and especially the concurrent buildup of the United States nuclear and military might, that would force the USSR to negotiate effectively for disarmament. Indeed, the lasting and positive memories of Reagan's presidency, especially in eastern Europe, reflect a belief, not shared by most historians, that Reagan's tough stance was responsible for the collapse of communism.

CHAPTER 41

# Soviet Society and Culture

A new sun he brings to the world,
He destroys thrones and prisons,
The nations he calls to eternal brotherhood,
He erases boundaries and borders.
With his crimson banner, symbol of struggle,
Beacon of salvation for the oppressed,
We will crush the yoke of fate,
And capture enchanting paradise.

> *VLADIMIR KIRILLOV,*
> *"THE IRON MESSIAH," 1918*

The Soviet people know that they are not working for the capitalists but for themselves, for the more and more complete satisfaction of their needs.... That is why the Soviet people put their heart and soul into their work.

> ALEXEI STAKHANOV, 1936

Socialist realism is the basic method of Soviet literature and literary criticism. It demands of the artist the truthful, historically concrete depiction of reality in its revolutionary development. Moreover, the truthfulness and historical concreteness of the artistic depiction of reality must be linked with the task of ideologically remolding and educating the working people in the spirit of socialism.

> STATUTE OF THE UNION OF SOVIET WRITERS, ADOPTED 1934

The moral and ethical significance of the emergence of the human rights movement in the USSR in the 1960s is huge, notwithstanding the small numbers of people involved and a certain apocalypticism. It changed the moral climate and created the mental preconditions for democratic transformation in the USSR and for the development of an ideology of human rights worldwide.

> ANDREI SAKHAROV

When the Bolsheviks came to power in Russia in October 1917, they were determined to remake the whole of society and culture. The impact of their efforts was considerable. Despite the enormous size, huge population, and tremendous ethnic and cultural variety among the peoples of the USSR, the Communist regime succeeded in imposing a remarkable degree of social and cultural homogeneity across this vast land. Thus, we can interpret Soviet social and cultural history as a story of totalitarian human engineering—in the 1930s, writers were actually called "engineers of human souls"—that embraced society and culture as well as politics and economics. While true, this picture oversimplifies Soviet history. For these years also saw sudden shifts in social and cultural policy, a great deal of imagination and experimentation, widespread enthusiasm for the new, the persistence of ethnic and cultural variety, and much disorientation, disappointment, and discontent. Indeed, it is precisely in social and cultural life that we begin to see signs of the disintegration of the Communist order that would contribute to its collapse in 1991.

## The Communist Party of the Soviet Union

The Communist Party played in fact, as well as in theory, the leading role in Soviet society. Its membership, estimated at the surprisingly low figure of less than 25,000 in 1917, passed the half million mark in 1921 and the million mark in the late 1920s. The number of Soviet Communists continued to rise, in spite of repeated purges that included the frightful great purge of the 1930s, and reached the total of almost 4 million full members and candidates when Germany invaded the USSR. While many Communists perished in the war, numerous new members were admitted into the party, especially from frontline units. Postwar recruitment drives further augmented party membership to between 7 and 9 million in the immediate postwar years, as many as 13 million in 1967, more than 16 million in 1978, and almost 20 million in the 1980s.

In addition to the party proper, there existed huge youth organizations: Little Octobrists for young children, Pioneers for those aged nine to fifteen, and the Union of Communist Youth, or Komsomol, with members between fourteen and twenty-six. The first two organizations, and eventually even the Komsomol, acted as party agencies for the general education of the younger Soviet generations, opening their doors wide to members. The party also worked with and directed countless institutions and groups: professional, social, cultural, athletic, and others. In fact, from the official standpoint, Soviet society had only one ideology and only one outlook, the Communist; citizens and groups of citizens differed solely in the degree to which they embodied it.

The word *partiinost*, usually translated as "party-mindedness," summarized the essential quality of a Communist's life and work. While the early emphasis on austerity was greatly relaxed after the 1930s, especially in the upper circles, the requirements of implicit obedience and hard work generally remained. In particular, party members were expected throughout their lives both to continue their own education in Marxism-Leninism and to utilize their knowledge in all their activities, carrying out party directives to the letter and influencing those with whom they came in contact. While exacting, the "party ticket" opened many doors. It constituted in effect the greatest single mark of status, importance, and, above all, of being an "insider" in the Soviet Union. Although, to be sure, many Soviet Communists were people of no special significance, virtually all prominent figures in the country were members of the party. After the Second World War special efforts were made to assure that such fields as university teaching and scientific research were largely in the hands of Communists. Conversely, it became much easier for outstanding people to join the party.

The social composition of the Communist Party of the Soviet Union changed over time. Before 1917, this party of the proletariat had a largely bourgeois leadership and a relatively small mass following. During and after the revolution, large numbers of workers entered its ranks, and special recruitment campaigns were organized to increase proletarian membership. With the stabilization of the Soviet system and the inauguration of the five-year plans, the "Soviet intelligentsia," in particular technical and administrative personnel of all sorts, became prominent. On the eve of the Second World War the party was described as composed of 50 percent workers, 20 percent peasants, and 30 percent intelligentsia, with the last group on the increase. That increase continued after the war, as social origin became less significant with time and the authorities tried to bring all prominent people into the party. It might be noted that, in relation to their numbers, peasants were poorly represented, indicating the difficulty the Communists experienced in permeating the countryside. The proportion of women increased up to about one-quarter of the membership of the party.

The Communist Party of the Soviet Union was thoroughly organized. Starting with primary units, or cells, which were established where three or more Communists could be found, that, is, in factories, collective farms, schools, military units, and so forth, the structure rose from level to level to culminate in periodic party congresses, which constituted important events in Soviet history, and in the permanently active Central Committee, Secretariat, and Politburo. At every step, from an individual factory/or collective farm to the ministries and other superior governing agencies, Communists were supposed to provide supervision and inspiration, making it their business to see that no undesirable trends developed and that production goals were fulfilled. At higher government levels, as already indicated, the entire personnel consisted of Communists, a fact that nevertheless did not eliminate party vigilance and control. In general, rotation between full-time government positions and party administrative positions was common. It should be noted that the guiding role of the party asserted itself with increased force after Stalin's death, for the late general secretary's dictatorial power had grown to such enormous proportions that it had even cast a shadow over the party itself.

## The Destruction of the Old Society

Whereas the October Revolution catapulted the Communist Party to power, it led to the destruction of entire social classes. The Revolution was in many ways inspired by a hatred of the old dominant classes, which led to widespread assaults on their property and position and sometimes on their persons. The result was a rapid and sweeping leveling of traditional Russian society. The landowning gentry, for centuries the top social group in Russia, disappeared rapidly in 1917 and 1918 as peasants seized their land and often demolished their homes. The upper bourgeoisie, financial, industrial, and commercial, was similarly eliminated when workers seized control of many businesses and then when the Bolsheviks nationalized finance, industry, and trade. The middle and especially the lower bourgeoisie, to be sure, staged a remarkable comeback during the years of the New Economic Policy. Their final destruction, however, came with the implementation of the five-year plans. If the gentry occupied the stage in Russia too long, the bourgeoisie was cut down before it came into its own. The clergy, the monks and nuns, and other people associated with the Church constituted yet another group to suffer harsh persecution, although in their case it stopped short of complete annihilation. Finally, the old intelligentsia was deeply fractured by the revolution. Many intellectuals and writers embraced the revolution and participated actively in building socialism—though many would perish in Stalin's terror. But many opposed the new regime as a violation of liberal and humanistic values—though also because the Communists distrusted and persecuted the old upper classes, from which most had come. Many highly educated Russians emigrated. Many others perished in the frightful years of civil war and famine. Indeed, we can say that the intelligentsia as an independent and critical force in Russian life was no more. There was no place outside the establishment for independent and intellectually engaged individuals who stood opposed, as a matter of absolute principle, to everything that restricted and harmed the human personality. Such individuals remained, of course, though always at risk. Yet, in time, especially after Stalin's death, we see again the rise of an independent and critical intelligentsia opposed to the status quo.

## Peasants

While traditional Marxism envisioned socialism coming to an urbanized and industrialized society, the Soviet Union was for most of its history a land of peasants. In 1926, 82 percent of the population lived in rural areas. Only in the mid-1960s did the number of city dwellers finally exceed the number living in the countryside. Even in the final years of the Soviet Union, the rural population still numbered almost a third of the total. Not surprisingly, peasants bore the brunt of the privations and sacrifices imposed by the Soviet "builders of socialism." In the two demographic catastrophes of Soviet history, one associated with collectivization and the famine and the other resulting from the Second World War, peasants—and peasants as soldiers—suffered the most, dying by the millions.

Of course, peasants carried such a heavy burden in the USSR not only because of their vast numbers, but also because of the policies pursued by the government. The Communist view of peasants was always ambivalent. On the one hand, Bolsheviks believed themselves to be acting in the name of "the people," that is, of the workers and the peasants. On the other hand, as Marxists, they viewed peasants (with the possible exception of semi-proletarianized "poor peasants") as petit bourgeois property owners who would support the building of communism only after they were fully proletarianized by leaving the countryside or once agriculture had been transformed along collective industrial lines. Initial policies reflected this ambivalence. Lenin's original endorsement of the peasant seizure of land had great appeal in the countryside, though Lenin understood this to be a necessary but temporary "compromise with peasant desires. Influenced by the Bolshevik land policy and by revolutionary soldiers returning home—a point effectively emphasized by Oliver Radkey—the rural masses proved reasonably well inclined toward the new regime and on the whole apparently preferred it to the Whites during the Civil War. But War Communism antagonized many of them. Besides, the Bolsheviks tried to split the peasants, inciting the poor against the better-off. During NEP, the official policy was one of *smychka*, of the "bond" uniting the proletariat (and the ruling party of the proletariat) with the peasants. But already, we see efforts to promote proletarianization. Rural soviets, staffed by urban Communists along with some poor peasants, competed with the traditional power of the peasant commune. Cooperatives and collective farms were organized. Communists tried to organize the poorer peasants against the richer kulaks, though this required greatly exaggerating the actual extent of social differentiation in the villages. And efforts were made to transform peasant manners and beliefs. But many Communists found this gentle approach to peasants distasteful and dangerous and called for a more aggressive policy toward the traditional peasantry.

The First Five-Year Plan resulted in such an all-out offensive against the peasantry, often framed in the language of class war and proletarianization. Millions of "kulaks" and members of their families disappeared. Countless peasants, recalcitrant or relatively prosperous or simply unlucky, populated forced-labor camps. Countless other peasants starved to death. Scenes of horror in once bounteous Ukraine defied description. But, as we know, the peasants, in spite of their resistance, were finally pushed and pulled into collectives. The typical member of a kolkhoz was a new phenomenon in Russian history. The novelty resided not in peasant poverty nor in the heavy exactions imposed on peasant labor, but in the minute state organization and control of work and life. While peasants profited from certain Soviet policies, notably the spread of education, and while some of them rose to higher stations in society, on the whole the condition of the rural masses, the bulk of the Soviet people, remained miserable and at times desperate. Largely supporting the five-year plans by their labor, as already explained, Soviet peasants received very little in return. After Stalin's death, Khrushchev and other leaders admitted the grave condition of the Soviet countryside, while writers presented

This 1925 poster, by the noted Russian painter Boris Kustodiev, is titled "Leningrad Society for the Smychka (Bond) between City and Country." An urban worker and a peasant and his son are shown in stereotypical dress. Note the differences. The worker is handing the boy a pamphlet of writings by Lenin, who is also quoted at the bottom of the poster: "Establishing connections between city and country is one of the fundamental tasks of the working class holding power." *(Gosizdat)*

some unforgettable pictures of it during the relative freedom of expression that prevailed for several months in 1956. Subsequent years, to be sure, witnessed an improvement. Yet rural Russia remained poor. Moreover, the party and the government continued their social engineering, as clearly indicated in such postwar measures and projects as the increase in the size of the collective farms, the abortive agrogoroda, the temporary emphasis on the sovkhoz form of agriculture, and the periodic campaigns against the private plots of kolkhoz members. Indeed—logically, from their point of view—Communists were not likely to relax until peasants disappeared as a separate group, having been integrated into a completely industrialized economy.

## Workers

Industrial workers in many ways profited most from the Bolshevik revolution. That revolution was made in their name, and they gave the new regime its greatest social support. Upward social mobility for workers was an essential part of the new system. There was even, especially during the 1920s and 1930s, a special term for promoted workers—and, to a lesser extent, promoted peasants—*vydvizhentsy* (those moving upward). Large numbers of workers and Communists of working-class origin were promoted into more responsible positions in the economy, the administration, the military, and the party. Many received special training to become engineers and other technical specialists. Proletarians also received special access to higher education. Many prominent people throughout Soviet life, including much of the post-Stalin ruling class, owed their positions to this policy of proletarian promotion.

Soviet industrialization created a much larger labor force than ever before in Russian history. In huge numbers, the peasants of yesterday became the workers of today. Society, as the Communists intended, was becoming proletarianized. Whether the condition of workers in the Soviet Union improved compared to tsarist times is difficult to measure; even more difficult is to judge how the conditions of working-class life would have developed had there been no revolution and capitalism survived. On the one hand, Soviet workers certainly benefited materially from communism, especially as the economy grew and stabilized. An extensive welfare state provided workers, and all Soviet citizens, with free medical care, subsidized prices for basic foods, job protection (there was virtually no unemployment), subsidized vacation and travel opportunities, increased educational and cultural opportunities, and guaranteed pensions. On the other hand, real wages were low, especially in the early years, for industrial development was made possible by directing resources toward production rather than consumption. For the same reason, through most of Soviet history, there was relatively little to buy in the stores. Workers also suffered from the inadequate supply and the low quality of urban housing. Yet, these areas too saw improvement as governments placed more emphasis on improving workers standards of living.

In the workplace, the revolutionary ideals of "workers' control" were quickly set aside as the needs of increasing production took precedence. The power of management over the everyday lives of workers was matched by trade unions made to serve the interests of the state more than the needs of individual workers. In contrast to tsarist days, workers could not strike or otherwise express their discontent. Perhaps a reflection of these conditions, alcoholism, indiscipline, and poor work habits persisted—and evidently increased in the late Soviet years—signs, much talked about, that many Soviet workers remained far from the model of conscious proletarians. The material condition of the Soviet proletariat did improve, however, after the death of Stalin. Still, it remained quite poor as the Soviet system came to its end.

## Privilege and the "New Class"

Whereas the initial impact of the Bolshevik revolution, coupled with famine and other catastrophes, did much to level Russian society, smashing the rigid class structure of imperial Russia and even destroying entire classes, before long social differentiation began to grow again. In particular, the five-year plans produced a tremendous expansion of administrative and technical personnel, which, together with the already existing party and government bureaucracies, became, broadly speaking, the leading class in the country. Scientists, writers, artists, professors, and other intellectuals, purged and integrated into the new system, became prominent members of the privileged group. Army and naval officers and their families provided additional members. Altogether, the privileged, distinguished primarily by their education and nonmanual occupations, came to compose about 15 percent of the total population.

As time passed, the benefits enjoyed by the elite grew. The Brezhnev era has been called the "golden age" of the Soviet elite, especially for the "nomenklatura"—appointed government, party, and managerial elites, in other words the bureaucracy, though this privileging of the elite began in the 1930s. There were special stores at which only members of the elite could shop (and the higher the rank, the better the store). Elite status meant access to better medical care, to better housing, and to scarce or better commodities. The Soviet Union, in other words, was becoming a class society, though determined, it has been argued, not by capitalist relations to the means of production, but by Communist relations to the means of power. Certainly, these measures did much to create a loyal managerial class.

## "Cultural Revolution" and the "Great Retreat"

As the new Soviet elite advanced to the fore, Soviet society lost many of its revolutionary traits and began to acquire in certain respects a strikingly conservative character. The transformation occurred essentially during the 1930s, but on the whole it continued and developed further during the Second World War and in the postwar years. While state laws and regulations were crucial in this process, they reflected, as well as contributed to, basic social and economic changes.

Soviet history began with radical experiments to transform society. Experiments such as the "Orchestra without a Conductor" or house communes and attacks on "bourgeois specialists" were meant to nurture a spirit of collectivism and egalitarianism. Iconoclasm and imagination were encouraged in the arts and literature, as will be discussed later. Perhaps most important, as part of an effort to liberate individuals, a sustained effort was made to undermine the family. Marriage was no longer a sacrament, but a simple legal agreement between two people, easily broken. A divorce could be obtained merely at the request of one of the partners—a postcard was enough. Children were optional and abortions were legal and quite common. Some Bolshevik leaders even spoke of "free love." Efforts were made to establish collective kitchens and day care centers.

In the 1930s, all that changed. Artistic and literary expression, as will be seen, was made more uniform and conventional than ever before. The discourse of egalitarianism was overturned: attacks on engineers and other professionals were halted, Stalin explicitly repudiated wage equality as "silly chatter" and "fashionable leftism," and inequality and privilege were allowed to grow. Discipline was reinforced in the army and other institutions. Ranks, titles, decorations, and other distinctions, whether bureaucratic, military, or academic, were restored and acquired vast importance. Traditional uniforms blossomed everywhere, reminding observers of tsarist Russia. Generalissimo Stalin toasting his marshals at a gargantuan Kremlin reception presented a far different picture from Lenin in his worn-out coat haranguing workers in squares and factory yards. In schools, the experiments of the 1920s were halted and classroom discipline reinstated along with uniforms, formal lecturing, learning by rote, standardized textbooks, and homework. The content of education also shifted. While instruction in Marxism-Leninism and party history remained obligatory, traditional academic subjects were reemphasized. And glorification of the party and its leaders was joined by a new emphasis on patriotism and Russian national tradition. In family policy, greater ceremony was restored to marriage, divorce became difficult and expensive, homosexuality was made a criminal offense, and abortion was outlawed. Especially after the losses of the Second World War, particular emphasis was placed on having many children. Mothers with five or six living offspring received the Motherhood Medal, those with seven or eight were awarded a decoration known as Motherhood Glory, while those with ten achieved the status of Heroine Mother. Financial grants to large families helped further the implementation of the new policy. Throughout these years, the press extolled family life and the role of women as mothers as mainstays of the socialist order.

In the post-Stalin years, especially, other signs of social and cultural "retreat" were noticed, though these were less the result of official policy than of gradual changes in everyday life and mentalities, which often ran against the grain of party policy. Most often mentioned at the time was the widespread retreat into private life. Soviet sociologists, around the 1970s, began documenting what one researcher called a "drift toward domesticity." Opinion surveys showed that Soviet citizens valued family above work, social recognition, or participation in organizations. Making "cozy" private spaces for oneself and one's family became of prime importance. No less value was placed on friendship. Scholars have argued that family and friends in the late Soviet years became "private institutions" that offered bases of loyalty and cultural value that functioned as alternatives, and even as subtle opposition, to the official order. These same years also saw the growth of wider alternative networks of affinity and values, especially among the young: devotees of various trends in Western rock music, sports fan gangs known as *fanaty*, counter-cultural identities such as "hippies" or "punks" (the English words were used), and, among the intelligentsia, private cultural circles where new poetry or prose was read, art displayed, and ideas discussed. It was precisely in these expanding semi-private spaces where the dissident movement developed from the late 1960s into the 1980s. Drinking, of course, was pervasive throughout this bourgeoning private and unofficial civic life. That so much of this was at odds with official ideology led sociologists and party officials to worry about the "lack of Soviet consciousness" among the youth in the 1970s and led Gorbachev in the mid-1980s to speak of a "spiritual crisis" in the Soviet Union in which much of the population had become alienated from the established order in their values, judgments, tastes, and beliefs.

## Women

The emancipation of women was a major goal of socialism. Women were to be liberated from social discrimination, domestic violence, and the drudgery of housework. Actual results were contradictory, though; and actual policies also varied in different periods. In general, as before 1917, economic development created new opportunities for women to work outside the home. Educational and cultural opportunities gave women both a space for personal development and the notion that their function could be more than only serving their families. And the party and state were officially committed to the principle of gender equality and women's liberation. Still, in various ways, patriarchal and conservative values persisted and even strengthened.

To realize their commitment to women, after 1917 a special branch of the party was established to address the condition of women, known as the Zhenotdel, or Women's Section. Leaders of the movement, such as Alexandra Kollontai, sought to create a "new woman": self-confident and bold, sexually liberated (a controversial point for many Bolshevik leaders, including Lenin, who mocked talk of free love), and dedicated to building socialism rather than limiting their lives to the domestic sphere. At the very least, women's activists tried to mobilize women for self-education and to defend their right to be treated as human beings. Many Communists, including Lenin, spoke of socializing domestic work and childcare in order to free women for more public roles. Yet, given the harsh economic conditions, the upheavals in family life caused by war and revolution, and the persistence of traditional attitudes toward women—including in the party—these goals were largely utopian. Indeed, even official political propaganda in the 1920s was as likely to portray women as happy mothers surrounded by their children as to show women factory workers or professionals.

During the great industrialization drive of the 1930s, women's emancipation was reduced mainly to participation in production. In 1930, the Zhenotdel was abolished, for separate advocacy of women's issues was seen as unnecessary and a distraction from allegedly more important concerns. On the other hand, industrialization opened the gates to women's employment as never before. Employment opportunities were not equal, however: not in the types of jobs available (notions of gender "suitability" for different types of work persisted and women were less often trained for highly skilled jobs), not in wage levels, and not in access to managerial positions. Still, women along with men benefitted from policies that promoted individuals from peasant

Young women and soldiers on a Moscow street in the 1980s. The freedom to visibly dissent from established tastes was a sign both of greater personal freedom in Russia after Stalin's death and of growing alienation from the system. (*I. Moukhin*)

and working-class backgrounds into higher education and thus into better and more responsible jobs. Another major source of inequality was the fact that women remained responsible for housework, cooking, and childcare. As Barbara Engel has written, "because the state failed to socialize domestic labor as promised, working women often did two jobs rather than one." As we have mentioned, motherhood was actively promoted and harnessed to social needs. In the interests of economic growth, the Soviet leaders believed it essential to support reproduction and women's role as mothers. Beginning in the Stalin era, the Soviet leadership viewed women's primary responsibility to society to be the bearing and raising of children. Numerous policies were enacted to strengthen the family, as we have seen. While the Second World War brought large numbers of women into the workforce and even into the army, wartime propaganda increasingly emphasized a view of women as the embodiment of the home and family for which men were fighting. After the war, the celebration of women's domestic role and the family became stronger than ever.

After Stalin, as part of the larger effort to improve standards of living, serious attention was paid to the status and condition of women. Still, especially due to the persistent effects of wartime population decline, a major focus of state concern was how to best mobilize women as a "demographic resource"—in a word, to have more children, but also raise them more effectively. The "double burden" of full-time employment and full-time work at home limited women's opportunities and satisfactions. Also, there was much public discussion of a crisis of masculinity, where men felt that their status and dignity were harmed when their wives worked outside the home. The position of women in late Soviet society was contradictory, as Gail Lapidus and other scholars have described. On the one hand, positive signs included not only high levels of women's employment but also a great increase in education, to the point that women came to be proportionately better represented as students in Soviet institutions of higher learning than men, as well as an increased proportion of women in the professions, such that the great majority of medical doctors in the late Soviet years were women. At the same time, few women reached the top rungs of their profession, medicine included, and they were strikingly absent at the highest levels of both party and government.

## The Nationalities

The multiplicity of nationalities, ethnicities, languages, and religions in the USSR defined Soviet society as a multinational state no less than it did that of the Russian Empire. For most of the Soviet period, ethnic Russians formed about half of the population of the country, and Ukrainians and Belorussians approximately another quarter. The rest of the population included a huge variety of peoples, ranging from groups with long national histories and strong national identities, such as the Armenians and Georgians, to tribal groups in Siberia. The census in 1989 listed about 150 languages still spoken in the Soviet Union, though, depending on how one defines a language as opposed to a dialect, linguists believe the number may be closer to 200. By religious confession or at least residual religious identity, the Soviet Union included not only a large population of Eastern Orthodox, but also many Catholics, Protestants, Jews, Muslims, Buddhists, and shamanists.

Soviet authorities developed several basic policies in dealing with national groups that were often quite contradictory. On the one hand, the Soviet state promoted education (including the creation of local intelligentsias), created opportunities for individuals from local nationalities to hold positions of local influence, and allowed the languages and cultures of local peoples to be preserved and taught. At the same time, the Soviet authorities allowed no independence in ideological, political, economic, or social matters, discouraged and sometimes punished religious practice (often closely tied to national identities), settled large numbers of ethnic Russians in the national republics and autonomous regions, and discriminated against minority nationalities in the recognized national republics (such as the Abkhaz in Georgia). Even cultural traditions were restricted by the stipulation that they be "national in form and socialist in content." All histories had to be interpreted in the simple terms of class struggle and the progressive march of secular civilization. Above all, the centralized unity of the USSR was an absolute principle and the single Communist Party of the Soviet Union was an important foundation and guarantee of that unity.

But this dual approach to nationality policy contained seeds of danger. The policy of favoring local elites, allowing the use of local mother tongues in schools and in public, and encouraging limited preservation and development of ethnic traditions had both benefits and risks. As long as the system was stable and the economy strong, these limited local privileges nurtured support for the system and even a certain "Soviet" identity. But these policies also kept alive—indeed, sometimes helped created—national and ethnic identities that could lead to demands for independence. In other words, cultural autonomy could become cultural nationalism, and that in turn could lead to separatism. Always suspicious, the Soviet leadership kept uncovering "bourgeois nationalists" in union republics and lesser subdivisions of the USSR. In the crucially important case of Ukraine, for example, the party apparatus itself suffered several sweeping purges because of its "deviations." Moreover, after a controlled measure of Great Russian patriotism and nationalism became respectable in the Soviet Union, Stalin and the Politburo began to stress the Russian language and the historical role of the Great Russian people as binding cement of their multinational state. This trend continued during the Second World War and in the postwar years. Eastern peoples of the USSR were made to use the Cyrillic in place of the Latin alphabet for their native tongues, while the Russian language received emphasis in all Soviet schools. Histories had to be rewritten again to demonstrate that the incorporation of minority nationalities into the Russian state was a positive good rather than merely the lesser evil as compared to other alternatives. Basically contrary to Marxism, the new interpretation was fitted into Marxist dress by such means as stress on the progressive nature of the Russian proletariat and the advanced character of the Russian revolutionary movement. But Stalin, and some other Soviet leaders as well, went further, giving violent expression to some of the worst kinds of prejudices.

Especially in the postwar years, Jews suffered particular persecution. Jews, especially Yiddish-speaking intellectuals, had been especially targeted in the Great Purge, with many thousands sent to the camps or executed. But while Jews shared in the fate of many persecuted individuals and groups during the terror, the immediate postwar years brought a new attack directed at Jews alone—particularly painful and ironic given the devastation inflicted on Soviet Jews by the Nazis. A fierce campaign against "cosmopolitanism"—which soon became a euphemism for Jews—led to a purge of Jews from many institutions, widespread arrests, and a general atmosphere of fear. Evidence suggests that Stalin was planning a mass deportation of all Jews to the Soviet east. Stalin's death brought this assault to an end. Although the post-Stalin years saw nothing comparable, continued and growing restrictions on Jewish religious and language education—restrictions that themselves sometimes helped nurture ethnic and religious identity among assimilated Soviet Jews—was one of the reasons many Jews sought to emigrate.

Stalinist repressions effectively limited nationalist protests in the Soviet Union. After Stalin, however, small nationalist movements began to emerge in the 1960s and 1970s, often connected to the larger underground dissident movement. Organizations were founded in Ukraine, Lithuania, Georgia, and elsewhere; samizdat publications appeared; and occasional street protests were mounted. Participants in these movements frequently faced waves of arrests. Generally, only handfuls of intellectuals engaged in these movements. The broader populations still generally showed little interest in the national question.

## Education

Education played an extremely important role in the development of the Soviet Union. Educational advances were a most important part of state planning and made the striking Soviet economic and technological progress possible. As already indicated, education also stood at the heart of the evolution of Soviet society.

Somewhat less than half of the Russian people were literate at the time of the Bolshevik revolution. Furthermore, the years of civil war, famine, epidemics, and general disorganization that followed the establishment of the Soviet regime resulted in a decline of literacy and in a general lowering of the educational level in the country. Beginning in 1922, however, the authorities began to implement a large-scale educational program, aiming not only at establishing schools for all children, but also at eliminating illiteracy among adults. By the end of the Second Five-Year Plan, that is, by 1938, a network of four-year elementary schools covered the USSR, while more advanced seven-year schools had been organized for urban children. The total elimination of illiteracy proved more difficult, although the government created more than 19,000 "centers for liquidating illiteracy" by 1925 and persevered in its efforts. The census of 1926 registered 51 percent of Soviet citizens, aged ten and above, as literate; that of 1939 81.1 percent. Projecting the increase, 85 percent of the Soviet people must have been literate at the time of the German invasion, and almost all at the end of the Communist regime.

The four-year and the seven-year schools became basic to the Soviet system. But ten-year schools also appeared in quantity. This type of school, for boys and girls from seven to seventeen, provided more class hours in its ten years than does the American educational system in twelve. Although in 1940 tuition was introduced in the last three years of the ten-year school, as well as in the institutions of higher learning—and repealed and restored since—an extremely widespread system of scholarships and stipends was used at all times to make advanced education available to those with ability.

After initial experimentation with some progressive education and certain quite radical methods of teaching the young and combining school and work, in the 1930s and after Soviet education returned to entirely traditional, disciplinarian, and academic practices. The emphasis centered on memorization and recitation, with a tremendous amount of homework. Soviet schools were especially strong in mathematics and science, that is, in physics, chemistry, biology, and astronomy, as well as in geography and drafting. But they also stressed language, literature, foreign languages, and history, together

"Literacy Is the Path to Communism," 1920. Note the mythic imagery with which the power of literacy was imagined. The book being held by the rider reads "proletarians of all countries, unite." (*Gosizdat*)

with certain other academic subjects. For instance, six years of a foreign language were taught in a ten-year school. There were no electives. The Soviet Union had special schools for children with musical and artistic gifts, military schools, also foreign language schools, and the like.

Beyond secondary schools were technical and other special schools, as well as full-fledged institutions of higher learning. The number of these higher schools was constantly growing. Soviet authorities developed the old university system, but they placed much more emphasis in higher education on institutes that concentrated on a particular field, such as technology, agriculture, medicine, pedagogy, or economics. Study in the institutes ranged from four to six years; a university course usually took five years. Applicants to universities and institutes had to take competitive entrance examinations, and it has been estimated that frequently as many as two out of three qualified candidates had to be rejected because of lack of space. Older Soviet students, as well as schoolchildren, were required to attend all their classes, were in general subject to strict discipline, and followed a rigidly prescribed course of study.

The educational effort of the party and the government extended beyond schools to libraries, museums, clubs, the theater, the cinema, radio, television, and even circuses. All of these, of course, were owned by the state, were constantly augmented, and were closely coordinated to serve the same purposes. More peculiarly Soviet was the practice of oral propaganda in squares and at street corners, with more than 2 million propagandists sponsored by the party. Education on the job and by correspondence was also extremely widespread in the USSR. Moreover, a further expansion and diffusion of education constituted an essential part of the later five-year plans, although the rate of educational advance slowed down compared to the earlier period.

Soviet education, and indeed Soviet culture in general, greatly profited from the prerevolutionary legacy. The high standards, the serious academic character, and even the discipline of Soviet schools dated from tsarist days. The main Communist contribution was the rapid dissemination of education at all levels and on a vast scale, though imperial Russia was slowly moving toward universal schooling. Many observers noted that Soviet students studied with remarkable diligence and determination. That probably stemmed both from cultural traditions that held education in high esteem and from contemporary conditions of life: education provided for Soviet citizens the only generally available escape from the poverty and drabness of the kolkhoz and the factory. If generous subsidization and energetic promotion constituted the main Soviet virtues in education, the all-pervasive emphasis on uniformity, memorization, and Marxist ideology was the chief vice. It has often been observed in critical histories of Soviet education that the closer a discipline was to the pronouncements of Soviet Marxism—philosophy, history, and sociology, for example— the more rigid, restrictive, and distorted it became. On the other hand, many scholars and teachers learned how to acknowledge Marx and Lenin deftly while working with a good measure of independence and honesty. Often, notably in history, this meant close attention to documentable facts and limited analysis and interpretation. Still, as a rule, there was more intellectual freedom in fields like mathematics and theoretical physics than in the social sciences and humanities, fields where ideological positions were well established and the essential skills of critical thinking were not encouraged.

## Soviet Culture

Soviet science, scholarship, literature, and arts did not stand outside the currents of Soviet history. The political drive to transform the country and its people, the traumas of civil war and world war, the dramatic shifts in policy, the idealism, and the repression were all reflected in Soviet culture. There was one constant, though: growing party control. Already in the first years after the October Revolution, Bolshevik cultural leaders were insisting that science, literature, and the arts must be "proletarian." While this often meant that priority was given to individuals of working-class backgrounds, "proletarian" was mainly understood in ideological terms as reflecting a properly understood Marxist point of view. In later years, the notion of *partiinost* (party-mindedness) served the same function. At the same time, the development of culture was valued as an essential part of socialist development. Thus, by the Stalin years, Soviet science, scholarship, literature, and the arts were well-funded, thoroughly organized, and closely tied to the policies of the party and the state. All Soviet intellectuals were in effect employed by the state. Even when their income depended primarily on royalties, their books could not be published nor their music played without official authorization. The quality of Soviet creative work varied enormously over time and by field. The experimentalism of the first years after the revolution and of the early 1920s, the radicalism of the First Five-Year Plan, the conservative rigidities of the 1930s, the "thaw" of the late 1950s and early 1960s, and the growth of underground dissent in the Brezhnev years, all created different opportunities and constraints for creative thought. And different fields were more or less subject to the demands of doctrine. Thus it was easier to do excellent work in science or to compose original music than to write the best possible history or literature. Still, in almost all fields, fruitful as well as barren, the influence of the party and its ideology left its mark.

## Science and Scholarship

For a variety of reasons, science was a privileged area of Soviet culture. It was obviously and immediately useful and, indeed, indispensable if the USSR were to become the military, technological, and economic leader of the world. It was fully endorsed by Marxism, which prided itself on its own scientific character. In fact, some writers have commented on an almost religious admiration of science and technology in the Soviet Union, an expression in part of the old revolutionary titanism and determination to transform the world. Yet science, while subject to the dialectic, lies on the whole outside Marxist doctrines, which concentrate on human society, and thus constituted a "safer" field in the Soviet Union than, for example, sociology or literature. Not that it escaped the party and ideology altogether. Communist interference with science included such important instances as Soviet difficulties in accepting Einstein's "petty bourgeois" theories, as well as Trofim Lysenko's virtual destruction of Soviet biology, particularly genetics, together with the elimination of a number of leading Soviet biologists, notably Nikolai Vavilov. Lysenko claimed to have disproved the basic laws of heredity and obtained party support for his claims: Lysenko's theories gave Marxist environmentalism a new dimension and made a Communist transformation of the world seem more feasible than ever—the only trouble was that Lysenko's theories were false. But Einstein's views had to be accepted, at least for practical purposes; and even Soviet biology staged a comeback, although it took many years and several turns of fortune finally to dispose of Lysenko's authority. Moreover, thousands of scientists, in contrast, for example, to writers, could continue working in their fields more or less undisturbed. And science especially profited from the large-scale financing and organization of effort provided by the state.

The Sputniks, the shot at the moon, the photographing of the far side of the moon, and Soviet astronauts' orbiting of the earth, together with atomic and hydrogen explosions, have emphasized the achievements of Soviet applied science, and in particular Soviet rockets, missiles, and atomic and space technology.* In these fields, as in others, the Soviet Union profited from the pre-revolutionary legacy, especially from the continuing work of such scholars as the pioneer in space travel Konstantin Tsiolkovsky, 1857–1935. The contributions made by espionage and by German scientists brought to the USSR after the Second World War are more difficult to assess. The state, of course, financed and promoted to the full all the extremely expensive technological programs referred to above. It also organized, in connection with the five-year plans, a great search for new natural resources, vast geographic expeditions, and other, similar projects. The work of Soviet scientists in the far north acquired special prominence. The Academy of Sciences continued to direct Soviet science as well as other branches of Soviet scholarship.

While Soviet applied science received perhaps too much praise in the world press, the overall excellence of Soviet science was on the whole not sufficiently appreciated. With theoretical physicists like Lev Landau, experimental physicists like Abram Ioffe and Petr Kapitza, chemists like Nikolai Semenov, mathematicians like Ivan Vinogradov, astronomers like Viktor Ambartsumian, geochemists like Vladimir Vernadsky, and botanists like Vladimir Komarov—to select only a very few out of many names—the Soviet Union had outstanding scientific talent, while the scope of its scientific effort exceeded that of all other countries except the United States.

Soviet social sciences and humanities did not compare with the sciences. The imperatives of Soviet Marxism stifled virtually all growth in such fields as philosophy and sociology, although the 1920s, the "thaw" years, and, to a

---

* Soviet "firsts" in space include: first earth satellite, Sputnik I, launched October 4, 1957; first satellite with animal aboard. Sputnik II, November 3, 1957; first moon rocket, Lunik I, January 2, 1959; first photographs of hidden side of moon, October 18, 1959; first retrieval of animal from orbit, August 20, 1960; first launching from orbit, Venus probe, February 12, 1961; first human in space, Lieut. Col. Iurii A. Gagarin, April 12, 1961; first double launching with humans. Major Andrian Nikolaev, August 11, 1961, Lieut. Col. Pavel Popovich, August 12, 1962; First woman in space, Valentina Tereshkova, June 16, 1963; first triple-manned launching, Col. Vladimir Komarov, space commander, Konstantin Feoktistov, scientist, Dr. Boris Egorov, physiologist, October 12, 1964; first person to walk in cosmic space, Lieut. Col. Aleksei A. Leonov from Voskhod II (flight commander, Col. Pavel Beliaev) March 19, 1965; first flight around the moon and return of an automatic space craft, Zond 5, September 15–22; 1968; establishment of first orbital experimental station during flight of Soyuz 4 and Soyuz 5 spaceships, January 1969; first self-propelled automatic laboratory on the surface of the moon, Lunokhod-1, November 17, 1970; first manned research station, Salyut, in circumterrestrial orbit, June 7, 1971; first soft landing on the surface of Mars and transmission of video signal to Earth by Mars-3 probe, December 2, 1971; first soft landing on the sunward surface of Venus by Venera-8 probe and transmission to Earth of atmospheric and surface measurements for 50 minutes, July 22,1972. The Soviet Union also announced the first loss of a person in actual space flight, Col. Vladimir Komarov, Soyuz 1, April 24, 1967.

lesser extent, the later Brezhnev years, were more open to work that made gestures toward official ideology but was not entirely constrained by it. Official ideology itself, especially after the 1920s and before the brief Gorbachev era, proved to be remarkably barren, with the result that even Marxist thought in the USSR was crude and undeveloped compared to certain Western and eastern European varieties.

In history, until the early and middle 1930s Mikhail Pokrovsky's negativistic school held sway. Pokrovsky took an extremely critical and bitter view of the Russian past, in effect declaring it of no importance. With the Soviet consolidation and turn to cultural conservatism in the 1930s, Pokrovsky and his school were denounced, and the authorities began to promote intense work in the field of history and in such related disciplines as archaeology. In particular, Soviet historians turned to collecting and editing sources. Some valuable work was also done in social and economic history, with at least one Soviet historian, Boris Grekov, originally a prerevolutionary specialist, making contributions of the first rank. Yet in general, in spite of the change in the 1930s and a certain further liberalization following Stalin's death, Soviet historiography suffered enormously from the party straitjacket, most especially in such fields as intellectual history and international relations.

Linguistic studies followed a somewhat different pattern. There Nikolai Marr, 1864–1934, an outstanding scholar of Caucasian languages who apparently fell prisoner to some weird theories of his own invention, played the same sad role that Trofim Lysenko had played in biology. Endorsed by the party, Marr's strange views almost destroyed philology and linguistics in the Soviet Union, denying as they did the established families of languages in favor of a ubiquitous and multiform evolution of four basic sounds. The new doctrine seemed Marxist because it related, or at least could relate, different families of languages to different stages in the material development of a people, but its implications proved so confusing and even dangerous that Stalin himself turned against the Marr school in 1950, much to the relief and benefit of Soviet scholarship.

Most areas of Soviet scholarship, however, profited much more by Stalin's death than by his dicta. From the spring of 1953, Soviet scholars enjoyed more contact with the outside world and somewhat greater freedom in their own work. In particular, they no longer had to praise Stalin at every turn, prove that most things were invented first by Russians, or deny Western influences in Russia—as they had had to do in the worst days of Zhdanov. Entire disciplines or sub-disciplines, such as cybernetics and certain kinds of economic analysis, were eventually permitted and even promoted. Yet, while some of the excesses of Stalinism were gone, compulsory Marxism-Leninism and *partiinost* remained.

## Literature and the Arts

Like other educated Russians, writers and artists responded to the Communist revolution differently. A large number felt like outsiders in the new Russia.

Socially, most were from the despised upper classes. Politically, most had been vaguely liberal or quite apolitical. And as artists, many felt aesthetically alienated from the new proletarian standards for culture. As a result, many fled Soviet Russia, frequently enriching European and American culture. But many artists and writers remained. The least political tried to ignore the new order—to create art outside official channels, to write or paint for art's sake alone, and for oneself and one's friends. Other writers and artists sought to be part of the revolution, as they understood it, to produce "revolutionary" art and literature. It helped that in the early years the Soviet government tolerated a variety of artistic currents and positively encouraged avant-garde artists. Many received paid government positions as cultural officials. More commonly, writers and artists benefited from a state that provided subsidies, studio space, and publishing and exhibition opportunities. This attachment to the cause of the party and the state, however, and this dependence on official aid, would soon prove to be increasingly constraining.

Literature in the early Soviet years continued in certain ways the trends of the "silver age," in spite of the heavy losses of the revolutionary and civil war years and the large-scale emigration of intellectuals. Symbolists like Blok and Bely and acmeists like Mandelshtam and Akhmatova continued publishing excellent poetry and developing their work in new directions. Futurists like Mayakovsky crafted modernist odes to the revolution. And many brilliant new writers emerged, often elaborating on prerevolutionary traditions. Important authors whose first major works appeared after 1917 (though some had begun publishing just before the revolution) included Isaak Babel, Mikhail Bulgakov, Iurii Olesha, Boris Pasternak, Boris Pilnyak, Andrei Platonov, Evgenii Zamiatin, and Mikhail Zoshchenko. Formalist criticism rose and flourished, as did the highly original work of the literary critic and language theorist Mikhail Bakhtin. Non-Communist writers created numerous groups and movements, tolerated by the party as "fellow travelers," a term coined to denote nonproletarian or nonrevolutionary writers who were willing to accept Soviet power and work constructively within the socialist order. At the same time, organizations of "left" or "proletarian" authors competed for influence and state support. Starting in 1918 and continuing through the 1920s, the Proletcult established studios to promote literary and artistic creativity among workers. Proletcult leaders insisted on creating a pure, class art. In practice, however, workers in the studios often studied with such nonproletarian writers as Bely and Briusov, and many worker writers, developed quite distinctive and heterodox voices (to the great dismay of Proletcult leaders). Among professional "proletarian" writers, conflicts over literary style and content (for example, was lyricism and inwardness tolerable?) and over party policy produced a whole series of proletarian writers' organizations, beginning in 1920 with the All-Union Association of Proletarian Writers (VAPP) and ending during the First Five-Year Plan with the militant Russian Association of Proletarian Writers (RAPP), which often viciously condemned the existence of all approaches but their own. Until the late 1920s, in part due to the influence of Anatolii Lunacharsky, the commissar of enlightenment until 1929, diverse approaches were tolerated. Even RAPP's demands for proletarian hegemony were largely ignored.

Signs of trouble were already looming in the late 1920s. The voices of orthodox Marxist critics of deviant literary trends were becoming shriller and more influential. A number of suicides could be read as marks of disillusionment or even protest. The celebrated "peasant" poet Sergei Esenin hanged himself in 1925, writing that "there's nothing new in dying/But living is no newer," and the leftist Mayakovsky took his own life in 1930, observing in a last poem that he had been made to "step on the throat of my own song." But the greater change came in 1932, when all literary groupings were abolished, along with all independent publishing houses and journals, replaced by a single Union of Soviet Writers. In 1934, at the first All-Union Congress of Soviet Writers, party leaders proclaimed that there was only one correct approach in literature: "socialist realism." In effect, Soviet literature now literally became an organ of the government and writers employees of the state. Members of the Writers' Union enjoyed secure incomes and potential privileges but were required to write according to official standards. And when writings did not conform, or when standards changed, authors had to be ready to rewrite the offending texts. Many writers—including Akhmatova, Mandelshtam, Pasternak, Olesha, Babel, and Bulgakov—withdrew into public literary silence.

The official definition of socialist realism as "the truthful, historically concrete depiction of reality in its revolutionary development," already indicates a particular ideological understanding of "truth" and "reality." This was elaborated with the further explanation that "the truthfulness and historical concreteness" of these realistic depictions of the world must serve the purpose of "ideologically remolding and educating the working people in the spirit of socialism." Other doctrinal notions were soon added. Literature, it was said, must by guided by *partiinost* (accord with the policies of the party), *ideinost* (being inspired by lofty ideas and principles), and *narodnost* (being comprehensible to ordinary people—the *narod*— and serving their needs). Sufficiently vague in theory, socialist realism often meant in practice that Stalin and his associates dictated proper literary form and content. Indeed, writers were urged to study Stalin's works for inspiration. The result was a flood of novels, stories, poems, and plays, as well as movies (a genre much valued by the party for its propaganda value), idealizing Soviet life, portraying the Russian past in a patriotic light, glorifying individual heroism (in the revolution, in production, in history), and highlighting the high idealism of the new Soviet man and woman. The socialist realist hero was always a paragon of both moral and physical beauty, with no fundamental inner conflicts and no psychological ambiguities. Instead of the grim world around them, authors were urged to see things as they should appear and will appear in the future. Pessimism was banned.

With artistry subordinated to revolutionary purpose and much of the complexity of life deliberately drained out of socialist realist literature, it is not surprising that the quality and lasting appeal of Stalinist literature was often very low. After Gorky's death in 1936, no writer of comparable stature rose in Soviet letters. A few gifted men, such as Alexei N. Tolstoy, 1883–1945, the author of popular historical and contemporary novels, and Mikhail Sholokhov, 1905–84, who wrote the novels *The Quiet Don* and *Virgin Soil Upturned*, describing Don cossacks in civil war and collectivization, managed to produce good works more or less in line with the requirements of the regime, although they too had to revise their writings from edition to edition to meet changing party demands. Other talented writers, for instance, Iurii Olesha, failed on the whole to adjust to "socialist realism." Soviet poetry, especially hampered by the injunction to be simple and easy to understand, as well as socialist and realist, proved to be inferior even to Soviet prose. The government no doubt contributed more to the enjoyment of its readers by publishing on a large scale the Russian classics and world classics in translation.

In the post-Stalin years, the Writers' Union continued to insist on the socialist realist principles of *partiinost, ideinost,* and *narodnost,* though greater flexibility was allowed. Forbidden themes such as Stalin's purges and labor camps were briefly allowed. And greater objectivity was accepted in writing about everyday Soviet life. Literary critics openly admitted that much socialist realist literature was emotionally shallow and false. Still, strong limits remained in place. For example, when Pasternak was offered the Nobel Prize in 1958 for his novel, *Doctor Zhivago* (completed in 1955), which was rejected for publication in the Soviet Union but was published abroad to great acclaim, he was forbidden to travel abroad to accept the prize and was excoriated in the Soviet press for the novel's ideologically incorrect perspective on the Soviet past.

The post-Khrushchev years saw increasing demands to depict Soviet achievements, but also increasing variety and even subtle deviance. Many writers avoided heroic topics to focus on the complexities of everyday human relationships. The "village prose" school of writers offered readers more realistic portraits of the hardships of rural life that emphasized traditional values such as closeness to nature, simplicity, and moral decency. We see a similar emphasis on individual experience and feelings in the songs of popular bards like Vladimir Vysotsky and Bulat Okudzhava. While classic socialist realism continued to be produced, studies of readers' tastes make it clear that most Soviet readers preferred books about individuals, feelings, and relationships to accounts of heroic labor or revolutionary devotion. Works about the war, crime and detection, and espionage were especially popular. The limits of tolerance were regularly reasserted, however. For example, Alexander Solzhenitsyn, whose story about the forced labor camps, *One Day in the Life of Ivan Denisovich* (published in 1962 with Khrushchev's direct approval), one of the hallmarks of the literature of the "thaw," was forbidden after 1965 to publish anything. All of his later works were published abroad and smuggled back into the Soviet Union. In 1969, he was expelled from the Writers' Union and in 1973 he was expelled from the USSR. The poet Iosif Brodsky, whose works, publishable only in the West or in samizdat, are pervaded by sadness and nostalgia derived from contemplating the human condition, was sentenced to five years' hard labor in 1964 (released after a year in the face of protests by Russian authors and the world) and forced to leave the Soviet Union in 1972. Many writers similarly found themselves forbidden to publish or even on trial for sedition. In fact, much of the best Russian literature in the Soviet era was written abroad. Some of the outstanding expatriate authors of the "first wave" of emigration were the novelist, story writer, and poet Ivan Bunin and the highly original prose writer with a unique style, Alexei Remizov, who both died in Paris, in 1953 and 1957, respectively. Some émigré Russian writers, notably the novelist Vladimir Nabokov and later the poet Brodsky, wrote influential works in English or other languages. In recent years, especially since the fall of communism, émigré literature had been reclaimed as an essential part of the whole of Russian literature.

The Soviet record in the arts paralleled that in literature. Again, the first postrevolutionary decade was closely linked to the silver age and to contemporary trends in the West. Most of the artists who embraced the revolution viewed it as essentially about freedom and possibility, often expressed artistically in art fully freed from the conventions ("bourgeois conventions") of representational art. Many artists insisted that revolutionary art had to be useful to the revolution as well. "Art into Life!" became a popular slogan. Artists designed monuments and festival decorations for public squares, clothing, books, and other objects, using the most modern designs. As a rule, whatever the style adopted—and in the first Soviet decade diverse styles thrived, ranging from Kazimir Malevich's transcendental abstractions to Marc Chagall's nostalgic and magical portraits to Vladimir Tatlin's fantastic constructions to traditional paintings of revolutionary leaders and events—imagination thrived. The same applied to architecture in these early years, in which revolutionary visions of flying cities and towering iron skyscrapers with revolving glass interiors (which could not be built) coexisted with modernist functionalism (which did produce a number of lasting buildings).

However, once "socialist realism" established its hold on Soviet culture, arts in the Soviet Union acquired a most conservative and indeed antiquated character. Stalin-era painting and sculpture restored traditional realism to visual representation but always in a heroic and positive mood, always to at least imply progress and success in the building of socialism. Brightly colored paintings of happy and healthy peasants laboring in sunny fields of grain or of strong and joyous factory workers became commonplace, alongside endless portraits of Stalin and other Soviet leaders. Soviet architecture also turned away from the avant-garde creativity of the early Soviet years toward the design of heavily ornamented apartment and office buildings, grand boulevards and squares suitable for parades (replacing old neighborhoods and churches), extensive public decorative art such the traditionalist mosaics and chandeliers of the Moscow metro, and the notorious Moscow skyscrapers of Stalin's declining years, which combined the styles of the early Western skyscraper with baroque and gothic elements. After Stalin's death, uninspired realism dominated mainstream painting, while architecture became modest and functional.

Soviet music in the 1920s and 1930s followed a similar trajectory: avant-garde experimentalism gave way to socialist realism. The emotional power of music made the party's cultural guardians concerned to ensure that music also contributed to the building of socialism. Creativity and originality were much more pronounced in music than in painting, however, partly because music stood further from Marxist and "realistic" injunctions and partly because of accidents of talent. The most notorious incident of state control was an official attack in the Communist Party newspaper *Pravda* in 1936 on Dmitrii Shostokovich's new opera, *The Lady Macbeth of the Mtsensk District*, which was chastised as not "natural, human music," but merely modernist "noise," a "musical racket" that could "only whip up passion" and that suited the "degenerate" tastes of the bourgeoisie, not the simple and pure tastes of the proletariat. This was one of many such attacks on "formalism" and "left-ism" in music. Music thrived, nonetheless. The contributions of the Sergei Prokofiev (who spent many of the early Soviet years abroad, ironically because he found that his revolutionary music was not appreciated but also because of poor financial support for music) and Shostakovich are recognized world-wide. In later years, Aram Khachaturian and Alfred Schnittke would again demonstrate the potential of Soviet classical music to achieve international recognition. Jazz also had an important role to play in Soviet musical life, though it too faced regular repression by the state, especially during the late Stalin years—it is worth recalling that when criticizing Shostakovich's opera, *Pravda* noted that he had borrowed "his nervous, frenetic, and epileptic music from jazz." In the 1960s and 1970s, singer-songwriters such as Vysotsky and Okudzhava created a genre of performed folk poetry that drew on various song traditions in both prerevolutionary and Soviet Russia to create an important and original musical form.

The history of the performing arts—music, ballet, theater—was contradictory, like so much else. As critics have noted, these arts were short on creativity and development, but long on execution and performance. The high standards were continuations from tsarist days, aided by increased state subsidies and a very developed system of artistic education and training. Soviet musical education produced a series of brilliant classical musicians, especially violinists and pianists, who performed to great acclaim at international competitions, including the violinist David Oistrakh and the pianists Sviatoslav Richter and Emil Gilels, who were among the first to be allowed to tour abroad. Ballet was largely stagnant in the realm of choreography, the clock having stopped for most purposes in 1917. But performance technique was among the highest in the world. Also, the ballet was backed by more funds and a better system of schools and selection than in any other country. Nonetheless, the rigid traditionalism of Russian ballet (along with the many other restrictions in Soviet life), combined with new possibilities for touring abroad, led some of its best dancers to defect to the West, notably Rudolf Nureyev in 1961 and Mikhail Baryshnikov in 1974. The Moscow Art Theater remained one of the most remarkable centers of acting anywhere, although the long monopoly that its approach to theater had in the Soviet Union effectively proscribed more

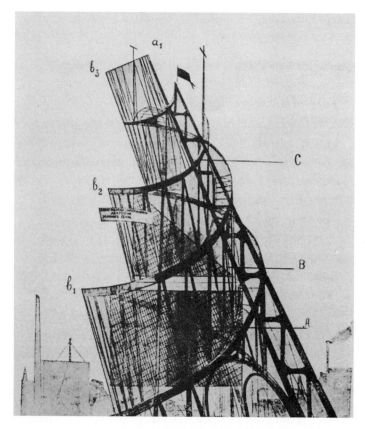

Vladimir Tatlin's design for a Monument to the Third International, 1919–20. Although never built, Tatlin's utopian design for a headquarters for the Communist International was a massive symbol of revolutionary modernism. Envisioned as the tallest manmade structure in the world, its spiral iron structure was to contain interior halls made of glass, each above the other and rotating in harmony with nature: a bottom cube revolving on its axis once a year, a cone making a full circle monthly, and a top cylinder making one revolution each day. The building was to provide meeting space, offices, and a communications center. (Punin, *Pamiatnik III Internatsionala*).

innovative approaches to performance. Film was perhaps the most popular of the arts. While selected imports were a continual presence in Soviet cinemas, Soviet filmmaking had its own rich history—and its own trajectory of experimentalism, socialist realism, and traditionalist realism. Sergei Eisenstein, 1898–1948, was perhaps the most artistically brilliant Soviet filmmaker of the revolutionary and Stalinist epochs (though there were others, such as Alexander Dovzhenko), and the one facing the most difficult political relations with Stalin's regime. Audiences, however, were more interested in light and entertaining films, notwithstanding their heavy-handed ideology, such as Grigorii Alexandrov's cheery musical comedy films of the 1930s.

Moscow State University. Built after the war on the Lenin hills, the university was one of a series of towers in Moscow built in a style sometimes called "Stalinist gothic." Classical columns, large exterior ornaments, grand entryways, and marble interiors decorated with chandeliers in the main public spaces were characteristic of these buildings, which were meant to convey the grandeur and power of socialism. *(World Wide Photos)*

With the coming of the "thaw" after Stalin's death, and the development of a dissident movement, alternative artistic approaches again surfaced, sometimes tolerated but often criticized and forbidden public display—as in 1962, when Khrushchev visited an exhibit of modern art in Moscow only to mock it with crude humor, and especially in 1974 when bulldozers were sent to destroy an informal exhibit in a park outside Moscow. Unofficial art differed from the dictates of party ideology in almost every respect: it might be melancholy and even pessimistic in mood (with dark colors predominant), hint at religious belief or suggest existential doubt, favor abstraction or symbolism over representational realism, or be subtly ironic. In film too, a new period of innovation in form and a focus on less ideological themes began in the more liberal 1960s, as can be seen in the work of Andrei Tarkovsky— though audiences were still more likely to prefer light comedies or heroic adventure films. In theater, as well, innovation and iconoclasm thrived, though less on the main official stages than in smaller theaters such as Iurii Liubimov's Taganka in Moscow and the many informal "studio-theaters." Although effectively marginalized, nonconformist artistic currents were

among the many signs of growing alienation, especially among the educated, from official ideology.

## Religion

Religion in the Soviet Union constituted an anomaly, a threat, and a challenge
from the Communist point of view. Bolshevik efforts to "modernize" Russia
necessarily meant, as they saw it, replacing the superstition, mysticism, and
fictions of religion with a scientific worldview. Initially, this campaign was
directed mainly against the Orthodox Church as an institution. Immediately
after coming to power, the Bolsheviks disestablished the Orthodox Church,
which had been closely linked to the imperial regime, ended financial support
for the Church, confiscated vast amounts of property, and transferred control
of thousands of parish schools to the state. During the Civil War, revolutionaries frequently arrested and sometimes summarily executed priests and monks,
confiscated or destroyed sacramental objects, and closed many churches and
monasteries. Once victorious in the Civil War, the government moved even
more vigorously, if less violently, against the Church. The government ordered
the seizure of all Church valuables, temporarily imprisoned Patriarch Tikhon
(elected by a Church council in 1918 to resume the patriarchal form of ecclesiastical organization that had been discontinued by Peter the Great), tried to
break up the Church from within by assisting a modernist "Renovationist"
or "Living Church" group within it, and began to assault popular religious
belief directly through a "militant atheist" movement. After Tikhon's death in
1925, the government prevented any new patriarch being elected and Church
leadership fell to provisional appointees.

Although atheism indeed grew in the Soviet Union, this antireligious
movement was far from successful. Attacks on the Church often inspired
resistance and solidarity with Church and clergy and local efforts to ensure
that religion thrived even.without state support. Also, the disestablishment of
the Orthodox Church enabled "sectarian" Christian faiths to grow as well as
other religions. More generally, in the turmoil and uncertainties of these revolutionary years, faith and spirituality flourished as a source of meaning and
hope. During the radical upheavals of the First Five-Year Plan and during the
bloody terror of the late 1930s, persecution of religion was particularly intense.
However, the assumption that severely restricting religious institutions and
promoting rationalist thought would lead religion to disappear proved vain.
According to an official report based on the unpublished census of 1936, 55
percent of Soviet citizens still identified themselves as religious—while many
others presumably concealed their belief.

That stubborn fact in conjunction with the general social stabilization
of the 1930s made Stalin and the Politburo assume a more tolerant attitude
toward religion. The war and the patriotic behavior of the Church in the war
added to its acceptance and standing. In 1943 the Church was permitted to
elect a patriarch, the statesmanlike Metropolitan Sergius obtaining that position. After his death in 1945, Sergius was succeeded by Alexis, who continued

The seventeenth-century Simeon Stolpnik church on Moscow's Kalinin Prospect in front of a Soviet housing project. Huge numbers of churches in Russia were shut down and often demolished. Some churches continued to function, but most of the church buildings that survived, such as this one, were put to secular uses as factories, warehouses, and museums or simply stood empty, their ritual objects removed and their walls whitewashed, but "protected by the state" as monuments of architecture. *(Sovfoio)*

as "Patriarch of Moscow and All Russia" for a quarter of a century. In 1971, following Alexis's death, Pimen was elected patriarch, followed in 1990 by Alexis II. The ecclesiastical authorities were also allowed to establish a few theological schools, required to prepare students for the priesthood, and to open a limited number of new churches. The activities of the League of the Militant Godless and antireligious propaganda in general were curtailed. In return the patriarchal Church declared complete loyalty to the regime, and supported, for example, its international peace campaigns and its attempts to influence the Balkan Orthodox. More unfortunately, the two cooperated in bringing the 2 or 3 million Uniates of former eastern Poland into Orthodoxy. The Church in the USSR, however, remained restricted to strictly religious, rather than more general social and educational, functions—even the constitution proclaimed merely the freedom of religious confession, as against the freedom of antireligious propaganda—and, while temporarily tolerated within limits, it remained a designated enemy of Marxist ideology and Communist society. In fact, Khrushchev especially, as well as his successors, increased the pressures against religion even when "liberalizing" other aspects of Soviet life. It should be added that other Soviet Christians, such as Baptists, and other religious groups, such as Jews and the numerous Muslims, shared their histories with the Orthodox. They, too, led a constricted and precarious existence within a fundamentally hostile system, profiting from relaxations when they occurred. Even before Gorbachev's policy of glasnost and the collapse of Communist rule enabled a new renaissance of religion in Russia, its revival in the growing unofficial space in everyday social and cultural life was another visible sign of the weakening hold of the Communist regime over people's lives. The 1970s and 1980s, in particular, saw a proliferation of religious prayer and study groups (Orthodox, Protestant, Jewish, and others), the rediscovery among young people of their family's religious traditions, and growing attendance at religious services. In this sense too, as Gorbachev worried aloud when he came to power in 1985, Communist rule in the Soviet Union was facing a "spiritual crisis."

# CHAPTER 42

# The Gorbachev Years, 1985–91, and the Collapse of the Soviet Union

We want a type of socialism that has been cleansed of the encrusted layers and perversions of past eras but retains everything that is best from the founders of socialist teaching....We see socialism as a system of high culture and morality...a society in which the life of working people is saturated with material and spiritual fulfillment, rejecting consumerism, lack of spirituality, and cultural primitiveness.

MIKHAIL, GORBACHEV, 1988

The most perilous moment for a bad government is when it seeks to mend its ways. Only consummate statecraft can enable a king to save his throne when, after a long spell of oppressive rule, he sets to improving the lot of his subjects.

ALEXIS DE TOCQUEVILLE

The river of time in its flow
Carries away all the works of human beings...

GAVRIIL DERZHAVIN

In the years leading to the collapse of the Soviet Union and Communist rule in 1991, no scholars predicted its imminent demise. Many Russians themselves in the 1980s were predicting that the Communist regime would last at least as long as the 300-year reign of the Romanov dynasty. As the preceding chapters have described, the system was pervaded by problems, both structural and in people's attitudes. But there was nothing inevitable about the outcome of this situation. As most Russians who lived through these years readily acknowledged, though variously with blame or appreciation, Mikhail Gorbachev was a primary cause of that historic collapse. To be sure, the Soviet leader was not in control of his country and its citizens, and, indeed, he had been repeatedly obtaining results opposite to those intended—after all, Nicholas II also made important contributions to the revolutions of 1917. And as many scholars remind us, it is dangerous to personalize major historical issues, and another Gorbachev or still other lines of development might have produced similar results. But as long as history is an account of what happened and is happening rather than of the logical alternatives, the period of glasnost and perestroika will remain linked to its extraordinary protagonist, a contradictory man of intelligence, optimism, insatiable energy, intensity, and self-confidence, but a man also noted for his prudence and even conservatism, his glibness, and his remarkable political agility and adroitness in the face of the unexpected and often unwanted results of his own reforms.

## Gorbachev and Reform

Exactly what Gorbachev and his original associates, such as Eduard Shevardnadze and Alexander Yakovlev, had in mind when they began reforming the Soviet Union may never become clear, even to them. Suppositions and explanations of their intent abound, but the overwhelming factors in what transpired appear to have been a sincere desire to address the Soviet Union's deepening problems, a persistent effort to balance transformation with traditional values and political stability, a gap between plans and real accomplishments, the dizzying power of contradictory forces unchained by even slight reform, and continual improvisation in the face of the unexpected. The unfolding events in the USSR and eastern Europe stunned everyone, especially those who had any regard for the communist system, and that includes by definition the entire Soviet leadership. There may well be, however, one quite major exception to this almost total disjunction between purpose and accomplishment. Gorbachev, Shevardnadze especially, and other prominent Soviet figures insisted that one of the pillars of their new thinking was the absolute realization of the inadmissibility of nuclear war in human affairs and, therefore, of the necessity for at least a minimum of international cooperation, in particular between the Soviet Union and the United States. With all qualifications, it can be argued that Soviet foreign policy came to reflect that realization. If so, the gain to the world was incalculable, although the realization itself is elementary and its roots even in the Soviet Union largely preceded Gorbachev. Otherwise, one hardly needs reminding that in his book *Perestroika*—published in English as well as in Russian in October 1987 and a good way to become acquainted with its author—and even later Gorbachev emphasized the supreme importance of Lenin and the Communist Party in the Soviet Union, rejected privatization and political pluralism in communist states, and praised Soviet solutions to social and nationality problems. And it should be remembered that the Warsaw Pact was renewed and extended for twenty years on April 26, 1985; it was abolished, following the complete collapse of communism in eastern Europe, on February 25, 1991. The river of time does carry away the works of human beings.

At the foundation of Gorbachev's reform lay the recognition that the Soviet Union was facing a crisis. Slowing rates of economic growth combined with growing disillusionment and pessimism. When Gorbachev was named general secretary, his mandate was to address this crisis, first by admitting it publicly. The government and the party spoke openly about economic problems: the slowing of economic growth, the negative effects on the standard of living, the dismal condition of agriculture, the poor quality of manufactured products, the failure to keep up with world developments in science and technology (including computing), and the huge proportion of the gross national product devoured by military needs (more than twice the percentage in the United States). Recognition of deepening "stagnation"—the term widely used to speak of the 1970s and early 1980s—was matched by recognition of cultural and ideological crisis. Gorbachev and other party leaders acknowledged the widespread withdrawal from public life, the spread of alcoholism and drug addiction, the growth of crime, "weakened respect for work," pessimism, and cynicism. In a word, Gorbachev pronounced, the Soviet Union was facing a "spiritual crisis" (*dukhovnyi krizis*) along with an economic one, and it needed structural and spiritual reconstruction (perestroika).

Gorbachev's actions—which had such profound consequences for history—were also shaped by a fairly well developed set of ideological beliefs, evident in his many speeches as he rose through the ranks as Komsomol activist, party chief in the Stavropol region near the Caucasus, young new recruit to the Politburo, and then general secretary. Most important, Gorbachev believed strongly in the ideals of Leninist socialism, so much so that he found it difficult to accept the widespread cynicism he found throughout much of Soviet life, including in the party, not to mention the very tangible decline of Soviet society. Often echoing Lenin's statements during the first Soviet years (the Lenin Gorbachev most admired), Gorbachev argued that the country could be revitalized through a combination of "democratization" and an improved vanguard. Democratization was key to revitalizing the economy and people's faith in the socialist system. Thus, Gorbachev constantly appealed to citizens to become more involved in public life and to take more initiative. At the same time, he also believed, following Lenin as well as a longer Russian political tradition, that strong central authority was essential in times of change. For both democracy and strong power to be effective, however, certain qualities were necessary. Strong power is of no use, he insisted, if leaders are not of the highest quality, are not a true vanguard. Thus, even before he came to power, he fought to improve the behavior of local leaders, to eradicate what he called bureaucratic boorishness, self-satisfaction, red-tapeism (*volokita*), inertia, careerism, and incompetence. In turn, for socialist democracy, in all of its potential dynamism, to work, ordinary people must also rid themselves of the sins of passivity, irresponsibility, indiscipline, drunkenness, acquisitiveness, materialism, and cultural vulgarity (*poshlost*).

For Gorbachev, these were practical ideas. If economic stagnation was to be overcome, citizens and leaders alike would have to play a more active, committed, and responsible role in the country's development. Democracy, Gorbachev liked to say, "must not be understood abstractly" but as "an instrument for the development of the economy" (1985). But there were also deeper moral notions at work in Gorbachev's thinking about democracy and reform. His language, as can be seen, was full of disgust for undisciplined and irresponsible behavior. Personally, we know, Gorbachev was exceptionally hard working and refused to drink hard liquor. More complexly, Gorbachev's moralism was ideological. When speaking of socialism he often spoke of its essential "humanism," its commitment to seeking the fullest development of the "human person" (*lichnost*), its defense and promotion of "universal human values." These were clichés in Soviet ideology, though the emphasis on universal as opposed to class values was not entirely orthodox. More to the point, every indication is that Gorbachev took these clichés quite seriously and sought to make them real.

The first two or three years of the Gorbachev regime, inaugurated on March 11, 1985, displayed a fairly "traditional" cast. The new party secretary, then the youngest man in the Politburo, had to concentrate on strengthening his position, and, indeed, over a period of time he effected a major turnover of ruling and high administrative personnel. Thus on July 1, 1985, Shevardnadze became a member of the Politburo, and on the following day he was appointed foreign minister, replacing Andrei Gromyko, who was moved to a more ceremonial high office. Other new men entered the Politburo, while Viktor Grishin, Gorbachev's original rival for the position of party secretary, retired. These reorganizations of leadership notwithstanding, Gorbachev continued in the coming years to face opposition in the Central Committee and the Politburo: from "puritans" such as Yegor Ligachev, whose interest in reform was limited to ending the corruption of the Brezhnev era; to "technocrats" like Prime Minister Nikolai Ryzhkov, who sought only more scientific expertise and rational procedures in Soviet administrative and economic life; to radicals like Boris Yeltsin, who were increasingly disillusioned with Gorbachev's hesitations (which were partly a function of a desire to avoid a split in the ruling party).

In fact, while Gorbachev's early talk about the need for reform was relatively bold, actual policy was cautious and relatively traditional. Some have suggested he was biding his time until his power base was strong enough. Others argue he was responding to his growing knowledge of the depth of the problems and the failure of his earliest measures. In any case, from March 1985 to the fall of 1986, his policies were quite similar to the proposals and exhortations of earlier Soviet reformers. The draft plan, as presented by Gorbachev in October 1985, called for doubling the national income in fifteen years, with special emphasis on the modernization of equipment and an increase in labor productivity. This was to be realized by an economic policy of "acceleration," which involved a major campaign against alcoholism, a struggle against absenteeism, increased pressure on managers to economize on materials and balance their books, and an anticorruption campaign. As the months passed, Gorbachev began to talk of more radical change. At the Twenty-seventh Party Congress in February 1986, he first used the phrase "radical reform," and in July he spoke of perestroika as a "real revolution." But this radicalism remained mainly rhetorical. The policies of glasnost, in these early months, were closely linked to economic acceleration. Allowing greater freedom of criticism in print and speech, though an important policy shift, was treated not as an end in itself but as a way to expose incompetent and corrupt managers or bureaucrats and to begin mobilizing society to participate in developing the economy. Similarly, in foreign policy, Gorbachev combined talk of improving relations with the Western powers, developing more respectful relations with other Communist countries, and acknowledging that the war in Afghanistan was a disaster (a "bleeding wound," he called it in 1986) with continued criticism of "U.S. imperialism."

Unfortunately, almost none of Gorbachev's initial effects made any difference. The economy would not respond to mere exhortations. Indeed, the government's own economic, especially financial, policies led to budget deficits and inflation and thus made matters worse. Even the anti-alcohol campaign proved to be a disaster, its only incontrovertible result a great increase in the illegal production of spirits, to the extent that sugar disappeared from stores in parts of the USSR. Before long under the new administration and its vacillating and confusing direction, the economy began to lose what cohesion it had had under Brezhnev without gaining anything to replace it. The war in Afghanistan continued to take its toll. On April 28, 1986, a nuclear reactor exploded in Chernobyl; the resulting medical and environmental catastrophe threw a glaring light on multiple Soviet deficiencies, from those in engineering to those in the news media. Indeed, that tragic episode, treated at first in the firm tradition of Stalinist secrecy, eventually became both an opening into a more radical glasnost and a strong argument in its favor.

Leaders of the communist world in Moscow, 1986. From left: Kadar of Hungary, Ceausescu of Romania, Honecker of East Germany, Gorbachev of the Soviet Union, Chinh of Vietnam, Jaruzelski of Poland, Castro of Cuba, Zhivkov of Bulgaria, Husak of Czechoslovakia, Tsedenbal of Mongolia. (*World Wide Photos*)

In 1986 and 1987, Gorbachev's policies became more radical—though opposition to his reforms within the party leadership also began to grow as did pressures from Communists like Yeltsin who wanted reform to go faster and further. The meaning of glasnost expanded. In late 1986, Gorbachev made it clear that censorship would be relaxed and journals would be given much greater freedom to criticize and offer solutions to problems. Reform-minded editors were put at the helm of leading publications and journals began discussing political and social problems, past and present, as never before. Newly daring and previously banned works of literature and history were published. Movies with critical social perspectives were shown. Political prisoners were released—especially after the definition of anti-Soviet propaganda was greatly narrowed in a 1987 law—and dissident exiles like Andrei Sakharov (forced to live in isolation in the city of Gorky) were allowed to return home and be active in politics. Gorbachev and his allies also openly encouraged Soviet citizens to form voluntary civic associations, called "informals." In the economy, in 1987, directors of enterprises were given greater autonomy in setting prices, wages, and output targets, thus beginning a turn away from centralized planning. Laws on "individual labor activity" (1986) and cooperatives (1988) resulted in the emergence of the first private businesses since the 1920s, usually small service enterprises like cafes, but also distribution companies and even a few private banks. These new entrepreneurs, many of whom would make great fortunes after 1991, were mainly individuals who already had access to material and political resources, which meant primarily officials of the state and the party. "Joint-ventures" with foreign firms were also authorized. Gorbachev insisted that these changes were consistent with "the socialist choice" the Soviet Union had made and would adhere to, though this was to be a middle ground between the failed system of planned Communist economics and the exploitative economics of capitalism. These measures also created opportunities for corrupt officials and organized crime to extort money from this emerging, but still fragile, private sector.

Political reform followed an even bolder course beginning with the dramatic Nineteenth Party Conference in June 1988. The entire meeting was televised—an unprecedented level of openness and publicity for the party. Speeches detailed the worsening economic conditions in the country, the problems in education and health care, the past lies about achievements, and some of the crimes of the past. Divisions in the party also became clear, as conservatives castigated the press for excessive criticism and radicals like Yeltsin attacked the continuing privileges of the old party elite who, he said, were to blame for many of the country's problems. The most dramatic moment came when Gorbachev announced his plan to create a new national parliamentary body, the Congress of People's Deputies, to be chosen in part through multi-candidate elections, which would be the "supreme body of power." The old Supreme Soviet would be made into a smaller, full-time legislative body elected by the Congress. This was the beginning of a process, it seemed, of shifting power away from the often distrustful and divided party and toward a reformed state. This shift continued during the next couple of years, though not all of it was controlled. The elections to the new Congress in March 1989 saw unprecedented public mobilization and many official party candidates defeated, including by mavericks like Yeltsin. In 1990, to link his own power more to the reformed state than to the troublesome party, Gorbachev created the new post of president of the USSR, to which the Congress of People's Deputies elected him in March 1990. At the same time, Article 6 of the Constitution, which made the Communist Party the "leading and guiding force" through-out Soviet society and all Soviet organizations, was repealed at Gorbachev's suggestion, but also in response to great public pressure. Gorbachev was even, by 1989, distancing himself from one of the hallmarks of Leninist ideology: the Communist monopoly on truth. "We no longer think that we are the best and that we are always right, and that those who disagree with us are our enemies."

This was not entirely a revolution from above nor an entirely coherent one. Gorbachev continually hesitated before more radical steps. Trying to maintain a centrist position, he vacillated between allying himself with party radicals and conservatives, eventually alienating both. In any case, the party was less and less in control of society. Reform was spinning out of Gorbachev's con-trol, often forcing him to leap forward to keep up with the changes or lead-ing him onto the defensive. The party's humiliation in the 1989 elections was a dramatic sign of this loss of control. The rise of nationalist and secession-ist movements in the various republics, to be discussed later, was another. Finally, the public sphere of the press and even the streets became an arena

"We shall look at things realistically" declares this typical glasnost poster from 1987, which shows rose-colored glasses having been removed.  (*Sovetskii khudozhnik*)

of civic political activity such as had not been seen in Russia since the first years after the 1917 Revolution. Intellectuals, journalists, and literary writers were publishing increasingly bold works in which no issue or argument seemed taboo. Mass demonstrations in favor of greater reform were organized, especially in Moscow, often by "informal" democratic organizations such as the Democratic Union, the Moscow Popular Front, Memorial (formed to document past Communist crimes), and Democratic Russia (a national electoral bloc that would win many seats in the new parliament), but also by neocommunist organizations such as the Russian United Workers' Front. In 1989, thousands of coal miners struck, first demanding improved living conditions but soon escalating their demands to include a new constitution and a ban on Communist Party activity in the workplace. Most dangerously, these years saw the revival of numerous nationalisms, suppressed but still alive in the Marxist superstate. The new time of troubles, like the original one at the end of the sixteenth century and the beginning of the seventeenth, was to have its national phase.

## The Rise of Nationalisms and the Breakup of the Soviet Union

Because of the diversity, richness, and specificity of national and ethnic experiences and actions in the last years of the Soviet Union, it is impossible to present in a brief general account an adequate summary of the rise of nationalism and national movements. It is generally true, though, that these histories began before Gorbachev's rule, that nationalist feeling and organization intensified as centralized control was lessened by Gorbachev's reforms, and that these identities and movements contributed to the collapse of the USSR (along with, and partly stimulated by, the "loss" of eastern Europe in 1989, which was also due to national resentment of Soviet rule). It is important to recall here that Soviet nationality policies themselves contributed to the rise of nationalism, or rather nationalisms, in the Soviet Union, not only as a response and protest to Moscow's rule but also as a consequence of the official ideal that the USSR was a multinational state and of its consequent policies to encourage national cultures and identities. Economic development, urbanization, and education also contributed to the rise of national and ethnic leaders. As long as the economy was strong, national elites found good reason to feel loyal to the Soviet Union. The economic crisis made continued alliance seem less and less essential.

Once Gorbachev loosened the bonds on public expression, it became clear that Soviet policies had not eradicated national identities and aspirations. At the same time, demands for greater autonomy were also often about local power and independence from the stifling Soviet state. Nationalism was not simply a revival of the past, a return of the repressed. For many Soviet citizens, alienated from the Soviet system and even from Gorbachev's idealistic promises to make Soviet socialism work, nationalism offered an alternative faith, and an alternative path to prosperity and freedom. Four types of national or ethnic upheaval arose in these last years of the Soviet Union: resistance by self-conscious national groups such as Lithuanians, Ukrainians, or Georgians to continued rule by the Soviet Russian imperial center; protests by ethnic minorities against the dominant nationalities in the union republics, as in the case of Armenians living in the Nagorno-Karabakh region of Azerbaijan; the rise of Russian nationalism or at least of a movement favoring Russian secession from the USSR; and the problem of diasporas living outside their ethnic homelands or lacking a territory of their own, including large numbers of Russians living outside the Russian republic who were facing national movements that excluded them.

The three Baltic republics—Estonia, Latvia, and Lithuania—led the way. Independent states between the two world wars (and in the case of Lithuania, of course, with a long and rich historical past as a nation-state), they had been forced to join the Soviet Union only at the start of the Second World War. Greater freedom of expression under glasnost allowed memories of independence and resentment of Soviet domination to come to the surface. Demands for independence became more and more frequent. It was in Estonia that the first large-scale noncommunist political coalition, the People's Front, received recognition, in June 1988, and it was Estonia that proclaimed on November 17, 1988, the right to reject Soviet laws when they infringed on its autonomy. On January 18, 1989, Estonian became the official language of the republic; legislation was enacted in an even more rigorous form a week later for the Lithuanian language in Lithuania, and still later, after mass demonstrations, for the Latvian language in Latvia. In May 1989, the Lithuanian legislature adopted a resolution seeking independence. In August 1989, on the fiftieth anniversary of the Nazi-Soviet Pact that ended the independence of the Baltic states, a million Estonians, Latvians, and Lithuanians created a human chain stretching across the three republics. By the end of that year, the governments of the Baltic republics had all declared Soviet occupation and annexation of their countries to have been illegal. In early December 1989, Lithuania became the first republic to abolish the Communist Party's guaranteed monopoly of power, while later that month the Communist Party in Lithuania voted to break away from Moscow, thus becoming the first local and independent Communist Party in the USSR, and to endorse political separation. On March 11, 1990, Lithuania, led by its president, Vytautas Landsbergis, proclaimed full independence. Events in Estonia and Latvia followed a similar course. It is worth noting that whereas Lithuanians constituted at least three-quarters of the total population of their republic, Latvians and Estonians composed only a little more than half of theirs, and that all three new states tended toward rather exclusive policies that mandated a single official language and, for citizenship, a residential or familial connection with the pre-Soviet period to eliminate Russian newcomers. Yet in spite of the resulting built-in opposition, which claimed discrimination, in February 1991, 91 percent of the voters in Lithuania approved independence; in March, referendums in Estonia and Latvia gave independence a three to one majority—clearly, not only the Balts, but also many Russians and people of still other ethnic backgrounds wanted above all to escape the Soviet system.

Gorbachev drastically underestimated the power of nationalism in the Baltic area, as well as elsewhere, and at first tried to ignore or dismiss the demands for recognition and independence. Once the crisis became obvious, he attempted persuasion, political maneuvering with the many elements involved, including different kinds of communists, and coercion, although never to the extent of mass military repression. Thus on January 11, 1990, he went to Vilnius, the capital of Lithuania, hoping to convince both leaders and milling crowds to check the nationalist course of development, but his trip was in vain. More successful was the oil blockade, a great reduction in the supply of oil to Lithuania, which began in mid-April 1990 and forced the republic to suspend, although not repeal, its declaration of independence on May 16. More violent coercion consisted of such incidents as army intervention in Vilnius, resulting in the death of fourteen people, and the assault by Black Berets on a Latvian government ministry building in Riga, both in January 1991—aborted coups d'état in the opinion of some—as well as repeated attacks on border posts and customs personnel of the nationalist republics, the signs of their new independence. Gorbachev emphasized that he objected to the aggressiveness and impatience of the movement in the Baltic republics, not to their goal of independence, which could be legitimately obtained in time, although personally he retained the hope that they would decide to remain in a reformed Soviet Union.

While nationalisms developed in a parallel and cooperative way among the Baltic states, they were on a collision course in Transcaucasia. Armenia, Georgia, and Azerbaijan have quite different cultures and histories. Armenia and Georgia represent two of the oldest cultures of the world. Azerbaijan, not a distinct nation-state until Soviet times, represented the Turkic element so prominent in the past and present life of the area. Most Georgians are Orthodox, most Armenians are Eastern Christians but not Orthodox, and most Azerbaijanis (especially the ethnic Azeris) are Turkic-speaking Muslims. Also, while the people of the Baltic republics could agree on 1940 as the dark year when Soviet power crushed their independence, the different peoples of the Caucasus each had particular experiences and memories of recent history.

The central event in the Georgian revolution was a Georgian "Bloody Sunday." On April 9, 1989, the particularly brutal suppression of a nationalist demonstration in Tbilisi led to the death of 20 participants and more than 200 left injured. Although authorities in Moscow blamed local officials and started an investigation, Communist control could not in effect be restored. The local party, which, as in Lithuania, tried to play an independent role, lost the crucial ensuing election, and Georgia emerged with a noncommunist government headed by Zviad Gamsakhurdia. On April 1, 1991, Georgians responded to the question of whether they agreed "that the state independence of Georgia should be restored on the basis of the independence act of May 26, 1918," with a turnout, according to official sources, of 90.53 percent of the 3.4 million Georgian voters and the affirmative reply of 98.93 percent of them. Whatever their exact political future, Georgians, like the Baltic peoples, definitely wanted to live outside the Soviet Union. In the summer of 1991, there even existed widespread interest in restoring the ancient Georgian monarchy, although in a modern constitutional form, in the person of Giorgi Bagration, a racecar driver then living in Spain who was recognized as heir to the throne and invited by President Gamsakhurdia and the parliament to visit Georgia. Yet in Georgia, too, nationalism brought no easy solutions. In particular, while asserting their own rights, Georgians did their best to limit and control those of the constituent minority groups in their state—the Adzharians, the Abkhazians, and perhaps especially the Ossetians—sometimes to the point of fighting on a considerable scale.

But the most extensive fighting in Transcaucasia, and indeed in the entire Soviet Union, took place between the Armenians and the Azerbaijanis and their respective republics. The hostility of the two peoples came to center on Nagorno-Karabakh, an Armenian-populated area within the republic of Azerbaijan. The Armenians claimed it for themselves on grounds of nationality and of alleged mistreatment of its inhabitants. The Azerbaijanis refused to give up what they considered part of their national homeland. Demonstrations and violence broke out on both sides, notably in Sumgait where anti-Armenian crowds rioted for two days. Azerbaijan blockaded railroads carrying vital supplies into Armenia and Armenia deported Azeris. Especially traumatic were assaults in Baku, the capital of Azerbaijan, on Armenians and some Russians in January 1990 which resulted in at least twenty-five deaths. On January 20, the Soviet army intervened against the Azerbaijani rioters, who were also seeking independence. The central government was blamed both for intervening and for intervening late and was accused by both sides of inflaming hostility among nationalities for its own purposes. The Armenian-Azerbaijani border was transformed into front lines, with the opponents remarkably well provided with weapons and matériel stolen or otherwise obtained from the Soviet army. Although active fighting gradually abated, the situation remained volatile. Masses of people migrated between the two republics and even to Moscow and other distant points. Some Armenians were brutally moved by the Soviet army into the Armenian republic from their native villages in Azerbaijan.

Slower to develop popular nationalist movements were the five "Muslim" republics of the USSR located in Central Asia: the Turkic Kazakh, Kirghiz, Turkmen, and Uzbek republics and the Iranian Tajik republic. Deeply affected by the political and nationalist turmoil, affirming in the train of other republics their "rights" and their "sovereignty," and in constant conflict with central authorities, their own minorities, and at times one another, they proved among the less self-assertive major components of the former Soviet Union. The party and the administration were relatively successful in maintaining their positions in Soviet Central Asia. The explanation for that success may well lie in the comparative underdevelopment of the area, with its extreme reliance on a single crop (cotton), its poverty, its population explosion, and especially its dependence on huge government subsidies vital to the economy and even to the existence of its peoples. Kazakhstan, by far the largest republic of the five, represents a special case: it is little more than half Kazakh, the southern half, while the north is predominantly Russian.

From the Russian point of view, the struggles for independence in the Baltic, the Caucasus, and Central Asia were less emotionally fraught—and of less economic and social consequence—than the struggles of Slavs to free themselves from Moscow's rule. This was especially the case with Ukraine, whose history was so intimately intertwined with Russia's history; indeed, as we know, Russian history can be said to have begun in what later became Ukraine. In July 1990, a newly elected parliament, which included many nationalistically minded Communists and noncommunist dissidents, notably the nationalist movement known as Rukh, proclaimed Ukraine's "state sovereignty," which gave precedence to Ukraine's own laws over Soviet laws on Ukrainian territory and declared that "the Ukrainian Soviet Socialist Republic is independent in determining any issue of its state affairs." In contrast to more exclusive Baltic nationalists, Ukrainian politicians appealed to all the inhabitants of the republic. As to its relation to Soviet and, later, Russian governments, Ukraine gave some indication of willingness to participate in certain kinds of associations but always with reservations and conflicting problems. The problems included Ukrainian sovereignty over the Crimea, the management and disposal of atomic weapons, and the division and control of the armed forces, in particular of the Black Sea fleet. The eastern and the smaller western parts of Ukraine are sharply different from each other. It was especially in the latter, Soviet only since 1939 or 1945, that the many-sided religious revival included the restoration, at times a militant restoration, of the formerly prohibited Uniate Church, a Catholic jurisdiction, while anticommunism and anti-Russian nationalism thrived. Belorussians, whose history and culture were closely connected to that of Ukraine and Russia, had a much less developed nationalist movement. In any case, the leaders of the republic tended to be more loyal to Moscow and more willing to compromise with Moscow's desires. Still, in July 1990, Belorussia too issued a resounding declaration of "sovereignty."

If the USSR began to collapse as minority national republics asserted their sovereignty, when the gigantic and central Russian Soviet Federated Socialist Republic did this in March 1990, it became all but inevitable that the USSR was doomed. Gorbachev and his government received no support from the Russian republic as they were trying to control the non-Russian nationalities of the Soviet Union. To the contrary, before long the leaders of the Russian government began to treat the "center"—Soviet authorities in Moscow—as standing in the way of Russia's progress, and insisted on Russian "autonomy" and even "sovereignty," supported other republics doing the same, and initiated a "war of laws," in which new Russian laws countermanded Soviet laws on Russian territory. To be sure, Russians enjoyed certain advantages within the Soviet Union, such as the privileged position of their language and a greater acceptance of their cultural and historical past. But they remained poor, even poorer than the inhabitants of a number of other republics, and, all in all, they bore their full share of the deprivation, suffering, and oppression characteristic of the Soviet system. They were even denied such "local" institutions, granted to other republics, as their own branch of the Communist Party and their own academy of sciences, apparently, at least in part, because of the fear that these organizations might become too powerful and compete with the central Soviet ones.

The Russian republic acquired a remarkable, idiosyncratic leader in the person of Boris Yeltsin, whom Gorbachev had brought to leadership positions in Moscow in 1985 from provincial Sverdlovsk (now Yekaterinburg), where Yeltsin had been party boss. Gorbachev saw in him a fellow reformer but soon found him to be a most difficult ally, bridling at authority and demanding a faster pace of change. Gorbachev would also find in Yeltsin a man completely unlike him in his extravagant manner (including heavy drinking) and populist leadership style (riding buses and subways as Moscow party chief, personally raiding stores in search of hidden goods, and forcing officials to face the public in open discussions of problems). In October 1987, Yeltsin delivered a harsh speech before the Central Committee criticizing the slow pace of reform, the obstructionism of the central party apparatus and especially the Politburo, and Gorbachev's complacent and hesitant leadership. He asked to resign from the Politburo. In turn, he was denounced by Gorbachev and the Politburo and dismissed as head of the Moscow party organization. This only fueled Yeltsin's ambitions and popularity. In 1989, he won a landslide victory to the new Congress of People's Deputies from the city of Moscow,

Patriarch Alexis II of the Russian Orthodox Church blessing Yeltsin, the first freely elected president of the Russian Soviet Federated Socialist Republic. (*World Wide Photos*)

the largest electoral district in the Soviet Union, though the party leaders had openly backed another candidate and regularly smeared Yeltsin in the press. In the Congress, the meetings of which were televised, he continued to speak out boldly against privilege and corruption and for a faster pace of economic and political reform. He began to focus his efforts on the emerging Russian rather than Soviet political arena, however. In March 1990, he won election to the newly created parliament of the Russian republic and was elected head of its Supreme Soviet. He then convinced the Russian parliament to hold a referendum that approved creating a new post of president directly elected by the citizens of the Russian republic, an election Yeltsin won on June 12, 1991, a stunning display of democratic procedure and popular support that neither Gorbachev nor any other leader in the central government could claim. Elections had already brought other liberals to office in the Russian republic, especially in its great cities, with Anatolii Sobchak becoming mayor of Leningrad and Gavriil Popov, of Moscow. It is worth noting that Yeltsin had resigned from the Communist Party on July 12, 1990, and Sobchak and Popov on the following day. Liberalism was combined with nationalism and a religious revival as historic towns, places, and streets regained their old names, the white-blue-red flag and double-headed eagle of the tsarist state were restored, and religious services, including public religious services, multiplied. The day Yeltsin was elected president, the Leningrad voters also decided that their city should again become St. Petersburg. At the same time, Russian leaders made it clear that their vision of Russian statehood was based not on ethnic Russian nationalism—though this was on the rise in the Russian population and associated with a number of right-wing nationalist groups—but on a concept of Russia as a multinational federation. Immense problems, of course, continued; indeed, the entire dazzling change acquired a certain operatic quality, while the basic processes of economic and social life were grinding down. The mere administration of the RSFSR became a near impossibility, with everyone from the Tatars on the Volga to the Yakuts in eastern Siberia and the nomadic tribes of the far north laying claim to their historic rights, their diamonds, or their reindeer. The excruciating interplay between Gorbachev and Yeltsin, with its repeated reversals of positions, ranging from close collaboration to determined attempts by each to drive the other out of politics, came to occupy center stage on the Soviet scene.

## Eastern Europe and the World

If we view the unraveling of the Soviet system in a broader context, we can see that it was in eastern Europe that this disintegration, especially subject nations pulling away from Moscow's control, began and moved most rapidly toward its climax. In retrospect, there appear to be two main explanations for the stunning events of the miraculous year of 1989: the enormous extent of the opposition—indeed, hatred—the peoples of the satellite states felt for their Communist system and regimes, and Gorbachev's decision against any Soviet army intervention in defense of his Communist allies. It was the extent to which communism was bankrupt and despised in eastern Europe that most outside observers failed to take into account. As to Gorbachev's decision, this was a matter of both political principle and reasoned pragmatism. The Soviet leader apparently initially naively believed that there should be perestroika in the satellite countries, as well as in the Soviet Union, and that restructuring would only strengthen the system. But once the system began unravelling, and at a terrifying speed, he concluded that nothing could be done to save the old order. As he thundered against Soviet hardliners who accused him of betrayal, only tanks could block change in eastern Europe, which would have violated Gorbachev's often stated opposition to foreign military intervention in the internal politics of sovereign nations; in any case, he understood that tanks could not be used forever.

Thus 1989 witnessed the collapse of communism in Poland, Czechoslovakia, Hungary, Romania, Bulgaria, and, of course, East Germany, which was to disappear entirely through absorption into the Federal Republic of Germany. Masses of refugees crossing newly opened frontiers, the once-formidable Berlin Wall acquiring souvenir status as it was disassembled piece by piece, the corpses of Ceausescu and his wife, executed immediately after the overturn in Romania, and so many other episodes and details will be enshrined in history books and human memory for ages to come. While each national case had its own peculiarities, such as the tremendous importance of West Germany for what happened in and to East Germany or the unique role of Solidarity and the Catholic Church in Poland, there were also common characteristics. Above all, Communist regimes proved unable to survive intellectual and political freedom—glasnost, if you will—and, especially, free elections, beginning with the election in Poland on June 4, 1989. Even in the controversial cases of Romania and Bulgaria—perhaps especially relevant for the Russian future— where much of the establishment survived the fall of communism, the issues were the continuation of privilege and the brakes that old personnel might put on the democratic development of these countries, not the fear of a return to the days of Ceausescu and Zhivkov.

Gorbachev reacted to the events rapidly and imaginatively. Instead of mounting any kind of rearguard action, especially on the central issue of the unification of Germany, Gorbachev fully accepted the unification, earning German gratitude—in particular, that of Chancellor Helmut Kohl—as well as advantageous financial provisions for the withdrawal and relocation at home of Soviet troops and some other German aid. Moreover, the solution of the German problem and the Soviet abandonment of troublesome eastern Europe meshed well with Gorbachev's policy of peace and international cooperation.

Gorbachev's foreign policy, crafted together with his foreign minister Eduard Shevardnadze, shifted in a more liberal direction after 1987. Doctrinally, he began to argue that Soviet world power in the future would be based not mainly on military might but on cooperating with other world powers in developing solutions to international problems and respecting national sovereignties. The ruling principles of his "new thinking" were multilateralism, cooperation, nonintervention, and, as he often repeated, a recognition of "common human values." In 1989, Soviet army troops finally left Afghanistan, although the Soviet Union continued to provide massive military aid to the government forces in the seemingly endless civil war. Extremely complex and long-drawn-out negotiations with the United States resulted, at the end of July 1991, in an agreement to reduce certain kinds of armaments. Commentators noted at the time that the new spirit of cooperation was even more significant than the particular provisions of the treaty. Although some disagreements and tensions remained, for example, in connection with the Japanese determination to regain some small islands in the Kurile chain seized by the Soviet Union toward the end of the Second World War or the American pressure to have the USSR dump Castro and Cuba altogether, Gorbachev and his country were rapidly becoming respected supporters of world order. They played that role successfully in 1990 in the crisis and war following the Iraqi occupation of Kuwait, although the Soviet Union did not intervene militarily, and in 1991 in the aftermath of that war when international attention shifted to the continuous Arab-Israeli conflict. It should be added that in October 1990, Gorbachev was awarded the Nobel Peace Prize. Gorbachev's foreign policy could thus be considered a catastrophe, a great success, or both, depending largely on the point of view. In any case, at this point, Gorbachev was certainly more popular outside Russia than within it.

## The Final Crisis

At home, the situation was becoming catastrophic. The optimism and confidence of the early Gorbachev years were gone. Gorbachev had hoped and believed that glasnost would unleash popular enthusiasm for his efforts at reform, which would, as he put it in 1987, "multiply the good and combat the bad" and help cure the "spiritual crisis" in the country. Instead, that crisis seemed only to deepen. The flood of open discussion about the evils of the past seemed to produce not new optimism about reform but derision for all the ideals of the socialist project. The fact that the present was filled with high idealism and greater opportunities to make one's voice heard but only decline in everyday material life seemed part of the same long and tragic story of Soviet history. In both the press and everyday conversation, glasnost produced not optimism and commitment to the good cause but growing anger about both past and present, cynicism (especially about the rhetoric and promises of leaders), and what observers in those years called a pervasive discourse of lament, disintegration, and "the dead end."

Russians had good reasons to despair. The economy kept deteriorating. By 1990, gross domestic product and industrial growth rates were declining while retail prices were on the rise. In 1991, industrial decline and inflation were beginning to spin out of control. Shortages of consumer goods were more severe than in recent memory, producing long lines at stores, and there was even fear of famine. In the spring of 1990, miners in the Ural region, Siberia, and Ukraine went on strike again, first over intolerable material conditions but soon denouncing Gorbachev and the Soviet government, while expressing support for Yeltsin and the new Russian government. Meanwhile crime, prostitution, and other social problems were on the rise. A growing budget deficit and intensive printing of new money (one of the few things not in short supply) only made matters worse. Many attempts to solve problems, such as the decree of January 23, 1991, withdrawing 50- and 100-ruble notes from circulation and compelling the exchange of these notes under highly restrictive conditions, turned into disasters. Very poorly managed, that decree failed to check inflation or limit crime, while it hit hard the average working citizens and pensioners. In fact, proliferating decrees and directives only led to utter confusion. With the new self-assertion of the union republics and of lesser jurisdictions, it was not at all clear who owned or managed what. The same piece of property or sphere of economic activity could be claimed by the central government, a union republic, a regional administration, or a municipality. Reforming measures by all kinds of authorities were at best partial, haphazard, and difficult, if not impossible, to implement. Major general economic reform, while repeatedly promised, kept being postponed.

Natural and human-made catastrophes together with their aftermaths, whether in the case of the earthquake in Armenia in December 1988, which killed some 25,000 people and left another half a million homeless, or in that of the train collision and gas explosion near Asha in the Urals in June 1989, served to underline the manifold deficiencies, including the incompetence, of the Soviet system. Ecological issues loomed ever larger as the nature and extent of the ecological damage in the country became better known. Perhaps even more damaging to the government and system were repeated discoveries of mass graves: some 102,000 bodies found near Minsk in Belorussia in October 1988; between 200,000 and 300,000 burials outside Kiev which a special commission determined in March 1989 to contain victims of Stalin, not of the Nazis; about 300,000 more bodies in mass graves near Cheliabinsk and Sverdlovsk in the Urals, uncovered on October 2, 1989; and still others. Glasnost not only provided information about all these matters and contributed to the rehabilitation of many Communists executed in the purges of the 1930s as well as of Russian cultural figures abroad, but also led to a great diversity of opinion and variety of criticism. Gorbachev and his policies were attacked from the right, from the left, and from every direction.

Meanwhile, Gorbachev's formal power was growing. That Gorbachev was leader of both the party and the state was nothing new for Soviet leaders; the novelty of the latest arrangement consisted in the fact that the state position could now be used against the party. Gorbachev had prepared his state base of power well, succeeding Gromyko to the title of president in October 1988, obtaining election to that office by the 2,250-member Congress of People's Deputies on April 25, 1989, and being elected by the Congress to the newly enhanced post of president of the USSR in 1990. As the sway of the Politburo and the party declined, close advisory bodies to the president, such as the eighteen-member Presidential Council, which lasted from March to December 1990, and then the eight-member Security Council of the USSR, which succeeded it, acquired greater significance. The latter was composed mainly of the more important ministers of state. Gorbachev was granted greater powers to appoint ministers, conduct international negotiations, and control executive organs. He was given special authority to deal with economic problems and strengthen "law and order" in the country, including by executive decree. In the summer of 1991, speculation was rife that Gorbachev might abandon the party altogether and stake everything on the state administration and reform. Actually, he turned in the opposite direction, winning once more sufficient party support and apparently determined to carry it with him on his way-ward way.

It is not easy to evaluate or even simply present Gorbachev's policy. Often it seems impossible to distinguish his own projects, plans, and aims from the political and other tactical concessions and compromises he had to make, and even from extraneous elements imposed on him by other political forces in the Soviet Union. The net result was a tortuous course most notable for its meandering between reform and restraint. To mention only some of his last turnings, in October 1990 Gorbachev endorsed the so-called Shatalin plan, associated with the economist Stanislav Shatalin and meant to establish within 500 days a market economy in the USSR. But soon, feeling pressure from con-servatives, Gorbachev retreated, moderating the plan by borrowing from less radical market-reform proposals, and soon gutting it of all its key measures, while relying ever more strongly on the old administrative system and his own powers to manage the economy. Gorbachev was also seen to be retreat-ing from radical reform and to be making common cause with party con-servatives. In December 1990, he purged from his government many liberals and centrists, placing conservatives in some of the most powerful government positions, and granted new powers to the police and the army acting as police. Many democrats became convinced that cooperation with Gorbachev was no longer possible. It was at just this time that Shevardnadze, one of Gorbachev's closest allies, resigned as foreign minister in protest and warning. Yet spring and summer brought another turning, with Gorbachev more enthusiastic than ever in the cause of economic and general reform, although still without specifics or a timetable. In July 1991, Gorbachev proposed that the Communist Party, which had already lost its legal claim to a monopoly on power, drop Marxism-Leninism as its official ideology and transform itself into a party committed to a market economy and multiparty politics. This revolutionary new party program was to be considered at the Twenty-ninth Party Congress scheduled for November.

It may be most appropriate to end this brief discussion of deepening cri-sis where it began, that is, with the economic crisis, and for that to turn to Gregory Grossman's compelling presentation of the nature and the problem of the Soviet economic collapse in his testimony to congressional committees on June 25, 1991.*

---

*Abridged statement of Gregory Grossman (Berkeley) submitted at the Joint Hearing of the Subcommittee on Europe and the Middle East of the Committee on Foreign Affairs of the U.S. House of Representatives and of the Joint Economic Committee of the U.S. Congress.

One can hardly recall an instance in modern history in which—major war or its effects apart—the economic condition of an important country plunged so deep so fast as has that of the Soviet Union in the last few years. Less than a decade ago, serious Western observers could still seriously consider whether the global economic competition would eventually be "won" by the East, with all that implied for the world's future. Today, equally serious people equally seriously advocate Marshall-like assistance from the West in the hundreds of billions of dollars lest the Soviet economy (and polity and society) fall even deeper into destitution and disorder, with all *that* would imply for the world's future.

Although the present economic condition is indeed catastrophic, it has not been quite as unexpected as one might have assumed from appearances alone. In fact, the underlying forces of rot and ruin have been at work for decades, albeit concealed by the secretiveness of the dictatorial regime and the silence of an intimidated population (but for a relatively few dissidents). Among such long-term, corrosive trends one might mention the huge diversion of national resources to military and imperial ends; heedlessly wasteful depletion of natural and human reserves for economic growth and progress, combined with lags in civilian technological advance and improvement in quality; inability to feed the population without massive imports; enormous physical degradation and contamination of the environment with major effects on human health; growing sclerosis of the centralized system of economic planning and governance, aggravated by rigid price-wage controls and monetary mismanagement; steady growth of a large underground economy intimately linked with widespread official corruption and (with time) major organized crime; deterioration of work incentives and work morale, not to say initiative, enterprise (except in the underground), and sense of responsibility. And consequent steady retardation of economic growth, and actual decline.

One could extend this dismal list of the underlying economic factors (not to mention the political, social, and ethnic ones) that have been propelling the Soviet economy for decades towards its historic moment of deep crisis. That moment arrived under Gorbachev, not because Gorbachev is the most skilled economic reformer the USSR could have sooner or later produced—very likely he is not—but because it is difficult to imagine another communist leader, and it would have to be one, who could have more quickly and thoroughly discredited the shams of the past.

This situation of economic, social, and political crisis and uncertainty was the setting for the final drama, which brought down the whole Soviet system. But it was the specific question of preserving the Soviet Union that provoked this last act. Following a referendum in March 1991 that showed majority support for keeping the Soviet Union together but on new terms in which the "sovereignty" of each republic is guaranteed—though Lithuania, Latvia, Estonia, Armenia, Georgia, and Moldavia refused to participate in the voting—Gorbachev set out to write a new Union Treaty. On July 11, the Congress of People's Deputies approved a plan to create a Union of Soviet Sovereign States in which a great deal of economic and administrative authority devolved to the constituent states. Communist conservatives were determined not to allow this weakening of the Soviet Union, though this was only the final straw in their growing dismay with Gorbachev's reforms. On August 19, one day before the treaty was to be signed, a State Committee for the State of Emergency (GKChP), composed of leading officials Gorbachev had himself appointed in trying to make peace with the conservatives, arrested Gorbachev at his vacation house (though they told the country he was ill and incapacitated and had voluntarily relinquished power to them), placed tanks and soldiers in the center of Moscow, and vowed to protect the Soviet Union against "political adventurers" who were destroying it. The coup collapsed within three days in the face of mass demonstrations in the streets, resistance by republic governments (including Yeltsin's daring speech from the top of a tank in front of the Moscow parliament building), the refusal of key military and police units to obey the orders of the coup leaders, and poor planning and organization.

In the wake of the coup, Gorbachev returned to his post, but little remained of his power. The dissolution of the USSR gathered great momentum. Lithuania, Latvia, and Estonia declared immediate independence, which received international and even Soviet recognition. Most other republics, including Ukraine, also proclaimed independence. Meanwhile, Yeltsin's Russian government proceeded to take over the offices of the union government and outlaw the Communist Party of the Soviet Union, seizing

A young Lithuanian woman sits on a toppled statue of Lenin in Lithuania following the failed Kremlin coup, August 1991.  (AFP/Getty Images)

its property. On December 9, the leaders of the Russian, Ukrainian, and Belorussian republics met to declare the USSR abolished and replaced by a loose association of states to be called the Commonwealth of Independent States. Within the next couple of weeks, the remaining republics declared their independence as well. On December 25, 1991, Gorbachev went on television to announce his resignation as president of a country that, in reality, no longer existed. A triumphant Boris Yeltsin stood out as the central figure in a new and highly unsettled situation.

## Concluding Remarks

The disappearance of the Soviet Union proved to be at least as unexpected and sudden as its appearance, and as controversial. Bitterly hated as well as enthusiastically admired during three-quarters of a century of its existence, the USSR seemed to receive a universal recognition of its might and its durability after the victory over Germany in the Second World War and its attaining the position of one of only two superpowers in the world. Worshipful communists aside, numerous observers interpreted Soviet history in terms of continuity and stabilization bringing it closer to Western nations whether after the inauguration of NEP, the cultural "great retreat" of the 1930s, the gigantic war itself and the victory over Germany and Japan, the death of Stalin, or the ascendancy of Khrushchev. Although none of these varied developments proved a decisive turning point, it was within that framework that many in the West welcomed perestroika and glasnost: The Soviet Union would join democratic states as a major partner, perhaps even with much to offer. Very few expected total unraveling and collapse.

There were plenty of signs that the Soviet system was failing, however. Gorbachev admitted as much himself when he spoke of a "spiritual crisis" in Soviet society. Widespread pessimism and cynicism, disillusionment with the promises of Marxist rhetoric, social problems such as alcoholism and crime, the widespread retreat into private life, and the rise of cultural values and tastes at odds with socialist norms, together with the stagnating economy, were among many signs that the Soviet Union was a mammoth power with clay feet. The same can be said for the illusion that "the blossoming of nations and nationalities" in the Soviet Union brought diverse peoples ever closer together as a "single family—the Soviet people." Gorbachev's reforms were premised on the optimistic faith that the Soviet people could be inspired again by the humanistic ideals of socialism and that the system itself needed only to be improved not scrapped. Or as Yeltsin argued after Gorbachev's fall, "He thought he could unite the impossible: communism with the market, ownership by the people with private ownership, a multiparty system with the Communist Party of the Soviet Union." One can admire Gorbachev for his idealism and recognize him as one in a long line of Communist visionaries. But his dream appears to have been an impossible one.

Economists had been warning that this system was flawed for a long time. As early as the first years of the Soviet regime, certain economists pointed to the basic flaws of the Soviet economic system, and that initial critique was continued by such specialists as János Kornai, who worked within the system in Hungary, and Gregory Grossman and Vladimir Treml, who studied the second, unofficial, Soviet economy from the vantage point of American universities. Indeed it became a commonplace to claim that whereas the Soviet Union did well in terms of a traditional industrialization based on coal and iron, it could not keep up with the West in cybernetics, computers, and in general the new communication technology. And modern technology made isolation always more difficult, and Soviet citizens better acquainted with the rest of the world. The arms race continued to cost the Soviet Union twice the percentage of its much smaller productive capacity than was the case for the United States. Grossman pointed out repeatedly that only the massive export

of oil and natural gas kept the Soviet economy for fifteen years, 1970–85, from sliding downhill rather than remaining merely in a kind of cul-de-sac.

The mistakes were many. Possibly the worst was the inability to see reality through the prism of ideology. Nationalism was misjudged until it destroyed the Soviet Union. Indeed Gorbachev apparently believed that he could go to Vilnius and persuade the Lithuanians not to secede. But the understanding of Russia itself was not much better, and Russian interests and Russian nationalism played a major role in the abolition of the USSR. As to Gorbachev's contribution, it was extremely important from any point of view, although it was not what Gorbachev had planned. It was most impressive for those who believe in the great power of totalitarianism and the inability of a fragmented society to challenge it successfully. If so, a totalitarian system can unravel only from the top down. In the Soviet Union it did. In any case, there glasnost and other measures meant to strengthen the system led to a complete collapse. To cite, as a counterpoint to Derzhavin's, Heraclites' even more famous statement: "τά πάνταρ ει" ("Everything flows").

# CHAPTER 43

# Politics and the Economy after Communism: Yeltsin, Putin, and Beyond

Our country has not been lucky....It was decided to carry out this Marxist experiment on us—fate pushed us in precisely this direction. Instead of some country in Africa, they began this experiment with us. In the end, we proved that there is no place for this idea. It has simply pushed us off the road that the world's civilized countries have taken.

BORIS YELTSIN, JUNE 1991

Revolution is usually followed by counter-revolution, reforms by counter-reforms, and then by the search for those guilty of revolutionary misdeeds and by punishment....Russia's historical experience is rich in such examples. But I think it is time to say firmly that this cycle has ended. There will be no revolution or counter-revolution. Firm and economically supported state stability is a good thing for Russia and its people and it is long overdue that we learn to live according to this normal human logic.

VLADIMIR PUTIN, MARCH 2001

Democracy is a historical term and at the same time completely supranational....But there is another thing: for many of our citizens, the very difficult political, and especially economic, processes of the 1990s were combined with the arrival of basic democratic institutions in our country, and this was for them a very difficult time. This left its mark on how this term is comprehended.

DMITRII MEDVEDEV, APRIL 2009

Russia's history after the collapse of the Soviet Union and communist rule has most often been viewed as an era of "transition." But toward what? Has the transition period ended, as some political leaders in Russia have recently argued? From the perspective of the United States and western Europe, the idea of transition usually has been assumed to mean market capitalism and liberal democracy, and many Russians have hoped for the same. The passage of time is still too brief to be able confidently to define the political, social, and cultural shape of Russia after communism. The pervasiveness of "posts" in speaking of Russia since 1991—postcommunist, postsocialist, post-Soviet, post-totalitarian—reminds us of the uncertainty of the present and the weight of the past. So do the often paradoxical definitions that scholars in both Russia and the West have offered to define recent history: "managed democracy," "liberal authoritarianism," "illiberal democracy," or "managed pluralism," in speaking of the hybrid political order, and "crony capitalism," "oligarchical corporatism," "industrial feudalism," "bureaucratic capitalism," or "state corporatist capitalism," in characterizing the emergent economic system. Beyond political and economic structures, many other questions have remained unsettled and often preoccupying in these years, none of them new in Russian history: the meaning of Russia as a nation (the "Russian idea," which was explicitly declared by the state as a social project), the place of national minorities in Russia's multinational state, Russia's political but also cultural relation to the West, and the moral values that should guide everyday public and private life. As will be seen, Russians themselves have been divided and uncertain about where they are as a country and often even where they want to go, though most have spoken of a desire for Russia to become a "normal" society, though even that category has meant different things to different people. At the center of this history of change and uncertainty have stood Russia's first two elected presidents, Boris Yeltsin (1991–99) and Vladimir Putin (2000–2008, appointed prime minister in 2008). Though these two former communists both valued state power and individual leaders as makers of history, neither was ever completely in control of the situation around them—they experienced daily what Karl Marx long ago observed: "Men make their own history, but they do not make it just as they please, under conditions of their own choosing." This may partly explain the deep contradictions in both politics and economics in these years.

## Yeltsin's Presidency

Boris Nikolaevich Yeltsin (1931–2007), a construction engineer by profession and a party administrator by occupation, rose by dint of hard and diligent work to the top ranks of the party. Like Gorbachev, he evidently believed in the system and was skilled at making it work. But then, he fell out with both Gorbachev and the party over the slowness of reform. Yeltsin's career, as well as his pronouncements and his writings (especially the two autobiographical books he produced with his friend the young journalist Valentin Yumashev), depict an extremely high-strung individual, a courageous fighter, and a very poor loser, on occasion volatile and unpredictable. Those who have worked with Yeltsin have described him as energetic, impulsive, temperamental, easy

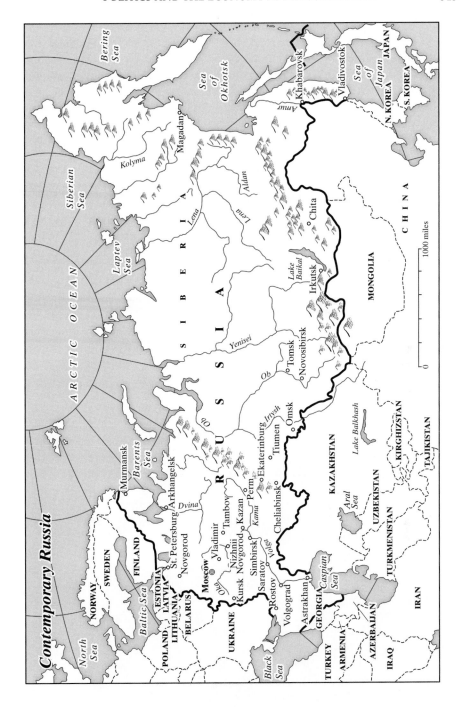

Contemporary Russia

to offend, a risk-taker, relatively uncorrupt, and always preferring to be in charge—he was long a local party "boss," whether in Sverdlovsk from the mid-1970s or in Moscow in the late 1980s. Frequent and at times very serious illnesses and heavy drinking further complicate evaluations of his actions and aims. Still, it is worth remembering that Yeltsin surged past Gorbachev as a radical, i.e., favoring the breakup of the Soviet Union and a major reform of Russia. Even more a Soviet and a party product than Gorbachev, for he came from a still poorer, indeed semi-starving, background, and had no cultural baggage except that provided by the Soviet system, Yeltsin broke with that system more sharply and decisively. No adjusted Leninism or nostalgia for him. On the other hand, Yeltsin's ideological reorientation did not change his career-long political manner of an authoritarian communist boss. Notably, as one studies his battle with his legislatures, one has to recognize that time and again both sides acted illegally. Timothy Colton, a political scientist who has written the best biography of Yeltsin, described him as a "paradoxical hero": extravagant and inconsistent, both too daring and too cautious, and acting out of intuition more than a master vision or plan. But the bottom line in Colton's evaluation focuses on Yeltsin's historic role: "For what he wrought, and for pulling it off in the main by ballots rather than bullets, he belongs with the instigators of the global trend away from authoritarianism and statism and toward democratic politics and market-based economics. As a democratizer, he is in the company of Nelson Mandela, Lech Watesa, Mikhail Gorbachev,

Russian President Boris Yeltsin climbs on a tank in August 1991 to call on the army and citizens to defy the coup.  (*Associated Press*)

and Václav Havel." It is telling that among Russian leaders of the past, Peter the Great had long been his favorite.

Yeltsin came to power with a program for changing Russia in which negative goals were much clearer than positive aims. Indeed, he was not an ideological militant, but a disillusioned communist. By his own account, he was moved above all by communism's failure. By the end of the 1980s he concluded, as so many out of power already had, that the unitary rule of the Communist Party and state control of the economy did not work. It was, therefore, a practical necessity to introduce a market economy, multiparty democracy, and the freedoms of press and speech that these required. He wished to see Russia become a "normal" and "civilized" nation, respected in the world, and integrated into the global capitalist economy. These new convictions made him oppose Gorbachev's efforts as too hesitant. Indeed, he became intensely impatient for change and willing to personally challenge the establishment. He was convinced, especially after his election as president of the Russian republic in a contested election on June 12, 1991 (defeating Gorbachev's preferred candidate), that he embodied popular opinion. His heroic defiance of the August 1991 coup, standing on a tank in front of the Russian parliament, was a symbolic moment cementing his popularity as a figure leading Russians in their effort to break with the bankrupt Soviet system.

Yeltsin's years in power, from 1991 to the final day of 1999, can be divided into several key periods: August 1991 to October 1993 (sometimes referred to as the "first Russian republic"), which began with radical reform from above and ended with growing polarization and open conflict; October 1993 to August 1998, a period marked by Yeltsin's growing power but also by deepening problems, even crisis, in the course of reform; and August 1998 to December 1999, which saw retreat from reform and growing emphasis on social stability and Yeltsin's own personal power and security. His own administrative style complicated all this. Yeltsin put economic change at the top of his agenda, but since he had little understanding of economics, he repeatedly put his confidence in such economic reformers as Anatolii Chubais, Yegor Gaidar, or Sergei Kiriyenko. Only this confidence did not last long. The enormous difficulties of the reform process and the opposition of the increasingly powerful interests that did not want economic reform, or at least that particular kind of economic reform, made the president retreat repeatedly and try something else. In this tortuous process, Yeltsin, like Gorbachev before him, was vilified from all sides. Once the most acclaimed politician in Russia, Yeltsin's support in opinion polls would drop to as low as 2 or even 1 percent. Yet Yeltsin refused to die either physically, in spite of a very dangerous bypass operation and constant illness, or even politically, but actively reemerged, greatly assisted by the extremely strong position of the president in the Russian constitution, often to fire leading figures in the government and change its course somewhat. The Russian president's ability to survive and even to remain, at least in a sense, on top of Russian politics, continuously baffled many observers, and it even led some of them to despair. Survivability, however, exacted a heavy price. Most commentators came to interpret Yeltsin's behavior simply in terms of his determination to hold on to his position rather than as a pursuit of any economic or political principles.

The year 1992 began with a radical economic program of "shock therapy," developed by Gaidar, Chubais, and other young Russian economists brought into the government, and influenced by Western economic advisors. Shock therapy was intended to "cure" the Russian economy of its attachments to central state planning and Russian citizens of their passivity as economic individuals and to create the foundation of a self-sustaining market system by quickly ending price controls, cutting subsidies to industry and agriculture (which would also help balance the budget), and privatizing industry, finance, commerce, agriculture, and real estate. It has been argued that like Stalin's economic revolution from above, shock therapy was as much a political and cultural as an economic program—as much, or more, about destroying the communist economy as about building the foundations for an effective capitalist one. In any case, Yeltsin was attracted to this breakthrough strategy and to promises of rapid success. He repeatedly assured the population—evidently sincerely—that the pain from shock therapy would last no more than six months to a year. The chief economist of the World Bank would later observe that Yeltsin's reforms were inspired by a nearly mystical faith in the market, which underplayed the role of the state in economic transition and ignored the need first to create institutional frameworks for effective markets.

In practice, the course of reform was uneven, protracted, and created much suffering—though some economists argued that it was the incompleteness of reform that was the main source of problems, while others proposed a still more gradual course to allow social institutions and attitudes to adapt. In any case, faced with opposition in parliament by communists and nationalists (though Yeltsin sometimes got around them by ruling by decree), the powerful interests of vested elites (especially industrial managers and officials), and public discontent and even unrest in the face of the suffering caused by the reforms and the still declining economy, Yeltsin often modified the radical proposals for reform he was given. The pace of change was slowed, plans to cut subsidies to some industries were lessened or scrapped, and most agricultural property remained nationalized. Still, economic reform was dramatic. Price controls were lifted on almost all goods as were many subsidies for industry. Most important, privatization moved forward rapidly. Starting in 1992, state firms were turned into joint-stock companies and citizens were given vouchers to help buy shares, though it was mainly insider managers and workers of firms who purchased these shares. In practice, directors continued to control most enterprises, ownership began to accumulate in a smaller number of hands as shares were re-sold, and organized criminal "mafias" gained growing influence in the economy. A second round of privatization, which started in July 1994, has been described by political scientist George Breslauer as "one of the largest and most blatant cases of plutocratic favoritism imaginable." Huge industries were sold by the government to influential wealthy individuals at a fraction of their value—most often through "loans" by banks and individuals to the government, which were not paid back. Again, the logic was more political than economic: to speed up the transition to capitalism and create a potentially loyal and supportive class of wealthy property owners.

The results of these reforms were contradictory. On the one hand, private enterprise spread rapidly in Russia, ranging from the activities of leading international companies to those of the uncounted and often miserably poor local entrepreneurs. Commercial banks and stock exchanges were established and foreign investment grew. Gradually, Moscow and to a lesser extent St. Petersburg and other cities acquired a great variety of consumer goods of every kind, mostly imported, impossible even to imagine in Soviet times. A new class of prosperous Russians, mocked for their crass materialism as "new Russians," appeared. Because Russians now faced no restrictions on travel abroad, tourism grew, as did new colonies of rich Russians abroad. At the same time, however, terrible inflation in the first years of reform (at least 300 percent in the month of January 1992 alone, though declining to 800 percent annually in 1993 and then to only 22 percent in 1996) quickly wiped out the savings of millions, devalued salaries, and made the pensions of the elderly worthless. GDP dropped a staggering 43 percent from 1991 to the end of 1997 (when the economy finally began again to grow). Investment fell 92 percent between 1989 and 1997. Agriculture was in shambles, with the old structure in disarray and no effective substitute in place. As Russian manufacturing declined, imports grew, though the majority of the population could not afford them. In fact, in cities like Moscow, whole streets were lined with people selling off personal goods. Homelessness and unemployment rose.

Citizens, with good reason, complained that reform was all shock and no therapy. Scholars continue to debate how to interpret these changes. Many critics, both in Russia and internationally, argued that gradual reform was not only possible but would have been less disruptive. Some describe Yeltsin's radical reforms as equivalent in brutality and damage to Stalin's revolution from above, though encouraged by the United States and global capitalist institutions like the International Monetary Fund (IMF): a "market Bolshevism" in tune with that older "self-confident, almost vanguard mentality of a self-appointed elite that sees itself entitled to impose 'progress' and 'development'...on the 'backward' majority," according to political scientists Peter Reddaway and Dmitri Glinski. The result was ultimately a reduction of both democracy and modernization—even an unnecessary "tragedy." By contrast, other scholars blame the disruptions and chaos on the difficult circumstances under which the reforms were enacted, not least being an economy already in rapid decline, and see these actions as a "de-monopolizing revolution" (according to Timothy Colton) that aligned Russia with the rest of the world and created the foundations for the almost miraculous levels of economic growth seen in the 2000s, the first signs of which were already evident by 1997. The same arguments can be seen in the Russian population, though Yeltsin's very low approval ratings by the late 1990s, even as the economy was improving, indicate that the critical view was predominant. Especially in the early 1990s, discontented citizens took to the streets. The Russian capital and other cities saw mass anti-government demonstrations, some of them leading to violent clashes with police. These marches and rallies were usually organized by the new Communist Party of the Russian Federation, various neo-communist groups such as Working Russia, and nationalist organizations; cooperation between communists and nationalists, as in the National Salvation Front organized in 1992, was derisively called the "Red-Brown" alliance. Strikes became more frequent. Indeed, it was common in 1992 and the years following to hear Russians talk of impending catastrophe, an anti-reform coup d'état, and possibly civil war.

The government itself seemed to become a victim of its own policies. The declining economy hurt tax revenues; in any case, the disorder in the country meant that taxes were often left uncollected or deliberately unpaid. The government kept borrowing money to stay afloat and sought large foreign loans. Short of funds, the government fell months behind in paying wages and salaries, and this lack of payments and lack of money spread throughout the economy. Pensioners were among the obvious sufferers. The situation was made worse by the fact that the Soviet Union had never had a strong social security system, especially if we exclude the social services of the very enterprises that were collapsing. Because of a drastic shortage of funds, such state institutions as the prison system and the armed forces themselves reached a desperate state. Prisoners' conditions, political persecution and punishment aside, declined compared to the Soviet period. Soldiers and officers were "advised" by their superiors to fish, hunt, farm, and gather mushrooms in order to survive until the federal government accumulated enough cash to pay military wage arrears. At times uniformed servicemen begged in the streets. As usual, the situation was more complicated than a very brief summary can indicate. Thus the penury of the army resulted partly because the high command and certain other elements were blocking its effective reduction in size. Similarly other, and sometimes the same, interests kept hanging on to the heavy and largely obsolete defense industry. And it proved very difficult to close mines, even when they operated at a loss or became superfluous. Entrenched administrators on top had a common cause with workers who were losing their jobs, often with nothing to replace them. Yet with all the variations and qualifications, the financial catastrophe loomed ever larger.

The central Russian government found it very difficult or impossible to control and sometimes simply to influence the component parts of the huge Russian state even after the fourteen non-Russian republics had separated themselves. Eventually eighty-nine distinct autonomous units, these component parts claimed often far-reaching rights and privileges, stopping in the case of Tatarstan just short of full sovereignty, although so far only Chechnya has fought a major war for independence. As regional interests and electoral democracy gained ground, local officials had all the less reason to obey Moscow. Most of the directives from the center were simply ignored. Corruption and crime grew rapidly. Exploiting privatization or exporting oil, gas, metals, and other valuable materials abroad, often with the aid of special permissions or even illegally, as well as profiting in other ways from the unhinged economy, some people quickly became enormously rich. Often compared to the robber barons of the early stage of capitalism in other countries, the Russian barons unfortunately proved to be different in that they took their enormous fortunes abroad rather than use them to develop the economy of their native land. In fact, very much more capital left Russia than came in the form of loans, aid, and investments put together.

Political life in these first years of Yeltsin's leadership (1991–96) was also increasingly marked by crisis. Indeed, economic problems greatly exacerbated Yeltsin's efforts to create a working democratic political order, while political conflict often made effective economic reform difficult. The Russian Congress of People's Deputies and its Supreme Soviet, the legislature, still had a majority communist presence and its members, even many noncommunists, were increasingly opposed to Yeltsin's radical reforms of the economy, troubled by the deepening social disorder, and offended by Yeltsin's authoritarian style of rule. They were also fully aware of public suffering and discontent. The legislators, therefore, had some reason to believe that in a showdown with Yeltsin they would be supported by the army and the people. A very mixed group or, perhaps better, combination of groups, their leaders included the vice president, Alexander Rutskoi, whom Yeltsin had hastily appointed to that position probably because of his military record and impressive appearance, and the leader of the legislature Ruslan Khasbulatov. By the end of 1992, under pressure, Yeltsin had to let Gaidar go, and the more generally acceptable Viktor Chernomyrdin became prime minister. The Congress succeeded in limiting Yeltsin's power to rule by decree and passed a number of laws limiting the president's power, though legislators failed in their efforts to impeach him or to limit drastically his powers by law, although on one occasion by a very narrow margin. All sides recognized that the legislature was determined to shift the balance of power away from the president and was making progress. Yeltsin responded by holding a popular referendum in April 1993—though he had to threaten the legislature to approve this—on support for his authority and a number of other key issues (although not on that of private property). The results were gratifying for Yeltsin: 59 percent affirming their "trust" in the president, 53 percent supporting the social and economic policies of the government, 49.5 percent favoring an early election for president, but 67.2 percent favoring an early election for parliament.

Yeltsin—convinced of the need for strong central authority and of his own personal role as guarantor of Russia's progress away from communism and satisfied that the 1993 referendum had given him a new popular mandate—was determined to increase his power and freedom to act at the expense of the legislature. His advisors drafted a constitution that enhanced presidential power over the courts, the bureaucracy, and the legislature. The legislature, meanwhile, drafted its own constitution limiting the power of the president. Yeltsin decided to rid himself of this obstacle. On September 21, he dissolved the Congress of People's Deputies and announced that elections would be held in December to ratify a new constitution and to elect representatives to a new bicameral parliament, leaving him to rule by decree in the meantime. The parliament fought back: they barricaded themselves in the building, declared

Yeltsin unfit to govern for having violated the constitution, swore in Rutskoi as the new Russian president, and handed out arms to civilians willing to guard the parliament. Supplies of armaments and a great variety of rebellious individuals and groups flocked toward the White House, where Rutskoi and others tried to organize them into an effective military force. Witnesses remember the standard of the Romanov family flying next to the red flag of communism; the cossacks and even the neo-Nazis were also prominent. The showdown soon became violent. On October 3, having gained more followers and some crowd support, Rutskoi and Khasbulatov endorsed attacks on the Ostankino television center and the headquarters of the mayor of the city, i.e., tactics of a classical military rebellion and takeover. On the fourth, troops, with tanks, arrived to bombard the White House rebels into submission and to arrest them. More than a hundred people were killed, many of them bystanders; the building itself presented a picture of utter devastation. Russians had not seen such use of military force in politics, or this level of bloodshed on the streets, since the Civil War. The violence further deepened the political divisions in the country and alienated even many democrats from Yeltsin.

The parliamentary catastrophe of 1993 was followed in 1994 by a still greater disaster, the Chechen war. One of the 89 units of the new Russian Federation, the Chechens constituted less than 1 percent of its population and were located on a far Caucasian periphery, important perhaps only for oil and gas transport. An Islamic people, the Chechens had fought under Shamil against the imposition of Russian rule in the mid-nineteenth century and resisted Soviet power after 1917. Stalin considered them disloyal in the Second World War and had them transported, under atrocious conditions, to Central Asia, from which they were allowed to return to their native land only after the supreme dictator's death. At the time of the 1991 coup, as the Soviet Union was collapsing as states declared their independence, a general in the Soviet air force, Dzhokar Dudayev, was elected leader of Chechnya by a council of elders and declared independence. He was then elected president of the Chechen republic, though in quite uncertain elections. Dudayev regularly defied Moscow's authority and allowed his country to become a base for much criminal activity in Russia. Several covert attempts by Russian agents to overthrow Dudayev failed. Yeltsin decided to invade (he called it a "peacemaking mission"), though the new parliament, the State Duma, and even many military leaders opposed military intervention. On December 11, 1994, 40,000 troops were sent to Chechnya. No doubt, Yeltsin grossly underestimated the military preparedness and the fighting quality of the Chechens, as did Minister of Defense Pavel Grachev, who promised a very quick and easy victory. Also, the president did not want to antagonize Russian nationalists and wished to assure himself and all others that a component unit could not simply leave the Russian Federation at will. Pride and stubbornness certainly entered the picture on both sides. When the initial military effort failed, the Chechen capital city of Grozny and the land of Chechnya became a battlefield, often compared to Vietnam, or, to keep the analogy closer, to Afghanistan.

Perhaps not so unexpectedly to those who followed the evolution of Russia in the Gorbachev and Yeltsin years, but to the great surprise of the world, the Russian army proved to be in an appalling condition and totally unprepared for a war with the Chechens. Tank assaults on Grozny without the necessary infantry support and even without maps of the city led to the isolation and annihilation of the attackers. Massive bombardment eventually reduced much of the city to rubble, but probably killed mostly its peaceful ethnic Russian inhabitants, for the Chechen urbanites were much quicker to take to the hills. As to the Chechen fighters, they proved remarkably elusive, usually escaping with ease and striking suddenly from all sides. Some 40,000 people perished in Grozny. To be sure, the Russian army did capture, or recapture, the city, but only to abandon it again. And the total Russian military casualties in Chechnya were estimated as exceeding those of the Soviet army in Afghanistan. The unavoidable death and destruction of war were underlined by particular acts of deliberate cruelty, such as the massacre of civilians in the village of Samashki by the special forces of the ministry of the interior on the sixth through the eighth of April 1995. In general, there was much cruelty on both sides, but it was the Russians who were the aggressors. About a year after the assassinations in Samashki they even succeeded in killing by a rocket from a Russian aircraft, which had homed in on a satellite telephone in Chechen headquarters, President Dudayev. Yet the bitter war, although deadlocked, continued. It was only several months later, in August 1996, that Aleksandr Lebed, representing Russia, and Aslan Maskhadov, a more moderate Chechen leader, signed a peace pact. Victorious, the Chechens had in effect gained their independence and retained all their land for themselves, although the formulation of their exact relationship to Russia was left for the future.

One great fear of Yeltsin and his government, associated with the Chechen war, did not materialize: The inability to suppress the Chechens did not lead, in a domino effect, to other nationalities or parts of the country separating themselves from Moscow. But in other major respects the war was indeed a disaster. The utterly miserable performance of the Russian army was a shame and a scandal for patriotic Russians, and even Russians in general, and it was blamed directly on Yeltsin, Grachev, and their assistants. Perhaps an even more significant divide came to separate the president from the liberals who could not pardon him the stubborn pursuit of the Chechen war and its cruelty. In the Duma, only nationalists and communists supported the war. Indeed, most of the population was against this disastrous war: a national poll in January 1995 showed 71 percent opposed. The war also damaged Yeltsin's already declining popularity. By January 1995, fully 80 percent of the population expressed disapproval of Yeltsin as president. The much respected Sergei Kovalev's resignation from his position as head of the president's human rights commission was more than an individual gesture. Yeltsin's humanitarian and progressive mystique was no more. Abroad, too, the Chechen war produced a most painful impression, even if no state rushed to recognize the new Chechen government.

Yeltsin's bloody victory over the parliament in October 1993 did not establish either cooperation or a stable balance between the executive and the legislative branches of the Russian government. Yeltsin seemed to have become even more convinced that his own personal role was essential to keep Russia on the path to civilization and that all opposition to him represented the threat of a return to communism. The successful referendum on the new constitution of December 12, 1993, further strengthened the president's powerful position. In full charge of the executive, he could appoint and dismiss ministers and even pass measures by executive decree, when legislative approval was not available. Yeltsin's constitution gave the central government greater power over the regions. It also made it virtually impossible to impeach the president or amend the constitution. Specialists have described the constitution as "super-presidentialist." Yet ultimately he needed the agreement of the two-house legislature—the Upper House, the Federation Council, representing the federal units of the state, and the Lower House, the State Duma, representing the people at large—to enact a budget and a full legislative program. The parliament could also reject the proposed prime minister, although a third rejection would lead to the dissolution of the legislature and new elections, a threat that was to be effective in obtaining approval.

The victory of Yeltsin's constitution in the December 1993 election was undermined by the startling outcome of the simultaneous elections to the new Duma. Yeltsin had expected liberal parties loyal to his reforms, like Gaidar's Russia's Choice (widely treated as "the president's party") or Grigorii Yavlinsky's Yabloko (the Russian word for "apple," constructed of the first letters in the names of the party's original founders), to win a majority of seats. Instead, the largest unified bloc of seats went to a variety of nationalist and communist parties, increasingly allied in their opposition to radical market reforms and to Yeltsin personally. The largest share of the vote (23 percent) was won by Vladimir Zhirinovsky's paradoxically named Liberal Democratic Party of Russia (LDPR). The closely allied Communist Party of the Russian Federation (KPRF, led by Gennady Zyuganov) and the Agrarian Party won 12 percent and 8 percent respectively. Many smaller nationalist and communist deputies were also elected, though many deputies, elected directly rather than from party lists in the complicated procedures Yeltsin set up, declared themselves independents. The two largest centrist parties, the Democratic Party of Russia and Women of Russia, won about 15 percent of the votes. Meanwhile, Russia's Choice and Yabloko won only 23 percent of the vote.

Many explanations have been offered for the failure of the reformists to win a majority. As has been repeatedly noted, neither Gorbachev nor Yeltsin made a determined effort to establish and lead a strong political party. They had little appreciation of party politics and preferred to think of themselves as national leaders on a presumably higher plane. Moreover, through the years Russian liberals and moderates could not create an effective united party, but stayed divided into quarreling factions. The main reason for the poor showing of the liberals, however, was likely the unpopularity of the policies introduced under the banner of liberalism. By contrast, communists and nationalists sought to capitalize on widespread discontent in Russia over the results of postcommunist reform, though it should be noted that about half of all eligible voters refrained from voting at all. The new Duma remained hostile to Yeltsin throughout his tenure in office. Symbolically, one of the Duma's first acts was a declaration of amnesty for Yeltsin's opponents in the conflict of October 1993 as well as for those who attempted the coup in August 1991. The December 1995 Duma elections brought more bad news. Reformers, organized around the moderate new party Our Home Is Russia, associated with Prime Minister Chernomyrdin, and with Yavlinsky's more liberal Yabloko, ended up with even fewer seats than before while communists and nationalists gained additional seats—together winning nearly 54 percent of the vote. The biggest losers were the moderate centrists. The country was ever more deeply divided. Not surprisingly, the new Duma was more oppositional than the previous.

Two political figures who would remain key players in Russian national politics for a number of years to come became especially prominent as a result of the 1993 elections: Zhirinovsky and Zyuganov. Zhirinovsky became politically prominent rather suddenly in 1991, when he came in third in the first Russian presidential election won by Yeltsin. Much of Zhirinovsky's support was a protest vote for a man who challenged the government, the establishment, and even the world in a most extreme and vulgar manner, including physical assault on his opponents in the Duma, who promised everything to all, and who never hesitated to lie or to deny well-known facts. Yet beyond that amazing behavior—similar in some important ways to that of Zhirinovsky's friend, the French right-wing leader Jean-Marie Le Pen—many observers seemed to detect a fundamental fanaticism in Zhirinovsky's proposals, which included restoring the nineteenth-century Russian Empire, Russian expansion to the Indian ocean, taking back Alaska from the United States, and such solutions for establishing peace in the world as another major war, which would destroy Turkey and the Turks and ensure the legitimate Russian expansion to the south. Zhirinovsky certainly made his contribution to the frequently drawn analogy between Yeltsin's Russia and the Weimar Republic in Germany. At the same time, Zhirinovsky was not opposed to market economics and accepted the new political structures Yeltsin had established, especially the strong presidential system. Still, it was his persona as audacious and charismatic nationalist rebel, as well as his party's superb grassroots organizing, that attracted voters to his party, though he gradually lost popularity to more serious opposition politicians like Zyuganov. Unlike such virulent communists as Viktor Anpilov, Zyuganov also accepted the necessity of a market economy and the new political principles—he insisted that communists may come to power only through the ballot box. In fact, he admitted that Soviet communism failed because of its impossible attempt to maintain a monopoly on political and economic power. He also combined traditional communist concern for the material suffering of ordinary citizens with nationalist ideology. He often spoke of fighting to protect Russia's "spiritual heritage" against the degrading effects of postcommunist change in Russia. He even avoided speaking of socialism or communism, preferring instead to talk of "the

Russian tradition of community and collectivism." Meanwhile, Yeltsin himself backed away from liberalism—leading some liberals, such as Gaidar, to quit his administration. In 1994–95, Yeltsin began to talk less about structural transformation (notwithstanding the new round of privatization about to take place) than about "normalization" and "stability" as what Russia needed most, adding (as he wrote in his 1994 memoir) that "the only guarantor of calm is the president himself." In policy, he began to pay more attention to social programs, improving the legal system, and fighting crime. He also began making more use of nationalist discourse, talking of Russia's cultural and religious rebirth and of the Motherland; at the same time, in 1995, he cracked down on nationalist movements by banning all "fascist" organizations and activities.

As the June 1996 presidential elections approached, Yeltsin's chances of political survival looked minimal. After five years of his rule, most of the Russian people were in dire and still worsening economic straits, with no end to their tribulations in sight. Agriculture was in shambles, industrial output kept declining, the government went on borrowing money, but did not even provide wages or social security payments to its millions of employees and retirees who had to survive somehow for weeks, months, and sometimes years on their own. The war in Chechnya continued. Enormous corruption and organized crime held sway in the country. The polls indicated that popular approval and support of Yeltsin had fallen to several percentage points. Yeltsin's main challenger the communist leader Zyuganov, while deficient in charisma and even in simple personal appeal, had a huge nationwide party behind him and aimed to mobilize all discontent, including the nationalist variety. There was widespread anxiety among Russia democrats and in the West that Zyuganov might win this election, bringing the communists back to power.

Yeltsin, who always relished a fight, was determined to do battle, despite his own deteriorating health. To be sure, he had certain advantages in the election, and he utilized them to the full and even beyond the legally proper and permissible. Notably the government had a virtual monopoly on television and used this opportunity to display communists' oppression and atrocities during their seventy-five years of rule, to denigrate Yeltsin's opponents, and to portray the campaign as a fundamental struggle to prevent the return of communism. Repeatedly, Yeltsin depicted himself as the candidate of peace, order, stability, and progress—not radical reform—and depicted Zyuganov as totalitarian restorationist. The entire administrative and bureaucratic apparatus was urged to do everything possible to turn out the right vote. The fabulously wealthy "oligarchs," such as Boris Berezovsky and Vladimir Gusinsky, naturally feared the return to power of communists and agreed to end their rivalries and support Yeltsin's campaign with their influence and millions of dollars. The press was also heavily in favor of the incumbent president, though the stance of the media was complex. The Russian press was generally pluralistic and free, though the oligarchs controlled a great deal of it (often at a loss, but they saw this as the best means to influence public opinion and the public). Many journalists themselves, however, were highly professional and had been quite critical of the government. However, the fear of Zyuganov and the communists made it rally solidly behind Yeltsin, including some publications that switched from sharp criticism to support, only to return to criticism after the election. The communists had their advantages, too. They represented the only huge, well-organized, and territorially comprehensive political party in Russia, while Yeltsin in effect had no party of his own. Candidates could have their representatives at the polling places, but only the communists provided them everywhere.

The first round of voting, on June 16, gave Yeltsin 35 percent of the vote, Zyuganov 32 percent, Aleksandr Lebed (a charismatic retired general credited with preventing civil war in Moldova, who campaigned as a moderate national patriot) 15 percent, Yavlinsky 7 percent, Zhirinovsky 6 percent, and so on down the line, with Gorbachev getting one-half of 1 percent. Because no one obtained a majority of votes, the two leading candidates had to compete in a second round. In the end, it appears to have been public distaste for the communists, however reformed Zyuganov appeared to have been, that ensured Yeltsin's victory. In the final election, on July 3, Yeltsin gained 53.8 percent of the vote against Zyuganov's 40.3 percent. Sixty-nine percent of the electorate voted. The support for Zyuganov was impressive. However, the communists had great difficulty expanding their electorate in the second round after they had gathered the faithful and the susceptible protesters in the first. Later analyses indicated that the party relied very heavily for support on the elderly and the retired, and had little acceptance among the young.

Encouraged by his election and by some signs of growing economic activity, but also continuously beset by mounting indebtedness, the increasing poverty, even penury, of the people, widespread problems of crime and corruption, the inability of the government to collect most of the taxes and of industry to increase production, Yeltsin turned to one more burst of economic reform. In his State of the Federation speech of March 1997, Yeltsin warned that "the people's patience is at a breaking point." He blamed high officials and promised to bring into the government "competent and energetic people." However, he spoke of "reform" not as further structural transformation but, as he had begun to do since 1995, as improving tax collection, raising pensions, fighting corruption, enhancing social services, and strengthening the armed forces. He fired a number of ministers and deputy ministers close to Chernomyrdin and brought Chubais back to government along with Boris Nemtsov, the reformist young governor of the Nizhnii Novgorod region. Both were determined to weaken the political influence of the oligarchs as a class (though some individual oligarchs remained influential). By the end of 1997, Chernomyrdin, seen by many as the protector of the oligarchs, convinced Yeltsin to dismiss Chubais and Nemtsov. In Yeltsin's State of the Federation speech in February 1998, however, he repeated his concerns about widespread social problems in the country, warning again that if the government failed to solve these problems "we shall have a different government." Again he fired ministers, including, this time, the prime minister, Chernomyrdin. The new leader was a relatively little-known economist Sergei Kiriyenko, who after a long battle was finally endorsed by the Duma and became prime minister in March 1998.

The Kiriyenko government developed an anti-crisis austerity plan of reduced government expenditures and increased tax collections (though the Duma rejected increasing personal income taxes) and effectively convinced the International Monetary Fund to release part of its multi-billion-dollar rescue package of loans. The situation was dire: indebtedness was growing, wage payments to state workers were often unpaid, hard currency and gold reserves were being depleted, investment was minimal, capital continued to flee the country, and the Russian stock market was plummeting as was the value of the ruble. The problems were not entirely internal to Russia. For one thing, Russia became embroiled in the world financial crisis, which began in Asia but was spreading to other continents. Another devastating factor outside Russian control was the plunge in the price of natural gas and oil, which constituted over 50 percent in value of Russian exports. But, probably more important, Russia was paying for a failure to restructure effectively its economy and operating a kind of a pyramid scheme where only ever-new international loans kept the economic machinery going. On August 17, 1998, "Black Monday," the government defaulted on billions of dollars of short-term, high-interest treasury bills that the government had issued to meet its expenses and devalued the ruble by 50 percent. The stock market collapsed, many of Russia's largest banks failed, small businesses were wiped out, and real wages fell severely. Most of the foreigners working in the country left faster than they had come in and the International Monetary Fund refused further loans. Kiriyenko was dismissed. Yeltsin again proposed Chernomyrdin as prime minister, but this time he could not push him through the Duma, because of the obvious long-term connection between the candidate and the system that had failed so disastrously.

Yeltsin was clearly losing influence. His feeble health was also becoming more and more visible. Under pressure from the Duma, he nominated as prime minister Evgenii Primakov, the foreign minister, who was perceived as politically neutral and a pragmatist but who also had an important past in the Communist Party and the police establishment. Yeltsin's prestige sank lower than ever, and it was expected that he would be promptly forced to resign or at least become unmistakably a mere figurehead. But Yeltsin was not ready to give up. His State of the Federation speech in April 1999 was often feebly presented, disjointed, and defensive, but his message was clear enough: Russia needed order, stability, and security, in both economic and political life; he warned against communists and nationalists whose goals were "revenge" and the return of "directives and plans in the economy, censorship in media, and another round of the Cold War and refusal to integrate into the global economy." A month later, he fired Primakov (viewed, it has been argued, as too popular and too independent) and appointed Sergei Stepashin, the former head of the interior ministry, as prime minister. And he implicitly warned the Duma that if they rejected Stepashin—who represented the security services, after all—he might use force against the Duma. In the words of a leading political scientist, Yeltsin was again "ready to rumble." The Duma accepted Stepashin, who worked hard to stabilize the economy and win more Western economic aid, not without some success. A few months later, however, amidst new violence in Chechnya, Yeltsin announced that he was replacing Stepashin with another veteran of the security services, the relatively unknown former KGB officer from St. Petersburg, forty-six-year-old Vladimir Putin, whom Yeltsin effusively described as representing the new generation of leaders for Russia's future. Together they faced a new crisis in Chechnya. Armed militants invaded neighboring Dagestan, perhaps, some Chechen leaders suggested, to set up an independent Islamic republic uniting Chechnya and Dagestan. That summer, bombs destroyed two apartment buildings in Moscow and two in southern Russia, killing more than 300 people. Chechen terrorists were blamed and in September 1999, a massive Russian invasion opened the second Chechen war. The still shadowy Putin showed his style by declaring "we will wipe them out in their outhouses" and authorizing extreme force.

Initial successes in this war, along with improvements in the economy, helped the government achieve a rare victory in the Duma elections in December 1999. A new pro-government party, Unity—whose platform was limited to supporting the government and ensuring Russia's "territorial integrity and national greatness"—benefited from massive financial and media support from the oligarchs and won 23.8 percent of the party-list vote. With the support of individual deputies and other reformist parties, the government found itself with a likely working majority in the Duma for the first time. Also for the first time, the communist and nationalist opposition was in a minority, though still a strong one. Putin's approval ratings in polls soared to 50 percent, while Yeltsin, increasingly incoherent in his public statements and seemingly more preoccupied with his own power and personal security than with the politics of the country, was left with a mere 1.7 percent approval. Even Yeltsin now recognized that the time had come for him to step aside. In his New Year's address on December 31, 1999, Yeltsin announced his resignation as president, effective immediately. Putin was named acting president. He immediately showed his gratitude: he guaranteed Yeltsin and his family a lifetime of immunity from legal prosecution and a generous pension. In the presidential elections held in March 2000, Putin won 53 percent of the votes in the first round, twice as many votes as his only serious opponent, the communist Zyuganov. It seemed to many that a new age of stability—the goal Yeltsin had been talking of for the last few years—was now truly underway. Huge social and economic problems remained, though these were easing. Most important, politics was evidently outgrowing its years of tumult and uncertainty. Or, at least, it has been argued, that was what most Russians were voting for.

## Putin's Russia

Vladimir Vladimirovich Putin was born in Leningrad in October 1952, so that neither the Second World War nor Stalin were part of his immediate experience. He was also not one of the "sixties generation" (*shestidesyatniki*) inspired by Khrushchev's secret speech, de-Stalinization, and reform communism in eastern Europe (as Gorbachev and Yeltsin were). He was, scholars like the British political scientist Richard Sakwa have argued (whose study of Putin is one of the best), a typical person of the 1970s (the *semidesyatniki*): deeply patriotic but not especially ideological, neither in the dissident mold nor as a committed communist. As he told an interviewer after being appointed acting president, "I was a pure and utterly successful product of Soviet patriotic education"—note the emphasis on patriotic not communist. From the time of his youth, according to his own account, he dreamed of working in Soviet intelligence (inspired by "romantic spy stories") and showed up as a ninth grader at the KGB headquarters in Leningrad to ask what would be the best preparation. Advised to study law, he later entered law school at Leningrad State University and was accepted into the KGB after graduation. He was posted to East Germany, in Dresden, though was never a major spy. Perhaps the most dramatic moment in his career in foreign intelligence came when he helped the East German secret police, the Stasi, burn files as the Berlin Wall came down. He also discovered how weak the system was, teaching him, he later told an interviewer, that a system "built on walls and dividers cannot last." Putin returned home to work briefly at Leningrad State University in the office watching foreigners. In 1990, when the liberal reformer Antolii Sobchak (one of Putin's former law professors) was elected mayor, Putin became his assistant for international affairs, building a reputation as an excellent administrator. When Sobchak led the resistance in Leningrad to the 1991 coup, Putin resigned from the KGB and sided with the mayor. In 1995, at Sobchak's request, Putin organized and led the St. Petersburg branch of the moderate reformist party Our Home Is Russia in preparation for the Duma elections. When Sobchak lost the mayoral election in 1996, Putin also resigned. Putin's loyalty and his reputation as a man who could get things done impressed Yeltsin, who brought him to Moscow that same year to work in his administration. In 1999, Yeltsin named Putin, though a virtual unknown, his new prime minister and then acting president. While his election in 2000 with 53 percent of the vote can be seen as a vote for stability and hope, his reelection with 71 percent in 2004 suggests real popularity. Throughout Putin's eight years as president, opinion polls continually gave him approval ratings of more than 70 percent, an exceptional rating for any national leader. Forbidden by the constitution from holding more than two consecutive terms, Putin retained his influence by nominating his own successor, Dmitrii Medvedev, who was elected in 2008 with 71 percent of the vote and immediately named Putin prime minister. It is too soon to say (in 2010) whether Medvedev, as many hope but few expect, will put his own stamp on Russian politics, though his tone has been softer and more generous with critics. Of course, Putin still remains exceptionally active as prime minister. The deeper effects of the world economic crisis that began in 2008, which has been felt very deeply in Russia, must also be a question for the future.

Putin's extraordinary popularity—especially in the face of intense criticism for eroding democracy by an increasingly marginalized opposition but

also by international human rights organizations and media—has been attributed in part to the population's weariness with political turmoil and desire
for stable government and a strong individual leader. Steady improvements
in the economy from 1998 to 2008 were also very important (though this was
not entirely within Putin's control). But Putin's own personality and efforts as
a political leader have been essential. What do we know of Putin's thinking,
of his approach to politics? As Yeltsin appreciated, and many observers have
agreed, Putin is a problem solver, a pragmatist, a rational thinker. Analysts
have describe his approach to decision making as gradual, incremental, and
structured but also "hands-on." He has insisted that he is nonideological and
opposed to the establishment of any official state dogma. This has also meant,
as he often said, an end to revolutionary attempts at transformation: as he
quipped in 2001, "Russia in the past century over-fulfilled its plan for revolutions." In other words, it was time to restore "normal" politics to Russia.

It is not entirely accurate, though, to say Putin lacks ideology. As many
specialists have argued, Putin is inspired by at least one "ism," one with a
long history in Russia and the Soviet Union: "statism" (*gosudarstvennichestvo*
in Putin's use), the belief that a strong state is the necessary means for Russia's
progress and part of the definition of that progress. Especially after the state's

Vladimir Putin speaking with American journalists, 2001.   *(Associated Press)*

weakness in the 1990s—in the public mind and in Putin's view, the state effectively yielded real political power to oligarchic and criminal interests— Putin insisted on the need for relegitimizing and reconcentrating state power. "Russians are alarmed by the obvious weakening of state power," he wrote at the end of 1999; "the public looks forward to a certain restoration of the guiding and regulating rule of the state." Putin's statism is not without contradictions. His talk, during his 2000 election campaign, about "dictatorship of the law" and "the stronger the state, the freer the individual" may seem like oxymorons. So too might ideas about "managed democracy" or "guided democracy"—sometimes used in government circles, though largely replaced by "sovereign democracy" after 2006 (meaning that other countries have no right to criticize political practices within Russia for each country must adapt international values to its distinctive needs and traditions). Yet this paradoxical thinking is a key to understanding what some call Putinism. Consistently, Putin insisted on the need to overcome traditional dichotomies such as authoritarianism vs. liberalism, statism vs. democracy, order vs. freedom, universalism vs. nationalism. Richard Sakwa has written of the "dual nature" of Putin's approach: a neo-Soviet Putin that tends toward administrative methods and a post-Soviet Putin that favors assimilation of Western political norms. There is also an attempt to unite these contradictions in a Putinist "third way," combining the values of liberal individualism with statist collectivism. He calls Putin a "liberal conservative," such as was often found in Russian life before 1917. Critics see not paradox or even contradiction but simply hypocrisy: liberal fig leafs used to justify policies that have largely re-created autocracy by recentralizing the federal state (at the expense of the regions), asserting state control over the economy (especially the energy sector), reigning in the press, and co-opting or sidelining the opposition.

Closely connected to Putin's statism is his "patriotism"–even "nationalism," for it is often tied to talk of Russia's distinctive history and culture. His statements as president regularly feature patriotic and nationalist language, notably his famous "programmatic essay" on Russia's development, "Russia at the Turn of the Millennium," posted online at the government's Web site and then reprinted in the press in December 1999, and in his annual addresses to the Federal Assembly (both houses of parliament, hence this is sometimes called the "state of the nation" speech). His patriotism, typically, is complex, even contradictory. On the one hand, he is a Westernizer: he regularly insists that "we are Europeans" and that Russia, including its east and south, is part of the West. In talking of the "Russian idea" in his "Turn of the Millennium" manifesto he insisted that the Russian people "have begun to assimilate and embrace supranational universal values" such as "freedom of expression, freedom to travel abroad, and fundamental political rights and human liberties." When talking of "modernization," he framed this in Western terms as not merely a developed economy but a "market economy," "civil society," "rule of law," and "democracy." But he cast these in a Russian mold, or at least, his critics would argue, tried to justify renewed authoritarianism and even "autocracy" with rhetoric about Russia's distinctive traditions. In his millennium essay he linked Russian embrace of universal values to a second "foundation" for national development: "the indigenous [*iskonnye*], traditional values of the Russians" (though here he carefully used the nonethnic term *rossiyane*, whereas in some speeches he used the ethnic designation *russkii*, for example when speaking of "Russian patriotism"). Indeed, he continually spoke of Russia's *samobytnost*—a term that is variously translated as distinctive character, uniqueness, traditions. Insistently, he argued that hand in hand with a strong state Russia needed to be united around a "civic consensus" where the "main social groups and political forces" share "basic values and fundamental ideological orientations" (as he stated in "Russia at the Turn of the Millenium"). In his final address to the Federal Assembly in April 2007, he continued to argue that the "spiritual unity of the nation" and respect for Russia's "unique distinctive values" are no less important for Russia's development than "political and economic stability." He warned bluntly against "blindly following foreign models." This is part of the meaning of "sovereign democracy."

These arguments have shaped Putin's views about Soviet history, which differ considerably from those of Yeltsin and many radical reformers. In speeches, to much sympathetic applause, he has often said that "anyone who does not regret the collapse of the Soviet Union has no heart, but anyone who wants it restored has no brain." He acknowledged that there were "very harsh, dark periods" in the Soviet past, but he insisted this is Russia's heritage, part of people's experiences and memories and contains many moments to be proud of. Indeed, he continually rejected calls for the state to accept responsibility and apologize for the crimes of the Soviet era (and his government harassed human rights organizations like Memorial that focused on documenting these crimes). Instead, he insisted on the value of pride in Soviet accomplishments. Putin tried to reconcile the many Russian pasts—by focusing on the positive—in order to create a unified sense of nation. Symbolically, while it was Yeltsin who brought back the imperial flag and crowned double-headed eagle as Russia's national symbols, Putin restored as the national anthem the Stalin-era Soviet hymn (a wordless melody by Glinka had been used during the 1990s) with new words by the original author and gave the red star back to the army.

What is "managed democracy"? Most Western analysts use this term in defining Putin's politics, though the Putin government eventually came up with "sovereign democracy" as the preferred term. Critics—including the Western media, international human rights organizations, Russian oppositionists, and most Western political scientists—have argued that Putin weakened democracy and civil society. The most generous accounts have defined the state under Putin as more effective but less accountable. Harsher critics have questioned even the effectiveness, pointing to widespread corruption, still powerful oligarchs, failure to make much progress in modernizing the country, and deep social problems for the majority. Or as one Russian oppositionist ironically put it in 2008 in an analysis of Putin's presidency, paraphrasing Stalin's famous slogan. Life has become . . . better, but worse [or, more repugnant]" (*zhit' stalo luchshe, no protivnee*). Certain facts are generally recognized, especially the reduced role of the independent media and other nongovernmental civic institutions, a more "vertical" structure of government, and a more "orderly" electoral and party system. Still, it has been argued, if "democracy" is defined as inclusion of the majority of the adult population in political life and competition among different points of view in the public sphere (a common definition in Western political science), de-democratization in Putin's Russia has mainly involved only reducing competition, not eliminating participation or all competition. In a word, it has been "managed."

Analysts often mark the beginning of Putin's new approach to democracy with his efforts to reign in the independent media, though Putin's defenders have seen this as taking the media out of the hands of the rich oligarchs. In 1993, Vladimir Gusinsky established the first private television network in Russia, NTV (Independent Television). Its news shows, political talk shows, and satirical puppet show, *Kukly*, were enormously popular and influential; in particular, NTV was valued (and reviled) for revealing the suffering on both sides in the war in Chechnya. Gusinsky also published his own widely read newspaper and weekly magazine, both admired for their critical independence, and he funded an influential radio station. Other financial tycoons established media outlets or took control of state-owned media—Berezovsky acquired control of the state television network ORT and founded his own smaller channel. Most of Russia's national newspapers fell under the control of a small circle of banks or energy companies. Though clearly connected to the world of oligarchical wealth, the press under Yeltsin was relatively free and used this freedom to report on both every pathology of contemporary life—crime, violence, prostitution, rape, child abuse—as well as the "crimes" of the communist past. Some critics felt that the media was making life itself more horrible with its unceasing nightmare narrative. Both for cultural and political reasons, Putin and his allies were determined to clean up and rein in the media. After his victory in the March 2000 presidential elections, Putin announced a new press policy. He believed in the principle of a free press, he insisted, but this should not allow the media to become "means of mass disinformation and tools of struggle against the state." He also insisted that state-owned media must dominate the market in order to ensure that the population had "objective" information. A mixture of police raids, arrests (allegedly about financial corruption, not media control), new laws governing the content of mass media, and relentless government pressure largely muzzled critical television. Comparisons to Soviet television became common, especially once all networks were in the hands of the state or of state corporations and news broadcasts again became filled with lengthy and uncritical reports on the leader. Major newspapers and radio outlets were similarly bought by individuals or companies loyal to the Kremlin and brought under control. According the international Committee to Protect Journalists, by 2007 "the process of squeezing critical journalism out of the public space is now near complete." Laws against incitmg hatred or enmity, stimulating "extremism," or libeling public officials have regularly been used against journalists, according to an Amnesty International report of February 2008. The most disturbing development has been the violent assaults on many investigative journalists—most notoriously the murders of *Forbes Russia* editor Paul Klebnikov in 2004 and of Anna Politkovskaya, a writer renowned for her critical coverage of the Chechen conflict, and whose newspaper, *Novaya Gazeta*, is said to be one of the last independent media outlets, in 2006 (on Putin's birthday). Almost all of these attacks remain unsolved, some critics arguing that this is because the state itself is involved. Whoever is to blame, the state has not been able to prevent Russia from becoming what Amnesty International and the Committee to Protect Journalists have defined as one of the most dangerous places in the world for critical journalism.

Pressure on nongovernmental organizations (NGOs) and other civic movements, especially those with foreign ties and support, has also grown. The NGO sector burgeoned in the 1990s and early 2000s, with scholars estimating around 600,000 nongovernmental, noncommercial organizations operating in the Russian federation by 2004, including social service providers, educational organizations, policy think-tanks, gender-based groups, credit unions, and international rights organizations. A large percentage of these organizations have received foreign funds from organizations and governments wishing to promote democracy and civil society in Russia. Government concerns were evident even before the outbreak of the "color revolutions" in former Soviet lands—notably the "Rose Revolution" in Georgia in late 2003 and especially the "Orange Revolution" in Ukraine at the end of 2004, which the Russian government blamed on Western-funded NGOs—and the terrorist attack on a school in Beslan in the north Caucasus in September 2004, when hundreds of hostages, many of them children, died when the government attempted to liberate them, which led to new efforts to strengthen state authority. As early as his May 2004 annual address to the Federal Assembly, at the very start of his generally more authoritarian second term, Putin warned of the conflict with national interests posed by nongovernmental organizations who are receiving foreign funding and are naturally unwilling to "bite the hand that feeds them." In his final speech in 2008 he was even more blunt, suggesting a type of NGO-colonialism threatening Russia: "The flood of money from abroad used for direct interference in our internal affairs has grown. If we look at what happened in the distant past we can see that even in the epoch of colonialism they spoke of the so-called civilizing role of colonizing states. Now they arm themselves with slogans about democratization. But the goal is the same—to secure unilateral preeminence and one's own advantage." These concerns were reflected in a 2005 law that required all NGOs to reregister after a careful vetting process. The culling process was not as severe as many expected, but some large Russian NGOs, especially those involved in human rights work, were closed, access to foreign support became much more complicated, and bureaucratic obstacles discouraged many organizations. In general, critics have complained of growing harassment of human rights activists, environmentalists, religious groups, gay activists, and others. Many civil rights and election-monitoring organizations have been subject to at least temporary suspension—sometimes in accord with the NGO law, sometimes for alleged fire-code violations. In its efforts to manage civil society, the government has also sponsored its own civic movements, variously called by critics GONGOs, MANGOs, and GRINGOs (government-organized NGOs; manipulated NGOs, and government-regulated and initiated NGOs). Among the most reviled has been the pro-government, nationalist youth movement *Nashi* (Our Own)—its full name is the Youth Democratic Anti-Fascist Movement "Our Own," established in 2005. Public civic opposition to Putin persists, both on the Right and the Left, though it has largely been marginalized. A 2002 law against "inciting enmity" and "extremist activity" has been applied broadly against civic organizations deemed extreme, especially on the nationalist far Right, though also against liberal critics of the Church. The most important antiestablishment movement is The Other Russia, a coalition of civil society groups and political opponents of the regime. Their most visible public presence has been in annual nationwide Marches of Dissenters (*nesoglasnykh*—literally, of those who do not agree), which the government has vigorously tried to prevent and limit in scope. Summing up all these trends, an Amnesty International report of February 2008 concluded that "the space for dissenting views, independent media, and independent organizations to operate is shrinking in the Russian Federation."

In the structure of the government itself, Putin's government sought to "strengthen the vertical of power" (*vertikal vlasti*), to use an often-heard phrase. This included, starting in 2000, a reform of the Federation Council (the upper house of the legislature) that replaced elected officials from the regions with representatives appointed by regional administrations, a process overseen by the Kremlin; and the establishment in 2000 of seven supraregional governments with appointed supergovernors to provide greater oversight and control of local administration. Critics have noted the dominant role government of the so-called *siloviki* (from the Russian *sila*, meaning might or force)—individuals with past or present associations with the intelligence services, the Ministry of the Interior, the military, and other agencies of armed state power—whom Putin has often promoted in his government and relied on for advice. The government under Putin also became bigger, even though Putin regularly railed against the bloated "bureaucracy." The entire Soviet administration bureaucracy in 1990 numbered 662,700 individuals, according to a recent study; by 2000 the Russian Federation's bureaucracy numbered about a million people and had risen to a million and a half by 2006. After the Beslan school siege in September 2004 (sometimes described as Russia's 9/11 in its effects on politics), Putin began what Richard Sakwa has called a "constitutional coup" (others have made comparisons to Alexander III's "counterreforms" following the assassination of Alexander II). This has meant a sharp escalation in strengthening the vertical of power, including replacing the direct election of regional governors with officials appointed by the president himself, subject to the approval of regional parliaments, and creating alternative deliberative national structures separate from parliament that were representative, though by appointment, and only consultative. The political scientist Thomas

Remington has called these "extraconstitutional 'parallel parliaments'...that divert policy making expertise and debate from the parliament itself to alternative arenas, which the president can consult at his pleasure." These included the State Council (already formed in 2000) and especially the Public Chamber (2005) and the Council for the Realization of Priority National Projects (2005).

The Putin years also produced a streamlined and loyal structure of political parties that has much reduced conflict and criticism and enabled Putin to enact his legislative program. The electoral law of 2001, which required parties to have relatively large nationwide constituencies, began a series of electoral reforms that created a system of far fewer parties competing for power. In 2003, the United Russia party, established in 2001 largely to support the government, won its first large majority in parliamentary elections. From then on, observers have defined United Russia as the "party of power" and seen the start of a new pattern of postcommunist politics in which parliament largely did the bidding of the president. At the same time, political scientists argue, Russia remained a "hybrid regime" in which a powerful president and a loyal parliament left room for organized electoral opposition, though "managed" through restrictive electoral rules and effective media control. Indeed, after the December 2007 Duma elections, when the barrier for electoral entry was raised from 5 to 7 percent, only four parties received enough votes to be represented: United Russia (64.3 percent); the Communist Party of the Russian Federation (11.7 percent), which supported Putin's statism but criticized social inequalities; the Liberal Democratic Party (8.1 percent), which favors a very strong state and nationalist defense of Russian sovereignty in everything from politics to culture; and Just Russia (*Spravedlivaya Rossiya*, also translated as Fair Russia [7.7 percent]), a party formed in 2006 that describes itself as "social-democratic" and "patriotic" and has been openly praised by Putin—indeed political scientists have labeled Just Russia a "parastatal" opposition (a loyal opposition effectively controlled by the state). Liberal parties, notably Yabloko and the Union of Right Forces, both of which included many prominent Russian liberals, a number of whom had been active in Yeltsin's government, were effectively excluded after 2003—due partly to their own fractiousness, but also to ideological and tactical differences, and thus an inability to form a party large enough to compete (even to cross the earlier 5 percent threshold). Their absence from the parliament has dramatically narrowed the range of debate. As Richard Sakwa observed in his 2008 book, "The spirit of managed democracy inhibited the development of a genuinely competitive political marketplace. It was not clear that Putin was quite ready for that—or indeed whether the country was."

The effectiveness of the message of Putin and United Russia is an important factor in this consolidation of power. Polls suggest that they continued to win elections due to a mixture of personal appeal (citizens find Putin to be exceptionally intelligent, knowledgeable, honest, and caring) and because they attribute economic growth to his policies (President Dmitrii Medvedev seems to have been able to tap the same perceptions, at least until the dramatic economic collapse that began in 2008). No less, Putin has been admired for his adherence to core popular principles, including support of a market economy and the desire to integrate Russia into Western civilization but without "humiliation." Thus, in the critical 2003 parliamentary elections, the party's message—or what some specialists have called its carefully crafted "non-message"—was a key to success with voters (along with overwhelmingly favorable news coverage). Few specific programs were proposed and candidates refused to be drawn into televised debates over issues. Instead the party conveyed an upbeat and patriotic message of a country moving "together with the president" along a path toward increasing stability and prosperity, inspired by the vague but compelling idea of "Russia united and strong." Advertisements and speeches regularly reminded voters that the economy was improving, political stability restored, and Russia's stature in the world growing. Images used in the campaign conveyed this message as strongly as words: figures from Russian and Soviet history, happy families, gleaming new buildings, beautiful rural scenes. Pride in country, a desire for respect in the world, prosperity, a "decent life" for every person, stability, honesty, and happiness—these were the themes that inspired, and continue to inspire, so many voters.

Evaluations of Putin's actual accomplishments vary. Some speak admiringly of stabilization, normalization, and progress, especially in the economy. Others view claims—and most popular opinion—that the majority of Russians were better off than in the 1990s, and that Putin's policies deserve the credit, as the reigning "myth of Putinism." Certainly, Putin can point with pride to an impressive legislative record. Concerning the economy and society, major successful legislative initiatives included a pro-business reform of the tax code, laws lowering the regulatory burden for businesses, a Land Code allowing private ownership of land, a new Labor Code giving employers more authority over workers, improvements in the pension system, and expansion of the jury system and the rights of defense lawyers in trials—many of these quite "liberal" reforms. He also, defenders argue, increased the effectiveness of government by strengthening the "vertical of power," as we have already described.

Most important, the economy expanded enormously. While signs of recovery were evident in the late 1990s—indeed, Putin entered office amidst a mini-boom in 2000—the performance of the Russian economy continued apace (at least until the world financial crisis that began in 2008). During the Putin years, GDP rose consistently in the vicinity of between 6 and 7 percent annually; real disposable incomes rose between 8 and 14 percent annually, as did household saving; inflation slowed from 36 percent in 1999 to 9 percent in 2006; the international debt burden was reduced and some debts paid off entirely; investment in manufacturing grew (from 1 percent in 1999 to 13 percent in 2006); Russian-made consumer products became more common as domestic industry and agriculture expanded (partly helped by the devaluation of the ruble after the crisis of 1998, which made imports more expensive and thus stimulated domestic production and export); capital flight to offshore banks and other foreign havens slowed; the number of small and medium businesses grew, though very slowly; wages were paid more regularly and in cash, replacing widespread payment in kind in the early reform years; and the percentage living in poverty declined. Policies certainly made a difference. The radical reforms of the 1990s, which focused on neo-liberal privatization, fiscal discipline, and price and trade liberalization (sometimes called the "Washington consensus"), which had both laid the groundwork for growth and spread enormous economic chaos, criminality, and suffering, shifted to a newer "Moscow consensus" that did not reject market-oriented reform but favored a policy of developing productive resources, maintaining high employment, and increasing the role of the state in managing the economy. No less important, of course, was the windfall of extraordinarily high oil and gas prices between 1998 and 2008—Russia is the world's largest exporter of natural gas and the second largest exporter of oil. The market price for Russian oil increased dramatically between the beginning of 1999 (about ten dollars a barrel) and the beginning of 2008 (over ninety dollars a barrel). These "petrodollars" were a key fuel for the economy. Also, to prepare for eventual collapse of the oil bubble (which indeed began in the middle of 2008), the government created a gigantic "stabilization fund." Still, economists all agreed, as a World Bank report put it in 2006, that "future textbooks on Russian history will likely evaluate the economic policies of the current government on how effectively it manages the country's growing oil wealth."

Indeed, critics have argued that the Putin government did not made good use of these opportunities to push forward the reforms needed to sustain economic development. Many structural problems persisted behind the encouraging macroeconomic indicators. Manufacturing was still concentrated in large firms rather than in the small- and medium-sized firms that have been so critical to growth in eastern Europe. Too much of the recovery was centered in Moscow, such that the economic gap between the capital and the rest of the country grew as the economy improved. The banking system was still poorly developed and overly concentrated. New laws to adjudicate disputes were far from effective. Wages, for most of the population, were too low to allow much spending beyond necessities. Inflation remained a drain on real earnings. Low productivity in agriculture and profound rural poverty continued to hold back the economy. And Russia remained poorly integrated into the global economy, though moving in that direction. Measures were adopted to address some of these problems: taxes were cut to a flat rate of 13 percent and business taxes reduced; the government reassured business owners that no review of past privatization would be undertaken; most state and collective farms were privatized. The harshest critics, such as Boris Nemtsov (a deputy prime minister under Yeltsin and a leader of the liberal Union of Right Forces), who coauthored a 2008 overview of the Putin years, judged the "oil windfall" to have been squandered: growth rates should have been higher; restrictions on private business limited investment and growth; business finance, and property was concentrated in too few hands; corruption was not reigned in; too much state money was diverted to the growing state bureaucracy and the security apparatus; roads and other infrastructure, especially away from the major cities, were allowed to erode; public health suffered; and social welfare and education were neglected. Above all, critics have argued, the greatest remaining problem is economic inequality—a double inequality of both class and region—which contains many hazards for continued economic progress and political stability.

Among the most serious obstacles to effective government has been bureaucratization and corruption. After 1991, the Russian state was a dual state (and not for the first time in Russian history)—a new constitutional and elected government sitting atop the enormous Soviet administrative apparatus. As we have noted, the size of the bureaucracy grew after 1991. A key challenge for Russian politics, as the journalist Vitalii Tretyakov put it at the start of Putin's presidency, is for "Leviathan (the state bureaucracy) to be subordinated to Goliath (the president)." Putin continually worried, as so many Russian rulers have, about the "vast" size of the Russian bureaucracy and its low "quality," even calling "our bureaucracy" (he often used, as here, the old and slightly contemptuous word *chinovnichestvo*), in his 2005 national address, a "closed caste, sometimes quite arrogant, that views state service as a type of business." The problem remains unresolved. As always, it is closely connected to corruption, which has been a soaring problem. Putin continually railed against the way private and business interests undermined public interest. He came to power promising to free Russia from the power of the "oligarchs" who, in his words, had dangerously "merged power with capital." Toward the end of his term in office, in his 2006 national address, he was still expressing frustration that "despite all our efforts we have still not managed to remove one of the most serious obstacles on the path of our development: corruption." President Medvedev echoed this in his own 2008 address: "for a free, democratic, and just society, enemy number one is corruption." Indeed, in Transparency International's corruption index Russia has consistently been ranked among the worst offenders in Europe (and sometimes the single most corrupt) and generally on par with the most corrupt African nations. Critics argue that corruption is inescapable in a system where the state has so much power over society and the economy.

Putin's main line of attack, apart from speeches, was a series of targeted investigations, raids of business offices, arrests, and legal actions against some of the most politically influential moguls, who were accused of tax evasion, fraud, and embezzlement. Critics countered that the goal was mainly to rid the government of political competition, often as part of a renationalization of both media and the powerful oil and natural resource companies. Certainly, the major oligarchs who were targeted—Vladimir Gusinsky (arrested in 2000), Boris Berezovsky (fled the country in 2001 to avoid arrest), and Mikhail Khodorkovsky (sentenced in 2005 to nine years in prison)—were fierce critics of Putin's regime and used their wealth to finance critical organizations and media. It remains quite plausible—and polls showed this is what most Russians thought—that these men were crooks. No one became rich honestly in the postcommunist 1990s, it was widely said. As Berezovsky told the *Moscow Times* in July 2000: "everyone who hasn't been asleep for the past 10 years has willingly or unwillingly broken the law." The selective nature of the attacks convinced critics that the main goal was political. Indeed, Putin publicly made it clear to other oligarchs, and to the foreign investors who were often partners in their firms, that their fortunes and property were safe as long as they paid their taxes and kept out of national politics, a promise in stark contrast with the communists who continued to talk of renationalizing property to undo the corrupt privatizations of the 1990s. And Putin's years have been economically good for most of Russia's biggest capitalists. But more than silencing opponents may have been at stake in these campaigns. A number of political scientists have also described a complex process of reasserted state control over the economy, creating a new corporatist system in which the state was the dominant player: as Sakwa summarized these "new rules of the game," the final years of Putin's presidency saw the emergence of a "new model of political economy in which the line between public and private was no less blurred than in the 1990s, but now state capture [by the oligarchs] gave way to business capture [by the state]." Some would even argue that while economic wealth and power remain highly concentrated, the "oligarchs," as key political actors, are no more.

One of the major responsibilities of a government is national security. For Putin and his allies, there were two key and related challenges and measures of success: Chechnya and terrorism. From the first, in his Millennium speech, Putin made it clear that "the future of Russia is being decided" in Chechnya. Failure would mean the disintegration of Russia, for the loss of Chechnya would only be the beginning. This failure would, in turn, mean that "the state has become weak, and it ought to be strong." The second Chechen war, which followed a series of apartment house bombings in Moscow, was launched in late 1999 as a "counterterrorism operation," insisting that the war was not a response to an independence movement but a fight against "religious extremists and international terrorists." Western specialists and Russian critics have recognized a measure of internationalization and Islamicization of the conflict, though they interpreted this as a result of this unsettled war rather than its cause. The war was long and brutal, even after the capital Grozny was largely destroyed and a pro-Russian government established. In the ongoing insurgency and counterinsurgency, there were recurrent charges against Russian soldiers for illegal beatings, abductions, torture, and summary executions. Chechen rebels, in turn, regularly ambushed soldiers and undertook car bombings, suicide bombings, and kidnappings against Russians in Chechnya as well as in neighboring Dagestan. And terrorist assaults continued to reach into the Russian capital and other cities, with many people maimed and killed, including an attack on a Moscow theater in 2002, when a large group of armed young Chechen men and women took hostage an entire audience watching a popular musical; an attack by two female suicide bombers at a rock concert in Moscow in July 2003; a bomb near Red Square in December 2003; a bomb in the Moscow metro in February 2004; and two evident bombings of airplanes leaving Moscow in August 2004. Gradually, however, the insurgency was marginalized, though international human rights organizations accused the Chechen president, Ramzan Kadyrov, who is loyal to Moscow, of severe human rights abuses and tyrannical rule, and many questions about Russian war crimes remain. But Moscow's policies did produce a measure of pacification. Though sporadic attacks in the region continued, the Russian government formally declared on April 17, 2009, that the "counterterrorism operation" was over. The statement insisted that the "terrorists" alone were to blame for all the "grief and suffering of thousands of people." No one doubted the great human costs of this war. But critics argued that there was plenty of blame to go around and plenty of problems remaining.

A related concern—and perhaps even more entwined throughout Russian history with the stature and legitimacy of the Russian state—was the condition of the military. The end of communism was devastating for the Russian army. The Russian defense budget decreased steadily from 1994 until 2000. As a result, according to official reports, weapons and equipment were in short supply, the strategic missile system was becoming obsolete and ill-repaired, and most of the navy's ships were in need of modernization and often simple maintenance (dramatized for the world when internal explosions led to the loss of the nuclear submarine *Kursk* and its entire crew in the Arctic circle in August 2000). No less, serious problems plagued the army's human resources. Pay and prestige of officers was so low that recruitment was difficult. Avoidance of the draft, which remained universal, was endemic, and many of those who did join were physically or socially unfit. Hazing of soldiers by senior enlisted men was pervasive, reaching extremes of theft, beatings, rape, and even murder. Suicide was pervasive among both officers and men. Rates of desertion, by individuals and whole units, were growing. Alcoholism, drugs, and AIDS were growing problems. Food was sometimes in short supply and often of low quality. And effective training exercises became increasingly difficult due to the lack of funds. Finally, many officers were guilty of selling off valuable military assets for their own personal benefit, though sometimes for the good of their hungry and ill-equipped troops. Although there was much talk of "military reform" under Yeltsin, little was done.

Openly acknowledging these problems, Putin increased the military budget significantly. In his final speech to the Federal Assembly, Putin could tally his government's successes in improving both the salaries and living condition of soldiers and the supply and quality of matériel—including a reduction of the term of service and improvements in training. In 2003, he supported plans to gradually shift from a draft to a professional "contract army." Specialists have described these reforms as the first serious effort to address the military's problems since the collapse of the Soviet Union. Russian critics highlight the persistent problems: continued degradation of the strategic nuclear arsenal, the technological backwardness of military-industrial production, corruption, inadequate housing, and continued violent hazing of recruits. Certainly, the quick victory in the war against Georgia in 2008 (see later) and the eventual success in Chechnya seem to convince most Russians that their army has been restored to some measure of its historic might.

## Foreign Policy

The willingness to let eastern Europe go and to allow the Soviet Union to break up, in which Gorbachev and Yeltsin both played key roles, ended the Cold War and radically transformed international relations and even the world's political map. Not least, the dread of a catastrophic nuclear war between competing superpowers, which had hovered over the world for decades, vanished. In general, Yeltsin, Putin, Medvedev, and their foreign ministers and policy advisors continued the work Gorbachev began, though with varying emphases. In general, the tense play of hostile perception and interests of the Cold War gave way to a relatively normal and orderly process of negotiation and often shared interest. Conflicts certainly remained among international actors—interests differed and values continued to shape how interests were perceived. But the dominant orientation that emerged in the first postcommunist decades has been what scholars have variously dubbed "great power pragmatism," a "new realism," "normality," and "centrism." This emerging Russian approach to international relations begins with the argument, almost universally shared across the political spectrum, that Russia is a "great power." As Putin argued at the end of 1999, this is an "inseparable characteristic of [Russia's] geopolitical, economic, and cultural existence" and has "defined the mentality [*umonastroenie*] of Russians and the policies of the state throughout the whole history of Russia." But, it was clear to the new Russian rulers, the actual conditions of the world demanded new practices. Russia's power could not be limited to the exercise of military might alone. Nor should it have "imperial ambitions." Above all, it is best realized in a cooperative international arena in which the "sovereignty" and interests of every country are recognized and joint solutions are sought to the world's problems. Given Russia's loss of territory, the severe economic decline in the 1990s, and growing Western criticism of Putin's retreat from democracy after 2000, some analysts have argued that this insistence that Russia be treated as an autonomous great power is itself a type of idealism. But this "new thinking," as Gorbachev called his version of it, was becoming the new standard, not without argument and inconsistencies, however—not least in response to how Russia was actually treated by its potential partners and as particular conflicts and dangers arose in the region.

At least three visions for foreign policy have competed in post-Soviet Russia (the terminologies are varied and generally invented by political scientists seeking to systematize often overlapping points of view): liberals or Westernizers, who favor complete alignment with the United States and the West; conservatives or neo-Slavophiles (though Pan-Slavs would be a more historically accurate term), who favor a combative stance against the West (and thus alliance with any countervailing powers) and restoration of Russia's power in its traditional imperial space, including the defense of all Slavs (a variant, neo-Eurasianism, emphasized the common history and destiny of the ethnically mixed civilization of European and Asian Russia); and a centrism or realism that tries to balance Russian autonomy with international integration, especially through participation in multilateral institutions. In the early

Yeltsin years, the liberal perspective dominated and foreign policy was pro-Western to the point of capitulation, his critics complained; even some sympathetic analysts defined this as a "pragmatism of the weak." By the late Yeltsin years—especially under Yevgeny Primakov (foreign minister 1996–98, prime minister 1998–99), who had great authority and experience as a leader in the KGB and its successor and government leader under Gorbachev—policy turned "hard-line," in the language of the Western press. Primakov viewed the world in competitive terms and saw Russia as a needed alternative pole to growing Western power. Thus, Russia sought multilateral alliances that could counterbalance the seemingly unilateral might of the United States, especially. For the same reason, "integration" of the former Soviet region into a strong strategic and economic alliance was a high priority. Under Putin, the balance shifted again: Russia should be an autonomous actor but not an alternative one. The idea of a "rivalry" was explicitly rejected. In practice, these choices between Russia as an alternative force to Western hegemony, as an imperial regional power, or as an "autonomous" but cooperating power have often overlapped. Still, it is the fundamental shift in Russian international thinking that should be emphasized. As the foreign minister Igor Ivanov declared, at a celebration of the two-hundredth anniversary of the Russian foreign ministry in 2002, "Russia has consciously given up the global Messianic ideology that had been intrinsic to the former USSR," for it became clear, at least in the late Soviet years, that this no longer served the "national interests of our country."

Russia's relations within the former Soviet sphere have been especially fraught. Although nationalists, communists, and even some members of the pro-government United Russia party have publicly talked of someday reuniting the lost parts of the Russian Empire and the Soviet Union—the so-called "near abroad"—most political elites have recognized that complete reintegration is impossible. There are good reasons for insisting that these newly independent countries have a special place in Russian foreign policy: as borderlands, and thus for security reasons; because of extensive economic ties built over many years; and because of the large Russian diaspora, numbering perhaps 30 million. Putin's policy has been decidedly pragmatic, though always focused on Russia's own national interests. The early post-Soviet hope, strong through most of the Yeltsin years, of using the Commonwealth of Independent States as a basis for regional integration, foundered on mutual suspicions and practical failures. Under Putin, this yielded to a less sweeping policy of bilateral relations with individual post-Soviet states in which mutual interests were recognized, though Russia's special role needed to be preserved and strengthened. Russian policies focused on economic ties, the treatment of Russians, and limiting the expansion of NATO and the European Union (EU) into the post-Soviet space. Particular attention was paid to strengthening Russian economic influence in the region, especially through control of oil pipelines (and the construction of new ones) and energy prices. The most successful relationship has been with Belarus, whose authoritarian president, Alexander Lukashenko, has favored very close ties with Russia, including the creation of a unified economic zone. By contrast, relations with Ukraine and

Georgia exemplify some of the most difficult aspects of relations in the post-Soviet sphere.

In Russian-Ukrainian relations, the sources of potential conflict are considerable. Millions of ethnic Russians live in Ukraine, especially in the eastern parts of the country and in Crimea, where Russians are the majority and the historical intertwining of their economies made separation difficult. No less, hostility to Russian dominance—nurtured by strong historical memories of crimes like the Holodomor, the famine of 1932—33, which Ukrainians almost universally view as deliberate "genocide" by Stalin's government against the Ukrainian nation—had become an essential component of Ukrainian national identity, matched by a certain nationalist "Ukrainophobia" in Russia, which failed to understand how Ukrainians could imagine themselves to be a separate nation, minimized Russian dominance, and worried about vehement pro-Westernism. Thus, it is impressive that Russia and Ukraine managed during the 1990s to settle amicably a series of disputes over borders, military bases, and energy supplies. Then came the conflict around the 2004 presidential elections in Ukraine. Russian actions were shaped in part by growing anxieties about Western intentions in the former Soviet world, especially around the expansion of NATO. Many Western powers openly supported the pro-Western opposition candidate, Viktor Yushchenko; many Russians viewed this support as an attack on Russian influence. Russia openly backed the pro-Russian candidate, Viktor Yanukovych; many Ukrainians and Westerners viewed this support as a sign of Russian neo-imperialism in the region. Yanukovych's declared victory, which critics attributed to fraud, led to a well coordinated moment of public protest, supported by many Western organizations and governments, and ultimately resulted in Yushchenko's election in a new vote December 2004. Problems escalated in the wake of this "Orange Revolution": both Russian aggravation at the West for "meddling" and tense relations with Yushchenko's government, including serious conflicts over gas supplies and pricing, over trade, over Ukraine's desire to join the EU and NATO, and about the status of the Russian language in Ukraine. Still, both governments avoided a complete break and the Russian leadership did all it could to prevent the conflict from damaging their relations with the West. Putin also recognized the diplomatic blunder of openly backing a candidate in another country's elections.

With Georgia there were tensions even before the "Rose Revolution" of 2003, during which President Eduard Shevardnadze, Gorbachev's former foreign minister, resigned to avoid a bloody conflict arising over alleged abuses in parliamentary elections, bringing to power the very pro-Western opposition leader, Mikheil Saakashvili. The complexity of ethnicities and borders in the Caucasus, the result of a long history of Russian and Soviet rule and reorganization, continued to produce serious conflicts over territory, local authority, and influence throughout the region, especially in the north Caucasus: both within the borders of the Russian Federation, notably Chechnya, Dagestan, and North Ossetia, and across the border in Abkhazia and South Ossetia, which Georgia considers parts of its sovereign territory, while Russia supported secessionist movements in both regions throughout the 1990s. These conflicts grew under President Saakashvili, who insisted on the territorial integrity of Georgia against independence movements in Abkhazia and South Ossetia, made Georgian membership in NATO a high priority (which the United States endorsed), and welcomed extensive American military assistance (and sent Georgian troops to support U.S. efforts in the Iraq war). Meanwhile, Russia continued to support independence, including by offering South Ossetians Russian citizenship. These conflicts culminated in the Russian-Georgian war in the summer of 2008, mainly over the fate of South Ossetia. Although the two sides dispute who began the conflict, Georgia, determined to reclaim the independent region, bombarded the capital, Tskhinvali, while Russia sent thousands of troops into South Ossetia and extended bombing raids into the rest of Georgia. Russia quickly crushed Georgia's army and recognized Abkhazia and South Ossetia as independent states, which Georgia rejected as outright annexation. This recognition was also condemned by NATO, the United States, and other Western powers.

The withdrawal of Soviet dominance and troops from eastern Europe allowed dramatic changes in the region—indeed, the tendency of Poles, Czechs, Hungarians, and others to identify their location as "central Europe" indicates the extent of the geopolitical reorientation. Particular experiences in the region varied and shifted over time, including East Germany's absorption into a larger Germany and the breakup of Czechoslovakia and Yugoslavia into smaller ethnic nation states; radical and liberal capitalist and democratic reform (notably in early postcommunist Poland and the Czech Republic) but also hesitance and even persistent, or returning, communist influence (as in Romania, Bulgaria, and Serbia); and different degrees of economic breakdown and revival. Most important, though, from a Russian perspective, has been the profound turn of the former communist bloc in eastern Europe away from the East and the remarkable acceptance of this by post-Soviet Russian governments. Throughout eastern Europe, the period preceding the collapse of 1989 was regarded as that of Russian, as well as communist, oppression, and, once that oppression ended, the inhabitants of the area were at best indifferent, if not hostile, to the Russians and their fate. This has worked out most tangibly in the eastward "enlargement" of the EU and NATO. In 1999, NATO expanded to include Poland, Hungary, and the Czech Republic. In 2004, the former Soviet Baltic states (Estonia, Latvia, and Lithuania), Slovakia, Bulgaria, Romania, and Slovenia were admitted. In 2009, Croatia and Albania joined, and active negotiations are underway to include Bosnia and Herzegovina, Montenegro, Georgia, and Ukraine, all of whom have expressed a desire for accession. The EU similarly expanded to absorb much of the former East Bloc, though this process was protracted by demands that new members adhere to certain political and economic standards. In 2004, eight former communist countries were admitted as new members: Estonia, Latvia, Lithuania, Poland, the Czech Republic, Slovakia, Hungary, and Slovenia, "finally ending," as EU officials put it, "the division of Europe decided by the Great Powers 60 years earlier at Yalta." In 2007, Romania and Bulgaria joined, and Croatia and the

Former Yugoslav Republic of Macedonia became candidate states. Critics warned about the excessive speed of incorporation as well as the strategic danger of constructing a Europe without a meaningful role for Russia. For their part, Russian leaders were initially fearful and hostile to NATO and EU expansion but also continued to assert that Russia is a European nation and inseparable from Europe. Talk among some Russian diplomats of a "primitive Russophobia" in the expanded EU continued to signal Russia's concern, but Putin avoided making this a major source of tension. As Putin told David Frost in an interview in March 2000, "Russia is a part of European culture and I cannot imagine my own country cut off from Europe, from what we often call the 'civilized world.' Therefore it is difficult to imagine NATO as an enemy." The insistence that Russia is part of Europe, of course, was also a demand for respect and inclusion, an expectation that would sometimes be disappointed.

In practice, direct relations with the European Union, NATO, individual western European countries, and with global financial institutions like the International Monetary Fund, the World Bank, and the World Trade Organization—and, of course, the gigantic presence in all of these of the United States, about which more later—have been a high priority, not least to fight against a tendency to treat Russia as either outside the West or as a junior partner. As mentioned, Yeltsin favored a strongly pro-Western foreign policy. He unilaterally destroyed many ballistic missiles, negotiated further reductions, cut subsidies to Cuba and Afghanistan, and maintained warm personal relations with Western leaders, such as Chancellor Kohl and President Clinton, whom he liked to refer to as "my friend Helmut" and "my friend Bill." But tensions were growing. In return for Russia's cooperative relations with the Western powers, Yeltsin expected respect for Russia's "national interests and national pride" (as he said in his 1994 State of the Federation address) and financial aid. On both counts, Yeltsin would be increasingly disappointed, making political criticisms of Yeltsin's subservience before the West increasingly effective. In the pursuit of loans and aid from Western states, the World Bank, and the International Monetary Fund, Yeltsin found himself as early as 1992 reminding Western leaders, who made strong demands about the domestic economic policies that would be required before Russia would be given aid, that Russia is a great power in the midst of a great transition away from communism, not a "charity case."

NATO expansion into eastern Europe was a particular source of tension. Judged, not without reason, to be anti-Russian, these moves produced a strong negative reaction in Russia. In March 1997, the Duma voted 300–1 against expansion, a rare example of political unanimity. Yeltsin's anti-Western critics insisted that expansion proved that the West wanted a weakened and isolated Russia. Compromises were offered to help Russians accept this growth of a former anti-Soviet military alliance closer to Russian borders—which, in any case, they knew they could not prevent—including membership in a vague "Partnership for Peace" with the Western powers and a slowed pace of enlargement. But, as we have seen, the direction of change was unstoppable.

Between 1999 and 2009, every member of the former Soviet-led Warsaw Pact, founded in 1955 as a counterweight to NATO, became a NATO member— apart from Russia, of course.

The conflict in the former Yugoslavia further damaged Russian-NATO relations. The Yeltsin government insisted on its special relationship with the Serbs, for practical as well as sentimental reasons: Serbs were Slavic and Orthodox and, before the Bolshevik revolution, Russia had considered itself a protector of the Serbs. When the United States bombed the Bosnian Serbs in 1994 for failing to respect UN warnings, though without UN sanction, the Russians were furious, including at what was seen as the hypocritical unilateralism of the world's one remaining superpower, which seemingly did not have to follow the rules it set for others. Russian troops were soon invited to serve beside NATO forces under UN command, however, and Russia was able to broker a cease-fire that prevented further U.S. air strikes. But relations remained tense. By the end of 1994, Yeltsin was warning that a "cold peace" was replacing the cold war, and his foreign minister, Andrei Kozyrev, soon declared that "the honeymoon is over." The Kosovo tragedy was a milestone. As what was left of Yugoslavia continued to disintegrate—a problem the Russians could well sympathize with—the Serbian-Yugoslav leader Slobodan Milosevic sought to prevent the largely Muslim Albanian province of Kosovo from seceding. Arguing that violent atrocities and "ethnic cleansing" made intervention necessary, NATO, led by the United States (again without UN sanction), bombed Serbia in March 1999. Both the public and the government in Russia were outraged. Many argued that the United States was the main "rogue" state in the world, determined to intervene whenever and wherever it wished. The Russian government denounced the aggression and pointedly refused to attend as a guest the celebration of NATO's fiftieth anniversary. Still, Yeltsin and his government maintained essential ties with the West, and Russia went on to participate in the occupation and restoration of the devastated areas, enhancing Russia's international position. Most important, it was becoming clear that even when conflicts arose, these no longer represented the dreaded confrontations of the cold war.

Putin, too, continued to strike a balance between demanding respect for Russia's regional authority, warning against signs of anti-Russianness in EU and NATO, and persisting in pragmatic engagement. Indeed, Russian demands for inclusion, and warnings against dismissing or provoking Russia, grew stronger under Putin. But cooperation remained the dominant method of pursuing Russian interests and self-identity as a "European" power. Throughout the post-Soviet years, Russia participated in numerous agreements and institutions designed to facilitate cooperative relations with the European powers, including the EU-Russia Partnership and Cooperation Agreement of 1997, biannual EU-Russia summits, a NATO-Russia Council formed in 2002, and a plan for "Common Spaces" of EU-Russia cooperation after 2005 (after Russia demonstratively refused to participate in the new "European Neighborhood Policy," seeing it as too biased toward dominant EU authority). Of course, and perhaps most important, the European Union has overwhelmingly been

Russia's largest international trading partner, both for export (especially energy supplies) and for imported manufactures and food.

Russian relations with the United States have been more fraught, especially as both countries became more assertive in world affairs during the presidencies of George W. Bush (2001–8) and Vladimir Putin (2000–2008). The underlying problem, argued liberal critics of U.S. foreign policy, such as the political scientist Stephen Cohen, was that "the cold war ended in Moscow, but not in Washington." The United States pursued, in Cohen's words, "a relentless, winner-take-all exploitation of Russia's post-1991 weakness." The effect was "growing military encirclement" of Russia by U.S. and NATO bases and a tacit denial that Russia has any legitimate national interests outside its own territory or the strength to pursue these. Even Yeltsin, as we have seen, warned Western leaders not to humiliate Russia. When Yeltsin and Clinton met in Moscow in 1994, Yeltsin complained of many deficiencies in U.S. policy toward Russia, including tangible material support. In fact, billions would be loaned to Russia in the 1990s, mainly through the IMF and the World Bank, but frustration remained. Many Russians felt deceived in their expectations of a much larger sponsorship. Clinton (speaking in 1998) agreed the effort had been limited: "a forty-watt bulb in a damned big darkness." As already noted, U.S. bombing of Serbia and the expansion of NATO added to these tensions.

When Putin came to power, relations with the United States were relatively stable, but he also faced continued condescension toward postcommunist Russia. It had become common in the Yeltsin years to hear Western commentators dismiss Russia as a political has-been on the world stage with a basket-case economy, a declining population, a chaotic and corrupt political order, and a deteriorating military. After 2000, charges of democratic backsliding were added to the reasons not to treat Russia as a partner. For Putin, as for most Russians citizens and politicians, it was essential to restore Russia's place in the world as a respected and influential power. This meant the same combination we have seen in his domestic policy: a mixture of patriotic assertiveness and pragmatic Realpolitik. Putin was determined to assert Russia's global role, while remaining quite aware that this must be done in a world in which "when the Russian bear growls" few any longer worried. The exceptionally powerful position of the United States in the post–cold war world was a key concern. An official foreign policy concept paper in June 2000 highlighted Putin's emerging approach: given limited resources Russia must concentrate on areas of vital interest but must insist on these interests; while NATO expansion is undesirable, Russian cooperation in both security and economic partnerships is more important; and, for the longer term, the present unipolar economic and political domination by the United States must be replaced by a "multipolar world." Putin continued negotiating reductions of strategic weapons, showed willingness to compromise on U.S. plans to modify the anti-ballistic missile (ABM) treaty so that it could begin testing the U.S. national missile defense system (NMD) in return for deep mutual cuts in strategic weapons, and signed other agreements. Tensions persisted. Conflicts over the NMD continued and there was little personal rapport between presidents Clinton and

Putin. When George W. Bush was elected U.S. president in November 2000, relations further chilled. Bush advisors like Condoleezza Rice, a former Soviet specialist, argued openly that Russia's weakness made cooperation unnecessary and unwise: its economic problems were its own to solve, sharing security information was dangerous due to the risks of leaks, and Russia remained "a threat to the West."

Russia, in turn, continued to look to reduce U.S. unipolar power in the world and minimize its own isolation. Putin nurtured bilateral ties in Europe, especially with Germany, whose leaders shared Russian anxieties about the United States. Although the 1990s idea of building an Indian-Chinese-Russian alliance to counterbalance the United States and NATO was largely abandoned, Putin's government vigorously pursued economic relations with China, especially as a market for Russian arms and energy supplies. In the Middle East, Russia directly intervened in peace negotiations despite being formally excluded by the United States (though Russia had been a cosponsor of the 1993 Oslo accords). Russia rebuilt relations with Iran, even resuming arms sales, and with Iraq. Putin traveled to North Korea, where he believed that he convinced the Koreans to give up their nuclear weapons program (they denied any pledge), and to Vietnam and South Korea to improve business opportunities for Russian companies. And he visited Castro in Havana to pledge continued economic relations and joined the Cuban president in deploring U.S. efforts to dominate Latin America and the world.

But Putin's pragmatism led him to resist the temptation—and to resist much of the advice of his own foreign policy and military establishment—to continue too far along the path of challenging the United States in the world. After all, Russia's goal was a seat at the table of world politics, not the stance of outsider and spoiler. And the realities of U.S. power could not be ignored. The personal chemistry between Bush and Putin helped. After their first meeting, in the summer of 2001, Bush famously observed, "I was able to get a sense of his soul." Several months later, after their meeting at the presidential ranch in Texas, Bush would add, "the more I get to see his heart and soul, the more I know we can work together in a positive way." Discussions on allowing a U.S. missile defense system, to which Bush was strongly committed, revived, and Bush promised to support Russia's entry into the World Trade Organization, a Putin priority. Most important (even prophetic), they found strong common interest in fighting what they viewed as the threat of Islamic fundamentalism. Bush's comments after their meetings showed that he did understand Putin in some ways: "I found a man who realizes his future lies with the West.... On the other hand, he doesn't want to be diminished by America." The terrorist attacks in the United States on September 11, 2001, facilitated further warming of U.S.-Russian relations. Putin was the first world leader to call President Bush with sympathy and shared outrage against what Putin called "barbarous terrorist acts aimed against wholly innocent people." Obviously, the Chechen conflict was in Putin's mind, for he had already been linking it to Islamic fundamentalism and international terrorism and was now likely to find more sympathy for Russia's brutal fight there. More subtly, many Russians saw

The political relationship and balance of power between Dmitrii Medvedev (elected president in 2008) and Vladimir Putin (president 2000–2008, then appointed prime minister) has been the subject of much speculation. Most specialists believe that Putin remains the dominant figure in Russia.    (Dmitry Astakhov/AFP/Getty Images)

September 11 as bursting the illusion of a unipolar world and as likely to lead the United States into more cooperative engagement with other nations in the common struggle for security and peace. By offering Russian "solidarity" with America in the fight against world terrorism, Russia was again inviting itself to the table. Putin offered to share intelligence and (though against much internal government resistance) to support U.S. plans to go after Al Qaeda and the Taliban in Afghanistan, including by tacitly accepting U.S. troops on former Soviet bases in Central Asia. When, in December 2001, the U.S. Secretary of State informed Moscow that they were pulling out of the ABM treaty, the Russian response was muted. During the following months, Russia actively cooperated with the United States in a number of areas: as a full member of the newly expanded Group of Eight (G8) industrialized nations; as coauthor with the United States, the United Nations, and the European Union (the "Quartet") of a Road Map for peace between Israel and the Palestinians; in negotiating world energy policies and technological exchanges; in measures to stem the proliferation of "weapons of mass destruction"; and in cooperating in the "war on terrorism."

Relations again began to deteriorate, however. Distrust ran deep, and Russia seemed to be gaining little from its concessions to U.S. power. Many Russian political leaders were troubled by U.S. policies: tearing up the ABM treaty, stationing troops in Central Asia and Georgia, and continued movement toward incorporating East European nations and the former Soviet Baltic states into NATO and the European Union. Above all, critics complained and Putin himself likely wondered, what had all these concessions gained for Russia? Many Russian elites felt they were seeing a repeat of Gorbachevian capitulationism, made worse by an increasingly unilateralist America. In this light, it is not surprising that Russia opposed the U.S.-led invasion of Iraq in March

2003: whereas the 2001 invasion of Afghanistan was consistent with Russia's long hostility against the Taliban and their own concerns about the dangers of terrorism, there was little evidence that Iraq was connected to international terrorism, the war threatened Russia economic ties with Iraq, and this seemed yet another sign of American unilateralism. It helped that Russia could stand side by side with France and Germany in opposing the war. Still, Russian defiance did not derail relations with the United States. In fact, some specialists have seen this conflict as marking a still higher stage in improving these relations: "Moscow dared to disagree and Washington grudgingly accepted its right to do so." But sources of tension remained. If anything, they intensified during Putin's and Bush's second terms. U.S. officials regularly criticized the Russian government for arrests of business moguls and attacks on the independent media and publicly voiced dismay over the lack of a stable system of competing political parties and a still rudimentary "civil society." In turn, Russian officials criticized many recent U.S. a policies as threatening Russia: the expansion of NATO; American efforts to promote democratic "color revolutions" in Georgia, Ukraine, and Kyrgyzstan; U.S. troop presence in the near abroad and eastern Europe; plans, announced in 2007, to establish an ABM defense system in Poland and the Czech republic; and U.S. support for Georgia during the 2008 war. Russia's assistance to Iran in building a nuclear power plant and use of oil supplies as bargaining tool with neighbors provoked strong U.S. criticism. That trade with the United States remained quite low added to a sense of disengagement and distance. Some of the rhetoric could be quite hostile, with U.S. Vice President Cheney rebuking Russia at a meeting in Vilnius in 2006 for restricting rights in Russia and trying to dominate its neighbors and Putin in 2007 admonishing foreign governments who "need a weak and feeble state" in Russia. Nonetheless, both sides continued to insist that the relationship between Russia and the United States was founded on "friendship" and "trust," that talk of a "new cold war" was absurd. For Russian leaders like Putin, this was a friendship based on both pragmatism and idealism. As one Russian foreign policy advisor put it, "Many in the Russian leadership resent the United States, but they have decided it is better to adapt to American power." In any case, although the United States may often do "stupid" and harmful things in the world, it is "the only steamship we can hitch ourselves to and go in the direction of modernity." While continuing to complain of American unilateralism and even ideological messianism, the Russians refused to be provoked. After the defeat of the Republicans in the 2008 U.S. presidential elections with the election of Barack Obama as president, Russian diplomats welcomed official American statements that, as Vice President Joseph Biden put it in 2009, "it is time to press the reset button and to revisit the many areas where we can and should work together." Important steps included abandoning the plan, which Russians vigorously opposed, to station anti-ballistic missiles in Central Europe. At the same time, Russian leaders have continued to keep their options open that U.S. power would decline as new centers of global wealth and power continue to rise. As President Medvedev observed at a meeting of the BRIC nations (Brazil, Russia, India, and China) in 2009, it may be in just such an alliance of emerging economies that will be built "a more just world order."

# CHAPTER 44

# Society and Culture since 1991

Where are you racing, troika? Where does your path lie?
The coachman's drunk again on vodka....
As the saints foretold, everything is hanging by a thread.
I look at it all with ancient Russian sorrow and longing.
                                    BORIS GREBENSHCHIKOV, 1996

When the collective farm was here you could get a sled or roofing
or any kind of nail you wanted. Now everything is coming apart.
That's all. Little by little it's all coming apart. That's my story.
Nothing good about it.
        V. BYKOV, 76-YEAR-OLD RESIDENT OF THE VILLAGE OF ISUPOVA, 2004

Uncertainty may have been the defining experience of social and cultural
life after the fall of communist rule in 1991. Yeltsin's unfulfilled promises of
a quick transition to a prosperous market democracy, and widespread hope
for what freedom would bring, were followed less by simple disillusionment
and anger than by a subtle disorientation. Polls during the 1990s repeatedly
showed that citizens were troubled less by material suffering (this was not
new, after all) than by the pervasive instability (*nestabil'nost'*), disintegration, and uncertainty about the future. Scholars have defined these years in
historically negative terms as the "unmaking of Soviet life." We have seen
that the aim of dismantling past economic, social, and political structures
was precisely what inspired much radical reform. This historical destruction
could be an exhilarating experience and offer new opportunities and hope,
but it was more likely to be frightening and depressing. For many, it could be
both at once. This history may also help explain the growing public acceptance of new forms of order and control, a nostalgia for the past, a desire for
"normalcy." This chapter surveys this contradictory social experience, but it
also considers how people tried to make sense of the world around them, to
figure out where Russia was heading, and to decide how they fit in and what
they believe.

## Poverty and Wealth

One of the most visible effects of the unmaking of communism has been the intense restratification of Russian society. Socialist leveling—though always more ideological ideal than real social fact—was wholly thrown out in favor of relentless acquisition of property and wealth by private entrepreneurs, new freedom for individuals to struggle and compete, and rapidly growing social inequality. Many Russians found this change personally and morally offensive. The privatization of the economy was widely stigmatized as prikhvatization (changing the normal, if new, word *privatizatsiia* into the mocking neologism *prikhvatizatsiia*, adding the meanings of snatching or grabbing), and Russians began to speak with contempt (though also derisive humor) of the *nouveau riche* "New Russians," a class defined not only by their recent and rapid acquisition of wealth but also by their presumed dishonesty, selfish greed, links with corrupt political privilege and underground crime, showy consumerism, and low cultural level. Other terms used, by Russians and in the Western press, to describe the new Russian rich reflected the same mixture of social analysis and moral judgment: robber barons, crony capitalists, kleptocrats. A more generous interpretation of the rise of this new economic elite, favored by liberal social scientists, sees them, like other historical bourgeoisies, contributing to the development of market democracy in Russia, especially given the presumably natural tendency of educated, urbanized, propertied groups to support individual initiative, economic and political freedom, and citizen participation in public life. Other analysts have noted the many obstacles entrepreneurship has faced in postcommunist Russia, hindering and distorting normal business in many ways: the Soviet legacy in which private entrepreneurship was a criminal activity; the inadequacy of institutional, legal, and fiscal conditions; the strong place of corruption, crime, and even violence in the creation and conduct of Russian business; and widespread negative or ambivalent attitudes among the Russian public toward private business. What is certain is that a powerful new class emerged virtually overnight, though it did not emerge out of the blue: most of the leading capitalists of the 1990s already had access to resources and power, though they were also individuals with personal drive and motivation—viewed by some as vision and by others as greed. According to specialists, five of the seven powerful financial-industrial groups in the mid-1990s, headed by businessmen known as "oligarchs" for their fabulous wealth and close ties to political power, had been established with the direct political and financial support of Soviet-era officials and institutions. Mikhail Khodorkovsky (widely believed to be one of the richest men in the world at the start of the new century) had been an official in the Communist Youth League, the Komsomol. Vladimir Vinogradov had been an economist at a government bank and a Komsomol official. Boris Berezovsky had been an information management specialist in the Academy of Sciences working as a consultant for the largest Soviet automobile manufacturer. There were exceptions. Roman Abramovich, for example, often at the top of the list of the richest Russians during the Putin years, was neither well educated nor well connected, but began his rise in black-market commerce and small-scale enterprise during the Gorbachev years. Looking beyond this super-elite, studies have found that the majority of large-scale entrepreneurs of the mid-1990s had been managers or enterprise directors, typically members of the Communist Party, and often well educated, though some entrepreneurs, such as Vladimir Gusinsky, enjoyed good educations (typically humanistic rather than technical) but felt themselves to be outsiders to the system—Gusinsky, for example, was a minor theater director and a cab driver before beginning his rise to wealth by helping to establish a Soviet-American joint venture. During the Putin years, this class continued to grow in wealth, though their direct political influence was gradually restricted. *Forbes* magazine estimated that the number of Russian billionaires (measured in U.S. dollars) had increased from thirty-six individuals in 2004 (all men apart from the billionaire wife of the Moscow mayor) to eighty-seven in 2008, a national total second in the world after the United States.

Notwithstanding all the attention paid the oligarchs, who indeed managed to concentrate exceptional wealth in their hands, Russia's new entrepreneurial class was diverse. Most "New Russians" were not oligarchs, though they had much in common with them. They were young and rich and made their fortunes not in manufacturing—a more respectable area of the economy in public opinion, though a stagnant one—but in finance,

Demonstrator at the "People's Veche (Assembly)" in Moscow in 1992. Poster reads "The Goal of Perestroika in the USSR: To Each Their Own? Prikhvatizatsiia" (Privatization as Grabbing). The drawing shows enterprise directors and bureaucrats taking control of factories while ordinary citizens are given only "vouchers." In the background, demonstrators carry red flags. *(Mark Steinberg)*

commerce, services, and crime. Most had some connection to criminal organizations, if only in needing to pay for protection-patronage "roofs" for their
businesses. Much attention has been paid to the "New Russians" not only
because of their wealth but also because they were most demonstrative in
standing for a new economic ethos. Their Mercedes and Land Cruisers, their
expensive Western clothing, their styling salons and gyms, their brick vil-
las (*kottedzhi*) decked out with imported furnishings and Jacuzzis inspired
by Western magazines, and their women (the "New Russian" was always
male—the role of a woman, whether as wife or the ubiquitous mistress, was
to be possessed, cared for, and to ornament the man's life), as well as their
occupations and wealth, all marked them as profoundly different from the
old Soviet elite. This was only the visible tip of the capitalist-entrepreneurial
iceberg, however. Various groups of new business operators, both men and
very often women, emerged after 1991, including top managers of privatized
firms, officials who became business directors, founders of new media and
small businesses, and leaders of "mafia" protection rackets. Despite conditions far from conducive to rational capitalism, tens of thousands of entrepreneurs entered and conducted business throughout the country. The 1998
financial collapse drove many out of business. On the other hand, the devalued ruble created new possibilities for domestic production, leading to a
rise in small and medium businesses engaged in domestic manufacturing
as well as services and trade. Indeed, by 1999, small businesses were proliferating, though they remained concentrated in Moscow, St. Petersburg, and
other large cities.

   Sociologists and economists have argued that the major challenge facing
businesspeople in the new Russia has not been public attitudes—the often
described "traditional" moral disdain for wealth not earned through direct
labor—but the legacy of the structural conditions in which Russia's new capitalism arose: the massive and often corrupt transfer of state and public assets
into private hands, which created, in the words of the sociologist Victoria
Bonnell, a "mode of acquisitiveness" that is less the rationalist model of modern capitalism described by Max Weber (though this "civilized" state of business and society is precisely what many entrepreneurs long for) than a system
based on "personalistic ties, political influence, crime, corruption, and violent
entrepreneurship." And yet, individuals have been ready to take part in this
uncertain system. Indeed, not only entrepreneurs but also growing numbers
of consultants, stockbrokers, commodity traders, and employees in all sorts
of businesses have embraced capitalist behaviors and values. More broadly,
a growing number of salary- and wage-earning Russians began to identify
themselves as "middle class," by virtue of their education, professional skills,
and occupations; limited but still increased ability to buy consumer goods,
both domestic and imported and acceptance of the new economic order.
Between 1999 and 2004, polls; indicate, the proportion of Russians identifying themselves as "middle class" more than doubled from about 20 percent
to 43 percent of the population: most were young, educated, lived in large cities, felt they had good incomes, and were optimistic about the future. Indeed,

objective measurements suggest that the actual percentage of middle-class Russians today is much lower.

The growth of wealth in Russia has been inseparable from the persistence and growth of poverty. The 1990s were devastating in this respect, and the effects have lasted. Average real wages declined, variously affected by extreme inflation, direct pay cuts, reduced working hours, temporary layoffs, and wages paid in kind rather than in cash (widespread in the early 1990s); throughout the 1990s, huge numbers of workers, perhaps the majority, did not receive their wages on time, sometimes waiting months for a paycheck. Most enterprises preferred wage reductions to unemployment—fearing social disorder but also reflecting the notion that firms should care for their workers, a heritage of Soviet paternalism—thus limiting this scourge. Still, official unemployment data, which most specialists agree were too conservative, recorded steadily rising joblessness, from about 5 percent in 1992 to 13 percent in 1999. These structural degradations strongly affected standards of living, already low in Soviet times. The everyday diet for the majority of the population declined throughout the 1990s. Per capita consumption of meat and dairy products fell, such that the overall caloric intake reached a level well below the minimum established by the World Health Organization. And all of this, at least in the major cities, occurred while shops filled with imported luxury foods and expensive new restaurants proliferated.

In the early years of free trade after 1991, small sales booths like this one in Moscow in 1994 proliferated. As here, alcohol, cigarettes, and snack food, almost all of it imported, were particularly common items. Also note the German advertisement, the plastic shopping bags (one decorated with an American flag), and the bra. (*Mark Steinberg*)

A small grocery store and currency exchange in Moscow in 1999. A picture of Pushkin is in the window. Such mixing of commerce, Russian national cultural pride, and foreign advertising been common.  *(Mark Steinberg)*

Conditions were even worse, of course, for those who could not work. Scholars spoke of a growing class of "dispossessed," including the jobless, the disabled, refugees from post-Soviet successor states, economic migrants, and people living in cities without proper residence permits. Desperate rural poverty produced a mass migration out of the countryside, turning tens of thousands of villages into ghost towns with no more than a handful of usually elderly residents; in 2004, 13,000 villages stood officially empty. The declining value of government pensions relative to the cost of living pushed the huge class of the elderly into poverty. Homelessness—including the "dispossessed" as well as abandoned, orphaned, and runaway children who formed gangs of waifs—became endemic in larger cities. That many Russians were not surviving the transition was often literally true. Compared to 1985, when life expectancy for Soviet men had reached 65 years, by the end of the 1990s men were likely to live on average only 59 years (women's life expectancy declined more modestly from 74 to 70 years). Rising mortality (a growth of 30 percent from 1990 to 2000, giving Russia the highest rate of any major nation) combined with a falling birthrate (many families, given the insecurities of the age, chose to have few children or forego them altogether) resulted in a declining national population. As the twenty-first century began, Russia's population was falling by about a million people a year. And many Russians, including some of the ablest, were emigrating.

Under Putin, these conditions were ameliorated as the economy expanded, but everyone agreed that poverty and ill health remained persistent problems. According to World Bank criteria, poverty peaked in Russia in 1999 at 41.5

The existence of dire poverty and homelessness beside growing wealth for part of the urban population is one of the persistent and troubling features of postcommunist life in Russia, as reflected in this photograph from the center of Moscow in 2007. *(Maxim Marmur/AFP/Getty Images)*

percent and declined by as much as 20 percent in the following decade, though interrupted by the severe economic crisis that began in 2008. But extensive poverty remained. In 2008, the new president, Dmitrii Medvedev, defined poverty, along with corruption, as the greatest internal threat facing Russia. Nongovernmental studies and opinion polls of people's subjective sense of living conditions suggest that as much as 40 percent of the population still lived in poverty in 2008, before the new recession. News reports and sociological studies continued to find that most people could afford to purchase little more than essential food. Conditions were especially dire in rural areas—such that scholars began to speak of a "ruralization of poverty"—and in the southern regions of the Russian Federation. The catastrophic condition of public health also remained a persistent concern. A slight increase in life expectancy (about two additional years for men from 1999 to 2008) and a decline in infant mortality were positive signs of progress, though Russia remained far behind European norms. Indeed, the continued shrinking of the national population may be a sign of continued social damage. This continued decline in population has alarmed many Russians: not only for the economic risks it poses, but also as a sign of a suffering "nation." That birthrates have been higher among ethnic minorities has been one of many conditions stimulating growing ethnic and racial enmity in recent years.

Surprisingly, perhaps, the deepening stratification of Russian society did not lead to open social polarization or mass protest—apart from a series of sometimes violent anti-government demonstrations led by communists and nationalists in the early 1990s and growing violence against minorities in the late 2000s. To be sure, opinion polls have shown much contempt for the immoral and illegal means by which the new rich aggrandized themselves and for their corrupt links to political power. And the success of both communists and nationalists in elections throughout the 1990s reflected what has been called a "politics of *ressentiment*" that combined relatively abstract feelings of political loss over the demise of the Soviet Union with very tangible and personal feelings of material suffering. But acceptance of the new social conditions—shaped, many have argued, by disillusionment with socialism, so that no plausible alternatives seem to exist—and a focus on survival rather than on the struggle for change, has been the most visible response to hardship. Strikes have been rare. Trade unions have not enjoyed a revival. And polls of workers show hope that more and more ordinary Russians will be able to take advantage of the greater availability of goods and the new possibilities for upward mobility. But most of all, individuals and families have focused their energies on finding ways to survive. Especially during the devastating 1990s, people took multiple jobs, supplemented impossibly low pensions and disability payments by finding menial jobs, cultivated garden plots for food, obtained help from relatives when possible, and sold goods they no longer needed (or purchased to resell) in markets and on street corners. In the early 1990s, especially, the sight of long rows of individuals selling handfuls of goods in the street became common. And begging has remained ubiquitous. Women, in particular, both as individuals and as key figures in the family economy, have been in the forefront of these strategies of survival. Ordinary Russians have not been passive in the face of the economic hardships of post-socialism, but they also seem to have been more patient with the "transition" than many expected.

## Decay, Disintegration, and Disorder

Decay and disintegration pervaded public perceptions of social life after the fall of communism. Newspapers and government commissions regularly reported, and citizens were able to easily witness, decaying and malfunctioning machinery, deteriorating roads and buildings, collapsing buildings (old ones due to disrepair and new ones due to faulty construction), accidents and explosions caused by the age and ill repair of equipment of all sorts, gas and oil pipeline ruptures, fires, electricity failures, toxic spills, airplane crashes, and other signs that Russia in the 1990s was becoming "a perpetual calamity zone." Lenin had declared that communism equaled Soviet power plus the electrification of the whole country; now newspapers reported an epidemic of looting of electric wires and equipment to sell as metal scrap, resulting not only in power interruptions but many electrocutions. The tragic sinking in August 2000 of the nuclear submarine *Kursk*, which resulted in the death of its entire crew, shortly followed by a devastating fire in the Ostankino television tower in Moscow, both symbols of Soviet technological prowess (the tower had been erected to celebrate the fiftieth anniversary of the Bolshevik Revolution), seemed symbolic. As one Russian scholar put it, "The dark television screens seemed to say that Russia was entering an age of catastrophes." The country has seen some improvements since the 1990s. The physical condition of buildings and roads began to improve first in Moscow, where a concentration of new wealth led to intensive reconstruction and modernization, and gradually in other cities. Still, the coexistence of deteriorating apartment buildings and new luxury residences, of dilapidated neighborhoods and shining new shopping malls or gated communities, remains characteristic of Russia's new urban landscape. Likewise, statistics on public safety show progress in reducing fires and other accidents, though these still claim far more lives in Russia, even in Moscow, than in other industrial countries, underscoring what a foreign journalist in 2007 described as the "enduring disorder beneath Russia's partial revival."

Human bodies were also suffering. The 1990s, especially, saw a dramatic rise in infectious diseases as well as of heart attacks, strokes, and cancer. Tuberculosis reached epidemic proportions. Rates of hepatitis, syphilis, and AIDS skyrocketed, and there were severe outbreaks of diphtheria, encephalitis, typhoid fever, malaria, polio, pneumonia, and influenza. A large percentage of military recruits were found to be physically unfit; the head of the draft, General Alexander Galkin, declared the health condition of recruits in the late 1990s to be "catastrophic." Part of the problem was the healthcare system, which staggered under the pressures of low salaries for doctors and healthcare workers, shortages of medicines and other supplies, and backward and decaying technologies. Limited privatization benefited only a tiny minority. But social conditions were the primary cause, especially widespread poverty, stress, alcoholism, smoking, overcrowding, unprotected sex (especially with prostitutes), and intravenous drug use. The prison system, in particular, was described as an "epidemiological pump." Rising mortality rates and a declining population—and suicide rates that reached among the highest levels in the world in the mid-1990s—made it seem that Russia, in the common phrase of critics on both the Left and the Right, was "dying." There were improvements under Putin, but they remained incremental. The World Health Organization reported improvements in almost all statistical measures of public health but still defined Russia as one of the sickest countries in the world. Thirty percent of draftees in the 2007 recruitment year were judged "unsuitable" and 50 percent as limited in capacity. Even younger Russians continued to suffer physically. In 2008, President Medvedev, in his first annual speech to the nation, admitted that the health condition of schoolchildren was "simply horrible." Critics bitterly noted that well into the twenty-first century, Russians remained anchorless, alienated, and vulnerable; uncertain about their futures while still in school; and finding material success elusive after entering the workforce. Drug use, prostitution, and AIDS have been most widespread among teenagers and youths—and the fact that these problems were relatively "unknown" in Soviet times, which is to say that they were not officially reported, is as much parts the perception of their meaning as that these problems have increased. As will be discussed later, popular culture among the young—music, clothing styles, and leisure activities (summarized by some youths as limited to "buying beer, sitting with friends, and listening to music")—was seen as another sign that Russian society was heading in the wrong direction. Indeed, polls throughout the 1990s found that many Russians viewed the whole course of postcommunist economic, social, and cultural development in Russia as leading to a "dead end."

The spread of crime after 1991 represented for many the surest sign of Russia's social and moral fall and the inability of the state to maintain needed order and normalcy, notwithstanding Yeltsin's and especially Putin's declarations of war on crime. Rates of assault, homicide, corruption, poaching, and trafficking (including internationally) in narcotics, arms, and people (especially women and children) have been disturbingly widespread. Organized crime the—"mafia"—has loomed larger in the imagination of both foreigners and Russians than in reality; a 1997 poll found that more Russians believed organized crime ran the country than those who felt the government was in charge. Nonetheless, crime was a real and persistent problem, taking a variety of forms. With the collapse of the Soviet economy and the rise of private enterprise, "protection rackets" proliferated. At its most simple, a protection racket involved extorting regularly paid dues in return for a "roof" (*krysha*) of protection against other gangs, street bandits, police, and politicians (all of whom competed in offering "roofs"). At their best, these rackets offered real protection and even the enforcement of contracts and property rights between businesses and individuals at a time when state and legal structures remained weak. At their worse, rackets engaged in unambiguous extortion: pay us or we will make you pay, even with your lives. Often, they were a mixture of both. Criminal groups, often styled as "mafias," also became involved in smuggling, the drug trade, counterfeiting, and organized prostitution, but they also invested in banks, casinos, and other businesses. Indeed, specialists have described a large criminal "shadow economy." This criminal economy has often been entwined with the legal economy, including illegal and sometimes violent means in the pursuit of legal economic activities, illegal privatizations left uncontested by law, criminals involved in entirely legal legal activities, and ordinary citizens engaged in illegal activities without connections to mobs. Indeed, while true gangsters are said to adhere to certain criminal cultural conventions—a recognized thieves' "law"—the problem of thugs who lack any moral or rational restraint made even the criminal underworld a dangerous and uncertain order. Worse still were "social black holes" where state authority, legal order, and a functioning civil society were replaced by lawlessness, invisible social networks that rule a locality through predation and violence, and the breakdown of confidence and social norms in favor of an ethos of individual survival by any means. Emerging social black holes were described in the north Caucasus and the Russian North and Far East.

Perhaps the most spectacularly disturbing criminal activity is contract assassinations of public figures. Politicians (such as the noted liberal reformer

Galina Starovoitova in St. Petersburg in 1998), journalists (most famously, the investigative reporter Anna Politkovskaya in 2006), human rights activists, lawyers, bankers, and businessmen have been gunned down, often on the streets in broad daylight, and many others have had their lives threatened for challenging local authorities, for overly zealous investigations of criminals, for violating agreements with racketeers, for refusing to agree to extortionist protection or patronage demands, or for reasons unknown. Many of these crimes remain unsolved. A less brutal, but ubiquitous, scourge has been official corruption, ranging from local police officers to Kremlin officials. For ordinary citizens, the bribery of public officials became a familiar experience, ranging from payments to expedite matters that were otherwise quite legal, to secure access (such as entry into university), and to secure an exception to some rule or law, to outright purchase of an official's ongoing support. Complicating all of this have been ambiguous definitions of what is "crime" and what is simply necessary "reciprocity," especially in a context in which laws and legal norms were still evolving.

## Beliefs and Ideologies

How Russians have understood and interpreted the realities around them has been as important as the facts themselves. Perceptions, desires, and ideals have shaped responses to social and economic conditions. Since 1991, Russians have been struggling to decide what they believe about such crucial questions as the meaning of freedom and democracy, the cultural values and ethics that should guide everyday life, and the character and future of the Russian nation. A useful source has been regular public opinion polls, especially by such professional and independent organizations as the All-Russian Center for the Study of Public Opinion (VTsIOM) and the Levada Center. These polls, along with other social research, have revealed much uncertainty about Russia's "transition." By the end of the 1990s, the overwhelming majority of Russians (70 percent) believed they had lost more than they had gained from the changes of that decade. Polls also found most Russians dismayed with Russia's humiliation as a world power, the perceived moral breakdown in society, and the invasion of the country by Western popular culture—sentiments, as we have seen, that political leaders regularly echoed. Disillusionment was widespread, not only because of the tangible results of reform, but also because of an awareness that there were no better alternatives than the difficult present. Thus, at the end of the 1990s, the vast majority of Russians continued to believe that dismantling the Soviet Union was a mistake and to view a "democratized" version of the Soviet system as the preferred political form for Russia (only 9 percent spoke of desiring "Western-type democracy"). Of course, success in the new order shaped different judgments. Partly because age and likelihood of success in the new Russia were connected, young people were more positive: half of men and women over the age of sixty-nine in 1999 voiced a preference for the old Soviet system, compared to only 10 percent of those under thirty. As the economy recovered and grew, beginning in the late 1990s,

Russians' sense of "satisfaction" with the present and confidence in the future also grew. Still, even on the eve of the new economic crisis that began in 2008, which dramatically depressed social confidence, a poll by the Levada Center found that half the people who identified themselves as "middle class" (and were aged twenty-four to thirty-nine, so most likely to have good prospects) doubted the stability of the present and were thinking of emigration.

"Democracy" found strong support in the population. Indeed, scholars have argued, Russians appear to have "assimilated democratic values" faster than the elite established democratic institutions or ensured that democracy had made most people's lives tangibly better. In polls taken between 1996 and 2003, most Russians—though not all, it bears remembering—agreed that the life and rights of the individual are more important than any other value (and that this is a "universal" truth), that laws should apply equally to everyone, that property rights are inviolable, that freedom of thought and expression is as necessary to Russians as to people in the West, and that citizens should elect their leaders in a free and competitive environment. To be sure, half the population, according to a 2000 survey, insisted that order is more important than personal freedom. And most Russians professed to value a "strong leader" and a "strong state." But even in the name of "restoring Russia's great power potential" or restoring "order," most Russians rejected curtailing freedom of speech and the press and democratic elections. Better to "know the truth," it was agreed, even when the media is filled with frightening "problems and scandals," than return to a time when the media focused only on "good things." No less important, opinion studies showed deep skepticism about the utopian promise that the state or leaders can create a perfect society.

On the other hand, belief in democracy has been paired with disillusionment. As President Medvedev told a newspaper interviewer in 2009, because "the very difficult political, and especially economic, processes of the 1990s were combined with the arrival of basic democratic institutions in our country... this left its mark on how this term is comprehended." Observers noted pervasive skepticism, fatalism, and passivity in public opinion—also reflected in declining participation in elections. This has worried both public officials and specialists. As Lilia Shevtsova, a leading Russian political scientist, observed in 1999, "hopelessness breeds frustration, despair, and violence. How strong can a government be that is built on the disenchantment of the population?... Who can guarantee that at some moment the desire for violent revenge will not overtake those who feel they have been betrayed? Russia has a long and tragic history of attempts to find justice." And yet the dominant mood, even in the harsh 1990s, seems to have been a determination to endure. And enduring has continued to mean, for most Russians, staying on the path of democracy. Still, specialists on Russian public opinion have warned that attitudes remain volatile. "Ambivalence" remains a most characteristic feature of public views on such critical issues as democracy, markets, and Westernizing reform. Indeed, opinion polls after 2005 found attachment to democracy and civil liberties yielding to a greater emphasis on economic prosperity and civil order.

Communists demonstrate on Red Square in Moscow in 1992.   (*P. Gorshkov*)

Nationalists and communists thrived in Russian civic life after 1991 partly because their rhetoric echoed widespread anxieties, discontents, and ideals. Important differences separated the communists of the Left from the nationalists of the Right: communists were more likely to speak of social justice for the common person while nationalists of the harm alien ideas and ethnicities have brought to the Russian people. But both took the stance, often in alliance, of offering a "national-patriotic" and "spiritual" opposition to liberal democratic reform, which was seen to have resulted in a loss of national and moral strength as well as personal suffering. A variety of militant nationalist groups formed during the crisis years of the early 1990s, often taking to the streets of Moscow and other cities in demonstrations and regularly clashing with police, leading many to speak of a Weimar-like situation: newspapers of "national and spiritual opposition" like Alexander Prokhorov's *Den* (Day, renamed *Zavtra*, Tomorrow, in 1993); anti-Semitic and anti-Western organizations like Pamyat (Memory), which had formed in 1987; numerous small-scale publishers of scurrilously anti-Semitic and anti-government pamphlets and newspapers (easily found for sale on the street corners of major cities); neo-Stalinist groups like Viktor Anpilov's Working Russia; movements openly laying claim to the prerevolutionary legacy of the "Black-Hundred" Union of the Russian People; monarchists who looked to a restoration of the empire and the Romanovs; neo-fascists like Russian National Unity, with their uniformed storm troopers and use of a slightly modified swastika as their symbol; the writer Eduard Limonov's somewhat

bizarre "left-fascist" National Bolshevik Party; "statist" and "national-patriotic" groupings of parliamentary deputies; gatherings such as the "People's
*Veche*" (a term invoking a medieval Russian political tradition) of 1992; the
nationalist Union of Officers; a revived cossack movement; and the National
Salvation Front, which united nationalists and communists. Socially, these
radical groups attracted a mixture of unskilled workers, pensioners, and
military men—in other words, those who felt they had lost the most after
the end of communism—though leaders were often intellectuals attracted
by the idea of restoring a "Russian idea" to public life. While Yeltsin banned
some of the most extreme groups in the wake of the October 1993 battle
over parliament, and many groups remained marginal, the movement of
"patriotic" opposition also had a strong national and legislative presence.
By the late 1990s, two groups stood out: the Communist Party of the Russian
Federation, led by Gennady Zyuganov since its establishment in 1993, and
Vladimir Zhirinovsky's Liberal Democratic Party. Both parties remained
active in Russian politics—able to cross the electoral threshold for representation in parliament and tolerated by the government—throughout the
Yeltsin and Putin years.

Ideologically, the "patriotic" critique of postcommunism focused on
two interrelated concerns: Russia's crisis of national strength and its moral
("spiritual") crisis. Nationalists and communists alike echoed and encouraged
widespread feelings that Russia had been humiliated in the world. Russia's
loss of political space (the Soviet Union, which was largely coextensive with
the Russian Empire), the decline of Russia's military might, and the weakness of the economy were seen as resulting in the loss of status as a great
power. Symbolic of the loss of sovereignty and dignity was the flood of foreign
goods pouring into Russia in the early 1990s—Fords and Mercedes, Barbie
dolls, food, even vodka, not to mention the ubiquitous use of dollars—along
with foreign popular culture, including popular music, imported television
shows and movies, McDonald's, and MTV. Russia's weakness was also seen
to result from its moral disintegration. Pornography and prostitution, garish
gambling parlors in city centers, a new economy marked more by trade than
productive work, conspicuous consumption by rich "New Russians" and their
imitators, sexual explicitness and violence in films and television, a decadent
youth culture, and pervading materialism were all seen as bleeding Russia of
its sources of spiritual and hence national strength.

Various enemies were blamed for Russia's fall. Right-wing nationalists castigated "democrats" as traitors who "stabbed the Fatherland in the
back" in alliance with foreign powers who conspired to weaken a once
mighty nation, accused reformers of "subservience to the West" and even of
"economic genocide," and condemned the mass media for "Russophobia."
Communists, too, tended to attack capitalism less in class terms as the
exploitation of the proletariat than in national terms as the exploitation of
peripheral nations like Russia by the "new world order." In all cases, the
language of nationalism has been emotional. At its most positive, this has
been a language of love for the Russian motherland, its nature and history,

its people, and its "spiritual heritage"—a rhetoric also adopted by Yeltsin, Putin, Medvedev, and the ruling party. The unique "Russian idea," it has been said, is characterized by collectivism (*sobornost*), a statist ideal that links the interests of the individual to the strength of the state, and a "spiritual" commitment to truth, goodness, and justice. But nationalist and communist movements have also often expressed great resentment, anger, and hatred. The most extreme voices have spoken of Russia's "spiritual occupation" by an alien Western culture and called for uniting the "simple people" in "holy struggle" against the "parasites" and "Judases." The language has sometimes been virulently anti-Western and anti-Semitic: "a foreign 'for sale' sign has been affixed to the body of our country with patented, American-made nails," wrote one influential writer; others have blamed Jews for all of Russia's problems (noting, in particular, the Jewish ancestry of a number of the oligarchs) and branded the government a "Yidocracy." Many alienated urban youths were attracted to Nazi paraphernalia, violent attacks on non-Russians, skinhead dress and groups, and tough right-wing and racist talk about "yids" and "democrashit" (*dermokratiia*). More socially minded movements, mainly on the communist and socialist Left, have added the suffering of the common people to this critique and advocated a reborn nation characterized by egalitarianism, social justice, and care for the unprotected poor. Social grievance and emotional nationalism have been strongly interconnected in all this. The popular success of Zhirinovsky and Zyuganov throughout the 1990s and 2000s has been due to their abilities to voice people's socioeconomic resentments as well as to their emotional appeals. Communists and nationalists alike, scholars have argued, effectively tapped into a "politics of *ressentiment*," which has been central to nationalist ideologies in many parts of the world in recent times. It is the harsh truth that the end of communism resulted in much suffering, alienation, and perceived humiliation. Nationalists and communists offered both explanations and promises of redemption or revenge.

Especially in Putin's Russia, it has been argued, nationalism became mainstream—as official rhetoric, in popular culture, and in public opinion. Rhetorically, the three main "opposition" parties in the parliament—the Communist Party, the Liberal Democrats, and Just Russia (formed in 2006 as a coalition of the Motherland [Rodina], Pensioners', and Life parties)—regularly speak of the continuing "misfortunes of the Russian people," the need to address social problems in order to create a unified "national" community, and the need for a renaissance of the "Russian nation." The ruling party, United Russia, says much the same. After 2000, Putin was as likely as any nationalist to speak of the essential need for Russia's "spiritual unity" around distinctive national "values." His restoration of the Soviet national anthem (with new words) and the army's red star were part of a larger campaign to appropriate nationalism for the state. Putin's government also supported demands to impose traditional cultural values on Russia's disordered freedom and to stem the tide of cultural decadence, ranging from slightly comical and ineffective actions, like an attempt to ban Halloween celebrations in schools, to a gradual but sustained effort to require mandatory religious instruction in schools and a massive shutdown of casinos in Moscow and other central cities in 2009. Government officials pursued other cultural "reforms" such as restoring to the history textbooks approved for schools a view of the past uncorrupted by "pseudo-liberalism" and constructing (or rebuilding) statues commemorating Russia's imperial and Soviet past. The government also helped establish, in 2005, a patriotic youth movement, *Nashi* (translatable literally as "Our Own," though it implies "we Russians"), which critics dubbed Putin-Jugend in reference to the Hitler-Jugend in Nazi Germany. Insistently optimistic and patriotic, the movement envisioned Russia, due to its strong cultural traditions, as "the global leader of the 21st century," though only if foreign and non- Russian influences in the country are limited.

The teaching of history, especially, developed again into an account of positive national achievement. Putin regularly called on teachers to instill feelings of pride in the whole of the Russian and Soviet past. Textbooks dwelling on past crimes, such as the Stalinist Terror or the gulag, were replaced by more positive accounts. Pavel Danilin, one of the authors of an influential guide for history teachers, written at the government's request and published in 2007, stated that teachers must present Russian history "not as a depressing sequence of misfortunes and mistakes but as something to instill pride in one's country." Likewise, civic organizations that documented and publicized political repression in Soviet history, notably Memorial, were criticized and harassed. In 2009, President Medvedev went still further and established a commission to investigate the "falsification" of history that sought to "disparage the international prestige of the Russian Federation." Popular films and books, as we will see later, were also increasingly filled with a new idealization of Russianness, past and present. Public opinion polls indicate that the public largely shares this preference for a patriotic telling of Russian history.

The dark side of this patriotic and nationalist revival was a new rise under Putin of "radical nationalism and xenophobia"—the phrase used by Russian human rights organizations, like the SOVA (OWL) Center in Moscow, that have documented this trend. Reports have described, especially since 2004 (possibly stimulated by a series of terrorist attacks in Russia, notably the bloody Beslan school siege in 2004), the proliferation of right-wing groups; violent and often murderous attacks by "neo-Nazi skinheads" on minorities, especially migrants from the Caucasus and Central Asia, but also students from Africa and east Asia; anti-Jewish and anti-Muslim vandalism and violence; and the general tendency of police authorities to minimize racist violence as mere "hooliganism" rather than as hate crimes. Rights organizations have also noted the revival of xenophobic and racist language in the media and the use of "xenophobia as an electoral strategy" by almost every political party. Public opinion surveys in the late 2000s similarly showed a rise in hostility to non-Russians. In particular, polls showed strong public support for deporting non-Slavic migrants from Russia's central cities. It is not surprising, in this context, that a UN official found in 2006 an exceptional "feeling of fear and solitude" among foreign communities and ethnic minorities in the main Russian cities.

## Religion

Since 1991, we have seen a new prominence of religious institutions and belief, a revived link between national identity and religion, and the ubiquity of religious ideas and vocabularies in public discourse. This sudden resurgence should make us question any simple understanding of Soviet society as purely secular and atheist (though also of modernization as inevitably displacing religion). As we now know, the actual history of religion under communism was a mixture of secularization, often brutally enforced, and persistent belief and practice. Since the fall of communism, religion has provided many people with a powerful source of identity, community, and morality. Many religions and denominations have revived—Russian Orthodoxy, Old Belief, Protestantism, Catholicism, Islam, Judaism, Buddhism, and others. But the Orthodox Church has been the main beneficiary. The Church has been openly favored by presidents Yeltsin, Putin, and Medvedev and by almost all political parties; even Zyuganov and his communists have proclaimed religion to be part of Russia's essential heritage and declared the party open to believers. A large majority of the population of the Russian Federation now identify themselves as Orthodox (a percentage that increased steadily after 1991)—though a smaller majority say they believe in God, and only a small minority regularly attend services.

The Church sought and gained a large role in the country's civil and moral life. Patriarch Alexis II (enthroned 1990, died 2008) was close to the government and actively spoke out on public issues. His successor, Kirill I (enthroned 2009), has continued this public role. The Church believes it has an essential interest in guiding Russia's social and moral development but also in supporting a strong state. In 2000, the Church hierarchs adopted a social doctrine condemning abortion, homosexuality, euthanasia, and genetic engineering; warning against the new capitalist ethos of selfish materialism; and endorsing ecumenical engagement (though this was opposed by the Church's right wing and even the majority made it clear that they were offended by other religions' efforts to convert Orthodox Russians), support for the military (though acknowledging that war is an evil), and the concept of private property. The role of the state in civic life grew dramatically after Putin became president, and the Church, in turn, endorsed the state's leaders and policies. These efforts have been complicated by ideological divisions in the Russian Orthodox Church. There exists a strong right wing, characterized among its other qualities by anti-Westernism, anti-Semitism, and isolationism, and headed until his death in 1995 by the second-ranking hierarch of the Church, the Metropolitan of St. Petersburg John (Ioann). Patriarch Alexis II managed to contain Metropolitan John and his followers and to continue a rather moderate and flexible policy, but the tension between the two points of view remains unresolved. At the other end of the spectrum, dissident priests and laypeople

A woman crosses herself in a former church in 1991. Many church buildings, which had been turned into storage buildings or factories during Soviet times, were reclaimed by the Church, re-sanctified, and restored. (*M. Rogozin*)

have organized movements within the Church—though some clerical leaders have been defrocked—favoring a new, more relevant, liturgy in the vernacular; greater lay participation in services; regular Bible study; ecumenicalism; and an active social mission. In 2007, the Russian Church ended an eighty-year schism and reunited with the two émigré branches, the agreement signed in the presence of President Putin, the mayor of Moscow, and other government officials.

The question of Church-state relations has been a complex one, as in much of Russian history. Article 14 of the constitution of 1993 declares that "The Russian Federation is a secular state. No religion may be established as a state or obligatory one. Religious associations shall be separated from the state and shall be equal before the law." But this division has been steadily eroded in practice. This has been justified by Russian traditions, notably arguments about the unbreakable trinity of "Faith, Fatherland, and Nation," which almost literally revived the nineteenth-century ideal of Official Nationality, with its unity of "Orthodoxy, Autocracy, Nationality." Symbolically, property was returned to the Church and new churches built with state support. When former President Yeltsin died in 2007, his funeral—including a lying in state in the rebuilt Cathedral of Christ the Savior in Moscow—was the first state-sanctioned Orthodox funeral for a Russian leader since the death of Emperor Alexander III in 1894. In state-run schools, the requirement since 2002 that a course on the "Foundations of Orthodox Culture" be included in the curriculum, though formally only a course *about* Orthodoxy, has been criticized as amounting to state establishment of religion.

Many critics worry about declining tolerance for other faiths as Orthodoxy is treated as the national religion. A key step was the 1997 law on religion that, on the one hand, guaranteed "freedom of conscience and religious confession" and "tolerance and respect" for all beliefs, while, with the other hand, declared Christianity, Islam, Judaism, and Buddhism to be the historically traditional religions of Russia, giving them various legal privileges and requiring complicated registration procedures for other religious groups to operate. "Christianity" has meant, in practice, Orthodoxy, which was recognized in the law for its "special contribution ... to the history of Russia and to the establishment and development of Russia's spirituality and culture. Although the bill was internationally denounced as an infraction of the freedom of religion, its defenders insisted that this move was necessary to prevent well-funded and organized movements from unfairly filling a vacuum created by decades of Soviet oppression of native religions. Many Orthodox churches posted at their entrances a long list of "false faiths," ranging from Catholicism to Krishna Consciousness, against which Orthodox believers were to guard themselves. In practice, Catholics and some mainstream Protestant groups were tacitly recognized and nontraditional denominations persisted, though obstacles and restrictions grew under Putin's presidency. A *New York Times* journalist summarized a common view of the situation in a report in 2008: "Just as the government has tightened control over political life, so, too, has it intruded in matters of faith. The Kremlin's surrogates in many areas have turned the Russian Orthodox Church into a de facto official religion, warding off other Christian denominations that seem to offer the most significant competition for worshipers.... This close alliance between the government and the Russian Orthodox Church has become a defining characteristic of Mr. Putin's tenure, a mutually reinforcing choreography that is usually described here as working 'in symphony.'" Certainly, Putin was quite clear in insisting that Russianness is linked to Orthodoxy. "Of course, by law the Church in Russia is separate from the state," Putin declared in January 2004 while on a Christmas tour of ancient monasteries and churches, "but in our souls as well as in our history, we are together. So it is and shall be forever."

The rise of the Orthodox Church is not the only sign of revived religion. The aftermath of 1991 also witnessed a rich and diverse flourishing of religious and spiritual beliefs and practices, much reminiscent of (and sometimes

Christ the Savior cathedral in Moscow being rebuilt in 1997. To commemorate the Russian victory over Napoleon, Alexander I ordered the construction of a great cathedral in Moscow, dedicated to Christ the Savior. Consecrated by Alexander III in 1883, it was destroyed on Stalin's orders in 1931, in order to build in its place a massive Palace of Soviets. Due to unstable ground, the Palace could not be built; believers saw divine intervention in this failure. A public swimming pool was built instead. With the support of the government of the city of Moscow, the cathedral was reconstructed according to the original plans as a symbol of defeated communism and resurrected faith. The completed cathedral was consecrated in 2000, though many believers expressed discomfort that so much money was spent on this project while material suffering in the country remained so great. *(Mark Steinberg)*

explicitly a revival of) trends during Russia's prerevolutionary religious renaissance. Influential poets, writers, artists, and even rock musicians made religion, sometimes tied to ideas of nation, central to their work, though references to pre-Christian Slavic elements, vague mysticism, and illusions to Christ, Mary, saints, and the Church were often ambiguously intertwined. Intellectuals often wrote about a unique Russian spirituality that is central to the "Russian idea" and the "Russian soul." Many prerevolutionary and émigré religious authors, such as Vladimir Solovyov and Nikolai Berdyaev, were widely republished and reread. And, as we have noted, most nationalist movements linked their notions of the nation to Orthodox faith and defined Russia's salvation as fundamentally "spiritual." But many who have rediscovered Christian faith also found themselves uncomfortable with the Church as an institution.

Despite obstacles, other religions also enjoyed a revival. Among Buddhists, Muslims, and Jews, various new organizations, religious and communal festivals, study groups, and temples and synagogues developed. Protestants, evangelical Christians, Mormons, Hare Krishnas, the Unification Church, Scientology, Jehovah's Witnesses, and other religious groups also became increasingly active in Russia in search of converts, to the great dismay of the established Church and many Russians. But the "threat" to the Church was not limited to foreign imports. These postcommunist years have also seen a proliferation of original domestic "cults." New religious movements like the Great White Brotherhood of Maria Devi Khristos, which has been described as a "New Age goulash of chakras, karma, Kabbalah, and music theory" combined with belief in the incarnation of Christ and Mary in one person, as well as the popularity of astrology, mysticism, ESP, and spiritualism, have been variously seen as evidence of Russia's spiritual degeneration and crisis or signs of new postcommunist freedom and creativity. For most Russians, however, spirituality has been a simpler and more personal matter. If anything, religion in Russia is becoming normalized along European lines. Recent data suggest that regular Church attendance has been declining since the revival of the early 1990s—to only 10 percent of the population according to a 2008 poll—though professed belief in God has continued to grow. For many Russians, especially given the economic, social, and moral dislocations of postcommunism, religious belief and affiliation have offered a source of community, stable truth, and faith in the future.

## Literature, the Arts, and Popular Culture

The immediate impact of the collapse of communism was as sweeping in culture as in politics and society. Censorship was abolished (shortly before the end of the Soviet Union, on August 1, 1990), ending a long history of government control of the printed word. Marxism-Leninism disappeared from sight—whatever its underground residue—both as a massive presence in schools and other academic institutions and as the universal guiding doctrine; even the new Communist Party, as we have seen, distanced itself from this one-time sacred canon. Instead Russia became immediately open to every conceivable idea and doctrine, with Russian intellectuals reveling in the latest Western views and teachings, but also in the accomplishments of their own prerevolutionary Silver Age. Unfortunately, the new intellectual richness coincided with a diminishing support from the state and general economic decline and even disaster. Ballet, opera, classical music, painting, theater, film, and literature, along with institutions of science and scholarship, all found themselves foundering financially, forced to function in a suddenly market-oriented society. Another phenomenon of these early postcommunist years was the return of dissenters and other émigrés for a visit, a few performances, or permanently. In a deeper sense, a "myth of return" has been characteristic of much postcommunist culture: nostalgic return to the "Russia we have lost" (the title of a popular documentary film in the early 1990s), return to "Western civilization," or return to suppressed or forgotten values. As social conditions worsened during the 1990s, this was joined by a nostalgia for the remembered orderliness, security, and achievements of Soviet times.

The landscape of literature, the arts, and popular culture after 1991 has been diverse and changing, a mixture of unbounded liberty, competing values, a sense of crisis, and new structures of authority. Any summary is necessarily too simple. In any case, it is still too soon to define postcommunist culture in Russia—or the rest of the post-Soviet experience, for that matter. But key trends suggest something of this complex experience. In literature—which Russians have long viewed as a mirror of contemporary life—the virtually unbridled freedom along with the social and political uncertainties and turmoil after 1991 combined to offer readers choices such as they had never seen before. Almost immediately, bookstores and especially book tables and stalls on busy streets were crowded with a phenomenal mixture: translated foreign works, ranging from pornography to detective novels to literary classics; long-forbidden émigré fiction, such as the works of Bunin, Nabokov, and Solzhenitsyn (who himself returned from exile to live in Russia, and criticize what he witnessed, in 1994); previously restricted Soviet writers, such as Babel, Bulgakov, Olesha, and Pasternak (sometimes called "returned literature"); and bibles along with occult writings. The rise of a commercial market in publishing, however, has been the biggest change in literary life, and the source of much dismay among intellectuals, who have complained that the public seems to prefer literature marked by excesses of violence and sex to serious writing about big existential questions and that poets and writers have lost their status as figures of inspiration and become merely entertainers in the cultural marketplace. Literary scholars have similarly spoken of "the wholesale displacement of the cult of high culture." During the 1990s, sex and violence became particularly pervasive in popular culture, and this trend has persisted. Naked bodies adorned the covers of magazines, movies regularly featured graphic sex, pornographic videos and Web sites proliferated, "erotic festivals" became common, and pornographic as well as serious erotic literature could be found everywhere. Sex, in much of this new work, tended to be extravagant, transgressive, and amoral. Even more popular, however, was crime fiction, or *detektivy*, and violent action stories, or *boeviki*. Gratuitous violence, social and moral chaos, and bad writing characterized most crime literature: "Take a look at any bookstand," a reviewer commented with disgust in 1996, "and you'll be dazzled by the distorted physiognomies and black muzzles of pistols aimed right at the forehead of the potential reader." Worse still, a great deal of popular literature through the 1990s, the literary historian Eliot Borenstein has argued, was marked by "a logic of cultural pessimism":

The often extravagant mixture of sex and violence has been both a defining feature of post-Soviet popular culture and a source of much public concern. The illustration here is the cover of a popular detective novel by Alexandra Marinina, *Death and a Little Love*, 1995 *(Izdatel'stvo "Eksmo")*

images of disorder, disintegration, and degradation supplanted traditional (and mandatory) Soviet optimism and cheeriness with dark anxiety about the present and the future.

Though commercial success was elusive for many of the best writers, the work of fiction writers like Lyudmila Petrushevskaya, Viktor Erofeyev, Tatyana Tolstaya, Vladimir Sorokin, and Viktor Pelevin and of poets like Dmitrii Prigov offer clear evidence of both the vitality and originality of Russian writing and the troubled cultural mood. In the view of Viktor Erofeyev, a literary critic as well as a fiction writer, much postcommunist prose abandoned the humanism and hope that inspired both Soviet and dissident authors in favor of an uncertain outlook that rejected any causes or universal truths. Suffering was recognized, but not valued as ennobling. Hope was abandoned as an illusion. Faith in reason was repudiated. Moralism was replaced by postmodern doubt and irony. Every value was called into question. The mood alternated between despair and indifference. And there was even a certain smell in this literature, Erofeev suggested: no longer the "perfume of wild flowers and hay," which pervaded older Russian and Soviet literature, but the "stench" of "death, sex, old-age, bad food, everyday life." Other critics similarly noted the centrality in the new literature of chaos, betrayal, physical need, sexuality, social degeneration (crime, prostitution, violence, crass materialism), moral transgression (or the absence of moral boundaries altogether), the deconstruction of subjectivity, an iconoclastic tendency to shock, skepticism, personal failure (though also, more optimistically, survival, but rarely personal fulfillment), and existential despair. This was reflected in the slang term *chernukha*, from the Russian word for "black," to describe the harsh naturalism and pessimism of most early post-Soviet fiction—which itself echoed widespread journalistic *chernukha* and, one might add, the dark realities that both journalism and literature reflected.

Some of this work is richly creative and complex. Lyudmila Petrushevskaya (b. 1938), for example, has been described as "an existentialist who conceives of human life as an unrelievedly punitive condition," who "charts the daily psychic monstrosities of a spiritual wasteland populated by victims and victimizers bound by an endless chain of universal suffering and abuse." Viktor Pelevin (b. 1962), who has been both critically acclaimed and relatively successful commercially and internationally, writes ironic, surreal, and often quite funny works filled with uncertainties, shadows, ambiguous metaphors, the fantastic, and the absurd. His work explores the unleashed imagination and universal questions about human existence, but also, it has been said, the "dark chaos of New Russia." His stories and novels are about the myth of individual freedom, unrealized love and longing, the ubiquity of money and materialism, mindless conformity (with television and the obsession with imitating and consuming Western things central to this theme), and the unending and unsatisfied search for existential and metaphysical meaning. Perhaps the most disturbing contemporary writer has been Vladimir Sorokin (b. 1955), whose works have been praised by some critics for their decadent and transgressive themes and reviled by Russian nationalists and moralists for the same reasons—in 2002 members of the pro-Putin youth group "Walking Together" (*Idushchie vmeste*) flushed his work down a giant toilet they constructed in front of the Bolshoy Theater in Moscow. Sorokin's work features extravagant sex and especially violence (which, he says, is the essence of human nature) and treats the present, the past, and the future with a dark sensibility but also with humor, satire, and surrealism.

In this light, and in concert with other changes after 2000, it is perhaps not surprising that literature in the Putin era, especially bestsellers, has been marked by a growing taste for nostalgic settings, fantasy, and heroic tales of good defeating evil. This was already evident in the late 1990s, for example, in the popular detective novels of Boris Akunin (the pen name of Grigorii Chkhartishvili), set in the nineteenth century, when, in the words of advertisements, "literature was great, faith in progress was unlimited, and crimes were committed and investigated with grace and refinement." And this trend has become increasingly dominant. As Eliot Borenstein has observed, a good deal of Putin-era popular literature "rejected the violent excess and bleak cynicism of the previous decade in favor of domesticity, comfort, and the continuity of family ties." The most popular new fiction tends toward sentimentality, coziness (*uiutnost'*), intimacy, and family life. But even artistic literature is often inclined toward nostalgia, or at least a melancholy sense of irremediable loss. Naturalistic *chernukha* is being pushed aside and the "perfume of wild flowers and hay" is back.

We see similar patterns in Russian cinema. The early 1990s was mainly a period of decline and chaos in the Russian film industry—the vacuum being filled by a flood of American and other foreign movies (often the worst of them), though foreign films remain a dominant presence in movie houses. But Russian filmmaking, which had a rich tradition in the Soviet era, despite the many artistic and ideological restrictions, revived dramatically by the late 1990s. Although the decline of serious artistic films during the 1990s was decried as further evidence that high art and culture had been dethroned by entertainment, this anxiety was countered by the work of talented directors such as Alexei Balabanov, Pavel Lungin, Kira Muratova, and Alexander Sokurov. Post-Soviet film has been enormously diverse in genre, including urban crime dramas (very popular and perhaps the dominant form in the 1990s), historical-costume dramas, romantic melodramas, and (often dark) comedies. Stylistically, films have ranged from the harshly naturalistic, to the fantastic or romantic, to the abstract and symbolic. But almost all of these films contain ideas and arguments about the present (or about the past as helping to define the present) and especially about "Russia." As the director and studio head Sergei Livnev explained in 1996, the purpose is "not to introduce innovations in film language," but to engage in a discussion with Russian audiences, through film, of "those questions that mutually concern us."

This search for meanings and ideals has often revolved around the question of Russia and Russianness. (This has also been a central concern in the theater, which, like film, experienced a renaissance following an initial collapse in the early 1990s.) The answers have evolved but also remain largely

Viacheslav Mikhailov, "Metaphysical Icon," 1994. A leading St. Petersburg artist, Mikhailov's works are filled with spiritual and philosophical reflections on both beauty and suffering. In this painting, part of a series called "The Russian Home," one sees both a simple domestic reference to a window and echoes of Kazimir Malevich's famous black square (see page 456), which also echoed the icon as an opening to a spiritual sphere. Here the color of the square is red, long a sacred color. *(V. Mikhailov)*

unresolved. During the 1990s, especially, critics and audiences complained that too much of Russia's new cinema offered audiences bleak and cynical portraits of Russian life rather than needed comfort and hope. Balabanov's *Brother* (1997), for example, dwelled on urban decay, organized crime, violence, murder, and youthful alienation. Other "dark" films (*chernukha*) similarly highlighted the brutality and suffering of everyday life—whether in the Chechen wars or on the streets of Moscow. A dominant theme in artistic films of the Yeltsin era was deep anxiety about social, cultural, and moral collapse, often read as national humiliation and crisis: nostalgia for what had been "lost" (perhaps in the imperial past, but also in the Soviet past), the rise of materialism and decadence and the search for a countering spirituality and morality, a crisis of masculinity and the suffering of women, love and especially its absence, death (including suicide), and survival.

In the Putin years—though many films continued to portray, and condemn, a contemporary world filled with consumerism, corruption, crime, and ruin—film often tried to suggest a way out. Patriotism, sometimes elaborated as Russian nationalism (including with hints of xenophobia), has been a growing theme in Russian film. Some directors, such as Nikita Mikhalkov, have been defined, well before the Putin era, by this national project. Films like *Burnt by the Sun* (1994) or the *Barber of Siberia* (1998) viewed both the tsarist imperial and Soviet pasts through a rosy lens of idealized Russianness rooted in tradition, nature, and patriarchal family values. Movies like Balabanov's *Brother 2* (2000) presented new heroes who violently avenge national humiliation and cleanse the world of evil. Sokurov's *Russian Ark* (*Russkii kovcheg*, 2002) saw salvation in Russia's cultural heritage, though this heritage, exemplified by the film's setting in the Hermitage Museum, is inseparably linked to the West. Other films, like Lungin's *Island* (2006), suggested a revived Orthodox spirituality as the answer to the problems of suffering and sin; the Orthodox Church recommended the film and some showings opened with prayers. Still other movies dwelled on the redeeming qualities of ordinary family life or in bucolic rural or provincial settings that evoked a less modern age. The rise of commercially successful Russian "blockbusters" (*blokbastery*) has been a new phenomenon in Russian cinema, beginning with the fantasy-action film *Night Watch* in 2004 and including films based on Akunin's novels and a number of historical epics. In style and content, these movies tended to fit with other trends in popular culture in the Putin years, especially escapism (most were set in other times or places), the heroic struggle of good against evil, and patriotic heroism and victory.

Television may well be the most important of the postcommunist visual arts in terms of audience and influence. During the 1990s, every critical event and trend—the 1991 coup, the 1993 battle over parliament, wealth and poverty, crime, cultural debates—was seen on TV. Political satires like *Kukly* (Puppets), sex talk shows like *Pro eto* (About that), game shows in which materialist consumption was idealized, music television, extremely popular crime dramas and soap operas, discussions with philosophers and writers, and historical documentaries and debates about the past—all put Russian television at the center of how Russians thought about the experience of postcommunism. In the words of one scholar, Russian TV was "largely responsible for the production of the new post-Soviet culture." No wonder, then, that television became a battleground. In the Putin years—though largely government controlled and often self-censoring—television fit with the general tenor of the times: mainly positive news reporting with much coverage of government leaders, escapist and often nostalgic comedy, melodramatic soap operas, crime dramas that emphasized the successful detective, series based on Russian literary classics, and heroic war and military spy dramas (especially around the sixtieth anniversary of victory in the Second World War). Even commercials often used national and patriotic imagery to sell products.

The more traditional forms of visual art—especially painting—also thrived after 1991, even if audiences remained small. In many ways, Russian art after communism became fully a part of world art. As in other countries, contemporary work has been variously abstract and philosophical, performative (an *aktsionizm* in which the reactions of viewers are part of the work), symbolic, magical, pop-artistic, nostalgic kitsch, primitivist, technological, and sensual. Some artists have been preoccupied with texture and form, but almost all have been concerned with meaning, even if meaning remains obscure and uncertain. Philosophically, however, painting has emphasized many of the same themes we see in the best of postcommunist literature. Spirituality—as a search for spiritual feeling if not certain meaning or faith—has been pervasive (as in the often abstract and semi-abstract work of the St. Petersburg painter Viacheslav Mikhailov). Memory and nostalgia—though much of it tinged with a knowing irony that the past can never be restored—has been no less ubiquitous (notably in the influential work of émigré Moscow conceptual artists like Ilya Kabakov or of Timur Novikov's New Academy of Fine Arts in St. Petersburg, which played with classical-imperial reminiscences). Many other themes have been noted in post-Soviet art, such as a desire magically to transcend the everyday (Nikolai Sazhin, for example), expressions of artistic inwardness, playful and ironic reworkings of images from the Soviet past (Larisa Zvezdochetova), urban dreams and phantoms (the theme of the St. Petersburg "master class" exhibition of 1997), the heroism of the individual artist, and catastrophe and cataclysm (Mikhailov). In almost all of this work, we see what the Russian art historian Alexei Kurbanovsky has called a characteristically Russian "logocentrism" in which intellectual and verbal associations—implied words and ideas—pervade the visual. In Moscow, this has taken a more conceptualist turn, working intellectually with language and images, and in St. Petersburg a more painterly and semi-abstract form, though rich in religious, literary, and historical illusions. Still, postcommunist art has rarely been art for art's sake but rather is most often art that seeks to make viewers think and feel about the world around them.

Young people and their culture have often been seen as a bellwether of Russia's cultural direction. Especially in the post-Soviet years—though the roots reached back to the late-Soviet era—rampant consumerism, cultural imitativeness, loss of ideological and moral bearing, and enormous uncertainty about the future, but also the flourishing of new opportunities, affected teenagers and young adults with particular force. Journalists, public officials, and scholars described new and much less restrictive attitudes among young people about such questions as premarital sex, gender roles, homosexuality, and drug use. Trends in rock and popular music were viewed as evidence of a decadent youth culture. Overwhelmingly, from the 1990s to today, the popular music heard on Russian radio, available for purchase on tapes and CDs, and visible on Russian MTV and its equivalents has been Western, especially American. Two styles were particularly popular among youths during the 1990s and 2000s: techno-trance (described as "give me a space to forget about the rest of the world") and hard rock ("I am pained and angry and don't really know why"). A number of Russian bands adapted popular music styles, including by giving greater weight to lyrics than most recent Western music. The popularity of groups like Alisa or Kino, whose songs often evoked a despondent gloom and alienation, suggest a disturbed and dark youth culture, as do songs like Agata Kristi's "Opium" (1995), with its dark romanticization of drugs and explicit decadence. A more recent and very popular trend has been "Russian chanson." With its naturalistic portrayals of everyday Russian life and its romantic take on crime and punishment, a Western reporter described chanson in 2006 as "the soundtrack of contemporary Russia." Complicating all this, spirituality has also been pervasive in contemporary Russian rock, ranging from Boris Grebenshikov's folk-rock explorations of ancient saints, Christ's passion, pre-Christian Slavic spiritual traditions, and "ancient Russian sorrow" (*drevnerusskaia toska*), to Alisa's hard rock images of "the blood on the Cross" that leads toward "love." To be sure, for most young people, the literary side of rock music has been less important—if noticed at all—than the danceable rhythms and compelling tunes of the music itself. Consuming music, like consuming fashionable clothing styles, has been about pleasure and fun above all. Indeed, much recent music has eschewed complex lyrics or dark melodic styles in favor of upbeat tunes and light lyrics. Still, cultural conservatives continue to worry about the decadent tendencies in youth culture, while recognizing that this is an apolitical culture. That the Russian president since 2008, Dmitrii Medvedev, is a huge fan of British hard rock (especially Deep Purple), seems to have had no effect on his political views.

Notwithstanding the anxieties popular youth culture has continued to provoke, one can see a great deal of ordinariness and normalcy. Studies suggest that throughout the 1990s and still today, most young Russians share the same concerns and values as older Russians: they care about Russia's character as a nation (including the place of ethnic difference and religious belief); they are troubled by the spread of poverty on the one hand and the selfishness and greed of the new rich on the other; they find crime and corruption disturbing; they distrust the promises of politicians and the passions of political movements of both the Left and the Right (though they tend to be more liberal than older generations); they are ambivalent about mere imitation and borrowing of Western culture; they want Russia to be a "normal" and stable society; and they are concerned first and foremost with making decent lives for themselves. According to the research of anthropologists and sociologists who have worked with young Russians, the pursuit of normalcy is what most defines the lives of youth. Young people have responded to Russia's jolting transition by being, in the words of one specialist, "neither inspired nor defeated, not happy or sad, encouraged or frustrated, creative or rebellious." They have simply been getting on with the task of making a life for themselves. They have dreamed, not of the "bright future" of communism nor the similar promises of what capitalism would bring, but simply of "living well, living at ease."

Russian history has been filled with efforts to create a bright and happy world. This idealism has been variously heroic, brutal, and tragic. Putin's frequent declarations that Russia has had its fill of revolutions echoes both this history and a widespread weariness with it. Perhaps it is a sign of change that goals have become more modest, even for Russia's historically ambitious state. Certainly, as polls and other research show, most people's greatest desire has been for "normalcy." What most Russians want for themselves and for their country is nothing more nor less than a "normal life" (*normal'naia zhizn'*). When asked, most have defined normalcy in terms that most people in the world would share: economic stability and security, public safety, an effective government respected in the world, freedom, and a moral and just society in which both social needs and individual rights are protected. In many ways, Russia remains far from "normal." But most of the population now believes that such a life is possible in Russia, though as recently as the 1990s most did not. This renewed but still fragile confidence, amidst all the contradictions and uncertainties that surround it, may be one of the most encouraging developments in the still brief history of Russia after communism.

# Appendix

RUSSIAN RULERS
TABLE 1

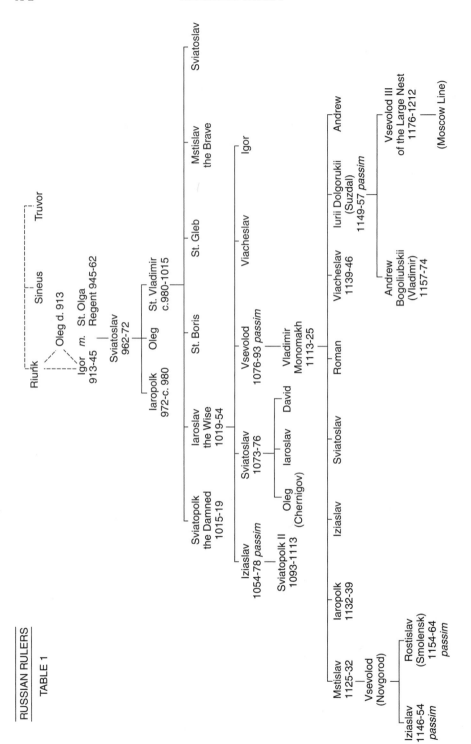

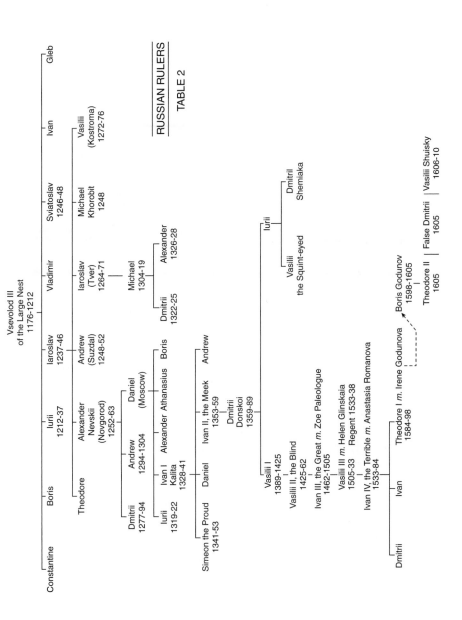

RUSSIAN RULERS

TABLE 2

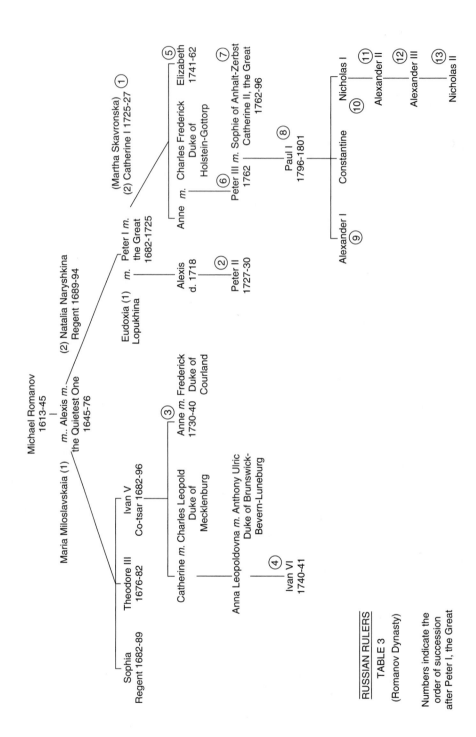

RUSSIAN RULERS

TABLE 3

(Romanov Dynasty)

Numbers indicate the
order of succession
after Peter I, the Great

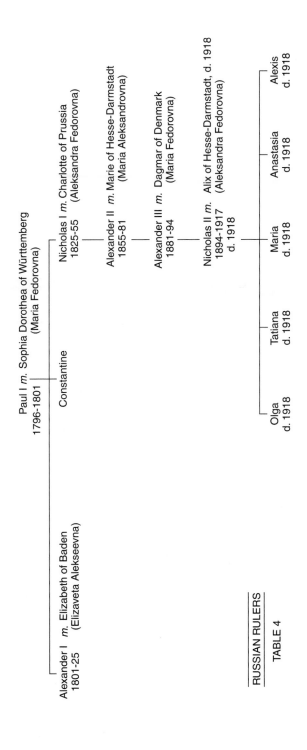

RUSSIAN RULERS

TABLE 4

# A Bibliography of Readings in English on Russian History

## Books Covering Multiple Periods

### A. Bibliography and Historiography

*American Bibliography of Slavic* (previously *Russian*) *and East European Studies (ABSEES)*. Bloomington, Ind., and Urbana-Champaign, Ill., since 1957 (now on-line).

Brumfield, W. *A History of Russian Architecture*. New York, 1993.

Horak, S. M. *Russia, the USSR, and Eastern Europe: A Bibliographic Guide to English-Language Publications*. Littleton, Colo. *(1964–74—1979; 1975–40—1982; 1981–85—1987)*.

Horecky, P., ed. *Basic Russian Publications: A Selected and Annotated Bibliography on Russia and the Soviet Union*. Chicago and London, 1965.

Horecky, P., ed. *Russia and the Soviet Union: A Bibliographic Guide lo Western-Language Publications*. Chicago and London, 1965.

Kaiser, D. H., ed. "Rus', Russia, and the Russian Empire." Section 34 of the American Historical Association's *Guide to Historical Literature*. 3rd ed. New York, 1995.

Konn, T., ed. *Soviet Studies Guide*. London, 1992.

Maichel, K. *Guide to Russian Reference Books*. Stanford, 1962.

Mazour, A. G. *Modern Russian Historiography*. Princeton, N.J., 1958.

Orlovsky, D. T., ed. "Soviet Union." Section 35 of the American Historical Association's *Guide to Historical Literature*. 3rd ed. New York, 1995.

Pierce, R. A. *Soviet Central Asia. A Bibliography: Part 1: 1558–1866. Part 2: 1867–1917. Part 3: 1917–1966*. Berkeley, 1966.

Pushkarev, S. G. *A Source Book for Russian History from Early Times to 1917*. Edited by A. Ferguson et al. 3 vols. New Haven, Conn., 1972.

Pushkarev, S. G., comp. *Dictionary of Russian Historical Terms from the Eleventh Century to 1917*. Edited by G. Vernadsky and R. Fisher, Jr., New Haven, Conn., 1970.

Sanders, T., ed. *Historiography of Imperial Russia: The Profession and Writing of History in a Multinational State*. Armonk, N.Y., 1999.

Shapiro, D. *A Selected Bibliography of Works in English on Russian History, 1801–1917*. New York and London, 1962.

Sullivan, H. F. and R. Burger. *Russia and the Former Soviet Union: A Bibliographic Guide to English Language Publications, 1986–1991*. Englewood, Colo., 1994.

Szeftel, M. *Russia before 1917, in Bibliographical Introduction to Legal History and Ethnology.* Edited by J. Glissen. Brussels, 1966.

## B. Encyclopedias

Brown, A., et al., eds. *The Cambridge Encyclopedia of Russia and the Soviet Union.* Cambridge, 1982.

Florinsky, M. T., ed. *McGraw-Hill Encyclopedia of Russia and the Soviet Union.* New York, 1961.

Kubijovyč, V., et al., eds. *Ukraine: A Concise Encyclopedia.* Vol. 1. Toronto, 1963.

Utechin, S. V. *Everyman's Concise Encyclopedia of Russia.* New York, 1961.

Wieczynski, J. L., ed. *The Modern Encyclopedia oj Russian and Soviet History.* 54 vols. Gulf Breeze, Fla., 1976. Continued by *The Supplement to the Modern Encyclopedia of Russian, Soviet, and Eurasian History.* Gulf Breeze, Fla., 1995–.

## C. Geography and Demography

Chew, A. F. *An Atlas of Russian History: Eleven Centuries of Changing Borders.* New Haven, Conn., 1970.

Gilbert, M. *Atlas of Russian History.* New York, 1993.

Hooson, D. J. *The Soviet Union: People and Regions.* Belmont, Calif., 1966.

Jorré, G. *The Soviet Union: The Land and Its People.* Translated by E. D. Laborde. London, 1950. 3rd ed., 1967.

Kaiser, R.J. *The Geography of Nationalism in Russia and the USSR.* Princeton, N.J., 1994.

Milner-Gulland, R. R., and N. Dejevsky. *Cultural Atlas of Russia and the Soviet Union.* New York, 1989.

## D. Nationalities and Empire

Allen, W. E. D. *A History of the Georgian People.* New York, 1971.

Allworth, E. A. *The Modern Uzbeks from the Fourteenth Century to the Present: A Cultural History.* Stanford, 1990.

Baron, S. W. *The Russian Jew under Tsars and Soviet.* New York, 1964.

Becker, S. *Russia's Protectorates in Central Asia: Bukhara and Khiva, 1865–1924.* Cambridge, Mass., 1968.

Breyfogle, N., A. Schrader, and W. Sunderland, eds. *Peopling the Russian Periphery: Borderland Colonization in Eurasian History.* New York, 2007.

Brower, D. and E. Lazzerini, eds. *Russia's Orient: Imperial Borderlands and Peoples, 1700–1917.* Bloomington, Ind., 1997.

Chase, T. *The Story of Lithuania,* New York, 1946.

Chirovsky, N. L. *Old Ukraine: Its Socio-Economic History Prior to 1781.* Madison, N.J., 1963.

Doroshenko, D. *History of the Ukraine.* Edmonton, Alberta, 1941.

Dubnow, S. M. *History of the Jews in Russia and Poland.* 3 vols. Philadelphia, 1916.

d'Encausse, H. C. *Islam and the Russian Empire: Reform and Revolution in Central Asia.* Berkeley, 1988.

Greenberg, L. S. *The Jews in Russia,* 2 vols. New Haven, Conn., 1944, 1951.

Grousset, R. *The Empire of the Steppes: A History of Central Asia.* Translated by N. Walford. New Brunswick, N.J., 1970.

Hosking, G. *Russia: People and Empire, 1552–1917.* Cambridge, Mass., 1997.

Hosking, G. and R. Service, eds. *Russian Nationalism, Past and Present.* New York, 1997.

Halecki, O. *A History of Poland.* New York, 1943.

Hrushevskyi, M. *A History of the Ukraine.* New Haven, Conn., 1941.

Kappeler, A. *The Russian Empire: A Multiethnic History.* Harlow, Eng., 2001.

Kubijovyč, V., et al., eds. *Ukraine: A Concise Encyclopedia.* Vol. 1. Toronto, 1963.

Lang, D. M. *A Modern History of Georgia.* London, 1962.

Lantzeff, G. V., and R. A. Pierce. *Eastward to Empire: Exploration and Conquest on the Russian Open Frontier to 1750.* Montreal and London, 1973.

Lewis, R. A., R. H. Rowland, and R. S. Clem, eds. *Nationality and Population Change in Russia and the USSR: An Evaluation of Census Data, 1870–1970.* New York, 1976.

Nelbandian, L. *The Armenian Revolutionary Movement.* Berkeley, 1967.

Nowak, A. *History and Geopolitics: A Contest for Eastern Europe.* Warsaw, 2008.

Olcott, M. B. *The Kazakhs.* 2d ed. Stanford, 1995.

Potichnyj, P. J., and H. Aster, eds. *Ukrainian-Jewish Relations in Historical Perspective.* Edmonton, Alberta, 1988.

Raun, T. U. *Estonia and the Estonians.* Stanford, 1987.

Rorlich, A-A. *The Volga Tatars: A Profile in National Resilience.* Stanford, 1986.

Senn, A. E. *The Emergence of Modern Lithuania.* New York, 1959.

Senn, A. E. *Lithuania Awakening.* Berkeley, 1990.

Slezkine, Y. *Arctic Mirrors: Russia and the Small Peoples of the North.* Ithaca, N.Y., 1994.

Sunderland, W. *Taming the Wild Field: Colonization and Empire on the Russian Steppe.* Ithaca, N.Y., 2004.

Suny, R. G. *The Making of the Georgian Nation.* Bloomington, Ind., 1988.

Suny, R. G., ed. *Transcaucasia: Nationalism and Social Change. Essays in the History of Armenia, Azerbaijan, and Georgia.* Ann Arbor, Mich., 1983.

Swietochowski, T. *Russian Azerbaijan, 1905–1920: The Shaping of National Destiny in a Muslim Community.* Cambridge, 1985.

Vakar, N. *Belorussia: The Making of a Nation.* Cambridge, Mass., 1956.

Wheeler, G. *The Modern History of Soviet Central Asia.* London, 1964.

Zenkovsky, S. A. *Pan-Turkism and Islam in Russia.* Cambridge, Mass., 1960.

## E. General Histories

Auty, R., and D. Obolensky, eds. *An Introduction to Russian History.* Vol 1. *Companion to Russian Studies.* Cambridge, 1976.

Charques, R. *A Short History of Russia.* London, 1959.

Clarkson, J. *A History of Russia.* New York, 1961.

Evtuhov, C., D. Goldfrank, L. Hughes, and R. Stites. *A History of Russia: Peoples, Legends, Events, Forces.* Boston, 2004.

Florinsky, M. T. *Russia: A History and an Interpretation.* 2 vols. New York, 1953.

Freeze, G. L., ed. *Russia: A History.* New York, 1997. Rev. ed. 2002.

Harcave, S. *Russia: A History.* Chicago, 1956.

Hosking, G. *Russia and Russians: A History.* Cambridge, Mass., 2001.

Klyuchevsky (Kliuchevsky), V. O. *Course of Russian History.* Translated by C. J. Hogarth. 5 vols. New York, 1911–31.

Lievan, D., ed. *Cambridge History of Russia.* Vol. 2: *Imperial Russia, 1989–1917.* Cambridge, Eng., 2006.

Miliukov, P., C. Seignobos, L. Eisenmann, et al. *History of Russia.* Translated by C. L. Markmann. 3 vols. New York, 1968.

Pares, B. *A History of Russia.* London, 1926.

Perrie, M., ed. *Cambridge History of Russia.* Vol. 1: *From Early Rus' to 1689.* Cambridge, Eng., 2006.

Pipes, R E. *Russia Under the Old Regime.* New York, 1974.

Pokrovsky, M. N. *Brief History of Russia*. 2 vols. London, 1933.

Sumner, B. H. *Survey of Russian History*. London, 1944.

Suny, R., ed. *Cambridge History of Russia*. Vol. 3: *The Twentieth Century*. Cambridge, Eng., 2006.

Vernadsky, G. *A History of Russia*. New Haven, Conn., 1929. 5th rev. ed., 1961.

Vernadsky, G., and M. Karpovich. *A History of Russia*. Vol. 1, *Ancient Russia*. Vol. 2, *Kievan Russia*. Vol. 3, *The Mongols and Russia*. Vol. 4, *Russia at the Dawn of the Modern Age*. Vol. 5, *Tsardom of Moscow, 1547–1682*. 2 books. New Haven, Conn., 1943, 1948, 1953, 1959, 1968.

## F. Specialized Histories and Interpretative Essays

Avrich, P. *Russian Rebels, 1600–1800*. New York, 1972.

Beumers, B. *A History of Russian Cinema*. Oxford, 2009.

Billington, J. *The Icon and the Axe: An Interpretative History of Russian Culture*. New York, 1966.

Blum, J. *Lord and Peasant in Russia from the Ninth to the Nineteenth Century*. Princeton, N.J., 1961.

Brumfield, W. *A History of Russian Architecture*. New York, 1993.

Bulgakov, S. N. *The Orthodox Church*. New York and London, 1935.

Cherniavsky, M. *Tsar and People: Studies in Russian Myths*. New Haven, Conn., 1961.

Chyzhevskyi, D. *History of Russian Literature from the Eleventh Century to the End of the Baroque*. New York and The Hague, 1960.

Fennell, J., and A. Stokes. *Early Russian Literature*. Berkeley, 1974.

Gasiorowska, X. *The Image of Peter the Great in Russian Fiction*. Madison, Wis., 1979.

Gerschenkron, A. *Continuity in History and Other Essays*. Cambridge, Mass., 1968.

Gerschenkron, A. *Europe in the Russian Mirror: Four Lectures in Economic History*. Cambridge, Mass., 1970.

Hans, N. *History of Russian Educational Policy, 1701–1917*. London, 1931.

Hans, N. *The Russian Tradition in Education*. London, 1963.

Haxthausen, A. von. *The Russian Empire, Its People, Institutions, and Resources*. Translated by R. Farie. New York, 1970.

Hingley, R. *The Russian Secret Police: Muscovite, Imperial Russian and Soviet Political Security Operations, 1565–1970*. New York, 1970.

Hunczak, T., ed. *Russian Imperialism from Ivan the Great to the Revolution*. New Brunswick, N-J., 1974.

Iswolsky, H. *Christ in Russia: The History, Tradition and Life of the Russian Church*. Milwaukee, 1960.

Kelly, C. *Children's World: Growing Up in Russia, 1890–1991*. New Haven, Conn. 2007.

Kerner, R. J. *The Urge to the Sea: The Course of Russian History*. New York, 1971.

Kochan, L., and J. Keep. *The Making of Modern Russia: Fom Kiev Rus' to the Collapse of the Soviet Union*. 3rd ed. London, 1997.

Lewin, M. *Russia—USSR—Russia: The Drive and Drift of a Superstate*. New York, 1995.

Leonard, R. *A History of Russian Music*. London, 1956.

Liashchenko, P. I. *A History of the National Economy of Russia to the 1917 Revolution*. Translated from Russian. New York, 1949.

Lincoln, W. B. *The Romanovs: Autocrats of All the Russias*. New York, 1981.

Lincoln, W. B. *Between Heaven and Hell: The Story of a Thousand Years of Artistic Life in Russia*. New York, 1998.

Lincoln, W. B. *The Conquest of a Continent: Siberia and the Russians*. New York, 1994.

Longworth, P. *The Cossacks: Five Centuries of Turbulent Life on the Russian Steppes.* New York, 1970.

Lossky, N. O. *History of Russian Philosophy.* New York, 1951.

Masaryk, T. G. *The Spirit of Russia.* Translated from German. 3 vols. New York, 1955–67.

Miliukov, P. N. *Outlines of Russian Culture.* Edited by M. Karpovich. Translated and abridged from Russian. 4 vols. Philadelphia, 1942–75.

Miliukov, P. N. *Russia and Its Crisis.* Chicago, 1905.

Mirsky, D. S. *A History of Russian Literature.* New York, 1927.

Mirsky, D. S. *Russia: A Social History.* London, 1931.

Obolensky, D. *The Byzantine Commonwealth.* New York, 1971.

Pokrovsky, M. N. *Russia in World History: Selected Essays.* Edited by R. Szporluk. Translated by R. Szporluk and M. Szporluk. Ann Arbor, Mich., 1970.

Pushkareva, N. *Women in Russian History from the Tenth to the Twentieth Century.* Ed. Eve Levin. Armonk, N.Y., 1997.

Ragsdale, H. *The Russian Tragedy: The Burden of History.* Armonk, N.Y., 1996.

Riasanovsky, N. *Russian Identities: A Historical Survey.* Oxford, 2005.

Rice, T. T. *Russian Art.* London, 1949.

Schmemann, A. *The Historical Road of Eastern Orthodoxy.* New York, 1963.

Soloviev, A. V. *Holy Russia: The History of a Religious-Social Idea.* New York, 1959.

Stephan, J. J. *Sakhalin. A History.* New York, 1971.

Stokes, A. D. (with John Fennell). *Early Russian Literature.* Berkeley, 1974.

Thaden, E. C. *Russia since 1801: The Making of a New Society.* New York, 1971.

Treadgold, D. W. *The West in Russia and China: Religion and Secular Thought in Modern Times.* Vol. 1, *Russia, 1472–1917.* Cambridge, Mass., 1973.

Utechin, S. V. *Russian Political Thought: A Concise History.* New York and London, 1964.

Volin, L. *A Century of Russian Agriculture: From Alexander II to Khrushchev.* Cambridge, Mass., 1970.

Vucinich, A. S. *Science in Russian Culture: A History to 1860.* Stanford, 1963.

Vucinich, A. S. *Science in Russian Culture (1861–1917).* Stanford, 1970.

Weidle, V. *Russia Absent and Present.* New York, 1952.

Wren, M. C. *The Western Impact upon Tsarist Russia.* Chicago, 1971.

Zenkovsky, V. V. *A History of Russian Philosophy.* 2 vols. New York, 1953.

## G. Collected Essays

Atkinson, D., A. Dallin, and G. W. Lapidus, eds. *Women in Russia.* Stanford, 1977.

Cherniavsky, M., ed. *The Structure of Russian History.* New York, 1970.

Clements, B., B. Engel, and C. Worobec, eds. *Russia's Women: Accommodation, Resistance, Transformation.* Berkeley, 1991.

Curtiss, J. S., ed. *Essays in Russian and Soviet History in Honor of G. T. Robinson.* Leiden, 1963.

Edmondson, L., ed., *Women and Society in Russia and the Soviet Union.* Cambridge, 1992.

Ferguson, A. D., and A. Levin, eds. *Essays in Russian History: A Collection Dedicated to George Vernadsky.* Hamden, Conn., 1964.

Gleason, A., ed. *A Companion to Russian History.* Oxford, 2009.

Kivelson, V., and J. Neuberger, eds. *Picturing Russia: Explorations in Visual Culture.* New Haven, Conn., 2008.

McLean, H., M. Malia, and G. Fischer, eds. *Russian Thought and Politics.* Harvard Slavic Studies, vol 4. Cambridge, Mass., 1957.

Mendelsohn, E., and M. S. Shatz, eds. *Imperial Russia, 1700–1917: Essays in Honor of Marc Raeff.* DeKalb, Ill., 1988.

Oberlander, E., et al., eds. *Russia Enters the Twentieth Century, 1894–1917.* Translated by G. Onn. New York, 1971.

Oliva, L. Jay, ed. *Russia and the West from Peter to Khrushchev.* Boston, 1965.

Pipes, R., ed. *Revolutionary Russia.* Cambridge, Mass., 1968.

Pipes, R., ed. *The Russian Intelligentsia.* New York, 1961.

Rabinowitch, A., J. Rabinowitch, and L. Kristof, eds. *Revolution and Politics in Russia: Essays in Memory of B. I. Nicolaevsky.* Bloomington, Ind., 1972.

Treadgold, D. W., ed. *Soviet and Chinese Communism: Similarities and Differences.* Seattle, 1967.

Vucinich, W. S., ed. *The Peasant in Nineteenth Century Russia.* Stanford, 1968.

Vucinich, W. S., ed. *Russia and Asia; Essays on the Influence of Russia on the Asian Peoples.* Stanford, 1972.

## H. Readings, Anthologies

Harcave, S., ed. *Readings in Russian History.* 2 vols. New York, 1962.

Kaiser, D. and G. Marker, eds. *Reinterpreting Russian History: Readings, 860–1860s.* New York, 1994.

Kollman, N., ed. *Major Problems in Early Modern Russian History.* New York, 1992.

Page, S. W., ed. *Russia in Revolution: Selected Readings in Russian Domestic History since 1855.* Princeton, N.J., 1965.

Raeff, M., ed. *Russian Intellectual History: An Anthology.* New York, 1966.

Riha, T., ed. *Readings in Russian Civilization.* 3 vols. Chicago, 1964.

Schmemann, A., ed. *Ultimate Questions: An Anthology of Modern Russian Religious Thought.* New York, 1965.

Vernadsky, G., R. Fisher, A. Ferguson, A. Lossky, and S. Pushkarev, eds. *A Source Book for Russian History from Early Times to 1917,* 3 vols. New Haven, Conn., 1972.

## Pre-Petrine Russia (to 1682)

### A. Source Materials

Avvakum. *The Life of the Archpriest Avvakum by Himself.* Translated by V. Nabokov. New York, 1960.

Baron, S. H., ed. and trans. *The Travels of Olearius in Seventeenth-Century Russia.* Stanford, 1967.

Berry, L. E., and R. O. Crummey, eds. *Rude and Barbarous Kingdom: Russia in the Accounts of Sixteenth-Century English Voyagers.* Madison, Wisc., 1968.

Cross, S. H., and O. P. Sherbovitz-Wetzor, trans and eds. *The Russian Primary Chronicle, Laurentian Text.* Cambridge, Mass., 1953.

Dewey, H. W. "The White Lake Chapter: A Medieval Russian Administrative Statute." *Speculum* 32 (1957).

Dmytryshyn, B., ed. *Medieval Russia: A Source Book, 900–1700.* New York, 1967.

Esper, T., ed. and trans. *Heinrich von Staden: The Land and Government of Muscovy: A Sixteenth-Century Account.* Stanford, 1967.

Fedotov, G. P. *A Treasury of Russian Spirituality.* New York, 1948.

Fennell, J., ed. and trans. *The Correspondence between Prince A. M. Kurbsky and Tsar Ivan IV of Russia, 1564–1579, with Russian Text.* New York, 1955.

Fennell, J., ed. and trans. *Prince A. M. Kurbsky's History of Ivan IV.* Cambridge, Eng., 1965.

Fletcher, G. *Of the Russe Commonwealth, 1591.* Facsimile ed. Introduction by R. Pipes. Cambridge, Mass., 1966.

Hellie, R., ed. and trans. *The Muscovite Law Code (Ulozhenie) of 1649.* Irvine, Calif., 1988.

Heppell, M., trans, and ed. *The Paterik of the Kievan Caves Monastery.* Cambridge, Mass., 1989.

Hollingsworth, P., trans, and ed. *The Hagiography of Kievan Rus.* Cambridge, Mass., 1992.

Howes, R. C., ed. and trans. *The Testaments of the Grand Princes of Moscow.* Ithaca, N.Y., 1967.

Kaiser, D., ed. and trans. *The Laws of Rus': Tenth to Fifteenth Centuries.* Salt Lake City, 1992.

Michell, R., and N. Forbes, trans. *The Chronicle of Novgorod, 1016–1471.* In *Royal Historical Society Publications,* Camden 3rd ser., vol. 25. London, 1914.

Palmer, W. *The Patriarch and the Tsar.* 6 vols. London, 1871–76.

Pouncy, C., ed. *Domostroi: The Rules for Russian Households in the Time of Ivan the Terrible.* Ithaca, N.Y., 1994.

Vernadsky, G., trans. *Medieval Russian Laws.* In *Records of Civilization,* no. 41, edited by A. P. Evans. New York, 1947.

Zenkovsky, S. A. *Medieval Russian Epics, Chronicles and Tales.* New York, 1963.

## B. Specialized Studies

Alexander, J. *Bubonic Plague in Early Modern Russia: Public Health and Urban Disaster.* Baltimore, 1980.

Anderson, M. S. *Britain's Discovery of Russia, 1555–1815.* London, 1958.

Baron, S. H. *Muscovite Russia.* London, 1980.

Baron, S. H., and N. S. Kollmann, eds. *Religion and Culture in Early Modern Russia and Ukraine.* DeKalb, Ill., 1997.

Bogatyrev, S. *The Sovereign and His Counsellors. Ritualized Consultations in Muscovite Culture 1350s–1570s.* Helsinki, 2000.

Bushkovitch, P. *Religion and Society in Russia: The Sixteenth and Seventeenth Centuries.* New York, 1992.

Cherniavsky, M. "Old Believers and the New Religion." *Slavic Review* 25 (March 1966).

Cherniavsky, M. *Tsar and People: Studies in Russian Myths.* New Haven, Conn., 1961.

Chyzhevskyi, D. *History of Russian Literature from the Eleventh Century to the End of the Baroque.* New York and The Hague, 1960.

Conybeare, F. C. *Russian Dissenters.* Cambridge, Mass., 1921.

Crummey, R. O. *Aristocrats and Servitors: The Boyar Elite in Russia, 1613–1689.* Princeton, N.J., 1983.

Crummey, R. O. *The Formation of Muscovy, 1304–1613.* London and New York, 1987.

Davies, Brian. *Warfare, State and Society on the Black Sea Steppe, 1500–1700.* New York, 2007.

Dewey, H. W. "The 1497 Sudebnik: Muscovite Russia's First National Law Code." *American Slavic and East European Review* 29 (1951).

Dukes, P. *The Making of Russian Absolutism, 1613–1801.* London and New York, 1990.

Dunlop, D. M. *The History of the Jewish Khazars.* Princeton, N.J., 1954.

Dunning, C. S. L. *Russia's First Civil War: The Time of Troubles and the Founding of the Romanov Dynasty.* University Park, Pa., 2001.

Dvornik, F. *The Slavs, Their Early History and Civilization.* Boston, 1956.

Fedotov, G. *The Russian Religious Mind.* Vol. I, *Kievan Christianity: The Tenth to the Thirteenth Centuries.* Vol. 2, *The Middle Ages: The Thirteenth to the Fifteenth Centuries.* Edited by J. Meyendorff. Cambridge, Mass., 1946, 1966.

Fennell, J. *The Crisis of Medieval Russia, 1200–1304.* London and New York, 1983.

Fennell, J. *The Emergence of Moscow, 1304–1359.* Berkeley, 1968.

Fennell, J. *A History of the Russian Church to 1448.* London, 1995.

Fennell, J. *Ivan the Great of Moscow.* London, 1961.

Flier, M. S. and D. Rowland, eds. *Medieval Russian Culture,* Berkeley, 1994.

Florovsky, G. "The Problem of Old Russian Culture." *Slavic Review* 21 (March 1962).

Franklin, S. *Writing, Society, and Culture in Early Rus, c. 950–1300.* Cambridge, 2002.

Franklin, S. and J. Shepard. *The Emergence of Rus, 750–1200.* London, 1996.

Fuhrmann, J. T. *The Origins of Capitalism in Russia: Industry and Progress in the Sixteenth and Seventeenth Centuries.* Chicago, 1972.

Graham, S. *Boris Godunov.* London, 1933.

Grekov, B. *Kiev Rus.* Translated from Russian. Moscow, 1959.

Grey, I. *Ivan III and the Unification of Russia.* New York, 1964.

Halperin, C. *Russia and the Golden Horde: The Mongol Impact on Russian History.* Bloomington, Ind., 1985.

Hellie, R. *Enserfment and Military Change in Muscovy.* Chicago, 1971.

Hellie, R. *Slavery in Russia, 1450–1725.* Chicago, 1982.

Hughes, L. *Sophia, Regent of Russia, 1657–1704.* New Haven, Conn., 1990.

Kaiser, D. H. *The Growth of the Law in Medieval Russia.* Princeton, N.J., 1980.

Kaminski, A. *Republic vs. Autocracy: Poland-Lithuania and Russia, 1686–1697.* Cambridge, Mass., 1993.

Keenan, E. "Muscovite Political Folkways." *Russian Review* 45, no. 2 (1986). Discussions in *Russian Review* 46, no. 2 (1987).

Keep, J. "The Decline of the Zemsky Sobor." *Slavonic and East European Review* 36 (1957).

Keep, J. "The Regime of Filaret." *Slavonic and East European Review* 38 (1960).

Kivelson, V. A. *Autocracy in the Provinces: The Muscovite Gentry and Political Culture in the Seventeenth Century.* Stanford, 1996.

Kivelson, V. *Cartographies of Tsardom: The Land and Its Meanings in Seventeenth-Century Russia.* Ithaca, N.Y., 2006.

Kliuchevsky, V. O. *A Course in Russian History: The Seventeenth Century* (translation of Vol. 3 of the 1957 Soviet edition of his *Collected Works*). Translated by N. Duddington. Introduction by A. Rieber. Chicago, 1968.

Kliuchevsky, V. O. *Peter the Great.* New York, 1959 (part of Vol. 4 of his *Course of Russian History*).

Kliuchevsky, V. O. *The Rise of the Romanovs.* Edited and translated by L. Archibald. New York, 1970.

Kliuchevsky, V. O. "St. Sergius: The Importance of His Life and Work." *Russian Review* (London) 2 (1913).

Kollmann, N. S. *By Honor Bound. State and Society in Early Modern Russia.* Ithaca, N.Y., 1999.

Kollmann, N. S. *Kinship and Politics: The Making of the Muscovite Political System, 1345–1547.* Stanford, 1987.

Kondakov, N. P. *The Russian Icon.* Translated from Russian. Oxford, 1927.

Lantzeff, G. *Siberia in the Seventeenth Century: A Study of Colonial Administration.* Berkeley, 1943.

Leatherbarrow, W. J., and D. C. Offord, eds. *A Documentary History of Russian Thought: From the Enlightenment to Marxism.* Ann Arbor, Mich., 1987.

Levin, E. *Sex and Society in the World of the Orthodox Slavs, 900–1700.* Ithaca, N.Y., 1989.

Madariaga, I. de. *Ivan the Terrible: First Tsar of Russia.* New Haven and London, 2005.

Martin, J. *Medieval Russia, 980–1584.* Cambridge, 1995.

Medlin, W. K. *Moscow and East Rome: A Political Study of the Relation of Church and State in Muscovite Russia.* New York and Geneva, 1952.

Medlin, W. K., and C. G. Patrinelis. *Renaissance Influences and Religious Reforms in Russia: Western and Post-Byzantine Impacts on Culture and Education (16th–17th Centuries).* Geneva, 1971.

Michels, G. B. *At War with the Church: Religious Dissent in Seventeenth Century Muscovy.* Stanford, 1999.

Norretranders, B. *The Shaping of Tsardom under Ivan Grozny.* Copenhagen, 1964.

Nowak, F. *Medieval Slavdom and the Rise of Russia.* New York, 1970.

Obolensky, D. *The Byzantine Commonwealth: Eastern Europe, 500–1453.* London, 1971.

O'Brien, C. B. *Muscovy and the Ukraine: From the Pereiaslavl Agreement to the Truce of Andrusovo.* Berkeley, 1963.

Ostrowski, D. *Muscovy and the Mongols: Cross-Cultural Influences on the Steppe Frontier, 1304–1589.* Cambridge, 1998.

Paszkiewicz, H. *The Making of the Russian Nation.* London, 1963.

Paszkiewicz, H. *The Origin of Russia.* London, 1954.

Payne, R., and N. Romanoff. *Ivan the Terrible.* New York, 1975.

Pelenski, J. *Russia and Kazan: Conquest and Imperial Ideology (1438–1560's).* The Hague and Paris, 1974.

Perrie, M. *The Image of Ivan the Terrible in Russian Folklore.* Cambridge, Eng., 1987.

Pierre, M. *Pretenders and Popular Monorchism in Early Modern Russia: The False Tsars of the Time of Troubles.* Cambridge, Eng., 1995.

Platonov, S. F. *Moscow and the West.* Edited and translated by J. Wieczynski. Hattiesburg, Miss., 1972.

Platonov, S. F. *The Time of Troubles: A Historical Study of the Internal Crisis and Social Struggle in Sixteenth- and Seventeenth-Century Muscovy.* Translated by J. Alexander. Lawrence, Kans., 1970.

Plokhii, S. *The Cossacks and Religion in Early Modern Ukraine.* Oxford, 2001.

Plokhii, S. *The Origins of the Slavic Nations: Premodern Identities in Russia, Ukraine and Belarus.* Cambridge, Eng., 2006.

Poe, M. *"A People Born to Slavery": Russia in Early Modern Ethnography, 1476–1748.* Ithaca, N.Y., 2000.

Poe, M. *The Russian Elite in the Seventeenth Century.* 2 Vols. Helsinki, 2003.

Pokrovsky, M. N. *History of Russia from the Earliest Times to the Rise of Commercial Capitalism.* Translated and edited by J. D. Clarkson and M. R. Griffiths. New York, 1931.

Prawdin, M. *The Mongol Empire: Its Rise and Legacy.* Translated by E. Paul and C. Paul. New York and London, 1940. 2nd ed., 1967.

Presniakov, A. E. *The Formation of the Great Russian State: A Study of Russian History in the Thirteenth to Fifteenth Centuries.* Translated by A. E. Moorhouse. Chicago, 1970.

Raeff, M. "An Early Theorist of Absolutism: Joseph of Volokolamsk." *American Slavic and East European Review* 8 (1949).

Riasanovsky, N. V. "The Norman Theory of the Origin of the Russian State." *Russian Review* (Autumn 1947).

Ševčenko, I. "Byzantine Cultural Influences." In *Rewriting Russian History*, edited by
    C. Black. Princeton, N.J., 1962.
Ševčenko, I. "A Neglected Byzantine Source of Muscovite Ideology." *Harvard Slavic
    Studies* 2 (1945).
Skrynnikov, R. *The Time of Troubles*. Gulf Breeze, Fla., 1988.
Soloviev, A. V. *Holy Russia: The History of a Religious-Social Idea*. New York, 1959.
Spinka, M. "Patriarch Nikon and the Subjection of the Russian Church to the State."
    *Church History* 10 (1941).
Stevens, C. *Soldiers on the Steppe: Army Reform and Social Change in Early Modern Russia*.
    DeKalb, Ill., 1995.
Stremoukhoff, D. "Moscow, the Third Rome: Sources of the Doctrine." *Speculum*
    (1953).
Szeftel, M. *Russian Institutions and Culture up to Peter the Great*. London, 1975.
Thomsen, V. *Relations Between Ancient Russia and Scandinavia and the Origins of the
    Russian State*. Oxford, 1877.
Thyret, I. *Between God and the Tsar: Religious Symbolism and the Royal Women of Muscovite
    Russia*. DeKalb, Ill., 2001.
Tikhomirov, M. N. *The Towns of Ancient Rus*. Translated from Russian. Moscow,
    1959.
Vasiliev, A. A. *The Goths in the Crimea*. Cambridge, Mass., 1936.
Vernadsky, G. *Ancient Russia*. New Haven, Conn., 1943.
Vernadsky, G. *Bohdan, Hetman of Ukraine*. New Haven, Conn., 1941.
Vernadsky, G. *Kievan Russia*. New Haven, Conn., 1948.
Vernadsky, G. *The Mongols and Russia*. New Haven, Conn., 1953.
Vernadsky, G. *The Origins of Russia*. Oxford, 1959.
Vernadsky, G. *Russia at the Dawn of the Modern Age*. New Haven, Conn., 1959.
Vernadsky, G. *The Tsardom of Moscow, 1547–1682*. New Haven, Conn., 1959.
Voyce, A. *The Art and Architecture of Medieval Russia*. Norman, Okla., 1967.
Voyce, A. *Moscow and the Roots of Russian* Culture. Norman, Okla., 1964.
Voyce, A. *The Moscow Kremlin*. Berkeley, 1954.
Wolff, R. L. "The Three Romes: The Migration of an Ideology and the Making of an
    Autocrat." *Daedolus* (Spring 1959).
Zernov, N. *St. Sergius, Builder of Russia*. London, 1938.
Zernov, N. "Vladimir and the Origin of the Russian Church." *Slavonic and East European
    Review* 28 (1949–50).

## Imperial Russia, 1682–1917

### A. Source Materials

Afanasiev, A. *Russian Fairy Tales Collected by Aleksandr Afanasiev*. New York, 1945.
Annenkov, P. *The Extraordinary Decade: Literary Memoirs by P. V. Annenkov*. Edited by
    A. P. Mendel. Ann Arbor, Mich., 1968.
Bakunin, M. *Selected Writings*. Edited by A. Lehning. New York, 1974.
Barratt, G. R. V. *Voices in Exile: The Decembrist Memoirs*. Montreal and London, 1974.
Bisha, R., J. Gheith, C. Holden, and W. Wagner, eds. *Russian Women, 1698–1917:
    Experience and Expression: An Anthology of Sources*. Bloomington, Ind., 2002.
Bing, E. J., ed. *The Letters of Tsar Nicholas and Empress Marie*. London, 1937.
Bock, M. P. von. *Reminiscences of My Father, Peter A. Stolypin*. Edited and translated by
    M. Patoski. Metuchen, N.J., 1970.
Buchanan, G. *My Mission to Russia*. 2 vols. Boston, 1923.

Catherine the Great. *The Memoirs of Catherine the Great.* Edited by D. Maroger. Translated by M. Budberg. New York, 1961.

Chaadaev, P. *The Major Works of Peter Chaadaev.* Translated and with commentary by R. T. McNally. Notre Dame, Ind., 1969.

Chernyshevsky, N. G. *Selected Philosophical Essays.*

Chernyshevsky, N. G. *What Is to Be Done?* Translated by M. Katz and annotated by W. Wagner. Ithaca, N.Y., 1989.

Dostoevsky, F. M. *The Diary of a Writer.* Translated by R. Brasol. New York, 1954.

Engel, B. A. and C. Rosenthal, *Five Sisters: Women Against the Tsar.* New York, 1975.

Freeze, G. L. *From Supplication to Revolution: A Documentary Social History of Imperial Russia.* New York, 1988.

Geldern, J. von and L. McReynolds, eds. *Entertaining Tsarist Russia, 1779–1917.* Bloomington, Ind., 1998.

Giers, N. K. *The Education of a Russian Statesman: The Memoirs of N. K. Giers.* Edited by C. Jelavich and B. Jelavich. Berkeley, 1962.

Golder, F. A., ed. *Documents of Russian History, 1914–1917.* New York and London, 1927.

Gurko, V. I. *Features and Figures of the Past. Government and Opinion in the Reign of Nicholas II.* Stanford, 1939.

Herzen, A. I. *My Past and Thoughts.* Translated by C. Garnett. 6 vols. New York, 1924–28; abridged edition by D. Macdonald, 1973.

Izvolsky, A. P. *Recollections of a Foreign Minister.* Garden City, N.Y., 1921.

Karamzin, N. M. *Letters of a Russian Traveler, 1789–1790: An Account of a Young Russian Gentleman's Tour through Germany, Switzerland, France and England.* Translated by F. Jonas. Edited by E. Simmons. New York, 1957.

Karamzin, N. M. *Memoir on Ancient and Modern Russia.* Translated and analysis by R. Pipes. Edited by R. Pipes. Cambridge, Mass., 1959.

Kokovtsov, V. N. *Out of My Past.* Edited by H. H. Fisher. Stanford, 1935.

Kravchinsky, S. M. (Stepniak) *Underground Russia: Revolutionary Profiles and Sketches from Life.* Preface by P. L. Lavrov. New York, 1883.

Kropotkin, P. A. *Memoirs of a Revolutionist.* New York, 1899.

Kropotkin, P. A. *Modern Science and Anarchism.* London, 1913.

Kropotkin, P. A. *The State: Its Part in History.* London, 1898, 1943.

Lavrov, P. *Historical Letters.* Edited and translated by J. P. Scanlan. Berkeley, 1967.

Maklakov, V. A. *Memoirs of V. A. Maklakov: The First State Duma: Contemporary Reminiscences.* Edited by M. Belkin. Bloomington, Ind., 1964.

Maximoff, G. P., ed. *The Political Philosophy of Bakunin: Scientific Anarchism.* Chicago, 1953.

Miliukov, P. *Political Memoirs, 1905–1917.* Edited by A. P. Mendel. Ann Arbor, Mich., 1967.

Paleologue, G. *An Ambassador's Memoirs.* 3 vols. London, 1925.

Pares, B. "Conversations with Mr. Stolypin." *Russian Review* (London) 2 (1913).

Pares, B. *My Russian Memoirs.* London, 1931

Pares, B., ed. *Letters of the Tsaritsa to the Tsar, 1914–1916.* London, 1923.

Pobedonostsev, K. P. *Reflections of a Russian Statesman.* London, 1898.

Radishchev, A. N. *A Journey from St. Petersburg to Moscow.* Edited with an introduction and notes by R. P. Thaler. Cambridge, Mass., 1958.

Raeff, M., ed.. *The Decembrist Movement.* Englewood Cliffs, N.J., 1966.

Raeff, M., ed. *Plans for Political Reform in Russia, 1730–1905.* Englewood Cliffs, N.J., 1966.

Read, H., ed. *Kropotkin: Selections from His Writings.* London, 1942.

Reddaway, W. F., ed. *Documents of Catherine the Great*. Cambridge, 1931.

Rieber, A. *The Politics of Autocracy: Letters of Alexander II to Prince A. I. Bariatinskii, 1857–1864*. Paris, 1966.

Rosen, R. R. *Forty Years of Diplomacy*. 2 vols. New York, 1922.

Rozanov, V. V. *Fallen Leaves*. Translated by S. S. Koletiansky. London, 1920.

Rozanov, V. V. *Selected Works*. Edited by G. Ivask. New York, 1956.

Sazonov, S. D. *Fateful Years, 1909–1916*. New York, 1928.

*Signposts*. See *Vekhi*.

Soloviev, V. S. *Lectures on Godmanhood*. Poughkeepsie, N.Y., 1944. London, 1948.

Soloviev, V. S. *Russia and the Universal Church*. Translated by H. Rees. London, 1948.

Soloviev, V. S. *A Soloviev Anthology*. Edited by S. L. Frank. London, 1950.

Soloviev, V. S. *War, Progress and the End of History*. Translated by A. Bakstry. London, 1915.

Tikhomiroff, L. *Russia: Political and Social*. Translated by E. Aveling. 2 vols. London, 1888.

Tolstoy, L. *Works*. Translated by L. Maude and A. Maude. 21 vols. London and New York, 1928–37.

*Vekhi: Landmarks: A Collection of Articles about the Russian Intelligentsia* . Translated and edited by M. Shatz and J. Zimmerman. Armonk, N.Y., 1994.

Wallace, D. M. *Russia*. New York, 1880.

Watrous, S. D., ed. *John Ledyard's Journey through Russia and Siberia, 1787–1788: The Journal and Selected Letters*. Madison, Wis., 1966.

Witte, S. *The Memoirs of Count Witte*. Edited by A. Yarmolinsky. Garden City, N.Y., 1921.

## B. General Studies

Benois, A. *The Russian School of Painting*. London, 1916.

Bird, A. *A History of Russian Painting*. Boston, 1987.

Burbank, J. and D. L. Ransel, eds. *Imperial Russia: New Histories for the Empire*. Bloomington, Ind., 1998.

Dmytryshyn, B., ed. *Modernization of Russia under Peter I and Catherine II*. New York and Toronto, 1974.

Figes, O. *Natasha's Dance: A Cultural History of Russia*. New York, 2002.

Florinsky, M. T. *The End of the Russian Empire*. New Haven, Conn., 1931.

Harcave, S. *Years of the Golden Cockerel: The Last Romanov Tsars, 1814–1917*. New York, 1968.

Ivanits, L. J. *Russian Folk Belief*. Armonk, N.Y., 1989.

Karpovich, M. *Imperial Russia, 1801–1917*. New York, 1932.

Kornilov, A. *Modern Russian History from the Age of Catherine the Great to the End of the Nineteenth Century*. Translated by A. Kaun. Bibliography by J. Curtiss. 2 vols. New York, 1970.

Lincoln, W. B. *In War's Dark Shadow: The Russians before the Great War*. New York, 1983.

Maynard, J. *Russia in Flux*. New York, 1948.

Miliukov, P. *Russia and Its Crisis*. Chicago, 1905; New York, 1962.

Mirsky, D. S. *History of Russian Literature*. New York, 1927.

Pares, B. *The Fall of the Russian Monarchy: A Study of the Evidence*. New York, 1939.

Pares, B. *Russia: Between Reform and Revolution*. Edited by F. B. Randall. New York, 1962.

Pavlovsky, G. *Agricultural Russia on the Eve of the Revolution*. London, 1930.

Pushkarev, S. *The Emergence of Modern Russia.* Translated from Russian. New York, 1963.

Raeff, M. *Imperial Russia, 1652–1825: The Coming of Age of Modern Russia.* New York, 1971.

Robinson, G. T. *Rural Russia under the Old Regime: A History of the Landlord-Peasant World and a Prologue to the Peasant Revolution of 1917.* New York, 1932.

Rogger, H. *Russia in the Age of Modernization and Revolution, 1881–1917.* London, 1983.

Seton-Watson, H. *The Russian Empire, 1801–1917.* Oxford, 1967.

Treadgold, D. W. *Twentieth Century Russia.* Chicago, 1959.

Vucinich, A. S. *Science in Russian Culture: A History to 1860.* Stanford, 1963.

Vucinich, A. S. *Science in Russian Culture (1861–1917).* Stanford, 1970.

Vucinich, W. S., ed. *The Peasant in Nineteenth Century Russia.* Stanford, 1968.

Wallace, D. M. *Russia on the Eve of War and Revolution.* New York, 1961.

Westwood, J. N. *Endurance and Endeavour: Russian History, 1812–1980.* 3rd ed. The Short Oxford History of the Modern World. Oxford, 1987.

## C. Specialized Studies: Government, Institutions, Society, and Culture

Alexander, J. *Emperor of the Cossacks: Pugachev and the Frontier Jacquerie of 1773–1775.* Lawrence, Kans., 1973.

Alexander, J. T. *Catherine the Great: Life and Legend.* New York, 1989.

Anderson, B. *Internal Migration during Modernization in Late Nineteenth Century Russia.* Princeton, N.J., 1980.

Anisimov, E. V. *The Reforms of Peter the Great: Progress through Coercion in Russia.* Armonk, N.Y., 1993.

Ascher, A. *P. A. Stolypin: The Search for Stability in Late Imperial Russia.* Stanford, 2001.

Ascher, A. *The Revolution of 1905.* 2 vols. Stanford, 1988, 1992.

Becker, S. *Nobility and Privilege in Late Imperial Russia.* DeKalb, Ill., 1985.

Black, C, ed. *Aspects of Social Change since 1861: The Transformation of Russian Society.* Cambridge, Mass., 1960.

Bonnell, V. *Roots of Rebellion: Workers' Politics and Organizations in St. Petersburg and Moscow, 1900–1914.* Berkeley, 1983.

Blum, J. *Lord and Peasant in Russia from the Ninth to the Nineteenth Century.* Princeton, N.J., 1961.

Bradley, J. *Muzhik and Muscovite: Urbanization in Late Imperial Russia.* Berkeley, 1985.

Brooks, J. *When Russia Learned to Read: Literacy and Popular Literature, 1861–1917.* Princeton, N.J., 1985.

Bushkovitch, P. *Peter the Great: The Struggle for Power, 1671–1725.* Cambridge, Eng., 2001.

Clausewitz, Carl von. *The Campaign of 1812 in Russia.* London, 1843.

Clowes, E., S. Kassow, and J. West, eds. *Between Tsar and People: Educated Society and the Quest for Public Identity in Late Imperial Russia.* Princeton, N.J., 1991.

Cracraft, J. *The Petrine Revolution in Russian Architecture.* Chicago, 1990.

Cracraft, J. *The Petrine Revolution in Russian Imagery.* Chicago, 1997.

Crisp, O., and L. Edmonson, eds. *Civil Rights in Imperial Russia.* New York, 1989.

Crummey, R. O. *The Old Believers and the World of the Anti-Christ; The Vyg Community and the Russian State, 1864–1855.* Madison, Wisc., 1970.

Curtiss, J. S. *Church and State in Russia, 1900–1917.* New York, 1940.

Curtiss, J. S. *The Russian Army under Nicholas I, 1825–1855.* Durham, N.C., 1965.

Dukes, P. *Catherine the Great and the Russian Nobility: A Study Based on the Materials of the Legislative Commission of 1767.* Cambridge, 1968.

Edelman, R. *Gentry Politics on the Eve of the Russian Revolution: The Nationalist Party, 1907–1917.* New Brunswick, N.J., 1980.

Edelman, R. *Proletarian Peasants: The Revolution of 1905 in Russia's Southwest.* Ithaca, N.Y., 1987.

Eklof, B. *Russian Peasant Schools: Officialdom, Village Culture, and Popular Pedagogy, 1864–1914.* Berkeley, 1986.

Eklof, B. and S. Frank, eds. *The World of the Russian Peasant: Post-emancipation Culture and Society.* Boston, 1990.

Eklof, B., J. Bushnell, and L. Zakharova, eds. *Russia's Great Reforms, 1855–1881.* Bloomington, Ind., 1994.

Ely, C. *This Meager Nature: Landscape and National Identity in Imperial Russia,* DeKalb, Ill., 2002.

Emmons, T. *The Russian Landed Gentry and the Peasant Emancipation of 1861.* Cambridge, 1967.

Emmons, T., ed. *Emancipation of the Russian Serfs.* New York, 1970.

Emmons, T. and W. Vucinich, eds. *The Zemstvo in Russia: An Experiment in Local Self-Government.* Cambridge, 1982.

Engel, B, A. *Between the Fields and the City: Women, Work, and Family in Russia, 1861–1914.* Cambridge, 1994.

Engelstein, L. *The Keys to Happiness: Sex and the Search for Modernity in Fin-de-Siècle Russia.* Ithaca, N.Y., 1992.

Field, D. *The End of Serfdom: Nobility and Bureaucracy in Russia, 1855–1861.* Cambridge, Mass., 1976.

Frank, S. P. *Crime, Cultural Conflict, and Justice in Rural Russia, 1856–1914.* Berkeley, 1999.

Frank, S. P. and M. D. Steinberg, eds., *Cultures in Flux: Lower-Class Values, Practices, and Resistance in Late Imperial Russia.* Princeton, N.J., 1994.

Freeze, G. *The Parish Clergy in Nineteenth Century Russia: Crisis, Reform, Counter-Reform.* Princeton, N.J., 1983.

Freeze, G. *The Russian Levites: The Parish Clergy in the Eighteenth Century.* Cambridge, Mass., 1977.

Frierson, C. *Peasant Icons: Representations of Rural People in Late Nineteenth Century Russia.* New York, 1993.

Fuhrmann, J. *Rasputin: A Life.* New York, 1990.

Glickman, R. L. *Russian Factory Women: Workplace and Society, 1880–1914.* Berkeley, 1984.

Golovin, N. N. *The Russian Army in the World War.* New Haven, Conn., 1931.

Gooch, G. P. *Catherine the Great and Other Studies.* London, 1954.

Gronsky, P., and N. Astrov. *The War and the Russian Government.* New Haven, Conn., 1929.

Haimson, L. H., ed. *The Politics of Rural Russia, 1905–1914.* Bloomington, Ind., 1979.

Hamm, M. F. *The City in Russian History.* Lexington, Ky., 1976.

Hartley, J. M. *Alexander I.* New York, 1994.

Heretz, L. *Russia on the Eve of Modernity: Popular Religion and Traditional Culture under the Last Tsars.* Cambridge, Eng., 2008.

Hoch, S. *Serfdom and Social Control in Russia.* Chicago, 1986.

Hosking, G. *The Russian Constitutional Experiment: Government and Duma, 1907–1914.* Cambridge, 1973.

Hughes, L. *Russia in the Age of Peter the Great*. New Haven, Conn., 1998.

Hutchinson, J. F. *Politics and Public Health in Revolutionary Russia, 1890–1918*. Baltimore, 1990.

Jones, R. E. *The Emancipation of the Russian Nobility, 1762–85*. Princeton, N.J., 1973.

Kassow, S. D. *Students, Professors, and the State in Tsarist Russia*. Berkeley, 1989.

Keep, J. *Soldiers of the Tsar: Army and Society in Russia, 1462–1874*. Oxford, 1985.

Kelly, C. and D. Shepherd, eds. *Constructing Russian Culture in the Age of Revolution: 1881–1940*. Oxford, 1998.

Kennan, G. *Siberia and the Exile System*. 2 vols. New York, 1891.

Kliuchevsky, V. O. *Peter the Great*. New York, 1959.

Kolchin, P. *Unfree Labor: American Slavery and Russian Serfdom*. Cambridge, Mass., 1987.

Kovalevsky, M. M. *Russian Political Institutions*. Chicago, 1902.

Kucherov, S. *Courts, Lawyers and Trials under the Last Three Tsars*. New York, 1953.

LeDonne, J. P. *Absolutism and Ruling Class: The Formation of the Russian Political Order, 1700–1825*. New York, 1991.

LeDonne, J. P. *Ruling Russia: Politics and Administration in the Age of Absolutism, 1762–1796*. Princeton, N.J., 1984.

Levin, A. *The Second Duma: A Study of the Social-Democratic Parly and the Russian Constitutional Experiment*. New Haven, Conn., 1940.

Lieven, D. C. B. *Nicholas II: Twilight of the Empire*. New York, 1994.

Lincoln, W. B. *The Great Reforms: Autocracy, Bureaucracy, and the Politics of Change in Imperial Russia*. DeKalb, Ill., 1990.

Lincoln, W. B. *In the Vanguard of Reform: Russia's Enlightened Bureaucrats, 1825–1861*. DeKalb, Ill., 1986.

Lincoln, W. B *.Nicholas I: Emperor and Autocrat of All the Russias*. Bloomington, Ind., 1978.

Lincoln, W. B. *The Romanovs: Autocrats of All the* Russias. New York, 1981.

MacDaniel, T. *Autocracy, Capitalism, and Revolution in Russia*. Berkeley, 1988.

MacKenzie, D. *The Lion of Tashkent: The Career of General M. G. Cherniaev*. Athens, Ga., 1974.

Madariaga, I. de. *Politics and Culture in Eighteenth-Century Russia*. Harlow, Eng., 1998.

Madariaga, I. de. *Russia in the Age of Catherine the Great*. New Haven, Conn., 1981.

Manning, R. *The Crisis of the Old Order in Russia*: Gentry and Government. Princeton, N J., 1982.

Martin, A. *Romantics, Reformers, Reactionaries: Russian Conservative Thought and Politics in the Reign of Alexander I*. DeKalb, Ill., 1997.

McClelland, J. C. *Autocrats and Academics: Education, Culture, and Society in Tsarist Russia*. Chicago and London, 1979.

McGrew, R. E. *Russia and the Cholera, 1823–1832*. Madison, Wis., 1965.

Mehlinger, H. D. and J. M. Thompson. *Count Witte and the Tsarist Government in the 1905 Revolution*. Bloomington, Ind., 1972.

Miller, E. *Dimitrii Miliutin and the Reform Era in Russia*. Nashville, Tenn., 1968.

Mironov, B., with Ben Eklof. *The Social History of Imperial Russia, 1700–1917*. 2 vols. Boulder, Colo., 2000.

Monas, S. *The Third Section: Police and Society under Nicholas I*. Cambridge, Mass., 1961.

Neuberger, J. *Hooliganism: Crime, Culture, and Power in St. Petersburg, 1900–1914*. Berkeley, 1993.

Nichols, R. L. and T. G. Stavrou, eds. *Russian Orthodoxy under the Old Regime*. Minneapolis, 1978.

O'Brien, C. B. *Russia under Two Tsars, 1682–1689.* Berkeley, 1952.

Orlovsky, D. T. *The Limits of Reform: The Ministry of Internal Affairs in Imperial Russia, 1802–1881.* Cambridge, Mass., 1981.

Paleologue, G. M. *The Enigmatic Tsar: The Life of Alexander I of Russia.* London, 1938.

Papmehl, K. A. *Freedom of Expression in Eighteenth Century Russia.* The Hague, 1971.

Pearson, T. S. *Russian Officialdom in Crisis: Autocracy and Local Self-Government, 1861–1900.* Cambridge, 1989.

Pintner, W. M., and D. K. Rowney, eds. *Russian Officialdom: The Bureaucratization of Russian Society from the Seventeenth to the Twentieth Century.* Chapel Hill, N.C., 1980.

Pipes, R. ed. *Revolutionary Russia.* Cambridge, Mass., 1968.

Raeff, M. *Michael Speransky: Statesman of Imperial Russia.* The Hague, 1957.

Raeff, M. *Siberia and the Reforms of 1822.* Seattle, 1956.

Raeff, M. *The Well-Ordered Police State: Social and Institutional Change through Law in the Germanies and Russia, 1600–1800.* New Haven, Conn., 1983.

Raeff, M., ed. *Peter the Great: Reformer or Revolutionary?* Boston, 1963.

Ransel, D. L. *Mothers of Misery: Child Abandonment in Russia.* Princeton, N.J., 1988.

Ransel, D. L. *The Politics of Catherinean Russia: The Panin Party.* New Haven, Conn., 1975.

Rheinelander, A. *Prince Michael Vorontsov: Viceroy to the Tsar.* Montreal, 1990.

Rodzianko, M. V. *Reign of Rasputin: An Empire's Collapse.* New York, 1927.

Rogger, H. *National Consciousness in 18th Century Russia.* Cambridge, Mass., 1960.

Roosevelt, P. R. *Life on the Russian Country Estate: A Social and Cultural History.* New Haven, Conn., 1995.

Ruud, C. A. *Fighting Words: Imperial Censorship and the Russian Press, 1804–1906.* Toronto, 1982.

Sablinsky, W. *The Road to Bloody Sunday: Father Gapon and the St. Petersburg Massacre of 1905.* Princeton, N.J., 1976.

Schneiderman, J. *Sergei Zubatov and Revolutionary Marxism: The Struggle for the Working Class in Tsarist Russia.* Ithaca, N.Y., 1976.

Schrader, A. *The Languages of the Lash: Corporal Punishment and Identity in Imperial Russia.* DeKalb, Ill., 2002.

Schwarz, S. M. *The Russian Revolution of 1905: The Workers' Movement and the Formation of Bolshevism and Menshevism.* Chicago and London, 1967.

Seregny, S. *Russian Teachers and Peasant Revolution: The Politics of Education in 1905.* Bloomington, Ind., 1989.

Shevzov, V. *Russian Orthodoxy on the Eve of Revolution.* New York, 2003.

Sinel, A. *The Classroom and the Chancellery: State Education Reform in Russia under Count Dimitrii Tolstoy.* Cambridge, Mass., 1973.

Starr, S. F. *Decentralization and Self-Government in Russia, 1830–1870.* Princeton, N.J., 1972.

Steinberg, M. D. *Proletarian Imagination: Self, Modernity, and the Sacred in Russia, 1910–1925.* Ithaca, N.Y., 2002.

Steinberg, M. D. and H. Coleman eds. *Sacred Stories: Religion and Spirituality in Modern Russia.* Bloomington, Ind. 2007.

Sumner, B. H. *Peter the Great and the Emergence of Russia.* New York, 1962.

Surh, G. D. *1905 in St. Petersburg: Labor, Society, and Revolution.* Stanford, 1989.

Treadgold, D. W. *The Great Siberian Migration: Government and Peasant in Resettlement from Emancipation to the First World War.* Princeton, N.J., 1957.

Troyat, H. *Catherine the Great.* Translated by J. Pinkham. New York, 1980.

Verner, A. *The Crisis of Russian Autocracy: Nicholas II and the 1905 Revolution.* Princeton, N.J., 1990.

Wade, R. A., and S. J. Seregny, eds. *Politics and Society in Provincial Russia: Saratov, 1590–1917.* Columbus, Ohio, 1989.

Wagner, W. *Marriage, Property, and Law in Late Imperial Russia.* New York, 1994.

Walkin, J. *The Rise of Democracy in Pre-Revolutionary Russia: Political and Social Institutions under the Last Three Tsars.* New York, 1962.

Wildman, A. *The Making of a Workers' Revolution: Russian Social Democracy, 1891–1903.* Chicago, 1967.

Wirtschafter, E. K. *From Serf to Russian Soldier.* Princeton, N.J., 1990.

Wirtschafter, E. K. *The Play of Ideas: Russian Enlightenment Theater.* DeKalb, Ill., 2003.

Wirtschafter, E. K. *Social Identity in Imperial Russia.* DeKalb, Ill., 1997.

Wirtschafter, E. K. *Structures of Society: Imperial Russia's "People of Various Ranks."* DeKalb, Ill., 1994.

Worobec, C. *Peasant Russia: Family and Community in the Post-Emancipation Period.* 1991.

Wortman, R. *Scenarios of Power: Myth and Ceremony in Russian Monarchy from Peter the Great to the Abdication of Nicholas II.* Princeton, N.J., 2006.

Wortman, R. S. *The Development of a Russian Legal Consciousness.* Chicago and London, 1976.

Yaney, G. *Systematization of Russian Government: Social Evolution in the Domestic Administration of Imperial Russia, 1711–1905.* Urbana, Ill., 1973.

Zaionchkovskii, P. A. *The Abolition of Serfdom in Russia.* Gulf Breeze, Fla., 1978.

Zaionchkovskii, P. A. *The Russian Autocracy in Crisis, 1878–1882.* Gulf Breeze, Fla., 1979.

Zaionchkovskii, P. A. *The Russian Autocracy under Alexander III.* Gulf Breeze, Fla., 1976.

Zaitsev, P. *Taras Shevchenko: A Life.* Edited, abridged, and translated with an introduction by G. S. N. Luckyj. Toronto, 1988.

Zelnik, R. E. *Labor and Society in Tsarist Russia: The Factory Workers of St. Petersburg, 1855–1870.* Stanford, 1971.

Zelnik, R. *Law and Disorder on the Narova River: The Kreenholm Strike of 1872.* Berkeley, 1995.

## D. Specialized Studies: Foreign Affairs, Empire, Nationalities

Aronson, I. M. *Troubled Waters: The Origins of the 1881 Anti-Jewish Progroms in Russia.* Pittsburgh, 1990.

Barker, A. J. *The War Against Russia, 1854–1856.* New York, 1971.

Bassin, M. *Imperial Visions: Nationalist Imagination and Geographical Expansion in the Russian Far East, 1840–1865.* Cambridge, Eng., 1999.

Bromley, J. S., ed. *The Rise of Great Britain and Russia, 1688–1715/25.* Vol. 6 of *The New Cambridge Modern History.* Cambridge, Mass., 1970.

Brower, D. *Turkestan and the Fate of the Russian Empire.* London, 2003.

Brower, D. and E. Lazzerini, eds. *Russia's Orient: Imperial Borderlands and Peoples, 1700–1917.* . Bloomington, Ind., 1997.

Burbank, J., and D. L. Ransel, eds. *Imperial Russia: New Histories of the Empire.* Bloomington, Ind., 1998.

Curtiss, J. S. *Russia's Crimean War.* Durham, N.C., 1979.

Dallin, D. J. *The Rise of Russia in Asia.* New Haven, Conn., 1949.

Donnelly, A. S. *The Russian Conquest of Bashkiria: A Case Study in Imperialism, 1552–1740.* New Haven, Conn., 1968.

Fisher, A. W. *The Russian Annexation of the Crimea, 1772–1783.* Cambridge, 1970.

Geraci, R. *Window on the East: National and Imperial Identities in Late Tsarist Russia.* Ithaca, N.Y., 2001.

Golder, F. A. *Russian Expansion on the Pacific, 1641–1850.* Cleveland, 1914.

Goldfrank, D. *The Origins of the Crimean War.* New York, 1994.

Jelavich, B. *A Century of Russian Foreign Policy, 1814–1914.* New York, 1964.

Jelavich, B. *Russia and Greece During the Regency of King Otton, 1832–1835.* Thessalonika, 1962.

Jelavich, B. *Russia and the Greek Revolution of 1843.* Munich, 1966.

Jelavich, B. *Russia and the Rumanian National Cause, 1858–1859.* Bloomington, Ind., 1959.

Jelavich, B., and C. Jelavich. *Russia in the East, 1876–1880.* Leiden, 1959.

Jelavich, C. *Tsarist Russia and Balkan Nationalism: Russian Influence in the Internal Affairs of Bulgaria and Serbia, 1879–1886.* Berkeley, 1958.

Jersild, A. *Orientalism and Empire: North Caucasus Mountain Peoples and the Georgian Frontier, 1845–1917.* Montreal, 2002.

Kaplan, H. H. *The First Partition of Poland.* New York, 1962.

Kennan, G. F. *The Decline of Bismarck's European Order: Franco-Russian Relations, 1875–1890.* Princeton, N.J., 1979.

Khalid, A. *Politics of Muslim Cultural Reform: Jadidism in Central Asia.* Berkeley, 2000.

Khodarkovsky, M. *Where Two Worlds Meet: The Russian State and the Kalmyk Nomads, 1600–1771.* Ithaca, N.Y., 1992.

Langer, W. L. *The Diplomacy of Imperialism, 1890–1902.* 2 vols. New York, 1935.

Langer, W. L. *The European Alliances and Alignments, 1871–1890.* New York, 1950.

Langer, W. L. *The Franco-Russian Alliance, 1890–1894.* Cambridge, Mass., 1929.

Layton, S. *Russian Literature and Empire: Conquest of the Caucasus from Pushkin to Tolstoy.* Cambridge, Eng., 1994

Lederer, I., ed. *Russian Foreign Policy: Essays in Historical Perspective.* New Haven, Conn., 1962.

LeDonne, J. P. *The Russian Empire and the World, 1700–1917: The Geopolitics of Expansion and Containment.* New York, 1997.

Lensen, G. A. *The Russian Push toward Japan: Russo-Japanese Relations, 1697–1875.* Princeton, N.J., 1959.

Lobanov-Rostovsky, A. *Russia and Asia.* Ann Arbor, Mich., 1951.

Lobanov-Rostovsky, A. *Russia and Europe, 1789–1825.* Durham, N.C., 1947.

Lobanov-Rostovsky, A. *Russia and Europe, 1825–1878.* Ann Arbor, Mich., 1954.

Lord, R. H. *The Second Partition of Poland.* Cambridge, Mass., 1915.

Madariaga, I. de. *Britain, Russia, and the Armed Neutrality of 1780: Sir James Harris's Mission to St. Petersburg During the American Revolution.* New Haven, Conn., 1962.

Malozemoff, A. *Russian Far Eastern Policy, 1881–1904.* Berkeley, 1958.

Montesquiou-Fezensac, R. *The Russian Campaign, 1812.* Translated by L. Kennett. Athens, Ga., 1970.

Mosely, P. *Russian Diplomacy and the Opening of the Eastern Question in 1838 and 1839.* Cambridge, Mass., 1934.

Mosse, W. E. *The European Powers and the German Question, 1848–1871.* Cambridge, 1958.

Nathans, B. *Beyond the Pale: The Jewish Encounter with Late Imperial Russia.* Berkeley, 2002

Okun, S. B. *The Russian-American Company.* Translated from Russian. Cambridge, Mass., 1951.

Pierce, R. A. *Russian Central Asia, 1867–1917: A Study in Colonial Rule.* Berkeley, 1960.

Pierce, R. A. *Russia's Hawaiian Adventure, 1815–1817.* Berkeley, 1965.

Puryear, V. J. *England, Russia and the Straits Question, 1844–1856.* Berkeley, 1931.

Ragsdale, H. *Détente in the Napoleonic Era: Bonaparte and the Russians.* Lawrence, Kans., 1980.

Romanov, B. *Russia in Manchuria, 1892–1906.* Translated by S. Jones. Ann Arbor, Mich., 1952.

Sahadeo, J. *Russian Colonial Society in Tashkent, 1865–1923.* Bloomington, Ind., 2007.

Saul, N. E. *Concord and Conflict: The United States and Russia, 1867–1914.* Lawrence, Kans., 1996.

Smith, C. J. *The Russian Struggle for Power, 1914–1917: A Study of Russian Foreign Policy During the First World War.* New York, 1956.

Sumner, B. H. *Peter the Great and the Ottoman Empire.* Oxford, 1949.

Sumner, B. H. *Russia and the Balkans, 1870–1880.* Oxford, 1937.

Sumner, B. H. *Tsardom and Imperialism in the Far East and Middle East, 1880–1914.* London, 1940.

Tarle, E. V. *Napoleon's Invasion of Russia, 1812.* Translated from Russian first edition. New York, 1942.

Taylor, A. J. P. *The Struggle for Mastery in Europe, 1848–1918.* Berkeley, 1931.

Thaden, E. C. *Russia and the Balkan Alliance of 1912.* University Park, Pa. 1965.

Thaden, E. C., ed. *Russification in the Baltic Provinces and Finland.* Princeton, N.J., 1981.

Thomson, G. S. *Catherine the Great and the Expansion of Russia.* London, 1947.

Warner, D., and P. Warner. *The Tide at Sunrise: A History of the Russo-Japanese War, 1904–1905.* New York, 1974.

Weeks, T. *Nation and State in Late Imperial Russia: Nationalism and Russification on the Western Frontier, 1863–1914.* DeKalb, Ill.,., 1996.

White J. A. *The Diplomacy of the Russo-Japanese War.* Princeton, N.J., 1964.

## E. Specialized Studies: Economic Development

Blackwell, W.L. *The Beginnings of Russian Industrialization, 1800–1860.* Princeton, N.J., 1968.

Gerschenkron, A. *Economic Backwardness in Historical Perspective.* Cambridge, Mass., 1962.

Kahan, A. *The Plow, the Hammer, and the Knout: An Economic History of Eighteenth-Century Russia.* Chicago, 1985.

Lih, L. *Bread and Authority in Russia, 1914–1921.* Berkeley, 1990.

Marks, S. G. *Road to Power: The Trans-Siberian Railroad and the Colonization of Asian Russia, 1850–1917.* Ithaca, N.Y., 1991.

McKay, J. P. *Pioneers for Profit: Foreign Entrepreneurship and Russian Industrialization, 1885–1913.* Chicago, 1970.

Owen, T. *Capitalism and Politics in Russia: A Social History of the Moscow Merchants, 1855–1905.* Cambridge, 1981.

Pintner, W. W. *Russian Economic Policy under Nicholas I.* Ithaca, N.Y., 1967.

Rieber, A. J. *Merchants and Entrepreneurs in Imperial Russia.* Chapel Hill, N.C., 1982.

Rozman, G. *Urban Networks in Russia, 1750–1800, and Premodern Periodization.* Princeton, N.J., 1976.

Smith, R. E. F., and D. Christian. *Bread and Salt: A Social and Economic History of Food and Drink in Russia.* New York, 1981.

Tugan-Baranovsky, M. I. *The Russian Factory in the 19th Century.* Translated by A. Levin, C. Levin, and G. Grossman. Homewood, Ill., 1970.

Von Laue, T. H. *Sergei Witte and the Industrialization of Russia.* New York, 1963.

## F. Specialized Studies: Intellectual History and the Intelligentsia

Ambler, E. *Russian Journalism and Politics 1861–1881: The Career of Aleksei S. Suvorin.* Detroit, 1972.

Andrew, J. *Women in Russian Literature, 1780–1863.* New York, 1988.

Avrich, P. *The Russian Anarchists.* Princeton, N.J., 1967.

Baron, S. H. *Plekhanov: The Father of Russian Marxism.* Stanford, 1963.

Berdiaev, N. *Constantin Leontieff.* Translated by H. Iswolsky. Paris, 1937.

Berdiaev, N. *The Russian Idea.* Translated by R. French. London, 1947.

Berlin, I. *Russian Thinkers.* Edited by H. Hardy and A. Kelly. New York, 1978.

Billington, J. *Mikhailovsky and Russian Populism.* New York, 1958.

Bowman, H. *Vissarion Belinskii, 1811–1848: A Study in the Origins of Social Criticism* in *Russia.* Cambridge, Mass., 1954.

Broido, E. *Memoirs of a Revolutionary.* Edited and translated by V. Broido. New York, 1967.

Brower, D. R. *Training the Nihilists: Education and Radicalism in Tsarist Russia.* Ithaca, N.Y., 1975.

Brown, E, J. *Stankevich and His Moscow Circle, 1830–1840.* Stanford, 1966.

Byrnes, R. F. *Pobedonostsev: His Life and Thought.* Bloomington, Ind., 1968.

Byrnes, R. F. *V. O. Kliuchevskii, Historian of Russia.* Bloomington, Ind., 1995.

Carr, E. H. *Michael Bakunin,* New York, 1961.

Carr, E. H. *The Romantic Exiles: A Nineteenth Century Portrait Gallery.* London, 1933.

Chmielewski, E. *Tribune of the Slavophiles: Konstantin Aksakov.* University of Florida Monograph. Social Sciences, no. 12. Gainesville, Fla., 1961.

Christoff, P. K. *An Introduction to Nineteenth-Century Russian Slavophilism: A Study in Ideas.* Vol. 1, *A. S. Xomjakov.* The Hague, 1961.

Christoff, P. K. *An Introduction to Nineteenth-Century Russian Slavophilism: A Study in Ideas.* Vol. 2, *I. V. Kireevskij.* The Hague, 1972.

Christoff, P. K. *An Introduction to Nineteenth-Century Russian Slavophilism.* Vol. 3, *K. S. Aksakov: A Study in Ideas.* Princeton, N.J., 1982.

Christoff, P. K. *An Introduction to Nineteenth-Century Russian Slavophilism.* Vol. 4, *Iu. F. Samarin.* Boulder, Colo., 1991.

Christoff, P. K. *Third Heart: Some Intellectual-Ideological Currents in Russia, 1800–1830.* The Hague, 1970.

Clark, K. *Petersburg: Crucible of Revolution.* Cambridge, Mass., 1986.

Engel, B. *Mothers and Daughters: Women of the Intelligentsia in 19th Century Russia.* Cambridge, 1983.

Evtuhov, C. *The Cross and the Sickle: Sergei Bulgakov and the Fate of Russian Religious Philosophy.* Ithaca, N.Y., 1997.

Fadner, F. *Seventy Years of Pan-Slavism: Karazin to Danilevskii, 1800–1870.* Washington, D.C., 1962.

Field, D. *Rebels in the Name of the Tsar.* Boston, 1976.

Fischer, G. *Russian Liberalism, from Gentry to Intelligentsia.* Cambridge, Mass., 1958.

Frank, J. *Dostoevsky: The Mantle of the Prophet, 1871–1881.* Princeton, N.J., 2002.

Frank, J. *Dostoevsky: The Miraculous Years, 1865–1871.* Princeton, N.J., 1995.

Frank, J. *Dostoevsky: The Seeds of Revolt, 1821–1849.* Princeton, N.J., 1976.

Frank, J. *Dostoevsky: The Stir of Liberation, 1860–1865*. Princeton, N.J., 1986.

Frank, J. *Dostoevsky: The Years of Ordeal, 1850–1859*. Princeton, N.J., 1983

Galai, S. *The Liberation Movement in Russia, 1900–1905*. Cambridge, 1973.

Gerstein, L. *Nikolai Strakhov*. Cambridge, Mass., 1971.

Getzler, I. *Martov: A Political Biography of a Russian Social Democrat*. New York, 1967.

Haimson, L. H. *The Russian Marxists and the Origins of Bolshevism*. Cambridge, Mass., 1955.

Hardy, D. *Land and Freedom: The Origins of Russian Terrorism, 1876–1879*. Westport, Conn. 1987.

Hare, R. *Portraits of Russian Personalities between Reform and Revolution*. New York, 1959.

Katz, M. *Mikhail N- Katkov: A Political Biography, 1818–1887*. The Hague, 1966.

Keep, J. L. H. *The Rise of Social Democracy in Russia*. Oxford, 1963.

Kelly, A. *Toward Another Shore: Russian Thinkers between Necessity and Chance*. New Haven, Conn., 1998.

Kindersley, R. *The First Russian Revisionists: A Study of legal Marxism in Russia*. Oxford, 1962.

Kline, G. *Religious and Anti-Religious Thought in Russia*. Chicago, 1968.

Kohn, H. *Pan Slavism: Its History and Ideology*. Notre Dame, Ind., 1953; New York, 1960.

Lampert, E. *Sons against Fathers: Studies in Russian Radicalism and Revolution*. London, 1965.

Lampert, E. *Studies in Rebellion*. London, 1957.

Lang, D. M. *The First Russian Radical: Alexander Radishchev, 1749–1802*. New York, 1960.

Lednicki, W. *Russia, Poland and the West: Essays in Literary and Cultural History*. London and New York, 1954.

Leslie, R. F. *Reform and Insurrection in Russian Poland, 1856–1865*. London, 1963.

Lukashevich, S. *Ivan Aksakov, 1823–1866: A Study in Russian Thought and Politics*. Cambridge, Mass., 1965.

Lukashevich,S. *Konstantin Leontev, 1831–1891: A Study in Russian "Heroic Vitalism."* New York, 1967.

Lukashevich, S. *N. F. Fedorov (1828–1903): A Study in Roman Eupsychian and Utopian Thought*. Newark, N.J., 1977.

Malia, M. *Alexander Herzen and the Birth of Russian Socialism, 1812–1855*. Cambridge, Mass., 1961.

Mazour, A. *The First Russian Revolution, 1825: The Decembrist Movement*. Stanford, 1937.

Mazour, A. G. *Women in Exile: Wives of the Decembrists*. Tallahassee, Fla., 1975.

McNally, R. T. *Chaadaev and His Friends: An Intellectual History of Peter Chaadaev and His Russian Contemporaries*. Tallahassee, Fla., 1971.

Mendel, A. P. *Dilemmas of Progress in Tsarist Russia: Legal Marxism and Legal Populism*. Cambridge, Mass., 1961.

Mendel, A. P. *Michael Balkunin: Roots of Apocalypse*. New York, 1981.

Mochulsky, K. *Dostoevsky: His Life and Work*. Translated by M. Minihan. Princeton, N.J., 1967.

Mohrenschildt, D. von. *Russia in the Intellectual Life of 18th Century France*. New York, 1936.

Paperno, I. *Chernyshevsky and the Age of Russian Realism*. Stanford, 1988.

Petrovich, M. B. *The Emergence of Russian Pan-Slavism, 1856–1870*. New York, 1956.

Pipes, R. *Social Democracy and the St. Petersburg Labor Movement, 1885–1897*. Cambridge, Mass., 1963.

Pipes, R. *Struve: Liberal on the Left, 1870–1905*. Cambridge, Mass., 1970.

Pipes, R. *Struve: Liberal on the Right, 1905–1944*. Cambridge, Mass., 1980.

Pipes, R., ed. *The Russian Intelligentsia*. New York, 1961.

Plamenatz, J. *German Marxism and Russian Communism*. London, 1954.

Pomper, P. *Peter Lavrov and the Russian Revolutionary Movement*. Chicago, 1972.

Pomper, P. *The Russian Revolutionary Intelligentsia*. Arlington Heights, Ill., 1970.

Putnam, G. F. *Russian Alternatives to Marxism: Christian Socialism and Idealistic Liberalism in Twentieth-Century Russia*. Knoxville, Tenn., 1977.

Raeff, M. *Origins of the Russian Intelligentsia: The Eighteenth Century Nobility*. New York, 1966.

Randall, F. *N. G. Chernyshevskii*. New York, 1967.

Randolph, J. *The House in the Garden: The Bakunin Family and the Romance of Russian Idealism*. Ithaca, N.Y., 2007.

Rawson, D., C. *Russian Rightists and the Revolution of 1905*. New York, 1995.

Read, C. *Religion, Revolution and the Russian Intelligentsia, 1900–1912*. Totowa, N.J., 1979.

Riasanovsky, N. V. *The Image of Peter the Great in Russian History and Thought*. New York, 1985.

Riasanovsky, N. V. *Nicholas I and Official Nationality in Russia, 1825–1855*. Berkeley, 1959.

Riasanovsky, N. V. *A Parting of Ways: Government and the Educated Public in Russia, 1801–1855*. Oxford, 1976.

Riasanovsky, N. V. *Russia and the West in the Teachings of the Slavophiles*. Cambridge, Mass., 1952.

Rogger, H. *National Consciousness in 18th Century Russia*. Cambridge, Mass., 1960.

Rosenthal, B. G., ed. *Nietzsche in Russia*. Princeton, N.J., 1986.

Schapiro, L. *Rationalism and Nationalism in Russian Nineteenth Century Political Thought*. New Haven, Conn., 1967.

Serge, V. *Memoirs of a Revolutionary, 1901–1941*. Translated by P. Sedgwick. London, 1963.

Service, R. *Lenin: a Political Life*. Vols. 1–2. Bloomington, Ind., 1985, 1991.

Stites, R. *The Women's Liberation Movement in Russia: Feminism, Nihilism, and Bolshevism, 1860–1930*. Princeton, N.J., 1978.

Thaden, E. C. *Conservative Nationalism in 19th Century Russia*. Seattle, 1964.

Treadgold, D. W. *Lenin and His Rivals: The Struggle far Russia's Future, 1898–1906*. New York, 1955.

Trotsky, L. *1905*. Translated by A. Bostock. New York, 1971.

Ulam, A. B. *The Bolsheviks*. New York, 1965.

Venturi, F. *Roots of Revolution: A History of the Populist and Socialist Movements in Nineteenth Century Russia*. Translated by F. Haskell. New York, 1960.

Vucinich, A. *Social Thought in Tsarist Russia: The Quest for a General Science of Society 1861–1917*. Chicago and London, 1976.

Walicki, A. *The Controversy Over Capitalism*. Oxford, 1969.

Walicki, A. *A History of Russian Thought from the Enlightenment to Marxism*. Stanford, 1979.

Walicki, A. *The Slavophile Controversy. History of a Conservative Utopia in Nineteenth Century Russian Thought*. Translated by H. Andrews-Rusiecka. Oxford, 1975.

Weeks, A. L. *The First Bolshevik: A Political Biography of Peter Tkachev*. New York, 1968.

Wilson, E. *To the Finland Station*. New York, 1940.

Woehrlin, W. F. *Chernyshevsky: The Man and the Journalist*. Cambridge, Mass., 1971.

Wolfe, B. E. *Three Who Made a Revolution: A Biographical History*. New York, 1948.

Wortman, R. *The Crisis of Russian Populism*. Cambridge, Eng., 1967.

Yarmolinsky, A. *Road to Revolution: A Century of Russian Radicalism.* London, 1957.

Zenkovsky, V. V. *Russian Thinkers and Europe.* Translated from Russian. Ann Arbor, Mich., 1953.

Zetlin, M. *The Decembrists.* Translated by G. Panin. New York, 1958.

## Soviet Russia, 1917–1991

### A. Revolution and Civil War

#### 1. GENERAL STUDIES, INCLUDING WORKS BY PARTICIPANTS

Acton, E., V. Iu. Cherniaev, and W. G. Rosenberg, eds. *Critical Companion to the Russian Revolution.* Bloomington, Ind., 1997.

Carr, E. H. *A History of Soviet Russia.* Vols. 1–3, *The Bolshevik Revolution, 1917–1923.* Vol. 4, *The Interregnum, 1923–1924.* Vols. 5–7, *Socialism in One Country, 1924–1926.* Vols. 8–9, *Foundations of a Planned Economy, 1926–1929* (Vol. 8 with R. W. Davies). New York, 1951–53, 1954, 1958, 1971–72.

Chamberlin, W. N. *The Russian Revolution, 1917–1921.* 2 vols. New York, 1935.

Chernov, V., *The Great Russian Revolution.* New Haven, Conn., 1936.

Curtiss, J. S. *The Russian Revolutions of 1917.* Princeton, N.J., 1957.

Denikin, A. I. *The Russian Turmoil.* London, 1922.

Figes, O. *A People's Tragedy: The Russian Revolution, 1891–1924.* New York, 1997.

Fitzpatrick, S. *The Russian Revolution.* New York, 1994.

Footman, D. *Civil War in Russia.* New York, 1961.

Footman, D. *The Russian Revolution.* New York, 1962.

Gorky, M. *Untimely Thoughts: Essays on Revolution, Culture, and the Bolsheviks, 1917–1918.* Translated by H. Ermolaev. Introduction by M. Steinberg. New Haven, Conn., 1995.

Katkov, G. *Russia, 1917: The February Revolution.* New York, 1967.

Kerensky, A. *The Catastrophe: Kerensky's Own Story of the Russian Revolution.* New York, 1927.

Kerensky, A. *The Crucifixion of Liberty.* New York, 1934.

Kerensky, A. *Russia and History's Turning Point.* London, 1965.

Liebman, M. *The Russian Revolution.* Translated by A. Pomerans. New York, 1970.

Lincoln, W. B. *Passage Through Armageddon: The Russians in War and Revolution, 1914–1918.* New York, 1986.

Mawdsley, E. *The Russian Civil War.* New York, 1996.

Steinberg, M. D. *Voices of Revolution, 1917.* New Haven, Conn., 2001.

Sukhanov, N. N. *The Russian Revolution of 1917.* New York, 1955.

Trotsky, L. *The History of the Russian Revolution,* 3 vols. New York, 1932–57.

Tucker, R. C., ed. *The Lenin Anthology.* New York, 1975.

Von Mohrenschildt, D., ed. *The Russian Revolution of 1917: Contemporary Accounts.* New York, 971.

Woytinsky, W. S. *Stormy Passage. A Personal History through Two Russian Revolutions to Democracy and Freedom: 1905–1960.* New York, 1961.

#### 2. READINGS ON SPECIAL TOPICS

Adams, A. E. *Bolsheviks in the Ukraine: The Second Campaign.* New Haven, Conn., 1963.

Adams, A. E., ed. *The Russian Revolution and Bolshevik Victory: Why and How?* Boston, 1960.

Anweiler, O. *The Soviets: The Russian Workers, Peasants, and Soldiers Councils, 1905–1921.* Translated by R. Hein. New York, 1974.

Avrich, P. *Kronstadt 1921.* Princeton, N.J., 1970.

Badcock, S. *Politics and the People in Revolutionary Russia: A Provincial History.* New York, 2007.

Browder, R., and F. Kerensky, eds. *The Russian Provisional Government, 1917.* 3 vols. Stanford, 1961.

Bunyan, J., ed. *Intervention, Civil War and Communism in Russia, April-December, 1918: Documents.* Baltimore, 1936.

Bunyan, J., and H. H. Fisher, eds. *The Bolshevik Revolution, 1917–1918: Documents.* Stanford, 1934.

Burdzhalov, E. N. *Russia's Second Revolution: The February Uprising in Petrograd.* Translated and edited by D. J. Raleigh. Bloomington, Ind., 1987.

Carr, E. H. *The October Revolution: Before and After.* New York, 1969.

Dan, Th. *The Origins of Bolshevism.* London, 1964.

Daniels, R. V. *Red October. The Bolshevik Revolution of 1917.* London, 1968.

Deutscher, I. ed. *The Age of Permanent Revolution: A Trotsky Anthology.* New York, 1964.

Farnsworth, B. *Alexandra Kollontai: Socialism, Feminism, and the Bolshevik Revolution.* Stanford, 1980.

Ferro, M. *The Russian Revolution of February 1917.* Translated by J. L. Richards. Englewood Cliffs, N.J., 1972.

Figes, O. *Peasant Russia, Civil War: The Volga Countryside in Revolution, 1917–1921.* Oxford, 1989.

Figes, O. and B. Kolonitskii. *Interpreting the Russian Revolution: The Language and Symbols of 1917.* New Haven, Conn., 1999.

Fischer, Louis. *The Life of Lenin.* New York, 1964.

Galili, Z. *The Menshevik Leaders in the Russian Revolution: Social Realities and Political Struggles.* Princeton, N.J., 1989.

Gankin, O. H., and H. H. Fisher, eds. *The Bolsheviks and the World War: Documents.* Stanford, 1940.

Getzler, I. *Kronstadt, 1917–1921: Fate of a Soviet Democracy.* Cambridge, 1983.

Haimson, L. H., ed. *The Mensheviks: From the Revolution of 1917 to the Second World War.* Chicago, 1974.

Hasegawa, T. *The February Revolution: Petrograd, 1917.* Seattle, 1981.

Holquist, P. *Making War, Forging Revolution: Russia's Continuum of Crisis, 1914–1921.* Cambridge, Mass., 2002.

Hunczak, T., ed. *The Ukraine, 1917–1921: A Study in Revolution.* Cambridge, Mass., 1977.

Keep, J. *The Russian Revolution: A Study in Mass Mobilization.* New York, 1976.

Kennan, G. F. *Soviet-American Relations, 1917–1920.* Vol. 1, *Russia Leaves the War.* Vol. 2, *The Decision to Intervene.* Princeton, N.J., 1956, 1958.

Koenker, D. P. *Moscow Workers and the 1917 Revolution.* Princeton, N.J., 1981.

Koenker, D. P. and W. G. Rosenberg. *Strikes and Revolution in Russia, 1917.* Princeton, N.J., 1989.

Koenker, D. P., W. G. Rosenberg, and R. G. Suny, eds. *Party, State, and Society in the Russian Civil War.* Bloomington, Ind., 1989.

Laqueur, W. *The Fate of the Revolution: Interpretations of Soviet History.* New York, 1967.

Lehovich, D. V. *White Against Red: The Life of General Anton Denikin.* New York, 1974.

Lenin, V. I. *Collected Works.* New York, 1927–42.

Lenin, V. I. *Imperialism: The Highest Stage of Capitalism.* New York, 1927.

Lenin, V. I. *The State and Revolution.* New York, 1927.

Lenin, V. I. *What Is to Be Done?* Moscow, 1947.

Lewin, M. *Lenin's Last Struggle.* New York, 1968.

Luckett, R. *The White Generals: An Account of the White Movement and the Russian Civil War.* New York, 1987.

Mally, L. *Culture of the Future: The Proletkult Movement in Revolutionary Russia.* Berkeley, 1990.

McAuley, M. *Bread and Justice: State and Society in Petrograd, 1917–1922.* Oxford, 1991.

Medvedev, R. A. *The October Revolution.* Translated by G. Saunders. Foreword by H. G. Salisbury. New York, 1979.

Melgunov, S. P. *The Bolshevik Seizure of Power.* Edited by S. G. Pushkarev and B. S. Pushkarev. Translated by J. Beaver. Santa Barbara, Calif., 1972.

Payne, R. *The Life and Death of Lenin.* New York, 1964.

Pipes, R. *The Formation of the Soviet Union: Communism and Nationalism, 1917–1923.* Cambridge, Mass., 1954.

Pipes, R., ed. *Revolutionary Russia: A Symposium.* 2nd ed. rev. Cambridge, Mass., 1968.

Possony, S. T. *Lenin: The Compulsive Revolutionary.* Chicago, 1964. Rabinowitch, A. *The Bolsheviks Come to Power. The Revolution of 1917 in Petrograd.* New York, 1976.

Rabinowitch, A. *Prelude to Revolution: The Petrograd Bolsheviks and the July 1917 Uprising.* Bloomington, Ind., 1968.

Radkey, O. H. *The Agrarian Foes of Bolshevism: Promise and Default of the Russian Socialist Revolutionaries, February to October, 1917.* New York, 1958.

Radkey, O. H. *The Election to the Russian Constituent Assembly of 1917.* Cambridge, Mass., 1950.

Radkey, O. H. *The Sickle under the Hammer: The Russian Socialist Revolutionaries in the Early Months of Soviet Rule.* New York, 1963.

Raleigh, D. J. *Revolution on the Volga: 1917 in Saratov.* Ithaca, N.Y., 1986.

Raskolnikov, F. F. *Kronstadt and Petrograd in 1917.* Translated and annotated by B. Pearce. London, 1982.

Reed, J. *Ten Days That Shook the World.* New York, 1960.

Reshetar, J. S. *The Ukrainian Revolution, 1917–1920.* Princeton, N.J., 1952.

Rosenberg, A. *A History of Bolshevism.* Garden City, N.Y., 1967.

Rosenberg, W. G. *A. I. Denikin and the Anti-Bolshevik Movement in South Russia.* Amherst, Mass., 1961.

Rosenberg, W. G. *Liberals in the Russian Revolution: The Constitutional Democratic Party, 1917–1921.* Princeton, N.J., 1974.

Rosmer, A. *Moscow under Lenin.* Translated by I. Birchall. New York, 1972.

Serge, V. *Year One of the Russian Revolution.* Translated by P. Sedgwick. New York, 1972.

Shapiro, L. *The Origins of the Communist Autocracy: Political Opposition in the Soviet State: First Phase, 1917–1922.* Cambridge, Mass., 1955.

Smith, E. E. *The Young Stalin.* New York, 1967.

Smith, S. A. *Red Petrograd: Revolution in the Factories.* Cambridge, 1983.

Stewart, G. *The White Armies of Russia.* New York, 1933.

Stites, R. *Revolutionary Dreams: Utopian Vision and Experimental Life in the Russian Revolution.* New York, 1989.

Suny, R. G. *The Baku Commune, 1917–1918: Class and Nationality in the Russian Revolution.* Princeton, N.J., 1972.

Tirado, I. A. *Young Guard! The Communist Youth League, Petrograd 1917–1920.* New York, 1988.

Varnock, E., and H. H. Fisher. *The Testimony of Kolchak and Other Siberian Materials and Documents.* Stanford, 1935.

Wade, R. *The Russian Revolution, 1917.* Cambridge, 2000.

Wheeler-Bennett, J. W. *The Forgotten Peace: Brest-Litovsk.* New York, 1939.

Wildman, A. K. *The End of the Russian Imperial Army.* 2 vols. Princeton, N.J., 1980, 1987.

## B. Soviet Period: General

Abramovitch, R. *The Soviet Revolution, 1917–1939.* New York, 1962.

Alliluyeva, S. *Twenty Letters to a Friend.* New York, 1967.

Amalrik, A. *Involuntary Journey to Siberia.* New York, 1970.

Amalrik, A. *Notes of a Revolutionary.* Translated by G. Daniels. New York, 1982.

Amalrik, A. *Will the Soviet Union Survive until 1984?* New York, 1970.

Benet, S., ed. and trans. *The Village of Viriatino: An Ethnographic Study of a Russian Village from before the Revolution to the Present.* Garden City, N.Y., 1970.

Berdiaev, N. *The Origins of Russian Communism.* London, 1948.

Berdiaev, N. *The Russian Revolution: Two Essays on Its Implications in Religion and Psychology.* London, 1931.

Bialer, S. *Stalin's Successors: Leadership, Stability, and Change in the Soviet Union.* Cambridge, 1980.

Breslauer, G. W. *Khrushchev and Brezhnev as Leaders: Building Authority in Soviet Politics.* London, 1982.

Chalidze, V. *To Defend These Rights: Human Rights and the Soviet Union.* Translated by G. Daniels. New York, 1974.

Cohen, S. F. *Bukharin and the Bolshevik Revolution.* New York, 1973.

Cohen, S. F. *Rethinking the Soviet Experience: Politics and History since 1917.* New York, 1985.

Conquest, R. *Stalin and the Kirov Murder.* New York, 1989.

Crossman, R. ed. *The God That Failed.* London, 1950.

Daniels, R. V. *A Documentary History of Communism.* New York, 1960.

Daniels, R. V. *Russia: The Roots of Confrontation.* Cambridge, Mass., 1985.

Daniels, R. V., ed. *The Stalin Revolution: Fulfillment or Betrayal of Communism?* Boston, 1965.

Davies, S. *Popular Opinion in Stalin's Russia: Terror, Propaganda and Dissent, 1934–1941.* New York, 1997.

Deutscher, I. *The Prophet Armed: Trotsky, 1879–1921.* New York, 1954.

Deutscher, I. *The Prophet Outcast: Trotsky, 1929–1940.* New York, 1963.

Deutscher, I. *The Prophet Unarmed: Trotsky, 1921–1929.* New York, 1959.

Deutscher, I. *Stalin: A Political Biography.* New York, 1949. 2nd ed., 1966.

Dmytryshyn, B. *USSR: A Concise History.* New York, 1971.

Dornberg, J. *Brezhnev: The Masks of Power.* New York, 1974.

Dunn, S., and E. Dunn. *The Peasants of Central Russia.* New York, 1967.

Farnsworth, B. *Alexandra Kollontai: Socialism, Feminism, and the Bolshevik Revolution.* Stanford, 1980.

Feshbach, M., with A. Friendly, Jr. *Ecocide in the USSR: Health and Nature under Siege.* New York, 1992.

Fischer, G. *Soviet Opposition to Stalin: A Case Study in World War II.* Westport, Conn., 1970.

Fitzpatrick, S., A. Rabinowitch, and R. Stites, eds. *Russia in the Era of NEP*. Bloomington, Ind., 1991.

Friedrich, C. J., and Z. K. Brzezinski. *Totalitarian Dictatorship and Autocracy*. Cambridge, Mass., 1956.

Galanskov, I., et al. *The Trial of the Four: A Collection of Materials on the Case of Galanskov, Ginzberg, Dobrovolsky and Lashkova, 1967–68*. Edited by P. Reddaway. Translated by J. Saprets, H. Sternberg, and D. Weissbort. New York, 1972.

Geiger, H. K. *The Family in Soviet Russia*. Cambridge, Mass., 1968.

Gerstenmaier, C. *The Voices of the Silent*. Translated by S. Hecker. New York, 1972.

Geyer, M. and S. Fitzpatrick, eds. *Beyond Totalitarianism: Stalinism and Nazism Compared*. Cambridge, Eng., 2009

Harding, N. *Leninism*. Durham, N.C., 1996.

Heller, M., with A. Nekrich. *Utopia in Power: The History of the Soviet Union from 1917 to the Present*. New York, 1986.

Hindus, M. *Red Bread: Collectivization in a Russian Village*. Foreword by R. G. Suny. Bloomington, Ind., 1988.

Hosking, G. *The First Socialist Society: A History of the Soviet Union from Within*. Cambridge, Mass., 1985.

Jones, P., ed. *The Dilemmas of De-Stalinisation: Negotiating Cultural and Social Change in the Khrushchev Era*. London, 2006.

Khrushchev, N. S. *Khrushchev Remembers*. Vol. 1, edited and translated by S. Talbott. Introduction and Commentary by E. Crankshaw. Vol. 2. *The Last Testament*. Edited and translated by S. Talbott. Foreword by E. Crankshaw. Introduction by J. L. Schecter. Boston and Toronto, 1970, 1974.

Knight, A. *Beria: Stalin's First Lieutenant*. Princeton, N.J., 1996.

Lapidus, G. W. *Women in Soviet Society: Equality, Development, and Social Change*. Berkeley, 1978.

Lapidus, G. W. ed. *Women, Work and Family in the Soviet Union*. Armonk, N.Y., 1982.

Mandelshtam, N. *Hope Abandoned*. Translated by M. Hayward. New York, 1974.

Mandelshtam, N. *Hope Against Hope*. Translated by M. Hayward. New York, 1970.

Marcuse, H. *Soviet Marxism*. New York, 1958.

McNeal, R. H. *Stalin: Man and Ruler*. New York, 1988.

McNeal, R. H. *The Bolshevik Tradition: Lenin, Stalin, Khrushchev*. Englewood Cliffs, N.J., 1963.

McNeal, R. H., ed. *Lenin, Stalin, Khrushchev: Voices of Bolshevism*. Englewood Cliffs, N.J., 1963.

Medvedev, R. *Let History Judge. The Origins and Consequences of Stalinism*. Edited by D. Joravsky and G. Haupt. Translated by C. Taylor. New York, 1971.

Medvedev, R. *On Socialist Democracy*. Edited and translated by E. de Kadt. New York, 1975.

Medvedev, Zh. A., and R. A. Medvedev. *A Question of Madness*. New York, 1971.

Meyer, A. *Communism*. New York, 1960.

Meyer, A. *Leninism*. Cambridge, Mass., 1957.

Meyer, A. *Marxism*. Cambridge, Mass., 1954.

Nettl, J. P. *The Soviet Achievement*. London, 1967.

*On Trial: The Case of Sinyavsky (Tertz) and Daniel (Arzhak)*. Documents edited by L. Labedz and M. Hayward. Russian text translated by M. Harari and M. Hayward. French texts translated by M. Villiers. London, 1967.

Pankratova, A. M., ed. *A History of the USSR.* Compiled by K. V. Bazilevich et al. 3 vols. New York, 1970.

Rabinowitch, A., and J. Rabinowitch, eds. *Revolution and Politics in Russia. Essays in Memory of B. I. Nicolaevsky.* Bloomington, Ind., 1972.

Ratushinskaya, I. *In the Beginning.* Translated by A. Kojevnikov. New York, 1991.

Rauch, B. von. *A History of Soviet Russia.* New York, 1957.

Reddaway, P., ed. and trans. *Uncensored Russia: Protest and Dissent in the Soviet Union. The unofficial Moscow Journal A Chronicle of Current Events.* London, 1972.

Reve, K. van het, ed. *Dear Comrade: Pavel Litvinov and the Voices of Soviet Citizens in Dissent.* New York, 1969.

Rieber, A. J., and R. C. Nelson. *A Study of the USSR and Communism: An Historical Approach.* Chicago, 1962.

Rostow, W. W. *The Dynamics of Soviet Society.* New York, 1963.

Rothberg, A. *The Heirs of Stalin: Dissidence and the Soviet Regime, 1953–1970.* Ithaca, N.Y., 1972.

Ruder, C. A. *Making History for Stalin: The Story of the Belomor Canal.* Gainesville, Fla., 1998.

Schlesinger, R. *Changing Attitudes in Soviet Russia: The Family.* London, 1949.

Service, R. *Lenin: a Political Life.* Vol, 3. Bloomington, Ind., 1995.

Shatz, M. S. *Soviet Dissent in Historical Perspective.* Cambridge, 1981. '

Shentalinskii, V. *Arrested Voices: Resurrecting the Disappeared Writers of the Soviet Regime.* New York, 1996.

Siegelbaum, L. H. *The Soviet State and Society between Revolutions, 1918–1929.* Cambridge, 1992.

Souvarine, B. *Stalin, A Critical Survey of Bolshevism.* New York, 1939.

Suny, R. G. *The Soviet Experiment: Russia, the USSR, and the Successor States.* New York, 1998.

Treadgold, D. W. *Twentieth-Century Russia.* Chicago, 1959. 6th ed., 1987.

Trotsky, L. *The Revolution Betrayed.* New York, 1937.

Trotsky, L. *Stalin: An Appraisal of the Man and His Influence.* New York, 1941.

Tucker, R. C. *Stalin as Revolutionary, 1879–1929: A Study in History and Personality.* New York, 1973.

Tucker, R. C. *Stalin in Power: The Revolution from Above, 1929–1941.* New York, 1990.

Ulam, A. B. *Stalin: The Man and His Era.* New York, 1973.

Von Laue, T. H. *The Global City.* Philadelphia and New York, 1969.

Von Laue, T. H. *Why Lenin? Why Stalin?* Philadelphia and New York, 1964.

Webb, S., and B. Webb. *Soviet Communism. A New Civilization?* 2 vols. New York, 1936.

Werth, A. *Russia: The Post-War Years.* New York, 1972.

Westwood, J. N. *Endurance and Endeavour: Russian History, 1812–1980.* 3rd ed. The Short Oxford History of the Modern World. Oxford, 1987.

Zubkova, E. *Russia after the War: Hopes, Illusions, and Disappointments, 1945–1957.* Armonk, N.Y., 1998.

## C. Ideology, Government, Administration, and Law

Armstrong, J. A. *The Politics of Totalitarianism: The Communist Party of the Soviet Union.* New York, 1961.

Armstrong, J. A. *The Soviet Bureaucratic Elite: A Case Study of the Ukrainian Apparatus.* New York, 1961.

Avtorkhanov, A. *Stalin and the Soviet Communist Party.* Munich, 1959.

Azrael, J. R. *Managerial Power and Soviet Politics.* Cambridge, Mass., 1966.

Barghoorn, F. C. *Soviet Russian Nationalism.* New York, 1956.

Barron, J. *KGB: The Secret Work of Soviet Agents.* New York, 1974.

Berman, H. J. *Justice in Russia.* Cambridge, Mass., 1950. Rev. ed., 1963.

Berman, H. J., and M. Kerner. *Soviet Military Law and Administration.* Cambridge, Mass., 1955.

Berman, H. J., and P. B. Maggs. *Disarmament Inspection under Soviet Law.* Dobbs Ferry, N.Y., 1967.

Berman, H. J., and J. W. Spindler, trans. *Soviet Criminal Law and Procedure: The RSFSR Code.* Introduction and analysis by H. J. Berman. Cambridge, Mass., 1965.

Brzezinski, Z. K. *The Permanent Purge.* Cambridge, Mass., 1956.

Conquest, R. *The Great Terror: A Reassessment.* New York, 1990.

Conquest, R. *The Great Terror: Stalin's Purge of the Thirties.* New York, 1971.

Dallin, A., and T. B. Larson, eds. *Soviet Politics since Khrushchev.* Englewood Cliffs, N. J., 1968.

Daniels, R. V. *The Conscience of the Revolution: Communist Opposition in Soviet Russia.* Cambridge, Mass., 1960.

Deacon, R. *A History of the Russian Secret Service.* New York, 1972.

Dinerstein, H. S., and L. Goure. *Communism and the Russian Peasant.* Glencoe, Ill., 1955.

Dinerstein, H. S., and L. Goure. *War and the Soviet Union.* New York, 1962.

Dobson, M. *Khrushchev's Cold Summer: Gulag Returnees, Crime, and the Fate of Reform after Stalin.* Ithaca, N.Y., 2009.

Erickson, J. *The Soviet High Command: A Military-Political History, 1918–1941.* New York, 1962.

Fainsod, M. *How Russia Is Ruled.* Cambridge, Mass., 1953.

Fainsod, M. *Smolensk under Soviet Rule.* Cambridge, Mass., 1958.

Fischer, G. *Soviet Opposition to Stalin.* Cambridge, Mass., 1952.

Getty, J. A. and R. Manning, eds. *Stalinist Terror: New Perspectives.* Cambridge, 1993.

Goldman, W. Z. *Terror and Democracy in the Age of Stalin: The Social Dynamics of Repression.* New York, 2007.

Gorlizki, Y. and O. Khlevniuk. *Cold Peace: Stalin and the Soviet Ruling Circle, 1945–1953.* Oxford, 2004.

Graham, L. R. *The Soviet Academy of Sciences and the Communist Party, 1927–1932.* Princeton, N.J., 1967.

Gregory, P. R. and N. Naimark, eds. *The Lost Politburo Transcripts: From Collective Rule to Stalin's Dictatorship.* New Haven, Conn., 2008.

Gsovsky, V. *Soviet Civil Law.* 2 vols. Ann Arbor, Mich., 1948, 1949.

Gsovsky, V., and K. Grybowski. *Government, Law and Courts in the Soviet Union and Eastern Europe.* New York, 1959.

Hahn, W. G. *Postwar Soviet Politics: The Fall of Zhdanov and the Defeat of Moderation, 1946–1953.* Ithaca, N.Y., 1982.

Hammer, D. P. *USSR: The Politics of Oligarchy.* Hinsdale, Ill., 1974.

Harvey, M. L., L. Goure, and V. Prokofieff. *Science and Technology as an Instrument of Soviet Policy.* Washington, D.C., 1972.

Hazard, J. N. *The Soviet System of Government.* Chicago, 1957.

Hendel, S., ed. *The Soviet Crucible: Soviet Government in Theory and Practice.* Princeton, N.J., 1960.

Inkeles, A., and R. A. Bauer. *The Soviet Citizen.* Cambridge, Mass., 1959.

Inkeles, A., R. Bauer, and C. Kluckhohn. *How the Soviet System Works*. Cambridge, Mass., 1956.

Karcz, J., ed. *Soviet and East European Agriculture*. Berkeley, 1967.

Kassof, A., ed. *Prospects for Soviet Society*. New York, 1968.

Khlevniuk, O. V. *Master of the House: Stalin and His Inner Circle*. New Haven, Conn., 2009.

Kotkin, S. *Magnetic Mountain: Stalinism as a Civilization*. Berkeley, 1995.

Kucherov, S. *The Organs of Soviet Administration of Justice: Their History and Operation*. London, 1970.

Kuromiya, Hiroaki. *The Voices of the Dead: Stalin's Great Terror in the 1930s*. New Haven, Conn., 2008.

Leites, N., and E. Bernaut. *Ritual of Liquidation: The Case of the Moscow Trials*. Glencoe, Ill., 1954.

Leonard, W. *The Kremlin since Stalin*. New York, 1962.

Levytsky. B. *The Uses of Terror. The Soviet Secret Police, 1917–1970*. Translated by H. Piehler. New York, 1972.

Malia, M. E. *The Soviet Tragedy: A History of Socialism in Russia, 1917–1991*. New York, 1994.

Matthews, M. *Class and Society in Soviet Russia*. New York, 1972.

Matthews, M., ed. *Soviet Government: A Selection of Official Documents on Internal Policies*. New York, 1974.

Meissner, B. *The Communist Party of the Soviet Union: Party Leadership*. New York, 1956.

Moore, B. *Soviet Politics: The Dilemma of Power*. Cambridge, Mass., 1950.

Odom, W. E. *The Soviet Volunteers: Modernization and Bureaucracy in a Public Mass Organization*. Princeton, N.J., 1973.

Pipes, R. *Russia under the Bolshevik Regime*. New York, 1994.

Reshetar, J. S. *A Concise History of the Communist Party of the Soviet* Union. New York, 1960.

Rigby, T. H. *Communist Party Membership in the USSR, 1917–1967*. Princeton, N.J., 1968

Schapiro, L. B. *The Communist Party of the Soviet Union*. New York, 1971.

Schlesinger, R. *Soviet Legal Theory*. London, 1945.

Solomon, P. H., Jr. *Soviet Criminal Justice under Stalin*. Cambridge, 1996.

Sorenson, R. *The Life and Death of Soviet Trade Unionism*. New York, 1969.

Stone, D. R. *Hammer and Rifle: The Militarization of the Soviet Union, 1926–1933*. Lawrence, Kans., 2000

Swearer, H. R, and M. Rush. *The Politics of Succession in the USSR: Materials on Khrushchev's Rise to Leadership*. Boston, 1964.

Tucker, R. C. *The Soviet Political Mind*. New York, 1963.

Tucker, R. C., ed. *Stalinism: Essays in Historical Interpretation*. New York, 1977.

Ulam, A. *The New Face of Soviet Totalitarianism*. Cambridge, Mass., 1963.

Ulam, A. *The Unfinished Revolution: An Essay on the Sources of Influence of Marxism and Communism*. New York, 1960.

Viola, L. *The Unknown Gulag: The Lost World of Stalin's Special Settlements*. Oxford, 2007.

Vyshinsky, A. *The Law of the Soviet State. New York, 1948*.

Walicki, A. *Marxism and the Leap to the Kingdom of Freedom: The Rise and Fall of the Communist Utopia*. Stanford, 1995.

Weinberg, E. A. *The Development of Sociology in the Soviet Union*. Boston, 1974.

Wolin, S., and R. Slusser, eds. *The Soviet Secret Police*. New York, 1957.

## D. Economic Development

Ball, A. M. *Russia's Last Capitalists: The Nepmen, 1921–1929.* Berkeley, 1987.

Baykov, A. *The Development of the Soviet Economic System.* Cambridge, 1947.

Bergson, A. *The Economics of Soviet Planning.* New Haven, Conn., 1964.

Bergson, A. *Planning and Productivity under Soviet Socialism.* New York, 1968.

Bergson, A. *Real National Income of Soviet Russia since 1928.* Cambridge, Mass., 1961.

Bergson, A. *Soviet Economic Growth.* Evanston, Ill., 1953.

Bergson, A. *The Structure of Soviet Wages.* Cambridge, Mass., 1944.

Bergson, A., and S. Kuznets, eds. *Economic Trends in the Soviet Union.* Cambridge, Mass., 1963.

Campbell, R. *Soviet Economic Power: Its Organization, Growth and Challenge.* Boston, 1960.

Dallin, D. J., and B. I. Nicolaevsky. *Forced Labor in Soviet Russia.* New Haven, Conn., 1947.

Davies, R. W. *The Industrialization of Soviet Russia.* 2 vols. Cambridge, Mass., 1980.

Davies, R. W. *The Socialist Offensive: The Collectivization of Soviet Agriculture, 1929–30,* Cambridge, Mass., 1980.

Davies, R. W. and S. G. Wheatcroft. *The Years of Hunger: Soviet Agriculture, 1931–1933.* New York, 2004.

Davies, R. W., M. Harrison, and S. G. Wheatcroft, eds. *The Economic Transformation of the Soviet Union, 1913–1945.* Cambridge, Eng., 1994.

Deutscher, I. *Soviet Trade Unions.* London, 1950.

De Witt, N. *Education and Professional Employment in the USSR.* Washington, D.C., 1961.

Dobb, M. *Soviet Economic Development Since the 1917 Revolution.* London, 1948.

Erlich, A. *The Soviet Industrialization Debate, 1924–28.* Cambridge, Mass., I960.

Gregory, P. R., and R. C. Stuart. *Soviet Economic Structure and Performance.* New York, 1974.

Grossman, G. "The Economy at Middle Age." *Problems of Communism* (March–April 1976).

Grossman, G. "The Solitary Society: A Philosophical Issue in Communist Economic Reforms." In *Essays in Socialism and Planning in Honor of Carl Landauer,* edited by G. Grossman. Englewood Cliffs, N.J., 1970.

Grossman, G. "Subverted Sovereignty: Historic Role of the Soviet Underground." *The Tunnel at the End of the Light: Privatization, Business Networks, and Economic Transformation in Russia,* edited by Stephen S. Cohen, Andrew Schwartz, and John Zysman. Berkeley, 1998.

Grossman, G., ed. *Money and Plan: Financial Aspects of East European Economic Reforms.* Berkeley, 1968.

Jasny, N. *The Socialized Agriculture of the USSR.* Stanford, 1949.

Jasny, N. *Soviet Economy during the Plan Era.* Stanford, 1951.

Jasny, N. *Soviet Industrialization, 1928–1932.* Chicago, 1961.

Laird, R. D., ed. *Soviet Agricultural and Peasant Affairs.* Lawrence, Kans., 1963.

Lewin, M. *Russian Peasants and Soviet Power: A Study of Collectivization.* Translated by I. Nove. Evanston, Ill., 1968.

Moskoff, W. *The Bread of Affliction: The Food Supply in the USSR during World War II.* Cambridge, 1990.

Nove, A. *An Economic History of the USSR, 1917–1991,* 3rd ed. London, 1992.

Pryde, P. R. *Conservation in the Soviet Union.* Cambridge, 1972.

Quigley, J. *The Soviet Foreign Trade Monopoly: Institutions and Laws.* Columbus, Ohio, 1974.

Schwartz, H. *The Soviet Economy since Stalin.* Philadelphia, 1965.

Schwarz, S. *Labor in the Soviet Union.* New York, 1952.


## E. Foreign Affairs

Adams, A. E. *Readings in Soviet Foreign Policy: Theory and Practice.* Boston, 1961.

Barber, J. and M. Harrison. *The Soviet Home Front 1941–1945: A Social and Economic History of the USSR in World War* II. London, 1991.

Barghoorn, F. C. *The Soviet Cultural Offensive: The Role of Cultural Diplomacy in Soviet Foreign Policy.* Princeton, N.J., 1960.

Barghoorn, F. C. *Soviet Foreign Propaganda.* Princeton, N.J., 1964.

Beloff, M. *The Foreign Policy of Soviet Russia, 1929–1941.* 2 vols. New York, 1947, 1949.

Beloff, M. *Soviet Foreign Policy in the Far East, 1944–1951.* London, 1953.

Bishop. D. G., ed. *Soviet Foreign Relations: Documents and Readings.* Syracuse, N.Y., 1952.

Borzecky, J. *The Soviet-Polish Peace of 1921 and the Creation of Interwar Europe.* New Haven, Conn., 2008.

Brandt, C. *Stalin's Failure in China, 1924–1927.* Cambridge, Mass., 1958.

Brzezinski, Z. K. *The Soviet Bloc: Unity and Conflict.* Cambridge, Mass., 1960. Rev. ed., 1967.

Carell, P. *Scorched Earth: The Russian-German War, 1943–1944.* Translated by E. Osers. Boston, 1970.

Carr, E. H. *The Soviet Impact on the Western World.* London, 1946.

Carr, E. H. *Twilight of the Comintern, 1930–1935.* New York, 1982.

Cattell, D. T. *Communism and the Spanish Civil War.* Berkeley, 1955.

Chew, A. F. *The White Death: The Epic of the Soviet-Finnish Winter* War. East Lansing, Mich., 1971.

Dallin, A. *German Rule in Russia, 1941–1945: A Study of Occupation Policies.* New York, 1957.

Dallin, D. J. *Soviet Russia and the Far East.* New Haven, Conn., 1948.

Dallin, D. J. *Soviet Russia's Foreign Policy, 1939–1942.* New Haven, Conn., 1942.

Degras, J. *The Communist International, 1919–1943.* New York, 1956.

Degras, J. *Soviet Documents on Foreign Policy, 1917–1941.* 3 vols. New York, 1951–53.

Degras, J., ed. *Calendar of Soviet Documents on Foreign Policy, 1917–1941.* London, 1948.

Erickson, J. *The Road* to *Stalingrad: Stalin's War with Germany.* New York, 1975.

Eudin, X., and H. H. Fisher. *Soviet Russia and the West, 1920–1927.* Stanford, 1957.

Eudin, X., and R. C. North, eds. *Soviet Russia and the East, 1920–1927.* Stanford, 1957.

Farnsworth, B. *William C. Bullitt and the Soviet Union.* Bloomington, Ind., 1967.

Fischer, L. *The Soviets in World Affairs, 1917–1929.* Princeton, N.J., 1951.

Fischer, R. *Stalin and German Communism.* Cambridge, Mass., 1948.

Floyd, D. *Mao against Khrushchev: A Short History of the Sino-Soviet Conflict.* New York, 1963.

Gaddis, J. L. *We Now Know: Rethinking Cold War History.* New York, 1997.

Garthoff. R. L. *Soviet Strategy in the Nuclear Age.* New York, 1962.

Glantz, D. M. and J. M. House. *When Titans Clashed: How the Red Army Stopped Hitler.* Lawrence, Kans., 2001.

Gleason, A. *Totalitarianism: The Inner History of the Cold War.* New York, 1995.

Gorodetsky, G. *Grand Illusion: Stalin and the* German *Invasion of Russia*, New Haven, Conn., 1999.

Griffith, W. E. *Communism in Europe: Continuity, Change and the Sino-Soviet Dispute.* Cambridge, Mass., 1966.

Gruber, H. *International Communism in the Era of Lenin: A Documentary History.* Greenwich, Conn., 1967.

Harvey, D. L., and L. C. Ciccoritti. *U.S.-Soviet Cooperation in Space.* Washington, D.C., 1974.

Hasegawa, T. *Racing the Enemy: Stalin, Truman, and the Surrender of Japan.* Cambridge, Mass., 2005.

Holloway, D. *Stalin and the Bomb: The Soviet Union and Atomic Energy, 1939–1956.* New Haven, Conn., 1994.

Hopf, T. *Social Construction of International Politics: Identities & Foreign Policies, Moscow 1955 and 1999.* Ithaca, N.Y., 2002.

Jamgotch, N., Jr. *Soviet-East European Dialogue: International Relations of a New Type.* Stanford, 1968.

Kapur, H. *Soviet Russia and Asia, 1917–1927: A Study of Soviet Policy towards Turkey, Iran and Afghanistan.* London, 1966; New York, 1967.

Kennan, G. F. *Russia and the West under Lenin and Stalin.* Boston, 1961.

Kennan, G. F. *Soviet Foreign Policy, 1917–1941.* Princeton, N.J., 1960.

Laqueur, W. Z. *The Soviet Union and the Middle East.* New York, 1959.

Laserson, M. M., ed. *The Development of Soviet Foreign Policy in Europe, 1917–1942: A Selection of Documents.* International Conciliation, no. 386 (January 1943).

Leach, B. A. *German Strategy Against Russia, 1939–1941.* Oxford, 1973.

Leffler, M. P. *For the Soul of Mankind: The United States, the Soviet Union, and the Cold War.* New York, 2007.

Lüthi, L. M. *The Sino-Soviet Split: Cold War in the Communist World.* Princeton, N. J., 2008.

Mackintosh, J. *Strategy and Tactics of Soviet Foreign Policy.* New York, 1962.

Maisky, I. *Memoirs of a Soviet Ambassador: The War 1939–1943.* New York, 1968.

Menon, R. *Soviet Power and the Third World.* New Haven, Conn., and London, 1986.

Merridale, C. *Ivan's War. Life and Death in the Red Army, 1939–1945.* New York, 2006.

Moore, H. L. *Soviet Far Eastern Policy, 1931–1945.* Princeton, N.J., 1945.

Mosely, P. E. *The Kremlin and World Politics.* New York, 1961.

Mosely, P. E. *Russia after Stalin.* New York, 1955.

Mosely, P. E., ed. *The Soviet Union, 1922–1962: A Foreign Affairs Reader.* New York and London, 1963.

Nation, R. *Black Earth, Red Star: A History of Soviet Security Policy.* Ithaca, N.Y., 1992.

Nekrich, A. M. *Pariahs, Partners, Predators: German-Soviet Relations, 1922–1941.* Edited and translated by Gregory L. Freeze; with a foreword by Adam B. Ulam. New York, 1997.

North, R. C. *Moscow and Chinese Communists.* 2nd ed. Stanford, 1962.

O'Connor, T. *Diplomacy and Revolution: G. V. Chicherin and Soviet Foreign Affairs, 1918–1930.* Ames, Ia., 1988.

Pethybridge, R., ed. *The Development of the Communist Bloc.* Boston, 1965.

Ro'i, Y. *From Encroachment to Involvement: A Documentary Study of Soviet Policy in the Middle East, 1945–1973.* New York, 1974.

Rubinstein, A. Z. *Soviet Foreign Policy Since World War II: Imperial and Global.* Cambridge, Mass., 1981.

Rubinstein, A. Z., ed. *The Foreign Policy of the Soviet Union*. New York, 1960.

Rubinstein, A. Z., ed. *Soviet and Chinese Influence* in *the Third World*. New York, 1975.

Seton-Watson, H. *The East European Revolution*. 3rd ed. New York, 1956.

Seton-Watson, H. *From Lenin to Khrushchev: The History of World Communism*. New York, 1951.

Shotwell, J. T., and M. M. Laserson. *Poland and Russia, 1919–1945*. New York, 1945.

Shulman, M. D. *Beyond the Cold War*. New Haven, Conn., 1966.

Shulman, M. D. *Stalin's Foreign Policy Reappraised*. Cambridge, Mass., 1963.

Slepyan, K. *Stalin's Guerrillas: Soviet Partisans in World War II*. Lawrence, Kans., 2006.

Sontag, R. J., and J. S. Beddie, eds. *Nazi-Soviet Relations, 1939–1941: Documents from the Archives of the German Foreign Office*. Washington, D.C., 1948.

Swearingen, A. R., and P. Langer, *Red Flag in Japan*. Cambridge, Mass., 1952.

Thurston, R. W. and B. Bonwetsch, eds. *The People's War: Responses to World War II in the Soviet Union*. Urbana, Ill., 2000.

Ulam, A. B. *Expansion and Coexistence: A History of Soviet Foreign Policy, 1917–1967*. New York, 1968.

Ulam, A. B. *Titoism and the Cominform*. Cambridge, Mass., 1952.

Ullman, R. H. *Anglo-Soviet Relations, 1917–21*. Vol. 1, *Intervention and the War*. Vol. 2, *Britain and the Russian Civil War, November 1918–February 1920*. Vol. 3, *Anglo-Soviet Accord*. Princeton, N.J., 1961, 1968, 1973.

Villmow, J. R. *The Soviet Union and Eastern Europe*. Englewood Cliffs, N.J., 1965.

Warth, R. *Soviet Russia in World Politics*. New York, 1963.

Weinberg, G. *Germany and the Soviet Union, 1939–1942*. Leiden, 1954.

Weiner, A. *Making Sense of War: The Second World* War *and the Fate of the Bolshevik Revolution*. Princeton, N.J., 2001.

Werth, A. *Russia at War, 1941–1945*. New York, 1964.

Zinner, Paul E. *Communist Strategy and Tactics in Czechoslovkia, 1918–1948*. New York, 1963.

Zubok, V. M. *A Failed Empire: The Soviet Union in the Cold War from Stalin to Gorbachev*. Chapel Hill, N.C., 2007.

## F. Nationalities

Armstrong, J. A. *Ukrainian Nationalism, 1939–1945*. New York, 1955.

Brown, K. *A Biography of No Place: From Ethnic Borderland to Soviet Heartland*. Cambridge, Mass., 2004.

Browne, M., ed. *Ferment in the Ukraine: Documents by V. Chornovil, I. Kandyba, L. Lukyanenko, V. Moroz and Others*. New York, 1971.

Carrere d'Encausse, H. *Decline of an Empire: Soviet Socialist Republics in Revolt*. New York, 1980.

Carrere d'Encausse, H. *The Great Challenge: Nationalities and the Bolshevik State, 1917–1930*. New York, 1992.

Carve, Sir O. *Soviet Empire: The Turks of Central Asia and Stalinism*. London, 1967.

Comrie, B. *The Languages of the Soviet Union*. Cambridge, 1981.

Conquest, R. *The Nation Killers: The Soviet Deportation of Nationalities*. London, 1970.

Dmytryshyn, B. *Moscow and the Ukraine, 1918–1952: A Study of Russian Bolshevik Nationality Policy*. New York, 1956.

Dunlop, J. B. *The Faces of Contemporary Russian Nationalism*. Princeton, N.J., 1983.

Dunn, S. P. *Cultural Processes in the Baltic Area under Soviet Rule*. Berkeley, 1967.

Fedyshyn, O. S. *Germany's Drive to the East and the Ukrainian Revolution, 1917–1918.* New Brunswick, N.J., 1971.

Gitelman, Z. Y. *Jewish Nationality and Soviet Politics: The Jewish Sections of the CPSU, 1917–1930.* Princeton, N.J., 1972.

Goldhagen, E., ed. *Ethnic Minorities in the Soviet Union.* New York, 1967.

Hirsch, F. *Empire of Nations: Ethnographic Knowledge and the Making of the Soviet Union.* Ithaca, N.Y., 2005.

Hovannisian, R. G. *The Republic of Armenia.* Vol. 1, *The First Year, 1918–1919.* Berkeley, 1971.

Israel, G. *The Jews in Russia.* Translated by S. L. Chernoff. New York, 1975.

Katz, Z., R. Rogers, and F. Harned, eds. *Handbook of Major Soviet Nationalities.* New York and London, 1975.

Kazemzadeh, F. *The Struggle for Transcaucasia, 1917–1921.* New York, 1961.

Kirchner, W. *The Rise of the Baltic Question.* Westport, Conn., 1970.

Kolarz, W. *Russia and Her Colonies.* New York, 1953.

Kolasky, J. *Education in the Soviet Ukraine.* Toronto, 1968.

Levin, N. *The Jews in the Soviet Union Since 1917: Paradox of Survival.* 2 vols. New York and London, 1990.

Lubachko, I. S. *Belorussia under Soviet Rule, 1917–1957.* Lexington, Ky., 1972.

Martin, T. *The Affirmative Action Empire: Nations and Nationalism in the Soviet Union, 1923–1939.* Ithaca, N.Y., 2001.

Massell, G. J. *The Surrogate Proletariat: Moslem Women and Revolutionary Strategies in Soviet Central Asia, 1919–1929.* Princeton, N.J., 1974.

Nahaylo, B., and V. Swoboda. *Soviet Disunion: A History of the Nationalities Problem in the USSR.* New York, 1991.

Northrop, D. *Veiled Empire: Gender and Power in Stalinist Central Asia.* Ithaca, N.Y., 2004.

Nove, A., and J. A. Newth. *The Soviet Middle East.* London, 1967.

Peters, V. *Nestor Makhno: The Life of an Anarchist.* Winnipeg, 1970.

Ro'i, Y. and A. Beker. *Jewish Culture and Identity in the Soviet Union.* New York, 1991.

Rumer, B. Z. *Soviet Central Asia: "A Tragic Experiment."* Boston, 1989.

Schwarz, S. *The Jews in the Soviet Union.* Syracuse, N.Y., 1951.

Sullivant, R. S. *Soviet Politics and the Ukraine, 1917–1957.* New York, 1962.

Tarulis, A. N. *Soviet Policy toward the Baltic States, 1918–1940.* Notre Dame, Ind., 1959.

von Rauch, G. *The Baltic States: The Years of Independence: Estonia, Latvia, Lithuania, 1917–1940.* Translated by G. Onn. Berkeley, 1974.

## G. Society, Culture, Education, Religion

Bailes, K. E. *Technology and Society under Lenin and Stalin: Origins of the Soviet Technical Intelligentsia, 1917–1941.* Princeton, N.J., 1978.

Bereday, G., and J. Pennar, eds. *The Politics of Soviet Education.* New York, 1960.

Bonnell, V. *Iconography of Power: Soviet Political Posters under Lenin and Stalin.* Berkeley, 1997.

Borenstein, E. *Men without Women: Masculinity and Revolution in Russian Fiction, 1917–1929.* Durham, N.C., 2000

Bowlt, J. E., ed. and trans. *Russian Art of the Avant-garde: Theory and Criticism, 1902–1934.* New York, 1988.

Boym, S. *Common Places: Mythologies of Everyday Life in Russia.* Cambridge, Mass., 1994.

Brooks, J. *Thank You, Comrade Stalin! Soviet Public Culture from Revolution to Cold War.* Princeton, N.J., 2000.

Brown, E. J. *The Proletarian Episode in Soviet Literature, 1929–1932.* New York, 1953.

Brown, E. J. *Russian Literature since the Revolution.* New York, 1963, 1982.

Churchward, L. G. *The Soviet Intelligentsia: An Essay on the Social Structure and Roles of Soviet Intellectuals during the 1960's.* London and Boston, 1973.

Clark, K. *Petersburg: Crucible of Cultural Revolution.* Cambridge, Mass., 1995.

Clark, K. *The Soviet Novel: History as Ritual.* Chicago, 1981.

Clark, K. and E. Dobrenko, eds. *Soviet Culture and Power: A History in Documents, 1917–1953.* New Haven, Conn., 2007.

Clements, B. E. *Bolshevik Women.* Cambridge, 1997.

Curtiss, J. S. *The Russian Church and the Soviet State, 1917–1950.* Boston, 1953.

Danilov, V. P. *Rural Russia under the New Regime.* Translated by O. Figes. Bloomington, Ind., 1988.

Dunham, V. S. *In Stalin's Time: Middle-Class Values in Soviet Fiction.* New York, 1976.

Dunlop, J. B., R. Haugh, and A. Klimoff, eds. *Aleksandr Solzhenitsyn: Critical Essays and Documentary Materials.* Belmont, Mass., 1973.

Edele, M. *Soviet Veterans of World War II: A Popular Movement in an Authoritarian Society, 1941–1991.* Oxford, 2009.

Edmondson, L., ed. *Women and Society in Russia and the Soviet Union.* Cambridge, 1992.

Ehrenburg, I. *Memoirs: 1921–1941.* Translated by T. Shebunina. New York, 1963.

Ellis, J. *The Russian Orthodox Church: A Contemporary History.* Bloomington, Ind., 1986.

Enteen, G. M. *The Soviet Scholar-Bureaucrat: M. N. Pokrovskii and the Society of Marxist Historians.* University Park, Pa., 1978.

Evtushenko, E. *A Precocious Autobiography.* New York, 1963.

Figes, O. *The Whisperers: Private Life in Stalin's Russia.* New York, 2007.

Fitzpatrick, S. *The Cultural Front: Power and Culture in Revolutionary Russia.* Ithaca, N.Y., 1992.

Fitzpatrick, S. *Education and Social Mobility in the Soviet Union, 1921–1934.* Cambridge, 1979.

Fitzpatrick, S. *Everyday Stalinism: Ordinary Life in Extraordinary Times: Soviet Russia in the 1930s.* New York, 1999.

Fitzpatrick, S. *Stalin's Peasants: Resistance and Survival in the Russian Village after Collectivization.* New York, 1994-

Fitzpatrick, S., ed. *Cultural Revolution in Russia, 1928–1931.* Bloomington, Ind., 1978.

Fletcher, W. C. *A Study in Survival: The Church in Russia, 1927–1943.* New York, 1965.

Geldern, J. von and R. Stites. *Mass Culture in Soviet Russia.* Bloomington, Ind., 1995.

Gleason, A., P. Kenez, and R. Stites, eds. *Bolshevik Culture: Experiment and Order in the Russian Revolution.* Bloomington, Ind., 1985.

Goldman, W. Z. *Women at the Gates: Gender and Industry in Stalin's Russia.* New York, 2002.

Goldman, W. Z. *Women, the State, and Revolution: Soviet Family Policy and Social Life, 1917–1936.* Cambridge, 1993.

Gorsuch, A. *Youth in Revolutionary Russia: Enthusiasts, Bohemians, Delinquents.* Bloomington, Ind., 2000.

Graham, L. *Science and Philosophy in the Soviet Union.* New York, 1972.

Groys, B. *The Total Art of Stalinism: Avant-garde, Aesthetic Dictatorship, and Beyond.* Translated by Charles Rougle. Princeton, N.J., 1992.

Hansson, C., and K. Linden. *Moscow Women: Thirteen Interviews by Carola Hansson and Karin Linden.* Translated by G. Bothmer, G. Blechler, and L. Blechler. Introduction by G. W. Lapidus. New York, 1983.

Hayward, M., and W. C. Fletcher, eds. *Religion and the Soviet State: A Dilemma of Power.* New York, 1969.

Healy, D. *Bolshevik Sexual Forensics: Diagnosing Disorder in the Clinic and Courtroom, 1917–1939.* DeKalb, Ill., 2009.

Hellbeck, J. *Revolution on My Mind: Writing a Diary under Stalin.* Cambridge, Mass., 2006.

Heller, M. *Cogs in the Soviet Wheel: The Formation of Soviet Man.* New York, 1988.

Hosking, G. *Beyond Socialist Realism: Soviet Fiction Since "Ivan Denisovich."* New York, 1980.

Jacoby, S. *Inside Soviet Schools.* New York, 1974.

Johnson, P. *Khrushchev and the Arts: The Politics of Soviet Culture, 1962–1964.* Cambridge, Mass., 1965.

Josephson, P. R. *New Atlantis Revisited: Akademgorodok, the Siberian City of Science.* Princeton, N.J., 1997.

Keep, J., ed. *Contemporary History in the Soviet Mirror.* New York, 1964.

Kenez, P. *The Birth of the Soviet Propaganda State: Soviet Methods of Mass Mobilization, 1917–1930.* Cambridge, 1985.

Kenez, P. *Cinema and Soviet Society, 1917–1953.* Cambridge, 1992.

Koenker, D. P. *Republic of Labor: Russian Printers and Soviet Socialism, 1918–1930.* Ithaca, N.Y., 2005.

Kozlov, V. *Mass Uprisings in the USSR: Protest and Rebellion in the Post-Stalin Years.* Armonk, N.Y., 2002.

Lewin, M. *Russian Peasants and Soviet Power: A Study of Collectivization.* New York, 1968.

Lewin, M. *The Making of the Soviet System: Essays in the Social History of Interwar Russia.* London, 1985.

Lowe, D. *Russian Writing Since 1953: A Critical Survey.* Cambridge, 1987.

Luckyj, G. *Literary Politics in the Soviet Ukraine, 1917–1934.* New York, 1955.

McLean, H., and W. N. Vickery. *The Year of Protest, 1956: An Anthology of Soviet Literary Materials.* New York, 1961.

Medvedev, Zh. A. *The Rise and Fall of T. D. Lysenko.* Translated by I. M. Lerner. New York, 1969.

Pospielovsky, D. *The Russian Church Under the Soviet Regime, 1917–1982.* 2 vols. Crestwood, N.Y., 1984.

Reese, R. R. *Stalin's Reluctant Soldiers: A Social History of the Red Army, 1925–1941.* Lawrence, Kans., 1996.

Rosenberg, W. G. ed, *Bolshevik Visions: First Phase of the Cultural Revolution in Soviet Russia.* Ann Arbor, Mich., 1984.

Sakharov, A. D. *Progress, Coexistence and Intellectual Freedom.* Translated and introduction by H. Salisbury. New York, 1968.

Shlapentokh, V. *Public and Private Life of the Soviet People: Changing Values in Post-Stalin Russia.* New York, 1989.

Siegelbaum, L. H. *Cars for Comrades: The Life of the Soviet Automobile.* Ithaca, N.Y., 2008.

Siegelbaum, L. H. *Stakhanovism and the Politics of Productivity in the USSR, 1935–1941.* Cambridge, 1988.

Siegelbaum, L. H. and Ronald Grigor Suny, ed. *Making Workers Soviet: Power, Class, and Identity.* Ithaca, N.Y., 1994.

Simon, G. *Church, State and Opposition in the USSR.* Translated by K. Matett. Berkeley, 1974.

Slonim, M. *Soviet Russian Literature: Writers and Problems.* New York, 1964.

Solzhenitsyn, A. *The Cancer Ward.* Translated by R. Frank. New York, 1968.

Solzhenitsyn, A. *The First Circle.* Translated by M. Guydon. London, 1968.

Solzhenitsyn, A. *The Gulag Archipelago.* 3 vols. Vols. 1 and 2 translated by T. Whitney; vol. 3 translated by H. Willetts. New York, 1974–1978.

Starr, S. F. *Red and Hot: The Fate of Jazz in the Soviet Union, 1917–1980.* New York, 1994.

Steinberg, M. D. *Proletarian Imagination: Self, Modernity, and the Sacred in Russia, 1910–1925.* Ithaca, N.Y., 2002.

Stites, R. *Russian Popular Culture: Entertainment and Society since 1900.* Cambridge, 1992.

Stroyen, W. *Communist Russia and the Russian Orthodox Church, 1943–1962.* Washington, D.C., 1967.

Struve, G. *Russian Literature under Lenin and Stalin, 1917–1953.* Norman, Okla., 1971.

Struve, N. *Christians in Contemporary Russia.* Translated by L. Sheppard and A. Manson. New York, 1967.

Swayze, H. *Political Control of Literature in the USSR, 1946–1959.* Cambridge, Mass., 1962.

Timasheff, N. *The Great Retreat.* New York, 1946.

Tumarkin, N. *Lenin Lives!: The Lenin Cult in Soviet Russia.* Cambridge, Mass., 1983.

Viola, L. *Peasant Rebels under Stalin: Collectivization and the Culture of Peasant Resistance.* New York, 1996.

Vucinich, A. *Empire of Knowledge: The Academy of Sciences of the USSR, 1917–1970.* Berkeley, 1984.

Weiner, D. *A Little Corner of Freedom: Russian Nature Protection from Stalin to Gorbachev.* Berkeley, 1999.

Weiner, D. R. *Models of Nature: Ecology, Conservation, and Cultural Revolution in Soviet Russia.* Bloomington, Ind., 1988.

Wood, E. *The Baba and the Comrade: Gender and Politics in Revolutionary Russia.* Bloomington, Ind., 1997.

## H. Gorbachev and the Collapse of the Soviet Union

Breslauer, G. W. *Gorbachev and Yeltsin as Leaders.* Cambridge, 2002.

Brown, A. *The Gorbachev Factor.* Oxford; New York, 1996.

Carrere d'Encausse, H. *The End of the Soviet Empire: The Triumph of the Nations.* New York, 1993.

Castells, M., with E. Kiselyova. *The Collapse of Soviet Communism: A View from the Information Society.* Berkeley, 1995.

Dunlop, J. *The Rise of Russia and the Fall of the Soviet Union.* Princeton, N.J., 1995.

Fowkes, B. *The Disintegration of the Soviet Union: A Study in the Rise and Triumph of Nationalism.* New York, 1997.

Goldman, M. *What Went Wrong with Perestroika.* New York, 1992.

Hough, J. F. *Democratization and Revolution in the U.S.S.R., 1985–1991.* Washington, D.C., 1997.

Kaiser, R. G. *Why Gorbachev Happened: His Triumphs and His Failure.* New York, 1991.

Kotkin, S. *Armageddon Averted: The Soviet Collapse, 1970–2000.* New York, 2001.

Kotkin, S. *Steeltown, USSR: Soviet Society in the Gorbachev Era.* Berkeley, 1991.

Kotz, D. M., with F. Weir. *Revolution from Above: The Demise of the Soviet System.* New York, 1997.

Lewin, M. *The Gorbachev Phenomenon: A Historical Interpretation*. Berkeley: University of California Press, 1991.

Lieven, A. *The Baltic Revolution: Estonia, Latvia, Lithuania, and the Path to Democracy*. New Haven, Conn., 1993.

Remnick, D. *Lenin's Tomb: The Last Days of the Soviet Empire*. New York, 1993.

Ries, N. *Russian Talk: Culture and Conversation during Perestroika*. Ithaca, N.Y., 1997.

Strayer, R. W. *Why Did the Soviet Union Collapse?: Understanding Historical Change*. Armonk, N.Y., 1998.

Suny, R. G. *The Revenge of the Past: Nationalism, Revolution, and the Collapse of the Soviet Union*. Stanford, 1993.

Walicki, A. *Marxism and the Leap to The Kingdom of Freedom: The Rise and Fall of the Communist Utopia*. Stanford, 1995.

White, S. *Gorbachev and After*. 3rd ed. Cambridge, 1992.

Yurchak, A. *Everything Was Forever, Until It Was No More: The Last Soviet Generation*. Princeton, N.J., 2006.

## Russian Federation, 1991–

Barker, A. M., ed. *Consuming Russia: Popular Culture, Sex, and Society since Gorbachev*. Durham, N.C., 1999.

Bonnell, V. E. and G. W. Breslauer. *Russia in the New Century: Stability or Disorder?* Boulder, Colo., 2001.

Borenstein, E. *Overkill: Sex and Violence in Contemporary Russian Popular Culture*. Ithaca, N.Y., 2008.

Brown, A., ed. *Contemporary Russian Politics: A Reader*. Oxford, 2001.

Colton, T. *Yeltsin: A Life*. New York, 2008.

Condee, N. *The Imperial Trace: Recent Russian Cinema*. Oxford, 2009.

Ellis, J. *The Russian Orthodox Church: Triumphalism and Defensiveness*. New York, 1996.

Feshbach, M. *Ecological Disaster: Cleaning Up the Hidden Legacy of the Soviet Regime*. New York, 1995.

Gessen, M. *Dead Again: The Russian Intelligentsia after Communism*. New York, 1997.

Goldman, M. *Lost Opportunity: Why Economic Reforms in Russia Have Not Worked*. New York, 1994.

Handelman, S. *Comrade Criminal: Russia's New Mafiya*. New Haven, Conn., 1995.

Herspring, D. R., ed. *Putin's Russia: Past Imperfect, Future Uncertain*. New York, 2007.

Humphrey, C. *The Unmaking of Soviet Life: Everyday Economies after Socialism*. Ithaca, N.Y., 2002.

Kampfner, J. *Inside Yeltsin's Russia: Corruption, Conflict, Capitalism*. London, 1994.

Khazanov. A. M. *After the USSR: Ethnicity, Nationalism, and Politics in the Commonwealth of Independent States*. Madison, Wisc., 1995.

Knight, A. *Spies without Cloaks: The KGB's Successors*. Princeton, N.J., 1998.

Ledeneva, A. *How Russia Really Works: The Informal Practices That Shaped Post-Soviet Politics and Business*. Ithaca, N.Y., 2006.

Lieven, A. *Chechnya: Tombstone of Russian Power*. New Haven, Conn., 1998.

McFaul, M. *Russia's Unfinished Revolution: Political Change from Gorbachev to Putin*. Ithaca, N.Y., 2001.

Mikheyev, D. *Russia Transformed*. Indianapolis, 1996.

Remnick, D. *Resurrection: The Struggle for a New Russia*. New York, 1997.

Sakwa, R. *Putin: Russia's Choice*. Second edition. London, 2008.

Shevtsova, L. *Putin's Russia*. Washington, D C., 2003.

Steinberger, M. D. and Wanner. C. Religion Morality, and *Community in Post-Soviet Societies. Bloomington*, Ind. 2008.

Shevtsova, L. *Yeltsin's Russia: Myths and Reality*. Washington, D.C., 1999.

Volkov, V. *Violent Entrepreneurs: The Role of Force in the Making of Russian Capitalism*. Ithaca, N.Y., 2002.

Woodruff, D. *Money Unmade: Barter and the Fate of Russian Capitalism*. Ithaca, N.Y., 1999.

# Index